lleno *adj* full (**de** of); *pared* cc with); *de lleno* fully

D1358861

debatir ⟨3a⟩ **1** *v/t* debate, discuss **2** *v/i* struggle **3** *v/r* debatirse: *debatirse entre la vida y la muerte* fight for one's life

Entries divided into grammatical categories
División de artículo en categorías gramaticales

fiambre *m* cold cut, *Br* cold meat; P (*cadáver*) stiff P

Register labels
Marcas de registro

sablear ⟨1a⟩ *v/t & v/i L.Am.* F scrounge (*a* from)

Latin American Spanish
Español latinoamericano

rotonda *f* traffic circle, *Br* roundabout

British variants
Variantes del inglés británico

A
B
C
D
E
F
G
H
I
J
K
L
M
N
Ñ
O
P
Q
R
S
T
U
V
W
X
Y
Z

Langenscheidt

Pocket Spanish Dictionary

**Spanish – English
English – Spanish**

edited by the
Langenscheidt editorial staff

Langenscheidt

Berlin · Munich · Vienna · Zurich
London · Madrid · New York · Warsaw

Neither the presence nor the absence of a designation indicating that any entered word constitutes a trademark should be regarded as affecting the legal status thereof.

Compiled by LEXUS
with
José A. Gálvez · Roy Russell
Jane Goldie · Peter Terrell
Monica Tamariz-Martel Mirêlis · Rafael Alarcón Gaeta
Andrew Wilkes · Stephanie Parker
Mike Gonzalez

© 2011 Langenscheidt KG, Berlin and Munich
Printed in Germany

11010 (98139)

Preface

Here is a new dictionary of English and Spanish, a tool with some 50,000 references for those who work with the English and Spanish languages at beginner's or intermediate level.

Focusing on modern usage, the dictionary offers coverage of everyday language – and this means including vocabulary from areas such as computer use and business. English means both American and British English; Spanish means both Latin American and European Spanish.

The editors have provided a reference tool to enable the user to get straight to the translation that fits a particular context of use. Indicating words are given to identify senses. Is the *mouse* you need for your computer, for example, the same in Spanish as the *mouse* you don't want in the house? Is *flimsy* referring to furniture the same in Spanish as *flimsy* referring to an excuse? This dictionary is rich in sense distinctions like this – and in translation options tied to specific, identified senses.

Vocabulary needs grammar to back it up. So in this dictionary you'll find irregular verb forms, in both English and Spanish, irregular English plural forms, guidance on Spanish feminine endings and on prepositional usage with verbs.

Since some vocabulary items are often only clearly understood when contextualized, a large number of idiomatic phrases are given to show how the two languages correspond in particular contexts.

All in all, this is a book full of information, which will, we hope, become a valuable part of your language toolkit.

Contents

How to use the dictionary

To get the most out of your dictionary you should understand how and where to find the information you need. Whether you are yourself writing text in a foreign language or wanting to understand text that has been written in a foreign language, the following pages should help.

1. How and where do I find a word?

1.1 Spanish and English headwords. The word list for each language is arranged in alphabetical order and also gives irregular forms of verbs and nouns in their correct alphabetical order.

Sometimes you might want to look up terms made up of two separate words, for example **shooting star**, or hyphenated words, for example **absent-minded**. These words are treated as though they were a single word and their alphabetical ordering reflects this.

The only exception to this strict alphabetical ordering is made for English phrasal verbs - words like **go off**, **go out**, **go up**. These are positioned in a block directly after their main verb (in this case **go**), rather than being scattered around in alphabetical positions.

Spanish words beginning with **ch** and **ll** are positioned in their alphabetical position in letters C and L. Words beginning with **ñ** are listed after N.

1.2 Spanish feminine headwords are shown as follows:

> **abogado** *m*, **-a** *f* lawyer
> **fumador** *m*, **~a** *f* smoker
> **bailarín** *m*, **-ina** *f* dancer
> **pibe** *m*, **-a** *f* *Rpl* F kid F
> **edil** *m*, **~a** *f* council(l)or

The feminine forms of these headwords are: **abogada**, **fumadora**, **bailarina**, **piba** and **edila**.

When a Spanish headword has a feminine form which translates differently from the masculine form, the feminine is entered as a separate headword in alphabetical order:

> **empresaria** *f* businesswoman; **empresario** *m* businessman

1.3 Running heads

If you are looking for a Spanish or English word you can use the **running heads** printed in bold in the top corner of each page. The running head on the left tells you the *first* headword (either blue or black) on the left-hand page and the one on the right tells you the *last* headword (either blue or black) on the right-hand page.

1.4 How is the word spelt?

You can look up the spelling of a word in your dictionary in the same way as you would in a spelling dictionary. British spelling variants are marked *Br.* If just a single letter is omitted in the American spelling, this is put between round brackets:

colo(u)r – hono(u)r – travel(l)er

2. How do I split a word?

Spanish speakers find English hyphenation very difficult. All you have to do with this dictionary is look for the bold dots between syllables. These dots show you where you can split a word at the end of a line but you should avoid having just one letter before or after the hyphen as in **a•mend** or **thirst•y**. In such cases it is better to take the entire word over to the next line.

3. Swung dashes and long dashes

3.1 A swung dash (~) replaces the entire headword, when the headword is repeated within an entry:

face [feɪs] **1** *n* cara *f*; **~ *to* ~** cara a cara

Here **~ *to* ~** means **face to face**.

rencor *m* resentment; ***guardar* ~ *a alguien*** bear s.o. a grudge

Here ***guardar* ~ *a alguien*** means ***guardar rencor a alguien***.

3.2 When a headword changes form in an entry, for example if it is put in the past tense or in the plural, then the past tense or plural ending is added to the swung dash – but only if the rest of the word doesn't change:

flame [fleɪm] *n* llama *f*; ***go up in* ~*s*** ser pasto de las llamas
parch [pɑːrtʃ] *v/t* secar; ***be* ~*ed*** F *of person* estar muerto de sed F

But:

sur•vive [sərˈvaɪv] **1** *v/i* sobrevivir; ***how are you? – I'm surviving***
¿cómo estás? – voy tirando
saltón *adj*: ***ojos saltones*** bulging eyes

3.3 Double headwords are replaced by a single swung dash:

Pan•a•ma Ca'nal *n*: ***the* ~** el Canal de Panamá
one-track 'mind *hum*: ***have a* ~** ser un obseso

3.4 In the Spanish-English part of the dictionary, when a headword is repeated in a phrase or compound with an altered form, a long dash is used:

escaso *adj* ... **-*as posibilidades de*** not much chance of, little chance of

Here **-*as posibilidades*** means **escasas posibilidades**.

4. What do the different typefaces mean?

4.1 All Spanish and English headwords and the Arabic numerals differentiating between parts of speech appear in **bold**:

> **neoyorquino 1** *adj* New York *atr* **2** *m*, **-a** New Yorker
> **splin·ter** ['splɪntər] **1** *n* astilla *f* **2** *v/i* astillarse

4.2 *Italics* are used for:

a) abbreviated grammatical labels: *adj, adv, v/i, v/t* etc

b) gender labels: *m, f, mpl* etc

c) all the indicating words which are the signposts pointing to the correct translation for your needs:

> **sport·y** ['spɔːrtɪ] *adj person* deportista; *clothes* deportivo
> ♦ **work out 1** *v/t problem, puzzle* resolver; *solution* encontrar, hallar
> **2** *v/i at gym* hacer ejercicios; *of relationship etc* funcionar, ir bien
> **completo** *adj* complete; *autobús, teatro* full
> **grano** *m* grain; *de café* bean; *en la piel* pimple, spot

4.3 All phrases (examples and idioms) are given in ***secondary bold italics***:

> **sym·pa·thet·ic** [sɪmpə'θetɪk] *adj* (*showing pity*) compasivo;
> (*understanding*) comprensivo; ***be ~ toward a person / an idea***
> simpatizar con una persona / idea
> **salsa** *f* GASTR sauce; *baile* salsa; ***en su ~*** *fig* in one's element

4.4 The normal typeface is used for the translations.

4.5 If a translation is given in italics, and not in the normal typeface, this means that the translation is more of an *explanation* in the other language and that an explanation has to be given because there just is no real equivalent:

> **'walk-up** *n apartamento en un edificio sin ascensor*
> **adobera** *f Méx type of mature cheese*

5. Stress

To indicate where to put the **stress** in English words, the stress marker ' appears before the syllable on which the main stress falls:

> **mo·tif** [mou'tiːf] motivo *m*
> **rec·ord**[1] ['rekɔːrd] *n* MUS disco *m*; SP *etc* récord *m*
> **re·cord**[2] [rɪ'kɔːrd] *v/t electronically* grabar; *in writing* anotar

Stress is shown either in the pronunciation or, if there is no pronunciation given, in the actual headword or compound itself:

> **'rec·ord hold·er** plusmarquista *m/f*

6. What do the various symbols and abbreviations tell you?

6.1 A solid blue diamond is used to indicate a phrasal verb:

> ♦ **call off** *v/t* (*cancel*) cancelar; *strike* desconvocar

6.2 A white diamond is used to divide up longer entries into more easily digested chunks of related bits of text:

> **de** *prp* ◊ *origen* from; **~ Nueva York** from New York; **~ ... a** from ... to ◊ *posesión* of; **el coche ~ mi amigo** my friend's car ◊ *material* (made) of; **un anillo ~ oro** a gold ring ◊ *contenido* of; **un vaso ~ agua** a glass of water ◊ *cualidad*: **una mujer ~ 20 años** a 20 year old woman ◊ *causa* with; **temblaba ~ miedo** she was shaking with fear ...

6.3 The abbreviation F tells you that the word or phrase is used colloquially rather than in formal contexts. The abbreviation V warns you that a word or phrase is vulgar or taboo. Words or phrases labeled P are slang. Be careful how you use these words.

These abbreviations, F, V and P, are used both for headwords and phrases (placed after) and for the translations of headwords and phrases (placed after). If there is no such label given, then the word or phrase is neutral.

6.4 A colon before an English or Spanish word or phrase means that usage is restricted to this specific example (at least as far as this dictionary's translation is concerned):

> **catch-22** [kætʃtwentɪˈtuː]: **it's a ~ situation** es como la pescadilla que se muerde la cola
> **co·au·thor** [ˈkoʊ|θər] ... **2** *v/t*: **~ a book** escribir un libro conjuntamente
> **decantarse** <1a> *v/r*: **~ por** opt for

7. Does the dictionary deal with grammar too?

7.1 All English headwords are given a part of speech label:

> **tooth·less** [ˈtuːθlɪs] *adj* desdentado
> **top·ple** [ˈtɑːpl] **1** *v/i* derrumbarse **2** *v/t government* derrocar

But if a headword can only be used as a noun (in ordinary English) then no part of speech is given, since none is needed:

> **'tooth·paste** pasta *f* de dientes, dentífrico *m*

7.2 Spanish headwords have part of speech labels. Spanish gender markers are given:

> **barbacoa** *f* barbecue
> **bocazas** *m/f inv* F loudmouth F
> **budista** *m/f & adj* Buddhist

7.3 If an English translation of an Spanish adjective can only be used in front of a noun, and not after it, this is marked with *atr*:

> **bursátil** *adj* stock market *atr*
> **campestre** *adj* rural, country *atr*

7.4 If the Spanish, unlike the English, doesn't change form if used in the plural, this is marked with *inv*:

> **cortacircuitos** *m inv* circuit breaker
> **metrópolis** *f inv* metropolis

7.5 If the English, in spite of appearances, is not a plural form, this is marked with *nsg*:

> **bil·li·ards** ['bɪljərdz] *nsg* billar *m*
> **mea·sles** ['miːzlz] *nsg* sarampión *m*

English translations are given a *pl* or *sg* label (for plural or singular) in cases where this does not match the Spanish:

> **acciones** *pl* COM stock *sg*, *Br* shares
> **entarimado** *m* (*suelo*) floorboards *pl*

7.6 Irregular English plurals are identified:

> **the·sis** ['θiːsɪs] (*pl* **theses** ['θiːsiːz]) tesis *f inv*
> **thief** [θiːf] (*pl* **thieves** [θiːvz]) ladrón(-ona) *m(f)*
> **trout** [traʊt] (*pl* **trout**) trucha *f*

7.7 Words like **physics** or **media studies** have not been given a label to say if they are singular or plural for the simple reason that they can be either, depending on how they are used.

7.8 Irregular and semi-irregular verb forms are identified:

> **sim·pli·fy** ['sɪmplɪfaɪ] *v/t* (*pret & pp* **-ied**) simplificar
> **sing** [sɪŋ] *v/t & v/i* (*pret* **sang**, *pp* **sung**) cantar
> **la·bel** ['leɪbl] **1** *n* etiqueta *f* **2** *v/t* (*pret & pp* **-ed**, *Br* **-led**) bags etiquetar

7.9 Cross-references are given to tables of Spanish conjugations:

> **gemir** <3l> *v/i* moan, groan
> **esconder** <2a> **1** *v/t* hide, conceal ...

7.10 Grammatical information is provided on the prepositions you'll need in order to create complete sentences:

> **'switch·o·ver** to new system cambio *m* (**to** a)
> **sneer** [snɪːr] **1** *n* mueca *f* desdeñosa **2** *v/i* burlarse (**at** de)
> **escindirse** <3a> *v/r* (*fragmentarse*) split (**en** into); (*segregarse*) break away (**de** from)
> **enviciarse** <1b> *v/r* get addicted (**con** to)

Abbreviations

and	&	y	electronics,	ELEC	electrónica,
see	→	véase	electronic		electrotecnia
registered	®	marca	engineering		
trademark		registrada	Spain	*Esp*	España
abbreviation	*abbr*	abreviatura	especially	*esp*	especialmente
abbreviation	*abr*	abreviatura	euphemistic	*euph*	eufemismo
adjective	*adj*	adjetivo	familiar,	F	familiar
adverb	*adv*	adverbio	colloquial		
agriculture	AGR	agricultura	feminine	*f*	femenino
anatomy	ANAT	anatomía	feminine noun	*f/adj*	sustantivo
architecture	ARCHI	arquitectura	and adjective		femenino y
Argentina	*Arg*	Argentina			adjetivo
architecture	ARQUI	arquitectura	railroad	FERR	ferrocarriles
article	*art*	artículo	figurative	*fig*	figurativo
astronomy	AST	astronomía	financial	FIN	finanzas
astrology	ASTR	astrología	physics	FÍS	física
attributive	*atr*	atributivo	formal	*fml*	formal
motoring	AUTO	automóvil	photography	FOT	fotografía
civil aviation	AVIA	aviación	feminine plural	*fpl*	femenino
biology	BIO	biología			plural
Bolivia	*Bol*	Bolivia	feminine	*fsg*	femenino
botany	BOT	botánica	singular		singular
British English	*Br*	inglés	gastronomy	GASTR	gastronomía
		británico	geography	GEOG	geografía
Central	*C.Am.*	América	geology	GEOL	geología
America		Central	geometry	GEOM	geometría
chemistry	CHEM	química	grammatical	GRAM	gramática
Chile	*Chi*	Chile	historical	HIST	histórico
Colombia	*Col*	Colombia	humorous	*hum*	humorístico
commerce,	COM	comercio	IT term	INFOR	informática
business			interjection	*int*	interjección
comparative	*comp*	comparativo	interrogative	*interr*	interrogativo
computers,	COMPUT	informática	invariable	*inv*	invariable
IT term			ironic	*iron*	irónico
conjunction	*conj*	conjunción	ironic	*irón*	irónico
Southern Cone	*CSur*	Cono Sur	law	JUR	jurisprudencia
sports	DEP	deporte	Latin	*L.Am.*	América
contemptuous	*desp*	despectivo	America		Latina
determiner	*det*	determinante	law	LAW	jurisprudencia
Ecuador	*Ecuad*	Ecuador	linguistics	LING	lingüística
education	EDU	educación,	literary	*lit*	literario
(schools,		enseñanza	masculine	*m*	masculino
universities)		(sistema	masculine	*m/adj*	sustantivo
		escolar y	noun and		masculino y
		universitario)	adjective		adjetivo
electronics,	EL	electrónica,	nautical	MAR	navegación,
electronic		electrotecnia			marina
engineering			mathematics	MAT	matemáticas

mathematics	MATH	matemáticas	preterite (past tense)	*pret*	pretérito
medicine	MED	medicina	pronoun	*pron*	pronombre
meteorology	METEO	meteorología	preposition	*prp*	preposición
Mexico	*Mex*	México	psychology	PSI	psicología
Mexico	*Méx*	México	psychology	PSYCH	psicología
masculine and feminine	*m/f*	masculino y femenino	chemistry	QUÍM	química
masculine and feminine plural	*m/fpl*	masculino y femenino plural	radio	RAD	radio
			railroad	RAIL	ferrocarriles
military	MIL	militar	relative	*rel*	relativo
mineralogy	MIN	mineralogía	religion	REL	religión
motoring	MOT	automóvil	River Plate	*Rpl*	Río de la Plata
masculine plural	*mpl*	masculino plural	South America	S.Am.	América del Sur
music	MUS	música	singular	*sg*	singular
music	MÚS	música	someone	s.o.	alguien
mythology	MYTH	mitología	sports	SP	deporte
noun	*n*	sustantivo	Spain	*Span*	España
nautical	NAUT	navegación, náutica	something	*sth*	algo, alguna cosa
negative	*neg*	negativo	subjunctive	*subj*	subjuntivo
noun plural	*npl*	sustantivo plural	superlative	*sup*	superlativo
noun singular	*nsg*	sustantivo singular	bullfighting	TAUR	tauromaquia
			also	*tb*	también
ornithology	ORN	ornitología	theater, theatre	TEA	teatro
oneself	o.s.	sí mismo	technology	TÉC	técnica
popular, slang	P	popular	technology	TECH	técnica
painting	PAINT	pintura	telecommunications	TELEC	telecomunicaciones
Paraguay	*Parag*	Paraguay	theater	THEA	teatro
past participle	*part*	participio pasado	typography, typesetting	TIP	tipografía
Peru	*Pe*	Perú	transportation	TRANSP	transportes
pejorative	*pej*	peyorativo	television	TV	televisión
photography	PHOT	fotografía	vulgar	V	vulgar
physics	PHYS	física	auxiliary verb	*v/aux*	verbo auxiliar
painting	PINT	pintura	verb	*vb*	verbo
plural	*pl*	plural	Venezuela	*Ven*	Venezuela
politics	POL	política	intransitive verb	*v/i*	verbo intransitivo
possessive	*pos*	posesivo	impersonal verb	*v/impers*	verbo impersonal
possessive	*poss*	posesivo			
past participle	*pp*	participio pasado	reflexive verb	*v/r*	verbo reflexivo
predicative usage	*pred*	predicativo	transitive verb	*v/t*	verbo transitivo
prefix	*pref*	prefijo	West Indies	W.I.	Antillas
preposition	*prep*	preposición	zoology	ZO	zoología

The pronunciation of Spanish

Stress

1. If a word ends in a vowel, or in *n* or *s*, the penultimate syllable is stressed: **espada, biblioteca, hablan, telefonean, edificios.**

2. If a word ends in a consonant other than *n* or *s*, the last syllable is stressed: **dificultad, hablar, laurel, niñez.**

3. If a word is to be stressed in any way contrary to rules 1 and 2, an acute accent is written over the stressed vowel: **rubí, máquina, crímenes, carácter, continúa, autobús.**

4. Diphthongs and syllable division. Of the 5 vowels *a, e, o* are considered "strong" and *i* and *u* "weak":

  a) A combination of weak + strong forms a diphthong, the stress falling on the stronger element: **reina, baile, cosmonauta, tiene, bueno.**

  b) A combination of weak + weak forms a diphthong, the stress falling on the second element: **viuda, ruido.**

  c) Two strong vowels together remain two distinct syllables, the stress falling according to rules 1 and 2: **ma/estro, atra/er.**

  d) Any word having a vowel combination not stressed according to these rules has an accent: **traído, oído, baúl, río.**

Sounds

Since the pronunciation of Spanish is (unlike English) adequately represented by the spelling of words, Spanish headwords have not been given a phonetic transcription. The sounds of Spanish are described below.

The pronunciation described is primarily that of the educated Spaniard. But the main features of Latin American pronunciation are also covered.

Vowels

a　As in English *father*: **paz, pata.**

e　Like *e* in English *they* (but without the following sound of *y*): **grande, pelo.** A shorter sound when followed by a consonant in the same syllable, like *e* in English *get*: **España, renta.**

i　Like *i* in English *machine*, though somewhat shorter: **pila, rubí.**

o　As in English *November*, *token*: **solo, esposa.** A shorter sound when followed by a consonant in the same syllable, like *au* in English *fault* or the *a* in *fall*: **costra, bomba.**

u　Like *oo* in English *food*: **pura, luna.** Silent after **q** and in **gue, gui,** unless marked with a dieresis (**antigüedad, argüir**).

y　when occurring as a vowel (in the conjunction **y** or at the end of a word), is pronounced like *i*.

Diphthongs

ai like *i* in English *right*: **baile, vaina**.

ei like *ey* in English *they*: **reina, peine**.

oi like *oy* in English *boy*: **boina, oigo**.

au like *ou* in English *bout*: **causa, audacia**.

eu like the vowel sounds in English *may-you*, without the sound of the *y*: **deuda, reuma**.

Semiconsonants

i, y like *y* in English *yes*: **yerno, tiene**; in some cases in *L.Am.* this *y* is pronounced like the *s* in English *measure*: **mayo, yo**.

u like *w* in English *water*: **huevo, agua**.

Consonants

b, v These two letters represent the same value in Spanish. There are two distinct pronunciations:

    1. At the start of a word and after *m* and *n* the sound is like English *b*: **batalla, ventaja; tromba, invierno**.

    2. In all other positions the sound is what is technically a "bilabial fricative". This sound does not exist in English. Go to say a *b* but do not quite bring your lips together: **estaba, cueva, de Vigo**.

c 1. *c* before *a, o, u* or a consonant is like English *k*: **café, cobre**.

    2. *c* before *e, i* is like English *th* in *thin*: **cédula, cinco**. In *L.Am.* this is pronounced like an English *s* in *chase* .

ch like English *ch* in *church*: **mucho, chocho**.

d Three distinct pronunciations:

    1. At the start of a word and after *l* and *n*, the sound is like English *d*: **doy, aldea, conde**.

    2. Between vowels and after consonants other than *l* and *n* the sound is relaxed and approaches English *th* in *this*: **codo, guardar**; in parts of Spain it is further relaxed and even disappears, particularly in the **-ado** ending.

    3. In final position, this type 2 is further relaxed or omitted altogether: **usted, Madrid**.

f like English *f*: **fuero, flor**.

g Three distinct pronunciations:

    1. Before *e* and *i* it is the same as the Spanish j (below): **coger, general**.

    2. At the start of a word and after *n*, the sound is that of English *g* in *get*: **granada, rango**.

    3. In other positions the sound is like 2 above, but much softer, the *g* almost disappearing: **agua, guerra**. N.B. In the group **gue, gui** the **u** is silent (**guerra, guindar**) unless marked with a dieresis (**antigüedad, argüir**). In the group **gua** all letters are sounded.

h	always silent: **honor**, **búho**.
j	A strong guttural sound not found in English, but like the *ch* in Scots *loch*, German *Achtung*: **jota**, **ejercer**.
k	like English *k*: **kilogramo**, **ketchup**.
l	like English *l*: **león**, **pala**.
ll	approximating to English *lli* in *million*: **millón**, **calle**. In *L. Am.* like the *s* in English *measure*.
m	like English *m*: **mano**, **como**.
n	like English *n*: **nono**, **pan**; except before **v**, when the group is pronounced like *mb*: **enviar**, **invadir**.
ñ	approximating to English *ni* in *onion*: **paño**, **ñoño**.
p	like English *p*: **Pepe**, **copa**.
q	like English *k*; always in combination with **u**, which is silent: **que**, **quiosco**.
r	a single trill stronger than any *r* in English, but like Scots *r*: **caro**, **querer**. Somewhat relaxed in final position. Pronounced like **rr** at the start of a word and after **l**, **n**, **s**: **rata**.
rr	strongly trilled: **carro**, **hierro**.
s	like *s* in English *chase*: **rosa**, **soso**. But before **b**, **d**, hard **g**, **l**, **m** and **n** it is like English *s* in *rose*: **desde**, **mismo**, **asno**. Before "impure **s**" in recent loan-words, an extra *e*-sound is inserted in pronunciation: **e-sprint**, **e-stand**.
t	like English *t*: **patata**, **tope**.
v	see **b**.
w	found in a few recent loan-words only and pronounced pretty much as the English *w*, but sometimes with a very slight *g* sound before it: **whisky**, **windsurf**. In one exceptional case it is pronounced like an English *v* or like Spanish **b** and **v**: **wáter**.
x	like English *gs* in *big sock*: **máximo**, **examen**. Before a consonant like English *s* in *chase*: **extraño**, **mixto**.
z	like English *th* in *thin*: **zote**, **zumbar**. In *L. Am.* like English *s* in *chase*.

The Spanish Alphabet

a [ah]	g [Heh]	m ['emeh]	rr ['erreh]	x ['ekees]
b [beh]	h ['acheh]	n ['eneh]	s ['eseh]	y [eegree-'eh-ga]
c [theh]	i [ee]	ñ ['en-yeh]	t [teh]	z ['theh-ta]
ch [cheh]	j ['Hota]	o [oh]	u [oo]	
d [deh]	k [ka]	p [peh]	v ['ooveh]	*H is pronounced*
e [eh]	l ['eleh]	q [koo]	w ['ooveh	*as in the Scottish*
f ['ef-feh]	ll ['el-yeh]	r ['ereh]	doh-bleh]	*way of saying loch*

Written Spanish

I. Capitalization

The rules for capitalization in Spanish largely correspond to those for the English language. In contrast to English, however, adjectives derived from proper nouns are not capitalized (*americano* American, *español* Spanish).

II. Word division

Spanish words are divided according to the following rules:

1. If there is a **single consonant** between two vowels, the division is made between the first vowel and the consonant (*di-ne-ro, Gra-na-da*).

2. **Two consecutive consonants** may be divided (*miér-co-les, dis-cur-so*). If the second consonant is an *l* or *r*, however, the division comes before the two consonants (*re-gla, nie-bla; po-bre, ca-bra*). This also goes for ch, ll and rr (*te-cho, ca-lle, pe-rro*).

3. In the case of **three consecutive consonants** (usually including an *l* or *r*), the division comes after the first consonant (*ejem-plo, siem-pre*). If the second consonant is an *s*, however, the division comes after the *s* (*cons-tan-te, ins-ti-tu-to*).

4. In the case of **four consecutive consonants** (the second of these is usually an *s*), the division is made between the second and third consonants (*ins-tru-men-to*).

5. **Diphthongs** and **triphthongs** may not be divided (*bien, buey*). Vowels which are part of different syllables, however, may be divided (*frí-o, acre-e-dor*).

6. **Compounds**, including those formed with prefixes, are divided morphologically (*nos-otros, des-ali-ño, dis-cul-pa*).

III. Punctuation

In Spanish a comma is often placed after an adverbial phrase introducing a sentence (*sin embargo, todos los esfuerzos fueron inútiles* however, all efforts were in vain). A subsidiary clause beginning a sentence is also followed by a comma (*si tengo tiempo, lo haré* if I have time, I'll do it, **but:** *lo haré si tengo tiempo* I'll do it if I have time).

Questions and exclamations are introduced by an inverted question mark and exclamation point respectively, which immediately precedes the question or exclamation (*Dispense usted, ¿está en casa el señor Pérez?* Excuse me, is Mr. Pérez at home?; *¡Que lástima!* What a shame!).

English pronunciation

Vowels

[ɑː]	*father*	['fɑːðər]
[æ]	*man*	[mæn]
[e]	*get*	[get]
[ə]	*about*	[ə'baut]
[ɜː]	*absurd*	[əb'sɜːrd]
[ɪ]	*stick*	[stɪk]
[iː]	*need*	[niːd]
[ɒː]	*in-laws*	['ɪnlɒːz]
[ɔː]	*more*	[mɔːr]
[ʌ]	*mother*	['mʌðər]
[ʊ]	*book*	[bʊk]
[uː]	*fruit*	[fruːt]

Diphthongs

[aɪ]	*time*	[taɪm]
[au]	*cloud*	[klaud]
[eɪ]	*name*	[neɪm]
[ɔɪ]	*point*	[pɔɪnt]
[ou]	*oath*	[ouθ]

Consonants

[b]	*bag*	[bæg]
[d]	*dear*	[dɪr]
[f]	*fall*	[fɒːl]
[g]	*give*	[gɪv]
[h]	*hole*	[houl]
[j]	*yes*	[jes]
[k]	*come*	[kʌm]
[l]	*land*	[lænd]
[m]	*mean*	[miːn]
[n]	*night*	[naɪt]
[p]	*pot*	[pɑːt]
[r]	*right*	[raɪt]
[s]	*sun*	[sʌn]
[t]	*take*	[teɪk]
[v]	*vain*	[veɪn]
[w]	*wait*	[weɪt]
[z]	*rose*	[rouz]
[ŋ]	*bring*	[brɪŋ]
[ʃ]	*she*	[ʃiː]
[tʃ]	*chair*	[tʃer]
[dʒ]	*join*	[dʒɔɪn]
[ʒ]	*leisure*	['liːʒər]
[θ]	*think*	[θɪŋk]
[ð]	*the*	[ðə]
[']	means that the following syllable is stressed: *ability* [ə'bɪlətɪ]

a *prp* ◇ *dirección* to; **al este de** to the east of; **a casa** home; **ir a la cama / al cine** go to bed / to the movies; **vamos a Bolivia** we're going to Bolivia; **voy a casa de Marta** I'm going to Marta's (house)
◇ *situación* at; **a la mesa** at the table; **al lado de** next to; **a la derecha** on the right; **al sol** in the sun; **a treinta kilómetros de Quito** thirty kilometers (*Br* kilometres) from Quito; **está a cinco kilómetros** it is five kilometers (*Br* kilometres) away
◇ *tiempo*: **¿a qué hora llegas?** what time do you arrive?; **a las tres** at three o'clock; **estamos a quince de febrero** it's February fifteenth; **a los treinta años** at the age of thirty
◇ *modo*: **a la española** the Spanish way; **a mano** by hand; **a pie** on foot; **a 50 kilómetros por hora** at fifty kilometers (*Br* kilometres) an hour
◇ *precio*: **¿a cómo** *or* **cuánto está?** how much is it?
◇ *objeto indirecto*: **dáselo a tu hermano** give it to your brother
◇ *objeto directo*: **vi a mi padre** I saw my father
◇ *en perífrasis verbal*: **empezar a** begin to; **jugar a las cartas** play cards; **a decir verdad** to tell the truth
◇ *para introducir pregunta*: **¿a que no lo sabes?** I bet you don't know; **a ver ... OK ...**, right ...

ábaco *m* abacus

abadía *f* abbey

abajo 1 *adv situación* below, underneath; *en edificio* downstairs; **ponlo ahí abajo** put it down there; **el cajón de abajo** *siguiente* the drawer below; *último* the bottom drawer ◇ *dirección* down; *en edificio* downstairs; **cuesta abajo** downhill; **empuja hacia abajo** push down
◇ *con cantidades*: **de diez para abajo** ten or under, ten or below **2** *int*: **¡abajo**

los traidores! down with the traitors!

abalanzarse ⟨1f⟩ *v/i* rush *o* surge forward; **abalanzarse sobre algo / alguien** leap *o* pounce on sth/s.o.

abalear ⟨1a⟩ *v/t S. Am.* shoot

abandonar ⟨1a⟩ **1** *v/t lugar* leave; *objeto, a alguien* abandon; *a esposa, hijos* desert; *idea* give up, abandon; *actividad* give up **2** *v/r* **abandonarse** let o.s. go; **abandonarse a** abandon o.s. to

abanicar ⟨1g⟩ **1** *v/t* fan **2** *v/r* **abanicarse** *v/r* fan o.s.

abanico *m* fan; *fig* range; **abanico eléctrico** *Méx* electric fan

abaratar ⟨1a⟩ *v/t* reduce or lower the price of; *precio* reduce, lower

abarcar ⟨1g⟩ *v/t territorio* cover; *fig* comprise, cover; *L.Am.* (*acaparar*) hoard, stockpile; **el libro abarca desde ... hasta ...** the book covers the period from ... to ...; **abarcar con la vista** take in

abarrotado *adj* packed

abarrotar ⟨1a⟩ **1** *v/t lugar* pack; *L.Am.* com buy up, stockpile **2** *v/r* **abarrotarse** *L.Am. del mercado* become glutted

abarrotes *mpl L.Am.* (*mercancías*) groceries; (**tienda de**) **abarrotes** grocery store, *Br* grocer's

abarrotería *f Méx, C.Am.* grocery store, *Br* grocer's

abarrotero *m*, **-a** *f Méx, C.Am.* storekeeper, shopkeeper

abastecer ⟨2d⟩ **1** *v/t* supply (**de** with) **2** *v/r* **abastecerse** stock up (**de** *o* with)

abastecimiento *m* supply

abasto *m*: **no dan abasto** they can't cope (**con** with)

abatí *m Rpl* corn, *Br* maize; *Parag*: fermented maize drink

abatible *adj* collapsible, folding *atr*

abatido *adj* depressed

abatimiento *m* gloom

abatir ⟨3a⟩ *v/t edificio* knock *o* pull down; *árbol* cut down, fell; AVIA shoot *o* bring

down; *fig* kill; (*deprimir*) depress
abdicación *f* abdication
abdicar ⟨1g⟩ *v/t* abdicate
abdomen *m* abdomen
abdominal *adj* abdominal
abdominales *mpl* sit-ups
abecedario *m* alphabet
abedul *m* birch
abeja *f* zo bee
abejorro *m* bumblebee
aberración *f* aberration
abertura *f* opening
abeto *m* fir (tree)
abiertamente *adv* openly
abierto 1 *part* → **abrir 2** *adj tb persona*
open; **está abierto a nuevas ideas** *fig*
he's open to new ideas
abigarrado *adj* multicolo(u)red
abismo *m* abyss; *fig* gulf
ablandar ⟨1a⟩ **1** *v/t tb fig* soften **2** *v/r*
ablandarse soften, get softer; *fig* relent
ablande *m Arg* AUTO running in
abnegación *f* self-denial
abnegado *adj* selfless
abocado *adj* doomed; **abocado al fracaso** doomed to failure, destined to fail
abochornar ⟨1a⟩ **1** *v/t* embarrass **2** *v/r*
abochornarse feel embarrassed
abogacía *f* law
abogaderas *fpl L.Am.* F (*discusiones*) ar-
guments
abogado *m*, **-a** *f* lawyer; *en tribunal superior* attorney, *Br* barrister; **no le faltaron
abogados** *fig* there were plenty of people who defended him
abogar ⟨1h⟩ *v/i*: **abogar por alguien** defend; *algo* advocate
abolición *f* abolition
abolir ⟨3a⟩ *v/t* abolish
abollado *adj* dented
abolladura *f* dent
abollar ⟨1a⟩ *v/t* dent
abombado *adj S. Am.* F *comida* rotten,
bad; F (*tonto*) dopey F
abombarse *S. Am. de comida* go off, go
bad
abominable *adj* abominable
abominar ⟨1a⟩ *v/t* detest, loathe
abonado *m*, **-a** *f* subscriber; *a teléfono,*

gas, electricidad customer; *a ópera, teatro*
season-ticket holder
abonar ⟨1a⟩ **1** *v/t* COM pay; AGR fertilize;
Méx pay on account; **abonar el terreno**
fig sow the seeds **2** *v/r* **abonarse** *a espectáculo* buy a season ticket (**a** for); *a
revista* take out a subscription (**a** to)
abono *m* COM payment; AGR fertilizer; *para espectáculo, transporte* season ticket
abordar ⟨1a⟩ *v/t* MAR board; *tema, asunto*
broach, raise; *problema* tackle, deal
with; *a una persona* approach
aborigen 1 *adj* native, indigenous **2** *m/f*
native
aborrecer ⟨2d⟩ *v/t* loathe, detest
abortar ⟨1a⟩ **1** *v/i* MED *espontáneamente*
miscarry; *de forma provocada* have an
abortion **2** *v/t plan* foil
abortivo *adj* abortion *atr*; **píldora -a** abortion pill
aborto *m espontáneo* miscarriage; *provocado* abortion; *fig* F freak F; **tener un
aborto** have a miscarriage
abotonar ⟨1a⟩ *v/t* button up
abra *f L.Am.* clearing
abrasador *adj* scorching (hot)
abrasar ⟨1a⟩ **1** *v/t* burn **2** *v/i del sol* burn,
scorch; *de bebida, comida* be boiling hot
3 *v/r* **abrasarse**: **abrasarse de sed** F be
parched F; **abrasarse de calor** F be swel-
tering F; **abrasarse de pasión** *lit* be
aflame with passion *lit*
abrazar ⟨1f⟩ **1** *v/t* hug **2** *v/r* **abrazarse** embrace
abrazo *m* hug; **dar un abrazo a alguien**
hug s.o., give s.o. a hug; **un abrazo** *en
carta* best wishes; *más íntimo* love
abrebotellas *m inv* bottle opener
abrelatas *m inv* can opener, *Br tb* tin
opener
abreviar ⟨1b⟩ *v/t* shorten; *palabra* abbre-
viate; *texto* abridge
abreviatura *f* abbreviation
abridor *m* bottle opener
abrigado *adj* warmly dressed
abrigar ⟨1h⟩ **1** *v/t* wrap up; *esperanzas*
hold out; *duda* entertain **2** *v/r* **abrigarse**
wrap up warm; **abrigarse del frío** (take)
shelter from the cold

abrigo *m* coat; (*protección*) shelter; ***ropa de abrigo*** warm clothes; ***al abrigo de*** in the shelter of

abril *m* April

abrir ⟨3a; *part* ***abierto*** ⟩ **1** *v/t* open; *túnel* dig; *grifo* turn on; ***le abrió el apetito*** it gave him an appetite **2** *v/i de persona* open up; *de ventana, puerta* open; ***en un abrir y cerrar de ojos*** in the twinkling of an eye **3** *v/r* **abrirse** open; ***abrirse a algo*** *fig* open up to sth; ***abrirse paso entre*** make one's way through

abrochar ⟨1a⟩ **1** *v/t* do up; *cinturón de seguridad* fasten **2** *v/r* **abrocharse** do up; *cinturón de seguridad* fasten; ***tendremos que abrocharnos el cinturón*** we'll have to tighten our belts

abrumador *adj* overwhelming

abrumar ⟨1a⟩ *v/t* overwhelm (***con*** *o* ***de*** with); ***abrumado de*** *o* ***con trabajo*** snowed under with work

abrupto *adj terreno* rough; *pendiente* steep; *tono, respuesta* abrupt; *cambio* sudden

absentismo *m* absenteeism; ***absentismo escolar*** truancy

absolución *f* absolution

absolutamente *adv* absolutely; ***no entendió absolutamente nada*** he didn't understand a thing

absolutismo *m* absolutism

absoluto *adj* absolute; ***en absoluto*** not at all

absolver ⟨2h; *part* ***absuelto*** ⟩ *v/t* JUR acquit; REL absolve

absorbente *adj* absorbent

absorber ⟨2a⟩ *v/t* absorb; (*consumir*) take; (*cautivar*) absorb

absorto *adj* absorbed (***en*** in), engrossed (***en*** in)

abstemio 1 *adj* teetotal **2** *m*, **-a** *f* teetotal(l)er

abstención *f* abstention

abstenerse ⟨2l⟩ *v/r* refrain (***de*** from); POL abstain

abstinencia *f* abstinence; ***síndrome de abstinencia*** MED withdrawal symptoms *pl*

abstracto *adj* abstract

abstraerse ⟨2p; *part* ***abstraido*** ⟩ *v/r* shut o.s. off (***de*** from)

abstraído 1 *adj* preoccupied; ***abstraído en algo*** engrossed in sth **2** *part* → **abstraerse**

absuelto *part* → **absolver**

absurdo 1 *adj* absurd **2** *m*: ***es un absurdo que*** it's absurd that

abuchear ⟨1a⟩ *v/t* boo

abucheo(s) *m* (*pl*) booing *sg*, boos *pl*

abuela *f* grandmother; F *persona mayor* old lady; ***¡cuéntaselo a tu abuela!*** F don't try to put one over on me! F, *Br* pull the other one! F

abuelo *m* grandfather; F *persona mayor* old man; ***abuelos*** grandparents

abultado *adj* bulging; *derrota* heavy

abultamiento *m* bulge

abultar ⟨1a⟩ *v/i* be bulky; ***no abulta casi nada*** it takes up almost no room at all

abundancia *f* abundance; ***había comida en abundancia*** there was plenty of food

abundante *adj* plentiful, abundant

abundar ⟨1a⟩ *v/i* be plentiful *o* abundant

aburguesarse ⟨1a⟩ *v/r desp* become bourgeois *o* middle class

aburrido *adj* (*que aburre*) boring; (*que se aburre*) bored; ***aburrido de algo*** bored *o* fed up F with sth

aburrimiento *m* boredom

aburrir ⟨3a⟩ **1** *v/t* bore **2** *v/r* **aburrirse** get bored; ***aburrirse de algo*** get bored *o* fed up F with sth; ***aburrirse como una ostra*** F get bored stiff F

abusado *adj Méx* F smart, clever; ***¡abusado!*** look out!

abusar ⟨1a⟩ *v/i*: ***abusar de*** *poder, confianza* abuse; *persona* take advantage of; ***abusar del alcohol*** drink too much; ***abusar sexualmente de alguien*** sexually abuse s.o.

abusivo *adj* JUR unfair

abuso *m* abuse; ***abusos*** *pl* ***deshonestos*** indecent assault *sg*

A.C. *abr* (= *antes de Cristo*) BC (= before Christ)

acá *adv* here; ***de acá para allá*** from here to there; ***de entonces para acá*** since then acabado *m* finish

acabar ⟨1a⟩ **1** *v/t* finish **2** *v/i de persona* finish; *de función, acontecimiento* finish, end; *acabé haciéndolo yo* I ended up doing it myself; *acabar con* put an end to; *caramelos* finish off; *persona* destroy; *acabar de hacer algo* have just done sth; *va a acabar mal F persona* he'll come to no good; *esto va a acabar mal* F this is going to end badly **3** *v/r acabarse de actividad* finish, end; *de pan, dinero* run out; *se nos ha acabado el azúcar* we've run out of sugar; *¡se acabó!* that's that!

acacia *f* acacia

academia *f* academy; *academia de idiomas* language school; *academia militar* military academy

académico **1** *adj* academic **2** *m*, *-a f* academician

acalenturarse ⟨1a⟩ *v/r L.Am. (afiebrarse)* get a temperature *o* fever

acallar ⟨1a⟩ *v/t tb fig* silence

acalorarse ⟨1a⟩ *v/r (enfadarse)* get worked up; *(sofocarse)* get embarrassed

acampada *f* camp; *ir de acampada* go camping

acampar ⟨1a⟩ *v/i* camp

acantilado *m* cliff

acaparar ⟨1a⟩ *v/t* hoard, stockpile; *tiempo* take up; *interés* capture; *(monopolizar)* monopolize

acápite *m L.Am.* section; *(párrafo)* paragraph

acaramelado *adj fig* F lovey-dovey F

acariciar ⟨1b⟩ *v/t* caress; *perro* stroke; *acariciar una idea fig* contemplate an idea

acarrear ⟨1a⟩ *v/t* carry; *fig* give rise to, cause

acaso *adv* perhaps; *por si acaso* just in case

acatar ⟨1a⟩ *v/t* comply with, obey

acatarrarse ⟨1a⟩ *v/r* catch a cold

acaudalado *adj* wealthy, well-off

acceder ⟨2a⟩ *v/i (ceder)* agree (*a* to), accede (*a* to) *fml*; *acceder a lugar* gain access to; *cargo* accede to *fml*

accesible *adj* accessible

acceso *m tb* INFOR access; *de fiebre* attack, bout; *de tos* fit; *de difícil acceso* inaccessible

accesorio **1** *adj* incidental **2** *m* accessory

accidentado **1** *adj terreno, camino* rough; *viaje* eventful **2** *m*, *-a f* casualty

accidental *adj (no esencial)* incidental; *(casual)* chance *atr*

accidente *m* accident; *(casualidad)* chance; GEOG feature; *accidente de tráfico or de circulación* road traffic accident, RTA; *accidente laboral* industrial accident

acción *f* action; *acciones pl* COM stock *sg*, *Br* shares; *poner en acción* put into action

accionar ⟨1a⟩ *v/t* activate

accionista *m/f* stockholder, *Br* shareholder

acebo *m* holly

acechar ⟨1a⟩ *v/t* lie in wait for

acecho *m*: *al acecho* lying in wait

aceite *m* oil; *aceite de girasol / oliva* sunflower / olive oil; *aceite lubricante* lubricating oil

aceitera *f* TÉC oilcan; GASTR cruet

aceitoso *adj* oily

aceituna *f* olive

aceleración *f* acceleration

acelerador *m* accelerator

acelerar ⟨1a⟩ **1** *v/t motor* rev up; *fig* speed up; *aceleró el coche* she accelerated **2** *v/i* accelerate **3** *v/r acelerarse L.Am.* F *(enojarse)* lose one's cool

acelgas *fpl* BOT Swiss chard *sg*

acento *m en ortografía, pronunciación* accent; *(énfasis)* stress, emphasis; *poner el acento en fig* stress, emphasize

acentuar ⟨1e⟩ **1** *v/t* stress; *fig* accentuate, emphasize **2** *v/r acentuarse* become more pronounced

acepción *f* sense, meaning

aceptable *adj* acceptable

aceptación *f* acceptance; *(éxito)* success

aceptar ⟨1a⟩ *v/t* accept

acequia *f* irrigation ditch

acera *f* sidewalk, *Br* pavement; *ser de la otra acera, ser de la acera de enfrente* F be gay

acerca *adv*: **acerca de** about

acercar ⟨1g⟩ **1** *v/t* bring closer; **acercar a alguien a un lugar** give s.o. a ride (*Br* lift) somewhere **2** *v/r* **acercarse** approach; (*ir*) go; *de grupos, países* come closer together; *de fecha* draw near; **se acercó a mí** she came up to me *o* approached me; **acércate** come closer; **no te acerques a la pared** don't get close to the wall

acero *m* steel; **acero inoxidable** stainless steel

acertado *adj comentario* apt; *elección* good, wise; **estar muy acertado** be dead right

acertar ⟨1k⟩ **1** *v/t respuesta* get right; *al hacer una conjetura* guess **2** *v/i* be right; **acertar con algo** get sth right

acertijo *m* riddle, puzzle

achacar ⟨1g⟩ *v/t* attribute (**a** to)

achantarse ⟨1a⟩ *v/r* F keep quiet, keep one's mouth shut F

achaque *m* ailment

achatado *adj* flattened

achatarse ⟨1a⟩ *v/r* be flattened

achicharrar ⟨1a⟩ **1** *v/t* burn **2** *v/r* **achicharrarse** *fig* F roast F

achinado *adj L.Am.* oriental-looking

achinero *m C.Am. vendedor* peddler

achiquitarse ⟨1a⟩ *v/r L.Am.* become frightened *o* scared

achisparse ⟨1a⟩ *v/r* F get tipsy F

acholar ⟨1a⟩ *v/t S. Am.* embarrass

achuchar ⟨1a⟩ *v/t fig* F pester, nag

achuchón *m* F squeeze, hug; (*empujón*) push; **le dio un achuchón** *desmayo* she felt faint

achuras *fpl S. Am.* variety meat *sg*, *Br* offal *sg*

aciago *adj* fateful

acicalarse ⟨1a⟩ *v/r* get dressed up

acidez *f* acidity; **acidez de estómago** heartburn

ácido 1 *adj tb fig* sour, acid **2** *m* acid

acierto *m idea* good idea; *respuesta* correct answer; *habilidad* skill

aclamación *f* acclaim

aclamar ⟨1a⟩ *v/t* acclaim

aclaración *f* clarification

aclarar ⟨1a⟩ **1** *v/t duda, problema* clarify, clear up; *ropa, vajilla* rinse **2** *v/i de día* break, dawn; *del tiempo* clear up **3** *v/r* **aclararse**: **aclararse la voz** clear one's throat; **no me aclaro** F I don't understand; *por cansancio, ruido etc* I can't think straight

aclimatarse ⟨1a⟩ *v/r* acclimatize, become acclimatized

acné *m* acne

ACNUR *abr* (= **Alto Comisionado de las Naciones Unidas para los Refugiados**) UNHCR (= United Nations High Commission for Refugees)

acobardar ⟨1a⟩ **1** *v/t* daunt **2** *v/r* **acobardarse** get frightened, lose one's nerve

acodarse ⟨1a⟩ *v/r* lean (one's elbows) (**en** on)

acogedor *adj* welcoming; *lugar* cozy, *Br* cosy

acoger ⟨2c⟩ **1** *v/t* receive; *en casa* take in; **acoger con satisfacción** welcome, greet with satisfaction **2** *v/r* **acogerse**: **acogerse a algo** have recourse to sth

acogida *f* reception; **tener buena acogida** get a good reception, be well received

acojonar ⟨1a⟩ **1** *v/t* V (*asustar*) scare the shit out of P; (*asombrar*) knock out F, blow away P **2** *v/r* **acojonarse** V be shit scared P

acolchado *adj Rpl* quilted

acolchonar ⟨1a⟩ *v/t Rpl* quilt

acomedido *adj L.Am.* obliging, helpful

acomedirse ⟨3l⟩ *v/r Méx* offer to help

acometer ⟨2a⟩ **1** *v/t attack; tarea, proyecto* undertake, tackle **2** *v/i* attack; **acometer contra algo** attack sth

acomodado *adj* well-off

acomodador *m* usher

acomodadora *f* usherette

acomodar ⟨1a⟩ **1** *v/t* (*adaptar*) adapt; *a alguien* accommodate **2** *v/r* **acomodarse** make o.s. comfortable; (*adaptarse*) adapt (**a** to)

acompañamiento *m* accompaniment

acompañante *m/f* companion; MÚS accompanist

acompañar ⟨1a⟩ *v/t* (*ir con*) go with, accompany *fml*; (*permanecer con*) keep company; MÚS, GASTR accompany

acompaño m C.Am. (reunión) meeting

acomplejar ⟨1a⟩ **1** v/t: **acomplejar a alguien** give s.o. a complex **2** v/r **acomplejarse** get a complex

acondicionar ⟨1a⟩ v/t un lugar equip, fit out; pelo condition

acongojar ⟨1a⟩ v/t lit grieve lit, distress

aconsejable adj advisable

aconsejar ⟨1a⟩ v/t advise

acontecer ⟨2d⟩ v/i take place, occur

acontecimiento m event

acopio m: **hacer acopio de** gather, muster

acoplar ⟨1a⟩ **1** v/t piezas fit together **2** v/r **acoplarse** de persona fit in (**a** with); de nave espacial dock (**a** with); de piezas fit together

acorazado adj armo(u)red

acordar ⟨1m⟩ **1** v/t agree **2** v/r **acordarse** v/r remember; **¿te acuerdas de él?** do you remember him?

acorde **1** adj: **acorde con** appropriate to, in keeping with **2** m MÚS chord

acordeón m accordion

acordeonista m/f accordionist

acordonar ⟨1a⟩ v/t cordon off

acorralar ⟨1a⟩ v/t tb fig corner

acortar ⟨1a⟩ **1** v/t shorten **2** v/i take a short cut **3** v/r **acortarse** get shorter

acosar ⟨1a⟩ v/t hound, pursue; con preguntas bombard (**con** with)

acosijar ⟨1a⟩ v/t Méx badger, pester

acoso m fig hounding, harassment; **acoso sexual** sexual harrassment

acostar ⟨1m⟩ **1** v/t put to bed **2** v/r **acostarse** go to bed; (tumbarse) lie down; **acostarse con alguien** go to bed with s.o., sleep with s.o.

acostumbrado adj (habitual) usual; **estar acostumbrado a algo** be used to sth

acostumbrar ⟨1a⟩ **1** v/t get used (**a** to) **2** v/i: **acostumbraba a venir a este café todas las mañanas** he used to come to this café every morning **3** v/r **acostumbrarse** get used (**a** to); **se acostumbró a levantarse temprano** he got used to getting up early

ácrata m/f & adj anarchist

acre adj olor acrid; crítica biting

acrecentar ⟨1k⟩ **1** v/t increase **2** v/r **acrecentarse** increase, grow

acreditar ⟨1a⟩ **1** v/t diplomático etc accredit (**como** as); (avalar) prove; **un documento que lo acredita como el propietario** a document that is proof of his ownership **2** v/r **acreditarse** acquire a good reputation

acreedor m, acreedora f creditor

acreencia f L.Am. credit

acribillar ⟨1a⟩ v/t: **acribillar a alguien a balazos** riddle s.o. with bullets; **acribillar a alguien a preguntas** bombard s.o. with questions

acrílico m/adj acrylic

acristalar ⟨1a⟩ v/t glaze

acróbata m/f acrobat

acrobático adj acrobatic; **vuelo acrobático** stunt flight

acta(s) f (pl) minutes pl

actitud f (disposición) attitude; (posición) position

activar ⟨1a⟩ v/t activate; (estimular) stimulate

actividad f activity

activista m/f POL activist

activo **1** adj active; **en activo** on active service; **población -a** labo(u)r force **2** m COM assets pl

acto m (acción), TEA act; ceremonia ceremony; **acto sexual** sexual intercourse; **acto seguido** immediately afterward(s); **en el acto** instantly, there and then

actor m actor

actriz f actress

actuación f TEA performance; (intervención) intervention

actual adj present, current; **un tema muy actual** a very topical issue

actualidad f current situation; **en la actualidad** at present, presently; (hoy en día) nowadays; **actualidades** current affairs

actualizar ⟨1f⟩ v/t bring up to date, update

actualmente adv currently

actuar ⟨1e⟩ v/i (obrar, ejercer), TEA act; MED work, act

acuarela *f* watercolo(u)r
acuario *m* aquarium
Acuario *m/f inv* ASTR Aquarius
acuático *adj* aquatic; *deporte acuático* water sport
acuchillar ⟨1a⟩ *v/t* stab
acuciante *adj* pressing, urgent
acudir ⟨3a⟩ *v/i* come; *acudir a alguien* turn to s.o.; *acudir a las urnas* go to the polls
acueducto *m* aqueduct
acuerdo *m* agreement; *estar de acuerdo con* agree with; *llegar a un acuerdo, ponerse de acuerdo* come to *o* reach an agreement (*con* with); *de acuerdo con algo* in accordance with sth; *¡de acuerdo!* all right!, OK!
acumulación *f* accumulation
acumular ⟨1a⟩ 1 *v/t* accumulate 2 *v/r* acumularse accumulate
acunar ⟨1a⟩ *v/t* rock
acuñar ⟨1a⟩ *v/t monedas* mint; *término, expresión* coin
acuoso *adj* watery
acupuntura *f* acupuncture
acurrucarse ⟨1g⟩ *v/r* curl up
acusación *f* accusation
acusado *m*, **-a** *f* defendant
acusar ⟨1a⟩ *v/t* accuse (*de* of); JUR charge (*de* with); (*manifestar*) show; *acusar recibo de* acknowledge receipt of
acuse *m*: *acuse de recibo* acknowledg(e)ment
acusetas *m/f inv S. Am.* F tattletale F, *Br* tell-tale F
acusica *m/f* F tattletale F, *Br* tell-tale F
acústica *f* acoustics
adaptable *adj* adaptable
adaptación *f* adaptation; *adaptación cinematográfica* screen *o* movie version
adaptador *m* adaptor
adaptar ⟨1a⟩ 1 *v/t* adapt 2 *adaptarse v/r* adapt (*a* to)
A. de C. *abr* (= *año de Cristo*) AD (= Anno Domini)
adecentar ⟨1a⟩ *v/t* straighten up, tidy up
adecuadamente *adv* properly
adecuado *adj* suitable, appropriate
adecuar ⟨1d⟩ 1 *v/t* adapt (*a* to) 2 *v/r* ade-

cuarse fit in (*a* with)
adefesio *m fig* F monstrosity F; *persona* freak F; *estar hecho un adefesio* look a sight
a. de J.C. *abr* (= *antes de Jesucristo*) BC (= before Christ)
adelantado *adj* advanced; *por adelantado* in advance; *ir adelantado de un reloj* be fast
adelantamiento *m* AUTO passing maneuver, *Br* overtaking manoeuvre
adelantar ⟨1a⟩ 1 *v/t mover* move forward; *reloj* put forward; AUTO pass, *Br* overtake; *dinero* advance; (*conseguir*) achieve, gain 2 *v/i de un reloj* be fast; (*avanzar*) make progress; AUTO pass, *Br* overtake 3 *v/r* **adelantarse** *mover* move forward; (*ir delante*) go on ahead; *de estación, cosecha* be early; *de un reloj* gain; *se me adelantó* she beat me to it, she got there first
adelante *adv en espacio* forward; *seguir adelante* carry on, keep going; *¡adelante!* come in; *más adelante en tiempo* later on; *de ahora o de aquí en adelante* from now on; *salir adelante fig: de persona* succeed; *de proyecto* go ahead
adelanto *m tb* COM advance
adelfa *f* BOT oleander
adelgazante *adj* weight-reducing, slimming *atr*
adelgazar ⟨1f⟩ 1 *v/t* lose 2 *v/i* lose weight
ademán *m* gesture; *hacer ademán de* make as if to
además 1 *adv* as well, besides 2 *prp*: *además de* as well as
adentrarse ⟨1a⟩ *v/r*: *adentrarse en territorio* penetrate; *tema* go into
adentro 1 *adv* inside; *¡adentro!* get inside!; *mar adentro* out to sea; *adentro de L.Am.* inside 2 *mpl*: *para sus adentros* to oneself
adepto *m* follower; *fig* supporter
aderezar ⟨1f⟩ *v/t con especias* season; *ensalada* dress; *fig* liven up
adeudar ⟨1a⟩ *v/t* owe
adherente *adj* adhesive
adherir ⟨3i⟩ 1 *v/i* stick, adhere *fml* 2 *v/t* stick 3 *v/r* **adherirse** *a superficie* stick

(*a* to), adhere (*a* to) *fml*; **adherirse a una organización** become a member of *o* join an organization; **adherirse a una idea** support an idea

adhesivo *m/adj* adhesive

adicción *f* addiction; **adicción a las drogas** drug addiction

adicional *adj* additional

adictivo *adj* addictive

adicto 1 *adj* addicted (*a* to); **ser adicto al régimen** be a supporter of the regime **2** *m*, **-a** *f* addict

adiestrar ⟨1a⟩ *v/t* train

adinerado *adj* wealthy

adiós 1 *int* goodbye, bye; *al cruzarse* hello **2** *m* goodbye; **decir adiós** say goodbye (*a* to)

aditivo *m* additive

adivinanza *f* riddle

adivinar ⟨1a⟩ *v/t* guess; *de adivino* foretell

adjetivo *m* adjective

adjudicar ⟨1g⟩ **1** *v/t* award **2** *v/r* **adjudicarse** win

adjuntar ⟨1a⟩ *v/t* enclose

adm. *abr* (= **administración**) admin (= administration)

administración *f* administration; *de empresa etc* management; (*gobierno*) administration, government; **administración pública** civil service

administrador *m*, **administradora** *f* administrator; *de empresa etc* manager

administrar ⟨1a⟩ *v/t medicamento, sacramentos* administer, give; *empresa* run, manage; *bienes* manage

administrativo 1 *adj* administrative **2** *m*, **-a** *f* administrative assistant

admirable *adj* admirable

admiración *f* admiration; **signo de admiración** exclamation mark

admirador *m*, **admiradora** *f* admirer

admirar ⟨1a⟩ **1** *v/t* admire; (*asombrar*) amaze **2** *v/r* **admirarse** be amazed (*de* at *o* by)

admisible *adj* admissible

admisión *f* admission; **derecho de admisión** right of admission

admitir ⟨3a⟩ *v/t* (*aceptar*) accept; (*reconocer*) admit

admón. *abr* (= **administración**) admin (= administration)

ADN *abr* (= **ácido desoxirribonucleico**) DNA (= deoxyribonucleic acid)

adobar ⟨1a⟩ *v/t* GASTR marinate

adobera *f Méx type of mature cheese*

adobo *m* GASTR marinade

adoctrinar ⟨1a⟩ *v/t* indoctrinate

adolecer ⟨2d⟩ *v/t* suffer (*de* from)

adolescencia *f* adolescence

adolescente *m/f* adolescent

adonde *adv* where

adónde *interr* where

adopción *f* adoption

adoptar ⟨1a⟩ *v/t* adopt

adoptivo *adj padres* adoptive; *hijo* adopted

adoquín *m* paving stone

adorable *adj* lovable, adorable

adoración *f* adoration

adorar ⟨1a⟩ *v/t* love, adore; REL worship

adormecer ⟨2d⟩ **1** *v/t* make sleepy **2** *v/r* **adormecerse** doze off

adormidera *f* BOT poppy

adormilado *adj* sleepy

adormilarse ⟨1a⟩ *v/r* doze off

adornar ⟨1a⟩ *v/t* decorate

adorno *m* ornament; *de Navidad* decoration

adosar ⟨1a⟩ *v/t*: **adosar algo a algo** put sth (up) against sth

adquirir ⟨3i⟩ *v/t* acquire; (*comprar*) buy

adquisición *f* acquisition; **hacer una buena adquisición** make a good purchase

adquisitivo *adj*: **poder adquisitivo** purchasing power

adrede *adv* on purpose, deliberately

adrenalina *f* adrenaline

aduana *f* customs

aduanero 1 *adj* customs *atr* **2** *m*, **-a** *f* customs officer

aducir ⟨3o⟩ *v/t razones, argumentos* give, put forward; (*alegar*) claim

adueñarse ⟨1a⟩ *v/r*: **adueñarse de** take possession of

adulación *f* flattery

adular ⟨1a⟩ *v/t* flatter

adulón 1 *adj S. Am.* fawning **2** *m*, **-ona** *f*

flatterer
adultera f adulteress
adulterar ⟨1a⟩ v/t adulterate
adulterio m adultery; *cometer adulterio* commit adultery
adúltero 1 adj adulterous **2** m adulterer
adultez f adulthood
adulto 1 adj adult; *edad -a* adulthood **2** m, **-a** f adult
adusto adj paisaje harsh; persona stern, severe; L.Am. (inflexible) stubborn
adverbio m adverb
adversario m, **-a** f adversary, opponent
adverso adj adverse
advertencia f warning
advertir ⟨3i⟩ v/t warn (de about, of); (notar) notice
adyacente adj adjacent
aéreo adj air atr; vista, fotografía aerial; *compañía -a* airline
aerobic, aeróbic m aerobics
aerodinámico adj aerodynamic
aeroespacial adj aerospace atr
aerolínea f airline
aeromozo m, **-a** f L.Am. flight attendant
aeronáutico adj aeronautical
aeropuerto m airport
aerosol m aerosol
afable adj pleasant, affable
afamado adj famous
afán m (esfuerzo) effort; (deseo) eagerness; *sin afán de lucro* organización not-for-profit, non-profit (making)
afanar ⟨1a⟩ **1** v/i C.Am. (ganar dinero) make money **2** v/t C.Am. dinero make; Rpl F (robar) pinch F **3** v/r **afanarse** make an effort
afección f MED complaint, condition
afectado adj (afligido) upset (por by); (amanerado) affected
afectar ⟨1a⟩ v/t (producir efecto en) affect; (conmover) upset, affect; (fingir) feign
afectivo adj emotional
afecto m affection; *tener afecto a alguien* be fond of s.o.
afectuoso adj affectionate
afeitada f shave
afeitado m shave

afeitadora f electric razor
afeitar ⟨1a⟩ v/t shave; barba shave off **2** v/r **afeitarse** shave, have a shave
afeminado adj effeminate
aferrarse ⟨1k⟩ v/r fig cling (**a** to)
Afganistán Afghanistan
afianzar ⟨1f⟩ **1** v/t fig strengthen **2** v/r **afianzarse** become consolidated
afición f love (por of); (pasatiempo) pastime, hobby; *la afición* DEP the fans
aficionado 1 adj: *ser aficionado a* be interested in, Br tb be keen on **2** m, **-a** f enthusiast; no profesional amateur; *un partido de aficionados* an amateur game
aficionarse ⟨1a⟩ v/r become interested (**a** in)
afiebrarse ⟨1a⟩ v/r L.Am. develop a fever
afilado adj sharp
afilador m sharpener
afilalápices m inv pencil sharpener
afilar ⟨1a⟩ **1** v/t sharpen; L.Am. F (halagar) flatter, butter up F; S. Am. (seducir) seduce **2** v/r **afilarse** S. Am. F (prepararse) get ready
afiliarse ⟨1a⟩ v/r: *afiliarse a un partido* become a member of a party, join a party
afinar ⟨1a⟩ v/t MÚS tune; punta sharpen; fig perfect, fine-tune
afincarse ⟨1g⟩ v/r settle
afinidad f affinity
afirmación f statement; declaración positiva affirmation
afirmar ⟨1a⟩ v/t state, declare
afirmativo adj affirmative
afligido adj upset
afligir ⟨3c⟩ **1** v/t afflict; (apenar) upset; L.Am. F (golpear) beat up **2** v/r **afligirse** get upset
aflojar ⟨1a⟩ **1** v/t nudo, tornillo loosen; F dinero hand over **2** v/i de tormenta abate; de viento, fiebre drop **3** v/r **aflojarse** come o work loose
afluente m tributary
afmo. abr (= afectísimo): *su afmo* Yours truly
afónico adj: *está afónico* he has lost his voice
aforo m capacity

afortunado *adj* lucky, fortunate

afrecho *f Arg* bran

África Africa; ***África del Sur*** South Africa

africano 1 *adj* African **2** *m*, **-a** *f* African

afrodisíaco *m* aphrodisiac

afrontar ⟨1a⟩ *v/t* face (up to)

afuera *adv* outside

afueras *fpl* outskirts

agachar ⟨1a⟩ **1** *v/i* duck **2** *v/r* **agacharse** bend down; (*acuclillarse*) crouch down; *L.Am.* (*rendirse*) give in

agalla *f* zo gill; ***tener agallas*** F have guts F

agarrado *adj fig* F mean, stingy F

agarrar ⟨1a⟩ **1** *v/t* (*asir*) grab; *L.Am.* (*tomar*) take; *L.Am.* (*atrapar, pescar*), *resfriado* catch; *L.Am. velocidad* gather, pick up; ***agarrar una calle*** *L.Am.* go up *o* along a street **2** *v/i* (*asirse*) hold on; *de planta* take root; *L.Am. por un lugar* go; ***agarró y se fue*** he upped and went **3** *v/r* **agarrarse** (*asirse*) hold on; *L.Am. a golpes* get into a fight

agarrón *m Rpl* P (*pleito*) fight, argument; *L.Am.* (*tirón*) pull, tug

agarrotado *adj* stiff

agarrotarse ⟨1a⟩ *v/r de músculo* stiffen up; TÉC seize up

agasajar ⟨1a⟩ *v/t* fête

agazaparse ⟨1a⟩ *v/r* crouch (down); (*ocultarse*) hide

agencia *f* agency; ***agencia inmobiliaria*** real estate office, *Br* estate agency; ***agencia de viajes*** travel agency

agenciarse ⟨1b⟩ *v/r* F get hold of

agenda *f diario* diary; *programa* schedule; *de mitin* agenda

agente 1 *m* agent **2** *m/f* agent; ***agente de cambio y bolsa*** stockbroker; ***agente de policía*** police officer

ágil *adj* agile

agilidad *f* agility

agilizar ⟨1f⟩ *v/t* speed up

agitación *f* POL unrest

agitar ⟨1a⟩ **1** *v/t* shake; *brazos, pañuelo* wave; *fig* stir up **2** *v/r* **agitarse** become agitated *o* worked up

aglomeración *f de gente* crowd

aglomerar ⟨1a⟩ *v/t* pile up

aglutinar ⟨1a⟩ *v/t fig* bring together

agobiante *adj* oppresssive

agobiar ⟨1b⟩ **1** *v/t de calor* oppress; *de problemas* get on top of, overwhelm **2** *v/r* **agobiarse** F feel overwhelmed

agobio *m*: ***es un agobio*** it's unbearable, it's a nightmare F

agolparse ⟨1a⟩ *v/r* crowd together

agonía *f* agony; ***la espera fue una agonía*** the wait was unbearable

agonizante *adj* dying

agonizar ⟨1f⟩ *v/i de persona* be dying; *de régimen* be crumbling

agorero *adj* ominous

agosto *m* August; ***hacer su agosto*** F make a fortune

agotado *adj* (*cansado*) exhausted, worn out; (*terminado*) exhausted; (*vendido*) sold out

agotador *adj* exhausting

agotar ⟨1a⟩ **1** *v/t* (*cansar*) wear out, exhaust; (*terminar*) use up, exhaust **2** *v/r* **agotarse** (*cansarse*) get worn out, exhaust o.s.; (*terminarse*) run out, become exhausted; (*venderse*) sell out

agraciado *adj persona* attractive

agradable *adj* pleasant, nice

agradar ⟨1a⟩ *v/i*: ***me agrada la idea*** *fml* I like the idea; ***nos agradaría mucho que ...*** *fml* we would be delighted *o* very pleased if ...

agradecer ⟨2d⟩ *v/t*: ***agradecer algo a alguien*** thank s.o. for sth; ***te lo agradezco*** I appreciate it

agradecimiento *m* appreciation

agrado *m*: ***ser del agrado de alguien*** be to s.o.'s liking

agrandar ⟨1a⟩ **1** *v/t* make bigger **2** *v/r* **agrandarse** get bigger

agrario *adj* land *atr*, agrarian; *política* agricultural

agravar ⟨1a⟩ **1** *v/t* make worse, aggravate **2** *v/r* **agravarse** get worse, deteriorate

agravio *m* offense, *Br* offence

agredir ⟨3a⟩ *v/t* attack, assault

agregado *m*, **-a** *f en universidad* senior lecturer; *en colegio* senior teacher; POL attaché; ***agregado cultural*** cultural attaché

agregar ⟨1h⟩ v/t add
agresión f aggression
agresividad f aggression
agresivo adj aggressive
agresor m, **agresora** f aggressor
agreste adj terreno rough; paisaje wild
agriarse ⟨1b or 1c⟩ v/r de vino go sour; de carácter become bitter
agrícola adj agricultural, farming atr
agricultor m, **agricultora** f farmer
agricultura f agriculture
agridulce adj bittersweet
agriera f L.Am. heartburn
agrietarse ⟨1a⟩ v/r crack; de manos, labios chap
agringarse ⟨1h⟩ v/r L.Am. become Americanized
agrio adj fruta sour; disputa, carácter bitter
agrios mpl BOT citrus fruit sg
agropecuario adj farming atr, agricultural
agrupar ⟨1a⟩ 1 v/t group, put into groups 2 v/r **agruparse** gather
agua f water; **agua corriente** running water; **agua dulce** fresh water; **agua mineral** mineral water; **agua oxigenada** (hydrogen) peroxide; **agua potable** drinking water; **es agua pasada** it's water under the bridge; **está con el agua al cuello** con problemas he's up to his neck in problems F; con deudas he's up to his neck in debt F; **se me hace la boca agua** it makes my mouth water
aguas waters; **aguas** pl **residuales** effluent sg, sewage sg
aguacate m BOT avocado
aguacero m downpour
aguachento adj CSur watery
aguafiestas m/f inv partypooper F, killjoy
aguaitar ⟨1a⟩ v/t S. Am. spy on
aguamala f S. Am. jellyfish
aguamiel f L.Am. mixture of water and honey; Méx (jugo de maguey) agave sap
aguanieve f sleet
aguantar ⟨1a⟩ 1 v/t un peso bear, support; respiración hold; (soportar) put up with; **no lo puedo aguantar** I can't stand o bear it 2 v/i hang on, hold out 3 v/r

aguantarse contenerse keep quiet; **me tuve que aguantar** conformarme I had to put up with it
aguante m patience; física stamina, endurance
aguar ⟨1a⟩ v/t fiesta spoil
aguardar ⟨1a⟩ 1 v/t wait for, await 2 v/i wait
aguardiente m fruit-based alcoholic spirit
aguarrás m turpentine, turps F
aguatero m, **-a** f S. Am. water-seller
agudeza f de voz, sonido high pitch; MED intensity; (perspicacia) sharpness; **agudeza visual** sharp-sightedness
agudizar ⟨1f⟩ 1 v/t un sentido sharpen; **agudizar un problema** make a problem worse 2 v/r **agudizarse** MED get worse; de un sentido become sharper
agudo adj acute; (afilado) sharp; sonido high-pitched; (perspicaz) sharp
agüero m omen; **ser de mal agüero** be an ill omen
aguijón m ZO sting; fig spur
águila f eagle; **¿águila o sol?** Méx heads or tails?; **ser un águila** fig be very sharp
aguilucho m eaglet
agüita f L.Am. F (agua) water; (infusión) infusion
aguja f needle; de reloj hand; **buscar una aguja en un pajar** fig look for a needle in a haystack
agujerear ⟨1a⟩ 1 v/t make holes in 2 v/r **agujerearse** develop holes
agujero m hole
agujetas fpl stiffness sg; **tener agujetas** be stiff
aguzar ⟨1f⟩ v/t sharpen; **aguzar el ingenio** sharpen one's wits; **aguzar el oído** prick up one's ears
ah int ah!
ahí adv there; **está por ahí** it's (somewhere) over there; dando direcciones it's that way
ahijada f goddaughter
ahijado m godson
ahínco m effort; **trabajar con ahínco** work hard
ahogado adj en agua drowned
ahogar ⟨1h⟩ 1 v/t (asfixiar) suffocate; en

agua drown; AUTO flood; *protestas* stifle **2** *v/r* **ahogarse** choke; (*asfixiarse*) suffocate; *en agua* drown; AUTO flood; *ahogarse en un vaso de agua* fig F get in a state over nothing

ahondar ⟨1a⟩ *v/i*: *ahondar en algo* go into sth in depth

ahora *adv* (*en este momento*) now; (*pronto*) in a moment; *ahora mismo* right now; *por ahora* for the present, for the time being; *ahora bien* however; *desde ahora, de ahora en adelante* from now on; *¡hasta ahora!* see you soon

ahorcar ⟨1g⟩ **1** *v/t* hang **2** *v/r* **ahorcarse** hang o.s.

ahorita *adv* L.Am. (*en este momento*) (right) now; *Méx, C.Am.* (*pronto*) in a moment; *Méx, C.Am.* (*hace poco*) just now

ahorrar ⟨1a⟩ **1** *v/t* save; *ahorrar algo a alguien* save s.o. (from) sth **2** *v/i* save (up) **3** *v/r* **ahorrarse** *dinero* save; *fig* spare o.s., save s.o.

ahorro *m* saving; *ahorros pl* savings; *caja de ahorros* savings bank

ahulado *m* C.Am., *Méx* oilskin

ahumar ⟨1a⟩ *v/t* smoke

ahuyentar ⟨1a⟩ **1** *v/t* scare off *o* away **2** *v/r* **ahuyentarse** L.Am. run away

AI *abr* (= *Amnistía Internacional*) AI (= Amnesty International)

airado *adj* angry

airbag *m* AUTO airbag

aire *m* air; *aire acondicionado* air-conditioning; *al aire libre* in the open air; *a mi aire* in my own way; *estar en el aire* fig F be up in the air F; *hace mucho aire* it is very windy

airear ⟨1a⟩ *v/t tb fig* air

airoso *adj*: *salir airoso de algo* do well in sth

aislado *adj* isolated

aislante 1 *adj* insulating, insulation *atr* **2** *m* insulator

aislar ⟨1a⟩ **1** *v/t* isolate; EL insulate **2** *v/r* **aislarse** cut o.s. off

ajardinado *adj* landscaped; *zona -a* area with parks and gardens

a. J.C. *abr* (= *antes de Jesucristo*) BC (= before Christ)

ajedrez *m* chess

ajeno *adj propiedad, problemas etc* someone else's; *me era totalmente ajeno* it was completely alien to me; *estar ajeno a* be unaware of, be oblivious to; *por razones -as a nuestra voluntad* for reasons beyond our control

ajete *m* BOT young garlic

ajetreo *m* bustle

ají *m S. Am.* chili, *Br* chilli

ajiaco *m Col* spicy potato stew

ajillo *m*: *al ajillo* with garlic

ajo *m* BOT garlic; *estar o andar en el ajo* F be in the know F

ajuar *m de novia* trousseau

ajustar ⟨1a⟩ **1** *v/t máquina etc* adjust; *tornillo* tighten; *precio* set; *ajustar cuentas* fig settle a score **2** *v/i* fit **3** *v/r* **ajustarse** *el cinturón* tighten; *ajustarse a algo* fig keep within sth; *ajustarse a la ley* comply with the law

ajuste *m*: *ajuste de cuentas* settling of scores

ajusticiar ⟨1b⟩ *v/t* execute

al *prp* **a** *y art* **el**; **al entrar** on coming in, when we / they *etc* came in

ala *f* wing; MIL flank; *ala delta* hang glider; *cortar las alas a alguien* clip s.o.'s wings

alabanza *f* acclaim

alabar ⟨1a⟩ *v/t* praise, acclaim

alacena *f* larder

alacrán *m* ZO scorpion

alambrada *f* wire fence

alambrar ⟨1a⟩ *v/t* fence

alambre *m* wire; *alambre de espino or de púas* barbed wire

álamo *m* BOT poplar; *álamo temblón* aspen

alarde *m* show, display; *hacer alarde de* make a show of

alardear ⟨1a⟩ *v/i* show off (*de* about)

alargador *m* TÉC extension cord, *Br* extension lead

alargar ⟨1h⟩ **1** *v/t* lengthen; *prenda* let down; *en tiempo* prolong; *mano, brazo* stretch out **2** *v/r* **alargarse** *de sombra, día* get longer, lengthen

A

alarido *m* shriek; **dar alaridos** shriek

alarma *f* (*mecanismo, miedo*) alarm; **dar la voz de alarma** raise the alarm

alarmante *adj* alarming

alarmar ⟨1a⟩ **1** *v/t* alarm **2** *v/r* **alarmarse** become alarmed

alba *f* dawn

albahaca *f* BOT basil

Albania Albania

albañil *m* bricklayer

albaricoque *m* BOT apricot

albatros *m inv* ZO albatross

albedrío *m*: **libre albedrío** free will

alberca *f* reservoir; *Méx* (swimming) pool

albergar ⟨1h⟩ *v/t* (*hospedar*) put up; (*contener*) house; *esperanzas* hold out

albergue *m* refuge, shelter; **albergue juvenil** youth hostel

albino *m*, **-a** *f* albino

albóndiga *f* meatball

albornoz *m* bathrobe

alborotador *m*, **alborotadora** *f* rioter

alborotar ⟨1a⟩ **1** *v/t* stir up; (*desordenar*) disturb **2** *v/i* make a racket **3** *v/r* **alborotarse** get excited; (*inquietarse*) get worked up

alboroto *m* commotion

álbum *m* album

alcachofa *f* BOT artichoke; *de ducha* shower head

alcalde *m*, **-esa** *f* mayor

alcalino *adj* alkaline

alcance *m* reach; *de arma etc* range; *de medida* scope; *de tragedia* extent, scale; **al alcance de la mano** within reach; **¿está al alcance de tu bolsillo?** can you afford it?; **dar alcance a alguien** catch up with s.o.; **poner al alcance de alguien** put within s.o.'s reach

alcancía *f* L.Am. piggy bank

alcantarilla *f* sewer; (*sumidero*) drain

alcanzar ⟨1f⟩ **1** *v/t a alguien* catch up with; *lugar* reach, get to; *en nivel* reach; *cantidad* amount to; *objetivo* achieve **2** *v/i en altura* reach; *en cantidad* be enough; **alcanzar a oír / ver** manage to hear / see

alcaparra *f* BOT caper

alcayata *f* hook

alcázar *m* fortress

alce *m* ZO elk

alcista *adj en bolsa* rising, bull *atr*; **tendencia alcista** upward trend

alcoba *f* S. Am. bedroom

alcohol *m* alcohol; MED rubbing alcohol, *Br* surgical spirit; **alcohol de quemar** denatured alcohol, *Br* methylated spirits *sg*

alcoholemia *f* blood alcohol level; **prueba de alcoholemia** drunkometer test, *Br* Breathalyzer® test

alcohólico 1 *adj* alcoholic **2** *m*, **-a** *f* alcoholic

alcoholismo *m* alcoholism

alcornoque *m* BOT cork oak; **pedazo de alcornoque** F blockhead F

alcurnia *f* ancestry

aldea *f* (small) village

aleación *f* alloy

aleatorio *adj* random

aleccionar ⟨1a⟩ *v/t* instruct; (*regañar*) lecture

aledaños *mpl* surrounding area *sg*; *de ciudad* outskirts

alegador *adj* L.Am. argumentative

alegar ⟨1h⟩ **1** *v/t motivo, razón* cite; **alegar que** claim *o* allege that **2** *v/i* L.Am. (*discutir*) argue; (*quejarse*) moan, gripe

alegrar ⟨1a⟩ **1** *v/t* make happy; (*animar*) cheer up **2** *v/r* **alegrarse** cheer up; F *bebiendo* get tipsy; **alegrarse por alguien** be pleased for s.o. (**de** about)

alegre *adj* (*contento*) happy; *por naturaleza* happy, cheerful; F *bebido* tipsy

alegría *f* happiness

alejar ⟨1a⟩ **1** *v/t* move away **2** *v/r* **alejarse** move away (**de** from); *de situación, ámbito* get away (**de** from); **¡no te alejes mucho!** don't go too far away!

alelar ⟨1a⟩ *v/t* stupefy

aleluya *m & int* hallelujah

alemán 1 *m/adj* German **2** *m*, **-ana** *f persona* German

Alemania Germany

alentado *adj* L.Am. encouraged

alentar ⟨1k⟩ **1** *v/t* (*animar*) encourage; *esperanzas* cherish **2** *v/r* **alentarse** L.Am. get better

alergia *f* allergy

alérgico *adj* allergic (**a** to)

alerta 1 *adv:* ***estar alerta*** be on the alert **2** *f* alert; ***dar la alerta*** raise the alarm; ***poner en alerta*** alert

alertar ⟨1a⟩ *v/t* alert (**de** to)

aleta *f* zo fin; *de buzo* flipper; *de la nariz* wing

aletargarse ⟨1h⟩ *v/r* feel lethargic

aletear ⟨1a⟩ *v/i* flap one's wings

alevosía *f* treachery

alfabético *adj* alphabetical

alfabetizar ⟨1f⟩ *v/t lista etc* put into alphabetical order; ***alfabetizar a alguien*** teach s.o. to read and write

alfabeto *m* alphabet

alfalfa *f* BOT alfalfa

alfanumérico *adj* alphanumeric

alfarero *m,* **-a** *f* potter

alfil *m* bishop

alfiler *m* pin; ***alfiler de gancho*** *Arg* safety pin; ***no cabe un alfiler*** *fig* F there's no room for anything else

alfiletero *m* (*cojín*) pincushion; (*estuche*) needlecase

alfombra *f* carpet; *más pequeña* rug

alfombrado *m* L.Am. carpeting, carpets *pl*

alfombrar ⟨1a⟩ *v/t* carpet

alfombrilla *f* mouse mat

alga *f* BOT alga; *marina* seaweed

álgebra *f* algebra

álgido *adj fig* decisive

algo 1 *pron en frases afirmativas* something; *en frases interrogativas o condicionales* anything; ***algo es algo*** it's something, it's better than nothing **2** *adv* rather, somewhat

algodón *m* cotton; ***criado entre algodones*** F mollycoddled, pampered

alguacil *m,* **alguacilesa** *f* bailiff

alguien *pron en frases afirmativas* somebody, someone; *en frases interrogativas o condicionales* anybody, anyone

algún *adj en frases afirmativas* some; *en frases interrogativas o condicionales* any; ***algún día*** some day

alguno 1 *adj en frases afirmativas* some; *en frases interrogativas o condicionales* any; ***no la influyó de modo alguno*** it

didn't influence her in any way; ***¿has estado alguna vez en …?*** have you ever been to …? **2** *pron: persona* someone, somebody; ***algunos opinan que …*** some people think that …; ***alguno se podrá usar*** *objeto* we'll be able to use some of them

alhaja *f* piece of jewel(le)ry; *fig* gem; ***alhajas*** jewelry *sg*

alhelí *m* BOT wallflower

aliado *m,* **-a** *f* ally

alianza *f* POL alliance; (*anillo*) wedding ring

aliarse ⟨1c⟩ *v/r* form an alliance (**con** with)

alias *m inv* alias

alicaído *adj* F down F

alicatar ⟨1a⟩ *v/t* tile

alicates *mpl* pliers

aliciente *m* (*estímulo*) incentive; (*atractivo*) attraction

alienar ⟨1a⟩ *v/t* alienate

alienígena *m/f* alien

aliento *m* breath; *fig* encouragement

aligerar ⟨1a⟩ *v/t carga* lighten; ***aligerar el paso*** quicken one's pace

alijo *m* MAR consignment

alimentación *f* (*dieta*) diet; *acción* feeding; EL power supply

alimentar ⟨1a⟩ **1** *v/t tb* TÉC, *fig* feed; EL power **2** *v/i* be nourishing **3** *v/r* **alimentarse** feed o.s.; ***alimentarse de algo*** de *persona, animal* live on sth; *de máquina* run on sth

alimento *m* (*comida*) food; ***tiene poco alimento*** it has little nutritional value; ***alimentos dietéticos*** (**de régimen**) slimming aids

alineación *f* DEP line-up

alinear ⟨1a⟩ **1** *v/t* align **2** *v/r* **alinearse** (*ponerse en fila*) line up; POL align o.s. (**con** with)

aliñar ⟨1a⟩ *v/t* dress

aliño *m* dressing

alioli *m* GASTR garlic mayonnaise

alisar ⟨1a⟩ *v/t* smooth

alistarse ⟨1a⟩ *v/r* MIL enlist

aliviar ⟨1b⟩ *v/t* alleviate, relieve

alivio *m* relief

allá adv de lugar (over) there; **allá por los años veinte** back in the twenties; **más allá** further on; **más allá de** beyond; **el más allá** the hereafter; **allá él / ella** F that's up to him / her

allanamiento m: **allanamiento de morada** JUR breaking and entering

allanar ⟨1a⟩ v/t (alisar) smooth; (aplanar) level (out); **obstáculos** overcome

allegado m, -a f relation, relative

allí adv there; **por allí** over there; **dando direcciones** that way; **¡allí está!** there it is!

alma f soul; **se me cayó el alma a los pies** F my heart sank; **llegar al alma** conmover move deeply; **herir** hurt deeply; **no se ve un alma** there isn't a soul to be seen; **lo siento en el alma** I am truly sorry

almacén m warehouse; (tienda) store, shop; **grandes almacenes** pl department store sg

almacenamiento m storage; **almacenamiento de datos** data storage

almacenar ⟨1a⟩ v/t tb INFOR store

almacenero m, -a f storekeeper, shopkeeper

almanaque m almanac

almeja f zo clam

almenas fpl battlements

almendra f almond

almendro m almond tree

almíbar m syrup; **en almíbar** in syrup

almibarado adj fig syrupy

almidón m starch

almirante m admiral

almirez m mortar

almohada f pillow; **consultarlo con la almohada** sleep on it

almohadilla f small cushion; TÉC pad

almohadón m large cushion

almorranas fpl piles

almorzada f Méx lunch

almorzar ⟨1f & 1m⟩ 1 v/i al mediodía have lunch; a media mañana have a mid-morning snack 2 v/t: **almorzar algo** al mediodía have sth for lunch; a media mañana have sth as a mid-morning snack

almuerzo m al mediodía lunch; a media mañana mid-morning snack; **almuerzo de trabajo** working lunch

¿alo? L.Am. hello?

alocado 1 adj crazy **2** m, -a f crazy fool

áloe m BOT aloe

alojamiento m accommodations pl, Br accommodation

alojar ⟨1a⟩ **1** v/t accommodate **2** v/r alojarse stay (**en** in)

alojo m L.Am. → **alojamiento**

alondra f zo lark

alopecia f MED alopecia

alpaca f animal, lana alpaca

alpargata f Esp espadrille

alpinismo m mountaineering

alpinista m/f mountaineer, climber

alpiste m birdseed

alquilar ⟨1a⟩ v/t de usuario rent; de dueño rent out

alquiler m acción: de coche etc rental; de casa renting; dinero rental, Br tb rent; **alquiler de coches** car rental, Br tb car hire

alquitrán m tar

alrededor 1 adv around **2** prp: **alrededor de** around

alrededores mpl surrounding area sg

alta f MED discharge; **dar de alta** MED discharge; **darse de alta** en organismo register

altanero adj arrogant

altar m altar; **llevar al altar** marry

altavoz m loudspeaker

alteración f alteration

alterar ⟨1a⟩ **1** v/t (cambiar) alter; a alguien upset; **alterar el orden público** cause a breach of the peace **2** v/r alterarse get upset (**por** because of)

altercado m argument, altercation fml

alternar ⟨1a⟩ **1** v/t alternate; **alternar el trabajo con el descanso** alternate work and study **2** v/i mix **3** v/r alternarse alternate, take turns

alternativa f alternative

alternativo adj alternative

alterno adj alternate; **corriente -a** EL alternating current; **en días alternos** on alternate days

Alteza f título Highness

altibajos *mpl* ups and downs

altillo *m* (*desván*) attic; *en armario* top (part of the) closet

altiplano *m* high plateau

altisonante *adj* high-flown

altitud *f* altitude

altivo *adj* haughty

alto[1] **1** *adj persona* tall; *precio, número, montaña* high; *-as presiones* high pressure; *alto horno* blast furnace; *clase -a* high class; *en -a mar* on the high seas; *en voz -a* out loud **2** *adv volar, saltar* high; *hablar alto* speak loudly; *pasar por alto* overlook; *poner más alto* TV, RAD turn up; *por todo lo alto* F lavishly **3** *m* (*altura*) height; *Chi* pile

alto[2] *m* halt; (*pausa*) pause; *hacer un alto* stop; *alto el fuego* ceasefire; *¡alto!* halt!

altoparlante *m L.Am.* loudspeaker

altozano *m* hillock

altramuz *m planta* lupin; *semilla* lupin seed

altruismo *m* altruism

altruista *adj* altruistic

altura *f* MAT height; MÚS pitch; AVIA altitude, height; GEOG latitude; *a estas alturas* by this time, by now; *estar a la altura de algo* be up to sth F

alubia *f* BOT kidney bean

alucinación *f* hallucination

alucinado *adj* F gobsmacked F

alucinante *adj* F incredible

alucinar ⟨1a⟩ **1** *v/i* hallucinate **2** *v/t* F amaze

alucine *m*: *de alucine* F amazing

alucinógeno *m* hallucinogen

alud *m* avalanche

aludir ⟨3a⟩ *v/i*: *aludir a algo* allude to sth

aludido: *darse por aludido* take it personally

alumbrar ⟨1a⟩ **1** *v/t* (*dar luz a*) light (up) **2** *v/i* give off light

aluminio *m* aluminum, *Br* aluminium; *papel de aluminio* aluminum (*Br* aluminium) foil

alumno *m*, **-a** *f* student

alusión *f* allusion (*a* to); *hacer alusión a* refer to, allude to

aluvión *m* barrage

alza *f* rise; *en alza en bolsa* rising

alzado *m*, **-a** *f L.Am.* insurgent

alzar ⟨1f⟩ **1** *v/t barrera, brazo* lift, raise; *precios* raise **2** *v/r* alzarse rise; *en armas* rise up

alzo *m C.Am.* theft

a. m. *abr* (= *ante meridiem*) a. m. (= ante meridiem)

ama *f* (*dueña*) owner; *ama de casa* housewife, homemaker; *ama de llaves* housekeeper; *ama de leche or cría L.Am.* wetnurse

amabilidad *f* kindness

amable *adj* kind (*con* to)

amaestrar ⟨1a⟩ *v/t* train

amago *m* threat; *hizo amago de levantarse* she made as if to get up; *amago de infarto* minor heart attack

amainar ⟨1a⟩ *v/i de lluvia, viento* ease up, slacken off

amalgamar ⟨1a⟩ **1** *v/t fig* combine **2** *v/r* amalgamarse amalgamate

amamantar ⟨1a⟩ *v/t bebé* breastfeed; *cría* feed

amanecer 1 ⟨2d⟩ *v/i* get light; *de persona* wake up **2** *m* dawn

amanerado *adj* affected

amante 1 *adj* loving; *es amante de la buena vida* he's fond of good living **2** *m/f en una relación* lover; *los amantes de la naturaleza* nature lovers

amañar ⟨1a⟩ *v/t* F rig F; *partido* fix F

amapola *f* BOT poppy

amar ⟨1a⟩ *v/t* love

amargar ⟨1h⟩ **1** *v/t día, ocasión* spoil; *amargar a alguien* make s.o. bitter **2** *v/r* amargarse get bitter; *amargarse la vida* get upset

amargo *adj tb fig* bitter

amargura *f tb fig* bitterness

amarillento *adj* yellowish

amarillo *m/adj* yellow

amarrar ⟨1a⟩ *v/t L.Am.* (*atar*) tie

amasar ⟨1a⟩ *v/t pan* knead; *fortuna* amass

amatista *f* amethyst

amazona *f* horsewoman

amazónico *adj* GEOG Amazonian

Amazonas: *el Amazonas* the Amazon

ambages *mpl*: *decirlo sin ambages* say

it straight out

ámbar *m* amber; *el semáforo está en ámbar* the lights are yellow, *Br* the lights are at amber

ambición *f* ambition

ambicioso *adj* ambitious

ambidextro, ambidiestro *adj* ambidextrous

ambientador *m* air freshener

ambiental *adj* environmental

ambientar ⟨1a⟩ *v/t película, novela* set **2** *v/r* **ambientarse** be set

ambiente 1 *adj*: *medio ambiente* environment; *temperatura ambiente* room temperature **2** *m* (*entorno*) environment; (*situación*) atmosphere

ambigüedad *f* ambiguity

ambiguo *adj* ambiguous

ámbito *m* area; (*límite*) scope

ambo *m* *Arg* two-piece suit

ambos, ambas *adj* both **2** *pron* both (of us / you / them)

ambulancia *f* ambulance

ambulante 1 *adj* travel(l)ing; *venta ambulante* peddling, hawking **2** *m/f* *L.Am.* (*vendedor*) street seller

ambulatorio 1 *adj* MED out-patient atr **2** *m* out-patient clinic

amedrentar ⟨1a⟩ *v/t* terrify

amén 1 *m* amen **2** *prp*: *amén de* as well as

amenaza *f* threat; *amenaza de bomba* bomb scare

amenazador *adj* threatening

amenazante *adj* threatening

amenazar ⟨1f⟩ **1** *v/t* threaten (*con, de* with) **2** *v/i*: *amenazar con* threaten to; *amenaza tempestad* there's a storm brewing

amenizar ⟨1f⟩ *v/t*: *amenizar algo* make sth more entertaining *o* enjoyable

ameno *adj* enjoyable

América America; *América del Norte* North America; *América del Sur* South America

americana *f* American (woman); *prenda* jacket

americano *m/adj* American

amerizar ⟨1f⟩ *v/i* de nave espacial splash down

ametralladora *f* machine gun

amianto *m* MIN asbestos

amígdala *f* ANAT tonsil

amigdalitis *f* MED tonsillitis

amigo 1 *adj* friendly; *ser amigo de algo* be fond of sth **2** *m*, *-a f* friend; *hacerse amigos* make friends

aminorar ⟨1a⟩ *v/t* reduce; *aminorar la marcha* slow down

amistad *f* friendship; *amistades* friends

amistosamente *adv* amicably

amistoso *adj* friendly; *partido amistoso* DEP friendly (game)

amnesia *f* amnesia

amnistía *f* amnesty

amo *m* (*dueño*) owner; HIST master

amoblado *S. Am.* **1** *adj* furnished **2** *m* furniture

amodorrarse ⟨1a⟩ *v/r* feel sleepy

amoldarse ⟨1a⟩ *v/r* adapt (*a* to)

amonestación *f* warning; DEP caution

amonestar ⟨1a⟩ *v/t* reñir reprimand; DEP caution

amoníaco, amoniaco *m* ammonia

amontonar ⟨1a⟩ **1** *v/t* pile up **2** *v/r* **amontonarse** de objetos, problemas pile up; de gente crowd together

amor *m* love; *amor mío* my love, darling; *amor propio* self-respect; *por amor al arte* fig just for the fun of it; *por amor de Dios* for God's sake; *hacer el amor* make love

amoral *adj* amoral

amoratado *adj* bruised

amordazar ⟨1f⟩ *v/t* gag; *animal, la prensa* muzzle

amorfo *adj* shapeless

amoroso *adj* amorous

amortajar ⟨1a⟩ *v/t* shroud

amortiguador *m* AUTO shock absorber

amortiguar ⟨1i⟩ *v/t impacto* cushion; *sonido* muffle

amortizar ⟨1f⟩ *v/t* pay off; COM *bienes* charge off, *Br* write off

amotinarse ⟨1a⟩ *v/r* rebel

amp. *abr* (= *amperios*) amp (= amperes)

amparar ⟨1a⟩ **1** *v/t* protect; (*ayudar*) help **2** *v/r* **ampararse** seek shelter (*de* from); *ampararse en algo* seek protection in sth

amparo *m* protection; *(cobijo)* shelter; *al amparo de* under the protection of

ampliación *f de casa, carretera* extension; FOT enlargement; *ampliación de capital* COM increase in capital

ampliadora *f* FOT enlarger

ampliamente *adv* widely

ampliar ⟨1c⟩ *v/t plantilla* increase; *negocio* expand; *plazo, edificio* extend; FOT enlarge **2** *v/r ampliarse* broaden

amplificador *m* amplifier

amplificar ⟨1g⟩ *v/t* amplify

amplio *adj casa* spacious; *gama, margen* wide; *falda* full

amplitud *f* breadth

ampolla *f* MED blister; *(botellita)* vial, *Br* phial

ampolleta *f Arg, Chi* light bulb

ampuloso *adj* pompous

amputación *f* amputation

amputar ⟨1a⟩ *v/t brazo, pierna* amputate

amueblar ⟨1a⟩ *v/t* furnish

amuermar ⟨1a⟩ *v/t* F bore

amuleto *m* charm

anabolizante *m* anabolic steroid

anacardo *m* BOT cashew

anaconda *f* ZO anaconda

anacoreta *m/f* hermit

anacrónico *adj* anachronistic

ánade *m* ZO duck

anagrama *m* anagram

anal *adj* anal

anales *mpl* annals

analfabeto 1 *adj* illiterate **2** *m*, -a *f* illiterate

analgésico 1 *adj* painkilling, analgesic **2** *m* painkiller, analgesic

análisis *m inv* analysis; *análisis de mercado* market research; *análisis de sangre* blood test; *análisis de sistemas* INFOR systems analysis

analista *m/f* analyst

analizar ⟨1f⟩ *v/t* analyze

analogía *f* analogy

analógico *adj* analog, *Br* analogue

análogo *adj* analogous

ananá(s) *m S. Am.* BOT pineapple

anarquía *f* anarchy

anárquico *adj* anarchic

anarquista 1 *adj* anarchist atr **2** *m/f* anarchist

anatema *m* anathema

anatomía *f* anatomy

anatómico *adj* anatomical; *asiento anatómico* AUTO anatomically designed seat

anca *f* haunch; *ancas pl de rana* GASTR frogs' legs

ancestral *adj* ancestral

ancho 1 *adj* wide, broad; *a sus -as* at ease, relaxed; *quedarse tan ancho* F carry on as if nothing had happened **2** *m* width; *ancho de vía* FERR gauge; *dos metros de ancho* two meters (*Br* metres) wide

anchoa *f* anchovy

anchura *f* width

anciana *f* old woman

anciano 1 *adj* old **2** *m* old man

ancla *f* MAR anchor

anclar ⟨1a⟩ *v/i* MAR anchor

andadas *fpl: volver a las andadas* F fall back into one's old ways

andador *m para bebé* baby walker; *para anciano* walker, Zimmer®

andamio *m* scaffolding

andanzas *fpl* adventures

andar ⟨1q⟩ **1** *v/i (caminar)* walk; *(funcionar)* work; *andando* on foot; *andar bien / mal fig* go well / badly; *andar con cuidado* be careful; *andar en algo (buscar)* rummage in sth; *andar tras algo* be after sth F; *andar haciendo algo* be doing sth; *¡anda!* come on! **2** *v/t* walk **3** *v/r andarse: andarse con bromas* kid around F

andas *fpl: llevar en andas* carry on one's shoulders

andén *m* platform; *L.Am.* sidewalk, *Br* pavement

Andes *mpl* Andes

andinismo *m L.Am.* mountaineering, climbing

andinista *m/f L.Am.* mountaineer, climber

andino *adj* Andean

Andorra Andorra

andrajoso *adj* ragged

andurriales *mpl*: *por estos andurriales* F around here

anécdota *f* anecdote

anegar ⟨1h⟩ **1** *v/t* flood **2** *v/r* **anegarse de campo, terreno** be flooded; **anegarse en llanto** dissolve into tears

anemia *f* MED an(a)emia

anémico *adj* an(a)emic

anestesia *f* MED an(a)esthesia

anestesiado *adj* an(a)esthetized, under F

anestesiar ⟨1b⟩ *v/t* an(a)esthetize

anexión *f* POL annexation

anexionar ⟨1a⟩ *v/t* POL annex

anexo 1 *adj* attached **2** *m edificio* annex, *Br* annex(e)

anfeta F, **anfetamina** *f* MED amphetamine

anfibio *m/adj* amphibian

anfiteatro *m* TEA amphitheater, *Br* amphitheatre; *de teatro* dress circle

anfitrión *m* host

anfitriona *f* hostess

ánfora *f* *L.Am.* POL ballot box; HIST amphora

ángel *m* angel; **ángel custodio** *or* **de la guarda** guardian angel

angelical *adj* angelic

angina *f* MED: **anginas** *pl* sore throat *sg*, strep throat *sg*; **angina de pecho** angina

anglicano 1 *adj* Anglican **2** *m*, **-a** *f* Anglican

anglicismo *m* Anglicism

anglófono *adj* English-speaking

anglosajón 1 *adj* Anglo-Saxon **2** *m*, **-ona** *f* Anglo-Saxon

angora *f* angora

angosto *adj* narrow

anguila *f* ZO eel

angula *f* ZO, GASTR elver

ángulo *m* MAT, *fig* angle

angustia *f* anguish

angustiado *adj* distraught

angustiante *adj* distressing

angustiar ⟨1b⟩ **1** *v/t* distress **2** *v/r* **angustiarse** agonize (*por* over)

angustioso *adj* agonizing

anhelar ⟨1a⟩ *v/t* long for

anhelo *m* longing, desire (**de** for)

anhídrido *m* QUÍM anhydride; **anhídrido carbónico** carbon dioxide

anidar ⟨1a⟩ *v/i* nest

anilla *f* ring; **cuaderno de anillas** ring binder; **anillas** *pl* DEP rings

anillo *m* ring; **te viene como anillo al dedo** F it suits you perfectly

animación *f* liveliness; *en películas* animation; **hay mucha animación** it's very lively

animado *adj* lively

animador *m* host; **animador turístico** events organizer

animadora *f* hostess; DEP cheerleader

animal 1 *adj* animal *atr*; *fig* stupid **2** *m tb fig* animal; **animal doméstico** *mascota* pet; *de granja* domestic animal

animalada *f*: **decir / hacer una animalada** F say / do something nasty

animar ⟨1a⟩ **1** *v/t* cheer up; (*alentar*) encourage **2** *v/r* **animarse** cheer up

anímico *adj* mental; **estado anímico** state of mind

ánimo *m* spirit; (*coraje*) encouragement; **estado de ánimo** state of mind; **con ánimo de** with the intention of; **¡ánimo!** cheer up!

animosidad *f* animosity

aniquilar ⟨1a⟩ *v/t* annihilate

anís *m* BOT aniseed; *bebida* anisette

aniversario *m* anniversary

ano *m* ANAT anus

anoche *adv* last night; **antes de anoche** the night before last

anochecer ⟨2d⟩ **1** *v/i* get dark; **anocheció** night fell, it got dark **2** *m* dusk

anodino *adj* anodyne; *fig* bland

anómalo *adj* anomalous

anonadar ⟨1a⟩ *v/t*: **anonadar a alguien** take s.o. aback

anónimo 1 *adj* anonymous **2** *m* poison pen letter

anorak *m* anorak

anorexia *f* MED anorexia

anoréxico *adj* anorexic

anormal *adj* abnormal

anotar ⟨1a⟩ *v/t* note down

anquilosarse ⟨1a⟩ *v/r* get stiff

ansia *f* yearning; (*inquietud*) anxiousness

ansiar ⟨1b⟩ *v/t* yearn for, long for

ansiedad *f* anxiety

ansioso *adj* anxious; *está ansioso por verlos* he's longing to see them

anta *f L.Am.* zo tapir

antagonista *m/f* antagonist

antaño *adv* long ago

antártico *adj* Antarctic

Antártida Antarctica

ante¹ *m* suede; zo moose; *Méx (postre)* egg and coconut dessert

ante² *prp posición* before; *dificultad* faced with; *ante todo* above all

anteayer *adv* the day before yesterday

antebrazo *m* forearm

antecedente *m* precedent; *antecedentes penales* previous convictions; *poner a alguien en antecedentes* put s.o. in the picture

antecesor *m*, antecesora *f* predecessor

antediluviano *adj* prehistoric *hum*

antelación *f*: *con antelación* in advance

antemano: *de antemano* beforehand

antena *f de radio, televisión* antenna, *Br* aerial; zo antenna; *antena parabólica* satellite dish

anteojos *mpl* binoculars

antepasado *m*, -a *f* ancestor

antepenúltimo *adj* third last

anteponer ⟨2r⟩ *v/t*: *anteponer algo a algo* put sth before sth

anteproyecto *m* draft

anterior *adj* previous, former

antes 1 *adv* before; *cuanto antes, lo antes posible* as soon as possible; *poco antes* shortly before; *antes que nada* first of all 2 *prp*: *antes de* before

antesala *f* lobby

antiadherente *adj* non-stick

antiaéreo *adj* anti-aircraft *atr*

antibala(s) *adj* bulletproof

antibelicista *adj* anti-war

antibiótico *m* antibiotic

anticiclón *m* anticyclone

anticipado *adj pago* advance *atr; elecciones* early; *por anticipado* in advance

anticipar ⟨1a⟩ 1 *v/t sueldo* advance; *fecha, viaje* move up, *Br* bring forward; *información, noticias* give a preview of 2 *v/r anticiparse de suceso* come early; *anticiparse a alguien* get there ahead of s.o.

anticonceptivo 1 *adj* contraceptive *atr* 2 *m* contraceptive

anticongelante *m* antifreeze

anticonstitucional *adj* unconstitutional

anticuado *adj* antiquated

anticuario *m* antique dealer

anticuerpo *m* BIO antibody

antideslizante *adj* non-slip

antidisturbios *adj*: *policía antidisturbios* riot police

antidoping *adj*: *control antidoping* dope test, drug test

antídoto *m* MED antidote; *fig* cure

antifaz *m* mask

antiguamente *adv* in the past

antigüedad *f* age; *en el trabajo* length of service; *antigüedades* antiques

antiguo *adj* old; *del pasado remoto* ancient; *su antiguo novio* her old *o* former boyfriend

antiinflamatorio *adj* MED anti-inflammatory

Antillas *fpl* West Indies

antílope *m* zo antelope

antinatural *adj* unnatural

antinuclear *adj* anti-nuclear

antioxidante *m/adj* antioxidant

antipatía *f* antipathy, dislike

antipático *adj* disagreeable, unpleasant

antípodas *mpl* antipodes

antirreglamentario *adj* DEP *posición* offside; *una jugada -a* a foul

antirrobo *m* AUTO antitheft device

antisemitismo *m* anti-Semitism

antiséptico *m/adj* antiseptic

antisocial *adj* antisocial

antiterrorista *adj brigada* antiterrorist; *la lucha antiterrorista* the fight against terrorism

antítesis *f inv* antithesis

antojarse ⟨1a⟩ *v/r*: *se le antojó salir* he felt like going out; *se me antoja que ...* it seems to me that ...

antojo *m* whim; *de embarazada* craving; *a mi antojo* as I please

antología *f* anthology; *de antología fig F* fantastic, incredible F

antonomasia *f*: *por antonomasia* par excellence

antorcha f torch

antro m F dive F, dump F

antropófago m, **-a** f cannibal

antropología f anthropology

anual adj annual

anualidad f annual payment

anualmente adv yearly

anudar ⟨1a⟩ v/t knot

anular[1] ⟨1a⟩ v/t cancel; matrimonio annul; gol disallow

anular[2] adj ring-shaped; dedo anular ring finger

anunciante m COM advertiser

anunciar ⟨1b⟩ v/t announce; COM advertise

anuncio m announcement; (presagio) sign; COM advertisement; anuncios luminoso illuminated sign; anuncios por palabras, pequeños anuncios classified advertisements

anzuelo m (fish) hook; morder or tragar el anzuelo fig F take the bait

añadidura f: por añadidura in addition

añadir ⟨3a⟩ v/t add

añejo adj mature

añicos mpl: hacer añicos F smash to smithereens F

año m year; año bisiesto leap year; año fiscal fiscal year, Br financial year; año luz light year; año nuevo New Year; ¿cuándo cumples años? when's your birthday?; ¿cuántos años tienes? how old are you?; a los diez años at the age of ten; los años veinte the twenties

añorar ⟨1a⟩ v/t miss

aorta f ANAT aorta

apabullante adj overwhelming

apabullar ⟨1a⟩ v/t overwhelm

apacible adj mild-mannered

apaciguar ⟨1i⟩ **1** v/t pacify, calm down **2** v/r apaciguarse calm down

apadrinar ⟨1a⟩ v/t be godparent to; político support, back; artista etc sponsor; apadrinar a la novia give the bride away

apagado adj fuego out; luz off; persona dull; color subdued

apagar ⟨1h⟩ **1** v/t televisor, luz turn off; fuego put out **2** v/r apagarse de luz go off; de fuego go out

apagón m blackout

apaisado adj landscape atr

apalabrar ⟨1a⟩ v/t agree (verbally)

apalancar ⟨1g⟩ **1** v/t lever **2** v/r apalancarse F settle

apalear ⟨1a⟩ v/t beat

apañar ⟨1a⟩ **1** v/t tidy up; aparato repair; resultado rig F, fix F; estamos apañados F we've had it F **2** v/r apañarse manage; apañárselas manage, get by

apaño m fig F makeshift repair

aparador m sideboard; Méx (escaparate) shop window

aparato m piece of equipment; doméstico appliance; BIO, ANAT system; de partido político machine; aparato respiratorio respiratory system; al aparato TELEC speaking

aparatoso adj spectacular

aparcacoches m inv valet

aparcamiento m parking lot, Br car park; aparcamiento subterráneo underground parking garage, Br underground car park

aparcar ⟨1g⟩ **1** v/t park; tema, proyecto shelve **2** v/i park

aparearse ⟨1a⟩ v/r ZO mate

aparecer ⟨2d⟩ **1** v/i appear **2** v/r aparecerse turn up

aparejador m, **aparejadora** f architectural technician, Br quantity surveyor

aparejo m: aparejos pl de pesca fishing gear sg

aparentar ⟨1a⟩ v/t pretend; no aparenta la edad que tiene she doesn't look her age

aparente adj (evidente) apparent; L.Am. (fingido) feigned

aparentemente adv apparently

aparición f appearance; (fantasma) apparition; hacer su aparición make one's appearance

apariencia f appearance; en apariencia outwardly; las apariencias engañan appearances can be deceptive

apartado m section; apartado de correos PO box

apartamento m apartment, Br flat

apartamiento *m* separation; *L.Am.* (*apartamento*) apartment, *Br* flat

apartar ⟨1a⟩ **1** *v/t* separate; *para después* set *o* put aside; *de un sitio* move away (**de** from); **apartar a alguien de hacer algo** dissuade s.o. from doing sth **2** *v/r* **apartarse** move aside (**de** from); **apartarse del tema** stray from the subject

aparte *adv* to one side; (*por separado*) separately; **aparte de** aside from, *Br* apart from; **punto y aparte** new paragraph

apasionado 1 *adj* passionate **2** *m/f* enthusiast

apasionante *adj* fascinating

apasionar ⟨1a⟩ *v/t* fascinate

apatía *f* apathy

apático *adj* apathetic

apdo. *abr* (= **apartado (de correos)**) PO Box (= Post Office Box)

apearse ⟨1a⟩ *v/r* get off, alight *fml*; **apearse de algo** get off sth, alight from sth *fml*

apechugar ⟨1h⟩ *v/i*: **apechugar con algo** cope with sth

apego *m* attachment

apelación *f* JUR appeal

apelar ⟨1a⟩ *v/t tb* JUR appeal (**a** to)

apellidarse ⟨1a⟩ *v/r*: **¿cómo se apellida?** what's your / his / her surname?; **se apellida Ocaña** his / her surname is Ocaña

apellido *m* surname; **apellido de soltera** maiden name

apelmazarse ⟨1f⟩ *v/r de lana* get matted; *de arroz* stick together

apelotonarse ⟨1a⟩ *v/r* crowd together

apenado *adj* sad; *L.Am.* (*avergonzado*) ashamed; *L.Am.* (*incómodo*) embarrassed; *L.Am.* (*tímido*) shy

apenar ⟨1a⟩ **1** *v/t* sadden **2** *v/r* **apenarse** be upset *o* distressed; *L.Am.* (*avergonzarse*) be ashamed; *L.Am.* (*sentir incómodo*) be embarrassed; *L.Am.* (*ser tímido*) be shy

apenas 1 *adv* hardly, scarcely **2** *conj* as soon as

apéndice *m* appendix

apendicitis *f* MED appendicitis

apercibirse ⟨3a⟩ *v/r*: **apercibirse de algo** notice sth

apergaminado *adj fig* wrinkled

aperitivo *m comida* appetizer; *bebida* aperitif

apero *m utensilio* implement; *L.Am.* (*arneses*) harness; **aperos de labranza** farming implements

apertura *f* opening; FOT aperture; POL opening up

apesadumbrado *adj* heavy-hearted

apestar ⟨1a⟩ **1** *v/t* stink out F **2** *v/i* reek (**a** of); **huele que apesta** it reeks

apestoso *adj* smelly

apetecer ⟨2d⟩ *v/i*: **me apetece ir a dar un paseo** I feel like going for a walk; **¿qué te apetece?** what do you feel like?

apetito *m* appetite

apetitoso *adj* appetizing

apiadarse ⟨1a⟩ *v/r* take pity (**de** on)

ápice *m*: **ni un ápice** *fig* not an ounce; **no ceder ni un ápice** *fig* not give an inch

apicultura *f* beekeeping

apilar ⟨1a⟩ *v/t* pile up

apiñarse ⟨1a⟩ *v/r* crowd together

apio *m* BOT celery

apisonadora *f* steamroller

aplacar ⟨1g⟩ *v/t hambre* satisfy; *sed* quench; *a alguien* calm down, placate *fml*

aplanar ⟨1a⟩ *v/t* level, flatten; **aplanar las calles** *C.Am., Pe* hang around the streets **2** *v/r* **aplanarse** *fig* (*descorazonarse*) lose heart

aplastante *adj* overwhelming; *calor* suffocating

aplastar ⟨1a⟩ *v/t tb fig* crush

aplaudida *f L.Am.* applause

aplaudir ⟨3a⟩ **1** *v/i* applaud, clap **2** *v/t tb fig* applaud

aplauso *m* round of applause

aplazamiento *m de visita, viaje* postponement

aplazar ⟨1f⟩ *v/t visita, viaje* put off, postpone; *Arg* fail

aplicación *f* application

aplicar ⟨1g⟩ **1** *v/t* apply; *sanciones* impose **2** *v/r* **aplicarse** apply o.s.

aplomo *m* composure, aplomb *fml*

apocalíptico *adj* apocalyptic

apócrifo *adj* apocryphal

apodar ⟨1a⟩ v/t nickname, call
apoderado m COM agent
apoderar ⟨1a⟩ **1** v/t authorize **2** v/r apoderarse take possession o control (**de** of)
apodo m nickname
apogeo m fig height, peak; **estar en su apogeo** be at its height
apolillarse ⟨1a⟩ v/r get moth-eaten
apolítico adj apolitical
apología f defense, Br defence
apoltronarse ⟨1a⟩ v/r en asiento settle down; en trabajo, rutina get into a rut
apoplejía f MED apoplexy; **ataque de apoplejía** MED stroke
aporrear ⟨1a⟩ v/t pound on
aportación f contribution; COM investment
aportar ⟨1a⟩ v/t contribute; **aportar pruebas** JUR provide evidence
apósito m dressing
aposta adv on purpose, deliberately
apostar ⟨1m⟩ **1** v/t bet (**por** on) **2** v/i bet; **apostar por algo** opt for sth **3** v/r apostarse bet; MIL position o.s.
apóstata m/f apostate
apóstol m apostle
apóstrofe, apóstrofo m apostrophe
apoteosis f fig climax
apoyar ⟨1a⟩ **1** v/t lean (**en** against), rest (**en** against); (respaldar, confirmar) support **2** v/r apoyarse lean (**en** on; **contra** against); en persona rely (**en** on); ¿**en qué te apoyas para decir eso?** what are you basing that comment on?
apoyo m fig support
apreciable adj (visible) appreciable, noticeable; (considerable) considerable, substantial
apreciar ⟨1b⟩ v/t appreciate; (sentir afecto por) be fond of, think highly of
aprecio m respect
apremiar ⟨1b⟩ v/t pressure, put pressure on **2** v/i: **el tiempo apremia** time is pressing
aprender ⟨2a⟩ **1** v/t learn **2** v/r aprenderse learn; **aprenderse algo de memoria** learn sth (off) by heart
aprendiz m, **aprendiza** f apprentice, trainee

aprendizaje m apprenticeship
aprensión f (miedo) apprehension; (asco) squeamishness
apresar ⟨1a⟩ v/t nave seize; ladrón, animal catch, capture
aprestarse ⟨1a⟩ v/r: **aprestarse a** get ready to
apresurar ⟨1a⟩ **1** v/t hurry **2** v/r apresurarse hurry up; **apresurarse a hacer algo** hurry o rush to do sth
apretado adj tight; **iban muy apretados en el coche** they were very cramped o squashed in the car
apretar ⟨1k⟩ **1** v/t botón press; (pellizcar, pinzar) squeeze; tuerca tighten; **apretar el paso** quicken one's pace; **apretar los puños** clench one's fists **2** v/i de ropa, zapato be too tight **3** v/r apretarse squeeze o squash together; **apretarse el cinturón** fig tighten one's belt
apretón m squeeze; **apretón de manos** handshake
apretujar ⟨1a⟩ **1** v/t F squeeze, squash **2** v/r apretujarse F squash o squeeze together
aprieto m predicament
aprisa adv quickly
aprisionar ⟨1a⟩ v/t fig trap
aprobación f approval; de ley passing
aprobado m EDU pass
aprobar ⟨1m⟩ v/t approve; comportamiento, idea approve of; examen pass
apropiado adj appropriate, suitable
apropiarse ⟨1b⟩ v/r: **apropiarse de algo** take sth
aprovechado 1 adj desp opportunistic **2** m, -a f desp opportunist
aprovechar ⟨1a⟩ **1** v/t take advantage of; tiempo, espacio make good use of; **quiero aprovechar la ocasión para ...** I would like to take this opportunity to ... **2** v/i take the opportunity (**para** to); **¡que aproveche!** enjoy your meal! **3** v/r aprovecharse take advantage (**de** of)
aprovisionarse ⟨1a⟩ v/r stock up (**de** on)
aproximadamente adv approximately
aproximado adj approximate
aproximar ⟨1a⟩ **1** v/t bring closer **2** v/r aproximarse approach

aptitud f aptitude (*para* for), flair (*para* for)

apto adj suitable (*para* for); *para servicio militar* fit; EDU pass

apuesta f bet

apuesto adj handsome

apunado adj Pe, Bol suffering from altitude sickness

apunarse ⟨1a⟩ v/r S. Am. get altitude sickness

apuntador m, **apuntadora** f TEA prompter

apuntalar ⟨1a⟩ v/t *edificio* shore up; *fig* prop up

apuntar ⟨1a⟩ **1** v/t (*escribir*) note down, make a note of; TEA prompt; *en curso, para viaje etc* put down (**en**, **a** on; **para** for); *apuntar con el dedo* point at *o* to **2** v/i con arma aim **3** v/r **apuntarse** put one's name down (**para**, **en** *or* **a** for); *¡me apunto!* count me in!

apunte m note

apuñalar ⟨1a⟩ v/t stab

apurado adj L.Am. (con prisa) in a hurry; (pobre) short (of cash)

apurar ⟨1a⟩ **1** v/t *vaso* finish off; *a alguien* pressure, put pressure on **2** v/i Chi: **no me apura** I'm not in a hurry for it **3** v/r **apurarse** worry; L.Am. (darse prisa) hurry (up)

apuro m predicament, tight spot F; *vergüenza* embarrassment; L.Am. rush; *me da apuro* I'm embarrassed

aquejado adj: *estar aquejado de* be suffering from

aquel, aquella, aquellos, aquellas det singular that; plural those

aquél, aquélla, aquéllos, aquéllas pron singular that (one); plural those (ones)

aquello pron that

aquí adv en el espacio here; en el tiempo now; *desde aquí* from here; *por aquí* here

árabe 1 m/f & adj Arab **2** m idioma Arabic **Arabia Saudí** Saudi Arabia

arado m plow, Br plough

arancel m tariff

arancelario adj tariff atr

arándano m blueberry

arandela f washer

araña f zo spider; *lámpara* chandelier

arañar ⟨1a⟩ v/t scratch

arañazo m scratch

arar ⟨1a⟩ v/t plow, Br plough

arbitraje m arbitration

arbitrar ⟨1a⟩ v/t en fútbol, boxeo referee; en tenis, béisbol umpire; en conflicto arbitrate

arbitrario adj arbitrary

árbitro m en fútbol, boxeo referee; en tenis, béisbol umpire; en conflicto arbitrator

árbol m tree; *árbol genealógico* family tree

arboleda f grove

arbusto m shrub, bush

arca f chest; *arca de Noé* Noah's Ark

arcada f MED: *me provocó arcadas* it made me retch *o* heave F

arcaico adj archaic

arce m BOT maple

arcén m shoulder, Br hard shoulder

archidiócesis f inv archdiocese

archipiélago m archipelago

archivador m filing cabinet

archivar ⟨1a⟩ v/t papeles, documentos file; asunto shelve

archivo m archive; INFOR file

arcilla f clay

arco m ARQUI arch; MÚS bow; L.Am. DEP goal; *arco iris* rainbow

arder ⟨2a⟩ v/i burn; *estar muy caliente* be exceedingly hot; *la reunión está que arde* F the meeting is about to erupt F

ardilla f zo squirrel

ardor m entusiasmo fervo(u)r; *ardor de estómago* heartburn

arduo adj arduous

área f area; DEP *área de castigo or de penalty* penalty area; *área de descanso* pull-in (at the side of the road); *área de servicio* service area

arena f sand; *arenas pl movedizas* quicksand sg

arenga f morale-boosting speech; (sermón) harangue

arenque m herring

arepa f C.Am., Ven cornmeal roll

arete m L.Am. joya earring

Argelia Algeria

Argentina Argentina

argentino 1 *adj* Argentinian **2** *m*, **-a** *f* Argentinian

argolla *f L.Am.* ring

argot *m* slang

argucia *f* clever argument

argüir ⟨3g⟩ *v/t & v/i* argue

argumentar ⟨1a⟩ *v/t* argue

argumento *m razón* argument; *de libro, película etc* plot

árido *adj* arid, dry; *fig* dry

Aries *m/f inv* ASTR Aries

arisco *adj* unfriendly

aristocracia *f* aristocracy

aristócrata *m/f* aristocrat

aristocrático *adj* aristocratic

aritmética *f* arithmetic

arma *f weapon;* ***arma blanca*** knife; ***arma de doble filo*** *or* ***de dos filos*** *fig* two-edged sword; ***arma de fuego*** firearm; ***alzarse en armas*** rise up in arms

armada *f* navy

armadillo *m* ZO armadillo

armado *adj* armed

armadura *f* armo(u)r

armamento *m* armaments *pl*

armar ⟨1a⟩ **1** *v/t* MIL arm; TÉC assemble, put together; ***armar un escándalo*** F kick up a fuss F, make a scene F **2** *v/r* **armarse** arm o.s.; ***la que se va a armar*** F all hell will break loose F; ***armarse de valor*** pluck up courage

armario *m* closet, *Br* wardrobe; *de cocina* cabinet, *Br* cupboard

armazón *f* skeleton, framework

armisticio *m* armistice

armonía *f* harmony

armónica *f* harmonica, mouth organ

armonioso *adj* harmonious

armonizar ⟨1f⟩ **1** *v/t* harmonize; *diferencias* reconcile **2** *v/i de color, estilo* blend (**con** with); *de persona* get on (**con** with)

arnés *m* harness; *para niños* leading strings *pl*, *Br* leading reins *pl*

aro *m* hoop; *L.Am.* (*pendiente*) earring; ***entrar*** *or* ***pasar por el aro*** *fig* F bite the bullet, take the plunge

aroma *m* aroma; *de flor* scent

arpa *f* harp

arpía *f* harpy

arpón *m* harpoon

arquear ⟨1a⟩ *v/t espalda* arch; *cejas* raise

arqueología *f* arch(a)eology

arqueológico *adj* arch(a)eological

arqueólogo *m*, **-a** *f* arch(a)eologist

arquero *m* archer; *L.Am. en fútbol* goalkeeper

arquetipo *m* archetype

arquitectónico *adj* architectural

arquitecto *m*, **-a** *f* architect

arquitectura *f* architecture

arrabal *m* poor outlying area

arraigado *adj* entrenched

arraigar ⟨1h⟩ **1** *v/i* take root **2** *v/r* **arraigarse** *de persona* settle (**en** in); *de costumbre, idea* take root

arramblar ⟨1a⟩ *v/t* (*destruir*) destroy

arrancar ⟨1g⟩ **1** *v/t planta, página* pull out; *vehículo* start (up); (*quitar*) snatch **2** *v/i de vehículo, máquina* start (up); INFOR boot (up); *Chi* (*huir*) run away **3** *v/r* **arrancarse** *Chi* run away

arranque *m* AUTO starting mechanism; (*energía*) drive; (*ataque*) fit

arrasar ⟨1a⟩ **1** *v/t* devastate **2** *v/i* F be a big hit

arrastrar ⟨1a⟩ **1** *v/t por el suelo*, INFOR drag (**por** along); (*llevarse*) carry away **2** *v/i por el suelo* trail on the ground **3** *v/r* **arrastrarse** crawl; *fig* (*humillarse*) grovel (**delante de** to)

arrastre *m*: ***estar para el arrastre*** *fig* F be fit to drop F

arreada *f Rpl* round-up

arrebatar ⟨1a⟩ *v/t* snatch (**a** from)

arrebato *m* fit

arrebujarse ⟨1a⟩ *v/r* F wrap o.s. up; *en cama* snuggle up

arreciar ⟨1b⟩ *v/i* get worse; *de viento* get stronger

arrecife *m* reef

arredrarse ⟨1a⟩ *v/r* be intimidated (**ante** by)

arreglar ⟨1a⟩ **1** *v/t* (*reparar*) fix, repair; (*ordenar*) tidy (up); (*solucionar*) sort out; MÚS arrange; ***arreglar cuentas*** settle up; *fig* settle scores **2** *v/r* **arreglarse**

get (o.s.) ready; *de problema* get sorted out; (*apañarse*) manage; **arreglárselas** manage

arreglo *m* (*reparación*) repair; (*solución*) solution; (*acuerdo*) agreement; MÚS arrangement; **arreglo de cuentas** settling of scores; **con arreglo a** in accordance with; **esto no tiene arreglo** there's nothing to be done

arrellanarse ⟨1a⟩ *v/r* settle

arremangarse ⟨1h⟩ *v/r* roll up one's sleeves

arremeter ⟨2a⟩ *v/i:* **arremeter contra** charge (at); *fig* (*criticar*) attack

arremolinarse ⟨1a⟩ *v/r* mill around

arrendamiento *m* renting

arrendar ⟨1k⟩ *v/t L.Am.* (*dar en alquiler*) rent (out), let; (*tomar en alquiler*) rent; **se arrenda** for rent

arreo *m Rpl* driving, herding; (*manada*) herd

arrepentimiento *m* repentance; (*cambio de opinión*) change of heart

arrepentirse ⟨3i⟩ *v/r* be sorry; (*cambiar de opinión*) change one's mind; **arrepentirse de algo** regret sth

arrestar ⟨1a⟩ *v/t* arrest

arresto *m* arrest

arriba 1 *adv* ◇ *situación* up; *en edificio* upstairs; **ponlo ahí arriba** put it up there; **el cajón de arriba** *siguiente* the next drawer up, the drawer above; *último* the top drawer; **arriba del todo** right at the top

◇ *dirección* up; *en edificio* upstairs; **sigan hacia arriba** keep going up; **me miró de arriba abajo** *fig* she looked me up and down

◇ *con cantidades*: **de diez para arriba** ten or above **2** *int* long live

arribeño *m*, **-a** *f L.Am.* uplander, highlander

arribista *m/f* social climber

arriesgado *adj* adventurous

arriesgar ⟨1h⟩ **1** *v/t* risk **2** *v/r* **arriesgarse** take a risk; **arriesgarse a hacer algo** risk doing sth

arrimar ⟨1a⟩ **1** *v/t* move closer; **arrimar el hombro** F pull one's weight **2** *v/r* **arri-**

marse move closer (**a** to)

arrinconar ⟨1a⟩ *v/t* (*acorralar*) corner; *libros etc* put away; *persona* cold-shoulder

arroba *f* INFOR 'at' symbol, @

arrodillarse ⟨1a⟩ *v/r* kneel (down)

arrogancia *f* arrogance

arrogante *adj* arrogant

arrojar ⟨1a⟩ **1** *v/t* (*lanzar*) throw; *resultado* produce; (*vomitar*) throw up **2** *v/r* **arrojarse** throw o.s.

arrollador *adj* overwhelming

arropar ⟨1a⟩ *v/t* wrap up; *fig* protect

arrope *m Rpl, Chi, Pe* fruit syrup

arroyo *m* stream; **sacar a alguien del arroyo** *fig* lift s.o. out of the gutter

arroz *m* rice; **arroz con leche** rice pudding

arruga *f* wrinkle

arrugar ⟨1h⟩ **1** *v/t* wrinkle; **2** *v/r* **arrugarse** *de piel, ropa* get wrinkled

arruinado *adj* ruined, broke F

arruinar ⟨1a⟩ **1** *v/t* ruin **2** *v/r* **arruinarse** be ruined

arrullo *m de paloma* cooing; *para niño* lullaby

arsenal *m* arsenal

arsénico *m* arsenic

art *abr* (= **artículo**) art. (= article)

art.° *abr* (= **artículo**) art. (= article)

arte *m* (*pl f*) art; **arte dramático** dramatic art; **bellas artes** *pl* fine art *sg*; **malas artes** *pl* guile *sg*

artefacto *m* (*dispositivo*) device

arteria *f* artery

arterio(e)sclerosis *f* arteriosclerosis

artesana *f* craftswoman

artesanía *f* (handi)crafts *pl*

artesano *m* craftsman

Ártico *zona, océano* Arctic

articulación *f* ANAT, TÉC joint; *de sonidos* articulation

artículo *m de periódico*, GRAM, JUR article; COM product, item

artificial *adj* artificial

artillería *f* artillery; **artillería ligera / pesada** light / heavy artillery

artilugio *m aparato* gadget

artimaña *f* trick

artista *m/f* artist

artístico *adj* artistic

artritis *f* MED arthritis

arveja *f Rpl, Chi, Pe* BOT pea

arzobispo *m* archbishop

as *m tb fig* ace

asa *f* handle

asado 1 *adj* roast *atr* **2** *m* roast

asalariado *m*, **-a** *f* wage earner; *de empresa* employee

asaltante *m/f* assailant

asaltar ⟨1a⟩ *v/t persona* attack; *banco* rob

asalto *m a persona* attack (**a** on); *robo* robbery, raid; *en boxeo* round

asamblea *f reunión* meeting; *ente* assembly

asar ⟨1a⟩ **1** *v/t* roast; *asar a la parrilla* broil, *Br* grill **2** *v/r asarse fig* F be roasting F

ascender ⟨2g⟩ **1** *v/t a empleado* promote **2** *v/i de precios, temperatura etc* rise; *de montañero* climb; DEP, *en trabajo* be promoted (**a** to)

ascensión *f* ascent

ascenso *m de temperatura, precios* rise (**de** in); *de montaña* ascent; DEP, *en trabajo* promotion

ascensor *m* elevator, *Br* lift

ascético *adj* ascetic

asco *m* disgust; *me da asco* I find it disgusting; *¡qué asco!* how revolting *o* disgusting!

ascua *f* ember; *estar en or sobre ascuas* be on tenterhooks

asearse ⟨1a⟩ *v/r* wash up, *Br* have a wash

asediar ⟨1b⟩ *v/t tb fig* besiege

asedio *m* MIL siege, blockade; *a alguien* hounding

aseguradora *f* insurance company

asegurar ⟨1a⟩ **1** *v/t (afianzar)* secure; *(prometer)* assure; *(garantizar)* guarantee; COM insure **2** *v/r asegurarse* make sure

asentamiento *m* settlement

asentarse ⟨1k⟩ *v/r* settle

asentir ⟨3i⟩ *v/i* agree (**a** to), consent (**a** to); *con la cabeza* nod

aseo *m* cleanliness; *(baño)* restroom, toilet

aséptico *adj* aseptic

asequible *adj precio* affordable; *obra* accessible

aserrar ⟨1k⟩ *v/t* saw

aserrín *m L.Am.* sawdust

asesinar ⟨1a⟩ *v/t* murder; POL assassinate

asesinato *m* murder; POL assassination

asesino *m*, **-a** *f* murderer; POL assassin

asesor *m*, **asesora** *f* consultant, advisor, *Br* adviser; *asesor fiscal* financial advisor (*Br* adviser); *asesor de imagen* public relations consultant

asesorar ⟨1a⟩ *v/t* advise

asesoría *f* consultancy

asestar ⟨1a⟩ *v/t golpe* deal (**a** to); *me asestó una puñalada* he stabbed me

asfaltar ⟨1a⟩ *v/t* asphalt

asfalto *m* asphalt

asfixia *f* asphyxiation

asfixiante *adj* asphyxiating, suffocating

asfixiar ⟨1b⟩ **1** *v/t* asphyxiate, suffocate **2** *v/r asfixiarse* asphyxiate, suffocate

así 1 *adv (de este modo)* like this; *(de ese modo)* like that; *así no más S. Am.* just like that; *así pues* so; *así que* so; *así de grande* this big **2** *conj: así como al igual que* while, whereas

Asia Asia

asiático 1 *adj* Asian **2** *m*, **-a** *f* Asian

asiduidad *f* frequency; *con asiduidad con frecuencia* regularly

asiduo *adj* regular

asiento *m* seat; *tomar asiento* take a seat

asignación *f acción* allocation; *dinero* allowance

asignar ⟨1a⟩ *v/t* allocate; *persona, papel* assign

asignatura *f* subject

asilarse ⟨1a⟩ *v/r* take refuge, seek asylum

asilo *m* home, institution; POL asylum; *asilo de ancianos* old people's home

asimétrico *adj* asymmetrical

asimilar ⟨1a⟩ *v/t* assimilate

asimismo *adv (también)* also; *(igualmente)* in the same way, likewise

asistencia *f (ayuda)* assistance; *a lugar* attendance (**a** at); *asistencia en carretera* AUTO roadside assistance; *asistencia médica* medical care

asistenta *f* cleaner, cleaning woman

asistente *m/f* (*ayudante*) assistant; **asistente social** social worker; **los asistentes** those present

asistir ⟨3a⟩ **1** *v/t* help, assist **2** *v/i* be present; **asistir a una boda** attend a wedding

asma *f* asthma

asmático *adj* asthmatic

asno *m* zo donkey; *persona* idiot

asociación *f* association

asociar ⟨1b⟩ **1** *v/t* associate; **asociar a alguien con algo** associate s.o. with sth **2** *v/r* asociarse team up (**con** with), go into partnership (**con** with); **asociarse a grupo, club** become a member of

asolar ⟨1m⟩ *v/t* devastate

asoleada *f*: **pegarse una asoleada** *Bol*, *Pe* sunbathe

asomar ⟨1a⟩ **1** *v/t* put o stick out **2** *v/i* show **3** *v/r* asomarse lean out; **asomarse a** or **por la ventana** lean out of the window

asombrado *adj* amazed

asombrar ⟨1a⟩ **1** *v/t* amaze, astonish **2** *v/r* asombrarse be amazed o astonished

asombro *m* amazement, astonishment

asombroso *adj* amazing

asomo *m*: **ni por asomo** no way

asorocharse ⟨1a⟩ *v/r* *Pe*, *Bol* get altitude sickness

aspecto *m* de persona, cosa look, appearance; (*faceta*) aspect; **tener buen aspecto** look good

áspero *adj superficie* rough; *sonido* harsh; *persona* abrupt

aspersor *m* sprinkler

aspiraciones *fpl* aspirations

aspirador *m*, aspiradora *f* vacuum cleaner

aspirante *m/f a cargo* candidate (**a** for); *a título* contender (**a** for)

aspirar ⟨1a⟩ **1** *v/t* suck up; *al respirar* inhale, breathe in **2** *v/i*: **aspirar a** aspire to

aspirina *f* aspirin

asqueado *adj* disgusted

asquear ⟨1a⟩ *v/t* disgust

asqueroso **1** *adj* (*sucio*) filthy; (*repugnante*) revolting, disgusting **2** *m*, -a *f* creep

asterisco *m* asterisk

astigmatismo *m* astigmatism

astilla *f* splinter; **astillas** *pl para fuego* kindling *sg*; **hacer astillas algo** *fig* smash sth to pieces

astillero *m* shipyard

astral *adj* astral

astringente *m/adj* astringent

astro *m* AST, *fig* star

astrología *f* astrology

astrólogo *m*, -a *f* astrologer

astronauta *m/f* astronaut

astronave *f* spaceship

astronomía *f* astronomy

astronómico *adj* astronomical

astrónomo *m*, -a *f* astronomer

astucia *f* shrewdness, astuteness

astuto *adj* shrewd, astute

asumir ⟨3a⟩ *v/t* assume; (*aceptar*) accept, come to terms with

asunto *m* matter; F (*relación*) affair; **asuntos exteriores** foreign affairs; **no es asunto tuyo** it's none of your business

asustar ⟨1a⟩ **1** *v/t* frighten, scare **2** *v/r* asustarse be frightened o scared

atacar ⟨1g⟩ *v/t* attack

atajar ⟨1a⟩ **1** *v/t* check the spread of, contain; *L.Am. pelota* catch **2** *v/i* take a short cut

atajo *m L.Am.* short cut

atañer ⟨2f⟩ *v/i* concern

ataque *m* (*agresión*) attack; (*acceso*) fit; **ataque cardíaco** or **al corazón** MED heart attack; **le dio un ataque de risa** she burst out laughing

atar ⟨1a⟩ *v/t* tie (up); *fig* tie down

atardecer ⟨2d⟩ **1** *v/i* get dark **2** *m* dusk

atareado *adj* busy

atascar ⟨1g⟩ **1** *v/t* block **2** *v/r* atascarse *de cañería* get blocked; *de mecanismo* jam, stick; *al hablar* dry up

atasco *m* traffic jam

ataúd *m* coffin, casket

atemorizar ⟨1f⟩ *v/t* frighten

atención *f* attention; (*cortesía*) courtesy; **¡atención!** your attention, please!; **llamar la atención a alguien** *reñir* tell s.o. off; *por ser llamativo* attract s.o.'s attention; **prestar atención** pay attention

A

(*a* to)

atender ⟨2g⟩ **1** *v/t a enfermo* look after; *en tienda* attend to, serve **2** *v/i* pay attention (*a* to)

atenerse ⟨2l⟩ *v/r:* **atenerse a** *normas* abide by; *consecuencias* face, accept; *saber a qué atenerse* know where one stands

atentado *m* attack (*contra, a* on); **atentado terrorista** terrorist attack

atentamente *adv* attentively; *en carta* sincerely, *Br* Yours sincerely

atentar ⟨1k⟩ *v/i:* **atentar contra** *vida* make an attempt on; *moral etc* be contrary to

atento *adj* attentive; **estar atento a algo** pay attention to sth

atenuante *adj* JUR extenuating; **circunstancia atenuante** JUR extenuating circumstance

atenuar ⟨1e⟩ *v/t* lessen, reduce

ateo 1 *adj* atheistic **2** *m*, **-a** *f* atheist

aterciopelado *adj tb fig* velvety

aterido *adj* frozen

aterrador *adj* frightening

aterrar ⟨1a⟩ *v/t* terrify

aterrizaje *m* AVIA landing; **aterrizaje forzoso** *or* **de emergencia** emergency landing

aterrizar ⟨1f⟩ *v/i* land

aterrorizado *adj* terrified, petrified F

aterrorizar ⟨1f⟩ *v/t* terrify; (*amenazar*) terrorize

atestado *adj* overcrowded

atestiguar ⟨1i⟩ *v/t* JUR testify; *fig* bear witness to

atiborrarse ⟨1a⟩ *v/r* F stuff o.s. F (*de* with)

ático *m piso* top floor; *apartamento* top floor apartment (*Br* flat); (*desván*) attic

atinar ⟨1a⟩ *v/i* manage (*a* to); **no atinó con la respuesta correcta** she couldn't come up with the right answer

atípico *adj* atypical

atisbo *m* sign

atizar ⟨1f⟩ *v/t fuego* poke; *pasiones* stir up; **le atizó un golpe** she hit him

Atlántico *m/adj:* **el (océano) Atlántico** the Atlantic (Ocean)

atlas *m inv* atlas

atleta *m/f* athlete

atlético *adj* athletic

atletismo *m* athletics

atmo. *abr* (= *atentísimo*): **su atmo** Yours truly

atmósfera *f* atmosphere

atole *m Méx flavored hot drink made with maize flour*

atolladero *m:* **sacar a alguien del atolladero** *fig* F get s.o. out of a tight spot

atolondrado *adj* scatterbrained

atómico *adj* atomic

átomo *m* atom; **ni un átomo de** *fig* not an iota of

atónito *adj* astonished, amazed

atontar ⟨1a⟩ *v/t* make groggy *o* dopey; *de golpe* stun, daze; (*volver tonto*) turn into a zombie

atorar ⟨1a⟩ *L.Am.* **1** *v/t cañería etc* block (up) **2** *v/r* **atorarse** choke; *de cañería etc* get blocked (up)

atormentar ⟨1a⟩ *v/t* torment

atornillar ⟨1a⟩ *v/t* screw on

atorrante *m Rpl, Chi* F bum F, *Br* tramp; (*holgazán*) layabout

atosigar ⟨1h⟩ *v/t* pester

atrabancado *adj Méx* clumsy

atracar ⟨1g⟩ **1** *v/t banco, tienda* hold up; *a alguien* mug; *Chi* F make out with F, neck with *Br* F **2** *v/i* MAR dock

atracción *f* attraction

atraco *m de banco, tienda* robbery; *de persona* mugging

atracón *m:* **darse un atracón de** stuff o.s. with F

atractivo 1 *adj* attractive **2** *m* appeal, attraction

atraer ⟨2p⟩ *v/t* attract

atragantarse ⟨1a⟩ *v/r* choke (*con* on); **se le ha atragantado** *fig* she can't stand *o* stomach him

atrancar ⟨1g⟩ **1** *v/t puerta* barricade **2** *v/r* **atrancarse** *fig* get stuck

atrapar ⟨1a⟩ *v/t* catch, trap

atrás *adv para indicar posición* at the back, behind; *para indicar movimiento* back; **años atrás** years ago *o* back; **hacia atrás** back, backwards; **quedarse atrás** get left behind atrasado *adj en estudios, pago* behind (**en** in *o* with); *reloj* slow; *pueblo* backward; *ir atrasado de un reloj* be slow

atrasar ⟨1a⟩ **1** *v/t reloj* put back; *fecha* postpone, put back **2** *v/i de reloj* lose time

atraso *m* backwardness; COM **atrasos** arrears

atravesar ⟨1k⟩ *v/t* cross; (*perforar*) go through, pierce; *crisis* go through

atrevido *adj* daring

atreverse ⟨2a⟩ *v/r* dare

atribuir ⟨3g⟩ **1** *v/t* attribute (**a** to) **2** *v/r* **atribuirse** claim

atrincherarse ⟨1a⟩ *v/r* MIL dig o.s. in, entrench o.s.; *se atrincheró en su postura fig* he dug his heels in

atrocidad *f* atrocity

atrofiado *adj* atrophied

atrofiarse ⟨1b⟩ *v/r* atrophy

atropellar ⟨1a⟩ *v/t* knock down

atroz *adj* appalling, atrocious

ATS *abr* (= *ayudante técnico sanitario*) registered nurse

atte. *abr* (= *atentamente*) sincerely (yours)

atuendo *m* outfit

atufar ⟨1a⟩ *v/t* F stink out F

atún *m* tuna (fish)

aturdido *adj* in a daze

aturdir ⟨3a⟩ **1** *v/t de golpe, noticia* stun, daze; (*confundir*) bewilder, confuse **2** *v/r* **aturdirse** be stunned *o* dazed; (*confundirse*) be bewildered *o* confused

aturullar ⟨1a⟩ **1** *v/t* confuse **2** *v/r* **aturullarse** get confused

audacia *f* audacity

audaz *adj* daring, bold, audacious

audición *f* TEA audition; JUR hearing

audiencia *f* audience; JUR court; *índice de audiencia* TV ratings *pl*

audífono *m para sordos* hearing aid

audiovisual *adj* audiovisual

auditivo *adj* auditory; *problema* hearing *atr*

auditor *m*, auditora *f* auditor

auditoría *f* audit

auditorio *m* (*público*) audience; *sala auditoria*

auge *m* peak; *estar en auge aumento* be enjoying a boom

augurar ⟨1a⟩ *v/t de persona* predict, foretell; *de indicio* augur

augurio *m* omen, sign; *un buen / mal augurio* a good / bad omen

aula *f* classroom; *en universidad* lecture hall, *Br* lecture theatre

aullido *m* howl

aumentar ⟨1a⟩ **1** *v/t* increase; *precio* increase, raise, put up **2** *v/i de precio, temperatura* rise, increase, go up

aumento *m de precios, temperaturas etc* rise (**de** in), increase (**de** in); *de sueldo* raise, *Br* rise; *ir en aumento* be increasing

aun *adv* even; *aun así* even so

aún *adv en oraciones no negativas* still; *en oraciones negativas* yet; *en comparaciones* even; *aún no* not yet

aunar ⟨1a⟩ *v/t* combine

aunque *conj* although, even though; + *subj* even if

auricular *m de teléfono* receiver; *auriculares* headphones, earphones

aurora *f* dawn; *aurora boreal* northern lights *pl*

auscultar ⟨1a⟩ *v/t*: *auscultar a alguien* listen to s.o.'s chest

ausencia *f de persona* absence; *no existencia* lack (**de** of); *brillaba por su ausencia* he was conspicuous by his absence

ausente *adj* absent

auspicio *m* sponsorship; *bajo los auspicios de* under the auspices of

austeridad *f* austerity

austero *adj* austere

austral *adj* southern

Australia Australia

australiano **1** *adj* Australian **2** *m*, -a *f* Australian

Austria Austria

austriano **1** *adj* Austrian **2** *m*, -a *f* Austrian

auténtico *adj* authentic

autentificar ⟨1g⟩ *v/t* authenticate

autismo *m* autism

auto *m* JUR order; *L.Am.* AUTO car

autoadhesivo *adj* self-adhesive

autoayuda f self-help
autobiografía f autobiography
autobombo m F self-glorification
autobús m bus
autocar m bus
autocaravana f camper van
autocontrol m self-control
autocrítica f self-criticism
autóctono adj indigenous, native
autodefensa f self-defense, Br self-defence
autodeterminación f self-determination
autodidacta 1 adj self-taught **2** m/f self-taught person
autoedición f desktop publishing, DTP
autoescuela f driving school
autoestima f self-esteem
autoestop m hitchhiking
autoestopista m/f hitchhiker
autógrafo m autograph
automático adj automatic
automatizar ⟨1f⟩ v/t automate
automedicación f self-medication
automóvil m car, automobile
automovilismo m driving
automovilista m/f motorist
autonomía f autonomy; *en España* autonomous region
autónomo adj autonomous
autopista f freeway, Br motorway; **autopista de la información** or **de la comunicación** INFOR information (super)highway
autopsia f post mortem, autopsy
autor m, **autora** f author; *de crimen* perpetrator
autoridad f authority
autoritario adj authoritarian
autorización f authority
autorizar ⟨1f⟩ v/t authorize
autorradio m car radio
autorretrato m self-portrait
autoservicio m supermarket; *restaurante* self-service restaurant
autostop m hitchhiking; **hacer autostop** hitch(hike)
autosuficiencia f self-sufficiency; *desp* smugness
autosuficiente adj self-sufficient; *desp*
smug
autovía f divided highway, Br dual carriageway
auxiliar 1 adj auxiliary; *profesor* assistant **2** m/f assistant; **auxiliar f de vuelo** stewardess, flight attendant **3** ⟨1b⟩ v/t help
auxilio m help; **primeros auxilios** pl first aid sg
Av. abr (= **Avenida**) Ave (= Avenue)
aval m guarantee; **aval bancario** bank guarantee
avalancha f avalanche
avalar ⟨1a⟩ v/t guarantee; *fig* back
avance m advance
avanzado adj advanced
avanzar ⟨1f⟩ **1** v/t move forward, advance **2** v/i advance, move forward; MIL advance (**hacia** on); *en trabajo* make progress
avaricia f avarice
avaro 1 adj miserly **2** m, -a f miser
avasallar ⟨1a⟩ v/t subjugate; **no dejes que te avasallen** *fig* don't let them push you around
Av.da abr (= **Avenida**) Ave (= Avenue)
ave f bird; *S. Am. (pollo)* chicken; **ave de presa** or **de rapiña** bird of prey
avecinarse ⟨1a⟩ v/r approach
avejentar ⟨1a⟩ v/t age
avellana f BOT hazelnut
avellano m BOT hazel
avena f oats pl
avenida f avenue
avenirse ⟨3s⟩ v/r agree (**a** to)
aventajar ⟨1a⟩ v/t be ahead of
aventura f adventure; *riesgo* venture; *amorosa* affair
aventurar ⟨1a⟩ **1** v/t risk; *opinión* venture **2** v/r **aventurarse** venture; **aventurarse a hacer algo** dare to do sth
aventurero adj adventurous
avergonzar ⟨1n & 1f⟩ **1** v/t (*abochornar*) embarrass; **le avergüenza** algo *reprensible* she's ashamed of it **2** v/r **avergonzarse** be ashamed (**de** of)
avería f TÉC fault; AUTO breakdown
averiarse ⟨1c⟩ v/r break down
averiguar ⟨1i⟩ v/t find out
aversión f aversion

avestruz *m* ZO ostrich; *del avestruz polí-tica, táctica* head-in-the-sand
aviación *f* aviation; MIL air force
avicultor *m*, **avicultora** *f* poultry farmer
avidez *f* eagerness
ávido *adj* eager (*de* for), avid (*de* for)
avinagrarse ⟨1a⟩ *v/r de vino* turn vine-gary; *fig* become bitter *o* sour
avión *m* plane; *por avión mandar una carta* (by) airmail
avioneta *f* light aircraft
avisar ⟨1a⟩ *v/t notificar* let know, tell; *de peligro* warn; (*llamar*) call, send for
aviso *m comunicación* notice; (*adverten-cia*) warning; *L.Am.* (*anuncio*) advertise-ment; *hasta nuevo aviso* until further notice; *sin previo aviso* unexpectedly, without any warning
avispa *f* ZO wasp
avivar ⟨1a⟩ *v/t fuego* revive; *interés* arouse
avizor *adj*: *estar ojo avizor* be alert
axila *f* armpit
axioma *m* axiom
ay *int de dolor* ow!, ouch!; *de susto* oh!
ayer *adv* yesterday; *ayer por la mañana* yesterday morning
ayuda *f* help; *ayuda al desarrollo* devel-opment aid *o* assistance
ayudante *m/f* assistant
ayudar ⟨1a⟩ *v/t* help
ayunas: *estoy en ayunas* I haven't eaten anything

ayuno *m* fast
ayuntamiento *m* city council, town coun-cil; *edificio* city hall
azabache *m* MIN jet
azadón *m* mattock
azafata *f* flight attendant; *azafata de congresos* hostess
azafrán *m* BOT saffron
azalea *f* BOT azalea
azar *m* fate, chance; *al azar* at random
azorarse ⟨1a⟩ *v/r* be embarrassed
azotar ⟨1a⟩ *v/t con látigo* whip, flog; *con mano* smack; *de enfermedad, hambre* grip; *Méx puerta* slam
azote *m con látigo* lash; *con mano* smack; *fig* scourge; *dar un azote a alguien* F smack s.o.
azotea *f* flat roof; *estar mal de la azotea fig* F be crazy F
azteca *m/f* & *adj* Aztec
azúcar *m* (*also f*) sugar; *azúcar glas* con-fectioner's sugar, *Br* icing sugar; *azúcar moreno, Méx puerta* slam
azucarero *m* sugar bowl
azucena *f* BOT Madonna lily
azufre *m* sulfur, *Br* sulphur
azul 1 *adj* blue; *azul celeste* sky-blue; *azul marino* navy(-blue) **2** *m* blue
azulejo *m* tile
azuzar ⟨1f⟩ *v/t*: *azuzar los perros a al-guien* set the dogs on s.o.; *fig* egg s.o. on

B

B.A. *abr* (= *Buenos Aires*) Buenos Aires
baba *f* drool, dribble; *se le caía la baba* F he was drooling F (*con* over)
babear ⟨1a⟩ *v/i* dribble
babero *m* bib
Babia *f*: *estar en Babia* be miles away
babor *m* MAR port
babosa *f* ZO slug

babosada *f L.Am.* F stupid thing to do / say
baboso *adj L.Am.* F stupid
baca *f* AUTO roof rack
bacalao *m* cod; *cortar el bacalao* F call the shots F
bache *m* pothole; *fig* rough patch
bachicha 1 *m/f Rpl, Chi desp* wop *desp* **2** *f*

Méx cigarette stub

bachillerato *m Esp high school leaver's certificate*

bacón *m* bacon

bacteria *f* bacteria

bádminton *m* badminton

bafle *m* loudspeaker

bahía *f* bay

bailaor *m*, **bailaora** *f* flamenco dancer

bailar ⟨1a⟩ **1** *v/i* dance; *de zapato* be loose **2** *v/t* dance; *se lo bailó Méx* F he pinched F *o* swiped F it

bailarín *m*, **-ina** *f* dancer

baile *m* dance; *fiesta formal* ball; *baile de salón* ballroom dancing; *baile de San Vito fig* St. Vitus's dance

baja *f descenso* fall, drop; *estar de baja (por enfermedad)* be off sick; *bajas* MIL casualties

bajada *f* fall

bajar ⟨1a⟩ **1** *v/t voz, precio* lower; *escalera* go down; *bajar algo de arriba* get sth down **2** *v/i* go down; *de intereses* fall, drop **3** *v/r bajarse* get down; *de automóvil* get out (*de* of); *de tren, autobús* get off (*de* sth)

bajío *m L.Am.* lowland

bajo 1 *adj* low; *persona* short; *por lo bajo* at least **2** *m* MÚS bass; *piso* first floor, *Br* ground floor **3** *adv cantar, hablar* quietly, softly; *volar* low **4** *prp* under; *tres grados bajo cero* three degrees below zero

bajón *m* sharp decline; *dar un bajón* decline sharply, slump

bala *f* bullet; *como una bala* like lightning; *ni a bala L.Am.* F no way

balaceo *m L.Am.*, **balacera** *f L.Am.* shooting

balada *f* ballad

balance *m* COM balance

balancearse ⟨1a⟩ *v/r* swing, sway

balanza *f* scales *pl*; *balanza comercial* balance of trade; *balanza de pagos* balance of payments

balaustrada *f* balustrade

balazo *m* shot

balbucear ⟨1a⟩, **balbucir** ⟨3f; *defective*⟩ **1** *v/i* stammer; *de niño* babble **2** *v/t* stammer

Balcanes *mpl* Balkans

balcánico *adj* Balkan

balcón *m* balcony

baldado *adj fig* F bushed F

balde *adv*: *de balde* for nothing; *en balde* in vain

baldosa *f* floor tile

balear ⟨1a⟩ *v/t L.Am.* shoot

baleo *m L.Am.* shooting

Baleares *fpl* Balearic Islands

baleárico *adj* Balearic

baliza *f* MAR buoy

ballena *f* ZO whale

ballet *m* ballet

balneario *m* spa

balón *m* ball

baloncesto *m* basketball

balonmano *m* handball

balonvolea *m* volleyball

balsa *f* raft; *como una balsa de aceite fig* like a mill pond

bálsamo *m* balsam

baluarte *m* stronghold; *persona* pillar, stalwart

balumba *f L.Am.* F heap, pile; F (*ruido*) noise, racket F

bambolearse ⟨1a⟩ *v/r* sway

bambolla *f L.Am.* F fuss

bambú *m* BOT bamboo

banal *adj* banal

banana *f L.Am., Rpl, Pe, Bol* banana

banca *f actividad* banking; *conjunto de bancos* banks *pl; en juego* bank; DEP, *Méx* (*asiento*) bench

bancal *m* terrace; *división de terreno* plot

bancario *adj* bank *atr*

bancarrota *f* bankruptcy; *estar en bancarrota* be bankrupt

banco *m* COM bank; *para sentarse* bench; *banco de arena* sand bank; *banco de datos* data bank

banda *f* MÚS, (*grupo*) band; *de delincuentes* gang; (*cinta*) sash; *en fútbol* touchline; *banda sonora* soundtrack

bandada *f de pájaros* flock

bandazo *m*: *dar bandazos de coche* swerve

bandeja *f* tray; *servir en bandeja* hand on a plate

bandera *f* flag; (*lleno*) **hasta la bandera** packed (out); **bajar la bandera** de taxi start the meter running

banderilla *f* TAUR banderilla (*dart stuck into bull's neck during bullfight*)

bandido *m*, -a *f* bandit

bando *m* edict; *en disputa* side

bandolero *m*, -a *f* bandit

banjo *m* MÚS banjo

banquero *m*, -a *f* banker

banqueta *f* L.Am. stool; L.Am. (*acera*) sidewalk, *Br* pavement; **banqueta trasera** AUTO back seat

banquete *m* banquet; **banquete de bodas** wedding reception

banquillo *m* JUR dock; DEP bench

bañadera *f* Rpl (*baño*) bath

bañador *m* swimsuit

bañar ⟨1a⟩ **1** *v/t de sol, mar* bathe; *a un niño, un enfermo* bathe, *Br* bath; GASTR coat (**con** with, **en** in) **2** *v/r* **bañarse** have a bath; *en el mar* go for a swim

bañera *f* (bath)tub, bath

bañista *m/f* swimmer

baño *m* bath; *en el mar* swim; *esp* L.Am. bathroom; TÉC plating; **baño de sangre** blood bath; **baño María** bain-marie

baptisterio *m* baptistry

baquiano L.Am. **1** *adj* expert *atr* **2** *m*, -a *f* guide

bar *m* bar

baraja *f* deck of cards

barandilla *f* handrail, banister

barata *f* Méx bargain counter; (*saldo*) sale

baratero *m*, -a *f* Chi *tendero* junk-shop owner

baratija *f* trinket

barato *adj* cheap

barba *f* tb BOT beard; **por barba** F a head, per person

barbacoa *f* barbecue

barbaridad *f* barbarity; **costar una barbaridad** cost a fortune; **decir barbaridades** say outrageous things; **¡qué barbaridad!** what a thing to say / do!

bárbaro **1** *adj* F tremendous, awesome F; **¡qué bárbaro!** amazing!, wicked! F **2** *m*, -a *f* F punk F

barbería *f* barber's shop

barbero *m* barber

barbilla *f* chin

barbitúrico *m* barbiturate

barbo *m pescado* barbel

barca *f* boat

barcaza *f* MAR barge

barco *m* boat; *más grande* ship; **barco de vela** sailing ship

baremo *m* scale

barniz *m para madera* varnish

barnizar ⟨1f⟩ *v/t* varnish

barómetro *m* barometer

barquero *m* boatman

barquillo *m* wafer; Méx, C.Am. ice-cream cone

barra *f de metal, en bar* bar; *de cortinas* rod; **barra de labios** lipstick; **barra de pan** baguette; **barra espaciadora** space-bar; **barra de herramientas** INFOR tool bar; **barra invertida** backslash

barraca *f* (*chabola*) shack; *de tiro* stand; *de feria* stall; L.Am. (*deposito*) shed; **barracas** *pl* L.Am. shanty town *sg*

barracón *m* MIL barrack room

barranco *m* ravine

barrenar ⟨1a⟩ *v/t* drill

barrendero *m*, -a *f* street sweeper

barreno *m* drill hole

barreño *m* washing up bowl

barrer ⟨2a⟩ *v/t* sweep

barrera *f* barrier; **barrera del sonido** sound barrier

barriada *f* C.Am. (*barrio marginal*) slum, shanty town

barrial *m* L.Am. bog

barricada *f* barricade

barrida *f* L.Am. sweep; L.Am. (*redada*) police raid

barriga *f* belly; **rascarse la barriga** *fig* F sit on one's butt F

barrigón *adj* F pudgy F

barril *m* barrel

barrio *m* neighbo(u)rhood, area; **barrio de chabolas** Esp shanty town; **irse al otro barrio** F kick the bucket P

barro *m* mud

barroco *m/adj* baroque

barrote *m* bar

bártulos *mpl* F things, gear *sg* F

barullo *m* uproar, racket

basar⟨1a⟩ **1** *v/t* base (*en* on) **2** *v/r* **basarse** be based (*en* on)

báscula *f* scales

base *f* QUÍM, MAT, MIL base; *base de datos* INFOR database; *bases de concurso etc* conditions; *a base de* by dint of

básico *adj* basic

basílica *f* basilica

básquetbol *m L.Am.* basketball

bastante **1** *adj* enough; *número o cantidad considerable* plenty of; *quedan bastantes plazas* there are plenty of seats left **2** *adv* quite, fairly; *bebe bastante* she drinks quite a lot

bastar⟨1a⟩ *v/i* be enough; *basta con uno* one is enough; *¡basta!* that's enough!

bastardo **1** *adj* bastard *atr* **2** *m* bastard

bastidor *m*: *entre bastidores* F behind the scenes

bastión *m* bastion

basto **1** *adj* rough, coarse **2** *mpl*: *bastos* (*en naipes*) suit in Spanish deck of cards

bastón *m* stick

basura *f tb fig* trash, *Br* rubbish; *cubo de la basura* trash can, *Br* rubbish bin

basural *m L.Am.* dump, *Br* tip

basurero *m* garbage collector, *Br* dustman

bata *f* robe, *Br* dressing gown; MED (white) coat; TÉC lab coat

batacazo *m* F bump

batalla *f* battle

batallón *m* battalion

batata *f* BOT sweet potato

bate *m* DEP bat

batería *f* MIL, EL, AUTO battery; MÚS drums, drum kit; *batería de cocina* set of pans; *aparcar en batería* AUTO parallel park

batido **1** *adj* camino well-trodden **2** *m* GASTR milkshake

batidora *f* mixer

batir⟨3a⟩ *v/t* beat; *nata* whip; *récord* break

baúl *m* chest, trunk; *L.Am.* AUTO trunk, *Br* boot

bautismo *m* baptism, christening; *bautismo de fuego* baptism of fire

bautizar⟨1f⟩ *v/t* baptize, christen; *barco* name; *vino* F water down

bautizo *m* baptism, christening

baya *f* berry

bayeta *f* cloth

bayoneta *f* bayonet

bayunco *adj C.Am.* P silly, stupid

baza *f en naipes* trick; *fig* trump card; *meter baza* F interfere

bazar *m* hardware and fancy goods store; *mercado* bazaar

bazo *m* ANAT spleen

bazofia *f fig* F load of trash F

beatífico *adj* beatific

beatitud *f* beatitude

beato **1** *adj desp* overpious **2** *m*, -*a f desp* over-pious person

bebé *m* baby

bebedor *m*, bebedora *f* drinker

beber⟨2a⟩ **1** *v/i & v/t* drink **2** *v/r* **beberse** drink up

bebida *f* drink

beca *f* scholarship; (*del estado*) grant

becerro *m* calf

béchamel *f* GASTR béchamel (sauce)

bedel *m* porter

beige *adj* beige

béisbol *m* baseball

belén *m* nativity scene

belga *m/f & adj* Belgian

Bélgica Belgium

Belice Belize

belicista *m/f* warmonger

bélico *adj* war *atr*

beligerante *adj* belligerent

bellaco *m*, -*a f Arg* rascal

belleza *f* beauty

bello *adj* beautiful

bellota *f* BOT acorn

bemol *m* MÚS flat; *mi bemol* E flat; *tener bemoles* *fig* F be tricky F

bencina *f* benzine; *Pe, Bol* (*gasolina*) gas, *Br* petrol

bendecir⟨3p⟩ *v/t* bless

bendición *f* blessing

bendito *adj* blessed

benefactor *adj* charitable

beneficencia *f* charity

beneficiar⟨1b⟩ **1** *v/t* benefit; *Rpl ganado* slaughter **2** *v/r* **beneficiarse** benefit (*de,*

con from)

beneficio *m* benefit; COM profit; *Rpl* slaughterhouse; *C.Am.* coffee-processing plant; **en beneficio de** in aid of

beneficioso *adj* beneficial

benéfico *adj* charity *atr*; **función -a** charity function *o* event

beneplácito *m* approval

benévolo *adj* benevolent, kind; (*indulgente*) lenient

bengala *f* flare

benigno *adj* MED benign

benjamín *m* youngest son

benjamina *f* youngest daughter

beodo *adj* drunk

berberecho *m* ZO cockle

berenjena *f* BOT egg plant, *Br* aubergine

berenjenal *m*: **meterse en un berenjenal** *fig* F get o.s. into a jam F

bermudas *mpl*, *fpl* Bermuda shorts

berrear ⟨1a⟩ *v/i* bellow; *de niño* bawl, yell

berrido *m* bellow; *de niño* yell

berrinche *m* F tantrum; **coger un berrinche** F throw a tantrum

berro *m* BOT watercress

berza *f* BOT cabbage

besamel *f* GASTR béchamel (sauce)

besar ⟨1a⟩ **1** *v/t* kiss **2** *v/r* **besarse** kiss

beso *m* kiss

bestia 1 *f* beast **2** *m/f/fig* F brute F, swine F; *mujer* bitch F; **conducir a lo bestia** F drive like a madman

besugo *m* ZO bream; *fig* F idiot

betún *m* shoe polish

biberón *m* baby's bottle

Biblia *f* Bible

bibliografía *f* bibliography

biblioteca *f* library; *mueble* bookcase

bibliotecario *m*, **-a** *f* librarian

bicarbonato *m*: **bicarbonato (de sodio)** bicarbonate of soda, bicarb F

bíceps *mpl* biceps

bicho *m* bug, *Br tb* creepy-crawly; (*animal*) creature; *fig* F *persona* nasty piece of work; **¿qué bicho te ha picado?** what's eating you?

bici *f* F bike

bicicleta *f* bicycle; **ir** *or* **montar en bicicleta** go cycling; **bicicleta de montaña** mountain bike

BID *abr* (= **Banco Interamericano de Desarollo**) IADB (= Inter-American Development Bank)

bidé *m* bidet

bidón *m* drum

bien 1 *m* good; **por tu bien** for your own good; **bienes** *pl* goods, property *sg*; **bienes de consumo** consumer goods *o* durables; **bienes inmuebles** real estate *sg* **2** *adv* well; (*muy*) very; **más bien** rather; **o bien ... o ...** either ... or ...; **¡está bien!** it's OK!, it's alright!; **estoy bien** I'm fine, I'm OK; **¿estás bien aquí?** are you comfortable here?; **¡bien hecho!** well done!

bienestar *m* well-being

bienvenida *f* welcome; **dar la bienvenida a alguien** welcome s.o.

bienvenido *adj* welcome

bife *m* *Rpl* steak

bifocal *adj* bifocal

bifurcación *f* fork; *de línea férrea* junction

bifurcarse ⟨1g⟩ *v/r* fork

bigamia *f* bigamy

bigote *m* m(o)ustache; **bigotes de gato** *etc* whiskers

bikini *m* bikini

bilateral *adj* bilateral

bilingüe *adj* bilingual

bilis *f* bile; *fig* F bad mood

billar *m* billiards; **billar americano** pool

billete *m* ticket; **billete abierto** open ticket; **billete de autobús** bus ticket; **billete de banco** bill, *Br* banknote; **billete de ida, billete sencillo** one-way ticket, *Br* single (ticket); **billete de ida y vuelta** round-trip ticket, *Br* return (ticket)

billetera *f* *L.Am.*, **billetero** *m* billfold, *Br* wallet

billón *m* trillion

binario *adj* binary

bingo *m* bingo; *lugar* bingo hall

biodegradable *adj* biodegradable

biodiversidad *f* biodiversity

biografía *f* biography

biología *f* biology

biológico *adj* biological; AGR organic

biólogo *m*, **-a** *f* biologist

biombo *m* folding screen

biopsia f MED biopsy
bioquímica f biochemistry
bipartidismo m POL two-party system
biquini m bikini
birlar ⟨1a⟩ v/t F lift F, swipe F
birome m Rpl ballpoint (pen)
birria f F piece of junk F; *va hecha una birria* she looks a real mess
bis m encore; *9 bis* 9A
bisabuela f great-grandmother
bisabuelo m great-grandfather
bisagra f hinge
biscote m rusk
bisexual adj bisexual
bisiesto adj: *año bisiesto* leap year
bisnieta f great-granddaughter
bisnieto m great-grandson
bisonte m ZO bison
bisoñé m hairpiece, toupee
bisté, bistec m steak
bisturí m MED scalpel
bisutería f costume jewel(le)ry
bit m INFOR bit
bizco adj cross-eyed
bizcocho m sponge (cake)
blanca f persona white; MÚS half-note, Br minim; *estar sin blanca* fig F be broke F
blanco 1 adj white; (sin escrito) blank; *arma -a* 2 m persona white; (diana), fig target; *dar en el blanco* hit the nail on the head; *ser el blanco de todas las miradas* be the center (Br centre) of attention
blando adj soft
blanquear ⟨1a⟩ v/t whiten; *pared* whitewash; *dinero* launder
blanqueo m whitewashing; *blanqueo de dinero* money laundering
blanquillo m Méx egg
blasfemar ⟨1a⟩ v/i curse, swear; REL blaspheme
blasfemia f REL blasphemy
blindado adj armo(u)red; *puerta* reinforced; EL shielded
bloc m pad
blof m L.Am. bluff
bloque m block; POL bloc; *bloque de apartamentos* apartment building, Br block of flats; *en bloque* en masse

bloquear ⟨1a⟩ v/t block; DEP obstruct; (atascar) jam; MIL blockade; COM freeze
bloqueo m blockade
blusa f blouse
boa f ZO boa constrictor
bobada f piece of nonsense
bobina f bobbin; FOT reel, spool; EL coil
bobo 1 adj silly, foolish 2 m, -a f fool
boca f mouth; *boca a boca* mouth to mouth; *boca de metro* subway entrance; *boca abajo* face down; *boca arriba* face up; *dejar con la boca abierta* leave open-mouthed; *se me hace la boca agua* my mouth is watering
bocacalle f side street
bocadillo m sandwich
bocado m mouthful, bite
bocana f river mouth
bocanada f mouthful; *de viento* gust
bocata m F → *bocadillo*
bocazas m/f inv F loudmouth F
boceto m sketch
bochar ⟨1a⟩ v/t Rpl F *en examen* fail, flunk F; Méx cold-shoulder, rebuff
bochinche m Méx uproar
bochorno m sultry weather; fig embarrassment
bocina f MAR, AUTO horn
bocio m MED goiter, Br goitre
boda f wedding
bodega f wine cellar; MAR, AVIA hold; L.Am. bar; C.Am., Pe, Bol grocery store
bodeguero m, -a f C.Am., Pe, Ven storekeeper
body m prenda body
bofetada f slap
bofetear ⟨1a⟩ v/t L.Am. slap
bofia f F cops pl F
boga f: *estar en boga* fig be in fashion
bogavante m ZO lobster
bohemio 1 adj bohemian 2 m, -a f bohemian
bohío m Cuba, Ven hut
boicot m boycott
boicotear ⟨1a⟩ v/t boycott
boicoteo m boycotting
boina f beret
bojote m L.Am. fig bundle
bol m bowl

bola f ball; TÉC ball bearing; *de helado* scoop; F (*mentira*) fib F; *bola de nieve* snowball; *no dar pie con bola* get everything wrong

bolada f L.Am. throw; (*suerte*) piece of luck

bolado m S. Am. deal; L.Am. F (*mentira*) fib F

boleada f Arg hunt

boleador m, **boleadora** f Méx bootblack

boleadoras fpl L.Am. bolas

bolear ⟨1a⟩ **1** v/i L.Am. DEP have a knockabout **2** v/t L.Am. DEP bowl; Rpl con boleadoras bring down; Méx zapatos shine **3** v/r bolearse Rpl fall; (*aperarse*) get embarrassed

bolera f bowling alley

bolero 1 m MÚS bolero **2** m/f Méx F bootblack

boleta f L.Am. ticket; L.Am. (*pase*) pass, permit; L.Am. (*voto*) ballot paper

boletería f L.Am. ticket office; *en cine, teatro* box office

boletero m, -a f L.Am. ticket clerk; *en cine, teatro* box office employee

boletín m bulletin, report; *boletín de evaluación* report card; *boletín meteorológico* weather report

boleto m L.Am. ticket; *boleto de autobús* L.Am. bus ticket; *boleto de ida y vuelta* L.Am., *boleto redondo* Méx round-trip ticket, Br return

boliche m AUTO jack; CSur grocery store, Br grocer's

bólido m fig racing car

bolígrafo m ball-point pen

bolillo m bobbin; Méx bread roll; *encaje de bolillos* handmade lace

Bolivia Bolivia

boliviano 1 adj Bolivian **2** m, -a f Bolivian

bollo m bun; (*abolladura*) bump

bolo m pin; C.Am., Méx christening present

bolos mpl bowling sg

bolsa f bag; COM stock exchange; L.Am. (*bolsillo*) pocket; *bolsa de agua caliente* hot-water bottle

bolsero m, -a f Méx F scrounger

bolsillo m pocket; *meterse a alguien en*

el bolsillo F win s.o. over

bolso m purse, Br handbag

bolsón m Arg, Pe traveling bag, Br holdall

bomba f bomb; TÉC pump; S. Am. gas station; *bomba de relojería* time bomb; *caer como una bomba* fig F come as a bombshell; *pasarlo bomba* F have a great time

bombacha f Arg panties pl, Br tb knickers pl

bombacho m: *bombachos* pl, *pantalón bombacho* baggy pants pl

bombardear ⟨1a⟩ v/t bomb

bombero m, -a f firefighter; *llamar a los bomberos* call the fire department

bombilla f light bulb; Rpl metal straw for the mate gourd

bombillo m C.Am., Pe, Bol light bulb

bombita f Arg light bulb

bombo m MÚS bass drum; TÉC drum

bombón m chocolate; fig F babe F

bombona f cylinder

bonaerense 1 adj of Buenos Aires, Buenos Aires atr **2** m/f native of Buenos Aires

bonanza f fig boom, bonanza

bondad f goodness, kindness; *tenga la bondad de* please be so kind as to

bondadoso adj caring

bongo m L.Am. bongo

boniato m BOT sweet potato

bonito 1 adj pretty **2** m ZO tuna

bono m voucher; COM bond

bonsái m bonsai

boñiga f dung

boom m boom

boquerón m ZO anchovy

boquete m hole

boquiabierto adj fig F speechless

borbotón m: *salir a borbotones de agua* gush out; *hablaba a borbotones* fig it all came out in a rush; *hablar borbotón* burble, splutter

borda f MAR gunwale; *echar* or *tirar por la borda* throw overboard

bordado 1 adj embroidered **2** m embroidery

bordar ⟨1a⟩ v/t embroider; *bordar algo* fig do sth brilliantly borde[1] *adj* F rude, uncouth

borde[2] *m* edge; **al borde de** *fig* on the verge *o* brink of

bordear ⟨1a⟩ *v/t* border

bordillo *m* curb, *Br* kerb

bordo *m*: **a bordo** MAR, AVIA on board

borona *f* corn, *Br* maize

borrachera *f* drunkenness; **agarrar una borrachera** get drunk

borrachería *f Méx, Rpl* → **borrachera**

borracho **1** *adj* drunk **2** *m*, **-a** *f* drunk

borrador *m* eraser; *de texto* draft; *(boceto)* sketch

borrar ⟨1a⟩ *v/t* erase; INFOR delete; *pizarra* clean; *recuerdo* blot out

borrasca *f* area of low pressure

borrego *m* ZO lamb; *fig: persona* sheep

borrico *m*, **-a** *f* donkey; *fig* dummy

borrón *m* blot; *mancha extendida* smudge; **hacer borrón y cuenta nueva** *fig* wipe the slate clean

borroso *adj* blurred, fuzzy

Bosnia Bosnia

bosque *m* wood; *grande* forest

bosquejo *m* sketch; *fig* outline

bostezar ⟨1f⟩ *v/i* yawn

bostezo *m* yawn

bota *f* boot; **bota de montar** riding boot; **ponerse las botas** *fig* F coin it F, rake it in F; *(comer mucho)* make a pig of o.s. F

botado *L.Am.* F **1** *adj (barato)* dirt cheap **2** *m*, **-a** *f* abandoned child

botana *f Méx* snack

botánica *f* botany

botar ⟨1a⟩ **1** *v/t* MAR launch; *pelota* bounce; *L.Am. (echar)* throw; *L.Am. (desechar)* throw out; *L.Am. (despedir)* fire **2** *v/i de pelota* bounce

bote *m (barco)* boat; *L.Am. (lata)* can, *Br tb* tin; *(tarro)* jar; **pegar un bote** jump; **bote de la basura** *Méx* trash can, *Br* rubbish bin; **bote salvavidas** lifeboat; **chupar del bote** *fig* F line one's pockets F; **tener a alguien en el bote** F have s.o. in one's pocket F; **de bote en bote** packed out

botella *f* bottle

botijo *m container with a spout for drinking from*

botín *m* loot; *calzado* ankle boot

botiquín *m* medicine chest; *estuche* first-aid kit

botón *m en prenda*, TÉC button; BOT bud

botones *m inv en hotel* bellhop, bellboy

boutique *f* boutique

bóveda *f* vault

bovino *adj* bovine

boxeador *m*, boxeadora *f* boxer

boxear ⟨1a⟩ *v/i* box

boxeo *m* boxing

boya *f* buoy; *de caña* float

boyante *adj fig* buoyant

bragas *fpl* panties, *Br tb* knickers

bragueta *f* fly

bramido *m* roar, bellow

brandy *m* brandy

branquia *f* ZO gill

brasa *f* ember; **a la brasa** GASTR charbroiled, *Br* char-grilled

brasero *m* brazier; *eléctrico* electric heater

Brasil Brazil

brasileño **1** *adj* Brazilian **2** *m*, **-a** *f* Brazilian

bravata *f* boast; *(amenaza)* threat

bravo *adj animal* fierce; *mar* rough, choppy; *persona* brave; *L.Am. (furioso)* angry; **¡bravo!** well done!; *en concierto etc* bravo!

bravucón *m*, **-ona** *f* F boaster, blowhard F

braza *f* breaststroke

brazalete *m* bracelet; *(banda)* armband

brazo *m* arm; **brazo de gitano** GASTR jelly roll, *Br* Swiss roll; **con los brazos abiertos** with open arms; **dar su brazo a torcer** give in

brebaje *m desp* concoction

brecha *f* breach; *fig* F gap; MED gash; **seguir en la brecha** F hang on in there F

brécol *m* broccoli

breva *f* BOT early fig; **no caerá esa breva** *fig* F no such luck!

breve *adj* brief; **en breve** shortly

brevedad *f* briefness, shortness

brevemente *adv* briefly

brezo *m* BOT heather

bribón *m*, **-ona** *f* rascal

bricolaje *m* do-it-yourself, DIY

brigada *f* MIL brigade; *en policía* squad

brillante 1 *adj* bright; *fig* brilliant **2** *m* diamond

brillar ⟨1a⟩ *v/i fig* shine

brillo *m* shine; *de estrella, luz* brightness; ***dar*** *or* ***sacar brillo a algo*** polish sth

brincar ⟨1g⟩ *v/i* jump up and down

brinco *m* F leap, bound; ***dar brincos*** jump

brindar ⟨1a⟩ **1** *v/t* offer **2** *v/i* drink a toast (***por*** to)

brindis *m inv* toast

brío *m fig* verve, spirit

brisa *f* MAR breeze

brisera *f L.Am.* windshield, *Br* windscreen

británico 1 *adj* British **2** *m*, **-a** *f* Briton, Brit F

broca *f* TÉC drill bit

brocha *f* brush

broche *m* brooch; (*cierre*) fastener; *L.Am.* (*pinza*) clothes pin

brocheta *f* skewer

brócoli *m* broccoli

broma *f* joke; ***en broma*** as a joke; ***gastar bromas*** play jokes; ***tomar algo a broma*** take sth as a joke

bromear ⟨1a⟩ *v/i* joke

bromista *m/f* joker

bronca *f* F telling off F; *Méx* P fight; ***armar una bronca*** *Méx* get into a fight; ***echar bronca a alguien*** F give s.o. a telling off, tell s.o. off

bronce *m* bronze

bronceado 1 *adj* tanned **2** *m* suntan

bronceador *m* suntan lotion

broncearse ⟨1a⟩ *v/r* get a tan

bronquitis *f* MED bronchitis

brotar ⟨1a⟩ *v/i* BOT sprout, bud; *fig* appear, arise

brote *m* BOT shoot; MED, *fig* outbreak; ***brotes de bambú*** bamboo shoots; ***brotes de soja*** beansprouts

bruces: ***caer de bruces*** F fall flat on one's face

bruja *f* witch

brujo *m* wizard

brújula *f* compass

bruma *f* mist

bruñir ⟨3h⟩ *v/t* burnish, polish; *C.Am.* F (*molestar*) annoy

brusco *adj* sharp, abrupt; *respuesta, tono* brusque, curt

Bruselas Brussels

brutalidad *f* brutality

bruto 1 *adj* brutish; (*inculto*) ignorant; (*torpe*) clumsy; COM gross **2** *m*, **-a** *f* brute, animal

buceador *m*, **buceadora** *f* diver

bucear ⟨1a⟩ *v/i* dive; *fig* delve (***en*** into)

bucólico *adj* bucolic

budista *m/f* & *adj* Buddhist

buen *adj* → **bueno**

buenaventura *f* fortune

bueno *adj* good; (*bondadoso*) kind; (*sabroso*) nice; ***por las -as*** willingly; ***de -as a primeras*** without warning; ***ponerse bueno*** get well; ***¡bueno!*** well!; ***¿bueno?*** *Méx* hello; **-a voluntad** goodwill; ***¡-as!*** hello!; ***buenos días*** good morning; **-as noches** good evening; **-as tardes** good evening

buey *m* ZO ox

búfalo *m* ZO buffalo

bufanda *f* scarf; *fig* F perk

bufete *m* lawyer's office

buffet *m* GASTR buffet

bufón *m* buffoon, fool

buganvilla *f* BOT bougainvillea

buhardilla *f* attic, loft

búho *m* ZO owl

buitre *m* ZO vulture

bulbo *m* BOT bulb

bulevar *m* boulevard

Bulgaria Bulgaria

bulimia *f* MED bulimia

bulla *f* din, racket

bullicio *m* hubbub, din; (*actividad*) bustle

bullir ⟨3h⟩ *v/i fig*: *de sangre* boil; *de lugar* swarm, teem (***de*** with)

bulo *m* F rumo(u)r

bulto *m* package; MED lump; *en superficie* bulge; (*silueta*) vague shape; (*pieza de equipaje*) piece of baggage

bumerán *m* boomerang

buque *m* ship; ***buque de guerra*** warship

burbuja *f* bubble

burdel *m* brothel

C

burdo *adj* rough
burgués 1 *adj* middle-class, bourgeois **2** *m*, **-esa** *f* middle-class person, member of the bourgeoisie
burguesía *f* middle class, bourgeoisie
burla *f* joke; (*engaño*) trick; ***hacer burla de alguien*** F make fun of s.o.
burlar ⟨1a⟩ **1** *v/t* F get round **2** *v/r* **burlarse** make fun (*de* of)
burlete *m* L.Am. draft excluder, Br draught excluder
buró *m* bureau
burocracia *f* bureaucracy
burócrata *m/f* bureaucrat
burocrático *adj* bureaucratic
burrada *f fig* F piece of nonsense; ***hay una burrada*** there's loads F; ***costar una burrada*** cost a packet F
burro *m* zo donkey; ***no ver tres en un bu-***

rro be as blind as a bat
bursátil *adj* stock market *atr*
bus *m* bus
busca 1 *f* search; ***en busca de*** in search of **2** *m* F pager
buscador *m* searcher; INFOR search engine
buscapersonas *m inv* pager
buscapleitos *m/f inv* F troublemaker
buscar ⟨1a⟩ *v/t* search for, look for
búsqueda *f* search
busto *m* bust
butaca *f* armchair; TEA seat
butano *m* butane
butifarra *f* type of sausage
buzo *m* diver
buzón *m* mailbox, Br postbox; ***buzón de voz*** TELEC voicemail
byte *m* INFOR byte

C

C *abr* (= ***Centígrado***) C (= Centigrade); (= ***compañía***) Co. (= Company); c (= ***calle***) St. (= Street); (= ***capítulo***) ch. (= chapter)
cabal *adj*: **no estar en sus cabales** not be in one's right mind
cabalgar ⟨1h⟩ *v/i* ride
cabalgata *f* procession
caballa *f* zo mackerel
caballada *f* Rpl: **decir / hacer una caballada** say / do sth stupid
caballería *f* MIL cavalry; (*caballo*) horse
caballero 1 *adj* gentlemanly, chivalrous **2** *m hombre* gentleman, man; *hombre educado* gentleman; HIST knight; *trato* sir; (**servicio de**) **caballeros** *pl* men's room, gents; *en tienda de ropa* menswear
caballeroso *adj* gentlemanly, chivalrous
caballito *m*: **caballito del diablo** zo dragonfly; **caballito de mar** zo seahorse; **caballitos** *pl* carousel *sg*, merry-go-round *sg*

caballo *m* horse; *en ajedrez* knight; **caballo balancín** rocking horse; **a caballo entre** halfway between; **montar** *or* **andar** Rpl **a caballo** ride (a horse); **me gusta montar a caballo** I like riding; **ir a caballo** go on horseback
cabaña *f* cabin
cabaret *m* cabaret
cabecear ⟨1a⟩ **1** *v/i* nod **2** *v/t el balón* head
cabecera *f de mesa, cama* head; *de periódico* masthead; *de texto* top
cabecero *m de cama* headboard
cabecilla *m/f* ringleader
cabello *m* hair
caber ⟨2m⟩ *v/i* fit; **caben tres litros** it holds three liters *o* Br litres; **cabemos todos** there's room for all of us; **no cabe duda** *fig* there's no doubt; **no me cabe en la cabeza** I just don't understand
cabestrillo *m* MED sling
cabeza 1 *f* ANAT head; **cabeza de ajo** bulb

C

of garlic; **cabeza (de ganado)** head (of cattle); **cabeza nuclear** nuclear warhead; **el equipo a la cabeza** or **en cabeza** the team at the top; **por cabeza** per head, per person; **estar mal** or **no estar bien de la cabeza** F not be right in the head F **2** m/f: **cabeza de familia** head of the family; **cabeza de turco** scapegoat; **cabeza rapada** skinhead

cabezada f: **echar una cabezada** have a nap

cabezonería f pigheadedness

cabezota **1** adj pig-headed **2** m/f pig--headed person

cabida f capacity; **dar cabida a** hold

cabildo m POL council

cabina f cabin; **cabina telefónica** phone booth

cabizbajo adj dejected, downhearted

cable m EL cable; MAR line, rope; **echar un cable a alguien** give s.o. a hand

cabo m end; GEOG cape; MAR rope; MIL corporal; **al cabo de** after; **de cabo a rabo** F from start to finish; **atar cabos** F put two and two together F; **llevar a cabo** carry out

cabra f zo goat; **estar como una cabra** F be nuts F

cabrear ⟨1a⟩ **1** v/t bug F **2** v/r cabrearse P get mad F

cabriola f: **hacer cabriolas** de niño jump around

cabro m Chi boy; **cabro chico** Chi baby

cabrón m V bastard P, son of a bitch V

caca f F poop F, Br pooh F; **cosa mala** piece of trash F; **hacer caca** F poop F, Br do a pooh F

cacahuate m Méx peanut

cacahuete m peanut

cacalote m C.Am., Cuba, Méx crow

cacao m cocoa; **de labios** lip salve; **no valer un cacao** L.Am. fig F not be worth a bean F

cacatúa f zo cockatoo

cacería f hunt

cacerola f pan

cachar ⟨1a⟩ v/t L.Am. (engañar) trick; L.Am. (sorprender) catch out; **¿me cachas?** Chi get it?

cacharro m pot; Méx, C.Am. F (trasto) piece of junk; Méx, C.Am. F coche junkheap; **lavar los cacharros** Méx, C.Am. wash the dishes

cachas adj: **estar cachas** F be a real hunk F

cachear ⟨1a⟩ v/t frisk

cachemira f cashmere

cachetada f L.Am. slap

cachete m cheek

cachetear ⟨1a⟩ v/t L.Am. slap

cachimba f pipe

cachivache m thing; **cachivaches** pl (cosas) things, stuff sg F; (basura) junk sg

cacho m F bit; Rpl (cuerno) horn; Ven, Col F (marijuana) joint F; **jugar al cacho** Bol, Pe play dice; **ponerle cachos a alguien** cheat on sb

cachondeo m: **estar de cachondeo** F be joking; **tomar a cachondeo** F take as a joke; **¡vaya cachondeo!** F what a laugh! F

cachondo adj F (caliente) horny F; (gracioso) funny

cachorro m zo pup

cacique m chief; POL local political boss; fig F tyrant

cacle m Méx shoe

caco m F thief

cactus m inv BOT cactus

cada adj considerado por separado each; con énfasis en la totalidad every; **cada cosa en su sitio** everything in its place; **cada uno, cada cual** each one; **cada vez** every time, each time; **cada vez más** more and more, increasingly; **cada tres días** every three days; **uno de cada tres** one out of every three

cadáver m (dead) body, corpse

cadena f chain; de perro leash, Br lead; TV channel; **cadena perpetua** life sentence

cadencia f MÚS rhythm, cadence

cadera f hip

caducado adj out of date

caducar ⟨1g⟩ v/i expire

caducidad f: **fecha de caducidad** expiry date; de alimentos, medicinas use-by date

caer ⟨2o⟩ **1** v/i fall; **me cae bien / mal** fig I

like / don't like him; **dejar caer algo**
drop sth; **estar al caer** be about to arrive; **caer enfermo** fall ill; **caer en lunes**
fall on a Monday; **¡ahora caigo!** *fig* now
I get it! **2** *v/r* **caerse** fall (down)

café *m* coffee; (*bar*) café; **café con leche**
white coffee; **café descafeinado** decaffeinated coffee; **café instantáneo** instant coffee; **café solo** black coffee

cafeína *f* caffeine

cafetera *f* coffee maker; *para servir* coffee
pot

cafetería *f* coffee shop

cagar ⟨1h⟩ V **1** *v/i* have a shit P **2** *v/r* **cagarse** shit o.s. P; **cagarse de miedo** shit
o.s. P

caguama *f Méx* (*tortuga*) turtle

caída *f* fall

caigo *vb* → **caer**

caimán *m* zo alligator; *Méx, C.Am. útil*
monkey wrench

Cairo: **El Cairo** Cairo

caja *f* box; *de reloj, ordenador* case, cas-
ing; COM cash desk; *en supermercado*
checkout; **caja de ahorros** savings bank;
caja de cambios gearbox; **caja de cau-
dales, caja fuerte** safe, strongbox; **caja
de cerillas** matchbox; **caja de música**
music box; **caja postal** post office savings bank; **caja registradora** cash register; **echar a alguien con cajas destem-
pladas** F send s.o. packing

cajero *m*, -a *f* cashier; *de banco* teller; **cajero automático** ATM, *Br tb* cash point

cajeta *f Méx* caramel spread

cajón *m* drawer; *L.Am.* casket, coffin

cajuele *f Méx* AUTO trunk, *Br* boot

cal *f* lime

cala *f* cove

calabacín *m* BOT zucchini, *Br* courgette

calabaza *f* pumpkin; **dar calabazas a alguien** F *en examen* fail s.o., flunk s.o. F;
en relación give s.o. the brush off F

calabozo *m* cell

calada *f* puff

calado *adj* soaked; **calado hasta los
huesos** soaked to the skin

calamar *m* zo squid

calambre *m* EL shock; MED cramp

calamidad *f* calamity

calaña *f desp* sort, type

calar ⟨1a⟩ **1** *v/t* (*mojar*) soak; *techo, tela*
soak through; *persona, conjura* see
through **2** *v/i de zapato* leak; *de ideas,
costumbres* take root; **calar hondo en**
make a big impression on **3** *v/r* **calarse
de motor** stall; **calarse hasta los huesos**
get soaked to the skin

calato *adj Chi, Pe* naked

calavera *f* skull

calcar ⟨1g⟩ *v/t* trace

calceta *f:* **hacer calceta** knit

calcetín *m* sock

calcinado *adj* burnt

calcio *m* calcium

calcomanía *f* decal, *Br* transfer

calculador *adj fig* calculating

calculadora *f* calculator

calcular ⟨1a⟩ *v/t tb fig* calculate

cálculo *m* calculation; MED stone; **cálculo
biliar** gallstone; **cálculo renal** kidney
stone

caldear ⟨1a⟩ *v/t* warm up; *ánimos* inflame

caldera *f* boiler; *Rpl, Chi* kettle

calderilla *f* small change

caldero *m* (small) boiler

caldillo *m Méx* GASTR stock

caldo *m* GASTR stock; **caldo de cultivo** *fig*
breeding ground

caldoso *adj* watery

calefacción *f* heating; **calefacción central** central heating

calefactor *m* heater

calendario *m* calendar; (*programa*)
schedule

caléndula *f* BOT marigold

calentador *m* heater; **calentador de
agua** water heater

calentamiento *m:* **calentamiento global**
global warming

calentar ⟨1k⟩ **1** *v/t* heat (up); **calentar a
alguien** *fig* provoke s.o. **2** *v/i* DEP warm
up **3** *v/r* **calentarse** warm up; *fig: de discusión, disputa* become heated

calentura *f* fever

calibrar ⟨1a⟩ *v/t* gauge; *fig* weigh up

calibre *m tb fig* caliber, *Br* calibre

calidad *f* quality; **calidad de vida** quality

of life; **en calidad de médico** as a doctor

cálido adj tb fig warm

caliente adj hot; F (cachondo) horny F; **en caliente** in the heat of the moment

calificable adj gradable

calificación f description; EDU grade, Br mark

calificar ⟨1g⟩ v/t describe, label (**de** as); EDU grade, Br mark

caligrafía f calligraphy

caliza f limestone

callado adj quiet

callar ⟨1a⟩ **1** v/i (dejar de hablar) go quiet; (guardar silencio) be quiet, keep quiet; **¡calla!** be quiet!, shut up! **2** v/t silence **3** v/r **callarse** (dejar de hablar) go quiet; (guardar silencio) be quiet, keep quiet; **callarse algo** keep sth quiet

calle f street; DEP lane; **echar a alguien a la calle** fig throw s.o out onto the street

callejón m alley; **callejón sin salida** blind alley; fig dead end

callo m callus; **callos** pl GASTR tripe sg

calma f calm

calmante 1 adj soothing **2** m MED sedative

calmar ⟨1a⟩ **1** v/t calm (down) **2** v/r **calmarse** calm down

calor m heat; fig warmth; **hace mucho calor** it's very hot; **tengo calor** I'm hot

caloría f calorie

calumnia f oral slander; por escrito libel

calumniar ⟨1b⟩ v/t oralmente slander; por escrito libel

caluroso adj hot; fig warm

calva f bald patch

calvario m fig calvary

calvicie f baldness

calvo 1 adj bald **2** m bald man

calzada f road (surface)

calzado m footwear

calzador m shoe horn

calzar ⟨1f⟩ **1** v/t zapato, bota etc put on; mueble, rueda wedge **2** v/r **calzarse** zapato, bota etc put on

calzón m DEP shorts pl; L.Am. de hombre shorts pl, Br (under)pants pl; L.Am. de mujer panties pl; **calzones** L.Am. shorts, Br (under)pants

calzoncillos mpl shorts, Br (under)pants

cama f bed; **cama de matrimonio** double bed; **hacer la cama** make the bed; **irse a la cama** go to bed

camaleón m chameleon

cámara f FOT, TV camera; (sala) chamber; **cámara de comercio e industria** chamber of commerce and industry; **a cámara lenta** in slow motion; **cámara de vídeo** video camera

camarada m/f comrade; de trabajo colleague, co-worker

camaradería f camaraderie, comradeship

camarera f waitress

camarero m waiter

camarógrafo m, -a f L.Am. camera operator

camarón m L.Am. ZO shrimp, Br prawn

camarote m MAR cabin

camarotero m L.Am. steward

cambalache m Arg F second-hand shop

cambiar ⟨1b⟩ **1** v/t change (**por** for); compra exchange (**por** for) **2** v/i change; **cambiar de lugar** change places; **cambiar de marcha** AUTO shift gear, Br change gear **3** v/r **cambiarse** change; **cambiarse de ropa** change (one's clothes)

cambio m change; COM exchange rate; **cambio climático** climate change; **cambio de marchas** AUTO gear shift, Br gear change; **cambio de sentido** U-turn; **a cambio de** in exchange for; **en cambio** on the other hand

camelia f BOT camellia

camello 1 m ZO camel **2** m/f (vendedor de drogas) pusher F, dealer

camelo m F con F; (broma) joke

camilla f stretcher

caminar ⟨1a⟩ **1** v/i walk; fig move; **caminando** on foot **2** v/t walk

camino m (senda) path; (ruta) way; **a medio camino** halfway; **de camino a** on the way to; **por el camino** on the way; **abrirse camino** fig make one's way; **ir por buen/mal camino** fig be on the right / wrong track; **ponerse en camino** set out

camión m truck, Br tb lorry; Méx bus

camionero m, -a f truck driver, Br tb lorry

driver; *Méx* bus driver
camioneta *f* van
camisa *f* shirt
camiseta *f* T-shirt
camisón *m* nightdress
camorra *f* F fight; *armar camorra* F cause trouble
campal *adj*: *batalla campal* pitched battle
campamento *m* camp
campana *f* bell; *campana extractora* extractor hood
campanada *f* chime; *dar la campanada* cause a stir
campanario *m* bell tower
campanazo *m* *L.Am.* warning
campanilla *f* small bell; ANAT uvula
campante *adj*: *tan campante* F as calm as anything F
campaña *f* campaign; *campaña electoral* election campaign
campechano *adj* down-to-earth
campeón *m*, **-ona** *f* champion
campeonato *m* championship; *de campeonato* F terrific F
campera *f* *L.Am.* jacket
campesino 1 *adj* peasant *atr* **2** *m*, **-a** *f* peasant
campestre *adj* rural, country *atr*
camping *m* campground, *Br tb* campsite
campo *m* field; DEP field, *Br tb* pitch; (*estadio*) stadium, *Br tb* ground; *el campo* (*área rural*) the country; *campo de batalla* battlefield; *campo de concentración* concentration camp; *campo de golf* golf course; *campo visual* MED field of vision; *a campo traviesa, campo a través* cross-country
campus *m inv*: *campus universitario* university campus
camuflaje *m* camouflage
camuflar ⟨1a⟩ *v/t* camouflage
cana *f* gray (*Br* grey) hair
Canadá Canada
canadiense *m/f* & *adj* Canadian
canal *m* channel; TRANSP canal
canalete *m* paddle
canalizar ⟨1f⟩ *v/t* channel
canalla *m* swine F, rat F

canalón *m* gutter
canapé *m* (*sofá*) couch; *para cama* base; GASTR canapé
Canarias *fpl* Canaries
canario 1 *adj* Canary *atr* **2** *m* ZO canary
canasta *f* basket; *juego* canasta
cancela *f* (wrought-iron) gate
cancelación *f* cancellation
cancelar ⟨1a⟩ *v/t* cancel; *deuda, cuenta* settle, pay
cáncer *m* MED, *fig* cancer; *Cáncer* *m/f inv* ASTR Cancer
cancerígeno *adj* carcinogenic
canceroso *adj* cancerous
cancha *f* DEP court; *L.Am. de fútbol* field, *Br tb* pitch; *cancha de tenis* tennis court; *¡cancha! Rpl* F gangway! F; *abrir* or *hacer cancha Rpl* make room
canchear ⟨1a⟩ *v/i L.Am.* climb
canciller *m* Chancellor; *S. Am. de asuntos exteriores* Secretary of State, *Br* Foreign Minister
canción *f* song; *siempre la misma canción* F the same old story F
candado *m* padlock
candela *f L.Am.* fire; *¿me das candela?* have you got a light?
candelabro *m* candelabra
candelero *m*: *estar en el candelero de persona* be in the limelight
candente *adj* red-hot; *tema* topical
candidato *m*, **-a** *f* candidate
candidatura *f* candidacy
cándido *adj* naive
candor *m* innocence; (*franqueza*) cando(u)r
canela *f* cinnamon
canelones *mpl* GASTR cannelloni *sg*
cangrejo *m* ZO crab
canguro 1 *m* ZO kangaroo **2** *m/f* F baby-sitter
caníbal 1 *adj* cannibal *atr* **2** *m/f* cannibal
canica *f* marble
caniche *m* poodle
canícula *f* dog days *pl*
canijo *adj* F puny
canilla *f L.Am.* faucet, *Br* tap
canillita *m/f Arg* newspaper vendor
canjear ⟨1a⟩ *v/t* exchange (*por* for)

C

canoa f canoe
canónico adj canonical
canónigo m canon
canonizar ⟨1f⟩ v/t canonize
cansado adj tired
cansancio m tiredness
cansar ⟨1a⟩ **1** v/t tire; (*aburrir*) bore **2** v/r cansarse get tired; (*aburrirse*) get bored; *cansarse de algo* get tired of sth
cantante m/f singer
cantar ⟨1a⟩ **1** v/i sing; *de delincuente* squeal P **2** v/t sing **3** m: *ése es otro cantar* fig F that's a different story
cántaro m pitcher; *llover a cántaros* F pour (down)
cantautor m, cantautora f singer-songwriter
cante m: *cante hondo* or *jondo* flamenco singing
cantera f quarry
cantidad f quantity, amount; *había cantidad de* there was (*pl* were) a lot of
cantimplora f water bottle
cantina f canteen
canto¹ m singing; *de pájaro* song
canto² m edge; (*roca*) stone; *canto rodado* boulder; *darse con un canto en los dientes* count o.s. lucky
canturrear ⟨1a⟩ v/t sing softly
canutas: *las pasé canutas* F it was really tough F
caña f BOT reed; (*tallo*) stalk; *cerveza* small glass of beer; *L.Am.* straw; *muebles de caña* cane furniture; *caña de azúcar* sugar cane; *caña de pescar* fishing rod; *dar* or *meter caña a alguien* F wind s.o. up F; *¡dale caña!* F get off your butt! F
cañada f ravine; *L.Am.* (*arroyo*) stream
cáñamo m hemp; *L.Am.* marijuana plant
cañería f pipe
cañero adj *L.Am.* sugar-cane atr
caño m pipe; *de fuente* spout
cañón m HIST cannon; *antiaéreo, antitanque etc* gun; *de fusil* barrel; GEOG canyon **2** adj F great, fantastic F
cañonazo m gunshot
caoba f mahogany
caos m chaos

caótico adj chaotic
cap abr (= *capítulo*) ch. (= chapter)
capa f layer; *prenda* cloak; *capa de ozono* ozone layer; *capa de pintura* coat of paint
capacidad f capacity; (*aptitud*) competence; *capacidad de memoria / de almacenamiento* INFOR memory / storage capacity
capacitar ⟨1a⟩ v/t prepare; *capacitar alguien para hacer algo* qualify s.o. to do sth
capar ⟨1a⟩ v/t castrate
caparazón m zo shell
capataz m foreman
capataza f forewoman
capaz adj able (*de* to); *ser capaz de* be capable of
capcioso adj: *pregunta -a* trick question
capear ⟨1a⟩ v/t temporal weather
capellán m chaplain
capicúa adj: *número capicúa* reversible number
capilar **1** adj capillary atr; *loción* hair atr **2** m capillary
capilla f chapel; *capilla ardiente* chapel of rest
capirotada f *Méx* type of French toast with honey, cheese, raisins etc
capital **1** adj importancia prime; *pena capital* capital punishment **2** f de país capital **3** m COM capital
capitalismo m capitalism
capitalista **1** adj capitalist atr **2** m/f capitalist
capitán m captain
capitanear ⟨1a⟩ v/t captain
capitel m ARQUI capital
Capitolio m Capitol
capitulación f capitulation, surrender; (*pacto*) agreement
capitular ⟨1a⟩ v/i surrender, capitulate
capítulo m chapter
capó m AUTO hood, Br bonnet
capón m Rpl mutton
capota f AUTO top, Br hood
capote m cloak; MIL greatcoat
capotera f *L.Am.* coat stand
capricho m whim

caprichoso *adj* capricious

Capricornio *m/f inv* ASTR Capricorn

cápsula *f* capsule; **cápsula espacial** space capsule

captar ⟨1a⟩ *v/t* understand; RAD pick up; *negocio* take

capturar ⟨1a⟩ *v/t* capture

capucha *f* hood

capuchino *m* cappuccino

capullo *m* ZO cocoon; BOT bud

caqui 1 *adj* khaki **2** *m* BOT persimmon

cara *f* face; (*expresión*) look; *fig* nerve; **cara a algo** facing sth; **cara a cara** face to face; **de cara a** facing; *fig* with regard to; **dar la cara** face the consequences; **echar algo en cara a alguien** remind s.o. of sth; **tener cara dura** have a nerve; **tener buena / mala cara** *de comida* look good / bad; *de persona* look well / sick; **cara o cruz** heads or tails

carabinero *m* GASTR (large) shrimp, *Br* prawn; (*agente de aduana*) border guard

caracol *m* snail; **¡caracoles!** wow! F; *enfado* damn! F

caracola *f* ZO conch

carácter *m* character; (*naturaleza*) nature

característica *f* characteristic

característico *adj* characteristic (**de** of)

caracterizar ⟨1f⟩ **1** *v/t* characterize; TEA play (the part of) **2** *v/r* **caracterizarse** be characterized (**por** by)

caradura *m/f* F guy / woman with a nerve, *Br* cheeky devil F

carajillo *m* coffee with a shot of liquor

carajo *m*: **irse al carajo** F go down the tubes F

caramba *int* wow!; *enfado* damn! F

carambola *f billar* carom, *Br* cannon; **por or de carambola** F by sheer chance

caramelo *m dulce* candy, *Br* sweet; (*azúcar derretida*) caramel

carantoña *f* caress

caraqueño 1 *adj* of / from Caracas, Caracas *atr* **2** *m*, **-a** *f* native of Caracas

carátula *f de disco* jacket, *Br tb* sleeve; *L.Am. de reloj* face

caravana *f* (*remolque*) trailer, *Br* caravan; *de tráfico* queue of traffic, traffic jam; *Méx* (*reverencia*) bow

caray *int* F wow! F; *enfado* damn! F

carbón *m* coal

carboncillo *m* charcoal

carbonizar ⟨1f⟩ *v/t* char

carbono *m* QUÍM carbon

carburador *m* AUTO carburet(t)or

carburante *m* fuel

carca *m/f & adj* F reactionary

carcajada *f* laugh, guffaw; **reír a carcajadas** roar with laughter

carcajearse ⟨1a⟩ *v/r* have a good laugh (**de** at)

cárcel *f* prison

carcelero *m*, **-a** *f* warder, jailer

carcinoma *f* MED carcinoma

carcoma *f* ZO woodworm

carcomer ⟨2a⟩ **1** *v/t* eat away; *fig: de envidia* eat away at, consume **2** *v/r* **carcomerse** be eaten away; **carcomerse de** *fig* be consumed with

cardamomo *m* BOT cardamom

cardenal *m* REL cardinal; (*hematoma*) bruise

cardíaco, cardiaco *adj* cardiac

cardinal *adj* cardinal; **número cardinal** cardinal number; **puntos cardinales** points of the compass, cardinal points

cardiólogo *m*, **-a** *f* cardiologist

cardo *m* BOT thistle

carecer ⟨2d⟩ *v/i*: **carecer de algo** lack sth

carencia *f* lack (**de** of)

carente *adj*: **carente de** lacking in

careta *f* mask

carga *f* load; *de buque* cargo; MIL, EL charge; (*responsabilidad*) burden; **carga explosiva** explosive charge; **carga fiscal** or **impositiva** tax burden; **ser una carga para alguien** be a burden to s.o.; **volver a la carga** return to the attack

cargado *adj* loaded (**de** with); *aire* stuffy; *ambiente* tense; *café* strong

cargamento *m* load

cargante *adj* F annoying

cargar ⟨1h⟩ **1** *v/t arma, camión* load; *batería, acusado* charge; COM charge (**en** to); *L.Am.* (*traer*) carry; **esto me carga** *L.Am.* I can't stand this **2** *v/i* (*apoyarse*) rest (**sobre** on); (*fastidiar*) be annoying; **cargar con algo** carry sth; **cargar con la**

culpa *fig* shoulder the blame; *cargar contra alguien* MIL, DEP charge (at) s.o. 3 v/r *cargarse con peso, responsabilidad* weigh o.s. down; F (*matar*) bump off F; F (*romper*) wreck F

cargo *m* position; JUR charge; *alto cargo* high-ranking position; *persona* high-ranking official; *a cargo de la madre* in the mother's care; *está a cargo de Gómez* Gómez is in charge of it; *hacerse cargo de algo* take charge of sth

cariarse ⟨1b⟩ v/r decay

Caribe *m* Caribbean

caribeño *adj* Caribbean

caricatura *f* caricature

caricaturizar ⟨1f⟩ v/t caricature

caricia *f* caress

caridad *f* charity

caries *f* MED caries

cariño *m* affection, fondness; *hacer cariño a alguien* L.Am. (*acariciar*) caress s.o.; (*abrazar*) hug s.o.; *¡cariño!* darling!; *con cariño* with love

cariñoso *adj* affectionate

carisma *m* charisma

carismático *adj* charismatic

caritativo *adj* charitable

cariz *m* look; *tomar mal cariz* start to look bad

carmín *m de labios* lipstick

carnaval *m* carnival

carne *f* meat; *de persona* flesh; *carne de gallina* *fig* goose bumps *pl*, *Br* gooseflesh; *carne picada* ground meat, *Br* mince; *de carne y hueso* flesh and blood; *sufrir algo en sus propias carnes* *fig* go through sth oneself

carné *m* → *carnet*

carnear ⟨1a⟩ v/t L.Am. slaughter

carnero *m* ram

carnet *m* card; *carnet de conducir* driver's license, *Br* driving licence; *carnet de identidad* identity card

carnicería *f* butcher's; *fig* carnage

carnicero *m*, *-a f* butcher

carnívoro *adj* carnivorous

carnoso *adj* fleshy

caro *adj* expensive, dear; *costar caro* *fig* cost dear

carozo *m* Chi, Rpl pit

carpa *f de circo* big top; zo carp; L.Am. *para acampar* tent; L.Am. *de mercado* stall

carpeta *f* file

carpintero *m* carpenter; *de obra* joiner; *pájaro carpintero* woodpecker

carpir ⟨3a⟩ v/t L.Am. hoe

carraspear ⟨1a⟩ v/i clear one's throat

carraspera *f* hoarseness

carrera *f* race; EDU degree course; *profesional* career; *carrera de armamento* arms race; *a las carreras* at top speed; *con prisas* in a rush; *hacer la carrera* F *de prostituta* turn tricks F; *carreras* *pl de coches* motor racing *sg*

carrerilla *f*: *tomar carrerilla* take a run up; *decir algo de carrerilla* reel sth off

carreta *f* cart

carrete *m* FOT (roll of) film; *carrete de hilo* reel of thread

carretera *f* highway, (main) road; *carretera de circunvalación* ring road

carretilla *f* wheelbarrow

carril *m* lane; *carril-bici* cycle lane; *carril-bus* bus lane

carrillo *m* cheek; *comer a dos carrillos* F stuff oneself F

carrito *m* cart, *Br* trolley; *carrito de bebé* buggy, *Br* pushchair

carro *m* cart; L.Am. car; L.Am. (*taxi*) taxi, cab; *carro de combate* tank; *carro-patrulla* L.Am. F patrol car

carrocería *f* AUTO bodywork

carroña *f* carrion

carruaje *m* carriage

carta *f* letter; GASTR menu; (*naipe*) playing card; (*mapa*) map; *carta certificada o registrada* registered letter; *carta urgente* special-delivery letter; *a la carta* a la carte; *dar carta blanca a alguien* give s.o. carte blanche *o* a free hand; *poner las cartas boca arriba* *fig* put one's cards on the table; *tomar cartas en el asunto* intervene in the matter

cartearse ⟨1a⟩ v/r write to each other

cartel *m* poster; *estar en cartel de película, espectáculo* be on

cártel *m* cartel

cartelera f billboard; de periódico listings, entertainments section

cartera f wallet; (maletín) briefcase; COM, POL portfolio; de colegio knapsack, Br satchel; L.Am. purse, Br handbag; mujer mailwoman, Br postwoman

carterista m/f pickpocket

cartero m mailman, Br postman

cartílago m cartilage

cartilla f reader; Méx identity card; *cartilla de ahorros* savings book; *leerle a alguien la cartilla* F give s.o. a telling off F

cartógrafo m, -a f cartographer

cartón m cardboard; de tabaco carton; *cartón piedra* pap(i)er- mâché

cartuchera f cartridge belt

cartucho m de arma cartridge

cartulina f sheet of card; *cartulina roja* DEP red card

casa f house; (hogar) home; *en casa* at home; *como una casa* F huge F; *casa cuna* children's home; *casa de huéspedes* rooming house, Br boarding house; *casa matriz* head office; *casa de socorro* first aid post; *casa adosada, casa pareada → chalet*

casaca f cassock

casado adj married; *recién casado* newly-wed

casamentero m, -a f matchmaker

casar ⟨1a⟩ 1 v/i fig match (up); *casar con* go with 2 v/r *casarse* get married; *casarse con alguien* marry s.o.; *no casarse con nadie* fig refuse to compromise

cascabel m small bell

cascada f waterfall

cascado adj voz hoarse; F persona worn out F

cascanueces m inv nutcracker

cascar ⟨1g⟩ v/t crack; algo quebradizo break; fig F whack F; *cascarla* peg out F

cáscara f de huevo shell; de naranja, limón peel

cascarón m shell; *salir del cascarón* hatch (out)

cascarrabias m inv F grouch F

casco m helmet; de barco hull; (botella vacía) empty (bottle); edificio empty building; de caballo hoof; de vasija fragment; *casco urbano* urban area; *cascos azules* MIL blue berets, UN peace-keeping troops

cascote m piece of rubble

casera f landlady

casero 1 adj home-made; *comida -a* home cooking 2 m landlord

caseta f hut; de feria stall

casete m (also f) cassette

casi adv almost, nearly; en frases negativas hardly

casilla f en formulario box; en tablero square; de correspondencia pigeon hole; S. Am. post office box; *sacar a alguien de sus casillas* drive s.o. crazy

casino m casino

caso m case; *en caso de que, caso de* in the event that, in case of; *hacer caso* take notice; *ser un caso* F be a real case F; *no venir al caso* be irrelevant; *en todo caso* in any case, in any event; *en el peor de los casos* if the worst comes to the worst; *en último caso* as a last resort

caspa f dandruff

caspiroleta f S. Am. eggnog

casquillo m de cartucho case; EL bulb holder; L.Am. horseshoe

cassette m (also f) cassette; *cassette virgen* blank cassette

casta f caste

castaña f chestnut; *sacar las castañas del fuego a alguien* fig F pull s.o.'s chestnuts out of the fire F

castaño 1 adj color chestnut, brown 2 m chestnut (tree); color chestnut, brown; *ya pasa de castaño oscuro* F it's gone too far, it's beyond a joke

castañuela f castanet; *estar como unas castañuelas* F be over the moon F

castellano m (Castilian) Spanish

castidad f chastity

castigar ⟨1h⟩ v/t punish

castigo m punishment

castillo m castle; *castillo de fuegos artificiales* firework display

castizo adj pure

casto adj chaste

castor m ZO beaver

castrar ⟨1a⟩ v/t castrate; fig emasculate

C

castrense adj army atr
casual adj chance atr
casualidad f chance, coincidence; **por** or **de casualidad** by chance
cataclismo m cataclysm, catastrophe
catalán 1 adj Catalan **2** m, **-ana** f Catalan
catalejo m telescope
catalizador m catalyst; AUTO catalytic converter
catalizar ⟨1f⟩ v/t catalyze
catalogar ⟨1h⟩ v/t catalog(ue); fig class
catálogo m catalog(ue)
catamarán m MAR catamaran
cataplasma f MED poultice; fig: persona bore
catapulta f slingshot, Br catapult
catapultar ⟨1a⟩ v/t catapult
catar ⟨1a⟩ v/t taste
catarata f GEOG waterfall; MED cataract
catarro m cold; inflamación catarrh
catástrofe f catastrophe
catastrófico adj catastrophic
cate m EDU F fail
catear ⟨1a⟩ v/t F flunk F
catecismo m catechism
catedral f cathedral; **una mentira como una catedral** F a whopping great lie F
catedrático m, **-a** f EDU head of department
categoría f category; social class; fig: de local, restaurante class; (estatus) standing; **actor de primera categoría** first-rate actor
categórico adj categorical
catequesis f catechesis
catéter m MED catheter
catolicismo m (Roman) Catholicism
católico 1 adj (Roman) Catholic **2** m, **-a** f (Roman) Catholic
catorce adj fourteen
catre m bed
cauce m riverbed; fig channel; **volver a su cauce** fig get back to normal
caucho m rubber; L.Am. (neumático) tire, Br tyre
caudal m de río volume of flow; fig wealth
caudillo m leader
causa f cause; (motivo) reason; JUR lawsuit; **a causa de** because of

causante m cause
causar ⟨1a⟩ v/t cause
cáustico adj tb fig caustic
cautela f caution
cauteloso adj cautious
cauterizar ⟨1f⟩ v/t cauterize
cautivar ⟨1a⟩ v/t fig captivate
cautiverio m, **cautividad** f captivity
cautivo 1 adj captive **2** m, **-a** f captive
cauto adj cautious
cava m cava, sparkling wine
cavar ⟨1a⟩ v/t dig
caverna f cavern
cavernícola m/f caveman; **mujer** cavewoman
caviar m caviar
cavidad f cavity
cavilar ⟨1a⟩ v/t meditate on
cayó vb → **caer**
caza1 f hunt; actividad hunting; **caza mayor / menor** big / small game; **andar a la caza de algo / alguien** be after sth/s.o. **2** m AVIA fighter
cazador m hunter
cazadora f hunter; prenda jacket
cazar ⟨1f⟩ **1** v/t animal hunt; fig: información track down; (pillar, captar) catch; **cazar un buen trabajo** get o.s. a good job **2** v/i hunt; **ir a cazar** go hunting
cazo m saucepan
cazuela f pan; de barro, vidrio casserole
cazurro adj stubborn; (basto) coarse; (lento de entender) dense F, thick F
c.c. abr (= **centímetro cúbico**) c.c. (= cubic centimeter)
c/c abr (= **cuenta corriente**) C/A(= checking account)
CD m (= **disco compacto**) CD (= compact disc); reproductor CD-player
CD-ROM m CD-ROM
cebada f barley
cebar ⟨1a⟩ **1** v/t fatten; anzuelo bait; TÉC prime; L.Am. mate prepare **2** v/r cebarse feed (en on); **cebar con alguien** vent one's fury on s.o.
cebo m bait
cebolla f onion
cebra f zebra; **paso de cebra** crosswalk, Br zebra crossing

ceceo *m* pronunciation of 's' with 'th' sound

cecina *f* cured meat

cedazo *m* sieve

ceder ⟨2a⟩ **1** *v/t* give up; (*traspasar*) transfer, cede; **ceder el paso** AUTO yield, *Br* give way **2** *v/i* give way, yield; *de viento, lluvia* ease off

cedro *m* BOT cedar

cédula *f* L.Am. identity document

cegar ⟨1h & 1k⟩ *v/t* blind; *tubería* block

ceguera *f tb fig* blindness

ceja *f* eyebrow; **lo tiene entre ceja y ceja** F she can't stand him F

cejar ⟨1a⟩ *v/i* give up; **no cejar en** not let up in

celador *m*, **celadora** *f* orderly; *de cárcel* guard; *de museo* attendant

celda *f* cell

celebración *f* celebration

celebrar ⟨1a⟩ *v/t misa* celebrate; *reunión, acto oficial* hold; *fiesta* have, hold

célebre *adj* famous

celeste *adj* light blue, sky blue

celestial *adj* celestial; *fig* heavenly

celibato *m* celibacy

celo *m* zeal; (*cinta adhesiva*) Scotch® tape, *Br* Sellotape®; **en celo** ZO in heat; **celos** *pl* jealousy *sg*; **tener celos de** be jealous of

celofán *m* cellophane

celoso *adj* jealous (**de** of)

célula *f* cell

celular *adj* cellular

celulitis *f* cellulite

celulosa *f* cellulose

cementerio *m* cemetery

cemento *m* cement

cena *f* dinner; *más tarde* supper

cenagoso *adj* boggy

cenar ⟨1a⟩ **1** *v/t*: **cenar algo** have sth for dinner **2** *v/i* have dinner

cencerro *m* cowbell

cenicero *m* ashtray

cenit *m* AST zenith; *fig* peak

ceniza *f* ash; **cenizas** ashes

censo *m* census; **censo electoral** voting register, electoral roll

censura *f* censorship

censurar ⟨1a⟩ *v/t* censor; *tratamiento* condemn

cent *abr* (= **céntimo**) cent

centavo *m* cent

centellear ⟨1a⟩ *v/i* sparkle; *de estrella* twinkle

centena *f* hundred

centenar *m* hundred; **regalos a centenares** hundreds of gifts

centenario 1 *adj* hundred-year-old *atr* **2** *m* centennial, *Br* centenary

centeno *m* BOT rye

centígrado *adj* centigrade; **dos grados centígrados** two degrees centigrade

centímetro *m* centimeter, *Br* centimetre

céntimo *m* cent; **estar sin un céntimo** not have a red cent F

centinela *m/f* sentry; *de banda criminal* lookout

central 1 *adj* central; (*principal*) main, central **2** *f* head office; **central atómica** or **nuclear** nuclear power station; **central eléctrica** power station; **central telefónica** telephone exchange; **central térmica** thermal power station

centralismo *m* POL centralism

centralita *f* TELEC switchboard

centralizar ⟨1f⟩ *v/t* centralize

centrar ⟨1a⟩ **1** *v/t tb* DEP center, *Br* centre; *esfuerzos* focus (**en** on) **2** *v/r* **centrarse** concentrate (**en** on)

céntrico *adj* central

centrifugar ⟨1h⟩ *v/t* spin

centro *m* center, *Br* centre; **centro comercial** (shopping) mall, *Br* shopping centre; **centro urbano** en señal town center (*Br* centre)

Centroamérica Central America

centroamericano *adj* Central American

ceñido *adj* tight

ceñirse ⟨3h & 3l⟩ *v/r*: **ceñirse a algo** *fig* stick to sth

ceño *m*: **fruncir el ceño** frown

cepa *f de vid* stock

cepillar ⟨1a⟩ **1** *v/t* brush **2** *v/r* **cepillarse** brush; F (*comerse*) polish off F; F (*matar*) kill, knock off F

cepillo *m* brush; **cepillo de dientes** toothbrush

cera f wax

cerámica f ceramics

cerca[1] f fence

cerca[2] adv near, close; **de cerca** close up; **cerca de** near, close to; (*casi*) nearly

cercanía f: **tren de cercanías** suburban train

cercano adj nearby; **cercano a** close to, near to

cercar ⟨1g⟩ v/t surround; **con valla** fence in

cerciorarse ⟨1a⟩ v/r make sure (**de** of)

cerco m ring; *de puerta* frame; *L.Am.* fence; **poner cerco a** lay siege to

cerda f *animal* sow; *fig* F *persona* pig F; *de brocha* bristle

cerdo m hog, *Br* pig; *fig* F *persona* pig F

cereal m cereal; **cereales** *pl* (breakfast) cereal *sg*

cerebro m ANAT brain; *fig: persona* brains *sg*

ceremonia f ceremony

cereza f cherry

cerezo m cherry (tree)

cerilla f match

cernerse ⟨2g⟩ v/r: **cernerse sobre** *fig* hang over

cernícalo m ZO kestrel

cero m EDU zero, *Br tb* nought; **en fútbol etc** zero, *Br* nil; **en tenis** love; **bajo / sobre cero** below / above zero; **empezar desde cero** start from scratch; **vencer por tres a cero** win three-zero (*Br* nil)

cerrado adj closed; *persona* narrow-minded; (*tímido*) introverted; *cielo* overcast; *curva -a* tight curve

cerradura f lock; **ojo de la cerradura** keyhole

cerrajero m, -a f locksmith

cerrar ⟨1k⟩ 1 v/t close; *para siempre* close down; *tubería* block; *grifo* turn off; **cerrar con llave** lock 2 v/i close; *para siempre* close down 3 v/r **cerrarse** close; *de cielo* cloud over; *de persona* shut o.s. off (**a** from); **cerrarse de golpe** slam shut

cerrazón f *fig* narrow-mindedness

cerrero adj *L.Am. persona* rough

cerril adj *animal* wild; (*terco*) stubborn,

pig-headed F; (*torpe*) F dense F

cerro m hill

cerrojo m bolt; **echar el cerrojo** bolt the door

certamen m competition

certeza f certainty

certidumbre f certainty

certificado 1 adj *carta* registered 2 m certificate

certificar ⟨1g⟩ v/t certify; *carta* register

cerval adj: **miedo cerval** terrible fear

cervecería f bar

cerveza f beer; **cerveza de barril** or **de presión** draft, *Br* draught (beer); **cerveza negra** stout; **cerveza rubia** lager; **fábrica de cerveza** brewery

cesante adj *Chi* unemployed, jobless; **dejar cesante a alguien** let s.o. go

cesar ⟨1a⟩ v/i stop; **no cesar de hacer algo** keep on doing sth; **sin cesar** non-stop

cesárea f MED C(a)esarean

cese m cessation

cesión f transfer

césped m lawn

cesta f basket; **cesta de la compra** shopping basket

cesto m large basket

C.F. *abr* (= **Club de Fútbol**) FC (= Football Club)

cfc *abr* (= **clorofluorocarbono**) CFC (= chlorofluorocarbon)

cg. *abr* (= **centigramo**) centigram

ch/ *abr* (= **cheque**) check

chabacano adj vulgar, tacky F

chabola f shack; **barrio de chabolas** shanty town

chacal m ZO jackal

chacarero m, -a f *Rpl, Chi* smallholder, farmer

chacha f F maid

chácharas fpl *L.Am.* junk *sg*, bits and pieces

chachi adj F great F

chacra f *L.Am.* AGR smallholding

chafar ⟨1a⟩ v/t squash; *cosa erguida* flatten; F *planes etc* ruin F

chaflán m corner

chal m shawl

chalado adj F crazy F (**por** about)

C

chalé *m* → **chalet**

chaleco *m de traje* waistcoat; *de sport* gilet, bodywarmer; **chaleco salvavidas** life vest; **chaleco antibalas** bulletproof vest

chalet *m* chalet; **chalet adosado** house sharing one or more walls with other houses; **chalet pareado** semi-detached house

chalupa *f* MAR small boat; *Méx* stuffed tortilla

chamaca *f* C.Am., *Méx* girl

chamaco *m* C.Am., *Méx* boy

chamarra *f Méx (saco)* (short) jacket

chamba *f Méx* F job

chambón *m*, **-ona** *f Méx* F clumsy idiot F

champán *m*, champaña *m* champagne

champiñón *m* BOT mushroom

champú *m* shampoo

chamuscar ⟨1g⟩ *v/t* scorch; *pelo* singe

chamusquina *f*: **oler a chamusquina** F smell fishy F

chance **1** *m* L.Am. chance; **dame chance** let me have a go **2** *conj Méx* perhaps, maybe

chanchería *f* L.Am. pork butcher's shop

chancho *m* L.Am. hog, *Br* pig; *carne* pork

chanchullo *m* F trick, scam F

chancla *f* thong, *Br* flip-flop; *Méx, C.Am. (zapato)* slipper

chancleta *f* thong, *Br* flip-flop; *S. Am.* F baby girl

chándal *m* tracksuit

changa *f Rpl* odd job

chango **1** *adj Méx* F sharp, smart **2** *m*, **-a** *f Méx* monkey

chanquetes *mpl* GASTR whitebait *sg*

chantaje *m* blackmail; **hacer chantaje a alguien** blackmail s.o.

chantajear ⟨1a⟩ *v/t* blackmail

chantajista *m/f* blackmailer

chanza *f* wisecrack

chao *int* bye

chapa *f (tapón)* cap; *(plancha)* sheet (of metal); *(insignia)* badge; AUTO bodywork

chapado *adj* plated; **chapado a la antigua** old-fashioned; **chapado en oro** gold-plated

chapar ⟨1a⟩ *v/t* plate; *Arg, Pe* catch

chaparro *adj Méx* small

chaparrón *m* downpour; *fig* F *de insultos* barrage

chapotear ⟨1a⟩ *v/i* splash

chapucero **1** *adj* shoddy, slapdash **2** *m*, **-a** *f* shoddy worker

chapurrear ⟨1a⟩ *v/t*: **chapurrear el francés** speak poor French

chapuza *f (trabajo mal hecho)* shoddy piece of work; *(trabajo menor)* odd job

chapuzón *m* dip; **darse un chapuzón** go for a dip

chaqué *m* morning coat

chaqueta *f* jacket; **chaqueta de punto** cardigan

chaquetero *m*, **-a** *f* F turncoat

chaquetón *m* three-quarter length coat

charango *m Pe, Bol* five string guitar

charca *f* pond

charco *m* puddle

charcutería *f* delicatessen

charla *f* chat; *organizada* talk

charlar ⟨1a⟩ *v/i* chat

charlatán **1** *adj* talkative **2** *m*, **-ana** *f* chatterbox

charol *m* patent leather; **zapatos de charol** patent leather shoes

charqui *m* L.Am. beef jerky

charro **1** *adj desp* garish, gaudy **2** *m Méx* (Mexican) cowboy

chasco *m* joke; **llevarse un chasco** be disappointed

chasis *m inv* AUTO chassis

chasquear ⟨1a⟩ *v/t* click; *látigo* crack

chasquido *m* click; *de látigo* crack

chatarra *f* scrap

chato *adj nariz* snub; *L.Am. nivel* low

chau *int Rpl* bye

chaucha *f Rpl* French bean

chaval *m* F kid F, boy

chavala *f* F kid F, girl

chavalo *m* C.Am. F kid F, boy

che *int Rpl* hey!, look!

checar ⟨1g⟩ *v/t Méx* check

checo **1** *adj* Czech **2** *m*, **-a** *f* Czech

chef *m* chef

chelo *m* MÚS cello

chepa *f* F hump; **subírsele a la chepa** get too familiar

cheque *m* check, *Br* cheque; **cheque cru-**

zado crossed check (*Br* cheque); ***cheque sin fondos*** bad check (*Br* cheque); ***cheque de viaje*** traveler's check, *Br* traveller's cheque

chequear ⟨1a⟩ *v/t* check; *C.Am. equipaje* check (in)

chequeo *m* MED check-up

chequera *f* checkbook, *Br* chequebook

chica *f* girl

chicha *f L.Am.* corn liquor; ***no ser ni chicha ni limonada*** F be neither one thing nor the other

chícharo *m Méx* pea

chiche 1 *adj C.Am.* F (*fácil*) easy **2** *m S. Am.* (*juguete*) toy; (*adorno*) trinket

chichera *f C.Am.* jail

chichería *f L.Am.* bar selling corn liquor

chichón *m* bump

chicle *m* chewing gum

chico 1 *adj* small, little **2** *m* boy

chifa *m Pe* Chinese restaurant; (*comida china*) Chinese food

chifla *f Méx* whistling

chiflado *adj* F crazy F (*por* about), nuts F (*por* about)

chiflar ⟨1a⟩ **1** *v/t* boo **2** *v/i* whistle; ***me chifla ...*** F I'm crazy about ... F

chile *m* chilli (pepper)

Chile Chile

chileno 1 *adj* Chilean **2** *m,* -a *f* Chilean

chillar ⟨1a⟩ *v/i* scream, shriek; *de cerdo* squeal

chillido *m* scream, shriek; *de cerdo* squeal

chillón 1 *adj voz* shrill; *color* loud **2** *m,* -ona *f* loudmouth

chilote *m C.Am.* baby corn

chimenea *f* chimney; *de salón* fireplace

chimichurri *m Rpl* hot sauce

chimpancé *m* zo chimpanzee

China China

china[1] *f* Chinese woman

china[2] *f piedra* small stone

chincheta *f* thumbtack, *Br* drawing pin

chinchorro *m* hammock

chinear ⟨1a⟩ *v/t C.Am. niños* look after

chingar ⟨1h⟩ *v/t Méx* V screw V, fuck V; ***¡chinga tu madre!*** screw you! V, fuck you! V; ***no chingues*** don't screw me around V

chino 1 *adj* Chinese **2** *m* Chinese man; *idioma* Chinese; *L.Am. desp* half-breed *desp*; ***trabajo de chinos*** F hard work; ***me suena a chino*** F it's all Chinese *o* double Dutch to me F

chip *m* INFOR chip

chipirón *m* baby squid

chiquilla *f* girl, kid

chiquillo *m* boy, kid

chirimoya *f* BOT custard apple

chiringuito *m* beach bar

chiripa *f*: ***de chiripa*** F by sheer luck

chirona *f*: ***en chirona*** F in the can F, inside F

chirriar ⟨1c⟩ *v/i* squeak

chirrido *m* squeak

chisme *m* F bit of gossip; *objeto* doodad F, *Br* doodah F

chismografía *f* F gossip

chismorrear ⟨1a⟩ *v/i* F gossip

chismoso 1 *adj* gossipy **2** *m,* -a *f* F gossip

chispa *f* spark; (*cantidad pequeña*) spot; *fig* wit

chispear ⟨1a⟩ *v/i* spark; *fig* sparkle; *de lluvia* spit

chistar ⟨1a⟩ *v/i*: ***sin chistar*** without saying a word

chiste *m* joke

chiva *f L.Am.* goat; *C.Am., Col* bus

chivarse ⟨1a⟩ *v/r* F rat F (*a* to)

chivato *m,* -a *f* F stool pigeon F

chivo *m* zo kid; *C.Am., Méx* wages *pl*

chocante *adj* (*sorprendente*) startling; *que ofende* shocking; (*extraño*) odd; *L.Am.* (*antipático*) unpleasant

chocar ⟨1g⟩ **1** *v/t*: ***¡choca esos cinco!*** P give me five! P, put it there! P **2** *v/i* crash (*con, contra* into), collide (*con* with); ***chocarle a alguien*** (*sorprender*) surprise s.o.; (*ofender*) shock s.o.; ***me choca ese hombre*** F that guy disgusts me; ***chocar con un problema*** come up against a problem

chocho *adj* F senile; ***estar chocho con*** dote on

choclo *m Rpl* corn, *Br* corn on the cob

chocolate *m* chocolate; F (*hachís*) hashish, hash F

chocolatina *f* chocolate bar

chófer, *L.Am.* **chofer** *m* driver

chollo *m* F bargain

cholo *m L.Am.* half-caste *desp*

chompa *f S. Am.* jumper, sweater

chop *m L.Am.* large beer

chopo *m* BOT poplar

choque *m* collision, crash; DEP, MIL clash; MED shock

chorizo *m* chorizo (*spicy cured sausage*); F thief; *Rpl* (*filete*) rump steak

chorlito *m*: **cabeza de chorlito** F featherbrain F

chorrada *f* F piece of junk; **decir chorradas** F talk garbage, *Br* talk rubbish

chorrear ⟨1a⟩ *v/i* gush out, stream; (*gotear*) drip

chorro *m líquido* jet, stream; *fig* stream; *C.Am.* faucet, *Br* tap

chovinista *m/f* chauvinist

choza *f* hut

chubasco *m* shower

chubasquero *m* raincoat

chuchería *f* knick-knack; (*golosina*) candy, *Br* sweet

chucho 1 *adj C.Am.* mean **2** *m* F (*perro*) mutt F, mongrel; *Chi* (*cárcel*) can F, prison

chueco *adj L.Am.* (*torcido*) twisted

chulería *f* bragging

chuleta *f* GASTR chop

chulo F **1** *adj* fantastic F, great F; *Méx* (*guapo*) attractive; (*presuntuoso*) cocky F **2** *m* pimp F

chumbera *f C.Am.* prickly pear

chumpipe *m C.Am.* turkey

chupa *f* jacket

chupado *adj* F (*delgado*) skinny F; F (*fácil*) dead easy F; *L.Am.* F drunk

chupar ⟨1a⟩ **1** *v/t* suck; (*absorber*) soak up **2** *v/r* chuparse: **chuparse algo** suck sth; *fig* F put up with sth; **chuparse los dedos** F lick one's fingers

chupete *m de bebé* pacifier, *Br* dummy; (*sorbete*) Popsicle®, *Br* ice lolly

chupi *adj* F great F, fantastic F

churrasco *m Rpl* steak

churro *m* fritter; (*chapuza*) botched job

chusma *f desp* rabble *desp*

chutar ⟨1a⟩ *v/i* DEP shoot; **esto va que**

chuta F this is working out fine; **y vas que chutas** F and that's your lot! F

chuzo *m Chi* F *persona* dead loss F; **caer chuzos de punta** F pelt down F

Cía. *abr* (= **Compañía**) Co. (= Company)

ciberespacio *m* cyberspace

cibernauta *m/f* Internet surfer

cibernética *f* cybernetics

cicatriz *f* scar

cicatrizar ⟨1f⟩ *v/t* scar

cíclico *adj* cyclical

ciclismo *m* cycling

ciclista *m/f* cyclist

ciclo *m* cycle; *de cine* season

ciclomotor *m* moped

ciclón *m* cyclone

cicloturismo *m* bicycle touring

ciega *f* blind woman

ciego 1 *adj* blind; *a -as* blindly **2** *m* blind man

cielito *m Rpl* folk dance

cielo *m* sky; REL heaven; **ser un cielo** F be an angel F; **cielo raso** ceiling

ciempiés *m inv* ZO centipede

cien *adj* a *o* one hundred

ciencia *f* science; **ciencia ficción** science fiction; **a ciencia cierta** for certain, for sure

científico 1 *adj* scientific **2** *m*, **-a** *f* scientist

ciento *pron* a *o* one hundred; **cientos de** hundreds of; **el cinco por ciento** five percent

ciernes *en ciernes* *fig* potential, in the making

cierre *m* fastener; *de negocio* closure; **cierre centralizado** AUTO central locking; **cierre relámpago** *L.Am.* zipper, *Br* zip

cierto *adj* certain; **hasta cierto punto** up to a point; **un cierto encanto** a certain charm; **es cierto** it's true; **cierto día** one day; **por cierto** incidentally; **estar en lo cierto** be right

ciervo *m* ZO deer; **ciervo volante** ZO stag beetle

c.i.f. *abr* (= **costo, seguro y flete**) cif (= cost, insurance, freight)

cifra *f* figure

cigala *f* ZO crayfish

cigarra *f* ZO cicada

cigarrería *f L.Am.* shop selling cigarettes etc

cigarrillo *m* cigarette

cigarro *m* cigar; *L.Am.* cigarette

cigüeña *f* ZO stork

cigüeñal *m* AUTO crankshaft

cilantro *m* BOT coriander

cilindrada *f* AUTO cubic capacity

cilíndrico *adj* cylindrical

cilindro *m* cylinder

cima *f* summit; *fig* peak

cimarrón *adj L.Am. animal* wild; *esclavo* runaway; *mate cimarrón Arg* unsweetened maté

cimentar ⟨1k⟩ *v/t* lay the foundations of; *fig* base (**en** on)

cimientos *mpl* foundations

cinc *m* zinc

cincel *m* chisel

cinco 1 *adj* five **2** *m* five; *no tener ni cinco* F not have a red cent F

cincuenta *adj* fifty

cincuentón *m* man in his fifties

cincuentona *f* woman in her fifties

cine *m* movies *pl*, cinema

cineasta *m/f* film-maker

cinéfilo *m*, **-a** *f* movie buff

cinematográfico *adj* movie *atr*

cinético *adj* kinetic

cínico 1 *adj* cynical **2** *m*, **-a** *f* cynic

cinismo *m* cynicism

cinta *f* ribbon; *de música, vídeo* tape; *cinta adhesiva* adhesive tape; *cinta aislante* electrical tape, friction tape, *Br* insulating tape; *cinta métrica* tape measure; *cinta de vídeo* video tape

cintura *f* waist

cinturón *m* belt; *cinturón de seguridad* AUTO seatbelt

cíper *m Méx* zipper, *Br* zip

ciprés *m* BOT cypress

circo *m* circus

circuito *m* circuit; *corto circuito* EL short circuit

circulación *f* movement; FIN, MED circulation; AUTO traffic; *poner en circulación* put into circulation

circular 1 *adj* circular **2** ⟨1a⟩ *v/i* circulate; AUTO drive, travel; *de persona* move (along)

círculo *m* circle; *círculo vicioso* vicious circle

circuncisión *f* circumcision

circundante *adj* surrounding

circunferencia *f* circumference

circunscribir ⟨3a; *part* **circunscrito** ⟩ *v/t* limit (**a** to)

circunscripción *f* POL electoral district, *Br* constituency

circunspecto *adj* circumspect, cautious

circunstancia *f* circumstance

circunstancial *adj* circumstantial

circunvalación *f*: *(carretera de) circunvalación* beltway, *Br* ring-road

cirio *m* candle; *armar or montar un cirio* F kick up a fuss F

ciruela *f* plum; *ciruela pasa* prune

cirugía *f* surgery; *cirugía estética* cosmetic surgery

cirujano *m*, **-a** *f* surgeon

cisco *m*: *hacer cisco* smash

cisne *m* ZO swan

cisterna *f de WC* cistern

cistitis *f* MED cystitis

cita *f* appointment; *de texto* quote, quotation

citar ⟨1a⟩ **1** *v/t a reunión* arrange to meet; *a juicio* summon; (*mencionar*) mention; *de texto* quote **2** *v/r* **citarse** arrange to meet

citología *f* smear test

cítrico *m* citrus fruit

ciudad *f* town; *más grande* city; *ciudad universitaria* university campus

ciudadano *m*, **-a** *f* citizen

cívico *adj* civic

civil *adj* civil; *casarse por lo civil* have a civil wedding

civilización *f* civilization

civismo *m* civility

cizaña *f*: *sembrar or meter cizaña* cause trouble

cl. *abr* (= *centilitro*) cl. (= centiliter)

clamar ⟨1a⟩ *v/i*: *clamar por algo* clamo(u)r for sth, cry out for sth

clamor *m* roar; *fig* clamo(u)r

clan *m* clan

clandestino *adj* POL clandestine, underground

claqué *m* tap-dancing

clara *f de huevo* white; *bebida* beer with lemonade, *Br* shandy

claraboya *f* skylight

claridad *f* light; *fig* clarity

clarificar ⟨1g⟩ *v/t* clarify

clarinete *m* clarinet

clarividente *m/f* clairvoyant

claro *adj; color* light; (*luminoso*) bright; *salsa* thin; *¡claro!* of course!); *hablar claro* speak plainly

clase *f* class; (*variedad*) kind, sort; *clase particular* private class; *dar clase (s)* teach

clásico *adj* classical

clasificación *f* DEP league table

clasificar ⟨1g⟩ **1** *v/t* classify **2** *v/r* **clasificarse** DEP qualify

claudicar ⟨1g⟩ *v/i* give in

claustro *m* ARQUI cloister

claustrofobia *f* claustrophobia

cláusula *f* clause

clausurar ⟨1a⟩ *v/t acto oficial* close; *por orden oficial* close down

clavadiste *m/f Méx* diver

clavado *adj: ser clavado a alguien* be the spitting image of s.o. F

clavar ⟨1a⟩ **1** *v/t* stick (**en** into); *clavos, estaca* drive (**en** into); *uñas* sink (**en** into); *clavar los ojos en alguien* fix one's eyes on s.o.; *clavar a alguien por algo* F overcharge s.o. for sth **2** *v/r* **clavarse**: *clavarse un cuchillo en la mano* stick a knife into one's hand

clave **1** *f* key; *en clave* in code **2** *adj* (*importante*) key

clavel *m* BOT carnation

clavícula *f* ANAT collarbone

clavija *f* EL pin

clavo *m de metal* nail; GASTR clove; *CSur F persona* dead loss F; *dar en el clavo* hit the nail on the head

claxon *m* AUTO horn

clemencia *f* clemency, mercy

clementina *f* BOT clementine

clérigo *m* priest, clergyman

clero *m* clergy

clic *m* INFOR click; *hacer clic en* click on

cliché *m* cliché

clienta, cliente *m/f de tienda* customer; *de empresa* client

clientela *f* clientele, customers *pl*

clima *m* climate

climatizado *adj* air-conditioned

climatizar ⟨1f⟩ *v/t* air-condition

clímax *m fig* climax

clínica *f* clinic

clínico *adj* clinical

clip *m para papeles* paperclip; *para el pelo* bobby pin, *Br* hairgrip

cloaca *f tb fig* sewer

clon *m* BIO clone

clonación *f* BIO cloning

clonar ⟨1a⟩ *v/t* clone

cloro *m* QUÍM chlorine

clóset *m L.Am.* closet, *Br* wardrobe

club *m* club; *club náutico* yacht club

cm *abr* (= *centímetro*) cm (= centimeter)

coacción *f* coercion

coaccionar ⟨1a⟩ *v/t* coerce

coagular ⟨1a⟩ **1** *v/t* coagulate; *sangre* clot **2** *v/r* **coagularse** coagulate; *de sangre* clot

coágulo *m* clot

coala *m* ZO koala

coalición *f* coalition

coaligarse ⟨1h⟩ *v/r tb* POL work together, join forces

coartada *f* JUR alibi

coba *f: dar coba a alguien* F soft-soap s.o. F

cobarde **1** *adj* cowardly **2** *m/f* coward

cobaya *m/f* guinea pig

cobertizo *m* shed

cobertor *m* (*manta*) blanket

cobertura *f* cover; TV *etc* coverage

cobija *f L.Am.* blanket

cobijar ⟨1a⟩ **1** *v/t* give shelter to; (*acoger*) take in **2** *v/r* **cobijarse** take shelter

cobijo *m* shelter, refuge

cobra *f* ZO cobra

cobrador *m*, cobradora *f a domicilio* collector

cobrar ⟨1a⟩ **1** *v/t* charge; *subsidio, pensión* receive; *deuda* collect; *cheque* cash; *salud, fuerzas* recover; *importancia* acquire **2** *v/i* be paid, get paid; *vas a cobrar*

C

F (*recibir un palo*) you're going to get it! F

cobre *m* copper

cobro *m* charging; *de subsidio* receipt; *de deuda* collection; *de cheque* cashing

coca *f* F *droga* coke F; **de coca** *Méx* free

cocacho *m* S. Am. F whack on the head F

cocada *f* L.Am. coconut cookie

cocaína *f* cocaine

cocainómano *m*, **-a** *f* cocaine addict

cocción *f* cooking; *en agua* boiling; *al horno* baking

cocer ⟨2b & 2h⟩ **1** *v/t* cook; *en agua* boil; *al horno* bake **2** *v/r* **cocerse** cook; *en agua* boil; *al horno* bake; *fig* F *de persona* be roasting F

cochambroso *adj* F filthy

coche *m* car; *Méx* (*taxi*) cab, taxi; **coche de caballos** horse-drawn carriage; **coche cama** sleeping car; **coche comedor** L.Am. dining car; **coche de línea** (long--distance) bus

cochecito *m*: **cochecito de niño** stroller, *Br* pushchair

cochera *f* garage; *de trenes* locomotive shed

cochina *f* sow; F *persona* pig F

cochino 1 *adj fig* filthy, dirty; (*asqueroso*) disgusting **2** *m* hog, *Br* pig; F *persona* pig F

cocido 1 *adj* boiled **2** *m* stew

cociente *m* quotient

cocina *f* *habitación* kitchen; *aparato* cooker, stove; *actividad* cooking; **cocina de gas** gas cooker *o* stove

cocinar ⟨1a⟩ **1** *v/t* cook; *fig* F plot **2** *v/i* cook

cocinero *m*, **-a** *f* cook

coco *m* BOT coconut; *monstruo* bogeyman F; **comer el coco a alguien** F softsoap s.o.; *más fuerte* brainwash s.o.

cocodrilo *m* crocodile

cocoliche *m* Arg pidgin Spanish

cocotazo *m* L.Am. F whack on the head F

cocotero *m* coconut palm

cóctel *m* cocktail; **cóctel Molotov** Molotov cocktail

cód *abr* (= **código**) code

codazo *m*: **darle a alguien un codazo** el-

bow s.o.

codearse ⟨1a⟩ *v/r*: **codearse con alguien** rub shoulders with s.o.

codicia *f* greed

codiciar ⟨1b⟩ *v/t* covet

codicioso *adj* greedy

codificado *adj* TV encrypted

código *m* code; **código de barras** COM barcode; **código postal** zip code, *Br* postcode

codo *m* ANAT elbow; **codo con codo** *fig* F side by side; **hablar por los codos** F talk nineteen to the dozen F

codorniz *f* ZO quail

coeficiente *m* coefficient

coetáneo *m*, **-a** *f* contemporary

coexistir ⟨3a⟩ *v/i* coexist (**con** with)

cofradía *f* fraternity; (*gremio*) guild

cofre *m de tesoro* chest; *para alhajas* jew-el(le)ry box

coger ⟨2c⟩ **1** *v/t* (*asir*) take (hold of); *del suelo* pick up; *ladrón, enfermedad* catch; TRANSP catch, take; (*entender*) get; L.Am. V screw V **2** *v/i en un espacio* fit; L.Am. V screw V; **coger por la primera a la derecha** take the first right **3** *v/r* **cogerse** hold on (tight); **cogerse de algo** hold on to sth

cogorza *f*: **agarrar una cogorza** F get plastered F

cogote *m* F nape of the neck

cohabitar ⟨1a⟩ *v/i* live together, cohabit

cohecho *m* JUR bribery

coherencia *f* coherence

coherente *adj* coherent; **ser coherente con** be consistent with

cohesión *f* cohesion

cohete *m* rocket

cohibir ⟨3a⟩ *v/t* inhibit

COI *abr* (= **Comité Olímpico Internacional**) IOC (= International Olympic Committee)

coima *f* L.Am. bribe

coincidencia *f* coincidence

coincidir ⟨3a⟩ *v/i* coincide

coito *m* intercourse

cojear ⟨1a⟩ *v/i de persona* limp, hobble; *de mesa, silla* wobble

cojera *f* limp

cojín m cushion

cojo adj persona lame; mesa, silla wobbly

cojón m V ball V

cojonudo adj P awesome F, brilliant

col. abr (= **columna**) col. (= column)

col f cabbage; **col de Bruselas** Brussels sprout

cola¹ f (pegamento) glue

cola² f (de animal) tail; de gente line, Br queue; L.Am. F de persona butt F, Br bum F; **hacer cola** stand in line, Br queue; **estar a la cola** be in last place

colaboración f collaboration

colaborador m, **colaboradora** f collaborator; en periódico contributor

colaborar ⟨1a⟩ v/i collaborate

colación f: **traer** or **sacar a colación** bring up

colada f: **hacer la colada** do the laundry o washing

colado adj: **estar colado por alguien** F be nuts about s.o. F

colador m colander; para té etc strainer

colapsar ⟨1a⟩ **1** v/t paralyze; **colapsar el tráfico** bring traffic to a standstill **2** v/r **colapsarse** grind to a halt

colapso m collapse; **provocar un colapso en la ciudad** bring the city to a standstill

colar ⟨1m⟩ **1** v/t líquido strain; billete falso pass; **colar algo por la aduana** F smuggle sth through customs **2** v/i fig F: **no cuela** I'm not buying it F **3** v/r **colarse** F en un lugar get in; en una fiesta gatecrash; en una cola cut in line, Br push in

colcha f L.Am. bedspread

colchón m mattress; fig buffer

colchoneta f DEP mat; hinchable air bed

cole m F school

colección f collection

coleccionar ⟨1a⟩ v/t collect

coleccionista m/f collector

colecta f collection

colectivero m, -a f Arg bus driver

colectivo 1 adj collective **2** m L.Am. bus; Méx, C.Am. taxi

colega m/f colleague; F pal

colegiado m, -a f DEP referee

colegial m student, schoolboy

colegiala f student, schoolgirl

colegio m school; **colegio electoral** electoral college; **colegio profesional** professional institute

cólera 1 f anger; **montar en cólera** get in a rage **2** m MED cholera

colesterol m cholesterol

coleta f ponytail; **coletas de pelo** bunches

colgado adj: **dejar colgado a alguien** F let s.o. down

colgador m L.Am. hanger

colgante 1 adj hanging **2** m pendant

colgar ⟨1h & 1m⟩ **1** v/t hang; TELEC put down **2** v/i hang (de from); TELEC hang up **3** v/r **colgarse** hang o.s.; INFOR F lock up; **colgarse de algo** hang from sth; **colgarse de alguien** hang onto s.o.

colibrí m ZO hummingbird

cólico m MED colic

coliflor f cauliflower

colilla f cigarette end

colina f hill

colindante adj adjoining

colirio m MED eye drops pl

colisión f collision; fig clash

colisionar ⟨1a⟩ v/i collide (**con** with)

colitis f MED colitis

collar m necklace; para animal collar

colleras fpl Chi cuff links

colmar ⟨1a⟩ v/t deseos, ambición etc fulfill; **colmar un vaso** fill a glass to the brim; **colmar a alguien de elogios** heap praise on s.o.

colmena f beehive

colmillo m ANAT eye tooth; de perro fang; de elefante, rinoceronte tusk

colmo m: **¡es el colmo!** this is the last straw!; **para colmo** to cap it all

colocación f positioning, placing; (trabajo) position

colocar ⟨1g⟩ **1** v/t put, place; **colocar a alguien en un trabajo** get s.o. a job **2** v/r **colocarse** de persona position o.s.; **se colocó a mi lado** he stood next to me; **se colocaron en primer lugar** they moved into first place

colofón m fig culmination

Colombia f Colombia

colombiano 1 adj Colombian **2** m, -a f

Colombian

Colón Columbus

colonia f colony; *de viviendas* subdivision, *Br* estate; *perfume* cologne; ***colonia de verano*** summer camp

colonial *adj* colonial

colonización f colonization

colonizar ⟨1f⟩ v/t colonize

coloquial *adj* colloquial

coloquio m talk

color m colo(u)r; ***color café*** coffee-colo(u)red; *L.Am.* brown

colorado *adj* red

colorante m colo(u)ring

colorear ⟨1a⟩ v/t colo(u)r

colorete m blusher

colorido m colo(u)rs *pl*

colosal *adj* colossal

columna f column; ***columna vertebral*** ANAT spinal column

columnista m/f columnist

columpiar ⟨1b⟩ **1** v/t swing **2** v/r **columpiarse** swing

columpio m swing

colza f BOT rape

coma **1** f GRAM comma **2** m MED coma

comadre f *L.Am.* godmother

comadrear ⟨1a⟩ v/i F gossip

comadrona f midwife

comandante m MIL commander; *rango* major; AVIA captain

comarca f area

comba f jump rope, *Br* skipping rope; ***jugar* or *saltar a la comba*** jump rope, *Br* skip

combate m *acción* combat; MIL engagement; DEP fight; ***fuera de combate*** out of action

combatir ⟨3a⟩ v/t & v/i fight

combi m *Méx* minibus

combinación f combination; *prenda* slip; ***hacer combinación*** TRANSP change

combinar ⟨1a⟩ v/t combine

combustible m fuel

combustión f combustion

comedia f comedy

comedianta f actress

comediante m actor

comedido *adj* moderate

comedor m dining room

comején m termite

comensal m/f diner

comentar ⟨1a⟩ v/t comment on

comentario m comment; ***comentario de texto*** textual analysis; ***comentarios*** *pl* gossip *sg*

comentarista m/f commentator

comenzar ⟨1f & 1k⟩ v/t begin

comer ⟨2a⟩ **1** v/t eat; *a mediodía* have for lunch **2** v/i eat; *a mediodía* have lunch; ***dar de comer a alguien*** feed s.o. **3** v/r **comerse** tb fig eat up; ***se comió una palabra*** she missed out a word; ***está para comértela*** F she's really tasty F

comercial 1 *adj* commercial; *de negocios* business *atr*; ***el déficit comercial*** the trade deficit **2** m/f representative

comercializar ⟨1f⟩ v/t market, sell; *desp* commercialize

comerciante m/f trader; ***comerciante al por menor*** retailer

comercio m *actividad* trade; *local* store, shop; ***comercio exterior*** foreign trade

comestible 1 *adj* eatable, edible **2** m foodstuff; ***comestibles*** *pl* food *sg*

cometa 1 m comet **2** f kite

cometer ⟨2a⟩ v/t commit; *error* make

cometido m task

comezón f itch

cómic m comic

comicios *mpl* elections *pl*

cómico 1 *adj* comical **2** m, *-a* f comedian

comida f *(comestibles)* food; *ocasión* meal

comienzo m beginning

comillas *fpl* quotation marks, inverted commas

comino m BOT cumin; ***me importa un comino*** F I don't give a damn F

comisaría f *precinct*, *Br* police station

comisario m commissioner; *de policía* captain, *Br* superintendent

comisión f committee; *de gobierno* commission; *(recompensa)* commission

comité m committee

comitiva f retinue

como 1 *adv* as; ***así como*** as well as; ***había como cincuenta*** there were about fifty **2**

conj if; **como si** as if; **como no bebas vas a enfermar** if you don't drink you'll get sick; **como no llegó, me fui solo** as *o* since she didn't arrive, I went by myself
cómo *adv* how; **¿cómo estás?** how are you?; **¡cómo me gusta!** I really like it; **me gusta cómo habla** I like the way he talks; **¿cómo dice?** what did you say?; **¡cómo no!** *Méx* of course!
cómoda *f* chest of drawers
comodidad *f* comfort
comodín *m en naipes* joker
cómodo *adj* comfortable
comp. *abr* (= **compárese**) cf (= confer)
compacto *adj* compact
compadecer ⟨2d⟩ **1** *v/t* feel sorry for **2** *v/r* **compadecerse** feel sorry (**de** for)
compadre *m L.Am.* F buddy F
compadrear ⟨1a⟩ *v/i Arg* F brag
compadrito *m Arg* F show-off
compaginar ⟨1a⟩ *v/t fig* combine
compañero *m*, **-a** *f* companion; *en una relación, un juego* partner; **compañero de trabajo** coworker, colleague; **compañero de clase** classmate
compañía *f* company; **hacer compañía a alguien** keep s.o. company
comparación *f* comparison; **en comparación con** in comparison with
comparado *adj*: **comparado con** compared with
comparar ⟨1a⟩ *v/t* compare
comparecencia *f* JUR appearance
comparecer ⟨2d⟩ *v/i* appear
compartir ⟨3a⟩ *v/t* share (**con** with)
compás *m* MAT compass; MÚS rhythm; **al compás** to the beat
compasión *f* compassion
compatibilidad *f* compatibility
compatible *adj* INFOR compatible
compatriota *m/f* compatriot
compendio *m* summary
compenetrado *adj*: **están muy compenetrados** they are very much in tune with each other
compenetrarse ⟨1a⟩ *v/r*: **compenetrarse con alguien** reach a good understanding with s.o.
compensación *f* compensation

compensar ⟨1a⟩ **1** *v/t* compensate (**por** for) **2** *v/i fig* be worthwhile
competencia *f* (*habilidad*) competence; *entre rivales* competition; (*incumbencia*) area of responsibility, competency; **competencia desleal** unfair competition
competente *adj* competent
competición *f* DEP competition
competir ⟨3l⟩ *v/i* compete (**con** with)
competitivo *adj* competitive
compilar ⟨1a⟩ *v/t* compile
compinche *m/f* F buddy F; *desp* crony F
complacencia *f* (*placer*) pleasure; (*tolerancia*) indulgence
complacer ⟨2x⟩ *v/t* please
complaciente *adj* obliging, helpful
complejidad *f* complexity
complejo 1 *adj* complex **2** *m* PSI complex; **complejo de inferioridad** inferiority complex
complementar ⟨1a⟩ *v/t* complement
complemento *m* complement; GRAM complement, object; **complementos de moda** fashion accessories
completar ⟨1a⟩ *v/t* complete
completo *adj* complete; *autobús, teatro* full; **por completo** completely
complicación *f* complication
complicado *adj* complicated
complicar ⟨1g⟩ **1** *v/t* complicate **2** *v/r* **complicarse** get complicated; **complicarse la vida** make things difficult for o.s.
cómplice *m/f* accomplice
complot *m* plot
componente *m* component
componer ⟨2r; *part* **compuesto**⟩ **1** *v/t* make up, comprise; *sinfonía, poema etc* compose; *algo roto* fix, mend **2** *v/r* **componerse** be made up (**de** of); *L.Am.* MED get better
comportamiento *m* behavio(u)r
comportarse ⟨1a⟩ *v/r* behave
composición *f* composition
compositor *m*, **compositora** *f* composer
compostura *f fig* composure
compota *f* compote
compra *f acción* purchase; (*cosa comprada*) purchase, buy; **ir de compras** go

C

shopping
comprar ⟨1a⟩ v/t buy, purchase
compraventa f buying and selling
comprender ⟨2a⟩ v/t understand; (abarcar) include
comprensión f understanding; de texto, auditiva comprehension
comprensivo adj understanding
compresa f sanitary napkin, Br sanitary towel
compresión f tb INFOR compression
comprimido m MED pill
comprimir ⟨3a⟩ v/t compress
comprobación f check
comprobar ⟨1m⟩ v/t check; (darse cuenta de) realize
comprometer ⟨2a⟩ 1 v/t compromise; (obligar) commit 2 v/r comprometerse promise (a to); a una causa commit o.s.; de novios get engaged
comprometido adj committed; estar comprometido en algo be implicated in sth; estar comprometido de novios be engaged
compromiso m commitment; (obligación) obligation; (acuerdo) agreement; (apuro) awkward situation; sin compromiso COM without commitment; soltero y sin compromiso F footloose and fancy-free
compuesto 1 part → componer 2 adj composed; estar compuesto de be composed of
compulsar ⟨1a⟩ v/t certify
compulsivo adj PSI compulsive
computación f L.Am. computer science
computadora f L.Am. computer; computadora de escritorio desktop (computer); computadora personal personal computer; computadora portátil laptop
computarizar ⟨1f⟩ v/t computerize
comulgar ⟨1h⟩ v/i take communion; comulgar con alguien (en algo) fig F think the same way as s.o. (on sth)
común adj common; por lo común generally
comuna f commune; L.Am. (población) town
comunicación f communication; TRANSP

link
comunicado 1 adj connected; el lugar está bien comunicado the place has good transport links 2 m POL press release, communiqué
comunicar ⟨1g⟩ 1 v/t TRANSP connect, link; comunicar algo a alguien inform s.o. of sth 2 v/i communicate; TELEC be busy, Br tb be engaged 3 v/r comunicarse communicate
comunidad f community; comunidad autónoma autonomous region
comunión f REL communion
comunismo m Communism
comunista m/f & adj Communist
comunitario adj POL EU atr, Community atr
con prp with; voy con ellos I'm going with them; pan con mantequilla bread and butter; con todo eso in spite of all that; con tal de que provided that, as long as; con hacer eso by doing that
conato m: conato de violencia minor outbreak of violence; conato de incendio small fire
cóncavo adj concave
concebir ⟨3l⟩ v/t conceive
conceder ⟨2a⟩ v/t concede; entrevista, permiso give; premio award
concejal m, concejala f council(l)or
concentración f concentration; de personas gathering
concentrar ⟨1a⟩ 1 v/t concentrate 2 v/r concentrarse concentrate (en on); de gente gather
concepto m concept; en concepto de algo COM (in payment) for sth; bajo ningún concepto on no account
concernir ⟨3i⟩ v/i concern; en lo que concierne a X as far as X is concerned
concertar ⟨1k⟩ v/t cita arrange; precio agree; esfuerzos coordinate
concesión f concession; COM dealership; hacer concesiones make concessions
concesionario m dealer
concha f ZO shell
conchabar ⟨1a⟩ 1 v/t L.Am. trabajador hire 2 v/r conchabarse F plot
conciencia f conscience; a conciencia

conscientiously; **con plena conciencia de** fully conscious of

concienciar ⟨1b⟩ **1** v/t: **concienciar a alguien de algo** make s.o. aware of sth **2** v/r **concienciarse** realize (**de** sth)

concienzudo *adj* conscientious

concierto *m* MÚS concert; *fig* agreement

conciliador *adj* conciliatory

conciliar ⟨1b⟩ v/t reconcile; **conciliar el sueño** get to sleep

conciso *adj* concise

concluir ⟨3g⟩ v/t & v/i conclude

conclusión *f* conclusion; **en conclusión** in short

concretar ⟨1a⟩ **1** v/t specify; (*hacer concreto*) realize **2** v/r **concretarse** materialize; *de esperanzas* be fulfilled

concreto **1** *adj* specific; (*no abstracto*) concrete; **en concreto** specifically **2** *m* L.Am. concrete

concurrencia *f* audience; *de circunstancias* combination

concurrido *adj* crowded

concursante *m/f* competitor

concursar ⟨1a⟩ v/i compete

concurso *m* competition; COM tender

conde *m* count

condecoración *f* decoration

condecorar ⟨1a⟩ decorate

condena *f* JUR sentence; (*desaprobación*) condemnation

condenar ⟨1a⟩ v/t JUR sentence (**a** to); (*desaprobar*) condemn

condensación *f* condensation

condensado *adj* condensed

condensar ⟨1a⟩ **1** v/t condense; *libro* abridge **2** v/r **condensarse** condense

condesa *f* countess

condescendiente *adj actitud* accommodating; *desp* condescending

condición *f* condition; **a condición de que** on condition that; **estar en condiciones de** be in a position to

condimentar ⟨1a⟩ flavo(u)r

condimento *m* seasoning

condón *m* condom

cóndor *m* ZO condor

conducir ⟨3o⟩ **1** v/t *vehículo* drive; (*dirigir*) lead (**a** to); EL, TÉC conduct **2** v/i

drive; *de camino* lead (**a** to)

conducta *f* conduct, behavio(u)r

conducto *m* pipe; *fig* channel; **por conducto de** through

conductor *m*, conductora *f* driver; **conductor de orquesta** L.Am. conductor

conduje *vb* → **conducir**

conectar ⟨1a⟩ v/t connect, link; EL connect

conejillo *m*: **conejillo de Indias** *tb fig* guinea pig

conejo *m* rabbit

conexión *f tb* EL connection

confabularse ⟨1a⟩ v/r plot

confección *f* making; *de vestidos* dressmaking; *de trajes* tailoring

confeccionar ⟨1a⟩ v/t make

confederación *f* confederation

conferencia *f* lecture; (*reunión*) conference; TELEC long-distance call

conferenciante *m/f* lecturer

conferencista *m/f* L.Am. lecturer

conferir ⟨3i⟩ v/t award

confesar ⟨1k⟩ **1** v/t REL confess; *delito* confess to, admit **2** v/i JUR confess **3** v/r **confesarse** confess; (*declararse*) admit to being

confesión *f* confession

confeti *m* confetti

confiado *adj* trusting

confianza *f* confidence; **confianza en sí mismo** self-confidence; **de confianza** *persona* trustworthy; **amigo de confianza** good friend

confiar ⟨1c⟩ v/t *secreto* confide (**a** to); **confiar algo a alguien** entrust s.o. with sth, entrust sth to s.o. **2** v/i trust (**en** in); (*estar seguro*) be confident (**en** of)

confidencia *f* confidence

confidencial *adj* confidential

configuración *f* configuration; INFOR set-up, configuration

configurar ⟨1a⟩ v/t shape; INFOR set up, configure

confinar ⟨1a⟩ v/t confine

confirmación *f* confirmation

confirmar ⟨1a⟩ v/t confirm

confiscar ⟨1g⟩ v/t confiscate

confitería *f* confectioner's

confitura *f* preserve

conflagración *f* conflagration; (*guerra*) war

conflicto *m* conflict

conformarse ⟨1a⟩ *v/r* make do (**con** with)

conforme 1 *adj* satisfied (**con** with) 2 *prp*: **conforme a** in accordance with

confortable *adj* comfortable

confrontación *f* confrontation

confundir ⟨3a⟩ 1 *v/t* confuse; (*equivocar*) mistake (**con** for) 2 *v/r* confundirse make a mistake; **confundirse de calle** get the wrong street

confusión *f* confusion

confuso *adj* confused

congelación *f* freezing; **congelación de precios / de salarios** price / wage freeze

congelado *adj* frozen

congelador *m* freezer

congelar ⟨1a⟩ 1 *v/t* freeze 2 *v/r* congelarse freeze

congeniar ⟨1b⟩ *v/i* get on well (**con** with)

congénito *adj* congenital

congestión *f* MED congestion; **congestión del tráfico** traffic congestion

congestionar ⟨1a⟩ *v/t* congest

congoja *f* anguish

congregar ⟨1h⟩ *v/t* bring together

congresal *m/f* L.Am., congresista *m/f* conference *o* convention delegate, conventioneer

congreso *m* conference, convention; **Congreso en EE.UU** Congress; **congreso de los diputados** lower house of Spanish parliament

congrio *m* ZO conger eel

conjetura *f* conjecture

conjugar ⟨1h⟩ *v/t* GRAM conjugate; *fig* combine

conjunción *f* GRAM conjunction

conjuntivitis *f* MED conjunctivitis

conjunto 1 *adj* joint 2 *m de personas, objetos* collection; *de prendas* outfit; MAT set; **en conjunto** as a whole

conllevar ⟨1a⟩ *v/t* entail

conmemorar ⟨1a⟩ *v/t* commemorate

conmigo *pron* with me

conmoción *f* shock; (*agitación*) upheaval

conmocionar ⟨1a⟩ *v/t* shock

conmovedor *adj* moving

conmover ⟨2h⟩ 1 *v/t* move 2 *v/r* conmoverse be moved

conmutador *m* EL switch; L.Am. TELEC switchboard

connotación *f* connotation

cono *m* cone

conocer ⟨2d⟩ 1 *v/t* know; *por primera vez* meet; *tristeza, amor etc* experience, know; (*reconocer*) recognize; **dar a conocer** make known 2 *v/r* conocerse know one another; *por primera vez* meet one another; *a sí mismo* know o.s.; **se conoce que** it seems that

conocido 1 *adj* well-known 2 *m*, -a *f* acquaintance

conocimiento *m* knowledge; MED consciousness; **perder el conocimiento** lose consciousness

conquista *f* conquest

conquistar ⟨1a⟩ *v/t* conquer; *persona* win over

consabido *adj* usual

consagrar ⟨1a⟩ 1 *v/t* REL consecrate; (*hacer famoso*) make famous; *vida* devote 2 *v/r* consagrarse devote o.s. (**a** to)

consciente *adj* MED conscious; **consciente de** aware of, conscious of

consecuencia *f* consequence; **a consecuencia de** as a result of; **en consecuencia** consequently

consecuente *adj* consistent

consecutivo *adj* consecutive; **tres años consecutivos** three years in a row

conseguir ⟨3l & 3d⟩ *v/t* get; *objetivo* achieve

consejero *m*, -a *f* adviser; COM director

consejo *m* piece of advice; **consejo de administración** board of directors; **consejo de ministros** *grupo* cabinet; *reunión* cabinet meeting

consenso *m* consensus

consentido *adj* spoilt

consentimiento *m* consent

consentir ⟨3i⟩ 1 *v/t* allow; *a niño* indulge 2 *v/i*: **consentir en algo** agree to sth

conserje *m/f* superintendent, Br caretaker

conserva *f*: **en conserva** canned, Br

tinned; **conservas** pl canned (Br tinned) food sg

conservación f de alimentos preservation; de edificios, especies conservation

conservador adj conservative

conservante m preservative

conservar ⟨1a⟩ **1** v/t conserve; alimento preserve **2** v/r **conservarse** survive

conservatorio m conservatory

considerable adj considerable

consideración f consideration

considerar ⟨1a⟩ v/t consider

consigna f order; de equipaje baggage room, Br left-luggage

consigo pron with him / her; (con usted, con ustedes) with you; (con uno) with you, with one fml

consiguiente adj consequent; **por consiguiente** and so, therefore

consistencia f consistency

consistente adj consistent; (sólido) solid

consistir ⟨3a⟩ v/i consist (**en** of)

consola f INFOR console

consolar ⟨1m⟩ v/t console

consolidar ⟨1a⟩ **1** v/t consolidate **2** v/r **consolidarse** strengthen

consomé m GASTR consommé

consonancia f: **en consonancia con** in keeping with

consonante f consonant

consorte m/f spouse

conspiración f conspiracy

conspirar ⟨1a⟩ v/i conspire

constancia f constancy; **dejar constancia de** leave a record of

constante adj constant

constar ⟨1a⟩ v/i be recorded; **constar de** consist of

constatación f verification

constatar ⟨1a⟩ v/t verify

constelación f AST constellation

consternar ⟨1a⟩ v/t dismay

constipado 1 adj: **estar constipado** have a cold **2** m cold

constiparse ⟨1a⟩ v/r get a cold

constitución f constitution

constituir ⟨3g⟩ v/t constitute, make up; empresa, organismo set up

construcción f construction; (edificio) building

construir ⟨3g⟩ v/t build, construct

consuelo m consolation

cónsul m/f consul

consulado m consulate

consulta f consultation; MED local office, Br surgery

consultar ⟨1a⟩ v/t consult

consultor m, **consultora** f consultant

consultoría f consultancy

consultorio m MED office, Br surgery

consumidor m, **consumidora** f COM consumer

consumir ⟨3a⟩ **1** v/t consume **2** v/r **consumirse** waste away

consumo m consumption; **de bajo consumo** economical

contabilidad f accountancy; **llevar la contabilidad** do the accounts

contable m/f accountant

contactar ⟨1a⟩ v/i: **contactar con alguien** contact s.o.

contacto m contact; AUTO ignition; **ponerse en contacto** get in touch (**con** with)

contado adj: **al contado** in cash

contador 1 m meter **2** m, **contadora** f L.Am. accountant

contagiar ⟨1b⟩ **1** v/t: **contagiar la gripe a alguien** give s.o. the flu; **nos contagió su entusiasmo** he infected us with his enthusiasm **2** v/r **contagiarse** become infected

contagioso adj contagious

contaminación f de agua etc contamination; de río, medio ambiente pollution

contaminar ⟨1a⟩ v/t contaminate; río, medio ambiente pollute

contar ⟨1m⟩ **1** v/t count; (narrar) tell **2** v/i count; **contar con** count on

contemplación f: **sin contemplaciones** without ceremony

contemplar ⟨1a⟩ v/t (mirar) look at, contemplate; posibilidad consider

contemporáneo 1 adj contemporary **2** m, **-a** f contemporary

contenedor m TRANSP container; **contenedor de basura** dumpster, Br skip; **contenedor de vidrio** bottle bank

C

contener ⟨2l⟩ 1 v/t contain; *respiración* hold; *muchedumbre* hold back 2 v/r contenerse control o.s.
contenido m content
contentarse ⟨1a⟩ v/r be satisfied (**con** with)
contento adj (*satisfecho*) pleased; (*feliz*) happy
contestación f answer
contestador m: **contestador automático** TELEC answer machine
contestar ⟨1a⟩ 1 v/t answer, reply to 2 v/i reply (**a** to), answer (**a** sth); *de forma insolente* answer back
contexto m context
contigo pron with you
contiguo adj adjoining, adjacent
continental adj continental
continente m continent
continuación f continuation; **a continuación** (*ahora*) now; (*después*) then
continuar ⟨1e⟩ 1 v/t continue 2 v/i continue; **continuar haciendo algo** continue o carry on doing sth
continuidad f continuity
continuo adj (*sin parar*) continuous; (*frecuente*) continual
contorno m outline
contra prp against; **en contra de** against
contraataque m counterattack
contrabajo m double bass
contrabandista m/f smuggler
contrabando m contraband, smuggled goods pl; *acción* smuggling; **hacer contrabando** smuggle; **pasar algo de contrabando** smuggle sth in
contracción f contraction
contraceptivo m/adj contraceptive
contradecir ⟨3p⟩ v/t contradict
contradicción f contradiction
contradictorio adj contradictory
contraer ⟨2p; part **contraído**⟩ 1 v/t contract; *músculo* tighten; **contraer matrimonio** marry 2 v/r contraerse contract
contraindicación f MED contraindication
contraluz f: **a contraluz** against the light
contrapartida f COM balancing entry; **como contrapartida** fig in contrast
contrapeso m counterweight

contraposición f: **en contraposición a** in comparison to
contraproducente adj counterproductive
contrariedad f setback; (*disgusto*) annoyance
contrario 1 adj contrary; *sentido* opposite; *equipo* opposing; **al contrario, por el contrario** on the contrary; **de lo contrario** otherwise; **ser contrario a algo** be opposed to sth; **llevar la -a a alguien** contradict s.o. 2 m, -a f adversary, opponent
contrarreloj f DEP time trial
contrarrestar ⟨1a⟩ v/t counteract
contraseña f password
contrastar ⟨1a⟩ v/t & v/i contrast (**con** with)
contraste m contrast
contratar ⟨1a⟩ v/t contract; *trabajadores* hire
contratiempo m setback
contrato m contract
contravenir ⟨3s⟩ v/i contravene
contribución f contribution; (*impuesto*) tax
contribuir ⟨3g⟩ v/t contribute (**a** to)
contribuyente m/f taxpayer
contrincante m/f opponent
control m control; (*inspección*) check; **control remoto** remote control
controlador m, controladora f: **controlador aéreo** air traffic controller
controlar ⟨1a⟩ 1 v/t control; (*vigilar*) check 2 v/r controlarse control o.s.
controversia f controversy
contundente adj *arma* blunt; *fig: derrota* overwhelming
contusión f MED bruise
convalecencia f convalescence
convaleciente m/f convalescent
convalidar ⟨1a⟩ v/t recognize
convencer ⟨2b⟩ v/t convince
convención f convention
convencional adj conventional
conveniencia f de hacer algo advisability; **hacer algo por conveniencia** do sth in one's own interest
conveniente adj convenient; (*útil*) useful;

(*aconsejable*) advisable

convenio *m* agreement

convenir ⟨3s⟩ **1** *v/t* agree **2** *v/i* be advisable; *no te conviene* it's not in your interest; *convenir a alguien hacer algo* be in s.o.'s interests to do sth

conventillo *m CSur* tenement

convento *m de monjes* monastery; *de monjas* convent

converger ⟨2c⟩ *v/i* converge

conversación *f* conversation

conversar ⟨1a⟩ *v/i* make conversation

conversión *f* conversion

convertible 1 *adj* COM convertible **2** *m L.Am.* convertible

convertir ⟨3i⟩ **1** *v/t* convert **2** *v/r* **convertirse: convertirse en algo** turn into sth

convexo *adj* convex

convicción *f* conviction

convidar ⟨1a⟩ *v/t* invite (*a* to)

convincente *adj* convincing

convivencia *f* living together

convivir ⟨3a⟩ *v/i* live together

convocar ⟨1g⟩ *v/t* summon; *huelga* call; *oposiciones* organize

convocatoria *f* announcement; *de huelga* call

convoy *m* convoy

convulsión *f* convulsion; *fig* upheaval

conyugal *adj* conjugal

cónyuge *m/f* spouse

coña *f*: *decir algo de coña* F say sth as a joke; *darle la coña a alguien* F bug s.o. F; *¡ni de coña!* F no way! F

coñac *m* (*pl* ⁓s) brandy, cognac

coño *m* V cunt V

cooperación *f* cooperation

cooperar ⟨1a⟩ *v/i* cooperate

cooperativa *f* cooperative

coordinación *f* coordination

coordinar ⟨1a⟩ *v/t* coordinate

copa *f de vino etc* glass; DEP cup; *tomar una copa* have a drink; *copas pl* (*en naipes*) suit in Spanish deck of cards

copia *f* copy; *copia pirata* pirate copy

copiar ⟨1b⟩ *v/t* copy

copiloto *m/f* copilot

copioso *adj* copious

copla *f* verse; (*canción*) popular song

copo *m* flake; *copo de nieve* snowflake; *copos de maíz* cornflakes

copropietario *m*, -a *f* co-owner, joint owner

coquetear ⟨1a⟩ *v/i* flirt

coquetería *f* flirtatiousness

coqueto *adj* flirtatious; *lugar* pretty

coraje *m* courage; *me da coraje* fig F it makes me mad F

corajudo *adj L.Am.* brave

coral[1] *m* ZO coral

coral[2] *f* MÚS choir

Corán *m* Koran

coraza *f* cuirasse; ZO shell; *fig* shield

corazón *m* heart; *de fruta* core

corazonada *f* hunch

corbata *f* tie

corcho *m* cork

cordel *m* string

cordero *m* lamb

cordial *adj* cordial

cordillera *f* mountain range

cordón *m* cord; *de zapato* shoelace; *cordón umbilical* ANAT umbilical cord

cordura *f* sanity; (*prudencia*) good sense

Corea Korea

coreano 1 *adj* Korean **2** *m*, -a *f* Korean

coreografía *f* choreography

cormorán *m* ZO cormorant

cornada *f* TAUR goring

corneja *f* ZO crow

córner *m en fútbol* corner (kick)

corneta *f* MIL bugle

cornisa *f* ARQUI cornice

cornudo 1 *adj* horned **2** *m* cuckold

coro *m* MÚS choir; *de espectáculo, pieza musical* chorus; *a coro* together, in chorus

corona *f* crown; *corona de flores* garland

coronar ⟨1a⟩ *v/t* crown

coronario *adj* MED coronary

coronel *m* MIL colonel

coronilla *f* ANAT crown; *estoy hasta la coronilla* F I've had it up to here F

corotos *mpl L.Am.* F bits and pieces

corporación *f* corporation

corporal *adj placer, estética* physical; *fluido* body *atr*

corpulento *adj* solidly built

corral *m* farmyard

correa *f* lead; *de reloj* strap

corrección *f* correction; *en el trato* correctness

correcto *adj* correct; (*educado*) polite

corredizo *adj* sliding

corredor 1 *m*, **corredora** *f* DEP runner; COM agent; **corredor de bolsa** stockbroker **2** *m* ARQUI corridor

corregir ⟨3c & 3l⟩ *v/t* correct

correlación *f* correlation

correligionario *m*, **-a** *f*: **sus correligionarios republicanos** his fellow republicans

correntada *f* L.Am. current

correntoso *adj* L.Am. fast-flowing

correo *m* mail, Br *tb* post; **correos** *pl* post office *sg*; **correo aéreo** airmail; **correo electrónico** e-mail; **por correo** by mail; **echar al correo** mail, Br *tb* post

correr ⟨2a⟩ **1** *v/i* run; (*apresurarse*) rush; *de tiempo* pass; *de agua* run, flow; **correr con los gastos** pay the expenses; **a todo correr** at top speed **2** *v/t* run; *cortinas* draw; *mueble* slide, move; **correr la misma suerte** suffer the same fate **3** *v/r* **correrse** move; *de tinta* run

correspondencia *f* correspondence; FERR connection (**con** with)

corresponder ⟨2a⟩ *v/i*: **corresponder a alguien** *de bienes* be for s.o., be due to s.o.; *de responsabilidad* be up to s.o.; *de asunto* concern s.o.; *a un favor* repay s.o. (**con** with); **actuar como corresponde** do the right thing

correspondiente *adj* corresponding

corresponsal *m/f* correspondent

corretear ⟨1a⟩ *v/i* run around

corrida *f*: **corrida de toros** bullfight

corrido *adj*: **decir algo de corrido** *fig* say sth parrot-fashion

corriente 1 *adj* (*actual*) current; (*común*) ordinary; **corriente y moliente** F run-of-the-mill; **estar al corriente** be up to date **2** *f* EL, *de agua* current; **corriente de aire** draft, Br draught

corro *m* ring

corroborar ⟨1a⟩ *v/t* corroborate

corroer ⟨2za⟩ *v/t* corrode; *fig* eat up

corromper ⟨2a⟩ **1** *v/t* corrupt **2** *v/r* **corromperse** become corrupted

corrosión *f* corrosion

corrosivo *adj* corrosive; *fig* caustic

corrupción *f* decay; *fig* corruption; **corrupción de menores** corruption of minors

corrupto *adj* corrupt

corsetería *f* lingerie store

cortacésped *m* lawnmower

cortacircuitos *m inv* circuit breaker

cortada *f* L.Am. cut

cortado 1 *adj* cut; *calle* closed; *leche* curdled; *persona* shy; **quedarse cortado** be embarrassed **2** *m* coffee with a dash of milk

cortar ⟨1a⟩ **1** *v/t* cut; *electricidad* cut off; *calle* close **2** *v/i* cut **3** *v/r* **cortarse** cut o.s.; *fig* F get embarrassed; **cortarse el pelo** have one's hair cut

cortaúñas *m inv* nail clippers *pl*

corte[1] *m* cut; **corte de luz** power outage; **corte de pelo** haircut; **corte de tráfico** F road closure; **me da corte** F I'm embarrassed

corte[2] *f* court; *L.Am.* JUR (law) court; **las Cortes** Spanish parliament

cortejar ⟨1a⟩ *v/t* court

cortés *adj* courteous

cortesía *f* courtesy

corteza *f* *de árbol* bark; *de pan* crust; *de queso* rind

cortina *f* curtain

corto *adj* short; **corto de vista** nearsighted; **ni corto ni perezoso** as bold as brass; **quedarse corto** fall short

cortocircuito *m* EL short circuit

corzo *m* ZO roe deer

cosa *f* thing; **como si tal cosa** as if nothing had happened; **decir a alguien cuatro cosas** give s.o. a piece of one's mind; **eso es otra cosa** that's another matter; **¿qué pasa? – poca cosa** what's new? – nothing much

coscorrón *m* bump on the head

cosecha *f* harvest

cosechar ⟨1a⟩ *v/t* harvest; *fig* gain, win

coser ⟨2a⟩ *v/t* sew; **ser coser y cantar** F be dead easy F cosmético *m/adj* cosmetic

cósmico *adj* cosmic

cosmonauta *m/f* cosmonaut

cosmopolita *adj* cosmopolitan

cosmos *m* cosmos

cosmovisión *f* L.Am. world view

cosquillas *fpl:* **hacer cosquillas a alguien** tickle s.o.; **tener cosquillas** be ticklish

cosquilleo *m* tickle

costa¹ *f:* **a costa de** at the expense of; **a toda costa** at all costs

costa² *f* GEOG coast

costado *m* side; **por los cuatro costados** *fig* throughout, through and through

costar ⟨1m⟩ **1** *v/t en dinero* cost; *trabajo, esfuerzo etc* take; **¿cuánto cuesta?** how much does it cost? **2** *v/i en dinero* cost; **me costó** it was hard work; **cueste lo que cueste** at all costs; **costar caro** *fig* cost dear

Costa Rica Costa Rica

costarricense *m/f & adj* Costa Rican

coste *m* → **costo**

costear ⟨1a⟩ *v/t* pay for

costero *adj* coastal

costilla *f* ANAT rib; GASTR sparerib

costo *m* cost; **costo de la vida** cost of living

costoso *adj* costly

costra *f* MED scab

costumbre *f* custom; *de una persona* habit; **de costumbre** usual

costura *f* sewing

costurear ⟨1a⟩ *v/t* L.Am. sew

cotarro *m:* **manejar el cotarro** F be the boss F

cotejar ⟨1a⟩ *v/t* compare

cotidiano *adj* daily

cotilla *m/f* F gossip

cotillear ⟨1a⟩ *v/i* F gossip

cotizado *adj* COM quoted; *fig* sought-after

cotizar ⟨1f⟩ *v/i de trabajador* pay social security, *Br* pay National Insurance; *de acciones, bonos* be listed (**a** at); **cotizar en bolsa** be listed on the stock exchange

coto¹ *m:* **coto de caza** hunting reserve; **poner coto a algo** *fig* put a stop to sth

coto² *m* S. Am. MED goiter, *Br* goitre

cotorra *f* ZO parrot; F *persona* motor-mouth F

coyote *m* ZO coyote

coyuntura *f* situation; ANAT joint

C.P. *abr* (= **código postal**) zip code, *Br* post code

cráneo *m* ANAT skull, cranium

cráter *m* crater

creación *f* creation

creador *m*, **creadora** *f* creator

crear ⟨1a⟩ *v/t* create; *empresa* set up

creativo *adj* creative

crecer ⟨2d⟩ *v/i* grow

creces *fpl:* **con creces** *superar* by a comfortable margin; *pagar* with interest

creciente *adj* growing; *luna* waxing

crecimiento *m* growth

credencial *f* document

credibilidad *f* credibility

crédito *m* COM credit; **a crédito** on credit; **no dar crédito a sus oídos / ojos** F not believe one's ears / eyes

credo *m* REL, *fig* creed

crédulo *adj* credulous

creencia *f* belief

creer ⟨2e⟩ **1** *v/i* believe (**en** in) **2** *v/t* think; *(dar por cierto)* believe; **no creo que esté aquí** I don't think he's here; **¡ya lo creo!** F you bet! F **3** *v/r* creerse: **creerse que ...** believe that ...; **se cree muy lista** she thinks she's very clever

crema *f* GASTR cream

cremallera *f* zipper, *Br* zip; TÉC rack

crematorio *m* crematorium

cremoso *adj* creamy

crepe *f* GASTR crêpe, pancake

crepitar ⟨1a⟩ *v/i* crackle

crepúsculo *m* tb *fig* twilight

cresta *f* crest

cretino *m*, **-a** *f* F cretin F, moron F

creyente **1** *adj:* **ser creyente** REL believe in God **2** *m* REL believer

creyó *vb* → **creer**

cría *f acción* breeding; *de zorro, león* cub; *de perro* puppy; *de gato* kitten; *de oveja* lamb; **sus crías** her young

criada *f* maid

criado *m* servant

criar ⟨1c⟩ **1** *v/t niños* raise, bring up; *ani-*

C

males breed **2** *v/r* **criarse** grow up
criatura *f* creature; F (*niño*) baby, child
crimen *m* crime
criminal *m/f* & *adj* criminal
crío *m*, -a *f* F kid F
criollo 1 *adj* Creole **2** *m*, -a *f* Creole
cripta *f* crypt
crisantemo *m* BOT chrysanthemum
crisis *f inv* crisis
crismas *m inv* Christmas card
crispar ⟨1a⟩ *v/t* irritate; *crisparle a alguien los nervios* get on s.o.'s nerves
cristal *m* crystal; (*vidrio*) glass; (*lente*) lens; *de ventana* pane; *cristal líquido* liquid crystal
cristalizar ⟨1f⟩ *v/i* crystallize; *de idea, proyecto* jell
cristianismo *m* Christianity
cristiano 1 *adj* Christian **2** *m*, -a *f* Christian
Cristo Christ
criterio *m* criterion; (*juicio*) judg(e)ment
crítica *f* criticism; *muchas críticas* a lot of criticism
criticar ⟨1g⟩ *v/t* criticize
crítico 1 *adj* crucial **2** *m*, -a *f* critic
Croacia Croatia
crol *m* crawl
cromo *m* QUÍM chrome; (*estampa*) picture card, trading card
crónica *f* chronicle; *en periódico* report
crónico *adj* MED chronic
cronológico *adj* chronological
cronometrar ⟨1a⟩ *v/t* DEP time
cronómetro *m* stopwatch
croqueta *f* GASTR croquette
croquis *m inv* sketch
cross *m* DEP cross-country (running); *con motocicletas* motocross
cruce *m* cross; *de carreteras* crossroads *sg*; *cruce en las líneas* TELEC crossed line
crucero *m* cruise
crucial *adj* crucial
crucificar ⟨1g⟩ *v/t* crucify
crucifijo *m* crucifix
crucigrama *m* crossword
crudo 1 *adj alimento* raw; *fig* harsh **2** *m* crude (oil)

cruel *adj* cruel
cruento *adj* bloody
crujiente *adj* GASTR crunchy
crujir ⟨3a⟩ *v/i* creak; *al arder* crackle; *de grava* crunch
cruz *f* cross; *Cruz Roja* Red Cross
cruzar ⟨1f⟩ **1** *v/t* cross **2** *v/r* **cruzarse** pass one another; *cruzarse de brazos* cross one's arms; *cruzarse con alguien* pass s.o.
c.s.f. *abr* (= *costo, seguro, flete*) cif (= cost, insurance, freight)
cta, c.ta *abr* (= *cuenta*) A/C (= account)
cuaderno *m* notebook; EDU exercise book
cuadra *f* stable; *L.Am.* (*manzana*) block
cuadrado 1 *adj* square **2** *m* square; *al cuadrado* squared
cuadrilla *f* squad, team
cuadro *m* painting; (*grabado*) picture; (*tabla*) table; DEP team; *cuadro de mandos or de instrumentos* AUTO dashboard; *de or a cuadros* checked
cuádruple, cuadruplo *m* quadruple
cuajada *f* GASTR curd
cuajar ⟨1a⟩ *v/i de nieve* settle; *fig: de idea, proyecto cosa* come together, jell F
cuajo *m*: *de cuajo* by the roots
cual 1 *pron rel*: *el cual, la cual* etc *cosa* which; *persona* who; *por lo cual* (and) so **2** *adv* like
cuál *interr* which (one)
cualidad *f* quality
cualificar ⟨1g⟩ *v/t* qualify
cualquier *adj* any; *cualquier día* any day; *cualquier cosa* anything; *de cualquier modo or forma* anyway
cualquiera *pron persona* anyone, anybody; *cosa* any (one); *un cualquiera* a nobody; *¡cualquiera lo comprende!* nobody can understand it!
cuando 1 *conj* when; *condicional* if; *cuando quieras* whenever you want **2** *adv* when; *de cuando en cuando* from time to time; *cuando menos* at least
cuándo *interr* when
cuantía *f* amount, quantity; *fig* importance
cuantificar ⟨1g⟩ *v/t* quantify
cuantioso *adj* substantial

cuanto 1 *adj*: **cuanto dinero quieras** as much money as you want; **unos cuantos chavales** a few boys 2 *pron* all, everything; **se llevó cuanto podía** she took all *o* everything she could; **le dio cuanto necesitaba** he gave her everything she needed; **unas -as** a few; **todo cuanto** everything 3 *adv*: **cuanto antes, mejor** the sooner the better; **en cuanto** as soon as; **en cuanto a** as for

cuánto 1 *interr adj* how much; *pl* how many; **¿cuánto café?** how much coffee?; **¿cuántos huevos?** how many eggs? 2 *pron* how much; *pl* how many; **¿cuánto necesita Vd.?** how much do you need?; **¿cuántos ha dicho?** how many did you say?; **¿a cuánto están?** how much are they?; **¿a cuántos estamos?** what's the date today? 3 *exclamaciones*: **¡cuánta gente había!** there were so many people!; **¡cuánto me alegro!** I'm so pleased!

cuarenta *adj* forty

Cuaresma *f* Lent

cuartear ⟨1a⟩ 1 *v/t* cut up, quarter 2 *v/r* **cuartearse** crack

cuartel *m* barracks *pl*; **cuartel general** headquarters *pl*

cuartelazo *m L.Am.* military uprising

cuartilla *f* sheet of paper

cuarto 1 *adj* fourth 2 *m* (*habitación*) room; (*parte*) quarter; **cuarto de baño** bathroom; **cuarto de estar** living room; **cuarto de hora** quarter of an hour; **cuarto de kilo** quarter of a kilo; **de tres al cuarto** F third-rate; **las diez y cuarto** quarter past ten, quarter after ten; **las tres menos cuarto** a quarter to *o* of three

cuarzo *m* quartz

cuatro *adj* four; **cuatro gotas** F a few drops

cuatrocientos *adj* four hundred

cuba *f*: **estar como una cuba** F be plastered F

Cuba Cuba

cubano 1 *adj* Cuban 2 *m*, **-a** *f* Cuban

cubierta *f* MAR deck; AUTO tire, *Br* tyre

cubierto 1 *part* → **cubrir** 2 *m* piece of cut-

lery; **en la mesa** place setting; **cubiertos** *pl* cutlery *sg*

cubito *m*: **cubito de hielo** ice cube

cubo *m* cube; *recipiente* bucket; **cubo de la basura** *dentro* garbage can, *Br* rubbish bin; *fuera* garbage can, *Br* dustbin

cubrir ⟨3a; *part* **cubierto** ⟩ 1 *v/t* cover (**de** with) 2 *v/r* **cubrirse** cover o.s.

cucaracha *f* zo cockroach

cuchara *f* spoon; **meter su cuchara** *L.Am.* F stick one's oar in F

cucharada *f* spoonful

cucharilla *f* teaspoon

cucharón *m* ladle

cuchichear ⟨1a⟩ *v/i* whisper

cuchilla *f* razor blade

cuchillo *m* knife

cuclillas: **en cuclillas** squatting

cuco 1 *m* zo cuckoo; **reloj de cuco** cuckoo clock 2 *adj* (*astuto*) sharp

cucurucho *m de papel etc* cone; *sombrero* pointed hat

cuece *vb* → **cocer**

cuelgo *vb* → **colgar**

cuello *m* ANAT neck; *de camisa etc* collar

cuelo *vb* → **colar**

cuenca *f* GEOG basin

cuenco *m* bowl

cuenta *f* (*cálculo*) sum; *de restaurante* check, *Br* bill; COM account; **cuenta atrás** countdown; **cuenta bancaria** bank account; **cuenta corriente** checking account, *Br* current account; **más de la cuenta** too much; **caer en la cuenta** realize; **darse cuenta de algo** realize sth; **pedir cuentas a alguien** ask s.o. for an explanation; **perder la cuenta** lose count; **tener** *or* **tomar en cuenta** take into account; **corre por mi** / **su cuenta** I'll / he'll pay for it

cuentagotas *m inv* dropper

cuentakilómetros *m inv* odometer, *Br* mileometer

cuentista *m/f* story-teller; F (*mentiroso*) fibber F

cuento *m* (short) story; (*pretexto*) excuse; **cuento chino** F tall story F; **venir a cuento** be relevant

cuerda *f* rope; *de guitarra, violín* string;

dar cuerda al reloj wind the clock up; **dar cuerda a algo** *fig* F string sth out F; **cuerdas vocales** ANAT vocal chords

cuerdo *adj* sane; (*sensato*) sensible

cuerno *m* horn; *de caracol* feeler; **irse al cuerno** F fall through, be wrecked; **poner los cuernos a alguien** F be unfaithful to s.o.

cuero *m* leather; *Rpl* (*fuete*) whip; **en cueros** F naked

cuerpo *m* body; *de policía* force; **cuerpo diplomático** diplomatic corps *sg*; **a cuerpo de rey** like a king; **en cuerpo y alma** body and soul

cuervo *m* ZO raven, crow

cuesta *f* slope; **cuesta abajo** downhill; **cuesta arriba** uphill; **a cuestas** on one's back

cuestión *f* question; (*asunto*) matter, question; **en cuestión de ...** in a matter of ...

cuestionar ⟨1a⟩ *v/t* question

cuestionario *m* questionnaire

cueva *f* cave

cuidado *m* care; **¡cuidado!** look out!; **andar con cuidado** tread carefully; **me tiene sin cuidado** I could *o* Br couldn't care less; **tener cuidado** be careful

cuidadora *f Méx* nursemaid

cuidadoso *adj* careful

cuidar ⟨1a⟩ **1** *v/t* look after, take care of **2** *v/i*: **cuidar de** look after, take care of **3** *v/r* **cuidarse** look after o.s., take care of o.s.; **cuidarse de hacer algo** take care to do sth

culebra *f* ZO snake

culebrón *m* TV soap

culinario *adj* cooking *atr*, culinary

culminación *f* culmination

culminante *adj*: **punto culminante** peak, climax

culminar ⟨1a⟩ **1** *v/i* culminate (**en** in); *fig* reach a peak *o* climax **2** *v/t* finish

culo *m* V ass V, *Br* arse V; F butt F, *Br* bum F; **ser culo de mal asiento** *fig* F be restless, have ants in one's pants F

culpa *f* fault; **echar la culpa de algo a alguien** blame s.o. for sth; **ser por culpa de alguien** be s.o.'s fault; **tener la culpa**

be to blame (**de** for)

culpabilidad *f* guilt

culpable 1 *adj* guilty **2** *m/f* culprit

culpar ⟨1a⟩ *v/t*: **culpar a alguien de algo** blame s.o. for sth

cultivar ⟨1a⟩ *v/t* AGR grow; *tierra* farm; *fig* cultivate

cultivo *m* AGR crop; BIO culture

culto 1 *adj* educated **2** *m* worship

cultura *f* culture

cultural *adj* cultural; **un nivel cultural muy pobre** a very poor standard of education

cumbre *f tb* POL summit

cumpleaños *m inv* birthday

cumplido *m* compliment; **no andarse con cumplidos** not stand on ceremony

cumplimentar ⟨1k⟩ *v/t trámite* carry out

cumplir ⟨3a⟩ **1** *v/t orden* carry out; *promesa* fulfill; *condena* serve; **cumplir diez años** reach the age of ten, turn ten **2** *v/i*: **cumplir con algo** carry sth out; **cumplir con su deber** do one's duty; **te invita sólo por cumplir** he's only inviting you out of politeness **3** *v/r* **cumplirse** *de plazo* expire

cúmulo *m* (*montón*) pile, heap

cuna *f tb fig* cradle

cundir ⟨3a⟩ *v/i* spread; (*dar mucho de sí*) go a long way

cuneta *f* ditch

cuñada *f* sister-in-law

cuñado *m* brother-in-law

cuota *f* share; *de club, asociación* fee

cupón *m* coupon

cúpula *f* dome; *esp* POL leadership

cura 1 *m* priest **2** *f* cure; (*tratamiento*) treatment; *Méx, C.Am.* F hangover; **tener cura** be curable

curado *adj Méx, C.Am.* F drunk

curandero *m*, **-a** *f* faith healer

curar ⟨1a⟩ **1** *v/t tb* GASTR cure; (*tratar*) treat; *herida* dress; *pieles* tan **2** *v/i* MED recover (**de** from) **3** *v/r* **curarse** MED recover; *Méx, C.Am.* F get drunk

curda *f*: **agarrarse una curda** F get plastered F

curiosidad *f* curiosity

curioso 1 *adj* curious; (*raro*) curious, odd,

strange **2** *m*, **-a** *f* onlooker
curita *f L.Am.* Band-Aid®, *Br* Elastoplast®
currar ⟨1a⟩ *v/i* F work
currículum vitae *m* résumé, *Br* CV, *Br* curriculum vitae
curry *m* GASTR curry
cursi *adj* F *persona* affected
cursillo *m* short course
cursiva *f* italics *pl*
curso *m* course; **curso a distancia** or **por correspondencia** correspondence course; **en el curso de** in the course of

cursor *m* INFOR cursor
curtir ⟨3a⟩ *v/t* tan; *fig* harden
curva *f* curve
curvo *adj* curved
cúspide *f de montaña* summit; *de fama etc* height
custodia *f* JUR custody
custodiar ⟨1b⟩ *v/t* guard
cususa *f C.Am.* corn liquor
cutre *adj* F shabby, dingy
cuyo, -a *adj* whose
CV *m* resumé, *Br* CV

D

D. *abr* (= **Don**) Mr
Dª. *abr* (= **Doña**) Mrs
dactilar *adj* finger *atr*
dadivoso *adj* generous
dado[1] *m* dice
dado[2] *part* → **dar 2** *adj* given; **ser dado a algo** be given to sth **3** *conj*: **dado que** since, given that
dalia *f* dahlia
daltónico *adj* colo(u)r-blind
daltonismo *m* colo(u)r-blindness
dama *f* lady; **dama de honor** bridesmaid; (**juego de**) **damas** checkers *sg*, *Br* draughts *sg*
damasco *m* damask; *L.Am. fruta* apricot
damnificado 1 *adj* affected **2** *m*, **-a** *f* victim
danés 1 *adj* Danish **2** *m*, **-esa** *f* Dane
danza *f* dance
danzar ⟨1f⟩ *v/i* dance
dañar ⟨1a⟩ **1** *v/t* harm; *cosa* damage **2** *v/r* **dañarse** harm o.s.; *de un objeto* get damaged
dañino *adj* harmful; *fig* malicious
daño *m* harm; *a un objeto* damage; **hacer daño** hurt; **daños** *pl* damage *sg*; **daños y perjuicios** damages

dar ⟨1r; *part* **dado**⟩ **1** *v/t* give; *beneficio* yield; *luz* give off; *fiesta* give, have; **dar un golpe a** hit; **dar un salto / una patada / miedo** jump / kick / frighten; **el jamón me dió sed** the ham made me thirsty **2** *v/i*: **dame** give it to me, give me it; **dar a de ventana** look onto; **dar con algo** come across sth; **dar de comer a alguien** feed s.o.; **dar de beber a alguien** give s.o. something to drink; **dar de sí** *de material* stretch, give; **le dio por insultar a su madre** F she started insulting her mother; **¡qué más da!** what does it matter!; **da igual** it doesn't matter **3** *v/r* **darse** *de una situación* arise; **darse a algo** take to sth; **esto se me da bien** I'm good at this; **dárselas de algo** make o.s. out to be sth, claim to be sth
dardo *m* dart
datar ⟨1a⟩ *v/i*: **datar de** date from
dátil *m* BOT date
dato *m* piece of information; **datos** *pl* information *sg*, data *sg*; **datos personales** personal details
D.C. *abr* (= **después de Cristo**) AD (= Anno Domini)
dcho, dcha *abr* (= **derecho, derecha**) r

D

(= right)

d. de J.C. *abr* (= *después de Jesucristo*) AD (= Anno Domini)

de *prp* ◇ *origen* from; *de Nueva York* from New York; *de ... a* from ... to
◇ *posesión* of; *el coche de mi amigo* my friend's car
◇ *material* (made) of; *un anillo de oro* a gold ring
◇ *contenido* of; *un vaso de agua* a glass of water
◇ *cualidad: una mujer de 20 años* a 20 year old woman
◇ *causa* with; *temblaba de miedo* she was shaking with fear
◇ *hora: de noche* at night, by night; *de día* by day
◇ *en calidad de* as; *trabajar de albañil* work as a bricklayer
◇ *agente* by; *de Goya* by Goya
◇ *condición* if; *de haberlo sabido* if I'd known

dé *vb* → *dar*

deambular ⟨1a⟩ *v/i* wander around

debajo 1 *adv* underneath 2 *prp*: (*por*) *debajo de* under; *un grado por debajo de lo normal* one degree below normal

debate *m* debate, discussion

debatir ⟨3a⟩ 1 *v/t* debate, discuss 2 *v/i* struggle 3 *v/r* debatirse: *debatirse entre la vida y la muerte* fight for one's life

deber 1 *m* duty; *deberes pl* homework *sg* 2 ⟨2a⟩ *v/t* owe 3 *v/i en presente* must, have to; *en pretérito* should have; *en futuro* (will) have to; *en condicional* should; *debe de tener quince años* he must be about 15 4 *v/r* deberse: *deberse a* be due to, be caused by

debido 1 *part* → *deber* 2 *adj: como es debido* properly; *debido a* owing to, on account of

débil *adj* weak

debilitar ⟨1a⟩ 1 *v/t* weaken 2 *v/r* debilitarse weaken, become weak; *de salud* deteriorate

debut *m* debut

década *f* decade

decadencia *f* decadence; *de un imperio* decline

decaer ⟨2o; *part decaído*⟩ *v/i tb* fig decline; *de rendimiento* fall off, decline; *de salud* deteriorate

decaído 1 *part* → *decaer* 2 *adj* fig depressed, down F

decantarse ⟨1a⟩ *v/r: decantarse por* opt for

decapitar ⟨1a⟩ *v/t* behead, decapitate

decenio *m* decade

decente *adj* decent

decepción *f* disappointment

decepcionado *adj* disappointed

decepcionante *adj* disappointing

decepcionar ⟨1a⟩ *v/t* disappoint

decidido 1 *part* → *decidir* 2 *adj* decisive; *estar decidido* be determined (*a* to)

decidir ⟨3a⟩ 1 *v/t* decide 2 *v/r* decidirse make up one's mind, decide

decimal *adj* decimal *atr*

décimo 1 *adj* tenth 2 *m de lotería* share of a lottery ticket

decir ⟨3p; *part dicho*⟩ 1 *v/t* say; (*contar*) tell; *querer decir* mean; *decir que sí* say yes; *decir que no* say no; *es decir* in other words; *no es rico, que digamos* let's say he's not really; *¡no me digas!* you're kidding!; *¡quién lo diría!* who would believe it!; *se dice que ...* they say that ..., it's said that ... 2 *v/i: ¡diga!, ¡dígame!* Esp TELEC hello

decisión *f* decision; *fig* decisiveness

decisivo *adj* critical, decisive

declaración *f* declaration; *declaración de la renta* or *de impuestos* tax return; *prestar declaración* JUR testify, give evidence

declarar ⟨1a⟩ 1 *v/t* state; *bienes* declare; *declarar culpable* find guilty 2 *v/i* JUR give evidence 3 *v/r* declararse declare o.s.; *de incendio* break out; *declararse a alguien* declare one's love for s.o.

declinar ⟨1a⟩ *v/t & v/i* decline

declive *m* fig decline; *en declive* in decline

decodificador *m* → *descodificador*

decodificar ⟨1g⟩ *v/t* → *descodificar*

decolaje *m* L.Am. takeoff

decolar ⟨1a⟩ *v/i* L.Am. take off

decolorar ⟨1a⟩ *v/t* bleach

decoración f decoration

decorado m TEA set

decorador m, decoradora f: *decorador (de interiores)* interior decorator

decorar ⟨1a⟩ v/t decorate

decorativo adj decorative

decreciente adj decreasing, diminishing

decrépito adj decrepit

decretar ⟨1a⟩ v/t order, decree

decreto m decree

dedicación f dedication

dedicar ⟨1g⟩ **1** v/t dedicate; *esfuerzo* devote **2** v/r *dedicarse* devote o.s. (*a* to); *¿a qué se dedica?* what do you do (for a living)?

dedicatoria f dedication

dedillo m: *conocer algo al dedillo* F know sth like the back of one's hand; *saber algo al dedillo* F know sth off by heart

dedo m finger; *dedo del pie* toe; *dedo gordo* thumb; *dedo índice* forefinger; *no tiene dos dedos de frente* F he doesn't have much commonsense

deducción f deduction

deducir ⟨3o⟩ v/t deduce; COM deduct

defecar ⟨1g⟩ v/i defecate

defecto m defect; *moral* fault; INFOR default

defectuoso adj defective, faulty

defender ⟨2g⟩ **1** v/t defend **2** v/r *defenderse* defend o.s. (*de* against); *fig* F manage, get by; *defenderse del frío* ward off the cold

defenestrar ⟨1a⟩ v/t fig F oust

defensa **1** f JUR, DEP defense, Br defence; *L.Am.* AUTO fender, Br bumper; *defensas* MED defenses, Br defences **2** m/f DEP defender

defensivo adj defensive

defensor m, defensora f defender, champion; JUR defense counsel, Br defending counsel; *defensor del pueblo en España* ombudsman

deficiente **1** adj deficient; (*insatisfactorio*) inadequate **2** m/f handicapped person

déficit m deficit

definición f definition; *de alta definición*

TV high definition

definir ⟨3a⟩ **1** v/t define **2** v/r *definirse* come down (*por* in favor of)

definitivo adj definitive; *respuesta* definite; *en -a* all in all

deforestación f deforestation

deformar ⟨1a⟩ v/t distort; MED deform

deforme adj deformed

defraudar ⟨1a⟩ v/t disappoint; (*estafar*) defraud; *defraudar a Hacienda* evade taxes

defunción f death, demise fml

degenerar ⟨1a⟩ v/i degenerate

degollar ⟨1n⟩ v/t cut the throat of

degradante adj degrading

degradar ⟨1a⟩ v/t degrade; MIL demote; PINT gradate **2** v/r *degradarse* demean o.s.

degustar ⟨1a⟩ v/t taste

dejadez f slovenliness; (*negligencia*) neglect

dejar ⟨1a⟩ **1** v/t leave; (*permitir*) let, allow; (*prestar*) lend; *beneficios* yield; *déjame en la esquina* drop me at the corner; *dejar para mañana* leave until tomorrow; *dejar caer algo* drop sth **2** v/i: *dejar de hacer algo* (*parar*) stop doing sth; *no deja de fastidiarme* he keeps (on) annoying me **3** v/r *dejarse* let o.s. go; *dejarse llevar* let o.s. be carried along

del prp *de* y art *el*

delantal m apron

delante adv in front; (*más avanzado*) ahead; (*enfrente*) opposite; *por delante* ahead; *se abrocha por delante* it does up at the front; *tener algo por delante* have sth ahead of o in front of one; *delante de* in front of; *el asiento de delante* the front seat

delantera f DEP forward line; *llevar la delantera* be ahead of, lead

delantero m, -a f DEP forward

delatar ⟨1a⟩ v/t: *delatar a alguien* inform on s.o.; fig give s.o. away

delegación f delegation; (*oficina*) local office; *delegación de Hacienda* tax office

delegado m, -a f delegate; COM representative

delegar ⟨1h⟩ v/t delegate

deleitar ⟨1a⟩ **1** v/t delight **2** v/r **deleitarse** take delight

deletrear ⟨1a⟩ v/t spell

delfín m ZO dolphin

delgado adj slim; *lámina, placa* thin

deliberado adj deliberate

deliberar ⟨1a⟩ v/i deliberate (**sobre** on)

delicadeza f gentleness; *de acabado, tallado* delicacy; (*tacto*) tact

delicado adj delicate

delicia f delight; *hacer las delicias de alguien* delight s.o.

delicioso adj delightful; *comida* delicious

delimitar ⟨1a⟩ v/t delimit

delincuente m/f criminal

delineante m/f draftsman, Br draughtsman; *mujer* draftswoman, Br draughtswoman

delinear ⟨1a⟩ v/t draft; *fig* draw up

delirar ⟨1a⟩ v/i be delirious; *¡tú deliras!* fig you must be crazy!

delirio m MED delirium; *tener delirio por el fútbol* fig be mad about soccer; *delirios de grandeza* delusions of grandeur

delito m offense, Br offence

demacrado adj haggard

demagógico adj demagogic

demanda f demand (**de** for); JUR lawsuit, claim

demandar ⟨1a⟩ v/t JUR sue

demás 1 adj remaining **2** adv: *lo demás* the rest; *los demás* the rest, the others; *por lo demás* apart from that

demasiado 1 adj too much; *antes de pl* too many; *demasiada gente* too many people; *hace demasiado calor* it's too hot **2** adv *antes de adj, adv* too; *con verbo* too much

demencia f MED dementia; *fig* madness; *demencia senil* MED senile dementia

demencial adj fig crazy, mad

demente 1 adj demented, crazy **2** m/f mad person

democracia f democracy

demócrata 1 adj democratic **2** m/f democrat

democrático adj democratic

demografía f demographics

demoler ⟨2h⟩ v/t demolish

demoníaco, demoníaco adj demonic

demonio m demon; *¡demoníos!* hell! F, damn! F

demora f delay; *sin demora* without delay

demorar ⟨1a⟩ **1** v/i stay on; *L.Am.* (*tardar*) be late; *no demores* don't be long **2** v/t delay **3** v/r **demorarse** be delayed; *¿cuánto se demora de Concepción a Santiago?* how long does it take to get from Concepción to Santiago?

demostración f proof; *de método* demonstration; *de fuerza, sentimiento* show

demostrar ⟨1m⟩ v/t prove; (*enseñar*) demonstrate; (*mostrar*) show

denegar ⟨1h & 1k⟩ v/t refuse

denigrante adj degrading; *artículo* denigrating

denigrar ⟨1a⟩ v/t degrade; (*criticar*) denigrate

denominación f name; *denominación de origen* guarantee of quality of a wine

denominador m: *denominador común* fig common denominator

denominar ⟨1a⟩ **1** v/t designate **2** v/r **denominarse** be called

denotar ⟨1a⟩ v/t show, indicate

densidad f density

denso adj *bosque* dense; *fig* weighty

dentadura f: *dentadura postiza* false teeth pl, dentures pl

dental adj dental

dentera f: *darle dentera a alguien* set s.o.'s teeth on edge

dentífrico m toothpaste

dentista m/f dentist

dentro 1 adv inside; *por dentro* inside; *de dentro* from inside **2** *dentro de* en *espacio* in, inside; *en tiempo* in, within

denuncia f report; *poner una denuncia* make a formal complaint

denunciar ⟨1b⟩ v/t report; *fig* condemn, denounce

departamento m department; *L.Am.* (*apartamento*) apartment, Br flat

depender ⟨2a⟩ v/i depend (**de** on); *depender de alguien* en *una jerarquía* report to s.o.; *eso depende* that all de-

pends
dependiente 1 *adj* dependent **2** *m*, **-a** *f*
sales clerk, *Br* shop assistant
depilación *f* hair removal; *con cera* waxing; *con pinzas* plucking
depilar ⟨1a⟩ *v/t con cera* wax; *con pinzas*
pluck
deplorar ⟨1a⟩ *v/t* deplore
deportar ⟨1a⟩ *v/t* deport
deporte *m* sport
deportista *m/f* sportsman; *mujer* sports-
woman
depositar ⟨1a⟩ *v/t tb fig* put, place; *dinero*
deposit (*en* in)
depósito *m* COM deposit; (*almacén*) store;
de agua, AUTO tank; ***depósito de cadáveres*** morgue, *Br* mortuary
depravado *adj* depraved
depravar ⟨1a⟩ *v/t* deprave
depreciación *f* depreciation
depreciar ⟨1b⟩ **1** *v/t* lower the value of **2**
v/r **depreciarse** depreciate, lose value
depredador 1 *adj* predatory **2** *m* ZO pred-
ator
depresión *f* MED depression
deprimente *adj* depressing
deprimir ⟨3a⟩ **1** *v/t* depress **2** *v/r* **deprimir-
se** get depressed
depuradora *f* purifier
depurar ⟨1a⟩ *v/t* purify; *agua* treat; POL
purge
derecha *f tb* POL right; *la derecha* the
right(-hand); *a la derecha posición* on
the right; *dirección* to the right
derecho 1 *adj lado* right; (*recto*) straight;
C.Am. fig straight, honest **2** *adv* straight
3 *m* (*privilegio*) right; JUR law; *del derecho* on the right side; *derecho de asilo*
right to asylum; *derechos de autor* roy-
alties; *derechos humanos* human
rights; *derecho de voto* right to vote;
no hay derecho it's not fair, it's not
right; *tener derecho a* have a right to
4 *mpl*: *derechos* fees; *derechos de inscripción* registration fee *sg*
derechura *f* straightness; *C.Am., Pe* (*suerte*) luck; *en derechura* straight away
deriva *f*: *ir a la deriva* MAR, *fig* drift
derivar ⟨1a⟩ **1** *v/i* derive (*de* from); *de bar-

co* drift **2** *v/r* **derivarse** be derived (*de*
from)
dermatólogo *m*, **-a** *f* dermatologist
derogar ⟨1h⟩ *v/t* repeal
derramar ⟨1a⟩ **1** *v/t* spill; *luz, sangre* shed;
(*esparcir*) scatter **2** *v/r* **derramarse** spill;
de gente scatter
derrame *m* MED: *derrame cerebral* stroke
derrapar ⟨1a⟩ *v/i* AUTO skid
derrengado *adj* exhausted
derretir ⟨3l⟩ **1** *v/t* melt **2** *v/r* **derretirse**
melt; *fig* be besotted (*por* with)
derribar ⟨1a⟩ *v/t edificio, persona* knock
down; *avión* shoot down; POL bring down
derrocar ⟨1g⟩ *v/t* POL overthrow
derrochador *m*, **derrochadora** *f* spendthrift
derrochar ⟨1a⟩ *v/t* waste; *salud, felicidad*
exude, burst with
derroche *m* waste
derrota *f* defeat
derrotar ⟨1a⟩ *v/t* MIL defeat; DEP beat, defeat
derruir ⟨3g⟩ *v/t edificio* demolish
derrumbar ⟨1a⟩ **1** *v/t* knock down **2** *v/r*
derrumbarse collapse, fall down; *de
una persona* go to pieces
desabrido *adj* (*soso*) tasteless; *persona*
surly; *tiempo* unpleasant
desabrochar ⟨1a⟩ *v/t* undo, unfasten
desacato *m* JUR contempt
desaceleración *f* deceleration
desacertado *adj* misguided
desaconsejar ⟨1a⟩ *v/t* advise against
desacreditado *adj* discredited
desacreditar ⟨1a⟩ *v/t* discredit
desactivar ⟨1a⟩ *v/t bomba etc* deactivate
desacuerdo *m* disagreement; *estar en
desacuerdo con* disagree with
desafiar ⟨1c⟩ *v/t* challenge; *peligro* defy
desafinar ⟨1a⟩ *v/t* MÚS be out of tune
desafío *m* challenge; *al peligro* defiance
desafortunado *adj* unfortunate, unlucky
desagradable *adj* unpleasant, disagreeable
desagradar ⟨1a⟩ *v/i*: *me desagrada tener que ...* I dislike having to ...
desagradecido *adj* ungrateful; *una tarea
-a* a thankless task

desagrado *m* displeasure

desagravio *m* apology

desagüe *m* drain; *acción* drainage; *(cañería)* drainpipe

desahogar ⟨1h⟩ **1** *v/t sentimiento* vent **2** *v/r* **desahogarse** *fig* F let off steam F, get it out of one's system F

desahogo *m* comfort; **con desahogo** comfortably

desahuciar ⟨1b⟩ *v/t*: **desahuciar a alguien** declare s.o. terminally ill; *(inquilino)* evict s.o.

desairar ⟨1a⟩ *v/t* snub

desajustar ⟨1a⟩ *v/t tornillo, pieza* loosen; *mecanismo, instrumento* affect, throw out of balance

desajuste *m* disruption; COM imbalance

desalentar ⟨1k⟩ *v/t* discourage

desaliento *m* discouragement

desalinización *f* desalination

desaliñado *adj* slovenly

desalojar ⟨1a⟩ *v/t ante peligro* evacuate; *(deshauciar)* evict; *(vaciar)* vacate

desamparar ⟨1a⟩ *v/t*: **desamparar a alguien** abandon s.o.

desangelado *adj lugar* soulless

desangrarse ⟨1a⟩ *v/r* bleed to death

desanimar ⟨1a⟩ **1** *v/t* discourage, dishearten **2** *v/r* **desanimarse** become discouraged *o* disheartened

desánimo *m* discouragement

desapacible *adj* nasty, unpleasant

desaparecer ⟨2d⟩ **1** *v/i* disappear, vanish **2** *v/t L.Am.* disappear F

desaparecido *m*, **-a** *f L.Am.*: **un desaparecido** one of the disappeared

desaparición *f* disappearance

desapego *m* indifference; *(distancia)* distance, coolness

desapercibido *adj* unnoticed; **pasar desapercibido** go unnoticed

desaprensivo *adj* unscrupulous

desaprobar ⟨1m⟩ *v/t* disapprove of

desaprovechar ⟨1a⟩ *v/t oportunidad* waste

desarmado *adj* unarmed

desarmar ⟨1a⟩ *v/t* MIL disarm; TÉC take to pieces, dismantle

desarme *m* MIL disarmament

desarraigo *m fig* rootlessness

desarreglar ⟨1a⟩ *v/t* make untidy; *horario* disrupt

desarrollar ⟨1a⟩ **1** *v/t* develop; *tema* explain; *trabajo* carry out **2** *v/r* **desarrollarse** develop, evolve; *(ocurrir)* take place

desarrollo *m* development

desarticular ⟨1a⟩ *v/t banda criminal* break up; MED dislocate

desaseado *adj* F scruffy

desasirse ⟨3a⟩ *v/r* get free, free o.s.

desasosiego *m* disquiet, unease

desastre *m tb fig* disaster

desastroso *adj* disastrous

desatar ⟨1a⟩ **1** *v/t* untie; *fig* unleash **2** *v/r* **desatarse** *de animal, persona* get free; *de cordón* come undone; *fig* be unleashed, break out

desatascar ⟨1g⟩ *v/t* unblock

desatender ⟨2g⟩ *v/t* neglect; *(ignorar)* ignore

desatino *m* mistake

desatornillador *m esp L.Am.* screwdriver

desatornillar ⟨1a⟩ *v/t* unscrew

desatrancar ⟨1g⟩ *v/t cañería* unblock

desavenencia *f* disagreement

desaventajado *adj* unfavo(u)rable

desayunar ⟨1a⟩ **1** *v/i* have breakfast **2** *v/t*: **desayunar algo** have sth for breakfast

desayuno *m* breakfast

desazón *f (ansiedad)* uneasiness, anxiety

desazonar ⟨1a⟩ *v/t* worry, make anxious

desbancar ⟨1g⟩ *v/t fig* displace, take the place of

desbandarse ⟨1a⟩ *v/r* disband; *de un grupo de personas* scatter

desbarajuste *m* mess

desbaratar ⟨1a⟩ *planes* ruin; *organización* disrupt

desbarrancar ⟨1g⟩ *L.Am.* **1** *v/t* push over the edge of a cliff **2** *v/r* **desbarrancarse** go over the edge of a cliff

desbocarse ⟨1g⟩ *v/r de un caballo* bolt

desbordante *adj energía, entusiasmo etc* boundless; **desbordante de** bursting with, overflowing with

desbordar ⟨1a⟩ **1** *v/t de un río* overflow, burst; *de un multitud* break through; *de un acontecimiento* overwhelm; *fig* exceed **2** v/i overflow **3** v/r desbordarse de un río burst its banks, overflow; fig get out of control

descabellado adj: **idea -a** F hare-brained idea F

descabellar⟨1a⟩ v/t TAUR kill with a knife-thrust in the neck

descabello m fatal knife thrust

descafeinado adj decaffeinated; fig watered-down

descalabro m calamity, disaster

descalificar ⟨1g⟩ v/t disqualify

descalzarse ⟨1f⟩ v/r take one's shoes off

descalzo adj barefoot

descaminado adj fig misguided; **andar** or **ir descaminado** be on the wrong track

descamisado adj shirtless; fig ragged

descampado m open ground

descansar ⟨1a⟩ v/i rest, have a rest; **¡que descanses!** sleep well

descansillo m landing

descanso m rest; DEP half-time; TEA interval; **sin descanso** without a break

descapotable m AUTO convertible

descarado adj rude, impertinent

descarga f EL, MIL discharge; de mercancías unloading

descargar ⟨1h⟩ v/t arma, EL discharge; fig: ira etc take out (**en, sobre** on); mercancías unload; de responsabilidad, culpa clear (**de** of)

descaro m nerve

descarriado adj: **ir descarriado** go astray

descarrilar ⟨1a⟩ v/t derail

descartar ⟨1a⟩ v/t rule out

descastado adj cold, uncaring

descender ⟨2g⟩ **1** v/i para indicar alejamiento go down, descend; para indicar acercamiento come down, descend; fig go down, decrease, diminish; **descender de** descend from **2** v/t escalera go down; para indicar acercamiento come down

descendiente 1 adj descended **2** m/f descendant

descenso m de precio etc drop; de montaña, AVIA descent; DEP relegation; **la prueba de descenso** en esquí the downhill (race o competition)

descentralizar ⟨1f⟩ v/t decentralize

descentrar ⟨1a⟩ v/t fig shake

descifrar ⟨1a⟩ v/t decipher; fig work out

descodificación f decoding

descodificador m decoder

descodificar ⟨1g⟩ v/t decode

descolgar ⟨1h & 1m⟩ **1** v/t take down; teléfono pick up **2** v/r descolgarse por una cuerda lower o.s.; de un grupo break away

descollar ⟨1m⟩ v/i stand out (**sobre** among)

descolonización f decolonization

descolorido adj faded; fig colo(u)rless

descomponer ⟨2r; part **descompuesto**⟩ **1** v/t (dividir) break down; (pudrir) cause to decompose; L.Am. (romper) break **2** v/r descomponerse (pudrirse) decompose, rot; TÉC break down; Rpl (emocionarse) break down (in tears); **se le descompuso la cara** he turned pale

descomposición f breaking down; putrefacción decomposition; (diarrea) diarrh(o)ea

descompuesto 1 part → **descomponer 2** adj alimento rotten; cadáver decomposed; persona upset; L.Am. tipsy; L.Am. máquina broken down

descomunal adj huge, enormous

desconcertar ⟨1k⟩ v/t a persona disconcert

desconchado, desconchón m place where the paint is peeling; en porcelana chip

desconcierto m uncertainty

desconectar ⟨1a⟩ **1** v/t EL disconnect **2** v/i fig switch off **3** v/r desconectarse fig lose touch (**de** with)

desconfiar ⟨1c⟩ v/i be mistrustful (**de** of), be suspicious (**de** of)

descongelar ⟨1a⟩ v/t comida thaw, defrost; refrigerador defrost; precios unfreeze

descongestionar ⟨1a⟩ v/t MED clear; **descongestionar el tráfico** relieve traffic congestion

desconocer ⟨2d⟩ v/t not know

desconocido 1 adj unknown **2** m, -a f stranger

desconsiderado adj inconsiderate

D

desconsolado *adj* inconsolable

desconsuelo *m* grief

descontado 1 *part* → **descontar** 2 *adj*: **dar por descontado** take for granted; **por descontado** certainly

descontaminar ⟨1a⟩ *v/t* decontaminate

descontar ⟨1m⟩ *v/t* com deduct, take off; *fig* exclude

descontento 1 *adj* dissatisfied 2 *m* dissatisfaction

descontrol *m* chaos

descontrolarse ⟨1a⟩ *v/r* get out of control

desconvocar ⟨1g⟩ *v/t* call off

descorazonar ⟨1a⟩ 1 *v/t* discourage 2 *v/r* descorazonarse get discouraged

descorchar ⟨1a⟩ *v/t botella* uncork

descortés *adj* impolite, rude

descoserse ⟨2a⟩ *v/r de costura, dobladillo etc* come unstitched; *de prenda* come apart at the seams

descosido *m*: **como un descosido** F like mad F

descoyuntar ⟨1a⟩ *v/t* dislocate

descremado *adj* skimmed

describir ⟨3a; *part* **descrito** ⟩ *v/t* describe

descripción *f* description

descrito *part* → **describir**

descuajaringarse ⟨1h⟩ *v/r* F fall apart, fall to bits

descuartizar ⟨1f⟩ *v/t* quarter

descubierto 1 *part* → **descubrir** 2 *adj* uncovered; *persona* bareheaded; *cielos* clear; *piscina* open-air; **al descubierto** in the open; **quedar al descubierto** be exposed 3 *m* com overdraft

descubrimiento *m* discovery; (*revelación*) revelation

descubrir ⟨3a; *part* **descubierto** ⟩ 1 *v/t* discover; *poner de manifiesto* uncover, reveal; *estatua* unveil 2 *v/r* descubrirse take one's hat off; *fig* give o.s. away

descuento *m* discount; DEP stoppage time

descuerar ⟨1a⟩ *v/t L.Am.* skin; **descuerar a alguien** *fig* tear s.o. to pieces

descuidado *adj* careless

descuidar ⟨1a⟩ 1 *v/t* neglect 2 *v/i*: **¡descuida!** don't worry! 3 *v/r* descuidarse get careless; *en cuanto al aseo* let o.s.

go; (*despistarse*) let one's concentration drop

descuido *m* carelessness; (*error*) mistake; (*omisión*) oversight; **en un descuido** *L.Am.* in a moment of carelessness

desde 1 *prp en el tiempo* since; *en el espacio* from; *en escala* from; **desde 1993** since 1993; **desde hace tres días** for three days; **desde ... hasta ...** from ... to ... 2 *adv*: **desde luego** of course; **desde ya** *Rpl* right away

desdén *m* disdain, contempt

desdeñable *adj* contemptible; **nada desdeñable** far from insignificant

desdeñar ⟨1a⟩ *v/t* scorn

desdibujado *adj* blurred

desdichado 1 *adj* unhappy; (*sin suerte*) unlucky 2 *m*, -a *f* poor soul

desdoblar ⟨1a⟩ *v/t* unfold; (*dividir*) split

desear ⟨1a⟩ *v/t* wish for; *suerte etc* wish; **¿qué desea?** what would you like?

desecar ⟨1g⟩ *v/t* dry

desechable *adj* disposable

desechar ⟨1a⟩ *v/t* (*tirar*) throw away; (*rechazar*) reject

desechos *mpl* waste *sg*

desembalar ⟨1a⟩ *v/t* unpack

desembarazarse ⟨1f⟩ *v/r*: **desembarazarse de** get rid of

desembarazo *m* ease

desembarcadero *m* MAR landing stage

desembarcar ⟨1g⟩ *v/t* disembark

desembocadura *f* mouth

desembocar ⟨1g⟩ *v/i* flow (**en** into); *de calle* come out (**en** into); *de situación* end (**en** in)

desembolsar ⟨1a⟩ *v/t* pay out

desembuchar ⟨1a⟩ *v/i fig* F spill the beans F, come out with it F

desempacar ⟨1g⟩ *v/t* unpack

desempaquetar ⟨1a⟩ *v/t* unwrap

desempatar ⟨1a⟩ *v/i* DEP, POL decide the winner

desempeñar ⟨1a⟩ *v/t deber, tarea* carry out; *cargo* hold; *papel* play

desempleado 1 *adj* unemployed 2 *m*, -a *f* unemployed person

desempleo *m* unemployment

desencadenar ⟨1a⟩ 1 *v/t fig* trigger 2 *v/r*

desencadenarse *fig* be triggered

desencajarse ⟨1a⟩ *v/r de una pieza* come out; *se me ha desencajado la mandíbula* I dislocated my jaw

desencantado *adj fig* disenchanted (*con* with)

desencanto *m fig* disillusionment

desenchufar ⟨1a⟩ *v/t* EL unplug

desenfadado *adj* self-assured; *programa* light, undemanding

desenfocado *adj* FOT out of focus

desenfrenado *adj* frenzied, hectic

desenfreno *m* frenzy

desenfundar ⟨1a⟩ *v/t arma* take out, draw

desengañarse ⟨1a⟩ *v/r* become disillusioned (*de* with); (*dejar de engañarse*) stop kidding o.s.

desengaño *m* disappointment

desenlace *m* outcome, ending

desenmascarar ⟨1a⟩ *v/t fig* unmask, expose

desenredar ⟨1a⟩ *v/t* untangle; *situación confusa* straighten out, sort out

desenrollar ⟨1a⟩ *v/t* unroll

desenroscar ⟨1g⟩ *v/t* unscrew

desentenderse ⟨2g⟩ *v/r* not want to know (*de* about)

desentendido *adj*: *hacerse el desentendido* F pretend not to notice

desentonar ⟨1a⟩ *v/i* MÚS go off key; *desentonar con fig* clash with; *decir algo que desentona* say sth out of place

desentrañar ⟨1a⟩ *v/t fig* unravel

desenvoltura *f* ease

desenvolverse ⟨2h; *part* desenvuelto ⟩ *v/r fig* cope

desenvuelto 1 *part* → desenvolverse 2 *adj* self-confident

deseo *m* wish

desequilibrar ⟨1a⟩ *v/t* unbalance; *desequilibrar a alguien* throw s.o. off balance

desequilibrio *m* imbalance; *desequilibrio mental* mental instability

desertar ⟨1a⟩ *v/i* MIL desert

desertor *m*, desertora *f* deserter

desértico *adj* desert *atr*

desertización *f* desertification

desesperación *f* despair

desesperado *adj* in despair

desesperante *adj* infuriating, exasperating

desesperar ⟨1a⟩ 1 *v/t* infuriate, exasperate 2 *v/i* give up hope (*de* of), despair (*de* of) 3 *v/r* desesperarse get exasperated

desestabilizar ⟨1f⟩ *v/t* POL destabilize

desfachatez *f* impertinence

desfalco *m* embezzlement

desfallecer ⟨2d⟩ *v/i* faint

desfase *m fig* gap

desfavorable *adj* unfavo(u)rable

desfavorecer ⟨2d⟩ *v/t* (*no ser favorable*) not favo(u)r, be disadvantageous to; *de ropa etc* not suit

desfigurar ⟨1a⟩ *v/t* disfigure

desfiladero *m* ravine

desfilar ⟨1a⟩ *v/i* parade

desfile *m* parade; *desfile de modelos* or *de modas* fashion show

desfogarse ⟨1h⟩ *v/r fig* vent one's emotions

desforestación *f* deforestation

desgana *f* loss of appetite; *con desgana fig* reluctantly, half-heartedly

desgañitarse ⟨1a⟩ *v/r* F shout one's head off F

desgarbado *adj* F ungainly

desgarrador *adj* heartrending

desgarrar ⟨1a⟩ *v/t* tear up; *fig: corazón* break

desgastar ⟨1a⟩ *v/t* wear out; *defensas* wear down

desgaste *m* wear (and tear)

desglose *m* breakdown, itemization

desgracia *f* misfortune; *suceso* accident; *por desgracia* unfortunately

desgraciadamente *adv* unfortunately

desgraciado 1 *adj* unfortunate; (*miserable*) wretched 2 *m*, -a *f* wretch; (*sinvergüenza*) swine F

desgravar ⟨1a⟩ 1 *v/t* deduct 2 *v/i* be tax-deductible

desguazar ⟨1f⟩ *v/t* scrap

deshabitado *adj* uninhabited

deshacer ⟨2s; *part* deshecho ⟩ 1 *v/t* undo; *maleta* unpack; *planes* wreck, ruin; *eso los obligó a deshacer todos sus planes* this forced them to cancel their plans **2** v/r **deshacerse** de nudo de corbata, lazo etc come undone; de hielo melt; **deshacerse de** get rid of

deshecho 1 part → **deshacer 2** adj F anímicamente devastated F; de cansancio beat F, exhausted

desheredar ⟨1a⟩ v/t disinherit

deshice vb → **deshacer**

deshidratar ⟨1a⟩ v/t dehydrate

deshielo m thaw

deshinchar ⟨1a⟩ **1** v/t globo deflate, let down **2** v/r **deshincharse** deflate, go down; fig lose heart

deshonesto adj dishonest

deshonra f dishono(u)r

deshonroso adj dishono(u)rable

deshora f: **a deshora** (**s**) at the wrong time

desidia f apathy, lethargy

desierto 1 adj lugar empty, deserted; **isla -a** desert island **2** m desert

designar ⟨1a⟩ v/t appoint, name; lugar select

designio m plan

desigual adj unequal; terreno uneven, irregular

desigualdad f inequality

desilusión f disappointment

desilusionado adj disappointed

desilusionar ⟨1a⟩ **1** v/t disappoint; (quitar la ilusión) disillusion **2** v/r **desilusionarse** be disappointed; (perder la ilusión) become disillusioned

desinfectante m disinfectant

desinfectar ⟨1a⟩ v/t disinfect

desinflar ⟨1a⟩ **1** v/t globo, neumático let the air out of, deflate **2** v/r **desinflarse** de neumático deflate; fig lose heart

desinformación f disinformation

desinhibir ⟨3a⟩ **1** v/t: **desinhibir alguien** get rid of s.o.'s inhibitions **2** v/r **desinhibirse** lose one's inhibitions

desintegrar ⟨1a⟩ **1** v/t cause to disintegrate; grupo de gente break up **2** v/r **desintegrarse** disintegrate; de grupo de gente break up

desinterés m lack of interest; (generosidad) unselfishness

desinteresado adj unselfish

desintoxicación f detoxification; **hacer una cura de desintoxicación** go into detox F, have treatment for drug / alcohol abuse

desistir ⟨3a⟩ v/i give up; **tuvo que desistir de hacerlo** I had to stop doing it

deslealtad f disloyalty

desligar ⟨1h⟩ **1** v/t separate (**de** from); fig persona cut off (**de** from) **2** v/r **desligarse** fig cut o.s. off (**de** from)

desliz m fig F slip-up F

deslizar ⟨1f⟩ **1** v/t slide, run (**por** along); idea, frase slip in **2** v/i slide **3** v/r **deslizarse** slide

deslomarse ⟨1a⟩ v/r fig kill o.s.

deslucido adj tarnished; colores dull, drab

deslucir ⟨3f⟩ v/t tarnish; fig spoil

deslumbrante adj dazzling

deslumbrar ⟨1a⟩ **1** v/t fig dazzle **2** v/r **deslumbrarse** fig be dazzled

desmadre m F chaos

desmandarse ⟨1a⟩ v/r de animal break loose

desmantelar ⟨1a⟩ v/t fortificación, organización dismantle

desmañado adj clumsy

desmaquillar ⟨1a⟩ **1** v/t remove makeup from **2** v/r **desmaquillarse** remove one's makeup

desmarcarse ⟨1g⟩ v/r DEP lose one's marker; **desmarcarse de** distance o.s. from

desmayarse ⟨1a⟩ v/r faint

desmayo m fainting fit; **sin desmayo** without flagging

desmedido adj excessive

desmelenarse ⟨1a⟩ v/r fig F let one's hair down F; (enfurecerse) hit the roof F

desmembrar ⟨1k⟩ v/t dismember

desmemoriado adj forgetful

desmentido m denial

desmentir ⟨3i⟩ v/t deny; a alguien contradict

desmenuzar ⟨1f⟩ v/t crumble up; fig break down

desmerecer ⟨2d⟩ **1** v/t not do justice to **2** v/i be unworthy (**con** of); **desmerecer de** not stand comparison with; **no desme-**

recer de be in no way inferior to
desmesurado *adj* excessive
desmilitarización *f* demilitarization
desmitificar ⟨1g⟩ *v/t* demystify, demythologize
desmontar ⟨1a⟩ **1** *v/t* dismantle, take apart; *tienda de campaña* take down **2** *v/i* dismount
desmoralizado *adj* demoralized
desmoralizar ⟨1f⟩ *v/t* demoralize
desmoronamiento *m tb fig* collapse
desmoronarse ⟨1a⟩ *v/r tb fig* collapse
desnatado *adj* skimmed
desnaturalizado *adj* QUÍM denatured
desnivel *m* unevenness; *entre personas* disparity
desnivelar ⟨1a⟩ *v/t* upset the balance of
desnucarse ⟨1g⟩ *v/r* break one's neck
desnudar ⟨1a⟩ **1** *v/t* undress; *fig* fleece **2** *v/r* **desnudarse** undress
desnudo 1 *adj* naked; *(sin decoración)* bare **2** *m* PINT nude
desnutrición *f* undernourishment
desobedecer ⟨2d⟩ *v/t* disobey
desobediencia *f* disobedience
desobediente *adj* disobedient
desocupación *f L.Am.* unemployment
desocupado 1 *adj apartamento* vacant, empty; *L.Am. sin trabajo* unemployed **2** *mpl:* **los desocupados** the unemployed
desocupar ⟨1a⟩ *v/t* vacate
desodorante *m* deodorant
desoído *part* → **desoír**
desoír ⟨3q; *part* desoído⟩ *v/t* ignore, turn a deaf ear to
desolado *adj* desolate; *fig* griefstricken, devastated
desolar ⟨1m⟩ *v/t tb fig* devastate
desollar ⟨1m⟩ *v/t* skin
desorbitado *adj* astronomical; **con ojos desorbitados** pop-eyed
desorden *m* disorder
desordenado *adj* untidy, messy F; *fig* disorganized
desordenar ⟨1a⟩ *v/t* make untidy
desorganización *f* lack of organization
desorganizado *adj* disorganized
desorientar ⟨1a⟩ **1** *v/t* disorient; *(confun-*

dir) confuse **2** *v/r* **desorientarse** get disoriented, lose one's bearings; *fig* get confused
despabilado *adj fig* bright
despabilar ⟨1a⟩ **1** *v/t* wake up; **¡despabila!** get your act together! **2** *v/r* **despabilarse** *fig* get one's act together
despachar ⟨1a⟩ **1** *v/t a persona, cliente* attend to; *problema* sort out; *(vender)* sell; *(enviar)* send, dispatch **2** *v/i* meet (**con** with) **3** *v/r* **despacharse** F polish off F; **despacharse a su gusto** speak one's mind
despacho *m* office; *diplomático* dispatch; **despacho de billetes** ticket office
despacio *adv* slowly; *L.Am. (en voz baja)* in a low voice
desparpajo *m* self-confidence
desparramar ⟨1a⟩ **1** *v/t* scatter; *líquido* spill; *dinero* squander **2** *v/r* **desparramarse** spill; *fig* scatter
despavorido *adj* terrified
despecho *m* spite; **a despecho de** in spite of
despectivo *adj* contemptuous; GRAM pejorative
despedazar ⟨1f⟩ *v/t* tear apart
despedida *f* farewell; **despedida de soltero** stag party; **despedida de soltera** hen party
despedir ⟨3l⟩ **1** *v/t* see off; *empleado* dismiss; *perfume* give off; *de jinete* throw **2** *v/r* **despedirse** say goodbye (**de** to)
despegar ⟨1h⟩ **1** *v/t* remove, peel off **2** *v/i* AVIA, *fig* take off **3** *v/r* **despegarse** come unstuck (**de** from), come off (**de** sth); *de persona* distance o.s. (**de** from)
despegue *m* AVIA, *fig* take-off
despeinar ⟨1a⟩ *v/t:* **despeinar a alguien** muss s.o.'s hair
despejado *adj cielo, cabeza* clear
despejar ⟨1a⟩ **1** *v/t* clear; *persona* wake up **2** *v/r* **despejarse** *de cielo* clear up; *fig* wake o.s. up
despellejar ⟨1a⟩ *v/t* skin; **despellejar a alguien** *fig* tear s.o. to pieces
despenalizar ⟨1f⟩ *v/t* decriminalize
despensa *f* larder

despeñarse ⟨1a⟩ v/r throw o.s. off a cliff
desperdiciar ⟨1b⟩ v/t *oportunidad* waste
desperdicio m waste; **desperdicios** pl
waste sg; **no tener desperdicio** be
worthwhile
desperdigar ⟨1h⟩ v/t scatter
despertador m alarm (clock)
despertar ⟨1k⟩ **1** v/t wake, waken; *apetito*
whet; *sospecha* arouse; *recuerdo* reawak-
en, trigger **2** v/i wake up **3** v/r **despertarse** wake (up)
despiadado adj ruthless
despido m dismissal
despierto adj awake; *fig* bright
despilfarrar ⟨1a⟩ v/t squander
despistado adj scatterbrained
despistarse ⟨1a⟩ v/r get distracted
despiste m distraction; **tener un despiste** become distracted
desplante m: **hacer un desplante a alguien** *fig* be rude to s.o.
desplazar ⟨1f⟩ **1** v/t move; (*suplantar*)
take over from **2** v/r **desplazarse** travel
desplegar ⟨1h & 1k⟩ v/t unfold, open out;
MIL deploy
despliegue m MIL deployment; **con gran
despliegue de** *fig* with a great show of
desplomarse ⟨1a⟩ v/r collapse
desplome m collapse
despojar ⟨1a⟩ **1** v/t strip (**de** of) **2** v/r despojarse: **despojarse de** *prenda* take off
despojos mpl (*restos*) left-overs; (*desperdicios*) waste sg; *fig* spoils; *de animal* offal sg
desposeídos mpl: **los desposeídos** the
dispossessed
déspota m/f despot
despotricar ⟨1g⟩ v/i F rant and rave F
(**contra** about)
despreciar ⟨1b⟩ v/t look down on; *propuesta* reject
desprecio m contempt; (*indiferencia*) disregard; *acto* slight
desprender ⟨2a⟩ **1** v/t detach, separate;
olor give off **2** v/r **desprenderse** come
off; **desprenderse de** *fig* part with; **de
este estudio se desprende que ...** what
emerges from the study is that ...
despreocupación f indifference

despreocuparse ⟨1a⟩ v/r not worry (**de**
about)
desprestigio m loss of prestige
desprevenido adj unprepared; **pillar** or
L.Am. **agarrar desprevenido** catch unawares
desproporcionado adj disproportionate
despropósito m stupid thing
desprotegido adj unprotected
desprovisto adj: **desprovisto de** lacking
in
después adv (*más tarde*) afterward, later;
seguido en orden next; *en el espacio* after; **yo voy después** I'm next; **después
de** after; **después de todo** after all; **después de que se vaya** after he's gone
desquiciar ⟨1b⟩ **1** v/t fig drive crazy **2** v/r
desquiciarse fig lose one's mind
desquitarse ⟨1a⟩ v/r get one's own back
(**de** for)
desrielar ⟨1a⟩ v/t Chi derail
destacado adj outstanding
destacar ⟨1g⟩ **1** v/i stand out **2** v/r **desta-
carse** stand out (**por** because of); (*ser excelente*) be outstanding (**por** because of)
destajo m: **a destajo** piecework
destapar ⟨1a⟩ **1** v/t open, take the lid off;
fig uncover **2** v/r **destaparse** take one's
coat off; *en cama* kick off the bedcovers;
fig strip (off)
destartalado adj *vehículo, casa* dilapidat-
ed
destello m *de estrella* twinkling; *de faros*
gleam; *fig* brief period, moment
destemplarse ⟨1a⟩ v/r fig become unwell
desteñir ⟨3h & 3l⟩ **1** v/t discolo(u)r, fade
2 v/r **desteñirse** fade
desternillante adj F hilarious
desterrar ⟨1k⟩ v/t exile
destiempo m: **a destiempo** at the wrong
moment
destierro m exile
destilar ⟨1a⟩ v/t distill; *fig* exude
destinar ⟨1a⟩ v/t allocate (**para** for); *a
persona* post (**a** to)
destino m fate; *de viaje etc* destination; *en
el ejército etc* posting
destituir ⟨3g⟩ v/t dismiss
destornillador m screwdriver

destornillar ⟨1a⟩ v/t unscrew

destreza f skill

destrozar ⟨1f⟩ v/t destroy; *emocionalmente* shatter, devastate

destrozos mpl damage sg

destrucción f destruction

destruir ⟨3g⟩ v/t destroy; (*estropear*) ruin, wreck

desunir ⟨3a⟩ v/t divide

desuso m disuse; *caer en desuso* fall into disuse

desvaído adj color, pintura faded

desvalido adj helpless

desvalijar ⟨1a⟩ v/t rob; *apartamento* burglarize, burgle

desván m attic

desvanecimiento m MED fainting fit

desvarío m delirium; *desvaríos* ravings

desvelar ⟨1a⟩ **1** v/t keep awake; *secreto* reveal **2** v/r **desvelarse** stay awake; *fig* do one's best (*por* for)

desvelo m sleeplessness; *desvelos* efforts

desventaja f disadvantage

desventura f misfortune

desvergonzado adj shameless

desvergüenza f shamelessness

desvestir ⟨3l⟩ **1** v/t undress **2** v/r **desvestirse** get undressed, undress

desviar ⟨1c⟩ **1** v/t golpe deflect, parry; *tráfico* divert; *río* alter the course of; *desviar la conversación* change the subject; *desviar la mirada* look away; *desviar a alguien del buen camino* lead s.o. astray **2** v/r **desviarse** (*girar*) turn off; (*bifurcarse*) branch off; (*apartarse*) stray (*de* from)

desvincular ⟨1a⟩ **1** v/t dissociate (*de* from) **2** v/r **desvincularse** dissociate o.s. (*de* from)

desvío m diversion

detallar ⟨1a⟩ v/t explain in detail, give details of; COM itemize

detalle m detail; *fig* thoughtful gesture; *al detalle* retail

detección f detection

detectar ⟨1a⟩ v/t detect

detective m/f detective; *detective privado* private detective

detector m detector; *detector de mentiras* lie detector

detención f detention; *orden de detención* arrest warrant

detener ⟨2l⟩ **1** v/t stop; *de policía* arrest, detain **2** v/r **detenerse** stop

detenido 1 adj held up; (*minucioso*) detailed **2** m, -a f person under arrest

detenimiento m: *con detenimiento* thoroughly

detentar ⟨1a⟩ v/t hold

detergente m detergent

deteriorar ⟨1a⟩ **1** v/t damage **2** v/r **deteriorarse** deteriorate

deterioro m deterioration

determinado adj certain

determinar ⟨1a⟩ v/t determine **2** v/r **determinarse** decide (*a* to)

detestar ⟨1a⟩ v/t detest

detonación f detonation

detonante m explosive; *fig* trigger

detonar ⟨1a⟩ **1** v/i detonate, go off **2** v/t detonate, set off

detractor m, **detractora** f detractor, critic

detrás adv behind; *por detrás* at the back; *fig* behind your / his etc back; *detrás de* behind; *uno detrás de otro* one after the other; *estar detrás de algo* fig be behind sth

detrimento m: *en detrimento de* to the detriment of

detritus m detritus

detuvo vb → **detener**

deuda f debt; *estar en deuda con alguien* fig be in s.o.'s debt, be indebted to s.o.

deudor m, **deudora** f debtor

devaluación f devaluation

devaluar ⟨1e⟩ v/t devalue

devanarse ⟨1a⟩ v/r: *devanarse los sesos* F rack one's brains F

devaneo m affair

devastar ⟨1a⟩ v/t devastate

devoción f tb fig devotion

devolver ⟨2h; *part* **devuelto** ⟩ **1** v/t give back, return; *fig: visita, saludo* return; F (*vomitar*) throw up F **2** v/r **devolverse** *L.Am.* go back, return

devorar ⟨1a⟩ v/t devour

devuelto *part* → **devolver**

D.F. *abr Méx* (= **Distrito Federal**) Mexico City

dg. *abr* (= **decigramo**) decigram

di *vb* → **dar**

día *m* day; **día de fiesta** holiday; **día festivo** holiday; **día hábil** *or* **laborable** work day; **poner al día** update, bring up to date; **a los pocos días** a few days later; **algún día, un día** some day, one day; **de día** by day, during the day; **de un día a or para otro** from one day to the next; **el día menos pensado** when you least expect it; **hace mal día** *tiempo* it's a nasty day; **hoy en día** nowadays; **todo el santo día** all day long; **todos los días** every day; **un día sí y otro no** every other day; **ya es de día** it's light already; **¡buenos días!** good morning

diabetes *f* diabetes

diabético 1 *adj* diabetic **2** *m*, -a *f* diabetic

diablesa *f* F she-devil

diablo *m* devil; **un pobre diablo** *fig* a poor devil; **mandar a alguien al diablo** tell s.o. to go to hell

diablura *f* prank, lark

diabólico *adj* diabolical

diadema *f* tiara; *para el pelo* hair-band

diáfano *adj* clear

diafragma *m* diaphragm

diagnosticar ⟨1g⟩ diagnose

diagnóstico 1 *adj* diagnostic **2** *m* diagnosis

diagonal 1 *adj* diagonal **2** *f* diagonal (line)

diagrama *m* diagram

dialecto *m* dialect

dialogar ⟨1h⟩ *v/i* talk (**sobre** about), discuss (**sobre** sth); *(negociar)* hold talks (**con** with)

diálogo *m* dialog(ue)

diamante *m* diamond

diametralmente *adv*: **diametralmente opuesto** diametrically opposed

diámetro *m* diameter

diana *f* MIL reveille; *(blanco)* target; *para jugar a los dardos* dartboard; *(centro de blanco)* bull's eye; **dar en la diana** *fig* hit the nail on the head

diantre *int* F hell! F

diapositiva *f* FOT slide, transparency

diariero *m*, -a *f Arg* newspaper vendor

diario 1 *adj* daily **2** *m* diary; *(periódico)* newspaper; **a diario** daily

diarrea *f* MED diarrh(o)ea

dibujante *m/f* draftsman, *Br* draughtsman; *mujer* draftswoman, *Br* draughtswoman; *de viñetas* cartoonist

dibujar ⟨1a⟩ **1** *v/t* draw; *fig* describe **2** *v/r* **dibujarse** *fig* appear

dibujo *m arte* drawing; *ilustración* drawing, sketch; *estampado* pattern; **dibujos animados** cartoons; **película de dibujos animados** animation

diccionario *m* dictionary

dic.ᵉ *abr* (= **diciembre**) Dec. (= December)

dice *vb* → **decir**

díceres *mpl L.Am.* sayings

dicharachero *adj* chatty; *(gracioso)* witty

dicho 1 *part* → **decir 2** *adj* said; **dicho y hecho** no sooner said than done; **mejor dicho** or rather **3** *m* saying

dichoso *adj* happy; F *(maldito)* damn F

diciembre *m* December

diciendo *vb* → **decir**

dictado *m* dictation

dictador *m*, **dictadora** *f* dictator

dictadura *f* dictatorship

dictaminar ⟨1a⟩ *v/t* state

dictar ⟨1a⟩ *v/t lección, texto* dictate; *ley* announce; **dictar sentencia** JUR pass sentence

didáctico *adj* educational

diecinueve *adj* nineteen

dieciocho *adj* eighteen

dieciséis *adj* sixteen

diecisiete *adj* seventeen

diente *m* tooth; **diente de ajo** clove of garlic; **diente de león** BOT dandelion; **poner los dientes largos a alguien** make s.o. jealous

diesel *m* diesel

diestro 1 *adj*: **a diestro y siniestro** *fig* F left and right **2** *m* TAUR bullfighter

dieta *f* diet; **estar a dieta** be on a diet; **dietas** travel(l)ing expenses

dietético *adj* dietary

diez *adj* ten

diezmar ⟨1a⟩ v/t decimate

difamar ⟨1a⟩ v/t slander, defame; *por escrito* libel, defame

difamatorio *adj* defamatory

diferencia *f* difference; *a diferencia de* unlike; *con diferencia* fig by a long way

diferenciar ⟨1b⟩ **1** v/t differentiate **2** v/r *diferenciarse* differ (*de* from); *no se diferencian en nada* there's no difference at all between them

diferente *adj* different

diferido *adj* TV: *en diferido* prerecorded

difícil *adj* difficult

dificultad *f* difficulty; *poner dificultades* make it difficult

dificultar ⟨1a⟩ v/t hinder

difundir ⟨3a⟩ **1** v/t spread; (*programa*) broadcast **2** v/r *difundirse* spread

difunto **1** *adj* late **2** *m*, **-a** *f* deceased

difuso *adj* idea, conocimientos vague, sketchy

digerir ⟨3i⟩ v/t digest; F noticia take in

digestión *f* digestion

digital *adj* digital

digitalizar ⟨1f⟩ v/t INFOR digitalize

dígito *m* digit

dignarse ⟨1a⟩ v/r deign

dignidad *f* dignity

digno *adj* worthy; *trabajo* decent; *digno de mención* worth mentioning

digo *vb* → *decir*

digresión *f* digression

dije *vb* → *decir*

dilación *f*: *sin dilación* without delay

dilapidar ⟨1a⟩ v/t waste

dilatar ⟨1a⟩ **1** v/t dilate; (*prolongar*) prolong; (*aplazar*) postpone **2** v/i *Méx* (*tardar*) be late; *no me dilato* I won't be long

dilema *m* dilemma

diligencia *f* diligence; *vehículo* stagecoach; *diligencias* JUR procedures, formalities

diligente *adj* diligent

dilucidar ⟨1a⟩ v/t clarify

diluir ⟨3g⟩ v/t dilute

diluviar ⟨1b⟩ v/i pour down

diluvio *m* downpour; fig deluge

dimensión *f* dimension; fig size, scale; *dimensiones* measurements

diminutivo *m* diminutive

diminuto *adj* tiny, diminutive

dimisión *f* resignation

dimitir ⟨3a⟩ v/t resign

Dinamarca Denmark

dinámico *adj* fig dynamic

dinamita *f* dynamite

dinastía *f* dynasty

dinero *m* money; *dinero en efectivo, dinero en metálico* cash

dinosaurio *m* dinosaur

dio *vb* → *dar*

Dios *m* God; *hazlo como Dios manda* do it properly; *¡Dios mío!* my God!; *¡por Dios!* for God's sake!; *sabe Dios lo que dijo* God knows what he said

dios *m* tb fig god

diosa *f* goddess

diploma *m* diploma

diplomacia *f* diplomacy

diplomático **1** *adj* diplomatic **2** *m*, **-a** *f* diplomat

diputado *m*, **-a** *f* representative, *Br* Member of Parliament

dique *m* dike, *Br* dyke

dirá *vb* → *decir*

diré *vb* → *decir*

dirección *f* tb TEA, de película direction; COM management; POL leadership; de coche steering; en carta address; *en aquella dirección* that way; *dirección asistida* AUTO power steering; *dirección de correo electrónico* e-mail address

directiva *f* board of directors; POL executive committee

directivo **1** *adj* governing; COM managing **2** *m*, **-a** *f* COM manager

directo *adj* direct; *en directo* TV, RAD live

director **1** *adj* leading **2** *m*, directora *f* manager; EDU principal, *Br* head (teacher); TEA, de película director; *director de orquesta* conductor

directriz *f* guideline

dirigir ⟨3c⟩ **1** v/t TEA, película direct; COM manage, run; MÚS conduct; *dirigir una carta a* address a letter to; *dirigir una pregunta a* direct a question to **2** v/r dirigirse make, head (*a, hacia* for)

discapacidad *f* disability

discapacitado 1 *adj* disabled **2** *m*, **-a** *f* disabled person

discar ⟨1g⟩ *v/t L.Am.* TELEC dial

discernir ⟨3i⟩ *v/t* distinguish, discern

disciplina *f* discipline

disciplinar ⟨1a⟩ *v/t* discipline

discípulo *m*, **-a** *f* REL, *fig* disciple

disco *m* disk, *Br* disc; MÚS record; (*discoteca*) disco; DEP discus; **disco compacto** compact disc; **disco duro**, *L.Am.* **disco rígido** INFOR hard disk

discordante *adj* discordant

discordia *f* discord; (*colección de discos*) record collection

discreción *f* discretion; **a discreción disparar** at will; **a discreción de** at the discretion of

discrepancia *f* discrepancy; (*desacuerdo*) disagreement

discrepar ⟨1a⟩ *v/i* disagree

discreto *adj* discreet

discriminación *f* discrimination

discriminar ⟨1a⟩ *v/t* discriminate against; (*diferenciar*) differentiate

disculpa *f* apology

disculpar ⟨1a⟩ **1** *v/t* excuse **2** *v/r* **disculparse** apologize

discurrir ⟨3a⟩ *v/i de tiempo* pass; *de acontecimiento* pass off; (*reflexionar*) reflect (**sobre** on)

discurso *m* speech; *de tiempo* passage, passing

discusión *f* discussion; (*disputa*) argument

discutir ⟨3a⟩ **1** *v/t* discuss **2** *v/i* argue (**sobre** about)

diseminar ⟨1a⟩ *v/t* scatter; *fig* spread

disentir ⟨3i⟩ *v/i* disagree (**de** with)

diseñador *m*, **diseñadora** *f* designer

diseñar ⟨1a⟩ *v/t* design

diseño *m* design; **diseño gráfico** graphic design

disfraz *m para ocultar* disguise; *para fiestas* costume, fancy dress

disfrazarse ⟨1f⟩ *v/r para ocultarse* disguise o.s. (**de** as); *para divertirse* dress up (**de** as)

disfrutar ⟨1a⟩ **1** *v/t* enjoy **2** *v/i* have fun, enjoy o.s.; **disfrutar de buena salud** be in *o* enjoy good health

disgregarse ⟨1h⟩ *v/r* disintegrate

disgustar ⟨1a⟩ **1** *v/t* upset **2** *v/r* **disgustarse** get upset

disgusto *m*: **me causó un gran disgusto** I was very upset; **llevarse un disgusto** get upset; **a disgusto** unwillingly

disidente *m/f* dissident

disimular ⟨1a⟩ **1** *v/t* disguise **2** *v/i* pretend

disimulo *m*: **con disimulo** unobtrusively

disipar ⟨1a⟩ **1** *v/t duda* dispel **2** *v/r* **disiparse** *de niebla* clear; *de duda* vanish

diskette *m* diskette, floppy (disk)

dislexia *f* dyslexia

dislocar ⟨1g⟩ *v/t* dislocate

disminución *f* decrease

disminuido 1 *adj* handicapped **2** *m*, **-a** *f* handicapped person; **disminuido físico** physically handicapped person

disminuir ⟨3g⟩ **1** *v/t gastos, costos* reduce, cut; *velocidad* reduce **2** *v/i* decrease, diminish

disociar ⟨1b⟩ *v/t* separate

disolvente *m* solvent

disolver ⟨1h; *part* **disuelto** ⟩ *v/t* dissolve; *manifestación* break up

disparada *f L.Am.*: **a la disparada** in a rush

disparar ⟨1a⟩ **1** *v/t tiro, arma* fire; *foto* take; *precios* send up **2** *v/i* shoot, fire **3** *v/r* **dispararse** *de arma, alarma* go off; *de precios* rise dramatically, rocket F

disparatado *adj* absurd

disparate *m* F piece of nonsense; **es un disparate hacer eso** it's crazy to do that

disparo *m* shot

dispendio *m* waste

dispensar ⟨1a⟩ *v/t* dispense; *recibimiento* give; (*eximir*) excuse (**de** from)

dispensario *m* MED clinic

dispersar ⟨1a⟩ **1** *v/t* disperse **2** *v/r* **dispersarse** disperse

disperso *adj* scattered

displicente *adj* disdainful

disponer ⟨2r; *part* **dispuesto** ⟩ *v/t* (*arreglar*) arrange; (*preparar*) prepare; (*ordenar*) stipulate **2** *v/i*: **disponer de algo** have sth at one's disposal **3** *v/r* **disponerse** get ready (**a** to)

disponibilidad *f* COM availability

disponible *adj* available

disposición *f* disposition; *de objetos* arrangement; **disposición de ánimo** state of mind; **estar a disposición de alguien** be at s.o.'s disposal

dispositivo *m* device

dispuesto 1 *part* → **disponer 2** *adj* ready (**a** to)

disputa *f* dispute

disputar ⟨1a⟩ **1** *v/t* dispute; *partido* play **2** *v/i* argue (**sobre** about) **3** *v/r* **disputarse** compete for

disquería *f L.Am.* record store

disquete *m* INFOR diskette, floppy (disk)

disquetera *f* disk drive

distancia *f tb fig* distance

distanciarse ⟨1b⟩ *v/r* distance o.s. (**de** from)

distante *adj tb fig* distant

distar ⟨1a⟩ *v/i* be far (**de** from)

distinción *f* distinction; **a distinción de** unlike

distinguido *adj* distinguished

distinguir ⟨3d⟩ *v/t* distinguish (**de** from); (*divisar*) make out; *con un premio* hono(u)r

distintivo *m* emblem; MIL insignia

distinto *adj* different; **distintos** (*varios*) several

distorsión *f* distortion

distracción *f* distraction; (*descuido*) absent-mindedness; (*diversión*) entertainment; (*pasatiempo*) pastime; **por distracción** out of absent-mindedness

distraer ⟨2p; *part* **distraído** ⟩ **1** *v/t* distract; **la radio la distrae** she enjoys listening to the radio **2** *v/r* **distraerse** get distracted; (*disfrutar*) enjoy o.s.

distraído 1 *part* → **distraer 2** *adj* absent-minded; *temporalmente* distracted

distribución *f* COM, *de película* distribution

distribuir ⟨3g⟩ *v/t* distribute; *beneficio* share out

distrito *m* district

disturbio *m* disturbance

disuadir ⟨3a⟩ *v/t* dissuade; POL deter; **disuadir a alguien de hacer algo** dissuade s.o. from doing sth

disuelto *part* → **disolver**

disyuntiva *f* dilemma

diurético *adj* diuretic

diurno *adj* day *atr*

divagar ⟨1h⟩ *v/i* digress

diván *m* couch

diversidad *f* diversity

diversión *f* fun; (*pasatiempo*) pastime; **aquí no hay muchas diversiones** there's not much to do around here

diverso *adj* diverse; **diversos** several, various

divertido *adj* funny; (*entretenido*) entertaining

divertir ⟨3i⟩ **1** *v/t* entertain **2** *v/r* **divertirse** have fun, enjoy o.s.

dividendo *m* dividend

dividir ⟨3a⟩ *v/t* divide

divinamente *adv fig* wonderfully

divinidad *f* divinity

divino *adj tb fig* divine

divisa *f* currency; **divisas** *pl* foreign currency *sg*

divisar ⟨1a⟩ *v/t* make out

división *f* MAT, MIL, DEP division; **hubo división de opiniones** there were differences of opinion

divorciado 1 *adj* divorced **2** *m*, -a *f* divorcee

divorciarse ⟨1b⟩ *v/r* get divorced

divorcio *m* divorce

divulgación *f* spread

divulgar ⟨1h⟩ **1** *v/t* spread **2** *v/r* **divulgarse** spread

d. J.C. *abr* (= **después de Jesucristo**) A.D. (= Anno Domini)

dl. *abr* (= **decilitro**) deciliter

dm. *abr* (= **decímetro**) decimeter

dobladillo *m* hem

doblado *adj película* dubbed

doblaje *m de película* dubbing

doblar ⟨1a⟩ **1** *v/t* fold; *cantidad* double; *película* dub; MAR round; *pierna, brazo* bend; *en una carrera* pass, *Br* overtake; **doblar la esquina** go round *o* turn the corner **2** *v/i* turn; **doblar a la derecha** turn right **3** *v/r* **doblarse** bend; *fig* give in

doble 1 *adj* double; *nacionalidad* dual; **doble clic** *m* double click **2** *m*: **el doble**

twice as much (**de** as); **el doble de gente** twice as many people; **dobles 3** *m/f* **en película** double

doblegar ⟨1h⟩ *v/t* fig: *voluntad* break; *orgullo* humble

doblez **1** *m* fold **2** *f* fig deceit

doce *adj* twelve

docena *f* dozen

docente *adj* teaching *atr*

dócil *adj* docile

doctor *m*, doctora *f* doctor; **doctor honoris causa** honorary doctor

doctorado *m* doctorate

doctrina *f* doctrine

documentación *f* documentation; *de una persona* papers

documental *m* documentary

documento *m* document; **documento nacional de identidad** national identity card

dogma *m* dogma

dogo *m* zo mastiff

dólar *m* dollar

dolencia *f* ailment

doler ⟨2h⟩ *v/t tb* fig hurt; **me duele el brazo** my arm hurts; **le dolió que le mintieran** fig she was hurt that they had lied to her

dolor *m tb* fig pain; **dolor de cabeza** headache; **dolor de estómago** stomach-ache; **dolor de muelas** toothache

dolorido *adj* sore, aching; fig hurt

doloroso *adj tb* fig painful

domador *m*, domadora *f* tamer

domesticar ⟨1g⟩ *v/t* domesticate

doméstico **1** *adj* domestic, household *atr* **2** *m*, -a *f* servant

domiciliación *f* **de sueldo** credit transfer; *de pagos* direct billing, *Br* direct debit

domicilio *m* address; **repartir a domicilio** do home deliveries

dominante *adj* dominant; *desp* domineering

dominar ⟨1a⟩ **1** *v/t* dominate; *idioma* have a good command of **2** *v/i* dominate **3** *v/r* dominarse control o.s.

domingo *m* Sunday; **domingo de Ramos** Palm Sunday

dominguero *m*, -a *f* F weekender, Sunday tripper

dominical *adj* Sunday *atr*

dominicano GEOG **1** *adj* Dominican **2** *m*, -a *f* Dominican

dominio *m* control; *fig* command; **ser del dominio público** be in the public domain

dominó *m* dominoes *pl*

don[1] *m* gift; **don de gentes** way with people

don[2] *m* Mr; **don Enrique** Mr Sanchez *English uses the surname while Spanish uses the first name*

donación *f* donation; **donación de sangre** blood donation; **donación de órganos** organ donation

donante *m/f* donor; **donante de sangre** blood donor

donar ⟨1a⟩ *v/t sangre, órgano, dinero* donate

donativo *m* donation

doncella *f* maid

donde **1** *adv* where **2** *prp esp L.Am.:* **fui donde el médico** I went to the doctor's

dónde *interr* where; **¿de dónde eres?** where are you from?; **¿hacia dónde vas?** where are you going?

dondequiera *adv* wherever

doña *f* Mrs; **doña Estela** Mrs Sanchez *English uses the surname while Spanish uses the first name*

dopaje, doping *m* doping

dorada *f* zo gilthead

dorado *adj* gold; *montura* gilt

dormido *adj* asleep; **quedarse dormido** fall asleep

dormir ⟨3k⟩ **1** *v/i* sleep; (*estar dormido*) be asleep **2** *v/t* put to sleep; **dormir a alguien** MED give s.o. a general an(a)esthetic **3** *v/r* dormirse go to sleep; (*quedarse dormido*) fall asleep; (*no despertarse*) oversleep; **no podía dormirme** I couldn't get to sleep

dormitorio *m* bedroom

dorso *m* back

dos *adj* two; **de dos en dos** in twos; **los dos** both; **anda con ojo con los dos** watch out for the pair of them; **cada dos por tres** all the time, continually

doscientos *adj* two hundred

dosificar ⟨1g⟩ *v/t* cut down on

dosis *f inv* dose

dotar ⟨1a⟩ *v/t* equip (**de** with); *fondos* provide (**de** with); *cualidades* endow (**de** with)

dote *f a novia* dowry; **tener dotes para algo** have a gift for sth

doy *vb* → **dar**

dpto. *abr* (**= departamento**) dept (= department)

Dr. *abr* (**= Doctor**) Dr (= Doctor)

Dra. *abr* (**= Doctora**) Dr (= Doctor)

dragar ⟨1h⟩ *v/t* dredge

dragón *m* dragon; MIL dragoon

drama *m* drama

dramático *adj* dramatic; **arte dramático** dramatic art

dramatizar ⟨1f⟩ *v/t* dramatize

drástico *adj* drastic

drenaje *m* drainage

droga *f* drug; **droga de diseño** designer drug

drogadicto 1 *adj*: **una mujer -a** a woman addicted to drugs 2 *m*, -a *f* drug addict

drogarse ⟨1h⟩ *v/r* take drugs

drogodependencia *f* drug dependency

droguería *f store selling cleaning and household products*

dromedario *m* zo dromedary

d.to *abr* (**= descuento**) discount

ducha *f* shower; **ser una ducha de agua fría** *fig* come as a shock

ducharse ⟨1a⟩ *v/r* have a shower, shower

duda *f* doubt; **sin duda** without doubt; **poner en duda** call into question

dudar ⟨1a⟩ 1 *v/t* doubt 2 *v/i* hesitate (**en** to)

dudoso *adj* doubtful; (*indeciso*) hesitant

duele *vb* → **doler**

duelo *m* grief; (*combate*) duel

duende *m* imp

dueño *m*, -a *f* owner

dulce 1 *adj* sweet; *fig* gentle 2 *m* candy, *Br* sweet

dulzura *f tb fig* sweetness

dumping *m* dumping

duna *f* dune

duo *m* MÚS duo

duodécimo *adj* twelfth

dúplex *m* duplex (apartment)

duplicado 1 *adj* duplicate; **por duplicado** in duplicate 2 *m* duplicate

duplicar ⟨1g⟩ *v/t* duplicate

duque *m* duke

duquesa *f* duchess

duración *f* duration

duradero *adj* lasting; *ropa*, *calzado* hard-wearing

durante *prp indicando duración* during; *indicando período* for; **durante seis meses** for six months

durar ⟨1a⟩ *v/i* last

duraznero *m L.Am.* BOT peach (tree)

durazno *m L.Am.* BOT peach

Durex® *m Méx* Scotch tape®, *Br* Sellotape®

duro 1 *adj* hard; *carne* tough; *clima*, *fig* harsh; **duro de oído** F hard of hearing; **ser duro de pelar** be a tough nut to crack 2 *adv* hard 3 *m* five peseta coin

DVD *abr* (**= Disco de Vídeo Digital**) DVD (= Digital Versatile *o* Video Disc)

E

E *abr* (**= este**) E (= East(ern))

e *conj* (*instead of* **y** *before words starting with* **i**, **hi**) and

ebanista *m* cabinetmaker

ébano *m* ebony

ebrio *adj* drunk

ebullición f: **punto de ebullición** boiling point

eccema m eczema

echar ⟨1a⟩ **1** v/t (*lanzar*) throw; (*poner*) put; *de un lugar* throw out; *humo* give off; *carta* mail, *Br tb* post; **lo han echado del trabajo** he's been fired; **echar abajo** pull down, destroy; **echar la culpa a alguien** blame s.o., put the blame on s.o.; **me echó 40 años** he thought I was 40 **2** v/i: **echar a** start to, begin to; **echar a correr** start o begin to run, start running **3** v/r **echarse** (*tirarse*) throw o.s.; (*tumbarse*) lie down; (*ponerse*) put on; **echarse a llorar** start o begin to cry, start crying

eclesiástico adj ecclesiastical, church atr

eclipsar ⟨1a⟩ v/t eclipse

eclipse m eclipse

eco m echo; **tener eco** fig make an impact

ecografía f (ultrasound) scan

ecología f ecology

ecológico adj ecological; *alimentos* orgánico

ecologista m/f ecologist

economato m co-operative store

economía f economy; *ciencia* economics; **economía de mercado** market economy; **economía sumergida** black economy

económico adj economic; (*barato*) economical

economista m/f economist

economizar ⟨1f⟩ v/t economize on, save

ecosistema m ecosystem

ecoturismo m ecotourism

ecuación f equation

ecuador m equator

Ecuador Ecuador

ecuánime adj (*sereno*) even-tempered; (*imparcial*) impartial

ecuatorial adj equatorial

ecuatoriano 1 adj Ecuadorean **2** m, -a f Ecuadorean

eczema m eczema

ed. abr (= **edición**) ed (= edition)

edad f age; **la Edad Media** the Middle Ages pl; **la tercera edad** the over 60s; **estar en la edad del pavo** be at that awkward age; **a la edad de** at the age of;

¿qué edad tienes? how old are you?

edición f edition

edificar ⟨1g⟩ v/t construct, build

edificio m building

edil m, **edila** f council(l)or

editar ⟨1a⟩ v/t edit; (*publicar*) publish

editor m, **editora** f editor

editorial 1 m editorial, leading article **2** f publishing company o house, publisher

edredón m eiderdown

educación f (*crianza*) upbringing; (*modales*) manners; **educación física** physical education, PE

educado adj polite, well-mannered; **mal educado** rude, ill-mannered

educar ⟨1g⟩ v/t educate; (*criar*) bring up; *voz* train

educativo adj educational

edulcorante m sweetener

EE. UU. abr (= **Estados Unidos**) US(A) (= United States (of America))

efectista adj theatrical, dramatic

efectivamente adv indeed

efectivo 1 adj effective; **hacer efectivo** COM cash **2** m: **en efectivo** (in) cash

efecto m effect; **efecto invernadero** greenhouse effect; **efectos secundarios** side effects; **en efecto** indeed; **surtir efecto** take effect, work

efectuar ⟨1e⟩ v/t carry out

efervescente adj effervescent; *bebida* carbonated, sparkling

eficacia f efficiency

eficaz adj (*efectivo*) effective; (*eficiente*) efficient

eficiencia f efficiency

eficiente adj efficient

efímero adj ephemeral, short-lived

efusivo adj effusive

egipcio 1 adj Egyptian **2** m, -a f Egyptian

Egipto Egypt

ego m ego

egocéntrico adj egocentric, self-centered (*Br* -centred)

egoísmo m selfishness, egoism

egoísta 1 adj selfish, egoistic **2** m/f egoist

egresar ⟨1a⟩ v/i L.Am. de universidad graduate; *de colegio* graduate from high school, *Br* leave school

egreso *m L.Am.* graduation

eh *int para llamar atención* hey!; **¿eh?** eh?

eje *m* axis; *de auto* axle; *fig* linchpin

ejecución *f (realización)* implementation, carrying out; *de condenado* execution; MÚS performance

ejecutar ⟨1a⟩ *v/t (realizar)* carry out, implement; *condenado* execute; INFOR run, execute; MÚS play, perform

ejecutiva *f* executive

ejecutivo 1 *adj* executive; **el poder ejecutivo** POL the executive **2** *m* executive; **el Ejecutivo** the government

ejemplar 1 *adj alumno, padre etc* model *atr*, exemplary **2** *m de libro* copy; *de revista* issue; *animal, planta* specimen

ejemplo *m* example; **dar buen ejemplo** set a good example; **por ejemplo** for example

ejercer ⟨2b⟩ **1** *v/t cargo* practice, *Br* practise; *influencia* exert **2** *v/i de profesional* practice, *Br* practise; **ejerce de médico** he's a practicing (*Br* practising) doctor

ejercicio *m* exercise; COM fiscal year, *Br* financial year; **hacer ejercicio** exercise

ejercitar ⟨1a⟩ **1** *v/t músculo, derecho* exercise **2** *v/r* **ejercitarse** train; **ejercitarse en** practice, *Br* practise

ejército *m* army

ejido *m Méx* traditional rural communal farming unit

ejote *m L.Am.* green bean

el 1 *art* the **2** *pron:* **el de ...** that of ...; **el de Juan** Juan's; **el más grande** the biggest (one); **el que está ...** the one who is ...

él *pron sujeto* he; *cosa* it; *complemento* him; *cosa* it; **de él** his

elaborar ⟨1a⟩ *v/t produce, make; metal etc* work; *plan* devise, draw up

elasticidad *f* elasticity

elástico 1 *adj* elastic **2** *m* elastic; (*goma*) elastic band, *Br* rubber band

elección *f* choice

eleccionario *adj L.Am.* election *atr*, electoral

elecciones *fpl* election *sg*

elector *m* voter

electorado *m* electorate

electoral *adj* election *atr*, electoral

electricidad *f* electricity

electricista *m/f* electrician

eléctrico *adj luz, motor* electric; *aparato* electrical

electrocutar ⟨1a⟩ **1** *v/t* electrocute **2** *v/r* **electrocutarse** be electrocuted, electrocute o.s.

electrodo *m* electrode

electrodoméstico *m* electrical appliance

electrón *m* electron

electrónica *f* electronics

electrónico *adj* electronic

elefante *m* ZO elephant; **elefante marino** elephant seal, sea elephant

elegancia *f* elegance, stylishness

elegante *adj* elegant, stylish

elegantoso *adj L.Am.* F stylish, classy F

elegía *f* elegy

elegible *adj* eligible

elegir ⟨3c & 3l⟩ *v/t* choose; *por votación* elect

elemental *adj (esencial)* fundamental, essential; (*básico*) elementary, basic

elemento *m* element

elevado *adj* high; *fig* elevated

elevador *m* hoist; *L.Am.* elevator, *Br* lift

elevar ⟨1a⟩ **1** *v/t* raise **2** *v/r* **elevarse** rise; *de monumento* stand

eliminación *f* elimination; *de desperdicios* disposal

eliminar ⟨1a⟩ *v/t* eliminate; *desperdicios* dispose of

eliminatoria *f* DEP qualifying round, heat

élite *f* elite

elitista *adj* elitist

elixir *m* elixir; **elixir bucal** mouthwash

ella *pron sujeto* she; *cosa* it; *complemento* her; *cosa* it; **de ella** her; **es de ella** it's hers

ellas *pron sujeto* they; *complemento* them; **de ellas** their; **es de ellas** it's theirs

ello *pron* it

ellos *pron sujeto* they; *complemento* them; **de ellos** their; **es de ellos** it's theirs

elocuente *adj* eloquent

elogiar ⟨1b⟩ *v/t* praise

elogio *m* praise

elote *m* *L.Am.* corncob; *granos* corn, *Br* sweetcorn

El Salvador El Salvador

eludir ⟨3a⟩ *v/t* evade, avoid

emanar ⟨1a⟩ **1** *v/i* *fml* emanate (**de** from) *fml*; *fig* stem (**de** from), derive (**de** from) **2** *v/t* exude, emit

emancipación *f* emancipation

emanciparse ⟨1a⟩ *v/r* become emancipated

embadurnar ⟨1a⟩ *v/t* smear (**de** with)

embajada *f* embassy

embajador *m*, embajadora *f* ambassador

embalaje *m* packing

embalar ⟨1a⟩ **1** *v/t* pack **2** *v/r* embalarse *de persona* get excited; **el coche se embaló** the car went faster and faster; **no te embales** don't go so fast

embalse *m* reservoir

embarazada **1** *adj* pregnant **2** *f* pregnant woman

embarazo *m* pregnancy; **interrupción del embarazo** termination, abortion

embarazoso *adj* awkward, embarrassing

embarcación *f* vessel, craft

embarcadero *m* wharf

embarcar ⟨1g⟩ *v/t* *pasajeros* board, embark; *mercancías* load **2** *v/i* board, embark **3** *v/r* embarcarse *en barco* board, embark; *en avión* board; **embarcarse en** *fig* embark on

embargo *m* embargo; JUR seizure; **sin embargo** however

embarque *m* boarding; *de mercancías* loading

embarrancar ⟨1g⟩ **1** *v/i* MAR run aground **2** *v/r* embarrancarse MAR run aground

embaucador **1** *adj* deceitful **2** *m*, embaucadora *f* trickster

embeberse ⟨2a⟩ *v/r* get absorbed *o* engrossed (**en** in)

embelesar ⟨1a⟩ *v/t* captivate

embestir ⟨3l⟩ **1** *v/t* charge **2** *v/i* charge (**contra** at)

emblema *m* emblem

embobar ⟨1a⟩ *v/t* fascinate

embolarse ⟨1a⟩ *v/r* *C.Am.*, *Méx* F get plastered F

émbolo *m* TÉC piston

embolsar ⟨1a⟩ **1** *v/t* pocket **2** *v/r* embolsarse pocket

emborrachar ⟨1a⟩ **1** *v/t* make drunk, get drunk **2** *v/r* emborracharse get drunk

emborronar ⟨1a⟩ *v/t* blot, smudge

emboscada *f* ambush

embotar ⟨1a⟩ *v/t* blunt

embotellamiento *m* traffic jam

embotellar ⟨1a⟩ *v/t* bottle

embrague *m* AUTO clutch

embriagar ⟨1h⟩ *v/t* *fig* intoxicate

embriaguez *f* intoxication

embrión *m* embryo; **en embrión** in an embryonic state, in embryo

embrollo *m* tangle; *fig* mess, muddle

embromar ⟨1a⟩ *v/t* *Rpl* F (*molestar*) annoy

embrujar ⟨1a⟩ *v/t* *tb* *fig* bewitch

embrutecer ⟨2d⟩ **1** *v/t* brutalize **2** *v/r* embrutecerse become brutalized

embudo *m* funnel

embustero **1** *adj* deceitful **2** *m*, -a *f* liar

embutido *m* GASTR *type of dried sausage*

emergencia *f* emergency

emerger ⟨2c⟩ *v/i* emerge

emigración *f* emigration

emigrante *m* emigrant

emigrar ⟨1a⟩ *v/i* emigrate; ZO migrate

eminente *adj* eminent

emirato *m* emirate

emisario *m* emissary

emisión *f* emission; COM issue; RAD, TV broadcast

emisora *f* radio station

emitir ⟨3a⟩ *v/t* *calor*, *sonido* give out, emit; *moneda* issue; *opinión* express, give; *veredicto* deliver; RAD, TV broadcast; *voto* cast

emoción *f* emotion; **¡qué emoción!** how exciting!

emocionado *adj* excited

emocionante *adj* (*excitante*) exciting; (*conmovedor*) moving

emocionarse ⟨1a⟩ *v/r* get excited; (*conmoverse*) be moved

emotivo *adj* emotional; (*conmovedor*) moving

empacar ⟨1g⟩ **1** *v/t* & *v/i* *L.Am.* pack **2** *v/r* empacarse *L.Am.* (*ponerse tozudo*) dig one's heels in; *tragar* devour

empacharse ⟨1a⟩ *v/r* F get an upset stomach (*de* from); *empacharse de* fig overdose on

empacho *m* F upset stomach; fig bellyful F; *sin empacho* unashamedly

empadronar ⟨1a⟩ *v/t* register 2 *v/r* empadronarse register

empalagoso *adj* sickly; fig sickly sweet, cloying

empalizada *f* palisade

empalmar ⟨1a⟩ 1 *v/t* connect, join 2 *v/i* connect (*con* with), join up (*con* with); *de idea, conversación* run *o* follow on (*con* from)

empanada *f* pie

empanadilla *f* pasty

empanar ⟨1a⟩ *v/t* coat in breadcrumbs

empantanarse ⟨1a⟩ *v/r* become swamped *o* waterlogged; fig get bogged down

empañado *adj* misty

empañar ⟨1a⟩ 1 *v/t* steam up, mist up; fig tarnish, sully 2 *v/r* empañarse *de vidrio* steam up, mist up

empapado *adj* soaked, dripping wet

empapar ⟨1a⟩ 1 *v/t* soak; (*absorber*) soak up; 2 *v/r* empaparse get soaked *o* drenched; *empaparse de algo* immerse o.s. in sth

empapelar ⟨1a⟩ *v/t* wallpaper

empaque *m* presence; (*seriedad*) solemnity

empaquetar ⟨1a⟩ *v/t* pack

emparedado *m* sandwich

emparejar ⟨1a⟩ *v/t personas* pair off; *calcetines* match up

emparentado *adj* related

empastador *m*, empastadora *f L.Am.* bookbinder

empastar ⟨1a⟩ *v/t muela* fill; *libro* bind

empaste *m* filling

empatar ⟨1a⟩ *v/i* tie, *Br* draw; (*igualar*) tie the game, *Br* equalize

empate *m* tie, draw; *gol del empate en fútbol* equalizer

empecinarse ⟨1a⟩ *v/r* get an idea into one's head; *empecinarse en algo* insist on sth

empedernido *adj* inveterate, confirmed

empedrado *m* paving

empeine *m* instep

empellón *m* shove; *entró a empellones* he shoved his way in

empelotarse ⟨1a⟩ *v/r L.Am.* P take one's clothes off, strip off

empeñado *adj* (*endeudado*) in debt; *estar empeñado en hacer algo* be determined to do sth

empeñar ⟨1a⟩ 1 *v/t* pawn 2 *v/r* empeñarse (*endeudarse*) get into debt; (*esforzarse*) strive (*en* to), make an effort (*en* to); *empeñarse en hacer/insinarse* insist on doing, be determined to do

empeñero Méx 1 *adj* determined 2 *m*, -a *f* determined person

empeño *m* (*obstinación*) determination; (*esfuerzo*) effort; *Méx* fig pawn shop

empeñoso *adj L.Am.* hard-working

empeorar ⟨1a⟩ 1 *v/t* make worse 2 *v/i* deteriorate, get worse

empequeñecer ⟨2d⟩ *v/t* fig diminish

emperador *m* emperor; *pez* swordfish

emperatriz *f* empress

emperrarse ⟨1a⟩ *v/r* F: *emperrarse en hacer algo* have one's heart set on doing sth; *emperrarse con algo* set one's heart on sth

empezar ⟨1f & 1k⟩ 1 *v/t* start, begin 2 *v/i* start, begin; *empezar a hacer algo* start to do sth, start doing sth; *empezar por hacer algo* start *o* begin by doing sth

empiezo *m S. Am.* start, beginning

empinado *adj* steep

empinar ⟨1a⟩ *v/t* raise; *empinar el codo* F raise one's elbow F

empírico *adj* empirical

emplazamiento *m* site, location; JUR subpoena, summons

empleado 1 *adj*: *le está bien empleado* it serves him right 2 *m*, -a *f* employee; *-a de hogar* maid

emplear ⟨1a⟩ *v/t* (*usar*) use; *persona* employ

empleo *m* employment; (*puesto*) job; (*uso*) use; *modo de empleo* instructions for use *pl*, directions *pl*

emplomar ⟨1a⟩ *v/t S. Am.* fill

empobrecer ⟨2d⟩ 1 *v/t* impoverish, make

poor 2 v/i become impoverished, become poor 3 v/r **empobrecerse** become impoverished, become poor

empobrecimiento m impoverishment

empollar ⟨1a⟩ v/i F cram F, Br swot F

empollón m F grind F, Br swot F

emporio m L.Am. almacén department store

empotrado adj built-in, fitted

empotrarse ⟨1a⟩ v/r crash (**contra** into)

emprendedor adj enterprising

emprender ⟨2a⟩ v/t embark on, undertake; **emprenderla con alguien** F take it out on s.o.

empresa f company; fig venture, undertaking; **empresa de trabajo temporal** temping agency

empresaria f businesswoman

empresarial adj business atr; **ciencias empresariales** business studies

empresario m businessman

empujar ⟨1a⟩ v/t push; fig urge on, spur on

empujón m push, shove; **salían a empujones** F they were pushing and shoving their way out

empuñar ⟨1a⟩ v/t grasp

emular ⟨1a⟩ v/t emulate

emulsión f emulsion

en prp (dentro de) in; (sobre) on; **en un mes** in a month; **en la mesa** on the table; **en inglés** in English; **en la calle** on the street, Br tb in the street; **en casa** at home; **en coche / tren** by car / train

enajenación f JUR transfer; **enajenación mental** insanity

enajenar ⟨1a⟩ v/t JUR transfer; (trastornar) drive insane

enamorado adj in love (**de** with)

enamorar ⟨1a⟩ 1 v/t: **lo enamoró** she captivated him 2 v/r **enamorarse** fall in love (**de** with)

enano 1 adj tiny; perro, árbol miniature, dwarf atr 2 m dwarf; **trabajar como un enano** fig F work like a dog F

enarbolar ⟨1a⟩ v/t hoist, raise

encabezamiento m heading

encabezar ⟨1f⟩ v/t head; movimiento, revolución lead

encabritarse ⟨1a⟩ v/r de caballo rear up

encadenar ⟨1a⟩ 1 v/t chain (up); fig link o put together 2 v/r **encadenarse** chain oneself (**a** to)

encajar ⟨1a⟩ 1 v/t piezas fit; golpe take 2 v/i fit (**en** in; **con** with)

encaje m lace

encalado m whitewashing

encalar ⟨1a⟩ v/t whitewash

encallar ⟨1a⟩ v/i MAR run aground

encaminarse ⟨1a⟩ v/r set off (**a** for), head (**a** for); fig be aimed o directed (**a** at)

encandilar ⟨1a⟩ v/t dazzle

encantado adj (contento) delighted; castillo enchanted; **¡encantado!** nice to meet you

encantador adj charming

encantar ⟨1a⟩ v/t: **me / le encanta** I love / he loves it

encanto m (atractivo) charm; **como por encanto** as if by magic; **eres un encanto** you're an angel

encapricharse ⟨1a⟩ v/r fall in love (**de** with)

encapuchado adj hooded

encaramarse ⟨1a⟩ v/r climb

encarar ⟨1a⟩ v/t approach; desgracia etc face up to

encarcelar ⟨1a⟩ v/t put in prison, imprison

encarecer ⟨2d⟩ 1 v/t put up the price of, make more expensive 2 v/r **encarecerse** become more expensive; de precios increase, rise

encarecidamente adv: **le ruego encarecidamente que ...** I beg o urge you to ...

encargado m, -a f person in charge; **de un negocio** manager

encargar ⟨1h⟩ 1 v/t (pedir) order; **le encargué que me trajera ...** I asked him to bring me ... 2 v/r **encargarse** (tener responsabilidad) be in charge; **yo me encargo de la comida** I'll take care of o see to the food

encargo m job, errand; COM order; **¿te puedo hacer un encargo?** can I ask you to do something for me?; **hecho por encargo** made to order

encariñarse ⟨1a⟩ v/r: **encariñarse con**

alguien / algo grow fond of s.o/sth, become attached to s.o./sth

encarnado *adj* red

encarnar ⟨1a⟩ *v/t cualidad etc* embody; TEA play

encarnizado *adj* bitter, fierce

encarrilar ⟨1a⟩ *v/t fig* direct, guide

encasillar ⟨1a⟩ *v/t* class, classify; *(estereotipar)* pigeonhole

encasquetar ⟨1a⟩ *v/t gorro etc* pull down; *me lo encasquetó* F he landed me with it F

encasquillarse ⟨1a⟩ *v/r de arma* jam

encauzar ⟨1f⟩ *v/t tb fig* channel

encefalopatía *f*: *encefalopatía espongiforme bovina* bovine spongiform encephalitis, BSE

encendedor *m* lighter

encender ⟨2g⟩ 1 *v/t fuego* light; *luz, televisión* switch on, turn on; *fig* inflame, arouse, stir up 2 *v/r encenderse de luz, televisión* come on

encendido 1 *adj luz, televisión* (switched) on; *fuego* lit; *cara* red 2 *m* AUTO ignition

encerado *m* blackboard

encerar ⟨1a⟩ *v/t* polish, wax

encerrar ⟨1k⟩ 1 *v/t* lock up, shut up; *(contener)* contain 2 *v/r encerrarse* shut o.s. up

encerrona *f tb fig* trap

encestar ⟨1a⟩ *v/i* score

encharcado *adj* flooded, waterlogged

enchicharse ⟨1a⟩ *v/r L.Am. (emborracharse)* get drunk; *Rpl* P *(enojarse)* get angry, get mad F

enchilada *f Méx* GASTR enchilada *(tortilla with a meat or cheese filling)*

enchiloso *adj C.Am., Méx* hot

enchufado *m*: *es un enchufado* F he has connections, he has friends in high places

enchufar ⟨1a⟩ *v/t* EL plug in

enchufe *m* EL *macho* plug; *hembra* socket; *tener enchufe fig* F have pull F, have connections F

enchufismo *m* string-pulling

encía *f* gum

enciclopedia *f* encyclop(a)edia

encierro *m protesta* sit-in; *de toros* bull running

encima *adv* on top; *encima de* on top of, on; *por encima de* over, above; *por encima de todo* above all; *lo ayudo, y encima se queja* I help him and then he goes and complains; *hacer algo muy por encima* do sth very quickly; *no lo llevo encima* I haven't got it on me; *ponerse algo encima* put sth on

encimera *f sábana* top sheet; *Esp mostrador* worktop

encina *f* BOT holm oak

encinta *adj* pregnant

enclaustrarse ⟨1a⟩ *v/r fig* shut o.s. away

enclave *m* enclave

enclenque 1 *adj* sickly, weak 2 *m/f* weakling

encoger ⟨2c⟩ 1 *v/t* shrink; *las piernas* tuck in 2 *v/i de material* shrink 3 *v/r encogerse de material* shrink; *fig: de persona* be intimidated, cower; *encogerse de hombros* shrug (one's shoulders)

encolar ⟨1a⟩ *v/t* glue, stick

encolerizarse ⟨1f⟩ *v/r* get angry

encomienda *f L.Am.* HIST grant of land and labor by colonial authorities after the Conquest

enconado *adj* fierce, heated

encontrar ⟨1m⟩ 1 *v/t* find 2 *v/r encontrarse (reunirse)* meet; *(estar)* be; *encontrarse con alguien* meet s.o., run into s.o.; *me encuentro bien* I'm fine, I feel fine

encontronazo *m* smash, crash

encorvar ⟨1a⟩ *v/t* hunch; *estantería* cause to buckle

encrespar ⟨1a⟩ 1 *v/t pelo* curl; *mar* make rough *o* choppy; *fig* arouse, inflame 2 *v/r encresparse del mar* turn choppy; *fig* become inflamed

encrucijada *f* crossroads; *fig* dilemma

encuadernar ⟨1a⟩ *v/t* bind

encuadrar ⟨1a⟩ *v/t en marco* frame; *en grupo* include, place

encuartelar ⟨1a⟩ *v/t L.Am.* billet

encubierto *part* → *encubrir*

encubrir ⟨3a; *part* **encubierto** ⟩ *v/t delincuente* harbo(u)r; *delito* cover up, conceal

encuentro *m* meeting, encounter; DEP game; *salir* or *ir al encuentro de alguien* meet s.o., greet s.o.

encuerado *adj L.Am.* naked

encuesta *f* survey; (*sondeo*) (opinion) poll

encuestar ⟨1a⟩ *v/t* poll

encumbrarse ⟨1a⟩ *v/r fig* rise to the top

encurtidos *mpl* pickles

ende *adv: por ende* therefore, consequently

endeble *adj* weak, feeble

endémico *adj* endemic

endemoniado *adj* possessed; *fig* F terrible, awful

enderezar ⟨1f⟩ **1** *v/t* straighten out **2** *v/r enderezarse* straighten up, stand up straight; *fig* straighten o.s. out, sort o.s out

endeudarse ⟨1a⟩ *v/r* get (o.s.) into debt

endiablado *adj fig* (*malo*) terrible, awful; (*difícil*) tough

endibia *f* BOT endive

endilgar ⟨1h⟩ *v/t: me lo endilgó a mí* F he landed me with it F; *endilgar un sermón a alguien* F lecture s.o., give s.o. a lecture

endosar ⟨1a⟩ *v/t* COM endorse; *me lo endosó a mí* F she landed me with it F

endrina *f* BOT sloe

endrogarse ⟨1h⟩ *v/r Méx, C.Am.* get into debt

endulzar ⟨1f⟩ *v/t* sweeten; (*suavizar*) soften

endurecer ⟨2d⟩ **1** *v/t* harden; *fig* toughen up **2** *v/r endurecerse* harden, become harder; *fig* become harder, toughen up

enebro *m* BOT juniper

enema *m* MED enema

enemigo 1 *adj* enemy *atr* **2** *m* enemy; *ser enemigo de fig* be opposed to, be against

enemistarse ⟨1a⟩ *v/r* fall out

energético *adj crisis* energy *atr*; *alimento* energy-giving

energía *f* energy; *energía eólica* wind power; *energía nuclear* nuclear power, nuclear energy; *energía solar* solar power, solar energy

enérgico *adj* energetic; *fig* forceful, strong

energúmeno *m* lunatic; *ponerse hecho un energúmeno* go crazy F, blow a fuse F

ene. *abr* (*= enero*) Jan. (= January)

enero *m* January

enervar ⟨1a⟩ *v/t* irritate, get on the nerves of

enésimo *adj* nth; *por -a vez* for the umpteenth time

enfadado *adj* annoyed (*con* with); (*encolerizado*) angry (*con* with)

enfadar ⟨1a⟩ **1** *v/t* (*molestar*) annoy; (*encolerizar*) make angry, anger **2** *v/r enfadarse* (*molestarse*) get annoyed (*con* with); (*encolerizarse*) get angry (*con* with)

enfado *m* (*molestia*) annoyance; (*cólera*) anger

enfangarse ⟨1h⟩ *v/r* get muddy; *enfangarse en fig* get (o.s.) mixed up in

énfasis *m* emphasis; *poner énfasis en* emphasize, stress

enfático *adj* emphatic

enfermar ⟨1a⟩ **1** *v/t* drive crazy **2** *v/i* get sick, *Br tb* get ill

enfermedad *f* illness, disease

enfermería *f sala* infirmary, sickbay; *carrera* nursing

enfermero *m*, *-a f* nurse

enfermizo *adj* unhealthy

enfermo 1 *adj* sick, ill **2** *m*, *-a f* sick person

enfermoso *adj L.Am.* sickly, unhealthy

enfiestarse ⟨1a⟩ *v/r L.Am.* F party F, live it up F

enfocar ⟨1g⟩ *v/t cámara* focus; *imagen* get in focus; *fig: asunto* look at, consider

enfoque *m fig* approach

enfrentamiento *m* clash, confrontation

enfrentar ⟨1a⟩ **1** *v/t* confront, face up to **2** *v/r enfrentarse* DEP meet; *enfrentarse con alguien* confront s.o.; *enfrentarse a algo* face (up to) sth

enfrente *adv* opposite; *enfrente del colegio* opposite the school, across (the street) from the school

enfriar ⟨1c⟩ **1** *v/t vino* chill; *algo caliente* cool (down); *fig* cool **2** *v/r enfriarse* (*perder calor*) cool down; (*perder demasiado calor*) get cold, go cold; *fig* cool, cool off;

MED catch a cold, catch a chill

enfurecer ⟨2d⟩ **1** v/t infuriate, make furious **2** v/r **enfurecerse** get furious, get into a rage **enfurecido** adj furious, enraged

enfurruñado adj F sulky

enfurruñarse ⟨1a⟩ v/r F go into a huff F

engalanar ⟨1a⟩ v/t decorate, deck

enganchar ⟨1a⟩ **1** v/t hook; F novia, trabajo land F **2** v/r **engancharse** get caught (en on); MIL sign up, enlist; **engancharse a la droga** F get hooked on drugs F

engañar ⟨1a⟩ **1** v/t deceive, cheat; (ser infiel a) cheat on, be unfaithful to; **te han engañado** you've been had **2** v/r **engañarse** (mentirse) deceive o.s., kid o.s. F; (equivocarse) be wrong

engaño m (mentira) deception, deceit; (ardid) trick

engarzar ⟨1f⟩ v/t joya set

engatusar ⟨1a⟩ v/t F sweet-talk F

engendrar ⟨1a⟩ v/t father; fig breed, engender fml

engendro m fig eyesore

englobar ⟨1a⟩ v/t include, embrace fml

engordar ⟨1a⟩ **1** v/t put on, gain **2** v/i de persona put on weight, gain weight; de comida be fattening

engorrar ⟨1a⟩ v/t Méx, W.I. F annoy

engorroso adj tricky

engranaje m TÉC gears pl; fig machinery

engrasar ⟨1a⟩ v/t grease, lubricate

engrase m greasing, lubrication

engreído adj conceited

engrosar ⟨1m⟩ **1** v/t swell, increase **2** v/i put on weight, gain weight

engrudo m (flour and water) paste

engullir ⟨3h⟩ v/t bolt (down)

enhebrar ⟨1a⟩ v/t thread, string

enhiesto adj lit persona erect, upright; torre, árbol lofty

enhorabuena f congratulations pl; **dar la enhorabuena** congratulate (por on)

enigma m enigma

enigmático adj enigmatic

enjabonar ⟨1a⟩ v/t soap

enjambre m tb fig swarm

enjoyado adj bejewel(l)ed

enjuagar ⟨1h⟩ v/t rinse

enjugar ⟨1h⟩ v/t deuda etc wipe out; líquido mop up; lágrimas wipe away

enjuiciar ⟨1b⟩ v/t JUR institute proceedings against; fig judge

enlace m link, connection; **enlace matrimonial** marriage

enlatar ⟨1a⟩ v/t can, Br tb tin

enlazar ⟨1f⟩ **1** v/t link (up), connect; L.Am. con cuerda rope, lasso **2** v/i de carretera link up (con with); AVIA, FERR connect (con with)

enloquecer ⟨2d⟩ **1** v/t drive crazy o mad **2** v/i go crazy o mad

enmarañar ⟨1a⟩ **1** v/t pelo tangle; asunto complicate, muddle **2** v/r **enmarañarse** de pelo get tangled; **enmarañarse en algo** get entangled o embroiled in sth

enmarcar ⟨1g⟩ v/t frame

enmascarar ⟨1a⟩ v/t hide, disguise

enmendar ⟨1k⟩ **1** v/t asunto rectify, put right; JUR, POL amend; **enmendarle la plana a alguien** find fault with what s.o. has done **2** v/r **enmendarse** mend one's ways

enmienda f POL amendment

enmicar ⟨1g⟩ v/t L.Am. laminate

enmudecer ⟨2d⟩ **1** v/t silence **2** v/i fall silent

ennoblecer ⟨2d⟩ v/t ennoble

enojado adj L.Am. angry

enojar ⟨1a⟩ **1** v/t (molestar) annoy; L.Am. (encolerizar) make angry **2** v/r **enojarse** L.Am. (molestarse) get annoyed; (encolerizarse) get angry

enojo m L.Am. anger

enojón adj L.Am. F irritable, touchy

enojoso adj (delicado) awkward; (aburrido) tedious, tiresome

enorgullecer ⟨2d⟩ **1** v/t make proud, fill with pride **2** v/r **enorgullecerse** be proud (de of)

enorme adj enormous, huge

enrarecido adj aire rarefied; relaciones strained

enredadera f BOT creeper, climbing plant

enredar ⟨1a⟩ **1** v/t tangle, get tangled; fig complicate, make complicated **2** v/i make trouble **3** v/r **enredarse** get tangled; fig get complicated; **enredarse**

en algo get mixed up *o* involved in sth
enredo *m* tangle; (*confusión*) mess, confusion; (*intriga*) intrigue; *amoroso* affair
enrevesado *adj* complicated, involved
enriquecer ⟨2d⟩ **1** *v/t* make rich; *fig* enrich **2** *v/r* **enriquecerse** get rich; *fig* be enriched
enrojecer ⟨2d⟩ **1** *v/t* turn red **2** *v/i* blush, go red
enrolarse ⟨1a⟩ *v/r* MIL enlist
enrollar ⟨1a⟩ **1** *v/t* roll up; *cable* coil; *hilo* wind; *me enrolla* F I like it, I think it's great **2** *v/r* **enrollarse** F *hablar* go on and on F; *se enrolló mucho con nosotros* (*se portó bien*) he was great to us; *¡no te enrolles!* F get to the point!; *enrollarse con alguien* *fig* F neck with s.o.
enroscar ⟨1g⟩ **1** *v/t tornillo* screw in; *cable, cuerda* coil **2** *v/r* **enroscarse** coil up
ensaimada *f* GASTR *pastry in the form of a spiral*
ensalada *f* GASTR salad
ensaladera *f* salad bowl
ensaladilla *f*: **ensaladilla rusa** GASTR Russian salad
ensalmo *m*: *como por ensalmo* as if by magic
ensalzar ⟨1f⟩ *v/t* extol, praise
ensamblar ⟨1a⟩ *v/t* assemble
ensanchar ⟨1a⟩ **1** *v/t* widen; *prenda* let out **2** *v/r* **ensancharse** widen, get wider; *de prenda* stretch
ensangrentar ⟨1k⟩ *v/t* stain with blood, cover with blood
ensañarse ⟨1a⟩ *v/r* show no mercy (*con* to)
ensartar ⟨1a⟩ **1** *v/t en hilo* string; *aguja* thread; *L.Am.* (*engañar*) trick, trap **2** *v/r* **ensartarse** *L.Am.* *en discusión* get involved, get caught up
ensayar ⟨1a⟩ *v/t* test, try (out); TEA rehearse
ensayo *m* TEA rehearsal; *escrito* essay; *ensayo general* dress rehearsal
enseguida *adv* immediately, right away
ensenada *f* inlet, cove
enseñanza *f* teaching; *enseñanza primaria* elementary education, *Br* primary education; *enseñanza secundaria o*

media secondary education; *enseñanza superior* higher education
enseñar ⟨1a⟩ *v/t* (*dar clases*) teach; (*mostrar*) show
ensillar ⟨1a⟩ *v/t* saddle
ensimismarse ⟨1a⟩ *v/r* become lost in thought; *L.Am.* F get conceited *o* big--headed F
ensombrecer ⟨2d⟩ *v/t* cast a shadow over
ensordecedor *adj* deafening
ensuciar ⟨1b⟩ **1** *v/t* get dirty; *fig* sully, tarnish **2** *v/r* **ensuciarse** get dirty; *fig* get one's hands dirty
ensueño *m*: *de ensueño fig* fairy-tale *o*, dream *atr*
entablar ⟨1a⟩ *v/t* strike up, start
entablillar ⟨1a⟩ *v/t* splint, put in a splint
entarimado *m* (*suelo*) floorboards *pl*; (*plataforma*) stage, platform
ente *m* (*ser*) being, entity; F (*persona rara*) oddball F; (*organización*) body
entender ⟨2g⟩ **1** *v/t* understand; *dar a entender a alguien* give s.o. to understand **2** *v/i* understand; *entender de algo* know about sth **3** *v/r* **entenderse** communicate; *a ver si nos entendemos* let's get this straight; *yo me entiendo* I know what I'm doing; *entenderse con alguien* get along with s.o., get on with s.o. **4** *m*: *a mi entender* in my opinion, to my mind
entendido 1 *adj* understood; *¿entendido?* do you understand?, understood?; *tengo entendido que* I gather *o* understand that **2** *m*, *-a f* expert, authority
entendimiento *m* understanding; (*inteligencia*) mind
enterado *adj* knowledgeable, well-informed; *estar enterado de* know about, have heard about; *darse por enterado* get the message, take the hint
enterarse ⟨1a⟩ *v/r* find out, hear (*de* about); *¡para que te enteres!* F so there! F; *¡se va a enterar!* F he's in for it!
entereza *f* fortitude
enternecer ⟨2d⟩ *v/t* move, touch
entero 1 *adj* (*completo*) whole, entire; (*no roto*) intact, undamaged; *por entero*

completely, entirely **2** *m* (*punto*) point

enterrar ⟨1k⟩ *v/t* bury; *enterrar a todos* *fig* outlive everybody

entidad *f* entity, body

entierro *m* burial; (*funeral*) funeral

entonar ⟨1a⟩ **1** *v/t* intone, sing; *fig* F perk up **2** *v/i* sing in tune **3** *v/r* **entonarse** *con bebida* get tipsy

entonces *adv* then; *desde entonces* since, since then; *por entonces, en aquel entonces* in those days, at that time

entornar ⟨1a⟩ *v/t puerta* leave ajar; *ojos* half close

entorno *m* environment

entorpecer ⟨2d⟩ *v/t* hold up, hinder; *paso* obstruct; *entendimiento* dull

entrada *f acción* entry; *lugar* entrance; *localidad* ticket; *pago* deposit, down payment; *de comida* starter; *de entrada* from the outset, from the start

entrañable *adj amistad* close, deep; *amigo* close, dear; *recuerdo* fond

entrañar ⟨1a⟩ *v/t* entail, involve

entrañas *fpl* entrails

entrar ⟨1a⟩ **1** *v/i para indicar acercamiento* come in, enter; *para indicar alejamiento* go in, enter; *caber* fit; *me entró frío / sueño* I got cold / sleepy, I began to feel cold / sleepy; *no me entra en la cabeza* I can't understand it **2** *v/t para indicar acercamiento* bring in; *para indicar alejamiento* take in

entre *prp dos cosas, personas* between; *más de dos* among(st); *expresando cooperación* between; *la relación entre ellos* the relationship between them; *entre nosotros* among us; *lo pagamos entre todos* we paid for it among *o* between us

entreabierto 1 *part* → **entreabrir 2** *adj* half-open; *puerta* ajar

entreabrir ⟨3a; *part* **entreabierto** ⟩ *v/t* half-open

entreacto *m* TEA interval

entrecejo *m*: *fruncir el entrecejo* frown

entrecomillar ⟨1a⟩ *v/t* put in quotation marks

entrecortado *adj habla* halting; *respira-*

ción difficult, labo(u)red

entrecot *m* entrecote

entredicho *m*: *poner en entredicho* call into question, question

entrega *f* handing over; *de mercancías* delivery; (*dedicación*) dedication, devotion; *entrega a domicilio* (home) delivery; *entrega de premios* prize-giving, presentation; *hacer entrega de algo a alguien* present s.o. with sth

entregar ⟨1h⟩ **1** *v/t* give, hand over; *trabajo, deberes* hand in; *mercancías* deliver; *premio* present **2** *v/r* **entregarse** give o.s. up; *entregarse a fig* devote o.s. to, dedicate o.s. to

entrelazar ⟨1f⟩ *v/t* interweave, intertwine

entremeses *mpl* GASTR appetizers, hors d'oeuvres

entremezclar ⟨1a⟩ **1** *v/t* intermingle, mix **2** *v/r* **entremezclarse** intermingle, mix

entrenador *m*, **entrenadora** *f* coach

entrenamiento *m* coaching

entrenar ⟨1a⟩ **1** *v/t* train **2** *v/r* **entrenarse** train

entrepierna *f* ANAT crotch

entresacar ⟨1g⟩ *v/t* extract, select

entresijos *mpl fig* details, ins and outs F

entresuelo *m* mezzanine; TEA dress circle

entretanto *adv* meanwhile, in the meantime

entretecho *m Arg, Chi* attic

entretener ⟨2l⟩ *v/t* (*divertir*) entertain, amuse; (*retrasar*) keep, detain; (*distraer*) distract **2** *v/i* be entertaining **3** *v/r* **entretenerse** (*divertirse*) amuse o.s.; (*distraerse*) keep o.s. busy; (*retrasarse*) linger

entretenido *adj* (*divertido*) entertaining, enjoyable; *estar entretenido ocupado* be busy

entretenimiento *m* entertainment, amusement

entrevero *m S. Am.* (*lío*) mix-up, mess; *Chi* (*discusión*) argument

entrevista *f* interview

entrevistar ⟨1a⟩ **1** *v/t* interview **2** *v/r* **entrevistarse:** *entrevistarse con alguien* meet (with) s.o.

entristecer ⟨2d⟩ **1** *v/t* sadden **2** *v/r* **entristecerse** grow sad entrometerse ⟨2a⟩ *v/r* meddle (**en** in)

entrometido 1 *part* → **entrometerse** 2 *adj* meddling *atr*, interfering 3 *m* meddler, busybody

entronizar ⟨1f⟩ *v/t fig* instal(l)

entumecer ⟨2d⟩ 1 *v/t* numb 2 *v/r* entumecerse go numb, get stiff

enturbiar ⟨1b⟩ *v/t tb fig* cloud

entusiasmado *adj* excited, delirious

entusiasmar ⟨1a⟩ *v/t* excite, make enthusiastic

entusiasmo *m* enthusiasm

entusiasta 1 *adj* enthusiastic 2 *m/f* enthusiast

enumerar ⟨1a⟩ *v/t* list, enumerate

enunciar ⟨1b⟩ *v/t* state

envalentonarse ⟨1a⟩ *v/r* become bolder *o* more daring; (*insolentarse*) become defiant

envanecerse ⟨2d⟩ *v/r* become conceited *o* vain

envasar ⟨1a⟩ *v/t en botella* bottle; *en lata* can; *en paquete* pack

envase *m* container; *botella* (empty) bottle; **envase de cartón** carton; **envase no retornable** nonreturnable bottle

envejecer ⟨2d⟩ 1 *v/t* age, make look older 2 *v/i* age, grow old

envejecimiento *m* aging, ageing

envenenar ⟨1a⟩ *v/t tb fig* poison

envergadura *f* AVIA wingspan; MAR breadth; *fig* magnitude, importance; **de gran** *or* **mucha envergadura** *fig* of great importance

enviado *m*, -a *f* POL envoy; *de un periódico* reporter, correspondent; **enviado especial** POL special envoy; *de un periódico* special correspondent

enviar ⟨1c⟩ *v/t* send

enviciarse ⟨1b⟩ *v/r* get addicted (**con** to)

envidia *f* envy, jealousy; **me da envidia** I'm envious *o* jealous; **tener envidia a alguien de algo** envy s.o. sth

envidiar ⟨1b⟩ *v/t* envy; **envidiar a alguien por algo** envy s.o. sth

envidioso *adj* envious, jealous

envilecer ⟨2d⟩ 1 *v/t* degrade, debase 2 *v/r* envilecerse degrade o.s., debase o.s.

envío *m* shipment

enviudar ⟨1a⟩ *v/i* be widowed

envoltorio *m* wrapper

envoltura *f* cover, covering; *de regalo* wrapping; *de caramelo* wrapper

envolver ⟨2h; *part* **envuelto** ⟩ 1 *v/t* wrap (up); (*rodear*) surround, envelop; (*involucrar*) involve; **envolver a alguien en algo** involve s.o. in sth 2 *v/r* envolverse wrap o.s. up; **envolverse en** *fig* become involved in

envuelto *part* → **envolver**

enyesado *m* plastering

enzarzarse ⟨1f⟩ *v/r* get involved (**en** in)

eólico *adj* wind *atr*

épico *adj* epic

epidemia *f* epidemic

epilepsia *f* MED epilepsy

epílogo *m* epilog(ue)

episcopal *adj* episcopal

episodio *m* episode

epistolar *adj* epistolary

epitafio *m* epitaph

época *f* time, period; *parte del año* time of year; GEOL epoch; **hacer época** be epoch-making

epopeya *f* epic, epic poem

equidad *f* fairness

equidistante *adj* equidistant

equilibrado *adj* well-balanced

equilibrar ⟨1a⟩ *v/t* balance

equilibrio *m* balance; FÍS equilibrium

equino *adj* equine

equinoccio *m* equinox

equipaje *m* baggage; **equipaje de mano** hand baggage

equipamiento *m*: **equipamiento de serie** AUTO standard features *pl*

equipar ⟨1a⟩ *v/t* equip (**con** with)

equiparar ⟨1a⟩ *v/t* put on a level (**a** *or* **con** with); **equiparar algo con algo** *fig* compare *o* liken sth to sth

equipo *m* DEP team; *accesorios* equipment; **equipo de música** *or* **de sonido** sound system

equitación *f* riding

equitativo *adj* fair, equitable

equivalente *m/adj* equivalent

equivaler ⟨2q⟩ *v/i* be equivalent (**a** to)

equivocación *f* mistake; **por equivoca-**

ción by mistake

equivocado *adj* wrong; *estar equivocado* be wrong, be mistaken

equivocar ⟨1g⟩ **1** *v/t*: *equivocar a alguien* make s.o. make a mistake **2** *v/r* equivocarse make a mistake; *te has equivocado* you are wrong o mistaken; *equivocarse de número* TELEC get the wrong number

equívoco 1 *adj* ambiguous, equivocal **2** *m* misunderstanding; *(error)* mistake

era *f* era

erección *f* erection

eres *vb* → *ser*

ergonómico *adj* ergonomic

erguir ⟨3n⟩ **1** *v/t* raise, lift; *(poner derecho)* straighten **2** *v/r* erguirse *de persona* stand up, rise; *de edificio* rise

erial *m* uncultivated land

erigir ⟨3c⟩ **1** *v/t* erect **2** *v/r* erigirse: *erigirse en* set o.s. up as

erizarse ⟨1f⟩ *v/r de pelo* stand on end

erizo *m* zo hedgehog; *erizo de mar* zo sea urchin

ermita *f* chapel

ermitaño 1 *m* zo hermit crab **2** *m*, -a *f* hermit

erogación *f Méx, S. Am.* expenditure, outlay

erógeno *adj* erogenous

erosión *f* erosion

erosionar ⟨1a⟩ *v/t* GEOL erode

erótico *adj* erotic

erotismo *m* eroticism

erradicar ⟨1g⟩ *v/t* eradicate, wipe out

errante *adj* wandering

errar ⟨1l⟩ **1** *v/t* miss; *errar el tiro* miss **2** *v/i* miss; *errar es humano* to err is human

equivocarse be wrong, be mistaken

errata *f* mistake, error; *de imprenta* misprint

erre *f*: *erre que erre* F doggedly, stubbornly

erróneo *adj* wrong, erroneous *fml*

error *m* mistake, error; *error de cálculo* error of judg(e)ment

eructar ⟨1a⟩ *v/i* belch F, burp F

eructo *m* belch F, burp F

erudito 1 *adj* learned, erudite **2** *m* scholar

erupción *f* GEOL eruption; MED rash

esbelto *adj* slim, slender

esbozar ⟨1f⟩ *v/t* sketch; *idea, proyecto etc* outline

esbozo *m* sketch; *de idea, proyecto etc* outline

escabeche *m* type of marinade

escabroso *adj* rough; *problema* tricky; *relato* indecent

escabullirse ⟨3h⟩ *v/r* escape, slip away

escala *f* tb MÚS scale; AVIA stopover; *escala de cuerda* rope ladder; *escala de valores* scale of values; *a escala* to scale, life-sized

escalada *f* DEP climb, ascent; *escalada de los precios* increase in prices, escalation of prices

escalador *m*, **escaladora** *f* climber

escalafón *m fig* ladder

escalar ⟨1a⟩ **1** *v/t* climb, scale **2** *v/i* climb

escaldar ⟨1a⟩ *v/t* GASTR blanch; *manos* scald

escalera *f* stairs *pl*, staircase; *escalera de caracol* spiral staircase; *escalera de incendios* fire escape; *escalera de mano* ladder; *escalera mecánica* escalator

escalfar ⟨1a⟩ *v/t* poach

escalofriante *adj* horrifying

escalofrío *m* shiver

escalón *m* step; *de escalera de mano* rung

escalonar ⟨1a⟩ *v/t en tiempo* stagger; *terreno* terrace

escalope *m* escalope

escama *f* zo scale; *de jabón, piel* flake

escamar ⟨1a⟩ **1** *v/t* scale, remove the scales from; *fig* make suspicious **2** *v/r* escamarse become suspicious

escamotear ⟨1a⟩ *v/t (ocultar)* hide, conceal; *(negar)* withhold

escampar ⟨1a⟩ *v/i* clear up, stop raining

escanciar ⟨1b⟩ *v/t fml* pour

escandalizar ⟨1f⟩ **1** *v/t* shock, scandalize **2** *v/r* escandalizarse be shocked

escándalo *m (asunto vergonzoso)* scandal; *(jaleo)* racket, ruckus; *armar un escándalo* make a scene

escandaloso *adj (vergonzoso)* scandalous, shocking; *(ruidoso)* noisy, rowdy

Escandinavia Scandinavia

escanear ⟨1a⟩ v/t scan

escáner m scanner

escaño m POL seat

escapar ⟨1a⟩ 1 v/i escape (**de** from); **dejar escapar** oportunidad pass up, let slip; suspiro let out, give 2 v/r **escaparse** (huir) escape (**de** from); de casa run away (**de** from); **escaparse de** situación get out of

escaparate m store window

escapatoria f: **no tener escapatoria** have no way out

escape m de gas leak; AUTO exhaust; **salir a escape** rush out

escarabajo m ZO beetle

escaramuza f skirmish

escarbadientes m inv toothpick

escarbar ⟨1a⟩ 1 v/i tb fig dig around (**en** in) 2 v/t dig around in

escarceos mpl forays, dabbling sg; **escarceos amorosos** romantic o amorous adventures

escarcha f frost

escardar ⟨1a⟩ v/t hoe

escarmentar ⟨1k⟩ 1 v/t teach a lesson to 2 v/i learn one's lesson; **escarmentar en cabeza ajena** learn from other people's mistakes

escarmiento m lesson; **le sirvió de escarmiento** it taught him a lesson

escarnio m ridicule, derision

escarola f endive, escarole

escarpado adj sheer, steep

escarpia f hook

escasear ⟨1a⟩ v/i be scarce, be in short supply

escasez f shortage, scarcity

escaso adj recursos limited; **andar escaso de algo** falto be short of sth; **-as posibilidades de** not much chance of, little chance of; **falta un mes escaso** it's barely a month away

escatimar ⟨1a⟩ v/t be mean with, be very sparing with; **no escatimar esfuerzos** be unstinting in one's efforts, spare no effort

escayola f (plaster) cast

escayolar ⟨1a⟩ v/t put in a (plaster) cast

escena f scene; escenario stage; **entrar en escena** come on stage; **hacer una escena** fig make a scene

escenario m stage; fig scene

escénico adj stage atr

escenificar ⟨1g⟩ v/t stage

escepticismo m skepticism, Br scepticism

escéptico 1 adj skeptical, Br sceptical 2 m, -a f skeptic, Br sceptic

escindirse ⟨3a⟩ v/r (fragmentarse) split (**en** into); (segregarse) break away (**de** from)

escisión f (fragmentación) split; (segregación) break

esclarecer ⟨2d⟩ v/t throw o shed light on; misterio clear up

esclarecimiento m clarification; de misterio solving

esclavitud f slavery

esclavizar ⟨1f⟩ v/t enslave; fig tie down

esclavo m slave

esclerosis f MED: **esclerosis múltiple** multiple sclerosis

escoba f broom

escobilla f small brush; AUTO wiper blade

escocer ⟨2b & 2h⟩ v/i sting, smart; **todavía escuece la derrota** he's still smarting from the defeat

escocés 1 adj Scottish 2 m Scot, Scotsman

escocesa f Scot, Scotswoman

Escocia Scotland

escoger ⟨2c⟩ v/t choose, select

escogido adj select

escolar 1 adj school atr 2 m/f student

escolarización f education, schooling; **escolarización obligatoria** compulsory education

escolarizar ⟨1f⟩ v/t educate, provide schooling for

escolástico adj scholarly

escollera f breakwater

escollo m MAR reef; (obstáculo) hurdle, obstacle

escolta 1 f escort 2 m/f motorista outrider; (guardaespaldas) bodyguard

escoltar ⟨1a⟩ v/t escort

escombros mpl rubble sg

esconder ⟨2a⟩ 1 v/t hide, conceal 2 v/r es-

conderse hide

escondidas *fpl S. Am.* hide-and-seek *sg*; **a escondidas** in secret, secretly

escondite *m lugar* hiding place; *juego* hide-and-seek

escondrijo *m* hiding place

escopeta *f* shotgun; **escopeta de aire comprimido** air gun, air rifle

escopetado *adj:* **salir escopetado** F shoot *o* dash off F

escopetazo *m* gunshot

escorbuto *m* scurvy

escoria *f* slag; *desp* dregs *pl*

Escorpio *m/f inv* ASTR Scorpio

escorpión *m* ZO scorpion

escotado *adj* low-cut

escote *m* neckline; *de mujer* cleavage

escotilla *f* MAR hatch

escozor *m* burning sensation, stinging; *fig* bitterness

escribir ⟨3a; *part* **escrito**⟩ *v/t* write; (*deletrear*) spell; **escribir a mano** hand-write, write by hand; **escribir a máquina** type

escrito 1 *part* → **escribir** 2 *adj* written; **por escrito** in writing 3 *m* document; **escritos** writings

escritor *m*, **escritora** *f* writer, author

escritorio *m* desk; **artículos de escritorio** stationery

escritura *f* writing; JUR deed; **Sagradas Escrituras** Holy Scripture

escrúpulo *m* scruple; **sin escrúpulos** unscrupulous

escrupuloso *adj* (*cuidadoso*) meticulous; (*honrado*) scrupulous; (*aprensivo*) fastidious

escrutar ⟨1a⟩ *v/t* scrutinize; *votos* count

escrutinio *m de votos* count; (*inspección*) scrutiny

escuadrón *m* squadron

escuálido *adj* skinny, emaciated

escucha *f:* **estar a la escucha** be listening out; **escuchas** *pl* **telefónicas** wire-tapping *sg*, *Br* tb phone-tapping *sg*

escuchar ⟨1a⟩ 1 *v/t* listen to; *L.Am.* (*oír*) hear 2 *v/i* listen

escuchimizado *adj* F puny F, scrawny F

escudarse ⟨1a⟩ *v/r fig* hide (**en** behind)

escudería *f* stable

escudilla *f* bowl

escudo *m arma* shield; *insignia* badge; *moneda* escudo; **escudo de armas** coat of arms

escudriñar ⟨1a⟩ *v/t* (*mirar de lejos*) scan; (*examinar*) scrutinize

escuela *f* school; **escuela de comercio** business school; **escuela de idiomas** language school; **escuela primaria** elementary school, *Br* primary school

escuelero 1 *adj L.Am.* school *atr* 2 *m*, -a *f L.Am.* (*maestro*) teacher; *Pe, Bol* (*alumno*) student

escueto *adj* succinct, concise

escuincle *m/f Méx, C.Am.* F kid

esculpir ⟨3a⟩ *v/t* sculpt

escultor *m*, **escultora** *f* sculptor

escultura *f* sculpture

escupidera *f* spitoon; *L.Am.* chamber pot

escupir ⟨3a⟩ 1 *v/i* spit 2 *v/t* spit out

escupitajo *m* F gob of spit F

escurreplatos *m inv* plate rack

escurridizo *adj* slippery; *fig* evasive

escurridor *m* (*colador*) colander; (*escurreplatos*) plate rack

escurrir ⟨3a⟩ 1 *v/t ropa* wring out; *platos, verduras* drain 2 *v/i de platos* drain; *de ropa* drip-dry 3 *v/r* **escurrirse** *de líquido* drain away; (*deslizarse*) slip; (*escaparse*) slip away

escusado *m* bathroom

ese, esa, esos, esas *det singular* that; *plural* those

ése, ésa, ésos, ésas *pron singular* that (one); *plural* those (ones); **le ofrecí dinero pero ni por ésas** I offered him money but even that wasn't enough; **no soy de ésos que** I'm not one of those who

esencia *f* essence

esencial *adj* essential

esfera *f* sphere; **esfera de actividad** *fig* field *o* sphere (of activity)

esférico 1 *adj* spherical 2 *m* DEP F ball

esfinge *f* sphinx

esforzarse ⟨1f & 1m⟩ *v/r* make an effort, try hard

esfuerzo *m* effort; **hacer un esfuerzo** make an effort; **sin esfuerzo** effortlessly

esfumarse ⟨1a⟩ v/r F tb fig disappear

esgrima f fencing

esgrimir ⟨3a⟩ v/t arma wield; fig: argumento put forward, use

esguince m sprain

eslabón m link; **el eslabón perdido** the missing link

eslavo 1 adj Slavic, Slavonic **2** m, -a f Slav

eslogan m slogan

eslora f length

Eslovaquia Slovakia

Eslovenia Slovenia

esmalte m enamel; **esmalte de uñas** nail polish, nail varnish

esmerado adj meticulous

esmeralda f emerald

esmerarse ⟨1a⟩ v/r take great care (**en** over)

esmerilado adj: **cristal esmerilado** frosted glass

esmero m care; **con esmero** carefully

esmirriado adj F skinny F, scrawny F

esmoquin m tuxedo, Br dinner jacket

esnifar ⟨1a⟩ v/t F pegamento sniff F; cocaína snort F

esnob 1 adj snobbish **2** m snob

esnobismo m snobbishness

eso pron that; **en eso** just then, just at that moment; **eso mismo, eso es** that's it, that's the way; **a eso de las dos** at around two; **por eso** that's why; **¿y eso?** why's that?; **y eso que le dije que no se lo contara** and after I told him not to tell her

esotérico adj esoteric

espabilado adj (listo) bright, smart; (vivo) sharp, on the ball F

espabilar ⟨1a⟩ **1** v/t (quitar el sueño) wake up, revive; **lo ha espabilado** (avivado) she's got him to wise up **2** v/i (darse prisa) hurry up, get a move on; (avivarse) wise up **3** v/r espabilarse del sueño wake oneself up; (darse prisa) hurry up, get a move on; (avivarse) wise up

espacial adj cohete, viaje space atr; FÍS, MAT spatial

espaciarse ⟨1a⟩ v/r become more (and more) infrequent

espacio m space; TV program, Br programme; **espacios verdes** green spaces; **espacio de tiempo** space of time; **espacio vital** living space

espacioso adj spacious, roomy

espada f sword; **espadas** pl (en naipes) suit in Spanish deck of cards; **estar entre la espada y la pared** be between a rock and a hard place

espadachín m skilled swordsman

espaguetis mpl spaghetti sg

espalda f back; **a espaldas de alguien** behind s.o.'s back; **de espaldas a** with one's back to; **por la espalda** from behind; **caerse de espaldas** fall flat on one's back; **no me des la espalda** don't sit with your back to me; **nadar a espalda** swim backstroke; **tener cubiertas las espaldas** fig keep one's back covered; **volver la espalda a alguien** fig turn one's back on s.o.

espaldarazo m slap on the back; (reconocimiento) recognition

espalderas fpl wall bars

espantajo m scarecrow; fig sight

espantapájaros m inv scarecrow

espantar ⟨1a⟩ **1** v/t (asustar) frighten, scare; (ahuyentar) frighten away, shoo away; F (horrorizar) horrify, appal(l) **2** v/r espantarse get frightened, get scared; F (horrorizarse) be horrified, be appal(l)ed

espanto m (susto) fright; L.Am. (fantasma) ghost; **nos llenó de espanto** desagrado we were horrified; **¡qué espanto!** how awful!; **de espanto** terrible

espantoso adj horrific, appalling; para enfatizar terrible, dreadful; **hace un calor espantoso** it's terribly hot, it's incredibly hot

España Spain

español 1 adj Spanish **2** m idioma Spanish **3** m, -a f Spaniard; **los españoles** the Spanish

esparadrapo m Band-Aid®, Br plaster

esparcimiento m relaxation

esparcir ⟨3b⟩ **1** v/t papeles scatter; rumor spread **2** v/r esparcirse de papeles be scattered; de rumor spread

espárrago m BOT asparagus; **espárrago**

triguero wild asparagus; *¡vete a freír espárragos!* F get lost! F

espartano *adj* spartan

esparto *m* BOT esparto grass

espasmo *m* spasm

espátula *f* spatula; *en pintura* palette knife

especia *f* spice

especial *adj* special; *(difícil)* fussy; *en especial* especially

especialidad *f* specialty, *Br* speciality

especialista *m/f* specialist, expert; *en cine* stuntman; *mujer* stuntwoman

especializarse ⟨1f⟩ *v/r* specialize (*en* in)

especie *f* BIO species; *(tipo)* kind, sort

especiero *m* spice rack

especificar ⟨1g⟩ *v/t* specify

específico *adj* specific

espectacular *adj* spectacular

espectáculo *m* TEA show; *(escena)* sight; *dar el espectáculo* fig make a spectacle of o.s.

espectador *m*, espectadora *f* en cine etc member of the audience; DEP spectator; *(observador)* on-looker, observer

espectro *m* FÍS spectrum; *(fantasma)* ghost

especulación *f* speculation

especular ⟨1a⟩ *v/i* speculate

especulativo *adj* speculative

espejismo *m* mirage

espejo *m* mirror; *espejo retrovisor* rear--view mirror

espeleólogo *m* spelunker, *Br* pot-holer

espeluznante *adj* horrific, horrifying

espera *f* wait; *sala de espera* waiting room; *en espera de* pending; *estar a la espera de* be waiting for

esperanza *f* hope; *esperanza de vida* life expectancy

esperar ⟨1a⟩ **1** *v/t (aguardar)* wait for; *con esperanza* hope; *(suponer, confiar en)* expect **2** *v/i (aguardar)* wait

esperma *f* sperm

espesar ⟨1a⟩ **1** *v/t* thicken **2** *v/r* espesarse thicken, become thick

espeso *adj* thick; *vegetación, niebla* thick, dense

espesor *m* thickness

espesura *f* dense vegetation

espía *m/f* spy

espiar ⟨1c⟩ **1** *v/t* spy on **2** *v/i* spy

espiga *f* BOT ear, spike

espina *f de planta* thorn; *de pez* bone; *espina dorsal* spine, backbone; *dar mala espina a alguien* F make s.o. feel uneasy

espinacas *fpl* BOT spinach *sg*

espinazo *m* spine, backbone; *doblar el espinazo* fig *(trabajar mucho)* work o.s. into the ground; *(humillarse)* kowtow (*ante* to)

espinilla *f de la pierna* shin; *en la piel* pimple, spot

espinoso *adj* thorny, prickly; *fig* thorny, knotty

espionaje *m* spying, espionage

espiral **1** *adj* spiral *atr* **2** *f* spiral

espirar ⟨1a⟩ *v/t & v/i* exhale

espiritismo *m* spiritualism

espíritu *m* spirit

espiritual *adj* spiritual

espléndido *adj* splendid, magnificent; *(generoso)* generous

esplendor *m* splendo(u)r

espliego *m* lavender

espolear ⟨1a⟩ *v/t* tb fig spur on

espolvorear ⟨1a⟩ *v/t* sprinkle

esponja *f* sponge

esponjoso *adj* bizcocho spongy; *toalla* soft, fluffy

espónsor *m/f* sponsor

esponsorizar ⟨1f⟩ *v/t* sponsor

espontáneo *adj* spontaneous

esporádico *adj* sporadic

esposa *f* wife

esposas *fpl (manillas)* handcuffs *pl*

esposar ⟨1a⟩ *v/t* handcuff

esposo *m* husband

esprint *m* sprint

espuela *f* spur

espuerta *f*: *ganar dinero a espuertas* F make money hand over fist F

espuma *f* foam; *de jabón* lather; *de cerveza* froth; *espuma de afeitar* shaving foam; *espuma moldeadora* styling mousse

espumadera *f* slotted spoon, skimmer

espumarajo *m* froth, foam

espumilla *f C.Am.* GASTR meringue

espumoso *adj* frothy, foamy; *caldo* sparkling

esqueje *m* cutting

esquela *f aviso* death notice, obituary

esquelético *adj* skeletal

esqueleto *m* skeleton; *Méx, C.Am., Pe, Bol fig* blank form; *mover o menear el esqueleto* F dance

esquema *m* (*croquis*) sketch, diagram; (*sinopsis*) outline, summary

esquemático *adj dibujo* schematic, diagrammatic; *resumen* simplified

esquí *m tabla* ski; *deporte* skiing; *esquí de fondo* cross-country skiing; *esquí náutico o acuático* waterskiing

esquiador *m*, esquiadora *f* skier

esquiar ⟨1a⟩ *v/i* ski

esquilar ⟨1a⟩ *v/t* shear

esquilmar ⟨1a⟩ *v/t* overexploit; *a alguien* suck dry

esquina *f* corner

esquinazo *m Arg, Chi* serenade; *dar esquinazo a alguien* F give s.o. the slip F

esquirol *m/f* strikebreaker, scab F

esquite *m C.Am., Méx* popcorn

esquivar ⟨1a⟩ *v/t* avoid, dodge F

esquivo *adj* (*huraño*) unsociable; (*evasivo*) shifty, evasive

esquizofrenia *f* schizophrenia

esquizofrénico *adj* schizophrenic

esta *det* this

está *vb* → *estar*

estabilidad *f* stability

estabilizante *m* stabilizer

estabilizar ⟨1f⟩ *v/t* stabilize

estable *adj* stable

establecer ⟨2d⟩ 1 *v/t* establish; *negocio* set up 2 *v/r* establecerse *en lugar* settle; *en profesión* set up

establecimiento *m* establishment

establo *m* stable

estaca *f* stake

estacada *f: dejar a alguien en la estacada* F leave s.o. in the lurch

estación *f* station; *del año* season; *estación espacial o orbital* space station; *estación de invierno o invernal* winter resort; *estación de servicio* service station; *estación de trabajo* INFOR work station

estacional *adj* seasonal

estacionamiento *m* AUTO parking; *L.Am.* parking lot, *Br* car park

estacionar ⟨1a⟩ 1 *v/t* AUTO park 2 *v/r* estacionarse stabilize

estacionómetro *m Méx* parking meter

estadio *m* DEP stadium

estadística *f cifra* statistic; *ciencia* statistics

estado *m* state; MED condition; *estado civil* marital status; *estado de guerra* state of war; *en buen estado* in good condition; *el Estado* the State; *estado del bienestar* welfare state; *los Estados Unidos (de América)* the United States (of America)

estadounidense 1 *adj* American, US *atr* 2 *m/f* American

estafa *f* swindle, cheat

estafador *m*, estafadora *f* con artist F, fraudster

estafar ⟨1a⟩ *v/t* swindle, cheat (*a* out of), defraud (*a* of)

estalactita *f* stalactite

estalagmita *f* stalagmite

estallar ⟨1a⟩ *v/i* explode; *de guerra* break out; *de escándalo* break; *estalló en llanto* she burst into tears

estallido *m* explosion; *de guerra* outbreak

estamento *m* stratum, class

estampa *f de libro* illustration; (*aspecto*) appearance; REL prayer card

estampado *adj tejido* patterned

estampar ⟨1a⟩ *v/t sello* put; *tejido* print; *pasaporte* stamp; *le estampó una bofetada en la cara* F she smacked him one F

estampido *m* bang

estampilla *f L.Am.* stamp

estancado *adj agua* stagnant; *fig* at a standstill

estancar ⟨1g⟩ 1 *v/t río* dam up, block; *fig* bring to a standstill 2 *v/r* estancarse stagnate; *fig* come to a standstill

estancia *f* stay; *Rpl* farm, ranch

estanciero *m*, -a *f Rpl* farmer, rancher

estanco 1 *adj* watertight 2 *m shop selling cigarettes etc*

estándar *m* standard

estandarizar ⟨1f⟩ *v/t* standardize

estandarte *m* standard, banner

estanque *m* pond

estante *m* shelf

estantería *f* shelves *pl*; *para libros* bookcase

estaño *m* tin

estar ⟨1p⟩ **1** *v/i* be; *¿está Javier?* is Javier in?; *estar haciendo algo* be doing sth; *estamos a 3 de enero* it's January 3rd; *el kilo está a cien pesetas* they're a hundred pesetas a kilo; *te está grande* it's too big for you; *estar con alguien* agree with s.o.; *(apoyar)* support s.o.; *ahora estoy con Vd.* I'll be with you in just a moment; *estar a bien / mal con alguien* be on good / bad terms with s.o.; *estar de ocupación* work as, be; *estar en algo* be working on sth; *estar para hacer algo* be about to do sth; *no estar para algo* not be in a mood for sth; *estar por algo* be in favo(u)r of sth; *está por hacer* it hasn't been done yet; *estar sin dinero* have no money; *¿cómo está Vd.?* how are you?; *estoy mejor* I'm (feeling) better; *¡ya estoy!* I'm ready!; *¡ya está!* that's it! **2** *v/r* estarse stay; *estarse quieto* keep still

estárter *m* choke

estatal *adj* state *atr*

estático *adj* static

estatua *f* statue

estatura *f* height

estatutario *adj* statutory

estatuto *m* statute; *estatutos* articles of association

estatus *m* status

este[1] *m* east

este[2], **esta**, **estos**, **estas** *det singular* this; *plural* these

éste, **ésta**, **éstos**, **éstas** *pron singular* this (one); *plural* these (ones)

estela *f* MAR wake; AVIA, *fig* trail

estelar *adj* star *atr*

estepa *f* steppe

estera *f* mat

estercolero *m* dunghill, dung heap

estéreo *adj* stereo

estereofónico *adj* stereophonic

estereotipo *m* stereotype

estéril *adj* MED sterile; *trabajo, esfuerzo etc* futile

esterilidad *f* sterility

esterilizar ⟨1f⟩ *v/t tb persona* sterilize

esterilla *f* mat

esterlina *adj*: *libra esterlina* pound sterling

esternón *m* breast bone, sternum

estero *m Rpl* marsh

estertor *m* death rattle

esteticista *m/f* beautician

estético *adj* esthetic, *Br* aesthetic

estetoscopio *m* MED stethoscope

estibador *m* stevedore

estiércol *m* dung; *(abono)* manure

estilarse ⟨1a⟩ *v/r* be fashionable

estilista *m/f* stylist; *de modas* designer

estilo *m* style; *al estilo de* in the style of; *algo por el estilo* something like that; *son todos por el estilo* they're all the same

estilográfica *f* fountain pen

estima *f* esteem, respect; *tener a alguien en mucha estima* hold s.o. in high regard *o* esteem

estimación *f* (*cálculo*) estimate; (*estima*) esteem, respect

estimar ⟨1a⟩ *v/t* respect, hold in high regard; *estimo conveniente que* I consider it advisable to

estimulante 1 *adj* stimulating **2** *m* stimulant

estimular ⟨1a⟩ *v/t* stimulate; (*animar*) encourage

estímulo *m* stimulus; (*incentivo*) incentive

estío *m lit* summertime

estipular ⟨1a⟩ *v/t* stipulate

estirado *adj* snooty F, stuck-up F

estirar ⟨1a⟩ *v/t* stretch; (*alisar*) smooth out; *dinero* stretch, make go further; *estirar la pata* F kick the bucket F; *estirar las piernas* stretch one's legs

estirpe *f* stock

estival *adj* summer *atr*

esto *pron* this; *esto es* that is to say; *por esto* this is why; *a todo esto (mientras* *tanto*) meanwhile; (*a propósito*) incidentally

estofa *f*: **de baja estofa** *desp* low-class *desp*

estofado *adj* stewed

estofar ⟨1a⟩ *v/t* stew

estoico 1 *adj* stoic(al) **2** *m*, **-a** *f* stoic

estómago *m* stomach

estor *m* blind

estorbar ⟨1a⟩ **1** *v/t* (*dificultar*) hinder; **nos estorbaba** he was in our way **2** *v/i* get in the way

estorbo *m* hindrance, nuisance

estornino *m* ZO starling

estornudar ⟨1a⟩ *v/i* sneeze

estornudo *m* sneeze

estoy *vb* → **estar**

estrado *m* platform

estrafalario *adj* F eccentric; *ropa* outlandish

estragón *m* BOT tarragon

estragos *mpl* devastation *sg*; **causar estragos entre** wreak havoc among

estrambótico *adj* F eccentric; *ropa* outlandish

estrangular ⟨1a⟩ *v/t* strangle

estraperlo *m* black market; **de estraperlo** on the black market

estratagema *f* stratagem

estrategia *f* strategy

estratégico *adj* strategic

estrato *m* fig stratum

estrechar ⟨1a⟩ **1** *v/t ropa* take in; *mano* shake; **estrechar entre los brazos** hug, embrace **2** *v/r* **estrecharse** narrow, get narrower

estrechez *f* fig hardship; **estrechez de miras** narrow-mindedness; **pasar estrecheces** suffer hardship

estrecho 1 *adj* narrow; (*apretado*) tight; *amistad* close; **estrecho de miras** narrow-minded **2** *m* strait, straits *pl*

estrella *f tb de cine etc* star; **estrella fugaz** falling star, shooting star; **estrella de mar** ZO starfish; **estrella polar** Pole star

estrellar ⟨1a⟩ **1** *v/t* smash; **estrellar algo contra algo** smash sth against sth; **estrelló el coche contra un muro** he smashed the car into a wall **2** *v/r* **estrellarse** crash

(**contra** into)

estrellón *m* Pe, Bol crash

estremecer ⟨2d⟩ **1** *v/t* shock, shake F **2** *v/r* **estremecerse** shake, tremble; *de frío* shiver; *de horror* shudder

estrenar ⟨1a⟩ **1** *v/t ropa* wear for the first time, christen F; *objeto* try out, christen F; TEA, *película* premiere; **a estrenar** brand new **2** *v/r* **estrenarse** make one's debut

estreno *m* TEA, *de película* premiere; *de persona* debut; **estar de estreno** be wearing new clothes

estreñimiento *m* constipation

estrépito *m* noise, racket

estrés *m* stress

estresar ⟨1a⟩ *v/t*: **estresar alguien** cause s.o. stress, subject s.o. to stress

estría *f en piel* stretch mark

estribar ⟨1a⟩ *v/i*: **estribar en** stem from, lie in

estribillo *m* chorus, refrain

estribo *m* stirrup; **perder los estribos** fig fly off the handle F

estrictez *f* S. Am. strictness

estricto *adj* strict

estridente *adj* shrill, strident

estrofa *f* stanza, verse

estropajo *m* scourer

estropajoso *adj persona* wiry; *boca* dry; *camisa* scruffy

estropeado *adj* (*averiado*) broken

estropear ⟨1a⟩ **1** *v/t aparato* break; *plan* ruin, spoil **2** *v/r* **estropearse** break down; *de comida* go off, go bad; *de plan* go wrong

estructura *f* structure

estructurar ⟨1a⟩ *v/t* structure, organize

estruendo *m* racket, din

estrujar ⟨1a⟩ *v/t* F crumple up, scrunch up F; *trapo* wring out; *persona* squeeze, hold tightly

estuario *m* estuary

estuche *m* case, box

estuco *m* stuccowork

estudiante *m/f* student

estudiantil *adj* student *atr*

estudiar ⟨1b⟩ *v/t* & *v/i* study

estudio *m disciplina* study; *apartamento*

studio, *Br* studio flat; *de cine, música* studio

estudioso *adj* studious

estufa *f* heater

estupefaciente *m* narcotic (drug)

estupefacto *adj* stupefied, speechless

estupendo *adj* fantastic, wonderful

estupidez *f cualidad* stupidity; *acción* stupid thing

estúpido **1** *adj* stupid **2** *m*, -a *f* idiot

estupor *m* astonishment, amazement; MED stupor

esturión *m* ZO sturgeon

estuve *vb* → **estar**

estuvo *vb* → **estar**

etapa *f* stage; *por etapas* in stages

etarra *m/f* member of ETA

etc *abr* (= *etcétera*) etc (= etcetera)

etcétera *m* etcetera, and so on; *y un largo etcétera de …* and a long list of …, and many other …

etéreo *adj* ethereal

eternidad *f* eternity

eterno *adj* eternal; *la película se me hizo -a* the movie seemed to go on for ever

ética *f en filosofía* ethics; *comportamiento* principles *pl*

ético *adj* ethical

etimología *f* etymology

Etiopía Ethiopia

etiqueta *f* label; (*protocolo*) etiquette

etiquetar ⟨1a⟩ *v/t tb fig* label

étnico *adj* ethnic

eucalipto *m* BOT eucalyptus

eucaristía *f* Eucharist

eufemismo *m* euphemism

euforia *f* euphoria

eufórico *adj* euphoric

euro *m* euro

eurodiputado *m*, -a *f* MEP, member of the European Parliament

Europa Europe

europeísta *m/f* pro-European

europeo **1** *adj* European **2** *m*, -a *f* European

eusquera *m/adj* Basque

eutanasia *f* euthanasia

evacuación *f* evacuation

evacuar ⟨1d⟩ *v/t* evacuate

evadir ⟨3a⟩ **1** *v/t* avoid; *impuestos* evade **2** *v/r* evadirse *tb fig* escape

evaluación *f* evaluation, assessment; (*prueba*) test

evaluar ⟨1e⟩ *v/t* assess, evaluate

evangelio *m* gospel

evangelizar ⟨1f⟩ *v/t* evangelize

evaporación *f* evaporation

evaporarse ⟨1a⟩ *v/r* evaporate; *fig* F vanish into thin air

evasión *f tb fig* escape; *evasión de capitales* flight of capital; *evasión fiscal* tax evasion

evasiva *f* evasive reply

evento *m* event

eventual *adj* possible; *trabajo* casual, temporary; *en el caso eventual de* in the event of

eventualidad *f* eventuality

evidencia *f* evidence, proof; *poner en evidencia* demonstrate; *poner a alguien en evidencia* show s.o. up

evidente *adj* evident, clear

evitar ⟨1a⟩ *v/t* avoid; (*impedir*) prevent; *molestias* save; *no puedo evitarlo* I can't help it

evocar ⟨1g⟩ *v/t* evoke

evolución *f* BIO evolution; (*desarrollo*) development

evolucionar ⟨1a⟩ *v/t* BIO evolve; (*desarrollar*) develop

ex **1** *pref* ex- **2** *m/f* F ex F

exabrupto *m* sharp remark

exacerbar ⟨1a⟩ *v/t* exacerbate, make worse; (*irritar*) exasperate

exacto *adj medida* exact, precise; *informe* accurate; *¡exacto!* exactly!, precisely!

exageración *f* exaggeration

exagerado *adj* exaggerated

exagerar ⟨1a⟩ *v/t* exaggerate

exaltación *f* (*alabanza*) exaltation; (*entusiasmo*) agitation, excitement

exaltar ⟨1a⟩ *v/t* excite, get worked up

examen *m* test, exam; MED examination; (*análisis*) study; *examen de conducir* driving test

examinar ⟨1a⟩ **1** *v/t* examine **2** *v/r* examinarse take an exam

exasperar ⟨1a⟩ **1** *v/t* exasperate **2** *v/r*

exasperarse get exasperated
excarcelar ⟨1a⟩ v/t release (from prison)
excavación f excavation
excavadora f digger
excavar ⟨1a⟩ v/t excavate; *túnel* dig
excedencia f extended leave of absence
excedente 1 *adj* surplus; *empleado* on extended leave of absence 2 *m* surplus
exceder ⟨2a⟩ 1 v/t exceed 2 v/r **excederse** go too far, get carried away
excelencia f excellence; *Su Excelencia la señora embajadora* Her Excellency the Ambassador; *por excelencia* par excellence
excelente *adj* excellent
excéntrico 1 *adj* eccentric 2 *m*, -a f eccentric
excepción f exception; *a excepción de* except for; *sin excepción* without exception
excepcional *adj* exceptional
excepto *prp* except
exceptuar ⟨1e⟩ v/t except; *exceptuando* with the exception of, except for
excesivo *adj* excessive
exceso *m* excess; *exceso de equipaje* excess baggage; *exceso de velocidad* speeding; *en exceso* in excess, too much
excitación f excitement, agitation
excitante 1 *adj* exciting; *una bebida excitante* a stimulant 2 *m* stimulant
excitar ⟨1a⟩ 1 v/t excite; *sentimientos, sexualmente* arouse 2 v/r **excitarse** get excited; *sexualmente* become aroused
exclamación f exclamation
exclamar ⟨1a⟩ v/t exclaim
excluir ⟨3g⟩ v/t leave out (*de* of), exclude (*de* from); *posibilidad* rule out
exclusiva f *privilegio* exclusive rights *pl* (*de* to); *reportaje* exclusive
exclusivo *adj* exclusive
excomunión f excommunication
excremento *m* excrement
exculpar ⟨1a⟩ v/t exonerate
excursión f trip, excursion
excursionista *m/f* excursionist
excusa f excuse; *excusas* apologies
excusado *m* bathroom
excusar ⟨1a⟩ v/t excuse

execrable *adj* abominable, execrable *fml*
exención f exemption; *exención fiscal* tax exemption
exento *adj* exempt (*de* from); *exento de impuestos* tax-exempt, tax-free
exhalación f: *salir como una exhalación* fig rush o dash out
exhaustivo *adj* exhaustive
exhausto *adj* exhausted
exhibición f display, demonstration; *de película* screening, showing
exhibicionista *m/f* exhibitionist
exhibir ⟨3a⟩ 1 v/t show, display; *película* screen, show; *cuadro* exhibit 2 v/r **exhibirse** show o.s., let o.s. be seen
exhumar ⟨1a⟩ v/t exhume
exigencia f demand
exigente *adj* demanding
exigir ⟨3c⟩ v/t demand; (*requerir*) call for, demand; *le exigen mucho* they ask a lot of him
exiguo *adj* meager, *Br* meagre
exiliado 1 *adj* exiled, in exile *pred* 2 *m*, -a f exile
exiliar ⟨1a⟩ 1 v/t exile 2 v/r **exiliarse** go into exile
exilio *m* exile; *en el exilio* in exile
eximir ⟨3a⟩ v/t exempt (*de* from)
existencia f existence; (*vida*) life; *existencias* COM supplies, stocks
existencialista *m/f* & *adj* existentialist
existir ⟨3a⟩ v/i exist; *existen muchos problemas* there are a lot of problems
éxito *m* success; *éxito de taquilla* box office hit; *tener éxito* be successful, be a success
exitoso *adj* successful
Exmo. *abr* (= *Excelentísimo*) Your / His Excellency
exonerar ⟨1a⟩ v/t exonerate; *exonerar a alguien de algo* exempt s.o. from sth
exorbitante *adj* exorbitant
exorcista *m/f* exorcist
exótico *adj* exotic
expandir ⟨3a⟩ 1 v/t expand 2 v/r **expandirse** expand; *de noticia* spread
expansión f expansion; (*recreo*) recreation
expatriarse ⟨1b⟩ v/r leave one's country

expectación f sense of anticipation

expectativa f (*esperanza*) expectation; **estar a la expectativa de algo** be waiting for sth; **expectativas** (*perspectivas*) prospects

expedición f expedition

expediente m file, dossier; (*investigación*) investigation, inquiry; **expediente académico** student record; **expediente disciplinario** disciplinary proceedings pl; **abrir un expediente a alguien** take disciplinary action against s.o.

expedir ⟨3l⟩ v/t documento issue; mercancías send, dispatch

expeditar ⟨1a⟩ v/t L.Am. (*apresurar*) hurry; (*concluir*) finish, conclude

expeditivo adj expeditious

expendedor adj: **máquina expendedora** vending machine

expendio m L.Am. store, shop

expensas fpl: **a expensas de** at the expense of

experiencia f experience

experimentado adj experienced

experimentar ⟨1a⟩ 1 v/t try out, experiment with 2 v/i experiment (**con** on)

experimento m experiment

experto 1 adj expert; **experto en hacer algo** expert o very good at doing sth **2** m expert (**en** on)

expiar ⟨1c⟩ v/t expiate, atone for

expirar ⟨1a⟩ v/i expire

explanada f open area; junto al mar esplanade

explayarse ⟨1a⟩ v/r speak at length; (*desahogarse*) unburden o.s.; (*distraerse*) relax, unwind; **explayarse sobre algo** expound on sth

explicación f explanation

explicar ⟨1g⟩ 1 v/t explain 2 v/r **explicarse** (*comprender*) understand; (*hacerse comprender*) express o.s.; **no me lo explico** I can't understand it, I don't get it F

explícito adj explicit

explorador m, **exploradora** f explorer; MIL scout

explorar ⟨1a⟩ v/t explore

explosión f explosion; **explosión demográfica** population explosion; **hacer**

explosión go off, explode

explosionar ⟨1a⟩ v/t & v/i explode

explosivo m/adj explosive

explotación f de mina, tierra exploitation, working; de negocio running, operation; de trabajador exploitation

explotar ⟨1a⟩ 1 v/t tierra, mina work, exploit; situación take advantage of, exploit; trabajador exploit 2 v/i go off, explode; fig explode, blow a fuse F

expoliar ⟨1b⟩ v/t plunder, pillage

exponente m exponent

exponer ⟨2r; part **expuesto** ⟩ 1 v/t idea, teoría set out, put forward; (*revelar*) expose; pintura, escultura exhibit, show; (*arriesgar*) risk 2 v/r **exponerse: exponerse a algo** (*arriesgarse*) lay o.s. open to sth

exportación f export

exportar ⟨1a⟩ v/t export

exposición f exhibition

expresar ⟨1a⟩ 1 v/t express 2 v/r **expresarse** express o.s.

expresión f expression

expresivo adj expressive

expreso 1 adj express atr; **tren expreso** express (train) **2** m tren express (train); café espresso

exprimidor m lemon squeezer; eléctrico m juicer

exprimir ⟨3a⟩ v/t squeeze; (*explotar*) exploit

ex profeso adv (*especialmente*) expressly; (*a propósito*) deliberately

expropiar ⟨1b⟩ v/t expropriate

expuesto part → **exponer**

expugnar ⟨1a⟩ v/t take by storm

expulsar ⟨1a⟩ v/t expel, throw out F; DEP expel from the game, Br send off

expulsión f expulsion; DEP sending off

exquisito adj comida delicious; (*bello*) exquisite; (*refinado*) refined

extasiarse ⟨1c⟩ v/r be enraptured, go into raptures

éxtasis m tb droga ecstasy

extender ⟨2g⟩ 1 v/t brazos stretch out; (*untar*) spread; tela, papel spread out; (*ampliar*) extend; **me extendió la mano** she held out her hand to me 2 v/r extenderse *de campos* stretch; *de influencia* extend; (*difundirse*) spread; (*durar*) last; *explayarse* go into detail

extendido 1 *part* → **extender** 2 *adj costumbre* widespread; *brazos* outstretched; *mapa* spread out

extensión *f tb* TELEC extension; *superficie* expanse, area; **por extensión** by extension

extenso *adj* extensive, vast; *informe* lengthy, long

extenuar ⟨1e⟩ 1 *v/t* exhaust, tire out 2 *v/r* **extenuarse** exhaust o.s., tire o.s. out

exterior 1 *adj aspecto* external, outward; *capa* outer; *apartamento* overlooking the street; POL foreign; **la parte exterior del edificio** the exterior *o* the outside of the building 2 *m* (*fachada*) exterior, outside; *aspecto* exterior, outward appearance; **viajar al exterior** (*al extranjero*) travel abroad

exteriorizar ⟨1f⟩ *v/t* externalize

exterminar ⟨1a⟩ *v/t* exterminate, wipe out

externo 1 *adj aspecto* external, outward; *influencia* external, outside; *capa* outer; *deuda* foreign 2 *m*, -a *f* EDU *student who attends a boarding school but returns home each evening,* Br day boy / girl

extinción *f*: **en peligro de extinción** in danger of extinction

extinguidor *m L.Am.*: **extinguidor** (**de incendios**) (fire) extinguisher

extinguir ⟨3d⟩ 1 *v/t* BIO, ZO wipe out; *fuego* extinguish, put out 2 *v/r* **extinguirse** BIO, ZO become extinct, die out; *de fuego* go out; *de plazo* expire

extintor *m* fire extinguisher

extirpar ⟨1a⟩ *v/t* MED remove; *vicio* eradicate, stamp out

extorsión *f* extortion

extorsionar ⟨1a⟩ *v/t* extort money from

extra 1 *adj excelente* top quality; *adicional* extra; **horas extra** overtime; **paga extra** extra month's pay 2 *m/f de cine* extra 3 *m gasto* additional expense

extracto *m* extract; (*resumen*) summary; GASTR, QUÍM extract, essence; **extracto**

de cuenta bank statement

extractor *m* extractor; **extractor de humos** extractor fan

extradición *f* extradition

extraditar ⟨1a⟩ *v/t* extradite

extraer ⟨2p⟩ *v/t* extract, pull out; *conclusión* draw

extrajudicial *adj* out-of-court

extralimitarse ⟨1a⟩ *v/r* go too far, exceed one's authority

extramatrimonial *adj* extramarital

extranjería *f*: **ley de extranjería** immigration laws *pl*

extranjero 1 *adj* foreign 2 *m*, -a *f* foreigner; **en el extranjero** abroad

extranjis: **de extranjis** F on the quiet F, on the sly F

extrañar ⟨1a⟩ 1 *v/t L.Am.* miss 2 *v/r* **extrañarse** be surprised (**de** at)

extraño 1 *adj* strange, odd 2 *m*, -a *f* stranger

extraordinario *adj* extraordinary

extrapolar ⟨1a⟩ *v/t* extrapolate

extrarradio *m* outlying districts *pl*, outskirts *pl*

extraterrestre *adj* extraterrestial, alien

extravagante *adj* outrageous

extravertido *adj* extrovert

extraviar ⟨1c⟩ 1 *v/t* lose, mislay 2 *v/r* **extraviarse** get lost, lose one's way

extremadamente *adv* extremely

extremado *adj* extreme

extremar ⟨1a⟩ *v/t* maximize

extremidad *f* end; **extremidades** extremities

extremista 1 *adj* extreme 2 *m/f* POL extremist

extremo 1 *adj* extreme 2 *m* extreme; *parte primera o última* end; *punto* point; **llegar al extremo de** reach the point of 3 *m/f*: **extremo derecho / izquierdo** DEP right / left wing; **en extremo** in the extreme

extrovertido *adj* extrovert

exuberante *adj* exuberant; *vegetación* lush

exultante *adj* elated

eyacular ⟨1a⟩ *v/t* ejaculate

F

fabada f GASTR *Asturian stew with pork sausage, bacon and beans*
fábrica f plant, factory
fabricación f manufacturing
fabricante m manufacturer, maker
fabricar ⟨1g⟩ v/t manufacture
fábula f fable; (*mentira*) lie
fabuloso *adj* fabulous, marvel(l)ous
facción f POL faction; *facciones pl* (*rasgos*) features
faceta f *fig* facet
facha 1 f look; (*cara*) face **2** m/f *desp* fascist
fachada f *tb fig* façade
facial *adj* facial
fácil *adj* easy; *es fácil que* it's likely that
facilidad f ease; *con facilidad* easily; *tener facilidad para algo* have a gift for sth; *facilidades de pago* credit facilities, credit terms
facilitar ⟨1a⟩ v/t facilitate, make easier; (*hacer factible*) make possible; *medios, dinero etc* provide
factible *adj* feasible
factor m factor
factoría f *esp* L.Am. plant, factory
factura f COM invoice; *de luz, gas etc* bill
facturación f COM invoicing; (*volumen de negocio*) turnover; AVIA check-in
facturar ⟨1a⟩ v/t COM invoice, bill; *volumen de negocio* turn over; AVIA check in
facultad f faculty; (*autoridad*) authority
faena f task, job; *hacer una faena a alguien* play a dirty trick on s.o.
fagot m MÚS bassoon
faisán m ZO pheasant
faja f *prenda interior* girdle
fajarse ⟨1a⟩ v/r Méx, Ven F get into a fight
fajo m wad; *de periódicos* bundle
falacia f fallacy; (*engaño*) fraud
falange f ANAT phalange; MIL phalanx
falda f skirt; *de montaña* side
faldero *adj*: *perro faldero* lap dog
falla f fault; *de fabricación* flaw

fallar ⟨1a⟩ **1** v/i fail; (*no acertar*) miss; *de sistema etc* go wrong; JUR find (*en favor de* for; *en contra de* against); *fallar a alguien* let s.o. down **2** v/t JUR pronounce judg(e)ment in; *pregunta* get wrong; *fallar el tiro* miss
fallecer ⟨2d⟩ v/i pass away
fallecimiento m demise
fallo m mistake; TÉC fault; JUR judg(e)ment; *fallo cardiaco* heart failure
falsedad f falseness; (*mentira*) lie
falsificación f *de moneda* counterfeiting; *de documentos, firma* forgery
falsificar ⟨1g⟩ v/t *moneda* counterfeit; *documento, firma* forge, falsify
falso *adj* false; *joyas* fake; *documento, firma* forged; *jurar en falso* commit perjury
falta f (*escasez*) lack, want; (*error*) mistake; (*ausencia*) absence; *en tenis* fault; *en fútbol* foul; (*tiro libre*) free kick; *hacerle falta a alguien* foul s.o.; *falta de* lack of, shortage of; *sin falta* without fail; *buena falta le hace* it's about time; *echar en falta a alguien* miss s.o.; *hacer falta* be necessary
faltar v/i be missing; *falta una hora* there's an hour to go; *faltan 10 kilómetros* there are 10 kilometers to go; *sólo falta hacer la salsa* there's only the sauce to do; *faltar a* be absent from; *faltar a clase* miss class, be absent from class; *faltar a alguien* be disrespectful to s.o.; *faltar a su palabra* not keep one's word
falto *adj*: *falto de* lacking in, devoid of; *falto de recursos* short of resources
fama f fame; (*reputación*) reputation; *tener mala fama* have a bad reputation
familia f family; *sentirse como en familia* feel at home
familiar 1 *adj* family *atr*; (*conocido*) familiar; LING colloquial **2** m/f relation, relative

familiaridad f familiarity

familiarizarse ⟨1f⟩ v/r familiarize o.s. (con with)

famoso 1 adj famous 2 m, -a f celebrity

fan m/f fan

fanático 1 adj fanatical 2 m, -a f fanatic

fanatismo m fanaticism

fanfarrón 1 adj boastful 2 m, -ona f boaster

fanfarronear ⟨1a⟩ v/i boast, brag

fango m tb fig mud

fantasear ⟨1a⟩ v/i fantasize

fantasía f fantasy; (imaginación) imagination; joyas de fantasía costume jewel(l)ery

fantasma m ghost

fantástico adj fantastic

farándula f show business

fardar ⟨1a⟩ v/i: fardar de algo F boast about sth, show off about sth

fardo m bundle

faringitis f MED inflammation of the pharynx, pharyngitis

fariña f S. Am. manioc flour, cassava

farmacéutico 1 adj pharmaceutical 2 m, -a f pharmacist, Br chemist

farmacia f pharmacy, Br chemist's; estudios pharmacy; farmacia de guardia 24-hour pharmacist, Br emergency chemist

fármaco m medicine

farmacología f pharmacology

faro m MAR lighthouse; AUTO headlight, headlamp; faro antiniebla fog light

farol m lantern; (farola) streetlight, streetlamp; en juegos de cartas bluff

farola f streetlight, streetlamp

farolillo m: ser el farolillo rojo fig F be bottom of the league

farragoso adj texto dense

farrear ⟨1a⟩ v/i L.Am. F go out on the town F

farrista adj L.Am. F hard-drinking

farsa f tb fig farce

farsante m/f fraud, fake

fascículo m TIP instal(l)ment

fascinación f fascination

fascinante adj fascinating

fascinar ⟨1a⟩ v/t fascinate

fascismo m fascism

fascista m/f & adj fascist

fase f phase

fastidiar ⟨1b⟩ 1 v/t annoy; F (estropear) spoil 2 v/r fastidiarse grin and bear it

fastidio m annoyance; ¡qué fastidio! what a nuisance!

fastuoso adj lavish

fatal 1 adj fatal; (muy malo) dreadful, awful 2 adv very badly

fatídico adj fateful

fatiga f tiredness, fatigue

fatigar ⟨1h⟩ 1 v/t tire 2 v/r fatigarse get tired

fatuo adj conceited; (necio) fatuous

fauces fpl zo jaws

fauna f fauna

favor m favo(u)r; a favor de in favo(u)r of; por favor please; hacer un favor do a favo(u)r

favorecer ⟨2d⟩ v/t favo(u)r; de ropa, color suit

favoritismo m favo(u)ritism

favorito 1 adj favo(u)rite 2 m, -a f favo(u)rite

fax m fax; enviar un fax a alguien send s.o. a fax, fax s.o.

fayuca f Méx smuggling

fayuquero m, -a f Méx dealer in smuggled goods

F.C. abr (= Fútbol Club) FC (= Football Club)

fdo. abr (= firmado) signed

fe f faith (en in); fe de erratas errata

fealdad f ugliness

feb. abr (= febrero) Feb. (= February)

febrero m February

fecal adj f(a)ecal

fecha f date; fecha límite de consumo best before date; fecha de nacimiento date of birth

fechador m Chi, Méx postmark

fécula f starch

fecundación f fertilization; fecundación in vitro MED in vitro fertilization

fecundar ⟨1a⟩ v/t fertilize

fecundo adj fertile

federación f federation

federal adj federal

felicidad *f* happiness; **¡felicidades!** congratulations!

felicitación *f* letter of congratulations; **¡felicitaciones!** congratulations!

felicitar ⟨1a⟩ *v/t* congratulate (**por** on)

felino *adj tb fig* feline

feliz *adj* happy; **¡feliz Navidad!** Merry Christmas!

felpa *f* towel(l)ing

felpudo *m* doormat

femenino **1** *adj* feminine; *moda, equipo* women's **2** GRAM feminine

femin(e)idad *f* femininity

feminismo *m* feminism

feminista *m/f & adj* feminist

fenomenal **1** *adj* F fantastic F, phenomenal F **2** *adv*: **lo pasé fenomenal** F I had a fantastic time F

fenómeno **1** *m* phenomenon; *persona* genius **2** *adj* F fantastic F, great F

feo **1** *adj* ugly; *fig* nasty **2** *m*: **hacer un feo a alguien** F snub s.o.

féretro *m* casket, coffin

feria *f* COM fair; *L.Am.* (*mercado*) market; *Méx* (*calderilla*) small change; **feria de muestras** trade fair

feriado **1** *adj L.Am.*: **día feriado** (public) holiday **2** *m L.Am.* (public) holiday; **abierto feriados** open on public holidays

ferial **1** *adj*: **recinto ferial** fairground **2** *m* fair

fermentación *f* fermentation

fermentar ⟨1a⟩ *v/t* ferment

fermento *m* ferment

ferocidad *f* ferocity

feroz *adj* fierce; (*cruel*) cruel

férreo *adj tb fig* iron *atr*; *del ferrocarril* rail *atr*

ferretería *f* hardware store

ferrocarril *m* railroad, *Br* railway

ferrocarrilero *m L.Am.* railroad *o Br* railway worker

ferroviario *adj* rail *atr*

ferry *m* ferry

fértil *adj* fertile

fertilidad *f* fertility

fertilizante *m* fertilizer

ferviente *adj fig* fervent

fervor *m* fervo(u)r

festejar ⟨1a⟩ *v/t persona* wine and dine; *L.Am.* celebrate

festejo *m* celebration; **festejos** festivities

festín *m* banquet

festival *m* festival; **festival cinematográfico** film festival

festividad *f* feast; **festividades** festivities

festivo *adj* festive

fetal *adj* fetal

fetiche *m* fetish

fétido *adj* fetid

feto *m* fetus

feudal *adj* feudal

feudo *m fig* domain

FF. AA. *abr* (= **fuerzas armadas**) armed forces

FF. CC. *abr* (= **ferrocarriles**) railroads

fiable *adj* trustworthy; *datos, máquina etc* reliable

fiambre *m* cold cut, *Br* cold meat; P (*cadáver*) stiff P

fiambrera *f* lunch pail, *Br* lunch box

fiambrería *f L.Am.* delicatessen

fianza *f* deposit; JUR bail; **bajo fianza** on bail

fiar ⟨1c⟩ **1** *v/i* give credit **2** *v/r* **fiarse: fiarse de alguien** trust s.o.; **no me fío** I don't trust him/ them *etc*

fiasco *m* fiasco

fibra *f en tejido, alimento* fiber, *Br* fibre; **fibra óptica** optical fiber (*Br* fibre); **fibra de vidrio** fiberglass, *Br* fibreglass

fibroso *adj* fibrous

ficción *f* fiction

ficha *f* file card, index card; *en juegos de mesa* counter; *en un casino* chip; *en damas* checker, *Br* draught; *en ajedrez* man, piece; TELEC token

fichar ⟨1a⟩ **1** *v/t* DEP sign; JUR open a file on **2** *v/i* DEP sign (**por** for)

fichero *m* file cabinet, *Br* filing cabinet; INFOR file

ficticio *adj* fictitious

fidedigno *adj* reliable

fidelidad *f* fidelity

fideo *m* noodle

fiebre *f* fever; (*temperatura*) temperature; **fiebre del heno** hay fever

fiel 1 *adj* faithful; (*leal*) loyal **2** *mpl*: *los fieles* REL the faithful *pl*

fieltro *m* felt

fiera *f* wild animal; *ponerse hecho una fiera* F go wild F

fiero *adj* fierce

fierro *m* L.Am. iron

fiesta *f* festival; (*reunión social*) party; (*día festivo*) public holiday; *estar de fiesta* be in a party mood

fifí *m* L.Am. P afeminado sissy F

figura *f* figure; (*estatuilla*) figurine; (*forma*) shape; *naipes* face card, *Br* picture card; *tener buena figura* have a good figure

figurado *adj* figurative; *sentido figurado* figurative sense

figurar ⟨1a⟩ **1** *v/i* appear (*en* in); *aquí figura como ...* she appears *o* is down here as ... **2** *v/r figurarse* imagine; *¡figúrate!* just imagine!

fijar ⟨1a⟩ **1** *v/t* fix; *cartel* stick; *fecha, objetivo* set; *residencia* establish; *atención* focus **2** *v/r fijarse* (*establecerse*) settle; (*prestar atención*) pay attention (*en* to); *fijarse en algo* (*darse cuenta*) notice sth

fijo *adj* fixed; *trabajo* permanent; *fecha* definite

fila *f* line, *Br* queue; *de asientos* row; *en fila india* in single file; *filas* MIL ranks

filatelia *f* philately, stamp collecting

filete *m* GASTR fillet

filial 1 *adj* filial **2** *f* COM subsidiary

Filipinas *fpl* Philippines

film(e) *m* movie, film

filmación *f* filming, shooting

filmar ⟨1a⟩ *v/t* film, shoot

filo *m* edge; *de navaja* cutting edge; *al filo de las siete* *fig* around 7 o'clock

filología *f* philology; *filología hispánica* EDU Spanish language and literature

filólogo *m*, *-a* *f* philologist

filón *m* vein, seam; *fig* goldmine

filoso *adj* L.Am. sharp

filosofía *f* philosophy

filosófico *adj* philosophical

filósofo *m*, *-a* *f* philosopher

filtración *f* leak

filtrar ⟨1a⟩ **1** *v/t* filter; *información* leak **2** *v/r filtrarse* filter (*por* through); *de agua, información* leak

filtro *m* filter

fin *m* end; (*objetivo*) aim, purpose; *fin de semana* weekend; *a fines de mayo* at the end of May; *al fin y al cabo* at the end of the day, after all; *en fin* anyway

final *f/adj* final

finalidad *f* purpose, aim

finalista 1 *adj*: *las dos selecciones finalistas* the two teams that reached the final **2** *m/f* finalist

finalización *f* completion

finalizado *adj* complete

finalizar ⟨1f⟩ *v/t & v/i* end, finish

finalmente *adv* eventually

financiación *f* funding

financiar ⟨1b⟩ *v/t* finance, fund

financista *m/f* L.Am. financier

finanzas *fpl* finances

finca *f* (*bien inmueble*) property; *L.Am.* (*granja*) farm

fingido *adj* false

fingir ⟨3c⟩ **1** *v/t* feign *fml*; *fingió no haberlo oído* I pretended I hadn't heard **2** *v/r fingirse*: *fingirse enfermo* pretend to be ill, feign illness *fml*

finlandés 1 *adj* Finnish **2** *m*, *-esa* *f* Finn

Finlandia Finland

fino *adj* *calidad* fine; *libro, tela* thin; (*esbelto*) slim; *modales, gusto* refined; *sentido de humor* subtle

firma *f* signature; *acto* signing; COM firm

firmamento *m* firmament

firmar ⟨1a⟩ *v/t* sign

firme *adj* firm; (*estable*) steady; *en firme* COM firm

fiscal 1 *adj* tax *atr*, fiscal **2** *m/f* district attorney, *Br* public prosecutor

fisgar ⟨1h⟩ *v/i* F snoop F; *fisgar en algo* snoop around in sth

fisgón *m*, *-ona* *f* snoop

fisgonear ⟨1a⟩ *v/i* F snoop around F (*en* in)

física *f* physics

físico 1 *adj* physical **2** *m*, *-a* *f* physicist **3** *m de una persona* physique

fisiología *f* physiology

fisión *f* fission

fisioterapeuta *m/f* physical therapist, *Br* physiotherapist

fisioterapia *f* physical therapy, *Br* physiotherapy

fisonomía *f* features *pl*

fisura *f* crack; MED fracture

flác(c)ido *adj* flabby

flaco *adj* thin; **punto flaco** weak point

flacuchento *adj* L.Am. F skinny

flagelar ⟨1a⟩ *v/t* flagellate

flagrante *adj* flagrant; **en flagrante delito** red-handed, in flagrante delicto

flamante *adj* (*nuevo*) brand-new

flamenco 1 *adj* MÚS flamenco 2 *m* MÚS flamenco; ZO flamingo

flan *m* crème caramel

flanco *m* flank

flaquear ⟨1a⟩ *v/i* weaken; *de entusiasmo* flag

flaqueza *f* fig weakness

flash *m* FOT flash

flato *m* MED stitch

flatulencia *f* MED flatulence

flauta *f* flute; *Méx* fried taco; **flauta dulce** recorder; **flauta travesera** (transverse) flute

flautista *m/f* flautist

flecha *f* arrow

flechazo *m* fig love at first sight

flecos *mpl* fringe *sg*

flema *f* fig phlegm

flemático *adj* phlegmatic

flemón *m* MED gumboil

flequillo *m del pelo* fringe

fletar ⟨1a⟩ *v/t* charter; (*embarcar*) load

flete *m* L.Am. freight, cost of transport

fletero *adj* L.Am. hire *atr*, charter *atr*

flexibilidad *f* flexibility

flexible *adj* flexible

flexión *f en gimnasia* push-up, *Br* press-up; *de piernas* squat; *de la voz* inflection

flexionar ⟨1a⟩ 1 *v/t* flex 2 *v/r* flexionarse bend

flexo *m* desk lamp

flipar ⟨1a⟩ *v/i*: **le flipa el cine** P he's mad about the movies F

flirtear ⟨1a⟩ *v/i* flirt (**con** with)

flojo *adj* loose; *café, argumento* weak; COM *actividad* slack; *novela, redacción* poor; L.Am. lazy

flojera *f* L.Am. laziness; **me da flojera** I can't be bothered

flor *f* flower

flora *f* flora

florear ⟨1a⟩ 1 *v/t* decorate with flowers; *Méx* (*halagar*) flatter, compliment 2 *v/i* flower, bloom

florecer ⟨2d⟩ *v/i* BOT flower. bloom; *de negocio, civilización* etc flourish

floreciente *adj* flourishing

florero *m* vase

florista *m/f* florist

floristería *f* florist's, flower shop

flota *f* fleet

flotación *f* flotation

flotador *m* float

flotar ⟨1a⟩ *v/i* float

flote MAR: **a flote** afloat

fluctuación *f* fluctuation

fluctuar ⟨1e⟩ *v/i* fluctuate

fluidez *f* fluidity

fluido 1 *adj* fluid; *tráfico* free-flowing; *lenguaje* fluent 2 *m* fluid

fluir ⟨3g⟩ *v/i* flow

flujo *m* flow

fluorescente 1 *adj* fluorescent 2 *m* strip light

fluvial *adj* river *atr*

FM *abr* (= **frecuencia modulada**) FM (= frequency modulation)

FMI *abr* (= **Fondo Monetario Internacional**) IMF (= International Monetary Fund)

fobia *f* phobia

foca *f* ZO seal

foco *m* focus; TEA, TV spotlight; *de infección* center, *Br* centre; *de incendio* seat; L.Am. (*bombilla*) lightbulb; *de auto* headlight; *de calle* streetlight

fofo *adj* flabby

fogata *f* bonfire

fogoso *adj* fiery, ardent

foie-gras *m* foie gras

folclore *m* folklore

fólico *adj*: **ácido fólico** folic acid

folio *m* sheet (of paper)

folklore *m* folklore

follaje *m* foliage

folleto *m* pamphlet

follón *m* argument; (*lío*) mess; **armar un follón** kick up a fuss

fomentar ⟨1a⟩ *v/t* foster; COM promote; *rebelión* foment, incite

fomento *m* COM promotion

fonda *f* L.Am. cheap restaurant; (*pensión*) boarding house

fondear ⟨1a⟩ 1 *v/t* MAR anchor 2 *v/r* fondearse L.Am. get rich

fondero *m*, -a *f* L.Am. restaurant owner

fondista *m/f* DEP long-distance runner

fondo *m* bottom; *de sala, cuarto* etc back; *de pasillo* end; (*profundidad*) depth; PINT, FOT background; *de un museo* etc collection; COM fund; **fondo de inversión** investment fund; **fondo de pensiones** pension fund; **Fondo Monetario Internacional** International Monetary Fund; **fondos** *pl* money *sg*, funds; **tiene buen fondo** he's got a good heart; **en el fondo** deep down; **tocar fondo** *fig* reach bottom

fonética *f* phonetics

fontanería *f* plumbing

fontanero *m* plumber

footing *m* DEP jogging; **hacer footing** go jogging, jog

forastero 1 *adj* foreign 2 *m*, -a *f* outsider, stranger

forcejear ⟨1a⟩ *v/i* struggle

forcejeo *m* struggle

forense 1 *adj* forensic 2 *m/f* forensic scientist

forestación *f* afforestation

forestal *adj* forest *atr*

forestar ⟨1a⟩ *v/t* L.Am. afforest

forjar ⟨1a⟩ *v/t metal* forge

forma *f* form; (*apariencia*) shape; (*manera*) way; **de todas formas** in any case, anyway; **estar en forma** be fit

formación *f* formation; (*entrenamiento*) training; **formación profesional** vocational training

formal *adj* formal; *niño* well-behaved; (*responsable*) responsible

formalizar ⟨1f⟩ *v/t* formalize; *relación* make official

formar ⟨1a⟩ 1 *v/t* form; (*educar*) educate 2

v/r formarse form

formatear ⟨1a⟩ *v/t* INFOR format

formato *m* format

formidable *adj* huge; (*estupendo*) tremendous

fórmula *f* formula

formular ⟨1a⟩ *v/t teoría* formulate; *queja* make, lodge

formulario *m* form

fornicar ⟨1g⟩ *v/i* fornicate

fornido *adj* well-built

foro *m* forum

forofo *m*, -a *f* F fan

forrado *adj prenda* lined; *libro* covered; *fig* F loaded F

forraje *m* fodder

forrar ⟨1a⟩ 1 *v/t prenda* line; *libro, silla* cover 2 *v/r* forrarse F make a fortune F

forro *m de prenda* lining; *de libro* cover

fortalecer ⟨2d⟩ 1 *v/t tb fig* strengthen 2 *v/r* fortalecerse strengthen

fortaleza *f* strength of character; MIL fortress

fortificar ⟨1g⟩ *v/t* MIL fortify

fortuito *adj* chance *atr*, accidental

fortuna *f* fortune; (*suerte*) luck; **por fortuna** fortunately, luckily

forzar ⟨1f & 1m⟩ *v/t* force; (*violar*) rape

forzoso *adj aterrizaje* forced

forzudo *adj* brawny

fosa *f* pit; (*tumba*) grave; **fosa común** common grave; **fosas nasales** nostrils

fósforo *m* QUÍM phosphorus; L.Am. (*cerilla*) match

fósil 1 *adj* fossilized 2 *m* fossil

foso *m* ditch; TEA, MÚS pit; *de castillo* moat

foto *f* photo

fotocopia *f* photocopy

fotocopiadora *f* photocopier

fotocopiar ⟨1a⟩ *v/t* photocopy

fotogénico *adj* photogenic

fotografía *f* photography

fotografiar ⟨1c⟩ *v/t* photograph

fotógrafo *m*, -a *f* photographer

FP *f* (= **formación profesional**) vocational training

frac *m* tail coat

fracasado 1 *adj* unsuccessful 2 *m*, -a *f* loser

fracasar ⟨1a⟩ v/i fail

fracaso m failure

fracción f fraction; POL faction

fraccionamiento m L.Am. (housing) project, Br estate

fraccionar ⟨1a⟩ v/t break up; FIN pay in instal(l)ments

fractura f MED fracture

fracturar ⟨1a⟩ v/t MED fracture

fragancia f fragrance

frágil adj fragile

fragmentar ⟨1a⟩ v/t fragment

fragmento m fragment; de novela, poema excerpt, extract

fraguar ⟨1i⟩ v/t forge; plan devise; complot hatch

fraile m friar, monk

frambuesa f raspberry

francés 1 adj French **2** m Frenchman; idioma French

francesa f Frenchwoman

Francia f France

franco adj (sincero) frank; (evidente) distinct, marked; COM free

francotirador m sniper

franela f flannel

franja f fringe; de tierra strip

franquear ⟨1a⟩ v/t carta pay the postage on; camino, obstáculo clear

franqueo m postage

franqueza f frankness

franquicia f (exención) exemption; COM franchise

frasco m bottle

frase f phrase; (oración) sentence; **frase hecha** set phrase

fraternal adj brotherly

fraternidad f brotherhood, fraternity

fraternizar ⟨1f⟩ v/i POL fraternize

fraude m fraud

fraudulento adj fraudulent

frazada f L.Am. blanket

frecuencia f frequency; **frecuencia modulada** RAD frequency modulation; **con frecuencia** frequently

frecuentar ⟨1a⟩ v/t frequent

frecuente adj frequent; (común) common

frecuentemente adv often, frequently

fregadero m sink

fregar ⟨1h & 1k⟩ v/t platos wash; el suelo mop; L.Am. F bug F

fregón 1 adj annoying **2** m L.Am. F nuisance, pain in the neck F

fregona f mop; L.Am. F nuisance, pain in the neck F

freidora f deep fryer

freidura f frying

freír ⟨3m; part **frito** ⟩ v/t fry; F (matar) waste P

frenada f esp L.Am.: **dar una frenada** F slam the brakes on, hit the brakes F

frenar ⟨1a⟩ **1** v/i AUTO brake **2** v/t fig slow down; impulsos check

frenazo m: **pegar** or **dar un frenazo** F slam the brakes on, hit the brakes F

frenesí m frenzy

frenético adj frenetic

freno m brake; **freno de mano** parking brake, Br handbrake

frente 1 f forehead **2** m MIL, METEO front; **de frente** colisión head-on; **de frente al grupo** L.Am. facing the group; **hacer frente a** face up to **3** prp: **frente a** opposite

fresa f strawberry

fresco 1 adj cool; pescado etc fresh; persona F fresh F, Br cheeky F **2** m, -a f: **¡eres un fresco!** F you've got nerve! F, Br you've got a cheek! F **3** m fresh air; C.Am. fruit drink

frescor m freshness

frescura f freshness; (frío) coolness; fig nerve

fresno m BOT ash tree

fresón m strawberry

frialdad f tb coldness

fricción f TÉC, fig friction

friccionar ⟨1a⟩ v/t rub

friega f L.Am. F hassle F, drag F

frígido adj MED frigid

frigorífico 1 adj refrigerated **2** m fridge

frío 1 adj tb fig cold **2** m cold; **tener frío** be cold

friolento L.Am., **friolero** adj: **es friolento** he feels the cold

fritar ⟨1a⟩ v/t L.Am. fry

F

frito 1 part → **freír 2** adj fried **3** mpl: **fritos** fried food sg

fritura f fried food

frívolo adj frivolous

frondoso adj leafy

frontal adj frontal; ataque etc head-on; (delantero) front atr

frontera f border

fronterizo adj border atr

frontón m DEP pelota; cancha pelota court

frotar ⟨1a⟩ v/t rub

fructífero adj fruitful, productive

frugal adj persona frugal

fruncir ⟨3b⟩ v/t material gather; **fruncir el ceño** frown

frustración f frustration

frustrante adj frustrating

frustrar ⟨1a⟩ **1** v/t frustrate; plan thwart **2** v/r frustrarse fail

fruta f fruit

frutal 1 adj fruit atr **2** m fruit tree

frutería f fruit store, Br greengrocer's

frutilla f S. Am. strawberry

fruto m tb fig fruit; nuez, almendra etc nut; **frutos secos** nuts

fucsia adj fuchsia

fue vb → **ir, ser**

fuego m fire; ¿tienes fuego? do you have a light?; **fuegos artificiales** fireworks; **pegar** or **prender fuego a** set fire to

fuel(-oil) m fuel oil

fuelle m bellows pl

fuente f fountain; recipiente dish; fig source

fuera 1 vb → **ir, ser 2** adv outside; (en otro lugar) away; (en otro país) abroad; **por fuera** on the outside; ¡fuera! get out! **3** prp: **fuera de** outside; ¡sal fuera de aquí! get out of here!; **está fuera del país** he's abroad, he's out of the country

fuero m: **en el fuero interno** deep down

fuerte 1 adj strong; dolor intense; lluvia heavy; aumento sharp; ruido loud; fig P incredible F **2** adv hard **3** m MIL fort

fuerza f strength; (violencia) force; EL power; **fuerza aérea** air force; **fuerza de voluntad** willpower; **fuerzas armadas** armed forces; **fuerzas de seguridad** security forces; **a fuerza de ...** by (dint of)

fuese vb → **ir, ser**

fuete m L.Am. whip

fuga f escape; de gas, agua leak; **darse a la fuga** flee

fugarse ⟨1h⟩ v/r run away; de la cárcel escape

fugaz adj fig fleeting

fugitivo 1 adj runaway atr **2** m, -a f fugitive

fui vb → **ir, ser**

fuimos vb → **ir, ser**

fulano m so-and-so

fulgor m brightness

fulgurante adj fig dazzling

fulminante adj sudden

fulminar ⟨1a⟩ v/t: **lo fulminó un rayo** he was killed by lightning; **fulminar a alguien con la mirada** look daggers at s.o. F

fumador m, **fumadora** f smoker

fumar ⟨1a⟩ **1** v/t smoke **2** v/i smoke; **prohibido fumar** no smoking **3** v/r fumarse smoke; **fumarse una clase** F skip a class F

fumigar ⟨1h⟩ v/t fumigate

función f purpose, function; en el trabajo duty; TEA performance; **en función de** according to

funcional adj functional

funcionamiento m working

funcionar ⟨1a⟩ v/i work; **no funciona** out of order

funcionario m, **-a** f government employee, civil servant

funda f cover; de gafas case; de almohada pillowcase

fundación f foundation

fundador m, **fundadora** f founder

fundamental adj fundamental

fundamentalismo m fundamentalism

fundamentalista m/f fundamentalist

fundamentalmente adv essentially

fundamento m foundation; **fundamentos** (nociones) fundamentals

fundar ⟨1a⟩ **1** v/t fig base (en on) **2** v/r fundarse be based (en on)

fundición f smelting; (fábrica) foundry

fundir ⟨3a⟩ **1** v/t hielo melt; metal smelt; COM merge **2** v/r fundirse melt; de bombilla fuse; de plomos blow; COM merge;

L.Am. fig: de empresa go under
fúnebre adj funeral atr; fig: ambiente gloomy
funeral m funeral
funeraria f funeral parlo(u)r, Br undertaker's
funesto adj disastrous
funicular m funicular; (teleférico) cable car
furcia f P whore P
furgón m van; FERR boxcar, Br goods van; **furgón de equipajes** baggage car, Br luggage van
furgoneta f van
furia f fury; **ponerse hecho una furia** go into a fury o rage
furibundo adj furious
furioso adj furious
furor m: **hacer furor** fig be all the rage F
furtivo adj furtive

fuselaje m fuselage
fusible m EL fuse
fusil m rifle
fusilar ⟨1a⟩ v/t shoot; fig F (plagiar) lift F
fusión f FÍS fusion; COM merger
fusionar ⟨1a⟩ **1** v/t COM merge **2** v/r **fusionarse** merge
fusta f riding crop
fútbol m soccer, Br football; **fútbol americano** football, Br American football; **fútbol sala** five-a-side soccer (Br football)
futbolín m Foosball®, table football
futbolista m/f soccer player, Br footballer, Br football player
fútil adj trivial
futre m Chi dandy
futuro 1 adj future atr **2** m future
futurólogo m, **-a** f futurologist

G

g. abr (= **gramo** (**s**)) gr(s) (= gram(s))
gabardina f prenda raincoat; material gabardine
gabinete m (despacho) office; en una casa study; POL cabinet; L.Am. de médico office, Br surgery
gacela f ZO gazelle
gaceta f gazette
gachas fpl porridge sg
gachupín m Méx desp Spaniard
gacilla f C.Am. safety pin
gafas fpl glasses; **gafas de sol** sunglasses
gafe 1 adj jinxed **2** m jinx **3** m/f: **es un gafe** he's jinxed
gaita f MÚS bagpipes pl
gajes mpl: **gajes del oficio** iron occupational hazard
gajo m segment
gala f gala; **traje de gala** formal dress
galante adj gallant

galápago m ZO turtle
galardonar ⟨1a⟩ v/t: **fue galardonado con ...** he was awarded ...
galaxia f galaxy
galería f gallery; **galería de arte** art gallery
Gales Wales
galés Welsh
galgo m grayhound
gallera f L.Am. cockpit
galleta f cookie, Br biscuit
gallina f hen **2** m F chicken
gallinazo m L.Am. turkey buzzard
gallo m rooster, Br cock
galón m adorno braid; MIL stripe; medida gallon
galope m gallop
galpón m L.Am. large shed; W.I. HIST slave quarters pl
gama f range

gamba *f* ZO GASTR shrimp, *Br* prawn

gamberro *m*, -a *f* troublemaker

gamín *m*, -ina *f* Col street kid

gamo *m* ZO fallow deer

gamonal *m* Pe, Bol desp chief

gamuza *f* chamois

gana *f*: **de mala gana** unwillingly, grudgingly; **no me da la gana** I don't want to; **... me da ganas de ...** makes me want to; **tener ganas de (hacer) algo** feel like (doing) sth

ganadería *f* stockbreeding

ganadero *m*, -a *f* stockbreeder

ganado *m* cattle *pl*

ganador *m* winner

ganancia *f* profit

ganar ⟨1a⟩ **1** win; *mediante el trabajo* earn **2** *v/i mediante el trabajo* earn; (*vencer*) win; (*mejorar*) improve **3** *v/r* **ganarse** earn; *a alguien* win over; **ganarse la vida** earn one's living

ganchillo *m* crochet

gancho *m* hook; *L.Am., Arg fig* F sex-appeal; **hacer gancho** *L.Am.* (*ayudar*) lend a hand; **tener gancho** F *de un grupo, una campaña* be popular; *de una persona* have that certain something

gandul *m* lazybones *sg*

gandulear ⟨1a⟩ *v/i* F loaf around F

ganga *f* bargain

gangrena *f* MED gangrene

gángster *m* gangster

ganso *m* goose; *macho* gander

garabatear ⟨1a⟩ *v/i & v/t* doodle

garabato *m* doodle

garaje *m* garage

garantía *f* guarantee

garantizar ⟨1f⟩ *v/t* guarantee

garapiña *f Cuba, Méx* pineapple squash

garbanzo *m* BOT chickpea

garbo *m al moverse* grace

gardenia *f* BOT gardenia

garete *m*: **irse al garete** *fig* F go to pot F

garfio *m* hook

gargajo *m* piece of phlegm

garganta *f* ANAT throat; GEOG gorge

gargantilla *f* choker

gárgaras *fpl*: **hacer gárgaras** gargle

garito *m* gambling den

garra *f* claw; *de ave* talon; **caer en las garras de alguien** *fig* fall into s.o.'s clutches; **tener garra** F be compelling

garrafa *f* carafe

garrafal *adj error etc* terrible

garrapata *f* ZO tick

garrote *m palo* club, stick; *tipo de ejecución* garrotte

garúa *f L.Am.* drizzle

garuar ⟨1e⟩ *v/i L.Am.* drizzle

garzón *m Rpl* (*mesero*) waiter

garza *f* ZO heron

gas *m* gas; **gas natural** natural gas; **gases** *pl* MED gas *sg*, wind *sg*; **con gas** sparkling, carbonated; **sin gas** still

gasa *f* gauze

gaseosa *f* lemonade

gasfitero *m Pe, Bol* plumber

gasoducto *m* gas pipeline

gasoil, gasóleo *m* oil; *para motores* diesel

gasolina *f* gas, *Br* petrol

gasolinera *f* gas station, *Br* petrol station

gastar ⟨1a⟩ **1** *v/t dinero* spend; *energía, electricidad etc* use; (*llevar*) wear; (*desperdiciar*) waste; (*desgastar*) wear out; **¿qué número gastas?** what size do you take?, what size are you? **2** *v/r* **gastarse** *dinero* spend; *gasolina, agua* run out of; *pila* run down; *ropa, zapatos* wear out

gasto *m* expense

gastronomía *f* gastronomy

gata *f* (female) cat; *Méx* servant, maid; **a gatas** F on all fours; **andar a gatas** F crawl

gatear ⟨1a⟩ *v/i* crawl

gatillo *m* trigger

gato *m* cat; AUTO jack; **aquí hay gato encerrado** F there's something fishy going on here F; **cuatro gatos** a handful of people

gaucho *m Rpl* gaucho

gaviota *f* (sea)gull

gay **1** *adj* gay **2** *m* gay (man)

gazpacho *m* gazpacho (*cold soup made with tomatoes, peppers, garlic etc*)

gel *m* gel

gelatina *f* gelatin(e); GASTR Jell-O®, *Br* jelly

gélido *adj* icy
gema *f* gem
gemelo 1 *adj* twin *atr*; **hermano gemelo** twin brother **2** *mpl*: **gemelos** twins; *de camisa* cuff links; *(prismáticos)* binoculars
gemido *m* moan, groan
Géminis *m/f inv* ASTR Gemini
gemir ⟨3l⟩ *v/i* moan, groan
gen *m* gene
genealógico *adj*: **árbol genealógico** family tree
generación *f* generation
generador *m* EL generator
general 1 *adj* general; **en general** in general; **por lo general** usually, generally **2** *m* general
generalización *f* generalization
generalizar ⟨1f⟩ **1** *v/t* spread **2** *v/i* generalize **3** *v/r* **generalizarse** spread
generalmente *adv* generally
generar ⟨1a⟩ *v/t* generate
género *m* *(tipo)* type; *de literatura* genre; GRAM gender; COM goods *pl*, merchandise
generosidad *f* generosity
generoso *adj* generous
genética *f* genetics
genético *adj* genetic
genial *adj* brilliant; F *(estupendo)* fantastic F, great F
genialidad *f* brilliance
genio *m* talento, persona genius; *(carácter)* temper; **tener mal genio** be bad-tempered
genital *adj* genital
genitales *mpl* genitals
genocidio *m* genocide
gente *f* people *pl*; *L.Am. (persona)* person
gentileza *f* kindness; **por gentileza de** by courtesy of
gentío *m* crowd
genuino *adj* genuine, real
geografía *f* geography
geográfico *adj* geographical
geología *f* geology
geológico *adj* geological
geólogo *m*, **-a** *f* geologist
geometría *f* geometry

geométrico *adj* geometric(al)
geranio *m* BOT geranium
gerente *m/f* manager
geriatría *f* geriatrics *sg*
germen *m* germ
germinar ⟨1a⟩ *v/i tb fig* germinate
gerundio *m* GRAM gerund
gestación *f* gestation
gesticular ⟨1a⟩ *v/i* gesticulate
gestión *f* management; **gestiones** *pl* *(trámites)* formalities, procedure *sg*
gestionar ⟨1a⟩ *v/t trámites* take care of; *negocio* manage
gesto *m* movimiento gesture; *(expresión)* expression
gestoría *f Esp* agency offering clients help with official documents
gigante 1 *adj* giant *atr* **2** *m* giant
gilipollas *m/f inv* P jerk P
gilipollez *f Esp* V bullshit V
gimnasia *f* gymnastics; **hacer gimnasia** do exercises
gimnasio *m* gym
gimnasta *m/f* gymnast
gimotear ⟨1a⟩ *v/i* whine, whimper
ginebra *f* gin
ginecólogo *m*, **-a** *f* gyn(a)ecologist
gin-tonic *m* gin and tonic, G and T F
gira *f* tour
girar ⟨1a⟩ **1** *v/i* *(dar vueltas, torcer)* turn; *alrededor de algo* revolve; *fig (tratar)* revolve **(en torno a** around) **2** *v/t* COM transfer
girasol *m* BOT sunflower
giro *m* turn; GRAM idiom; **giro postal** COM money order
gis *m L.Am.* chalk
gitano 1 *adj* gypsy *atr* **2** *m*, **-a** *f* gypsy
glacial *adj* icy
glaciar *m* glacier
glándula *f* ANAT gland
global *adj* *(de todo el mundo)* global; *visión, resultado* overall; *cantidad* total
globo *m aerostático, de niño* balloon; *terrestre* globe; **globo terráqueo** globe
gloria *f* glory; *(delicia)* delight; **estar en la gloria** F be in seventh heaven
gloriado *m Pe, Bol, Ecuad* type of punch
glorieta *f* traffic circle, *Br* roundabout

glorioso *adj* glorious

glosario *m* glossary

glotón 1 *adj* greedy 2 *m*, -ona *f* glutton

glucosa *f* glucose

gnomo *m* gnome

gobernador *m* governor

gobernante *m* leader

gobernar ⟨1k⟩ *v/t & v/i* rule, govern

gobierno *m* government

goce *m* pleasure, enjoyment

gofre *m* waffle

gol *m* DEP goal

goleador *m* DEP (goal-)scorer

golf *m* DEP golf

golfista *m/f* golfer

golfo 1 *m* GEOG gulf 2 *m*, -a *f* good-for-nothing; *niño* little devil

Golfo de México *m* Gulf of Mexico

golondrina *f* ZO swallow

golosina *f* candy, *Br* sweet

goloso *adj* sweet-toothed

golpe *m* knock, blow; *golpe de Estado* coup d'état; *de golpe* suddenly; *no da golpe* F she doesn't do a thing

golpear ⟨1a⟩ *v/t cosa* bang, hit; *persona* hit

goma *f* (*caucho*) rubber; (*pegamento*) glue; (*banda elástica*) rubber band; F (*preservativo*) condom, rubber P; *C.Am.* F (*resaca*) hangover; *goma (de borrar)* eraser; *goma espuma* foam rubber

gomina *f* hair gel

gominola *f* jelly bean

góndola *f* Chi bus

gong *m* gong

gordinflón *m*, -ona *f* F fatso F

gordo 1 *adj* fat; *me cae gordo* F I can't stand him; *se va a armar la -a* all hell will break loose F 2 *m*, -a *f* fat person 3 *m premio* jackpot

gorila *m* ZO gorilla

gorjeo *m de pájaro* chirping, warbling; *de niño* gurgling

gorra *f* cap; *de gorra* F for free F

gorrino *m* fig pig

gorrión *m* ZO sparrow

gorro *m* cap; *estar hasta el gorro de algo* F be fed up to the back teeth with sth F

gorrón *m*, -ona *f* F scrounger

gorronear ⟨1a⟩ *v/t & v/i* F scrounge F

gota *f* drop; *ni gota* F *de cerveza, leche etc* not a drop; *de pan* not a scrap

gotear ⟨1a⟩ *v/i* drip; *filtrarse* leak

gotera *f* leak; (*mancha*) stain

gotero *m* MED drip; *L.Am.* (eye)dropper

gozar ⟨1f⟩ *v/i* (*disfrutar*) enjoy o.s.; *gozar de* (*disfrutar de*) enjoy; (*poseer*) have, enjoy

gozo *m* (*alegría*) joy; (*placer*) pleasure

grabación *f* recording

grabado *m* engraving

grabadora *f* tape recorder

grabar ⟨1a⟩ *v/t* record, video etc record; PINT, fig engrave

gracia *f*: *tener gracia* (*ser divertido*) be funny; (*tener encanto*) be graceful; *me hace gracia* I think it's funny, it makes me laugh; *no le veo la gracia* I don't think it's funny; *dar las gracias a alguien* thank s.o.; *gracias* thank you

grácil *adj* dainty

gracioso *adj* funny

gradas *fpl* DEP stands, grandstand *sg*

graderío *m* stands *pl*

grado *m* degree; *de buen grado* with good grace, readily

graduación *f* TÉC etc adjustment; *de alcohol* alcohol content; EDU graduation; MIL rank

gradual *adj* gradual

gradualmente *adv* gradually

graduarse ⟨1e⟩ *v/r* graduate, get one's degree

gráfica *f* graph

gráfico 1 *adj* graphic; *artes -as* graphic arts 2 *m* MAT graph; INFOR graphic

gragea *f* tablet, pill

grajo *m* ZO rook

Gral. *abr* (= *General*) Gen (= General)

gramática *f* grammar

gramatical *adj* grammatical

gramo *m* gram

gran *short form of grande before a noun*

granada *f* BOT pomegranate; *granada de mano* MIL hand grenade

granangular *m* wide-angle lens

granate *adj* dark crimson

Gran Bretaña Great Britain
grande **1** *adj* big; *a lo grande* in style **2**
m/f L.Am. (*adulto*) grown-up, adult;
(*mayor*) eldest; *pasarlo en grande* F
have a great time
grandeza *f* greatness
grandiosidad *f* grandeur
grandioso *adj* impressive, magnificent
granel *m*: *vender a granel* COM sell in
bulk; *había comida a granel* F there
was loads of food F
granero *m* granary
granito *m* granite
granizada *f* hailstorm
granizado *m type of soft drink made with
crushed ice*
granizar ⟨1f⟩ *v/i* hail
granizo *m* hail
granja *f* farm
granjearse ⟨1a⟩ *v/r* win, earn
granjero *m*, -a *f* farmer
grano *m* grain; *de café* bean; *en la piel*
pimple, spot; *ir al grano* get (straight)
to the point
granuja *m* rascal
grapa *f* staple
grapadora *f* stapler
grapar ⟨1a⟩ staple
grasa *f* BIO, GASTR fat; *lubricante, suciedad*
grease
grasiento *adj* greasy, oily
graso *adj* greasy; *carne* fatty
gratificación *f* gratification
gratificar ⟨1g⟩ *v/t* reward
gratinar ⟨1a⟩ *v/t* cook au gratin
gratis *adj* & *adv* free
gratitud *f* gratitude
gratuito *adj* free
grava *f* gravel
gravar ⟨1a⟩ *v/t* tax
grave *adj* serious; *tono* grave, solemn; *nota* low; *voz* deep; *estar grave* be seriously ill
gravedad *f* seriousness, gravity; FÍS gravity
gravemente *adv* seriously
gravilla *f* grave
Grecia Greece
gremio *m* HIST guild; *fig* F (*oficio manual*)

trade; (*profesión*) profession
griego **1** *adj* Greek **2** *m*, -a *f* Greek
grieta *f* crack
grifo **1** *adj Méx* F high **2** *m* faucet, *Br* tap;
Pe (*gasolinera*) gas station, *Br* petrol station
grillo *m* ZO cricket
grima *f*: *me da grima Esp de ruido*, *material etc* it sets my teeth on edge; *de algo
asqueroso* it gives me the creeps F; *en
grima Pe* alone
gringo *m L.Am. desp* gringo *desp*, foreigner
gripe *f* flu, influenza
gris *adj* gray, *Br* grey
gritar ⟨1a⟩ *v/t* & *v/i* shout, yell
griterío *m* shouting
grito *m* cry, shout; *a grito pelado* at the
top of one's voice; *pedir algo a gritos* F
be crying out for sth
grosella *f* redcurrant
grosero **1** *adj* rude **2** *m*, -a *f* rude person
grosor *m* thickness
grotesco *adj* grotesque
grúa *f* crane; AUTO wrecker, *Br* breakdown
truck
grueso *adj* thick; *persona* stout
grulla *f* ZO crane
grumo *m* lump
gruñido *m* grunt; *de perro* growl
gruñir ⟨3h⟩ *v/i* (*quejarse*) grumble, moan
F; *de perro* growl; *de cerdo* grunt
gruñón **1** *adj* F grumpy **2** *m*, -ona *f* F
grouch F
grupo *m* group
gruta *f* cave; *artificial* grotto
guacamol, guacamole *m* guacamole
guachimán *m Chi* watchman
guacho **1** *adj S. Am.* (*sin casa*) homeless;
(*huérfano*) orphaned **2** *m*, -a *f S. Am. sin
casa* homeless person; (*huérfano*) orphan
guadaño *m Cuba*, *Méx* small boat
guagua *f W.I., Ven, Canaries* bus; *Pe, Bol,
Chi* (*niño*) baby
guajolote *m Méx*, *C.Am.* turkey
guanaco **1** *adj L.Am.* F dumb F, stupid **2**
m ZO guanaco **3** *m*, -a *f persona* idiot
guantazo *m* slap

guante *m* glove

guantera *f* AUTO glove compartment

guapo *adj hombre* handsome, good-looking; *mujer* beautiful; *S. Am.* gutsy

guaracha *f W.I.* street band

guarache → **huarache**

guarapo *m* L.Am. alcoholic drink made from sugar cane and herbs

guarda *m/f* keeper; **guarda jurado** security guard

guardabosques *m/f inv* forest ranger

guardacostas *m inv* coastguard vessel

guardaespaldas *m/f inv* bodyguard

guardameta *m/f* DEP goalkeeper

guardar ⟨1a⟩ 1 *v/t* keep; *poner en un lugar* put (away); *recuerdo* have; *apariencias* keep up; INFOR save; **guardar silencio** remain silent, keep silent 2 *v/r* **guardarse** keep; **guardarse de** refrain from

guardarropa *m* checkroom, *Br* cloakroom; *(ropa, armario)* wardrobe

guardería *f* nursery

guardia 1 *f* guard; **de guardia** on duty; **bajar la guardia** *fig* lower one's guard 2 *m/f* MIL guard; *(policía)* police officer; **guardia civil** Esp civil guard; **guardia de seguridad** security guard; **guardia de tráfico** traffic warden

guardián 1 *adj*: **perro guardián** guard dog 2 *m*, **-ana** *f* guard; *fig* guardian

guarecer ⟨2d⟩ 1 *v/t* shelter 2 *v/r* **guarecerse** shelter, take shelter (**de** from)

guarida *f* ZO den; *de personas* hideout

guarnición *f* GASTR accompaniment; MIL garrison

guaro *m* C.Am. sugar-cane liquor

guarro 1 *adj* F *sucio* filthy 2 *m tb fig* F pig

guarura *m* Méx *(guardaespaldas)* bodyguard; F *(gamberro)* thug

guasa *f* L.Am. joke; **de guasa** as a joke

guaso 1 *adj* S. Am. rude 2 *m* Chi peasant

guata *f* L.Am. F paunch

Guatemala Guatemala

guatemalteco 1 *adj* Guatemalan 2 *m*, **-a** *f* Guatemalan

guatón *adj* L.Am. F pot-bellied, big-bellied

guay *int* Esp F cool F, neat F

guayaba *f* L.Am. BOT guava

guayabera *f* Méx, C.Am., W.I. loose embroidered shirt

gubernamental *adj* governmental, government *atr*

guepardo *m* ZO cheetah

güero 1 *adj* Méx, C.Am. fair, light-skinned 2 *m*, **-a** *f* Méx, C.Am. blond(e)

guerra *f* war; **guerra civil** civil war; **guerra fría** cold war; **guerra mundial** world war; **dar guerra a alguien** F give s.o. trouble

guerrero 1 *adj* warlike 2 *m* warrior

guerrilla *f* guerillas *pl*

guerrillero *m* guerilla

gueto *m* ghetto

guevear *v/i* → **huevear**

guevón → **huevón**

guía 1 *m/f* guide; **guía turístico** tourist guide 2 *f libro* guide (book); **guía telefónica** or **de teléfonos** phone book

guiar ⟨1c⟩ 1 *v/t* guide 2 *v/r* **guiarse**: **guiarse por** follow

guijarro *m* pebble

guillotina *f* guillotine

güinche *m* L.Am. winch, pulley

guinda 1 *adj* L.Am. purple 2 *f fresca* morello cherry; **en dulce** glacé cherry

guindilla *f* GASTR chil(l)i

guiñar ⟨1a⟩ *v/t*: **le guiñó un ojo** she winked at him

guiño *m* wink

guion *m de película* script; GRAM *corto* hyphen; *largo* dash

guionista *m/f* scriptwriter

guiri *m* Esp P (light-skinned) foreigner

guirnalda *f* garland

guisante *m* pea

guisar ⟨1a⟩ *v/t* GASTR stew, casserole

guiso *m* GASTR stew, casserole

guitarra *f* guitar

guitarrista *m/f* guitarist

gula *f* gluttony

gusano *m* worm

gustar ⟨1a⟩ *v/i*: **me gusta viajar** I like to travel, I like travelling; **¿te gusta el ajo?** do you like garlic?; **no me gusta** I don't like it

gusto *m* taste; *(placer)* pleasure; **a gusto** at ease; **con mucho gusto** with pleas-

ure; *de buen gusto* in good taste, taste-
ful; *de mal gusto* in bad taste, tasteless;
da gusto ... it's a pleasure ...; *mucho or*
tanto gusto how do you do
gutural *adj* guttural

H

ha *vb* → **haber**
haba *f* broad bean; *en todas partes se*
cuecen habas it's the same the world
over
Habana: *La Habana* Havana
habanero *m*, -a *f* citizen of Havana
habano *m* Havana (cigar)
haber ⟨2k⟩ 1 *v/aux* have; *hemos llegado*
we've arrived; *he de levantarme pronto*
I have to o I've got to get up early; *de*
haberlo sabido if I'd known; *has de*
ver Méx you ought to see it 2 *v/impers*:
hay there is *sg*, there are *pl*; *hubo un in-*
cendio there was a fire; *¿qué hay?*, Méx
¿qué hubo? how's it going?, what's happening?; *hay que hacerlo* it has to be
done; *no hay de qué* not at all, don't
mention it; *no hay más que decir*
there's nothing more to be said 3 *m* asset;
pago fee; *tiene en su haber 50.000 ptas*
she's 50,000 pesetas in credit
habichuela *f* kidney bean
hábil *adj* skilled; (*capaz*) capable; (*astuto*)
clever, smart
habilidad *f* skill; (*capacidad*) ability; (*as-*
tucia) cleverness
habilitar ⟨1a⟩ *v/t lugar* fit out; *persona* authorize
habitación *f* room; (*dormitorio*) bedroom; *habitación doble / individual*
double / single room
habitante *m/f* inhabitant
habitar ⟨1a⟩ *v/i* live (*en* in)
hábitat *m* habitat
hábito *m tb* REL habit; (*práctica*) knack;
colgar los hábitos fig de sacerdote give
up the priesthood

habitual 1 *adj* usual, regular 2 *m/f* regular
habituar ⟨1e⟩ 1 *v/t*: *habituar a alguien a*
algo get s.o. used to sth 2 *v/r* habituarse:
habituarse a algo get used to sth
habla *f* speech; *¡al habla!* TELEC speaking;
quedarse sin habla fig be speechless
hablada *f* L.Am. piece of gossip; *habla-*
das pl gossip *sg*
hablador *adj* talkative; Méx boastful
habladurías *fpl* gossip *sg*
hablante *m/f* speaker
hablar ⟨1a⟩ 1 *v/i* speak; (*conversar*) talk;
hablar claro fig say what one means; *ha-*
blar con alguien talk to s.o., talk with
s.o.; *hablar de de libro etc* be about, deal
with; *hablar por hablar* talk for the sake
of it; *¡ni hablar!* no way! 2 *v/r* hablarse
speak to one another; *no se hablan*
they're not speaking (to each other)
hacendado 1 *adj* land-owing 2 *m*, -a *f*
land-owner
hacendoso *adj* hardworking
hacer ⟨2s; *part* hecho⟩ 1 *v/t* (*realizar*) do;
(*elaborar*, *crear*) make; *¡haz algo!* do
something!; *hacer una pregunta* ask a
question; *¡qué le vamos a hacer!* that's
life; *no hace más que quejarse* all he
does is complain; *le hicieron ir* they
made him go; *tengo que hacer los de-*
beres I have to do my homework 2 *v/i*:
haces bien / mal en ir you are doing
the right / wrong thing by going; *me ha-*
ce mal it's making me ill; *esto hará de*
mesa de objeto this will do as a table; *ha-*
cer como que or como si act as if; *no le*
hace L.Am. it doesn't matter; *se me ha-*
ce qué L.Am. it seems to me that 3

H

v/impers: *hace calor / frío* it's hot / cold; *hace tres días* three days ago; *hace mucho (tiempo)* a long time ago; *desde hace un año* for a year **4** *v/r* hacerse *traje* make; *casa* build o.s.; *(cocinarse)* cook; *(convertirse, volverse)* get, become; *hacerse viejo* get old; *hacerse de noche* get dark; *se hace tarde* it's getting late; *hacerse el sordo / el tonto* pretend to be deaf / stupid; *hacerse a algo* get used to sth; *hacerse con algo* get hold of sth

hacha *f* ax, *Br* axe; *ser un hacha para algo* F be brilliant at sth

hachís *m* hashish

hacia *prp* toward; *hacia adelante* forward; *hacia abajo* down; *hacia arriba* up; *hacia atrás* back(ward); *hacia las cuatro* about four (o'clock)

Hacienda *f ministerio* Treasury Department, *Br* Treasury; *oficina* Internal Revenue Service, *Br* Inland Revenue

hacienda *f L.Am. (granja)* ranch, estate

hacinar ⟨1a⟩ *v/t* stack

hada *f* fairy

haga *vb* → *hacer*

hago *vb* → *hacer*

Haití Haiti

hala *int* come on!; *sorpresa* wow!

halagar ⟨1h⟩ *v/t* flatter

halago *m* flattery

halar ⟨1a⟩ *v/t L.Am.* haul, pull

halcón *m* zo falcon

halitosis *f* MED halitosis, bad breath

hall *m* hall

hallar ⟨1a⟩ **1** *v/t* find; *(descubrir)* discover; *muerte, destino* meet **2** *v/r* hallarse be; *(sentirse)* feel

hallazgo *m* find; *(descubrimiento)* discovery

halógeno *adj* halogen

halterofilia *f* DEP weight-lifting

hamaca *f* hammock; *(tumbona)* deck chair; *L.Am. (mecedora)* rocking chair

hamacar ⟨1g⟩ *v/t L.Am.* swing

hamaquear ⟨1a⟩ *v/t L.Am.* swing

hambre *f* hunger; *morirse de hambre fig* be starving; *pasar hambre* be starving

hambriento *adj tb fig* hungry (*de* for)

hambruna *f* famine

hamburguesa *f* GASTR hamburger

hamburguesería *f* hamburger bar

hampa *f* underworld

hámster *m* zo hamster

hangar *m* hangar

haragán *m*, -ana *f* shirker

harapo *m* rag

hardware *m* INFOR hardware

haré *vb* → *hacer*

harina *f* flour

harinoso *adj* floury

hartar ⟨1a⟩ **1** *v/t*: *hartar a alguien con algo* tire s.o. with sth; *hartar a alguien de algo* give s.o. too much of sth **2** *v/r* hartarse get sick (*de* of) F, get tired (*de* of); *(llenarse)* stuff o.s. (*de* with)

harto **1** *adj* fed up F; *(lleno)* full (up); *había hartos pasteles* there were cakes in abundance; *hace harto frío L.Am.* it's very cold; *estar harto de algo* be sick of sth F, be fed up with sth F **2** *adv* very much; *delante del adjetivo* extremely; *me gusta harto L.Am.* F I like it a lot

hartón **1** *adj L.Am.* greedy **2** *m*: *darse un hartón de algo* overdose on sth

has *vb* → *haber*

hasta **1** *prp* until, till; *llegó hasta Bilbao* he went as far as Bilbao; *hasta ahora* so far; *hasta aquí* up to here; *¿hasta cuándo?* how long?; *hasta que* until; *¡hasta luego!* see you (later); *¡hasta la vista!* see you (later) **2** *adv* even

hastiar ⟨1c⟩ *v/t* tire; *(aburrir)* bore

hastío *m* boredom

hatajo *m* bunch

hato *m L.Am.* bundle

hay *vb* → *haber*

haya **1** *vb* → *haber* **2** *f* BOT beech

haz **1** *m* bundle; *de luz* beam **2** *vb* → *hacer*

hazaña *f* achievement

hazmerreír *m fig* F laughing stock

he *vb* → *haber*

hebilla *f* buckle

hechicero **1** *adj* bewitching, captivating **2** *m* sorcerer; *de tribu* witch-doctor

hechizado *adj* spellbound

hechizar ⟨1f⟩ *v/t fig* bewitch, captivate

hechizo *m* spell, charm

hecho **1** *part* → *hacer*; *hecho a mano*

hand-made; **¡bien hecho!** well done!; **muy hecho** *carne* well-done **2** *adj* finished; **un hombre hecho y derecho** a fully grown man **3** *m* fact; **de hecho** in fact

hectárea *f* hectare *(10,000 sq m)*

hedor *m* stink, stench

helada *f* frost

heladera *f Rpl* fridge

heladería *f* ice-cream parlo(u)r

helado 1 *adj* frozen; *fig* icy; **quedarse helado** be stunned **2** *m* ice cream

helar ⟨1k⟩ **1** *v/t* freeze **2** *v/i* freeze; **anoche heló** there was a frost last night **3** *v/r* **helarse** *tb fig* freeze

helecho *m* BOT fern

hélice *f* propeller

helicóptero *m* helicopter

hematoma *m* bruise

hembra *f* ZO, TÉC female

hemiplejía *f* MED hemiplegia

hemisferio *m* hemisphere

hemofilia *f* MED h(a)emophilia

hemorragia *f* MED h(a)emorrhage, bleeding

hemorroides *fpl* MED h(a)emorrhoids, piles

hendidura *f* crack

heno *m* hay

hepatitis *f* MED hepatitis

herbicida *m* herbicide, weed-killer

herboristería *f* herbalist

hercúleo *adj* Herculean

heredar ⟨1a⟩ *v/t* inherit *(de* from)

heredera *f* heiress

heredero *m* heir

hereditario *adj* hereditary

hereje *m* heretic

herencia *f* inheritance

herida *f de arma* wound; *(lesión)* injury; *mujer* wounded woman; *mujer lesionada* injured woman

herido 1 *adj de arma* wounded; *(lesionado)* injured **2** *m de bala* wounded man; *(lesionado)* injured man

herir ⟨3i⟩ *v/t con arma* wound; *(lesionar)* injure; *fig (ofender)* hurt

hermana *f* sister

hermanastra *f* stepsister

hermanastro *m* stepbrother

hermano *m* brother

hermético *adj* airtight, hermetic; *fig: persona* inscrutable

hermoso *adj* beautiful

hernia *f* MED hernia

héroe *m* hero

heroico *adj* heroic

heroína *f mujer* heroine; *droga* heroin

heroinómano *m*, **-a** *f* heroin addict

herpes *m* MED herpes

herradura *f* horseshoe

herramienta *f* tool

hervidero *m fig* hotbed

hervido *m S. Am.* stew

hervir ⟨3i⟩ **1** *v/i* boil; *fig* swarm, seethe *(de* with) **2** *v/t* boil

heterodoxo *adj* unorthodox

heterogéneo *adj* heterogeneous

hez *f* scum, dregs *pl*

hibernar ⟨1a⟩ *v/i* hibernate

híbrido 1 *adj* hybrid *atr* **2** *m* hybrid

hice *vb* → **hacer**

hicimos *vb* → **hacer**

hidratante *adj* moisturizing; **crema hidratante** moisturizing cream

hidratar ⟨1a⟩ *v/t* hydrate; *piel* moisturize

hidrato *m*: **hidrato de carbono** carbohydrate

hidráulico *adj* hydraulic

hidroavión *m* seaplane

hidroeléctrico *adj* hydroelectric

hidrógeno *m* hydrogen

hiedra *f* BOT ivy

hielo *m* ice; **romper el hielo** *fig* break the ice

hiena *f* ZO hyena

hierba *f* grass; **mala hierba** weed

hiere *vb* → **herir**

hierro *m* iron

hierve *vb* → **hervir**

hígado *m* liver; **ser un hígado** *C.Am., Méx* F be a pain in the butt F

higiene *f* hygiene

higiénico *adj* hygienic

higo *m* BOT fig

higuera *f* BOT fig tree

hija *f* daughter

hijastra *f* stepdaughter

hijastro *m* stepson

hijo *m* son; *hijos* children *pl*; *hijo de puta* P son of a bitch V, bastard P; *hijo único* only child

hilachos *mpl Méx* rags

hilera *f* row, line

hilo *m* thread; *hilo dental* dental floss; *sin hilos* TELEC cordless; *colgar or pender de un hilo fig* hang by a thread; *perder el hilo fig* lose the thread

himno *m* hymn; *himno nacional* national anthem

hincapié *m*: *hacer hincapié* put special emphasis (*en* on)

hincar ⟨1g⟩ 1 *v/t* thrust, stick (*en* into); *hincar el diente* F sink one's teeth (*en* into) 2 *v/r hincarse*: *hincarse de rodillas* kneel down

hincha *m* F fan, supporter

hinchado *adj* swollen

hinchar ⟨1a⟩ 1 *v/t* inflate, blow up; *Rpl* P annoy 2 *v/r hincharse* MED swell; *fig* stuff o.s (*de* with); (*mostrarse orgulloso*) swell with pride

hinchazón *f* swelling

hiperactivo *adj* hyperactive

hipermercado *m* hypermarket

hipertensión *f* MED high blood pressure, hypertension

hipertexto *m* hypertext

hípico *adj* equestrian; *concurso hípico* show-jumping event; *carrera -a* horse race

hipnosis *f* hypnosis

hipnotizar ⟨1f⟩ *v/t* hypnotize

hipo *m* hiccups *pl*, hiccoughs *pl*; *quitar el hipo* F take one's breath away

hipocondríaco 1 *adj* hypochondriac 2 *m*, -a *f* hypochondriac

hipocresía *f* hypocrisy

hipócrita 1 *adj* hypocritical 2 *m/f* hypocrite

hipódromo *m* racetrack

hipopótamo *m* ZO hippopotamus

hipoteca *f* COM mortgage

hipotecar ⟨1g⟩ *v/t* COM mortgage; *fig* compromise

hipótesis *f* hypothesis

hipotético *adj* hypothetical

hispánico *adj* Hispanic

hispano 1 *adj* (*español*) Spanish; (*hispanohablante*) Spanish-speaking; *en EE.UU.* Hispanic 2 *m*, -a *f* (*español*) Spaniard; (*hispanohablante*) Spanish speaker; *en EE.UU.* Hispanic

hispanohablante *adj* Spanish-speaking

histeria *f* hysteria

histérico *adj* hysterical

historia *f* history; (*cuento*) story; *una historia de drogas* F some drugs business; *déjate de historias* F stop making excuses

historiador *m*, historiadora *f* historian

historial *m* record

histórico *adj* historical; (*importante*) historic

historieta *f* anecdote; (*viñetas*) comic strip

hito *m tb fig* milestone

hizo *vb* → *hacer*

Hnos. *abr* (= *Hermanos*) Bros (= Brothers)

hobby *m* hobby

hocico *m* snout; *de perro* muzzle

hockey *m* field hockey, *Br* hockey; *hockey sobre hielo* hockey, *Br* ice hockey

hogar *m fig* home

hogareño *adj* home *atr*; *persona* home-loving

hoguera *f* bonfire

hoja *f* BOT leaf; *de papel* sheet; *de libro* page; *de cuchillo* blade; *hoja de afeitar* razor blade; *hoja de cálculo* INFOR spreadsheet

hojalata *f* tin

hojaldre *m* GASTR puff pastry

hojear ⟨1a⟩ *v/t* leaf through, flip through

hola *int* hello, hi F

Holanda Holland

holandés 1 *adj* Dutch 2 *m* Dutchman

holandesa *f* Dutchwoman

holding *m* holding company

holgado *adj* loose, comfortable; *estar holgado de tiempo* have time to spare

holgazán *m* idler

holgazanear ⟨1a⟩ *v/i* laze around

holgura *f* ease; *de ropa* looseness; TÉC play; *vivir con holgura* live comfortably

hollín *m* soot

holocausto *m* holocaust

hombre *m* man; *el hombre* (*la humanidad*) man, mankind; *hombre lobo* werewolf; *hombre de negocios* businessman; *hombre rana* frogman; *¡claro, hombre!* you bet!, sure thing!; *¡hombre, qué alegría!* that's great!

hombro *m* shoulder; *hombro con hombro* shoulder to shoulder; *encogerse de hombros* shrug (one's shoulders)

homenaje *m* homage; *rendir homenaje a alguien* pay tribute to s.o.

homeopatía *f* hom(o)eopathy

homicidio *m* homicide

homogéneo *adj* homogenous

homologación *f* approval; *de título, diploma* official recognition

homólogo *m*, -a *f* counterpart, opposite number

homosexual *m/f & adj* homosexual

hondo *adj* deep

Honduras Honduras

hondureño 1 *adj* Honduran 2 *m*, -a *f* Honduran

honesto *adj* hono(u)rable, decent

hongo *m* fungus

honor *m* hono(u)r; *en honor a* in hono(u)r of; *hacer honor a* live up to; *palabra de honor* word of hono(u)r

honorarios *mpl* fees

honra *f* hono(u)r; *¡a mucha honra!* I'm hono(u)red

honradez *f* honesty

honrado *adj* honest

honrar ⟨1a⟩ *v/t* hono(u)r

hora *f* hour; *horas pl extraordinarias* overtime *sg*; *hora local* local time; *hora punta* rush hour; *a la hora de ... fig* when it comes to ...; *a última hora* at the last minute; *¡ya era hora!* about time too!; *tengo hora con el dentista* I have an appointment with the dentist; *¿qué hora es?* what time is it?

horario *m* schedule, *Br* timetable; *horario comercial* business hours *pl*; *horario flexible* flextime, *Br* flexitime; *horario de trabajo* (working) hours *pl*

horca *f* gallows *pl*

horcajadas *fpl*: *a horcajadas* astride

horchata *f* drink made from tiger-nuts

horda *f* horde

horizontal *adj* horizontal

horizonte *m* horizon

hormiga *f* ant

hormigón *m* concrete; *hormigón armado* reinforced concrete

hormigueo *m* pins and needles *pl*

hormiguero *m* ant hill; *la sala era un hormiguero de gente* the hall was swarming with people

hormona *f* hormone

hornilla *f* ring

horno *m* oven; *de cerámica* kiln; *alto horno* blast furnace

horóscopo *m* horoscope

horqueta *f L.Am. de camino* fork

horquilla *f para pelo* hairpin

horrendo *adj* horrendous

horrible *adj* horrible, dreadful

horripilante *adj* horrible

horror *m* horror (*a* of); *tener horror a* be terrified of; *me gusta horrores* F I like it a lot; *¡qué horror!* how awful!

horrorizar ⟨1f⟩ *v/t* horrify

horroroso *adj* terrible; (*de mala calidad*) dreadful; (*feo*) hideous

hortaliza *f* vegetable

hortensia *f* BOT hydrangea

hortera 1 *F adj* tacky F 2 *m/f* F tacky person F

horterada *f* F tacky thing F; *es una horterada* it's tacky F

horticultor *m*, horticultora *f* horticulturist

horticultura *f* horticulture

hosco *adj* sullen

hospedaje *m* accommodations *pl*, *Br* accommodation; *dar hospedaje a alguien* put s.o. up

hospedarse ⟨1a⟩ *v/r* stay (*en* at)

hospital *m* hospital

hospitalario *adj* hospitable; MED hospital *atr*

hospitalidad *f* hospitality

hospitalizar ⟨1f⟩ *v/t* hospitalize

hostal *m* hostel

hostelera *f* landlady

hostelería *f* hotel industry

hostelero **1** adj hotel atr **2** m landlord

hostia f REL host; P (golpe) sock F, wallop F; ¡**hostias**! P Christ! P

hostigar ⟨1h⟩ v/t pester; MIL harass; caballo whip

hostil adj hostile

hostilidad f hostility

hotel m hotel

hotelero m, -a f hotelier

hoy adv today; **de hoy** of today; **los padres de hoy** today's parents, parents today; **de hoy en adelante** from now on; **por hoy** for today; **hoy por hoy** at the present time; **hoy en día** nowadays

hoya f hole; de tumba grave; GEOG plain; S. Am. river basin

hoyo m hole; (depresión) hollow

hoyuelo m dimple

hoz f sickle

huachafo adj Pe (cursi) affected, pretentious

huarache m Méx rough sandal

huayno m Pe, Bol Andean dance rhythm

hubo vb → **haber**

hucha f money box

hueco **1** adj hollow; (vacío) empty; fig: persona shallow **2** m gap; (agujero) hole; de ascensor shaft

huele vb → **oler**

huelga f strike; **huelga de celo** work-to-rule; **huelga general** general strike; **huelga de hambre** hunger strike; **declararse en huelga, ir a la huelga** go on strike

huelguista m/f striker

huella f mark; de animal track; **huellas dactilares** finger prints

huelo vb → **oler**

huérfano **1** adj orphan atr **2** m, -a f orphan

huero adj fig empty; L.Am. blond

huerta f truck farm, Br market garden

huerto m kitchen garden; **llevar a alguien al huerto** F put one over on s.o. F

huesear ⟨1a⟩ v/t C.Am. beg

huesillo m S. Am. sun-dried peach

hueso m bone; de fruta pit, stone; persona tough nut; Méx F cushy number F; Méx F (influencia) influence, pull F; **hueso duro de roer** fig F hard nut to crack; **estar en los huesos** be all skin and bone

huésped m/f guest

huesudo adj bony

huevas fpl roe sg

huevear ⟨1a⟩ v/i Chi P mess around F

huevo m egg; P (testículo) ball V; **huevo duro** hard-boiled egg; **huevo escalfado** poached egg; **huevo frito** fried egg; **huevo pasado por agua** soft-boiled egg; **huevos revueltos** scrambled eggs; **un huevo de** P a load of F

huevón m, -ona f Chi P idiot; L.Am. F (flojo) idler F

huida f flight, escape

huir ⟨3g⟩ v/i flee, escape (de from); **huir de algo** avoid sth

hulado m C.Am., Méx rubberized cloth

hule m oilcloth; L.Am. (caucho) rubber

humanidad f humanity; **humanidades** humanities

humanismo m humanism

humanitario adj humanitarian

humanizar ⟨1f⟩ v/t humanize

humano adj human

humareda f cloud of smoke

humear ⟨1a⟩ v/i con humo smoke; con vapor steam

humedad f humidity; de una casa damp (-ness)

humedecer ⟨2d⟩ v/t dampen

húmedo adj humid; toalla damp

humildad f humility

humilde adj humble; (sin orgullo) modest; clase social lowly

humillación f humiliation

humillante adj humiliating

humillar ⟨1a⟩ v/t humiliate

humita f S. Am. meat and corn paste wrapped in leaves

humo m smoke; (vapor) steam; **tener muchos humos** F be a real bighead F

humor m humo(u)r; **estar de buen / mal humor** be in a good / bad mood; **sentido del humor** sense of humo(u)r

humorista m/f humo(u)rist; (cómico) comedian

humus m GASTR hummus

hundido adj fig: persona depressed

hundir ⟨3a⟩ **1** v/t sink; fig: empresa ruin,

bring down; *persona* devastate **2** *v/r* hundirse sink; *fig: de empresa* collapse; *de persona* go to pieces

húngaro 1 *adj* Hungarian **2** *m*, **-a** *f* Hungarian

Hungría Hungary

huracán *m* hurricane

huraño *adj* unsociable

hurgar ⟨1h⟩ **1** *v/i* rummage (**en** in) **2** *v/r*

hurgarse: *hurgarse la nariz* pick one's nose

hurón *m* zo ferret

hurtadillas *fpl*: ***a hurtadillas*** furtively

hurtar ⟨1a⟩ *v/t* steal

hurto *m* theft

husmear ⟨1a⟩ *v/i* F nose around F (**en** in)

huy *int sorpresa* wow!; *dolor* ouch!

huyo *vb* → **huir**

I

I+D *abr* (= ***investigación y desarrollo***) R&D (= research and development)

iba *vb* → **ir**

ibérico *adj* Iberian

iberoamericano *adj* Latin American

iceberg *m* iceberg

icono *m tb* INFOR icon

ida *f outward journey;* (***billete de*) *ida y vuelta*** round trip (ticket), *Br* return (ticket)

idea *f* idea; ***hacerse a la idea de que ...*** get used to the idea that ...; ***no tener ni idea*** not have a clue

ideal *m/adj* ideal

idealista 1 *adj* idealistic **2** *m/f* idealist

idear *v/t* ⟨1a⟩ think up, come up with

idéntico *adj* identical

identidad *f* identity

identificación *f* identification

identificar ⟨1g⟩ **1** *v/t* identify **2** *v/r* **identificarse** identify o.s.

ideología *f* ideology

idílico *adj* idyllic

idilio *m* idyll; (*relación amorosa*) romance

idioma *m* language

idiota 1 *adj* idiotic **2** *m/f* idiot

idiotez *f* stupid thing to say / do

ido 1 *part* → **ir 2** *adj* (*chiflado*) nuts F; ***estar ido*** be miles away F

idolatrar ⟨1a⟩ *v/t tb fig* worship

ídolo *m tb fig* idol

idóneo *adj* suitable

iglesia *f* church

ignominioso *adj* ignominious

ignorancia *f* ignorance

ignorante *adj* ignorant

ignorar ⟨1a⟩ *v/t* not know, not be aware of; ***ignoro cómo sucedió*** I don't know how it happened

igual 1 *adj* (*idéntico*) same (***a, que*** as); (*proporcionado*) equal (***a*** to); (*constante*) constant; ***al igual que*** like, the same as; ***me da igual*** I don't mind **2** *m/f* equal; ***no tener igual*** have no equal

igualado *adj* even

igualar ⟨1a⟩ **1** *v/t precio, marca* equal, match; (*nivelar*) level off; ***igualar algo*** MAT make sth equal (**con, a** to) **2** *v/i* DEP tie the game, *Br* equalize

igualdad *f* equality; ***igualdad de oportunidades*** equal opportunities

igualitario *adj* egalitarian

igualmente *adv* equally

iguana *f zo* iguana

ilegal *adj* illegal

ilegible *adj* illegible

ilegítimo *adj* unlawful; *hijo* illegitimate

ileso *adj* unhurt

ilícito *adj* illicit

ilimitado *adj* unlimited

llmo. *abr* (= ***ilustrísimo***) His / Your Excellency

ilógico *adj* illogical

iluminación *f* illumination

iluminar ⟨1a⟩ *v/t edificio, calle etc* light, illuminate; *monumento* light up, illuminate; *fig* light up

ilusión *f* illusion; (*deseo, esperanza*) hope

ilusionarse ⟨1a⟩ *v/r* get one's hopes up; (*entusiasmarse*) get excited (**con** about)

ilustración *f* illustration

ilustrar ⟨1a⟩ *v/t* illustrate; (*aclarar*) explain

ilustre *adj* illustrious

imagen *f tb fig* image; ***ser la viva imagen de*** be the spitting image of

imaginable *adj* imaginable

imaginación *f* imagination

imaginar ⟨1a⟩ **1** *v/t* imagine **2** *v/r* imaginarse imagine; ***¡ya me lo imagino!*** I can just imagine it!

imaginativo *adj* imaginative

imán *m* magnet

imbatible *adj* unbeatable

imbécil 1 *adj* stupid **2** *m/f* idiot, imbecile

imbecilidad *f* stupidity; ***¡qué imbecilidad decir eso!*** what a stupid thing to say!

imitación *f* imitation

imitar ⟨1a⟩ *v/t* imitate

impaciencia *f* impatience

impacientar ⟨1a⟩ **1** *v/t* make impatient **2** *v/r* impacientarse lose (one's) patience

impaciente *adj* impatient

impactar ⟨1a⟩ *v/t* hit; (*impresionar*) have an impact on

impacto *m tb fig* impact; ***impacto de bala*** bullet wound; ***impacto ecológico*** ecological

impar *adj número* odd

imparcial *adj* impartial

imparcialidad *f* impartiality

impasible *adj* impassive

impávido *adj* fearless, undaunted

impecable *adj* impeccable

impedimento *m* impediment

impedir ⟨3l⟩ *v/t* prevent; (*estorbar*) impede

imperante *adj* ruling; *fig* prevailing

imperar ⟨1a⟩ *v/i* rule; *fig* prevail

imperativo 1 *adj* GRAM imperative; *obliga-*

ción pressing **2** *m* GRAM imperative

imperdible *m* safety pin

imperdonable *adj* unpardonable, unforgivable

imperfecto *m/adj* imperfect

imperial *adj* imperial

imperio *m* empire

imperioso *adj necesidad* pressing; *persona* imperious

impermeable 1 *adj* waterproof **2** *m* raincoat

impersonal *adj* impersonal

impertérrito *adj* unperturbed, unmoved

impertinente 1 *adj* impertinent **2** *m/f*: ***¡eres un impertinente!*** you've got nerve! F, *Br* you've got a cheek! F

ímpetu *m* impetus

impetuoso *adj* impetuous

implacable *adj* implacable

implemento *m* implement

implicar ⟨1g⟩ *v/t* mean, imply; (*involucrar*) involve; *en un delito* implicate (**en** in)

implícito *adj* implicit

implorar ⟨1a⟩ *v/t* beg for

imponente *adj* impressive, imposing; F terrific

imponer ⟨2r⟩ **1** *v/t* impose; *miedo, respeto* inspire; *impuesto* impose; *levy* **2** *v/i* be imposing *o* impressive **3** *v/r* imponerse (*hacerse respetar*) assert o.s.; DEP win; (*prevalecer*) prevail; (*ser necesario*) be imperative; ***imponerse una tarea*** set o.s. a task

importación *f* import, importation; *artículo* import

importancia *f* importance; ***dar importancia a*** attach importance to; ***darse importancia*** give o.s. airs; ***tener importancia*** be important

importante *adj* important

importar ⟨1a⟩ *v/i* matter; ***no importa*** it doesn't matter; ***eso a ti no te importa*** that's none of your business; ***¿qué importa?*** what does it matter?; ***¿le importa ...?*** do you mind ...?

importe *m* amount; (*coste*) cost

importuno *adj* inopportune;

imposibilitar ⟨1a⟩ *v/t*: ***imposibilitar algo***

make sth impossible, prevent sth
imposible *adj* impossible
impostor *m*, **impostora** *f* impostor
impotencia *f* impotence, helplessness;
MED impotence
impotente *adj* helpless, powerless, impotent; MED impotent
impreciso *adj* imprecise
impredecible *adj* unpredictable
impregnar ⟨1a⟩ *v/t* saturate (**de** with); TÉC impregnate (**de** with)
imprenta *f taller* printer's; *arte, técnica* printing; *máquina* printing press
imprescindible *adj* essential; *persona* indispensable
impresión *f* impression; *acto* printing; (*tirada*) print run; *la sangre le da impresión* he can't stand the sight of blood
impresionante *adj* impressive
impresionar ⟨1a⟩ *v/t*: *impresionarle a alguien* impress s.o.; (*conmover*) move s.o.; (*alterar*) shock s.o.
impresionismo *m* impressionism
impreso *m* form; *impresos pl* printed matter *sg*
impresora *f* INFOR printer; *impresora de chorro de tinta* inkjet (printer); *impresora de inyección de tinta* inkjet (printer); *impresora láser* laser (printer)
imprevisible *adj* unpredictable
imprevisto 1 *adj* unforeseen, unexpected **2** *m* unexpected event
imprimir ⟨3a⟩ *v/t tb* INFOR print; *fig* transmit
improbable *adj* unlikely, improbable
improcedente *adj* improper
improductivo *adj* unproductive
impropio *adj* inappropriate
improvisar ⟨1a⟩ *v/t* improvise
improviso *adj*: *de improviso* unexpectedly
imprudencia *f* recklessness, rashness
imprudente *adj* reckless, rash
impuesto *m* tax; *impuesto sobre el valor añadido* sales tax; *Br* value-added tax; *impuesto sobre la renta* income tax
impugnar ⟨1a⟩ *v/t* challenge
impulsar ⟨1a⟩ *v/t* TÉC propel; COM boost
impulsivo *adj* impulsive

impulso *m* impulse; (*empuje*) impetus; COM boost; *fig* urge, impulse; *tomar impulso* take a run up
impunidad *f* impunity
impureza *f* impurity
imputar ⟨1a⟩ *v/t* attribute
inacabable *adj* endless, never-ending
inaccesible *adj* inaccessible
inaceptable *adj* unacceptable
inactivo *adj* inactive
inadaptado *adj* maladjusted
inadecuado *adj* inadequate
inadmisible *adj* inadmissible
inadvertido *adj*: *pasar inadvertido* go unnoticed
inagotable *adj* inexhaustible
inaguantable *adj* unbearable
inalámbrico 1 *adj* TELEC cordless **2** *m* TELEC cordless telephone
inamovible *adj* immovable
inanición *f* starvation
inapreciable *adj* (*valioso*) priceless; (*insignificante*) negligible
inasequible *adj objetivo* unattainable; *precio* prohibitive;
inaudito *adj* unprecedented
inauguración *f* official opening, inauguration
inaugurar ⟨1a⟩ *v/t* (officially) open, inaugurate
inca *m/f & adj* HIST Inca
incalculable *adj* incalculable
incalificable *adj* indescribable
incandescente *adj* incandescent
incansable *adj* tireless
incapacidad *f* disability; (*falta de capacidad*) inability; (*ineptitud*) incompetence
incapacitar ⟨1a⟩ *v/t* JUR disqualify
incapaz *adj* incapable (**de** of)
incautarse ⟨1a⟩ *v/r*: *incautarse de* seize
incauto *adj* unwary
incendiar ⟨1b⟩ **1** *v/t* set fire to **2** *v/r* incendiarse burn
incendio *m* fire; *incendio forestal* forest fire
incentivo *m* incentive
incertidumbre *f* uncertainty
incesante *adj* incessant
incesto *m* incest

I

incidencia *f* (*efecto*) effect; (*frecuencia*) incidence; (*incidente*) incident

incidente *m* incident

incidir ⟨3a⟩ *v/i*: **incidir en** (*afectar*) have an effect on, affect; (*recalcar*) stress; **incidir en un error** make a mistake

incienso *m* incense

incierto *m* uncertain

incineración *f de cadáver* cremation

incinerador *adj* incinerator

incinerar ⟨1a⟩ *v/t* incinerate; *cadáver* cremate

incipiente *adj* incipient

incitante *adj* provocative

incitar ⟨1a⟩ *v/t* incite

inclemencia *f del tiempo* inclemency

inclinación *f* inclination; *de un terreno* slope; *muestra de respeto* bow; *fig* tendency

inclinar ⟨1a⟩ **1** *v/t* tilt; **inclinar la cabeza** nod (one's head); **me inclina a creer que ...** it makes me think that ... **2** *v/r* inclinarse bend (down); *de un terreno* slope; *desde la vertical* lean; *en señal de respeto* bow; **inclinarse a** *fig* tend to, be inclined to

incluido *prp* inclusive

incluir ⟨3g⟩ *v/t* include

inclusive *adv* inclusive

incluso *adv, prp & conj* even

incógnita *f* unknown factor; MAT unknown (quantity)

incógnito *adj*: **de incógnito** incognito

incoherente *adj* incoherent

incombustible *adj* fireproof

incomodidad *f* uncomfortableness; (*fastidio*) inconvenience

incómodo *adj* uncomfortable; (*fastidioso*) inconvenient

incomparable *adj* incomparable

incompatibilidad *f* incompatibility

incompatible *adj tb* INFOR incompatible

incompetencia *f* incompetence

incompetente *adj* incompetent

incompleto *adj* incomplete

incomprendido *adj* misunderstood

incomprensible *adj* incomprehensible

incomunicado *adj* isolated, cut off; JUR in solitary confinement

inconcebible *adj* inconceivable

incondicional *adj* unconditional;

inconexo *adj* unconnected

inconfesable *adj* shameful

inconformista *m/f* nonconformist

inconfundible *adj* unmistakable

incongruente *adj* incongruous

inconsciencia *f* MED unconsciousness; (*desconocimiento*) lack of awareness, unawareness; (*irreflexión*) thoughtlessness

inconsciente *adj* MED unconscious; (*ignorante*) unaware; (*irreflexivo*) thoughtless

inconsecuente *adj* inconsistent

inconsistente *adj* flimsy, weak

inconsolable *adj* inconsolable

inconstante *adj* fickle

incontable *adj* uncountable

incontinencia *f* MED incontinence

incontrolable *adj* uncontrollable

inconveniente 1 *adj* (*inoportuno*) inconvenient; (*impropio*) inappropriate **2** *m* (*desventaja*) drawback, disadvantage; (*estorbo*) problem; **no tengo inconveniente** I don't mind

incordiar ⟨1b⟩ *v/t* annoy

incordio *m* nuisance

incorporar ⟨1a⟩ **1** *v/t* incorporate **2** *v/r* incorporarse sit up; **incorporarse a** MIL join

incorrecto *adj* incorrect, wrong; *comportamiento* impolite

incorregible *adj* incorrigible

incorruptible *adj* incorruptible

incredulidad *f* disbelief, incredulity

incrédulo *adj* incredulous

increíble *adj* incredible

incrementar ⟨1a⟩ **1** *v/t* increase **2** *v/r* incrementarse increase

incremento *m* growth

incriminar ⟨1a⟩ *v/t* incriminate

incruento *adj* bloodless

incrustar ⟨1a⟩ **1** *v/t* incrust (**de** with) **2** *v/r* incrustarse *de la suciedad* become ingrained

incubación *f* incubation

incubadora *f* incubator

incubar ⟨1a⟩ *v/t* incubate

incuestionable *adj* unquestionable

inculcar ⟨1g⟩ *v/t* instil(l) (**en** in)

inculpar ⟨1a⟩ v/t JUR accuse;

inculto adj ignorant, uneducated

incultura f ignorance, lack of education

incumbencia f responsibility, duty; **no es de mi incumbencia** it's not my responsibility

incumplimiento m non-fulfillment (**de** of), non-compliance (**de** with)

incumplir ⟨3a⟩ v/t break

incurable adj incurable

incurrir ⟨3a⟩ v/i: **incurrir en un error** make a mistake; **incurrir en gastos** incur costs

incursión f MIL raid; fig foray

indagar ⟨1h⟩ v/i investigate

indecente adj indecent; película obscene

indecisión f indecisiveness

indeciso adj undecided; por naturaleza indecisive

indefenso adj defenseless, Br defenceless

indefinidamente adv indefinitely

indefinido adj (impreciso) vague; (ilimitado) indefinite

indemnización f compensation

indemnizar ⟨1f⟩ v/t compensate (**por** for)

independencia f independence

independentismo m POL pro-independence movement

independiente adj independent

independizarse ⟨1f⟩ v/r become independent

indescriptible adj indescribable

indeseable adj undesirable

indestructible adj indestructible

indeterminado adj indeterminate; (indefinido) indefinite

India: **la India** India

indiada f L.Am. group of Indians

indicación f indication; (señal) sign; **indicaciones** para llegar directions; (instrucciones) instructions

indicado adj (adecuado) suitable; **lo más / menos indicado** the best / worst thing; **hora -a** specified time

indicador m indicator

indicar ⟨1g⟩ v/t show, indicate; (señalar) point out; (sugerir) suggest

índice m index; **dedo índice** index finger; **índice de precios al consumo** consum-

er price index, Br retail price index

indicio m indication, sign; (vestigio) trace

indiferencia f indifference

indiferente adj indifferent; (irrelevante) immaterial

indígena 1 adj indigenous, native 2 m/f native

indigente adj destitute

indigestión f indigestion

indigesto adj indigestible

indignación f indignation

indignado adj indignant

indignar ⟨1a⟩ 1 v/t: **indignar a alguien** make s.o. indignant 2 v/r **indignarse** become indignant

indigno adj unworthy (**de** of)

indio 1 adj Indian 2 m, -a f Indian; **hacer el indio** F clown around F, play the fool F

indirecta f insinuation; (sugerencia) hint

indirecto adj indirect

indiscreción f indiscretion, lack of discretion; (declaración) indiscreet remark

indiscreto adj indiscreet

indiscriminado adj indiscriminate

indiscutible adj indisputable

indispensable adj indispensable

indisponerse ⟨2r⟩ v/r become unwell; **indisponerse con alguien** fall out with s.o.

indisposición f indisposition

indispuesto adj indisposed, unwell

indistinto adj forma indistinct, vague; noción vague; sonido faint

individual adj individual; cama, habitación single

individualismo m individualism

individualista m/f individualist

individuo m individual

indivisible adj indivisible

indocumentado adj: **un hombre indocumentado** a man with no identity papers

índole f nature

indolente adj lazy

indoloro adj painless

indómito adj indomitable

Indonesia Indonesia

inducir ⟨3o⟩ v/t (persuadir) lead, induce (**a** to); EL induce

indudable adj undoubted

indudablemente *adv* undoubtedly
indulgente *adj* indulgent
indultar ⟨1a⟩ *v/t* pardon
indulto *m* pardon
indumentaria *f* clothing
industria *f* industry; (*esfuerzo*) industriousness, industry
industrial 1 *adj* industrial **2** *m/f* industrialist
industrializar ⟨1f⟩ **1** *v/t* industrialize **2** *v/r* industrializarse industrialize
inédito *adj* unpublished; *fig* unprecedented
ineficacia *f* inefficiency; *de un procedimiento* ineffectiveness
ineficaz *adj* inefficient; *procedimiento* ineffective
ineficiencia *f* inefficiency
ineficiente *adj* inefficient
ineludible *adj* unavoidable
inepto 1 *adj* inept, incompetent **2** *m*, -a *f* incompetent fool
inequívoco *adj* unequivocal
inercia *f* inertia
inerte *adj fig* lifeless; *FÍS* inert
inesperado *adj* unexpected
inestabilidad *f* instability
inestable *adj* unstable; *tiempo* unsettled
inestimable *adj* invaluable
inevitable *adj* inevitable
inexacto *adj* inaccurate
inexcusable *adj* inexcusable
inexistente *adj* non-existent
inexperto *adj* inexperienced
inexplicable *adj* inexplicable
infalible *adj* infallible
infame *adj* vile, loathsome; (*terrible*) dreadful
infancia *f* infancy
infantería *f* MIL infantry
infantil *adj* children's *atr*; *naturaleza* childlike; *desp* infantile, childish
infarto *m* MED heart attack
infección *f* MED infection
infeccioso *adj* infectious
infectar ⟨1a⟩ **1** *v/t* infect **2** *v/r* infectarse become infected
infecundo *adj* infertile
infeliz 1 *adj* unhappy, miserable **2** *m/f* poor devil

inferior 1 *adj* inferior (*a* to); *en el espacio* lower (*a* than) **2** *m/f* inferior
inferioridad *f* inferiority
inferir ⟨3i⟩ *v/t* infer (*de* from); *daño* do, cause (*a* to)
infernal *adj ruido* infernal; (*muy malo*) diabolical
infertilidad *f* infertility
infestar ⟨1a⟩ *v/t* infest; (*invadir*) overrun
infidelidad *f* infidelity
infiel 1 *adj* unfaithful **2** *m/f* unbeliever
infierno *m* hell
infiltrarse ⟨1a⟩ *v/r*: **infiltrarse en** infiltrate; *de agua* seep into
infinidad *f*: **infinidad de** countless
infinitivo *m* GRAM infinitive
infinito 1 *adj* infinite **2** *m* infinity
inflación *f* COM inflation; **tasa de inflación** inflation rate
inflacionista *adj* inflationary
inflamable *adj* flammable
inflamación *f* MED inflammation
inflamar ⟨1a⟩ **1** *v/t tb fig* inflame **2** *v/r* inflamarse MED become inflamed
inflar ⟨1a⟩ **1** *v/t* inflate **2** *v/r* inflarse swell (up); *fig* F get conceited
infligir ⟨3c⟩ *v/t* inflict
inflexible *adj fig* inflexible
influencia *f* influence; **tener influencias** have contacts
influenciar ⟨1b⟩ *v/t* influence
influir ⟨3g⟩ *v/i*: **influir en alguien / algo** influence s.o./sth, have an influence on s.o./sth
influjo *m* influence
influyente *adj* influential
infografía *f* computer graphics *pl*
información *f* information; (*noticias*) news *sg*
informal *adj* informal; *persona* unreliable
informar ⟨1a⟩ **1** *v/t* inform (*de, sobre* about) **2** *v/r* informarse find out (*de, sobre* about)
informática *f* information technology
informático 1 *adj* computer *atr* **2** *m*, -a *f* IT specialist
informativo 1 *adj* informative; *programa* news *atr* **2** *m* TV, RAD news *sg*

informatizar ⟨1f⟩ *v/t* computerize
informe 1 *adj* shapeless **2** *m* report; *informes* (*referencias*) references
infracción *f* offense, *Br* offence
infraestructura *f* infrastructure
in fraganti *adv* F in the act F
infrahumano *adj* subhuman
infrarrojo *adj* infra-red
infravalorar ⟨1a⟩ *v/t* undervalue
infrecuente *adj* infrequent
infringir ⟨3c⟩ *v/t* JUR infringe, violate
infructuoso *adj* fruitless
infundado *adj* unfounded, groundless
infundir ⟨3a⟩ *v/t* inspire; *terror* instil(l); *sospechas* arouse
infusión *f* infusion; *de tila, manzanilla* tea
ingeniarse ⟨1b⟩ *v/r*: *ingeniárselas para* manage to
ingeniería *f* engineering
ingeniero *m*, **-a** *f* engineer
ingenio *m* ingenuity; (*aparato*) device; *ingenio azucarero* L.Am. sugar refinery
ingenioso *adj* ingenious
ingenuidad *f* naivety
ingenuo 1 *adj* naive **2** *m*, **-a** *f* naive person, sucker F
ingerir ⟨3i⟩ *v/t* swallow
Inglaterra England
ingle *f* groin
inglés 1 *adj* English **2** *m* Englishman; *idioma* English
inglesa *f* Englishwoman
ingrato *adj* ungrateful; *tarea* thankless
ingrediente *m* ingredient
ingresar ⟨1a⟩ **1** *v/i*: *ingresar en* en *universidad* go to; *en asociación, cuerpo* join; *en hospital* be admitted to **2** *v/t cheque* pay in, deposit
ingreso *m* entry; *en una asociación* joining; *en hospital* admission; COM deposit; *ingresos pl* income *sg*; *examen de ingreso* entrance exam
inhabitable *adj* uninhabitable
inhalar ⟨1a⟩ *v/t* inhale
inherente *adj* inherent
inhibición *f* inhibition; JUR disqualification
inhibir ⟨3a⟩ *v/t* inhibit
inhóspito *adj* inhospitable

inhumano *adj* inhuman
iniciación *f* initiation
inicial *f/adj* initial
iniciar ⟨1b⟩ *v/t* initiate; *curso* start, begin
iniciativa *f* initiative; *tomar la iniciativa* take the initiative
inicio *m* start, beginning
inigualable *adj* incomparable; *precio* unbeatable
inimaginable *adj* unimaginable
inimitable *adj* inimitable
ininteligible *adj* unintelligible
ininterrumpido *adj* uninterrupted
injerencia *f* interference
injertar ⟨1a⟩ *v/t* graft
injerto *m* graft
injuriar ⟨1b⟩ *v/t* insult
injusticia *f* injustice
injustificado *adj* unjustified
injusto *adj* unjust
inmaculado *adj* immaculate
inmaduro *adj* immature
inmediaciones *fpl* immediate area *sg* (*de* of), vicinity *sg* (*de* of)
inmediatamente *adv* immediately
inmediato *adj* immediate; *de inmediato* immediately
inmejorable *adj* unbeatable
inmenso *adj* immense
inmersión *f* immersion; *de submarino* dive
inmerso *adj fig* immersed (*en* in)
inmigración *f* immigration
inmigrante *m/f* immigrant
inmigrar ⟨1a⟩ *v/i* immigrate
inminente *adj* imminent
inmiscuirse ⟨3g⟩ *v/r* meddle
inmobiliaria *f* realtor's office, *Br* estate agency
inmoderado *adj* excessive, immoderate
inmoral *adj* immoral
inmoralidad *f* immorality
inmortal *adj* immortal
inmóvil *adj persona* motionless; *vehículo* stationary
inmovilizar ⟨1f⟩ *v/t* immobilize
inmueble *m* building
inmundo *adj* filthy
inmune *adj* immune

inmunidad *f* MED, POL immunity

inmunizar ⟨1f⟩ *v/t* immunize

inmutarse ⟨1a⟩ *v/r*: **no inmutarse** not bat an eyelid; **sin inmutarse** without batting an eyelid

innato *adj* innate, inborn

innecesario *adj* unnecessary

innegable *adj* undeniable

innovación *f* innovation

innumerable *adj* innumerable, countless

inocencia *f* innocence

inocente *adj* innocent

inocuo *adj* harmless, innocuous; *película* bland

inodoro *m* toilet

inofensivo *adj* inoffensive, harmless

inoficioso *adj* L.Am. (*inútil*) useless

inolvidable *adj* unforgettable

inopia *f*: **estar en la inopia** F (*distraído*) be miles away F; (*alejado de la realidad*) be on another planet F

inoportuno *adj* inopportune; (*molesto*) inconvenient

inorgánico *adj* inorganic

inoxidable *adj*: **acero inoxidable** stainless steel

inquietar ⟨1a⟩ **1** *v/t* worry **2** *v/r* inquietarse worry, get worried *o* anxious

inquietud *f* worry, anxiety; *intelectual* interest

inquilino *m* tenant

inquisitivo *adj* inquisitive

insaciable *adj* insatiable

insatisfacción *f* dissatisfaction

insatisfactorio *adj* unsatisfactory

insatisfecho *adj* dissatisfied

inscribir ⟨3a⟩ **1** *v/t* (*grabar*) inscribe; *en lista, registro* register, enter; *en curso, concurso* enrol(l), register **2** *v/r* inscribirse *en un curso* enrol(l), register; *en un concurso* enter

inscripción *f* inscription; *en lista, registro* registration, entry; *en curso, concurso* enrol(l)ment, registration;

insecticida *m* insecticide

insecto *m* insect

inseguro *adj* insecure; *estructura* unsteady; (*peligroso*) dangerous, unsafe

inseminación *f* insemination; **insemina-**

ción artificial artificial insemination

insensato *adj* foolish

insensible *adj* insensitive (**a** to)

inseparable *adj* inseparable

insertar ⟨1a⟩ *v/t* insert

inservible *adj* useless

insidia *f* treachery; **actuar con insidia** act treacherously

insignia *f* insignia

insignificante *adj* insignificant

insinuante *adj* suggestive

insinuar ⟨1e⟩ **1** *v/t* insinuate **2** *v/r* insinuarse: **insinuarse a alguien** make advances to s.o.

insípido *adj* insipid

insistencia *f* insistence

insistir ⟨3a⟩ *v/i* insist; **insistir en hacer algo** insist on doing sth; **insistir en algo** stress sth

insociable *adj* unsociable

insolación *f* MED sunstroke

insolente *adj* insolent

insólito *adj* unusual

insolvente *adj* insolvent

insomnio *m* insomnia

insondable *adj* unfathomable

insonorizar ⟨1f⟩ *v/t* soundproof

insoportable *adj* unbearable, intolerable

insospechado *adj* unexpected

inspección *f* inspection

inspeccionar ⟨1a⟩ *v/t* inspect

inspector *m*, inspectora *f* inspector

inspiración *f* inspiration; MED inhalation

inspirar ⟨1a⟩ *v/t* inspire; MED inhale

instalación *f* acto installation; **instalaciones deportivas** sports facilities

instalar ⟨1a⟩ **1** *v/t* install(l); (*colocar*) put; *un negocio* set up **2** *v/r* instalarse *en un sitio* install(l) o.s.

instancia *f* JUR petition; (*petición por escrito*) application; **a instancias de** at the request of

instantáneo *adj* immediate, instantaneous

instante *m* moment, instant; **al instante** right away, immediately

instar ⟨1a⟩ *v/t* urge, press

instaurar ⟨1a⟩ *v/t* establish

instigar ⟨1h⟩ *v/t* incite (**a** to)

instinto *m* instinct
institución *f* institution
instituto *m* institute; *Esp* high school, *Br* secondary school; **instituto de belleza** beauty salon; **instituto de educación secundaria** high school, *Br* secondary school
instrucción *f* education; (*formación*) training; MIL drill; INFOR instruction, statement; JUR hearing; **instrucciones de uso** instructions, directions (for use)
instructor *m*, instructora *f* instructor
instruido *adj* educated
instruir ⟨3g⟩ *v/t* educate; (*formar*) train; JUR *pleito* hear
instrumental 1 *adj* instrumental 2 *m* MED instruments *pl*
instrumento *m* instrument; (*herramienta*) tool, instrument; *fig* tool; **instrumento musical** musical instrument
insubordinación *f* insubordination
insubordinarse ⟨1a⟩ *v/r con un superior* be insubordinate; (*rebelarse*) rebel
insuficiente 1 *adj* insufficient, inadequate 2 *m* EDU *nota* fail
insufrible *adj* insufferable
insulina *f* insulin
insulso *adj* bland, insipid
insultada *f L.Am.* (*insultos*) string of insults
insultar ⟨1a⟩ *v/t* insult
insulto *m* insult
insumiso *m person who refuses to do military service*
insuperable *adj* insurmountable
insurrección *f* insurrection
insustancial *adj conferencia* lightweight; *estructura* flimsy
intachable *adj* faultless
intacto *adj* intact; (*sin tocar*) untouched
integración *f* integration
integral *adj* complete; *alimento* whole
integrar ⟨1a⟩ *v/t* integrate; *equipo* make up
íntegro *adj* whole, entire; **un hombre íntegro** *fig* a man of integrity
intelectual *m/f & adj* intellectual
inteligencia *f* intelligence
inteligente *adj* intelligent

inteligible *adj* intelligible
intemperie *f*: **a la intemperie** in the open air
intempestivo *adj* untimely
intención *f* intention; **doble** *or* **segunda intención** ulterior motive
intencionado *adj* deliberate
intendente *m Rpl* military governor; (*alcalde*) mayor
intensidad *f* intensity; (*fuerza*) strength
intensificar ⟨1g⟩ 1 *v/t* intensify 2 *v/r* intensificarse intensify
intensivo *adj* intensive
intenso *adj* intense; (*fuerte*) strong
intentar ⟨1a⟩ *v/t* try, attempt
intento *m* attempt, try; *Méx* (*intención*) aim
interacción *f* interaction
interactivo *adj* interactive
intercalar ⟨1a⟩ *v/t* insert
intercambiar ⟨1a⟩ *v/t* exchange, swap
intercambio *m* exchange, swap
interceder ⟨2a⟩ *v/i* intercede (**por** for)
interceptar ⟨1a⟩ *v/t tb* DEP intercept
intercesión *f* intercession
interés *m tb* COM interest; *desp* self-interest; **sin interés** interest free; **intereses** (*bienes*) interests
interesante *adj* interesting
interesar ⟨1a⟩ 1 *v/t* interest 2 *v/r* interesarse: **interesarse por** take an interest in
interface *m*, interfaz *f* INFOR interface
interferencia *f* interference
interferir ⟨3i⟩ 1 *v/t* interfere with 2 *v/i* interfere (**en** in)
interino *adj* substitute *atr*, replacement *atr*; (*provisional*) provisional, acting *atr*
interior 1 *adj* interior; *bolsillo* inside *atr*; COM, POL domestic 2 *m* interior; DEP inside-forward; **en su interior** *fig* inwardly
interiorista *m/f* interior designer
interjección *f* GRAM interjection
interlocutor *m*, interlocutora *f* speaker; **mi interlocutor** the person I was talking to
intermediario *m* COM intermediary, middle-man
intermedio 1 *adj nivel* intermediate; *tamaño* medium; *calidad* average, medium

2 *m* intermission

interminable *adj* interminable, endless

intermitente 1 *adj* intermittent **2** *m* AUTO turn signal, *Br* indicator

internacional *adj* international

internado *m* boarding school

internarse ⟨1a⟩ *v/r*: *internarse en* go into

internauta *m/f* INFOR Internet user, Net surfer

Internet *f* INFOR Internet

interno 1 *adj* internal; POL domestic, internal **2** *m*, -a *f* EDU boarder; (*preso*) inmate; MED intern, *Br* houseman

interpelar ⟨1a⟩ *v/t* question

interplanetario *adj* interplanetary

interpolar ⟨1a⟩ *v/t* insert, interpolate *fml*

interponerse ⟨2r⟩ *v/r* intervene

interpretación *f* interpretation; TEA performance (*de* as)

interpretar ⟨1a⟩ *v/t* interpret; TEA play

intérprete *m/f* interpreter

interrogación *f* interrogation; *signo de interrogación* question mark

interrogante 1 *adj* questioning **2** *m* (*also f*) question; *fig* question mark, doubt

interrogar ⟨1h⟩ *v/t* question; *de policía* interrogate, question

interrogatorio *m* questioning, interrogation

interrumpir ⟨3a⟩ **1** *v/t* interrupt; *servicio* suspend; *reunión, vacaciones* cut short, curtail **2** *v/i* interrupt

interrupción *f* interruption; *de servicio* suspension; *de reunión, vacaciones* curtailment; *sin interrupción* non-stop

interruptor *m* EL switch

intersección *f* intersection

intervalo *m tb* MÚS interval; (*espacio*) gap

intervención *f* intervention; *en debate, congreso* participation; *en película, espectáculo* appearance; MED operation

intervenir ⟨3s⟩ **1** *v/i* intervene; *en debate, congreso* take part, participate; *en película, espectáculo* appear **2** *v/t* TELEC tap; *contrabando* seize; MED operate on

intestino *m* intestine

intimar ⟨1a⟩ *v/i* (*hacerse amigos*) become friendly (*con* with); (*tratar*) mix (*con* with)

intimidad *f* intimacy; (*lo privado*) privacy; *en la intimidad* in private

intimidar ⟨1a⟩ *v/t* intimidate

íntimo *adj* intimate; (*privado*) private; *somos íntimos amigos* we're close friends

intolerable *adj* intolerable, unbearable

intolerante *adj* intolerant

intoxicación *f* poisoning

intranquilidad *f* unease; (*nerviosismo*) restlessness

intranquilo *adj* uneasy; (*nervioso*) restless

intransferible *adj* non-transferable

intransigente *adj* intransigent

intransitable *adj* impassable

intransitivo *adj* GRAM intransitive

intrascendente *adj* unimportant

intravenoso *adj* MED intravenous

intrépido *adj* intrepid

intriga *f* intrigue; *de novela* plot

intrigante 1 *adj* scheming; (*curioso*) intriguing **2** *m/f* schemer

intrigar ⟨1h⟩ **1** *v/t* (*interesar*) intrigue **2** *v/i* plot, scheme

intrincado *adj* intricate

intrínseco *adj* intrinsic

introducción *f* introduction; *acción de meter* insertion; INFOR input

introducir ⟨3o⟩ **1** *v/t* introduce; (*meter*) insert; INFOR input **2** *v/r*: *introducirse*: *introducirse en* get into; *introducirse en un mercado* gain access to *o* break into a market

intromisión *f* interference

introvertido *adj* introverted

intruso *m* intruder

intuición *f* intuition

intuir ⟨3g⟩ *v/t* sense

intuitivo *adj* intuitive

inundación *f* flood

inundadizo *adj* L.Am. prone to flooding

inundar ⟨1a⟩ *v/t* flood

inusitado *adj* unusual, uncommon

inusual *adj* unusual

inútil 1 *adj* useless; MIL unfit **2** *m/f*: *es un inútil* he's useless

inutilidad *f* uselessness

inutilizar ⟨1f⟩ *v/t*: *inutilizar algo* render

sth useless
inútilmente *adv* uselessly
invadir ⟨3a⟩ *v/t* invade; *de un sentimiento* overcome
invalidar ⟨1a⟩ *v/t* invalidate
invalidez *f* disability
inválido 1 *adj persona* disabled; *documento, billete* invalid 2 *m*, -a *f* disabled person
invasión *f* MIL invasion
invasor *m*, invasora *f* invader
invencible *adj* invincible; *miedo* insurmountable
invención *f* invention
inventar ⟨1a⟩ *v/t* invent
inventario *m* inventory
invento *m* invention
inventor *m* inventor
invernada *f Rpl* winter pasture
invernadero *m* greenhouse
invernal *adj* winter *atr*
inverosímil *adj* unlikely
inversión *f* reversal; COM investment
inverso *adj* opposite; *orden* reverse; *a la -a* the other way round
inversor *m*, inversora *f* investor
invertir ⟨3i⟩ *v/t* reverse; COM invest (*en* in)
invertebrado *m* invertebrate
investigación *f* investigation; EDU, TÉC research; *investigación y desarrollo* research and development
investigador *m*, investigadora *f* researcher
investigar ⟨1h⟩ *v/t* investigate; EDU, TÉC research
inviable *adj* nonviable
invidente *m/f* blind person
invierno *m* winter
inviolable *adj* inviolable
invisible *adj* invisible
invitación *f* invitation
invitado *m*, -a *f* guest
invitar ⟨1a⟩ *v/t* invite (*a* to); (*convidar*) treat (*a* to)
invocar ⟨1g⟩ *v/t* invoke
involucrar ⟨1a⟩ *v/t* involve (*en* in)
involuntario *adj* involuntary
invulnerable *adj* invulnerable
inyección *f* MED, AUTO injection

inyectar ⟨1a⟩ *v/t tb* TÉC inject
IPC *abr* (= *índice de precios al consumo*) CPI (= consumer price index), *Br* RPI (= retail price index)
ir ⟨3t⟩ 1 *v/i* go go (*a* to): *ir a pie* walk, go on foot; *ir en avión* fly; *¡ya voy!* I'm coming!; *ir a por algo* go and fetch sth; *ir bien / mal* go well / badly; *iba de amarillo / de uniforme* she was wearing yellow/a uniform; *van dos a dos* DEP the score is two all; *¿de qué va la película?* what's the movie about?; *¡qué va!* you must be joking! F; *¡vamos!* come on!; *¡vaya!* well! 2 *v/aux*: *va a llover* it's going to rain; *ya voy comprendiendo* I'm beginning to understand; *ir para viejo* be getting old 3 *v/r irse* go (away), leave; *¡vete!* go away!; *¡vámonos!* let's go
ira *f* anger
Irak Iraq, Irak
Irán Iran
iraní *m/f & adj* Iranian
iraquí *m/f & adj* Iraqi, Iraki
iris *m inv* ANAT iris; *arco iris* rainbow
Irlanda Ireland
irlandés 1 *adj* Irish 2 *m* Irishman
irlandesa *f* Irishwoman
ironía *f* irony
irónico *adj* ironic
irracional *adj tb* MAT irrational
irradiar ⟨1b⟩ *v/t* radiate; MED irradiate
irreal *adj* unreal
irrealizable *adj* unattainable; *proyecto* unfeasible
irreconciliable *adj* irreconcilable
irrecuperable *adj* irretrievable
irrefutable *adj* irrefutable
irregular *adj* irregular; *superficie* uneven
irregularidad *f* irregularity; *de superficie* unevenness
irrelevante *adj* irrelevant
irremediable *adj fig* irremediable
irreparable *adj* irreparable
irreprochable *adj* irreproachable
irresistible *adj* irresistible
irrespetuoso *adj* disrespectful
irresponsable *adj* irresponsible
irreverente *adj* irreverent
irreversible *adj* irreversible

irrevocable *adj* irrevocable
irrigar ⟨1h⟩ *v/t* MED, AGR irrigate
irrisorio *adj* laughable, derisory
irritación *f tb* MED irritation
irritante *adj tb* MED irritating
irritar ⟨1a⟩ **1** *v/t tb* MED irritate **2** *v/r* irritarse get irritated
irrompible *adj* unbreakable
irrumpir ⟨3a⟩ *v/i* burst in
irrupción *f*: **hacer irrupción en** burst into
isla *f* island
islám *m* Islam
islámico *adj* Islamic
islamismo *m* Islam
isleño **1** *adj* island *atr* **2** *m*, -a *f* islander
Israel Israel

israelí *m/f & adj* Israeli
Italia Italy
italiano **1** *adj* Italian **2** *m*, -a *f* Italian
itinerario *m* itinerary
ITV*abr Esp* (= **inspección técnica de vehículos**) *compulsory annual test of motor vehicles of a certain age, Br* MOT
IVA *abr* (= **impuesto sobre el valor añadido**) *sales tax, Br* VAT (= value-added tax)
izar ⟨1f⟩ *v/t* hoist
izdo., izda *abr* (= **izquierdo, izquierda**) l (= left)
izquierda *f tb* POL left; **por la izquierda** on the left
izquierdo *adj* left

J

jabalí *m* ZO wild boar
jabalina *f* javelin
jabón *m* soap; **jabón de afeitar** shaving soap
jabonera *f* soap dish
jabonoso *adj* soapy
jacinto *m* hyacinth
jactancia *f* boasting
jactancioso *adj* boastful
jactarse ⟨1a⟩ *v/r* boast (**de** about), brag (**de** about)
jacuzzi *m* jacuzzi®
jade *m* MIN jade
jadear ⟨1a⟩ *v/i* pant
jadeo *m* panting
jaguar *m* ZO jaguar
jalar ⟨1a⟩ **1** *v/t L.Am.* pull; *con esfuerza* haul; *(atraer)* attract; *Méx* F *(dar aventón)* give a ride *o Br* a lift to; **¿te jala el arte?** *Méx* do you feel drawn to art? **2** *v/i L.Am.* pull; *(trabajar mucho)* work hard; *Méx* F *(tener influencia)* have pull F; **jalar hacia** F head toward; **jalar para la casa** F clear off home F **3** *v/r* jalarse *Méx (irse)*

go, leave; F *(emborracharse)* get plastered F
jalea *f* jelly; **jalea real** royal jelly
jaleo *m (ruido)* racket, uproar; *(lío)* mess, muddle; **armar jaleo** F kick up a fuss F
jalón *m* pull; **dar un jalón a algo** pull sth; **de un jalón** *Méx fig* in one go
jalonar ⟨1a⟩ *v/t fig* mark out
Jamaica Jamaica
jamás *adv* never; **jamás te olvidaré** I'll never forget you; **¿viste jamás algo así?** did you ever see anything like it?; **nunca jamás** never ever; **por siempre jamás** for ever and ever
jamón *m* ham; **jamón de York** cooked ham; **jamón serrano** cured ham; **¡y un jamón!** F *(¡no!)* no way! F; *(¡bromeas!)* come off it! F
jangada *f S. Am.* F dirty trick
Japón Japan
japonés **1** *adj* Japanese **2** *m*, -esa *f* Japanese
jaque *m* check; **jaque mate** checkmate;

dar jaque a checkmate
jaqueca *f* MED migraine
jarabe *m* syrup; *Méx* type of folk dance
jardín *m* garden; **jardín botánico** botanic(al) gardens; **jardín de infancia** kindergarten
jardinería *f* gardening
jardinero *m*, -a *f* gardener
jarra *f* pitcher, *Br* jug; **en jarras** with hands on hips
jarro *m* pitcher, *Br* jug; **un jarro de agua fría** *fig* a total shock, a bombshell
jarrón *m* vase
jauja *f*: **¡esto es jauja!** this is the life!
jaula *f* cage
jauría *f* pack
jazmín *m* BOT jasmine
J.C. *abr* (= **Jesucristo**) J.C. (= Jesus Christ)
jefatura *f* headquarters; (*dirección*) leadership; **jefatura de policía** police headquarters
jefe *m*, -a *f de departamento, organización* head; (*superior*) boss; POL leader; *de tribu* chief; **jefe de cocina** (head) chef; **jefe de estado** head of state
jengibre *m* BOT ginger
jeque *m* sheik
jerarquía *f* hierarchy
jerez *m* sherry
jerga *f* jargon; (*argot*) slang
jeringa *f* MED syringe
jeringuilla *f* MED syringe; **jeringuilla desechable** *or* **de un solo uso** disposable syringe
jeroglífico *m* hieroglyphic; *rompecabezas* puzzle
jersey *m* sweater
Jesucristo *m* Jesus Christ
Jesús *m* Jesus; **¡Jesús!** good grief!; *por estornudo* bless you!
jet **1** *m* AVIA jet **2** *f*: **jet (set)** jet set
jeta *f* F face, mug F; **¡qué jeta tiene!** F he's got nerve! F, *Br* what a cheek! F
jibia *f* ZO cuttlefish
jícara *f Méx* drinking bowl
jícaro *m L.Am.* BOT calabash
jilguero *m* ZO goldfinch
jilote *m C.Am.*, *Méx* young corn

jineta *f* ZO civet
jinete *m* rider; *en carrera* jockey
jirafa *f* ZO giraffe
jitomate *m Méx* tomato
JJ.OO *abr* (= **Juegos Olímpicos**) Olympic Games
jocoso *adj* humorous, joking
joder ⟨2a⟩ **1** *v/i* V screw V, fuck V **2** *v/t* V (*follar*) screw V, fuck V; (*estropear*) screw up V, fuck up V; *L.Am.* F (*fastidiar*) annoy, irritate; **¡joder!** V fuck! V; **me jode un montón** V it really pisses me off P
jolgorio *m* F partying F
jolín *int* wow! F, jeez! F
jornada *f* (working) day; *distancia* day's journey; **media jornada** half-day; **jornada laboral** work day; **jornada partida** split shift
jornal *m* day's wage
jornalero *m*, -a *f* day labo(u)rer
joroba *f* hump; *fig* pain F, drag F
jorobado *adj* hump-backed; *fig* F in a bad way F
jorobar ⟨la⟩ *v/t* F (*molestar*) bug F; *planes* ruin
jorongo *m Méx* poncho
jota *f letter 'j'*; **no saber ni jota** F not have a clue F
joven **1** *adj* young **2** *m/f* young man; *mujer* young woman; **los jóvenes** young people
jovial *adj* cheerful
joya *f* jewel; *persona* gem; **joyas** *pl* jewelry *sg*, *Br* jewellery *sg*
joyería *f* jewelry store, *Br* jeweller's
joyero *m*, -a *f* jewel(l)er **2** *m* jewelry (*Br* jewellery) box
juanete *m* MED bunion
jubilación *f* retirement; **jubilación anticipada** early retirement
jubilado **1** *adj* retired **2** *m*, -a *f* retiree, *Br* pensioner
jubilar ⟨1a⟩ **1** *v/t* retire; (*desechar*) get rid of **2** *v/r* jubilarse retire; *C.Am.* play hooky F, play truant
júbilo *m* jubilation
jubiloso *adj* jubilant
judaísmo *m* Judaism
judía *f* BOT bean; **judía verde** green bean,

runner bean
judicial *adj* judicial
judío 1 *adj* Jewish **2** *m*, **-a** *f* Jew
judo *m* DEP judo
juego *m* game; *acción* play; *por dinero* gambling; *(conjunto de objetos)* set; *__juego de café__* coffee set; *__juego de manos__* conjuring trick; *__juego de mesa__* board game; *__juego de rol__* role-playing game; *__juego de sociedad__* game; *__Juegos Olímpicos__* Olympic Games; *__estar en juego__* fig be at stake; *__fuera de juego__* DEP offside; *__hacer juego con__* go with, match
juerga *f* F partying F; *__irse de juerga__* F go out on the town F, go out partying F
jueves *m inv* Thursday
juez *m/f* judge; *__juez de línea__* en fútbol assistant referee; *en fútbol americano* line judge
jueza *f* → **juez**
jugada *f* play, *Br* move; *en ajedrez* move; *__hacerle una mala jugada a alguien__* play a dirty trick on s.o.
jugador *m*, **jugadora** *f* player
jugar ⟨1o⟩ **1** *v/t* play **2** *v/i* play; *con dinero* gamble; *__jugar al baloncesto__* play basketball **3** *v/r* jugarse risk; *__jugarse la vida__* risk one's life; *__jugársela a alguien__* do the dirty on s.o. F
jugarreta *f* F dirty trick F
jugo *m* juice; *__sacar jugo a algo__* get the most out of sth
jugoso *adj tb fig* juicy
juguete *m* toy
juguetear ⟨1a⟩ *v/i* play
juicio *m* judg(e)ment; JUR trial; *(sensatez)* sense; *(cordura)* sanity; *__a mi juicio__* in my opinion; *__estar en su juicio__* be in one's right mind; *__perder el juicio__* lose one's mind
julio *m* July
junco *m* BOT reed
jungla *f* jungle

junio *m* June
júnior *adj tb* DEP junior
junta *f* POL (regional) government; *militar* junta; COM board; *(sesión)* meeting; TÉC joint; *__junta directiva__* board of directors; *__junta general anual__* annual general meeting
juntar ⟨1a⟩ **1** *v/t* put together; *gente* gather together; *bienes* collect, accumulate **2** *v/r* juntarse *(reunirse)* meet, assemble; *de pareja:* empezar a salir start going out; empezar a vivir juntos move in together; *de caminos, ríos* meet, join; *__juntarse con alguien__* socialmente mix with s.o.
junto 1 *adj* together **2** *prp:* *__junto a__* next to, near; *__junto con__* together with
juntura *f* TÉC joint
jupa *f* C.Am., *Méx fig* F head, nut F
jurado *m* JUR jury
juramento *m* oath; *__bajo juramento__* under oath
jurar ⟨1a⟩ *v/i* swear
jurídico *adj* legal
jurisdicción *f* jurisdiction
jurisprudencia *f* jurisprudence
justamente *adv* fairly; *(precisamente)* precisely
justicia *f* justice; *__la justicia__* (la ley) the law; *__hacer justicia a__* do justice to
justificable *adj* justifiable
justificación *f tb* TIP justification
justificante *m de pago* receipt; *de ausencia, propiedad* certificate
justificar ⟨1g⟩ *v/t tb* TIP justify; *mala conducta* justify, excuse
justo *adj* just, fair; *(exacto)* right, exact; *__lo justo__* just enough; *__¡justo!__* right!, exactly!
juvenil *adj* youthful
juventud *f* youth
juzgado 1 *part* → **juzgar 2** *m* court
juzgar ⟨1h⟩ *v/t* JUR try; *(valorar)* judge; *considerar* consider, judge; *__a juzgar por__* to judge by, judging by

K

kárate m DEP karate
kayak m DEP kayak
ketchup m ketchup
kg. abr (= **kilogramo**) kg (= kilogram)
kilo m kilo; fig F million
kilogramo m kilogram, Br kilogramme
kilómetro m kilometer, Br kilometre

kiosco m kiosk
kiwi m BOT kiwi (fruit)
kleenex® m kleenex, tissue
km. abr (= **kilómetro**) km (= kilometer)
km./h. abr (= **kilómetros por hora**) kph
 (= kilometers per hour)
kv. abr (= **kilovatio**) kw (= kilowatt)

L

la 1 art the 2 pron complemento directo sg
 her; a usted you; algo it; **la que está em-**
 barazada the one who is pregnant; **la**
 más grande the biggest (one); **dame la**
 roja give me the red one
laberinto m labyrinth, maze
labia f: **tener mucha labia** have the gift of
 the gab
labio m lip
labor f work; (tarea) task, job; **hacer labo-**
 res do needlework; **no estar por la labor**
 F not be enthusiastic about the idea
laborable adj: **día laborable** workday
laboral adj labo(u)r atr
laboratorio m laboratory, lab F
laborioso adj laborious; persona hard-
 working
labrador m farm labo(u)rer, farm worker
labranza f de la tierra cultivation
labrar ⟨1a⟩ v/t tierra work; piedra carve
labriego m farm labo(u)rer, farm worker
laca f lacquer; para el cabello hairspray;
 laca de uñas nail varnish o polish
lacear ⟨1a⟩ v/t Rpl lasso
lacio adj limp; pelo lank
lacónico adj laconic
lacra f scar; L.Am. (llaga) sore; **la corrup-**
 ción es una lacra social corruption is a

blot on society
lacre m sealing wax
lacrimógeno adj fig tear-jerking
lactancia f lactation
lácteo adj: **Vía Láctea** Milky Way; **pro-**
 ductos lácteos dairy products
ladear ⟨1a⟩ v/t tilt
ladera f slope
ladino 1 adj cunning, sly 2 m C.Am. Indian who has become absorbed into
 white culture
lado m side; (lugar) place; **al lado** nearby;
 al lado de beside, next to; **de lado** sideways; **ir por otro lado** go another way;
 por un lado ... por otro lado on the
 one hand ... on the other hand; **hacerse**
 a un lado tb fig stand aside
ladrar ⟨1a⟩ v/i bark
ladrillo m brick
ladrón m thief
lagartija f zo small lizard
lagarto m zo lizard
lago m lake
lágrima f tear
laguna f lagoon; fig gap
laico adj lay
lamentable adj deplorable
lamentablemente adv regretfully

lamentar ⟨1a⟩ **1** v/t regret, be sorry about; *muerte* mourn **2** v/r lamentarse complain (*de* about)

lamento m whimper; *por dolor* groan

lamer ⟨2a⟩ v/t lick

lámina f sheet

lámpara f lamp; *lámpara halógena* halogen lamp; *lámpara de pie* floor lamp, Br standard lamp

lamparón m F grease mark

lana f wool; *Méx* P dough F; *pura lana virgen* pure new wool

lancha f launch; *lancha fueraborda* outboard

langosta f zo *insecto* locust; *crustáceo* spiny lobster

langostino m zo king prawn

languidecer ⟨2d⟩ v/i languish

lánguido adj languid

lanza f lance

lanzadera f shuttle; *lanzadera espacial* space shuttle

lanzado **1** adj fig go-ahead; *es muy lanzado con las chicas* he's not shy with girls **2** part → lanzar

lanzamiento m MIL, COM launch; *lanzamiento de disco / de martillo* discus / hammer (throw); *lanzamiento de peso* shot put

lanzar ⟨1f⟩ **1** v/t throw; *cohete, producto* launch; *bomba* drop **2** v/r lanzarse throw o.s. (*en* into); (*precipitarse*) pounce (*sobre* on); *lanzarse a hacer algo* rush into doing sth

lapa f zo limpet

lapicera f *Rpl, Chi* (ballpoint) pen; *lapicera fuente* L.Am. fountain pen

lapicero m automatic pencil, Br propelling pencil

lápida f memorial stone

lapidario adj memorable

lápiz m pencil; *lápiz de ojos* eyeliner; *lápiz labial or de labios* lipstick; *lápiz óptico* light pen

lapso m *de tiempo* space, period

lapsus m inv slip; *tener un lapsus* have a momentary lapse

larga f: *poner la (s) larga (s)* put the headlights on full beam; *dar largas a al-*guien F put s.o. off

largar ⟨1h⟩ **1** v/t drive away **2** v/r largarse F clear off o out F

largo **1** adj long; *persona* tall; *a la -a* in the long run; *a lo largo del día* throughout the day; *a lo largo de la calle* along the street; *¡largo!* F scram! F; *esto va para largo* this will take some time; *pasar de largo* go (straight) past **2** m length

largometraje m feature film

larguero m DEP crossbar

laringe f larynx

laringitis f MED laryngitis

larva f zo larva

las **1** art fpl the **2** pron complemento directo pl them; *a ustedes* you; *llévate las que quieras* take whichever ones you want; *las de ...* those of ...; *las de Juan* Juan's; *las que llevan falda* the ones o those that are wearing dresses

lasaña f GASTR lasagne

lascivo adj lewd

láser m laser; *rayo láser* laser beam

lástima f pity, shame; *me da lástima no usarlo* it's a shame o pity not to use it; *¡qué lástima!* what a pity o shame!

lastimar ⟨1a⟩ **1** v/t (*herir*) hurt **2** v/r lastimarse hurt o.s.

lastimoso adj pitiful; (*deplorable*) shameful

lastre m ballast; fig burden

lata f can, Br tb tin; fig F drag F, pain F; *dar la lata* F be a drag F o a pain F

latente adj latent

lateral **1** adj side atr; *cuestiones laterales* side issues **2** m DEP: *lateral derecho / izquierdo* right / left back

latería f L.Am. tin works

latero m,-a f L.Am. tinsmith

latido m beat

latifundio m large estate

latigazo m lash; (*chasquido*) crack

látigo m whip

latín m Latin

latino adj Latin

Latinoamérica Latin America

latinoamericano **1** adj Latin American **2** m, -a f Latin American

latir ⟨3a⟩ v/i beat

latitud f GEOG latitude

latón m brass

laucha f S. Am. mouse

laurel m BOT laurel; *dormirse en los laureles* fig rest on one's laurels

lava f lava

lavable adj washable

lavabo m washbowl

lavada f L.Am. wash

lavado m washing; *lavado de cerebro* fig brainwashing

lavadora f washing machine

lavamanos m inv L.Am. → *lavabo*

lavanda f BOT lavender

lavandería f laundry

lavaplatos m inv dishwasher; L.Am. sink

lavar ⟨1a⟩ 1 v/t wash; *lavar los platos* wash the dishes; *lavar la ropa* do the laundry, Br tb do the washing; *lavar en seco* dry-clean 2 v/i (lavar los platos) do the dishes; *de detergente* clean 3 v/r *lavarse* wash up, Br have a wash; *lavarse los dientes* brush one's teeth; *lavarse las manos* wash one's hands; *yo me lavo las manos* fig I wash my hands of it

lavarropas m inv L.Am. washing machine

lavavajillas m inv líquido dishwashing liquid, Br washing-up liquid; *electrodoméstico* dishwasher

laxante m/adj MED laxative

laxo adj relaxed; (poco estricto) lax

lazada f bow

lazarillo m guide; *perro lazarillo* seeing eye dog, Br guide dog

lazo m knot; *de adorno* bow; *para atrapar animales* lasso

le pron sg complemento indirecto (to) him; (a ella) (to) her; (a usted) (to) you; (a algo) (to) it; complemento directo him; (a usted) you

leal adj loyal

lealtad f loyalty

lección f lesson; *esto le servirá de lección* that will teach him a lesson

lechar ⟨1a⟩ v/t L.Am. (ordeñar) milk

leche f milk; *leche condensada* condensed milk; *leche entera* whole milk; *leche en polvo* powdered milk; *estar de mala leche* P be in a foul mood; *tener mala leche* P be out to make trouble

lechería f dairy

lechero 1 adj dairy atr 2 m milkman

lecho m tb de río bed

lechón m suckling pig

lechuga f lettuce; *ser más fresco que una lechuga* F have a lot of nerve

lechuza f zo barn-owl; Cuba, Méx P hooker F

lectivo adj: *día lectivo* school day

lector m, ~a f reader

lectura f reading

leer ⟨2e⟩ v/t read

legado m legacy; persona legate

legal adj legal; fig F persona great F, terrific F

legalidad f legality

legalizar ⟨1f⟩ v/t legalize

legaña f: *tener legañas en los ojos* have sleep in one's eyes

legar ⟨1h⟩ v/t leave

legendario adj legendary

legible adj legible

legión f legion

legislación f legislation

legislar ⟨1a⟩ v/i legislate

legislativo adj legislative

legislatura f cuerpo legislature; periodo term of office

legitimar ⟨1a⟩ v/t justify; documento authenticate

legítimo adj legitimate; (verdadero) authentic

lego adj lay atr; fig ignorant

legua f: *se ve a la legua* fig F you can see it a mile off F; *hecho* it's blindingly obvious F

legumbre f BOT pulse

leída f L.Am. reading

lejanía f distance; *en la lejanía* in the distance

lejano adj distant

lejía f bleach

lejos 1 adv far, far away; *Navidad queda lejos* Christmas is a long way off; *a lo lejos* in the distance; *ir demasiado lejos* fig go too far, overstep the mark; *llegar lejos* fig go far 2 prp: *lejos de* far from

lele adj C.Am. stupid

lema m slogan

lencería f lingerie

lengua f tongue; **lengua materna** mother tongue; **con la lengua fuera** fig with one's tongue hanging out; **irse de la lengua** let the cat out of the bag; **sacar la lengua a alguien** stick one's tongue out at s.o.; **lo tengo en la punta de la lengua** it's on the tip of my tongue

lenguado m zo sole

lenguaje m language; **lenguaje de programación** INFOR programming language

lenguaraz adj foul-mouthed

lengüeta 1 f de zapato tongue **2** adj: **ser lengüeta** S. Am. F be a gossip

lenitivo m balm

lente f lens; **lentes de contacto** contact lenses, contacts

lentes mpl L.Am. glasses

lenteja f BOT lentil

lentejuela f sequin

lentillas fpl contact lenses

lentitud f slowness

lento adj slow; **a fuego lento** on a low heat

leña f (fire)wood; **echar leña al fuego** fig add fuel to the fire

leñador m woodcutter

leño m log

Leo m/f inv ASTR Leo

león m zo lion; L.Am. puma; **león marino** sealion

leona f lioness

leonera f lion's den; jaula lion's cage; Rpl, Chi fig F habitación desordenada etc pigsty F; L.Am. F para prisioneros bullpen F, Br communal cell for holding prisoners temporarily

leopardo m zo leopard

leotardo m de gimnasta leotard; **leotardos** tights, Br heavy tights

lépero adj C.Am., Méx coarse

lerdo adj (torpe) slow(-witted)

les pron pl complemento indirecto (to) them; (a ustedes) (to) you; complemento directo them; (a ustedes) you

lesbiana f lesbian

lesión f injury

lesionado adj injured

lesionar ⟨1a⟩ v/t injure

letal adj lethal

letanía f litany

letárgico adj lethargic

letra f letter; de canción lyrics pl; **letra de cambio** COM bill of exchange; **letra de imprenta** block capital; **letra mayúscula** capital letter; **al pie de la letra** word for word

letrero m sign

letrina f latrine

leucemia f MED leuk(a)emia

levadura f yeast

levantamiento m raising; (rebelión) rising; de embargo lifting

levantar ⟨1a⟩ **1** v/t raise; bulto lift (up); del suelo pick up; edificio, estatua put up, erect; embargo lift; **levantar sospechas** arouse suspicion; **¡levanta los ánimos!** cheer up!; **levantar la voz** raise one's voice **2** v/r **levantarse** get up; (ponerse de pie) stand up; de un edificio, una montaña rise; en rebelión rise up

levante m east

levar ⟨1a⟩ v/t: **levar anclas** weigh anchor

leve adj slight; sonrisa faint

levedad f lightness

levitar ⟨1a⟩ v/i levitate

léxico m lexicon

ley f law; **con todas las de la ley** fairly and squarely

leyenda f legend

leyendo vb → **leer**

leyó vb → **leer**

liana f BOT liana, creeper

liar ⟨1c⟩ **1** v/t tie (up); en papel wrap (up); cigarrillo roll; persona confuse **2** v/r **liarse** de una persona get confused; **liarse a hacer algo** get tied up doing sth; **liarse con alguien** F get involved with s.o.

Líbano Lebanon

libélula f zo dragonfly

liberación f release; de un país liberation

liberal adj liberal

liberalización f liberalization

liberalizar ⟨1f⟩ v/t liberalize

liberar ⟨1a⟩ **1** v/t (set) free, release; país

liberate; *energia* release **2** *v/r* **liberarse**: **liberarse de algo** free o.s. of sth

libertad *f* freedom, liberty; **libertad bajo fianza** JUR bail; **libertad condicional** JUR probation; **dejar a alguien en libertad** release s.o., let s.o. go

libertinaje *m* licentiousness

Libia Libya

líbido *f* libido

libio(-a) *m/f* & *adj* Libyan

libra *f* pound; **libra esterlina** pound (sterling)

Libra *m/f inv* ASTR Libra

librar ⟨1a⟩ **1** *v/t* free (**de** from); *cheque* draw; *batalla* fight **2** *v/i*: **libro los lunes** I have Mondays off **3** *v/r* **librarse**: **librarse de algo** get out of sth; **de buena nos hemos librado** F that was lucky

libre *adj* free; *tiempo* spare, free; **eres libre de** you're free to

librecambio *m* free trade

librera *f* bookseller

librería *f* book store

librero *m* bookseller; *L.Am. mueble* bookcase

libreta *f* notebook; **libreta de ahorros** bankbook, passbook

libro *m* book; **libro de bolsillo** paperback (book); **libro de cocina** cookbook, cookery book; **libro de familia** *booklet recording family births, marriages and deaths*; **libro de reclamaciones** complaints book

licencia *f* permit, license, *Br* licence; (*permiso*) permission; MIL leave; **licencia (de manejar or conducir)** *L.Am.* driver's license, *Br* driving licence; **tomarse demasiadas licencias** take liberties

licenciado *m*, **-a** *f* graduate

licenciar ⟨1b⟩ **1** *v/t* MIL discharge **2** *v/r* **licenciarse** graduate; MIL be discharged

licenciatura *f* EDU degree

liceo *m L.Am.* high school, *Br* secondary school

licitación *f L.Am.* bidding

licitador *m*, **licitadora** *f L.Am.* bidder

licitar ⟨1a⟩ *v/t L.Am. en subasta* bid for

lícito *adj* legal; (*razonable*) fair, reasonable

licor *m* liquor, *Br* spirits *pl*

licuado *m Méx* fruit milkshake

licuadora *f* blender

licuar ⟨1d⟩ *v/t* blend, liquidize

líder 1 *m/f* leader **2** *adj* leading

liderar ⟨1a⟩ *v/t* lead

liderazgo *m* leadership

lidia *f* bullfighting

lidiar ⟨1b⟩ **1** *v/i fig* do battle, struggle **2** *v/t toro* fight

liebre *f* zo hare

lienzo *m* canvas

liga *f* POL, DEP league; *de medias* garter

ligamento *m* ANAT ligament

ligar ⟨1h⟩ **1** *v/t* bind; (*atar*) tie **2** *v/i*: **ligar con** F pick up F

ligereza *f* lightness; (*rapidez*) speed; *de movimiento* agility; *de carácter* shallowness, superficiality

ligero 1 *adj* (*de poco peso*) light; (*rápido*) rapid, quick; *movimiento* agile, nimble; (*leve*) slight; **ligero de ropa** scantily clad; **a la -a** (*sin pensar*) lightly, casually; **tomar algo a la -a** not take sth seriously **2** *adv* quickly

ligón *m* F: **es un ligón** he's a real Don Juan F

ligue *m* F: **estar de ligue** be on the pick-up F, *Br* be on the pull F

liguero *m* garter belt, *Br* suspender belt

lija *f*: **papel de lija** sandpaper

lijar ⟨1a⟩ *v/t* sand

lila *f* BOT lilac

lima *f* file; BOT lime; **lima de uñas** nail file

limar ⟨1a⟩ *v/t* file; *fig* polish

limitado 1 *adj* limited **2** *part* → **limitar**

limitar ⟨1a⟩ **1** *v/t* limit **2** *v/i*: **limitar con** border on **3** *v/r* **limitarse** limit *o* restrict o.s. (**a** to)

límite 1 *m* limit; (*línea de separación*) boundary; **límite de velocidad** speed limit **2** *adj*: **situación límite** life-threatening situation

limítrofe *adj* neighbo(u)ring

limón *m* lemon

limonada *f* lemonade

limosna *f*: **una limosna, por favor** can you spare some change?

limpiabotas *m/f inv* bootblack

limpiacristales *m inv* window cleaner

limpiada *f L.Am.* clean

limpiamanos *m inv L.Am.* hand towel

limpiaparabrisas *m inv* AUTO windshield wiper, *Br* windscreen wiper

limpiar ⟨1b⟩ *v/t* clean; *con un trapo* wipe; *fig* clean up; **limpiar a alguien** F clean s.o. out F

limpieza *f estado* cleanliness; *acto* cleaning; **limpieza general** spring cleaning; **limpieza en seco** dry-cleaning; **hacer la limpieza** do the cleaning

limpio *adj* neat, tidy; *político* honest; **gana $5.000 limpios al mes** he takes home $5,000 a month; **quedarse limpio** *S. Am.* F be broke F; **sacar algo en limpio** *fig* make sense of sth

limusina *f* limousine

linaje *m* lineage

lince *m* zo lynx; **ojos** *or* **vista de lince** *fig* eyes like a hawk

linchar ⟨1a⟩ *v/t* lynch

lindar ⟨1a⟩ *v/i:* **lindar con algo** adjoin sth; *fig* border on sth

lindo *adj* lovely; **de lo lindo** a lot, a great deal

línea *f* line; **línea aérea** airline; **mantener la línea** watch one's figure; **de primera línea** *fig* first-rate; **tecnología de primera línea** state-of-the art technology; **entre líneas** *fig* between the lines

lineal *adj* linear

linfático *adj* lymphatic

lingote *m* ingot; **lingote de oro** gold bar

lingüista *m/f* linguist

lingüística *f* linguistics

lingüístico *adj* linguistic

linier *m* DEP assistant referee, linesman

lino *m* linen; BOT flax

linterna *f* flashlight, *Br* torch

lío *m* bundle; F *(desorden)* mess; F *(jaleo)* fuss; **lío amoroso** F affair; **estar hecho un lío** be all confused; **hacerse un lío** get into a muddle; **meterse en líos** get into trouble

liposucción *f* MED liposuction

lipotimia *f* MED blackout

liquen *m* BOT lichen

liquidación *f* COM *de cuenta, deuda* settlement; *de negocio* liquidation; **liquidación total** clearance sale

liquidar ⟨1a⟩ *v/t cuenta, deuda* settle; COM *negocio* wind up, liquidate; *existencias* sell off; F *(matar)* liquidate F, bump off F

liquidez *f* COM liquidity

líquido 1 *adj* liquid; COM net **2** *m* liquid

lira *f* lira

lírico *adj* lyrical

lirio *m* BOT lily

lirón *m* zo dormouse; **dormir como un lirón** *fig* F sleep like a log

lisiado 1 *adj* crippled **2** *m* cripple

liso *adj* smooth; *terreno* flat; *pelo* straight; *(sin adornos)* plain; **-a y llanamente** plainly and simply

lisonja *f* flattery

lista *f* list; **lista de boda** wedding list; **lista de espera** waiting list; **pasar lista** take the roll call, *Br* call the register

listado *m* INFOR printout

listín *m:* **listín (telefónico)** phone book

listo *adj (inteligente)* clever; *(preparado)* ready; **pasarse de listo** F try to be too smart F

listón *m de madera* strip; DEP bar; **poner el listón muy alto** *fig* set very high standards

lisura *f Rpl, Pe* curse, swearword

litera *f* bunk; *de tren* couchette

literal *adj* literal

literario *adj* literary

literatura *f* literature

litigante *m/f* & *adj* JUR litigant

litigar ⟨1h⟩ *v/i* JUR go to litigation

litigio *m* lawsuit

litografía *f* lithography

litoral 1 *adj* coastal **2** *m* coast

litro *m* liter, *Br* litre

liturgia *f* REL liturgy

liviano *adj* light; *(de poca importancia)* trivial

lívido *adj* pale

llaga *f* ulcer; **poner** *or* **meter el dedo en la llaga** *fig* put one's finger on it

llama *f* flame; zo llama

llamada *f* call; *en una puerta* knock; *en*

timbre ring; **llamada a cobro revertido** collect call; **llamada de auxilio** distress call

llamado *m L.Am.* call

llamador *m* (door) knocker

llamamiento *m* call; **hacer un llamamiento a algo** call for sth

llamar ⟨1a⟩ **1** *v/t* call; TELEC call, *Br tb* ring **2** *v/i* TELEC call, *Br tb* ring; **llamar a la puerta** knock at the door; **con timbre** ring the bell; **el fútbol no me llama nada** football doesn't appeal to me in the slightest **3** *v/r* **llamarse** be called; **¿cómo te llamas?** what's your name?

llamarada *f* flare-up

llamativo *adj* eyecatching; *color* loud

llamón *adj Méx* moaning

llano 1 *adj terreno* level; *trato* natural; *persona* unassuming **2** *m* flat ground

llanta *f* wheel rim; *C.Am., Méx* (*neumático*) tire, *Br* tyre

llanto *m* sobbing

llanura *f* plain

llave *f* key; *para tuerca* wrench, *Br tb* spanner; **llave de contacto** AUTO ignition key; **llave inglesa** TÉC monkey wrench; **llave de paso** stop cock; **llave en mano** available for immediate occupancy; **bajo llave** under lock and key; **cerrar con llave** lock

llavero *m* key ring

llegada *f* arrival

llegar ⟨1h⟩ **1** *v/i* arrive; (*alcanzar*) reach; **la comida no llegó para todos** there wasn't enough food for everyone; **me llega hasta las rodillas** it comes down to my knees; **el agua me llegaba a la cintura** the water came up to my waist; **llegar a saber** find out; **llegar a ser** get to be; **llegar a viejo** live to a ripe old age **2** *v/r* **llegarse: llégate al vecino** F run over to the neighbo(u)r's

llenar ⟨1a⟩ **1** *v/t* fill; *impreso* fill out *o* in **2** *v/i* be filling **3** *v/r* **llenarse** fill up; **me he llenado** I have had enough (to eat)

lleno *adj* full (**de** of); *pared* covered (**de** with); **de lleno** fully

llevadero *adj* bearable

llevar ⟨1a⟩ **1** *v/t* take; *ropa, gafas* wear; *rit-*

mo keep up; **llevar a alguien en coche** drive s.o., take s.o. in the car; **llevar dinero encima** carry money; **llevar las de perder** be likely to lose; **me lleva dos años** he's two years older than me; **llevo ocho días aquí** I've been here a week; **llevo una hora esperando** I've been waiting for an hour **2** *v/i* lead (**a** to) **3** *v/r* **llevarse** take; *susto, sorpresa* get; **llevarse bien / mal** get on well / badly; **se lleva el color rojo** red is fashionable

llorar ⟨1a⟩ *v/i* cry, weep

lloriquear ⟨1a⟩ *v/i* snivel, whine

lloro *m* weeping, crying

llorón 1 *adj:* **ser llorón** be a crybaby F **2** *m* F crybaby F

llovedera *f L.Am.,* **llovedero** *m L.Am.* rainy season

llover ⟨2h⟩ *v/i* rain; **llueve** it is raining

llovizna *f* drizzle

lloviznar ⟨1a⟩ *v/i* drizzle

llueve *vb* → **llover**

lluvia *f* rain; *Rpl* (*ducha*) shower; **lluvia ácida** acid rain

lluvioso *adj* rainy

lo 1 *art sg* the; **lo bueno** the good thing; **no sabes lo difícil que es** you don't know how difficult it is **2** *pron sg:* **a él** him; **a usted** you; **algo** it; **lo sé** I know **3** *pron rel sg:* **lo que** what; **lo cual** which

loable *adj* praiseworthy, laudable

lobo *m* wolf; **lobo marino** seal; **lobo de mar** *fig* sea dog

lóbrego *adj* gloomy

lóbulo *m* lobe; **lóbulo de la oreja** earlobe

loca *f* madwoman

locador *m S. Am.* landlord

local 1 *adj* local **2** *m* premises *pl*; **local comercial** commercial premises *pl*

localidad *f* town; TEA seat

localización *f* location

localizar ⟨1f⟩ *v/t* locate; *incendio* contain, bring under control

loción *f* lotion

loco 1 *adj* mad, crazy; **a lo loco** F (*sin pensar*) hastily; **es para volverse loco** it's enough to drive you mad *o* crazy **2** *m* madman

locomoción *f* locomotion; **medio de lo-**

L

comoción means of transport

locomotora f locomotive

locro m S. Am. stew of meat, corn and potatoes

locuaz adj talkative, loquacious fml

locución f phrase

locura f madness; **es una locura** it's madness

locutor m, **locutora** f RAD, TV presenter

locutorio m TELEC phone booth

lodazal m quagmire

lodo m mud

lógica f logic

lógico adj logical

logística f logistics

logopeda m/f speech therapist

logotipo m logo

logrado adj excellent

lograr ⟨1a⟩ v/t achieve; (obtener) obtain; **lograr hacer algo** manage to do sth; **lograr que alguien haga algo** (manage to) get s.o. to do sth

logrero m L.Am. F profiteer

logro m achievement

loma f L.Am. small hill

lombriz f: **lombriz de tierra** earthworm

lomo m back; GASTR loin; **a lomos de burro** on a donkey

lona f canvas

loncha f slice

lonche m L.Am. afternoon snack

lonchería f L.Am. diner, luncheonette

londinense 1 adj London atr **2** m/f Londoner

Londres London

longaniza f type of dried sausage

longevidad f longevity

longevo adj long-lived

longitud f longitude; (largo) length

longitudinal adj longitudinal

lonja f de pescado fish market; (loncha) slice

loquera f L.Am. F shrink F; enfermera psychiatric nurse

loquero m L.Am. F persona shrink F; enfermero psychiatric nurse; (manicomio) mental hospital, funny farm F

loro m parrot; **estar al loro** F (enterado) be clued up F, be on the ball F

los mpl **1** art the **2** pron complemento directo pl them; a ustedes you; **llévate los que quieras** take whichever ones you want; **los de …** those of …; **los de Juan** Juan's; **los que juegan** the ones o those that are playing

losa f flagstone

lote m en reparto share, part; L.Am. (solar) lot

lotería f lottery

loto 1 m BOT lotus **2** f F lottery

loza f china

lozano adj healthy-looking

lubina f ZO sea bass

lubri(fi)cación f lubrication

lubri(fi)cante 1 adj lubricating **2** m lubricant

lubri(fi)car ⟨1g⟩ v/t lubricate

lucero m bright star; (Venus) Venus

lucha f fight, struggle; DEP wrestling; **lucha libre** DEP all-in wrestling

luchador 1 adj espíritu fighting **2** m, luchadora f fighter

luchar ⟨1a⟩ v/i fight (por for)

lúcido adj lucid, clear

luciérnaga f ZO glow-worm

lucimiento m (brillo) splendo(u)r; **le ofrece oportunidades de lucimiento** it gives him a chance to shine

lucio m ZO pike

lucir ⟨3f⟩ **1** v/i shine; L.Am. (verse bien) look good **2** v/t ropa, joya wear **3** v/r lucirse tb irón excel o.s., surpass o.s.

lucrativo adj lucrative

lucro m profit; **afán de lucro** profit-making; **sin ánimo de lucro** non-profit (making), not-for-profit

ludopatía f compulsive gambling

luego 1 adv (después) later; en orden, espacio then; L.Am. (en seguida) right now; **luego luego** Méx straight away; **¡desde luego!** of course!; **¡hasta luego!** see you (later) **2** conj therefore; **luego que** L.Am. after

lugar m place; **lugar común** cliché; **en lugar de** instead of; **en primer lugar** in the first place, first(ly); **fuera de lugar** out of place; **yo en tu lugar** if I were you, (if I were) in your place; **dar lugar a** give rise to

to; **tener lugar** take place
lúgubre *adj* gloomy
lujo *m* luxury
lujoso *adj* luxurious
lujuria *f* lust
lujurioso *adj* lecherous
lumbago *m* MED lumbago
lumbre *f* fire
lumbrera *f* genius
luminoso *adj* luminous; *lámpara, habitación* bright
luna *f* moon; *de tienda* window; *de vehículo* windshield, *Br* windscreen; **luna de miel** honeymoon; **luna llena / nueva** full / new moon; **media luna** *L.Am.* GASTR croissant; **estar en la luna** F have one's head in the clouds F
lunar **1** *adj* lunar **2** *m en la piel* mole; **de lunares** spotted, polka-dot
lunático *adj* lunatic
lunes *m inv* Monday
luneta *f*: **luneta térmica** AUTO heated windshield, *Br* heated windscreen
lunfardo *m Arg* slang used in Buenos Aires

lupa *f* magnifying glass; **mirar algo con lupa** *fig* go through sth with a fine tooth-comb
lustrabotas *m/f inv L.Am.* bootblack
lustrador *m*, **lustradora** *f L.Am.* bootblack
lustrar ⟨1a⟩ *v/t* polish
lustre *m* shine; *fig* luster, *Br* lustre; **dar lustre a** *fig* give added luster (*Br* lustre) to
lustro *m* period of five years
lustroso *adj* shiny
luto *m* mourning; **estar de luto por alguien** be in mourning for s.o.
luxación *f* MED dislocation
luz *f* light; **luz trasera** AUTO rear light; **luces de carretera** *or* **largas** AUTO full *o* main beam headlights; **luces de cruce** *or* **cortas** AUTO dipped headlights; **luz verde** *tb fig* green light; **arrojar luz sobre algo** *fig* shed light on s.th.; **dar a luz** give birth to; **salir a la luz** *fig* come to light; **a todas luces** evidently, clearly; **de pocas luces** *fig* F dim F, not very bright

M

m *abr* (= **metro**) m (= meter); (= **minuto**) m (= minute)
macabro **1** *adj* macabre **2** *m*, **-a** *f* ghoul
macaco *m* ZO macaque
macana *f L.Am.* billyclub, *Br* truncheon; F (*mentira*) lie, fib F; **hizo / dijo una macana** he did / said something stupid; **¡qué macana!** *Rpl* P what a drag!
macanear ⟨1a⟩ *v/t L.Am.* (*aporrear*) beat
macanudo *S. Am.* F great F, fantastic F
macarra **1** *m* P pimp **2** *adj* F: **ser macarra** be a bastard P
macarrones *mpl* macaroni *sg*
macedonia *f*: **macedonia de frutas** fruit salad

macerar ⟨1a⟩ *v/t* GASTR soak
maceta *f* flowerpot
macetero *m* flowerpot holder; *L.Am.* flowerpot
machacar ⟨1g⟩ *v/t* crush; *fig* thrash
machete *m* machete
machismo *m* male chauvinism
machista **1** *adj* sexist **2** *m* sexist, male chauvinist
macho **1** *adj* male; (*varonil*) tough; *desp* macho **2** *m* male; *apelativo* F man F, *Br* mate F; *L.Am.* (*plátano*) banana
macizo **1** *adj* solid; **estar macizo** F be a dish F **2** *m* GEOG massif; **macizo de flores** flower bed

macuto *m* backpack

madeja *f* hank

madera *f* wood; **tener madera de** have the makings of

maderera *f* timber merchant

madero *m* P cop P

madrastra *f* step-mother

madre **1** *f* mother; **madre soltera** single mother; **dar en la madre a alguien** F hit s..o. where it hurts; **¡me vale madre!** *Méx* V I don't give a fuck! V **2** *adj Méx*, *C.Am.* F great F, fantastic

madreselva *f* BOT honeysuckle

Madrid Madrid

madriguera *f* (*agujero*) burrow; (*guarida*) *tb fig* den

madrileño **1** *adj* of / from Madrid, Madrid *atr* **2** *m*, -a *f* native of Madrid

madrina *f* godmother

madrugada *f* early morning; (*amanecer*) dawn; **de madrugada** in the small hours

madrugador *m*, madrugadora *f* early riser

madrugar ⟨1h⟩ *v/i L.Am.* (*quedar despierto*) stay up till the small hours; (*levantarse temprano*) get up early

madurar ⟨1a⟩ **1** *v/t fig: idea* think through **2** *v/i de persona* mature; *de fruta* ripen

madurez *f mental* maturity; *edad* middle age; *de fruta* ripeness

maduro *adj mentalmente* mature; *de edad* middle-aged; *fruta* ripe

maestría *f* mastery; *Méx* EDU master's (degree)

maestro **1** *adj* master *atr* **2** *m*, -a *f* EDU teacher; MÚS maestro

mafia *f* mafia

mafioso **1** *adj* mafia *atr* **2** *m* mafioso, gangster

magdalena *f* cupcake, *Br tb* fairy cake

magia *f tb fig* magic

mágico *adj* magic

magisterio *m* teaching profession

magistrado *m* judge

magistral *adj* masterly

magnanimidad *f* magnanimity

magnánimo *adj* magnanimous

magnate *m* magnate, tycoon

magnesio *m* magnesium

magnético *adj* magnetic

magnetofón *m* tape recorder

magnífico *adj* wonderful, magnificent

magnitud *f* magnitude

magnolia *f* BOT magnolia

mago *m tb fig* magician; **los Reyes Magos** the Three Wise Men, the Three Kings

magrear ⟨1a⟩ *v/t* F feel up F

Magreb Maghreb

magro *adj carne* lean

magulladura *f* bruise

magullar ⟨1a⟩ *v/t* bruise

magullón *m L.Am.* bruise

mahometano **1** *adj* Muslim **2** *m*, -a *f* Muslim

mahonesa *f* mayonnaise

maillot *m* DEP jersey

maíz *m* corn

majada *f* CSur flock of sheep

majaderear ⟨1a⟩ *L.Am.* F **1** *v/t* bug F **2** *v/i* keep going on F

majadería *f: decir / hacer una majadería* say / do something stupid

majadero F **1** *adj* idiotic, stupid **2** *m*, -a *f* idiot

majareta *adj* nutty F, screwy F

majestad *f* majesty

majestuoso *adj* majestic

majo *adj* F nice; (*bonito*) pretty

mal **1** *adj* → **malo 2** *adv* badly; **mal que bien** one way or the other; **¡menos mal!** thank goodness!; **ponerse a mal con alguien** fall out with s.o.; **tomarse algo a mal** take sth badly **3** *m* MED illness; **el mal menor** the lesser of two evils

malabar *m/adj:* (*juegos*) **-es** *pl* juggling *sg*

malabarista *m/f* juggler

malacrianza *f L.Am.* rudeness

malaria *f* MED malaria

malcriadez *f L.Am.* bad upbringing

malcriado *adj* spoilt

malcrianza *f L.Am.* rudeness

malcriar ⟨1c⟩ *v/t* spoil

maldad *f* evil; **es una maldad hacer eso** it's a wicked thing to do

maldecir ⟨3p⟩ **1** *v/i* curse; **maldecir de alguien** speak ill of s.o. **2** *v/t* curse maldición f curse

maldito adj F damn F; **¡-a sea!** (god)damn it!

maleante m/f & adj criminal

malecón m breakwater

maleducado adj rude, bad-mannered

maleficio m curse

maléfico adj evil

malentendido m misunderstanding

malestar m MED discomfort; *social* unrest

maleta f bag, suitcase; *L.Am.* AUTO trunk, *Br* boot; **hacer la maleta** pack one's bags

maletero m trunk, *Br* boot

maletín m briefcase

malévolo adj malevolent

maleza f undergrowth

malformación f MED malformation

malgastar ⟨1a⟩ v/t waste

malgenioso adj Méx bad-tempered

malhablado adj foul-mouthed

malhechor m, malhechora f criminal

malherir ⟨3i⟩ v/t hurt badly

malhumorado adj bad-tempered

malicia f (mala intención) malice; (astucia) cunning, slyness; **no tener malicia** F be very naive

malicioso adj (malintencionado) malicious; (astuto) cunning, sly

maligno adj harmful; MED malignant

malinchismo m Méx treason

malla f mesh; *Rpl* swimsuit

malo 1 adj bad; calidad poor; (enfermo) sick, ill; **por las buenas o por las -as** whether he / she etc likes it or not; **por las -as** by force; **lo malo es que** unfortunately; **ponerse malo** fall ill 2 m hum bad guy, baddy F

malogrado adj muerto dead before one's time

malograr ⟨1a⟩ **1** v/t waste; trabajo spoil, ruin **2** v/r malograrse fail; de plan come to nothing; fallecer die before one's time; *S. Am.* (descomponerse) break down; (funcionar mal) go wrong

maloliente adj stinking

malparado adj: **quedar** or **salir malparado de algo** come out badly from sth

malpensado adj: **ser malpensado** have a nasty mind

malsano adj unhealthy

malsonante adj rude

malta f malt

maltratar ⟨1a⟩ v/t mistreat

maltrato m abuse, harsh words pl

maltrecho adj weakened, diminished; cosa damaged

malva adj mauve

malvado adj evil

malversación f: **malversación de fondos** embezzlement

malversar ⟨1a⟩ v/t embezzle

Malvinas: **las Malvinas** the Falklands, the Falkland Islands

malvivir ⟨3a⟩ v/i scrape by

mamá f mom, *Br* mum

mama f breast

mamadera f L.Am. feeding bottle

mamar ⟨1a⟩ v/i suck; **dar de mamar** (breast)feed

mamarracho m: **vas hecho un mamarracho** F you look a mess F

mamífero m mammal

mamila f Méx feeding bottle

mamografía f MED mammography

mamón 1 adj Méx P cocky 2 m P bastard P

mamona f P bitch P

mamotreto m F libro hefty tome

mampara f screen

mamporro m F punch

mampostería f masonry

maná m fig manna

manada f herd; de lobos pack

manantial m spring

manar ⟨1a⟩ v/i flow

manatí m ZO manatee

manaza f: **ser un manazas** F be ham--handed F

mancebo m youth

Mancha: **Canal de la Mancha** English Channel

mancha f (dirty) mark; de grasa, sangre etc stain

manchar ⟨1a⟩ **1** v/t get dirty; de grasa, sangre etc stain **2** v/r mancharse get dirty

mancillar ⟨1a⟩ v/t fig sully

manco adj de mano one-handed; de brazo

one-armed

mancornas *fpl Pe, Bol* cufflinks

mancuernas *fpl C.Am.* cufflinks

mandamás *m inv* F big shot F

mandado *m Méx, C.Am.:* **los mandados** *pl* the shopping *sg*

mandamiento *m* order; JUR warrant; REL commandment

mandar ⟨1a⟩ **1** *v/t* order; (*enviar*) send; *a mí no me manda nadie* nobody tells me what to do; *mandar hacer algo* have sth done **2** *v/i* be in charge; *¿mande?* Méx can I help you?; *Méx* TELEC hallo?; (*¿cómo?*) what did you say?, excuse me?

mandarina *f* mandarin (orange)

mandatario *m* leader; *primer mandatario Méx* President

mandato *m* order; POL mandate

mandíbula *f* ANAT jaw; *reírse a mandíbula batiente* F laugh one's head off F

mandioca *f* cassava

mando *m* command; *alto mando* high command; *mando a distancia* TV remote control; *tablero de mandos* AUTO dashboard

mandolina *f* MÚS mandolin

mandón *adj* F bossy F

manecilla *f* hand

manejable *adj* easy to handle; *automovil* maneuverable, *Br* manoeuvrable

manejar ⟨1a⟩ **1** *v/t* handle; *máquina* operate; *L.Am.* AUTO drive **2** *v/i L.Am.* AUTO drive **3** *v/r manejarse* manage, get by

manejo *m* handling; *de una máquina* operation

manera *f* way; *esa es su manera de ser* that's the way he is; *maneras* manners; *lo hace a su manera* he does it his way; *de manera que* so (that); *de ninguna manera* certainly not; *no hay manera de* it is impossible to; *de todas maneras* anyway, in any case

manga *f* sleeve; *manga de riego* hosepipe; *en mangas de camisa* in shirtsleeves; *sin mangas* sleeveless; *sacarse algo de la manga* fig make sth up; *traer algo en la manga* F have sth up one's sleeve

manganeso *m* manganese

mangar ⟨1h⟩ *v/t* P swipe F, pinch F

mangle *m* BOT mangrove

mango *m* BOT mango; *CSur* F (*dinero*) dough F, cash; *estoy sin un mango CSur* F I'm broke F, I don't have a bean F

mangonear ⟨1a⟩ **1** *v/i* F boss people around; (*entrometerse*) meddle **2** *v/t* F: *mangonear a alguien* boss s.o. around

manguera *f* hose(pipe)

maní *m S. Am.* peanut

manía *f* (*costumbre*) habit, mania; (*antipatía*) dislike; (*obsesión*) obsession; *manía persecutoria* persecution complex; *tiene sus -s* she has her little ways; *tener manía a alguien* F have it in for s.o.

maniaco *m* maniac

maniatar ⟨1a⟩ *v/t:* *maniatar a alguien* tie s.o.'s hands

maniático *adj* F fussy

manicomio *m* lunatic asylum

manicura *f* manicure; *hacerse la manicura* have a manicure

manido *adj* fig clichéd, done to death F

manifestación *f de alguien* demonstration; (*muestra*) show; (*declaración*) statement

manifestante *m/f* demonstrator

manifestar ⟨1k⟩ **1** *v/t* (*demostrar*) show; (*declarar*) declare, state **2** *v/r manifestarse* demonstrate

manifiesto 1 *adj* clear, manifest; *poner de manifiesto* make clear **2** *m* manifesto

manigua *f* W.I. thicket, bush

manija *f L.Am.* (*asa*) handle

manillar *m* handlebars *pl*

maniobra *f* maneuver, *Br* manoeuvre; *hacer maniobras* maneuver, *Br* manoeuvre

maniobrar ⟨1a⟩ *v/i* maneuver, *Br* manoeuvre

manipulación *f* manipulation; (*manejo*) handling

manipular ⟨1a⟩ *v/t* manipulate; (*manejar*) handle

maniqui 1 *m* dummy **2** *m/f* model

manirroto 1 *adj* extravagant **2** *m*, *-a f* spendthrift

manisero *m*, *-a f W.I., S. Am.* peanut seller

manitas *fpl*: **ser un manitas** be handy
manito *m Méx* pal, buddy
manivela *f* handle
manjar *m* delicacy
mano 1 *f* hand; **mano de obra** labo(u)r, manpower; **mano de pintura** coat of paint; **¡manos arriba!** hands up!; **a mano derecha / izquierda** on the right/left; **atar las manos a alguien** *fig* tie s.o.'s hands; **de segunda mano** second-hand; **echar una mano a alguien** give s.o. a hand; **estar a manos** *L.Am.* F be even, be quits; **hecho a mano** handmade; **poner la mano en el fuego** *fig* swear to it; **poner manos a la obra** get down to work; **se le fue la mano con** *fig* he overdid it with; **tener a mano** have to hand; **traerse algo entre manos** be plotting sth **2** *m Méx* F pal, buddy F
manojo *m* handful; **manojo de llaves** bunch of keys; **manojo de nervios** *fig* bundle of nerves
manopla *f* mitten
manosear ⟨1a⟩ *v/t fruta* handle; *persona* F grope F
manotazo *m* slap
manotear ⟨1a⟩ **1** *v/t Arg, Méx* grab **2** *v/i Arg, Méx* wave one's hands around
mansalva *f*: **a mansalva** in vast numbers; *bebida, comida* in vast amounts
mansedumbre *f* docility; *de persona* mildness
mansión *f* mansion
manso *adj* docile; *persona* mild
manta *f* blanket; **tirar de la manta** *fig* uncover the truth
manteca *f* fat; *Rpl* butter; **manteca de cacao** cocoa butter; **manteca de cerdo** lard
mantel *m* tablecloth; **mantel individual** table mat
mantelería *f* table linen; **una mantelería** a set of table linen
mantención *f L.Am.* → **manutención**
mantener ⟨2l⟩ **1** *v/t (sujetar)* hold; *techo etc* hold up; *(preservar)* keep; *conversación, relación* have; *económicamente* support; *(afirmar)* maintain **2** *v/r* **mantenerse** *(sujetarse)* be held; *económica-*

mente support o.s.; **en forma** keep
mantenimiento *m* maintenance; *económico* support; **gimnasia de mantenimiento** gym
mantequilla *f* butter
mantequillera *f L.Am.* butter dish
mantilla *f de bebé* shawl; **estar en mantillas** *fig* F be in its infancy
mantuvo *vb* → **mantener**
manual *m/adj* manual
manualidades *fpl* handicrafts
manubrio *m* handle; *S. Am.* handlebars *pl*
manufacturar ⟨1a⟩ *v/t* manufacture
manuscrito 1 *adj* handwritten **2** *m* manuscrito
manutención *f* maintenance
manzana *f* apple; *de casas* block; **manzana de la discordia** *fig* bone of contention
manzanilla *f* camomile tea
manzano *m* apple tree
maña *f* skill; **darse** *or* **tener maña para** be good at; **tiene muchas mañas** *L.Am.* she's got lots of tricks up her sleeve F
mañana 1 *f* morning; **por la mañana** in the morning; **mañana por la mañana** tomorrow morning; **de la mañana a la noche** from morning until night; **de la noche a la mañana** *fig* overnight; **esta mañana** this morning; **muy de mañana** very early (in the morning) **2** *adv* tomorrow; **pasado mañana** the day after tomorrow
mañanita *f* shawl
mañero *adj Rpl (animal: terco)* stubborn; *(nervioso)* skittish, nervous
mañoso *adj* skil(l)ful; *L.Am.* animal stubborn
mapa *m* map; **mapa de carreteras** road map
mapache *m* raccoon
mapamundi *m* map of the world
maqueta *f* model
maquillador *m*, **maquilladora** *f* make-up artist
maquillaje *m* make-up
maquillar ⟨1a⟩ **1** *v/t* make up **2** *v/r* **maquillarse** put on one's make-up
máquina *f* machine; FERR locomotive;

M

C.Am., W.I. car; **máquina de afeitar** (electric) shaver; **máquina de coser** sewing machine; **máquina de fotos** camera; **máquina recreativa** arcade game; **pasar algo a máquina** type sth; **a toda máquina** at top speed

maquinaciones *fpl* scheming *sg*

maquinador **1** *adj* scheming **2** *m*, maquinadora *f* schemer

maquinal *adj fig* mechanical

maquinar ⟨1a⟩ *v/t* plot

maquinaria *f* machinery

maquinilla *f*: **maquinilla de afeitar** razor; **maquinilla eléctrica** electric razor

maquinista *m/f* FERR engineer, *Br* train driver

mar *m (also f)* GEOG sea; **sudaba a mares** *fig* F the sweat was pouring off him F; **llover a mares** *fig* F pour, bucket down F; **alta mar** high seas *pl*; **la mar de bien** *(muy bien)* really well

maraca *f* MÚS maraca

maraña *f de hilos* tangle; *(lío)* jumble

marasmo *m fig* stagnation

maratón *m (also f)* marathon

maratoniano *adj* marathon *atr*

maravilla *f* marvel, wonder; BOT marigold; **de maravilla** marvellously, wonderfully; **a las mil maravillas** marvellously, wonderfully

maravillar ⟨1a⟩ **1** *v/t* amaze, astonish **2** *v/r* maravillarse be amazed *o* astonished **(de** at)

maravilloso *adj* marvellous, wonderful

marca *f* mark; COM brand; **marca registrada** registered trademark; **de marca** brand-name *atr*

marcador *m* DEP scoreboard

marcaje *m* DEP marking

marcapasos *m inv* MED pacemaker

marcar ⟨1g⟩ *v/t* mark; *número de teléfono* dial; *gol* score; *res* brand; *de termómetro, contador etc* read, register

marcha *f (salida)* departure; *(avance)* progress; MIL march; AUTO gear; DEP walk; **marcha atrás** AUTO reverse (gear); **a marchas forzadas** *fig* flat out; **a toda marcha** at top speed; **hacer algo sobre la marcha** do sth as one goes

along; **ponerse en marcha** get started, get going; **tener mucha marcha** F be very lively

marchante *m L.Am.* regular customer

marchar ⟨1a⟩ **1** *v/i (progresar)* go; *(funcionar)* work; *(caminar)* walk; MIL march **2** *v/r* marcharse leave, go

marchitarse ⟨1a⟩ *v/r* wilt

marcial *adj* martial; **artes marciales** martial arts

marciano *m* Martian

marco *m moneda* mark; *de cuadro, puerta* frame; *fig* framework

marea *f* tide; **marea alta** high tide; **marea baja** low tide; **marea negra** oil slick

mareado *adj* dizzy

marear ⟨1a⟩ **1** *v/t* make feel nauseous, *Br* make feel sick; *fig (confundir)* confuse **2** *v/r* marearse feel nauseous, *Br* feel sick

marejada *f* heavy sea

maremoto *m* tidal wave

mareo *m* seasickness

marfil *m* ivory

margarina *f* margarine

margarita *f* BOT daisy

margen *m tb fig* margin; **al margen de eso** apart from that; **mantenerse al margen** keep out

marginación *f* marginalization

marginal *adj* marginal

marginar ⟨1a⟩ *v/t* marginalize

mariachi **1** *m* mariachi band **2** *m/f* mariachi player

marica *m* F fag P, *Br* poof P

maricón *m* P fag P, *Br* poof P

marido *m* husband

marihuana *f* marijuana

marimacho *m* F butch woman

marimba *f* Rpl MÚS marimba

marina *f* navy; **marina mercante** merchant navy

marinar ⟨1a⟩ *v/t* GASTR marinade

marinero **1** *adj* sea *atr* **2** *m* sailor

marino **1** *adj brisa* sea *atr; planta, animal* marine; **azul marino** navy blue **2** *m* sailor

marioneta *f tb fig* puppet

mariposa *f* butterfly

mariquita *f* ladybug, *Br* ladybird

marisco *m* seafood
marisma *f* salt marsh
marítimo *adj* maritime
marketing *m* marketing
marmita *f* pot, pan
mármol *m* marble
marmota *f*: **dormir como una marmota** F
sleep like a log
marqués *m* marquis
marquesa *f* marchioness
marquesina *f* marquee, *Br* canopy
marranada *f* F dirty trick
marrano **1** *adj* filthy **2** *m* hog, *Br* pig; F
persona pig F
marras *adv*: **el ordenador de marras** the
darned computer F
marrón *m/adj* brown
marroquinería *f* leather goods
Marruecos Morocco
marta *f* zo marten
Marte *m* AST Mars
martes *m inv* Tuesday
martillero *m S. Am.* auctioneer
martillo *m* hammer; **martillo neumático**
pneumatic drill
martín *m*: **martín pescador** zo kingfisher
mártir *m/f* martyr
martirio *m tb fig* martyrdom
martirizar ⟨1f⟩ *v/t tb fig* martyr
marzo *m* March
mas *conj* but
más **1** *adj* more **2** *adv comp* more; *sup*
most; MAT plus; **más grande / pequeño**
bigger / smaller; **el más grande / pequeño** the largest / smallest; **trabajar más**
work harder; **más bien** rather; **más
que, más de lo que** more than; **más o
menos** more or less; **¿qué más?** what
else?; **no más** *L.Am.* → **nomás**; **por
más que** however much; **sin más** without more ado; **más lejos** further
masa *f* mass; GASTR dough; **pillar a alguien con las manos en la masa** F
catch s.o. red-handed
masacrar ⟨1a⟩ *v/t* massacre
masacre *f* massacre
masaje *m* massage
masajista *m/f* masseur; *mujer* masseuse
mascar ⟨1g⟩ **1** *v/t* chew **2** *v/i L.Am.* chew

tobacco
máscara *f* mask
mascarilla *f* mask; *cosmética* face pack
mascota *f* mascot; *animal doméstico* pet
masculino *adj* masculine
mascullar ⟨1a⟩ *v/t* mutter
masificación *f* overcrowding
masilla *f* putty
masita *f L.Am. small sweet cake or bun*
masivo *adj* massive
masón *m* mason
masoquismo *m* masochism
masoquista **1** *adj* masochistic **2** *m/f* mas-
ochist
máster *m* master's (degree)
masticación *f* chewing
masticar ⟨1g⟩ *v/t* chew
mástil *m* mast; *de tienda* pole
mastín *m* zo mastiff
mastodóntico *adj* colossal, enormous
mastuerzo *m* BOT cress
masturbarse ⟨1a⟩ *v/r* masturbate
mata *f* bush
matadero *m* slaughterhouse
matador *m* TAUR matador
matanza *f de animales* slaughter; *de gente*
slaughter, massacre
matar ⟨1a⟩ **1** *v/t* kill; *ganado* slaughter **2**
v/r matarse kill o.s.; *morir* be killed; **matarse a trabajar** work o.s. to death
matarratas *m* rat poison
matasanos *m/f inv* F quack F
matasellos *m inv* postmark
mate **1** *adj* matt **2** *m en ajedrez* mate;
L.Am. (infusión) maté
matear ⟨1a⟩ **1** *v/t CSur* checkmate **2** *v/i*
L.Am. drink maté
matemáticas *fpl* mathematics
matemático **1** *adj* mathematical **2** *m*, -a *f*
mathematician
materia *f* matter; *(material)* material; *(tema)* subject; **materia prima** raw material; **en materia de** as regards
material *m/adj* material
materialismo *m* materialism
materializar ⟨1f⟩ *v/t*: **materializar algo**
make sth a reality
maternal *adj* maternal
matero *m*, -a *f L.Am.* maté drinker

matinal *adj* morning *atr*

matiz *m de ironía* touch; *de color* shade

matizar ⟨1f⟩ *v/t comentarios* qualify

matón *m* bully; *(criminal)* thug

matorral *m* thicket

matrícula *f* AUTO license plate, *Br* numberplate; EDU enrol(l)ment, registration

matricular ⟨1a⟩ **1** *v/t* register **2** *v/r* matricularse EDU enrol(l), register

matrimonial *adj* marriage *atr*, marital

matrimonio *m* marriage; *boda* wedding

matriz *f* matrix; ANAT womb

matrona *f (comadrona)* midwife

matutino *adj* morning *atr*

maullar ⟨1a⟩ *v/i* miaow

maullido *m* miaow

mausoleo *m* mausoleum

máxima *f* maxim

máxime *adv* especially

máximo *adj* maximum

mayo *m* May

mayonesa *f* GASTR mayonnaise

mayor **1** *adj comp: en tamaño* larger, bigger; *en edad* older; *en importancia* greater; **ser mayor de edad** be an adult; **al por mayor** COM wholesale **2** *adj sup: el mayor* the oldest *o* eldest; *en tamaño* the largest *o* biggest; *en importancia* the greatest; *los mayores* adults; *la mayor parte* the majority

mayordomo *m* butler

mayoreo *m:* **vender al mayoreo** *Méx* sell wholesale

mayoría *f* majority; *alcanzar la mayoría de edad* come of age; *la mayoría de* the majority of, most (of); *en la mayoría de los casos* in the majority of cases, in most cases

mayorista *m/f* wholesaler

mayoritario *adj* majority *atr*

mayúscula *f* capital (letter), upper case letter

mazamorra *f* S. Am. kind of porridge made from corn

mazapán *m* marzipan

mazmorra *f* dungeon

mazo *m* mallet

mazorca *f* cob

me *pron pers complemento directo* me;

complemento indirecto (to) me; *reflexivo* myself; **me dio el libro** he gave me the book, he gave the book to me

mear ⟨1a⟩ F **1** *v/i* pee F **2** *v/r* mearse pee o.s. F; **mearse de risa** wet o.s. (laughing) F

meca *f fig* mecca

mecachis *int* F blast! F

mecánica *f* mechanics

mecánico **1** *adj* mechanical **2** *m*, -a *f* mechanic

mecanismo *m* mechanism

mecanizar ⟨1f⟩ *v/t* mechanize

mecanógrafo *m*, -a *f* typist

mecanografiar ⟨1c⟩ *v/t* type

mecate *m Méx* string, cord

mecedora *f* rocking chair

mecenas *m inv* patron, sponsor

mecer ⟨2b⟩ **1** *v/t* rock **2** *v/r* mecerse rock

mecha *f* wick; *de explosivo* fuse; *del pelo* highlight; *Méx* F fear

mechero *m* cigarette lighter

mechón *m de pelo* lock

medalla *f* medal

medallista *m/f* medal(l)list

media *f* stocking; **medias** *pl* pantyhose *pl*, *Br* tights *pl*

mediación *f* mediation

mediado *adj:* **a mediados de junio** in mid-June, halfway through June

mediador *m*, mediadora *f* mediator

mediana *f* AUTO median strip, *Br* central reservation

mediano *adj* medium, average

medianoche *f* midnight

mediante *prp* by means of

mediar ⟨1b⟩ *v/i* mediate

mediático *adj* media *atr*

medicación *f* medication

medicamento *m* medicine, drug

medicina *f* medicine

medicinal *adj* medicinal

médico **1** *adj* medical **2** *m/f* doctor; **médico de cabecera** *o* **de familia** family physician, *Br* GP, *Br* general practitioner; **médico de urgencia** emergency doctor

medida *f* measure; *acto* measurement; *(grado)* extent; *hecho a medida* made

to measure; *a medida que* as; *tomar medidas* fig take measures o steps
medidor m S. Am. meter
medieval adj medi(a)eval
medio 1 adj half; *tamaño* medium; (*de promedio*) average; *las tres y -a* half past three, three-thirty **2** m environment; (*centro*) middle; (*manera*) means; *medio ambiente* environment; *por medio de* by means of; *en medio de* in the middle of; *medios* dinero means, resources; *medios de comunicación* or *de información* (mass) media; *medios de transporte* means of transport **3** adv half; *hacer algo a -as* half do sth; *ir a -as* go halves; *día por medio* L.Am. every other day; *quitar de en medio algo* F move sth out of the way
medioambiental adj environmental
mediocre adj mediocre
mediodía m midday; *a mediodía* (*a las doce*) at noon, at twelve o'clock; (*a la hora de comer*) at lunchtime
medir ⟨3l⟩ **1** v/t measure **2** v/i: *mide 2 metros de ancho / largo / alto* it's 2 meters (o Br metres) wide / long / tall
meditación f meditation
meditar ⟨1a⟩ **1** v/t ponder **2** v/i meditate
Mediterráneo m/adj: (*mar*) *Mediterráneo* Mediterranean (Sea)
médium m/f medium
médula f marrow; *médula espinal* spinal cord; *hasta la médula* fig through and through, to the core
medusa f zo jellyfish
megafonía f public-address o PA system
megáfono m bullhorn, Br loud-hailer
megalomanía f megalomania
mejicano 1 adj Mexican **2** m, -a f Mexican
Méjico Mexico; *Méx DF* Mexico City
mejilla f cheek
mejillón m zo mussel
mejor adj comp better; *el mejor* sup the best; *lo mejor* the best thing; *lo mejor posible* as well as possible; *a lo mejor* perhaps, maybe; *tanto mejor* all the better
mejora f improvement
mejorana f bot marjoram

mejorar ⟨1a⟩ **1** v/t improve **2** v/i improve; *¡que te mejores!* get well soon!
mejoría f improvement
mejunje m desp concoction
melancolía f melancholy
melancólico adj gloomy, melancholic
melena f long hair; *de león* mane
melindroso adj affected
mella f: *hacer mella en alguien* have an effect on s.o., affect s.o.
mellado adj gap-toothed
mellizo 1 adj twin atr **2** m, -a f twin
melocotón m peach
melocotonero m peach tree
melodía f melody
melodrama m melodrama
melón m melon
membrana f membrane
membrillo m quince; *dulce de membrillo* quince jelly
memela f Méx corn tortilla
memo 1 adj F dumb F **2** m, -a f F idiot
memorable adj memorable
memoria f tb infor memory; (*informe*) report; *de memoria* by heart; *memorias* (*biografía*) memoirs
memorizar ⟨1f⟩ v/t memorize
mención f: *hacer mención de* mention
mencionar ⟨1a⟩ v/t mention
mendigar ⟨1h⟩ v/t beg for
mendigo m beggar
menear ⟨1a⟩ v/t shake; *las caderas* sway; *menear la cola* wag its tail **2** v/r menearse fidget
menestra f vegetable stew
mengano m, -a f F so-and-so F
menguante adj decreasing, diminishing; *luna* waning
menguar ⟨1i⟩ v/i decrease, diminish; *de la luna* wane
meningitis f med meningitis
menopausia f med menopause
menor adj comp less; *en tamaño* smaller; *en edad* younger; *ser menor de edad* be a minor; *al por menor* com retail; *el menor* sup: *en tamaño* the smallest; *en edad* the youngest; *el número menor* the lowest number
menos 1 adj en cantidad less; *en número*

M

fewer **2** adv comp en cantidad less; sup en cantidad least; MAT minus; **es menos guapa que Ana** she is not as pretty as Ana; **tres menos dos** three minus two; **a menos que** unless; **al menos, por lo menos** at least; **echar de menos** miss; **eso es lo de menos** that's the least of it; **ni mucho menos** far from it; **son las dos menos diez** it's ten of two, it's ten to two

menoscabar ⟨1a⟩ v/t autoridad diminish; (dañar) harm

menospreciar ⟨1b⟩ v/t underestimate; (desdeñar) look down on

mensaje m message

mensajero m courrier

menstruación f menstruation

menstruar ⟨1h⟩ v/i menstruate

mensual adj monthly

mensualidad f monthly instal(l)ment, monthly payment

mensualmente adv monthly

menta f BOT mint

mental adj mental

mentalidad f mentality

mentalizar ⟨1f⟩ **1** v/t: **mentalizar a alguien** make s.o. aware **2** v/r **mentalizarse** mentally prepare o.s.

mente f mind

mentecato **1** adj F dim F **2** m F fool

mentir ⟨3i⟩ v/i lie

mentira f lie

mentiroso **1** adj: **ser muy mentiroso** tell a lot of lies **2** m, -a f liar

mentón m chin

mentor m mentor

menú m tb INFOR menu; **menú de ayuda** help menu

menudencias fpl Méx giblets

menudeo m L.Am. retail trade

menudo **1** adj small; **¡-a suerte!** fig F lucky devil!; **¡-as vacaciones!** irón F some vacation!; **a menudo** often **2** m L.Am. small change; **menudos** GASTR giblets

meñique m/adj: **(dedo) meñique** little finger

meollo m fig heart

mercader m trader

mercadería f L.Am. merchandise

mercadillo m street market

mercado m market; **Mercado Común** Common Market; **mercado negro** black market

mercadotecnia f marketing

mercancía f merchandise

mercantil adj commercial

merced f: **estar a merced de alguien** be at s.o.'s mercy

mercenario m/adj mercenary

mercería f notions pl, Br haberdashery

MERCOSUR abr (= **Mercado Común del Sur**) Common Market including Argentina, Brazil, Paraguay and Uruguay

mercurio m mercury

merecer ⟨2d⟩ v/t deserve; **no merecer la pena** it's not worth it

merecido m just deserts pl

merendar ⟨1k⟩ **1** v/t: **merendar algo** have sth as an afternoon snack **2** v/i have an afternoon snack

merengue m GASTR meringue

meridiano m/f meridian

meridional **1** adj southern **2** m southerner

merienda f afternoon snack

mérito m merit

merluza f ZO hake; **agarrar una merluza** fig F get plastered F

mermar ⟨1a⟩ **1** v/t reduce **2** v/i diminish

mermelada f jam

mero **1** adj mere; **el mero jefe** Méx F the big boss **2** m ZO grouper

merodear ⟨1a⟩ v/i loiter

mes m month

mesa f table; **mesa redonda** fig round table; **poner / quitar la mesa** set / clear the table

mesera f L.Am. waitress

mesero m L.Am. waiter

meseta f plateau

mesilla, mesita f: **mesilla (de noche)** night stand, Br bedside table

mesón m traditional restaurant decorated in rustic style

mestizo m person of mixed race

mesura f: **con mesura** in moderation

meta f en fútbol goal; en carrera finishing line; fig (objetivo) goal, objective

metabolismo *m* metabolism
metafísica *f* metaphysics
metáfora *f* metaphor
metal *m* metal
metálico 1 *adj* metallic 2 *m*: **en metálico** (in) cash
metalúrgico *adj* metallurgical
metamorfosis *f inv* transformation, metamorphosis
metedura *f*: **metedura de pata** F blunder
meteorito *m* meteorite
meteorológico *adj* weather *atr*, meteorological; **pronóstico meteorológico** weather forecast
meteorólogo *m*, -a *f* meteorologist
meter ⟨2a⟩ 1 *v/t gen* put (**en** in, into); (*involucrar*) involve (**en** in); **meter a alguien en un lío** get s.o. into a mess 2 *v/r* meterse: **meterse en algo** get into sth; (*involucrarse*) get involved in sth, get mixed up in sth; **meterse con alguien** pick on s.o.; **meterse de administrativo** get a job in admin; **¿dónde se ha metido?** where has he got to?
meticuloso *adj* meticulous
metido *adj* involved; *L.Am.* F nosy F; **estar muy metido en algo** be very involved in sth
metódico *adj* methodical
método *m* method
metomentodo *m/f* F busybody F
metralleta *f* sub-machine gun
métrico *adj* metric
metro *m medida* meter, *Br* metre; *para medir* rule; *transporte* subway, *Br* underground
metrópolis *f inv* metropolis
metropolitano *adj* metropolitan
mexicano 1 *adj* Mexican 2 *m*, -a Mexican
México Mexico; *Méx DF* Mexico City
mezcal *m Méx* mescal
mezcla *f sustancia* mixture; *de tabaco, café etc* blend; *acto* mixing; *de tabaco, café etc* blending
mezclar ⟨1a⟩ 1 *v/t* mix; *tabaco, café etc* blend; **mezclar a alguien en algo** get s.o. mixed up *o* involved in sth 2 *v/r* mezclarse mix; **mezclarse en algo** get mixed up *o* involved in sth

mezquinar ⟨1a⟩ *v/t L.Am.* skimp on
mezquino *adj* mean
mezquita *f* mosque
mg. *abr* (= *miligramo*) mg (= milligram)
mi, mis *adj pos* my
mí *pron* me; *reflexivo* myself; **¿y a mí qué?** so what?, what's it to me?
michelín *m* F spare tire, *Br* spare tyre
mico *m* zo monkey
micro *m or f Chi* bus
microbio *m* microbe
microbús *m* minibus
microchip *m* (micro)chip
microfilm(e) *m* microfilm
micrófono *m* microphone; **micrófono oculto** bug
microondas *m inv* microwave
microordenador *m* microcomputer
microprocesador *m* microprocessor
microscópico *adj* microscopic
microscopio *m* microscope
mide *vb* → **medir**
miedo *m* fear (**a** of); **dar miedo** be frightening; **me da miedo la oscuridad** I'm frightened of the dark; **tener miedo de que** be afraid that; **por miedo a** for fear of; **de miedo** F great F, awesome F
miedoso *adj* timid; **¡no seas tan miedoso!** don't be scared!
miel *f* honey
miembro *m* member; (*extremidad*) limb, member *fml*
mientras 1 *conj* while; **mientras que** whereas 2 *adv*: **mientras tanto** in the meantime, meanwhile
miércoles *m inv* Wednesday
mierda *f* P shit P, crap P; **una mierda de película** a crap movie P; **¡una mierda!** no way! F
miga *f de pan* crumb; **migas** crumbs; **hacer buenas / malas migas** *fig* F get on well / badly
migraña *f* MED migraine
migratorio *adj* migratory
mijo *m* BOT millet
mil *adj* thousand
milagro *m* miracle; **de milagro** miraculously, by a miracle
milagroso *adj* miraculous

milano *m* zo kite
milenio *m* millennium
mili *f* F military service
milicia *f* militia
milico *m* S. Am. desp soldier
milímetro *m* millimeter, Br millimetre
militante *m/f* & *adj* militant
militar **1** *adj* military **2** *m* soldier; *los militares* the military **3** ⟨1a⟩ *v/i* POL: *militar en* be a member of
milla *f* mile
millar *m* thousand
millón *m* million; (*mil millones*) billion
millonario *m* millionaire
milpa *f Méx, C.Am.* corn, Br maize; *terreno* cornfield, Br field of maize
mimar ⟨1a⟩ *v/t* spoil, pamper
mimbre *m* BOT willow; *muebles pl de mimbre* wicker furniture *sg*
mímica *f* mime
mimo *m* TEA mime
mimosa *f* BOT mimosa
mimoso *adj*: *ser mimoso* be cuddly
mina *f* MIN mine; *Rpl* F broad F, Br bird F; *mina antipersonal* MIL antipersonnel mine
minar ⟨1a⟩ *v/t* mine; *fig* undermine
mineral *m/adj* mineral
minería *f* mining
minero **1** *adj* mining **2** *m* miner
miniatura *f* miniature
minifalda *f* miniskirt
minimizar ⟨1f⟩ *v/t* minimize
mínimo **1** *adj* minimum; *como mínimo* at the very least **2** *m* minimum
minino *m* F puss F, pussy (cat) F
ministerio *m* POL department; *ministerio de Asuntos Exteriores, L.Am. ministerio de Relaciones Exteriores* State Department, Br Foreign Office; *ministerio de Hacienda* Treasury Department, Br Treasury; *ministerio del Interior* Department of the Interior, Br Home Office
ministro *m*, -a *f* minister; *ministro del Interior* Secretary of the Interior, Br Home Secretary; *primer ministro* Prime Minister
minoría *f* minority

minorista COM **1** *adj* retail *atr* **2** *m/f* retailer
minoritario *adj* minority *atr*
mintió *vb* → **mentir**
minucia *f* minor detail
minucioso *adj* meticulous, thorough
minúscula *f* small letter, lower case letter
minúsculo *adj* tiny, minute
minusvalía *f* disability
minusválido **1** *adj* disabled **2** *m*, -a *f* disabled person; *los minusválidos* the disabled
minutero *m* minute hand
minuto *m* minute
mío, mía *pron* mine; *el mío / la -a* mine
miope *adj* near-sighted, short-sighted
miopía *f* near-sightedness, short-sightedness
mira *f*: *con miras a* with a view to
mirada *f* look; *echar una mirada* take a look (*a* at)
mirador *m* viewpoint
mirar ⟨1a⟩ *v/t* look at; (*observar*) watch; *L.Am.* (*ver*) see; *¿qué miras desde aquí?* what can you see from here? **2** *v/i* look; *mirar al norte de una ventana etc* face north; *mirar por la ventana* look out of the window
mirilla *f* spyhole
mirlo *m* zo blackbird
misa *f* REL mass
misántropo *m* misanthropist
miserable *adj* wretched
miseria *f* poverty; *fig* misery
misericordia *f* mercy, compassion
mísero *adj* wretched; *sueldo* miserable
misil *m* missile
misión *f* mission
misionero *m*, -a *f* missionary
mismo **1** *adj* same; *lo mismo que* the same as; *yo mismo* I myself; *da lo mismo* it doesn't matter, it's all the same; *me da lo mismo* I don't care, it's all the same to me **2** *adv*: *aquí mismo* right here; *ahora mismo* right now, this very minute
misógino *adj* misogynistic
misterio *m* mystery
misterioso *adj* mysterious
místico *adj* mystic(al)

mitad f half; **a mitad del camino** halfway; **a mitad de la película** halfway through the movie; **a mitad de precio** half-price
mítico adj mythical
mitigar ⟨1h⟩ v/t mitigate; *ansiedad, dolor etc* ease
mitin m POL meeting
mito m myth
mitología f mythology
mixto adj mixed; *comisión* joint
mm. abr (= *milímetro*) mm (= millimeter)
mobiliario m furniture
mochila f backpack
mochilero m, **-a** f backpacker
mochuelo m ZO little owl
moción f POL motion; **moción de confianza** /**censura** vote of confidence / no confidence
moco m: **tener mocos** have a runny nose
mocoso m, **-a** f F snotty-nosed kid F
moda f fashion; **de moda** fashionable, in fashion; **estar pasado de moda** be out of fashion
modales mpl manners
modalidad f form; DEP discipline; **modalidad de pago** method of payment
modelar ⟨1a⟩ v/t model
modelismo m model making
modelo 1 m model 2 m/f persona model
módem m INFOR modem
moderado 1 adj moderate 2 m, **-a** f moderate
moderador m, **moderadora** f TV presenter
moderar ⟨1a⟩ 1 v/t moderate; *impulsos* control, restrain; *velocidad, gastos* reduce; *debate* chair 2 v/r **moderarse** control o.s., restrain o.s.
modernización f modernization
modernizar ⟨1f⟩ v/t modernize
moderno adj modern
modestia f modesty; **modestia aparte** though I say so myself
modesto adj modest
módico adj precio reasonable
modificación f modification
modificar ⟨1g⟩ v/t modify
modista m/f dressmaker; *diseñador* fashion designer

modo m way; **a modo de** as; **de modo que** so that; **de ningún modo** not at all; **en cierto modo** in a way o sense; **de todos modos** anyway
modorra f drowsiness
módulo m module
mofarse ⟨1a⟩ v/r: **mofarse de** make fun of
mofeta f ZO skunk
mofletes mpl chubby cheeks
mogollón m F (*discusión*) argument; **mogollón de** F loads of F
moho m mo(u)ld
moisés m inv Moses basket
mojado adj (*húmedo*) damp, moist; (*empapado*) wet
mojar ⟨1a⟩ 1 v/t (*humedecer*) dampen, moisten; (*empapar*) wet; *galleta* dunk, dip 2 v/r **mojarse** get wet
mojigato 1 adj prudish 2 m, **-a** f prude
mojón m tb fig milestone
molar ⟨2h⟩ 1 v/t: **me mola ese tío** P I like the guy a lot 2 v/i P be cool F
molcajete m Méx, C.Am. (*mortero*) grinding stone
molde m mo(u)ld; *para bizcocho* (cake) tin; **romper moldes** fig break the mo(u)ld
moldear ⟨1a⟩ v/t mo(u)ld
moldura f ARQUI mo(u)lding
mole 1 f mass 2 m Méx mole (*spicy sauce made with chilies and tomatoes*)
molécula f molecule
moler ⟨2h⟩ v/t grind; *fruta* mash; **carne molida** ground meat, Br mince; **moler a alguien a palos** fig beat s.o. to a pulp
molestar ⟨1a⟩ 1 v/t bother, annoy; (*doler*) trouble; **no molestar** do not disturb 2 v/r **molestarse** get upset; (*ofenderse*) take offense (*Br* offence); (*enojarse*) get annoyed; **molestar en hacer algo** take the trouble to do sth
molestia f nuisance; **molestias** pl MED discomfort sg
molesto adj annoying; (*incómodo*) inconvenient
molestoso adj L.Am. annoying
molido adj F bushed F
molinillo m: **molinillo de café** coffee

M

grinder o mill

molino m mill; **molino de viento** windmill

mollera f F head; **duro de mollera** F pigheaded F

molusco m ZO mollusk, Br mollusc

momento m moment; **al momento** at once; **por el momento, de momento** for the moment

momia f mummy

momificar ⟨1g⟩ v/t mummify

monada f: **su hija es una monada** her daughter is lovely; **¡qué monada!** how lovely!

monaguillo m altar boy

monarca m monarch

monarquía f monarchy

monasterio m monastery

mondadientes m inv toothpick

mondar ⟨1a⟩ **1** v/t peel; árbol prune **2** v/r mondarse: **mondarse de risa** F split one's sides laughing

mondongo m tripe

moneda f coin; (divisa) currency

monedero m change purse, Br purse

monetario adj monetary

monigote m rag doll; F (tonto) idiot

monitor[1] m TV, INFOR monitor

monitor[2] m, monitora f (profesor) instructor

monja f nun

monje m monk

mono **1** m ZO monkey; prenda coveralls pl, Br boilersuit **2** adj pretty, cute

monógamo adj monogamous

monólogo m monolog(ue)

monopatín m skateboard

monopolio m monopoly

monopolizar ⟨1f⟩ v/t tb fig monopolize

monosílabo adj monosyllabic

monotonía f monotony

monótono adj monotonous

monovolumen m AUTO minivan, Br people carrier, MPV

monsergas fpl: **déjate de monsergas** F stop going on F

monstruo m monster; (fenómeno) phenomenon

monstruosidad f eyesore, monstrosity

monstruoso adj monstrous

monta f: **de poca monta** unimportant

montacargas m inv hoist

montada f L.Am. mounted police

montaje m TÉC assembly; de película editing; TEA staging; fig F con F

montante m COM total

montaña f mountain; **montaña rusa** rollercoaster

montañero m, -a f mountaineer

montañismo m mountaineering

montañoso adj mountainous

montaplatos m inv dumb waiter

montar ⟨1a⟩ **1** v/t TÉC assemble; tienda put up; negocio set up; película edit; caballo mount; **montar la guardia** mount guard **2** v/i: **montar en bicicleta** ride a bicycle; **montar a caballo** ride a horse

monte m mountain; (bosque) woodland

montículo m mound

montón m pile, heap; **ser del montón** fig be average, not stand out; **montones de** F piles of F, loads of F

montura f de gafas frame

monumento m monument

moño m bun

moqueta f (wall-to-wall) carpet

mora f BOT de zarza blackberry; de morera mulberry

morada f dwelling

morado adj purple; **pasarlas -as** F have a rough time

moral **1** adj moral **2** f (moralidad) morals pl; (ánimo) morale

moraleja f moral

moralidad f morality

moralista m/f moralist

moratón m bruise

moratoria f moratorium

morbo m F perverted kind of pleasure

morboso adj perverted

morcilla f blood sausage, Br black pudding

mordaz adj biting

mordaza f gag

morder ⟨2h⟩ v/t bite

mordida f Méx F bribe

mordisco m bite

mordisquear ⟨1a⟩ v/t nibble

morena f zo moray eel

moreno adj pelo, piel dark; (bronceado) tanned

morera f BOT white mulberry tree

moretón m L.Am. bruise

morfina f morphine

morfología f morphology

moribundo adj dying

morir ⟨3k; part muerto⟩ 1 v/i die (de of); morir de hambre die of hunger, starve to death 2 v/r morirse die; morirse de fig die of; morirse por fig be dying for

morisco adj Moorish

mormón m Mormon

moro 1 adj North African 2 m North African; no hay moros en la costa F the coast is clear

morocho adj S. Am. persona dark

moronga f C.Am., Méx blood sausage, Br black pudding

morralla f Méx small change

morriña f homesickness

morro m zo snout; tener mucho morro F have a real nerve

morrongo m F pussycat F

morsa f zo walrus

mortaja f shroud; L.Am. cigarette paper

mortal 1 adj mortal; accidente, herida fatal; dosis lethal 2 m/f mortal

mortalidad f mortality

mortalmente adv fatally

mortero m tb MIL mortar

mortífero adj lethal

mortificar ⟨1g⟩ 1 v/t torment 2 v/r mortificarse distress o.s.; Méx (apenarse) be embarrassed o ashamed

mosaico m mosaic

mosca f fly; por si las moscas F just to be on the safe side

moscada adj: nuez moscada nutmeg

moscardón m hornet

Moscú Moscow

mosquear ⟨1a⟩ 1 v/t Esp F rile 2 v/r mosquearse F get hot under the collar F; (sentir recelo) smell a rat F

mosquitero m mosquito net

mosquito m mosquito

mostaza f mustard

mosto m grape juice

mostrador m counter; en bar bar; mostrador de facturación check-in desk

mostrar ⟨1m⟩ 1 v/t show 2 v/r mostrarse: mostrarse contento seem happy

mota f speck; en diseño dot

mote m nickname; S. Am. boiled corn o Br maize

motel m motel

motín m mutiny; en una cárcel riot

motivación f motivation

motivar ⟨1a⟩ v/t motivate

motivo m motive, reason; MÚS, PINT motif; con motivo de because of

moto f motorcycle, motorbike; moto acuática or de agua jet ski

motocicleta f motorcycle

motociclismo m motorcycle racing

motociclista m/f motorcyclist

motocross m motocross

motor m engine; eléctrico motor

motora f motorboat

motorista m/f motorcyclist

motosierra f chain saw

motriz adj motor

mover ⟨2h⟩ 1 v/t move; (agitar) shake; (impulsar, incitar) drive 2 v/r moverse move; ¡muévete! get a move on! F, hurry up!

movida f F scene

móvil 1 adj mobile 2 m TELEC cellphone, Br mobile (phone)

movilidad f mobility

movilizar ⟨1f⟩ v/t mobilize

movimiento m movement; COM, fig activity

moza f girl; camarera waitress

mozo 1 adj: en mis años mozos in my youth 2 m boy; camarero waiter

mucama f Rpl maid

mucamo m Rpl servant

muchacha f girl

muchachada f Arg group of youngsters

muchacho m boy

muchedumbre f crowd

mucho 1 adj cantidad a lot of, lots of; esp neg much; no tengo mucho dinero I don't have much money; muchos a lot of, lots of, many; esp neg many; no tengo muchos amigos I don't have many friends; **tengo mucho frío** I am very cold; **es mucho coche para mí** it's too big a car for me **2** *adv* a lot; *esp neg* much; **no me gustó mucho** I didn't like it very much; **¿dura / tarda mucho?** does it last / take long?; **como mucho** at the most; **ni mucho menos** far from it; **por mucho que** however much **3** *pron* a lot, much; **muchos** a lot of people, many people

muda *f de ropa* change of clothes

mudanza *f de casa* move

mudarse ⟨1a⟩ *v/r*: **mudarse de casa** move house; **mudarse de ropa** change (one's clothes)

mudo *adj* mute; *letra* silent

mueble *m* piece of furniture

mueca *f de dolor* grimace; **hacer muecas** make faces

muela *f* tooth; ANAT molar; **muela del juicio** wisdom tooth

muelle *m* TÉC spring; MAR wharf

muérdago *m* BOT mistletoe

muerde *vb* → **morder**

muere *vb* → **morir**

muermo *m fig* F boredom; **ser un muermo** *fig* F be a drag F

muerte *f* death; **de mala muerte** *fig* F lousy F, awful F

muerto 1 *part* → **morir 2** *adj* dead **3** *m*, -a *f* dead person

muestra *f* sample; (*señal*) sign; (*exposición*) show

muestrario *m* collection of samples

mueve *vb* → **mover**

mugir ⟨3c⟩ *v/i* moo

mugre *f* filth

mugriento *adj* filthy

mugroso *adj* dirty

mujer *f* woman; (*esposa*) wife

mujeriego *m* womanizer

mújol *m* ZO gray *o Br* grey mullet

mula *f* mule; *Méx* trash, *Br* rubbish

mulato *m* mulatto

muleta *f* crutch; TAUR cape

mullido *adj* soft

mullir ⟨3h⟩ *v/t almohada* plump up

multa *f* fine

multar ⟨1a⟩ *v/t* fine

multicine *m* multiscreen

multicolor *adj* multicolo(u)red

multilateral *adj* multilateral

multimedia *f/adj* multimedia

multimillonario *m* multimillionaire

multinacional *f* multinational

múltiple *adj* multiple

multiplicación *f* multiplication

multiplicar ⟨1g⟩ **1** *v/t* multiply **2** *v/r* **multiplicarse** multiply

múltiplo *m* MAT multiple

multipropiedad *f* timeshare

multitud *f* crowd; **multitud de** thousands of

multitudinario *adj* mass *atr*

multiuso *adj* multipurpose

mundano *adj* society *atr*; REL wordly

mundial 1 *adj* world *atr* **2** *m*: **el mundial de fútbol** the World Cup

mundo *m* world; **el otro mundo** the next world; **nada del otro mundo** nothing out of the ordinary; **todo el mundo** everybody, everyone

munición *f* ammunition

municipal *adj* municipal

municipio *m* municipality

muñeca *f* doll; ANAT wrist

muñeco *m* doll; *fig* puppet; **muñeco de nieve** snowman

muñón *m* MED stump

mural 1 *adj* wall *atr* **2** *m* mural

muralla *f de ciudad* wall

murciélago *m* ZO bat

murga *f*: **dar la murga a alguien** F bug s.o. F

murió *vb* → **morir**

murmullo *m* murmur

murmurar ⟨1a⟩ *v/i hablar* murmur; *criticar* gossip

muro *m* wall

musa *f* muse

musaraña *f* ZO shrew; **pensar en las musarañas** F daydream

muscular *adj* muscular

músculo *m* muscle

musculoso *adj* muscular

museo *m* museum; *de pintura* art gallery

musgo *m* BOT moss

música *f* music

musical *m/adj* musical
músico *m*, -a *f* musician
musitar ⟨1a⟩ *v/i* mumble
muslo *m* thigh
mustio *adj* withered; *fig* down F
musulmán 1 *adj* Muslim 2 *m*, -ana *f* Muslim

mutilado *m*, -a *f* disabled person
mutilar ⟨1a⟩ *v/t* mutilate
mutualidad *f* benefit society, *Br* friendly society
mutuo *adj* mutual
muy *adv* very; *(demasiado)* too; **muy valorado** highly valued13

N, Ñ

N *abr* (= *norte*) N (North(ern))
nabo *m* 1 *adj Arg* F dumb F 2 *m* turnip
nácar *m* mother-of-pearl
nacatamal *m C.Am., Méx* meat, rice and corn in a banana leaf
nacer ⟨2d⟩ *v/i* be born; *de un huevo* hatch; *de una planta* sprout; *de un río, del sol* rise; *(surgir)* arise (**de** from)
naciente *adj país, gobierno* newly formed; *sol* rising
nacimiento *m* birth; *de Navidad* crèche, nativity scene
nación *f* nation
nacional *adj* national
nacionalidad *f* nationality
nacionalismo *m* nationalism
nacionalización *f* COM nationalization
nacionalizar ⟨1f⟩ 1 *v/t* COM nationalize; *persona* naturalize 2 *v/r* **nacionalizarse** become naturalized
naco *m Col* purée
nada 1 *pron* nothing; **no hay nada** there isn't anything; **¡nada de eso!** F you can put that idea out of your head; **nada más** nothing else; **nada menos que** no less than; **lo dices como si nada** you talk about it as if it was nothing; **¡de nada!** you're welcome, not at all; **no es nada** it's nothing 2 *adv* not at all; **no ha llovido nada** it hasn't rained 3 *f* nothingness
nadador *m*, nadadora *f* swimmer
nadar ⟨1a⟩ *v/i* swim
nadería *f* trifle

nadie *pron* nobody, no-one; **no había nadie** there was nobody there, there wasn't anyone there
nado: **atravesar a nado** swim across
nafta *f Arg* gas(oline), *Br* petrol
naftalina *f* naphthalene
nailon *m* nylon
naipe *m* (playing) card
nalga *f* buttock
nana *f* lullaby; *Rpl* F *(abuela)* grandma
napias *fpl* F schnozzle *sg* F, *Br* hooter *sg* F
naranja 1 *f* orange; **media naranja** F *(pareja)* other half 2 *adj* orange
naranjada *f* orangeade
naranjo *m* orange tree
narciso *m* BOT daffodil
narcótico *m/adj* narcotic
narcotráfico *m* drug trafficking
nariz *f* nose; **¡narices!** F nonsense!; **estar hasta las narices de algo** F be sick of sth F, be up to here with sth F; **meter las narices en algo** F stick one's nose in sth F
narración *f* narration
narrador *m*, narradora *f* narrator
narrar ⟨1a⟩ *v/t*: **narrar algo** tell the story of sth
nasal *adj* nasal
nata *f* cream; **nata montada** whipped cream
natación *f* swimming
natal *adj* native; **ciudad natal** city of one's birth, home town
natalidad *f* birthrate

natillas *fpl* custard *sg*
nativo *m*, -a *f* native
nato *adj* born
natural **1** *adj* natural; *ser natural de* come from; *es natural* it's only natural **2** *m*: *fruta al natural* fruit in its own juice
naturaleza *f* nature
naturalidad *f* naturalness
naturalmente *adv* naturally
naturista **1** *adj* nudist, naturist; *medicina natural* **2** *m/f* nudist, naturist
naufragar ⟨1h⟩ *v/i* be shipwrecked; *fig* fail
naufragio *m* shipwreck
náufrago **1** *adj* shipwrecked **2** *m*, -a *f* shipwrecked person
náuseas *fpl* nausea *sg*
nauseabundo *adj* nauseating
náutico *adj* nautical
navaja *f* knife
navajazo *m* knife wound, slash
navajero *m*: *le asaltó un navajero* he was attacked by a man with a knife
naval *adj* naval
nave *f* ship; *de iglesia* nave; *nave espacial* spacecraft
navegación *f* navigation; *navegación a vela* sailing
navegador *m* INFOR browser
navegante *m/f* navigator
navegar ⟨1h⟩ **1** *v/i* sail; *por el aire, espacio* fly; *navegar por la red* or *por Internet* INFOR surf the Net **2** *v/t* sail
Navidad *f* Christmas
navideño *adj* Christmas *atr*
navío *m* ship
nazi *m/f* & *adj* Nazi
nazismo *m* Nazi(i)sm
N. B. *abr* (= *nótese bien*) NB (= nota bene)
neblina *f* mist
nebuloso *adj fig* hazy, nebulous
necesario *adj* necessary
neceser *m* toilet kit, *Br* toilet bag
necesidad *f* need; (*cosa esencial*) necessity; *de primera necesidad* essential; *en caso de necesidad* if necessary; *hacer sus -es* F relieve o.s.
necesitado *adj* needy
necesitar ⟨1a⟩ *v/t* need

necio *adj* brainless
necrológica *f* obituary
nefasto *adj* harmful
negación *f* negation; *de acusación* denial
negar ⟨1h & 1k⟩ **1** *v/t acusación* deny; (*no conceder*) refuse **2** *v/r negarse* refuse (*a* to)
negativa *f* refusal; *de acusación* denial
negativo **1** *adj* negative **2** *m* FOT negative
negligencia *f* JUR negligence
negociable *adj* negotiable
negociación *f* negotiation; *negociaciones* talks
negociador *m*, negociadora *f* negotiator
negociante *m/f* businessman; *mujer* businesswoman; *desp* money-grubber
negociar ⟨1b⟩ *v/t* negotiate
negocio *m* business; (*trato*) deal
negra *f* black woman; MÚS quarter note, *Br* crotchet; *L.Am.* (*querida*) honey, dear
negrita *f* bold
negro **1** *adj* black; *estar negro* F be furious **2** *m* black man; *L.Am.* (*querido*) honey, dear
nena *f* F little girl, kid F
nene *m* F little boy, kid F
nenúfar *m* BOT water lily
neocelandés *m*, -esa *f* New Zealander
neón *m* neon
neoyorquino **1** *adj* New York *atr* **2** *m*, -a *f* New Yorker
nepotismo *m* nepotism
nervio *m* ANAT nerve
nerviosismo *m* nervousness
nervioso *adj* nervous; *ponerse nervioso* get nervous; (*agitado*) get agitated; *poner a alguien nervioso* get on s.o.'s nerves
neto *adj* COM net
neumático **1** *adj* pneumatic **2** *m* AUTO tire, *Br* tyre
neumonía *f* MED pneumonia
neurocirujano *m*, -a *f* brain surgeon
neurólogo *m*, -a *f* neurologist
neurosis *f inv* neurosis
neurótico *adj* neurotic
neutral *adj* neutral
neutralidad *f* neutrality

neutralizar ⟨1f⟩ v/t neutralize
neutro adj neutral
nevada f snowfall
nevar ⟨1k⟩ v/i snow
nevazón f Arg, Chi snowstorm
nevera f refrigerator, fridge; **nevera portátil** cooler
nevería f Méx, C.Am. ice-cream parlo(u)r
nevero m snowdrift
nexo m link; GRAM connective
ni conj neither; **ni ... ni** neither ... nor; **ni siquiera** not even; **no di ni una** I made a real mess of things
Nicaragua Nicaragua
nicaragüense m/f & adj Nicaraguan
nicho m niche
nicotina f nicotine; **bajo en nicotina** low in nicotine
nido m nest
niebla f fog
nieta f granddaughter
nieto m grandson; **nietos** grandchildren
nieva vb → **nevar**
nieve f snow; Méx water ice, sorbet
nihilismo m nihilism
nimiedad f triviality
nimio adj trivial
ningún adj → **ninguno**
ninguno adj no; **no hay -a razón** there's no reason why, there isn't any reason why
niña f girl; forma de cortesía young lady
niñato m, -a f brat
niñera f nanny
niñería f: **una niñería** a childish thing
niñez f childhood
niño 1 adj young; desp childish 2 m boy; forma de cortesía young man; **niños** children pl; **niño de pecho** infant
níquel m nickel
níspero m BOT loquat
nítido adj clear; imagen sharp
nitrógeno m nitrogen
nitroglicerina f nitroglycerin
nivel m level; (altura) height; **nivel del mar** sea level; **nivel de vida** standard of living
nivelar ⟨1a⟩ v/t level
nixtamal m Méx, C.Am. dough from which corn tortillas are made

n.º abr (= **número**) No. (= number)
no adv no; para negar verbo not; **no entiendo** I don't understand, I do not understand; **no te vayas** don't go; **no bien** as soon as; **no del todo** not entirely; **ya no** not any more; **no más** L.Am. → nomás; **así no más** L.Am. just like that; **te gusta, ¿no?** you like it, don't you?; **te ha llamado, ¿no?** he called you, didn't he?; **¿a que no?** I bet you don't/can't etc
nobiliario adj noble
noble m/f & adj noble
nobleza f nobility
noche f night; **de noche, por la noche** at night; **de la noche a la mañana** fig overnight; **¡buenas noches!** saludo good evening; despedida good night
Nochebuena f Christmas Eve
nochecita f L.Am. evening
nochero m L.Am. night watchman
Nochevieja f New Year's Eve
noción f notion
nocivo adj harmful
noctámbulo m, -a f sleepwalker
nocturno adj night atr; ZO nocturnal; **clase -a** evening class
nogal m BOT walnut
nómada 1 adj nomadic 2 m/f nomad
nomás adv L.Am. just, only; **llévaselo nomás** just take it away; **nomás llegue, te avisaré** as soon as he arrives, I'll let you know; **siga nomás** just carry on; **nomás lo vio, echó a llorar** as soon as she saw him she started to cry
nombramiento m appointment
nombrar ⟨1a⟩ v/t mention; para un cargo appoint
nombre m name; GRAM noun; **nombre de pila** first name; **no tener nombre** fig be inexcusable
nomenclatura f nomenclature
nomeolvides m inv BOT forget-me-not
nómina f pay slip
nominal adj nominal
nominar ⟨1a⟩ v/t nominate
non adj odd
nono adj ninth
nopal m L.Am. BOT prickly pear
nor(d)este m northeast

noria *f de agua* waterwheel; *en feria* ferris wheel

norma *f* standard; *(regla)* rule, regulation

normal *adj* normal

normalidad *f* normality

normalizar ⟨1f⟩ *v/t* standardize

normativa *f* rules *pl*, regulations *pl*

noroeste *m* northwest

norte *m* north

Norteamérica North America

norteamericano 1 *adj* North American **2** *m*, **-a** *f* North American

norteño 1 *adj* northern **2** *m*, **-a** *f* northerner

Noruega Norway

noruego 1 *adj* Norwegian **2** *m*, **-a** *f* Norwegian

nos *pron complemento directo* us; *complemento indirecto* (to) us; *reflexivo* ourselves; *nos dio el dinero* he gave us the money, he gave the money to us

nosotros, nosotras *pron* we; *complemento* us; *ven con nosotros* come with us; *somos nosotros* it's us

nostalgia *f* nostalgia; *por la patria* homesickness

nostálgico *adj* nostalgic

nota *f tb* MÚS note; EDU grade, mark; *nota a pie de página* footnote; *tomar nota de algo* make a note of sth

notable *adj* remarkable, notable

notar ⟨1a⟩ *v/t* notice; *(sentir)* feel; *hacer notar algo a alguien* point sth out to s.o.; *se nota que* you can tell that; *hacerse notar* draw attention to o.s.

notaría *f* notary's office

notario *m*, **-a** *f* notary

noticia *f* piece of news; *en noticiario* news story, item of news; *noticias pl* news *sg*

noticiario *m* RAD, TV news *sg*

notificación *f* notification

notificar ⟨1g⟩ *v/t* notify

notorio *adj* famous, well-known

novatada *f* practical joke

novato *m*, **-a** *f* beginner, rookie F

novecientos *adj* nine hundred

novedad *f* novelty; *cosa* new thing; *(noticia)* piece of news; *acontecimiento* new development; *llegar sin novedad* arrive

safely

novedoso *adj* novel, new; *invento* innovative

novela *f* novel; *novela negra* crime novel; *novela rosa* romantic novel

novelista *m/f* novelist

noveno *adj* ninth

noventa *adj* ninety

novia *f* girlfriend; *el día de la boda* bride

noviazgo *m* engagement

noviembre *m* November

novillada *f* bullfight featuring novice bulls

novillero *m* novice (bullfighter)

novillo *m* ZO young bull; *vaca* heifer; *hacer novillos* F play hooky F, play truant

novio *m* boyfriend; *el día de la boda* bridegroom; *los novios* the bride and groom; *(recién casados)* the newly-weds

nube *f* cloud; *estar en las nubes* fig be miles away; *estar por las nubes* fig F be incredibly expensive

nublado 1 *adj* cloudy, overcast **2** *m* storm cloud

nublarse ⟨1a⟩ *v/r* cloud over

nuboso *adj* cloudy

nuca *f* nape of the neck

nuclear *adj* nuclear

núcleo *m* nucleus; *de problema* heart

nudillo *m* knuckle

nudista *m/f* nudist; *playa nudista* nudist beach

nudo *m* knot; *se me hace un nudo en la garganta* F I get a lump in my throat

nuera *f* daughter-in-law

nuestro 1 *adj pos* our **2** *pron* ours

nueva *f lit* piece of news

nuevamente *adv* again

Nueva York New York

Nueva Zelanda New Zealand

nueve *adj* nine

nuevo *adj* new; *(otro)* another; *de nuevo* again

nuez *f* BOT walnut; ANAT Adam's apple

nulidad *f* nullity; *fig* F dead loss F

nulo *adj* null and void; F *persona* hopeless; *(inexistente)* non-existent, zero

núm. *abr* (= *número*) No. (= number)

numerar ⟨1a⟩ *v/t* number

numérico *adj* numerical; *teclado numé-*

rico numeric keypad, number pad
número *m* number; *de publicación* issue; *de zapato* size; **número complementario** *en lotería* bonus number; **número secreto** PIN (number); **en números rojos** fig in the red; **montar un número** F make a scene
numeroso *adj* numerous
numismática *f* numismatics
nunca *adv* never; **nunca jamás** or **más** never again; **más que nunca** more than ever
nupcial *adj* wedding *atr*
nutria *f* zo otter
nutrición *f* nutrition
nutrido *adj* fig large
nutriente *m* nutrient

nutrir ⟨3a⟩ *v/t* nourish; *fig: esperanzas* cherish
nutritivo *adj* nutritious, nourishing
nylon *m* nylon
ñandú *m* zo rhea
ñandutí *m* *Parag* type of lace
ñapa *f S. Am.* extra, bonus; **le di dos de ñapa** I threw in an extra two
ñato *adj Rpl* snub-nosed
ñeque *m S. Am.* strength; **de ñeque** F gutsy F; **tener mucho ñeque** F have a lot of guts F
ñoñería *f* feebleness F, wimpish behavio(u)r F
ñoño 1 *adj* feeble F, wimpish F **2** *m*, -a *f* drip F, wimp F
ñu *m* zo gnu

O

O *abr* (= *oeste*) W (= West(ern))
o *conj* or; **o … o** either … or; **o sea** in other words
oasis *m inv* oasis
obcecación *f* obstinacy
obcecarse ⟨1g⟩ *v/r* stubbornly insist
obedecer ⟨2d⟩ **1** *v/t* obey **2** *v/i* obey; *de una máquina* respond; **obedecer a** fig be due to
obediencia *f* obedience
obediente *adj* obedient
obelisco *m* obelisk
obesidad *f* obesity
obeso *adj* obese
obispo *m* bishop
objeción *f* objection; **objeción de conciencia** conscientious objection
objetar ⟨1a⟩ **1** *v/t* object; **tener algo que objetar** have any objection **2** *v/i* become a conscientious objector
objetividad *f* objectivity
objetivo 1 *adj* objective **2** *m* objective; MIL target; FOT lens

objeto *m* object; **con objeto de** with the aim of
objetor *m*, **objetora** *f* objector; **objetor de conciencia** conscientious objector
oblicuo *adj* oblique, slanted
obligación *f* obligation, duty; COM bond
obligar ⟨1h⟩ *v/t*: **obligar a alguien** oblige o force s.o. (**a** to); *de una ley* apply to s.o.
obligatorio *adj* obligatory, compulsory
obnubilar ⟨1a⟩ *v/t* cloud
oboe *m* MÚS oboe
obra *f* work; **obras** *pl* **de construcción** building work *sg*; **en la vía pública** road works; **obra de arte** work of art; **obra maestra** masterpiece; **obra de teatro** play
obraje *m Méx* butcher's
obrar ⟨1a⟩ *v/i* act
obrero 1 *adj* working **2** *m*, -a *f* worker
obsceno *adj* obscene
obsequiar ⟨1b⟩ *v/t*: **obsequiar a alguien con algo** present s.o. with sth
obsequio *m* gift
obsequioso *adj* attentive

observación *f* observation; JUR observance

observador **1** *adj* observant **2** *m*, observadora *f* observer

observar ⟨1a⟩ *v/t* observe; (*advertir*) notice, observe; (*comentar*) remark, serve

observatorio *m* observatory

obsesión *f* obsession

obsesionar ⟨1a⟩ **1** *v/t* obsess **2** *v/r* obsesionarse become obsessed (**con** with)

obsesivo *adj* obsessive

obsoleto *adj* obsolete

obstaculizar ⟨1f⟩ *v/t* hinder, hamper

obstáculo *m* obstacle

obstante: **no obstante** nevertheless

obstetra *m/f* obstetrician

obstetricia *f* obstetrics

obstinación *f* obstinacy

obstinado *adj* obstinate

obstinarse ⟨1a⟩ *v/r* insist (**en** on)

obstrucción *f* obstruction, blockage

obstruir ⟨3g⟩ *v/t* obstruct, block

obtener ⟨2l; *part* obtuvo⟩ *v/t* get, obtain *fml*

obturador *m* shutter

obtuvo *vb* → **obtener**

obvio *adj* obvious

oca *f* goose

ocasión *f* occasion; (*oportunidad*) chance, opportunity; **con ocasión de** on the occasion of; **de ocasión** COM cut-price, bargain *atr*; **de segunda mano** second-hand, used

ocasional *adj* occasional

ocasionar ⟨1a⟩ *v/t* cause

ocaso *m del sol* setting; *de un imperio, un poder* decline

occidental **1** *adj* western **2** *m/f* Westerner

occidente *m* west

OCDE *abr* (= **Organización de Cooperación y Desarrollo Económico**) OECD (= Organization for Economic Cooperation and Development)

océano *m* ocean

oceanógrafo *m*, -a *f* oceanographer

ocelote *m* ZO ocelot

ochenta *adj* eighty

ocho *adj* eight

ochocientos *adj* eight hundred

ocio *m* leisure time, free time; *desp* idleness

ociosear ⟨1a⟩ *v/i S. Am.* laze around

ocioso *adj* idle

ocre *m/adj* ocher, *Br* ochre

oct.ᵉ *abr* (= **octubre**) Oct. (= October)

octavilla *f* leaflet

octavo **1** *adj* eighth **2** *m* eighth; DEP **octavos de final** last 16

octógono *m* octagon

octubre *m* October

ocular *adj* eye *atr*

oculista *m/f* ophthalmologist

ocultación *f* concealment

ocultar ⟨1a⟩ *v/t* hide, conceal

ocultismo *m* occult

oculto *adj* hidden; (*sobrenatural*) occult

ocupación *f tb* MIL occupation; (*actividad*) activity

ocupado *adj* busy; *asiento* taken

ocupante *m/f* occupant

ocupar ⟨1a⟩ **1** *v/t espacio* take up, occupy; (*habitar*) live in, occupy; *obreros* employ; *periodo de tiempo* spend, occupy; MIL occupy **2** *v/r* ocuparse: **ocuparse de** deal with; (*cuidar de*) look after

ocurrencia *f* occurrence; (*chiste*) quip, funny remark

ocurrir ⟨3a⟩ *v/i* happen, occur; **se me ocurrió** it occurred to me, it struck me

odiar ⟨1b⟩ *v/t* hate

odio *m* hatred, hate

odioso *adj* odious, hateful

odisea *f fig* odyssey

odontólogo *m* odontologist

OEA *abr* (= **Organización de los Estados Americanos**) OAS (= Organization of American States)

oeste *m* west

ofender ⟨2a⟩ **1** *v/t* offend **2** *v/r* ofenderse take offense (**por** at)

ofensa *f* insult

ofensiva *f* offensive

ofensivo *adj* offensive

oferta *f* offer; **oferta pública de adquisición** takeover bid

oficial **1** *adj* official **2** *m/f* MIL officer

oficialista *adj L.Am.* pro-government

oficina f office; **oficina de correos** post office; **oficina de empleo** employment office; **oficina de turismo** tourist office

oficinista m/f office worker

oficio m trabajo trade

oficioso adj unofficial

ofimática f INFOR office automation

ofrecer ⟨2d⟩ **1** v/t offer **2** v/r **ofrecerse** volunteer, offer one's services (**de** as); (*presentarse*) appear; **¿qué se le ofrece?** what can I do for you?

ofrecimiento m offer

ofrenda f offering

oftalmólogo m, -a f ophthalmologist

ofuscar ⟨1g⟩ v/t tb fig blind

ogro m tb fig ogre

oída f: **conocer algo de oídas** have heard of sth

oído m hearing; **hacer oídos sordos** turn a deaf ear; **ser todo oídos** fig be all ears

oigo vb → **oír**

oír ⟨3q⟩ v/t tb JUR hear; (*escuchar*) listen to; **¡oye!** listen!, hey! F; **como quien oye llover, salió sin él** F he turned a deaf ear and went off without it

OIT abr (= **Organización Internacional de Trabajo**) ILO (= International Labor Organization)

ojal m buttonhole

ojalá int: **¡ojalá!** let's hope so; **¡ojalá venga!** I hope he comes; **¡ojalá tuvieras razón!** I only hope you're right

ojeada f glance; **echar una ojeada a alguien** glance at s.o.

ojeras fpl bags under the eyes

ojo m ANAT eye; **¡ojo!** F watch out!, mind! F; **ojo de la cerradura** keyhole; **a ojo** roughly; **andar con ojo** F keep one's eyes open F; **costar un ojo de la cara** F cost an arm and a leg F; **no pegar ojo** F not sleep a wink F

ojota f C.Am., Méx sandal

okupa m/f Esp F squatter

ola f wave; **ola de calor** heat wave; **ola de frío** cold spell

oleada f fig wave, flood

oleaje m swell

óleo m oil

oleoducto m (oil) pipeline

oler ⟨2i⟩ **1** v/i smell (**a** of) **2** v/t smell **3** v/r: **me huelo algo** fig there's something fishy going on, I smell a rat

olfatear ⟨1a⟩ v/t sniff

olfato m sense of smell; fig nose

olimpíada, olimpiada f Olympics pl

olímpico adj Olympic

olisquear ⟨1a⟩ v/t sniff

oliva f BOT olive

olivo m olive tree

olla f pot; **olla exprés** or **a presión** pressure cooker

olmo m BOT elm

olor m smell; *agradable* scent; **olor corporal** body odo(u)r, BO

oloroso adj scented

OLP abr (= **Organización para la Liberación de Palestina**) PLO (= Palestine Liberation Organization)

olvidadizo adj forgetful

olvidar ⟨1a⟩ **1** v/t forget **2** v/r **olvidarse**: **olvidarse de algo** forget sth

olvido m oblivion

ombligo m ANAT navel

OMC abr (= **Organización Mundial de Comercio**) WTO (= World Trade Organization)

omisión f omission

omiso adj: **hacer caso omiso de algo** ignore sth

omitir ⟨3a⟩ v/t omit, leave out

omnipotente adj omnipotent

omóplato, omoplato m ANAT shoulder blade

OMS abr (= **Organización Mundial de la Salud**) WHO (= World Health Organization)

once adj eleven

oncología f MED oncology

onda f wave; **estar en la onda** F be with it F; **¿qué onda?** Méx F what's happening? F

ondulado adj wavy; *cartón* corrugated

ONG abr (= **Organización no Gubernamental**) NGO (= non-governmental organization)

onomatopeya f onomatopœia

ONU abr (= **Organización de las Naciones Unidas**) UN (= United Nations) onza *f* ounce

OPA *abr* (= **oferta pública de adquisición**) takeover bid

opaco *adj* opaque

opción *f* option, choice; (*posibilidad*) chance

opcional *adj* optional

OPEP *abr* (= **Organización de Países Exportadores de Petróleo**) OPEC (= Organization of Petroleum Exporting Countries)

ópera *f* MÚS opera; **ópera prima** first work

operación *f* operation

operador *m*, operadora *f* TELEC, INFOR operator; **operador turístico** tour operator

operar ⟨1a⟩ **1** *v/t* MED operate on; *cambio* bring about **2** *v/i* operate; COM do business (**con** with) **3** *v/r* **operarse** MED have an operation (**de** on); *de un cambio* occur

operario *m*, -a *f* operator, operative

operativo **1** *adj* operational; **sistema operativo** INFOR operating system **2** *m* L.Am. operation

opereta *f* MÚS operetta

opinar ⟨1a⟩ *v/t* think (**de** about) **2** *v/i* express an opinion

opinión *f* opinion; **la opinión pública** public opinion; **en mi opinión** in my opinion

opio *m* opium

opíparo *adj* sumptuous

oponente *m/f* opponent

oponer ⟨2r; *part* **opuesto**⟩ **1** *v/t resistencia* put up (**a** to), offer (**a** to); *razón, argumento* put forward (**a** against) **2** *v/r* **oponerse** be opposed (**a** to); (*manifestar oposición*) object (**a** to)

oporto *m* port

oportunidad *f* opportunity

oportunista **1** *adj* opportunistic **2** *m/f* opportunist

oportuno *adj* timely; *momento* opportune; *respuesta, medida* suitable, appropriate

oposición *f* POL opposition; **oposiciones** official entrance exams

opresión *f* oppression

opresor **1** *adj* oppressive **2** *m*, opresora *f* oppressor

oprimir ⟨3a⟩ *v/t* oppress; *botón* press; *de zapatos* be too tight for

optar ⟨1a⟩ *v/i* (*elegir*) opt (**por** for); **optar a** be in the running for; **optar por hacer algo** opt to do sth

optativo *adj* optional

óptica *f* optician's; FÍS optics; *fig* point of view

óptico **1** *adj* optical **2** *m*, -a *f* optician

optimismo *m* optimism

optimista **1** *adj* optimistic **2** *m/f* optimist

optimizar ⟨1f⟩ *v/t* optimize

óptimo *adj* ideal

opuesto **1** *part* → **oponer 2** *adj* opposite; *opinión* contrary

opulencia *f* opulence

opuso *vb* → **oponer**

oquedad *f* cavity

oración *f* REL prayer; GRAM sentence

orador *m*, oradora *f* orator

oral *adj* oral; **prueba de inglés oral** English oral (exam)

orangután *m* ZO orangutan

orar ⟨1a⟩ *v/i* pray (**por** for)

oratoria *f* oratory

órbita *f* orbit; **colocar** *or* **poner en órbita** put into orbit

orca *f* ZO killer whale

órdago *m*: **de órdago** F terrific F

orden **1** *m* order; **orden del día** agenda; **por orden alfabético** in alphabetical order; **poner en orden** tidy up **2** *f* (*mandamiento*) order; **¡a la orden!** yes, sir; **por orden de** by order of, on the orders of

ordenado *adj* tidy

ordenador *m* INFOR computer; **ordenador de escritorio** desktop (computer); **ordenador personal** personal computer; **ordenador portátil** portable (computer); laptop; **asistido por ordenador** computer aided

ordenanza **1** *f* by-law **2** *m* office junior, gofer F; MIL orderly

ordenar ⟨1a⟩ *v/t habitación* tidy up; *alfabéticamente* arrange; (*mandar*) order

ordeñar ⟨1a⟩ *v/t* milk

ordinario *adj* ordinary; *desp* vulgar; **de ordinario** usually, ordinarily orégano *m* BOT oregano

oreja *f* ear; **aguzar las orejas** L.Am. prick one's ears up; **ver las orejas al lobo** *fig* F wake up to the danger

orejeras *fpl* earmuffs

orfanato *m* orphanage

orfebrería *f* goldsmith / silversmith work

orfelinato *m* orphanage

orgánico *adj* organic

organigrama *m* flow chart; *de empresa* organization chart, tree diagram

organillo *m* barrel organ

organismo *m* organism; POL agency, organization; **organismo modificado genéticamente** genetically modified organism

organización *f* organization; **Organización de Cooperación y Desarrollo Económico** Organization for Economic Co-operation and Development; **Organización de las Naciones Unidas** United Nations; **Organización de los Estados Americanos** Organization of American States; **Organización del Tratado del Atlántico Norte** North Atlantic Treaty Organization; **Organización de Países Exportadores de Petróleo** Organization of Petroleum Exporting Countries; **Organización Internacional de Trabajo** International Labor Organization; **Organización Mundial de Comercio** World Trade Organization; **Organización Mundial de la Salud** World Health Organization; **Organización para la Liberación de Palestina** Palestine Liberation Organization

organizador 1 *adj* organizing 2 *m*, organizadora *f* organizer; **organizador personal** personal organizer

organizar ⟨1f⟩ 1 *v/t* organize 2 *v/r* organizarse *de persona* organize one's time

órgano *m* MÚS, ANAT, *fig* organ

orgasmo *m* orgasm

orgía *f* orgy

orgullo *m* pride

orgulloso *adj* proud (**de** of)

orientación *f* orientation; *(ayuda)* guidance; **sentido de la orientación** sense of direction

orientador *m*, orientadora *f* counsel(l)or

oriental 1 *adj* oriental, eastern 2 *m/f* Oriental

orientar ⟨1a⟩ 1 *v/t (aconsejar)* advise; **orientar algo hacia algo** turn sth toward sth 2 *v/r* orientarse get one's bearings; *de una planta* turn (**hacia** toward)

oriente *m* east; **Oriente** Orient; **Oriente Medio** Middle East; **Extremo** or **Lejano Oriente** Far East

orificio *m* hole; *en cuerpo* orifice

origen *m* origin; **dar origen a** give rise to

original *m/adj* original

originalidad *f* originality

originar ⟨1a⟩ 1 *v/t* give rise to 2 *v/r* originarse originate; *de un incendio* start

originario *adj* original; *(nativo)* native (**de** of)

orilla *f* shore; *de un río* bank

orina *f* urine

orinal *m* urinal

orinar ⟨1a⟩ *v/i* urinate

oriundo *adj* native (**de** to)

ornamental *adj* ornamental

ornitología *f* ornithology

ornitólogo *m*, -a *f* ornithologist

oro *m* gold; **guardar como oro en paño** *con mucho cariño* treasure sth; *con mucho cuidado* guard sth with one's life; **prometer el oro y el moro** promise the earth; **oros** *(en naipes)* suit in Spanish deck of cards

orondo *adj* fat; *fig* smug

oropéndola *f* ZO golden oriole

orquesta *f* orchestra

orquestar ⟨1a⟩ *v/t fig* orchestrate

orquídea *f* BOT orchid

ortiga *f* BOT nettle

ortodoncia *f* MED orthodontics

ortodoxo *adj* orthodox

ortografía *f* spelling

ortopédico 1 *adj* orthop(a)edic 2 *m*, -a *f* orthop(a)edist

oruga *f* ZO caterpillar; TÉC (caterpillar) track

orujo *m* liquor made from the remains of grapes

orzuelo *m* MED stye

os *pron complemento directo* you; *com-*

plemento indirecto (to) you; *reflexivo* yourselves; **os lo devolveré** I'll give you it back, I'll give it back to you

osa *f* AST: **Osa Mayor** Great Bear; **Osa Menor** Little Bear

osadía *f* daring; (*descaro*) audacity

osamenta *f* bones *pl*

osar ⟨1a⟩ *v/i* dare

oscilación *f* oscillation; *de precios* fluctuation

oscilar ⟨1a⟩ *v/i* oscillate; *de precios* fluctuate

oscurecer ⟨2d⟩ **1** *v/t* darken; *logro, triunfo* overshadow **2** *v/i* get dark **3** *v/r* **oscurecerse** darken

oscuridad *f* darkness

oscuro *adj* dark; *fig* obscure; **a -as** in the dark

óseo *adj* bone *atr*

osezno *m* cub

osito *m*: **osito de peluche** teddy bear

oso *m* bear; **oso hormiguero** anteater; **oso panda** panda; **oso polar** polar bear

ostensible *adj* obvious

ostentación *f* ostentation; **hacer ostentación de** flaunt

ostentar ⟨1a⟩ *v/t* flaunt; *cargo* hold

ostentoso *adj* ostentatious

osteoporosis *f* MED osteoporosis

ostra *f* ZO oyster; **¡ostras!** F hell! F

ostrero *m* ZO oyster-catcher

OTAN *abr* (= **Organización del Tratado del Atlántico Norte**) NATO (= North Atlantic Treaty Organization)

otitis *f* MED earache

otoño *m* fall, *Br* autumn

otorgar ⟨1h⟩ *v/t* award; *favor* grant

otorrino F, **otorrinolaringólogo** *m* MED

ear, nose and throat *o* ENT specialist

otro 1 *adj* (*diferente*) another; *con el, la* other; **otros** other; **otros dos libros** another two books **2** *pron* (*adicional*) another (one); (*persona distinta*) someone *o* somebody else; (*cosa distinta*) another one, a different one; **otros** others; **entre otros** among others **3** *siguiente*: **¡hasta -a!** see you soon **4** *pron recíproco*: **amar el uno al otro** love one another

ovación *f* ovation

ovacionar ⟨1a⟩ *v/t* cheer, give an ovation to

ovalado *adj* oval

óvalo *m* oval

ovario *m* ANAT ovary

oveja *f* sheep; **oveja negra** *fig* black sheep

overol *m* *Méx* overalls *pl*, *Br* dungarees *pl*

ovillo *m* ball; **hacerse un ovillo** *fig* curl up (into a ball)

ovino 1 *adj* sheep *atr* **2** *m* sheep; **ovinos** sheep *pl*

OVNI *abr* (= **objeto volante no identificado**) UFO (= unidentified flying object)

ovulación *f* ovulation

óvulo *m* egg

oxidado *adj* rusty

oxidar ⟨1a⟩ **1** *v/t* rust **2** *v/r* **oxidarse** rust, go rusty

óxido *m* QUÍM oxide; (*herrumbre*) rust

oxigenarse ⟨1a⟩ *v/r* *fig* get some fresh air

oxígeno *m* oxygen

oye *vb* → **oír**

oyendo *vb* → **oír**

oyente *m/f* listener

oyó *vb* → **oír**

ozono *m* ozone; **capa de ozono** ozone layer

P

pabellón *m* pavilion; *edificio* block; MÚS bell; MAR flag

pachanga *f*: **ir de pachanga** *Méx, W.I., C.Am.* F go on a spree F pachocha *L.Am.*, pachorra *f* F slowness

pachucho *adj* MED F poorly

paciencia *f* patience

paciente *m/f & adj* patient

pacificador *m*, pacificadora *f* peace-
-maker

pacificar ⟨1g⟩ *v/t* pacify

pacífico **1** *adj* peaceful; *persona* peacea-
ble; *el océano Pacífico* the Pacific
Ocean **2** *m*: *el Pacífico* the Pacific

pacifista **1** *adj* pacifist *atr* **2** *m/f* pacifist

paco *m*, -a *f L.Am.* F (*policía*) cop F

pacotilla *f*: *de pacotilla* third-rate, lousy F

pacotillero *m*, -a *f L.Am.* street vendor

pactar ⟨1a⟩ **1** *v/t* agree; *pactar un acuerdo* reach (an) agreement **2** *v/i* reach (an)
agreement

pacto *m* agreement, pact

padecer ⟨2d⟩ **1** *v/t* suffer **2** *v/i* suffer; *padecer de* have trouble with

padrastro *m* step-father

padre *m* father; REL Father; *de padre y
muy señor mío* terrible; *padres* parents;
¡qué padre! *Méx* F brilliant!

padrenuestro *m* Lord's Prayer

padrillo *m Rpl* stallion

padrino *m en bautizo* godfather; (*en boda*) man who gives away the bride

padrón *m* register of local inhabitants

paella *f* GASTR paella

pág. *abr* (= *página*) p. (= page)

paga *f* pay; *de niño* allowance, *Br* pocket
money

pagado *adj* paid

pagano *adj* pagan

pagar ⟨1h⟩ **1** *v/t* pay; *compra, gastos, crimen* pay for; *favor* repay; *¡me las pagarás!* you'll pay for this! **2** *v/i* pay; *pagar a escote* F go Dutch F

pagaré *m* IOU

página *f* page; *página web* web page;
páginas amarillas yellow pages

pago *m* payment; *Rpl* (*quinta*) piece of
land; *pago al contado or en efectivo*
payment in cash; *en pago de* in payment
for; *por estos pagos* F in this neck of the
woods F

país *m* country; *país en vías de desarrollo* developing country; *los Países Ba-*

jos the Netherlands

paisaje *m* landscape

paisano *m*: *de paisano* MIL in civilian
clothes; *policía* in plain clothes

paja *f* straw; *hacerse una paja* V jerk off V

pajar *m* hayloft

pajarería *f* pet shop

pajarita *f corbata* bow tie; *de papel* paper
bird

pájaro *m* bird; *fig* ugly customer F, nasty
piece of work F; *pájaro carpintero*
woodpecker; *matar dos pájaros de un
tiro* kill two birds with one stone

Pakistán Pakistan

pakistaní *m/f & adj* Pakistani

pala *f* spade; *raqueta* paddle; *para servir*
slice; *para recoger* dustpan

palabra *f tb fig* word; *palabra de honor*
word of hono(u)r; *bajo palabra* on parole; *en una palabra* in a word; *tomar
la palabra* speak

palabrota *f* swearword

palacete *m* small palace

palaciego *adj* palace *atr*

palacio *m* palace; *palacio de deportes*
sports center (*Br* centre); *palacio de justicia* law courts

paladar *m* palate

palanca *f* lever; *palanca de cambios* AU-
TO gearshift, *Br* gear lever; *tener palanca* *Méx fig* F have pull F *o* clout F

palangana *f plastic bowl for washing dishes*, *Br* washing-up bowl

palanganear ⟨1a⟩ *v/i S. Am.* show off

palanqueta *f* crowbar

palco *m* TEA box

palenque *m L.Am.* cockpit (*in cock fighting*)

Palestina Palestine

palestino **1** *adj* Palestinian **2** *m*, -a *f* Palestinian

palestra *f* arena; *salir or saltar a la palestra* *fig* hit the headlines

paleta *f* PINT palette; *téc* trowel

paletilla *f* GASTR shoulder

paleto F **1** *adj* hick *atr* F, provincial **2** *m*, -a
f hick F, *Br* yokel F

paliar ⟨1b⟩ *v/t* alleviate; *dolor* relieve

paliativo *m/adj* palliative

palidecer ⟨2d⟩ v/i de persona turn pale
palidez f paleness
pálido adj pale
palillo m para dientes toothpick; para comer chopstick
palique m: estar de palique F have a chat
paliza 1 f beating; (derrota) thrashing F,
drubbing F; (pesadez) drag F 2 m/f F drag
F
palma f palm; dar palmas clap (one's
hands)
palmada f pat; (manotazo) slap
palmar ⟨1a⟩ v/t: palmarla P kick the bucket F
palmera f BOT palm tree; (dulce) heart-
-shaped pastry
palmito m BOT palmetto; GASTR palm
heart; fig F attractiveness
palmo m hand's breadth; palmo a palmo
inch by inch
palo m de madera etc stick; MAR mast; de
portería post, upright; palo de golf golf
club; palo mayor MAR mainmast; a medio palo L.Am. F half-drunk; a palo seco whisky straight up; ser un palo
L.Am. F be fantastic; de tal palo tal astilla a chip off the old block F
paloma f pigeon; blanca dove; paloma
mensajera carrier pigeon
palomar m pigeon loft
palometa f ZO pez pompano
palomilla f C.Am., Méx F gang
palomita f Méx checkmark, Br tick; palomitas pl de maíz popcorn sg
palpable adj fig palpable
palpar ⟨1a⟩ v/t con las manos feel, touch;
fig feel
palpitación f palpitation
palpitante adj corazón pounding; cuestión burning
palpitar ⟨1a⟩ v/i del corazón pound; Rpl
fig have a hunch F, have a feeling
palta f S. Am. BOT avocado
palto m S. Am. jacket
paludismo m MED malaria
palurdo 1 adj F hick atr F, provincial 2 m,
-a f F hick F, Br yokel F
pamela f picture hat
pampa f GEOG pampa, prairie; a la pampa

Rpl in the open
pamplinas fpl nonsense sg
pan m bread; un pan a loaf; pan francés
L.Am. French bread; pan integral
wholemeal bread; pan de molde sliced
bread; pan de barra French bread;
pan rallado breadcrumbs pl; pan tostado toast; ser pan comido F be easy as
pie F
pana f corduroy
panacea f panacea
panadería f baker's shop
panadero m, -a f baker
panal m honeycomb
Panamá Panama; el Canal de Panamá
the Panama Canal; Ciudad de Panamá
Panama city
panameño 1 adj Panamanian 2 m, -a f
Panamanian
pancarta f placard
panceta f belly pork
páncreas m inv ANAT
panda m ZO panda
pandereta f tambourine
pandilla f group; de delincuentes gang
panecillo m (bread) roll
panel m tb grupo de personas panel; panel solar solar panel
panela f L.Am. brown sugar loaf
panera f bread basket
panfleto m pamphlet
pánico m panic; sembrar el pánico
spread panic
panocha, panoja f ear
panoli adj F dopey F
panorama m panorama
panorámico adj: vista -a panoramic view
panqueque m L.Am. pancake
pantalla f TV, INFOR screen; de lámpara
shade; pequeña pantalla fig small
screen
pantalón m, pantalones mpl pants pl, Br
trousers pl; llevar los pantalones fig F
wear the pants (Br trousers) F
pantano m reservoir
panteón m pantheon
pantera f ZO panther
pantomima f pantomime
pantorrilla f ANAT calf

pantufla *f* slipper

panty *m* pantyhose *pl*, *Br* tights *pl*

panza *f de persona* belly

pañal *m* diaper, *Br* nappy

paño *m* cloth; *paño de cocina* dishtowel

pañuelo *m* handkerchief; *el mundo es un pañuelo fig* F it's a small world

papa 1 *m* Pope 2 *f L.Am.* potato

papá *m* F pop F, dad F; *papás L.Am.* parents; *Papá Noel* Santa Claus

papada *f* double chin

papagayo *m* zo parrot

papal 1 *adj* papal 2 *m L.Am.* potato field

papalote *m Méx* kite

papanatas *m/f inv* F dope F, dimwit F

paparruchas *fpl* F baloney *sg* F

papaya *f* BOT papaya

papel *m* paper; *trozo* piece of paper; TEA, *fig* role; *papel de aluminio* foil; *papel de envolver* wrapping paper; *papel de regalo* giftwrap; *papel higiénico* toilet paper *o* tissue; *papel reciclado* recycled paper; *perder los papeles* lose control; *ser papel mojado fig* not be worth the paper it's written on

papelada *f L.Am.* farce

papeleo *m* paperwork

papelera *f* wastepaper basket

papelería *f* stationer's shop

papelerío *m L.Am.* F muddle, mess

papeleta *f de rifa* raffle ticket; *fig* chore; *papeleta de voto* ballot paper

paperas *fpl* MED mumps

papilla *f para bebés* baby food; *para enfermos* puree; *hacer papilla a alguien* F beat s.o. to a pulp F

papista *adj*: *ser más papista que el papa* hold extreme views

paquete *m* package, parcel; *de cigarrillos* packet; F *en moto* (pillion) passenger

Paquistán Pakistan

paquistaní *m/f* & *adj* Pakistani

par 1 *f* par; *es bella a la par que inteligente* she is beautiful as well as intelligent, she is both beautiful and intelligent 2 *m* pair; *abierto de par en par* wide open; *un par de* a pair of

para *prp* for ◇ *dirección* toward(s); *ir para* head for; *va para directora* she's going to end up as manager

◇ *tiempo* for; *listo para mañana* ready for tomorrow; *para siempre* forever; *diez para las ocho L.Am.* ten of eight, ten to eight

◇ *finalidad*: *lo hace para ayudarte* he does it (in order) to help you; *para que* so that; *¿para qué te marchas?* what are you leaving for?; *para mí* for me; *lo heredó todo para morir a los 30* he inherited it all, only to die at 30

parabólica *f* satellite dish

parabrisas *m inv* AUTO windshield, *Br* windscreen

paracaídas *m inv* parachute

paracaidista *m/f* parachutist; MIL paratrooper

parachoques *m inv* AUTO fender, *Br* bumper

parada *f* stop; *parada de autobús* bus stop; *parada de taxis* taxi rank

paradero *m* whereabouts *sg*; *L.Am.* → *parada*

parado 1 *adj* unemployed; *L.Am. (de pie)* standing (up); *salir bien / mal parado* come off well / badly 2 *m*, -a *f* unemployed person

paradoja *f* paradox

paradójico *adj* paradoxical

parador *m Esp* parador (*state-run luxury hotel*)

parafernalia *f* F paraphernalia

parafina *f* kerosene, *Br* paraffin

paraguas *m inv* umbrella

Paraguay Paraguay

paraguayo 1 *adj* Paraguayan 2 *m*, -a *f* Paraguayan

paraíso *m* paradise; *paraíso fiscal* tax haven

paralelismo *m* parallel

paralelo *m/adj* parallel

parálisis *f tb fig* paralysis

paralítico 1 *adj* paralytic 2 *m*, -a *f* person who is paralyzed

paralización *f tb fig* paralysis

paralizar ⟨1f⟩ *v/t* MED paralyze; *actividad* bring to a halt; *país, economía* paralyze, bring to a standstill

parámetro *m* parameter

paramilitar *adj* paramilitary
parangón *m*: **sin parangón** incomparable
paranoia *f* paranoia
paranoico **1** *adj* MED paranoid **2** *m*, -a *f* MED person suffering from paranoia
paranormal *adj* paranormal
parapente *m* hang glider; *actividad* hang gliding
parapeto *m* parapet
parapléjico **1** *adj* MED paraplegic **2** *m*, -a *f* paraplegic
parar ⟨1a⟩ **1** *v/t* stop; *L.Am. (poner de pie)* stand up **2** *v/i* stop; *en alojamiento* stay; **parar de llover** stop raining; **ir a parar** end up **3** *v/r* pararse stop; *L.Am. (ponerse de pie)* stand up
pararrayos *m inv* lightning rod
parásito *m* parasite
parcela *f* lot, *Br* plot
parchar ⟨1a⟩ *v/t L.Am.* patch; *(arreglar)* repair
parche *m* patch
parcial *adj (partidario)* bias(s)ed
pardo **1** *adj color* dun; *L.Am. desp* half-breed *desp*, *Br tb* half-caste *desp* **2** *m color* dun; *L.Am. desp* half-breed *desp*
parecer **1** *m* opinion, view; *al parecer* apparently **2** ⟨2d⟩ *v/i* seem, look; *me parece que* I think (that), it seems to me that; *me parece bien* it seems fine to me; *¿qué te parece?* what do you think? **3** *v/r* parecerse resemble each other; *parecerse a alguien* resemble s.o.
parecido **1** *adj* similar **2** *m* similarity
pared *f* wall; *subirse por las paredes* F hit the roof F
pareja *f (conjunto de dos)* pair; *en una relación* couple; *de una persona* partner; *de un objeto* other one
parejo *adj L.Am. suelo* level, even; *andar parejos* be neck and neck; *llegaron parejos* they arrived at the same time
paréntesis *m inv* parenthesis; *fig* break; *entre paréntesis fig* by the way
pareo *m* wrap-around skirt
parida *f* P stupid thing to say / do
pariente *m* relative
paripé *m*: *hacer el paripé* F put on an act

F
parir ⟨3a⟩ **1** *v/i* give birth **2** *v/t* give birth to
París París
parisino **1** *adj* Parisian **2** *m*, -a *f* Parisian
parka *f* parka
parking *m* parking lot, *Br* car park
parlamentario **1** *adj* parliamentary **2** *m*, -a *f* member of parliament
parlamento *m* parliament
parlanchín *adj* chatty
parlante *m L.Am.* loudspeaker
parlotear ⟨1a⟩ *v/i* chatter
parmesano *m/adj* Parmesan
paro *m* unemployment; *estar en paro* be unemployed; *paro cardíaco* cardiac arrest
parodia *f* parody
parpadear ⟨1a⟩ *v/i* blink
parpadeo *m* blinking
párpado *m* eye lid
parque *m* park; *para bebé* playpen; *parque de atracciones* amusement park; *parque de bomberos* fire station; *parque nacional* national park; *parque natural* nature reserve; *parque temático* theme park
parqué *m* → *parquet*
parquear ⟨1a⟩ *v/t L.Am.* park
parquet *m* parquet
parquímetro *m* parking meter
parra *f* (grape) vine
párrafo *m* paragraph
parranda *f*: *andar or irse de parranda* F go out on the town F
parricidio *m* parricide
parrilla *f* broiler, *Br* grill; *a la parrilla* broiled, *Br* grilled
parrillada *f L.Am.* barbecue
párroco *m* parish priest
parroquia *f* REL parish; COM clientele, customers *pl*
parsimonia *f* parsimony
parte **1** *m* report; *parte meteorológico* weather report; *dar parte a alguien* inform s.o. **2** *f trozo* part; JUR party; *alguna parte* somewhere; *ninguna parte* nowhere; *otra parte* somewhere else; *de parte de* on behalf of; *en parte* partly; *en or por todas partes* everywhere; *la*

mayor parte de the majority of, most of;
por otra parte moreover; ***estar de parte
de alguien*** be on s.o.'s side; ***formar parte de*** form part of; ***tomar parte en*** take
part in

participación *f* participation
participante *m/f* participant
participar ⟨1a⟩ **1** *v/t una noticia* announce
2 *v/i* take part (***en*** in), participate (***en*** in)
participio *m* GRAM participle
partícula *f* particle
particular 1 *adj clase, propiedad* private;
asunto personal; (*específico*) particular;
(*especial*) peculiar; ***en particular*** in particular **2** *m* (*persona*) individual; ***parti-
culares*** particulars
particularidad *f* peculiarity
partida *f en juego* game; (*remesa*) consignment; *documento* certificate; ***partida de nacimiento*** birth certificate
partidario 1 *adj*: ***ser partidario de*** be in
favo(u)r of **2** *m*, **-a** *f* supporter
partidismo *m* partisanship
partido *m* POL party; DEP game; ***sacar
partido de*** take advantage of; ***tomar
partido*** take sides
partir ⟨3a⟩ **1** *v/t* (*dividir, repartir*) split;
(*romper*) break open, split open; (*cortar*)
cut **2** *v/i* (*irse*) leave; ***a partir de hoy***
(starting) from today; ***a partir de ahora***
from now on; ***partir de*** *fig* start from **3** *v/r*
partirse (*romperse*) break; ***partirse de
risa*** F split one's sides laughing F
partitura *f* MÚS score
parto *m* birth; *fig* creation
parvulario *m* kindergarten
pasa *f* raisin
pasable *adj* passable
pasada *f con trapo* wipe; *de pintura* coat;
de pasada in passing; ***¡qué pasada!*** F
that's incredible! F
pasadizo *m* passage
pasado 1 *adj tiempo* last; ***el lunes pasado*** last Monday; ***pasado de moda*** old-
-fashioned **2** *m* past
pasaje *m* (*billete*) ticket; MÚS, *de texto* passage
pasajero 1 *adj* temporary; *relación* brief **2**
m, **-a** *f* passenger

pasamano(s) *m* handrail
pasamontañas *m inv* balaclava (helmet)
pasaporte *m* passport
pasar ⟨1a⟩ **1** *v/t* pass; *el tiempo* spend; *un
lugar* go past; *frontera* cross; *problemas,
dificultades* experience; AUTO (*adelantar*)
pass, *Br* overtake; *una película* show; ***para pasar el tiempo*** (in order) to pass the
time; ***pasar la mano por*** run one's hand
through; ***pasarlo bien*** have a good time
2 *v/i* (*suceder*) happen; *en juegos* pass;
pasar de alguien F not want anything
to do with s.o.; ***paso de coger el teléfono*** F I can't be bothered to pick up the
phone; ***pasé a visitarla*** I dropped by
to see her; ***pasar de moda*** go out of
fashion; ***pasar por*** go by; ***pasé por la
tienda*** I stopped off at the shop; ***pasa
por aquí*** come this way; ***dejar pasar
oportunidad*** pass o.s. off as; ***pasaré por tu casa*** I'll
drop by your house; ***¡pasa!*** come in;
¿qué pasa? what's happening?, what's
going on?; ***¿qué te pasa?*** what's the
matter?; ***pase lo que pase*** whatever
happens, come what may **3** *v/r pasarse
tb fig* go too far; *del tiempo* pass, go by;
(*usar el tiempo*) spend; *de molestia, dolor*
go away; ***pasarse al enemigo*** go over to
the enemy; ***se le pasó llamar*** he forgot
to call
pasarela *f* catwalk
pasatiempo *m* pastime
Pascua *f* Easter; ***¡felices Pascuas!*** Merry Christmas!
pase *m tb* DEP, TAUR pass; *en el cine* showing; ***pase de modelos*** fashion show
pasear ⟨1a⟩ **1** *v/t* take for a walk; (*exhibir*)
show off **2** *v/i* walk **3** *v/r* **pasearse** walk
paseo *m* walk; ***paseo marítimo*** seafront;
dar un paseo go for a walk; ***mandar a
alguien a paseo*** *fig* F tell s.o. to get lost
pasillo *m* corridor; *en avión, cine* aisle
pasión *f* passion
pasividad *f* passivity
pasivo *adj* passive
pasmar ⟨1a⟩ *v/t* amaze, astonish
paso *m* step; (*manera de andar*) walk; (*ritmo*) pace, rate; *de agua* flow; *de tráfico*

movement; (*cruce*) crossing; *de tiempo* passing; (*huella*) footprint; **paso a nivel** grade crossing, *Br* level crossing; **paso de peatones** crosswalk, pedestrian crossing; **a este paso** *fig* at this rate; **de paso** on the way; **estar de paso** be passing through

pasta *f sustancia* paste; GASTR pasta; P (*dinero*) dough P; **pasta de dientes** toothpaste; **pastas de té** type of cookie (*Br biscuit*)

pastel *m* GASTR cake; *pintura, color* pastel

pastelería *f* cake shop

pastelero *m*, **-a** *f* pastry cook

paste(u)rizar ⟨1f⟩ *v/t* pasteurize

pastilla *f* tablet; *de jabón* bar; **a toda pastilla** F at top speed F, flat out F

pasto *m* (*hierba*) grass; **a todo pasto** F for all one is worth F

pastor *m* shepherd; REL pastor; **pastor alemán** German shepherd

pata[1] *m/f* Pe F pal F, buddy F

pata[2] *f* leg; **a cuatro patas** on all fours; **meter la pata** F put one's foot in it F; **tener mala pata** F be unlucky

patada *f* kick; **dar una patada** kick

patalear ⟨1a⟩ *v/i* stamp one's feet; *fig* kick and scream

patata *f* potato; **patatas fritas** *de sartén* French fries, *Br* chips; *de bolsa* chips, *Br* crisps

patatús *m*: **le dio un patatús** F he had a fit F

paté *m* paté

patear ⟨1a⟩ *v/t & v/i L.Am. de animal* kick

patentar ⟨1a⟩ *v/t* patent

patente 1 *adj* clear, obvious **2** *f* patent; *L.Am.* AUTO license plate, *Br* numberplate

paternidad *f* paternity, fatherhood

paterno *adj* paternal

patético *adj* pitiful

patíbulo *m* scaffold

patilla *f de gafas* arm; **patillas** *barba* sideburns

patín *m* skate; **patín (de ruedas) en línea** rollerblade®, in-line skate

patinador *m*, **patinadora** *f* skater

patinaje *m* skating; **patinaje artístico** fig-

ure skating; **patinaje sobre hielo** ice-skating; **patinaje sobre ruedas** roller-skating

patinar ⟨1a⟩ *v/i* skate

patinazo *m* skid; *fig* F blunder; **dar un patinazo** skid

patinete *m* scooter

patio *m* courtyard, patio; **patio de butacas** TEA orchestra, *Br* stalls *pl*

pato *m* ZO duck; **pagar el pato** F take the rap F, *Br* carry the can F

patojo *adj Chi* F squat

patológico *adj* pathological

patoso *adj* clumsy

patraña *f* tall story

patria *f* homeland

patriarca *m* patriarch

patrimonio *m* heritage; **patrimonio artístico** artistic heritage

patriota *m/f* patriot

patriótico *adj* patriotic

patriotismo *m* patriotism

patrocinador *m*, **patrocinadora** *f* sponsor

patrocinar ⟨1a⟩ *v/t* sponsor

patrocinio *m* sponsorship

patrón *m* (*jefe*) boss; REL patron saint; *para costura* pattern; (*modelo*) standard; MAR skipper

patrona *f* (*jefa*) boss; REL patron saint

patronal employers *pl*

patrulla *f* patrol

patrullar ⟨1a⟩ *v/t* patrol

patrullero *m* patrolman

paulatino *adj* gradual

pausa *f* pause; *en una actividad* break; MÚS rest; **pausa publicitaria** commercial break

pausado *adj* slow, deliberate

pauta *f* guideline; **marcar la pauta** set the guidelines

pavimento *m* pavement, *Br* road surface

pavo 1 *adj L.Am.* F stupid **2** *m* ZO turkey; **pavo real** peacock

pavonearse ⟨1a⟩ *v/r* boast (**de** about)

pavor *m* terror; **me da pavor** it terrifies me

payada *f Rpl improvized* ballad

payador *m Rpl* gaucho singer

P

payasadas *fpl* antics; *hacer payasadas* fool *o* clown around

payaso *m* clown

paz *f* peace; *dejar en paz* leave alone

pe: *de pe a pa* F from start to finish

PC *abr* (= *Partido Comunista*) CP (= Communist Party)

P.D. *abr* (= *posdata*) PS (= postscript)

peaje *m dinero, lugar* toll

peatón *m* pedestrian

peatonal *adj* pedestrian *atr*

pebete *m, -a f Rpl* F kid F

peca *f* freckle

pecado *m* sin

pecador *m,* **pecadora** *f* sinner

pecaminoso *adj* sinful

pecar ⟨1g⟩ *v/i* sin; *pecar de ingenuo / generoso* be very naive / generous

pecera *f* fish tank, aquarium

pecho *m* (*caja torácica*) chest; (*mama*) breast; *tomar algo a pecho* take sth to heart

pechuga *f* GASTR breast; *L.Am. fig* F (*caradura*) nerve F

pecoso *adj* freckled

pectoral *adj* ANAT pectoral

peculiar *adj* peculiar, odd; (*característico*) typical

peculiaridad *f* (*característica*) peculiarity

pedagogía *f* education

pedagogo *m, -a f* teacher

pedal *m* pedal

pedalear ⟨1a⟩ *v/i* pedal

pedante **1** *adj* pedantic; (*presuntuoso*) pretentious **2** *m/f* pedant; (*presuntuoso*) pretentious individual

pedantería *f* pedantry; (*presunción*) pretentiousness

pedazo *m* piece, bit; *pedazo de bruto* F blockhead F; *hacer pedazos* F smash to bits F

pederasta *m* pederast

pedestal *m* pedestal

pediatra *m/f* p(a)ediatrician

pedicura *f* pedicure

pedicuro *m, -a f* pedicurist, *Br* chiropodist

pedido *m* order

pedigrí *m* pedigree

pedigüeño *m, -a f* person who is always asking to borrow things, moocher F

pedir ⟨3l⟩ **1** *v/t* ask for; (*necesitar*) need; *en bar, restaurante* order; *me pidió que no fuera* he asked me not to go **2** *v/i mendigar* beg; *en bar, restaurante* order

pedo **1** *adj* drunk **2** *m* F fart F; *agarrarse un pedo* F get plastered F; *tirarse* or *echar un pedo* F fart F

pedorreta *f* F Bronx cheer F, *Br* raspberry F

pedrada *f* blow with a stone; *me dio una pedrada en la cabeza* he hit me over the head with a stone

pedregal *m* stony ground

pedregoso *adj* stony

Pedro *m:* *como Pedro por su casa fig* F as if he / she owned the place

pega *f* F snag F, hitch F; *poner pegas* raise objections

pegadizo *adj* catchy

pegado *adj* (*adherido*) stuck (*a* to); *estar pegado a* (*cerca de*) be right up against; *estar pegado a alguien fig* follow s.o. around, be s.o.'s shadow

pegajoso *adj* sticky; *fig: persona* clingy

pegamento *m* glue

pegar ⟨1h⟩ **1** *v/t* (*golpear*) hit; (*adherir*) stick, glue; *bofetada, susto, resfriado* give; *pegar un grito* shout; *no me pega la gana Méx* F I don't feel like it **2** *v/i* (*golpear*) hit; (*adherir*) stick; *del sol* beat down; (*armonizar*) go (together) **3** *v/r* **pegarse** *resfriado* catch; *acento* pick up; *susto* give o.s.; *pegarse un golpe / un tiro* hit / shoot o.s.; *pegársela a alguien* F con s.o. F

pegatina *f* sticker

pegote *m* F (*cosa fea*) eyesore

peinado *m* hairstyle

peinador *m,* **peinadora** *f L.Am.* hairdresser

peinar ⟨1a⟩ **1** *v/t tb fig* comb; *peinar a alguien* comb s.o.'s hair **2** *v/r* peinarse comb one's hair

peine *m* comb

p. ej. *abr* (= *por ejemplo*) e.g. (= exempli gratia, for example)

Pekín Beijing

pela *f* F peseta

peladero *m* L.Am. vacant lot

peladilla *f* sugared almond

pelado *adj* peeled; *fig* bare; F (*sin dinero*) broke F

pelar ⟨1a⟩ **1** *v/t manzana, patata etc* peel; *hace un frío que pela* F it's freezing **2** *v/r pelarse* (*cortarse el pelo*) have a haircut; *Rpl* F (*chismear*) gossip

pelazón *f* C.Am. backbiting

peldaño *m* step

pelea *f* fight

pelear ⟨1a⟩ **1** *v/i* fight **2** *v/r pelearse* fight

pelele *m* puppet

peleón *adj* argumentative; *vino peleón* F jug wine, *Br* plonk F

peletería *f* furrier's

peliagudo *adj* tricky

pelícano *m* zo pelican

película *f* movie, film; fot film; *película del Oeste* Western; *de película* F awesome F, fantastic F

peligrar ⟨1a⟩ *v/i* be at risk

peligro *m* danger; *correr peligro* be in danger; *poner en peligro* endanger, put at risk

peligroso *adj* dangerous

pelillo *m*: *¡pelillos a la mar! fig* F let's bury the hatchet

pelín: *un pelín* F a (little) bit

pelirrojo *adj* red-haired, red-headed

pellejo *m de animal* skin, hide; *salvar el pellejo fig* F save one's (own) skin F

pellizcar ⟨1g⟩ *v/t* pinch

pellizco *m* pinch; *un buen pellizco* F a tidy sum F

pelma **1** *adj* annoying **2** *m/f* pain F

pelmazo *m*, -a *f* F pain F

pelo *m de persona, de perro* hair; *de animal* fur; *tiene el pelo muy largo* he has very long hair; *estar en pelo* (*sin preparación*) unprepared; *montar a pelo* ride bareback; *por los pelos* F by a whisker F, by the skin of one's teeth F; *tomar el pelo a alguien* F pull s.o.'s leg F

pelota **1** *f* ball; *pelotas* F nuts F, balls F; *en pelotas* P stark naked; *hacer la pelota a alguien* suck up to s.o. F **2** *m/f* F creep F

pelotazo *m*: *rompió el cristal de un pelotazo* he smashed the window with a ball

pelotero *m*, -a *f* L.Am. (base)ball player

pelotón *m* mil squad; dep bunch, pack

peluca *f* wig

peluche *m* soft toy; *oso de peluche* teddy bear

peludo *adj persona* hairy; *animal* furry

peluquearse ⟨1a⟩ *v/r* L.Am. get one's hair cut

peluquería *f* hairdresser's

peluquero *m*, -a *f* hairdresser

peluquín *m* toupee, hairpiece

pelusa *f* fluff

pelvis *f inv* anat pelvis

pena *f* (*tristeza*) sadness, sorrow; (*congoja*) grief, distress; (*lástima*) pity; jur sentence; *pena capital* death penalty, capital punishment; *pena de muerte* death penalty; *no vale or no merece la pena* it's not worth it; *¡qué pena!* what a shame o pity!; *a duras penas* with great difficulty; *me da pena* L.Am. I'm ashamed

penal *adj* penal; *derecho penal* criminal law

penalidad *f fig* hardship

penalización *f acción* penalization; dep penalty

penalizar ⟨1f⟩ *v/t* penalize

penalty *m* dep penalty

penca **1** *adj Chi* soft, weak **2** *f* L.Am. (*nopal*) leaf of the prickly pear plant

pendejada *f* L.Am. stupid thing to do

pendejo **1** *m* (*pelea*) fight **2** *m*, -a *f* L.Am. F dummy F

pendenciero *adj* troublemaker

pendiente **1** *adj* unresolved, unfinished; *cuenta* unpaid **2** *m* earring **3** *f* slope

pendón **1** *adj* swinging F **2** *m*, -ona *f* F swinger F

péndulo *m* pendulum

pene *m* anat penis

penetración *f* penetration

penetrante *adj mirada* penetrating; *sonido* piercing; *frío* bitter; *herida* deep; *análisis* incisive

penetrar ⟨1a⟩ *v/i* penetrate; (*entrar*) enter; *de un líquido* seep in penicilina f penicillin

península f peninsula; **península Ibérica** Iberian Peninsula

penique m penny

penitencia f penitence

penitenciado m L.Am. prisoner, convict

penitenciario adj penitentiary atr, prison atr

penoso adj distressing; trabajo laborious

pensamiento m thought; BOT pansy

pensar ⟨1k⟩ 1 v/t think about; (opinar) think; **¡ni pensarlo!** don't even think about it 2 v/i think (**en** about)

pensativo adj thoughtful

pensión f hotel rooming house, Br guest-house; dinero pension; **pensión alimenticia** child support, Br maintenance; **pensión completa** American plan, Br full board

pensionista m/f pensioner

pentagrama m MÚS stave

pentatlón m DEP pentathlon

penúltimo adj penultimate

penumbra f half-light

penuria f shortage (**de** of); (pobreza) poverty

peña f crag, cliff; (roca) rock; F **de amigos** group, circle

peñasco m boulder

peñón m: **el Peñón de Gibraltar** the Rock of Gibraltar

peón m en ajedrez pawn; trabajador labo(u)rer

peor adj comp worse; **de mal en peor** from bad to worse

pepa f L.Am. (semilla) seed; **soltar la pepa** F spill the beans

pepinillo m gherkin

pepino m cucumber; **me importa un pepino** F I don't give a damn F

pepita f pip

pequeño 1 adj small, little; **de pequeño** when I was small o little 2 m, -a f little one

pequinés m ZO Pekinese, Peke F

pera f pear

peral m pear tree

perca f pez perch

percance m mishap

percatarse ⟨1a⟩ v/r notice; **percatarse de algo** notice sth

percebe m ZO barnacle

percepción f perception; COM acto receipt

percha f coat hanger; gancho coat hook

perchero m coat rack

percibir ⟨3a⟩ v/t perceive; COM sueldo receive

percusión f MÚS percussion

perdedor m, perdedora f loser

perder ⟨2g⟩ 1 v/t objeto lose; tren, avión etc miss; el tiempo waste 2 v/i lose; **echar a perder** ruin; **echarse a perder** de alimento go bad 3 v/r perderse get lost

perdición f downfall

pérdida f loss

perdido adj lost; **ponerse perdido** get filthy

perdigón m pellet

perdiz f ZO partridge

perdón m pardon; REL forgiveness; **pedir perdón** say sorry, apologize; **¡perdón!** sorry

perdonar ⟨1a⟩ v/t forgive; JUR pardon; **perdonar algo a alguien** forgive s.o. sth; **¡perdone!** sorry; **perdone, ¿tiene hora?** excuse me, do you have the time?

perdurar ⟨1a⟩ v/i endure

perecedero adj perishable

perecer ⟨2d⟩ v/i perish

peregrinación f pilgrimage

peregrinar ⟨1a⟩ v/i go on a pilgrimage

peregrino m, -a f pilgrim

perejil m BOT parsley

perenne adj BOT perennial

perentorio adj (urgente) urgent, pressing; (apremiante) peremptory

pereza f laziness

perezoso 1 adj lazy 2 m ZO sloth

perfección f perfection; **a la perfección** perfectly, to perfection

perfeccionamiento m perfecting

perfeccionar ⟨1a⟩ v/t perfect

perfeccionista m/f perfectionist

perfecto adj perfect

pérfido adj treacherous

perfil m profile; **de perfil** in profile, from the side

perforación f puncture

perforadora f punch
perforar ⟨1a⟩ v/t pierce; *calle* dig up
perfumar ⟨1a⟩ v/t perfume
perfume m perfume
perfumería f perfume shop
pergamino m parchment
pergenio m, -a f Rpl F kid F
pericia f expertise
pericote m Chi, Pe zo large rat
periferia f periphery; *de ciudad* outskirts pl
perilla f goatee; *me viene de perilla* F that'll be very useful; *tu visita me viene de perilla* F you've come at just the right time
perímetro m perimeter
periódico 1 adj periodic 2 m newspaper
periodismo m journalism
periodista m/f journalist
período, periodo m period
peripecia f adventure
periquete m: *en un periquete* F in a second, in no time F
periquito m zo budgerigar
periscopio m periscope
perito 1 adj expert 2 m, -a f expert; COM *en seguros* loss adjuster
perjudicar ⟨1g⟩ v/t harm, damage
perjudicial adj harmful, damaging
perjuicio m harm, damage; *sin perjuicio de* without affecting
perjurio m perjury
perla f pearl; *nos vino de perlas* F it suited us fine F
permanecer ⟨2d⟩ v/i remain, stay
permanente 1 adj permanent 2 f perm
permeable adj permeable
permisible adj permissible
permisivo adj permissive
permiso m permission; *documento* permit; *permiso de conducir* driver's license, Br driving licence; *permiso de residencia* residence permit; *con permiso* excuse me; *estar de permiso* be on leave
permitir ⟨3a⟩ 1 v/t permit, allow 2 v/r *permitirse* afford; *permitirse el lujo de* permit o.s. the luxury of
pernicioso adj harmful

pernoctar ⟨1a⟩ v/i spend the night
pero 1 conj but 2 m flaw, defect; *no hay peros que valgan* no excuses
perogrullada f platitude
peronismo m Peronism
peronista m/f Peronist
perorata f F lecture
perpendicular adj perpendicular
perpetrar ⟨1a⟩ v/t *crimen* perpetrate, commit
perpetuar ⟨1e⟩ v/t perpetuate
perpetuidad f: *a perpetuidad* in perpetuity
perpetuo adj fig perpetual
perplejidad f perplexity
perplejo adj puzzled, perplexed
perra f dog; *el perro y la perra* the dog and the bitch; *perras* F pesetas
perrera f kennels pl
perrería f F dirty trick
perrito m: *perrito caliente* GASTR hot dog
perro m dog; *perro callejero* stray; *perro guardián* guard dog; *perro lazarillo* seeing eye dog, Br guide dog; *perro pastor* sheepdog; *llevarse como el perro y el gato* fig fight like cat and dog; *hace un tiempo de perros* F the weather is lousy F
persecución f pursuit; *(acoso)* persecution
perseguidor m, perseguidora f persecutor
perseguir ⟨3l & 3d⟩ v/t pursue; *delincuente* look for; *(molestar)* pester; *(acosar)* persecute
perseverancia f perseverance
perseverar ⟨1a⟩ v/i persevere (*en* with)
persiana f blind
pérsico adj Persian
persignarse ⟨1a⟩ v/r cross o.s.
persistente adj persistent
persistir ⟨3a⟩ v/i persist
persona f person; *quince personas* fifteen people
personaje m TEA character; *famoso* celebrity
personal 1 adj personal 2 m personnel, staff
personalidad f personality

personalizar ⟨1f⟩ v/t personalize
personificar ⟨1g⟩ v/t personify, embody
perspectiva f perspective; fig point of view; **perspectivas** pl outlook sg, prospects
perspicacia f shrewdness, perspicacity
persuadir ⟨3a⟩ v/t persuade
persuasión f persuasion
persuasivo adj persuasive
pertenecer ⟨2d⟩ v/i belong (**a** to)
pertenencias fpl belongings
pértiga f pole; **salto con pértiga** DEP pole vault
pertinaz adj persistent; (terco) obstinate
pertinente adj relevant, pertinent
pertrechos mpl MIL equipment sg
perturbar ⟨1a⟩ v/t disturb; reunión disrupt
Perú Peru
peruano 1 adj Peruvian 2 m, -a f Peruvian
perversión f perversion
perverso adj perverted
pervertido m, -a f pervert
pervertir ⟨3i⟩ v/t pervert
pesa f para balanza weight; DEP shot; C.Am., W.I. butcher's shop
pesadez f fig drag F
pesadilla f nightmare
pesado 1 adj objeto heavy; libro, clase etc tedious, boring; trabajo tough 2 m, -a f bore; **¡qué pesado es!** F he's a real pain F
pésame m condolences pl
pesar ⟨1a⟩ 1 v/t weigh 2 v/i be heavy; (influir) carry weight; fig weigh heavily (**sobre** on); **me pesa tener que informarle ... 3** m sorrow; **a pesar de** in spite of, despite
pesca f actividad fishing; (peces) fish pl
pescadería f fish shop
pescadero m, -a f fishmonger
pescadilla f pez whiting
pescado m GASTR fish
pescador m fisherman
pescar ⟨1g⟩ 1 v/t un pez, resfriado etc catch; (intentar tomar) fish for; trabajo, marido etc land F 2 v/i fish
pescuezo m neck
pese: **pese a** despite

pesero m L.Am. minibus; Méx (collective) taxi
peseta f peseta
pesetero adj F money-grubbing F
pesimismo m pessimism
pesimista 1 adj pessimistic 2 m/f pessimist
pésimo adj sup awful, terrible
peso m weight; moneda peso; **de peso** fig weighty
pesquero 1 adj fishing atr 2 m fishing boat
pesquisa f investigation
pestaña f eyelash
pestañear ⟨1a⟩ v/i flutter one's eyelashes; **sin pestañear** fig without batting an eyelid
peste f MED plague; F olor stink F; **echar pestes** F curse and swear
pesticida m pesticide
pestilente adj foul-smelling
pestillo m (picaporte) door handle; (cerradura) bolt
petaca f para tabaco tobacco pouch; para bebida hip flask; C.Am. F insecto ladybug, Br ladybird
pétalo m petal
petanca f type of bowls
petardo 1 m firecracker 2 m, -a f F nerd F
petate m kit bag; L.Am. F en el suelo mat
petición f request; **a petición de** at the request of
petirrojo m ZO robin
petiso L.Am. 1 m, -a f F shorty F 2 m pony
peto m bib; **pantalón de peto** overalls pl, Br dungarees pl
petrificado adj petrified
petróleo m oil, petroleum
petrolero 1 adj oil atr 2 m MAR oil tanker
petrolífero adj oil atr
petroquímica f petrochemical
petulante adj smug
peyorativo adj pejorative
pez m ZO fish; **pez espada** swordfish; **pez gordo** F big shot F; **estar pez en algo** F be clueless about sth F
pezón m nipple
pezuña f ZO hoof
piadoso adj pious

pianista *m/f* pianist

piano *m* piano; **piano de cola** grand piano

piar ⟨1c⟩ *v/i* tweet, chirrup

PIB *abr* (= **producto interior bruto**) GDP (= gross domestic product)

pibe *m*, **-a** *f Rpl* F kid F

picada *f de serpiente* bite; *de abeja* sting; *L.Am. para comer* snacks *pl*, nibbles *pl*; *Rpl* (*camino*) path

picadero *m escuela* riding school

picado 1 *adj diente* decayed; *mar* rough, choppy; *carne* minced; *Br* finely chopped; *verdura* minced; *Br* finely chopped; *fig* offended **2** *m L.Am.* dive; **caer en picado** *de precios* nosedive, plummet

picadora *f en cocina* mincer

picadura *f de reptil, mosquito* bite; *de avispa* sting; *tabaco* cut tobacco

picaflor *m L.Am.* zo hummingbird; *F* womanizer

picante 1 *adj* hot, spicy; *chiste* risqué **2** *m* hot spice

picaporte *m* door handle

picar ⟨1g⟩ **1** *v/t de mosquito, serpiente* bite; *de avispa* sting; *de ave* peck; *carne* grind; *Br* mince; *verdura* mince, *Br* finely chop; *TAUR* jab with a lance; (*molestar*) annoy; *la curiosidad* **pique 2** *v/i tb fig* take the bait; *L.Am. de la comida* be hot; (*producir picor*) itch; *del sol* burn

picardía *f* (*astucia*) craftiness, slyness; (*travesura*) mischievousness; *Méx* (*taco, palabrota*) swearing, swearwords *pl*

pícaro *adj persona* crafty, sly; *comentario* mischievous

picarón *m Méx, Chi, Pe* (*buñuelo*) fritter

picatoste *m* piece of fried bread

picha *f* V prick V

pichicato *m Pe, Bol* P coke P

pichincha *f L.Am.* bargain

pichón *m L.Am.* orn chick; *F* (*novato*) rookie F

Picio: más feo que Picio F as ugly as sin F

picnic *m* (*pl* ~s) picnic

pico *m* zo beak; *F* (*boca*) mouth; *de montaña* peak; *herramienta* pickax(e); **a las tres y pico** some time after three o'clock; **cerrar el pico** F shut one's mouth F

picor *m* itch

picota *f* bigarreau (*type of sweet cherry*)

picotazo *m* peck

picotear ⟨1a⟩ *v/t* peck

pido *vb* → **pedir**

pie *m* foot; *de estatua, lámpara* base; **a pie** on foot; **de pie** standing; **no tiene ni pies ni cabeza** it doesn't make any sense at all, I can't make head nor tail of it

piedad *f* pity; (*clemencia*) mercy

piedra *f tb* MED stone; **piedra preciosa** precious stone; **quedarse de piedra** *fig* F be stunned

piel *f de persona, fruta* skin; *de animal* hide, skin; (*cuero*) leather; **abrigo de pieles** fur coat

pienso[1] *vb* → **pensar**

pienso[2] *m* animal feed

pierdo *vb* → **perder**

pierna *f* leg; **dormir a pierna suelta** sleep like a log

pieza *f de un conjunto*, MÚS piece; *de aparato* part; TEA play; (*habitación*) room; **pieza de recambio** spare (part); **quedarse de una pieza** F be amazed

pifia *f* F (*error*) booboo F; *Chi, Pe, Rpl* defect

pigmento *m* pigment

pigmeo *m*, **-a** *f* pigmy

pijama *m* pajamas *pl*, *Br* pyjamas *pl*

pijo 1 *adj* posh **2** *m* V (*pene*) prick V **3** *m*, **-a** *f* F *persona* rich kid F

pila *f* EL battery; (*montón*) pile; (*fregadero*) sink

pilar *m tb fig* pillar

píldora *f* pill

pileta *f Rpl* sink; (*alberca*) swimming pool

pillaje *m* pillage

pillar ⟨1a⟩ *v/t* (*tomar*) seize; (*atrapar*) catch; (*atropellar*) hit; *chiste* get

pillo 1 *adj* mischievous **2** *m*, **-a** *f* rascal

pilón *m Méx*: **me dio dos de pilón** he gave me two extra

pilotar ⟨1a⟩ *v/t* AVIA fly, pilot; AUTO drive; MAR steer

piloto *m* AVIA, MAR pilot; AUTO driver; EL pilot light; **piloto automático** autopilot

piltrafa *f*: **piltrafas** rags; **estar hecho una**

piltrafa *fig* be a total wreck F

pimentón *m* paprika

pimienta *f* pepper

pimiento *m* pepper; *me importa un pimiento* F I couldn't care less F

pimpón *m* ping-pong

PIN *m* PIN

pinar *m* pine forest

pincel *m* paintbrush

pinchadiscos *m/f* F disc jockey, DJ

pinchar ⟨1a⟩ **1** *v/t* prick; AUTO puncture; TELEC tap; F (*molestar*) bug F, needle F; *pincharle a alguien* MED give s.o. a shot **2** *v/i* prick; AUTO get a flat tire, *Br* get a puncture **3** *v/r* **pincharse** *con aguja etc* prick o.s.; F (*inyectarse*) shoot up P; *se nos pinchó una rueda* we got a flat (tire) *o Br* a puncture

pinchazo *m herida* prick; *dolor* sharp pain; AUTO flat (tire), *Br* puncture; *Br* flop F

pinche[1] *m* cook's assistant

pinche[2] *adj Méx* F rotten F; *C.Am., Méx* (*tacaño*) tight-fisted

pincho *m* GASTR bar snack

pingajo *m* F rag

ping-pong *m* ping-pong

pingüino *m* ZO penguin

pino *m* BOT pine; *hacer el pino* do a handstand

pinol(e) *m* C.Am., Méx cornstarch, *Br* cornflour; *L.Am.* roasted corn

pinta *f* pint; *aspecto* looks *pl*; *tener buena pinta fig* look inviting

pintalabios *m* lipstick

pintar ⟨1a⟩ **1** *v/t* paint; *no pintar nada* F not count **2** *v/r* **pintarse** put on one's makeup

pintor *m*, **pintora** *f* painter; *pintor (de brocha gorda)* (house) painter

pintoresco *adj* picturesque

pintura *f sustancia* paint; *obra* painting

pinza *f* clothes pin, *Br* clothes peg; ZO claw; *pinzas* tweezers; *L.Am.* (*alicates*) pliers

piña *f del pino* pine cone; *fruta* pineapple

piñón *m* BOT pine nut; TÉC pinion

piojo *m* ZO louse; *piojos pl* lice *pl*

piola *f L.Am.* cord, twine

piolín *m Arg* cord, twine

pionero 1 *adj* pioneering **2** *m*, -a *f tb fig* pioneer

pipa *f* pipe; *pipas semillas* sunflower seeds; *pasarlo pipa* F have a great time

pipí *m* F pee F; *hacer pipí* F pee F

pipiolo *m C.Am., Méx* F kid F; *pipiolos pl C.Am.* F (*dinero*) cash *sg*

pique *m* resentment; (*rivalidad*) rivalry; *irse a pique fig* go under, go to the wall

piqueta *f herramienta* pickax(e); *en cámping* tentpeg

piquete *m* POL picket

pirado *adj* F crazy F

piragua *f* canoe

piragüista *m/f* DEP canoeist

pirámide *f* pyramid

piraña *f* ZO piranha

pirarse ⟨1a⟩ *v/r* F (*marcharse*) clear off F; *pirarse por alguien* F lose one's head over s.o. F

pirata *m/f* pirate; *pirata informático* hacker

piratear ⟨1a⟩ *v/t* INFOR pirate

pirenaico *adj* Pyrenean

Pirineos *mpl* Pyrenees

pirómano *m*, -a *f* pyromaniac; JUR arsonist

piropo *m* compliment

pirotécnico *adj* fireworks *atr*

piruleta *f*, **pirulí** *m* F lollipop

pis *m* F pee F; *hacer pis* F have a pee F

pisada *f* footstep; *huella* footprint

pisapapeles *m* paperweight

pisar ⟨1a⟩ *v/t* step on; *uvas* tread; *fig* (*maltratar*) walk all over; *idea* steal; *pisar a alguien* step on s.o.'s foot

piscifactoría *f* fish farm

piscina *f* swimming pool

Piscis *m/f inv* ASTR Pisces

piso *m* apartment, *Br* flat; (*planta*) floor

pisotear ⟨1a⟩ *v/t* trample

pista *f* track, trail; (*indicio*) clue; *de atletismo* track; *pista de aterrizaje* AVIA runway; *pista de baile* dance floor; *pista de tenis / squash* tennis / squash court; *seguir la pista a alguien* be on the trail of s.o.

pistacho *m* BOT pistachio

pisto *m* GASTR *mixture of tomatoes, pep-*

pers etc cooked in oil; *C.Am.*, *Méx* F (*dinero*) cash, dough F

pistola *f* pistol

pistón *m* piston

pitada *f* (*abucheo*) whistle; *S. Am. de cigarillo* puff

pitar ⟨1a⟩ *v/i* whistle; *con bocina* beep, hoot; *L.Am.* (*fumar*) smoke; **salir pitando** F dash off F 2 *v/t* (*abuchear*) whistle at; *penalti, falta etc* call, *Br* blow for; *silbato* blow

pitazo *m L.Am.* whistle

pitear ⟨1a⟩ *v/i L.Am.* blow a whistle

pitido *m* whistle; *con bocina* beep, hoot

pitillo *m* cigarette; *hecho a mano* roll-up

pito *m* whistle; (*bocina*) horn; **me importa un pito** F I don't give a hoot F

pitón *m* zo python

pitonisa *f* fortune-teller

pitorrearse ⟨1a⟩ *v/r*: **pitorrearse de alguien** F make fun of s.o.

pívot *m en baloncesto* center, *Br* centre

piyama *m L.Am.* pajamas *pl*, *Br* pyjamas *pl*

pizarra *f* blackboard; *piedra* slate

pizca *f* pinch; *Méx* AGR harvest; **ni pizca de** not a bit of

pizza *f* pizza

placa *f* (*lámina*) sheet; (*plancha*) plate; (*letrero*) plaque; *Méx* AUTO license plate, *Br* number plate; **placa madre** INFOR motherboard; **placa** (*dental*) plaque; **placa de matrícula** AUTO license plate, *Br* number plate

placer ⟨2x⟩ *v/i* please; **siempre hace lo que le place** he always does as he pleases 2 *m* pleasure

plácido *adj* placid

plaga *f* AGR pest; MED plague; *fig* scourge; (*abundancia*) glut

plagado *adj* infested; (*lleno*) full; **plagado de gente** swarming with people

plagiar ⟨1b⟩ *v/t* plagiarize; *L.Am.* (*secuestrar*) kidnap

plagio *m* plagiarism

plan *m* plan

plana *f*: **primera plana** front page

plancha *f para planchar* iron; *en cocina* broiler, *Br* grill; *de metal* sheet; F (*mete-*

dura de pata) goof F; **a la plancha** GASTR broiled, *Br* grilled

planchar ⟨1a⟩ *v/t* iron; *Méx* F (*dar plantón*) stand up F; *L.Am.* (*lisonjear*) flatter

planeador *m* glider

planear ⟨1a⟩ 1 *v/t* plan 2 *v/i* AVIA glide

planeta *m* planet

planetario *m* planetarium

planificación *f* planning; **planificación familiar** family planning

planificar ⟨1g⟩ *v/t* plan

plano 1 *adj* flat 2 *m* ARQUI plan; *de ciudad* map; *en cine* shot; MAT plane; *fig* level

planta *f* BOT plant; (*piso*) floor; **planta del pie** sole of the foot

plantación *f* plantation

plantado *adj*: **dejar a alguien plantado** F stand s.o. up F

plantar ⟨1a⟩ 1 *v/t árbol etc* plant; *tienda de campaña* put up; **plantar a alguien** F stand s.o. up F 2 *v/r* **plantarse** put one's foot down

planteamiento *m de problema* posing; (*perspectiva*) approach

plantear ⟨1a⟩ *v/t dificultad, problema* pose, create; *cuestión* raise

plantel *m* (*equipo*) team; *L.Am.* staff

plantilla *f para zapato* insole; (*personal*) staff; DEP squad; *para cortar*, INFOR template

plantón *m*: **dar un plantón a alguien** F stand s.o. up F

plasma *m* plasma

plasmar ⟨1a⟩ *v/t* (*modelar*) shape; *fig* (*representar*) express

plasta 1 *m/f* F pain F, drag F 2 *adj*: **ser plasta** F be a pain *o* drag F

plástica *f* EDU handicrafts

plástico *m* plastic

plastificado *adj* laminated

plastificar ⟨1g⟩ *v/t documento* laminate

plastilina *f* Plasticine®

plata *f* silver; *L.Am.* F (*dinero*) cash, dough F

plataforma *f tb* POL platform; **plataforma petrolífera** oil rig

platal *m L.Am.* fortune

plátano *m* banana

plateado *adj Méx* wealthy

plática *f Méx* chat, talk

platicar ⟨1g⟩ **1** *v/t L.Am.* tell **2** *v/i Méx* chat, talk

platillo *m: platillo volante* flying saucer; *platillos* MÚS cymbals

platino *m* platinum

plato *m* plate; GASTR dish; *plato principal* main course; *plato preparado / precocinado* ready meal; *plato sopero / hondo* soup dish; *pagar los platos rotos* F carry the can F

plató *m de película* set; TV studio

platónico *adj* platonic

platudo *adj Chi* rich

plausible *adj* plausible

playa *f* beach; *playa de estacionamiento L.Am.* parking lot, *Br* car park

playeras *fpl* canvas shoes

playo *adj Rpl* shallow

plaza *f* square; (*vacante*) job opening, *Br* vacancy; *en vehículo* seat; *de trabajo* position; *plaza de toros* bull ring

plazo *m* period; (*pago*) instal(l)ment; *a corto / largo plazo* in the short / long term; *a plazos* in instal(l)ments

plebiscito *m* plebiscite

plegable *adj* collapsible, folding

plegar ⟨1h & 1k⟩ **1** *v/t* fold (up) **2** *v/r* plegarse *fig* submit (*a* to)

plegaria *f* prayer

pleito *m* JUR lawsuit; *fig* dispute; *poner un pleito a alguien* sue s.o.

pleno **1** *adj* full; *en pleno día* in broad daylight **2** *m* plenary session

pliego *m* **1** *vb* ► *plegar* **2** *m* (*hoja de papel*) sheet (of paper); (*carta*) sealed letter *o* document

pliegue *m* fold, crease

plomería *f Méx* plumbing

plomero *m Méx* plumber

plomo *m* lead; EL fuse; *fig* F drag F; *sin plomo* AUTO unleaded

pluma *f* feather; *para escribir* fountain pen

plumaje *m* plumage

plumero *m para limpiar* feather duster; *CSur para maquillaje* powder puff; *vérsele el plumero a alguien fig* F see what s.o. is up to F

plumífero *m* F down jacket

plural **1** *adj* plural **2** *m* GRAM plural

pluralismo *m* POL pluralism

pluriempleo *m* having more than one job

plus *m* bonus

plusmarquista *m/f* record holder

plusvalía *f* COM capital gain

plutonio *m* QUÍM plutonium

pluviosidad *f* rainfall

PNB *abr* (= *producto nacional bruto*) GNP (= gross national product)

P.º *abr* (= *Paseo*) Ave (= Avenue)

p.o. *abr* (= *por orden*) p. p. (per procurationem, by proxy)

población *f gente* population; (*ciudad*) city, town; (*pueblo*) village; *Chi* shanty town

poblado **1** *adj* populated; *barba* bushy; *poblado de fig* full of **2** *m* (*pueblo*) settlement

poblador *m*, pobladora *f Chi* shanty town dweller

poblar ⟨1m⟩ *v/t* populate

pobre **1** *adj económicamente, en calidad* poor **2** *m/f* poor person; *los pobres* the poor

pobreza *f* poverty

pocilga *f* pigpen

pócima *f* concoction

poción *f* potion

poco **1** *adj sg* little, not much; *pl* few, not many; *un poco de* a little; *unos pocos* a few **2** *adv* little; *trabaja poco* he doesn't work much; *ahora se ve muy poco* it's seldom seen now; *estuvo poco por aquí* he wasn't around much; *poco conocido* little known; *poco a poco* little by little; *dentro de poco* soon, shortly; *hace poco* a short time ago, not long ago; *por poco* nearly, almost; *¡a poco no lo hacemos! Méx* don't tell me we're not doing it; *de a poco me fui tranquilizando Rpl* little by little I calmed down **3** *m: un poco* a little, a bit

podar ⟨1a⟩ *v/t* AGR prune

poder ⟨2t⟩ **1** *v/aux capacidad* can, be able to; *permiso* can, be allowed to; *posibilidad* may, might; *no pude hablar con ella* I wasn't able to talk to her; *¿puedo* *ir contigo?* can *o* may I come with you?; *¡podías habérselo dicho!* you could have *o* you might have told him **2** *v/i*: *poder con* (*sobreponerse a*) manage, cope with; *me puede* he can beat me; *es franco a más no poder* F he's as frank as they come F; *comimos a más no poder* F we ate to bursting point F; *no puedo más* I can't take any more, I've had enough; *puede ser* perhaps, maybe; *puede que* perhaps, maybe; *¿se puede?* can I come in?, do you mind if I come in? **3** *m tb* POL power; *en poder de alguien* in s.o.'s hands

poderoso *adj* powerful

podio *m* podium

podólogo *m*, -a *f* MED podiatrist, *Br* chiropodist

podrido *adj tb fig* rotten

poema *m* poem

poesía *f género* poetry; (*poema*) poem

poeta *m/f* poet

poético *adj* poetic

poetisa *f* poet

polaco 1 *adj* Polish **2** *m*, -a *f* Pole

polar *adj* polar

polea *f* TÉC pulley

polémica *f* controversy

polémico *adj* controversial

polen *m* BOT pollen

poleo *m* BOT pennyroyal

polera *f Chi* turtle neck (sweater)

poli *m/f* F cop F; *la poli* F the cops *pl* F

policía 1 *f* police **2** *m/f* police officer, policeman; *mujer* police officer, policewoman

policíaco, policiaco *adj* detective *atr*

policial *adj* police *atr*

polideportivo *m* sports center, *Br* sports centre

poliéster *m* polyester

polifacético *adj* versatile, multifaceted

poligamia *f* polygamy

políglota *m/f* polyglot

polígono *m* MAT polygon; *polígono industrial* industrial zone, *Br* industrial estate

polilla *f* ZO moth

polio *f* MED polio

poliomielitis *f* MED poliomyelitis

política *f* politics

políticamente *adv*: *políticamente correcto* politically correct

político 1 *adj* political **2** *m*, -a *f* politician

póliza *f* policy; *póliza de seguros* insurance policy

polizón *m/f* stowaway

polla *f* V prick V, cock V

pollera *f L.Am.* skirt

pollería *f* poulterer's

pollito *m* chick

pollo *m* ZO, GASTR chicken

polluelo *m* ZO chick

polo *m* GEOG, EL pole; *prenda* polo shirt; DEP polo; *Polo Norte* North Pole; *Polo Sur* South Pole

polola *f Chi* girlfriend

pololear ⟨1a⟩ *v/i Chi* be going steady

pololo *m Chi* boyfriend

Polonia Poland

poltrona *f* easy chair

polución *f* pollution; *polución atmosférica* air pollution, atmospheric pollution

polucionar ⟨1a⟩ *v/t* pollute

polvo *m* dust; *en química, medicina etc* powder; *polvos pl de talco* talcum powder *sg*; *echar un polvo* V have a screw V; *estar hecho polvo* F be all in F

pólvora *f* gunpowder

polvorín *m almacén* magazine; *fig* powder keg

polvorón *m* GASTR *type of small cake*

pomada *f* cream

pomelo *m* BOT grapefruit

pómez *f*: *piedra pómez* pumice stone

pomo *m* doorknob

pompa *f* pomp; *pompa de jabón* bubble; *pompas pl fúnebres ceremonia* funeral ceremony *sg*; *establecimiento* funeral parlo(u)r *sg*

pomposo *adj* pompous

pómulo *m* ANAT cheekbone

pon *vb* → *poner*

ponchadura *f Méx* flat, *Br* puncture

ponchar ⟨1a⟩ **1** *v/t L.Am.* puncture **2** *v/r* *poncharse Méx* get a flat *o Br* puncture

ponche *m* punch

poncho *m* poncho; *pisarse el poncho*

S. Am. be mistaken

ponderación *f mesura* deliberation; *en estadísticas* weighting

ponencia *f* presentation; EDU paper

poner ⟨2r; *part* **puesto** ⟩ **1** *v/t* put; *(añadir)* put in; RAD, TV turn on, switch on; *la mesa* set; *ropa* put on; *telegrama* send; *(escribir)* put down; *en periódico, libro etc* say; *negocio* set up; *huevos* lay; **poner a alguien furioso** make s.o. angry; **ponerle a alguien con alguien** TELEC put s.o. through to s.o.; **ponerle una multa a alguien** fine s.o.; **pongamos que** let's suppose *o* assume that **2** *v/r* **ponerse** *ropa* put on; **ponte en el banco** go and sit on the bench; **se puso ahí** she stood over there; **dile que se ponga** TELEC tell her to come to the phone; **ponerse pálido** turn pale; **ponerse furioso** get angry; **ponerse enfermo** become *o* fall ill; **ponerse a** start to

pongo[1] *vb* → **poner**

pongo[2] *m Pe* indentured Indian laborer

poni *m* ZO pony

poniente *m* west

pontífice *m* pontiff; **sumo pontífice** Pope

ponzoñoso *adj* poisonous

pop 1 *adj* pop; **música pop** pop music **2** *m* pop

popa *f* MAR stern

popular *adj* popular; *(del pueblo)* folk *atr*; *barrio* lower-class

popularidad *f* popularity

popularizar ⟨1f⟩ *v/t* popularize

póquer *m* poker

por *prp* ◇ *motivo* for, because of; **lo hizo por amor** she did it out of love; **luchó por sus ideales** he fought for his ideals
◇ *medio* by; **por avión** by air; **por correo** by mail, *Br tb* by post
◇ *tiempo:* **por un segundo** *L.Am.* for a second; **por la mañana** in the morning
◇ *movimiento:* **por la calle** down the street; **por un tunel** through a tunnel; **por aquí** this way
◇ *posición aproximada* around, about; **está por aquí** it's around here (somewhere)

◇ *cambio:* **por cincuenta pesos** for fifty pesos
◇ *otros usos:* **por hora** an *o* per hour; **dos por dos** two times two; **¿por qué?** why?; **el motivo por el cual** or **por el que ...** the reason why ...

porcelana *f* porcelain, china; **de porcelana** porcelain *atr*, china *atr*

porcentaje *m* percentage

porche *f* porch

porción *f* portion

pordiosero *m*, **-a** *f* beggar

porfiar ⟨1c⟩ *v/i* insist (**en** on)

pormenor *m* detail

porno 1 *adj* porn *atr* **2** *m* porn

pornografía *f* pornography

pornográfico *adj* pornographic

poro *m* pore

poroso *adj* porous

poroto *m Rpl, Chi* bean; **porotos verdes** *L.Am.* green beans

porque *conj* because; **porque sí** just because

porqué *m* reason

porquería *f (suciedad)* filth; F *cosa de poca calidad* piece of trash F

porra *f baton;* *(palo)* club; **¡vete a la porra!** F go to hell! F

porrazo *m:* **darle un porrazo a alguien** F hit s.o.; **darse** *or* **pegarse un porrazo** crash (**contra** into)

porro *m* F joint F

porrón *m* container from which wine is poured straight into the mouth

portaaviones *m inv* aircraft carrier

portada *f* TIP front page; *de revista* cover; ARQUI front

portafolios *m inv* briefcase

portal *m* foyer; *(entrada)* doorway

portaligas *m inv Arg, Chi* garter belt, *Br* suspender belt

portarse ⟨1a⟩ *v/r* behave

portátil *adj* portable

portavoz *m/f* spokesman; **mujer** spokeswoman

portazo *m:* **dar un portazo** F slam the door

porte *m (aspecto)* appearance, air; *(gasto de correo)* postage portento *m* wonder; *persona* genius

porteño *Arg* 1 *adj* of Buenos Aires, Buenos Aires *atr* 2 *m*,-a *f* native of Buenos Aires

portería *f* reception; *casa* superintendent's apartment, *Br* caretaker's flat; DEP goal

portero *m* doorman; *de edificio* superintendent, *Br* caretaker; DEP goalkeeper; *portero automático* intercom, *Br* entryphone

portón *m* large door

Portugal Portugal

portugués 1 *m/adj* Portuguese 2 *m*,-esa *f persona* Portuguese

porvenir *m* future

posada *f C.Am., Méx* Christmas party; *(fonda)* inn

posar ⟨1a⟩ 1 *v/t mano* lay, place *(sobre* on); *posar la mirada en* gaze at 2 *v/r posarse de ave, insecto,* AVIA land

posavasos *m inv* coaster

posdata *f* postscript

poseer ⟨2e⟩ *v/t* possess; *(ser dueño de)* own, possess

posesión *f* possession; *tomar posesión (de un cargo)* POL take up office

posguerra *f* postwar period

posibilidad *f* possibility

posibilitar ⟨1a⟩ *v/t* make possible

posible *adj* possible; *en lo posible* as far as possible; *hacer todo lo posible* do everything possible; *es posible que ...* perhaps ...

posición *f tb* MIL, *fig* position; *social* standing, status

positivo *adj* positive

posmoderno *adj* postmodern

poso *m* dregs *pl*

posología *f* dosage

posponer ⟨2r; *part* **pospuesto**⟩ *v/t* postpone

pospuesto *part* → *posponer*

posta *f: a posta* on purpose

postal 1 *adj* mail *atr*, postal 2 *f* postcard

poste *m* post

póster *m* poster

postergar ⟨1a⟩ *v/t* postpone

posteridad *f* posterity

posterior *adj* later, subsequent; *(trasero)* rear *atr*, back *atr*

postizo 1 *adj* false 2 *m* hairpiece

postor *m* bidder; *al mejor postor* to the highest bidder

postrar ⟨1a⟩ 1 *v/t: la gripe lo postró* he was laid up with flu 2 *v/r postrarse* prostrate o.s.

postre *m* dessert; *a la postre* in the end

postular ⟨1a⟩ *v/t hipótesis* put forward, advance

póstumo *adj* posthumous

postura *f tb fig* position

pos(t)venta *adj inv* after-sales *atr*

potable *adj* drinkable; *fig* F passable; *agua potable* drinking water

potaje *m* GASTR stew

potasio *m* potassium

potencia *f* power; *en potencia* potential

potencial *m/adj* potential

potenciar ⟨1b⟩ *v/t fig* foster, promote

potentado *m*, -a *f* tycoon

potente *adj* powerful

potestad *f* authority; *patria potestad* parental authority

potingue *m* F *desp* lotion, cream

potro *m* ZO colt

pozo *m* well; MIN shaft; *Rpl* pothole; *un pozo sin fondo fig* a bottomless pit

pozol *m C.Am.* corn liquor

pozole *m Méx* corn stew

práctica *f* practice

practicar ⟨1g⟩ *v/t* practice, *Br* practise; *deporte* play; *practicar la equitación / la esgrima* ride / fence

práctico *adj* practical

pradera *f* prairie, grassland

prado *m* meadow

pragmático *adj* pragmatic

pragmatismo *m* pragmatism

pral. *abr* (= *principal*) first

preámbulo *m* preamble

prebenda *f* sinecure

precalentamiento *m* DEP warm-up

precario *adj* precarious

precaución *f* precaution; *tomar precauciones* take precautions

precavido *adj* cautious

precedente 1 *adj* previous 2 *m* precedent

preceder ⟨2a⟩ v/t precede
preceptivo adj compulsory, mandatory
preciado adj precious
preciarse ⟨1b⟩ v/r: **cualquier fontanero que se precie** ... any self-respecting plumber ...
precinto m seal
precio m price; **precio de venta al público** recommended retail price
preciosidad f: **esa casa /chica es una preciosidad** that house / girl is gorgeous o beautiful
precioso adj (de valor) precious; (hermoso) beautiful
preciosura f L.Am. F → **preciosidad**
precipicio m precipice
precipitación f (prisa) hurry, haste; **precipitaciones** rain sg
precipitado adj hasty, sudden
precipitarse ⟨1a⟩ v/r rush; fig be hasty
precisamente adv precisely
precisión f precision
preciso adj precise, accurate; **ser preciso** be necessary
preconcebido adj preconceived
precoz adj early; niño precocious
precursor m, **precursora** f precursor, forerunner
predecesor m, **predecesora** f predecessor
predecir ⟨3p; part **predicho**⟩ v/t predict
predestinar ⟨1a⟩ v/t predestine
predicado m predicate
predicador m, **predicadora** f preacher
predicar ⟨1g⟩ v/t preach; **predicar con el ejemplo** F practice (Br practise) what one preaches
predicción f prediction, forecast
predicho part → **predecir**
predilecto adj favo(u)rite
predisponer ⟨2r⟩ v/t prejudice
predisposición f tb MED predisposition; (tendencia) tendency; **una predisposición en contra de** a prejudice against
predispuesto adj predisposed (**a** to)
predominante adj predominant
predominar ⟨1a⟩ v/t predominate
preeminente adj preeminent
preescolar adj preschool

preestreno m preview
preexistente adj pre-existing
prefabricado adj prefabricated
prefacio m preface, foreword
preferencia f preference
preferente adj preferential
preferible adj preferable (**a** to); **es preferible que** ... it's better if ...
preferido 1 part → **preferir** 2 adj favo(u)rite
preferir ⟨3i⟩ v/t prefer
prefijo m prefix; TELEC area code, Br dialling code
pregonar ⟨1a⟩ v/t proclaim, make public
pregunta f question
preguntar ⟨1a⟩ 1 v/t ask 2 v/i ask; **preguntar por algo** ask about sth; **preguntar por alguien** paradero ask for s.o.; salud etc ask about s.o. 3 v/r **preguntarse** wonder
prehistoria f prehistory
prehistórico adj prehistoric
prejuicio m prejudice
prelado m prelate
prelavado m prewash
preliminar 1 adj preliminary; DEP qualifying 2 m L.Am. qualifier
preludio m prelude
premamá adj maternity atr
prematrimonial adj premarital
prematuro 1 adj premature 2 m, -a f premature baby
premeditado adj premeditated
premeditación f premeditation; **con premeditación** deliberately
premiado 1 adj prizewinning 2 m, -a f prizewinner
premiar ⟨1b⟩ v/t award a prize to
premio m prize
premisa f premise
premonición f premonition
premura f haste
prenatal adj prenatal
prenda f item of clothing, garment; garantía security; en juegos forfeit; **no soltar prenda** not say a word (**sobre** about)
prender ⟨2a; part **preso**⟩ 1 v/t a fugitivo capture; sujetar pin up; L.Am. fuego light; L.Am. luz switch on, turn on;

prender fuego a set fire to **2** v/i de planta take; (empezar a arder) catch; de moda catch on

prendería f Esp pawnbroker's, pawn shop

prensa f press; **prensa amarilla** gutter press

prensar ⟨1a⟩ v/t press

preñado adj pregnant

preocupación f worry, concern

preocupado adj worried (**por** about), concerned (**por** about)

preocupante adj worrying

preocupar ⟨1a⟩ **1** v/t worry, concern **2** v/r **preocuparse** worry (**por** about); **preocuparse de** (encargarse) look after, take care of

preparación f preparation; (educación) education; para trabajo training

preparado adj ready, prepared

preparador m, **preparadora** f: **preparador físico** trainer

preparar ⟨1a⟩ **1** v/t prepare, get ready **2** v/r **prepararse** get ready (**para** for), prepare o.s. (**para** for); de tormenta, crisis be brewing

preparativos mpl preparations

preponderante adj predominant

preposición f preposition

prepotente adj arrogant

prerrogativa f prerogative

presa f (dique) dam; (embalse) reservoir; (víctima) prey; L.Am. para comer bite to eat

presagio m omen, sign; (premonición) premonition

prescindir ⟨3a⟩ v/i: **prescindir de** (privarse de) do without; (omitir) leave out, dispense with; (no tener en cuenta) disregard

prescribir ⟨3a; part prescrito⟩ v/i JUR prescribe

prescrito part → **prescribir**

presencia f presence; **buena presencia** smart appearance

presenciar ⟨1b⟩ v/t witness; (estar presente a) attend, be present at

presentación f presentation; COM launch; entre personas introduction

presentador m, **presentadora** f TV presenter

presentar ⟨1a⟩ **1** v/t present; a alguien introduce; producto launch; solicitud submit **2** v/r presentarse en sitio show up; (darse a conocer) introduce o.s.; a examen take; de problema, dificultad arise; a elecciones run

presente 1 adj present; **tener algo presente** bear sth in mind; **¡presente!** here! **2** m tiempo present **3** m/fpl: **los presentes** those present

presentimiento m premonition

presentir ⟨3i⟩ v/t foresee; **presiento que vendrá** I have a feeling he'll come

preservar ⟨1a⟩ v/t protect

preservativo m condom

presidencia f presidency; de compañía presidency, Br chairmanship; de comité chairmanship

presidencial adj presidential

presidente m, -a f president; de gobierno premier, prime minister; de compañía president, Br chairman, Br mujer chairwoman; de comité chair

presidiario m, -a f prisoner

presidir ⟨3a⟩ v/t be president of; reunión chair, preside over

presión f pressure; **presión sanguínea** blood pressure

presionar ⟨1a⟩ v/t botón press; fig put pressure on, pressure

preso 1 part → **prender 2** m, -a f prisoner

prestación f provision; **prestación social sustitutoria** MIL community service in lieu of military service

prestado adj: **dejar prestado algo** lend sth; **pedir prestado algo** borrow sth

prestamista m/f moneylender

préstamo m loan; **préstamo bancario** bank loan

prestar ⟨1a⟩ v/t dinero lend; ayuda give; L.Am. borrow; **prestar atención** pay attention

prestidigitador m, **prestidigitadora** f conjurer

prestigio m prestige

prestigioso adj prestigious

presumido adj conceited; (coqueto) vain

presumir ⟨3a⟩ **1** v/t presume **2** v/i show

off; **presumir de algo** boast o brag about
sth; **presume de listo** he thinks he's very
clever
presuntamente adv allegedly
presunto adj alleged, suspected
presuntuoso adj conceited
presuponer ⟨2r; part **presupuesto** ⟩ v/t
assume
presupuesto 1 part → **presuponer** 2 m
POL budget
presuroso adj hurried
pretencioso adj pretentious
pretender ⟨2a⟩ v/t: **pretendía conven-
cerlos** he was trying to persuade them
pretendiente m de mujer suitor
pretensión f L.Am. (arrogancia) vanity;
sin pretensiones unpretentious
pretérito m GRAM preterite
pretextar ⟨1a⟩ v/t claim
pretexto m pretext
prevalecer ⟨2d⟩ v/t prevail (**sobre** over)
prevaricación f corruption
prevención f prevention
prevenido 1 part → **prevenir** 2 adj well-
-prepared
prevenir ⟨3s⟩ v/t prevent; (avisar) warn
(**contra** against)
preventivo adj preventive, preventative
prever ⟨2v; part **previsto** ⟩ v/t foresee
previo adj previous; **sin previo aviso**
without (prior) warning
previsible adj foreseeable
previsión f (predicción) forecast; (preparación) foresight
previsor adj farsighted
previsto 1 part → **prever** 2 adj foreseen,
expected; **tener previsto** have planned
prieto adj L.Am. dark-skinned
prima f de seguro premium; (pago extra)
bonus
primacía f supremacy, primacy; (prioridad) priority
primario adj primary
primavera f spring; BOT primrose
primer adj first
primera f first class; AUTO first gear; **a la
primera** first-time; **de primera** F first-
-class, first-rate
primerizo adj inexperienced, green F; ma-

dre new, first-time
primero 1 adj first; **primeros auxilios** pl
first aid sg 2 m, -a f first (one) 3 adv first
primitivo adj primitive; (original) original
primo m, -a f cousin
primogénito 1 adj first 2 m, -a f first child
primordial adj fundamental
primoroso adj exquisite
princesa f princess
principal adj main, principal; **lo principal**
the main o most important thing
príncipe m prince
principiante 1 adj inexperienced 2 m/f
beginner
principio m principle; **en tiempo** beginning; **a principios de abril** at the beginning of April; **en principio** in principle
pringar ⟨1h⟩ 1 v/t ensuciar get greasy; fig
F get involved (**en** in) 2 v/r pringarse get
greasy; fig F get mixed up (**en** in)
pringoso adj greasy
prioridad f priority
prioritario adj priority atr
prisa f hurry, rush; **darse prisa** hurry
(up); **tener prisa** be in a hurry o rush
prisión f prison, jail
prisionero 1 adj captive 2 m, -a f prisoner
prismáticos mpl binoculars
priva f Esp F booze F
privacidad f privacy
privación f acción deprivation; **sufrir privaciones** sufffer privation(s) o hardship
privado 1 part → **privar** 2 adj private
privar ⟨1a⟩ 1 v/t: **privar a alguien de algo**
deprive s.o. of sth 2 v/r privarse deprive
o.s.; **privarse de algo** deprive o.s. of sth,
go without sth
privatización f privatization
privatizar ⟨1f⟩ v/t privatize
privilegiado adj privileged; (excelente)
exceptional
privilegio m privilege
pro 1 prp for, in aid of; **en pro de** for 2 m
pro; **los pros y los contras** the pros and
cons
proa f MAR bow
probabilidad f probability
probable adj probable, likely; **es probable que venga** she'll probably come

P

probador *m* fitting room

probar ⟨1m⟩ **1** *v/t teoría* test, try out; *(comer un poco de)* taste, try; *(comer por primera vez)* try **2** *v/i* try; **probar a hacer** try doing **3** *v/r* **probarse** try on

probeta *f* test tube

problema *m* problem

problemático *adj* problematic

procedencia *f* origin, provenance

proceder ⟨2a⟩ **1** *v/i* come *(de* from); *(actuar)* proceed; *(ser conveniente)* be fitting; **proceder a** proceed to; **proceder contra alguien** initiate proceedings against s.o. **2** *m* conduct

procedimiento *m* procedure, method; JUR proceedings *pl*

procesado *m*, -a *f* accused, defendant

procesador *m* INFOR processor; **procesador de textos** word processor

procesamiento *m*: **procesamiento de textos** word processing

procesar ⟨1a⟩ *v/t* INFOR process; JUR prosecute

procesión *f* procession

proceso *m* process; JUR trial; **proceso de datos / textos** INFOR data / word processing

proclamar ⟨1a⟩ *v/t* proclaim

proclive *adj* given *(a* to)

procrear ⟨1a⟩ *v/i* breed, procreate *fml*

procurar ⟨1a⟩ *v/t* try; **procura no llegar tarde** try not to be late

prodigar ⟨1h⟩ **1** *v/t* be generous with **2** *v/r* **prodigarse** *(aparecer)* be seen in public

prodigio *m* wonder, miracle; *persona* prodigy

prodigioso *adj* prodigious

pródigo *adj (generoso)* generous; *(derrochador)* extravagant

producción *f* production

producir ⟨3o⟩ **1** *v/t* produce; *(causar)* cause **2** *v/r* **producirse** happen, occur; **se produjo un ruido tremendo** there was a tremendous noise

productividad *f* productivity

productivo *adj* productive; *empresa* profitable

producto *m* product; **producto interior bruto** gross domestic product; **producto**

nacional bruto gross national product

productor *m*, productora *f* producer

produjo *vb* → **producir**

produzco *vb* → **producir**

proeza *f* feat, exploit

profana *f* laywoman

profanar ⟨1a⟩ *v/t* defile, desecrate

profano **1** *adj fig* lay *atr* **2** *m* layman

profecía *f* prophecy

profesar ⟨1a⟩ *v/t* REL profess; *fig* feel, have

profesión *f* profession

profesional *m/f & adj* professional

profesor *m*, profesora *f* teacher; *de universidad* professor, *Br* lecturer

profesorado *m* faculty, *Br* staff *pl*

profeta *m* prophet

profetizar ⟨1f⟩ *v/t* prophesy

profiláctico **1** *adj* preventive, prophylactic *fml* **2** *m* condom

prófugo *m*, -a *f* JUR fugitive

profundidad *f* depth

profundizar ⟨1f⟩ *v/i*: **profundizar en algo** go into sth in depth

profundo *adj* deep; *pensamiento, persona* profound

profuso *adj* abundant, plentiful

programa *m* program, *Br* programme; INFOR program; EDU syllabus; **programa de estudios** curriculum

programación *f* RAD, TV programs *pl*, *Br* programmes; INFOR programming

programador *m*, programadora *f* programmer

programar ⟨1a⟩ *v/t aparato* program, *Br* programme; INFOR program; *(planear)* schedule

progresar ⟨1a⟩ *v/i* progress, make progress

progresista *m/f & adj* progressive

progresivo *adj* progressive

progreso *m* progress

prohibición *f* ban *(de* on)

prohibido *adj* forbidden

prohibir ⟨3a⟩ *v/t* forbid; *oficialmente* ban

prohibitivo *adj precio* prohibitive

prójimo *m* fellow human being

prole *f* offspring

proletario **1** *adj* proletarian **2** *m*, -a *f* pro-

letarian
proliferación f proliferation
proliferar ⟨1a⟩ v/i proliferate
prolífico adj prolific
prolijo adj long-winded; (minucioso) detailed
prólogo m preface
prolongado adj prolonged, lengthy
prolongar ⟨1h⟩ 1 v/t extend, prolong 2 v/r prolongarse go o carry on; en espacio extend
promedio m average
promesa f promise
prometedor adj bright, promising
prometer ⟨2a⟩ 1 v/t promise 2 v/r prometerse get engaged
prometida f fiancée
prometido 1 part → prometer 2 adj engaged 3 m fiancé
prominente adj prominent
promiscuidad f promiscuity
promiscuo adj promiscuous
promoción f promotion; EDU year
promocionar ⟨1a⟩ v/t promote
promotor m, promotora f promoter; promotor inmobiliario developer
promover ⟨2h⟩ v/t promote; (causar) provoke, cause
promulgar ⟨1h⟩ v/t ley promulgate
pronombre m GRAM pronoun
pronosticar ⟨1g⟩ v/t forecast
pronóstico m MED prognosis; pronóstico del tiempo weather forecast
pronto 1 adj prompt 2 adv (dentro de poco) soon; (temprano) early; de pronto suddenly; tan pronto como as soon as
pronunciación f pronunciation
pronunciar ⟨1b⟩ v/t pronounce; (decir) say; pronunciar un discurso give a speech
propaganda f advertising; POL propaganda
propagar ⟨1h⟩ 1 v/t spread 2 v/r propagarse spread
propano m propane
propasarse ⟨1a⟩ v/r go too far
propenso adj prone (a to); ser propenso a hacer be prone to do, have a tendency to do

propiciar ⟨1b⟩ v/t (favorecer) promote; (causar) bring about
propicio adj favo(u)rable
propiedad f property
propietario m, -a f owner
propina f tip
propinar ⟨1a⟩ v/t golpe, paliza give
propio adj own; (característico) characteristic (de of), typical (de of); (adecuado) suitable (para for); la -a directora the director herself
proponer ⟨2r; part propuesto ⟩ v/t propose, suggest
proporción f proportion
proporcional adj proportional
proporcionar ⟨1a⟩ v/t provide, supply; satisfacción give
proposición f proposal, suggestion
propósito m (intención) intention; (objetivo) purpose; a propósito on purpose; (por cierto) by the way
propuesto part → proponer
propuesta f proposal
propugnar ⟨1a⟩ v/t advocate
propulsar ⟨1a⟩ v/t TÉC propel; fig promote
propulsor m (motor) engine
prórroga f DEP overtime, Br extra time
prorrogar ⟨1h⟩ v/t plazo extend
prorrumpir ⟨3a⟩ v/i burst (en into)
prosa f prose
prosaico adj mundane, prosaic
proseguir ⟨3d & 3l⟩ 1 v/t carry on, continue 2 v/i continue (con with)
proselitismo m proselytism
prospecto m directions for use pl; de propaganda leaflet
prosperar ⟨1a⟩ v/i prosper, thrive
prosperidad f prosperity
próspero adj prosperous, thriving
próstata f prostate
prostíbulo m brothel
prostitución f prostitution
prostituirse ⟨3g⟩ v/r prostitute o.s.
prostituta f prostitute
prostituto m male prostitute
protagonista m/f personaje main character; actor, actriz star; de una hazaña hero; mujer heroine
protagonizar ⟨1f⟩ v/t star in, play the lead

P

in; *incidente* play a leading role in

protección *f* protection

proteger ⟨2c⟩ *v/t* protect (**de** from)

proteína *f* protein

protésico *m*, **-a** *f*: **protésico dental** dental technician

prótesis *f* prosthesis

protesta *f* protest

protestante *m/f* Protestant

protestar ⟨1a⟩ **1** *v/t* protest **2** *v/i* (*quejarse*) complain (**por**, **de** about); (*expresar oposición*) protest (**contra**, **por** about, against)

protocolo *m* protocol

prototipo *m* TÉC prototype

protuberancia *f* protuberance

prov. *abr* (= **provincia**) province

provecho *m* benefit; **¡buen provecho!** enjoy (your meal); **sacar provecho de** benefit from

proveedor *m*, **proveedora** *f* supplier; **proveedor de** (**acceso a**) **Internet** Internet Service Provider, ISP

proveer ⟨2e; *part* **provisto** ⟩ *v/t* supply; **proveer a alguien de algo** supply s.o. with sth

provenir ⟨3s⟩ *v/i* come (**de** from)

proverbio *m* proverb

providencia *f* providence

provincia *f* province

provincial *adj* provincial

provinciano 1 *adj* provincial **2** *m*, **-a** *f* provincial

provisional *adj* provisional

provisiones *fpl* provisions

provisto 1 *part* → **proveer 2** *adj*: **provisto de** equipped with

provocación *f* provocation

provocador *adj* provocative

provocar ⟨1g⟩ *v/t* cause; *al enfado* provoke; *sexualmente* lead on; **¿te provoca un café?** *S. Am.* how about a coffee?

provocativo *adj* provocative

proxeneta *m* pimp

proxenetismo *m* procuring

proximidad *f* proximity

próximo *adj* (*siguiente*) next; (*cercano*) near, close

proyección *f* MAT, PSI projection; *de película* showing

proyectar ⟨1a⟩ *v/t* project; (*planear*) plan; *película* show; *sombra* cast

proyectil *m* missile

proyecto *m* plan; *trabajo* project; **proyecto de ley** bill; **tenir en proyecto hacer algo** plan to do sth

proyector *m* projector

prudencia *f* caution, prudence

prudente *adj* careful, cautious

prueba *f* tb TIP proof; JUR piece of evidence; DEP event; EDU test; **a prueba de bala** bulletproof; **poner algo a prueba** put sth to the test

P.S. *abr* (= **postscriptum** (**posdata**)) PS (= postscript)

pseudo... *pref* pseudo-

pseudónimo *m* pseudonym

psicoanálisis *f* (psycho)analysis

psicoanalista *m/f* (psycho)analyst

psicodélico *adj* psychedelic

psicología *f* psychology

psicológico *adj* psychological

psicólogo *m*, **-a** *f* psychologist

psicópata *m/f* psychopath

psicosis *f inv* psychosis

psicoterapia *f* psychotherapy

psiquiatra *m/f* psychiatrist

psiquiatría *f* psychiatry

psiquiátrico *adj* psychiatric

psíquico *adj* psychic

pta *abr* (= **peseta**) peseta

ptas *abr* (= **pesetas**) pesetas

púa *f* ZO spine, quill; MÚS plectrum, pick

pub *m* bar

pubertad *f* puberty

publicación *f* publication

publicar ⟨1g⟩ **1** *v/t* publish **2** *v/r* **publicarse** come out, be published

publicidad *f* (*divulgación*) publicity; COM advertising; (*anuncios*) advertisements *pl*

publicista *m/f* advertising executive

publicitario 1 *adj* advertising *atr* **2** *m*, **-a** *f* advertising executive

público 1 *adj* public; *escuela* public, *Br* state **2** *m* public; TEA audience; DEP spectators *pl*, crowd

pucho *m S. Am.* P cigarette butt, *Br* fag end F; **no valer un pucho** be completely worthless

pude *vb* → **poder**

púdico *adj* modest

pudín *m* pudding

pudo *vb* → **poder**

pudor *m* modesty

pudrir ⟨3a⟩ **1** *v/t* rot **2** *v/r* pudrirse rot; **pudrirse de envidia** be green with envy

pueblerino *m*, **-a** *f* hick *desp*

pueblero *m*, **-a** *f L.Am.* villager; *de pueblo más grande* townsman; *mujer* townswoman

pueblo *m* village; *más grande* town

puedo *vb* → **poder**

puente *m* bridge; **hacer puente** have a day off between a weekend and a public holiday

puenting *m* bungee jumping

puerco 1 *adj* dirty; *fig* filthy F **2** *m* zo pig; **puerco espín** porcupine

puerro *m* BOT leek

puerta *f* door; *en valla* gate; DEP goal; **puerta de embarque** gate

puerto *m* MAR port; GEOG pass

Puerto Rico Puerto Rico

puertorriqueño 1 *adj* Puerto Rican **2** *m*, **-a** *f* Puerto Rican

pues *conj* well; *fml* (*porque*) as, since; **pues bien** well; **¡pues sí!** of course!

puesta *f*: **puesta a punto** tune-up; **puesta de sol** sunset

puestero *m*, **-a** *f L.Am.* stall holder

puesto 1 *part* → **poner 2** *m lugar* place; *en mercado* stand, stall; **puesto (de trabajo)** job **3** *conj*: **puesto que** since, given that

pugnar ⟨1a⟩ *v/i* fight (*por* for; *por hacer* to do)

puja *f* (*lucha*) struggle; *en subasta* bid

pujar ⟨1a⟩ *v/i* (*luchar*) struggle; *en subasta* bid

pulcro *adj* immaculate

pulga *f* zo flea; **tener malas pulgas** *fig* F be bad-tempered

pulgada *f* inch

pulgar *m* thumb

pulimentar ⟨1a⟩ *v/t* polish

pulir ⟨3a⟩ *v/t* polish

pulla *f* gibe

pulmón *m* lung

pulmonía *f* MED pneumonia

pulpa *f* pulp

pulpería *f L.Am.* mom-and-pop store, *Br* corner shop

pulpero *m*, **-a** *f S. Am.* storekeeper, shopkeeper

púlpito *m* pulpit

pulpo *m* zo octopus

pulque *m Méx* pulque (*alcoholic drink made from cactus*)

pulquería *f Méx* pulque bar

pulsación *f* beat; *al escribir a máquina* key stroke

pulsar ⟨1a⟩ *v/t botón, tecla* press

pulsera *f* bracelet

pulso *m* pulse; *fig* steady hand; **tomar el pulso a alguien** take s.o.'s pulse; **tomar el pulso a algo** *fig* take the pulse of sth

pulular ⟨1a⟩ *v/i* mill around

pulverizador *m* spray

pulverizar ⟨1f⟩ *v/t* spray; (*convertir en polvo*) pulverize, crush

puma *m* zo puma, mountain lion

puna *f L.Am.* GEOG high Andean plateau; MED altitude sickness

pundonor *m* pride

punitivo *adj* punitive

punta *f* tip; (*extremo*) end; *de lápiz*, GEOG point; *L.Am.* (*grupo*) group; **sacar punta a** sharpen

puntada *f* stitch

puntapié *m* kick

puntera *f* toe

puntería *f* aim

puntero 1 *adj* leading **2** *m* pointer

puntiagudo *adj* pointed, sharp

puntilla *f*: **de puntillas** on tippy-toe, *Br* on tiptoe

puntilloso *adj* particular, punctilious *fml*

punto *m* point; *señal* dot; *signo de puntuación* period, *Br* full stop; *en costura, sutura* stitch; **dos puntos** colon; **punto muerto** AUTO neutral; **punto de vista** point of view; **punto y coma** semicolon; **a punto** (*listo*) ready; (*a tiempo*) in time; **de punto** knitted; **en punto** on the dot; **estar a punto de** be about to; **hacer**

punto knit; **hasta cierto punto** up to a point; **empresa** *f* **punto.com** dot.com (company)

puntuación *f* punctuation; DEP score; EDU grade, mark

puntual *adj* punctual

puntualidad *f* punctuality

puntualizar ⟨1f⟩ *v/t* (*señalar*) point out; (*aclarar*) clarify

punzada *f* sharp *o* stabbing pain

punzante *adj* stinging

puñado *m* handful

puñal *m* dagger

puñalada *f* stab wound

puñeta *f*: **¡puñeta(s)!** F for heaven's sake! F; **hacer la puñeta a alguien** F give s.o. a hard time F

puñetazo *m* punch; **dar un puñetazo** punch

puño *m* fist; *de camisa* cuff; *de bastón, paraguas* handle

pupa *f en labio* cold sore; **hacerse pupa** *lenguaje infantil* hurt o.s.

pupila *f* pupil

pupitre *m* desk

pupusa *f L.Am.* filled dumpling

purasangre *m* thoroughbred

puré *m* purée; *sopa* cream; **puré de patatas** *or* **papas** *L.Am.* mashed potatoes

pureza *f* purity

purga *f* POL purge

purgante *m/adj* laxative, purgative

purgatorio *m* REL purgatory

purificación *f* purification

purificar ⟨1g⟩ *v/t* purify

purista *m/f* purist

puritano 1 *adj* puritanical **2** *m,-a f* puritan

puro 1 *adj* pure; *casualidad, coincidencia* sheer; *Méx* (*único*) sole, only; **la -a verdad** the honest truth; **te sirven la -a comida** *Méx* they just serve food **2** *m* cigar

púrpura *f* purple

pus *m* pus

puse *vb* → **poder**

pusilánime *adj* fainthearted

puso *vb* → **poder**

puta *f* P whore P

putada *f* P dirty trick; **¡qué putada!** shit! P

putear ⟨1a⟩ *v/t L.Am.* P swear at; **putear a alguien** *Esp* give s.o. a hard time, make life difficult for s.o.

puto *adj* P goddamn F, *Br* bloody F; **de puta madre** P great F, fantastic F

putrefacción *f* putrefaction

puzzle *m* jigsaw (puzzle)

PVC *abr* (= **cloruro de polivinilo**) PVC (= polyvinyl chloride)

P.V.P. *abr* (= **precio de venta al público**) RRP (= recommended retail price)

pza. *abr* (= **plaza**) sq (= square)

Q

q.e.p. d. *abr* (= **que en paz descanse**) RIP (= requiescat in pace)

que 1 *pron rel sujeto*: *persona* who, that; *cosa* which, that; *complemento*: *persona* that, whom *fml*; *cosa* that, which; **el coche que ves** the car you can see, the car that *o* which you can see; **el que** the one that **2** *conj* that; **lo mismo que tú** the same as you; **¡que entre!** tell him to come in; **¡que descanses!** sleep well; **¡que sí!** I said yes; **¡que no!** I said no; **es que ...** the thing is ...; **yo que tú** if I were you

qué 1 *adj & pron interr* what; **¿qué pasó?** what happened?; **¿qué día es?** what day is it?; **¿qué vestido prefieres?** which dress do you prefer? **2** *adj & pron int*: **¡qué moto!** what a motorbike!; **¡qué**

de flores! what a lot of flowers! **3** *adv*:
¡qué alto es! he's so tall!; **¡qué bien!**
great!

quebrada *f L.Am.* stream

quebradero *m*: **quebraderos de cabeza**
F headaches

quebradizo *adj* brittle

quebrado 1 *adj* broken **2** *m* MAT fraction

quebrantahuesos *m inv* zo lammergeier

quebrantar ⟨1a⟩ *v/t* ley, contrato break

quebrar ⟨1k⟩ **1** *v/t* break **2** *v/i* COM go
bankrupt **3** *v/r* **quebrarse** break

quedar ⟨1a⟩ **1** *v/i* (permanecer) stay; en
un estado be; (sobrar) be left; **quedó
sin resolver** it remained unsolved, it
wasn't sorted out; **te queda bien / mal
de estilo** it suits you / doesn't suit you;
de talla it fits you / doesn't fit you; **quedar cerca** be nearby; **quedar con alguien** F arrange to meet (with) s.o.; **quedar en algo** agree to sth; **¿queda mucho
tiempo?** is there much time left? **2** *v/r*
quedarse stay; **quedarse ciego** go
blind; **quedarse con algo** keep sth;
me quedé sin comer I ended up not eating

quehaceres *mpl* tasks

queja *f* complaint

quejarse ⟨1a⟩ *v/r* complain (**a** to; **de**
about)

quejica *adj* F whining F

quejido *m* moan, groan

quejumbroso *adj* moaning

quemado *adj* burnt; *Méx (desvirtuado)*
discredited; **quemado por el sol** sun-
burnt; **oler a quemado** smell of burning

quemadura *f* burn

quemar ⟨1a⟩ **1** *v/t* burn; con agua scald; F
recursos use up; F dinero blow F **2** *v/i* be
very hot **3** *v/r* **quemarse** burn o.s.; de tostada, papeles burn; fig burn o.s. out; *Méx
(desvirtuarse)* become discredited

quena *f S. Am.* Indian flute

quepo *vb* → **caber**

queque *m L.Am.* cake

querella *f* JUR lawsuit

querellarse ⟨1a⟩ *v/r* JUR bring a lawsuit
(**contra** against)

querer ⟨2u⟩ *v/t (desear)* want; *(amar)*

love; **querer decir** mean; **sin querer** un-
intentionally; **quisiera ...** I would like ...

querido 1 *part* → **querer 2** *adj* dear **3** *m,-a*
f darling

queroseno *m* kerosene

querrá *vb* → **querer**

querría *vb* → **querer**

quesadilla *f* quesadilla *(folded tortilla)*

queso *m* cheese; **queso para untar**
cheese spread; **queso rallado** grated
cheese

quicio *m*: **sacar de quicio a alguien** F
drive s.o. crazy F

quid *m*: **el quid de la cuestión** the nub of
the question

quiebra *f* COM bankruptcy

quien *pron rel sujeto* who, that; *objeto*
who, whom *fml*, that; **no soy quien para
hacerlo** I'm not the right person to do it

quién *pron* who; **¿quién es?** who is it?;
¿de quién es este libro? whose is this
book?, who does this book belong to?

quienquiera *pron* whoever

quiero *vb* → **querer**

quieto *adj* still; **¡estáte quieto!** keep still!

quijotesco *adj* quixotic

quilate *m* carat

quilla *f* keel

quimera *f* pipe dream

química *f* chemistry

químico 1 *adj* chemical **2** *m,-a f* chemist

quimioterapia *f* MED chemotherapy

quimono *m* kimono

quincalla *f* junk

quince *adj* fifteen

quincena *f* two weeks, *Br* fortnight

quiniela *f* lottery where the winners are de-
cided by soccer results

quinientos *adj* five hundred

quinina *f* quinine

quinquenio *m* five-year period

quinta *f* MIL draft, *Br* call-up; **es de mi
quinta** he's my age

quinteto *m* MÚS quintet

quinto 1 *adj* fifth **2** *m* MIL conscript

quiosco *m* kiosk; **quiosco de prensa**
newsstand, *Br* newsagent's

quiosquero *m,-a f* newspaper vendor

quirófano *m* operating room, *Br* operat-

Q

ing theatre
quiromancia, quiromancía f palmistry
quirúrgico adj surgical
quise vb → querer
quisiera vb → querer
quiso vb → querer
quisque F: **todo quisque** everyone and
his brother F, Br the world and his wife F
quisquilla f zo shrimp
quisquilloso adj touchy
quiste m MED cyst
quitaesmalte m nail varnish remover

quitamanchas m inv stain remover
quitar ⟨1a⟩ **1** v/t ropa take off, remove;
obstáculos remove; **quitar algo a alguien** take sth (away) from s.o.; **quitar
la mesa** clear the table **2** v/i: **¡quita!**
get out of the way! **3** v/r quitarse ropa,
gafas take off; (apartarse) get out of
the way; **quitarse algo/a alguien de encima** get rid of s.o./sth; **¡quítate de en
medio!** F get out of the way!
quizá(s) adv perhaps, maybe
quórum m quorum

R

rabadilla f ANAT coccyx
rábano m BOT radish; **me importa un
rábano** F I don't give a damn F
rabia f MED rabies sg; **dar rabia a alguien**
make s.o. mad; **tener rabia a alguien**
have it in for s.o.
rabiar ⟨1b⟩ v/i: rabiar de dolor be in agony; **hacer rabiar a alguien** fig F jerk
s.o.'s chain F, pull s.o.'s leg F; **rabiar
por** be dying for
rabieta f tantrum
rabino m rabbi
rabioso adj MED rabid; fig furious
rabo m tail
rabón adj L.Am. animal short-tailed
rácano adj F stingy F, mean
racha f spell
racial adj racial
racimo m bunch
ración f share; (porción) serving, portion
racional adj rational
racionalizar ⟨1f⟩ v/t rationalize
racionamiento m rationing
racionar ⟨1a⟩ v/t ration
racismo m racism
racista m/f & adj racist
radar m radar
radiación f radiation

radiactividad f radioactivity
radiactivo adj radioactive
radiador m radiator
radiante adj radiant
radiar ⟨1b⟩ v/i radiate
radical m/f & adj radical
radicalismo m radicalism
radicar ⟨1g⟩ v/i stem (en from), lie (en in)
radio **1** m MAT radius; QUÍM radium; L.Am.
radio; **en un radio de** within a radius of;
radio de acción range **2** f radio; **radio
despertador** clock radio
radioaficionado m radio ham
radiocasete m radio cassette player
radiodifusión f broadcasting
radiofónico adj radio atr
radiografía f X-ray
radiografiar ⟨1c⟩ v/t X-ray
radiología f radiology
radiólogo m, -a f radiologist
radiotaxi m radio taxi
radiotelegrafista m/f radio operator
radioyente m/f listener
ráfaga f gust; de balas burst
rafia f raffia
rafting m rafting
ragú m GASTR ragout
raído adj threadbare

rail, raíl *m* rail

raíz *f* root; **raíz cuadrada /cúbica** MAT square / cube root; **a raíz de** as a result of; **echar raíces** de *persona* put down roots

raja *f* (*rodaja*) slice; (*corte*) cut; (*grieta*) crack

rajar ⟨1a⟩ **1** *v/t fruta* cut, slice; *cerámica* crack; *neumático* slash **2** *v/i* F gossip **3** *v/r* **rajarse** *fig* F back out F

rajatabla: **a rajatabla** strictly, to the letter

ralentí *m*: **al ralentí** AUTO idling; FOT in slow motion

ralentizar ⟨1f⟩ *v/t* slow down

rallador *m* grater

rallar ⟨1a⟩ *v/t* GASTR grate

rally(e) *m* rally

rama *f* branch; POL wing; **andarse por las ramas** beat about the bush

ramificación *f* ramification

ramo *m* COM sector; **ramo de flores** bunch of flowers

rampa *f* ramp; **rampa de lanzamiento** launch pad

ramplón *adj* vulgar

rana *f* ZO frog

ranchera *f* typical Mexican song

ranchero **1** *adj*: **canción -a** romantic ballad; **música -a** *music of northern Mexico* **2** *m L.Am.* rancher

rancho *m Méx* small farm; *L.Am.* (*barrio de chabolas*) shanty town

rancio *adj* rancid; *fig* ancient

rango *m* rank; **de alto rango** high-ranking

ranking *m* ranking

ranura *f* slot

rapapolvo *m* F telling-off F

rapar ⟨1a⟩ *v/t pelo* crop

rapaz **1** *adj* predatory; **ave rapaz** bird of prey **2** *m*, **-a** *f* F kid F

rape *m pescado* anglerfish; **al rape** *pelo* cropped

rapidez *f* speed, rapidity

rápido **1** *adj* quick, fast **2** *m* rapids *pl*

rapiña *f* pillage

raptar ⟨1a⟩ *v/t* kidnap

rapto *m* kidnap

raptor *m*, raptora *f* kidnapper

raqueta *f* racket

raquítico *adj fig* rickety

rareza *f* scarcity, rarity

raro *adj* rare

ras *m*: **a ras de tierra** at ground level

rasante *adj vuelo* low

rasca *f L.Am.*: **pegarse una rasca** F get plastered F

rascacielos *m inv* skyscraper

rascado *adj L.Am.* F plastered F

rascar ⟨1g⟩ *v/t* scratch; *superficie* scrape, scratch

rasero *m*: **medir por el mismo rasero** treat equally

rasgado *adj boca* wide; **ojos rasgados** almond-shaped eyes

rasgar ⟨1h⟩ *v/t* tear (up)

rasgo *m* feature; **a grandes rasgos** broadly speaking

rasguño *m* MED scratch

raso **1** *adj* flat, level; **soldado raso** private **2** *m material* satin; **al raso** in the open air

raspa *f* fishbone; *L.Am.* F (*reprimanda*) telling-off

raspado *m Méx* water ice

raspadura *f* scrape

raspar ⟨1a⟩ **1** *v/t* scrape; *con lija* sand **2** *v/i* be rough

rastra *f*: **entrar a rastras** drag o.s. in, crawl in

rastreador *adj*: **perro rastreador** tracker dog

rastrear ⟨1a⟩ **1** *v/t persona* track; *bosque, zona comb* **2** *v/i* rake

rastrero *adj* mean, low

rastrillo *m* rake

rastro *m* flea market; (*huella*) trace; **desaparecer sin dejar rastro** vanish without trace

rastrojo *m* stubble

rasurar ⟨1a⟩ *v/t* shave

rata *f* ZO rat

ratero *m*, **-a** *f* petty thief

raticida *m* rat poison

ratificar ⟨1g⟩ *v/t* POL ratify

rato *m* time, while; **ratos libres** spare time *sg*; **al poco rato** after a short time *o* while; **todo el rato** all the time; **un buen rato** a good while, a pretty long

R

time; **pasar el rato** pass the time; **he pasado un buen / mal rato** I've had a great / an awful time

ratón m zo, INFOR mouse

ratonera f mouse trap

raudal m: **tienen dinero a raudales** they've got loads of money F

raudo adj swift

raya f GRAM dash; zo ray; de pelo part, Br parting; **a** or **de rayas** striped; **pasarse de la raya** overstep the mark, go too far

rayado adj disco, superficie scratched

rayano adj bordering (**en** on)

rayar ⟨1a⟩ **1** v/t scratch; (tachar) cross out **2** v/i border (**en** on), verge (**en** on)

rayo m FÍS ray; METEO (bolt of) lightning; **rayo láser** laser beam; **rayo X** X-ray; **rayos ultravioleta** ultraviolet rays

raza f race; de animal breed

razón f reason; **a razón de precio** at; **dar la razón a alguien** admit that s.o. is right; **entrar en razón** see sense; **perder la razón** lose one's mind; **tener razón** be right

razonable adj precio reasonable

razonamiento m reasoning

razonar ⟨1a⟩ v/i reason

RDSI abr (= **Red Digital de Servicios Integrados**) ISDN (= Integrated Services Digital Network)

reacción f reaction (**a** to); **avión a reacción** jet (aircraft)

reaccionar ⟨1a⟩ v/i react (**a** to)

reaccionario 1 adj reactionary **2** m, -a f reactionary

reacio adj reluctant (**a** to)

reactivación f COM revival, upturn

reactivar ⟨1a⟩ v/t COM revive

reactor m reactor; (motor) jet engine

reafirmar ⟨1a⟩ **1** v/t reaffirm **2** v/r reafirmarse: **reafirmarse en** idea reassert

reajuste m adjustment; **reajuste ministerial** POL cabinet reshuffle

real adj (regio) royal; (verdadero) real

realeza f royalty

realidad f reality; **en realidad** in fact, in reality

realismo m realism

realista 1 adj realistic **2** m/f realist

realización f fulfil(l)ment; RAD, TV production

realizador m, **realizadora** f de película director; RAD, TV producer

realizar ⟨1f⟩ **1** v/t tarea carry out; RAD, TV produce; COM realize **2** v/r realizarse de persona fulfil(l) o.s.

realquilar ⟨1a⟩ v/t sublet

realzar ⟨1f⟩ v/t highlight

reanimación f revival

reanimar ⟨1a⟩ v/t revive

reanudación f resumption

reanudar ⟨1a⟩ v/t resume

reaparecer ⟨2d⟩ v/i reappear

reaparición f reappearance

reaseguro m reinsurance

rebaja f reduction; **rebajas de verano / invierno** summer / winter sale

rebajar ⟨1a⟩ **1** v/t precio lower, reduce; mercancías reduce **2** v/r rebajarse lower o.s., humble o.s.

rebanada f slice

rebanar ⟨1a⟩ v/t slice

rebañar ⟨1a⟩ v/t: **rebañar algo** wipe sth clean

rebaño m flock

rebasar ⟨1a⟩ v/t Méx AUTO pass, Br overtake

rebatir ⟨3a⟩ v/t razones rebut, refute

rebeca f cardigan

rebeco m zo chamois

rebelarse ⟨1a⟩ v/r rebel

rebelde 1 adj rebel atr **2** m/f rebel

rebeldía f rebelliousness

rebelión f rebellion

reblandecer ⟨2d⟩ v/t soften

rebobinar ⟨1a⟩ v/t rewind

rebosar ⟨1a⟩ v/i overflow

rebotar ⟨1a⟩ **1** v/t bounce; (disgustar) annoy **2** v/i bounce, rebound

rebote m bounce; **de rebote** on the rebound

rebozar ⟨1f⟩ v/t GASTR coat

rebuscado adj over-elaborate

rebuznar ⟨1a⟩ v/i bray

recado m errand; Rpl (arnés) harness; **dejar un recado** leave a message

recaída f MED relapse

recalar ⟨1a⟩ v/i MAR put in (**en** at), call (**en**

at)

recalcar ⟨1g⟩ *v/t* stress, emphasize

recalcitrante *adj* recalcitrant

recalentar ⟨1k⟩ *v/t comida* warm o heat up

recámara *f de arma de fuego* chamber; *L.Am. (dormitorio)* bedroom

recambio *m* COM spare part

recapacitar ⟨1a⟩ *v/t* think over, reflect on

recapitular ⟨1a⟩ *v/t* recap

recargar ⟨1h⟩ *v/t batería* recharge; *recipiente* refill; *recargar un 5%* charge 5% extra

recargo *m* surcharge

recatado *adj* modest; *(cauto)* cautious

recato *m* modesty; *(prudencia)* caution

recauchutar ⟨1a⟩ *v/t neumáticos* retread

recaudación *f acción* collection; *cantidad* takings *pl*

recaudar ⟨1a⟩ *v/t impuestos, dinero* collect

recaudo *m*: *poner a buen recaudo* put in a safe place

recelo *m* mistrust

recepción *f* en *hotel* reception

recepcionista *m/f* receptionist

receptivo *adj* receptive

receptor *m* receiver

recesión *f* recession

receta *f* GASTR recipe; *receta médica* prescription

recetar ⟨1a⟩ *v/t* MED prescribe

recetario *m* recipe book

rechazar ⟨1f⟩ *v/t* reject; MIL repel

rechazo *m* rejection

rechinar ⟨1a⟩ *v/i* creak, squeak

rechistar ⟨1a⟩ *v/i* protest; *sin rechistar* F without a murmur, without complaining

rechoncho *adj* F dumpy F

rechupete: *de rechupete* F delicious

recibidor *m* entrance hall

recibimiento *m* reception

recibir ⟨3a⟩ *v/t* receive

recibo *m* (sales) receipt

reciclable *adj* recyclable

reciclado, reciclaje *m* recycling

reciclar ⟨1a⟩ *v/t* recycle

recién *adv* newly; *L.Am. (hace poco)* just; *recién casados* newly-weds; *recién na-*

cido newborn; *recién pintado* wet paint; *recién llegamos* we've only just arrived

reciente *adj* recent

recinto *m* premises *pl; área* grounds *pl*

recio *adj* sturdy, tough

recipiente *m* container

recíproco *adj* reciprocal

recital *m* recital

recitar ⟨1a⟩ *v/t* recite

reclamación *f* complaint; POL claim, demand

reclamar ⟨1a⟩ **1** *v/t* claim, demand **2** *v/i* complain

reclame *m* L.Am. advertisement

reclamo *m* lure

reclinable *adj*: *asiento reclinable* reclining seat

reclinar ⟨1a⟩ **1** *v/t* rest **2** *v/r* **reclinarse** lean, recline (*contra* against)

recluir ⟨3g⟩ *v/t* imprison, confine

reclusión *f* JUR imprisonment, confinement

recluso *m*, *-a f* prisoner

recluta *m/f* recruit

reclutar ⟨1a⟩ *v/t tb* COM recruit

recobrar ⟨1a⟩ **1** *v/t* recover **2** *v/r* **recobrarse** recover (*de* from)

recogedor *m* dustpan

recogepelotas *m/f inv* ball boy; *niña* ball girl

recoger ⟨2c⟩ **1** *v/t* pick up, collect; *habitación* tidy up; AGR harvest; *(mostrar)* show **2** *v/r* **recogerse** go home

recogida *f* collection; *recogida de basuras* garbage collection, *Br* refuse collection; *recogida de equipajes* baggage reclaim

recolectar ⟨1a⟩ *v/t* AGR harvest, bring in

recomendación *f* recommendation

recomendar ⟨1k⟩ *v/t* recommend

recompensa *f* reward

recompensar ⟨1a⟩ *v/t* reward

recomponer ⟨2r; *part* **recompuesto** ⟩ *v/t* mend

reconciliación *f* reconciliation

reconciliar ⟨1b⟩ **1** *v/t* reconcile **2** *v/r* **reconciliarse** make up (*con* with), be reconciled (*con* with) recóndito *adj* remote

reconfortar ⟨1a⟩ *v/t* comfort

reconocer ⟨2d⟩ *v/t* recognize; *errores* admit, acknowledge; *area* reconnoiter, *Br* reconnoitre; MED examine

reconocimiento *m* recognition; *de error* acknowledg(e)ment; MED examination, check-up; MIL reconnaissance

reconquista *f* reconquest

reconquistar ⟨1a⟩ *v/t* reconquer

reconsiderar ⟨1a⟩ *v/t* reconsider

reconstrucción *f* reconstruction

reconstruir ⟨3g⟩ *v/t fig* reconstruct

reconvenir ⟨3s⟩ *v/i* JUR counterclaim

reconversión *f* COM restructuring

recopilación *f* compilation

recopilar ⟨1a⟩ *v/t* compile

récord 1 *adj* record(-breaking) 2 *m* record

recordar ⟨1m⟩ *v/t* remember, recall; **recordar algo a alguien** remind s.o. of sth

recordatorio *m* reminder

recorrer ⟨2a⟩ *v/t distancia* cover, do; *a pie* walk; *territorio, país* go around, travel around; *camino* go along, travel along

recorrido *m* route; DEP round

recortar ⟨1a⟩ *v/t* cut out; *fig* cut

recorte *m fig* cutback; **recorte de periódico** cutting, clipping; **recorte salarial** salary cut

recostarse ⟨1m⟩ *v/r* lie down

recoveco *m* nook, cranny; *en camino* bend

recrearse ⟨1a⟩ *v/r* amuse o.s.

recreativo *adj* recreational; **juegos recreativos** amusements

recreo *m* recreation; EDU recess, *Br* break

recriminar ⟨1a⟩ *v/t* reproach

recrudecerse ⟨2d⟩ *v/r* intensify

recta *f* DEP straight; **recta final** *tb fig* home straight

rectángulo *m* rectangle

rectificar ⟨1g⟩ *v/t* correct, rectify; *camino* straighten

rectitud *f* rectitude, probity

recto *adj* straight; *(honesto)* honest

rector *m* rector, *Br* vice-chancellor

rectorado *m* rector's office, *Br* vice-chancellor's office

recuadro *m* TIP inset, box

recubierto *part* → recubrir

recubrir ⟨3a; *part* recubierto⟩ *v/t* cover (*de* with)

recuento *m* count; **recuento de votos** recount

recuerdo *m* memory; **da recuerdos a Luís** give my regards to Luís

recuperación *f tb fig* recovery

recuperar ⟨1a⟩ 1 *v/t tiempo* make up; *algo perdido* recover 2 *v/r* recuperarse recover (*de* from)

recurrir ⟨3a⟩ 1 *v/t* JUR appeal against 2 *v/i*: **recurrir a** resort to, turn to

recurso *m* JUR appeal; *material* resource; **recursos humanos** human resources; **recursos naturales** natural resources

red *f* net; INFOR, *fig* network; **caer en las redes de** *fig* fall into the clutches of; **Red Digital de Servicios Integrados** Integrated Services Digital Network

redacción *f* writing; *de editorial* editorial department; EDU essay

redactar ⟨1a⟩ *v/t* write, compose

redactor *m*, redactora *f* editor

redada *f* raid

redentor *m*, redentora *f* COM redeemer; **el Redentor** REL the Savio(u)r

redoble *m* MÚS (drum)roll

redomado *adj* F total, out-and-out

redonda *f*: **a la redonda** around, round about

redondear ⟨1a⟩ *v/t para más* round up; *para menos* round down; *(rematar)* round off

redondo *adj* round; *negocio* excellent; **caer redondo** flop down

reducción *f* reduction; MED setting

reducido *adj precio* reduced; *espacio* small, confined

reducir ⟨3o⟩ 1 *v/t* reduce (*a* to); MIL overcome 2 *v/r* reducirse come down (*a* to)

reducto *m* redoubt

redujo *vb* → reducir

redundancia *f* tautology

redundar ⟨1a⟩ *v/i* have an impact (*en* on)

reeditar ⟨1a⟩ *v/t* republish, reissue

reelegir ⟨3c & 3l⟩ *v/t* re-elect

reembolsar ⟨1a⟩ *v/t* refund

reembolso *m* refund; **contra reembolso**

collect on delivery, *Br* cash on delivery, COD

reemplazar ⟨1f⟩ *v/t* replace

reencarnación *f* REL reincarnation

reestructurar ⟨1a⟩ *v/t* restructure

refacción *f* L.Am. de edificio refurbishment; AUTO spare part

referencia *f* reference; **hacer referencia a** refer to, make reference to; **referencias** COM references

referéndum *m* referendum

referente *adj*: **referente a** referring to, relating to

referirse ⟨3i⟩ *v/r* refer (**a** to)

refilón *m*: **mirar de refilón** glance at

refinado *adj tb fig* refined

refinar ⟨1a⟩ *v/t* TÉC refine

refinería *f* TÉC refinery

reflector *m* reflector; EL spotlight

reflejar ⟨1a⟩ **1** *v/t tb fig* reflect **2** *v/r* reflejarse be reflected

reflejo *m* reflex; *imagen* reflection

reflexión *f fig* reflection, thought

reflexionar ⟨1a⟩ *v/t* reflect on, ponder

reflexivo *adj* GRAM reflexive

reflotar ⟨1a⟩ *v/t* COM refloat

reforestar ⟨1a⟩ *v/t* reforest

reforma *f* reform; **reformas** *pl (obras)* refurbishment *sg*; *(reparaciones)* repairs

reformador *m*, **reformadora** *f* reformer

reformar ⟨1a⟩ **1** *v/t* reform; *edificio* refurbish; *(reparar)* repair **2** *v/r* reformarse mend one's ways, reform

reformatorio *m* reform school, reformatory

reformista 1 *adj* reformist, reform *atr* **2** *m/f* reformer

reforzar ⟨1f & 1m⟩ *v/t* reinforce; *vigilancia* increase, step up

refrán *m* saying

refrenar ⟨1a⟩ *v/t* restrain, contain

refrescante *adj* refreshing

refrescar ⟨1g⟩ **1** *v/t tb fig* refresh; *conocimientos* brush up **2** *v/i* cool down **3** *v/r* refrescarse cool down

refresco *m* soda, *Br* soft drink

refriega *f* MIL clash, skirmish

refrigerador *m* refrigerator

refrigerar ⟨1a⟩ *v/t* refrigerate

refrigerio *m* snack

refuerzo *m* reinforcement; **refuerzos** MIL reinforcements

refugiado *m*, **-a** *f* refugee

refugiarse ⟨1b⟩ *v/r* take refuge

refugio *m* refuge

refulgente *adj* dazzling

refunfuñar ⟨1a⟩ *v/i* grumble

refutar ⟨1a⟩ *v/t* refute

regadera *f* watering can; *Méx (ducha)* shower; **estar como una regadera** F be nuts F

regadío *m*: **tierra de regadío** irrigated land

regalar ⟨1a⟩ *v/t*: **regalar algo a alguien** give sth to s.o., give s.o. sth

regaliz *m* BOT licorice, *Br* liquorice

regalo *m* gift, present

regañadientes: **a regañadientes** reluctantly

regañar ⟨1a⟩ **1** *v/t* tell off **2** *v/i* quarrel

regañina *f* F telling off

regar ⟨1h & 1k⟩ *v/t* water; AGR irrigate

regata *f* regatta

regatear ⟨1a⟩ *v/t* DEP get past, dodge; **no regatear esfuerzos** spare no effort

regazo *m* lap

regenerar ⟨1a⟩ *v/t* regenerate

regente *m/f* regent

regidor 1 *adj* governing, ruling **2** *m*, regidora *f* TEA stage manager

régimen *m* POL regime; MED diet; **estar a régimen** be on a diet

regimiento *m* MIL regiment

regio *adj* regal, majestic; *S. Am.* F *(estupendo)* great F, fantastic F

región *f* region

regional *adj* regional

regionalismo *m* regionalism

regir ⟨3l & 3c⟩ **1** *v/t* rule, govern **2** *v/i* apply, be in force **3** *v/r* regirse be guided (**por** by)

registrar ⟨1a⟩ **1** *v/t* register; *casa* search **2** *v/r* registrarse be recorded; **se registró un máximo de 45°C** a high of 45°C was recorded

registro *m* register; *de casa* search; **registro civil** register of births, marriages and deaths

regla *f* (*norma*) rule; *para medir* ruler; MED period; *por regla general* as a rule

reglamentar ⟨1a⟩ *v/t* regulate

reglamentario *adj* regulation *atr*

reglamento *m* regulation

regocijarse ⟨1a⟩ *v/r* rejoice (*de* at), take delight (*de* in)

regocijo *m* delight

regodearse ⟨1a⟩ *v/r* gloat (*con* over), delight (*en* in)

regresar ⟨1a⟩ **1** *v/i* return **2** *v/t Méx* return, give back **3** *v/r* **regresarse** *L.Am.* return

regreso *m* return

regüeldo *m* F belch

reguero *m* trail; *como un reguero de pólvora* fig like wildfire

regulación *f* regulation; *de temperatura* control

regular 1 *adj sin variar* regular; (*común*) ordinary; (*habitual*) regular, normal; (*no muy bien*) so-so **2** ⟨1a⟩ *v/t* TÉC regulate; *temperatura* control

regularidad *f* regularity

regularizar ⟨1f⟩ *v/t* regularize

regusto *m* aftertaste

rehabilitación *f* MED, fig rehabilitation; ARQUI restoration

rehabilitar ⟨1a⟩ *v/t* ARQUI restore

rehacer ⟨2s; *part* **rehecho** ⟩ *v/t película, ropa, cama* remake; *trabajo, ejercicio* redo; *casa, vida* rebuild

rehén *m* hostage

rehice *vb* → **rehacer**

rehizo *vb* → **rehacer**

rehogar ⟨1h⟩ *v/t* GASTR fry

rehuir ⟨3g⟩ *v/t* shy away from

rehusar ⟨1a⟩ *v/t* refuse, decline

reimprimir ⟨3a⟩ *v/t* reprint

reina *f* queen

reinado *m* reign

reinante *adj tb fig* reigning

reinar ⟨1a⟩ *v/i tb fig* reign

reincidente 1 *adj* repeat **2** *m/f* repeat offender

reincidir ⟨3a⟩ *v/i* reoffend

reincorporarse ⟨1a⟩ *v/r* return (*a* to)

reino *m tb fig* kingdom; *el Reino Unido* the United Kingdom

reinserción *f*: *reinserción social* social rehabilitation

reinsertar ⟨1a⟩ *v/t* rehabilitate

reinstaurar ⟨1a⟩ *v/t* bring back

reintegrarse ⟨1a⟩ *v/r* return (*a* to)

reintegro *m* (*en lotería*) prize in the form of a refund of the stake money

reír ⟨3m⟩ **1** *v/i* laugh **2** *v/r* **reírse** laugh (*de* at)

reiterar ⟨1a⟩ *v/t* repeat, reiterate

reivindicación *f* claim

reivindicar ⟨1g⟩ *v/t* claim; *reivindicar un atentado* claim responsibility for an attack

reja *f* AGR plowshare, *Br* ploughshare; (*barrote*) bar, railing; *meter entre rejas* fig F put behind bars

rejilla *f* FERR luggage rack

rejuvenecer ⟨2d⟩ *v/t* rejuvenate

relación *f* relationship; *relaciones públicas pl* public relations, PR *sg*

relacionado *adj* related (*con* to)

relacionarse ⟨1a⟩ *v/r* be connected (*con* to), be related (*con* to)

relajación *f* relaxation

relajante *adj* relaxing

relajar ⟨1a⟩ **1** *v/t* relax **2** *v/r* **relajarse** relax

relajo *m C.Am., Méx* uproar

relamerse ⟨2a⟩ *v/r* lick one's lips

relámpago *m* flash of lightning; *viaje relámpago* flying visit

relatar ⟨1a⟩ *v/t* tell, relate

relatividad *f* relativity

relativo *adj* relative; *relativo a* regarding, about

relato *m* short story

relax *m* relaxation

releer ⟨2e⟩ *v/t* reread

relegar ⟨1h⟩ *v/t* relegate

relevante *adj* relevant

relevar ⟨1a⟩ *v/t* MIL relieve; *relevar a alguien de algo* relieve s.o. of sth

relevo *m* MIL change; (*sustituto*) relief, replacement; *carrera de relevos* relay (race); *tomar el relevo de alguien* take over from s.o., relieve s.o.

relicario *m* shrine

relieve *m* relief; *poner de relieve* highlight

religión f religion
religiosa f nun
religioso 1 adj religious 2 m monk
relinchar ⟨1a⟩ v/i neigh
reliquia f relic
rellano m landing
rellenar ⟨1a⟩ v/t fill; GASTR pollo, pimientos stuff; formulario fill out, fill in
relleno 1 adj GASTR pollo, pimientos stuffed; pastel filled 2 m tb en cojín stuffing; en pastel filling
reloj m clock; de pulsera watch, wristwatch; reloj de pared wall clock; reloj de sol sundial
relojería f watchmaker's
relojero m, -a f watchmaker
reluciente adj sparkling, glittering
remanso m backwater; remanso de paz fig haven of peace
remar ⟨1a⟩ v/i row
remarcar ⟨1g⟩ v/t stress, emphasize
rematar ⟨1a⟩ 1 v/t finish off; L.Am. COM auction 2 v/i en fútbol shoot
remate m L.Am. COM auction, sale; en fútbol shot; ser tonto de remate be a complete idiot
remediar ⟨1b⟩ v/t remedy; no puedo remediarlo I can't do anything about it
remedio m remedy; sin remedio hopeless; no hay más remedio que ... there's no alternative but to ...
rememorar ⟨1a⟩ v/t remember
remendar ⟨1k⟩ v/t con parche patch; (zurcir) darn
remesa f (envío) shipment, consignment; L.Am. dinero remittance
remezón m L.Am. earth tremor
remiendo m (parche) patch; (zurcido) darn
remilgado adj fussy, finicky
reminiscencia f reminiscence
remiso adj reluctant (a to)
remite m en carta return address
remitente m/f sender
remitir ⟨3a⟩ 1 v/t send, ship; en texto refer (a to) 2 v/i MED go into remission; de crisis ease (off)
remo m pala oar; deporte rowing
remodelar ⟨1a⟩ v/t redesign, remodel

remojar ⟨1a⟩ v/t soak; L.Am. F acontecimiento celebrate
remojo m: poner a o en remojo leave to soak
remojón m drenching, soaking; darse un remojón go for a dip
remolacha f beet, Br beetroot; remolacha azucarera sugar beet
remolcador m tug
remolcar ⟨1g⟩ v/t AUTO, MAR tow
remolino m de aire eddy; de agua whirlpool
remolón m, -ona f F slacker; hacerse el remolón slack (off)
remolque m AUTO trailer
remontarse ⟨1a⟩ v/r en el tiempo go back (a to)
remonte m ski lift
remorder ⟨2h⟩ v/t: me remuerde la conciencia I have a guilty conscience
remordimiento m remorse
remoto adj remote; no tengo ni la más -a idea I haven't the faintest idea
remover ⟨2h⟩ v/t (agitar) stir; L.Am. (destituir) dismiss; C.Am., Méx (quitar) remove
remplazar v/t → reemplazar
remuneración f remuneration
remunerar ⟨1a⟩ v/t pay
renacentista adj Renaissance atr
renacer ⟨2d⟩ v/i fig be reborn
Renacimiento m Renaissance
renacuajo m ZO tadpole; F persona shrimp F
renal adj ANAT renal, kidney atr
rencilla f fight, argument
rencor m resentment; guardar rencor a alguien bear s.o. a grudge
rencoroso adj resentful
rendición f surrender
rendija f crack; (hueco) gap
rendimiento m performance; FIN yield; (producción) output
rendir ⟨3l⟩ 1 v/t honores pay, do; beneficio produce, yield 2 v/i perform 3 v/r rendirse surrender
renegado 1 adj renegade atr 2 m renegade
renegar ⟨1h & 1k⟩ v/i: renegar de al-

R

guien disown s.o.; **renegar de algo** renounce sth

renegrido *adj* blackened

RENFE *abr* (= **Red Nacional de Ferrocarriles Españoles**) *Spanish rail operator*

renglón *m* line; **a renglón seguido** immediately after

rengo *adj CSur* lame

renguear ⟨1a⟩ *v/i CSur* limp, walk with a limp

reno *m* zo reindeer

renombre *m*: **de renombre** famous, renowned

renovación *f* renewal

renovador *adj*: **las fuerzas renovadores** the forces of renewal

renovar ⟨1m⟩ *v/t* renew

renta *f* income; *de casa* rent; **renta per cápita** income per capita

rentabilidad *f* profitability

rentable *adj* profitable

rentar ⟨1a⟩ *v/t* (*arrendar*) rent out; (*alquiler*) rent; *carro* hire

renuente *adj* reluctant, unwilling

renunciar ⟨1b⟩ *v/i*: **renunciar a** *tabaco, alcohol etc* give up; *puesto* resign; *demanda* drop

reñir ⟨3h & 3l⟩ **1** *v/t* tell off **2** *v/i* quarrel, fight F

reo *m*, **-a** *f* accused

reojo: **de reojo** out of the corner of one's eye

repantigarse ⟨1h⟩ *v/r* lounge, sprawl

reparación *f* repair; *fig* reparation

reparar ⟨1a⟩ **1** *v/t* repair **2** *v/i*: **reparar en algo** notice sth

reparo *m*: **poner reparos a** find problems with; **no tener reparos en** have no reservations about

repartición *f S. Am.* department

repartidor *m* delivery man

repartir ⟨3a⟩ *v/t* (*dividir*) share out, divide up; *productos* deliver

reparto *m* (*división*) share-out, distribution; TEA cast; **reparto a domicilio** home delivery

repasar ⟨1a⟩ *v/t trabajo* go over again; EDU revise

repecho *m* steep slope

repelente 1 *adj fig* repellent, repulsive; F *niño* horrible **2** *m* repellent

repelús *m*: **dar repelús a alguien** F give s.o. the creeps F

repente: **de repente** suddenly

repentino *adj* sudden

repercusión *f fig* repercussion

repercutir ⟨3a⟩ *v/i* have repercussions (**en** on)

repertorio *m* TEA, MÚS repertoire

repetición *f* repetition

repetido *adj* repeated

repetir ⟨3l⟩ **1** *v/t* repeat **2** *v/i de comida* repeat **3** *v/r* **repetirse** happen again

repetitivo *adj* repetitive

repipi *adj* F (*afectado*) affected; **es tan repipi** *niño* he's such a know-it-all F

repisa *f* shelf

replantear ⟨1a⟩ *v/t pregunta, problema* bring up again

replegarse ⟨1h & 1k⟩ *v/r* MIL withdraw

repleto *adj* full (**de** of)

réplica *f* replica

replicar ⟨1g⟩ *v/t* reply

repoblar ⟨1m⟩ *v/t* repopulate

repollo *m* BOT cabbage

reponerse ⟨2r; *part* **repuesto**⟩ *v/r* recover (**de** from)

reportaje *m* story, report

reportero *m*, **-a** *f* reporter; **reportero gráfico** press photographer

reposacabezas *m inv* AUTO headrest

reposar ⟨1a⟩ *v/i* rest; *de vino* settle

reposera *f L.Am.* lounger

reposición *f* TEA revival; TV repeat

reposo *m* rest

repostar ⟨1a⟩ *v/i* refuel

repostería *f* pastries *pl*

reprender ⟨2a⟩ *v/t* scold, tell off

represa *f* dam; (*embalse*) reservoir

represalia *f* reprisal

representación *f* representation; TEA performance; **en representación de** on behalf of

representante *m/f tb* COM representative

representar ⟨1a⟩ *v/t* represent; *obra* put on, perform; *papel* play; **representar menos años** look younger

represión *f* repression

reprimenda *f* reprimand

reprimir ⟨3a⟩ *v/t tb* PSI repress

reprobar ⟨1m⟩ *v/t* condemn; *L.Am.* EDU fail

reprochar ⟨1a⟩ *v/t* reproach

reproche *m* reproach

reproducción *f* BIO reproduction

reproducir ⟨3o⟩ 1 *v/t* reproduce 2 *v/r* **reproducirse** BIO reproduce, breed

reptil *m* ZO reptile

república *f* republic

republicano 1 *adj* republican 2 *m*, -a *f* republican

repudiar ⟨1b⟩ *v/t fml* repudiate; *herencia* renounce

repuesto 1 *part* → **reponerse** 2 *m* spare part, replacement; *de repuesto* spare

repugnancia *f* disgust, repugnance

repugnante *adj* disgusting, repugnant

repugnar ⟨1a⟩ *v/t* disgust, repel

repulsión *f* repulsion

repulsivo *adj* repulsive

repuse *vb* → **reponerse**

reputación *f* reputation

requerir ⟨3i⟩ *v/t* require; JUR summons

requesón *m* cottage cheese

requetebién *adv* F really well, brilliantly F

réquiem *m* requiem

requisar ⟨1a⟩ *v/t Arg, Chi* MIL requisition

requisito *m* requirement

res *f L.Am.* bull; *carne f de res* beef; *reses pl* cattle *pl*

resaca *f* MAR undertow, undercurrent; *de beber* hangover

resaltar ⟨1a⟩ 1 *v/t* highlight, stress 2 *v/i* ARQUI jut out; *fig* stand out

resarcirse ⟨3b⟩ *v/r* make up (*de* for)

resbaladizo *adj* slippery; *fig* tricky

resbalar ⟨1a⟩ *v/i* slide; *fig* slip (up)

resbalón *m* slip; *fig* F slip-up

resbaloso *adj L.Am.* slippery

rescatar ⟨1a⟩ *v/t persona, animal* rescue, save; *bienes* save

rescate *m de peligro* rescue; *en secuestro* ransom

rescindir ⟨3a⟩ *v/t* cancel; *contrato* terminate

rescisión *f* cancellation; *de contrato* termination

reseco *adj* (*seco*) parched; (*flaco*) skinny

resentimiento *m* resentment

resentirse ⟨3i⟩ *v/r* get upset; *de rendimiento, calidad* suffer; *resentirse de algo* suffer from the effects of sth

reseña *f de libro etc* review

reseñar ⟨1a⟩ *v/t* review

reserva 1 *f* reservation; *reserva natural* nature reserve; *sin reservas* without reservation 2 *m/f* DEP reserve

reservar ⟨1a⟩ 1 *v/t* (*guardar*) set aside, put by; *billete* reserve 2 *v/r* **reservarse** save o.s. (*para* for)

resfriado 1 *adj*: *estar resfriado* have a cold 2 *m* cold

resfriarse ⟨1c⟩ *v/r* catch cold

resfrío *m L.Am.* cold

resguardar ⟨1a⟩ 1 *v/t* protect (*de* from) 2 *v/r* **resguardarse** protect o.s. (*de* from)

resguardo *m* COM counterfoil

residencia *f* residence; *residencia de ancianos or para la tercera edad* retirement home

residencial 1 *adj* residential 2 *f Arg, Chi* boarding house

residente 1 *adj* resident 2 *m/f* resident

residir ⟨3a⟩ *v/i* reside; *residir en fig* lie in

residual *adj* residual; (*de desecho*) waste *atr*

residuo *m* residue; *residuos* waste *sg*

resignación *f actitud* resignation

resignarse ⟨1a⟩ *v/r* resign o.s. (*a* to)

resina *f* resin

resistencia *f* resistance; EL, TÉC resistor

resistir ⟨3a⟩ 1 *v/t* resist; (*aguantar*) hold out 2 *v/t tentación* resist; *frío, dolor etc* stand, bear 3 *v/r* **resistirse** be reluctant (*a* to)

resolución *f actitud* determination, decisiveness; *de problema* solution (*de* to); JUR ruling

resolver ⟨2h; *part* **resuelto**⟩ 1 *v/t problema* solve 2 *v/r* **resolverse** decide (*a* to; *por* on)

resonar ⟨1m⟩ *v/i* echo

resoplar ⟨1a⟩ *v/i* snort

resorte *m* spring

respaldar ⟨1a⟩ *v/t* back, support

respaldo *m de silla* back; *fig* backing, support

respectar ⟨1a⟩ *v/i: por lo que respecta a ...* as regards ..., as far as ... is concerned

respectivo *adj* respective

respecto *m: al respecto* on the matter; *con respecto a* regarding, as regards

respetable *adj* respectable

respetar ⟨1a⟩ *v/t* respect

respeto *m* respect

respetuoso *adj* respectful

respiración *f* breathing; *estar con respiración asistida* MED be on a respirator

respirar ⟨1a⟩ *v/t & v/i* breathe

respiratorio *adj* respiratory

respiro *m fig* breather, break

resplandeciente *adj* shining

resplandor *m* shine, gleam

responder ⟨2a⟩ **1** *v/t* answer **2** *v/i: responder a* answer, reply to; MED respond to; *descripción* fit, match; *(ser debido a)* be due to

responsabilidad *f* responsibility

responsabilizarse ⟨1f⟩ *v/r* take responsibility *(de* for)

responsable 1 *adj* responsible *(de* for) **2** *m/f* person responsible *(de* for); *los responsables del crimen* those responsible for the crime

respuesta *f (contestación)* reply, answer; *fig* response

resquebrajar ⟨1a⟩ **1** *v/t* crack **2** *v/r resquebrajarse* crack

resquicio *m* gap

resta *f* MAT subtraction

restablecer ⟨2d⟩ **1** *v/t* re-establish **2** *v/r restablecerse* recover

restablecimiento *m* re-establishment; *de enfermo* recovery

restante 1 *adj* remaining **2** *m/fpl: los / las restantes pl* the rest *pl*, the remainder *pl*

restar ⟨1a⟩ **1** *v/t* subtract; *restar importancia a* play down the importance of **2** *v/i* remain, be left

restauración *f* restoration

restaurante *m* restaurant

restaurar ⟨1a⟩ *v/t* restore

restituir ⟨3g⟩ *v/t* restore; *en cargo* reinstate

resto *m* rest, remainder; *los restos mor-*

tales the (mortal) remains

restregar ⟨1h & 1k⟩ *v/t* scrub

restricción *f* restriction

restringir ⟨3c⟩ *v/t* restrict, limit

resucitar ⟨1a⟩ **1** *v/t* resuscitate; *fig* revive **2** *v/i de persona* rise from *o* come back from the dead

resuello *m* puffing, heavy breathing

resuelto 1 *part → resolver* **2** *adj* decisive, resolute

resultado *m* result; *sin resultado* without success

resultar ⟨1a⟩ *v/i* turn out; *resultar caro* prove expensive, turn out to be expensive; *resulta que ...* it turns out that ...

resumen *m* summary; *en resumen* in short

resumir ⟨3a⟩ *v/t* summarize

resurgir ⟨3c⟩ *v/i* reappear, come back

resurrección *f* REL resurrection

retaguardia *f* MIL rearguard

retahíla *f* string

retar ⟨1a⟩ *v/t* challenge; *Rpl (regañar)* scold, tell off

retardar ⟨1a⟩ *v/t* delay

retazo *m fig* snippet, fragment

retención *f* MED retention; *de persona* detention; *retención fiscal* tax deduction

retener ⟨2l⟩ *v/t dinero etc* withhold, deduct; *persona* detain, hold

reticencia *f* reticence

reticente *adj* reticent

retintín *m: con retintín* F sarcastically

retirada *f* MIL retreat, withdrawal

retirado *adj (jubilado)* retired; *(alejado)* remote, out-of-the-way

retirar ⟨1a⟩ **1** *v/t* take away, remove; *acusación, dinero* withdraw **2** *v/r retirarse* MIL withdraw

retiro *m lugar* retreat

reto *m* challenge; *Rpl (regañina)* scolding, telling-off

retobado *adj L.Am.* unruly

retocar ⟨1g⟩ *v/t* retouch, touch up; *(acabar)* put the finishing touches to

retomar ⟨1a⟩ *v/t: retomar algo fig* take sth up again

retoque *m* FOT touching-up; *(acabado)* finishing touch

retorcer ⟨2b & 2h⟩ v/t twist

retorcido adj fig twisted

retorcijón m stomach cramp

retórica f rhetoric

retornar ⟨1a⟩ v/i return

retorno m return

retortijón m cramps pl, Br stomach cramp

retozar ⟨1f⟩ v/i frolic, romp

retractar ⟨1a⟩ v/t retract, withdraw

retraer ⟨2p; part **retraído**⟩ **1** v/t retract **2** v/r **retraerse** withdraw

retraído 1 part → **retraer 2** adj withdrawn

retransmisión f RAD, TV transmission, broadcast

retransmitir ⟨3a⟩ v/t transmit, broadcast

retrasado 1 part → **retrasar 2** adj tren, entrega late; con trabajo, pagos behind; **está retrasado en clase** he's lagging behind in class; **retrasado mental** mentally handicapped

retrasar ⟨1a⟩ **1** v/t hold up; reloj put back; reunión postpone, put back **2** v/i de reloj lose time; en los estudios be behind **3** v/r **retrasarse** (atrasarse) be late; de reloj lose time; con trabajo, pagos get behind

retraso m delay; **ir con retraso** be late

retratar ⟨1a⟩ v/t FOT take a picture of; fig depict

retrato m picture; **retrato-robot** composite photo, E-Fit®

retrete m bathroom

retribución f salary

retroactivo adj retroactive

retroceder ⟨2a⟩ v/i go back, move back; fig back down

retroceso m fig backward step

retrógrado adj retrograde

retroproyector m overhead projector

retrospectiva f retrospective

retrovisor m AUTO rear-view mirror; **retrovisor exterior** wing mirror

retumbar ⟨1a⟩ v/i boom

retuve vb → **retener**

reuma, reúma m MED rheumatism

reunificación f POL reunification

reunión f meeting; de amigos get-together

reunir ⟨3a⟩ **1** v/t personas bring together; requisitos meet, fulfil(l); datos gather (together) **2** v/r **reunirse** meet up, get together; COM meet

reutilizar ⟨1f⟩ v/t re-use

revalorizar ⟨1f⟩ **1** v/t revalue **2** v/r **revalorizarse** appreciate (**en** by), increase in value (**en** by)

revaluar vb → **revalorizar**

revancha f revenge

revelación f revelation

revelado m development

revelar ⟨1a⟩ v/t FOT develop

reventa f resale

reventar ⟨1k⟩ **1** v/i burst; **lleno a reventar** full to bursting **2** v/t puerta etc break down **3** v/r **reventarse** burst; **se reventó a trabajar** fig he worked his butt off F

reventón m AUTO blowout

reverberar ⟨1a⟩ v/i de sonido reverberate

reverencia f reverence; saludo: de hombre bow; de mujer curtsy

reverendo m REL reverend

reversible adj ropa reversible

reverso m reverse, back

revés m setback; tenis backhand; **al o del revés** back to front; con el interior fuera inside out

revestir ⟨3l⟩ v/t TÉC cover (**de** with); **revestir gravedad** be serious

revisación f L.Am. check-up

revisada f L.Am. → **revisión**

revisar ⟨1a⟩ v/t check, inspect

revisión f check, inspection; AUTO service; **revisión técnica** roadworthiness test, Br MOT (test); **revisión médica** check-up

revisor m, **revisora** f FERR (ticket) inspector

revista f magazine; **pasar revista a** MIL inspect, review; fig review

revivir ⟨3a⟩ **1** v/i revive **2** v/t relive

revocar ⟨1g & 1m⟩ v/t pared render; JUR revoke

revolcarse ⟨1g & 1m⟩ v/r roll around

revolcón m tumble; F de amantes roll in the hay F

revolotear ⟨1a⟩ v/t flutter

revoltijo, revoltillo m mess, jumble

revoltoso adj niño naughty

revolución f revolution

revolucionario 1 adj revolutionary **2** m, -a f revolutionary revólver *m* revolver

revolver ⟨2h; *part* **revuelto**⟩ 1 *v/t* GASTR stir; *estómago* turn; (*desordenar*) mess up 2 *v/i* rummage (*en* in) 3 *v/r* revolverse *del tiempo* worsen

revuelo *m* stir

revuelto 1 *part* → **revolver** 2 *adj* mar rough; *gente* restless

rey *m* king

reyerta *f* fight

rezagarse ⟨1h⟩ *v/r* drop back, fall behind

rezar ⟨1f⟩ 1 *v/t oración* say 2 *v/i* pray; *de texto* say

rezo *m* prayer

rezongar ⟨1h⟩ *v/i* grumble

rezumar ⟨1a⟩ *v/t & v/i* ooze

ría 1 *vb* → **reír** 2 *f* estuary

riachuelo *m* stream

riada *f* flood

ribera *f* shore, bank

riberano *L.Am.* 1 *adj L.Am.* coastal; *de río* riverside *atr* 2 *m*, -a *f* person who lives by the sea / river

ribereño: **ribereño** *de* bordering (on)

rica *f* rich woman

rico 1 *adj* rich; *comida* delicious; F *niño* cute, sweet; *rico en vitaminas* rich in vitamins 2 *m* rich man; *nuevo rico* nouveau riche

ridiculizar ⟨1f⟩ *v/t* ridicule

ridículo 1 *adj* ridiculous 2 *m* ridicule; *hacer el ridículo, quedar en ridículo* make a fool of o.s.

ríe *vb* → **reír**

riego 1 *vb* → **regar** 2 *m* AGR irrigation; *riego sanguíneo* blood flow

ríen *vb* → **reír**

rienda *f* rein; *dar rienda suelta a* give free rein to

riesgo *m* risk; *a riesgo de* at the risk of; *correr el riesgo* run the risk (*de* of)

riesgoso *adj L.Am.* risky

rifa *f* raffle

rifar ⟨1a⟩ 1 *v/t* raffle 2 *v/r* rifarse *fig* fight over

rifle *m* rifle

rige *vb* → **regir**

rigidez *f* rigidity; *de carácter* inflexibility; *fig* strictness

rígido *adj* rigid; *carácter* inflexible; *fig* strict

rigor *m* rigo(u)r

riguroso *adj* rigorous, harsh

rima *f* rhyme

rimar ⟨1a⟩ *v/i* rhyme (*con* with)

rimbombante *adj* ostentatious

rímel *m* mascara

rincón *m* corner

rinde *vb* → **rendir**

rinoceronte *m* zo rhino, rhinoceros

riña *f* quarrel, fight

riñe *vb* → **reñir**

riñón *m* ANAT kidney; *costar un riñón* F cost an arm and a leg F

riñonera *f* fanny pack, *Br* bum bag

río 1 *m* river; *río abajo / arriba* up / down river; *el Río de la Plata* the River Plate 2 *vb* → **reír**

rioplatense *adj* of / from the River Plate area, River Plate *atr*

riqueza *f* wealth

risa *f* laugh; *risas pl* laughter *sg*; *dar risa* be funny; *morirse de risa* kill o.s. laughing; *tomar algo a risa* treat sth as a joke

ristra *f* string

risueño *adj* cheerful

rítmico *adj* rhythmic(al)

ritmo *m* rhythm; *de desarrollo* rate, pace

rito *m* rite

ritual *m/adj* ritual

rival *m/f* rival

rivalidad *f* rivalry

rivalizar ⟨1f⟩ *v/i*: *rivalizar con* rival

rizado *adj* curly

rizar ⟨1f⟩ 1 *v/t* curl 2 rizarse *v/r* curl

rizo *m* curl

robar ⟨1a⟩ *v/t persona, banco* rob; *objeto* steal; *naipe* take, pick up

roble *m* BOT oak

robo *m* robbery; *en casa* burglary

robot *m* robot; *robot de cocina* food processor

robótica *f* robotics

robustecer ⟨2d⟩ 1 *v/t* strengthen 2 *v/r* robustecerse become stronger

robusto *adj* robust, sturdy

roca *f* rock

roce *m fig* friction; *tener roces con* come

into conflict with

rociar ⟨1c⟩ *v/t* spray

rocín *m* F nag

rocío *m* dew

rock *m* MÚS rock

rococó *adj* rococo

rocódromo *m* climbing wall

rocoto *m* S. Am. hot red pepper

rodaballo *m* ZO turbot

rodaja *f* slice

rodaje *m de película* shooting, filming; AUTO breaking in, *Br* running in

rodapié *m* baseboard, *Br* skirting board

rodar ⟨1m⟩ **1** *v/i* roll; *de coche* go, travel (*a* at); *sin rumbo fijo* wander **2** *v/t película* shoot; AUTO break in, *Br* run in

rodear ⟨1a⟩ **1** *v/t* surround **2** *v/r* **rodearse** surround o.s. (*de* with)

rodeo *m* detour; *con caballos y vaqueros etc* rodeo; *andarse con rodeos* beat about the bush; *hablar sin rodeos* speak plainly, not beat about the bush

rodilla *f* knee; *de rodillas* kneeling, on one's knees; *hincarse or ponerse de rodillas* kneel (down)

rodillo *m* rolling pin; TÉC roller

rododendro *m* BOT rhododendron

roedor *m* rodent

roer ⟨2za⟩ *v/t* gnaw; *fig* eat into

rogar ⟨1h & 1m⟩ *v/t* ask for; (*implorar*) beg for, plead for; *hacerse de rogar* play hard to get

rojizo *adj* reddish

rojo 1 *adj* red; *al rojo vivo* red hot **2** *m color* red **3** *m*, -a *f* POL red, commie F

rol *m* role

rollizo *adj* F chubby

rollo *m* FOT roll; *fig* F drag F; *buen / mal rollo* F good / bad atmosphere; *¡qué rollo!* F what a drag! F

Roma Rome

romance *m* romance

románico *m/adj* Romanesque

romano 1 *adj* Roman **2** *m*, -a *f* Roman

romántico 1 *adj* romantic **2** *m*, -a *f* romantic

rombo *m* rhombus

romero *m* BOT rosemary

rompecabezas *m* puzzle

rompehielos *m inv* icebreaker

romper ⟨2a; *part* **roto**⟩ **1** *v/t* break; (*hacer añicos*) smash; *tela, papel* tear **2** *v/i* break; *romper a* start to; *romper con alguien* break up with s.o. **3** *v/r* **romperse** break

rompopo *m* C.Am., Méx *bebida* eggnog

ron *m* rum

roncar ⟨1g⟩ *v/i* snore

roncha *f* MED bump, swelling

ronco *adj* hoarse; *quedarse ronco* go hoarse

ronda *f* round

rondar ⟨1a⟩ **1** *v/t* patrol; *me ronda una idea* I have an idea going around in my head **2** *v/i* F hang around

ronquido *m* snore; *ronquidos pl* snoring *sg*

ronronear ⟨1a⟩ *v/i de gato* purr

roña *f* grime

roñoso *adj* grimy, grubby

ropa *f* clothes *pl*; *ropa de cama* bedclothes *pl*; *ropa interior* underwear; *ropa íntima* L.Am. underwear

ropero *m* closet, *Br* wardrobe

rosa 1 *adj* pink **2** *f* BOT rose; *fresco como una rosa* fresh as a daisy; *ver algo de color de rosa* see sth through rose-col-o(u)red glasses

rosado 1 *adj* pink; *vino* rosé **2** *m* rosé

rosal *m* rosebush

rosario *m* REL rosary; *fig* string

rosbif *m* GASTR roast beef

rosca *f* TÉC thread; GASTR F *pastry similar to a donut*

rosco *m* GASTR *pastry similar to a donut*; *no comerse un rosco* P not get anywhere

roscón *m* GASTR large ring-shaped cake

rosquilla *f* *pastry similar to a donut*

rosticería *f* L.Am. *type of deli that sells roast chicken*

rostro *m* face

rotación *f* rotation

rotisería *f* L.Am. deli, delicatessen

roto 1 *part* → **romper 2** *adj pierna etc* broken; (*hecho añicos*) smashed; *tela, papel* torn **3** *m*, -a *f Chi* one of the urban poor

rotonda *f* traffic circle, *Br* roundabout

rotoso *adj Rpl* F scruffy

rotulador *m* fiber-tip, *Br* fibre-tip, felt-tip

rótulo *m* sign

rotundo *adj fig* categorical

rotura *f* breakage; *una rotura de cadera* MED a broken hip

rozadura *f* chafing, rubbing

rozagante *adj* healthy

rozar ⟨1f⟩ **1** *v/t* rub; (*tocar ligeramente*) brush; *fig* touch on **2** *v/i* rub **3** *v/r* rozarse rub; (*desgastarse*) wear

rte. *abr* (= *remitente*) sender

ruana *f Ecuad* poncho

rubeola, rubéola *f* MED German measles *sg*

rubí *m* ruby

rubicundo *adj* ruddy

rubio *adj* blond; *tabaco rubio* Virginia tobacco

ruborizarse ⟨1f⟩ *v/r* go red, blush

rúbrica *f* heading; *de firma* flourish

rubro *m L.Am.* category, heading

rudeza *f* roughness

rudimentario *adj* rudimentary

rudo *adj* rough

rueda *f* wheel; *rueda dentada* cogwheel; *rueda de prensa* press conference; *rueda de recambio* spare wheel

ruedo *m* TAUR bullring

ruego **1** *vb* → *rogar* **2** *m* request

rufián *m* rogue

rugby *m* rugby

rugido *m* roar

rugir ⟨3c⟩ *v/i* roar

rugoso *adj superficie* rough

ruido *m* noise; *hacer ruido* make a noise; *mucho ruido y pocas nueces* all talk and no action

ruidoso *adj* noisy

ruin *adj* despicable, mean; (*tacaño*) mean, miserly

ruina *f* ruin; *llevar a alguien a la ruina fig* bankrupt s.o.

ruiseñor *m* zo nightingale

ruleta *f* roulette

ruletero *m Méx* cab *o* taxi driver

rulo *m* roller

rumbeador *m Rpl* tracker

rumbear ⟨1a⟩ *v/i L.Am.* head (*para* for)

rumbo *m* course; *tomar rumbo a* head for; *perder el rumbo fig* lose one's way

rumboso *adj* lavish

rumiar ⟨1b⟩ *v/t fig* ponder

rumor *m* rumo(u)r

rumorearse ⟨1a⟩ *v/r* be rumo(u)red

rupestre *adj*: *pintura rupestre* cave painting

ruptura *f de relaciones* breaking off; *de pareja* break-up

rural **1** *adj* rural **2** *m Rpl* station wagon, *Br* estate car; *rurales Méx* (rural) police

Rusia Russia

ruso **1** *adj* Russian **2** *m*, -a *f* Russian

rústico *adj* rustic

ruta *f* route

rutina *f* routine

rutinario *adj* routine *atr*

S

S *abr* (= *sur*) S (= South(ern))

S.A. *abr* (= *sociedad anónima*) inc (= incorporated), *Br* plc (= public limited company)

sábado *m* Saturday

sábana *f* sheet; *sábana ajustable* fitted sheet

sabana *f* savanna(h)

sabandija *f* bug, creepy-crawly

sabañón *m* chilblain

sabelotodo *m* F know-it-all F, *Br* know-all F

saber ⟨2n⟩ **1** v/t know (*de* about); **saber hacer algo** know how to do sth, be able to do sth; *no lo supe hasta más tarde* I didn't find out till later; *hacer saber algo a alguien* let s.o. know sth; *¡qué sé yo!* who knows?; *que yo sepa* as far as I know; *sabérselas todas* F know every trick in the book **2** v/i taste (*a* of); *me sabe a quemado* it tastes burnt to me; *me sabe mal* fig it upsets me **3** *m* knowledge, learning

sabiduría *f* wisdom; (*conocimientos*) knowledge

sabiendas *fpl*: *a sabiendas* knowingly; *a sabiendas que* knowing full well that

sabio **1** *adj* wise; (*sensato*) sensible **2** *m*, -a *f* wise person; (*experto*) expert

sabiondo *m*, -a *f* know- it-all F, *Br* know-all F

sablazo *m*: *dar un sablazo a alguien* F scrounge money off s.o.

sable *m* saber, *Br* sabre

sablear ⟨1a⟩ v/t & v/i *L.Am.* F scrounge (*a* from)

sabor *m* flavo(u)r, taste; *dejar mal sabor de boca* fig leave a bad taste in the mouth

saborear ⟨1a⟩ v/t savo(u)r; *fig* relish

sabotaje *m* sabotage

saboteador *m*, saboteadora *f* saboteur

sabotear ⟨1a⟩ v/t sabotage

sabroso *adj* tasty; *fig* juicy; *L.Am.* (*agradable*) nice, pleasant

sabrosura *f L.Am.* tasty dish

sabueso *m* fig sleuth

sacacorchos *m inv* corkscrew

sacamuelas *m inv* desp F dentist

sacapuntas *m inv* pencil sharpener

sacar ⟨1g⟩ **1** v/t take out; *mancha* take out, remove; *información* get; *disco, libro* bring out; *fotocopias* make; *sacar a alguien a bailar* ask s.o. to dance; *sacar algo en claro* (*entender*) make sense of sth; *sacar de paseo* take for a walk **2** v/r *sacarse L.Am. ropa* take off

sacarina *f* saccharin(e)

sacerdote *m* priest

sacerdotisa *f* priestess

saciar ⟨1b⟩ v/t fig satisfy, fulfil

saciedad *f*: *repetir algo hasta la saciedad* fig repeat sth time and again, repeat sth ad nauseam

saco *m* sack; *L.Am.* jacket; *saco de dormir* sleeping bag; *entrar a saco en* F burst into, barge into F

sacramento *m* sacrament

sacrificar ⟨1g⟩ **1** v/t sacrifice; (*matar*) slaughter **2** v/r sacrificarse make sacrifices (*por* for)

sacrificio *m* sacrifice

sacrilegio *m* sacrilege

sacristán *m* sexton

sacristía *f* vestry

sacudida *f* shake, jolt; EL shock

sacudir ⟨3a⟩ **1** v/t tb fig shake; F *niño* beat, wallop F **2** v/r sacudirse shake off, shrug off; *sacudirse alguien (de encima)* get rid of s.o.

sádico **1** *adj* sadistic **2** *m*, -a *f* sadist

sadismo *m* sadism

safari *m* safari; *safari fotográfico* photographic safari

sagaz *adj* shrewd, sharp

Sagitario *m/f inv* ASTR Sagittarius

sagrado *adj* sacred, holy

sagrario *m* tabernacle

Sahara Sahara

sainete *m* TEA short farce, one-act play

sal **1** *f* salt; *sal común* cooking salt; *sal marina* sea salt **2** *vb* → *salir*

sala *f* room, hall; *de cine* screen; JUR court room; *sala de embarque* AVIA departure lounge; *sala de espera* waiting room; *sala de estar* living room; *sala de fiestas* night club; *sala de sesiones* or *de juntas* boardroom

saladero *m L.Am.* meat / fish salting factory

salado *adj* salted; (*con demasiada sal*) salty; (*no dulce*) savo(u)ry; *fig* funny, witty; *C.Am., Chi, Rpl* F pric(e)y F

salamandra *f* ZO salamander

salamanquesa *f* ZO gecko

salami *m* salami

salar ⟨1a⟩ **1** v/t add salt to, salt; *para conservar* salt **2** *m Arg* salt mine

salarial *adj* salary *atr*

salario *m* salary; *salario base* basic wage;

S

salario mínimo minimum wage

salazón f salted fish / meat; **en salazón** salt atr

salchicha f sausage

salchichón m type of spiced sausage

saldar ⟨1a⟩ v/t disputa settle; deuda settle, pay; géneros sell off

saldo m COM balance; (resultado) result; **saldo acreedor** credit balance; **saldo deudor** debit balance; **de saldo** reduced, on sale

saldré vb → **salir**

salero m salt cellar; fig wit

saleroso adj funny, witty

salga vb → **salir**

salgo vb → **salir**

salida f exit, way out; TRANSP departure; **de carrera** start; **salida de emergencia** emergency exit; **salida de tono** ill-judged remark

saliente adj projecting, protruding; presidente retiring, outgoing

salir ⟨3r⟩ 1 v/i leave, go out; (aparecer) appear, come out; **salir de** (ir fuera de) leave, go out of; (venir fuera de) leave, come out of; **salir a alguien** take after s.o.; **salir a 1000 pesetas** cost 1000 pesetas; **salir bien / mal** turn out well / badly; **el dibujo no me sale** FI can't get this drawing right; **no me salió el trabajo** I didn't get the job; **salir con alguien** date s.o., go out with s.o.; **salir perdiendo** end up losing 2 v/r **salirse de líquido** overflow; (dejar) leave; **salirse de la carretera** leave the road, go off the road; **salirse con la suya** get what one wants

salitre m saltpeter, Br saltpetre

saliva f saliva; **tragar saliva** hold one's tongue

salmo m psalm

salmón m ZO salmon; **color salmón** salmon

salmonete m ZO red mullet

salmuera f pickle, brine

salobre adj salt; (con demasiada sal) salty

salomónico adj just, fair

salón m living room; **salón de actos** auditorium, hall; **salón de baile** dance hall; **salón de belleza** beauty parlo(u)r, beautician's

salpicadera f Méx AUTO fender, Br mudguard

salpicadero m AUTO dash(board)

salpicadura f stain

salpicar ⟨1g⟩ v/t splash, spatter (**con** with); fig sprinkle, pepper

salpicón m GASTR vegetable salad with chopped meat or fish

salpimentar ⟨1k⟩ v/t season (with salt and pepper)

salsa f GASTR sauce; baile salsa; **en su salsa** fig in one's element

salsera f sauce boat

saltamontes m inv ZO grasshopper

saltar ⟨1a⟩ 1 v/i jump, leap; **saltar a la vista** fig be obvious, be clear; **saltar sobre** pounce on; **saltar a la comba** jump rope, Br skip 2 v/t valla jump 3 v/r **saltarse** (omitir) miss, skip

saltear ⟨1a⟩ v/t GASTR sauté

saltimbanqui m acrobat

salto m leap, jump; **salto de agua** waterfall; **salto de altura** high jump; **salto de longitud** long jump; **salto mortal** somersault

saltón adj: **ojos saltones** bulging eyes

salubridad f L.Am. health; **Salubridad** L.Am. Department of Health

salud f health; **¡(a tu) salud!** cheers!

saludable adj healthy

saludar ⟨1a⟩ v/t say hello to, greet; MIL salute

saludo m greeting; MIL salute; **saludos en** carta best wishes

salva f: **salva de aplausos** round of applause

salvación f REL salvation

salvado m bran

salvador m REL savio(u)r

salvadoreño 1 adj Salvador(e)an **2** m, -a f Salvador(e)an

salvaguardar ⟨1a⟩ v/t safeguard, protect

salvajada f atrocity, act of savagery; **decir una salvajada** say something outrageous

salvaje 1 adj wild; (bruto) brutal **2** m/f savage

salvajismo m savagery

salvamanteles *m inv* table mat

salvamento *m* rescue; *buque de salvamento* life boat

salvapantallas *m inv* INFOR screensaver

salvar ⟨1a⟩ **1** *v/t* save; *obstáculo* get round, get over **2** *v/r* *salvarse* escape, get out

salvavidas *m inv* life belt

salvedad *f* (*excepción*) exception

salvo **1** *adj*: *estar a salvo* be safe (and sound); *ponerse a salvo* reach safety **2** *adv & prp* except, save; *salvo error u omisión* errors and omissions excepted

sambenito *m*: *le han colgado el sambenito de vago* F they've got him down as idle F

sambumbia *f* *L.Am.* watery drink

San *adj* Saint

sanar ⟨1a⟩ **1** *v/t* cure **2** *v/i* *de persona* get well, recover; *de herida* heal

sanatorio *m* sanitarium, clinic

sanción *f* JUR penalty, sanction

sancionar ⟨1a⟩ *v/t* penalize; (*multar*) fine

sancocho *m* *W.I.* type of stew

sandalia *f* sandal

sándalo *m* BOT sandalwood

sandez *f* nonsense; *decir sandeces* talk nonsense

sandía *f* watermelon

sandunga *f* F wit

sandunguero *adj* *L.Am.* F witty

sandwich *m* *tostado* toasted sandwich; *L.Am. sin tostar* sandwich

saneamiento *m* cleaning up; COM restructuring, rationalization

sanear ⟨1a⟩ *v/t* clean up; COM restructure, rationalize

sangrar ⟨1a⟩ **1** *v/t* *sangrar a alguien* *fig* sponge off s.o. **2** *v/i* bleed

sangre *f* blood; *sangre fría* *fig* calmness, coolness; *a sangre fría* *fig* in cold blood; *no llegará la sangre al río* it won't come to that, it won't be that bad

sangría *f* GASTR sangria

sangriento *adj* bloody

sangrigordo *adj* *Méx* tedious, boring

sanguijuela *f* ZO, *fig* leech

sanguinario *adj* bloodthirsty

sanidad *f* health

sanitario *adj* (public) health *atr*

sanitarios *mpl* bathroom fittings

sano *adj* healthy; *sano y salvo* safe and well; *cortar por lo sano* take drastic measures

sanseacabó: *y sanseacabó* F and that's that F

santa *f* Saint

santiamén *m*: *en un santiamén* F in an instant

santidad *f*: *Su Santidad* His Holiness

santiguarse ⟨1i⟩ *v/r* cross o.s., make the sign of the cross

santo **1** *adj* holy **2** *m* saint; *santo y seña* F password; *¿a santo de qué?* F what on earth for? F; *no es santo de mi devoción* F I don't like him very much

santuario *m* *fig* sanctuary

santurrón *m*, *-ona f* sanctimonious person

saña *f* viciousness

sapo *m* ZO toad; *echar sapos y culebras* *fig* curse and swear

saque *m* en tenis serve; *saque de banda en fútbol* throw-in; *saque de esquina* corner (kick); *tener buen saque* F have a big appetite

saquear ⟨1a⟩ *v/t* sack, ransack

sarampión *m* MED measles

sarao *m* party

sarape *m* *Méx* poncho, blanket

sarcasmo *m* sarcasm

sarcástico *adj* sarcastic

sarcófago *m* sarcophagus

sardina *f* sardine; *como sardinas en lata* like sardines

sargento *m* sergeant

sarna *f* MED scabies

sarnoso *adj* scabby

sarpullido *m* MED rash

sarro *m* tartar

sarta *f* string, series

sartén *f* frying pan; *tener la sartén por el mango* *fig* be the boss, be in the driving seat

sastra *f* tailor(ess)

sastre *m* tailor

satán, satanás *m* Satan

S

satánico *adj* satanic

satélite *m* satellite; **ciudad satélite** satellite town

satén, satín *m* satin

sátira *f* satire

satírico *adj* satirical

satirizar ⟨1f⟩ *v/t* satirize

satisfacción *f* satisfaction

satisfacer ⟨2s; *part* **satisfecho**⟩ *v/t* satisfy; *requisito, exigencia* meet, fulfil(l); *deuda* settle, pay off

satisfactorio *adj* satisfactory

satisfecho *part* → **satisfacer 2** *adj* satisfied; (*lleno*) full; **darse por satisfecho** be satisfied (**con** with)

saturar ⟨1a⟩ *v/t* saturate

sauce *m* BOT willow; **sauce llorón** weeping willow

saúco *m* BOT elder

saudí *m/f & adj* Saudi

saudita *m/f* Saudi

sauna *f* sauna

savia *f* sap

saxofón, saxófono *m* saxophone, sax F

sazón *f*: **a la sazón** at that time

sazonar ⟨1a⟩ *v/t* GASTR season

scooter *m* motor scooter

se ◇ *pron complemento indirecto*: *a él* (to) him; *a ella* (to) her; *a usted, ustedes* (to) you; *a ellos* (to) them; **se lo daré** I will give it to him / her / you / them

◇ *reflexivo*: *con él* himself; *con ella* herself; *cosa* itself; *con usted* yourself; *con ustedes* yourselves; *con ellos* themselves; **se vistió** he got dressed, he dressed himself; **se lavó las manos** she washed her hands; **se abrazaron** they hugged each other

◇ *oración impersonal*: **se cree** it is thought; **se habla español** Spanish spoken

sé *vb* → **saber**

sea *vb* → **ser**

sebo *m* grease, fat

secador *m*: **secador (de pelo)** hair dryer

secadora *f* dryer

secar ⟨1g⟩ **1** *v/t* dry **2** *v/r* **secarse** dry

sección *f* section

secesión *f* POL secession

seco *adj* dry; *fig persona* curt, brusque; **parar en seco** stop dead

secreción *f* secretion

secretaria *f* secretary; **secretaria de dirección** executive secretary

secretaría *f* secretary's office; *de organización* secretariat

secretario *m tb* POL secretary

secreter *m mueble* writing desk

secretismo *m* secrecy

secreto **1** *adj* secret **2** *m* secret; **un secreto a voces** an open secret; **en secreto** in secret

secta *f* sect

sectario *adj* sectarian

sectarismo *m* sectarianism

sector *m* sector

secuaz *m/f* follower

secuela *f* MED after-effect

secuencia *f* sequence

secuencial *adj* INFOR sequential

secuestrador *m*, secuestradora *f* kidnapper

secuestrar ⟨1a⟩ *v/t barco, avión* hijack; *persona* abduct, kidnap

secuestro *m de barco, avión* hijacking; *de persona* abduction, kidnapping; **secuestro aéreo** hijacking

secundar ⟨1a⟩ *v/t* support, back

secundario *adj* secondary

sed *f tb fig* thirst; **tener sed** be thirsty

seda *f* silk; **como una seda** F as smooth as silk

sedal *m* fishing line

sedante *m* sedative

sede *f de organización* headquarters; *de acontecimiento* site; **sede social** head office

sedentario *adj* sedentary

sedición *f* sedition

sediento *adj* thirsty; **estar sediento de** *fig* thirst for

sedimentar ⟨1a⟩ *v/t* deposit

sedimento *m* sediment

sedoso *adj* silky

seducción *f* seduction; (*atracción*) attraction

seducir ⟨3o⟩ *v/t* seduce; (*atraer*) attract; (*cautivar*) captivate, charm

seductor **1** adj seductive; (atractivo) attractive; oferta tempting **2** m seducer
seductora f seductress
segadora f reaper, harvester
segar ⟨1h & 1k⟩ v/t reap, harvest
seglar adj secular, lay atr
segmento m segment
segregación f segregation; **segregación racial** racial segregation
segregar ⟨1h⟩ v/t segregate
seguida f: **en seguida** at once, immediately
seguido **1** adj consecutive, successive; **ir todo seguido** go straight on **2** adv L.Am. often, frequently
seguidor m, seguidora f follower, supporter
seguimiento m monitoring
seguir ⟨3l & 3d⟩ **1** v/t follow; **seguir a alguien** follow s.o. **2** v/i continue, carry on; **sigue enfadado conmigo** he's still angry with me; **seguir haciendo algo** go on doing sth, continue to do sth
según **1** prp according to; **según él** according to him **2** adv it depends
segunda f: **de segunda** fig second-rate
segundero m second hand
segundo m/adj second
seguridad f safety; contra crimen security; (certeza) certainty; **Seguridad Social** Esp Social Security
seguro **1** adj safe; (estable) steady; (cierto) sure; **es seguro** (cierto) it's a certainty; **seguro de sí mismo** self-confident, sure of o.s. **2** adv for sure **3** m COM insurance; de puerta, coche lock; L.Am. (imperdible) safety pin; **poner el seguro** lock the door; **ir sobre seguro** be on the safe side
seis adj six
seiscientos adj six hundred
seísmo m earthquake
selección f selection; **selección nacional** DEP national team
seleccionador m, seleccionadora f DEP: **seleccionador nacional** national team manager
seleccionar ⟨1a⟩ v/t choose, select
selectividad f en España university entrance exam
selecto adj select, exclusive
sellar ⟨1a⟩ v/t seal
sello m stamp; fig hallmark; **sello discográfico** record label
selva f (bosque) forest; (jungla) jungle
semáforo m traffic light
semana f week; **Semana Santa** Holy Week, Easter
semanal adj weekly
semanario m weekly
semblante m face
sembrado m sown field
sembrar ⟨1k⟩ v/t sow; fig: pánico, inquietud etc spread
semejante **1** adj similar; **jamás he oído semejante tontería** I've never heard such nonsense **2** m fellow human being, fellow creature
semejanza f similarity
semejarse ⟨1a⟩ v/r look alike, resemble each other
semen m BIO semen
semental m toro stud bull; caballo stallion
semestre m six-month period; EDU semester
semicírculo m semicircle
semiconductor m EL semiconductor
semifinal f DEP semifinal
semilla f seed
seminario m seminary
seminarista m seminarian
semítico adj Semitic
sémola f semolina
senado m senate
senador m, senadora f senator
sencillez f simplicity
sencillo **1** adj simple **2** m L.Am. small change
senda f path, track
senderismo m trekking, hiking
senderista m/f walker, hiker
sendero m path, track
sendos, -as adj pl: **les entregó sendos diplomas** he presented each of them with a diploma
senil adj senile
seno m tb fig bosom; **senos** breasts
sensación f feeling, sensation; **causar**

sensación fig cause a sensation
sensacional adj sensational
sensacionalista adj sensationalist
sensatez f good sense
sensato adj sensible
sensibilidad f feeling; (emotividad) sensitivity
sensibilizar ⟨1f⟩ v/t make aware (**sobre** of)
sensible adj sensitive; (apreciable) appreciable, noticeable
sensiblero adj sentimental, schmaltzy F
sensor m sensor
sensorial adj sensory
sensual adj sensual
sensualidad f sensuality
sentada f sit-down
sentado adj sitting, seated; **dar por sentado** fig take for granted, assume
sentar ⟨1k⟩ 1 v/t establish, create; **sentar las bases** lay the foundations, pave the way 2 v/i: **sentar bien a alguien** de comida agree with s.o.; **le sienta bien esa chaqueta** that jacket suits her, she looks good in that jacket 3 v/r **sentarse** sit down
sentencia f JUR sentence
sentenciar ⟨1b⟩ v/t JUR sentence
sentido m sense; (significado) meaning; **sentido común** common sense; **sentido del humor** sense of humo(u)r; **perder / recobrar el sentido** lose / regain consciousness
sentimental adj emotional; **ser sentimental** be sentimental
sentimentalismo m sentiment
sentimiento m feeling; **lo acompaño en el sentimiento** my condolences
sentir 1 m feeling, opinion 2 ⟨3i⟩ v/t feel; (percibir) sense; **lo siento** I'm sorry 3 v/r **sentirse** feel; L.Am. (ofenderse) take offense, Br take offence
seña f gesture, sign; **me hizo una seña para que entrara** he gestured to me to go in; **señas** pl address sg; **hacer señas** wave
señal f signal; fig sign, trace; COM deposit, down payment; **en señal de** as a token of, as a mark of

señalado adj special
señalar ⟨1a⟩ v/t indicate, point out
señalizar ⟨1f⟩ v/t signpost
Señor m Lord
señor 1 m gentleman; man; trato sir; escrito Mr; **el señor López** Mr López; **los señores López** Mr and Mrs López
señora f lady, woman; trato ma'am, Br madam; escrito Mrs, Ms; **la señora López** Mrs López; **mi señora** my wife; **señoras y señores** ladies and gentlemen
señoría f: **su señoría** your Hono(u)r
señorial adj lordly, noble
señorita f young lady, young woman; tratamiento miss; escrito Miss; **la señorita López** Ms López, Miss López
señuelo m decoy
sepa vb → **saber**
separación f separation; **separación de bienes** JUR division of property
separado adj separated; **por separado** separately
separar ⟨1a⟩ 1 v/t separate 2 v/r **separarse** separate, split up F
separatismo m separatism
separatista m/f & adj separatist
sepia f ZO cuttlefish
sept.ᵉ abr (= **septiembre**) Sept. (= September)
septentrional adj northern
septiembre m September
séptimo adj seventh
sepulcro m tomb
sepultar ⟨1a⟩ v/t bury
sepultura f burial; (tumba) tomb; **dar sepultura a alguien** bury s.o.
sequedad f fig curtness
sequía f drought
séquito m retinue, entourage
ser ⟨2w; part **sido**⟩ 1 v/i be; **ser de Sevilla** be from Seville; **ser de madera / plata** be made of wood / silver; **es de Juan** it's Juan's, it belongs to Juan; **ser para bo**; **a no ser que** unless; **¡eso es!** exactly!, that's right!; **es que ...** the thing is ...; **es de esperar** it's to be hoped; **¿cuánto es?** how much is it?; **¿qué es de ti?** how's life?, how're things?; **o sea** in other words 2 being

Serbia Serbia
serenarse ⟨1a⟩ v/r calm down; *del tiempo* clear up
serenata *f* MÚS serenade
serenidad *f* calmness, serenity
sereno **1** *m*: *dormir al sereno* sleep outdoors **2** *adj* calm, serene
serial *m* TV, RAD series
serie *f* series; *fuera de serie* out of this world, extraordinary
seriedad *f* seriousness
serio *adj* serious; *(responsable)* reliable; *en serio* seriously
sermón *m* sermon
sermonear ⟨1a⟩ v/i preach
seropositivo *adj* MED HIV positive
serpentina *f* streamer
serpiente *f* ZO snake; *serpiente de cascabel* rattlesnake
serranía *f* mountainous region
serrar ⟨1k⟩ v/t saw
serrín *m* sawdust
serrucho *m* handsaw
servicial *adj* obliging, helpful
servicio *m* service; *servicios pl* restroom *sg*, *Br* toilets; *servicio doméstico* domestic service; *servicio militar* military service; *servicio pos(t)venta* after-sales service; *servicio de atención al cliente* customer service; *estar de servicio* be on duty
servidor *m* INFOR server
servil *adj* servile
servilismo *m* servility
servilleta *f* napkin, serviette
servilletero *m* napkin ring
servir ⟨3l⟩ **1** v/t serve **2** v/i be of use; *¿para qué sirve esto?* what is this (used) for?; *no servir de nada* be no use at all **3** v/r servirse help o.s.; *comida* help oneself to
servodirección power steering
sésamo *m* sesame
sesenta *adj* sixty
sesgar ⟨1h⟩ v/t slant, skew
sesión *f* session; *en cine, teatro* show, performance
sesionar ⟨1a⟩ v/i *L.Am.* be in session
seso *m* ANAT brain; *fig* brains *pl*, sense;

sesos GASTR brains
set *m* tenis set
seta *f* BOT mushroom; *venenosa* toadstool
setecientos *adj* seven hundred
setenta *adj* seventy
seto *m* hedge
s.e.u.o. *abr* (= *salvo error u omisión*) E & OE (= errors and omissions excepted)
seudónimo *m* pseudonym
severo *adj* severe
sevillanas *fpl* folk dance from Seville
sexismo *m* sexism
sexista *m/f & adj* sexist
sexo *m* sex
sexto *adj* sixth
sexual *adj* sexual
sexualidad *f* sexuality
sexy *adj inv* sexy
shock *m* MED shock
si *conj* if; *si no* if not; *como si* as if; *por si* in case; *me pregunto si vendrá* I wonder whether he'll come
sí **1** *adv* yes **2** *pron tercera persona: singular masculino* himself; *femenino* herself; *cosa, animal* itself; *plural* themselves; *usted* yourself; *ustedes* yourselves; *por sí solo* by himself / itself, on his / its own
siamés *adj* Siamese
sibarita *m* bon vivant, epicure
Siberia Siberia
sicario *m* hired assassin
Sicilia Sicily
SIDA *abr* (= *síndrome de inmunidad deficiente adquirida*) Aids (= acquired immune-deficiency syndrome)
sidecar *m* sidecar
sideral *adj viajes* space *atr*; *espacio sideral* outer space
siderurgia *f* iron and steel making
sido *part* → *ser*
sidra *f* cider
siembra *f* sowing
siempre *adv* always; *siempre que* providing that, as long as; *lo de siempre* the same old story; *para siempre* for ever
sien *f* ANAT temple
siendo *vb* → *ser*
siento *vb* → *sentir*
sierra *f* saw; GEOG mountain range

siesta f siesta, nap; **dormir la siesta** have a siesta o nap

siete adj seven

sífilis f MED syphilis

siga vb → **seguir**

sigilo m secrecy, stealth

sigiloso adj stealthy

sigla f abbreviation, acronym

siglo m century; **hace siglos** or **un siglo que no le veo** fig I haven't seen him in a long long time

signatario m, **-a** f signatory

significado m meaning

significar ⟨1g⟩ v/t mean, signify

significativo adj meaningful, significant

signo m sign; **signo de admiración** exclamation mark; **signo de interrogación** question mark; **signo de puntuación** punctuation mark

sigo vb → **seguir**

siguiente 1 adj next, following **2** pron next (one)

sílaba f syllable

silbar ⟨1a⟩ v/i & v/t whistle

silbato m whistle

silbido m whistle

silenciador m AUTO muffler, Br silencer

silencio m silence; **en silencio** in silence, silently

silencioso adj silent

silicio m QUÍM silicon

silicona f silicone

silla f chair; **silla de montar** saddle; **silla de ruedas** wheelchair

sillín m saddle

sillón m armchair, easy chair

silueta f silhouette

silvestre adj wild

silvicultura f forestry

simbiosis f symbiosis

simbolismo m symbolism

simbolizar ⟨1f⟩ v/t symbolize

símbolo m symbol

simétrico adj symmetrical

similar adj similar

similitud f similarity

simio m ZO ape

simpatía f warmth, friendliness

simpático adj nice, lik(e)able

simpatizante m/f sympathizer, supporter

simpatizar ⟨1f⟩ v/i sympathize

simple 1 adj simple; (mero) ordinary **2** m simpleton

simplicidad f simplicity

simplificar ⟨1g⟩ v/t simplify

simplista adj simplistic

simposio m symposium

simulación f simulation

simulacro m (cosa falsa) pretense, Br pretense, sham; (simulación) simulation; **simulacro de incendio** fire drill

simulador m simulator

simular ⟨1a⟩ v/t simulate

simultanear ⟨1a⟩ v/t: **simultanear dos cargos** hold two positions at the same time

simultáneo adj simultaneous

sin prp without; **sin que** without; **sin preguntar** without asking

sinagoga f synagogue

sinceridad f sincerity

sincero adj sincere

síncope m MED blackout

sincronizar ⟨1f⟩ v/t synchronize

sindical adj (labor, Br trade) union atr

sindicalismo m (labor, Br trade) union movement

sindicalista m/f (labor, Br trade) union member

sindicato m (labor, Br trade) union

síndrome m syndrome

sinfín m: **un sinfín de ...** no end of ...

sinfonía f MÚS symphony

singular 1 adj singular; fig outstanding, extraordinary **2** m GRAM singular

siniestro 1 adj sinister **2** m accident; (catástrofe) disaster

sinnúmero m: **un sinnúmero de** no end of

sino 1 m fate **2** conj but; (salvo) except; **no cena en casa, sino en el bar** he doesn't have dinner at home, he has it in the bar

sinónimo 1 adj synonymous **2** m synonym

sinopsis f inv synopsis

sinsentido m nonsense

sintaxis f syntax

síntesis f inv synthesis; (resumen) sum-

mary
sintético *adj* synthetic
sintetizador *m* MÚS synthesizer
síntoma *m* symptom
sintonía *f melodía* theme tune, signature
tune; RAD tuning, reception; *estar en la
sintonía de* RAD be tuned to
sintonizar ⟨1f⟩ **1** *v/t radio* tune in **2** *v/i fig*
be in tune (*con* with)
sinuoso *adj* winding
sinusitis *f* MED sinusitis
sinvergüenza *m/f* swine; *¡qué sinvergüenza!* (*descarado*) what a nerve!
siquiera *adv*: *ni siquiera* not even; *siquiera bebe algo L.Am.* at least have
a drink
sirena *f* siren; MYTH mermaid
Siria Syria
sirve *vb* → **servir**
sirvienta *f* maid
sirviente *m* servant
sisar ⟨1a⟩ *v/t* F pilfer
sísmico *adj* seismic
sistema *m* system; *sistema operativo* operating system
sistemático *adj* systematic
sitiar ⟨1b⟩ *v/t* surround, lay siege to
sitio *m* place; (*espacio*) room; *hacer sitio*
make room; *en ningún sitio* nowhere;
sitio web web site
situación *f* situation
situar ⟨1e⟩ **1** *v/t* place, put **2** *v/r* **situarse**
be
S.L. *abr* (= *sociedad limitada*) Ltd (=
limited)
slip *m* underpants *pl*
s/n *abr* (= *sin número*) not numbered
sobaco *m* armpit
sobar ⟨1a⟩ *v/t* handle, finger; F *sexualmente* grope F
soberanía *f* sovereignty
soberano *m*, *-a f* sovereign
soberbia *f* pride, arrogance
soberbio *adj* proud, arrogant; *fig* superb
sobornar ⟨1a⟩ *v/t* bribe
soborno *m* bribe
sobra *f* surplus, excess; *hay de sobra*
there's more than enough; *sobras* left-
overs

sobradamente *adv conocido* well
sobrar ⟨1a⟩ *v/t*: *sobra comida* there's
food left over; *me sobró pintura* I had
some paint left over; *sobraba uno* there
was one left
sobre 1 *m* envelope **2** *prp* on; *sobre esto*
about this; *sobre las tres* about three
o'clock; *sobre todo* above all, especially
sobrecargar ⟨1h⟩ *v/t* overload
sobrecargo *m* AVIA chief flight attendant;
MAR purser
sobrecoger ⟨2c⟩ *v/t* (*asustar*) strike fear
into; (*impresionar*) have an effect on
sobredosis *f inv* overdose
sobrehumano *adj* superhuman
sobremesa *f*: *de sobremesa* afternoon
atr
sobrenatural *adj* supernatural
sobrenombre *m* nickname
sobrentenderse ⟨2g⟩ *v/r*: *se sobrentien-
de que ...* needless to say, ...
sobrepasar ⟨1a⟩ **1** *v/t* exceed, surpass; *me
sobrepasa en altura* he is taller than me
2 *v/r* sobrepasarse go too far
sobrepeso *m* excess weight
sobreponerse ⟨2r; *part* **sobrepuesto** ⟩
v/r: *sobreponerse a* overcome, get over
sobrepuesto *part* → **sobreponerse**
sobresaliente *adj* outstanding, excellent
sobresalir ⟨3r⟩ *v/t* stick out, protrude; *fig*
excel; *sobresalir entre* stand out among
sobresaltar ⟨1a⟩ **1** *v/t* startle **2** *v/r* sobre-
saltarse jump, start
sobresalto *m* jump, start
sobreseer ⟨2e⟩ *v/t* JUR dismiss
sobrestimar ⟨1a⟩ *v/t* overestimate
sobresueldo *m* bonus
sobrevalorar ⟨1a⟩ *v/t* overrate
sobrevenir ⟨3s⟩ *v/i* happen; *de guerra*
break out
sobrevivir ⟨3a⟩ *v/i* survive
sobrevolar ⟨1m⟩ *v/t* fly over
sobriedad *f* soberness; *de comida, decoración* simplicity; (*moderación*) restraint
sobrina *f* niece
sobrino *m* nephew
sobrio *adj* sober; *comida, decoración* simple; (*moderado*) restrained
socarrón *adj* sarcastic, snide F

S

socavar ⟨1a⟩ v/t tb fig undermine

socavón m hollow

sociable adj sociable

social adj social

socialismo m socialism

socialista m/f & adj socialist

sociedad f society; **sociedad anónima** public corporation, Br public limited company; **sociedad de consumo** consumer society

socio m, -a f de club, asociación etc member; COM partner

sociología f sociology

socorrer ⟨2a⟩ v/t help, assist

socorrista m/f life guard

socorro m help, assistance; **¡socorro!** help!

soda f soda (water)

sodio m sodium

sofá m sofa

sofisticación f sophistication

sofisticado adj sophisticated

sofocante adj suffocating

sofocar ⟨1g⟩ 1 v/t suffocate; incendio put out 2 v/r sofocarse fig get embarrassed; (irritarse) get angry

sofoco m fig embarrassment

sofreír ⟨3m⟩ v/t sauté

sofrito m GASTR mixture of fried onions, peppers etc

software m INFOR software

soga f rope; **estar con la soga al cuello** F be in big trouble F

sois vb → ser

soja f soy, Br soya

sol m sun; **hace sol** it's sunny; **tomar el sol** sunbathe

solamente adv only

solapa f lapel

solar m vacant lot

solariego adj: **casa -a** family seat

solario, solárium m solarium

soldado m/f soldier

soldador m welder

soldadura f welding, soldering

soldar ⟨1m⟩ v/t weld, solder

soleado adj sunny

soledad f solitude, loneliness

solemne adj solemn

soler ⟨2h⟩ v/i: **soler hacer algo** usually do sth; **suele venir temprano** he usually comes early; **solía visitarme** he used to visit me

solera f traditional character

solfeo m (tonic) sol-fa

solicitante m/f applicant

solicitar ⟨1a⟩ v/t request; empleo, beca apply for

solícito adj attentive

solicitud f application, request

solidaridad f solidarity

solidario adj supportive, understanding

solidarizarse ⟨1f⟩ v/r: **solidarizarse con alguien** support s.o., back s.o.

solidez f solidity; fig strength

sólido adj solid; fig sound

solista m/f soloist

solitaria f zo tapeworm

solitario 1 adj solitary; lugar lonely 2 m solitaire, Br patience; **actuó en solitario** he acted alone

soliviantar ⟨1a⟩ 1 v/t incite, stir up 2 v/r soliviantarse v/r rise up, rebel

sollozar ⟨1f⟩ v/i sob

sollozo m sob

solo adj single; **estar solo** be alone; **sentirse solo** feel lonely; **un solo día** a single day; **a solas** alone, by o.s.; **por sí solo** by o.s.

sólo adv only, just

solomillo m GASTR sirloin

solsticio m solstice

soltar ⟨1m⟩ 1 v/t let go of; (librar) release, let go; olor give off 2 v/r soltarse free o.s.; **soltarse a andar / hablar** begin o start to walk / talk

soltera f single o unmarried woman

soltero 1 adj single, not married 2 m bachelor, unmarried man

solterona f desp old maid

soltura f fluency, ease

soluble adj soluble

solución f solution

solucionar ⟨1a⟩ v/t solve

solventar ⟨1a⟩ v/t resolve, settle

solvente adj solvent

somanta f F beating

sombra f shadow; **a la sombra de un**

árbol in the shade of a tree; *a la sombra de* fig under the protection of; *sombra de ojos* eye shadow

sombrero *m* hat; *sombrero de copa* top hat

sombrilla *f* sunshade, beach umbrella

sombrío *adj* fig somber, *Br* sombre

someter ⟨2a⟩ **1** *v/t* subject; *someter algo a votación* put sth to the vote **2** *v/r* someterse yield (*a* to); *al ley* comply (*a* with); (*rendirse*) give in (*a* to); *someterse a tratamiento* undergo treatment

somier *m* bed base

somnífero *m* sleeping pill

somnolencia *f* sleepiness, drowsiness

somnoliento *adj* sleepy, drowsy

somos *vb* → **ser**

son[1] *m* sound; *al son de* to the sound of; *en son de paz* in peace

son[2] *vb* → **ser**

sonado *adj* F famous, well-known

sonajero *m* rattle

sonámbulo *m* sleep-walker

sonar ⟨1m⟩ **1** *v/i* ring out; *sonar a* sound like; *me suena esa voz* I know that voice, that voice sounds familiar **2** *v/r* sonarse: *sonarse (la nariz)* blow one's nose

sonata *f* MÚS sonata

sonda *f* MED catheter; *sonda espacial* space probe

sondaje *m* L.Am. poll, survey

sondear ⟨1a⟩ *v/t* fig survey, poll

sondeo *m*: *sondeo (de opinión)* survey, (opinion) poll

soneto *m* sonnet

sonido *m* sound

soniquete *m* droning

sonreír ⟨3m⟩ *v/i* smile

sonriente *adj* smiling

sonrisa *f* smile

sonrojar ⟨1a⟩ **1** *v/t*: *sonrojar a alguien* make s.o. blush **2** *v/r* sonrojarse blush

sonrojo *m* blush

sonsacar ⟨1g⟩ *v/t*: *sonsacar algo* worm sth out (*a* of), wheedle sth out (*a* of)

sonso *adj* L.Am. F silly

soñador 1 *adj* dreamy **2** *m* dreamer

soñar ⟨1m⟩ **1** *v/t* dream (*con* about) **2** *v/i*

dream; *¡ni soñarlo!* dream on! F

soñolencia *f* → **somnolencia**

soñoliento *adj* → **somnoliento**

sopa *f* soup; *estar hecho una sopa* F be sopping wet; *hasta en la sopa* F all over the place F

sopapo *m* F smack, slap

sopera *f* soup tureen

sopesar ⟨1a⟩ *v/t* fig weigh up

sopetón *m*: *de sopetón* unexpectedly

soplar ⟨1a⟩ **1** *v/i del viento* blow **2** *v/t vela* blow out; *polvo* blow away; *soplar algo a la policía* tip the police off about sth

soplete *m* welding torch

soplo *m*: *en un soplo* F in an instant

soplón *m* F informer, stool pigeon F

soponcio *m*: *le dio un soponcio* F he passed out

sopor *m* drowsiness, sleepiness

soporífero *adj* soporific

soportal *m* porch

soportar ⟨1a⟩ *v/t* fig put up with, bear; *no puedo soportar a José* I can't stand José

soporte *m* support, stand; *soporte lógico* INFOR software; *soporte físico* INFOR hardware

soprano MÚS **1** *m* soprano **2** *m/f* soprano

sorber ⟨2a⟩ *v/t* sip

sorbete *m* sorbet; *C.Am.* ice cream

sorbetería *f C.Am.* ice-cream parlo(u)r

sorbo *m* sip

sordera *f* deafness

sórdido *adj* sordid

sordo 1 *adj* deaf **2** *m*, *-a f* deaf person; *hacerse el sordo* turn a deaf ear

sordomudo 1 *adj* deaf and dumb **2** *m*, *-a f* deaf-mute

sorna *f* sarcasm; *con sorna* sarcastically, mockingly

sorocharse ⟨1a⟩ *v/r Pe, Bol* get altitude sickness

soroche *m Pe, Bol* altitude sickness

sorprendente *adj* surprising

sorprender ⟨2a⟩ *v/t* surprise

sorpresa *f* surprise; *de* or *por sorpresa* by surprise

sortear ⟨1a⟩ *v/t* draw lots for; *obstáculo* get round

S

sorteo m (*lotería*) lottery, (prize) draw

sortija f ring

sortilegio m spell, charm

SOS m SOS

sosa f QUÍM: **sosa cáustica** caustic soda

sosegado adj calm

sosegarse ⟨1h & 1k⟩ v/r calm down

sosería f insipidness, dullness

sosiego m calm, quiet

soslayo adj: **de soslayo** sideways

soso 1 adj tasteless, insipid; *fig* dull 2 m, -a f stick-in-the-mud F

sospecha f suspicion

sospechar ⟨1a⟩ 1 v/t suspect 2 v/i be suspicious; **sospechar de alguien** suspect someone

sospechoso 1 adj suspicious 2 m, -a f suspect

sostén m brassiere, bra; *fig* pillar, mainstay

sostener ⟨2l⟩ 1 v/t familia support; *opinión* hold o.s.; *de pie* stand up; *en el poder* stay, remain

sota f naipes jack

sotana f REL cassock

sótano m basement, *Br* cellar

soterrar ⟨1k⟩ v/t bury

soviético adj Soviet

soy vb → **ser**

soya f L.Am. soy, *Br* soya

spot m TV commercial

spray m spray

sprint m sprint

squash m DEP squash

Sr. abr (= **señor**) Mr

Sra. abr (= **señora**) Mrs

Sres. abr (= **Señores**) Messrs (= Messieurs)

Srta. abr (= **Señorita**) Miss

stand m COM stand

stock m stock; **tener en stock** have in stock

su, sus adj pos: *de él* his; *de ella* her; *de cosa* its; *de usted, ustedes* your; *de ellos* their; *de uno* one's

suave adj soft, smooth; *sabor, licor* mild

suavidad f softness, smoothness; *de sabor, licor* mildness

suavizante m de pelo, ropa conditioner

suavizar ⟨1f⟩ v/t tb fig soften

subacuático adj underwater

subalterno 1 adj subordinate 2 m, -a f subordinate

subasta f auction; **sacar a subasta** put up for auction

subastar ⟨1a⟩ v/t auction (off)

subcampeón m DEP runner-up

subconsciente m/adj subconscious

subcontrata(ción) f subcontracting

subdesarrollado adj underdeveloped

subdesarrollo m underdevelopment

subdirector m, subdirectora f deputy manager

súbdito m subject

subestimar ⟨1a⟩ v/t underestimate

subida f rise, ascent; **subida de los precios** rise in prices

subido 1 part → **subir** 2 adj: **subido de tono** fig risqué, racy

subir ⟨3a⟩ 1 v/t cuesta, escalera go up, climb; *montaña* climb; *objeto* raise, lift; *intereses, precio* raise 2 v/i para indicar acercamiento come up; *para indicar alejamiento* go up; *de precio* rise, go up; *a un tren, autobús* get on; *a un coche* get in 3 v/r subirse go up; *a un árbol* climb

súbito adj: **de súbito** suddenly, all of a sudden

subjetivo adj subjective

subjuntivo m GRAM subjunctive

sublevar ⟨1a⟩ 1 v/t incite to revolt; *fig* infuriate, get angry 2 v/r sublevarse rise up, revolt

sublimación f fig sublimation

sublime adj sublime, lofty

subliminal adj subliminal

submarinismo m scuba diving

submarinista m/f scuba diver

submarino 1 adj underwater 2 m submarine

subnormal adj subnormal

subordinado 1 adj subordinate 2 m, -a f subordinate

subproducto m by-product

subrayar ⟨1a⟩ v/t underline; *fig* underline, emphasize

subrepticio adj surreptitious

subsanar ⟨1a⟩ v/t put right, rectify

subsidiario adj subsidiary

subsidio m welfare, Br benefit; **subsidio de paro** or **desempleo** unemployment compensation (Br benefit)

subsistencia f subsistence, survival; de pobreza, tradición persistence

subsistir ⟨3a⟩ v/i live, survive; de pobreza, tradición live on, persist

subte m Rpl subway, Br underground

subterfugio m subterfuge

subterráneo 1 adj underground 2 m L.Am. subway, Br underground

subtítulo m subtitle

suburbio m slum area

subvención f subsidy

subvencionar ⟨1a⟩ v/t subsidize

subversivo adj subversive

subyacente adj underlying

subyugar ⟨1h⟩ v/t subjugate

succionar ⟨1a⟩ v/t suck

sucedáneo m substitute

suceder ⟨2a⟩ v/i happen, occur; **suceder a** follow; **¿qué sucede?** what's going on?

sucesión f succession; **sucesión al trono** succession to the throne

sucesivo adj successive; **en lo sucesivo** from now on

suceso m event

sucesor m, sucesora f successor

suciedad f dirt

sucio adj tb fig dirty

suculento adj succulent

sucumbir ⟨3a⟩ v/i succumb, give in

sucursal f COM branch

sudaca m/f desp South American

sudadera f sweatshirt

Sudáfrica South Africa

sudafricano 1 adj South African 2 m, -a f South African

Sudamérica South America

sudamericano 1 adj South American 2 m, -a f South American

sudar ⟨1a⟩ v/i sweat

sudario m REL shroud

sudeste m southeast

sudoeste m southwest

sudor m sweat

sudoración f perspiration

sudoroso adj sweaty

Suecia Sweden

sueco 1 adj Swedish 2 m, -a f Swede; **hacerse el sueco** F pretend not to hear, act dumb F

suegra f mother-in-law

suegro m father-in-law

suela f de zapato sole

sueldo m salary

suelo m en casa floor; en el exterior earth, ground; AGR soil; **estar por los suelos** F be at rock bottom F

suelto 1 adj loose, free; **un pendiente suelto** a single earring; **andar suelto** be at large 2 m loose change

sueño m (estado de dormir) sleep; (fantasía, imagen mental) dream; **tener sueño** be sleepy

suero m MED saline solution; sanguíneo blood serum

suerte f luck; **por suerte** luckily; **echar a suertes** toss for, draw lots for; **probar suerte** try one's luck

suertero m, -a f L.Am. F, suertudo m, -a f L.Am. F lucky devil F

suéter m sweater

suficiente 1 adj enough, sufficient 2 m EDU pass

sufragar ⟨1h⟩ v/t COM meet, pay

sufragio m: **sufragio universal** universal suffrage

sufrimiento m suffering

sufrir ⟨3a⟩ 1 v/t fig suffer, put up with 2 v/i suffer (de from)

sugerencia f suggestion

sugerir ⟨3i⟩ v/t suggest

sugestionar ⟨1a⟩ v/t influence

sugestivo adj suggestive

suicida 1 adj suicidal 2 m/f suicide victim

suicidarse ⟨1a⟩ v/r commit suicide

suicidio m suicide

suite f suite

Suiza Switzerland

suizo 1 adj Swiss 2 m, -a f Swiss 3 m GASTR sugar topped bun

sujetador m brassiere, bra

sujetapapeles m inv paperclip

sujetar ⟨1a⟩ v/t hold (down), keep in

place; (*sostener*) hold

sujeto 1 *adj* secure 2 *m* individual; GRAM subject

sulfurarse ⟨1a⟩ *v/r* F blow one's top F

suma *f* sum; **en suma** in short

sumamente *adv* extremely, highly

sumar ⟨1a⟩ 1 *v/t* add; **5 y 6 suman 11** 5 and 6 make 11 2 *v/i* add up 3 *v/r* **sumarse: sumarse a** join

sumario *m* summary; JUR indictment

sumergir ⟨3c⟩ 1 *v/t* submerge, immerse 2 *v/r* sumergirse *fig* immerse o.s. (**en** in), throw o.s. (**en** into)

sumidero *m* drain

suministrar ⟨1a⟩ *v/t* supply, provide

suministro *m* supply

sumir ⟨3a⟩ 1 *v/t fig* plunge, throw (**en** into) 2 *v/r* sumirse *fig* sink (**en** into)

sumisión *f* submission

sumiso *adj* submissive

sumo *adj* supreme; **con sumo cuidado** with the utmost care; **a lo sumo** at the most

suntuoso *adj* sumptuous

supe *vb* → **saber**

supeditar ⟨1a⟩ *v/t* make conditional (**a** upon)

súper *adj* F super F, great F

superable *adj* surmountable

superación *f* overcoming, surmounting

superar ⟨1a⟩ 1 *v/t persona* beat; *límite* go beyond, exceed; *obstáculo* overcome, surmount 2 *v/r* superarse surpass o.s., excel o.s.

superávit *m* surplus

superchería *f* trick, swindle

superdotado *adj* gifted

superficial *adj* superficial, shallow

superficialidad *f* superficiality, shallowness

superficie *f* surface

superfluo *adj* superfluous

superior 1 *adj* upper; *en jerarquía* superior; **ser superior a** be superior to 2 *m* superior

superiora *f* REL Mother Superior

superioridad *f* superiority

superlativo *adj* superlative

supermercado *m* supermarket

superpoblación *f* overpopulation

superponer ⟨2r⟩ *v/t* superimpose

superpotencia *f* POL superpower

superpuesto *adj* superimposed

supersónico *adj* supersonic

superstición *f* superstition

supersticioso *adj* superstitious

supervisar ⟨1a⟩ *v/t* supervise

supervisor *m*, supervisora *f* supervisor

supervivencia *f* survival

superviviente 1 *adj* surviving 2 *m/f* survivor

suplantar ⟨1a⟩ *v/t* replace, take the place of

suplementario *adj* supplementary

suplemento *m* supplement

suplente *m/f* substitute, stand-in

súplica *f* plea

suplicar ⟨1g⟩ *v/t cosa* plead for, beg for; *persona* beg

suplicio *m fig* torment, ordeal

suplir ⟨3a⟩ *v/t carencia* make up for; (*sustituir*) substitute

supo *vb* → **saber**

suponer ⟨2r⟩; *part* **supuesto** ⟩ *v/t* suppose, assume

suposición *f* supposition

supositorio *m* MED suppository

supremacía *f* supremacy

supremo *adj* supreme

supresión *f* suppression; *de impuesto, ley* abolition; *de restricción* lifting; *de servicio* withdrawal

suprimir ⟨3a⟩ *v/t* suppress; *ley, impuesto* abolish; *restricción* lift; *servicio* withdraw; *puesto de trabajo* cut

supuesto 1 *part* → **suponer** 2 *adj* supposed, alleged; **por supuesto** of course 3 *m* assumption

sur *m* south

surco *m* AGR furrow

sureño *adj* southern

surf(ing) *m* surfing

surfista *m/f* surfer

surgir ⟨3c⟩ *v/i fig* emerge; *de problema* come up; *de agua* spout

surrealismo *m* surrealism

surtido 1 *adj* assorted; **bien surtido** COM well stocked 2 *m* assortment, range surtidor *m*: **surtidor de gasolina** or **de nafta** gas pump, *Br* petrol pump

surtir ⟨3a⟩ **1** *v/t* supply; **surtir efecto** have the desired effect **2** *v/i* spout **3** *v/r* surtirse stock up (**de** with)

susceptible *adj* touchy; **ser susceptible de mejora** leave room for improvement

suscitar ⟨1a⟩ *v/t* arouse; *polémica* generate; *escándalo* provoke

suscribir ⟨3a; *part* **suscrito** ⟩ **1** *v/t* subscribe to **2** *v/r* **suscribirse** subscribe

suscripción *f* subscription

suscriptor *m*, suscriptora *f* subscriber

suscrito *part* → **suscribir**

suspender ⟨2a⟩ **1** *v/t* empleado, alumno suspend; objeto hang; reunión adjourn; examen fail **2** *v/i* EDU fail

suspense *m* fig suspense

suspensión *f* suspension

suspenso **1** *adj* **alumnos suspensos** students who have failed; **en suspenso** suspended **2** *m* fail

suspensores *mpl* L.Am. suspenders, *Br* braces

suspicacia *f* suspicion

suspicaz *adj* suspicious

suspirar ⟨1a⟩ *v/i* sigh; **suspirar por algo** yearn for sth, long for sth

suspiro *m* sigh

sustancia *f* substance

sustancial *adj* substantial

sustantivo *m* GRAM noun

sustentar ⟨1a⟩ *v/t* sustain; familia support; opinión maintain

sustento *m* means of support

sustitución *f* substitution

sustituir ⟨3g⟩ *v/t*: **sustituir X por Y** replace X with Y, substitute Y for X

sustituto *m* substitute

susto *m* fright, scare; **dar** or **pegar un susto a alguien** give s.o. a fright

sustraer ⟨2p; *part* **sustraido** ⟩ *v/t* subtract, take away; (robar) steal

sustraido *part* → **sustraer**

susurrar ⟨1a⟩ *v/t* whisper

susurro *m* whisper

sutil *adj* fig subtle

sutileza *f* fig subtlety

suyo, suya *pron pos*: de él his; de ella hers; de usted, ustedes yours; de ellos theirs; **los suyos** his / her etc folks, his / her etc family; **hacer de las -as** get up to one's old tricks; **salirse con la -a** get one's own way

T

tabaco *m* tobacco

tábano *m* zo horsefly

tabarra *f*: **dar la tabarra a alguien** F bug s.o. F

taberna *f* bar

tabernero *m* bar owner, *Br* landlord; (camarero) bartender

tabique *m* partition, partition wall

tabla *f* de madera board, plank; PINT panel; (cuadro) table; **tabla de multiplicar** multiplication table; **tabla de planchar** ironing board; **tabla de surf** surf board; **acabar** or **quedar en tablas** end in a tie

tablero *m* board, plank; de juego board; **tablero de mandos** or **de instrumentos** AUTO dashboard

tableta *f*: **tableta de chocolate** chocolate bar

tablón *m* plank; **tablón de anuncios** bulletin board, *Br* notice board

tabú *m* taboo

tabulador *m* tb INFOR tab key

taburete *m* stool

tacañería *f* F miserliness, stinginess F

tacaño **1** *adj* F miserly, stingy F **2** *m*, -a *f* F miser F, tightwad F

tacha f flaw, blemish; **sin tacha** beyond reproach

tachadura f crossing-out

tachar ⟨1a⟩ v/t cross out

tacho m Rpl (papelera) wastepaper basket; en la calle garbage can, Br litter basket

tachón m crossing-out

tachuela f thumbtack, Br drawing pin

tácito adj tacit

taciturno adj taciturn

taco m F (palabrota) swear word; L.Am. heel; GASTR taco (filled tortilla)

tacón m de zapato heel; **zapatos de tacón** high-heeled shoes

táctica f tactics pl

táctico adj tactical

tacto m (sense of) touch; fig tact, discretion

TAE abr (= tasa anual efectiva) APR (= annual percentage rate)

tahona f bakery

tahúr m gambler, card-sharp F

taita m S. Am. F dad, pop F; S. Am. (abuelo) grandfather

tajada f GASTR slice; **agarrar una tajada** F get drunk; **sacar tajada** take a cut F

tajamar m S. Am. (dique) dike

tajante adj categorical

tajo m cut

tal 1 adj such; **no dije tal cosa** I said no such thing; **el gerente era un tal Lucas** the manager was someone called Lucas **2** adv: **tal como** such as; **dejó la habitación tal cual la encontró** she left the room just as she found it; **tal para cual** two of a kind; **tal vez** maybe, perhaps; **¿qué tal?** how's it going?; **¿que tal la película?** what was the movie like?; **con tal de que** + subj as long as, provided that

tala f de árboles felling

taladrar ⟨1a⟩ v/t drill

taladro m drill

talante m (genio, humor) mood; **un talante bonachón** a kindly nature; **de mal talante** in a bad mood

talar ⟨1a⟩ v/t árbol fell, cut down

talco m talc, talcum; **polvos de talco** talcum powder

talego m P 1000 pesetas

talento m talent

talismán m talisman

talla f size; (estatura) height; C.Am. F (mentira) lie; **dar la talla** fig make the grade

tallar ⟨1a⟩ v/t carve; piedra preciosa cut

tallarín m noodle

taller m workshop; **taller mecánico** AUTO repair shop; **taller de reparaciones** repair shop

tallo m BOT stalk, stem

talón m ANAT heel; COM stub; **talón de Aquiles** fig Achilles' heel; **pisar los talones a alguien** be hot on s.o.'s heels

talonario m: **talonario de cheques** check book, Br cheque book

tamal m Méx, C.Am. tamale (meat wrapped in a leaf and steamed)

tamaño 1 adj: **tamaño fallo / problema** such a great mistake / problem **2** m size

tambalearse ⟨1a⟩ v/r stagger, lurch; de coche sway

tambarria f C.Am., Pe, Bol F party

también adv also, too, as well; **yo también** me too; **él también dice que ...** he also says that ...

tambo m Rpl dairy farm; Méx type of large container

tambor m drum; persona drummer

tamborilear ⟨1a⟩ v/i drum with one's fingers

tamiz m sieve

tampoco adv neither; **él tampoco va** he's not going either

tampón m tampon; de tinta ink-pad

tan adv so; **tan ... como ...** as ... as ...; **tan sólo** merely

tanatorio m funeral parlo(u)r

tanda f series, batch; (turno) shift; L.Am. (commercial) break; **tanda de penaltis** DEP penalty shootout

tanga m tanga

tangente f MAT tangent; **salir or irse por la tangente** F sidestep the issue, duck the question F

tangible adj fig tangible

tango m tango

tanque *m tb* MIL tank

tantear ⟨1a⟩ *v/t* feel; (*calcular a ojo*) work out roughly; *situación* size up; *persona* sound out; (*probar*) try out; *tantear el terreno fig* see how the land lies

tantito *adv* Méx a little

tanto 1 *pron* so much; *igual cantidad* as much; *un tanto* a little; *tantos pl* so many *pl*; *igual número* as many; *tienes tanto* you have so much; *no hay tantos como ayer* there aren't as many as yesterday; *a las -as de la noche* in the small hours 2 *adv* so much; *igual cantidad* as much; *periodo* so long; *tardó tanto como él* she took as long as him; *tanto mejor* so much the better; *no es para tanto* it's not such a big deal; *estar al tanto* be informed (*de* about); *por lo tanto* therefore, so 3 *m* point; *tanto por ciento* percentage

tapa *f* lid; *tapa dura* hardback

tapacubos *m inv* AUTO hub cap

tapadera *f* lid; *fig* front

tapadillo *m*: *de tapadillo* on the sly

tapado *m* Arg, Chi coat

tapar ⟨1a⟩ *v/t* cover; *recipiente* put the lid on 2 *v/r* taparse wrap up; *taparse los ojos* cover one's eyes

taparrabo *m* loincloth

tapete *m* tablecloth; *poner algo sobre el tapete* bring sth up for discussion

tapia *f* wall; *más sordo que una tapia* as deaf as a post

tapicería *f* upholstery

tapicero *m*, -a *f* upholsterer

tapioca *f* tapioca

tapir *m* tapir

tapiz *m* tapestry

tapizar ⟨1f⟩ *v/t* upholster

tapón *m* top, cap; *de baño* plug; *de tráfico* traffic jam

taponar ⟨1a⟩ *v/t* block; *herida* swab

tapujo *m*: *sin tapujos* openly

taquicardia *f* MED tachycardia

taquigrafía *f* shorthand

taquilla *f* ticket office; TEA box-office; *C.Am.* (*bar*) small bar

taquillero 1 *adj cantante* popular; *una película -a* a hit movie, a box-office hit 2 *m*,

-a *f* ticket clerk

tara *f* defect

tarado *adj* F stupid, dumb F

tarántula *f* zo tarantula

tararear ⟨1a⟩ *v/t* hum

tardar ⟨1a⟩ *v/i* take a long time; *tardamos dos horas* we were two hours overdue *o* late; *¡no tardes!* don't be late; *a más tardar* at the latest; *¿cuánto se tarda …?* how long does it take to …?

tarde 1 *adv* late; *tarde o temprano* sooner or later 2 *f hasta las 5 ó 6* afternoon; *desde las 5 ó 6* evening; *¡buenas tardes!* good afternoon / evening; *por la tarde* in the afternoon / evening; *de tarde en tarde* from time to time

tardón *adj* F slow; (*impuntual*) late

tarea *f* task, job; *tareas pl domésticas* housework *sg*

tarifa *f* rate; *de tren* fare; *tarifa plana* flat rate

tarima *f* platform; *suelo de tarima* wooden floor

tarjeta *f* card; *tarjeta amarilla* DEP yellow card; *tarjeta de crédito* credit card; *tarjeta de embarque* AVIA boarding card; *tarjeta de sonido* INFOR sound card; *tarjeta de visita* (business) card; *tarjeta gráfica* INFOR graphics card; *tarjeta inteligente* smart card; *tarjeta monedero* electronic purse; *tarjeta postal* postcard; *tarjeta roja* DEP red card; *tarjeta telefónica* phone card

tarro *m* jar; P (*cabeza*) head

tarta *f* cake; *plana* tart; *tarta helada* ice-cream cake

tartamudear ⟨1a⟩ *v/i* stutter, stammer

tartamudez *f* stuttering, stammering

tartamudo 1 *adj* stuttering, stammering; *ser tartamudo* stutter, stammer 2 *m*,

-a *f* stutterer, stammerer

tartera *f* lunch box

tarugo *m* F blockhead

tarumba F crazy F; *volverse tarumba* go crazy

tasa *f* rate; (*impuesto*) tax; *tasa de desempleo or paro* unemployment rate

tasar ⟨1a⟩ *v/t* fix a price for; (*valorar*) assess

tasca f F bar

tata m *L.Am.* F (*abuelo*) grandpa F

tatarabuela f great-great-grandmother

tatarabuelo m great-great-grandfather

tataranieta f great-great-granddaughter

tataranieto m great-great-grandson

tate int F (*ahora caigo*) oh I see; (*cuidado*) look out!

tatuaje m tattoo

taurino adj bullfighting atr

Tauro m/f inv ASTR Taurus

tauromaquia f bullfighting

taxi m cab, taxi

taxista m/f cab o taxi driver

taza f cup; *del wáter* bowl

tazón m bowl

te *pron directo* you; *indirecto* (to) you; *reflexivo* yourself

té m tea

teatral adj fig theatrical

teatro m tb fig theater, Br theatre

tebeo m children's comic

techar ⟨1a⟩ v/t roof

techo m ceiling; (*tejado*) roof; *techo solar* AUTO sun-roof; *los sin techo* the homeless; *tocar techo* fig peak

tecla f key

teclado m MÚS, INFOR keyboard

teclear ⟨1a⟩ v/t key

técnica f technique

técnico 1 adj technical **2** m/f technician; *de televisor, lavadora etc* repairman

tecnología f technology; *alta tecnología* hi-tech; *tecnología punta* state-of-the-art technology, leading-edge technology

tecolote m Méx, C.Am. (*búho*) owl

tedio m tedium

tedioso adj tedious

teja f roof tile; *a toca teja* in hard cash

tejado m roof

tejanos mpl jeans

tejemanejes mpl F scheming sg, plotting sg

tejer ⟨2a⟩ **1** v/t weave; (*hacer punto*) knit; F *intriga* devise **2** v/i L.Am. F plot, scheme

tejido m fabric; ANAT tissue

tejo m BOT yew; *tirar a alguien los tejos* F hit on s.o. F, come on to s.o. F

tejón m ZO badger

Tel. abr (= *teléfono*) Tel. (= telephone)

tela f fabric, material; *tela de araña* spiderweb; *poner en tela de juicio* call into question; *hay tela para rato* F there's a lot to be done

telar m loom

telaraña f spiderweb

tele f F TV, Br telly F

telearrastre m drag lift

telebanca f telephone banking

telecabina f cable car

telecomedia f sitcom

telecompra f home shopping

telecomunicaciones fpl telecommunications

telediario m TV (television) news sg

teledirigido adj remote-controlled

teléf. abr (= *teléfono*) tel. (= telephone)

teleférico m cable car

telefilm(e) m TV movie

telefonear ⟨1a⟩ v/t & v/i call, phone

telefonema m L.Am. (phone) message

telefónico adj (tele)phone atr

teléfono m (tele)phone; *teléfono inalámbrico* cordless (phone); *teléfono móvil* cellphone, Br mobile (phone)

telégrafo m telegraph

telegrama m telegram

telemando m remote control

telemática f data comms

telenovela f soap (opera)

teleobjetivo m FOT telephoto lens

telepatía f telepathy

telescópico adj telescopic

telescopio m telescope

teleserie f (television) series

telesilla f chair lift

telespectador m, **telespectadora** f (television) viewer

telesquí m drag lift

teletexto m teletext

teletienda f home shopping

teletrabajo m teleworking

teletrabajador m, **teletrabajadora** f teleworker

televidente m/f (television) viewer

televisar ⟨1a⟩ v/t televise

televisión f television; *televisión por ca-*

ble cable (television); **televisión digital** digital television; **televisión de pago** pay-per-view television; **televisión vía satélite** satellite television

televisivo adj television atr

televisor m TV, television (set); **televisor en color** color TV

télex m telex

telón m TEA curtain; **el telón de acero** POL the Iron Curtain; **telón de fondo** fig backdrop, background

telonero m, **-a** f supporting artist

tema m subject, topic; MÚS, de novela theme

temario m syllabus

temático adj thematic

temblar ⟨1k⟩ v/i tremble, shake; de frío shiver

temblor m trembling, shaking; de frío shivering; L.Am. (terremoto) earthquake; **temblor de tierra** earth tremor

tembloroso adj trembling, shaking; de frío shivering

temer ⟨2a⟩ **1** v/t be afraid of **2** v/r **temerse** be afraid; **me temo que no podrá venir** I'm afraid he won't be able to come; **temerse lo peor** fear the worst

temerario adj rash, reckless

temeridad f rashness, recklessness

temible adj terrifying

temor m fear

témpano m ice floe

temperamento m temperament

temperante adj Méx teetotal

temperatura f temperature

tempestad f storm

tempestuoso adj tb fig stormy

templado adj warm; clima temperate; fig moderate, restrained

templanza f restraint

templar ⟨1a⟩ v/t ira, nervios etc calm

templo m temple

temporada f season; **una temporada** a time, some time

temporal 1 adj temporary **2** m storm

temporizador m timer

tempranear ⟨1a⟩ v/i L.Am. get up early

temprano adj & adv early

ten vb → **tener**

tenacidad f tenacity

tenaz adj determined, tenacious

tenaza f pincer, claw; **tenazas** pincers; para las uñas pliers

tendedero m clotheshorse, airer

tendencia f tendency; (corriente) trend

tendencioso adj tendentious

tender ⟨2g⟩ **1** v/t ropa hang out; cable lay; **le tendió la mano** he held out his hand to her **2** v/i: **tender a** tend to **3** v/r **tenderse** lie down

tenderete m stall

tendero m, **-a** f storekeeper, shopkeeper

tendido m EL: **tendido eléctrico** power lines pl

tendón m ANAT tendon; **tendón de Aquiles** Achilles' tendon

tenebroso adj dark, gloomy

tenedor m fork

tener ⟨2l⟩ **1** v/t have; **tener 10 años** be 10 (years old); **tener un metro de ancho / largo** be one metre (Br meter) wide / long; **tener por** consider to be; **tengo que madrugar** I must get up early, I have to o I've got to get up early; **conque ¿esas tenemos?** so that's how it is, eh? **2** v/r **tenerse** stand up; fig stand firm; **se tiene por atractivo** he thinks he's attractive

tenga vb → **tener**

tengo vb → **tener**

tenia f ZO tapeworm

teniente m/f MIL lieutenant

tenis m tennis; **tenis de mesa** table tennis

tenista m/f tennis player

tenor m MÚS tenor; **a tenor de** along the lines of

tenorio m lady-killer

tensar ⟨1a⟩ v/t tighten; músculo tense, tighten

tensión f tension; EL voltage; MED blood pressure

tenso adj tense; cuerda, cable taut

tentación f temptation

tentáculo m ZO, fig tentacle

tentador adj tempting

tentar ⟨1k⟩ v/t tempt, entice

tentativa f attempt

tentempié m F snack

T

tenue *adj* faint

teñir ⟨3h & 3l⟩ *v/t* dye; *fig* tinge

teología *f* theology

teorema *m* theorem

teoría *f* theory; **en teoría** in theory

tequila *m* tequila

terapeuta *m/f* therapist

terapéutico *adj* therapeutic

terapia *f* therapy

tercer *adj* third; **Tercer Mundo** Third World

tercermundista *adj* Third-World *atr*

tercero *m/adj* third

terciarse ⟨1b⟩ *v/r de oportunidad* come up

tercio *m* third

terciopelo *m* velvet

terco *adj* stubborn

tergiversar ⟨1a⟩ *v/t* distort, twist

termas *fpl* hot springs

térmico *adj* heat *atr*

terminación *f* GRAM ending

terminal **1** *m* INFOR terminal **2** *f* AVIA terminal; **terminal de autobuses** bus station

terminante *adj* categorical

terminar ⟨1a⟩ **1** *v/t* end, finish **2** *v/i* end, finish; *(parar)* stop **3** *v/r* **terminarse** run out; *(finalizar)* come to an end; **se ha terminado la leche** we've run out of milk, the milk's all gone

término *m* end, conclusion; *(palabra)* term; **término municipal** municipal area; **por término medio** on average; **poner término a algo** put an end to sth

terminología *f* terminology

termita *f* ZO termite

termo *m* thermos® (flask)

termómetro *m* thermometer

termostato *m* thermostat

ternera *f* calf; GASTR veal

ternero *m* calf

terno *m* CSur suit

ternura *f* tenderness

terracota *f* terracotta

terraplén *m* embankment

terrateniente *m/f* landowner

terraza *f* terrace; *(balcón)* balcony; *(café)* sidewalk café

terremoto *m* earthquake

terrenal *adj* earthly, worldly

terreno *m* land; *fig* field; **un terreno** a plot *o* piece of land; **terreno de juego** DEP field

terrestre *adj* animal land *atr*; *transporte* surface *atr*; **la atmósfera terrestre** the earth's atmosphere

terrible *adj* terrible, awful

territorial *adj* territorial

territorio *m* territory

terrón *m* lump, clod; **terrón de azúcar** sugar lump

terror *m* terror

terrorífico *adj* terrifying

terrorismo *m* terrorism

terrorista **1** *adj* terrorist *atr* **2** *m/f* terrorist

terso *adj* smooth

tertulia *f* TV debate, round table discussion

tertuliar ⟨1b⟩ *v/i L.Am.* get together for a discussion

tesina *f* dissertation

tesis *f inv* thesis

tesitura *f* situation

tesón *m* tenacity, determination

tesorero *m*, -a *f* treasurer

tesoro *m* treasure; **tesoro público** treasury

test *m* test

testa *f* head

testaferro *m* front man

testamento *m* JUR will

testarudez *f* stubbornness

testarudo *adj* stubborn

testículo *m* ANAT testicle

testificar ⟨1g⟩ **1** *v/t (probar, mostrar)* be proof of; **testificar que** JUR testify that, give evidence that **2** *v/i* testify, give evidence

testigo **1** *m/f* JUR witness; **testigo de cargo** witness for the prosecution; **testigo ocular** *or* **presencial** eye witness **2** *m* DEP baton

testimonio *m* testimony, evidence

teta *f* F boob F; ZO teat, nipple

tétanos *m* MED tetanus

tetera *f* teapot

tetilla *f de hombre* nipple

tirabuzón

tetina *f de biberón* teat

tetrabrik® *m* carton

tétrico *adj* gloomy

textil **1** *adj* textile *atr* **2** *mpl*: **textiles** textiles

texto *m* text

textual *adj* textual

textura *f* texture

tez *f* complexion

ti *pron* you; *reflexivo* yourself; *¿y a ti qué te importa?* so what?, what's it to you?

tía *f* aunt; F *(chica)* girl, chick F; **¡tía buena!** F hey gorgeous! F

tianguis *m Méx, C.Am.* market

tibio *adj tb fig* lukewarm

tiburón *m* ZO, *fig* F shark

tic *m* MED tic

ticket *m* (sales) receipt

tictac *m* tick-tock

tiempo *m* time; *(clima)* weather; GRAM tense; **tiempo libre** spare time, free time; **tiempo real** INFOR real time; *a tiempo* in time; *a un tiempo, al mismo tiempo* at the same time; **antes de tiempo** *llegar* ahead of time, early; *celebrar victoria* too soon; **con tiempo** in good time, early; **desde hace mucho tiempo** for a long time'; *hace buen / mal tiempo* the weather's fine / bad; **hace mucho tiempo** a long time ago

tienda *f* store, shop; **tienda de campaña** tent; *ir de tiendas* go shopping

tiene *vb* → **tener**

tientas *fpl*: *andar a tientas fig* feel one's way

tiento *m*: **con tiento** *fig* carefully

tierno *adj* soft; *carne* tender; *pan* fresh; *persona* tender-hearted

tierra *f* land; *materia* soil, earth; *(patria)* native land, homeland; **la Tierra** the earth; **tierra firme** dry land, terra firma; **echar por tierra** ruin, wreck

tieso *adj* stiff, rigid

tiesto *m* flower pot

tifón *m* typhoon

tifus *m* MED typhus

tigre *m* ZO tiger; *L.Am.* puma; *L.Am.* *(leopardo)* jaguar

tigresa *f* tigress

tijeras *fpl* scissors

tila *f* lime blossom tea

tildar ⟨1a⟩ *v/t*: **tildar a alguien de** *fig* brand s.o. as

tilde *f* accent; *en ñ* tilde

tilín *m*: **me hizo tilín** F I took an immediate liking to her

timador *m*, timadora *f* cheat

timar ⟨1a⟩ *v/t* cheat

timba *f* F gambling den

timbal *m* MÚS kettle drum

timbre *m de puerta* bell; *Méx* (postage) stamp

timidez *f* shyness, timidity

tímido *adj* shy, timid

timo *m* confidence trick, swindle

timón *m* MAR, AVIA rudder

tímpano *m* ANAT eardrum

tina *f* large jar; *L.Am. (bañera)* (bath)tub

tinglado *m fig* F mess

tinieblas *fpl* darkness *sg*

tino *m* aim, marksmanship; *(sensatez)* judg(e)ment; **con mucho tino** wisely, sensibly

tinta *f* ink; **de buena tinta** *fig* on good authority; **medias tintas** *fig* half measures

tinte *m* dye; *fig* veneer, gloss

tinterillo *m L.Am.* F shyster F

tintero *m* inkwell; **dejarse algo en el tintero** leave sth unsaid

tintin(e)ar ⟨1a⟩ *v/t* jingle

tinto *adj*: **vino tinto** red wine

tintorería *f* dry cleaner's

tío *m* uncle; F *(tipo)* guy F; F *apelativo* pal F

tiovivo *m* carousel, merry-go-round

típico *adj* typical *(de* of)

tipo *m* type, kind; F *persona* guy F; COM rate; **tipo de cambio** exchange rate; **tipo de interés** interest rate; **tener buen tipo** be well built; *de mujer* have a good figure

tipográfico *adj* typographic(al)

tíquet, tiquete *m L.Am.* receipt

tiquismiquis *m/f* F fuss-budget F, *Br* fusspot F

tira *f strip*; **la tira de** F loads of F, masses of F; **tira y afloja** *fig* give and take

tirabuzón *m* curl; *(sacacorchos)* corkscrew

tirachinas *m inv* slingshot, *Br* catapult

tirada *f* TIP print run; **de una tirada** in one go

tiradero *m Méx* dump

tirado *adj* P (*barato*) dirt-cheap F; **estar tirado** F (*fácil*) be a walkover F *o* a piece of cake F

tiradores *mpl Arg* suspenders, *Br* braces

tiranía *f* tyranny

tirano **1** *adj* tyrannical **2** *m*, -a *f* tyrant

tirante **1** *adj* taut; *fig* tense **2** *m* strap; **tirantes** suspenders, *Br* braces

tirantez *f fig* tension

tirar ⟨1a⟩ **1** *v/t* throw; *edificio, persona* knock down; (*volcar*) knock over; *basura* throw away; *dinero* waste, throw away F; TIP print; F *en examen* fail **2** *v/i* pull, attract; (*disparar*) shoot; **tirar a** tend toward; **tirar a conservador** have conservative tendencies; **tirar de algo** pull sth; **ir tirando** F get by, manage **3** *v/r* **tirarse** throw o.s.; F *tiempo* spend; **tirarse a alguien** P screw s.o. P

tirita *f* MED Bandaid®, *Br* plaster

tiritar ⟨1a⟩ *v/i* shiver

tiro *m* shot; **tiro al blanco** target practice; **al tiro** *CSur* F at once, right away; **de tiros largos** F dressed up; **ni a tiros** F for love nor money; **le salió el tiro por la culata** F it backfired on him; **le sentó como un tiro** F he needed it like a hole in the head F

tirón *m* tug, jerk; **de un tirón** at a stretch, without a break

tiroteo *m* shooting

tirria *f*: **tener tirria a alguien** F have it in for s.o. F

tisana *f* herbal tea

títere *m tb fig* puppet; **no dejar títere con cabeza** F spare no-one

titiritero *m*, -a *f* acrobat

titubear ⟨1a⟩ *v/i* waver, hesitate

titubeo *m* wavering, hesitation

titular *m de periódico* headline

titularse ⟨1a⟩ *v/r* be entitled

título *m* title; *universitario* degree; JUR title; COM bond; **tener muchos títulos** be highly qualified; **a título de** as; **títulos de crédito** credits

tiza *f* chalk

tiznar ⟨1a⟩ *v/t* blacken

tizón *m* ember

tlapalería *f Méx* hardware store

TLC *abr* (= **Tratado de Libre Comercio**) NAFTA (= North American Free Trade Agreement)

toalla *f* towel; **tirar** *or* **arrojar la toalla** *fig* throw in the towel

toallero *m* towel rail

tobillo *m* ankle

tobogán *m* slide

tocadiscos *m inv* record player

tocado *adj*: **estar tocado** *fig* F be crazy F

tocador *m* dressing-table

tocante: **en lo tocante a …** with regard to …

tocar ⟨1g⟩ **1** *v/t* touch; MÚS play **2** *v/i* L.Am. *a la puerta* knock (on the door); L.Am. (*sonar la campanita*) ring the doorbell; **te toca jugar** it's your turn **3** *v/r* **tocarse** touch

tocateja: **a tocateja** in hard cash

tocayo *m*, -a *f* namesake

tocino *m* bacon

tocólogo *m*, -a *f* obstetrician

todavía *adv* still, yet; **todavía no ha llegado** he still hasn't come, he hasn't come yet; **todavía no** not yet

todo **1** *adj* all; **todos los domingos** every Sunday; **-a la clase** the whole *o* the entire class **2** *adv* all; **estaba todo sucio** it was all dirty; **con todo** all the same; **del todo** entirely, absolutely **3** *pron* all, everything; *pl* everybody, everyone; **ir a por -as** go all out

todoterreno *m* AUTO off-road *o* all-terrain vehicle

toldo *m* awning; L.Am. Indian hut

tolerancia *f* tolerance

tolerar ⟨1a⟩ *v/t* tolerate

toma *f* FOT shot, take; **toma de conciencia** realization; **toma de corriente** outlet, socket; **toma de posesión** POL taking office

tomado *adj Méx* F (*borracho*) drunk

tomadura *f*: **tomadura de pelo** F joke

tomar ⟨1a⟩ **1** *v/t* take; *decisión* make, take; *bebida, comida* have; **tomarla**

con alguien F have it in for s.o. F; **tomar
el sol** sunbathe; **¡toma!** here (you are);
toma y daca give and take **2** v/i L.Am.
drink; **tomar por la derecha** turn right
3 v/r **tomarse** take; *comida, bebida* have;
se lo tomó a pecho he took it to heart

tomate m tomato

tomavistas m inv movie camera, cine
camera

tomillo m BOT thyme

tomo m volume, tome; **un timador de tomo y lomo** F an out-and-out conman

ton m: **sin ton ni son** for no particular
reason

tonada f song

tonalidad f tonality

tonel m barrel, cask

tonelada f *peso* ton

tónica f tonic

tónico m MED tonic

tonificar ⟨1g⟩ v/t tone up

tono m MÚS, MED, PINT tone

tontería f fig stupid o dumb F thing; **tonterías** pl nonsense sg

tonto 1 adj silly, foolish **2** m, -a f fool, idiot; **hacer el tonto** play the fool; **hacerse
el tonto** act dumb F

top m prenda top

topacio m MIN topaz

toparse ⟨1a⟩ v/r: **toparse con alguien**
bump into s.o., run into s.o.

tope m limit; *pieza* stop; Méx *en la calle*
speed bump; **pasarlo a tope** F have a
great time; **estar hasta los topes** F be
bursting at the seams F

tópico m cliché, platitude

topo m ZO mole

toque m: **toque de queda** MIL, fig curfew;
dar los últimos toques put the finishing
touches (**a** to)

toquilla f shawl

tórax m ANAT thorax

torbellino m whirlwind

torcer ⟨2b & 2h⟩ **1** v/t twist; *(doblar)*
bend; *(girar)* turn **2** v/i turn; **torcer a
la derecha** turn right **3** v/r **torcerse**
twist, bend; fig go wrong; **torcerse un
pie** sprain one's ankle

torcido adj twisted, bent

toreador m esp L.Am. bullfighter

torear ⟨1a⟩ **1** v/i fight bulls **2** v/t fight; fig
dodge, sidestep

toreo m bullfighting

torera f: **saltarse algo a la torera** F flout
sth, disregard sth

torero m bullfighter

tormenta f storm

tormento m torture

tornado m tornado, twister F

tornarse ⟨1a⟩ v/r *triste, difícil etc* become

torneo m competition, tournament

tornillo m screw; **con tuerca** bolt; **le falta
un tornillo** F he's got a screw loose F

torniquete m turnstile; MED tourniquet

torno m *de alfarería* wheel; **en torno a**
around, about

toro m bull; **ir a los toros** go to a bullfight;
coger al toro por los cuernos take the
bull by the horns

toronja f L.Am. grapefruit

torpe adj clumsy; *(tonto)* dense, dim

torpedo m MIL torpedo

torpeza f clumsiness; *(necedad)* stupidity

torre f tower; **torre de control** AVIA control
tower

torrencial adj torrential

torrente m fig avalanche, flood

torrezno m GASTR fried rasher of bacon

tórrido adj torrid

torrija f GASTR French toast

torta f cake; *plana* tart; F slap

tortazo m F crash; *(bofetada)* punch

tortícolis m MED crick in the neck

tortilla f omelette; L.Am. tortilla

tortillera f V dyke F, lesbian

tortuga f ZO tortoise; *marina* turtle; **a paso de tortuga** fig at a snail's pace

tortuoso adj fig tortuous

tortura f tb fig torture

torturar ⟨1a⟩ v/t torture

tos f cough

tosco adj fig rough, coarse

toser ⟨2a⟩ v/i cough

tostada f piece of toast

tostado adj *(moreno)* brown, tanned

tostador m toaster

tostar ⟨1m⟩ **1** v/t toast; *café* roast; **al sol**
tan **2** v/r **tostarse** tan, get brown

T

tostón *m* F bore

total **1** *adj* total, complete; **en total** altogether, in total **2** *m* whole; **un total de 50 personas** a total of 50 people

totalidad *f* totality

totalitario *adj* totalitarian

tóxico *adj* toxic

toxicómano *m*, -a *f* drug addict

toxina *f* toxin

tozudo *adj* obstinate

trabajador **1** *adj* hard-working **2** *m*, trabajadora *f* worker; **trabajador eventual** casual worker

trabajar ⟨1a⟩ **1** *v/i* work **2** *v/t* work; *tema, músculos* work on

trabajo *m* work; **trabajo en equipo** team work; **trabajo temporal** temporary work; **trabajo a tiempo parcial** part-time work

trabajoso *adj* hard, laborious

trabalenguas *m inv* tongue twister

trabar ⟨1a⟩ **1** *v/t conversación, amistad* strike up **2** *v/r* trabarse get tangled up

trabucarse ⟨1g⟩ *v/r* get all mixed up

tracción *f* TÉC traction; **tracción delantera/ trasera** front / rear-wheel drive

tractor *m* tractor

tradición *f* tradition

tradicional *adj* traditional

traducción *f* translation

traducir ⟨3o⟩ *v/t* translate

traductor *m*, traductora *f* translator

traer ⟨2p; *part* traído ⟩ **1** *v/t* bring; **traer consigo** involve, entail; **este periódico la trae en portada** this newspaper carries it on the front page **2** *v/r* traerse: **este asunto se las trae** F it's a very tricky matter

traficante *m* dealer

traficar ⟨1g⟩ *v/i* deal (**en** in)

tráfico *m* traffic; **tráfico de drogas** drug trafficking, drug dealing

tragaperras *f inv* slot machine

tragar ⟨1h⟩ **1** *v/t* swallow; **no lo trago** I can't stand him *o* bear him **2** *v/r* tragarse *tb fig* F swallow

tragedia *f* tragedy

trágico *adj* tragic

tragicomedia *f* tragicomedy

trago *m* mouthful; F *bebida* drink; **de un trago** in one gulp; **pasar un mal trago** *fig* have a hard time

tragón *adj* greedy

traición *f* treachery, betrayal

traicionar ⟨1a⟩ *v/t* betray

traidor **1** *adj* treacherous **2** *m*, traidora *f* traitor

traido *part* → **traer**

traigo *vb* → **traer**

tráiler *m* trailer

traje **1** *m* suit; **traje de baño** swimsuit **2** *vb* → **traer**

trajín *m* hustle and bustle

trajo *vb* → **traer**

trama *f* (*tema*) plot

tramar ⟨1a⟩ *v/t complot* hatch

tramitar ⟨1a⟩ *v/t documento*: *de persona* apply for; *de banco etc* process

trámite *m* formality

tramo *m* section, stretch; *de escaleras* flight

trampa *f* trap; (*truco*) scam F, trick; **hacer trampas** cheat

trampilla *f* trapdoor

trampolín *m* diving board

tramposo *m*, -a *f* cheat, crook

tranca *f*: **llevaba una tranca increíble** F he was wasted F *o* smashed F; **a trancas y barrancas** with great difficulty

trancazo *m* F dose of flu

trance *m* (*momento difícil*) tough time; **en trance** in a trance

tranquilidad *f* calm, quietness

tranquilizante *m* tranquilizer, *Br* tranquilliser

tranquilizar ⟨1f⟩ *v/t*: **tranquilizar a alguien** calm s.o. down

tranquillo *m*: **coger el tranquillo de algo** F get the hang of sth F

tranquilo *adj* calm, quiet; **¡tranquilo!** don't worry; **déjame tranquilo** leave me alone

transacción *f* COM deal, transaction;

transar ⟨1a⟩ *v/i* L.Am. (*ser vendido*) sell out

transatlántico **1** *adj* transatlantic **2** *m* liner

transbordador *m* ferry; **transbordador espacial** space shuttle

transbordo *m*: **hacer transbordo** TRANSP transfer, change

transcendental *adj fig* momentous

transcurrir ⟨3a⟩ *v/i de tiempo* pass, go by

transcurso *m* course; **de tiempo** passing

transeúnte *m/f* passer-by

transexual *m/f* transsexual

transferencia *f* COM transfer

transformación *f* transformation

transformador *m* EL transformer

transformar ⟨1a⟩ *v/t* transform

transfronterizo *adj* cross-border

tránsfuga *m/f* POL defector

transfusión *f*: **transfusión de sangre** blood transfusion

transgénico *adj* genetically modified

transgredir ⟨3a⟩ *v/t* infringe

transición *f* transition

transigir ⟨3c⟩ *v/i* compromise, make concessions

transistor *m* transistor

transitivo *adj* GRAM transitive

tránsito *m* COM transit; *L.Am. (circulación)* traffic

translúcido *adj* translucent

transmisión *f* transmission; **transmisión de datos** data transmission; **enfermedad de transmisión sexual** sexually transmitted disease

transmitir ⟨3a⟩ *v/t* spread; RAD, TV broadcast, transmit

transparencia *f para proyectar* transparency, slide

transparente *adj* transparent

transpiración *f* perspiration

transpirar ⟨1a⟩ *v/i* perspire

transplantar ⟨1a⟩ *v/t* transplant

transportar ⟨1a⟩ *v/t* transport

transporte *m* transport

tranvía *m* streetcar, *Br* tram

trapecio *m* trapeze

trapecista *m/f* trapeze artist(e)

trapiche *m CSur* sugar mill *o* press

trapicheo *m* F shady deal F

trapo *m viejo* rag; *para limpiar* cloth; **trapos** F clothes

trapujear ⟨1a⟩ *v/t & v/i C.Am.* smuggle

tráquea *f* ANAT windpipe, trachea

traqueteo *m* rattle, clatter

tras *prp en el espacio* behind; *en el tiempo* after

trasero **1** *adj* rear *atr*, back *atr* **2** *m* F butt F, *Br* rear end F

trasiego *m fig* bustle

trasladar ⟨1a⟩ **1** *v/t* move; *trabajador* transfer **2** *v/r* **trasladarse** move (*a* to); **se traslada** *Méx: en negocio* under new management

traslado *m* move; *de trabajador* transfer; **traslado al aeropuerto** airport transfer

trasluz *m*: **al trasluz** against the light

trasnochar ⟨1a⟩ *v/i (acostarse tarde)* go to bed late, stay up late; *(no dormir)* stay up all night; *L.Am.* stay overnight, spend the night

traspapelar ⟨1a⟩ *v/t* mislay

traspasar ⟨1a⟩ *v/t (atravesar)* go through; COM transfer

traspié *m* trip, stumble; **dar un traspié** *fig* slip up, blunder

trasplantar ⟨1a⟩ *v/t* AGR, MED transplant

trasplante *m* AGR, MED transplant

trastada *f* F prank, trick; **hacer trastadas** get up to mischief

traste *m*: **irse al traste** F fall through, go down the tubes F

trastero *m* lumber room

trasto *m desp* piece of junk; *persona* good-for-nothing

trastornar ⟨1a⟩ *v/t* upset; *(molestar)* inconvenience

trastorno *m* inconvenience; MED disorder

tratado *m esp* POL treaty; **Tratado de Libre Comercio** North American Free Trade Agreement

tratamiento *m* treatment; **tratamiento de datos / textos** INFOR data / word processing

tratar ⟨1a⟩ **1** *v/t* treat; *(manejar)* handle; *(dirigirse a)* address (**de** as); *gente* come into contact with; *tema* deal with **2** *v/i*: **tratar con alguien** deal with s.o.; **tratar de** *(intentar)* try to **3** *v/r* **tratarse**: **¿de qué se trata?** what's it about?

trato *m de prisionero, animal* treatment; COM deal; **malos tratos** *pl* ill treatment *sg*, abuse *sg*,; **tener trato con alguien** have dealings with s.o.; **¡trato hecho!** it's a deal

trauma *m* trauma

traumatizar ⟨1f⟩ *v/t* traumatize

traumatólogo *m*, **-a** *f* trauma specialist, traumatologist

través *m*: **a través de** through

travesaño *m* **en fútbol** crossbar

travesía *f* crossing

travesti *m* transvestite, drag artist

travesura *f* bit of mischief, prank

travieso *adj niño* mischievous

trayecto *m* journey; **10 dólares por trayecto** 10 dollars each way

trayectoria *f fig* course, path

trazar ⟨1f⟩ *v/t* (*dibujar*) draw; *ruta* plot, trace; (*describir*) outline, describe

trazo *m* line

trébol *m* BOT clover

trece *adj* thirteen; **mantenerse** *or* **seguir en sus trece** stand firm, not budge

trecho *m* stretch, distance

tregua *f* truce, cease-fire; **sin tregua** relentlessly

treinta *adj* thirty

tremebundo *adj* horrendous, frightening

tremendo *adj* awful, dreadful; *éxito, alegría* tremendous

tren *m* FERR train; **tren de alta velocidad** high speed train; **tren de lavado** car wash; **vivir a todo tren** F live in style; **estar como un tren** F be absolutely gorgeous

trenca *f* duffel coat

trenza *f* plait

trepa *m* F *socialmente* social climber; **en el trabajo** careerist

trepar ⟨1a⟩ *v/i* climb (*a* up), scale (*a* sth)

trepidante *adj fig* frenetic

tres *adj* three

trescientos *adj* three hundred

tresillo *m* living-room suite, *Br* three-piece suite

treta *f* trick, ploy

triángulo *m* triangle

tribu *f* tribe

tribuna *f* grandstand

tribunal *m* court; **Tribunal Supremo** Supreme Court

tributo *m* tribute; (*impuesto*) tax

triciclo *m* tricycle

tricotar ⟨1a⟩ *v/i* knit

trifulca *f* F brawl, punch-up F

trigo *m* wheat

trillado *adj fig* hackneyed, clichéd

trillar ⟨1a⟩ *v/t* AGR thresh

trillizos *mpl* triplets

trillón *m* quintillion, *Br* trillion

trimestral *adj* quarterly

trimestre *m* quarter; *escolar* semester, *Br* term

trinar ⟨1a⟩ *v/i* trill, warble; **está que trina** *fig* F he's fuming F, he's hopping mad F

trincar ⟨1g⟩ *v/t* F *criminal* catch

trinchera *f* MIL trench

trineo *m* sled, sleigh

trino *m* trill, warble

trío *m* trio

tripa *f* F belly F, gut F; **hacer de tripas corazón** *fig* pluck up courage

triple *m*: **el triple que el año pasado** three times as much as last year

triplicar ⟨1g⟩ *v/t* triple, treble

trípode *m* tripod

tripulación *f* AVIA, MAR crew

tripular ⟨1a⟩ *v/t* man

triquiñuela *f* F dodge F, trick

tris *m*: **estuvo en un tris de caerse** F she came within an inch of falling

triste *adj* sad

tristeza *f* sadness

triturar ⟨1a⟩ *v/t* grind

triunfador 1 *adj* winning **2** *m*, **triunfadora** *f* winner, victor

triunfar ⟨1a⟩ *v/i* triumph, win

triunfo *m* triumph, victory; *en naipes* trump

trivial *adj* trivial

triza *f*: **hacer trizas** F *jarrón* smash to bits; *papel, vestido* tear to shreds

trocear ⟨1a⟩ *v/t* cut into pieces, cut up

troche: **había errores a troche y moche** F there were mistakes galore F

trofeo *m* trophy

troglodita *m/f* cave-dweller

troj(e) *f Arg* granary

trola *f* F fib

trolebús *m* trolley bus

tromba *f*: **tromba de agua** downpour

trombón *m* MÚS trombone

trombosis *f* MED thrombosis

trompa 1 *adj* F wasted F **2** *f* MÚS horn; zo trunk

trompazo *m* L.Am. F whack F; **darse un trompazo con algo** F bang into sth

trompearse ⟨1a⟩ L.Am. F fight, lay into each other F

trompeta *f* MÚS trumpet

trompetista *m/f* MÚS trumpeter

trompicón *m*: **a trompicones** in fits and starts

trompo *m* spinning top

trona *f* high chair

tronar ⟨1m⟩ *v/i* thunder

troncha *f* S. Am. slice, piece

tronchante *adj* F sidesplitting

troncharse ⟨1a⟩ *v/r*: **troncharse de risa** F split one's sides laughing

tronco *m* trunk; *cortado* log; **dormir como un tronco** sleep like a log

trono *m* throne

tropa *f* MIL (**soldado raso**) ordinary soldier; **tropas** troops

tropel *m*: **en tropel** in a mad rush; **salir en tropel** pour out

tropezar ⟨1f & 1k⟩ *v/i* trip, stumble

tropical *adj* tropical

trópico *m* tropic

tropiezo *m* *fig* setback

tropilla *f* L.Am. herd

trotar ⟨1a⟩ *v/i* *fig* gad around

trote *m* trot; **ya no estoy para esos trotes** I'm not up to it any more

trozo *m* piece

trucha *f* zo trout

truco *m* trick; **coger el truco a algo** F get the hang of sth F

truculento *adj* horrifying

trueno *m* thunder

trueque *m* barter

trufa *f* BOT truffle

truhán *m* rogue

Tte. *abr* (= **Teniente**) Lieut. (= Lieutenant)

tú *pron sg* you; **tratar de tú** address as 'tu'

tu, tus *adj pos* your

tuberculosis *f* MED TB, tuberculosis

tubería *f* pipe

tubo *m* tube; **tubo de escape** AUTO exhaust (pipe); **por un tubo** F an enormous amount

tucán *m* zo toucan

tuerca *f* TÉC nut

tulipán *m* BOT tulip

tullido *m* cripple

tumba *f* tomb, grave

tumbar ⟨1a⟩ **1** *v/t* knock down **2** *v/r* tumbarse lie down

tumbo *m* tumble; **ir dando tumbos** stagger along

tumbona *f* (sun) lounger

tumor *m* MED tumo(u)r

tumulto *m* uproar

tuna *f* Méx *fruta* prickly pear

tunda *f* F beating

tundra *f* GEOG tundra

túnel *m* tunnel; **túnel de lavado** car wash

Túnez Tunisia

túnica *f* tunic

tuntún: **decir algo al buen tuntún** say sth off the top of one's head

tupé *m* F quiff

tupido *adj* *pelo* thick; *vegetación* dense, thick

turbante *m* turban

turbar ⟨1a⟩ **1** *v/t* (*emocionar*) upset; *paz, tranquilidad* disturb; (*avergonzar*) embarrass **2** *v/r* turbarse (*emocionarse*) get upset; *de paz, tranquilidad* be disturbed; (*avergonzarse*) get embarrassed

turbina *f* turbine

turbio *adj* cloudy, murky; *fig* shady, murky

turbo *m* turbo

turbulencia *f* turbulence

turbulento *adj* turbulent

turco 1 *adj* Turkish **2** *m*, -a *f* Turk

turismo *m* tourism; *automóvil* sedan, Br saloon (car); **turismo rural** tourism in rural areas

turista *m/f* tourist

turístico *adj* tourist *atr*

turnarse ⟨1a⟩ *v/r* take it in turns

turno *m* turn; **turno de noche** night shift; **por turnos** in turns

T

turquesa *f piedra preciosa* turquoise; *azul turquesa* turquoise

Turquía Turkey

turrón *m* nougat

turulato *adj* F stunned, dazed

tute *m*: *darse un tute* F work like a dog F, slave F

tutear ⟨1a⟩ *v/t* address as 'tu'

tutiplén: *había comida a tutiplén* F there was loads *o* masses to eat F

tutor *m*, **tutora** *f* EDU tutor

tuve *vb* → **tener**

tuvo *vb* → **tener**

tuyo, tuya *pron pos* yours; *los tuyos* your folks, your family

TV *abr* (= *televisión*) TV (= television)

U

u *conj* (*instead of* **o** *before words starting with* o) or

ubicación *f* L.Am. location; (*localización*) finding

ubicado *adj* located, situated

ubicar ⟨1g⟩ **1** *v/t* L.Am. place, put; (*localizar*) locate **2** *v/r* **ubicarse** be located, be situated; *en un empleo* get a job

ubicuo *adj* ubiquitous

ubre *f* udder

UCI *abr* (= *Unidad de Cuidados Intensivos*) ICU (= Intensive Care Unit)

Ud. *pron* → **usted**

Uds. *pron* → **usted**

UE *abr* (= *Unión Europea*) EU (= European Union)

ufano *adj* conceited; (*contento*) proud

ujier *m* usher

úlcera *f* MED ulcer

ulcerarse ⟨1a⟩ *v/r* MED become ulcerous, ulcerate

ulterior *adj* subsequent

últimamente *adv* lately

ultimar ⟨1a⟩ *v/t* finalize; L.Am. (*rematar*) finish off

ultimátum *m* ultimatum

último *adj* last; (*más reciente*) latest; *piso* top *atr*; *-as noticias* latest news *sg*; *por último* finally; *está en las -as* he doesn't have long (to live)

ultra *m* POL right-wing extremist

ultraderecha *f* POL extreme right

ultrajante *adj* outrageous; *palabras* insulting

ultrajar ⟨1a⟩ *v/t* outrage; (*insultar*) insult

ultraje *m* outrage; (*insulto*) insult

ultraligero *m* AVIA microlight

ultramarinos *mpl* groceries; *tienda de ultramarinos* grocery store, *Br* grocer's (shop)

ultramoderno *adj* ultramodern

ultranza: *a ultranza* for all one is worth; *un defensor a ultranza de algo* an ardent defender of sth

ultrasónico *adj* ultrasonic

ultrasonido *m* ultrasound

ultratumba *f*: *la vida de ultratumba* life beyond the grave

ultravioleta *adj* ultraviolet

ulular ⟨1a⟩ *v/i de viento* howl; *de búho* hoot

umbilical *adj* ANAT umbilical

umbral *m fig* threshold; *en el umbral de fig* on the threshold of

umbrío *adj* shady

un, una *art* a; *antes de vocal y h muda* an; *unos coches / pájaros* some cars / birds

unánime *adj* unanimous

unanimidad *f* unanimity; *por unanimidad* unanimously

unción *f fig* unction

undécimo *adj* eleventh

ungir ⟨3c⟩ *v/t* REL anoint

ungüento *m* ointment

únicamente *adv* only

único *adj* only; (*sin par*) unique; **es único** it's unique; **hijo único** only child; **lo único que ...** the only thing that ...

unicornio *m* MYTH unicorn

unidad *f* MIL, MAT unit; (*cohesión*) unity; **unidad de cuidados intensivos, unidad de vigilancia intensiva** MED intensive care unit; **unidad de disco** INFOR disk drive; **unidad monetaria** monetary unity

unido *adj* united; **una familia -a** a close-knit family

unificación *f* unification

unificar ⟨1g⟩ *v/t* unify

uniformar ⟨1a⟩ *v/t fig* standardize

uniforme **1** *adj* uniform; *superficie* even **2** *m* uniform

unilateral *adj* unilateral

unión *f* union; **Unión Europea** European Union

unir ⟨3a⟩ **1** *v/t* join; *personas* unite; *características* combine (**con** with); *ciudades* link **2** *v/r* unirse join together; **unirse a** join

unisex *adj* unisex

unísono *adj*: **al unísono** in unison

unitario *adj* unitary; **precio unitario** unit price

universal *adj* universal

universidad *f* university; **universidad a distancia** university correspondence school, *Br* Open University

universitario **1** *adj* university *atr* **2** *m*, -a *f* (*estudiante*) university student

universo *m* universe

uno **1** *pron* one; **es la -a** it's one o'clock; **me lo dijo uno** someone *o* somebody told me; **uno a uno, uno por uno, de uno en uno** one by one; **no dar ni -a** F not get anything right; **unos cuantos** a few, some; **unos niños** some children; **-as mil pesetas** about a thousand pesetas **2** *m* one; **el uno de enero** January first, the first of January

untar ⟨1a⟩ *v/t* spread; **untar a alguien** F (*sobornar*) grease s.o.'s palm

untuoso *adj fig* oily

uña *f* ANAT nail; ZO claw; **defenderse con**

uñas y dientes *fig* F fight tooth and nail; **ser uña y carne** *personas* be extremely close

uperisado *adj*: **leche -a** UHT milk

uranio *m* uranium

urbanidad *f* civility

urbanismo *m* city planning, *Br* town planning

urbanización *f* (*urban*) development; (*colonia*) housing development, *Br* housing estate

urbanizar ⟨1f⟩ *v/t terreno* develop

urbano *adj* urban; (*cortés*) courteous; **guardia urbano** local police officer

urbe *f* city

urdir ⟨3a⟩ *v/t complot* hatch

urea *f* urea

uretra *f* ANAT urethra

urgencia *f* urgency; (*prisa*) haste; MED emergency; **urgencias** *pl* emergency room *sg*, *Br* casualty *sg*

urgente *adj* urgent

urgir ⟨3c⟩ *v/i* be urgent

urinario *m* urinal

urna *f* urn; **urna electoral** ballot box

urólogo *m* MED urologist

urraca *f* ZO magpie

URSS *abr* (= **Unión de las Repúblicas Socialistas Soviéticas**) USSR (= Union of Soviet Socialist Republics)

urticaria *f* MED hives

Uruguay Uruguay

uruguayo **1** *adj* Uruguayan **2** *m*, -a *f* Uruguayan

usado *adj* (*gastado*) worn; (*de segunda mano*) second hand

usar ⟨1a⟩ **1** *v/t* use; *ropa, gafas* wear **2** *v/i*: **listo para usar** ready to use **3** *v/r* usarse be used

uso *m* use; (*costumbre*) custom; **obligatorio el uso de casco** helmets must be worn; **en buen uso** still in use

usted *pron* you; **tratar de usted** address as 'usted'; **ustedes** *pl* you; **de usted / ustedes** your; **es de usted / ustedes** it's yours

usual *adj* common, usual

usuario *m*, -a *f* INFOR user

usufructo *m* JUR usufruct

usura f usury
usurero m, -a f usurer
usurpar ⟨1a⟩ v/t usurp
utensilio m tool; de cocina utensil; **utensilios** pl equipment sg; **utensilios** pl **de pesca** fishing tackle sg
útero m ANAT uterus
útil **1** adj useful **2** m tool; **útiles** pl **de pesca** fishing tackle sg
utilidad f usefulness
utilitario **1** adj functional, utilitarian **2** m AUTO compact

utilitarismo m utilitarianism
utilización f use
utilizar ⟨1f⟩ v/t use
utopía f utopia
utópico adj utopian
uva f BOT grape; **estar de mala uva** F be in a foul mood; **tener mala uva** F be a nasty piece of work F
UVI abr (= Unidad de Vigilancia Intensiva) ICU (= Intensive Care Unit)
úvula f ANAT uvula

V

va vb → **ir**
vaca f cow; GASTR beef; **vaca lechera** dairy cow; **vaca marina** manatee, sea cow; **mal** or **enfermedad de las vacas locas** F mad cow disease F
vacaciones fpl vacation sg, Br holiday sg; **de vacaciones** on vacation, Br on holiday
vacante **1** adj vacant, empty **2** f job opening, position, Br vacancy; **cubrir una vacante** fill a position
vaciar ⟨1b⟩ **1** v/t empty **2** v/r vaciarse empty
vacilación f hesitation
vacilante adj unsteady; (dubitativo) hesitant
vacilar ⟨1a⟩ **1** v/i hesitate; de fe, resolución waver; de objeto wobble, rock; de persona stagger; Méx F (divertirse) have fun **2** v/t F make fun of
vacío **1** adj empty **2** m FÍS vacuum; fig espacio void; **vacío de poder** power vacuum; **vacío legal** loophole; **dejar un vacío** fig leave a gap; **envasado al vacío** vacuum packed; **hacer el vacío a alguien** fig ostracize s.o.
vacuna f vaccine
vacunación f vaccination

vacunar ⟨1a⟩ v/t vaccinate
vacuno adj bovine; **ganado vacuno** cattle pl
vacuo adj fig vacuous
vadear ⟨1a⟩ v/t río ford; dificultad get around
vado m ford; en la calle entrance ramp; **vado permanente** letrero keep clear
vagabundear ⟨1a⟩ v/i drift around
vagabundo **1** adj perro stray **2** m, -a f hobo, Br tramp
vagancia f laziness, idleness
vagar ⟨1h⟩ v/i wander
vagido m de bebe cry
vagina f ANAT vagina
vago adj (holgazán) lazy; (indefinido) vague; **hacer el vago** laze around
vagón m de carga wagon; de pasajeros car, Br coach; **vagón restaurante** dining car, Br tb restaurant car
vaguear ⟨1a⟩ v/i laze around
vaguedad f vagueness
vahído m MED dizzy spell
vaho m (aliento) breath; (vapor) steam
vaina f BOT pod; S. Am. F drag F
vainilla f vanilla
vais vb → **ir**
vaivén m to-and-fro, swinging; **vaivenes**

fig ups and downs

vajilla *f* dishes *pl*; *juego* dinner service, set of dishes

vale *m* voucher, coupon

valedero *adj* valid

valentía *f* bravery

valer ⟨2q⟩ **1** *v/t* be worth; (*costar*) cost **2** *v/i de billete, carné* be valid; (*estar permitido*) be allowed; (*tener valor*) be worth; (*servir*) be of use; **no valer para algo** be no good at sth; **vale más caro** it's more expensive; **sus consejos me valieron de mucho** his advice was very useful to me; **más vale ...** it's better to ...; **más te vale ...** you'd better ...; **¡vale!** okay, sure **3** *v/r* **valerse** manage (by o.s.); **valerse de** make use of

valeriana *f* BOT valerian

valeroso *adj* valiant

valga *vb* → **valer**

valgo *vb* → **valer**

valía *f* worth

validar ⟨1a⟩ *v/t* validate

validez *f* validity

válido *adj* valid

valiente *adj* brave; *irón* fine

valija *f* (*maleta*) bag, suitcase; *Br tb* case; **valija diplomática** diplomatic bag

valioso *adj* valuable

valla *f* fence; DEP, *fig* hurdle; **valla publicitaria** billboard, *Br* hoarding; **carrera de vallas** DEP hurdles

vallado *m* fence

vallar ⟨1a⟩ *v/t* fence in

valle *m* valley

valor *m* value; (*valentía*) courage; **valor añadido**, *L.Am.* **valor agregado** value added; **valor nominal** *de acción* nominal value; *de título* par value; **objetos de valor** valuables; **valores** COM securities

valoración *f* (*tasación*) valuation

valorar ⟨1a⟩ *v/t* value (**en** at); (*estimar*) appreciate, value

vals *m* waltz

valuar ⟨1e⟩ *v/t* value

válvula *f* ANAT, EL valve; **válvula de escape** *fig* safety valve

vampiro *m fig* vampire

van *vb* → **ir**

vanagloriarse ⟨1b⟩ *v/r* boast (**de** about), brag (**de** about)

vandálico *adj* destructive

vandalismo *m* vandalism

vándalo *m*, **-a** *f* vandal

vanguardia *f* MIL vanguard; **de vanguardia** *fig* avant-garde

vanidad *f* vanity

vanidoso *adj* conceited, vain

vano *adj* futile, vain; **en vano** in vain

vapor *m* vapo(u)r; *de agua* steam; **cocinar al vapor** steam

vaporizar ⟨1f⟩ **1** *v/t* vaporize **2** *v/r* **vaporizarse** vaporize

vaporoso *adj* vaporous; *fig: vestido* gauzy, filmy

vapulear ⟨1a⟩ *v/t* beat up

vapuleo *m* beating

vaquería *f* dairy

vaquero 1 *adj tela* denim; **pantalones vaqueros** jeans **2** *m* cowboy, cowhand

vaquilla *f* heifer

vara *f* stick; TÉC rod; (*bastón de mando*) staff

varapalo *m* F (*contratiempo*) hitch F, setback

variable *adj* variable; *tiempo* changeable

variación *f* variation

variado *adj* varied

variar ⟨1c⟩ **1** *v/t* vary; (*cambiar*) change **2** *v/i* vary; (*cambiar*) change; **para variar** for a change

varice *f* MED varicose vein

varicela *f* MED chickenpox

variedad *f* variety; **variedades** *pl* vaudeville *sg*, *Br* variety *sg*

variopinto *adj* varied, diverse

varios *adj* several

varita *f:* **varita mágica** magic wand

variz *f* varicose vein

varón *m* man, male

varonil *adj* manly, virile

vas *vb* → **ir**

vasallo *m* vassal

vasco 1 *adj* Basque; **País Vasco** Basque country **2** *m idioma* Basque **3** *m*, **-a** *f* Basque

Vascongadas *fpl* Basque country *sg*

vascuence *m* Basque

vascular *adj* ANAT vascular
vasectomía *f* MED vasectomy
vaselina *f* Vaseline®
vasija *f* container, vessel
vaso *m* glass; ANAT vessel
vasto *adj* vast
Vaticano *m* Vatican
vaticinar ⟨1a⟩ *v/t* predict, forecast
vaticinio *m* prediction, forecast
vatio *m* EL watt
vaya 1 *vb* → *ir* **2** *int* well!
V.° B.° *abr* (= *visto bueno*) approved, OK
Vd. *pron* → *usted*
Vds. *pron* → *usted*
ve *vb* → *ir, ver*
vea *vb* → *ver*
vecindad *f Méx* poor area
vecindario *m* neighbo(u)rhood
vecino 1 *adj* neighbo(u)ring **2** *m*, -a *f* neighbo(u)r
vedado *m*: *vedado de caza* game reserve
vedar ⟨1a⟩ *v/t* ban, prohibit
vedette *f* star
vegetación *f* vegetation
vegetal 1 *adj* vegetable, plant *atr* **2** *m* vegetable
vegetar ⟨1a⟩ *v/i fig* vegetate
vegetariano 1 *adj* vegetarian **2** *m*, -a *f* vegetarian
vehemente *adj* vehement
vehículo *m tb fig* vehicle; MED carrier
veinte *m/adj* twenty
veintena *f* twenty; *aproximadamente* about twenty
vejación *f* humiliation
vejar ⟨1a⟩ *v/t* humiliate
vejestorio *m* F old fossil F, old relic F
vejez *f* old age
vejiga *f* ANAT bladder
vela *f para alumbrar* candle; DEP sailing; *de barco* sail; *a toda vela* F flat out F, all out F; *estar a dos velas* F be broke F; *pasar la noche en vela* stay up all night
velada *f* evening
velador *m L.Am. lámpara* bedlamp, *Br* bedside light; *Chi mueble* nightstand, *Br* bedside table
velar ⟨1a⟩ *v/i*: *velar por algo* look after sth

velatorio *m* wake
velcro® *m* Velcro
veleidad *f* fickleness
velero *m* MAR sailing ship
veleta 1 *f* weathervane **2** *m/f fig* weathercock
vello *m* (body) hair
velo *m* veil
velocidad *f* speed; *(marcha)* gear
velódromo *m* velodrome
veloz *adj* fast, speedy
ven *vb* → *venir*
vena *f* ANAT vein; *le dio la vena y lo hizo* F she just upped and did it F; *estar en vena* F be on form
venado *m* ZO deer
vencedor 1 *adj* winning **2** *m*, vencedora *f* winner
vencejo *m* ZO swift
vencer ⟨2b⟩ **1** *v/t* defeat; *fig (superar)* overcome **2** *v/i* win; COM *de plazo etc* expire
vencido *adj*: *darse por vencido* admit defeat, give in; *a la tercera va la -a* third time lucky
vencimiento *m* expiration, *Br* expiry; *de bono* maturity
venda *f* bandage
vendaje *m* MED dressing
vendar ⟨1a⟩ *v/t* MED bandage, dress; *vendar los ojos a alguien* blindfold s.o.
vendaval *m* gale
vendedor *m*, **vendedora** *f* seller
vender ⟨2a⟩ **1** *v/t* sell; *fig (traicionar)* betray **2** *v/r* **venderse** sell o.s.; *venderse al enemigo* sell out to the enemy
vendimia *f* grape harvest
vendimiar ⟨1b⟩ *v/t uvas* harvest, pick
vendré *vb* → *venir*
veneno *m* poison
venenoso *adj* poisonous
venerable *adj* venerable
venerar ⟨1a⟩ *v/t* venerate, worship
venéreo *adj* MED venereal
venezolano 1 *adj* Venezuelan **2** *m*, -a *f* Venezuelan
Venezuela Venezuela
venga *vb* → *venir*

venganza f vengeance, revenge

vengar ⟨1h⟩ **1** v/t avenge **2** v/r **vengarse** take revenge (**de** on; **por** for)

vengativo adj vengeful

vengo vb → **venir**

venir ⟨3s⟩ **1** v/i come; **venir de España** come from Spain; **venir bien** be convenient; **venir mal** be inconvenient; **le vino una idea** an idea occurred to him; **viene a ser lo mismo** it comes down to the same thing; **el año que viene** next year; **¡venga!** come on; **¿a qué viene eso?** why do you say that? **2** v/r **venirse**: **venirse abajo** collapse; fig: de persona fall apart, go to pieces

venta f sale; **venta por correo** or **por catálogo** mail order; **venta al detalle** or **al por menor** retail; **en venta** for sale

ventaja f advantage; DEP en carrera, partido lead; **ventaja fiscal** tax advantage

ventajoso adj advantageous

ventana f window; **ventana de la nariz** nostril

ventanilla f AVIA, AUTO, FERR window; MAR porthole

ventilación f ventilation

ventilador m fan

ventilar ⟨1a⟩ v/t air; fig: problema talk over; opiniones air

ventisca f blizzard

ventosa f ZO sucker

ventosidad f wind, flatulence

ventrílocuo m ventriloquist

veo vb → **ver**

ver ⟨2v; part **visto**⟩ **1** v/t see; televisión watch; JUR pleito hear; L.Am. (mirar) look at; **está por ver** it remains to be seen; **no puede verla** fig he can't stand the sight of her; **no tiene nada que ver con** it doesn't have anything to do with; **¡a ver!** let's see; **¡hay que ver!** would you believe it!; **ya veremos** we'll see **2** v/i L.Am. (mirar) look; **ve aquí dentro** L.Am. look in here **3** v/r verse see o.s.; (encontrarse) see one another; **¡habráse visto!** would you believe it!; **¡se las verá conmigo!** F he'll have me to deal with!

veranear ⟨1a⟩ v/i spend the summer vaca-

tion o Br holidays

veraniego adj summer atr

verano m summer

veras f: **de veras** really, truly

verbal adj GRAM verbal

verbena f (fiesta) party

verbo m GRAM verb

verborrea f desp verbosity

verdad f truth; **a decir verdad** to tell the truth; **de verdad** real, proper; **no te gusta, ¿verdad?** you don't like it, do you?; **vas a venir, ¿verdad?** you're coming, aren't you?; **es verdad** it's true, it's the truth

verdadero adj true; (cierto) real

verde 1 adj green; fruta unripe; F chiste blue, dirty; **viejo verde** dirty old man; **poner verde a alguien** F criticize s.o. **2** m green; **los verdes** POL the Greens

verdoso adj greenish

verdugo m executioner

verdulería f fruit and vegetable store, Br greengrocer's

verdura f: verdura(s) (hortalizas) greens pl, (green) vegetables pl

vereda f S. Am. sidewalk, Br pavement; **meter alguien en vereda** fig put s.o. back on the straight and narrow, bring s.o. into line

veredicto m JUR, fig verdict

verga f rod

vergel m orchard

vergonzoso adj disgraceful, shameful; (tímido) shy

vergüenza f shame; (escándalo) disgrace; **me da vergüenza** I'm embarrassed; **es una vergüenza** it's a disgrace; **no sé cómo no se te cae la cara de vergüenza** you should be ashamed (of yourself)

vericuetos mpl fig twists and turns

verídico adj true

verificar ⟨1g⟩ v/t verify

verja f railing; (puerta) iron gate

vermú, vermut m vermouth

verosímil adj realistic; (creíble) plausible

verruga f wart

versado adj well-versed (**en** in)

versar ⟨1a⟩ v/i: **versar sobre** deal with, be about

versátil *adj* fickle; *artista* versatile

versículo *m* verse

versión *f* version; **en versión original** *película* original language version

verso *m* verse

vértebra *f* ANAT vertebra

vertedero *m* dump, tip

verter ⟨2g⟩ *v/t* dump; (*derramar*) spill; *fig: opinión* voice

vertical *adj* vertical

vertido *m* dumping; **vertidos** *pl* waste *sg*

vertiente *f* L.Am. (*cuesta*) slope; (*lado*) side

vertiginoso *adj* dizzy; (*rápido*) frantic

vértigo *m* MED vertigo; **darle a alguien vértigo** make s.o. dizzy

vesícula *f* blister; **vesícula biliar** ANAT gall-bladder

vespa® *f* motorscooter

vestíbulo *m de casa* hall; *de edifico público* lobby

vestido *m* dress; *L.Am. de hombre* suit

vestigio *m* vestige, trace

vestir ⟨3l⟩ **1** *v/t* dress; (*llevar puesto*) wear **2** *v/i* dress; **vestir de negro** wear black, dress in black; **vestir de uniforme** wear a uniform **3** *v/r* **vestirse** get dressed; (*disfrazarse*) dress up; **vestirse de algo** wear sth

vestuario *m* DEP locker room; TEA wardrobe

veta *f* MIN vein

vetar ⟨1a⟩ *v/t* POL veto

veterano **1** *adj* veteran; (*experimentado*) experienced **2** *m*, **-a** *f* veteran

veterinario **1** *adj* veterinary **2** *m*, **-a** *f* veterinarian, vet

veto *m* veto

vetusto *adj* ancient

vez *f* time; **a la vez** at the same time; **a su vez** for his / her part; **cada vez que** every time that; **de vez en cuando** from time to time; **en vez de** instead of; **érase una vez** once upon a time, there was; **otra vez** again; **tal vez** perhaps, maybe; **una vez** once; **a veces** sometimes; **muchas veces** (*con frecuencia*) often; **hacer las veces de** *de objeto* serve as; *de persona* act as

vi *vb* → **ver**

vía **1** *f* FERR track; **vía estrecha** FERR narrow gauge; **darle vía libre a alguien** give s.o. a free hand; **por vía aérea** by air; **en vías de** *fig* in the process of **2** *prp* via

viable *adj plan, solución* viable, feasible

viaducto *m* viaduct

viajante *m/f* sales rep

viajar ⟨1a⟩ *v/i* travel

viaje *m* trip, journey; **viaje organizado** package tour; **viaje de ida** outward journey; **viaje de ida y vuelta** round trip; **viaje de novios** honeymoon; **viaje de vuelta** return journey

viajero *m*, **-a** *f* travel(l)er

viario *adj* road *atr*; **educación -a** instruction in road safety

víbora *f tb fig* viper

vibración *f* vibration

vibrante *adj fig* exciting

vibrar ⟨1a⟩ *v/t* vibrate

vicaría *f* pastor's house, vicarage; **pasar por la vicaría** F get married in church

vicecónsul *m* vice-consul

vicepresidente *m*, **-a** *f* POL vice-president; COM vice-president, *Br* deputy chairman

vicerrector *m* vice-rector

viceversa *adv*: **y viceversa** and vice versa

viciado *adj aire* stuffy

viciarse ⟨1b⟩ *v/r* fall into bad habits

vicio *m* vice; **pasarlo de vicio** F have a great time F

vicioso *adj* vicious; (*corrompido*) depraved

vicisitudes *fpl* ups and downs

víctima *f* victim

victimar ⟨1a⟩ *v/t L.Am.* kill

victoria *f* victory; **cantar victoria** claim victory

victorioso *adj* victorious

vicuña *f* ZO vicuna

vid *f* vine

vida *f* life; *esp* TÉC life span; **de por vida** for life; **en mi vida** never (in my life); **ganarse la vida** earn a living; **hacer la vida imposible a alguien** make s.o.'s life impossible; **vida mía** my love

vidente *m/f* seer, clairvoyant

vídeo *m* video

videocámara f video camera
videocas(s)et(t)e m video cassette
videoclip m pop video
videoconferencia f video conference
videojuego m video game
videotex(to) m videotext
vidriera f *L.Am.* shop window
vidrio m *L.Am.* glass; (*ventana*) window
vieira f zo scallop
vieja f old woman
viejo 1 adj old **2** m old man; *mis viejos* F my folks F
viendo vb → *ver*
viene vb → *venir*
viento m wind; *viento en popa* fig F splendidly; *contra viento y marea* fig come what may; *hacer viento* be windy; *proclamar a los cuatro vientos* fig shout from the rooftops
vientre m belly
viernes m inv Friday; *Viernes Santo* Good Friday
Vietnam Vietnam
vietnamita adj & m/f Vietnamese
viga f beam, girder
vigente adj *legislación* in force
vigésimo adj twentieth
vigilante 1 adj watchful, vigilant **2** m *L.Am.* policeman; *vigilante nocturno* night watchman; *vigilante jurado* security guard
vigilar ⟨1a⟩ **1** v/i keep watch **2** v/t watch; *a un preso* guard
vigor m vigo(u)r; *en vigor* in force
vigoroso adj vigorous
vil adj vile, despicable
vilipendiar ⟨1b⟩ v/t insult, vilify *fml*; (*despreciar*) revile
villa f town
villancico m Christmas carol
villano 1 adj villainous **2** m, -a f villain
vilo: *en vilo* in the air; fig in suspense, on tenterhooks; *levantar en vilo* lift off the ground; *tener a alguien en vilo* fig keep s.o. in suspense *o* on tenterhooks
vinagre m vinegar
vinagrera f vinegar bottle; *S. Am.* (*indigestión*) indigestion; *vinagreras* pl cruet sg

vinagreta f vinaigrette
vincha f *S. Am.* hairband
vinculante adj binding
vincular ⟨1a⟩ v/t link (*a* to); (*comprometer*) bind
vínculo m link; fig (*relación*) tie, bond
vindicar ⟨1g⟩ v/t vindicate
vine vb → *venir*
vinícola adj *región, país* wine-growing atr; *industria* wine-making atr
viniendo vb → *venir*
vinicultura f wine-growing
vino 1 m wine; *vino blanco* white wine; *vino de mesa* table wine; *vino tinto* red wine **2** vb → *venir*
viña f vineyard
viñatero m, -a f *S. Am.* wine grower
viñedo m vineyard
viñeta f tip vignette
vio vb → *ver*
viola f mús viola
violación f rape; *de derechos* violation
violador m, **violadora** f rapist
violar ⟨1a⟩ v/t rape
violencia f violence
violentar ⟨1a⟩ v/t *puerta* force; (*incomodar*) embarrass
violento adj violent; (*embarazoso*) embarrassing; *persona* embarrassed
violeta 1 f bot violet **2** m/adj violet
violín m violin
violinista m/f violinist
violonc(h)elo m cello
VIP m VIP
viperino adj malicious; *lengua -a* sharp tongue
viral adj viral
virar ⟨1a⟩ v/t mar, avia turn
virgen 1 adj virgin; *cinta* blank; *lana virgen* pure new wool **2** f virgin
virginidad f virginity
Virgo m/f inv astr Virgo
virguería f: *hace virguerías* P he's a whizz P
vírico adj viral
viril adj virile, manly
virtual adj virtual
virtud f virtue; *en virtud de* by virtue of
virtuoso 1 adj virtuous **2** m, -a f virtuoso

viruela f MED smallpox

virulento adj MED, fig virulent

virus m inv MED virus; ***virus informático*** computer virus

viruta f shaving

visa f L.Am. visa

visado m visa

vísceras fpl guts, entrails

visceral adj fig gut atr, visceral

viscoso adj viscous

visera f de gorra peak; de casco visor

visibilidad f visibility

visible adj visible; fig evident, obvious

visillo m sheer, Br net curtain

visión f vision, sight; fig vision; (opinión) view; ***tener visión de futuro*** be forward looking

visita f visit; ***visita a domicilio*** house call; ***visita guiada*** guided tour; ***hacer una visita a alguien*** visit s.o.

visitante 1 adj visiting; DEP away **2** m/f visitor

visitar ⟨1a⟩ v/t visit

vislumbrar ⟨1a⟩ v/t glimpse

visos mpl: ***tener visos de*** show signs of

visón m ZO mink

víspera f eve; ***en vísperas de*** on the eve of

vista f (eye)sight; JUR hearing; ***vista cansada*** MED tired eyes; ***a la vista*** COM at sight, on demand; ***a primera vista*** at first sight; ***con vistas a*** with a view to; ***en vista de*** in view of; ***hasta la vista*** bye!, see you!; ***hacer la vista gorda*** fig F turn a blind eye; ***tener vista para algo*** fig have a good eye for sth; ***volver la vista atrás*** tb fig look back

vistazo m look; ***echar un vistazo a*** take a (quick) look at

viste vb → ver, vestir

visto 1 part → ver **2** adj: ***está bien visto*** it's the done thing; ***está mal visto*** it's not done, it's not the done thing; ***está visto que*** it's obvious that; ***estar muy visto*** be old hat, not be original; ***por lo visto*** apparently **3** m check(mark), Br tick; ***dar el visto bueno*** give one's approval

vistoso adj eye-catching

visual adj visual

visualizar ⟨1f⟩ v/t visualize; en pantalla display

vital adj vital; persona lively

vitalicio adj life atr, for life; ***renta -a*** life annuity

vitalidad f vitality, liveliness

vitamina f vitamin

viticultor m, **viticultora** f wine grower

vítores mpl cheers, acclaim sg

vitorear ⟨1a⟩ v/t cheer

vítreo adj vitreous

vitrificar ⟨1g⟩ v/t vitrify

vitrina f display cabinet; L.Am. shop window

vitrocerámica f ceramic hob

vituperar ⟨1a⟩ v/t condemn

viuda f widow

viudedad f widowhood; ***pensión de viudedad*** widow's pension

viudo 1 adj widowed **2** m widower; ***quedarse viudo*** be widowed

viva int hurrah!; ***¡viva el rey!*** long live the king!

vivaz adj bright, sharp

vivencia f experience

víveres mpl provisions

vívido adj vivid

vivienda f housing; (casa) house

vivir ⟨3a⟩ **1** v/t live through, experience **2** v/i live; ***vivir de algo*** live on sth

vivo adj alive; color bright; ritmo lively; fig F sharp, smart

vocabulario m vocabulary

vocación f vocation

vocal 1 m/f member **2** f vowel

vocalista m/f vocalist

vocalizar ⟨1f⟩ v/i vocalize

voceador m, **voceadora** f Méx newspaper vendor

vocerío m uproar

vocero m, **-a** f esp L.Am. spokesperson

vociferar ⟨1a⟩ v/i shout

vodka m vodka

volador adj flying

volandas: en volandas fig in the air

volante 1 adj flying **2** m AUTO steering wheel; de vestido flounce; MED referral (slip)

volar ⟨1m⟩ **1** v/i fly; fig vanish **2** v/t fly;

edificio blow up

volátil *adj tb fig* volatile

volatilizarse ⟨1f⟩ *v/r fig* vanish into thin air

volcán *m* volcano

volcánico *adj* volcanic

volcar ⟨1g & 1m⟩ **1** *v/t* knock over; (*vaciar*) empty; *barco, coche* overturn **2** *v/i de coche, barco* overturn **3** *v/r* **volcarse** tip over; **volcarse por alguien** F bend over backwards for s.o., go out of one's way for s.o.; **volcarse en algo** throw o.s. into sth

volea *f tenis* volley

voleibol *m* volleyball

voleo *m*: **a voleo** at random

voley-playa *m* beach volleyball

voltaje *m* EL voltage

voltear ⟨1a⟩ **1** *v/t L.Am.* (*invertir*) turn over; *Rpl* (*tumbar*) knock over; **voltear el jersey** turn the sweater inside out; **voltear la cabeza** turn one's head **2** *v/i* roll over; *de campanas* ring out

voltereta *f* somersault

voltio *m* EL volt

voluble *adj* erratic, unpredictable

volumen *m* TIP, MÚS, RAD volume; **volumen de negocios** COM turnover

voluntad *f* will; **buena / mala voluntad** good / ill will

voluntario 1 *adj* volunteer **2** *m*, *-a f* volunteer

voluntarioso *adj* willing, enthusiastic

voluptuoso *adj* voluptuous

volver ⟨2h; *part* **vuelto** ⟩ **1** *v/t página, mirada etc* turn (**a** to; *hacia* toward); **volver loco** drive crazy **2** *v/i* return; **volver a hacer algo** do sth again **3** *v/r* **volverse** turn round; **volverse loco** go crazy

vomitar ⟨1a⟩ **1** *v/t* throw up; *lava* hurl, throw out **2** *v/i* throw up, be sick; **tengo ganas de vomitar** I feel nauseous, *Br* I feel sick

vómito *m* MED vomit

vorágine *f* (*remolino*) whirlpool; *fig* whirl

voraz *adj* voracious; *incendio* fierce

vos *pron pers sg Rpl, C.Am., Ven* you

vosotros, vosotras *pron pers pl* you

votación *f* vote, ballot

votar ⟨1a⟩ **1** *v/t* (*aprobar*) vote **2** *v/i* vote

voto *m* POL vote; **voto en blanco** spoiled ballot paper

voy *vb* → *ir*

voz *f* voice; *fig* rumo(u)r; **voz activa / pasiva** GRAM active / passive voice; **a media voz** in a hushed voice, in a low voice; **a voz en grito** at the top of one's voice; **en voz alta** aloud; **en voz baja** in a low voice; **correr la voz** spread the word; **llevar la voz cantante** *fig* call the tune, call the shots; **no tener voz ni voto** *fig* not have a say; **voz en off** voice-over

vuelco 1 *vb* → **volcar 2** *m*: **dar un vuelco** *fig* F take a dramatic turn; **me dio un vuelco el corazón** my heart missed a beat

vuelo 1 *vb* → **volar 2** *m* flight; **vuelo chárter** charter flight; **vuelo nacional** domestic flight; **al vuelo** *coger, cazar* in mid-air; **una falda con vuelo** a full skirt

vuelta *f* return; *en carrera* lap; **vuelta de carnero** *L.Am.* half-somersault; **vuelta al mundo** round-the- world trip; **a la vuelta** on the way back; **a la vuelta de la esquina** *fig* just around the corner; **dar la vuelta** *llave etc* turn; **dar media vuelta** turn round; **dar una vuelta** go for a walk; **dar cien vueltas a alguien** F be a hundred times better than s.o. F

vuelto 1 *part* → **volver 2** *m L.Am.* change

vuelvo *vb* → **volver**

vuestro 1 *adj pos* your **2** *pron* yours

vulgar *adj* vulgar, common; *abundante* common

vulgaridad *f* vulgarity

vulgo *m* lower classes *pl*

vulnerable *adj* vulnerable

V

W

w. *abr* (= **watio**) w (= watt)
walkman *m* personal stereo
wáter *m* bathroom, toilet
waterpolo *m* DEP water polo

WC *abr* WC
whisky *m* whiskey, *Br* whisky
windsurf(ing) *m* wind-surfing
windsurfista *m/f* windsurfer

X, Y

xenofobia *f* xenophobia
xilófono *m* MÚS xylophone
y *conj* and
ya *adv* already; (*ahora mismo*) now; **¡ya!**
incredulidad oh, yeah!, sure!; *compren-*
sión I know, I understand; *asenso* OK,
sure; *al terminar* finished!, done!; **ya**
no vive aquí he doesn't live here any
more, he no longer lives here; **ya que**
since, as; **ya lo sé** I know; **ya viene** she's
coming now; **¿lo puede hacer? – ¡ya lo**
creo! can she do it? – you bet!; **ya … ya**
… either … or …
yacaré *m L.Am.* ZO cayman
yacer ⟨2y⟩ *v/i* lie
yacimiento *m* MIN deposit
yanqui *m/f* Yankee
yapa *f L.Am.* bit extra (for free); *Pe, Bol*
(*propina*) tip
yate *m* yacht
yaya *f* grandma
yayo *m* grandpa
yedra *f* BOT ivy

yegua *f* ZO mare
yema *f* yolk; **yema del dedo** fingertip
yendo *vb* → **ir**
yerba *f L.Am.* grass; **yerba mate** maté
yerbatero *m*, **-a** *f Rpl* herbalist
yerno *m* son-in-law
yeso *m* plaster
yo *pron* I; **soy yo** it's me; **yo que tú** if I
were you
yodo *m* iodine
yoga *m* yoga
yogur *m* yog(h)urt
yonqui *m/f* F junkie
yuca *f* BOT yucca
yugo *m* yoke
Yugoslavia Yugoslavia
yugoslavo **1** *adj* Yugoslav(ian) **2** *m*, **-a** *f*
Yugoslav(ian)
yugular *adj* ANAT jugular
yute *m* jute
yuxtaposición *f* juxtaposition
yuyo *m L.Am.* weed

Z

zacatal *m C.Am., Méx* pasture

zacate *m C.Am., Méx* fodder

zafarse ⟨1a⟩ *v/r* get away (**de** from); (*soltarse*) come undone; **zafarse de algo** (*evitar*) get out of sth

zafio *adj* coarse

zafiro *m* sapphire

zaga *f*: **ir a la zaga** bring up the rear

zalamero 1 *adj* flattering; *empalagoso* syrupy, sugary 2 *m*, -a *f* flatterer, sweet talker

zamba *f Arg* (*baile*) Argentinian folkdance

zambomba *f* MÚS *type of drum*

zambullirse ⟨3h⟩ *v/r* dive (**en** into); *fig* throw o.s. (**en** into), immerse o.s. (**en** in)

zamparse ⟨1a⟩ *v/r* F wolf down F

zanahoria *f* carrot

zancada *f* stride

zancadilla *f fig* obstacle; **poner** *or* **echar la zancadilla a alguien** trip s.o. up

zancudo *m L.Am.* mosquito

zángano *m* zo drone; *fig* F lazybones *sg*

zanja *f* ditch

zanjar ⟨1a⟩ *v/t fig problemas* settle; *dificultades* overcome

zapatería *f* shoe store, shoe shop

zapatero *m*, -a *f* shoemaker; **zapatero remendón** shoe mender

zapatilla *f* slipper; *de deporte* sneaker, *Br* trainer

Zapatista *m/f Méx* member or supporter of the Zapatista National Liberation Army

zapato *m* shoe

zapear ⟨1a⟩ *v/i* TV F channel hop

zapeo, zapping *m* TV F channel hopping

zarandear ⟨1a⟩ *v/t* shake violently, buffet; **zarandear a alguien** *fig* give s.o. a hard time

zarpa *f* paw

zarpar ⟨1a⟩ *v/i* MAR set sail (**para** for)

zarza *f* BOT bramble

zarzamora *f* BOT blackberry

zarzuela *f* MÚS *type of operetta*

zascandilear ⟨1a⟩ *v/i* mess around

zigzaguear ⟨1a⟩ *v/i* zigzag

zinc *m* zinc

zócalo *m* baseboard, *Br* skirting board

zodíaco, zodiaco *m* AST zodiac

zona *f* area, zone

zoncería *f L.Am.* F stupid thing

zonzo *adj L.Am.* F stupid

zoo *m* zoo

zoológico 1 *adj* zoological 2 *m* zoo

zoom *m* FOT zoom

zopilote *m L.Am.* zo turkey buzzard

zorra *f* zo vixen; P whore P

zorro 1 *adj* sly, crafty 2 *m* zo fox; *fig* old fox

zozobrar ⟨1a⟩ *v/i* MAR overturn; *fig* go under

zueco *m* clog

zulo *m* hiding place

zumba *f L.Am., Méx* (*paliza*) beating

zumbar ⟨1a⟩ 1 *v/i* buzz; **me zumban los oídos** my ears are ringing *o* buzzing 2 *v/t golpe, bofetada* give

zumbido *m* buzzing

zumo *m* juice

zurcir ⟨3b⟩ *v/t calcetines* darn; *chaqueta, pantalones* patch

zurdo 1 *adj* left-handed 2 *m*, *f* left-hander

zurrar ⟨1a⟩ *v/t* TÉC tan; **zurrar a alguien** F tan s.o.'s hide F

A

a [ə] *stressed* [eɪ] *art* un(a); *$50 a ride* 50 dólares por viaje

a·back [ə'bæk] *adv*: *taken aback* desconcertado (*by* por)

a·ban·don [ə'bændən] *v/t* abandonar

a·bashed [ə'bæʃt] *adj* avergonzado

a·bate [ə'beɪt] *v/i of storm, flood* amainar

ab·at·toir ['æbətwɑːr] matadero *m*

ab·bey ['æbɪ] abadía *f*

ab·bre·vi·ate [ə'briːvɪeɪt] *v/t* abreviar

ab·bre·vi·a·tion [əbriːvɪ'eɪʃn] abreviatura *f*

ab·di·cate ['æbdɪkeɪt] *v/i* abdicar

ab·di·ca·tion [æbdɪ'keɪʃn] abdicación *f*

ab·do·men ['æbdəmən] abdomen *m*

ab·dom·i·nal [æb'dɑːmɪnl] *adj* abdominal

ab·duct [əb'dʌkt] *v/t* raptar, secuestrar

ab·duc·tion [əb'dʌkʃn] rapto *m*, secuestro *m*

♦ a·bide by [ə'baɪd] *v/t* atenerse a

a·bil·i·ty [ə'bɪlətɪ] capacidad *f*, habilidad *f*

a·blaze [ə'bleɪz] *adj* en llamas

a·ble ['eɪbl] *adj* (*skillful*) capaz, hábil; *be able to* poder; *I wasn't able to see* / *hear* no conseguí *or* pude ver / escuchar

a·ble-bod·ied [eɪbl'bɑːdiːd] *adj* sano

ab·nor·mal [æb'nɔːrml] *adj* anormal

ab·nor·mal·ly [æb'nɔːrməlɪ] *adv* anormalmente; *behave* de manera anormal

a·board [ə'bɔːrd] **1** *prep* a bordo de **2** *adv* a bordo; *be aboard* estar a bordo; *go aboard* subir a bordo

a·bol·ish [ə'bɑːlɪʃ] *v/t* abolir

ab·o·li·tion [æbə'lɪʃn] abolición *f*

a·bort [ə'bɔːrt] *v/t mission, launch* suspender, cancelar; COMPUT cancelar

a·bor·tion [ə'bɔːrʃn] aborto *m* (*provocado*); *have an abortion* abortar

a·bor·tive [ə'bɔːrtɪv] *adj* fallido

a·bout [ə'baʊt] **1** *prep* (*concerning*) acerca de, sobre; *what's it about?* *of book, movie* ¿de qué trata? **2** *adv* (*roughly*) más o menos; *be about to ...* (*be going to*) estar a punto de ...; *be about* (*somewhere near*) estar por ahí; *there are a lot of people about* hay un montón de gente por ahí

a·bove [ə'bʌv] **1** *prep* por encima de; *500 m above sea level* 500 m sobre el nivel del mar; *above all* por encima de todo, sobre todo **2** *adv*: *on the floor above* en el piso de arriba

a·bove-men·tioned [əbʌv'menʃnd] *adj* arriba mencionado

ab·ra·sion [ə'breɪʒn] abrasión *f*

ab·ra·sive [ə'breɪsɪv] *adj personality* abrasivo

a·breast [ə'brest] *adv* de frente, en fondo; *keep abreast of* mantenerse al tanto de

a·bridge [ə'brɪdʒ] *v/t* abreviar, condensar

a·broad [ə'brɔːd] *adv live* en el extranjero; *go* al extranjero

a·brupt [ə'brʌpt] *adj departure* brusco, repentino; *manner* brusco, rudo

a·brupt·ly [ə'brʌptlɪ] *adv* (*suddenly*) repentinamente; (*curtly*) bruscamente

ab·scess ['æbsɪs] absceso *m*

ab·sence ['æbsəns] *of person* ausencia *f*; (*lack*) falta *f*

ab·sent ['æbsənt] *adj* ausente

ab·sen·tee [æbsən'tiː] *n* ausente *m/f*

ab·sen·tee·ism [æbsən'tiːɪzm] absentismo *m*

ab·sent-mind·ed [æbsənt'maɪndɪd] *adj* despistado, distraído

ab·sent-mind·ed·ly [æbsənt'maɪndɪdlɪ] *adv* distraídamente

ab·so·lute ['æbsəluːt] *adj power* absoluto; *idiot* completo; *mess* total

ab·so·lute·ly ['æbsəluːtlɪ] *adv* (*completely*) absolutamente, completamente; *absolutely not!* ¡en absoluto!; *do you agree? - absolutely!* ¿estás de acuerdo? - ¡completamente!

ab·so·lu·tion [æbsə'luːʃn] REL absolución *f*

ab·solve [əb'zɑːlv] *v/t* absolver

ab·sorb [əb'sɔːrb] *v/t* absorber; *absor-*

bed in ... absorto en ...

ab·sorb·en·cy [əb'sɔːrbənsɪ] absorbencia f

ab·sorb·ent [əb'sɔːrbənt] adj absorbente

ab·sorb·ent 'cot·ton algodón m hidrófilo

ab·sorb·ing [əb'sɔːrbɪŋ] adj absorbente

ab·stain [əb'steɪn] v/i from voting abstenerse

ab·sten·tion [əb'stenʃn] in voting abstención f

ab·stract ['æbstrækt] adj abstracto

ab·struse [əb'struːs] adj abstruso

ab·surd [əb'sɜːrd] adj absurdo

ab·surd·i·ty [əb'sɜːrdətɪ] lo absurdo

a·bun·dance [ə'bʌndəns] abundancia f

a·bun·dant [ə'bʌndənt] adj abundante

a·buse¹ [ə'bjuːs] n (insults) insultos mpl; of thing maltrato m; **he shouted abuse at me** me insultó; (child) **abuse** physical malos tratos mpl a menores; sexual agresión f sexual a menores

a·buse² [ə'bjuːz] v/t (physically) abusar de; (verbally) insultar

a·bu·sive [ə'bjuːsɪv] adj language insultante, injurioso; **become abusive** ponerse a insultar

a·bys·mal [ə'bɪzml] adj F (very bad) desastroso F

a·byss [ə'bɪs] abismo m

AC ['eɪsiː] abbr (= **alternating current**) CA (= corriente f alterna)

ac·a·dem·ic [ækə'demɪk] 1 n académico(-a) m(f), profesor(a) m(f) 2 adj académico

a·cad·e·my [ə'kædəmɪ] academia f

ac·cede [ək'siːd] v/i accede; **accede to** acceder a

ac·cel·e·rate [ək'seləreɪt] v/t & v/i acelerar

ac·cel·e·ra·tion [əkselə'reɪʃn] aceleración f

ac·cel·e·ra·tor [ək'seləreɪtər] of car acelerador m

ac·cent ['æksənt] when speaking acento m; (emphasis) énfasis m

ac·cen·tu·ate [ək'sentʊeɪt] v/t acentuar

ac·cept [ək'sept] v/t & v/i aceptar

ac·cep·ta·ble [ək'septəbl] adj aceptable

ac·cept·ance [ək'septəns] aceptación f

ac·cess ['ækses] 1 n acceso m; **have access to** computer tener acceso a; child tener derecho a visitar 2 v/t also COMPUT acceder a

'ac·cess code COMPUT código m de acceso

ac·ces·si·ble [ək'sesəbl] adj accesible

ac·ces·sion [ək'seʃn] acceso m

ac·ces·so·ry [ək'sesərɪ] for wearing accesorio m, complemento m; LAW cómplice m/f

'ac·cess road carretera f de acceso

'ac·cess time COMPUT tiempo m de acceso

ac·ci·dent ['æksɪdənt] accidente m; **by accident** por casualidad

ac·ci·den·tal [æksɪ'dentl] adj accidental

ac·ci·den·tal·ly [æksɪ'dentlɪ] adv sin querer

ac·claim [ə'kleɪm] 1 n alabanza f, aclamación f; **meet with acclaim** ser alabado or aclamado 2 v/t alabar, aclamar

ac·cla·ma·tion [əklə'meɪʃn] aclamación f

ac·cli·mate, ac·cli·ma·tize [ə'klaɪmət, ə'klaɪmətaɪz] v/t aclimatarse

ac·com·mo·date [ə'kɑːmədeɪt] v/t alojar; requirements satisfacer, hacer frente a

ac·com·mo·da·tions [əkɑːmə'deɪʃnz] npl alojamiento m

ac·com·pa·ni·ment [ə'kʌmpənimənt] MUS acompañamiento m

ac·com·pa·nist [ə'kʌmpənɪst] MUS acompañante m/f

ac·com·pa·ny [ə'kʌmpənɪ] v/t (pret & pp **accompanied**) also MUS acompañar

ac·com·plice [ə'kʌmplɪs] cómplice m/f

ac·com·plish [ə'kʌmplɪʃ] v/t task realizar; goal conseguir, lograr

ac·com·plished [ə'kʌmplɪʃt] adj consumado

ac·com·plish·ment [ə'kʌmplɪʃmənt] of a task realización f; (talent) habilidad f; (achievement) logro m

ac·cord [ə'kɔːrd] acuerdo m; **of one's own accord** de motu propio

ac·cord·ance [ə'kɔːrdəns]: **in accordance with** de acuerdo con

ac·cord·ing [ə'kɔːrdɪŋ] adv: **according to** según

ac·cord·ing·ly [ə'kɔːrdɪŋlɪ] adv (consequently) por consiguiente; (*appropriately*) como corresponde

ac·cor·di·on [əˈkɔːrdɪən] acordeón *m*

ac·cor·di·on·ist [əˈkɔːrdɪənɪst] acordeonista *m/f*

ac·count [əˈkaʊnt] *financial* cuenta *f*; (*report, description*) relato *m*, descripción *f*; **give an account of** relatar, describir; **on no account** de ninguna manera, bajo ningún concepto; **be held accountable** ser considerado responsable

ac·count·ant [əˈkaʊntənt] contable *m/f*, *L.Am.* contador(a) *m(f)*

ac·count hold·er titular *m/f* de una cuenta

ac·count num·ber número *m* de cuenta

ac·counts [əˈkaʊnts] *npl* contabilidad *f*

ac·cu·mu·late [əˈkjuːmjʊleɪt] **1** *v/t* acumular **2** *v/i* acumularse

ac·cu·mu·la·tion [əkjuːmjʊˈleɪʃn] acumulación *f*

ac·cu·ra·cy [ˈækjʊrəsɪ] precisión *f*

ac·cu·rate [ˈækjʊrət] *adj* preciso

ac·cu·rate·ly [ˈækjʊrətlɪ] *adv* con precisión

ac·cu·sa·tion [ækjuːˈzeɪʃn] acusación *f*

ac·cuse [əˈkjuːz] *v/t*: **accuse s.o. of sth** acusar a alguien de algo; **be accused of** LAW ser acusado de

ac·cused [əˈkjuːzd] *n* LAW acusado(-a) *m(f)*

ac·cus·ing [əˈkjuːzɪŋ] *adj* acusador

ac·cus·ing·ly [əˈkjuːzɪŋlɪ] *adv say* en tono acusador; **he looked at me accusingly** me lanzó una mirada acusadora

ac·cus·tom [əˈkʌstəm] *v/t* acostumbrar; **get accustomed to** acostumbrarse a; **be accustomed to** estar acostumbrado a

ace [eɪs] *in cards* as *m*; (*in tennis: shot*) ace *m*

ache [eɪk] **1** *n* dolor *m* **2** *v/i* doler

a·chieve [əˈtʃiːv] *v/t* conseguir, lograr

a·chieve·ment [əˈtʃiːvmənt] *of ambition* consecución *f*, logro *m*; (*thing achieved*) logro *m*

ac·id [ˈæsɪd] *n* ácido *m*

a·cid·i·ty [əˈsɪdətɪ] acidez *f*; *fig* sarcasmo *m*

ac·id 'rain lluvia *f* ácida

'ac·id test *fig* prueba *f* de fuego

ac·knowl·edge [əkˈnɑːlɪdʒ] *v/t* reconocer; **acknowledge receipt of a letter** acusar recibo de una carta

ac·knowl·edg(e)·ment [əkˈnɑːlɪdʒmənt] reconocimiento *m*; *of a letter* acuse *m* de recibo

ac·ne [ˈæknɪ] MED acné *m*, acne *m*

a·corn [ˈeɪkɔːrn] BOT bellota *f*

a·cous·tics [əˈkuːstɪks] acústica *f*

ac·quaint [əˈkweɪnt] *v/t fml*: **be acquainted with** conocer

ac·quaint·ance [əˈkweɪntəns] *person* conocido(-a) *m(f)*

ac·qui·esce [ækwɪˈes] *v/i fml* acceder

ac·qui·es·cence [ækwɪˈesns] *fml* aquiescencia *f*

ac·quire [əˈkwaɪr] *v/t* adquirir

ac·qui·si·tion [ækwɪˈzɪʃn] adquisición *f*

ac·quis·i·tive [əˈkwɪzətɪv] *adj* consumista

ac·quit [əˈkwɪt] *v/t* LAW absolver

ac·quit·tal [əˈkwɪtl] LAW absolución *f*

a·cre [ˈeɪkər] acre *m* (4.047m2)

a·cre·age [ˈeɪkrɪdʒ] superficie *f* en acres

ac·ri·mo·ni·ous [ækrɪˈmoʊnɪəs] *adj* áspero, agrio

ac·ro·bat [ˈækrəbæt] acróbata *m/f*

ac·ro·bat·ic [ækrəˈbætɪk] *adj* acrobático

ac·ro·bat·ics [ækrəˈbætɪks] *npl* acrobacias *fpl*

ac·ro·nym [ˈækrənɪm] acrónimo *m*

a·cross [əˈkrɑːs] **1** *prep* al otro lado de; **she lives across the street** vive al otro lado de la calle; **sail across the Atlantic** cruzar el Atlántico navegando **2** *adv* de un lado a otro; **it's too far to swim across** está demasiado lejos como para cruzar a nado; **once you're across** cuando hayas llegado al otro lado; **10 m**

across 10 m de ancho

a·cryl·ic [ə'krılık] *adj* acrílico

act [ækt] **1** *v/i* THEA actuar; (*pretend*) hacer teatro; **act as** actuar *or* hacer de **2** *n* (*deed*), *of play* acto *m*; *in vaudeville* número *m*; (*law*) ley *f*; **it's just an act** (*pretense*) es puro teatro; **act of God** caso *m* fortuito

act·ing ['æktɪŋ] **1** *n in a play* interpretación *f*; *as profession* teatro *m* **2** *adj* (*temporary*) en funciones

ac·tion ['ækʃn] acción *f*; **out of action** *machine* sin funcionar; *person* fuera de combate; **take action** tomar medidas; **bring an action against** LAW demandar a

ac·tion 're·play TV repetición *f* (de la jugada)

ac·tive ['æktɪv] *adj also* GRAM activo; *party member* en activo

ac·tiv·ist ['æktɪvɪst] POL activista *m/f*

ac·tiv·i·ty [æk'tɪvətɪ] actividad *f*

ac·tor ['æktər] actor *m*

ac·tress ['æktrɪs] actriz *f*

ac·tu·al ['æktʃʊəl] *adj* verdadero, real

ac·tu·al·ly ['æktʃʊəlɪ] *adv* (*in fact, to tell the truth*) en realidad; **did you actually see her?** ¿de verdad llegaste a verla?; **he actually did it!** ¡aunque parezca mentira lo hizo!; **actually, I do know him** (*stressing converse*) pues sí, de hecho lo conozco; **actually, it's not finished yet** el caso es que todavía no está terminado

ac·u·punc·ture ['ækjəpʌŋktʃər] acupuntura *f*

a·cute [ə'kjuːt] *adj pain* agudo; *sense* muy fino

a·cute·ly [ə'kjuːtlɪ] *adv* (*extremely*) extremadamente; **acutely aware** plenamente consciente

ad [æd] → **advertisement**

ad·a·mant ['ædəmənt] *adj* firme

ad·a·mant·ly ['ædəməntlɪ] *adv* firmemente

Ad·am's ap·ple [ædæmz'æpəl] nuez *f*

a·dapt [ə'dæpt] **1** *v/t* adaptar **2** *v/i of person* adaptarse

a·dapt·a·bil·i·ty [ədæptə'bılətı] adaptabilidad *f*

a·dapt·a·ble [ə'dæptəbəl] *adj* adaptable

a·dap·ta·tion [ædæp'teɪʃn] *of play etc* adaptación *f*

a·dapt·er [ə'dæptər] *electrical* adaptador *m*

add [æd] **1** *v/t* añadir; MATH sumar **2** *v/i of person* sumar

◆ **add on** *v/t* 15% *etc* sumar

◆ **add up 1** *v/t* sumar **2** *v/i fig* cuadrar

ad·der ['ædər] víbora *f*

ad·dict ['ædıkt] adicto(-a) *m(f)*; **drug addict** drogadicto(-a) *m(f)*

ad·dict·ed [ə'dıktıd] *adj* adicto; **be addicted to** ser adicto a

ad·dic·tion [ə'dıkʃn] adicción *f*

ad·dic·tive [ə'dıktıv] *adj* adictivo

ad·di·tion [ə'dıʃn] MATH suma *f*; *to list, company etc* incorporación *f*; *of new drive etc* instalación *f*; **in addition** además; **in addition to** además de

ad·di·tion·al [ə'dıʃənl] *adj* adicional

ad·di·tive ['ædıtıv] aditivo *m*

add-on ['ædɑːn] extra *m*, accesorio *m*

ad·dress [ə'dres] **1** *n* dirección *f*; **form of address** tratamiento *m* **2** *v/t letter* dirigir; *audience* dirigirse a; **how do you address the judge?** ¿qué tratamiento se le da al juez?

ad·dress book agenda *f* de direcciones

ad·dress·ee [ædre'siː] destinatario(-a) *m(f)*

ad·ept ['ædept] *adj* experto; **be adept at** ser un experto en

ad·e·quate ['ædıkwət] *adj* suficiente; (*satisfactory*) aceptable

ad·e·quate·ly ['ædıkwətlɪ] *adv* suficientemente; (*satisfactorily*) aceptablemente

ad·here [əd'hır] *v/i* adherirse

◆ **adhere to** *v/t surface* adherirse a; *rules* cumplir

ad·he·sive [əd'hiːsıv] *n* adhesivo *m*

ad·he·sive 'plas·ter esparadrapo *m*

ad·he·sive 'tape cinta *f* adhesiva

ad·ja·cent [ə'dʒeɪsnt] *adj* adyacente

ad·jec·tive ['ædʒıktıv] adjetivo *m*

ad·join [ə'dʒɔın] *v/t* lindar con

ad·join·ing [ə'dʒɔınıŋ] *adj* contiguo

ad·journ [ə'dʒɜːrn] *v/i of court, meeting* aplazar

ad·journ·ment [ə'dʒɜːrnmənt] aplazamiento m

ad·just [ə'dʒʌst] v/t ajustar, regular

ad·just·a·ble [ə'dʒʌstəbl] adj ajustable, regulable

ad·just·ment [ə'dʒʌstmənt] ajuste m; psychological adaptación f

ad lib [æd'lɪb] 1 adj improvisado 2 adv improvisadamente 3 v/i (pret & pp **adbed**) improvisar

ad·min·is·ter [əd'mɪnɪstər] v/t administrar

ad·min·is·tra·tion [ədmɪnɪ'streɪʃn] administración f

ad·min·is·tra·tive [ədmɪnɪ'strətɪv] adj administrativo

ad·min·is·tra·tor [əd'mɪnɪstreɪtər] administrador(a) m(f)

ad·mi·ra·ble ['ædmərəbl] adj admirable

ad·mi·ra·bly ['ædmərəblɪ] adv admirablemente

ad·mi·ral ['ædmərəl] almirante m

ad·mi·ra·tion [ædmə'reɪʃn] admiración f

ad·mire [əd'maɪr] v/t admirar

ad·mir·er [əd'maɪrər] admirador(a) m(f)

ad·mir·ing [əd'maɪrɪŋ] adj de admiración

ad·mir·ing·ly [əd'maɪrɪŋlɪ] adv con admiración

ad·mis·si·ble [əd'mɪsəbl] adj admisible

ad·mis·sion [əd'mɪʃn] (confession) confesión f; **admission free** entrada gratis

ad·mit [əd'mɪt] v/t (pret & pp **admitted**) to a place dejar entrar; to school, organization admitir; to hospital ingresar; (confess) confesar; (accept) admitir

ad·mit·tance [əd'mɪtəns] admisión f; **no admittance** prohibido el paso

ad·mit·ted·ly [əd'mɪtedlɪ] adv: **he didn't use those exact words, admittedly** es verdad que no utilizó exactamente esas palabras

ad·mon·ish [əd'mɑːnɪʃ] v/t fml reprender

a·do [ə'duː]: **without further ado** sin más dilación

ad·o·les·cence [ædə'lesns] adolescencia f

ad·o·les·cent [ædə'lesnt] 1 n adolescente m/f 2 adj de adolescente

a·dopt [ə'dɑːpt] v/t child, plan adoptar

a·dop·tion [ə'dɑːpʃn] of child adopción f

a·dop·tive 'par·ents [ədɑːptɪv] npl padres mpl adoptivos

a·dor·a·ble [ə'dɔːrəbl] adj encantador

ad·o·ra·tion [ædə'reɪʃn] adoración f

a·dore [ə'dɔːr] v/t adorar; **I adore chocolate** me encanta el chocolate

a·dor·ing [ə'dɔːrɪŋ] adj expression lleno de adoración; **his adoring fans** sus entregados fans

a·dren·al·in [ə'drenəlɪn] adrenalina f

a·drift [ə'drɪft] adj a la deriva; fig perdido

ad·u·la·tion [ædʊ'leɪʃn] adulación f

ad·ult ['ædʌlt] 1 n adulto(-a) m(f) 2 adj adulto

ad·ult ed·u·ca·tion educación f para adultos

a·dul·ter·ous [ə'dʌltərəs] adj relationship adúltero

a·dul·ter·y [ə'dʌltərɪ] adulterio m

'a·dult film euph película f para adultos

ad·vance [əd'væns] 1 n money adelanto m; in science, MIL avance m; **in advance** con antelación; get money por adelantado; **48 hours in advance** con 48 horas de antelación; **make advances** (progress) avanzar, progresar; sexually insinuarse 2 v/i MIL avanzar; (make progress) avanzar, progresar 3 v/t theory presentar; sum of money adelantar; human knowledge, a cause hacer avanzar

ad·vance 'book·ing reserva f (anticipada)

ad·vanced [əd'vænst] adj country, level, learner avanzado

ad·vance 'no·tice aviso m previo

ad·vance 'pay·ment pago m por adelantado

ad·van·tage [əd'væntɪdʒ] ventaja f; **there's no advantage to be gained** no se gana nada; **it's to your advantage** te conviene; **take advantage of** aprovecharse de

ad·van·ta·geous [ædvən'teɪdʒəs] adj ventajoso

ad·vent ['ædvent] fig llegada f

'ad·vent cal·en·dar calendario m de Adviento

ad·ven·ture [əd'ventʃər] aventura f

ad·ven·tur·ous [əd'ventʃərəs] adj person

aventurero; *investment* arriesgado
ad·verb ['ædvɜːrb] adverbio *m*
ad·ver·sa·ry ['ædvɜrserɪ] adversario(-a) *m(f)*
ad·verse ['ædvɜːrs] *adj* adverso
ad·vert ['ædvɜːrt] → **advertisement**
ad·ver·tise ['ædvərtaɪz] **1** *v/t* anunciar **2** *v/i* anunciarse, poner un anuncio
ad·ver·tise·ment [ədvɜːr'taɪsmənt] anuncio *m*
ad·ver·tis·er ['ædvərtaɪzər] anunciante *m/f*
ad·ver·tis·ing ['ædvərtaɪzɪŋ] publicidad *f*
'ad·ver·tis·ing a·gen·cy agencia *f* de publicidad
'ad·ver·tis·ing budg·et presupuesto *m* para publicidad
'ad·ver·tis·ing cam·paign campaña *f* publicitaria
'ad·ver·tis·ing rev·e·nue ingresos *mpl* por publicidad
ad·vice [əd'vaɪs] consejo *m*; *he gave me some advice* me dio un consejo; *take s.o.'s advice* seguir el consejo de alguien
ad·vis·a·ble [əd'vaɪzəbl] *adj* aconsejable
ad·vise [əd'vaɪz] *v/t person, caution* aconsejar; *government* asesorar; *I advise you to leave* te aconsejo que te vayas
ad·vis·er [əd'vaɪzər] asesor(a) *m(f)*
ad·vo·cate ['ædvəkeɪt] *v/t* abogar por
aer·i·al ['erɪəl] *n* antena *f*
aer·i·al 'pho·to·graph fotografía *f* aérea
aer·o·bics [e'roubɪks] *nsg* aerobic *m*
aer·o·dy·nam·ic [eroudaɪ'næmɪk] *adj* aerodinámico
aer·o·nau·ti·cal [erou'nɒːtɪkl] *adj* aeronáutico
aer·o·plane ['eroupleɪn] *Br* avión *m*
aer·o·sol ['erəsɑːl] aerosol *m*
aer·o·space in·dus·try ['erəspeɪs] industria *f* aeroespacial
aes·thet·ic *etc Br* → **esthetic** *etc*
af·fa·ble ['æfəbl] *adj* afable
af·fair [ə'fer] (*matter, business*) asunto *m*; (*love affair*) aventura *f*, lío *m*; *foreign affairs* asuntos *mpl* exteriores; *have an affair with* tener una aventura *or* lío con
af·fect [ə'fekt] *v/t also* MED afectar
af·fec·tion [ə'fekʃn] afecto *m*, cariño

af·fec·tion·ate [ə'fekʃnət] *adj* afectuoso, cariñoso
af·fec·tion·ate·ly [ə'fekʃnətlɪ] *adv* con afecto, cariñosamente
af·fin·i·ty [ə'fɪnətɪ] afinidad *f*
af·fir·ma·tive [ə'fɜːrmətɪv] *adj* afirmativo; *answer in the affirmative* responder afirmativamente
af·flu·ence ['æfluəns] prosperidad *f*, riqueza *f*
af·flu·ent ['æfluənt] *adj* próspero, acomodado; *affluent society* sociedad *f* opulenta
af·ford [ə'fɔːrd] *v/t* permitirse; *be able to afford sth financially* poder permitirse algo; *I can't afford the time* no tengo tiempo; *it's a risk we can't afford to take* es un riesgo que no podemos permitirnos tomar
af·ford·a·ble [ə'fɔːrdəbl] *adj* asequible
a·float [ə'flout] *adj boat* a flote; *keep the company afloat* mantener la compañía a flote
a·fraid [ə'freɪd] *adj*: *be afraid* tener miedo; *be afraid of* tener miedo de; *I'm afraid of cats* tengo miedo a los gatos; *he's afraid of the dark* le da miedo la oscuridad; *I'm afraid of annoying him* me da miedo enfadarle; *I'm afraid expressing regret* me temo; *he's very ill, I'm afraid* me temo que está muy enfermo; *I'm afraid so* (me) temo que sí; *I'm afraid not* (me) temo que no
a·fresh [ə'freʃ] *adv* de nuevo
Af·ri·ca ['æfrɪkə] África
Af·ri·can ['æfrɪkən] **1** *adj* africano **2** *n* africano(-a) *m(f)*
af·ter ['æftər] **1** *prep* después de; *after all* después de todo; *after that* después de eso; *it's ten after two* son las dos y diez **2** *adv* después; *the day after* el día siguiente
af·ter·math ['æftərmæθ] *time* periodo *m* posterior (*of* a); *state of affairs* repercusiones *fpl*
afternoon [æftər'nuːn] tarde *f*; *in the afternoon* por la tarde; *this afternoon* esta tarde; *good afternoon* buenas tardes
'af·ter sales serv·ice servicio *m* posventa

'af·ter·shave loción f para después del afeitado, after shave m

'af·ter·taste regusto m

af·ter·ward ['æftərwərd] adv después

a·gain [ə'geɪn] adv otra vez; **I never saw him again** no lo volví a ver

a·gainst [ə'genst] prep lean contra; **the USA against Brazil** SP Estados Unidos contra Brasil; **I'm against the idea** estoy en contra de la idea; **what do you have against her?** ¿que tienes en contra de ella?; **against the law** ilegal

age [eɪdʒ] **1** n of person, object edad f; (era) era f; **at the age of ten** a los diez años; **under age** menor de edad; **she's five years of age** tiene cinco años; **I've been waiting for ages** llevo siglos esperando F; **I haven't seen him for ages** hace siglos que no lo veo F **2** v/i envejecer

aged[1] [eɪdʒd] adj: **aged 16** con 16 años de edad

a·ged[2] ['eɪdʒɪd] **1** adj: **her aged parents** sus ancianos padres **2** n: **the aged** los ancianos

'age group grupo m de edades

'age lim·it límite m de edad

a·gen·cy ['eɪdʒənsɪ] agencia f

a·gen·da [ə'dʒendə] orden m del día; **on the agenda** en el orden del día

a·gent ['eɪdʒənt] agente m/f, representante m/f

ag·gra·vate ['ægrəveɪt] v/t agravar; (annoy) molestar

ag·gre·gate ['ægrɪgət] n SP: **win on aggregate** ganar en el total de la eliminatoria

ag·gres·sion [ə'greʃn] agresividad f

ag·gres·sive [ə'gresɪv] adj agresivo; (dynamic) agresivo, enérgico

ag·gres·sive·ly [ə'gresɪvlɪ] adv agresivamente

a·ghast [ə'gæst] adj horrorizado

ag·ile ['ædʒəl] adj ágil

a·gil·i·ty [ə'dʒɪlətɪ] agilidad f

ag·i·tate ['ædʒɪteɪt] v/i: **agitate for** hacer campaña a favor de

ag·i·tat·ed ['ædʒɪteɪtɪd] adj agitado

ag·i·ta·tion [ædʒɪ'teɪʃn] agitación f

ag·i·ta·tor [ædʒɪ'teɪtər] agitador(a) m(f)

AGM [eɪdʒiː'em] abbr (= **annual general meeting**) junta f general annual

ag·nos·tic [æg'nɑːstɪk] n agnóstico(-a) m(f)

a·go [ə'gou] adv: **2 days ago** hace dos días; **long ago** hace mucho tiempo; **how long ago?** ¿hace cuánto tiempo?; **how long ago did he leave?** ¿hace cuánto se marchó?

a·gog [ə'gɑːg] adj: **be agog at sth** estar emocionado con algo

ag·o·nize ['ægənaɪz] v/i atormentarse (over por), angustiarse (over por)

ag·o·niz·ing ['ægənaɪzɪŋ] adj pain atroz; wait angustioso

ag·o·ny ['ægənɪ] agonía f

a·gree [ə'griː] **1** v/i estar de acuerdo; of figures coincidir; (reach agreement) ponerse de acuerdo; **I agree** estoy de acuerdo; **it doesn't agree with me** of food no me sienta bien **2** v/t price acordar; **agree that sth should be done** acordar que hay que hacer algo

a·gree·a·ble [ə'griːəbl] adj (pleasant) agradable; **be agreeable** fml (in agreement) estar de acuerdo

a·gree·ment [ə'griːmənt] (consent, contract) acuerdo m; **reach agreement on** llegar a un acuerdo sobre

ag·ri·cul·tur·al [ægrɪ'kʌltʃərəl] adj agrícola

ag·ri·cul·ture ['ægrɪkʌltʃər] agricultura f

a·head [ə'hed] adv position delante; movement adelante; in race por delante, en cabeza; **be ahead of** estar por delante de; **plan / think ahead** planear con antelación / pensar con anticipación

aid [eɪd] **1** n ayuda f; **come to s.o.'s aid** acudir a ayudar a alguien **2** v/t ayudar

aide [eɪd] asistente m/f

Aids [eɪdz] sida m

ail·ing ['eɪlɪŋ] adj economy débil, frágil

ail·ment ['eɪlmənt] achaque m

aim [eɪm] **1** n in shooting puntería f; (objective) objetivo m **2** v/i in shooting apuntar; **aim at doing sth, aim to do sth** tener como intención hacer algo **3** v/t remark dirigir; **he aimed the gun at me** me apuntó con la pistola; **be aimed at** *of remark etc* estar dirigido a; *of gun* estar apuntando a

aim·less ['eɪmlɪs] *adj* sin objetivos

air [er] **1** *n* aire *m*; **by air** *travel* en avión; *send mail* por correo aéreo; **in the open air** al aire libre; **on the air** RAD, TV en el aire **2** *v/t room* airear; *fig*: *views* airear, ventilar

'**air·bag** airbag *m*, bolsa *f* de aire

'**air·base** base *f* aérea

'**air·con·di·tioned** *adj* con aire acondicionado, climatizado

'**air·con·di·tion·ing** aire *m* acondicionado

'**air·craft** avión *m*, aeronave *f*

'**air·craft car·ri·er** portaaviones *m inv*

'**air fare** (precio *m* del) *Span* billete *m or L.Am.* boleto *m* de avión

'**air·field** aeródromo *m*, campo *m* de aviación

'**air force** fuerza *f* aérea

'**air host·ess** azafata *f*, *L.Am.* aeromoza *f*

'**air let·ter** aerograma *m*

'**air·lift 1** *n* puente *m* aéreo **2** *v/t* transportar mediante puente aéreo

'**air·line** línea *f* aérea

'**air·lin·er** avión *m* de pasajeros

'**air·mail**: **by airmail** por correo aéreo

'**air·plane** avión *m*

'**air·pock·et** bolsa *f* de aire

'**air pol·lu·tion** contaminación *f* del aire

'**air·port** aeropuerto *m*

'**air·sick**: **get airsick** marearse (*en avión*)

'**air·space** espacio *m* aéreo

'**air ter·mi·nal** terminal *f* aérea

'**air·tight** *adj container* hermético

'**air traf·fic** tráfico *m* aéreo

'**air·traf·fic con·trol** control *m* del tráfico aéreo

air-traf·fic con'trol·ler controlador(a) *m(f)* del tráfico aéreo

air·y ['eri] *adj room* aireado; *attitude* despreocupado, ligero

aisle [aɪl] pasillo *m*

'**aisle seat** asiento *m* de pasillo

a·jar [ə'dʒɑːr] *adj*: **be ajar** estar entreabierto

a·lac·ri·ty [ə'lækrətɪ] presteza *f*

a·larm [ə'lɑːrm] **1** *n* alarma *f*; **raise the alarm** dar la alarma **2** *v/t* alarmar

a'larm clock reloj *m* despertador

a·larm·ing [ə'lɑːrmɪŋ] *adj* alarmante

a·larm·ing·ly [ə'lɑːrmɪŋlɪ] *adv* de forma alarmante

al·bum ['ælbəm] *for photographs*, (*record*) álbum *m*

al·co·hol ['ælkəhɑːl] alcohol *m*

al·co·hol·ic [ælkə'hɑːlɪk] **1** *n* alcohólico(-a) *m(f)* **2** *adj* alcohólico

a·lert [ə'lɜːrt] **1** *n signal* alerta *f*; **be on the alert** estar alerta **2** *v/t* alertar **3** *adj* alerta

al·ge·bra ['ældʒɪbrə] álgebra *f*

al·i·bi ['ælɪbaɪ] coartada *f*

a·li·en ['eɪlɪən] **1** *n* (*foreigner*) extranjero(-a) *m(f)*; *from space* extraterrestre *m/f* **2** *adj* extraño; **be alien to s.o.** ser ajeno a alguien

a·li·en·ate ['eɪlɪəneɪt] *v/t* alienar, provocar el distanciamiento de

a·light [ə'laɪt] *adj* en llamas

a·lign [ə'laɪn] *v/t* alinear

a·like [ə'laɪk] **1** *adj*: **be alike** parecerse **2** *adv* igual; **old and young alike** viejos y jóvenes sin distinción

al·i·mo·ny ['ælɪmənɪ] pensión *f* alimenticia

a·live [ə'laɪv] *adj*: **be alive** estar vivo

all [ɒːl] **1** *adj* todo(s) **2** *pron* todo; **all of us/them** todos nosotros/ellos; **he ate all of it** se lo comió todo; **that's all, thanks** eso es todo, gracias; **for all I care** para lo que me importa; **for all I know** por lo que sé; **all at once** (*suddenly*) de repente; (*at the same time*) a la vez; **all but** (*except*) todos menos; (*nearly*) casi; **all the better** mucho mejor; **all the time** desde el principio; **they're not at all alike** no se parecen en nada; **not at all!** ¡en absoluto!; **two all** SP empate a dos; **all right** → **alright**

al·lay [ə'leɪ] *v/t* apaciguar

al·le·ga·tion [ælɪ'geɪʃn] acusación *f*

al·lege [ə'ledʒ] *v/t* alegar

al·leged [ə'ledʒd] *adj* presunto

al·leg·ed·ly [ə'ledʒɪdlɪ] *adv* presuntamente, supuestamente

al·le·giance [ə'liːdʒəns] lealtad *f*

al·ler·gic [ə'lɜːrdʒɪk] *adj* alérgico; **be allergic to s.o.** ser alérgico a

al·ler·gy ['ælərdʒɪ] alergia f

al·le·vi·ate [ə'liːvɪeɪt] v/t aliviar

al·ley ['ælɪ] callejón m

al·li·ance [ə'laɪəns] alianza f

al·lo·cate ['æləkeɪt] v/t asignar

al·lo·ca·tion [ælə'keɪʃn] asignación f

al·lot [ə'lɒːt] v/t (pret & pp **allotted**) asignar

al·low [ə'laʊ] v/t (permit) permitir; (calculate for) calcular; **they don't allow smoking** no está permitido fumar, está prohibido fumar; **it's not allowed** no está permitido; **he allowed us to leave** nos permitió salir

◆ **allow for** v/t tener en cuenta

al·low·ance [ə'laʊəns] (money) asignación f; (pocket money) paga f; **make allowances** for weather etc tener en cuenta; for person disculpar

al·loy ['ælɔɪ] aleación f

'**all-pur·pose** adj multiuso

'**all-round** adj completo

'**all-time**: **be at an all-time low** haber alcanzado un mínimo histórico

◆ **al·lude to** [ə'luːd] v/t aludir a

al·lur·ing [ə'lʊrɪŋ] adj atractivo, seductor

all-wheel 'drive adj con tracción a las cuatro ruedas

al·ly ['ælaɪ] n aliado(-a) m(f)

Al·might·y [ɒːl'maɪtɪ]: **the Almighty** el Todopoderoso

al·mond ['ɑːmənd] almendra f

al·most ['ɒːlmoʊst] adv casi

a·lone [ə'loʊn] adj solo

a·long [ə'lɒːŋ] 1 prep (situated beside) a lo largo de; **the shop is halfway along Baker Street** la tienda está a mitad de Baker Street; **walk along this path** sigue por esta calle 2 adv: **would you like to come along?** ¿te gustaría venir con nosotros?; **he always brings the dog along** siempre trae al perro; **along with** junto con; **all along** (all the time) todo el tiempo, desde el principio

a·long·side [əlɒːŋ'saɪd] prep (in co-operation with) junto a; (parallel to) al lado de

a·loof [ə'luːf] adj distante, reservado

a·loud [ə'laʊd] adv en voz alta

al·pha·bet ['ælfəbet] alfabeto m

al·pha·bet·i·cal [ælfə'betɪkl] adj alfabético

al·read·y [ɒːl'redɪ] adv ya

al·right [ɒːl'raɪt] adj (not hurt, in working order) bien; **is it alright to leave now?** (permitted) ¿puedo irme ahora?; **is it alright to take these out of the country?** ¿se pueden sacar éstos del país?; **is it alright with you if I …?** ¿te importa si …?; **alright, you can have one!** de acuerdo, ¡puedes tomar uno!; **alright, I heard you!** vale, ¡te he oído!; **everything is alright now between them** vuelven a estar bien; **that's alright** (don't mention it) de nada; (I don't mind) no importa

al·so ['ɒːlsoʊ] adv también

al·tar ['ɒːltər] altar m

al·ter ['ɒːltər] v/t alterar

al·ter·a·tion [ɒːltə'reɪʃn] alteración f

al·ter·nate 1 v/i ['ɒːltərneɪt] alternar **2** adj ['ɒːltərnət] alterno

al·ter·nat·ing cur·rent ['ɒːltərneɪtɪŋ] corriente f alterna

al·ter·na·tive [ɒːl'tɜːrnətɪv] **1** n alternativa f **2** adj alternativo

al·ter·na·tive·ly [ɒːl'tɜːrnətɪvlɪ] adv si no

al·though [ɒːl'ðoʊ] conj aunque, si bien

al·ti·tude ['æltɪtuːd] of plane, city altitud f; of mountain altura f

al·to·geth·er [ɒːltə'geðər] adv (completely) completamente; (in all) en total

al·tru·ism ['æltruːɪzm] altruismo m

al·tru·is·tic [æltruː'ɪstɪk] adj altruista

a·lu·min·i·um [æljʊ'mɪnɪəm] Br, **a·lu·mi·num** [ə'luːmənəm] aluminio m

al·ways ['ɒːlweɪz] adv siempre

a. m. ['eɪem] abbr (= **ante meridiem**) a. m.; **at 11 a.m** a las 11 de la mañana

a·mal·gam·ate [ə'mælgəmeɪt] v/i of companies fusionarse

a·mass [ə'mæs] v/t acumular

am·a·teur ['æmətʊr] n unskilled aficionado(-a) m(f); sp amateur m/f

am·a·teur·ish ['æmətʊrɪʃ] adj pej chapucero

a·maze [ə'meɪz] v/t asombrar

a·mazed [ə'meɪzd] adj asombrado; **we were amazed to hear …** nos asombró oír ...

a·maze·ment [ə'meɪzmənt] asombro *m*

a·maz·ing [ə'meɪzɪŋ] *adj* (*surprising*) asombroso; F (*very good*) alucinante F

a·maz·ing·ly [ə'meɪzɪŋlɪ] *adv* increíblemente

Am·a·zon ['æməzən] *n*: **the Amazon** el *Amazonas*

Am·a·zo·ni·an [æmə'zoʊnɪən] *adj* amazónico

am·bas·sa·dor [æm'bæsədər] embajador(a) *m(f)*

am·ber ['æmbər] *adj* ámbar; **at amber** en ámbar

am·bi·dex·trous [æmbɪ'dekstrəs] *adj* ambidiestro

am·bi·ence ['æmbɪəns] ambiente *m*

am·bi·gu·i·ty [æmbɪ'gju:ətɪ] ambigüedad *f*

am·big·u·ous [æm'bɪgjʊəs] *adj* ambiguo

am·bi·tion [æm'bɪʃn] *also pej* ambición *f*

am·bi·tious [æm'bɪʃəs] *adj* ambicioso

am·biv·a·lent [æm'bɪvələnt] *adj* ambivalente

am·ble ['æmbl] *v/i* deambular

am·bu·lance ['æmbjʊləns] ambulancia *f*

am·bush ['æmbʊʃ] **1** *n* emboscada *f* **2** *v/t* tender una emboscada a

a·mend [ə'mend] *v/t* enmendar

a·mend·ment [ə'mendmənt] enmienda *f*

a·mends [ə'mendz] *npl*: **make amends for** compensar

a·men·i·ties [ə'mi:nətɪz] *npl* servicios *mpl*

A·mer·i·ca [ə'merɪkə] *continent* América; *USA* Estados *mpl* Unidos

A·mer·i·can [ə'merɪkən] **1** *n North American* estadounidense *m/f* **2** *adj North American* estadounidense

A'mer·i·can plan pensión *f* completa

a·mi·a·ble ['eɪmɪəbl] *adj* afable, amable

a·mi·ca·ble ['æmɪkəbl] *adj* amistoso

a·mi·ca·bly ['æmɪkəblɪ] *adv* amistosamente

am·mu·ni·tion [æmjʊ'nɪʃn] munición *f*; *fig* argumentos *mpl*

am·ne·sia [æm'ni:zɪə] amnesia *f*

am·nes·ty ['æmnəstɪ] amnistía *f*

a·mong(st) [ə'mʌŋ(st)] *prep* entre

a·mor·al [eɪ'mɔːrəl] *adj* amoral

a·mount [ə'maʊnt] cantidad *f*; (*sum of money*) cantidad *f*, suma *f*

◆ **amount to** *v/t* ascender a; **his contribution didn't amount to much** su contribución no fue gran cosa

am·phib·i·an [æm'fɪbɪən] anfibio *m*

am·phib·i·ous [æm'fɪbɪəs] *adj animal, vehicle* anfibio

am·phi·the·a·ter, *Br* **am·phi·the·a·tre** ['æmfɪθɪətər] anfiteatro *m*

am·ple ['æmpl] *adj* abundante; **$4 will be ample** 4 dólares serán más que suficientes

am·pli·fi·er ['æmplɪfaɪr] amplificador *m*

am·pli·fy ['æmplɪfaɪ] *v/t* (*pret* & *pp* **amplified**) *sound* amplificar

am·pu·tate ['æmpjʊteɪt] *v/t* amputar

am·pu·ta·tion [æmpjʊ'teɪʃn] amputación *f*

a·muse [ə'mju:z] *v/t* (*make laugh etc*) divertir; (*entertain*) entretener

a·muse·ment [ə'mju:zmənt] (*merriment*) diversión *f*; (*entertainment*) entretenimiento *m*; **amusements** (*games*) juegos *mpl*; **what do you do for amusement?** ¿qué haces para entretenerte?; **to our great amusement** para nuestro regocijo

a'muse·ment ar·cade [ɑːr'keɪd] salón *m* de juegos recreativos

a'muse·ment park parque *m* de atracciones

a·mus·ing [ə'mju:zɪŋ] *adj* divertido

an·a·bol·ic ster·oid [ænə'bɑːlɪk] esteroide *m* anabolizante

a·nae·mi·a *etc Br →* **anemia** *etc*

an·aes·thet·ic *etc Br →* **anesthetic** *etc*

an·a·log ['ænəlɑːg] *adj* COMPUT analógico

a·nal·o·gy [ə'nælədʒɪ] analogía *f*

a·nal·y·sis [ə'næləsɪs] (*pl* **analyses** [ə'næləsi:z]) análisis *m inv*; (*psychoanalysis*) psicoanálisis *m inv*

an·a·lyst ['ænəlɪst] analista *m/f*; PSYCH psicoanalista *m/f*

an·a·lyt·i·cal [ænə'lɪtɪkl] *adj* analítico

an·a·lyze ['ænəlaɪz] *v/t* analizar; (*psychoanalyse*) psicoanalizar

an·arch·y ['ænərkɪ] anarquía *f*

a·nat·o·my [ə'nætəmɪ] anatomía *f*

an·ces·tor ['ænsestər] antepasado(-a) *m(f)*

an·chor ['æŋkər] **1** *n* NAUT ancla *f* ; TV presentador(a) *m(f)* **2** *v/i* NAUT anclar

an·cient ['eɪnʃənt] *adj* antiguo

an·cil·lar·y [æn'sɪlərɪ] *adj staff* auxiliar

and [ənd] *stressed* [ænd] *conj* y

An·de·an ['ændɪən] *adj* andino

An·des ['ændiːz] *npl*: **the Andes** los Andes

an·ec·dote ['ænɪkdout] anécdota *f*

a·ne·mia [ə'niːmɪə] anemia *f*

a·ne·mic [ə'niːmɪk] *adj* anémico

an·es·thet·ic [ænəs'θetɪk] *n* anestesia *f*

an·es·the·tist [ə'niːsθətɪst] anestesista *m/f*

an·gel ['eɪndʒl] REL ángel *m*; *fig* ángel *m*, cielo *m*

an·ger ['æŋgər] **1** *n* enfado *m*, enojo *m* **2** *v/t* enfadar, enojar

an·gi·na [æn'dʒaɪnə] angina *f* (de pecho)

an·gle ['æŋgl] *n* ángulo *m*

An·glo-Sax·on [æŋglou'sæksn] **1** *adj* anglosajón **2** *n person* anglosajón(-ona) *m(f)*

an·gry ['æŋgrɪ] *adj* enfadado, enojado; **be angry with s.o.** estar enfadado *or* enojado con alguien

an·guish ['æŋgwɪʃ] angustia *f*

an·gu·lar ['æŋgjulər] *adj* anguloso

an·i·mal ['ænɪml] animal *m*

an·i·mated ['ænɪmeɪtɪd] *adj* animado

an·i·ma·ted car·toon dibujos *mpl* animados

an·i·ma·tion [ænɪ'meɪʃn] (*liveliness*), *of cartoon* animación *f*

an·i·mos·i·ty [ænɪ'mɑːsətɪ] animosidad *f*

an·kle ['æŋkl] tobillo *m*

an·nex ['æneks] **1** *n building* edificio *m* anexo **2** *v/t state* anexionar

an·nexe ['æneks] *n Br* edificio *m* anexo

an·ni·hi·late [ə'naɪəleɪt] *v/t* aniquilar

an·ni·hi·la·tion [ənaɪə'leɪʃn] aniquilación *f*

an·ni·ver·sa·ry [ænɪ'vɜːrsərɪ] (*wedding anniversary*) aniversario *m*

an·no·tate ['ænəteɪt] *v/t report* anotar

an·nounce [ə'naʊns] *v/t* anunciar

an·nounce·ment [ə'naʊnsmənt] anuncio *m*

an·nounc·er [ə'naʊnsər] TV, RAD presentador(a) *m(f)*

an·noy [ə'nɔɪ] *v/t* molestar, irritar; **be annoyed** estar molesto *or* irritado

an·noy·ance [ə'nɔɪəns] (*anger*) irritación *f*; (*nuisance*) molestia *f*

an·noy·ing [ə'nɔɪɪŋ] *adj* molesto, irritante

an·nu·al ['ænʊəl] *adj* anual

an·nu·al gen·er·al 'meet·ing junta *f* general anual

an·nu·i·ty [ə'nuːətɪ] anualidad *f*

an·nul [ə'nʌl] *v/t* (*pret & pp* **annulled**) *marriage* anular

an·nul·ment [ə'nʌlmənt] anulación *f*

a·non·y·mous [ə'nɑːnɪməs] *adj* anónimo

a·no·rak ['ænəræk] *Br* anorak *m*

an·o·rex·i·a [ænə'reksɪə] anorexia *f*

an·o·rex·ic [ænə'reksɪk] *adj* anoréxico

an·oth·er [ə'nʌðər] **1** *adj* otro **2** *pron* otro(-a) *m(f)*; **they helped one another** se ayudaron (el uno al otro); **do they know one another?** ¿se conocen?

ans·wer ['ænsər] **1** *n to letter, person, question* respuesta *f*, contestación *f*; *to problem* solución *f* **2** *v/t letter, person, question* responder, contestar; **answer the door** abrir la puerta; **answer the telephone** responder *or Span* coger al teléfono

♦ **answer back** *v/t & v/i* contestar, replicar

♦ **answer for** *v/t* responder de

an·swer·ing ma·chine ['ænsərɪŋ] TELEC contestador *m* (automático)

ans·wer·phone ['ænsərfoun] TELEC contestador *m* (automático)

ant [ænt] hormiga *f*

an·tag·o·nism [æn'tægənɪzm] antagonismo *m*

an·tag·o·nis·tic [æntægə'nɪstɪk] *adj* hostil

an·tag·o·nize [æn'tægənaɪz] *v/t* antagonizar, enfadar

Ant·arc·tic [ænt'ɑːrktɪk] *n*: **the Antarctic** el Antártico

an·te·na·tal [æntɪ'neɪtl] *adj* prenatal

an·ten·na [æn'tenə] *of insect, for* TV antena *f*

an·thol·o·gy [æn'θɑːlədʒɪ] antología *f*

an·thro·pol·o·gy [ænθrə'pɑːlədʒɪ] antropología *f*

an·ti·bi·ot·ic [æntɪbaɪ'ɑːtɪk] *n* antibiótico *m*

an·ti·bod·y ['æntɪbɑːdɪ] anticuerpo *m*

an·tic·i·pate [æn'tɪsɪpeɪt] *v/t* esperar, prever

an·tic·i·pa·tion [æntɪsɪ'peɪʃn] expectativa *f*, previsión *f*

an·ti·clock·wise ['æntɪklɑːkwaɪz] *adv Br* en dirección contraria a las agujas del reloj

an·tics ['æntɪks] *npl* payasadas *fpl*

an·ti·dote ['æntɪdout] antídoto *m*

an·ti·freeze ['æntɪfriːz] anticongelante *m*

an·ti·pa·thy [æn'tɪpəθɪ] antipatía *f*

an·ti·quat·ed ['æntɪkweɪtɪd] *adj* anticuado

an·tique [æn'tiːk] *n* antigüedad *f*

an·tique dealer anticuario(-a) *m(f)*

an·tiq·ui·ty [æn'tɪkwətɪ] antigüedad *f*

an·ti·sep·tic [æntɪ'septɪk] **1** *adj* antiséptico **2** *n* antiséptico *m*

an·ti·so·cial [æntɪ'souʃl] *adj* antisocial, poco sociable

an·ti·vi·rus pro·gram [æntɪ'vaɪrəs] COMPUT (programa *m*) antivirus *m inv*

anx·i·e·ty [æŋ'zaɪətɪ] ansiedad *f*

anx·ious ['æŋkʃəs] *adj* preocupado; (*eager*) ansioso; *be anxious for for news etc* esperar ansiosamente

an·y ['enɪ] **1** *adj*: *are there any disk-ettes / glasses?* ¿hay disquetes / vasos?; *is there any bread / improvement?* ¿hay algo de pan / alguna mejora?; *there aren't any diskettes / glasses* no hay disquetes / vasos; *there isn't any bread / improvement* no hay pan / ninguna mejora; *have you any idea at all?* ¿tienes alguna idea?; *any one of them could win* cualquiera de ellos podría ganar **2** *pron* alguno(-a); *do you have any?* ¿tienes alguno(s)?; *there aren't any left* no queda ninguno; *any of them could be guilty* cualquiera de ellos podría ser culpable **3** *adv*: *is that any bet-ter / easier?* ¿es mejor / más fácil así?; *I* *don't like it any more* ya no me gusta

an·y·bod·y ['enɪbɑːdɪ] *pron* alguien; *the-re wasn't anybody there* no había nadie allí

an·y·how ['enɪhaʊ] *adv* en todo caso, de todos modos; *if I can help you anyhow, please let me know* si puedo ayudarte de alguna manera, por favor dímelo

an·y·one ['enɪwʌn] → *anybody*

an·y·thing ['enɪθɪŋ] *pron* algo; *with nega-tives* nada; *I didn't hear anything* no oí nada; *anything but* todo menos; *anyt-hing else?* ¿algo más?

an·y·way ['enɪweɪ] → *anyhow*

an·y·where ['enɪwer] *adv* en alguna par-te; *is Peter anywhere around?* ¿está Peter por ahí?; *he never goes anywhere* nunca va a ninguna parte; *I can't find it anywhere* no lo encuentro por ninguna parte

a·part [ə'pɑːrt] *adv* aparte; *the two cities are 250 miles apart* las dos ciudades están a 250 millas la una de la otra; *live apart* *of people* vivir separado; *apart from* aparte de

a·part·ment [ə'pɑːrtmənt] apartamento *m*, *Span* piso *m*, *Am* departamento *m*

a·part·ment block bloque *m* de aparta-mentos *or Span* pisos

ap·a·thet·ic [æpə'θetɪk] *adj* apático

ap·a·thy ['æpəθɪ] apatía *f*

ape [eɪp] simio *m*

a·pe·ri·tif [ə'perɪtiːf] aperitivo *m*

ap·er·ture ['æpərtʃər] PHOT apertura *f*

a·piece [ə'piːs] *adv* cada uno

a·pol·o·get·ic [əpɑːlə'dʒetɪk] *adj letter* de disculpa; *he was very apologetic about ...* pedía constantes disculpas por ...

a·pol·o·gize [ə'pɑːlədʒaɪz] *v/i* discul-parse, pedir perdón

a·pol·o·gy [ə'pɑːlədʒɪ] disculpa *f*

a·pos·tle [ə'pɑːsl] REL apóstol *m*

a·pos·tro·phe [ə'pɑːstrəfɪ] GRAM apóstro-fo *m*

ap·pall [ə'pɒːl] *v/t* horrorizar, espantar

ap·pal·ling [ə'pɒːlɪŋ] *adj* horroroso

ap·pa·ra·tus [æpə'reɪtəs] aparatos *mpl*

ap·par·ent [ə'pærənt] *adj* aparente, evi-dente; *become apparent that ...* hacerse evidente que …

ap·par·ent·ly [ə'pærəntlɪ] *adv* al parecer, por lo visto

ap·pa·ri·tion [æpə'rɪʃn] (*ghost*) aparición *f*

ap·peal [ə'piːl] **1** *n* (*charm*) atractivo *m*; *for funds etc* llamamiento *m*; LAW apelación *f* **2** *v/i* LAW apelar

◆ **appeal to** *v/t* (*be attractive to*) atraer a

◆ **appeal for** *v/t* solicitar

ap·peal·ing [ə'piːlɪŋ] *adj idea, offer* atractivo; *glance* suplicante

ap·pear [ə'pɪr] *v/i* aparecer; *in court* comparecer; (*look, seem*) parecer; *it appears that …* parece que …

ap·pear·ance [ə'pɪrəns] aparición *f*; *in court* comparecencia *f*; (*look*) apariencia *f*, aspecto *m*; *put in an appearance* hacer acto de presencia

ap·pease [ə'piːz] *v/t* apaciguar

ap·pen·di·ci·tis [əpendɪ'saɪtɪs] apendicitis *m*

ap·pen·dix [ə'pendɪks] MED, *of book etc* apéndice *m*

ap·pe·tite ['æpɪtaɪt] *also fig* apetito *m*

ap·pe·tiz·er ['æpɪtaɪzər] aperitivo *m*

ap·pe·tiz·ing ['æpɪtaɪzɪŋ] *adj* apetitoso

ap·plaud [ə'plɔːd] **1** *v/i* aplaudir **2** *v/t also fig* aplaudir

ap·plause [ə'plɔːz] aplauso *m*

ap·ple ['æpl] manzana *f*

ap·ple 'pie tarta *f* de manzana

ap·ple 'sauce compota *f* de manzana

ap·pli·ance [ə'plaɪəns] aparato *m*; *household* electrodoméstico *m*

ap·plic·a·ble [ə'plɪkəbl] *adj* aplicable; *it's not applicable to foreigners* no se aplica a extranjeros

ap·pli·cant ['æplɪkənt] solicitante *m/f*

ap·pli·ca·tion [æplɪ'keɪʃn] *for job, passport etc* solicitud *f*; *for university* solicitud *f* (de admisión)

ap·pli·ca·tion form *for passport* impreso *m* de solicitud; *for university* impreso *m* de solicitud de admisión

ap·ply [ə'plaɪ] **1** *v/t* (*pret & pp applied*) *rules, solution, ointment* aplicar **2** *v/i* (*pret & pp applied*) *of rule, law* aplicarse

◆ **apply for** *v/t job, passport* solicitar; *uni-*

versity solicitar el ingreso en

◆ **apply to** *v/t* (*contact*) dirigirse a; (*affect*) aplicarse a

ap·point [ə'pɔɪnt] *v/t to position* nombrar, designar

ap·point·ment [ə'pɔɪntmənt] *to position* nombramiento *m*, designación *f*; *meeting* cita *f*; *make an appointment with the doctor* pedir hora con el doctor

ap·point·ments di·a·ry agenda *f* de citas

ap·prais·al [ə'preɪz(ə)l] evaluación *f*

ap·pre·cia·ble [ə'priːʃəbl] *adj* apreciable

ap·pre·ci·ate [ə'priːʃɪeɪt] **1** *v/t* (*value*) apreciar; (*be grateful for*) agradecer; (*acknowledge*) ser consciente de; *thanks, I appreciate it* te lo agradezco **2** *v/i* FIN revalorizarse

ap·pre·ci·a·tion [əpriːʃɪ'eɪʃn] *of kindness etc* agradecimiento *m*; *of music etc* aprecio *m*

ap·pre·ci·a·tive [ə'priːʃətɪv] *adj* agradecido

ap·pre·hen·sive [æprɪ'hensɪv] *adj* aprensivo, temeroso

ap·pren·tice [ə'prentɪs] aprendiz(a) *m(f)*

ap·proach [ə'prəʊtʃ] **1** *n* aproximación *f*; (*proposal*) propuesta *f*; *to problem* enfoque *m* **2** *v/t* (*get near to*) aproximarse a; (*contact*) ponerse en contacto con; *problem* enfocar

ap·proach·a·ble [ə'prəʊtʃəbl] *adj person* accesible

ap·pro·pri·ate[1] [ə'prəʊprɪət] *adj* apropiado, adecuado

ap·pro·pri·ate[2] [ə'prəʊprɪeɪt] *v/t* apropiarse de; (*euph: steal*) apropiarse de

ap·prov·al [ə'pruːvl] aprobación *f*

ap·prove [ə'pruːv] **1** *v/i*: *my parents don't approve* a mis padres no les parece bien **2** *v/t* aprobar

◆ **approve of** *v/t* aprobar; *her parents don't approve of me* no les gusto a sus padres

ap·prox·i·mate [ə'prɑːksɪmət] *adj* aproximado

ap·prox·i·mate·ly [ə'prɑːksɪmətlɪ] *adv* aproximadamente

ap·prox·i·ma·tion [əprɑːksɪ'meɪʃn] aproximación *f*

APR [eɪpiː'ɑː] *abbr* (= *annual percentage rate*) TAE *f* (= tasa *f* anual equivalente)

a·pri·cot ['æprɪkɒt] albaricoque *m*, *L.Am.* damasco *m*

A·pril ['eɪprəl] abril *m*

apt [æpt] *adj remark* oportuno; **be apt to ...** ser propenso a ...

ap·ti·tude ['æptɪtuːd] aptitud *f*; **he has a natural aptitude for ...** tiene aptitudes naturales para ...

'ap·ti·tude test prueba *f* de aptitud

aq·ua·lung ['ækwəlʌŋ] escafandra *f* autónoma

a·quar·i·um [ə'kweriəm] acuario *m*

A·quar·i·us [ə'kweriəs] ASTR Acuario *m/f inv*

a·quat·ic [ə'kwætɪk] *adj* acuático

Ar·ab ['ærəb] **1** *adj* árabe **2** *n* árabe *m/f*

Ar·a·bic ['ærəbɪk] **1** *adj* árabe **2** *n* árabe *m*

ar·a·ble ['ærəbl] *adj* arable, cultivable

ar·bi·tra·ry ['ɑːrbɪtrerɪ] *adj* arbitrario

ar·bi·trate ['ɑːrbɪtreɪt] *v/i* arbitrar

ar·bi·tra·tion [ɑːrbɪ'treɪʃn] arbitraje *m*

ar·bi·tra·tor ['ɑːrbɪtreɪtər] árbitro(-a) *m(f)*

arch [ɑːrtʃ] *n* arco *m*

ar·chae·ol·o·gy *etc Br* → **archeology** *etc*

ar·cha·ic [ɑːr'keɪɪk] *adj* arcaico

ar·che·o·log·i·cal [ɑːrkɪə'lɑːdʒɪkl] *adj* arqueológico

ar·che·ol·o·gist [ɑːrkɪ'ɑːlədʒɪst] arqueólogo(-a) *m(f)*

ar·che·ol·o·gy [ɑːrkɪ'ɑːlədʒɪ] arqueología *f*

ar·cher ['ɑːrtʃər] arquero(-a) *m(f)*

ar·chi·tec·t ['ɑːrkɪtekt] arquitecto(-a) *m(f)*

ar·chi·tec·tur·al [ɑːrkɪ'tektʃərəl] *adj* arquitectónico

ar·chi·tec·ture ['ɑːrkɪtektʃər] arquitectura *f*

ar·chives ['ɑːrkaɪvz] *npl* archivos *mpl*

arch·way ['ɑːrtʃweɪ] arco *m*

Arc·tic ['ɑːrktɪk] *n:* **the Arctic** el Ártico

ar·dent ['ɑːrdənt] *adj* ardiente, ferviente

ar·du·ous ['ɑːrdjuəs] *adj* arduo

ar·e·a ['erɪə] área *f*, zona *f*; *of activity, study etc* área *f*, ámbito *m*

'ar·e·a code TELEC prefijo *m*

a·re·na [ə'riːnə] SP estadio *m*

Ar·gen·ti·na [ɑːrdʒən'tiːnə] Argentina

Ar·gen·tin·i·an [ɑːrdʒən'tɪnɪən] **1** *adj* argentino **2** *n* argentino(-a) *m(f)*

ar·gu·a·bly ['ɑːrgjuəblɪ] *adv* posiblemente

ar·gue ['ɑːrgjuː] **1** *v/i* (*quarrel*) discutir; (*reason*) argumentar **2** *v/t:* **argue that ...** argumentar que ...

ar·gu·ment ['ɑːrgjumənt] (*quarrel*) discusión *m*; (*reasoning*) argumento *m*

ar·gu·men·ta·tive [ɑːrgjuˈmentətɪv] *adj* discutidor

a·ri·a ['ɑːrɪə] MUS aria *f*

ar·id ['ærɪd] *adj land* árido

Ar·i·es ['eriːz] ASTR Aries *m/f inv*

a·rise [ə'raɪz] *v/i* (*pret* **arose**, *pp* **arisen**) *of situation, problem* surgir

a·ris·en [ə'rɪzn] *pp* → **arise**

ar·is·toc·ra·cy [ærɪ'stɑːkrəsɪ] aristocracia *f*

ar·is·to·crat [ə'rɪstəkræt] aristócrata *m/f*

ar·is·to·crat·ic [ærɪstə'krætɪk] *adj* aristocrático

a·rith·me·tic [ə'rɪθmətɪk] aritmética *f*

arm[1] [ɑːrm] *n of person, chair* brazo *m*

arm[2] [ɑːrm] *v/t* armar

ar·ma·ments ['ɑːrməmənts] *npl* armamento *m*

arm·chair ['ɑːrmtʃer] sillón *m*

armed [ɑːrmd] *adj* armado

armed 'forc·es *npl* fuerzas *fpl* armadas

armed 'rob·ber·y atraco *m* a mano armada

ar·mor, *Br* **ar·mour** ['ɑːrmər] armadura *f*

ar·mored 've·hi·cle, *Br* **ar·moured 've·hi·cle** ['ɑːrmərd] vehículo *m* blindado

'arm·pit ['ɑːrmpɪt] sobaco *m*

arms [ɑːrmz] *npl* (*weapons*) armas *fpl*

ar·my ['ɑːrmɪ] ejército *m*

a·ro·ma [ə'roumə] aroma *m*

a·rose [ə'rouz] *pret* → **arise**

a·round [ə'raund] **1** *prep* (*enclosing*) alrededor de; **it's around the corner** está a la vuelta de la esquina **2** *adv* (*in the area*) por ahí; (*encircling*) alrededor; (*roughly*) alrededor de, aproximadamente; (*with expressions of time*) en torno a; **he lives**

around here vive por aquí; **walk around** pasear; **she has been around** (*has traveled, is experienced*) tiene mucho mundo; **he's still around** F (*alive*) todavía está rondando por ahí F

a·rouse [ə'rauz] *v/t* despertar; *sexually* excitar

ar·range [ə'reɪndʒ] *v/t* (*put in order*) ordenar; *furniture* ordenar, disponer; *flowers, music* arreglar; *meeting, party etc* organizar; *time and place* acordar; **I've arranged to meet her** he quedado con ella
◆ **arrange for** *v/t:* **I arranged for Jack to collect it** quedé para que Jack lo recogiera

ar·range·ment [ə'reɪndʒmənt] (*plan*) plan *m*, preparativo *m*; (*agreement*) acuerdo *m*; (*layout: of furniture etc*) orden *m*, disposición *f*; *of flowers, music* arreglo *m*; **I've made arrangements for the neighbors to water my plants** he quedado con los vecinos para que rieguen mis plantas

ar·rears [ə'rɪərz] *npl* atrasos *mpl*; **be in arrears** *of person* ir atrasado

ar·rest [ə'rest] **1** *n* detención *f*, arresto *m*; **be under arrest** estar detenido *or* arrestado **2** *v/t* detener, arrestar

ar·riv·al [ə'raɪvl] llegada *f*; **on your arrival** al llegar; **arrivals** *at airport* llegadas *fsg*

ar·rive [ə'raɪv] *v/i* llegar
◆ **arrive at** *v/t place, decision etc* llegar a

ar·ro·gance ['ærəgəns] arrogancia *f*

ar·ro·gant ['ærəgənt] *adj* arrogante

ar·ro·gant·ly ['ærəgəntlɪ] *adv* con arrogancia

ar·row ['ærou] flecha *f*

arse [ɑːrs] *Br* P culom P

ar·se·nic ['ɑːrsənɪk] arsénico *m*

ar·son ['ɑːrsn] incendio *m* provocado

ar·son·ist ['ɑːrsənɪst] pirómano(-a) *m(f)*

art [ɑːrt] arte *m*; **the arts** las artes

ar·te·ry ['ɑːrtərɪ] MED arteria *f*

'art gal·ler·y *public* museo *m*; *private* galería *f* de arte

ar·thri·tis [ɑːr'θraɪtɪs] artritis *f*

ar·ti·choke ['ɑːrtɪʃouk] alcachofa *f*, *L.Am.* alcaucil *m*

ar·ti·cle ['ɑːrtɪkl] artículo *m*

ar·tic·u·late [ɑːr'tɪkjulət] *adj person* elocuente

ar·ti·fi·cial [ɑːrtɪ'fɪʃl] *adj* artificial

ar·ti·fi·cial in'tel·li·gence inteligencia *f* artificial

ar·til·le·ry [ɑːr'tɪlərɪ] artillería *f*

ar·ti·san ['ɑːrtɪzæn] artesano(-a) *m(f)*

ar·tist ['ɑːrtɪst] (*painter, artistic person*) artista *m/f*

ar·tis·tic [ɑːr'tɪstɪk] *adj* artístico

'arts de·gree licenciatura *f* en letras

as [æz] **1** *conj* (*while, when*) cuando; (*because, like*) como; **as if** como si; **as usual** como de costumbre; **as necessary** como sea necesario **2** *adv* como; **as high / pretty as …** tan alto / guapa como …; **as much as that?** ¿tanto? **3** *prep* como; **work as a team** trabajar en equipo; **as a child / schoolgirl** cuando era un niño / una colegiala; **work as a teacher / translator** trabajar como profesor / traductor; **as for** por lo que respecta a; **as Hamlet** en el papel del Hamlet

asap ['eɪzæp] *abbr* (= **as soon as possible**) cuanto antes

as·bes·tos [æz'bestɑːs] amianto *m*, asbesto *m*

As·cen·sion [ə'senʃn] REL Ascensión *f*

ash [æʃ] ceniza *f*; **ashes** *of person* cenizas *fpl*

a·shamed [ə'ʃeɪmd] *adj* avergonzado, *L.Am.* apenado; **be ashamed of** estar avergonzado *or L.Am.* apenado de; **you should be ashamed of yourself** debería darte vergüenza *or L.Am.* pena; **it's nothing to be ashamed of** no tienes por qué avergonzarte *or L.Am.* apenarte

'ash bin, 'ash can cubo *m* de la basura

a·shore [ə'ʃɔːr] *adv* en tierra; **go ashore** desembarcar

ash·tray ['æʃtreɪ] cenicero *m*

A·sia ['eɪʃə] Asia

A·sian ['eɪʃn] **1** *adj* asiático **2** *n* asiático(-a) *m(f)*

a·side [ə'saɪd] *adv* a un lado; **move aside please** apártense, por favor; **he took me aside** me llevó aparte; **aside from** aparte de ask [æsk] **1** v/t *person, question* preguntar; *question* hacer; *(invite)* invitar; *favor* pedir; **can I ask you something?** ¿puedo hacerle una pregunta?; **ask s.o. for sth** pedir algo a alguien; **he asked me to leave** me pidió que me fuera; **ask s.o. about sth** preguntar por algo a alguien **2** v/i: **all you need to do is ask** no tienes más que pedirlo

◆ **ask after** v/t *person* preguntar por

◆ **ask for** v/t pedir; *person* preguntar por

◆ **ask out** v/t *for a drink, night out* invitar a salir

ask·ing price ['æskɪŋ] precio *m* de salida

a·sleep [ə'sliːp] *adj* dormido; **be (fast) asleep** estar (profundamente) dormido; **fall asleep** dormirse, quedarse dormido

as·par·a·gus [ə'spærəgəs] espárragos *mpl*

as·pect ['æspekt] aspecto *m*

as·phalt ['æsfælt] *n* asfalto *m*

as·phyx·i·ate [æ'sfɪksɪeɪt] v/t asfixiar

as·phyx·i·a·tion [əsfɪksɪ'eɪʃn] asfixia *f*

as·pi·ra·tion [æspə'reɪʃn] aspiración *f*

as·pi·rin ['æsprɪn] aspirina *f*

ass[1] [æs] *(idiot)* burro(-a) *m(f)*

ass[2] [æs] P *(backside)* culo P; *(sex)* sexo *m*

as·sai·lant [ə'seɪlənt] asaltante *m/f*

as·sas·sin [ə'sæsɪn] asesino(-a) *m(f)*

as·sas·sin·ate [ə'sæsɪneɪt] v/t asesinar

as·sas·sin·a·tion [əsæsɪ'neɪʃn] asesinato *m*

as·sault [ə'sɔːlt] **1** *n* agresión *f*; *(attack)* ataque *m* **2** v/t atacar, agredir

as·sem·ble [ə'sembl] **1** v/t *parts* montar **2** v/i *of people* reunirse

as·sem·bly [ə'semblɪ] *of parts* montaje *m*; POL asamblea *f*

as·sem·bly line cadena *f* de montaje

as·sem·bly plant planta *f* de montaje

as·sent [ə'sent] v/i asentir, dar el consentimiento

as·sert [ə'sɜːrt] v/t afirmar, hacer valer; **assert o.s.** mostrarse firme

as·ser·tive [ə'sɜːrtɪv] *adj person* seguro y firme

as·sess [ə'ses] v/t *situation* evaluar; *value* valorar

as·sess·ment [ə'sesmənt] evaluación *f*

as·set ['æset] FIN activo *m*; *fig* ventaja *f*; **she's an asset to the company** es un gran valor para la compañía

ass·hole ['æshoʊl] V ojete *m* V; *(idiot)* Span gilipollas *m/f inv* V, *L.Am.* pendejo(-a) *m(f)* V

as·sign [ə'saɪn] v/t *person, thing* asignar

as·sign·ment [ə'saɪnmənt] *(task, study)* trabajo *m*

as·sim·i·late [ə'sɪmɪleɪt] v/t *information* asimilar; *person into group* integrar

as·sist [ə'sɪst] v/t ayudar

as·sist·ance [ə'sɪstəns] ayuda *f*, asistencia *f*

as·sis·tant [ə'sɪstənt] ayudante *m/f*; *Br in store* dependiente(-a) *m(f)*

as·sis·tant di·rec·tor director(a) *m(f)* adjunto

as·sis·tant 'man·ag·er *of business* subdirector(a) *m(f)*; *of hotel, restaurant, store* subdirector(a) *m(f)*, subgerente *m/f*

as·so·ci·ate 1 v/t [ə'soʊʃɪeɪt] asociar; **he has long been associated with the Royal Ballet** ha estado vinculado al Royal Ballet durante mucho tiempo **2** v/i [ə'soʊʃɪeɪt]: **associate with** relacionarse con **3** *n* [ə'soʊʃɪət] colega *m/f*

as·so·ci·ate pro·fes·sor profesor(a) *m(f)* adjunto(a)

as·so·ci·a·tion [əsoʊsɪ'eɪʃn] asociación *f*; **in association with** conjuntamente con

as·sort·ed [ə'sɔːrtɪd] *adj* surtido, diverso

as·sort·ment [ə'sɔːrtmənt] *of food* surtido *m*; *of people* diversidad *f*

as·sume [ə'suːm] v/t *(suppose)* suponer

as·sump·tion [ə'sʌmpʃn] suposición *f*

as·sur·ance [ə'ʃʊrəns] garantía *f*; *(confidence)* seguridad *f*

as·sure [ə'ʃʊr] v/t *(reassure)* asegurar

as·sured [ə'ʃʊrd] *adj (confident)* seguro

as·ter·isk ['æstərɪsk] asterisco *m*

asth·ma ['æsmə] asma *f*

asth·mat·ic [æs'mætɪk] *adj* asmático

as·ton·ish [ə'stɑːnɪʃ] v/t asombrar, sorprender; **be astonished** estar asombrado *or* sorprendido

as·ton·ish·ing [ə'stɑːnɪʃɪŋ] *adj* asombroso, sorprendente

as·ton·ish·ing·ly [ə'stɑːnɪʃɪŋlɪ] *adv*

A

asombrosamente

as·ton·ish·ment [əˈstɒnɪʃmənt] asombro *m*, sorpresa *f*

as·tound [əˈstaʊnd] *v/t* pasmar

as·tound·ing [əˈstaʊndɪŋ] *adj* pasmoso

a·stray [əˈstreɪ] *adv*: *go astray* extraviarse; *morally* descarriarse

a·stride [əˈstraɪd] **1** *adv* a horcajadas **2** *prep* a horcajadas sobre

as·trol·o·ger [əˈstrɑːlədʒər] astrólogo(-a) *m(f)*

as·trol·o·gy [əˈstrɑːlədʒɪ] astrología *f*

as·tro·naut [ˈæstrənɔːt] astronauta *m/f*

as·tron·o·mer [əˈstrɑːnəmər] astrónomo(-a) *m(f)*

as·tro·nom·i·cal [æstrəˈnɑːmɪkl] *adj price etc* astronómico

as·tron·o·my [əˈstrɑːnəmɪ] astronomía *f*

as·tute [əˈstuːt] *adj* astuto, sagaz

a·sy·lum [əˈsaɪləm] *(mental asylum)* manicomio *m*; *political* asilo *m*

at [ət] *stressed* [æt] *prep with places* en; *at Joe's house* en casa de Joe; *bar* en el bar de Joe; *at the door* a la puerta; *at 10 dollars* a 10 dólares; *at the age of 18* a los 18 años; *at 5 o'clock* a las 5; *at 150 km/h* a 150 km./h.; *be good / bad at sth* ser bueno / malo haciendo algo

ate [eɪt] *pret* → *eat*

a·the·ism [ˈeɪθɪɪzm] ateísmo *m*

a·the·ist [ˈeɪθɪɪst] ateo(-a) *m(f)*

ath·lete [ˈæθliːt] atleta *m/f*

ath·let·ic [æθˈletɪk] *adj* atlético

ath·let·ics [æθˈletɪks] atletismo *m*

At·lan·tic [ətˈlæntɪk] *n*: *the Atlantic* el Atlántico

at·las [ˈætləs] atlas *m inv*

ATM [eɪtiːˈem] *abbr* (= *automatic teller machine*) cajero *m* automático

at·mos·phere [ˈætməsfɪr] *of earth* atmósfera *f*; *(ambiance)* ambiente *m*

at·mos·pher·ic pol'lu·tion [ætməsˈferɪk] contaminación *f* atmosférica

at·om [ˈætəm] átomo *m*

'at·om bomb bomba *f* atómica

a·tom·ic [əˈtɑːmɪk] *adj* atómico

a·tom·ic 'en·er·gy energía *f* atómica *or* nuclear

a·tom·ic 'waste desechos *mpl* radiactivos

a·tom·iz·er [ˈætəmaɪzər] atomizador *m*

a·tone [əˈtoʊn] *v/i*: *atone for* expiar

a·tro·cious [əˈtroʊʃəs] *adj* atroz, terrible

a·troc·i·ty [əˈtrɑːsəti] atrocidad *f*

at·tach [əˈtætʃ] *v/t* sujetar, fijar; *importance* atribuir; *be attached to* (*fond of*) tener cariño a

at·tach·ment [əˈtætʃmənt] (*fondness*) cariño *m* (*to* por)

at·tack [əˈtæk] **1** *n* ataque *m* **2** *v/t* atacar

at·tempt [əˈtempt] **1** *n* intento *m*; *an attempt on the world record* un intento de batir el récord del mundo **2** *v/t* intentar

at·tend [əˈtend] *v/t* acudir a

♦ **attend to** *v/t* ocuparse de; *customer* atender

at·tend·ance [əˈtendəns] asistencia *f*

at·tend·ant [əˈtendənt] *in museum etc* vigilante *m/f*

at·ten·tion [əˈtenʃn] atención *f*; *bring sth to s.o.'s attention* informar a alguien de algo; *your attention please* atención, por favor; *pay attention* prestar atención

at·ten·tive [əˈtentɪv] *adj listener* atento

at·tic [ˈætɪk] ático *m*

at·ti·tude [ˈætɪtuːd] actitud *f*

attn *abbr* (= *for the attention of*) atn (= a la atención de)

at·tor·ney [əˈtɜːrnɪ] abogado(-a) *m(f)*; *power of attorney* poder *m* (notarial)

at·tract [əˈtrækt] *v/t* atraer; *attract attention* llamar la atención; *attract s.o.'s attention* atraer la atención de alguien; *be attracted to s.o.* sentirse atraído por alguien

at·trac·tion [əˈtrækʃn] atracción *f*, atractivo *m*; *romantic* atracción *f*

at·trac·tive [əˈtræktɪv] *adj* atractivo

at·trib·ute¹ [əˈtrɪbjuːt] *v/t* atribuir; *attribute sth to …* atribuir algo a …

at·trib·ute² [ˈætrɪbjuːt] *n* atributo *m*

au·ber·gine [ˈoʊbɜːrʒiːn] *Br* berenjena *f*

auc·tion [ˈɒːkʃn] **1** *n* subasta *f*, *L.Am.* remate *m* **2** *v/t* subastar, *L.Am.* rematar

♦ **auction off** *v/t* subastar, *L.Am.* rematar

auc·tio·neer [ɒːkʃəˈnɪr] subastador(a) *m(f)*, *L.Am.* rematador(a) *m(f)*

au·da·cious [ɒː'deɪʃəs] adj plan audaz
au·dac·i·ty [ɒː'dæsətɪ] audacia f
au·di·ble ['ɒːdəbl] adj audible
au·di·ence ['ɒːdɪəns] in theater, at show público m, espectadores mpl; TV audiencia f
au·di·o ['ɒːdɪʊ] adj de audio
au·di·o·vi·su·al [ɒːdɪʊ'vɪʒʊəl] adj audiovisual
au·dit ['ɒːdɪt] 1 n auditoría f 2 v/t auditar; course asistir de oyente a
au·di·tion [ɒː'dɪʃn] 1 n audición f 2 v/i hacer una prueba
au·di·tor ['ɒːdɪtər] auditor(a) m(f)
au·di·to·ri·um [ɒːdɪ'tɔːrɪəm] of theater etc auditorio m
Au·gust ['ɒːgəst] agosto m
aunt [ænt] tía f
au pair [oʊ'per] au pair m/f
au·ra ['ɒːrə] aura f
aus·pic·es ['ɒːspɪsɪz] npl auspicios mpl; under the auspices of bajo los auspicios de
aus·pi·cious [ɒː'spɪʃəs] adj propicio
aus·tere [ɒː'stɪr] adj interior austero
aus·ter·i·ty [ɒːs'terətɪ] economic austeridad f
Aus·tra·li·a [ɒː'streɪlɪə] Australia
Aus·tra·li·an [ɒː'streɪlɪən] 1 adj australiano 2 n australiano(-a) m(f)
Aus·tri·a ['ɒːstrɪə] Austria
Aus·tri·an ['ɒːstrɪən] 1 adj austriaco 2 n austriaco(-a) m(f)
au·then·tic [ɒː'θentɪk] adj auténtico
au·then·tic·i·ty [ɒːθen'tɪsətɪ] autenticidad f
au·thor ['ɒːθər] of story, novel escritor(a) m(f); of text autor(a) m(f)
au·thor·i·tar·i·an [əθɑːrɪ'terɪən] adj autoritario
au·thor·i·ta·tive [ɒː'θɑːrɪtətɪv] adj autorizado
au·thor·i·ty [ə'θɑːrətɪ] autoridad f; (permission) autorización f; be an authority on ser una autoridad en; the authorities las autoridades
au·thor·i·za·tion [ɒːθəraɪ'zeɪʃn] autorización f
au·thor·ize ['ɒːθəraɪz] v/t autorizar; be

authorized to ... estar autorizado para ...
au·tis·tic [ɒː'tɪstɪk] adj autista
au·to·bi·og·ra·phy [ɒːtəbaɪ'ɑːgrəfɪ] autobiografía f
au·to·crat·ic [ɒːtə'krætɪk] adj autocrático
au·to·graph ['ɒːtəgræf] autógrafo m
au·to·mate ['ɒːtəmeɪt] v/t automatizar
au·to·mat·ic [ɒːtə'mætɪk] 1 adj automático 2 n car (coche m) automático m; gun pistola f automática; washing machine lavadora f automática
au·to·mat·i·cal·ly [ɒːtə'mætɪklɪ] adv automáticamente
au·to·ma·tion [ɒːtə'meɪʃn] automatización f
au·to·mo·bile ['ɒːtəmoʊbiːl] automóvil m, coche m, L.Am. carro m, Rpl auto m
'au·to·mo·bile in·dus·try industria f automovilística
au·ton·o·mous [ɒː'tɑːnəməs] adj autónomo
au·ton·o·my [ɒː'tɑːnəmɪ] autonomía f
au·to·pi·lot ['ɒːtoʊpaɪlət] piloto m automático
au·top·sy ['ɒːtɑːpsɪ] autopsia f
au·tumn ['ɒːtəm] Br otoño m
aux·il·ia·ry [ɒːg'zɪljərɪ] adj auxiliar
a·vail [ə'veɪl] 1 n: to no avail en vano 2 v/t: avail o.s. of aprovechar
a·vai·la·ble [ə'veɪləbl] adj disponible
av·a·lanche ['ævəlænʃ] avalancha f, alud m
av·a·rice ['ævərɪs] avaricia f
av·e·nue ['ævənuː] avenida f; fig camino m
av·e·rage ['ævərɪdʒ] 1 adj medio; (of mediocre quality) regular 2 n promedio m, media f; above / below average por encima / por debajo del promedio; on average como promedio, de media 3 v/t: I average six hours of sleep a night duermo seis horas cada noche como promedio or de media
◆ average out v/t calcular el promedio or la media de
◆ average out at v/t salir a
a·verse [ə'vɜːrs] adj: not be averse to no ser reacio a

a·ver·sion [əˈvɜːrʃn] aversión f; **have an aversion to** tener aversión a

a·vert [əˈvɜːrt] v/t one's eyes apartar; crisis evitar

a·vi·a·tion [eɪvɪˈeɪʃn] aviación f

av·id [ˈævɪd] adj ávido

av·o·ca·do [ɑːvəˈkɑːdoʊ] aguacate m, S. Am. palta f

a·void [əˈvɔɪd] v/t evitar; **you've been avoiding me** has estado huyendo de mí

a·void·a·ble [əˈvɔɪdəbl] adj evitable

a·wait [əˈweɪt] v/t aguardar, esperar

a·wake [əˈweɪk] adj despierto; **it kept me awake** no me dejó dormir

a·ward [əˈwɔːrd] 1 n (prize) premio m 2 v/t prize, damages conceder

a·ware [əˈwer] adj: **be aware of sth** ser consciente de algo; **become aware of sth** darse cuenta de algo

a·ware·ness [əˈwernɪs] conciencia f

a·way [əˈweɪ] adv: **look away** mirar hacia otra parte; **I'll be away until …** traveling voy a estar fuera hasta …; sick no voy a ir hasta …; **it's 2 miles away** está a 2 millas; **Christmas is still six weeks away** todavía quedan seis semanas para Navidad; **take sth away from s.o.** quitar algo a alguien; **put sth away** guardar algo

a'way match sp partido m fuera de casa

awe·some [ˈɒːsəm] adj F (terrific) alucinante F

aw·ful [ˈɒːfəl] adj horrible, espantoso; **I feel awful** me siento fatal

aw·ful·ly [ˈɒːfəlɪ] adv F (very) tremendamente; **awfully bad** malísimo

awk·ward [ˈɒːkwərd] adj (clumsy) torpe; (difficult) difícil; (embarrassing) embarazoso; **feel awkward** sentirse incómodo

awn·ing [ˈɒːnɪŋ] toldo m

ax, Br axe [æks] 1 n hacha f 2 v/t project etc suprimir; budget, job recortar

ax·le [ˈæksl] eje m

B

BA [biːˈeɪ] abbr (= **Bachelor of Arts**) Licenciatura f en Filosofía y Letras

ba·by [ˈbeɪbɪ] n bebé m

'ba·by boom explosión f demográfica

'ba·by car·riage [ˈkærɪdʒ] cochecito m de bebé

ba·by·ish [ˈbeɪbɪɪʃ] adj infantil

'ba·by-sit v/i (pret & pp **baby-sat**) hacer de Span canguro or L.Am. babysitter

'ba·by-sit·ter [ˈsɪtər] Span canguro m/f, L.Am. babysitter m/f

bach·e·lor [ˈbætʃələr] soltero m

back [bæk] 1 n of person, clothes espalda f; of car, bus, house parte f trasera or de atrás; of paper, book dorso m; of drawer fondo m; of chair respaldo m; sp defensa m/f; **in back** in store en la trastienda; **in the back (of the car)** atrás (del coche); **at the back of the bus** en la parte trasera or de atrás del autobús; **back to front** del revés; **at the back of beyond** en el quinto pino 2 adj trasero; **back road** carretera f secundaria 3 adv atrás; **please stand back** pongase más para atrás 2 **meters back from the edge** a 2 metros del borde; **back in 1935** allá por el año 1935; **give sth back to s.o.** devolver algo a alguien; **she'll be back tomorrow** volverá mañana; **when are you coming back?** ¿cuándo volverás?; **take sth back to the store** because unsatisfactory devolver alguien a la tienda; **they wrote / phoned back** contestaron a la carta/a la llamada; **he hit me back** me devolvió el golpe 4 v/t (support) apoyar, respaldar; horse apostar por 5 v/i **he backed into the garage** entró en el garaje marcha atrás

◆ **back away** v/i alejarse (hacia atrás)

◆ **back down** v/i echarse atrás

◆ **back off** v/i echarse atrás

◆ **back onto** v/t dar por la parte de atrás a

◆ **back out** v/i of commitment echarse atrás

◆ **back up 1** v/t (support) respaldar; file hacer una copia de seguridad de; *traffic was backed up all the way to ...* el atasco llegaba hasta ... **2** v/i in car dar marcha atrás; of drains atascarse

'back·ache dolor m de espalda

'back·bit·ing cotilleo m, chismorreo m

'back·bone ANAT columna f vertebral, espina f dorsal; (fig: courage) agallas fpl; (fig: mainstay) columna f vertebral

'back·break·ing adj extenuante, deslomador

back 'burn·er: *put sth on the back burner* aparcar algo

'back·date v/t: *a salary increase backdated to 1st January* una subida salarial con efecto retroactivo a partir del 1 de enero

'back·door puerta f trasera

back·er ['bækər]: *the backers of the movie* financially las personas que financiaron la película

back'fire v/i fig: *it backfired on us* nos salió el tiro por la culata

'back·ground n fondo m; of person origen m, historia f personal; of situation contexto m; *she prefers to stay in the background* prefiere permanecer en un segundo plano

'back·hand n in tennis revés m

back·ing ['bækɪŋ] n (support) apoyo m, respaldo m; MUS acompañamiento m

'back·ing group MUS grupo m de acompañamiento

'back·lash reacción f violenta

'back·log acumulación f

'back·pack **1** mochila f **2** v/i viajar con la mochila a cuestas

'back·pack·er mochilero(-a) m(f)

'back·pack·ing viajes mpl con la mochila a cuestas

'back·ped·al v/i fig echarse atrás, dar marcha atrás

'back seat of car asiento m trasero or de atrás

back-seat 'driv·er: *he's a terrible back-seat driver* va siempre incordiando al conductor con sus comentarios

'back·space (key) (tecla f de) retroceso m

'back·stairs npl escalera f de servicio

'back street callejuela f

'back streets npl callejuelas fpl; *poorer, dirtier part of a city* zonas fpl deprimidas

'back·stroke SP espalda f

'back·track v/i volver atrás, retroceder

'back·up (support) apoyo m, respaldo m; for police refuerzos mpl; COMPUT copia f de seguridad; *take a backup* COMPUT haz una copia de seguridad

'back·up disk COMPUT disquete m con la copia de seguridad

back·ward ['bækwərd] **1** adj child retrasado; society atrasado; glance hacia atrás **2** adv hacia atrás

'back·yard jardín m trasero; *in s.o.'s backyard* fig en la misma puerta de alguien

ba·con ['beɪkn] tocino m, Span bacon m

bac·te·ri·a [bæk'tɪrɪə] npl bacterias fpl

bad [bæd] adj malo; before singular masculine noun mal; cold, headache etc fuerte; mistake, accident grave; *I've had a bad day* he tenido un mal día; *smoking is bad for you* fumar es malo; *it's not bad* no está mal; *that's really too bad* (shame) es una verdadera pena; *feel bad about* (guilty) sentirse mal por; *I'm bad at math* se me dan mal las matemáticas; *Friday's bad, how about Thursday?* el viernes me viene mal, ¿qué tal el jueves?

bad 'debt deuda f incobrable

badge [bædʒ] insignia f, chapa f; of policeman placa f

bad·ger ['bædʒər] v/t acosar, importunar

bad 'lan·guage palabrotas fpl

bad·ly ['bædlɪ] adv injured gravemente; damaged seriamente; work mal; *I did really badly in the exam* el examen me salió fatal; *he hasn't done badly in life, business etc* no le ha ido mal; *you're badly in need of a haircut* necesitas urgentemente un corte de pelo; **he is badly off** poor anda mal de dinero

bad-man·nered [bæd'mænərd] adj: **be bad-mannered** tener malos modales

bad-min·ton ['bædmɪntən] bádminton m

bad-tem·pered [bæd'tempərd] adj malhumorado

baf·fle ['bæfl] v/t confundir, desconcertar; **be baffled** estar confundido or desconcertado; **I'm baffled why she left** no consigo entender por qué se fue

baf·fling ['bæflɪŋ] adj mystery, software desconcertante, incomprensible

bag [bæg] bolsa f; for school cartera f; (purse) bolso m, S. Am. cartera f, Mex bolsa f

bag·gage ['bægɪdʒ] equipaje m

'**bag·gage car** RAIL vagón m de equipajes

'**bag·gage check** consigna f

'**bag·gage re·claim** ['riːkleɪm] recogida f de equipajes

bag·gy ['bægɪ] adj ancho, holgado

'**bag·pipes** npl gaita f

bail [beɪl] n LAW libertad f bajo fianza; (money) fianza f; **on bail** bajo fianza

◆ **bail out 1** v/t LAW pagar la fianza de **2** v/i of airplane tirarse en paracaídas

bait [beɪt] n cebo m

bake [beɪk] v/t hornear, cocer al horno

baked 'beans [beɪkt] npl alubias con salsa de tomate

baked po'ta·to Span patata f or L.Am. papa f asada (con piel)

bak·er ['beɪkər] panadero(-a) m(f)

bak·er·y ['beɪkərɪ] panadería f

bak·ing pow·der ['beɪkɪŋ] levadura f

bal·ance ['bæləns] **1** n equilibrio m; (remainder) resto m; of bank account saldo m **2** v/t poner en equilibrio; **balance the books** cuadrar las cuentas **3** v/i mantenerse en equilibrio; of accounts cuadrar

bal·anced ['bælənst] adj (fair) objetivo; diet, personality equilibrado

bal·ance of 'pay·ments balanza f de pagos

bal·ance of 'trade balanza f comercial

'**bal·ance sheet** balance m

bal·co·ny ['bælkənɪ] of house balcón m; in theater anfiteatro m

bald [bɔːld] adj calvo; **he's going bald** se está quedando calvo; **bald spot** calva f

bald·ing ['bɔːldɪŋ] adj medio calvo

Bal·kan ['bɔːlkən] adj balcánico

Bal·kans ['bɔːlkənz] npl: **the Balkans** los Balcanes

ball [bɔːl] tennis-ball size pelota f; football size balón m, pelota f; billiard-ball size bola f; **on the ball** despierto; **play ball** fig cooperar; **the ball's in his court** le toca actuar a él, la pelota está en su tejado

bal·lad ['bæləd] balada f

ball 'bear·ing rodamiento m de bolas

bal·le·ri·na [bælə'riːnə] bailarina f

bal·let [bæ'leɪ] ballet m

'**bal·let danc·er** bailarín (-ina) m(f)

'**ball game** (baseball game) partido m de béisbol; **that's a different ball game** F esa es otra cuestión F

bal·lis·tic mis·sile [bə'lɪstɪk] misil m balístico

bal·loon [bə'luːn] globo m

bal·loon·ist [bə'luːnɪst] piloto m de globo aerostático

bal·lot ['bælət] **1** n voto m **2** v/t members consultar por votación

'**bal·lot box** urna f

'**bal·lot pa·per** papeleta f

'**ball·park** (baseball) campo m de béisbol; **you're in the right ballpark** F no vas descaminado

'**ball·park fig·ure** F cifra f aproximada

'**ball·point (pen)** bolígrafo m, Mex pluma f, Rpl birome m

balls [bɔːlz] npl V huevos mpl V; (courage) huevos mpl V; (nonsense) tonterías fpl, paridas fpl F

bam·boo [bæm'buː] n bambú m

ban [bæn] **1** n prohibición f **2** v/t (pret & pp **banned**) prohibir; **ban s.o. from doing sth** prohibir a alguien que haga algo

ba·nal [bə'næl] adj banal

ba·na·na [bə'nænə] plátano m, Rpl banana f

band [bænd] banda f; pop grupo m

ban·dage ['bændɪdʒ] **1** n vendaje m **2** v/t vendar

'Band-Aid® *Span* tirita *f*, *L.Am.* curita *f*
B&B [biːnˈbiː] *abbr* (= **bed and breakfast**) hostal *m* familiar
ban·dit ['bændɪt] bandido *m*
'band·wag·on: **jump on the bandwagon**
subirse al carro
ban·dy ['bændɪ] *adj legs* arqueado
bang [bæŋ] **1** *n noise* estruendo *m*, estrépito *m*; *(blow)* golpe *m*; **the door closed
with a bang** la puerta se cerró de un portazo **2** *v/t door* cerrar de un portazo; *(hit)*
golpear; **bang o.s. on the head** gol-
pearse la cabeza **3** *v/i* dar golpes; **the
door banged shut** la puerta se cerró
de un portazo
ban·gle ['bæŋgl] brazalete *m*, pulsera *f*
bangs [bæŋz] flequillo *m*
ban·is·ters ['bænɪstərz] *npl* barandilla *f*
ban·jo ['bændʒoʊ] banjo *m*
bank¹ [bæŋk] *of river* orilla *f*
bank² [bæŋk] **1** *n* FIN banco *m* **2** *v/i*: **I bank
with ...** mi banco es el ... **3** *v/t money* ingresar, depositar
◆ **bank on** *v/t* contar con; **don't bank on
it** no cuentes con ello
'bank ac·count cuenta *f* (bancaria)
'bank bal·ance saldo *m* bancario
'bank bill billete *m*
bank·er ['bæŋkər] banquero *m*
'bank·er's card tarjeta *f* bancaria
bank·ing ['bæŋkɪŋ] banca *f*
'bank loan préstamo *m* bancario
'bank man·ag·er director(a) *m(f)* de banco
'bank rate tipo *m* de interés bancario
'bank·roll *v/t* financiar
bank·rupt ['bæŋkrʌpt] **1** *adj* en bancarrota *or* quiebra; **go bankrupt** quebrar, ir a
la quiebra; *of person* arruinarse **2** *v/t* llevar a la quiebra
bank·rupt·cy ['bæŋkrʌpsɪ] *of person,
company* quiebra *f*, bancarrota *f*
'bank state·ment extracto *m* bancario
ban·ner ['bænər] pancarta *f*
banns [bænz] *npl* amonestaciones *fpl*
ban·quet ['bæŋkwɪt] *n* banquete *m*
ban·ter ['bæntər] *n* bromas *fpl*
bap·tism ['bæptɪzm] bautismo *m*
bap·tize [bæp'taɪz] *v/t* bautizar

bar¹ [baːr] *n of iron* barra *f*; *of chocolate*
tableta *f*; *for drinks* bar *m*; *(counter)* barra *f*; **a bar of soap** una pastilla de jabón;
be behind bars *(in prison)* estar entre
barrotes
bar² [baːr] *v/t (pret & pp barred) from
premises* prohibir la entrada a; **bar s.o.
from doing sth** prohibir a alguien que
haga algo
bar³ [baːr] *prep (except)* excepto
bar·bar·i·an [baːr'berɪən] bárbaro(-a)
m(f)
bar·bar·ic [baːr'bærɪk] *adj* brutal, inhumano
bar·be·cue ['baːrbɪkjuː] **1** *n* barbacoa *f* **2**
v/t cocinar en la barbacoa
barbed 'wire [baːrbd] alambre *f* de espino
bar·ber ['baːrbər] barbero *m*
bar·bi·tu·rate [baːr'bɪtʃərət] barbitúrico
m
'bar code código *m* de barras
bare [ber] *adj (naked)* desnudo; *(empty:
room)* vacío; *mountainside* pelado, raso;
floor descubierto; **in one's bare feet** descalzo
'bare·foot *adj* descalzo
bare·head·ed [ber'hedɪd] *adj* sin sombrero
'bare·ly ['berlɪ] *adv* apenas; **he's barely
five** acaba de cumplir cinco años
bar·gain ['baːrgɪn] **1** *n (deal)* trato *m*;
(good buy) ganga *f*; **into the bargain**
además **2** *v/i* regatear, negociar
◆ **bargain for** *v/t (expect)* imaginarse, esperar
barge [baːrdʒ] *n* NAUT barcaza *f*
◆ **barge into** *v/t person* tropezarse con;
room irrumpir en
bar·i·tone ['bærɪtoʊn] *n* barítono *m*
bark¹ [baːrk] **1** *n of dog* ladrido *m* **2** *v/i*
ladrar
bark² [baːrk] *of tree* corteza *f*
bar·ley ['baːrlɪ] cebada *f*
'bar·maid *Br* camarera *f*, *L.Am.* mesera *f*,
Rpl moza *f*
'bar·man camarero *m*, *L.Am.* mesero *m*,
Rpl mozo *m*
barn [baːrn] granero *m*
ba·rom·e·ter [bə'raːmɪtər] *also fig* baró-

metro *m*

Ba·roque [bə'rɑːk] *adj* barroco

bar·racks ['bærəks] *npl* MIL cuartel *m*

bar·rage [bə'rɑː3] MIL barrera *f* (de fuego); *fig* aluvión *m*

bar·rel ['bærəl] (*container*) tonel *m*, barril *m*

bar·ren ['bærən] *adj* land yermo, árido

bar·ri·cade [bærɪ'keɪd] *n* barricada *f*

bar·ri·er ['bærɪər] *also fig* barrera *f*; *language barrier* barrera *f* lingüística

bar·ring ['bɑːrɪŋ] *prep* salvo, excepto; *barring accidents* salvo imprevistos

bar·ris·ter ['bærɪstər] *Br* abogado(-a) *m(f)* (*que aparece en tribunales*)

bar·row ['bærou] carretilla *f*

'bar ten·der camarero(-a) *m(f)*, *L.Am.* mesero(-a) *m(f)*, *Rpl* mozo(-a) *m(f)*

bar·ter ['bɑːrtər] **1** *n* trueque *m* **2** *v/t* cambiar, trocar (*for* por)

base [beɪs] **1** *n* bottom, center base *f*; *base camp* campamento *m* base **2** *v/t* basar (*on* en); *be based in* of soldier estar destinado en; of company tener su sede en

'base·ball ball pelota *f* de béisbol; *game* béisbol *m*

'base·ball bat bate *m* de béisbol

'base·ball cap gorra *f* de béisbol

'base·ball play·er jugador(a) *m(f)* de béisbol, *L.Am.* pelotero(-a) *m(f)*

'base·board rodapié *m*

base·less ['beɪslɪs] *adj* infundado

base·ment ['beɪsmənt] of house, store sótano *m*

'base rate FIN tipo *m* de interés básico

bash [bæʃ] **1** *n* F porrazo *m* F **2** *v/t* F dar un porrazo a F

ba·sic ['beɪsɪk] *adj* (*rudimentary*) básico; *room* modesto, sencillo; *language skills* elemental; (*fundamental*) fundamental; *basic salary* sueldo *m* base

ba·sic·al·ly ['beɪsɪklɪ] *adv* básicamente

ba·sics ['beɪsɪks] *npl*: *the basics* lo básico, los fundamentos; *get down to basics* centrarse en lo esencial

bas·il ['bæzɪl] albahaca *f*

ba·sil·i·ca [bə'zɪlɪkə] basílica *f*

ba·sin ['beɪsn] for washing barreño *m*; in bathroom lavabo *m*

ba·sis ['beɪsɪs] (*pl bases* ['beɪsiːz]) base *f*; *on the basis of what you've told me* de acuerdo con lo que me has dicho

bask [bæsk] *v/i* tomar el sol

bas·ket ['bæskɪt] cesta *f*; in basketball canasta *f*

'bas·ket·ball *game* baloncesto *m*, *L.Am.* básquetbol *m*; *ball* balón *m* or pelota *f* de baloncesto; *basketball player* baloncestista *m/f*, *L.Am.* basquebolista *m/f*

Basque [bæsk] **1** *adj* vasco **2** *n person* vasco(-a) *m(f)*; *language* vasco *m*

bass [beɪs] **1** *n part, singer* bajo *m*; *instrument* contrabajo *m* **2** *adj* bajo

bas·tard ['bæstərd] ilegítimo(-a) *m(f)*, bastardo(-a) *m(f)*; P cabrón(-ona) *m(f)* P; *poor bastard* pobre desgraciado; *stupid bastard* desgraciado

bat¹ [bæt] **1** *n for baseball* bate *m*; *for table tennis* pala *f* **2** *v/i* (*pret & pp batted*) in baseball batear

bat² [bæt] *v/t* (*pret & pp batted*): *he didn't bat an eyelid* no se inmutó

bat³ [bæt] (*animal*) murciélago *m*

batch [bætʃ] *n of students* tanda *f*; of data conjunto *m*; of bread hornada *f*; of products lote *m*

ba·ted ['beɪtɪd] *adj*: *with bated breath* con la respiración contenida

bath [bæθ] baño *m*; *have a bath, take a bath* darse *or* tomar un baño

bathe [beɪð] *v/i* (*swim, have a bath*) bañarse

bath·ing cost·ume, bathing suit ['beɪðɪŋ] bañador *m*, traje *m* de baño

'bath mat alfombra *f* de baño

'bath·robe albornoz *m*

'bath·room for bath, washing hands, cuarto *m* de baño; (*toilet*) servicio *m*, *L.Am.* baño *m*

'bath tow·el toalla *f* de baño

'bath·tub bañera *f*

bat·on [bə'tɑːn] of conductor batuta *f*

bat·tal·i·on [bə'tæljən] MIL batallón *m*

bat·ter ['bætər] *n* masa *f*; in baseball bateador(a) *m(f)*

bat·tered ['bætərd] *adj* maltratado

bat·ter·y ['bætərɪ] in watch, flashlight pila *f*; in computer, car batería *f*

'bat·ter·y charg·er ['tʃɑːrdʒər] cargador *m* de pilas / baterías

bat·ter·y-op·er·at·ed [bætərɪ'ɑːpəreɪtɪd] *adj* que funciona con pilas

bat·tle ['bætl] **1** *n also fig* batalla *f* **2** *v/i against illness etc* luchar

'bat·tle·field, **'bat·tle·ground** campo *m* de batalla

'bat·tle·ship acorazado *m*

bawd·y ['bɔːdɪ] *adj* picante, subido de tono

bawl [bɔːl] *v/i* (*shout*) gritar, vociferar; (*weep*) berrear

◆ **bawl out** *v/t* F echar la bronca a F

bay [beɪ] (*inlet*) bahía *f*

bay·o·net ['beɪənət] *n* bayoneta *f*

bay 'win·dow ventana *f* en saliente

BC [biː'siː] *abbr* (= *before Christ*) a.C. (= antes de Cristo)

be [biː] ◇ *v/i* (*pret* **was** / **were**, *pp* **been**) *permanent characteristics, profession, nationality* ser; *position, temporary condition* estar; **was she there?** ¿estaba allí?; **it's me** soy yo; **how much is** / **are ...?** ¿cuánto es / son ...?; **there is, there are** hay; **be careful** ten cuidado; **don't be sad** no estés triste

◇ **has the mailman been?** ¿ha venido el cartero?; **I've been to Japan** no he estado en Japón; **I've been here for hours** he estado aquí horas

◇ *tags:* **that's right, isn't it?** eso es, ¿no?; **she's Chinese, isn't she?** es china, ¿verdad?

◇ *v/aux:* **I am thinking** estoy pensando; **he was running** corría; **you're being stupid** estás siendo un estúpido

◇ *obligation:* **you are to do what I tell you** harás lo que yo te diga; **I was to help him escape** se suponía que le iba a ayudar a escaparse; **you are not to tell anyone** no debes decírselo a nadie

◇ *passive:* **he was arrested** fue detenido, lo detuvieron; **they have been sold** se han vendido

◆ **be in for** *v/t:* **he's in for a big disappointment** se va a llevar una gran desilusión

beach [biːtʃ] *n* playa *f*

'beach ball pelota *f* de playa

'beach·wear ropa *f* playera

beads [biːdz] *npl* cuentas *fpl*

beak [biːk] pico *m*

'be-all: **the be-all and end-all** lo más importante del mundo

beam [biːm] **1** *n in ceiling etc* viga *f* **2** *v/i* (*smile*) sonreír de oreja a oreja **3** *v/t* (*transmit*) emitir

bean [biːn] judía *f*, alubia *f*, *L.Am.* frijol *m*, *S. Am.* poroto *m*; **green beans** judías *fpl* verdes, *Mex* ejotes *mpl*, *S. Am.* porotos *mpl* verdes; **coffee beans** granos *mpl* de café; **be full of beans** F estar lleno de vitalidad

'bean·bag cojín relleno de bolitas

bear¹ [ber] *animal* oso(-a) *m(f)*

bear² [ber] **1** *v/t* (*pret* **bore**, *pp* **borne**) *weight* resistir; *costs* correr con; (*tolerate*) aguantar, soportar; *child* dar a luz; **she bore him six children** le dio seis hijos **2** *v/i* (*pret* **bore**, *pp* **borne**): **bring pressure to bear on** ejercer presión sobre

◆ **bear out** *v/t* (*confirm*) confirmar

bear·a·ble ['berəbl] *adj* soportable

beard [bɪrd] barba *f*

beard·ed ['bɪrdɪd] *adj* con barba

bear·ing ['berɪŋ] *in machine* rodamiento *m*, cojinete *m*; **that has no bearing on the case** eso no tiene nada que ver con el caso

'bear mar·ket FIN mercado *m* a la baja

beast [biːst] *animal* bestia *f*; *person* bestia *m/f*

beat [biːt] **1** *n of heart* latido *m*; *of music* ritmo *m* **2** *v/i* (*pret* **beat**, *pp* **beaten**) *of heart* latir; *of rain* golpear; **beat about the bush** andarse por las ramas **3** *v/t* (*pret* **beat**, *pp* **beaten**) *in competition* derrotar, ganar a; (*hit*) pegar a; (*pound*) golpear; **beat it!** F ¡lárgate! F; **it beats me** no logro entender

◆ **beat up** *v/t* dar una paliza a

beat·en ['biːtən] **1** *adj:* **off the beaten track** retirado **2** *pp* → **beat**

beat·ing ['biːtɪŋ] (*physical*) paliza *f*

beat-up *adj* F destartalado F

beau·ti·cian [bjuː'tɪʃn] esteticista *m/f*

beau·ti·ful ['bjuːtəfəl] *adj woman, house,*

day, story, movie bonito, precioso, *L.Am.* lindo; *smell, taste, meal* delicioso, *L.Am.* rico; *vacation* estupendo; **thanks, that's just beautiful!** ¡muchísimas gracias, está maravilloso!

beau·ti·ful·ly ['bjuːtɪfəlɪ] *adv cooked, done* perfectamente, maravillosamente

beaut·y ['bjuːtɪ] *of woman, sunset* belleza *f*

'beaut·y par·lor ['puːrlər] salón *m* de belleza

◆ **bea·ver away** *v/i* F trabajar como un burro F

be·came [bɪ'keɪm] *pret* → **become**

be·cause [bɪ'kɑːz] *conj* porque; **because it was too expensive** porque era demasiado caro; **because of** debido a, a causa de; **because of you, we can't go** gracias a ti, no podemos ir

beck·on ['bekn] *v/i* hacer señas

be·come [bɪ'kʌm] *v/i* (*pret* **became**, *pp* **become**) hacerse, volverse; **it became clear that ...** quedó claro que ...; **he became a priest** se hizo sacerdote; **she's becoming very forgetful** cada vez es más olvidadiza; **what's become of her?** ¿qué fue de ella?

be·com·ing [bɪ'kʌmɪŋ] *adj* favorecedor, apropiado

bed [bed] *n* cama *f*; *of flowers* macizo *m*; *of sea* fondo *m*; *of river* cauce *m*, lecho *m*; **go to bed** ir a la cama; **he's still in bed** aún está en la cama; **go to bed with s.o.** irse a la cama *or* acostarse con alguien

'bed·clothes *npl* ropa *f* de cama

bed·ding ['bedɪŋ] ropa *f* de cama

bed·lam ['bedləm] F locura *f*, jaleo *m*

bed·rid·den ['bedrɪdən] *adj*: **be bedridden** estar postrado en cama

'bed·room dormitorio *m*, *L.Am.* cuarto *m*

'bed·side: **be at the bedside of** estar junto a la cama de

'bed·spread colcha *f*

'bed·time hora *f* de irse a la cama

bee [biː] abeja *f*

beech [biːtʃ] haya *f*

beef [biːf] **1** *n* carne *f* de vaca *or* vacuna; F (*complaint*) queja *f* **2** *v/i* F (*complain*) quejarse

◆ **beef up** *v/t* reforzar, fortalecer

'beef·bur·ger hamburguesa *f*

'bee·hive colmena *f*

'bee·line: **make a beeline for** ir directamente a

been [bɪn] *pp* → **be**

beep [biːp] **1** *n* pitido *m* **2** *v/i* pitar **3** *v/t* (*call on pager*) llamar con el buscapersonas

beep·er ['biːpər] buscapersonas *m inv*, *Span* busca *m*

beer [bɪr] cerveza *f*

beet [biːt] remolacha *f*

bee·tle ['biːtl] escarabajo *m*

be·fore [bɪ'fɔːr] **1** *prep* (*time*) antes de; (*space, order*) antes de, delante de **2** *adv* antes; **I've seen this movie before** ya he visto esta película; **have you been to Japan before?** ¿habías estado antes *or* ya en Japón?; **the week / day before** la semana / el día anterior **3** *conj* antes de que

be·fore·hand *adv* de antemano

be·friend [bɪ'frend] *v/t* hacerse amigo de

beg [beg] **1** *v/i* (*pret & pp* **begged**) mendigar, pedir **2** *v/t* (*pret & pp* **begged**): **beg s.o. to sth** rogar *or* suplicar a alguien que haga algo

began [bɪ'gæn] *pret* → **begin**

beg·gar ['begər] *n* mendigo(-a) *m(f)*

be·gin [bɪ'gɪn] **1** *v/i* (*pret* **began**, *pp* **begun**) empezar, comenzar; **to begin with** (*at first*) en un primer momento, al principio; (*in the first place*) para empezar **2** *v/t* (*pret* **began**, *pp* **begun**) empezar, comenzar; **begin to do sth, begin doing sth** empezar *or* comenzar a hacer algo

be·gin·ner [bɪ'gɪnər] principiante *m/f*

be·gin·ning [bɪ'gɪnɪŋ] principio *m*, comienzo *m*; (*origin*) origen *m*

be·grudge [bɪ'grʌdʒ] *v/t* (*envy*) envidiar; (*give reluctantly*) dar a regañadientes

be·gun [bɪ'gʌn] *pp* → **begin**

be·half [bɪ'hɑːf]: **on behalf of, in behalf of** en nombre de; **on my / his behalf** en nombre mío / suyo

be·have [bɪ'heɪv] *v/i* comportarse, portarse; **be·have (o.s.)** comportarse *or* portarse bien; **behave (yourself)!** ¡pórtate bien!

be·hav·ior [bɪˈheɪvɪər] comportamiento *m*, conducta *f*

be·hind [bɪˈhaɪnd] **1** *prep in position, order* detrás de; *in progress* por detrás de; *be behind …* (*responsible for*) estar detrás de …; (*support*) respaldar … **2** *adv* (*at the back*) detrás; *be behind in match* ir perdiendo; *be behind with sth* estar atrasado con algo; *leave sth behind* dejarse algo

beige [beɪʒ] *adj* beige, *Span* beis

be·ing [ˈbiːɪŋ] *existence, creature* ser *m*

be·lat·ed [bɪˈleɪtɪd] *adj* tardío

belch [beltʃ] **1** *n* eructo *m* **2** *v/i* eructar

Bel·gian [ˈbeldʒən] **1** *adj* belga **2** *n* belga *m/f*

Bel·gium [ˈbeldʒəm] Bélgica

be·lief [bɪˈliːf] creencia *f*; *it's my belief that* creo que …

be·lieve [bɪˈliːv] *v/t* creer

◆ **believe in** *v/t* creer en

be·liev·er [bɪˈliːvər] REL creyente *m/f*; *fig* partidario(a) *m(f)* (*in* de)

be·lit·tle [bɪˈlɪtl] *v/t* menospreciar

Be·lize [beˈliːz] Belice

bell [bel] *of bike, door, school* timbre *m*; *of church* campana *f*

'**bell·hop** botones *m inv*

bel·lig·er·ent [bɪˈlɪdʒərənt] *adj* beligerante

bel·low [ˈbeloʊ] **1** *n* bramido *m* **2** *v/i* bramar

bel·ly [ˈbeli] *of person* estómago *m*, barriga *f*; (*fat stomach*) barriga *f*, tripa *f*; *of animal* panza *f*

'**bel·ly·ache** *v/i* F refunfuñar

be·long [bɪˈlɒŋ] *v/i*: *where does this belong?* ¿dónde va esto?; *I don't belong here* no encajo aquí

◆ **belong to** *v/t of object, money* pertenecer a; *club* pertenecer a, ser socio de

be·long·ings [bɪˈlɒŋɪŋz] *npl* pertenencias *fpl*

be·loved [bɪˈlʌvd] *adj* querido

be·low [bɪˈloʊ] **1** *prep* debajo de; *in amount, rate, level* por debajo de **2** *adv* abajo; *in text* más abajo; *see below* véase más abajo; *10 degrees below* 10 grados

bajo cero

belt [belt] *n* cinturón *m*; *tighten one's belt fig* apretarse el cinturón

bench [bentʃ] *seat* banco *m*; (*workbench*) mesa *f* de trabajo

'**bench·mark** punto *m* de referencia

bend [bend] **1** *n* curva *f* **2** *v/t* (*pret & pp bent*) doblar **3** *v/i* (*pret & pp bent*) torcer, girar; *of person* flexionarse

◆ **bend down** *v/i* agacharse

bend·er [ˈbendər] F parranda *f* F

be·neath [bɪˈniːθ] **1** *prep* debajo de; *she thinks a job like that is beneath her* cree que un trabajo como ése le supondría rebajarse **2** *adv* abajo

ben·e·fac·tor [ˈbenɪfæktər] benefactor(a) *m(f)*

ben·e·fi·cial [benɪˈfɪʃl] *adj* beneficioso

ben·e·fi·ci·a·ry [benɪˈfɪʃəri] beneficiario(-a) *m(f)*

ben·e·fit [ˈbenɪfɪt] **1** *n* beneficio *m*, ventaja *f* **2** *v/t* beneficiar **3** *v/i* beneficiarse

be·nev·o·lence [bɪˈnevələns] benevolencia *f*

be·nev·o·lent [bɪˈnevələnt] *adj* benevolente

be·nign [bɪˈnaɪn] *adj* agradable; MED benigno

bent [bent] *pret & pp* → **bend**

be·queath [bɪˈkwiːð] *v/t also fig* legar

be·quest [bɪˈkwest] legado *m*

be·reaved [bɪˈriːvd] **1** *adj*: *the bereaved parents* los padres del difunto **2** *n*: *the bereaved* los familiares del difunto

be·ret [ˈbereɪ] boina *f*

ber·ry [ˈberi] baya *f*

ber·serk [bərˈsɜːrk] *adv*: *go berserk* F volverse loco

berth [bɜːrθ] *on ship* litera *f*; *on train* camarote *m*; *for ship* amarradero *m*; *give s.o. a wide berth* evitar a alguien

be·seech [bɪˈsiːtʃ] *v/t*: *beseech s.o. to do sth* suplicar a alguien que haga algo

be·side [bɪˈsaɪd] *prep* al lado de, junto a; *be beside o.s.* estar fuera de sí; *that's beside the point* eso no tiene nada que ver

be·sides [bɪˈsaɪdz] **1** *adv* además **2** *prep* (*apart from*) aparte de, además de be·siege [bɪˈsiːdʒ] v/t fig asediar, cercar

best [best] **1** adj mejor **2** adv mejor; **which did you like best?** ¿cuál te gustó más?; **it would be best if ...** sería mejor si ...; **I like her best** ella es la que más me gusta **3** n: **do one's best** hacer todo lo posible; **I did my best to convince her** hice todo lo posible por convencerla; **the best** person, thing el / la mejor; **we insist on the best** insistimos en lo mejor; **we'll just have to make the best of it** tendremos que arreglárnoslas; **all the best!** ¡buena suerte!, ¡que te vaya bien!

best be'fore date fecha f de caducidad

best 'man at wedding padrino m

'best-sell·er éxito m de ventas, best-seller m

bet [bet] **1** n apuesta f; **place a bet** hacer una apuesta **2** v/i also fig apostar; **I bet he doesn't come** apuesto a que no viene; **you bet!** ¡ya lo creo!

be·tray [bɪˈtreɪ] v/t traicionar; husband, wife engañar

be·tray·al [bɪˈtreɪəl] traición f; of husband, wife engaño m

bet·ter [ˈbetər] **1** adj mejor; **get better** in skills, health mejorar; **he's better** in health está mejor **2** adv mejor; **you'd better ask permission** sería mejor que pidieras permiso; **I'd really better not** mejor no; **all the better for us** tanto mejor para nosotros; **I like her better** me gusta más ella

bet·ter 'off adj (wealthier) más rico

be·tween [bɪˈtwiːn] prep entre; **between you and me** entre tú y yo

bev·er·age [ˈbevərɪdʒ] fml bebida f

be·ware [bɪˈwer] v/t: **beware of** tener cuidado con

be·wil·der [bɪˈwɪldər] v/t desconcertar

be·wil·der·ment [bɪˈwɪldərmənt] desconcierto m

be·yond [bɪˈjɑːnd] **1** prep in space más allá de; **she has changed beyond recognition** ha cambiado tanto que es difícil reconocerla; **it's beyond me** (don't understand) no logro entender; (can't do it) me es imposible **2** adv más allá

bi·as [ˈbaɪəs] n against prejuicio m; in favor of favoritismo m

bi·as(s)ed [ˈbaɪəst] adj parcial

bib [bɪb] for baby babero m

Bi·ble [ˈbaɪbl] Biblia f

bib·li·cal [ˈbɪblɪkl] adj bíblico

bib·li·og·ra·phy [bɪblɪˈɑːɡrəfɪ] bibliografía f

bi·car·bon·ate of so·da [baɪˈkɑːrbəneɪt] bicarbonato m sódico

bi·cen·ten·ni·al [baɪsenˈtenɪəl] bicentenario m

bi·ceps [ˈbaɪseps] npl bíceps mpl

bick·er [ˈbɪkər] v/i reñir, discutir

bi·cy·cle [ˈbaɪsɪkl] bicicleta f

bid [bɪd] **1** n at auction puja f; (attempt) intento m **2** v/i (pret & pp **bid**) at auction pujar

bid·der [ˈbɪdər] postor(a) m(f); **the highest bidder** el mejor postor

bi·en·ni·al [baɪˈenɪəl] adj bienal

bi·fo·cals [baɪˈfoukəlz] npl gafas fpl or L.Am. lentes mpl bifocales

big [bɪg] **1** adj grande; before singular nouns gran; **my big brother / sister** mi hermano / hermana mayor; **big name** nombre m importante **2** adv: **talk big** alardear, fanfarronear

big·a·mist [ˈbɪɡəmɪst] bígamo(-a) m(f)

big·a·mous [ˈbɪɡəməs] adj bígamo

big·a·my [ˈbɪɡəmɪ] bigamia f

'big·head F creído(-a) m(f) F

big·head·ed [bɪɡˈhedɪd] adj F creído F

big·ot [ˈbɪɡət] fanático(-a) m(f), intolerante m/f

bike [baɪk] **1** n F bici f F; motorbike moto f F **2** v/i ir en bici

bik·er [ˈbaɪkər] motero(-a) m(f)

bi·ki·ni [bɪˈkiːnɪ] biquini m

bi·lat·er·al [baɪˈlætərəl] adj bilateral

bi·lin·gual [baɪˈlɪŋgwəl] adj bilingüe

bill [bɪl] **1** n for gas, electricity factura f, recibo m; Br in hotel, restaurant cuenta f; (money) billete m; POL proyecto m de ley; (poster) cartel m **2** v/t (invoice) enviar la factura a

'bill·board valla f publicitaria

'bill·fold cartera f, billetera f

bil·li·ards [ˈbɪljərdz] nsg billar m

bil·li·on ['bɪljən] mil millones *mpl*, millardo *m*

bill of ex'change FIN letra *f* de cambio

bill of 'sale escritura *f* de compraventa

bin [bɪn] *n* cubo *m*

bi·na·ry ['baɪnərɪ] *adj* binario

bind [baɪnd] *v/t* (*pret & pp* **bound**) (*connect*) unir; (*tie*) atar; (LAW: *oblige*) obligar

bind·ing ['baɪndɪŋ] **1** *adj agreement, promise* vinculante **2** *n of book* tapa *f*

bi·noc·u·lars [bɪ'nɑːkjʊlərz] *npl* prismáticos *mpl*

bi·o·chem·ist [baɪoʊ'kemɪst] bioquímico(-a) *m(f)*

bi·o·chem·is·try [baɪoʊ'kemɪstrɪ] bioquímica *f*

bi·o·de·gra·da·ble [baɪoʊdɪ'greɪdəbl] *adj* biodegradable

bi·og·ra·pher [baɪ'ɑːgrəfər] biógrafo(-a) *m(f)*

bi·og·ra·phy [baɪ'ɑːgrəfɪ] biografía *f*

bi·o·log·i·cal [baɪoʊ'lɑːdʒɪkl] *adj* biológico; *biological parents* padres *mpl* biológicos; *biological detergent* detergente *m* biológico

bi·ol·o·gist [baɪ'ɑːlədʒɪst] biólogo(-a) *m(f)*

bi·ol·o·gy [baɪ'ɑːlədʒɪ] biología *f*

bi·o·tech·nol·o·gy [baɪoʊtek'nɑːlədʒɪ] biotecnología *f*

bird [bɜːrd] ave *f*, pájaro *m*

'bird·cage jaula *f* para pájaros

bird of 'prey ave *f* rapaz

'bird sanc·tu·a·ry reserva *f* de aves

bird's eye 'view vista *f* panorámica; *get a bird's eye view of sth* ver algo a vista de pájaro

bi·ro® ['baɪroʊ] *Br* bolígrafo *m*, *Mex* pluma *f*, *Rpl* birome *m*

birth [bɜːrθ] *also fig* nacimiento *m*; (*labor*) parto *m*; *give birth to child* dar a luz; *of animal* parir; *date of birth* fecha *f* de nacimiento; *the land of my birth* mi tierra natal

'birth cer·tif·i·cate partida *f* de nacimiento

'birth con·trol control *m* de natalidad

'birth·day cumpleaños *m inv*; *happy birthday!* ¡feliz cumpleaños!

'birth·day cake tarta *f* de cumpleaños

'birth·mark marca *f* de nacimiento, antojo *m*

'birth·place lugar *m* de nacimiento

'birth·rate tasa *f* de natalidad

bis·cuit ['bɪskɪt] bollo *m*, panecillo *m*; *Br* galleta *f*

bi·sex·u·al ['baɪsekʃʊəl] **1** *adj* bisexual **2** *n* bisexual *m/f*

bish·op ['bɪʃəp] obispo *m*

bit¹ [bɪt] *n* (*piece*) trozo *m*; (*part*) parte *f*; *of puzzle* pieza *f*; COMPUT bit *m*; *a bit* (*a little*) un poco; *let's sit down for a bit* sentémonos un rato; *you haven't changed a bit* no has cambiado nada; *a bit of* (*a little*) un poco de; *a bit of news* una noticia; *a bit of advice* un consejo; *bit by bit* poco a poco; *I'll be there in a bit* estaré allí dentro de un rato

bit² [bɪt] *pret* → **bite**

bitch [bɪtʃ] **1** *n of dog* perra *f*; F *woman* zorra *f* F **2** *v/i* F (*complain*) quejarse

bitch·y ['bɪtʃɪ] *adj F person* malicioso; *remark* a mala leche F

bite [baɪt] **1** *n of dog* mordisco *m*; *of spider, mosquito* picadura *f*; *of snake* mordedura *f*, picadura *f*; *of food* bocado *m*; *let's have a bite* (*to eat*) vamos a comer algo **2** *v/t* (*pret bit*, *pp bitten*) *of dog* morder; *of mosquito, flea* picar; *of snake* picar, morder; *bite one's nails* morderse las uñas **3** *v/i* (*pret bit*, *pp bitten*) *of dog* morder; *of mosquito, flea* picar; *of snake* morder, picar; *of fish* picar

bit·ten ['bɪtn] *pp* → **bite**

bit·ter ['bɪtər] *adj taste* amargo; *person* resentido; *weather* helador; *argument* agrio

bit·ter·ly ['bɪtərlɪ] *adv resent* amargamente; *it's bitterly cold* hace un frío helador

bi·zarre [bɪ'zɑːr] *adj* extraño, peculiar

blab [blæb] *v/i* (*pret & pp* **blabbed**) F irse de la lengua F

blab·ber·mouth ['blæbərmaʊθ] F bocazas *m/f inv* F

black [blæk] **1** *adj* negro; *coffee* solo; *tea* sin leche; *fig* negro, aciago **2** *n* (*color*) negro m; (person) negro(-a) m(f); **be in the black** FIN no estar en números rojos; **in black and white** en blanco y negro; **in writing** por escrito

◆ **black out** v/i perder el conocimiento

'black·ber·ry mora f

'black·bird mirlo m

'black·board pizarra f, encerado m

black 'box caja f negra

black 'cof·fee café m solo

black e'con·o·my economía f sumergida

black·en ['blækn] v/t fig: person's name manchar

black 'eye ojo m morado

'black·head espinilla f, punto m negro

black 'ice Br placas fpl de hielo

'black·list 1 n lista f negra 2 v/t poner en la lista negra

'black·mail 1 n chantaje m; **emotional blackmail** chantaje m emocional 2 v/t chantajear

'black·mail·er chantajista m/f

black 'mar·ket mercado m negro

black·ness ['blæknɪs] oscuridad f

'black·out ELEC apagón m; MED desmayo m; **have a blackout** desmayarse

'black·smith herrero m

blad·der ['blædər] vejiga f

blade [bleɪd] of knife, sword hoja f; of propeller pala f; of grass brizna f

blame [bleɪm] 1 n culpa f; **I got the blame for it** me echaron la culpa 2 v/t culpar; **blame s.o. for sth** culpar a alguien de algo

bland [blænd] adj smile insulso; food insípido, soso

blank [blæŋk] 1 adj (not written on) en blanco; tape virgen; look inexpresivo 2 n (empty space) espacio m en blanco; **my mind's a blank** tengo la mente en blanco

blank 'check, Br blank 'cheque cheque m en blanco

blan·ket ['blæŋkɪt] n manta f, L.Am. frazada f; **a blanket of snow** un manto de nieve

blare [bler] v/i retumbar

◆ **blare out 1** v/i retumbar 2 v/t emitir a todo volumen

blas·pheme [blæs'fi:m] v/i blasfemar

blas·phe·my ['blæsfəmɪ] blasfemia f

blast [blæst] 1 n (explosion) explosión f; (gust) ráfaga f 2 v/t tunnel abrir (con explosivos); rock volar; **blast!** F ¡mecachis! F

◆ **blast off** v/i of rocket despegar

'blast fur·nace alto horno m

'blast-off despegue m

bla·tant ['bleɪtənt] adj descarado

blaze [bleɪz] 1 n (fire) incendio m; **a blaze of color** una explosión de color 2 v/i of fire arder

◆ **blaze away** v/i with gun disparar sin parar

blaz·er ['bleɪzər] americana f

bleach [bli:tʃ] 1 n for clothes lejía f; for hair decolorante m 2 v/t hair aclarar, desteñir

bleak [bli:k] adj countryside inhóspito; weather desapacible; future desolador

blear·y-eyed ['blɪrɪaɪd] adj con ojos de sueño

bleat [bli:t] v/i of sheep balar

bled [bled] pret & pp → **bleed**

bleed [bli:d] 1 v/i (pret & pp bled) sangrar; **he's bleeding internally** tiene una hemorragia interna; **bleed to death** desangrarse 2 v/t (pret & pp bled) fig sangrar

bleed·ing ['bli:dɪŋ] n hemorragia f

bleep [bli:p] 1 n pitido m 2 v/i pitar 3 v/t (call on pager) llamar con el buscapersonas

bleep·er ['bli:pər] buscapersonas m inv, Span busca m

blem·ish ['blemɪʃ] 1 n imperfección f 2 v/t reputation manchar

blend [blend] 1 n of coffee etc mezcla f; fig combinación f 2 v/t mezclar

◆ **blend in** v/i of person in environment pasar desapercibido; of animal with surroundings etc confundirse; of furniture etc combinar 2 v/t in cooking añadir

blend·er ['blendər] machine licuadora f

bless [bles] v/t bendecir; (God) **bless you!** ¡que Dios te bendiga!; in response to sneeze ¡Jesús!; **be blessed with** tener la suerte de

bless·ing ['blesɪŋ] *also fig* bendición *f*

blew [bluː] *pret* → **blow²**

blind [blaɪnd] **1** *adj* ciego; *corner* sin visibilidad; **be blind to sth** *fig* no ver algo **2** *npl:* **the blind** los ciegos, los invidentes **3** *v/t of sun* cegar; **she was blinded in an accident** se quedó ciega a raíz de un accidente; **love blinded her to his faults** el amor le impedía ver sus defectos

blind 'al·ley callejón *m* sin salida

blind 'date cita *f* a ciegas

'blind·fold 1 *n* venda *f* **2** *v/t* vendar los ojos a **3** *adv* con los ojos cerrados

blind·ing ['blaɪndɪŋ] *adj light* cegador; *headache* terrible

blind·ly ['blaɪndlɪ] *adv* a ciegas; *fig* ciegamente

'blind spot *in road* punto *m* sin visibilidad; *in driving mirror* ángulo *m* muerto; *(ability that is lacking)* punto *m* flaco

blink [blɪŋk] *v/i* parpadear

blink·ered ['blɪŋkərd] *adj fig* cerrado

blip [blɪp] *on radar screen* señal *f*, luz *f*; **it's just a blip** *fig* es algo momentáneo

bliss [blɪs] felicidad *f*; **it was bliss** fue fantástico

blis·ter ['blɪstər] **1** *n* ampolla *f* **2** *v/i* ampollarse; *of paint* hacer burbujas

bliz·zard ['blɪzərd] ventisca *f*

bloat·ed ['bloʊtɪd] *adj* hinchado

blob [blɑːb] *of liquid* goterón *m*

bloc [blɑːk] POL bloque *m*

block [blɑːk] **1** *n* bloque *m*; *buildings* manzana *f*, *L.Am.* cuadra *f*; *of shares* paquete *m*; *(blockage)* bloqueo *m* **2** *v/t* bloquear; *sink* atascar

◆ **block in** *v/t with vehicle* bloquear el paso a

◆ **block out** *v/t light* impedir el paso de

◆ **block up** *v/t sink etc* atascar

block·ade [blɑːˈkeɪd] **1** *n* bloqueo *m* **2** *v/t* bloquear

block·age ['blɑːkɪdʒ] obstrucción *f*

block·bust·er ['blɑːkbʌstər] gran éxito *m*

block 'let·ters *npl* letras *fpl* mayúsculas

blond [blɑːnd] *adj* rubio

blonde [blɑːnd] *n woman* rubia *f*

blood [blʌd] sangre *f*; **in cold blood** a sangre fría

'blood al·co·hol lev·el nivel *m* de alcohol en sangre

'blood bank banco *m* de sangre

'blood bath baño *m* de sangre

'blood do·nor donante *m/f* de sangre

'blood group grupo *m* sanguíneo

blood·less ['blʌdlɪs] *adj coup* incruento, pacífico

'blood poi·son·ing septicemia *f*

'blood pres·sure tensión *f* (arterial), presión *f* sanguínea

'blood re·la·tion: she's not a blood relation of mine no nos unen lazos de sangre

'blood sam·ple muestra *f* de sangre

'blood·shed derramamiento *m* de sangre

'blood·shot *adj* enrojecido

'blood·stain mancha *f* de sangre

'blood·stain·ed *adj* ensangrentado, manchado de sangre

'blood·stream flujo *m* sanguíneo

'blood test análisis *m inv* de sangre

'blood·thirst·y *adj* sanguinario; *movie* macabro

'blood trans·fu·sion transfusión *f* sanguínea

'blood ves·sel vaso *m* sanguíneo

blood·y ['blʌdɪ] *adj hands etc* ensangrentado; *battle* sangriento; *Br F* maldito F, *Span* puñetero F; **bloody hell!** ¡ostras! F

bloom [bluːm] **1** *n* flor *f*; **in bloom** en flor **2** *v/i also fig* florecer

blos·som ['blɑːsəm] **1** *n* flores *fpl* **2** *v/i also fig* florecer

blot [blɑːt] **1** *n* mancha *f*, borrón *m*; **be a blot on the landscape** estropear el paisaje **2** *v/t* (*pret & pp* **blotted**) (*dry*) secar

◆ **blot out** *v/t* borrar; *sun, view* ocultar

blotch [blɑːtʃ] *on skin* erupción *f*, mancha *f*

blotch·y ['blɑːtʃɪ] *adj:* **blotchy skin** piel con erupciones

blouse [blaʊz] blusa *f*

blow¹ [bloʊ] *n* golpe *m*

blow² [bloʊ] **1** *v/t* (*pret* **blew**, *pp* **blown**) *smoke* exhalar; *whistle* tocar; F (*spend*) fundir F; *opportunity* perder, desaprovechar; **blow one's nose** sonarse (la nariz) **2** *v/i* (*pret* **blew**, *pp* **blown**) *of wind, person* soplar; *of whistle* sonar; *of fuse* fundirse; *of tire* reventarse

◆ **blow off 1** *v/t* llevarse **2** *v/i* salir volando

◆ **blow out 1** *v/t candle* apagar **2** *v/i of candle* apagarse

◆ **blow over 1** *v/t* derribar, hacer caer **2** *v/i* caerse, derrumbarse; *of storm* amainar; *of argument* calmarse

◆ **blow up 1** *v/t with explosives* volar; *balloon* hinchar; *photograph* ampliar **2** *v/i* explotar; F *(become angry)* ponerse furioso

'**blow-dry** *v/t (pret & pp* **blow-dried)** secar *(con secador)*

'**blow-job** V mamada *f* V

'**blow-out** *of tire* reventón *m*; F *(big meal)* comilona *f* F

'**blow-up** *of photo* ampliación *f*

blown [bloun] *pp* → **blow²**

blue [bluː] **1** *adj* azul; F *movie* porno *inv* F **2** *n* azul *m*

'**blue-ber-ry** arándano *m*

blue 'chip *adj* puntero, de primera fila

blue-'col·lar work·er trabajador(a) *m(f)* manual

'**blue-print** plano *m*; *(fig: plan)* proyecto *m*, plan *m*

blues [bluːz] *npl* MUS blues *m inv*; **have the blues** estar deprimido

'**blues sing·er** cantante *m/f* de blues

bluff [blʌf] **1** *n (deception)* farol *m* **2** *v/i* ir de farol

blun·der ['blʌndər] **1** *n* error *m* de bulto, metedura *f* de pata **2** *v/i* cometer un error de bulto, meter la pata

blunt [blʌnt] *adj pencil* sin punta; *knife* desafilado; *person* franco

blunt·ly ['blʌntlɪ] *adv speak* francamente

blur [blɜːr] **1** *n* imagen *f* desenfocada; **everything is a blur** todo está desenfocado **2** *v/t (pret & pp* **blurred)** desdibujar

blurb [blɜːrb] *on book* nota *f* promocional

◆ **blurt out** [blɜːrt] *v/t* soltar

blush [blʌʃ] **1** *n* rubor *m*, sonrojo *m* **2** *v/i* ruborizarse, sonrojarse

blush·er ['blʌʃər] *cosmetic* colorete *m*

blus·ter ['blʌstər] *v/i* protestar encolerizadamente

blus·ter·y ['blʌstərɪ] *adj* tempestuoso

BO [biːˈou] *abbr (= body odor)* olor *m*

corporal

board [bɔːrd] **1** *n* tablón *m*, tabla *f*; *for game* tablero *m*; *for notices* tablón *m*; **board (of directors)** consejo *m* de administración; **on board** *on plane, boat, train* a bordo; **take on board** *comments etc* aceptar, tener en cuenta; *(fully realize truth of)* asumir; **across the board** de forma general **2** *v/t airplane etc* embarcar; *train* subir a **3** *v/i of passengers* embarcar; **board with** *as lodger* hospedarse con

◆ **board up** *v/t* cubrir con tablas

board·er ['bɔːrdər] huésped *m/f*

'**board game** juego *m* de mesa

'**board·ing card** tarjeta *f* de embarque

'**board·ing house** hostal *m*, pensión *f*

'**board·ing pass** tarjeta *f* de embarque

'**board·ing school** internado *m*

'**board meet·ing** reunión *m* del consejo de administración

'**board room** sala *f* de reuniones *or* juntas

'**board·walk** paseo *m* marítimo con tablas

boast [boust] **1** *n* presunción *f*, jactancia *f* **2** *v/i* presumir, alardear *(about* de)

boat [bout] barco *m*; *small, for leisure* barca *f*; **go by boat** ir en barco

bob¹ [baːb] *haircut* corte *m* a lo chico

bob² [baːb] *v/i (pret & pp* **bobbed)** *of boat etc* mecerse

◆ **bob up** *v/i* aparecer

'**bob·sleigh**, '**bob·sled** bobsleigh *m*

bod·ice ['baːdɪs] cuerpo *m*

bod·i·ly ['baːdɪlɪ] **1** *adj* corporal; *needs* físico; *function* fisiológico **2** *adv eject* en volandas

bod·y ['baːdɪ] cuerpo *m*; *dead* cadáver *m*; **body of water** masa *f* de agua

'**body·guard** guardaespaldas *m/f inv*

'**body lan·guage** lenguaje *m* corporal

'**body o·dor** olor *m* corporal

'**body pierc·ing** piercing *m*, perforaciones *fpl* corporales

'**body·shop** MOT taller *m* de carrocería

'**body stock·ing** malla *f*

'**body suit** body *m* '**body·work** MOT carrocería *f*

bog·gle ['baːgl] *v/i*: **the mind boggles!** ¡no quiero ni pensarlo!

bo·gus ['bougəs] *adj* falso

boil[1] [bɔɪl] *n* (*swelling*) forúnculo

boil[2] [bɔɪl] **1** *v/t liquid* hervir; *egg, vegetables* cocer **2** *v/i* hervir

◆ **boil down to** *v/t* reducirse a

◆ **boil over** *v/i* of milk etc salirse

boil·er ['bɔɪlər] caldera *f*

boil·ing point ['bɔɪlɪŋ] of liquid punto *m* de ebullición; **reach boiling point** fig perder la paciencia

bois·ter·ous ['bɔɪstərəs] *adj* escandaloso

bold [bould] **1** *adj* valiente, audaz; *text* en negrita **2** *n* (*print*) negrita *f*; **in bold** en negrita

Bo·liv·i·a [bə'lɪvɪə] *n* Bolivia

Bo·liv·i·an [bə'lɪvɪən] **1** *adj* boliviano **2** *n* boliviano(-a) *m(f)*

bol·ster ['boulstər] *v/t confidence* reforzar

bolt [boult] **1** *n* on door cerrojo *m*, pestillo *m*; with nut perno *m*; of lightning rayo *m*; **like a bolt from the blue** de forma inesperada **2** *adv*: **bolt upright** erguido **3** *v/t* (*fix with bolts*) atornillar; *close* cerrar con cerrojo *or* pestillo **4** *v/i* (*run off*) fugarse, escaparse

bomb [bɑːm] **1** *n* bomba *f* **2** *v/t* MIL bombardear; of terrorist poner una bomba en

bom·bard [bɑːm'bɑːrd] *v/t* (*attack*) bombardear; **bombard s.o. with questions** bombardear alguien con preguntas

'**bomb attack** atentado *m* con bomba

bomb·er ['bɑːmər] *airplane* bombardero *m*; terrorista *m/f* (*que pone bombas*)

'**bomb·er jack·et** cazadora *f* de aviador

'**bomb-proof** *adj* a prueba de bombas

'**bomb scare** amenaza *f* de bomba

'**bomb·shell** (*fig: news*) bomba *f*

bond [bɑːnd] **1** *n* (*tie*) unión *f*; FIN bono *m* **2** *v/i* of glue adherirse

bone [boun] **1** *n* hueso *m*; of fish espina *f* **2** *v/t meat* deshuesar; fish quitar las espinas a

bon·fire ['bɑːnfaɪr] hoguera *f*

bon·net Br of car MOT capó *m*

bo·nus ['bounəs] money plus *m*, bonificación *f*; (*something extra*) ventaja *f* adicional; **a Christmas bonus** un plus por Navidad

boo [buː] **1** *n* abucheo *m* **2** *v/t & v/i* abuchear

boob [buːb] *n* P (*breast*) teta *f* P

boo·boo ['buːbuː] *n* F metedura *f* de pata

book [buk] **1** *n* libro *m*; of matches caja *f* (*de solapa*) **2** *v/t* (*reserve*) reservar; of policeman multar **3** *v/i* (*reserve*) reservar, hacer una reserva

'**book-case** estantería *f*, librería *f*

booked up [bukt'ʌp] *adj* lleno, completo; *person* ocupado

book·ie ['bukɪ] F corredor(a) *m(f)* de apuestas

book·ing ['bukɪŋ] (*reservation*) reserva *f*

'**book·ing clerk** taquillero(-a) *m(f)*

'**book-keep·er** tenedor(a) *m(f)* de libros

'**book-keep·ing** contabilidad *f*

'**book·let** ['buklɪt] folleto *m*

'**book-mak·er** corredor(a) *m(f)* de apuestas

books [buks] *npl* (*accounts*) contabilidad *f*; **do the books** llevar la contabilidad; **cook the books** F falsificar las cuentas

'**book-sell·er** librero(-a) *m(f)*

'**book·shelf** estante *m*

'**book·store** librería *f*

'**book·stall** puesto *m* de venta de libros

'**book to·ken** vale *m* para comprar libros

boom[1] [buːm] **1** *n* boom *m* **2** *v/i* of business desarrollarse, experimentar un boom

boom[2] [buːm] *n noise* estruendo *m*

boon·ies ['buːnɪz] *npl* F: **they live out in the boonies** viven en el quinto pino F

boor [bur] basto *m*, grosero *m*

boor·ish ['burɪʃ] *adj* basto, grosero

boost [buːst] **1** *n to sales, economy* impulso *m*; **your confidence needs a boost** necesitas algo que te dé más confianza **2** *v/t production, prices* estimular; *morale* levantar

boot [buːt] *n* bota *f*; Br of car maletero *m*, C.Am., Mex cajuela *f*, Rpl baúl *m*

◆ **boot out** *v/t* F echar

◆ **boot up** *v/t & v/i* COMPUT arrancar

booth [buːð] at market, fair cabina *f*; (*in restaurant*) mesa rodeada por bancos fijos

booze [buːz] n F bebida f, Span priva f F

bor·der ['bɔːrdər] **1** n between countries frontera f; (edge) borde m; on clothing ribete m **2** v/t country limitar con; river bordear

◆ **border on** limitar con; (be almost) rayar en

'**bor·der·line** adj: **a borderline case** un caso dudoso

bore¹ [bɔːr] **1** v/t hole taladrar; **bore a hole in sth** taladrar algo

bore² [bɔːr] **1** n (person) pesado(-a) m(f), pelma m/f inv F; **it's such a bore** ¡qué pesadez or Span lata! **2** v/t aburrir

bore³ [bɔːr] pret → **bear²**

bored [bɔːrd] adj aburrido; **I'm bored** me aburro, estoy aburrido

bore·dom ['bɔːrdəm] aburrimiento m

bor·ing ['bɔːrɪŋ] adj aburrido; **be boring** ser aburrido

born [bɔːrn] adj: **be born** nacer; **where were you born?** ¿dónde naciste?; **be a born teacher** haber nacido para ser profesor

borne [bɔːrn] pp → **bear²**

bor·row ['bɑːrou] v/t tomar prestado

bos·om ['buzm] of woman pecho m

boss [bɑːs] jefe(-a) m(f)

◆ **boss about** v/t dar órdenes a

boss·y ['bɑːsɪ] adj mandón

bo·tan·i·cal [bə'tænɪkl] adj botánico

bo·tan·ic(·al) gar·dens npl jardín m botánico

bot·a·nist ['bɑːtənɪst] botánico(-a) m(f)

bot·a·ny ['bɑːtənɪ] botánica f

botch [bɑːtʃ] v/t arruinar, estropear

both [bouθ] **1** adj & pron ambos, los dos; **I know both (of the) brothers** conozco a ambos hermanos, conozco a los dos hermanos; **both of them** ambos, los dos **2** adv: **both my mother and I** tanto mi madre como yo; **he's both handsome and intelligent** es guapo y además inteligente; **is it business or pleasure? - both** ¿es de negocios o de placer? - las dos cosas

both·er ['bɑːðər] **1** n molestias fpl; **it's no bother** no es ninguna molestia **2** v/t (disturb) molestar; (worry) preocupar **3** v/i

preocuparse; **don't bother!** (you needn't do it) ¡no te preocupes!; **you needn't have bothered** no deberías haberte molestado

bot·tle ['bɑːtl] **1** n botella f; for baby biberón m **2** v/t embotellar

◆ **bottle up** v/t feelings reprimir, contener

'**bot·tle bank** contenedor m de vidrio

bot·tled wa·ter ['bɑːtld] agua f embotellada

'**bot·tle·neck** n in road embotellamiento m, atasco m; in production cuello m de botella

'**bot·tle-o·pen·er** abrebotellas m inv

bot·tom ['bɑːtəm] **1** adj inferior, de abajo **2** n of drawer, case, pan fondo m; of hill, page pie m; of pile parte f inferior; (underside) parte f de abajo; of street final m; of garden fondo m; (buttocks) trasero m; **at the bottom of the screen** en la parte inferior de la pantalla

◆ **bottom out** v/i tocar fondo

bot·tom 'line (fig: financial outcome) saldo m final; (real issue) realidad f

bought [bɔːt] pret & pp → **buy**

boul·der ['bouldər] roca f redondeada

bounce [bauns] **1** v/t ball botar **2** v/i of ball botar, rebotar; on sofa etc saltar; of rain rebotar; of check ser rechazado

bounc·er ['baunsər] portero m, gorila m

bounc·y ['baunsɪ] adj ball que bota bien; cushion, chair mullido

bound¹ [baund] adj: **be bound to do sth** (obliged to) estar obligado a hacer algo; **she's bound to call an election soon** (sure to) seguro que convoca elecciones pronto

bound² [baund] adj: **be bound for** of ship llevar destino a

bound³ [baund] **1** n (jump) salto m **2** v/i saltar

bound⁴ [baund] pret & pp → **bind**

bound·a·ry ['baundərɪ] límite m; between countries frontera f

bound·less ['baundlɪs] adj ilimitado, infinito

bou·quet [bu'keɪ] (flowers) ramo m

bour·bon ['bɜːrbən] bourbon m

bout [baut] MED ataque m; in boxing combate *m*

bou·tique [buːˈtiːk] boutique *f*

bow¹ [bau] **1** *n as greeting* reverencia *f* **2** *v/i* saludar con la cabeza **3** *v/t head* inclinar

bow² [bou] (*knot*) lazo *m*; MUS, *for archery* arco *m*

bow³ [bau] *of ship* proa *f*

bow·els [ˈbauəlz] *npl* entrañas *fpl*

bowl¹ [boul] *for rice, cereals etc* cuenco *m*; *for soup* plato *m* sopero; *for salad* ensaladera *f*; *for washing* barreño *m*, palangana *f*

bowl² [boul] **1** *n* (*ball*) bola *f* **2** *v/i in bowling* lanzar la bola

♦ bowl over *v/t* (fig: *astonish*) impresionar, maravillar

bowl·ing [ˈboulɪŋ] bolos *mpl*

ˈbowl·ing al·ley bolera *f*

bow ˈtie [bou] pajarita *f*

box¹ [baːks] *n container* caja *f*; *on form* casilla *f*

box² [baːks] *v/i* boxear

box·er [ˈbaːksər] boxeador(a) *m(f)*

ˈbox·er shorts *npl* calzoncillos *mpl*, boxers *mpl*

box·ing [ˈbaːksɪŋ] boxeo *m*

ˈbox·ing glove guante *m* de boxeo

ˈbox·ing match combate *m* de boxeo

ˈbox·ing ring cuadrilátero *m*, ring *m*

ˈbox num·ber *at post office* apartado *m* de correos

ˈbox of·fice taquilla *f*, *L.Am.* boletería *f*

boy [bɔɪ] niño *m*, chico *m*; (*son*) hijo *m*

boy·cott [ˈbɔɪkaːt] **1** *n* boicot *m* **2** *v/t* boicotear

ˈboy·friend novio *m*

boy·ish [ˈbɔɪɪʃ] *adj* varonil

ˈboy scout boy scout *m*

bra [braː] *Br* sujetador *m*, sostén *m*

brace [breɪs] *on teeth* aparato *m*

brace·let [ˈbreɪslɪt] pulsera *f*

brack·et [ˈbrækɪt] *for shelf* escuadra *f*; (*square*) **bracket** *in text* corchete *m*

brag [bræg] *v/i* (*pret & pp* **bragged**) presumir, fanfarronear

braid [breɪd] *n in hair* trenza *f*; *trimming* trenzado *m*

braille [breɪl] braille *m*

brain [breɪn] cerebro *m*; *use your brain* utiliza la cabeza

ˈbrain dead *adj* MED clínicamente muerto

brain·less [ˈbreɪnlɪs] *adj* F estúpido

brains [breɪnz] *npl* (*intelligence*) inteligencia *f*; *the brains of the operation* el cerebro de la operación

ˈbrain·storm idea *f* genial

brain·storm·ing [ˈbreɪnstɔːrmɪŋ] tormenta *f* de ideas

ˈbrain sur·geon neurocirujano(-a) *m(f)*

ˈbrain sur·ger·y neurocirugía *f*

ˈbrain tu·mor tumor *m* cerebral

ˈbrain·wash *v/t* lavar el cerebro a

ˈbrain·wave (*brilliant idea*) idea *f* genial

brain·y [ˈbreɪnɪ] *adj* F: *be brainy* tener mucho coco F, ser una lumbrera

brake [breɪk] **1** *n* freno *m*; *act as a brake on* frenar **2** *v/i* frenar

ˈbrake flu·id MOT líquido *m* de frenos

ˈbrake light MOT luz *f* de frenado

ˈbrake ped·al MOT pedal *m* del freno

branch [bræntʃ] *n of tree* rama *f*; *of bank, company* sucursal *f*

♦ branch off *v/i of road* bifurcarse

♦ branch out *v/i* diversificarse; *they've branched out into furniture* han empezado a trabajar también con muebles

brand [brænd] **1** *n* marca *f* **2** *v/t*: *be branded a liar* ser tildado de mentiroso

ˈbrand im·age imagen *f* de marca

bran·dish [ˈbrændɪʃ] *v/t* blandir

ˈbrand lead·er marca *f* líder del mercado

ˈbrand loy·al·ty lealtad *f* a una marca

ˈbrand name nombre *m* comercial

brand-ˈnew *adj* nuevo, flamante

bran·dy [ˈbrændɪ] brandy *m*, coñac *m*

brass [bræs] *alloy* latón *m*; *the brass* MUS los metales

brass ˈband banda *f* de música

bras·sière [brəˈzɪr] sujetador *m*, sostén *m*

brat [bræt] *pej* niñato(-a) *m(f)*

bra·va·do [brəˈvaːdou] bravuconería *f*

brave [breɪv] *adj* valiente, valeroso

brave·ly [ˈbreɪvlɪ] *adv* valientemente, valerosamente

brav·er·y [ˈbreɪvərɪ] valentía *f*, valor *m*

brawl [brɔːl] **1** *n* pelea *f* **2** *v/i* pelearse

brawn·y [ˈbrɔːnɪ] *adj* fuerte, musculoso

Bra·zil [brə'zɪl] Brasil
Bra·zil·ian [brə'zɪlɪən] **1** *adj* brasileño **2** *n* brasileño(-a) *m(f)*
breach [briːtʃ] *n* (*violation*) infracción *f*, incumplimiento; *in party* ruptura *f*
breach of 'con·tract LAW incumplimiento *m* de contrato
bread [bred] *n* pan *m*
'**bread·crumbs** *npl for cooking* pan *m* rallado; *for birds* migas *fpl*
'**bread knife** cuchillo *m* del pan
breadth [bredθ] *of road* ancho *m*; *of knowledge* amplitud *f*
'**bread·win·ner**: **be the breadwinner** ser el que gana el pan
break [breɪk] **1** *n in bone etc* fractura *f*, rotura *f*; (*rest*) descanso *m*; *in relationship* separación *f* temporal; **give s.o. a break** F (*opportunity*) ofrecer una oportunidad a alguien; **take a break** descansar; **without a break** *work, travel* sin descanso **2** *v/t* (*pret* **broke**, *pp* **broken**) *machine, device* romper, estropear; *stick* romper, partir; *arm, leg* fracturar, romper; *glass, egg* romper; *rules, law* violar, incumplir; *promise* romper; *news* dar; *record* batir **3** *v/i* (*pret* **broke**, *pp* **broken**) *of machine, device* romperse, estropearse; *of glass, egg* romperse; *of stick* partirse, romperse; *of news* saltar; *of storm* estallar, comenzar; *of boy's voice* cambiar
◆ **break away** *v/i* (*escape*) escaparse; *from family* separarse; *from organization* escindirse; *from tradition* romper (**from** con)
◆ **break down 1** *v/i of vehicle* averiarse, estropearse; *of machine* estropearse; *of talks* romperse; *in tears* romper a llorar; *mentally* venirse abajo **2** *v/t door* derribar; *figures* detallar, desglosar
◆ **break even** *v/i* COM cubrir gastos
◆ **break in** *v/i* (*interrupt*) interrumpir; *of burglar* entrar
◆ **break off 1** *v/t* partir; *relationship* romper; **they've broken it off** han roto **2** *v/i* (*stop talking*) interrumpirse
◆ **break out** *v/i* (*start up*) comenzar; *of fighting* estallar; *of disease* desatarse; *of prisoners* escaparse, darse a la fuga; **he bro-**

ke out in a rash le salió un sarpullido
◆ **break up 1** *v/t into component parts* descomponer; *fight* poner fin a **2** *v/i of ice* romperse; *of couple* terminar, separarse; *of band* separarse; *of meeting* terminar
break·a·ble ['breɪkəbl] *adj* rompible, frágil
break·age ['breɪkɪdʒ] rotura *f*
'**break·down** *of vehicle, machine* avería *f*; *of talks* ruptura *f*; (*nervous breakdown*) crisis *f inv* nerviosa; *of figures* desglose *m*
break·'e·ven point punto *m* de equilibrio
break·fast ['brekfəst] *n* desayuno *m*; **have breakfast** desayunar
'**break·fast tel·e·vi·sion** televisión *f* matinal
'**break-in** entrada *f* (*mediante la fuerza*); *robbery* robo *m*; **we've had a break-in** han entrado a robar
'**break·through** *in plan, negotiations* paso *m* adelante; *of science, technology* avance *m*
'**break·up** *of marriage, partnership* ruptura *f*, separación *f*
breast [brest] *of woman* pecho *m*
'**breast-feed** *v/t* (*pret & pp* **breastfed**) amamantar
'**breast·stroke** braza *f*
breath [breθ] respiración *f*; **get your breath back** recobrar el aliento; **be out of breath** estar sin respiración; **take a deep breath** respira hondo
Breath·a·lyz·er® ['breθəlaɪzər] alcoholímetro *m*
breathe [briːð] **1** *v/i* respirar **2** *v/t* (*inhale*) aspirar, respirar; (*exhale*) exhalar, espirar
◆ **breathe in** *v/t & v/i* aspirar, inspirar
◆ **breathe out** *v/i* espirar
breath·ing ['briːðɪŋ] *n* respiración *f*
breath·less ['breθlɪs] *adj*: **arrive breathless** llegar sin respiración, llegar jadeando
breath·less·ness ['breθlɪsnɪs] dificultad *f* para respirar
breath·tak·ing ['breθteɪkɪŋ] *adj* impresionante, sorprendente
bred [bred] *pret & pp* → **breed**
breed [briːd] **1** *n* raza *f* **2** *v/t* (*pret & pp* **bred**) criar; *plants* cultivar; *fig* causar,

generar **3** v/i (pret & pp **bred**) of animals reproducirse

breed·er ['briːdər] of animals criador(a) m(f); of plants cultivador(a) m(f)

breed·ing ['briːdɪŋ] of animals cría f; of plants cultivo m; of person educación f

breed·ing ground fig caldo m de cultivo

breeze [briːz] brisa f

breez·i·ly ['briːzɪlɪ] adv fig jovialmente, tranquilamente

breez·y ['briːzɪ] adj ventoso; fig jovial, tranquilo

brew [bruː] **1** v/t beer elaborar; tea preparar, hacer **2** v/i of storm avecinarse; of trouble fraguarse

brew·er ['bruːər] fabricante m/f de cerveza

brew·er·y ['bruːərɪ] fábrica f de cerveza

bribe [braɪb] **1** n soborno m, Mex mordida f, S. Am. coima f **2** v/t sobornar

brib·er·y ['braɪbərɪ] soborno m, Mex mordida f, S. Am. coima f

brick [brɪk] ladrillo m

'**brick·lay·er** albañil m/f

brid·al suite ['braɪdl] suite f nupcial

bride [braɪd] novia f (en boda)

'**bride·groom** novio m (en boda)

'**brides·maid** dama f de honor

bridge¹ [brɪdʒ] **1** n puente m; of nose caballete m **2** v/t gap superar, salvar

bridge² [brɪdʒ] card game bridge m

bri·dle [braɪdl] brida f

brief¹ ['briːf] adj breve, corto

brief² [briːf] **1** n (mission) misión f **2** v/t: **brief s.o. on sth** informar a alguien de algo

'**brief·case** maletín m

brief·ing ['briːfɪŋ] reunión f informativa

brief·ly ['briːflɪ] adv (for a short period of time) brevemente; (in a few words) en pocas palabras; (to sum up) en resumen

briefs [briːfs] npl for women bragas fpl; for men calzoncillos mpl

bright [braɪt] adj color vivo; smile radiante; future brillante, prometedor; (sunny) soleado, luminoso; (intelligent) inteligente

◆ **bright·en up** ['braɪtn] **1** v/t alegrar **2** v/i of weather aclararse; of face, person ale-

grarse, animarse

bright·ly ['braɪtlɪ] adv shine intensamente, fuerte; smile alegremente

bright·ness ['braɪtnɪs] of light brillo m; of weather luminosidad f; of smile alegría f; (intelligence) inteligencia f

bril·liance ['brɪljəns] of person genialidad f; of color resplandor m

bril·liant ['brɪljənt] adj sunshine etc resplandeciente, radiante; (very good) genial; (very intelligent) brillante

brim [brɪm] of container borde m; of hat ala f

brim·ful ['brɪmfəl] adj rebosante

bring [brɪŋ] v/t (pret & pp **brought**) traer; **bring it here, will you** tráelo aquí, por favor; **can I bring a friend?** ¿puedo traer a un amigo?, ¿puedo venir con un amigo?

◆ **bring about** v/t ocasionar; **bring about peace** traer la paz

◆ **bring around** v/t from a faint hacer volver en sí; (persuade) convencer, persuadir

◆ **bring back** v/t (return) devolver; (re-introduce) reinstaurar; memories traer

◆ **bring down** v/t fence, tree tirar, echar abajo; government derrocar; bird, airplane derribar; rates, inflation, price reducir

◆ **bring in** v/t interest, income generar; legislation introducir; verdict pronunciar

◆ **bring on** v/t illness provocar

◆ **bring out** v/t book, video, new product sacar

◆ **bring to** v/t from a faint hacer volver en sí

◆ **bring up** v/t child criar, educar; subject mencionar, sacar a colación; (vomit) vomitar

brink [brɪŋk] borde m; **be on the brink of sth** fig estar a punto de hacer algo

brisk [brɪsk] adj person, voice enérgico; walk rápido; trade animado

bris·tle ['brɪsl] v/i: **the streets are bristling with policemen** las calles están atestadas de policías

brist·les ['brɪslz] npl on chin pelos mpl; of brush cerdas fpl

Brit [brɪt] F británico(-a) m(f)

Brit·ain ['brɪtn] Gran Bretaña

Brit·ish ['brɪtɪʃ] **1** *adj* británico **2** *n: the British* los británicos

Brit·on ['brɪtn] británico(-a) *m(f)*

brit·tle ['brɪtl] *adj* frágil, quebradizo

broach [brəʊtʃ] *v/t subject* sacar a colación

broad [brɔːd] **1** *adj* ancho; *smile* amplio; (*general*) general; *in broad daylight* a plena luz del día; *in broad terms* en líneas generales **2** *n* F (*woman*) tía *f* F

'broad·cast 1 *n* emisión *f*; *a live broadcast* una retransmisión en directo **2** *v/t* emitir, retransmitir

'broad·cast·er presentador(a) *m(f)*

'broad·cast·ing televisión *f*

broad·en ['brɔːdn] **1** *v/i* ensancharse, ampliarse **2** *v/t* ensanchar; *broaden one's horizons* ampliar los horizontes

'broad·jump salto *m* de longitud

broad·ly ['brɔːdlɪ] *adv* en general; *broadly speaking* en términos generales

broad·mind·ed [brɔːd'maɪndɪd] *adj* tolerante, abierto

broad·mind·ed·ness [brɔːd'maɪndɪdnɪs] mentalidad *f* abierta

broc·co·li ['brɑːkəlɪ] brécol *m*, brócoli *m*

bro·chure ['brəʊʃər] folleto *m*

broil [brɔɪl] *v/t* asar a la parrilla

broil·er ['brɔɪlər] *on stove* parrilla *f*; *chicken* pollo *m* (para asar)

broke [brəʊk] **1** *adj* F: *be broke* temporarily estar sin blanca F; *long term* estar arruinado; *go broke* (*go bankrupt*) arruinarse **2** *pret* → *break*

bro·ken ['brəʊkn] **1** *adj* roto; *home* deshecho; *they talk in broken English* chapurrean el inglés **2** *pp* → *break*

bro·ken-heart·ed [brəʊkn'hɑːrtɪd] *adj* desconsolado, destrozado

bro·ker ['brəʊkər] corredor(a) *m(f)*, agente *m/f*

bron·chi·tis [brɑːŋ'kaɪtɪs] bronquitis *f*

bronze [brɑːnz] *n* bronce *m*

brooch [brəʊtʃ] broche *m*

brood [bruːd] *v/i of person* darle vueltas a las cosas; *brood about sth* darle vueltas a algo

broom [bruːm] escoba *f*

broth [brɑːθ] *soup* sopa *f*; *stock* caldo *m*

broth·el ['brɑːθl] burdel *m*

broth·er ['brʌðər] hermano *m*

'broth·er-in-law (*pl brothers-in-law*) cuñado *m*

broth·er·ly ['brʌðərlɪ] *adj* fraternal

brought [brɔːt] *pret & pp* → *bring*

brow [braʊ] (*forehead*) frente *f*; *of hill* cima *f*

brown [braʊn] **1** *n* marrón *m*, *L.Am.* color *m* café **2** *adj* marrón; *eyes, hair* castaño; (*tanned*) moreno **3** *v/t in cooking* dorar **4** *v/i in cooking* dorarse

'brown·bag *v/t* (*pret & pp brown-bagged*) F: *brownbag it* llevar la comida al trabajo

Brown·ie ['braʊnɪ] escultista *f*

'Brown·ie points *npl* tantos *mpl*; *earn Brownie points* anotarse tantos

brown·ie ['braʊnɪ] (*cake*) pastel *m* de chocolate y nueces

'brown-nose *v/t* P lamer el culo a P

brown 'pa·per papel *m* de estraza

brown 'pa·per 'bag bolsa *f* de cartón

brown 'sug·ar azúcar *m or f* moreno(-a)

browse [braʊz] *v/i in store* echar una ojeada; *browse through a book* hojear un libro

brows·er ['braʊzər] COMPUT navegador *m*

bruise [bruːz] **1** *n* magulladura *f*, cardenal *f*; *on fruit* maca *f* **2** *v/t arm, fruit* magullar; (*emotionally*) herir **3** *v/i of person* hacerse cardenales; *of fruit* macarse

bruis·ing ['bruːzɪŋ] *adj fig* doloroso

brunch [brʌntʃ] combinación de desayuno y almuerzo

bru·nette [bruː'net] *n* morena *f*

brunt [brʌnt]: *this area bore the brunt of the flooding* esta zona fue la más castigada por la inundación; *we bore the brunt of the layoffs* fuimos los más perjudicados por los despidos

brush [brʌʃ] **1** *n* cepillo *m*; *conflict* roce *m* **2** *v/t* cepillar; (*touch lightly*) rozar; (*move away*) quitar

◆ **brush against** *v/t* rozar

◆ **brush aside** *v/t* hacer caso omiso a, no hacer caso a

◆ **brush off** *v/t* sacudir; *criticism* no hacer caso a

◆ **brush up** *v/t* repasar

'**brush·work** PAINT pincelada *f*

brusque [brʊsk] *adj* brusco

Brus·sels ['brʌslz] Bruselas

Brus·sels sprouts *npl* coles *fpl* de Bruselas

bru·tal ['bruːtl] *adj* brutal

bru·tal·i·ty [bruː'tælətɪ] brutalidad *f*

bru·tal·ly ['bruːtəlɪ] *adv* brutalmente; *be brutally frank* ser de una sinceridad aplastante

brute [bruːt] bestia *m/f*

brute 'force fuerza *f* bruta

bub·ble ['bʌbl] *n* burbuja *f*

'**bub·ble bath** baño *m* de espuma

'**bub·ble gum** chicle *m*

'**bub·ble wrap** *n* plástico *m* para embalar (*con burbujas*)

bub·bly ['bʌblɪ] *n* F (*champagne*) champán *m*

buck[1] [bʌk] *n* F (*dollar*) dólar *m*

buck[2] [bʌk] *v/i of horse* corcovear

buck[3] [bʌk] *n*: *pass the buck* escurrir el bulto

buck·et ['bʌkɪt] *n* cubo *m*

buck·le[1] ['bʌkl] **1** *n* hebilla *f* **2** *v/t belt* abrochar

buck·le[2] ['bʌkl] *v/i of wood, metal* combarse

◆ **buckle down** *v/i* ponerse a trabajar

bud [bʌd] *n* BOT capullo *m*, brote *m*

bud·dy ['bʌdɪ] F amigo(-a) *m(f)*, Span colega *m/f* F; *form of address Span* colega *m/f* F, *L.Am.* compadre *m/f* F

budge [bʌdʒ] **1** *v/t* mover; (*make reconsider*) hacer cambiar de opinión **2** *v/i* moverse; (*change one's mind*) cambiar de opinión

bud·ger·i·gar ['bʌdʒərɪgaːr] periquito *m*

bud·get ['bʌdʒɪt] **1** *n* presupuesto *m*; *be on a budget* tener un presupuesto limitado **2** *v/i* administrarse

◆ **budget for** *v/t* contemplar en el presupuesto

bud·gie ['bʌdʒɪ] F periquito *m*

buff[1] [bʌf] *adj color* marrón claro

buff[2] [bʌf] *n* aficionado(-a) *m(f)*; *a movie buff* un cinéfilo

buf·fa·lo ['bʌfələʊ] búfalo *m*

buff·er ['bʌfər] RAIL tope *m*; COMPUT búfer *m*; *fig* barrera *f*

buf·fet[1] ['bʊfeɪ] *n* (*meal*) bufé *m*

buf·fet[2] ['bʌfɪt] *v/t of wind* sacudir

bug [bʌg] **1** *n insect* bicho *m*; *virus* virus *m inv*; (*spying device*) micrófono *m* oculto; COMPUT error *m* **2** *v/t* (*pret & pp bugged*) *room* colocar un micrófono en; F (*annoy*) fastidiar F, jorobar F

bug·gy ['bʌgɪ] *for baby* silla *f* de paseo

bu·gle ['bjuːgl] corneta *f*, clarín *m*

build [bɪld] **1** *n of person* constitución *f*, complexión *f* **2** *v/t* (*pret & pp built*) construir, edificar

◆ **build up 1** *v/t strength* aumentar; *relationship* fortalecer; *collection* acumular **2** *v/i of dirt* acumularse; *of pressure, excitement* aumentar

'**build·er** ['bɪldər] albañil *m/f*; *company* constructora *f*

'**build·ing** ['bɪldɪŋ] edificio *m*; *activity* construcción *f*

'**build·ing blocks** *npl for child* piezas *fpl* de construcción

'**build·ing site** obra *f*

'**build·ing so·ci·e·ty** *Br* caja *f* de ahorros

'**build·ing trade** industria *f* de la construcción

'**build-up** (*accumulation*) accumulación *f*; *after all the build-up publicity* después de tantas expectativas

built [bɪlt] *pret & pp* → **build**

built-in ['bɪltɪn] *adj cupboard* empotrado; *flash* incorporado

built-up '**ar·e·a** zona *f* urbanizada

bulb [bʌlb] BOT bulbo *m*; (*light bulb*) bombilla *f*, *L.Am.* foco *m*

bulge [bʌldʒ] **1** *n* bulto *m*, abultamiento *m* **2** *v/i of eyes* salirse de las órbitas; *of wall* abombarse

bu·lim·i·a [buˈlɪmɪə] bulimia *f*

bulk [bʌlk]: *the bulk of* el grueso *or* la mayor parte de; *in bulk* a granel

'**bulk·y** ['bʌlkɪ] *adj* voluminoso

bull [bʊl] *animal* toro *m*

bull·doze ['bʊldəʊz] *v/t* (*demolish*) demoler, derribar; *bulldoze s.o. into sth fig* obligar a alguien a hacer algo

bull·doz·er ['bʊldəʊzər] bulldozer *m*

bul·let ['bʊlɪt] bala f

bul·le·tin ['bʊlɪtɪn] boletín m

'**bul·le·tin board** *on wall* tablón m de anuncios; COMPUT tablón m de anuncios, BBS f

'**bul·let-proof** adj antibalas inv

'**bull fight** corrida f de toros

'**bull fight·er** torero(-a) m(f)

'**bull fight·ing** tauromaquia f, los toros

'**bull mar·ket** FIN mercado m al alza

'**bull ring** plaza f de toros

'**bull's-eye** diana f, blanco m; *hit the bull's-eye* dar en el blanco

'**bull·shit 1** n V *Span* gilipollez f V, *L.Am.* pendejada f V **2** v/i (pret & pp *bullshitted*) V decir *Span* gilipolleces V or *L.Am.* pendejadas V

bul·ly ['bʊlɪ] **1** n matón(-ona) m(f); *child* abusón(-ona) m(f) **2** v/t (pret & pp *bullied*) intimidar

bul·ly·ing ['bʊlɪɪŋ] n intimidación f

bum [bʌm] **1** n F (*tramp*) vagabundo(-a) m(f); (*worthless person*) inútil m/f **2** adj F (*useless*) inútil **3** v/t (pret & pp *bummed*) F *cigarette etc* gorronear

◆ **bum around, bum about** v/i F (*travel*) vagabundear (*in* por); (*be lazy*) vaguear

bum·ble·bee ['bʌmblbiː] abejorro m

bump [bʌmp] **1** n (*swelling*) chichón m; *on road* bache m; *get a bump on the head* darse un golpe en la cabeza **2** v/t golpear

◆ **bump into** v/t *table* chocar con; (*meet*) encontrarse con

◆ **bump off** v/t F (*murder*) cargarse a F

◆ **bump up** v/t F (*prices*) aumentar

bump·er ['bʌmpər] **1** n MOT parachoques m inv; *the traffic was bumper to bumper* el tráfico estaba colapsado **2** adj F (*extremely good*) excepcional, extraordinario

'**bump-start** v/t *car* arrancar un coche empujándolo; *fig: economy* reanimar

bump·y ['bʌmpɪ] adj con baches; *flight* movido

bun [bʌn] *hairstyle* moño m; *for eating* bollo m

bunch [bʌntʃ] *of people* grupo m; *of keys* manojo m; *of flowers* ramo m; *of grapes* racimo m; *thanks a bunch* ironic no

sabes lo que te lo agradezco

bun·dle ['bʌndl] *of clothes* fardo m; *of wood* haz m

◆ **bundle up** v/t liar; (*dress warmly*) abrigar

bung [bʌŋ] v/t Br F echar

bun·gee jump·ing ['bʌndʒɪdʒʌmpɪŋ] puenting m

bun·gle ['bʌŋgl] v/t echar a perder

bunk [bʌŋk] litera f

bunk beds npl literas fpl

buoy [bɔɪ] n NAUT boya f

buoy·ant ['bɔɪənt] adj animado, optimista; *economy* boyante

bur·den ['bɜːrdn] **1** n *also fig* carga f **2** v/t: *burden s.o. with sth fig* cargar a alguien con algo

bu·reau ['bjʊroʊ] (*chest of drawers*) cómoda f; (*office*) departamento m, oficina f; *a translation bureau* una agencia de traducción

bu·reauc·ra·cy [bjʊ'rɑːkrəsɪ] burocracia f

bu·reau·crat ['bjʊrəkræt] burócrata m/f

bu·reau·crat·ic [bjʊrə'krætɪk] adj burocrático

burg·er ['bɜːrgər] hamburguesa f

'**bur·glar** ['bɜːrglər] ladrón(-ona) m(f)

'**bur·glar a·larm** alarma f antirrobo

bur·glar·ize ['bɜːrgləraɪz] v/t robar

bur·glar·y ['bɜːrglərɪ] robo m

bur·gle ['bɜːrgl] v/t Br robar

bur·i·al ['berɪəl] entierro m

bur·ly ['bɜːrlɪ] adj corpulento, fornido

burn [bɜːrn] **1** n quemadura f **2** v/t (pret & pp *burnt*) quemar; *be burned to death* morir abrasado **3** v/i (pret & pp *burnt*) of *wood, meat, in sun* quemarse

◆ **burn down 1** v/t incendiar **2** v/i incendiarse

◆ **burn out** v/t: *burn o.s. out* quemarse; *a burned-out car* un coche carbonizado

'**burn-out** F (*exhaustion*) agotamiento m

burnt [bɜːrnt] pret & pp → *burn*

burp [bɜːrp] **1** n eructo m **2** v/i eructar **3** v/t *baby* hacer eructar a

burst [bɜːrst] **1** n *in water pipe* rotura f; *of gunfire* ráfaga f; *in a burst of energy* en un arrebato de energía **2** adj *tire* reventado **3** v/t (pret & pp **burst**) balloon reventar **4** v/i (pret & pp **burst**) of balloon, tire reventar; **burst into a room** irrumpir en una habitación; **burst into tears** echarse a llorar; **burst out laughing** echarse a reír

bur·y ['beri] v/t (pret & pp **buried**) enterrar; **be buried under** (covered by) estar sepultado por; **bury o.s. in work** meterse de lleno en el trabajo

bus [bʌs] **1** n local autobús m, Mex camión m, Arg colectivo m, C.Am. guagua f; long distance autobús m, Span autocar m; **school bus** autobús m escolar **2** v/t (pret & pp **bussed**) llevar en autobús

'bus·boy ayudante m de camarero

'bus driv·er conductor(a) m(f) de autobús

bush [buʃ] plant arbusto m; type of countryside monte m

bushed [buʃt] adj F (tired) molido F

bush·y ['buʃɪ] adj beard espeso

busi·ness ['bɪznɪs] negocios mpl; (company) empresa f; (sector) sector m; (affair, matter) asunto m; as subject of study empresariales fpl; **on business** de negocios; **that's none of your business!** ¡no es asunto tuyo!; **mind your own business!** ¡no te metas en lo que no te importa!

busi·ness card tarjeta f de visita

'busi·ness class clase f ejecutiva

'busi·ness hours npl horario m de oficina

busi·ness·like ['bɪznɪslaɪk] adj eficiente

'busi·ness lunch almuerzo m de negocios

'busi·ness·man hombre m de negocios, ejecutivo m

'busi·ness meet·ing reunión f de negocios

'busi·ness school escuela f de negocios

'busi·ness stud·ies nsg course empresariales mpl

'busi·ness trip viaje m de negocios

'busi·ness·wom·an mujer f de negocios, ejecutiva f

'bus lane carril m bus

'bus shel·ter marquesina f

'bus sta·tion estación f de autobuses

'bus stop parada f de autobús

'bus tick·et billete m or L.Am. boleto m de autobús

bust¹ [bʌst] n of woman busto m

bust² [bʌst] **1** adj F (broken) escacharrado F: **go bust** quebrar **2** v/t F escacharrar F

◆ bus·tle about ['bʌsl] v/i trajinar

'bust-up F corte m F

bust·y ['bʌstɪ] adj pechugona

bus·y ['bɪzɪ] **1** adj also TELEC ocupado; full of people abarrotado; of restaurant etc: making money ajetreado; **the line was busy** estaba ocupado, Span comunicaba; **she leads a very busy life** lleva una vida muy ajetreada; **be busy doing sth** estar ocupado or atareado haciendo algo **2** v/t (pret & pp **busied**): **busy o.s. with** entretenerse con algo

'bus·y·bod·y metomentodo m/f, entrometido(-a) m(f)

'bus·y sig·nal señal f de ocupado or Span comunicando

but [bʌt] unstressed [bət] **1** conj pero; **it's not me but my father you want** no me quieres a mí sino a mi padre; **but then** (again) pero **2** prep: **all but him** todos excepto él; **the last but one** el penúltimo; **the next but one** el próximo no, el otro; **the next page but one** la página siguiente a la próxima; **but for you** si no hubiera sido por ti; **nothing but the best** sólo lo mejor

butch·er ['buʧər] carnicero(-a) m(f); murderer asesino(-a) m(f)

butt [bʌt] **1** n of cigarette colilla f; of joke blanco m; F (buttocks) trasero m F **2** v/t dar un cabezazo a; of goat, bull embestir

◆ butt in v/i inmiscuirse, entrometerse

but·ter ['bʌtər] **1** n mantequilla f **2** v/t untar de mantequilla

◆ butter up v/t F hacer la pelota a F

'but·ter·fly insect mariposa f

but·tocks ['bʌtəks] npl nalgas fpl

but·ton ['bʌtn] **1** n on shirt, machine botón m; (badge) chapa f **2** v/t abotonar

◆ button up v/t abotonar

'but·ton·hole **1** n in suit ojal m **2** v/t acorralar

but·tress ['bʌtrəs] contrafuerte m

bux·om ['bʌksəm] adj de amplios senos

buy [baɪ] **1** n compra f, adquisición f **2** v/t (pret & pp **bought**) comprar; **can I buy you a drink?** ¿quieres tomar algo?; **$5 doesn't buy much** con 5 dólares no se puede hacer gran cosa

◆ **buy off** v/t (bribe) sobornar

◆ **buy out** v/t COM comprar la parte de

◆ **buy up** v/t acaparar

buy·er [baɪr] comprador(a) m(f)

buzz [bʌz] **1** n zumbido m; **she gets a real buzz out of it** F (thrill) le vuelve loca, le entusiasma **2** v/i of insect zumbar; **with buzzer** llamar por el interfono **3** v/t **with buzzer** llamar por el interfono a

◆ **buzz off** v/i F largarse F, Span pirarse F

buz·zard ['bʌzərd] ratonero m

buzz·er ['bʌzər] timbre m

'buzz·word palabra f de moda

by [baɪ] **1** prep to show agent por; (near, next to) al lado de, junto a; (no later than) no más tarde de; mode of transport en; **she rushed by me** pasó rápidamente por mi lado; **as we drove by the church** cuando pasábamos por la iglesia; **side by side** uno junto al otro; **by day / night** de día / noche; **by bus / train** en autobús / tren; **by the dozen** por docenas; **by the hour / ton** por hora / por tonelada; **by my watch** en mi reloj; **by nature** por naturaleza; **a play by ...** una obra de ...; **by o.s.** without company solo; **I did it by myself** lo hice yo solito; **by a couple of minutes** por un par de minutos; **2 by 4** measurement 2 por 4; **by this time tomorrow** mañana a esta hora; **by this time next year** el año que viene por estas fechas; **go by, pass by** pasar **2** adv; **by and by** (soon) dentro de poco

bye (**-bye**) [baɪ] adiós

by·gones ['baɪgɑːnz]: **let bygones be bygones** lo pasado, pasado está

'by·pass 1 n road circunvalación f; MED bypass m **2** v/t sortear

'by-prod·uct subproducto m

by·stand·er ['baɪstændər] transeúnte m/f

byte [baɪt] byte m

'by·word: **be a byword for** ser sinónimo de

C

cab [kæb] (taxi) taxi m; of truck cabina f; **cab driver** taxista m/f

cab·a·ret ['kæbəreɪ] cabaret m

cab·bage ['kæbɪdʒ] col f, repollo m

cab·in ['kæbɪn] of plane cabina f; of ship camarote m

'cab·in at·tend·ant auxiliar m/f de vuelo

'cab·in crew personal m de a bordo

cab·i·net ['kæbɪnɪt] armario m; POL gabinete m; **drinks cabinet** mueble m bar; **medicine cabinet** botiquín m; **display cabinet** vitrina f

'cab·i·net mak·er ebanista m/f

ca·ble ['keɪbl] cable m; **cable (TV)** televisión f por cable

'ca·ble car teleférico m

'ca·ble tel·e·vi·sion televisión f por cable

'cab rank, 'cab stand parada f de taxis

cac·tus ['kæktəs] cactus m inv

ca·dav·er [kə'dævər] cadáver m

CAD [kæd] abbr (= **computer assisted design**) CAD m (= diseño asistido por Span ordenador or L.Am. computadora)

cad·die ['kædɪ] **1** n in golf caddie m/f **2** v/i hacer de caddie

ca·det [kə'det] cadete m

cadge [kædʒ] v/t F: **cadge sth from s.o.** gorronear algo a alguien

Cae·sar·e·an Br → **Cesarean**

caf·é ['kæfeɪ] café m, cafetería f

caf·e·te·ri·a [kæfɪ'tɪrɪə] cafetería f, cantina f

caf·feine ['kæfiːn] cafeína f

cage [keɪdʒ] jaula f

ca·gey ['keɪdʒɪ] adj cauteloso, reservado;
he's cagey about how old he is es muy
reservado con respecto a su edad

ca·hoots [kə'huːts] npl F: **be in cahoots
with** estar conchabado con

ca·jole [kə'dʒoul] v/t engatusar, persuadir

cake [keɪk] **1** n big tarta f; small pastel m;
be a piece of cake F estar chupado F **2** v/i
endurecerse

ca·lam·i·ty [kə'læmətɪ] calamidad f

cal·ci·um ['kælsɪəm] calcio m

cal·cu·late ['kælkjuleɪt] v/t calcular

cal·cu·lat·ing ['kælkjuleɪtɪŋ] adj calculador

cal·cu·la·tion [kælkju'leɪʃn] cálculo m

cal·cu·la·tor ['kælkjuleɪtər] calculadora f

cal·en·dar ['kælɪndər] calendario m

calf[1] [kæf] (pl **calves** [kævz]) (young
cow) ternero(-a) m(f), becerro(-a) m(f)

calf[2] [kæf] (pl **calves** [kævz]) of leg pantorrilla f

'calf·skin n piel f de becerro

cal·i·ber, Br cal·i·bre ['kælɪbər] of gun
calibre m; **a man of his calibre** un hombre de su calibre

Cal·i·for·ni·an [kælɪ'fɔːnɪən] **1** adj califor-
niano **2** n californiano(-a) m(f)

call [kɔːl] **1** n llamada f; (demand) llamamiento m; **there's a call for** tienes
una llamada, te llaman; **I'll give you a
call tomorrow** te llamaré mañana; **make a call** hacer una llamada; **a call for
help** una llamada de socorro; **be on call**
estar de guardia **2** v/t also TELEC llamar;
meeting convocar; **he called him a liar**
le llamó mentiroso; **what have they called the baby?** ¿qué nombre le han
puesto al bebé?; **but we call him Tom**
pero le llamamos Tom; **call s.o. names**
insultar a alguien; **I called his name** lo
llamé **3** v/t also TELEC llamar; (visit) pasarse; **can I tell him who's calling?**
¿quién le llama?; **call for help** pedir

◆ call at v/t (stop at) pasarse por; of train
hacer parada en

◆ call back **1** v/t (phone again) volver a
llamar; (return call) devolver la llamada;
(summon) hacer volver **2** v/i on phone
volver a llamar; (make another visit) volver a pasar

◆ call for v/t (collect) pasar a recoger; (demand) pedir, exigir; (require) requerir

◆ call in **1** v/t (summon) llamar **2** v/i (phone) llamar; **he called in sick** llamó para
decir que estaba enfermo

◆ call off v/t (cancel) cancelar; strike desconvocar

◆ call on v/t (urge) instar; (visit) visitar

◆ call out v/t (shout) gritar; (summon) llamar

◆ call up v/t (on phone) llamar; COMPUT
abrir, visualizar

'call cen·ter centro m de atención telefónica

call·er ['kɔːlər] on phone persona f que
llama; (visitor) visitante m/f

'call girl prostituta f (que concierta sus citas por teléfono)

cal·lous ['kæləs] adj cruel, desalmado

cal·lous·ly ['kæləslɪ] adv cruelmente

cal·lous·ness ['kæləsnɪs] crueldad f

calm [kɑːm] **1** adj sea tranquilo; weather
apacible; person tranquilo, sosegado;
please keep calm por favor mantengan
la calma **2** n calma f; **call for calm** pedir
calma

◆ calm down **1** v/t calmar, tranquilizar **2**
v/i of sea, weather calmarse; of person
calmarse, tranquilizarse

calm·ly ['kɑːmlɪ] adv con calma, tranquilamente

cal·o·rie ['kælərɪ] caloría f

cam·cor·der ['kæmkɔːrdər] videocámara f

came [keɪm] pret → **come**

cam·e·ra ['kæmərə] cámara f

'cam·e·ra·man cámara m, camarógrafo m

cam·i·sole ['kæmɪseʊl] camisola f

cam·ou·flage ['kæməfluːʒ] **1** n camuflaje
m **2** v/t camuflar

camp [kæmp] **1** n campamento m; **make**

camp acampar; *refugee camp* campo *m* de refugiados **2** *v/i* acampar

cam·paign [kæm'peɪn] **1** *n* campaña *f* **2** *v/i* hacer campaña (*for* a favor de)

cam·paign·er [kæm'peɪnər] defensor(a) *m(f)* (*for* de); *a campaigner against racism* una persona que hace campaña contra el racismo

camp·er ['kæmpər] *person* campista *m/f*; *vehicle* autocaravana *f*

camp·ing ['kæmpɪŋ] acampada *f*; *on campsite* camping *m*; *go camping* ir de acampada *or* camping

'camp·site camping *m*

cam·pus ['kæmpəs] campus *m*

can[1] [kæn] *unstressed* [kən] *v/aux* (*pret could*) ◇ (*ability*) poder; *can you swim?* ¿sabes nadar?; *can you hear me?* ¿me oyes?; *I can't see* no veo; *can you speak French?* ¿hablas francés?; *can he call me back?* ¿me podría devolver la llamada?; *as fast / well as you can* tan rápido / bien como puedas; *I can't go any further - you can and you will!* no puedo más - ¡ya lo creo que puedes!

◇ (*permission*) poder; *can I help you?* ¿te puedo ayudar?; *can you help me?* ¿me puedes ayudar?; *can I have a beer / coffee?* ¿me pones una cerveza / un café?; *that can't be right* debe haber un error

can[2] [kæn] **1** *n for drinks etc* lata *f* **2** *v/t* (*pret & pp canned*) enlatar

Can·a·da ['kænədə] Canadá

Ca·na·di·an [kə'neɪdɪən] **1** *adj* canadiense **2** *n* canadiense *m/f*

ca·nal [kə'næl] *waterway* canal *m*

ca·nar·y [kə'nerɪ] canario *m*

can·cel ['kænsl] *v/t* cancelar

can·cel·la·tion [kænsə'leɪʃn] cancelación *f*

can·cel·la·tion fee tarifa *f* de cancelación de reserva

can·cer ['kænsər] cáncer *m*

Can·cer ['kænsər] ASTR Cáncer *m/f inv*

can·cer·ous ['kænsərəs] *adj* canceroso

c & f *abbr* (= *cost and freight*) C&F (= costo y flete)

can·did ['kændɪd] *adj* sincero, franco

can·di·da·cy ['kændɪdəsɪ] candidatura *f*

can·di·date ['kændɪdət] *for position* candidato(-a) *m(f)*; *in exam* candidato(-a) *m(f)*, examinando(-a) *m(f)*

can·did·ly ['kændɪdlɪ] *adv* sinceramente, francamente

can·died ['kændiːd] *adj* confitado

can·dle ['kændl] vela *f*

'can·dle·stick candelero *m*; *short* palmatoria *f*

can·dor, *Br* **can·dour** ['kændər] sinceridad *f*, franqueza *f*

can·dy ['kændɪ] (*sweet*) caramelo *m*; (*sweets*) dulces *mpl*; *a box of candy* una caja de caramelos *or* dulces

cane [keɪn] caña *f*; *for walking* bastón *m*

can·is·ter ['kænɪstər] bote *m*

can·na·bis ['kænəbɪs] cannabis *m*, hachís *m*

canned [kænd] *adj fruit, tomatoes* enlatado, en lata; (*recorded*) grabado

can·ni·bal·ize ['kænɪbəlaɪz] *v/t* canibalizar

can·not ['kænɑːt] → *can*[1]

can·ny ['kænɪ] *adj* (*astute*) astuto

ca·noe [kə'nuː] canoa *f*, piragua *f*

'can o·pen·er abrelatas *m inv*

can't [kænt] → *can*[1]

can·tan·ker·ous [kæn'tæŋkərəs] *adj* arisco, cascarrabias

can·teen [kæn'tiːn] *in plant* cantina *f*, cafetería *f*

can·vas ['kænvəs] *for painting* lienzo *m*; *material* lona *f*

can·vass ['kænvəs] **1** *v/t* (*seek opinion of*) preguntar **2** *v/i* POL hacer campaña (*for* en favor de)

can·yon ['kænjən] cañón *m*

cap [kæp] *n hat* gorro *m*; *with peak* gorra *f*; *of bottle, jar* tapón *m*; *of pen, of lens* tapa *f*

ca·pa·bil·i·ty [keɪpə'bɪlətɪ] capacidad *f*; *it's beyond my capabilities* no entra dentro de mis posibilidades

ca·pa·ble ['keɪpəbl] *adj* (*efficient*) capaz, competente; *be capable of* ser capaz de

ca·pac·i·ty [kə'pæsətɪ] capacidad *f*; *of car engine* cilindrada *f*; *a capacity crowd* un

C

lleno absoluto; *the job is well within your capacity* el trabajo está dentro de tus posibilidades; *in my capacity as ...* en mi calidad de ...

cap·i·tal ['kæpɪtl] *n* of country capital *f*; (*capital letter*) mayúscula *f*; *money* capital *m*

cap·i·tal ex'pend·i·ture inversión *f* en activo fijo

cap·i·tal 'gains tax impuesto *m* sobre las plusvalías

cap·i·tal 'growth crecimiento *m* del capital

cap·i·tal·ism ['kæpɪtəlɪzm] capitalismo *m*

'cap·i·tal·ist ['kæpɪtəlɪst] **1** *adj* capitalista **2** *n* capitalista *m/f*

♦ **cap·i·tal·ize on** ['kæpɪtəlaɪz] *v/t* aprovecharse de

cap·i·tal 'let·ter letra *f* mayúscula

cap·i·tal 'pun·ish·ment pena *f* capital, pena *f* de muerte

ca·pit·u·late [kə'pɪtʊleɪt] *v/i* capitular

ca·pit·u·la·tion [kəpɪtʊ'leɪʃn] capitulación *f*

Cap·ri·corn ['kæprɪkɔːrn] ASTR Capricornio *m/f* inv

cap·size [kæp'saɪz] **1** *v/i* volcar **2** *v/t* hacer volcar

cap·sule ['kæpsʊl] of medicine cápsula *f*; (*space capsule*) cápsula *f* espacial

cap·tain ['kæptɪn] *n* of ship, team, MIL capitán(-ana) *m(f)*; of aircraft comandante *m/f*

cap·tion ['kæpʃn] *n* pie *m* de foto

cap·ti·vate ['kæptɪveɪt] *v/t* cautivar, fascinar

cap·tive ['kæptɪv] **1** *adj* prisionero **2** *n* prisionero(-a) *m(f)*

cap·tive 'mar·ket mercado *m* cautivo

cap·tiv·i·ty [kæp'tɪvətɪ] cautividad *f*

cap·ture ['kæptʃər] **1** *n* of city toma *f*; of criminal, animal captura *f* **2** *v/t* person, animal capturar; city, building tomar; market share ganar; (*portray*) captar

car [kɑːr] coche *m*, L.Am. carro *m*, Rpl auto *m*; of train vagón *m*; *by car* en coche

ca·rafe [kə'ræf] garrafa *f*, jarra *f*

car·at ['kærət] quilate *m*

car·bo·hy·drate [kɑːrbou'haɪdreɪt] car-

bohidrato *m*

'car bomb coche *m* bomba

car·bon mon·ox·ide [kɑːrbənmən'ɑːk-saɪd] monóxido *m* de carbono

car·bu·ret·er, car·bu·ret·or [kɑːrbu're-tər] carburador *m*

car·cass ['kɑːrkəs] cadáver *m*

car·cin·o·gen [kɑːr'sɪnədʒen] agente *m* cancerígeno *or* carcinógeno

car·cin·o·genic [kɑːrsɪnə'dʒenɪk] *adj* cancerígeno, carcinógeno

card [kɑːrd] to mark occasion, COMPUT, business tarjeta *f*; (*postcard*) (tarjeta *f*) postal *f*; (*playing card*) carta *f*, naipe *m*; *game of cards* partida *f* de cartas

'card·board cartón *m*

card·board 'box caja *f* de cartón

car·di·ac ['kɑːrdɪæk] *adj* cardíaco

car·di·ac ar'rest paro *m* cardíaco

car·di·gan ['kɑːrdɪgən] cárdigan *m*

car·di·nal ['kɑːrdɪnl] *n* REL cardenal *m*

'card in·dex fichero *m*

'card key llave *f* tarjeta

'card phone tarjeta *f* telefónica

care [ker] **1** *n* cuidado *m*; (*medical care*) asistencia *f* médica; (*worry*) preocupación *f*; *care of →* c/o; *take care* (*be cautious*) tener cuidado; *take care* (*of yourself*)! (goodbye) ¡cuídate!; *take care of* dog, tool, house, garden cuidar; baby cuidar (de); (*deal with*) ocuparse de; *I'll take care of the bill* yo pago la cuenta; (*handle*) *with care!* on label frágil **2** *v/i* preocuparse; *I don't care!* ¡me da igual!; *I couldn't care less* ¡me importa un pimiento!; *if you really cared ...* si de verdad te importara ...

♦ **care about** *v/t* preocuparse por

♦ **care for** *v/t* (*look after: person*) cuidar (de); (*look after: plant*) cuidar; *he doesn't care for me the way he used to* ya no le gusto como antes; *would you care for a drink?* ¿le apetece tomar algo?

ca·reer [kə'rɪr] carrera *f*; *career prospects* perspectivas *fpl* profesionales

ca'reers of·fi·cer asesor(a) *m(f)* de orientación profesional

'care·free *adj* despreocupado

care·ful ['kerfəl] *adj (cautious, thorough)* cuidadoso; *be careful* tener cuidado; *(be) careful!* ¡(ten) cuidado!

care·ful·ly ['kerfəlɪ] *adv (with caution)* con cuidado; *worded etc* cuidadosamente

care·less ['kerlɪs] *adj* descuidado; *you are so careless!* ¡qué descuidado eres!

care·less·ly ['kerlɪslɪ] *adv* descuidadamente

car·er ['kerər] *persona que cuida de un familiar o enfermo*

ca·ress [kə'res] **1** *n* caricia *f* **2** *v/t* acariciar

care·tak·er ['kerteɪkər] conserje *m*

'care-worn *adj* agobiado

'car fer·ry ferry *m*, transbordador *m*

car·go ['kɑːrgou] cargamento *m*

'car hire alquiler *m* de coches *or* automóviles

'car hire com·pa·ny empresa *f* de alquiler de coches *or* automóviles

car·i·ca·ture ['kærɪkətʃər] *n* caricatura *f*

car·ing ['kerɪŋ] *adj person* afectuoso, bondadoso; *society* solidario

'car me·chan·ic mecánico(-a) *m(f)* de coches *or* automóviles

car·nage ['kɑːrnɪdʒ] matanza *f*, carnicería *f*

car·na·tion [kɑːr'neɪʃn] clavel *m*

car·ni·val ['kɑːrnɪvl] feria *f*

car·ol ['kærəl] *n* villancico *m*

car·ou·sel [kærə'sel] *at airport* cinta *f* transportadora de equipajes; *for slide projector* carro *m*; *(merry-go-round)* tiovivo *m*

'car park *Br* estacionamiento *m*, *Span* aparcamiento *m*

car·pen·ter ['kɑːrpɪntər] carpintero(-a) *m(f)*

car·pet ['kɑːrpɪt] alfombra *f*

'car phone teléfono *m* de coche

'car·pool *n acuerdo para compartir el vehículo entre varias personas que trabajan en el mismo sitio*

'car port estacionamiento *m* con techo

'car ra·di·o autorradio *m*

car·ri·er ['kærɪər] *company* transportista *m*; *airline* línea *f* aérea; *of disease* portador(a) *m(f)*

car·rot ['kærət] zanahoria *f*

car·ry ['kærɪ] **1** *v/t (pret & pp carried) of person* llevar; *disease* ser portador de; *of ship, plane, bus etc* transportar; *proposal* aprobar; *be carrying a child (of pregnant woman* estar embarazada; *get carried away* dejarse llevar por la emoción, emocionarse **2** *v/i (pret & pp carried) of sound* oírse

◆ **carry on 1** *v/i (continue)* seguir, continuar; *(make a fuss)* organizar un escándalo; *(have an affair)* tener un lío **2** *v/t (conduct)* mantener; *business* efectuar

◆ **carry out** *survey etc* llevar a cabo

'car seat *for child* asiento *m* para niño

cart [kɑːrt] carro *m*

car·tel [kɑːr'tel] cartel *m*

car·ton ['kɑːrtn] *for storage, transport* caja *f* de cartón; *for milk etc* cartón *m*, tetrabrik *m* ®; *for eggs, of cigarettes* cartón *m*

car·toon [kɑːr'tuːn] *in newspaper, magazine* tira *f* cómica; *on* TV, *movie* dibujos *mpl* animados

car·toon·ist [kɑːr'tuːnɪst] dibujante *m/f* de chistes

car·tridge ['kɑːrtrɪdʒ] *for gun* cartucho *m*

carve [kɑːrv] *v/t meat* trinchar; *wood* tallar

carv·ing ['kɑːrvɪŋ] *figure* talla *f*

'car wash lavado *m* de coches

case¹ [keɪs] *container* funda *f*; *of scotch, wine* caja *f*; *(suitcase)* maleta *f*

case² [keɪs] *n instance, criminal,* MED caso *m*; LAW causa *f*; *I think there's a case for dismissing him* creo que hay razones fundadas para despedirlo; *the case for the prosecution* (los argumentos jurídicos de) la acusación; *make a case for sth* defender algo; *in case ...* por si ...; *in case of emergency* en caso de emergencia; *in any case* en cualquier caso; *in that case* en ese caso

'case his·to·ry MED historial *m* médico

'case·load número *m* de casos

cash [kæʃ] **1** *n (dinero m en)* efectivo *m*; *I'm a bit short of cash* no tengo mucho dinero; *cash down* al contado; *pay (in) cash* pagar en efectivo; *cash on delivery → COD* **2** *v/t check* hacer efectivo

◆ **cash in on** *v/t* sacar provecho de

'cash cow fuente f de ingresos
'cash desk caja f
cash 'dis·count descuento m por pago al contado
'cash di·spens·er Br cajero m automático
'cash flow flujo m de caja, cash-flow m; **cash flow problems** problemas fpl de liquidez
cash·ier [kæˈʃɪr] n in store etc cajero(-a) m(f)
'cash·mere [ˈkæʃmɪr] adj cachemir m
'cash-point cajero m automático
'cash re·gis·ter caja f registradora
ca·si·no [kəˈsiːnou] casino m
cas·ket [ˈkæskɪt] (coffin) ataúd m
cas·se·role [ˈkæsəroul] n meal guiso m; container cacerola f, cazuela f
cas·sette [kəˈset] cinta f, casete f
cas'sette play·er, cas'sette re·cord·er casete m
cast [kæst] **1** n of play reparto m; (mold) molde m **2** v/t (pret & pp **cast**) doubt, suspicion proyectar; metal fundir; play seleccionar el reparto de; **they cast Alan as …** le dieron a Alan el papel de …
◆ cast off v/i of ship soltar amarras
caste [kæst] casta f
cast·er [ˈkæstər] on chair etc ruedecita f
Cas·til·ian [kæsˈtɪljən] **1** adj castellano **2** n person castellano(-a) m(f); language castellano m
cast 'i·ron n hierro m fundido
cast-'i·ron adj de hierro fundido
cas·tle [ˈkæsl] castillo m
'cast·or [ˈkæstər] → caster
cas·trate [kæˈstreɪt] v/t castrar
cas·tra·tion [kæˈstreɪʃn] castración f
cas·u·al [ˈkæʒuəl] adj (chance) casual; (offhand) despreocupado; (not formal) informal; (not permanent) eventual; **it was just a casual remark** no era más que un comentario hecho de pasada; **he was very casual about the whole thing** parecía no darle mucha importancia al asunto; **casual sex** relaciones fpl sexuales (con parejas) ocasionales
cas·u·al·ly [ˈkæʒuəlɪ] adv dressed de manera informal; say a la ligera

cas·u·al·ty [ˈkæʒuəltɪ] víctima f
'cas·u·al wear ropa f informal
cat [kæt] gato m
Cat·a·lan [ˈkætələn] **1** adj catalán **2** n person catalán(-ana) m(f); language catalán m
cat·a·log, Br cat·a·logue [ˈkætəlɔːg] n catálogo m
cat·a·lyst [ˈkætəlɪst] catalizador m
cat·a·lyt·ic con'vert·er [kætəˈlɪtɪk] catalizador m
cat·a·pult [ˈkætəpʌlt] **1** v/t fig to fame, stardom catapultar, lanzar **2** n catapulta f; toy tirachinas m inv
cat·a·ract [ˈkætərækt] MED catarata f
ca·tas·tro·phe [kəˈtæstrəfɪ] catástrofe f
cat·a·stroph·ic [kætəˈstrɑːfɪk] adj catastrófico
catch [kætʃ] **1** n parada f (sin que la pelota toque el suelo); of fish captura f, pesca f; (locking device) cierre m; (problem) pega f; **there has to be a catch** tiene que haber una trampa **2** v/t (pret & pp **caught**) ball agarrar, Span coger; animal atrapar; escaped prisoner capturar; (get on: bus, train) tomar, Span coger; (not miss: bus, train) alcanzar, Span coger; fish pescar; in order to speak to alcanzar, pillar; (hear) oír; illness agarrar, Span coger; **catch (a) cold** agarrar or Span coger un resfriado, resfriarse; **catch s.o.'s eye** of person, object llamar la atención de alguien; **catch sight of, catch a glimpse of** ver; **catch s.o. doing sth** atrapar or Span coger a alguien haciendo algo
◆ catch on v/i (become popular) cuajar, ponerse de moda; (understand) darse cuenta
◆ catch up v/i: **catch up with s.o.** alcanzar a alguien; **he's having to work hard to catch up** tiene que trabajar muy duro para ponerse al día
◆ catch up on v/t: **catch up on one's sleep** recuperar sueño; **there's a lot of work to catch up on** hay mucho trabajo atrasado
catch-22 [kætʃtwentɪˈtuː]: **it's a catch-22 situation** es como la pescadilla que se

muerde la cola

catch·er ['kætʃər] *in baseball* cácher *m*, cácher *m*

catch·ing ['kætʃɪŋ] *adj also fig* contagioso

catch·y ['kætʃɪ] *adj tune* pegadizo

cat·e·gor·ic [kætə'gɑːrɪk] *adj* categórico

cat·e·gor·i·cal·ly [kætə'gɑːrɪklɪ] *adv* categóricamente

cat·e·go·ry ['kætəgɔːrɪ] categoría *f*

◆ **ca·ter for** ['keɪtər] *v/t (meet the needs of)* cubrir las necesidades de; *(provide food for)* organizar la comida para

ca·ter·er ['keɪtərər] hostelero(-a) *m(f)*

ca·ter·pil·lar ['kætərpɪlər] oruga *f*

ca·the·dral [kə'θiːdrl] catedral *f*

Cath·o·lic ['kæθəlɪk] **1** *adj* católico **2** *n* católico(-a) *m(f)*

Ca·thol·i·cism [kə'θɑːlɪsɪzm] catolicismo *m*

'cat·nap 1 *n* cabezada *f* **2** *v/i (pret & pp* **catnapped)** echarse una cabezada *f*

'cat's eyes *on road* captafaros *mpl (en el centro de la calzada)*

cat·sup ['kætsʌp] ketchup *m*, catchup *m*

cat·tle ['kætl] *npl* ganado *m*

cat·ty ['kætɪ] *adj* malintencionado

'cat·walk pasarela *f*

caught [kɔːt] *pret & pp* → **catch**

cau·li·flow·er ['kɒːlɪflaʊər] coliflor *f*

cause [kɒːz] **1** *n* causa *f; (grounds)* motivo *m*, razón *f* **2** *v/t* causar, provocar

caus·tic ['kɔːstɪk] *adj fig* cáustico

cau·tion ['kɔːʃn] **1** *n (carefulness)* precaución *f*, prudencia *f;* **caution is advised** se recomienda prudencia **2** *v/t (warn)* prevenir **(against** contra)

cau·tious ['kɔːʃəs] *adj* cauto, prudente

cau·tious·ly ['kɔːʃəslɪ] *adv* cautelosamente, con prudencia

cav·al·ry ['kævəlrɪ] caballería *f*

cave [keɪv] cueva *f*

◆ **cave in** *v/i of roof* hundirse

cav·i·ar ['kævɪɑːr] caviar *m*

cav·i·ty ['kævətɪ] caries *f inv*

cc[1] [siː'siː] **1** *abbr (=* **carbon copy)** copia *f* **2** *v/t memo* enviar una copia de; *person* enviar una copia a

cc[2] [siː'siː] *abbr (=* **cubic centimeters)** cc (centímetros *mpl* cúbicos); MOT cilindra-

da *f*

CD [siː'diː] *abbr (=* **compact disc)** CD *m* (= disco *m* compacto)

CD play·er (reproductor *m* de) CD *m*

CD-ROM [siːdiː'rɑːm] CD-ROM *m*

CD-ROM drive lector *m* de CD-ROM

cease [siːs] **1** *v/i* cesar **2** *v/t* suspender; *cease doing sth* dejar de hacer algo

'cease-fire alto *m* el fuego

cei·ling ['siːlɪŋ] *of room* techo *m; (limit)* tope *m*, límite *m*

cel·e·brate ['selɪbreɪt] **1** *v/i: let's celebrate with a bottle of champagne* celebrémoslo con una botella de champán **2** *v/t* celebrar, festejar; *(observe)* celebrar

cel·e·brat·ed ['selɪbreɪtɪd] *adj* célebre; *be celebrated for* ser célebre por

cel·e·bra·tion [selɪ'breɪʃn] celebración *f*

ce·leb·ri·ty [sɪ'lebrətɪ] celebridad *f*

cel·e·ry ['selərɪ] apio *m*

cel·i·ba·cy ['selɪbəsɪ] celibato *m*

cel·i·bate ['selɪbət] *adj* célibe

cell [sel] *for prisoner, in spreadsheet* celda *f;* BIO célula *f*

cel·lar ['selər] *of house* sótano *m; for wine* bodega *f*

cel·list ['tʃelɪst] violonchelista *m/f*

cel·lo ['tʃelou] violonchelo *m*

cel·lo·phane ['seləfeɪn] celofán *m*

'cell phone, cel·lu·lar phone ['seljələr] (teléfono *m*) móvil *m, L.Am.* (teléfono *m*) celular *m*

cel·lu·lite ['seljuːlaɪt] celulitis *f*

ce·ment [sɪ'ment] **1** *n* cemento *m* **2** *v/t* colocar con cemento; *friendship* consolidar

cem·e·tery ['semətərɪ] cementerio *m*

cen·sor ['sensər] *v/t* censor(a) *m(f)*

cen·sus ['sensəs] censo *m*

cent [sent] céntimo *m*

cen·te·na·ry [sen'tiːnərɪ] centenario *m*

cen·ter ['sentər] **1** *n* centro *m; in the center of* en el centro de **2** *v/t* centrar

◆ **center on** *v/t* centrarse en

cen·ter of 'grav·i·ty centro *m* de gravedad

cen·ti·grade ['sentɪgreɪd] *adj* centígrado; *10 degrees centigrade* 10 grados centígrados

cen·ti·me·ter, *Br* **cen·ti·me·tre** ['sentɪmiːtər] centímetro *m*

C

cen·tral ['sentrəl] *adj* central; *location, apartment* céntrico; ***central Chicago*** el centro de Chicago; ***be central to sth*** ser el eje de algo

Cen·tral A'mer·i·ca *n* Centroamérica, América Central

Cen·tral A'mer·i·can **1** *adj* centroamericano, de (la) América *f* Central **2** *n* centroamericano(-a) *m(f)*

cen·tral 'heat·ing calefacción *f* central

cen·tral·ize ['sentrəlaɪz] *v/t* centralizar

cen·tral 'lock·ing MOT cierre *m* centralizado

cen·tral 'pro·ces·sing u·nit unidad *f* central de proceso

cen·tre *Br* → center

cen·tu·ry ['sentʃərɪ] siglo *m*

CEO [siːiː'əʊ] *abbr* (= ***Chief Executive Officer***) consejero(-a) *m(f)* delegado

ce·ram·ic [sɪ'ræmɪk] *adj* de cerámica

ce·ram·ics [sɪ'ræmɪks] (*pl: objects*) objetos *mpl* de cerámica; (*sing: art*) cerámica *f*

ce·re·al ['sɪrɪəl] (*grain*) cereal *m*; (*breakfast cereal*) cereales *mpl*

cer·e·mo·ni·al [serɪ'məʊnɪəl] **1** *adj* ceremonial **2** *n* ceremonial *m*

cer·e·mo·ny ['serɪmənɪ] (*event, ritual*) ceremonia *f*

cer·tain ['sɜːrtn] *adj* (*sure*) seguro; (*particular*) cierto; ***I'm certain*** estoy seguro; ***it's certain that ...*** es seguro que ...; ***a certain Mr S.*** un cierto Sr. S.; ***make certain*** asegurarse; ***know / say for certain*** saber / decir con certeza

cer·tain·ly ['sɜːrtnlɪ] *adv* (*definitely*) claramente; (*of course*) por supuesto; ***certainly not!*** ¡por supuesto que no!

cer·tain·ty ['sɜːrtntɪ] (*confidence*) certeza *f*, certidumbre *f*; (*inevitability*) seguridad *f*; ***it's a certainty*** es seguro; ***he's a certainty for the gold medal*** va a ganar seguro la medalla de oro

cer·tif·i·cate [sər'tɪfɪkət] (*qualification*) título *m*; (*official paper*) certificado *m*

cer·ti·fied pub·lic ac·count·ant ['sɜːrtɪfaɪd] censor(a) *m(f)* jurado de cuentas

cer·ti·fy ['sɜːrtɪfaɪ] *v/t* (*pret & pp **certified***) certificar

Ce·sar·e·an [sɪ'zerɪən] *n* cesárea *f*

ces·sa·tion [se'seɪʃn] cese *m*

c/f *abbr* (= ***cost and freight***) CF (= costo y flete)

CFC [siːef'siː] *abbr* (= ***chlorofluorocarbon***) CFC *m* (= clorofluorocarbono *m*)

chain [tʃeɪn] **1** *n also of hotels etc* cadena *f* **2** *v/t* encadenar: ***chain sth / s.o. to sth*** encadenar algo/a alguien a algo

chain re'ac·tion reacción *f* en cadena

'chain-smoke *v/i* fumar un cigarrillo tras otro, fumar como un carretero

'chain-smok·er *persona que fuma un cigarrillo tras otro*

'chain store *store* tienda *f* (de una cadena); *company* cadena *f* de tiendas

chair [tʃer] **1** *n* silla *f*; (*armchair*) sillón *m*; *at university* cátedra *f*; ***the chair*** (*electric chair*) la silla eléctrica; *at meeting* la presidencia; ***go to the chair*** ser ejecutado en la silla eléctrica; ***take the chair*** ocupar la presidencia **2** *v/t meeting* presidir

'chair lift telesilla *f*

'chair·man presidente *m*

chair·man·ship ['tʃermənʃɪp] presidencia *f*

'chair·per·son presidente(-a) *m(f)*

'chair·wom·an presidenta *f*

'cham·ber mu·sic música *f* de cámara

Cham·ber of 'Com·merce Cámara *f* de Comercio

cham·ois (leath·er) ['ʃæmɪ] ante *m*

cham·pagne [ʃæm'peɪn] champán *m*

cham·pi·on ['tʃæmpɪən] **1** *n* SP campeón(-ona) *m(f)*; *of cause* abanderado(-a) *m(f)* **2** *v/t* (*cause*) abanderar

cham·pi·on·ship ['tʃæmpɪənʃɪp] campeo-

C

nato *m*

chance [tʃæns] (*possibility*) posibilidad *f*; (*opportunity*) oportunidad *f*; (*risk*) riesgo *m*; (*luck*) casualidad *f*, suerte *f*; *there's not much chance of that happening* no es probable que ocurra; *leave nothing to chance* no dejar nada a la improvisación; *by chance* por casualidad; *take a chance* correr el riesgo; *I'm not taking any chances* no voy a correr ningún riesgo

Chan·cel·lor ['tʃænsələr] *in Germany* canciller *m*; *Chancellor (of the Exchequer) in Britain* Ministro(-a) *m(f)* de Hacienda

chan·de·lier [ʃændə'lɪr] araña *f* (de luces)

change [tʃeɪndʒ] **1** *n* cambio *m*; (*small coins*) suelto *m*; *from purchase* cambio *m*, *Span* vuelta *f*, *L.Am.* vuelto *m*; *a change is as good as a rest* a veces cambiar es lo mejor; *that makes a nice change* eso es una novedad bienvenida; *for a change* para variar; *a change of clothes* una muda **2** *v/t* cambiar; *change trains* hacer transbordo; *change one's clothes* cambiarse de ropa **3** *v/i* cambiar; (*put on different clothes*) cambiarse; (*take different train/bus*) hacer transbordo; *the lights changed to green* el semáforo se puso verde

change·a·ble ['tʃeɪndʒəbl] *adj* variable, cambiante

'change·o·ver transición *f* (*to* a); *in relay race* relevo *m*

chang·ing room ['tʃeɪndʒɪŋ] SP vestuario *m*; *in shop* probador *m*

chan·nel ['tʃænl] *on* TV, *at sea* canal *m*

chant [tʃænt] **1** *n* REL canto *m*; *of fans* cántico *m*; *of demonstrators* consigna *f* **2** *v/i* gritar **3** *v/t* corear

cha·os ['keɪɑːs] caos *m*; *it was chaos at the airport* la situación en el aeropuerto era caótica

cha·ot·ic [keɪ'ɑːtɪk] *adj* caótico

chap [tʃæp] *n Br* F tipo *m* F, *Span* tío *m* F

chap·el ['tʃæpl] capilla *f*

chapped [tʃæpt] *adj lips* cortado; *hands* agrietado

chap·ter ['tʃæptər] *of book* capítulo *m*; *of organization* sección *f*

char·ac·ter ['kærɪktər] *nature, personality, in printing* carácter *m*; *person, in book, play* personaje *m*; *he's a real character* es todo un personaje

char·ac·ter·is·tic [kærɪktə'rɪstɪk] **1** *n* característica *f* **2** *adj* característico

char·ac·ter·is·ti·cal·ly [kærɪktə'rɪstɪklɪ] *adv* de modo característico; *he was characteristically rude* fue grosero como de costumbre

char·ac·ter·ize ['kærɪktəraɪz] *v/t* (*be typical of*) caracterizar; (*describe*) describir, clasificar

cha·rade [ʃə'rɑːd] *fig* farsa *f*

char·broil·ed ['tʃɑːrbrɔɪld] *adj* a la brasa

char·coal ['tʃɑːrkoʊl] *for barbecue* carbón *m* vegetal; *for drawing* carboncillo *m*

charge [tʃɑːrdʒ] **1** *n* (*fee*) tarifa *f*; LAW cargo *m*, acusación *f*; *free of charge* gratis; *bank charges* comisiones *fpl* bancarias; *will that be cash or charge?* ¿pagará en efectivo o con tarjeta?; *be in charge* estar a cargo; *take charge* hacerse cargo **2** *v/t sum of money* cobrar; (*put on account*) pagar con tarjeta; LAW acusar (*with* de); *battery* cargar; *please charge it to my account* cárguelo a mi cuenta **3** *v/i* (*attack*) cargar

'charge ac·count cuenta *f* de crédito

'charge card tarjeta *f* de compra

cha·ris·ma [kə'rɪzmə] carisma *m*

char·is·ma·tic [kærɪz'mætɪk] *adj* carismático

char·i·ta·ble ['tʃærɪtəbl] *adj institution, donation* de caridad; *person* caritativo

char·i·ty ['tʃærətɪ] *assistance* caridad *f*; *organization* entidad *f* benéfica

char·la·tan ['ʃɑːrlətən] charlatán(-ana) *m(f)*

charm [tʃɑːrm] **1** *n* (*appealing quality*) encanto *m*; *on bracelet etc* colgante *m* **2** *v/t* (*delight*) encantar

charm·ing ['tʃɑːrmɪŋ] *adj* encantador

charred [tʃɑːrd] *adj* carbonizado

chart [tʃɑːrt] (*diagram*) gráfico *m*; (*map*) carta *f* de navegación; *the charts* MUS las listas de éxitos

'chart flight vuelo *m* chárter

chase [tʃeɪs] **1** *n* persecución *f* **2** *v/t* perse-

C

guir
◆ **chase away** v/t ahuyentar
chas·sis ['ʃæsɪ] of car chasis m inv
chat [tʃæt] **1** n charla f, Mex plática f **2** v/i (pret & pp **chatted**) charlar, Mex platicar
'**chat show** tertulia f televisiva
'**chat show host** presentador(a) m(f) de tertulia televisiva
chat·ter ['tʃætər] **1** n cháchara f **2** v/i talk parlotear; of teeth castañetear
'**chat·ter·box** charlatán(-ana) m(f)
chat·ty ['tʃætɪ] adj person hablador
chauf·feur ['ʃoufər] n chófer m, L.Am. chofer m
'**chauf·feur-driv·en** adj con chófer or L.Am. chofer
chau·vin·ist ['ʃoʊvɪnɪst] n (male chauvinist) machista m
chau·vin·ist·ic [ʃoʊvɪ'nɪstɪk] adj chovinista; (sexist) machista
cheap [tʃiːp] adj (inexpensive) barato; (nasty) chabacano; (mean) tacaño
cheat [tʃiːt] **1** n (person) tramposo(-a) m(f) **2** v/t engañar; **cheat s.o. out of sth** estafar algo a alguien **3** v/i in exam copiar; in cards etc hacer trampa; **cheat on one's wife** engañar a la esposa
check¹ [tʃek] **1** adj shirt a cuadros **2** n cuadro m
check² [tʃek] FIN cheque m; in restaurant etc cuenta f; **the check please** la cuenta, por favor
check³ [tʃek] **1** n to verify sth comprobación f; **keep in check, hold in check** mantener bajo control; **keep a check on** llevar el control de **2** v/t (verify) comprobar; machinery inspeccionar; (restrain, stop) contener, controlar; with a checkmark poner un tic en; coat dejar en el guardarropa; package dejar en consigna **3** v/i comprobar; **check for** comprobar
◆ **check in** v/i at airport facturar; at hotel registrarse
◆ **check off** v/t marcar (como comprobada)
◆ **check on** v/t vigilar
◆ **check out 1** v/i of hotel dejar el hotel **2** v/t (look into) investigar; club, restaurant

etc probar
◆ **check up on** v/t hacer averiguaciones sobre, investigar
◆ **check with** v/t of person hablar con; (tally: of information) concordar con
'**check·book** talonario m de cheques, L.Am. chequera f
checked [tʃekt] adj material a cuadros
'**check·er·board** ['tʃekərbɔːrd] tablero m de ajedrez
check·ered ['tʃekərd] adj pattern a cuadros; career accidentado
'**check·ers** ['tʃekərz] nsg damas fpl
'**check-in (coun·ter)** mostrador m de facturación
'**check·ing ac·count** ['tʃekɪŋ] cuenta f corriente
'**check-in time** hora f de facturación
'**check·list** lista f de verificación
'**check mark** tic m
'**check·mate** n jaque m mate
'**check·out** caja f
'**check-out time** from hotel hora f de salida
'**check·point** control m
'**check·room** for coats guardarropa m; for baggage consigna f
'**check-up** medical chequeo m (médico), revisión f (médica); dental revisión f (en el dentista)
cheek [tʃiːk] ANAT mejilla f
'**cheek·bone** pómulo m
cheer [tʃɪr] **1** n ovación f; **cheers!** toast ¡salud!; **the cheers of the fans** los vítores de los aficionados **2** v/t ovacionar, vitorear **3** v/i lanzar vítores
◆ **cheer on** v/t animar
◆ **cheer up 1** v/i animarse; **cheer up!** ¡anímate! **2** v/t animar
cheer·ful ['tʃɪrfəl] adj alegre, contento
cheer·ing ['tʃɪrɪŋ] n vítores mpl
cheer·i·o [tʃɪrɪ'oʊ] Br F ¡chao! F
'**cheer·lead·er** animadora f
cheese [tʃiːz] queso m
'**cheese·burg·er** hamburguesa f de queso
'**cheese·cake** tarta f de queso
chef [ʃef] chef m, jefe m de cocina
chem·i·cal ['kemɪkl] **1** adj químico **2** n producto m químico

chem·i·cal 'war·fare guerra *f* química

chem·ist ['kemɪst] *in laboratory* quími·co(-a) *m(f)*; *Br dispensing* farmacéuti·co(-a) *m(f)*

chem·is·try ['kemɪstrɪ] química *f*; *fig* sin·tonía *f*, química *f*

chem·o·ther·a·py [kiːmouˈθerəpɪ] qui·mioterapia *f*

cheque [tʃek] *Br* → **check²**

cher·ish ['tʃerɪʃ] *v/t photo etc* apreciar mucho, tener mucho cariño a; *person* querer mucho; *hope* albergar

cher·ry ['tʃerɪ] *fruit* cereza *f*; *tree* cerezo *m*

cher·ub ['tʃerəb] *in painting, sculpture* querubín *m*

chess [tʃes] ajedrez *m*

'**chess·board** tablero *m* de ajedrez

'**chess·man**, '**chess·piece** pieza *f* de aje·drez

chest [tʃest] *of person* pecho *m*; *box* cofre *m*; *get sth off one's chest* desahogarse

chest·nut ['tʃesnʌt] castaña *f*; *tree* castaño *m*

chest of '**draw·ers** cómoda *f*

chew [tʃuː] *v/t* mascar, masticar; *of dog, rats* mordisquear

♦ **chew out** *v/t* F echar una bronca a F

chew·ing gum ['tʃuːɪŋ] chicle *m*

chic [ʃiːk] *adj* chic, elegante

chick [tʃɪk] *young chicken* pollito *m*; *young bird* polluelo *m*; F *girl* nena *f* F

chick·en ['tʃɪkɪn] **1** *n* gallina *f*; *food* pollo *m*; F (*coward*) gallina *f* F **2** *adj* F (*co·wardly*) cobarde; *be chicken* ser un(a) gallina F

♦ **chicken out** *v/i* F acobardarse

'**chick·en·feed** F calderilla *f*

chief [tʃiːf] **1** *n* jefe(-a) *m(f)* **2** *adj* princi·pal

chief ex·ec·u·tive 'of·fi·cer consejero(-a) *m(f)* delegado

chief·ly ['tʃiːflɪ] *adv* principalmente

chil·blain ['tʃɪlbleɪn] sabañón *m*

child [tʃaɪld] (*pl children* ['tʃɪldrən]) ni·ño(-a) *m(f)*; *son* hijo *m*; *daughter* hija *f*; *pej* niño(-a) *m(f)*, crío(-a) *m(f)*

'**child a·buse** malos tratos *mpl* a menores

'**child·birth** parto *m*

child·hood ['tʃaɪldhʊd] infancia *f*

child·ish ['tʃaɪldɪʃ] *adj pej* infantil

child·ish·ness ['tʃaɪldɪʃnɪs] *pej* infantilis·mo *m*

child·ish·ly ['tʃaɪldɪʃlɪ] *adv pej* de manera infantil

child·less ['tʃaɪldlɪs] *adj* sin hijos

child·like ['tʃaɪldlaɪk] *adj* infantil

'**child·mind·er** niñero(-a) *m(f)*

'**child·ren** ['tʃɪldrən] *pl* → **child**

Chil·e ['tʃɪlɪ] *n* Chile

Chil·e·an ['tʃɪlɪən] **1** *adj* chileno **2** *n* chile·no(-a) *m(f)*

chill [tʃɪl] **1** *n illness* resfriado *m*; *there's a chill in the air* hace bastante fresco **2** *v/t wine* poner a enfriar

♦ **chill out** *v/i* P tranquilizarse

chil·(l)i (**pep·per**) ['tʃɪlɪ] chile *m*, *Span* guindilla *f*

chill·y ['tʃɪlɪ] *adj weather, welcome* fresco; *I'm feeling a bit chilly* tengo fresco

chime [tʃaɪm] *v/i* campanada *f*

chim·ney ['tʃɪmnɪ] chimenea *f*

chim·pan·zee [tʃɪmˈpænzi] chimpancé *m*

chin [tʃɪn] barbilla *f*

Chi·na ['tʃaɪnə] China

chi·na ['tʃaɪnə] porcelana *f*

Chi·nese [tʃaɪˈniːz] **1** *adj* chino **2** *n* (*lan·guage*) chino *m*; (*person*) chino(-a) *m(f)*

chink [tʃɪŋk] *gap* resquicio *m*; *sound* tinti·neo *m*

chip [tʃɪp] **1** *n of wood* viruta *f*; *of stone* lasca *f*; *damage* mella *f*; *in gambling* fi·cha *f*; *chips* patatas *fpl* fritas **2** *v/t* (*pret & pp chipped*) (*damage*) mellar

♦ **chip in** *v/i* (*interrupt*) interrumpir; *with money* poner dinero

chip·munk ['tʃɪpmʌŋk] ardilla *f* listada

chi·ro·prac·tor ['kaɪroʊpræktər] quiro·práctico(-a) *m(f)*

chirp [tʃɜːrp] *v/i* piar

chis·el ['tʃɪzl] *n for stone* cincel *m*; *for wood* formón *m*

chit·chat ['tʃɪtʃæt] charla *f*

chiv·al·rous ['ʃɪvlrəs] *adj* caballeroso

chive [tʃaɪv] cebollino *m*

chlo·rine ['klɔːriːn] cloro *m*

chlor·o·form ['klɔːrəfɔːrm] *n* cloroformo *m*

choc·a·hol·ic [tʃɑːkəˈhɑːlɪk] *n* F adicto(-a) al chocolate

chock-a-block [ʧɑːkəˈblɑːk] *adj* F abarrotado F

chock-full [ʧɑːkˈfʊl] *adj* F de bote en bote F

choc·o·late [ˈʧɑːkələt] chocolate *m*; *a box of chocolates* una caja de bombones; *hot chocolate* chocolate *m* caliente

'**choc·o·late cake** pastel *m* de chocolate

choice [ʧɔɪs] **1** *n* elección *f*; *(selection)* selección *f*; *you have a choice of rice or potatoes* puedes elegir entre arroz y patatas; *the choice is yours* tú eliges; *I had no choice* no tuve alternativa **2** *adj* *(top quality)* selecto

choir [kwaɪr] coro *m*

'**choir·boy** niño *m* de coro

choke [ʧoʊk] **1** *n* мот estárter *m* **2** *v/i* ahogarse; *choke on sth* atragantarse con algo **3** *v/t* estrangular; *screams* ahogar

cho·les·te·rol [kəˈlestəroʊl] colesterol *m*

choose [ʧuːz] *v/t* & *v/i* (*pret* **chose**, *pp* **chosen**) elegir, escoger

choos·ey [ˈʧuːzɪ] *adj* F exigente

chop [ʧɑːp] **1** *n* *meat* chuleta *f*; *with one chop of the ax* con un hachazo **2** *v/t* (*pret* & *pp* **chopped**) *wood* cortar; *meat* trocear; *vegetables* picar

♦ **chop down** *v/t* *tree* talar

chop·per [ˈʧɑːpər] F *(helicopter)* helicóptero *m*

'**chop·sticks** *npl* palillos *mpl* (chinos)

cho·ral [ˈkɔːrəl] *adj* coral

chord [kɔːrd] мus acorde *m*

chore [ʧɔːr] tarea *f*

chor·e·o·graph [ˈkɔːrɪəgræf] *v/t* coreografiar

chor·e·og·ra·pher [kɔːrɪˈɑːgrəfər] coreógrafo(-a) *m(f)*

chor·e·og·ra·phy [kɔːrɪˈɑːgrəfɪ] coreografía *f*

cho·rus [ˈkɔːrəs] *singers* coro *m*; *of song* estribillo *m*

chose [ʧoʊz] *pret* → **choose**

cho·sen [ˈʧoʊzn] *pp* → **choose**

Christ [kraɪst] Cristo; *Christ!* ¡Dios mío!

chris·ten [ˈkrɪsn] *v/t* bautizar

chris·ten·ing [ˈkrɪsnɪŋ] bautizo *m*

Chris·tian [ˈkrɪsʧən] **1** *n* cristiano(-a) *m(f)* **2** *adj* cristiano

Chris·ti·an·i·ty [krɪstɪˈænətɪ] cristianismo *m*

'**Chris·tian name** nombre *m* de pila

Christ·mas [ˈkrɪsməs] Navidad(es) *f(pl)*; *at Christmas* en Navidad(es); *Merry Christmas!* ¡Feliz Navidad!

'**Christ·mas card** crismas *m inv*, tarjeta *f* de Navidad

Christ·mas 'Day día *f* de Navidad

Christ·mas 'Eve Nochebuena *f*

'**Christ·mas present** regalo *m* de Navidad

'**Christ·mas tree** árbol *m* de Navidad

chrome, chro·mi·um [kroʊm, ˈkroʊmɪəm] cromo *m*

chro·mo·some [ˈkroʊməsoʊm] cromosoma *m*

chron·ic [ˈkrɑːnɪk] *adj* crónico

chron·o·log·i·cal [krɑːnəˈlɑːdʒɪkl] *adj* cronológico; *in chronological order* en orden cronológico

chrys·an·the·mum [krɪˈsænθəməm] crisantemo *m*

chub·by [ˈʧʌbɪ] *adj* rechoncho

chuck [ʧʌk] *v/t* F tirar

♦ **chuck out** *v/t* F *object* tirar; *person* echar

chuck·le [ˈʧʌkl] **1** *n* risita *f* **2** *v/i* reírse por lo bajo

chum [ʧʌm] amigo(-a) *m(f)*

chum·my [ˈʧʌmɪ] *adj* F: *be chummy with* ser amiguete de F

chunk [ʧʌŋk] trozo *m*

chunk·y [ˈʧʌŋkɪ] *adj* *sweater* grueso; *person, build* cuadrado, fornido

church [ʧɜːrʧ] iglesia *f*

church 'hall *sala parroquial empleada para diferentes actividades*

church 'serv·ice oficio *m* religioso

'**church·yard** cementerio *m* (al lado de iglesia)

churl·ish [ˈʧɜːrlɪʃ] *adj* maleducado, grosero

chute [ʃuːt] rampa *f*; *for garbage* colector *m* de basura

CIA [siːaɪˈeɪ] *abbr* (= *Central Intelligence Agency*) CIA *f* (= Agencia *f* Central de Inteligencia)

C

ci·der ['saɪdər] sidra *f*

CIF [siːaːˈef] *abbr* (= *cost, insurance, freight*) CIF (= costo, seguro y flete)

ci·gar [sɪˈgɑːr] (cigarro *m*) puro *m*

cig·a·rette, cig·a·ret [sɪgəˈret] cigarrillo *m*

cig·a·rette end colilla *f*

cig·a·rette light·er encendedor *m*, mechero *m*

cig·a·rette pa·per papel *m* de fumar

cin·e·ma ['sɪnɪmə] cine *m*

cin·na·mon ['sɪnəmən] canela *f*

cir·cle ['sɜːrkl] **1** *n* círculo *m*; *sit in a circle* sentarse en círculo **2** *v/t* (*draw circle around*) poner un círculo alrededor de; *his name was circled in red* su nombre tenía un círculo rojo alrededor **3** *v/i* of plane, bird volar en círculo

cir·cuit ['sɜːrkɪt] circuito *m*; (*lap*) vuelta *f*

'cir·cuit board COMPUT placa *f* or tarjeta *f* de circuitos

'cir·cuit break·er ELEC cortacircuitos *m inv*

'cir·cuit train·ing SP: *do circuit training* hacer circuitos de entrenamiento

cir·cu·lar ['sɜːrkjʊlər] **1** *n* (*giving information*) circular *f* **2** *adj* circular

cir·cu·late ['sɜːrkjʊleɪt] **1** *v/i* circular **2** *v/t* memo hacer circular

cir·cu·la·tion [sɜːrkjʊˈleɪʃn] circulación *f*; of newspaper, magazine tirada *f*

cir·cum·fer·ence [sərˈkʌmfərəns] circunferencia *f*

cir·cum·stances ['sɜːrkəmstənsɪs] *npl* circunstancias *fpl*; *financial* situación *f* económica; *under no circumstances* en ningún caso, de ninguna manera; *under the circumstances* dadas las circunstancias

cir·cus ['sɜːrkəs] circo *m*

cir·rho·sis (of the liv·er) [sɪˈroʊsɪs] cirrosis *f* (hepática)

cis·tern ['sɪstɜːrn] cisterna *f*

cite [saɪt] *v/t* citar

cit·i·zen ['sɪtɪzn] ciudadano(-a) *m(f)*

cit·i·zen·ship ['sɪtɪznʃɪp] ciudadanía *f*

cit·rus ['sɪtrəs] *adj* cítrico; *citrus fruit* cítrico *m*

cit·y ['sɪtɪ] ciudad *f*

city 'cen·ter centro *m* de la ciudad

city 'hall ayuntamiento *m*

civ·ic ['sɪvɪk] *adj* cívico

civ·il ['sɪvl] *adj* civil; (*polite*) cortés

civ·il en·gi'neer ingeniero(-a) *m(f)* civil

ci·vil·i·an [sɪˈvɪljən] **1** *n* civil *m/f* **2** *adj* clothes de civil

ci·vil·i·ty [sɪˈvɪlɪtɪ] cortesía *f*

civ·i·li·za·tion [sɪvəlaɪˈzeɪʃn] civilización *f*

civ·i·lize ['sɪvəlaɪz] *v/t* person civilizar

civ·il 'rights *npl* derechos *mpl* civiles

civ·il 'ser·vant funcionario(-a) *m(f)*

civ·il 'ser·vice administración *f* pública

civ·il 'war guerra *f* civil

claim [kleɪm] **1** *n* (*request*) reclamación *f* (*for* de); (*right*) derecho *m*; (*assertion*) afirmación *f* **2** *v/t* (*ask for as a right*) reclamar; (*assert*) afirmar; *lost property* reclamar; *they have claimed responsibility for the attack* se han atribuido la responsabilidad del ataque

claim·ant ['kleɪmənt] reclamante *m/f*

clair·voy·ant [klerˈvɔɪənt] *n* clarividente *m/f*, vidente *m/f*

clam [klæm] almeja *f*

◆ **clam up** *v/i* (*pret & pp clammed*) F cerrarse, callarse

clam·ber ['klæmbər] *v/i* trepar (*over* por)

clam·my ['klæmɪ] *adj* húmedo

clam·or, Br clam·our ['klæmər] *noise* griterío *m*; *outcry* clamor *m*

◆ **clamor for** *v/t* justice clamar por; *ice cream* pedir a gritos

clamp [klæmp] **1** *n fastener* abrazadera *f*, mordaza *f* **2** *v/t fasten* sujetar con abrazadera; *car* poner un cepo a

◆ **clamp down** *v/i* actuar contundentemente

◆ **clamp down on** *v/t* actuar contundentemente contra

clan [klæn] clan *m*

clan·des·tine [klænˈdestɪn] *adj* clandestino

clang [klæŋ] **1** *n* sonido *m* metálico **2** *v/i* resonar; *the metal door clanged shut* la puerta metálica se cerró con gran estrépito

clap [klæp] *v/t & v/i* (*pret & pp clapped*)

C

(applaud) aplaudir

clar·et ['klærɪt] *wine* burdeos *m inv*

clar·i·fi·ca·tion [klærɪfɪ'keɪʃn] aclaración *f*

clar·i·fy ['klærɪfaɪ] *v/t (pret & pp **clarified**)* aclarar

clar·i·net [klærɪ'net] clarinete *m*

clar·i·ty ['klærətɪ] claridad *f*

clash [klæʃ] **1** *n* choque *m*, enfrentamiento *m*; *of personalities* choque *m* **2** *v/i* chocar, enfrentarse; *of colors* desentonar; *of events* coincidir

clasp [klæsp] **1** *n* broche *m*, cierre *m* **2** *v/t in hand* estrechar; *he clasped the precious documents to him* agarró firmemente los valiosos documentos

class [klæs] **1** *n lesson, students* clase *f*; *social class* clase *f* social **2** *v/t* clasificar *(as* como)

clas·sic ['klæsɪk] **1** *adj* clásico **2** *n* clásico *m*

clas·si·cal ['klæsɪkl] *adj music* clásico

clas·si·fi·ca·tion [klæsɪfɪ'keɪʃn] clasificación *f*

clas·si·fied ['klæsɪfaɪd] *adj information* reservado

'**clas·si·fied ad(ver·tise·ment)** anuncio *m* por palabras

clas·si·fy ['klæsɪfaɪ] *v/t (pret & pp **classified**)* clasificar

'**class·mate** compañero(-a) *m(f)* de clase

'**class·room** clase *f*, aula *f*

'**class war·fare** lucha *f* de clases

class·y ['klæsɪ] *adj* F con clase

clat·ter ['klætər] **1** *n* estrépito *m* **2** *v/i* hacer ruido

clause [klɔːz] *in agreement* cláusula *f*; GRAM cláusula *f*, oración *f*

claus·tro·pho·bi·a [klɔːstrə'foʊbɪə] claustrofobia *f*

claw [klɔː] **1** *n also fig* garra *f*; *of lobster* pinza *f* **2** *v/t (scratch)* arañar

clay [kleɪ] arcilla *f*

clean [kliːn] **1** *adj* limpio **2** *adv* F *(completely)* completamente **3** *v/t* limpiar; *clean one's teeth* limpiarse los dientes; *I must have my coat cleaned* tengo que llevar el abrigo a la tintorería

◆ **clean out** *v/t room, closet* limpiar por

completo; *fig* desplumar

◆ **clean up 1** *v/t also fig* limpiar; *papers* recoger **2** *v/i* limpiar; *(wash)* lavarse; *on stock market etc* ganar mucho dinero

clean·er ['kliːnər] *person* limpiador(a) *m(f)*; *(dry)* **cleaner** tintorería *f*

clean·ing wom·an ['kliːnɪŋ] señora *f* de la limpieza

cleanse [klenz] *v/t skin* limpiar

cleans·er ['klenzər] *for skin* loción *f* limpiadora

cleans·ing cream ['klenzɪŋ] crema *f* limpiadora

clear [klɪr] **1** *adj* claro; *weather, sky* despejado; *water* transparente; *conscience* limpio; *I'm not clear about it* no lo tengo claro; *I didn't make myself clear* no me expliqué claramente **2** *adv* **stand clear of the doors** apartarse de las puertas; *steer clear of* evitar **3** *v/t roads etc* despejar; *(acquit)* absolver; *(authorize)* autorizar; *(earn)* ganar, sacar; *the guards cleared everybody out of the room* los guardias sacaron a todo el mundo de la habitación; *you're cleared for takeoff* tiene autorización *or* permiso para despegar; *clear one's throat* carraspear **4** *v/i of sky, mist* despejarse; *of face* alegrarse

◆ **clear away** *v/t* quitar

◆ **clear off** *v/i* F largarse F

◆ **clear out 1** *v/t closet* ordenar, limpiar **2** *v/i* marcharse

◆ **clear up 1** *v/i* ordenar; *of weather* despejarse; *of illness, rash* desaparecer **2** *v/t (tidy)* ordenar; *mystery, problem* aclarar

clear·ance ['klɪrəns] *space* espacio *m*; *(authorization)* autorización *f*

clear·ance sale liquidación *f*

clear·ing ['klɪrɪŋ] claro *m*

clear·ly ['klɪrlɪ] *adv* claramente, **she is clearly upset** está claro que está disgustada

cleav·age ['kliːvɪdʒ] escote *m*

cleav·er ['kliːvər] cuchillo *m* de carnicero

clem·en·cy ['klemənsɪ] clemencia *f*

clench [klentʃ] *v/t teeth, fist* apretar

cler·gy ['klɜːrdʒɪ] clero *m*

cler·gy·man ['klɜːrdʒɪmæn] clérigo *m*

clerk [klɜːrk] *administrative* oficinista *m/f*; *in store* dependiente(-a) *m/f*
clev·er ['klevər] *adj person, animal* listo; *idea, gadget* ingenioso
clev·er·ly ['klevərlɪ] *adv designed* ingeniosamente
cli·ché ['kliːʃeɪ] tópico *m*, cliché *m*
cli·chéd ['kliːʃeɪd] *adj* estereotipado
click [klɪk] **1** *n* COMPUT clic *m* **2** *v/i* hacer clic
◆ **click on** *v/t* COMPUT hacer clic en
cli·ent ['klaɪənt] cliente *m/f*
cli·en·tele [kliːən'tel] clientela *f*
cli·mate ['klaɪmət] *also fig* clima *m*
'**cli·mate change** cambio *m* climático
cli·mat·ic [klaɪ'mætɪk] *adj* climático
cli·max ['klaɪmæks] *n* clímax *m*, punto *m* culminante
climb [klaɪm] **1** *n up mountain* ascensión *f*, escalada *f* **2** *v/t hill, ladder* subir; *mountain* subir, escalar; *tree* trepar a **3** *v/i* subir (**into** a); *up mountain* subir, escalar; *of inflation etc* subir
◆ **climb down** *v/i from ladder etc* bajar
climb·er ['klaɪmər] *person* escalador(a) *m(f)*, alpinista *m/f*, *L.Am.* andinista *m/f*
climb·ing ['klaɪmɪŋ] escalada *f*, alpinismo *m*, *L.Am.* andinismo *m*
'**climb·ing wall** rocódromo *m*
clinch [klɪntʃ] *v/t deal* cerrar; *that clinches it* ¡ahora sí que está claro!
cling [klɪŋ] *v/i (pret & pp clung) of clothes* pegarse al cuerpo
◆ **cling to** *v/t person, idea* aferrarse a
'**cling·film** plástico *m* transparente (para alimentos)
cling·y ['klɪŋɪ] *adj child, boyfriend* pegajoso
clin·ic ['klɪnɪk] clínica *f*
clin·i·cal ['klɪnɪkl] *adj* clínico
clink [klɪŋk] **1** *n noise* tintineo *m* **2** *v/i* tintinear
clip[1] [klɪp] **1** *n fastener* clip *m* **2** *v/t (pret & pp clipped)*: *clip sth to sth* sujetar algo a algo
clip[2] [klɪp] **1** *n extract* fragmento *m* **2** *v/t (pret & pp clipped) hair, grass* cortar; *hedge* podar
clip·pers ['klɪpərz] *npl for hair* maquinilla

f; *for nails* cortaúñas *m inv*; *for gardening* tijeras *fpl* de podar
clip·ping ['klɪpɪŋ] *from newspaper* recorte *m*
clique [kliːk] camarilla *f*
cloak *n* capa *f*
'**cloak·room** *Br* guardarropa *m*
clock [klɑːk] reloj *m*
'**clock ra·di·o** radio *m* despertador
'**clock·wise** *adv* en el sentido de las agujas del reloj
'**clock·work**: *it went like clockwork* salió a la perfección
◆ **clog up** [klɑːg] **1** *v/i (pret & pp clogged)* bloquearse **2** *v/t (pret & pp clogged)* bloquear
clone [kloun] **1** *n* clon *m* **2** *v/t* clonar
close[1] [klous] **1** *adj family* cercano; *friend* íntimo; *bear a close resemblance to* parecerse mucho a; *the closest town* la ciudad más cercana; *be close to s.o. emotionally* estar muy unido a alguien **2** *adv* cerca; *close to the school* cerca del colegio; *close at hand* a mano; *close by* cerca
close[2] [klouz] **1** *v/t* cerrar **2** *v/i of door, shop* cerrar; *of eyes* cerrarse
◆ **close down** *v/t & v/i* cerrar
◆ **close in** *v/i of fog* echarse encima; *of troops* aproximarse, acercarse
◆ **close up 1** *v/t building* cerrar **2** *v/i (move closer)* juntarse
closed [klouzd] *adj store, eyes* cerrado
closed-cir·cuit 'tel·e·vi·sion circuito *m* cerrado de televisión
'**close-knit** *adj* muy unido
close·ly ['klouslɪ] *adv listen, watch* atentamente; *cooperate* de cerca
clos·et ['klɑːzɪt] armario *m*
close-up ['klousʌp] primer plano *m*
clos·ing date ['klouzɪŋ] fecha *f* límite
'**clos·ing time** hora *f* de cierre
clo·sure ['klouʒər] cierre *m*
clot [klɑːt] **1** *n of blood* coágulo *m* **2** *v/i (pret & pp clotted) of blood* coagularse
cloth [klɑːθ] *(fabric)* tela *f*, tejido *m*; *for cleaning* trapo *m*
clothes [klouðz] *npl* ropa *f*
'**clothes brush** cepillo *m* para la ropa

C

'clothes hang·er percha f

'clothes·horse tendedero m plegable

'clothes·line cuerda f de tender la ropa

'clothes peg, 'clothes·pin pinza f (de la ropa)

cloth·ing ['kloʊðɪŋ] ropa f

cloud [klaʊd] n nube f; **a cloud of dust** una nube de polvo

◆ cloud over v/i of sky nublarse

'cloud·burst chaparrón m

cloud·less ['klaʊdlɪs] adj sky despejado

cloud·y ['klaʊdɪ] adj nublado

clout [klaʊt] (fig: influence) influencia f

clove of 'gar·lic [kloʊv] diente m de ajo

clown [klaʊn] also fig payaso m

club [klʌb] n weapon palo m, garrote m; in golf palo m; organization club m; **clubs** in cards tréboles

clue [kluː] pista f; **I haven't a clue** F (don't know) no tengo idea F; **he hasn't a clue** F (is useless) no tiene ni idea F

clued-up [kluːd'ʌp] adj F puesto F; **be clued-up on sth** F estar puesto sobre algo F

clump [klʌmp] n of earth terrón m; of flowers etc grupo m

clum·si·ness ['klʌmzɪnɪs] torpeza f

clum·sy ['klʌmzɪ] adj person torpe

clung [klʌŋ] pret & pp → **cling**

clus·ter ['klʌstər] 1 n grupo m 2 v/i of people apiñarse; of houses agruparse

clutch [klʌtʃ] 1 n MOT embrague m 2 v/t agarrar

◆ clutch at v/t: **clutch at sth** agarrarse a algo

clut·ter ['klʌtər] 1 n desorden m; **all the clutter on my desk** la cantidad de cosas que hay encima de mi mesa 2 v/t (also: clutter up) abarrotar

Co. abbr (= **Company**) Cía. (= Compañía f)

c/o abbr (= **care of**) en el domicilio de

coach [koʊtʃ] 1 n (trainer) entrenador(a) m(f); of singer, actor profesor(a) m(f); on train vagón m; Br (bus) autobús m 2 v/t footballer entrenar; singer preparar

coach·ing ['koʊtʃɪŋ] entrenamiento m

co·ag·u·late [koʊ'ægjʊleɪt] v/i of blood coagularse

coal [koʊl] carbón m

co·a·li·tion [koʊə'lɪʃn] coalición f

'coal·mine mina f de carbón

coarse [kɔːrs] adj áspero; hair basto; (vulgar) basto, grosero

coarse·ly ['kɔːrslɪ] adv (vulgarly) de manera grosera; **coarsely ground coffee** café molido grueso

coast [koʊst] n costa f; **at the coast** en la costa

coast·al ['koʊstl] adj costero

coast·er ['koʊstər] posavasos m inv

'coast·guard organization servicio m de guardacostas; person guardacostas m/f inv

'coast·line litoral m, costa f

coat [koʊt] 1 n chaqueta f, L.Am. saco m; (overcoat) abrigo m; of animal pelaje m; of paint etc capa f, mano f 2 v/t (cover) cubrir (**with** de)

'coat·hang·er percha f

coat·ing ['koʊtɪŋ] capa f

co·au·thor ['koʊɔːθər] 1 n coautor(a) m(f) 2 v/t: **co-author a book** escribir un libro conjuntamente

coax [koʊks] v/t persuadir; **coax sth out of s.o.** sonsacar algo a alguien

cob·bled ['kɑːbld] adoquinado

cob·ble·stone ['kɑːblstoʊn] adoquín m

'cob·web ['kɑːbweb] telaraña f

co·caine [kə'keɪn] cocaína f

cock [kɑːk] n (chicken) gallo m; (any male bird) macho m

cock·eyed [kɑːk'aɪd] adj F idea etc ridículo

'cock·pit of plane cabina f

cock·roach ['kɑːkroʊtʃ] cucaracha f

'cock·tail cóctel m (bebida)

'cock·tail par·ty cóctel m (fiesta)

'cock·tail shak·er coctelera f

cock·y ['kɑːkɪ] adj F creído, chulo

co·coa ['koʊkoʊ] drink cacao m

co·co·nut ['koʊkənʌt] coco m

'co·co·nut palm cocotero m

COD [siːoʊ'diː] abbr (= **collect on delivery**) entrega f contra reembolso

cod·dle ['kɑːdl] v/t sick person cuidar; pej: child mimar

code [koʊd] n código m; **in code** cifrado

co·ed·u·ca·tion·al [koʊedʊˈkeɪʃnl] *adj*
mixto

co·erce [koʊˈɜːrs] *v/t* coaccionar

co·ex·ist [koʊɪgˈzɪst] *v/i* coexistir

co·ex·ist·ence [koʊɪgˈzɪstəns] coexisten-
cia *f*

cof·fee [ˈkɑːfɪ] café *m*; *a cup of coffee* un
café

'cof·fee bean grano *m* de café

'cof·fee break pausa *f* para el café

'cof·fee cup taza *f* de café

'cof·fee grind·er [ˈɡraɪndər] molinillo *m*
de café

'cof·fee mak·er cafetera *f* (para preparar)

'cof·fee pot cafetera *f* (para servir)

'cof·fee shop café *m*, cafetería *f*

'cof·fee ta·ble mesa *f* de centro

cof·fin [ˈkɑːfɪn] féretro *m*, ataúd *m*

cog [kɑːɡ] diente *m*

co·gnac [ˈkɑːnjæk] coñac *m*

'cog·wheel rueda *f* dentada

co·hab·it [koʊˈhæbɪt] *v/i* cohabitar

co·her·ent [koʊˈhɪrənt] *adj* coherente

coil [kɔɪl] 1 *n* of rope rollo *m*; of smoke
espiral *f*; of snake anillo *m* 2 *v/t*: *coil
(up)* enrollar

coin [kɔɪn] *n* moneda *f*

co·in·cide [koʊɪnˈsaɪd] *v/i* coincidir

co·in·ci·dence [koʊˈɪnsɪdəns] coincidencia *f*

coke [koʊk] P (cocaine) coca *f*

Coke® [koʊk] Coca-Cola® *f*

cold [koʊld] 1 *adj* also fig frío; *I'm (feeling) cold* tengo frío; *it's cold* of weather
hace frío; *in cold blood* a sangre fría; *get
cold feet* F ponerse nervioso 2 *n* frío *m*;
MED resfriado *m*; *I have a cold* estoy resfriado, tengo un resfriado

cold-blood·ed [koʊldˈblʌdɪd] *adj* de sangre fría; *fig: murder* a sangre fría

cold 'call·ing [ˈkɔːlɪŋ] COM visitas o llamadas comerciales hechas sin cita previa

'cold cuts *npl* fiambres *mpl*

cold·ly [ˈkoʊldlɪ] *adv* fríamente, con frialdad

'cold·ness [ˈkoʊldnɪs] frialdad *f*

'cold sore calentura *f*

cole·slaw [ˈkoʊlslɔː] ensalada de col, cebolla, zanahoria y mayonesa

col·ic [ˈkɑːlɪk] cólico *m*

col·lab·o·rate [kəˈlæbəreɪt] *v/i* colaborar
(*on* en)

col·lab·o·ra·tion [kəlæbəˈreɪʃn] colaboración *f*

col·lab·o·ra·tor [kəˈlæbəreɪtər] colabora-
dor(a) *m(f)*; *with enemy* colaboracionis-
ta *m/f*

col·lapse [kəˈlæps] *v/i* of roof, building
hundirse, desplomarse; of person desplomarse

col·lap·si·ble [kəˈlæpsəbl] *adj* plegable

col·lar [ˈkɑːlər] cuello *m*; for dog collar *m*

'col·lar·bone clavícula *f*

col·league [ˈkɑːliːɡ] colega *m/f*

col·lect [kəˈlekt] 1 *v/t* recoger; *as hobby*
coleccionar 2 *v/i* (*gather together*) reunirse 3 *adv*: *call collect* llamar a cobro
revertido

col·lect call llamada *f* a cobro revertido

col·lect·ed [kəˈlektɪd] *adj works, poems
etc* completo; *person* sereno

col·lec·tion [kəˈlekʃn] colección *f*; *in
church* colecta *f*

col·lec·tive [kəˈlektɪv] *adj* colectivo

col·lec·tive 'bar·gain·ing negociación *f*
colectiva

col·lec·tor [kəˈlektər] coleccionista *m/f*

col·lege [ˈkɑːlɪdʒ] universidad *f*

col·lide [kəˈlaɪd] *v/i* chocar, colisionar
(*with* con *or* contra)

col·li·sion [kəˈlɪʒn] choque *m*, colisión *f*

col·lo·qui·al [kəˈloʊkwɪəl] *adj* coloquial

Co·lom·bi·a [kəˈlʌmbɪə] Colombia

Co·lom·bi·an [kəˈlʌmbɪən] 1 *adj* colombiano 2 *n* colombiano(-a) *m(f)*

co·lon [ˈkoʊlən] *punctuation*) dos puntos
mpl; ANAT colon *m*

colo·nel [ˈkɜːrnl] coronel *m*

co·lo·ni·al [kəˈloʊnɪəl] *adj* colonial

co·lo·nize [ˈkɑːlənaɪz] *v/t country* colonizar

co·lo·ny [ˈkɑːlənɪ] colonia *f*

col·or [ˈkʌlər] 1 *n* color *m*; *in color movie
etc* en color; *colors* MIL bandera *f* 2 *v/t
one's hair* teñir 3 *v/i* (*blush*) ruborizarse

'col·or-blind *adj* daltónico

col·ored [ˈkʌlərd] *adj person* de color

'col·or fast *adj* que no destiñe

col·or·ful ['kʌlərfəl] *adj* lleno de colores; *account* colorido

col·or·ing ['kʌlərɪŋ] color *m*

'col·or pho·to·graph fotografía *f* en color

'col·or scheme combinación *f* de colores

'col·or TV televisión *f* en color

co·los·sal [kə'lɑːsl] *adj* colosal

col·our *etc Br* → color *etc*

colt [koult] potro *m*

Co·lum·bus [kə'lʌmbəs] Colón

col·umn ['kɑːləm] *architectural, of text* columna *f*

col·umn·ist ['kɑːləmɪst] columnista *m/f*

co·ma ['koumə] coma *m*; *be in a coma* estar en coma

comb [koum] **1** *n* peine *m* **2** *v/t hair, area* peinar; *comb one's hair* peinarse

com·bat ['kɑːmbæt] **1** *n* combate *m* **2** *v/t* combatir

com·bi·na·tion [kɑːmbɪ'neɪʃn] combinación *f*

com·bine [kəm'baɪn] **1** *v/t* combinar; *ingredients* mezclar **2** *v/i* combinarse

com·bine har·vest·er [kɑːmbaɪn'hɑːrvɪstər] cosechadora *f*

com·bus·ti·ble [kəm'bʌstɪbl] *adj* combustible

com·bus·tion [kəm'bʌstʃn] combustión *f*

come [kʌm] *v/i (pret came, pp come) toward speaker* venir; *toward listener* ir; *of train, bus* llegar, venir; *don't come too close* no te acerques demasiado; *you'll come to like it* llegará a gustarte; *how come?* F ¿y eso?; *how come you've stopped going to the club?* ¿cómo es que has dejado de ir al club?

◆ come about *v/i (happen)* pasar, suceder

◆ come across **1** *v/t (find)* encontrar **2** *v/i*: *his humor comes across as ...* su humor da la impresión de ser ...; *she comes across as ...* da la impresión de ser ...

◆ come along *v/i (come too)* venir; *(turn up)* aparecer; *(progress)* marchar; *why don't you come along?* ¿por qué no te vienes con nosotros?

◆ come apart *v/i* desmontarse; *(break)* romperse

◆ come around *v/i to s.o.'s home* venir, pasarse; *(regain consciousness)* volver en sí

◆ come away *v/i (leave)* salir; *of button etc* caerse

◆ come back *v/i* volver; *it came back to me* lo recordé

◆ come by **1** *v/i* pasarse **2** *v/t (acquire)* conseguir; *how did you come by that bruise?* ¿cómo te has dado ese golpe?

◆ come down **1** *v/i* bajar; *of rain, snow* caer **2** *v/t*: *he came down the stairs* bajó las escaleras

◆ come for *v/t (attack)* atacar; *(collect thing)* venir a por; *(collect person)* venir a buscar a

◆ come forward *v/i (present o.s.)* presentarse

◆ come from *v/t (travel from)* venir de; *(originate from)* ser de

◆ come in *v/i* entrar; *of train* llegar; *of tide* subir; *come in!* ¡entre!, ¡adelante!

◆ come in for *v/t* recibir; *come in for criticism* recibir críticas

◆ come in on *v/t*: *come in on a deal* participar en un negocio

◆ come off *v/i of handle etc* soltarse, caerse; *of paint etc* quitarse

◆ come on *v/i (progress)* marchar, progresar; *come on!* ¡vamos!; *oh come on, you're exaggerating* ¡vamos, hombre!, estás exagerando

◆ come out *v/i* salir; *of book* publicarse; *of stain* irse, quitarse; *of gay* declararse homosexual públicamente

◆ come to **1** *v/t place* llegar a; *of hair, dress, water* llegar hasta; *that comes to $70* eso suma 70 dólares **2** *v/i (regain consciousness)* volver en sí

◆ come up *v/i* subir; *of sun* salir; *something has come up* ha surgido algo

◆ come up with *v/t solution* encontrar; *John came up with a great idea* a John se le ocurrió una idea estupenda

'come·back regreso *m*; *make a comeback* regresar

co·me·di·an [kə'miːdɪən] humorista *m/f*; *pej* payaso(-a) *m(f)*

'come·down gran decepción *f*

com·e·dy ['kɑːmədɪ] comedia f

com·et ['kɑːmɪt] cometa m

come·up·pance [kʌm'ʌpəns] n F: **he'll get his comeuppance** tendrá su merecido

com·fort ['kʌmfərt] **1** n comodidad f, confort m; (consolation) consuelo m **2** v/t consolar

com·for·ta·ble ['kʌmfərtəbl] adj chair cómodo; house, room cómodo, confortable; **be comfortable** of person estar cómodo; financially estar en una situación holgada

com·ic ['kɑːmɪk] **1** n to read cómic m; (comedian) cómico(-a) m(f) **2** adj cómico

com·i·cal ['kɑːmɪkl] adj cómico

'**com·ic book** cómic m

'**com·ics** ['kɑːmɪks] npl tiras fpl cómicas

'**com·ic strip** tira f cómica

com·ma ['kɑːmə] coma f

com·mand [kə'mænd] **1** n orden f **2** v/t ordenar, mandar

com·man·deer [kɑːmən'dɪr] v/t requisar

com·mand·er [kə'mændər] comandante m/f

com·mand·er·in·'chief comandante m/f en jefe

com·mand·ing of·fi·cer [kə'mændɪŋ] oficial m/f al mando

com·mand·ment [kə'mændmənt] mandamiento m: **the Ten Commandments** REL los Diez Mandamientos

com·mem·o·rate [kə'meməreɪt] v/t conmemorar

com·mem·o·ra·tion [kəmemə'reɪʃn]: **in commemoration of** en conmemoración de

com·mence [kə'mens] v/t & v/i comenzar

com·mend [kə'mend] v/t encomiar, elogiar

com·mend·a·ble [kə'mendəbl] adj encomiable

com·men·da·tion [kəmen'deɪʃn] for bravery mención f

com·men·su·rate [kə'menʃərət] adj: **commensurate with** acorde con

com·ment ['kɑːment] **1** n comentario m; **no comment!** ¡sin comentarios! **2** v/i hacer comentarios (**on** sobre)

com·men·ta·ry ['kɑːməntɪ] comentarios mpl

com·men·tate ['kɑːməntert] v/i hacer de comentarista

com·men·ta·tor ['kɑːməntertər] comentarista m/f

com·merce ['kɑːmɜːrs] comercio m

com·mer·cial [kə'mɜːrʃl] **1** adj comercial **2** n (advert) anuncio m (publicitario)

com·mer·cial 'break pausa f publicitaria

com·mer·cial·ize [kə'mɜːrʃlaɪz] v/t Christmas comercializar

com·mer·cial 'trav·el·er viajante m/f de comercio

com·mis·e·rate [kə'mɪzəreɪt] v/i: **she commiserated with me on my failure to get the job** me dijo cuánto sentía que no hubiera conseguido el trabajo

com·mis·sion [kə'mɪʃn] **1** n (payment, committee) comisión f; (job) encargo m **2** v/t: **she has been commissioned ...** se le ha encargado ...

com·mit [kə'mɪt] v/t (pret & pp **committed**) crime cometer; money comprometer; **commit o.s.** comprometerse

com·mit·ment [kə'mɪtmənt] compromiso m (**to** con); **he's afraid of commitment** tiene miedo de comprometerse

com·mit·tee [kə'mɪtɪ] comité m

com·mod·i·ty [kə'mɑːdətɪ] raw material producto m básico; product bien m de consumo

com·mon ['kɑːmən] adj común; **in common** al igual (**with** que); **have sth in common with s.o.** tener algo en común con alguien

com·mon·er ['kɑːmənər] plebeyo(-a) m(f)

com·mon 'law wife esposa f de hecho

com·mon·ly ['kɑːmənlɪ] adv comúnmente

Com·mon 'Mar·ket Mercado m Común

'**com·mon·place** adj común

Com·mons ['kɑːmənz] npl: **the Commons** in Britain la Cámara de los Comunes

com·mon 'sense sentido m común

com·mo·tion [kə'moʊʃn] alboroto m

com·mu·nal [kə'mjuːnl] adj comunal

com·mu·nal·ly [kəm'juːnəlɪ] *adv* en comunidad

com·mu·ni·cate [kə'mjuːnɪkeɪt] **1** *v/i* comunicarse **2** *v/t* comunicar

com·mu·ni·ca·tion [kəmjuːnɪ'keɪʃn] comunicación *f*

com·mu·ni·ca·tions *npl* comunicaciones *fpl*

com·mu·ni·ca·tions sat·el·lite satélite *m* de telecomunicaciones

com·mu·ni·ca·tive [kə'mjuːnɪkətɪv] *adj person* comunicativo

Com·mu·nion [kə'mjuːnjən] REL comunión *f*

com·mu·ni·qué [kə'mjuːnɪkeɪ] comunicado *m*

Com·mu·nism ['kɑːmjunɪzəm] comunismo *m*

Com·mu·nist ['kɑːmjunɪst] **1** *adj* comunista **2** *n* comunista *m/f*

com·mu·ni·ty [kə'mjuːnətɪ] comunidad *f*

com'mu·ni·ty cen·ter centro *m* comunitario

com'mu·ni·ty serv·ice servicios *mpl* a la comunidad (como pena)

com·mute [kə'mjuːt] **1** *v/i* viajar al trabajo; **commute to work** viajar al trabajo **2** *v/t* LAW conmutar

com·mut·er [kə'mjuːtər] *persona que viaja al trabajo*

com'mut·er traf·fic *tráfico generado por los que se desplazan al trabajo*

com'mut·er train *tren de cercanías que utilizan los que se desplazan al trabajo*

com·pact **1** *adj* [kəm'pækt] compacto **2** *n* ['kɑːmpækt] MOT utilitario *m*

com·pact 'disc (disco *m*) compacto *m*

com·pan·ion [kəm'pænjən] compañero(-a) *m(f)*

com·pan·ion·ship [kəm'pænjənʃɪp] compañía *f*

com·pa·ny ['kʌmpənɪ] COM empresa *f*, compañía *f*; (*companionship, guests*) compañía *f*; **keep s.o. company** hacer compañía a alguien

com·pa·ny 'car coche *m* de empresa

com·pa·ny 'law derecho *m* de sociedades

com·pa·ra·ble ['kɑːmpərəbl] *adj* comparable

com·par·a·tive [kəm'pærətɪv] **1** *adj* (*relative*) relativo; *study* comparado; GRAM comparativo; **comparative form** GRAM comparativo *m* **2** *n* GRAM comparativo *m*

com·par·a·tive·ly [kəm'pærətɪvlɪ] *adv* relativamente

com·pare [kəm'per] **1** *v/t* comparar; **compared with ...** comparado con ...; **you can't compare them** no se pueden comparar **2** *v/i* compararse

com·pa·ri·son [kəm'pærɪsn] comparación *f*; **there's no comparison** no hay punto de comparación

com·part·ment [kəm'pɑːrtmənt] compartimento *m*

com·pass ['kʌmpəs] brújula *f*; (*a pair of*) **compasses** GEOM un compás

com·pas·sion [kəm'pæʃn] compasión *f*

com·pas·sion·ate [kəm'pæʃənət] *adj* compasivo

com·pas·sion·ate 'leave *permiso laboral por muerte o enfermedad grave de un familiar*

com·pat·i·bil·i·ty [kəmpætə'bɪlɪtɪ] compatibilidad *f*

com·pat·i·ble [kəm'pætəbl] *adj* compatible; **we're not compatible** no somos compatibles

com·pel [kəm'pel] *v/t* (*pret & pp* **compelled**) obligar

com·pel·ling [kəm'pelɪŋ] *adj argument* poderoso; *movie, book* fascinante

com·pen·sate ['kɑːmpənseɪt] **1** *v/t with money* compensar **2** *v/i* **compensate for** compensar

com·pen·sa·tion [kɑːmpən'seɪʃn] (*money*) indemnización *f*; (*reward, comfort*) compensación *f*

com·pete [kəm'piːt] *v/i* competir (*for* por)

com·pe·tence ['kɑːmpɪtəns] competencia *f*

com·pe·tent ['kɑːmpɪtənt] *adj* competente; *I'm not competent to judge* no estoy capacitado para juzgar

com·pe·tent·ly ['kɑːmpɪtəntlɪ] *adv* competentemente

com·pe·ti·tion [kɑːmpə'tɪʃn] (*contest*) concurso *f*; SP competición *f*; (*competi-

tors) competencia *f*; **the government wants to encourage competition** el gobierno quiere fomentar la competencia

com·pet·i·tive [kəm'petətɪv] *adj* competitivo

com·pet·i·tive·ly [kəm'petətɪvlɪ] *adv* competitivamente: **competitively priced** con un precio muy competitivo

com·pet·i·tive·ness [kəm'petɪtɪvnɪs] COM competitividad *f*; *of person* espíritu *m* competitivo

com·pet·i·tor [kəm'petɪtər] *in contest* concursante *m/f*; SP competidor(a) *m(f)*, contrincante *m/f*; COM competidor(a) *m(f)*

com·pile [kəm'paɪl] *v/t* compilar

com·pla·cen·cy [kəm'pleɪsənsɪ] complacencia *f*

com·pla·cent [kəm'pleɪsənt] *adj* complaciente

com·plain [kəm'pleɪn] *v/i* quejarse, protestar; *to shop, manager* quejarse; **complain of** MED estar aquejado de

com·plaint [kəm'pleɪnt] queja *f*, protesta *f*; MED dolencia *f*

com·ple·ment ['kɑːmplɪmənt] *v/t* complementar; **they complement each other** se complementan

com·ple·men·ta·ry [kɑːmplɪ'mentərɪ] *adj* complementario; **the two are complementary** los dos se complementan

com·plete [kəm'pliːt] **1** *adj* (*total*) absoluto, total; (*full*) completo; (*finished*) finalizado, terminado; **I made a complete fool of myself** quedé como un verdadero tonto **2** *v/t task, building etc* finalizar, terminar; *course* completar; *form* rellenar

com·plete·ly [kəm'pliːtlɪ] *adv* completamente

com·ple·tion [kəm'pliːʃn] finalización *f*, terminación *f*

com·plex ['kɑːmpleks] **1** *adj* complejo **2** *n also* PSYCH complejo *m*

com·plex·ion [kəm'plekʃn] *facial* tez *f*

com·plex·i·ty [kəm'pleksɪtɪ] complejidad *f*

com·pli·ance [kəm'plaɪəns] cumplimiento (**with** de)

com·pli·cate ['kɑːmplɪkeɪt] *v/t* complicar

com·pli·cat·ed ['kɑːmplɪkeɪtɪd] *adj* complicado

com·pli·ca·tion [kɑːmplɪ'keɪʃn] complicación *f*; **complications** MED complicaciones *fpl*

com·pli·ment ['kɑːmplɪmənt] **1** *n* cumplido *m* **2** *v/t* hacer un cumplido a (**on** por)

com·pli·men·ta·ry [kɑːmplɪ'mentərɪ] *adj* elogioso; (*free*) de regalo, gratis

'com·pli·ments slip nota *f* de cortesía

com·ply [kəm'plaɪ] *v/i* (*pret & pp* **complied**) cumplir; **comply with** cumplir

com·po·nent [kəm'pounənt] pieza *f*, componente *m*

com·pose [kəm'pouz] *v/t also* MUS componer; **be composed of** estar compuesto de; **compose o.s.** serenarse

com·posed [kəm'pouzd] *adj* (*calm*) sereno

com·pos·er [kəm'pouzər] MUS compositor(a) *m(f)*

com·po·si·tion [kɑːmpə'zɪʃn] *also* MUS composición *f*; (*essay*) redacción *f*

com·po·sure [kəm'pouʒər] compostura *f*

com·pound ['kɑːmpaund] *n* CHEM compuesto *m*

com·pound 'in·ter·est interés *m* compuesto *or* combinado

com·pre·hend [kɑːmprɪ'hend] *v/t* (*understand*) comprender

com·pre·hen·sion [kɑːmprɪ'henʃn] comprensión *f*

com·pre·hen·sive [kɑːmprɪ'hensɪv] *adj* detallado

com·pre·hen·sive in·sur·ance seguro *m* a todo riesgo

com·pre·hen·sive·ly [kɑːmprɪ'hensɪvlɪ] *adv* detalladamente

com·press **1** *n* ['kɑːmpres] MED compresa *f* **2** *v/t* [kəm'pres] *air, gas* comprimir; *information* condensar

com·prise [kəm'praɪz] *v/t* comprender; **be comprised of** constar de

com·pro·mise ['kɑːmprəmaɪz] **1** *n* solución *f* negociada; **I've had to make compromises all my life** toda mi vida he tenido que hacer concesiones **2** *v/i* transigir, efectuar concesiones **3** *v/t principles* traicionar; (*jeopardize*) poner en peligro;

C

compromise o.s. ponerse en un compromiso

com·pul·sion [kəm'pʌlʃn] PSYCH compulsión *f*

com·pul·sive [kəm'pʌlsɪv] *adj behavior* compulsivo; *reading* absorbente

com·pul·so·ry [kəm'pʌlsərɪ] *adj* obligatorio

com·put·er [kəm'pju:tər] *Span* ordenador *m, L.Am.* computadora *f;* **have sth on computer** tener algo en el *Span* ordenador *or L.Am.* computadora

com·put·er-aid·ed de'sign [kəmpju:tər-'eɪdɪd] diseño *m* asistido por *Span* ordenador *or L.Am.* computadora

com·put·er-aid·ed man·u'fac·ture fabricación *f* asistida por *Span* ordenador *or L.Am.* computadora

com·put·er-con'trolled *adj* controlado por *Span* ordenador *or L.Am.* computadora

com'puter game juego *m* de *Span* ordenador *or L.Am.* computadora

com·put·er·ize [kəm'pju:təraɪz] *v/t* informatizar, *L.Am.* computarizar

com·put·er 'lit·er·ate *adj* con conocimientos de informática *or L.Am.* computación

com·put·er 'sci·ence informática *f, L.Am.* computación *f*

com·put·er 'sci·en·tist informático(-a) *m(f)*

com·put·ing [kəm'pju:tɪŋ] *n* informática *f, L.Am.* computación *f*

com·rade ['kɑ:mreɪd] *(friend)* compañero(-a) *m(f);* POL camarada *m/f*

com·rade·ship ['kɑ:mreɪdʃɪp] camaradería *f*

con [kɑ:n] **1** *n* F timo *m* F **2** *v/t (pret & pp* **conned)** F timar F

con·ceal [kən'si:l] *v/t* ocultar

con·ceal·ment [kən'si:lmənt] ocultación *f*

con·cede [kən'si:d] *v/t (admit)* admitir, reconocer; *goal* encajar

con·ceit [kən'si:t] engreimiento *m,* presunción *f*

con·ceit·ed [kən'si:tɪd] *adj* engreido, presuntuoso

con·cei·va·ble [kən'si:vəbl] *adj* concebible

con·ceive [kən'si:v] *v/i of woman* concebir; *conceive of (imagine)* imaginar; *I can't conceive of that happening* no puedo imaginar que eso vaya a pasar

con·cen·trate ['kɑ:nsəntreɪt] **1** *v/i* concentrarse **2** *v/t one's attention, energies* concentrar

con·cen·trat·ed ['kɑ:nsəntreɪtɪd] *adj juice etc* concentrado

con·cen·tra·tion [kɑ:nsən'treɪʃn] concentración *f*

con·cept ['kɑ:nsept] concepto *m*

con·cep·tion [kən'sepʃn] *of child* concepción *f*

con·cern [kən'sɜ:rn] **1** *n (anxiety, care)* preocupación *f; (business)* asunto *m; (company)* empresa *f; it's none of your concern* no es asunto tuyo; *cause concern* preocupar, inquietar **2** *v/t (involve)* concernir, incumbir; *(worry)* preocupar, inquietar; *concern o.s. with* preocuparse de

con·cerned [kən'sɜ:rnd] *adj (anxious)* preocupado, inquieto (*about* por); *(caring)* preocupado (*about* por); *(involved)* en cuestión; *as far as I'm concerned* por lo que a mí respecta

con·cern·ing [kən'sɜ:rnɪŋ] *prep* en relación con, sobre

con·cert [kən'sərt] concierto *m*

con·cert·ed [kən'sɜ:rtɪd] *adj (joint)* concertado, conjunto

'con·cert·mas·ter primer violín *m/f*

con·cer·to [kən'tʃertoʊ] concierto *m*

con·ces·sion [kən'seʃn] *(compromise)* concesión *f*

con·cil·i·a·to·ry [kənsɪlɪ'eɪtərɪ] *adj* conciliador

con·cise [kən'saɪs] *adj* conciso

con·clude [kən'klu:d] *v/t & v/i (deduce, end)* concluir (*from* de)

con·clu·sion [kən'klu:ʒn] *(deduction)* conclusión *f; (end)* conclusión *f; in conclusion* en conclusión

con·clu·sive [kən'klu:sɪv] *adj* concluyente

con·coct [kən'kɑ:kt] *v/t meal, drink* preparar; *excuse, story* urdir

con·coc·tion [kənˈkɑːkʃn] *food* mejunje *m*; *drink* brebaje *m*, pócima *f*

con·crete [ˈkɑːŋkriːt] **1** *adj* concreto; **concrete jungle** jungla *f* de asfalto **2** *n* hormigón *m*, *L.Am.* concreto *m*

con·cur [kənˈkɜːr] *v/i* (*pret & pp* **concurred**) coincidir

con·cus·sion [kənˈkʌʃn] conmoción *f* cerebral

con·demn [kənˈdem] *v/t* condenar; *building* declarar en ruina; **condemn s.o. to a life of poverty** condenar a alguien a vivir en la miseria

con·dem·na·tion [kɑːndəmˈneɪʃn] *of action* condena *f*

con·den·sa·tion [kɑːndenˈseɪʃn] *on walls, windows* condensación *f*

con·dense [kənˈdens] **1** *v/t* (*make shorter*) condensar **2** *v/i of steam* condensarse

con·densed 'milk [kənˈdensd] leche *f* condensada

con·de·scend [kɑːndɪˈsend] *v/i*: **he condescended to speak to me** se dignó a hablarme

con·de·scend·ing [kɑːndɪˈsendɪŋ] *adj* (*patronizing*) condescendiente

con·di·tion [kənˈdɪʃn] **1** *n* (*state*) condiciones *fpl*; *of health* estado *m*; *illness* enfermedad *f*; (*requirement, term*) condición *f*; **conditions** (*circumstances*) condiciones *fpl*; **on condition that ...** a condición de que ...; **you're in no condition to drive** no estás en condiciones de conducir **2** *v/t* PSYCH condicionar

con·di·tion·al [kənˈdɪʃnl] **1** *adj* *acceptance* condicional **2** *n* GRAM condicional *m*

con·di·tion·er [kənˈdɪʃnər] *for hair* suavizante *m*, acondicionador *m*; *for fabric* suavizante *m*

con·di·tion·ing [kənˈdɪʃnɪŋ] PSYCH condicionamiento *m*

con·do [ˈkɑːndoʊ] F *apartment* apartamento *m*, *Span* piso *m*; *building* bloque de apartamentos

con·do·lenc·es [kənˈdoʊlənsɪz] *npl* condolencias *fpl*

con·dom [ˈkɑːndəm] condón *m*, preservativo *m*

con·do·min·i·um [kɑːndəˈmɪniəm] → **condo**

con·done [kənˈdoʊn] *v/t actions* justificar

con·du·cive [kənˈduːsɪv] *adj*: **conducive to** propicio para

con·duct 1 *n* [ˈkɑːndʌkt] (*behavior*) conducta *f* **2** *v/t* [kənˈdʌkt] (*carry out*) realizar, hacer; ELEC conducir; MUS dirigir; **conduct o.s.** comportarse

con·duct·ed 'tour [kənˈdʌktɪd] visita *f* guiada

con·duc·tor [kənˈdʌktər] MUS director(a) *m(f)* de orquesta; *on train* revisor(-a) *m(f)*; PHYS conductor *m*

cone [koʊn] GEOM, *on highway* cono *m*; *for ice cream* cucurucho *m*; *of pine tree* piña *f*

con·fec·tion·er [kənˈfekʃənər] pastelero(-a) *m(f)*

con·fec·tion·ers' sug·ar azúcar *m or f* glas

con·fec·tion·e·ry [kənˈfekʃənərɪ] (*candy*) dulces *mpl*

con·fed·e·ra·tion [kənfedəˈreɪʃn] confederación *f*

con·fer [kənˈfɜːr] **1** *v/t* (*pret & pp* **conferred**): **confer sth on s.o.** (*bestow*) conferir *or* otorgar algo a alguien **2** *v/i* (*pret & pp* **conferred**) (*discuss*) deliberar

con·fe·rence [ˈkɑːnfərəns] congreso *m*; *discussion* conferencia *f*

'con·fe·rence room sala *f* de conferencias

con·fess [kənˈfes] **1** *v/t* confesar; **I confess I don't know** confieso que no lo sé **2** *v/i* confesar; REL confesarse; **confess to a weakness for sth** confesar una debilidad por algo

con·fes·sion [kənˈfeʃn] confesión *f*; **I've a confession to make** tengo algo que confesar

con·fes·sion·al [kənˈfeʃnl] REL confesionario *m*

con·fes·sor [kənˈfesər] REL confesor *m*

con·fide [kənˈfaɪd] **1** *v/t* confiar **2** *v/i*: **confide in s.o.** confiarse a alguien

con·fi·dence [ˈkɑːnfɪdəns] confianza *f*; (*secret*) confidencia *f*; **in confidence** en confianza, confidencialmente

con·fi·dent [ˈkɑːnfɪdənt] *adj* (*self-as-*

C

sured) seguro de sí mismo; (*convinced*) seguro

con·fi·den·tial [kɑːnfɪˈdenʃl] *adj* confidencial, secreto

con·fi·den·tial·ly [kɑːnfɪˈdenʃlɪ] *adv* confidencialmente

con·fi·dent·ly [ˈkɑːnfɪdəntlɪ] *adv* con seguridad

con·fine [kənˈfaɪn] *v/t* (*imprison*) confinar, recluir; (*restrict*) limitar; **be confined to one's bed** tener que guardar cama

con·fined [kənˈfaɪnd] *adj space* limitado

con·fine·ment [kənˈfaɪnmənt] (*imprisonment*) reclusión *f*; MED parto *m*

con·firm [kənˈfɜːrm] *v/t* confirmar

con·fir·ma·tion [kɑːnfərˈmeɪʃn] confirmación *f*

con·firmed [kɑːnˈfɜːrmd] *adj* (*inveterate*) empedernido; **I'm a confirmed believer in ...** creo firmemente en ...

con·fis·cate [ˈkɑːnfɪskeɪt] *v/t* confiscar

con·flict **1** *n* [ˈkɑːnflɪkt] conflicto *m* **2** *v/i* [kənˈflɪkt] (*clash*) chocar; **conflicting loyalties** lealtades *fpl* encontradas

con·form [kənˈfɔːrm] *v/i* ser conformista; **conform to** *to standards etc* ajustarse a

con·form·ist [kənˈfɔːrmɪst] *n* conformista *m/f*

con·front [kənˈfrʌnt] *v/t* (*face*) hacer frente a, enfrentarse; (*tackle*) hacer frente a

con·fron·ta·tion [kɑːnfrənˈteɪʃn] confrontación *f*, enfrentamiento *m*

con·fuse [kənˈfjuːz] *v/t* confundir; **confuse s.o. with s.o.** confundir a alguien con alguien

con·fused [kənˈfjuːzd] *adj person* confundido; *situation, piece of writing* confuso

con·fus·ing [kənˈfjuːzɪŋ] *adj* confuso

con·fu·sion [kənˈfjuːʒn] (*muddle, chaos*) confusión *f*

con·geal [kənˈdʒiːl] *v/i of blood* coagularse; *of fat* solidificarse

con·gen·ial [kənˈdʒiːnɪəl] *adj person* simpático, agradable; *occasion, place* agradable

con·gen·i·tal [kənˈdʒenɪtl] *adj* MED congénito

con·gest·ed [kənˈdʒestɪd] *adj roads* congestionado

con·ges·tion [kənˈdʒestʃn] *also* MED congestión *f*; **traffic congestion** congestión *f* circulatoria

con·grat·u·late [kənˈɡrætʃuleɪt] *v/t* felicitar

con·grat·u·la·tions [kənɡrætʃuˈleɪʃnz] *npl* felicitaciones *fpl*; **congratulations on ...** felicidades por ...; **let me offer my congratulations** permita que le dé la enhorabuena

con·grat·u·la·to·ry [kənɡrætʃuˈleɪtərɪ] *adj* de felicitación

con·gre·gate [ˈkɑːnɡrɪgeɪt] *v/i* (*gather*) congregarse

con·gre·ga·tion [kɑːnɡrɪˈgeɪʃn] REL congregación *f*

con·gress [ˈkɑːnɡres] (*conference*) congreso *m*; **Congress** *in US* Congreso *m*

Con·gres·sion·al [kənˈɡreʃnl] *adj* del Congreso

Con·gress·man [ˈkɑːnɡresmən] congresista *m*

Con·gress·wo·man [ˈkɑːnɡreswumən] congresista *f*

co·ni·fer [ˈkɑːnɪfər] conífera *f*

con·jec·ture [kənˈdʒektʃər] *n* (*speculation*) conjetura *f*

con·ju·gate [ˈkɑːndʒugeɪt] *v/t* GRAM conjugar

con·junc·tion [kənˈdʒʌŋkʃn] GRAM conjunción *f*; **in conjunction with** junto con

con·junc·ti·vi·tis [kəndʒʌŋktɪˈvaɪtɪs] conjuntivitis *f*

◆ con·jure up [ˈkʌndʒər] *v/t* (*produce*) hacer aparecer; (*evoke*) evocar

con·jur·er, con·jur·or [ˈkʌndʒərər] (*magician*) prestidigitador(a) *m(f)*

con·jur·ing tricks [ˈkʌndʒərɪŋ] *npl* juegos *mpl* de manos

con man [ˈkɑːnmæn] F timador *m* F

con·nect [kəˈnekt] *v/t* conectar; (*link*) relacionar, vincular; *to power supply* enchufar

con·nect·ed [kəˈnektɪd] *adj*: **be well-connected** estar bien relacionado; **be connected with** estar relacionado con

con·nect·ing flight [kəˈnektɪŋ] vuelo *m* de conexión

con·nec·tion [kəˈnekʃn] conexión *f*; *when traveling* conexión *f*, enlace; (*personal contact*) contacto *m*; *in connection with* en relación con

con·nois·seur [kɑːnəˈsɜːr] entendido(-a) *m*(*f*)

con·quer [ˈkɑːŋkər] *v/t* conquistar; *fig: fear etc* vencer

con·quer·or [ˈkɑːŋkərər] conquistador(a) *m*(*f*)

con·quest [ˈkɑːŋkwest] *of territory* conquista *f*

con·science [ˈkɑːnʃəns] conciencia *f*; *a guilty conscience* un sentimiento de culpa; *it was on my conscience* me remordía la conciencia

con·sci·en·tious [kɑːnʃɪˈenʃəs] *adj* concienzudo

con·sci·en·tious·ness [kɑːnʃɪˈenʃəsnəs] aplicación *f*

con·sci·en·tious ob'ject·or objetor(a) *m*(*f*) de conciencia

con·scious [ˈkɑːnʃəs] *adj* consciente; *be conscious of* ser consciente de

con·scious·ly [ˈkɑːnʃəslɪ] *adv* conscientemente

con·scious·ness [ˈkɑːnʃəsnəs] (*awareness*) conciencia *f*; MED con(s)ciencia *f*; *lose / regain consciousness* quedar inconsciente / volver en sí

con·sec·u·tive [kənˈsekjʊtɪv] *adj* consecutivo

con·sen·sus [kənˈsensəs] consenso *m*

con·sent [kənˈsent] **1** *n* consentimiento *m* **2** *v/i* consentir (*to* en)

con·se·quence [ˈkɑːnsɪkwəns] (*result*) consecuencia *f*; *as a consequence of* como consecuencia de

con·se·quent·ly [ˈkɑːnsɪkwəntlɪ] *adv* (*therefore*) por consiguiente

con·ser·va·tion [kɑːnsərˈveɪʃn] (*preservation*) conservación *f*, protección *f*

con·ser·va·tion·ist [kɑːnsərˈveɪʃnɪst] ecologista *m/f*

con·ser·va·tive [kənˈsɜːrvətɪv] **1** *adj* (*conventional*) conservador; *estimate* prudente **2** *n Br* POL *Conservative* Con-

servador(a) *m*(*f*)

con·ser·va·to·ry [kənˈsɜːrvətɔːrɪ] MUS conservatorio *m*

con·serve 1 *n* [ˈkɑːnsɜːrv] (*jam*) compota *f* **2** *v/t* [kənˈsɜːrv] conservar

con·sid·er [kənˈsɪdər] *v/t* (*regard*) considerar; (*show regard for*) mostrar consideración por; (*think about*) considerar; *it is considered to be ...* se considera que es ...

con·sid·e·ra·ble [kənˈsɪdrəbl] *adj* considerable

con·sid·e·ra·bly [kənˈsɪdrəblɪ] *adv* considerablemente

con·sid·er·ate [kənˈsɪdərət] *adj* considerado

con·sid·er·ate·ly [kənˈsɪdərətlɪ] *adv* con consideración

con·sid·e·ra·tion [kənsɪdəˈreɪʃn] (*thoughtfulness, concern*) consideración *f*; (*factor*) factor *m*; *take sth into consideration* tomar algo en consideración; *after much consideration* tras muchas deliberaciones; *your proposal is under consideration* su propuesta está siendo estudiada

con·sign·ment [kənˈsaɪnmənt] COM envío *m*

♦ **con·sist of** [kənˈsɪst] *v/t* consistir en

con·sis·ten·cy [kənˈsɪstənsɪ] (*texture*) consistencia *f*; (*unchangingness*) coherencia *f*, consecuencia *f*; *of player* regularidad *f*, constancia *f*

con·sis·tent [kənˈsɪstənt] *adj person* coherente, consecuente; *improvement*, *change* constante

con·sis·tent·ly [kənˈsɪstəntlɪ] *adv* perform con regularidad *or* constancia; *improve* continuamente; *he's consistently late* llega tarde sistemáticamente

con·so·la·tion [kɑːnsəˈleɪʃn] consuelo *m*; *if it's any consolation* si te sirve de consuelo

con·sole [kənˈsoul] *v/t* consolar

con·sol·i·date [kənˈsɑːlɪdeɪt] *v/t* consolidar

con·so·nant [ˈkɑːnsənənt] *n* GRAM consonante *f*

con·sor·ti·um [kənˈsɔːrtɪəm] consorcio

C

m

con·spic·u·ous [kənˈspɪkjʊəs] *adj* llamativo; **he felt very conspicuous** sentía que estaba llamando la atención

con·spi·ra·cy [kənˈspɪrəsɪ] conspiración *f*

con·spi·ra·tor [kənˈspɪrətər] conspirador(a) *m(f)*

con·spire [kənˈspaɪr] *v/i* conspirar

con·stant [ˈkɑːnstənt] *adj (continuous)* constante

con·stant·ly [ˈkɑːnstəntlɪ] *adv* constantemente

con·ster·na·tion [kɑːnstərˈneɪʃn] consternación *f*

con·sti·pat·ed [ˈkɑːnstɪpeɪtɪd] *adj* estreñido

con·sti·pa·tion [kɑːnstɪˈpeɪʃn] estreñimiento *m*

con·sti·tu·ent [kənˈstɪtjʊənt] *n (component)* elemento *m* constitutivo, componente *m*

con·sti·tute [ˈkɑːnstɪtuːt] *v/t* constituir

con·sti·tu·tion [kɑːnstɪˈtuːʃn] constitución *f*

con·sti·tu·tion·al [kɑːnstɪˈtuːʃnl] *adj* POL constitucional

con·straint [kənˈstreɪnt] *(restriction)* restricción *f*, límite *m*

con·struct [kənˈstrʌkt] *v/t building etc* construir

con·struc·tion [kənˈstrʌkʃn] construcción *f*; **under construction** en construcción

conˈstruc·tion in·dus·try sector *m* de la construcción

conˈstruc·tion site obra *f*

conˈstruc·tion work·er obrero(-a) *m(f)* de la construcción

con·struc·tive [kənˈstrʌktɪv] *adj* constructivo

con·sul [ˈkɑːnsl] cónsul *m/f*

con·su·late [ˈkɑːnsʊlət] consulado *m*

con·sult [kənˈsʌlt] *v/t (seek the advice of)* consultar

con·sul·tan·cy [kənˈsʌltənsɪ] *company* consultoría *f*, asesoría *f*; *(advice)* asesoramiento *m*

con·sul·tant [kənˈsʌltənt] *n (adviser)* asesor(a) *m(f)*, consultor(a) *m(f)*

con·sul·ta·tion [kɑːnslˈteɪʃn] consulta *f*; **have a consultation with** consultar con

con·sume [kənˈsuːm] *v/t* consumir

con·sum·er [kənˈsuːmər] *(purchaser)* consumidor(a) *m(f)*

con·sum·er ˈcon·fi·dence confianza *f* de los consumidores

con·sum·er goods *npl* bienes *mpl* de consumo

con·sum·er so·ci·e·ty sociedad *f* de consumo

con·sump·tion [kənˈsʌmpʃn] consumo *m*

con·tact [ˈkɑːntækt] **1** *n* contacto; **keep in contact with s.o.** mantenerse en contacto con alguien; **come into contact with s.o.** entrar en contacto con alguien **2** *v/t* contactar con, ponerse en contacto con

ˈcon·tact lens lentes *fpl* de contacto, *Span* lentillas *fpl*

ˈcon·tact num·ber número *m* de contacto

con·ta·gious [kənˈteɪdʒəs] *adj also fig* contagioso

con·tain [kənˈteɪn] *v/t (hold, hold back)* contener; **contain o.s.** contenerse

con·tain·er [kənˈteɪnər] *(recipient)* recipiente *m*; COM contenedor *m*

conˈtain·er ship buque *m* de transporte de contenedores

con·tam·i·nate [kənˈtæmɪneɪt] *v/t* contaminar

con·tam·i·na·tion [kəntæmɪˈneɪʃn] contaminación *f*

con·tem·plate [ˈkɑːntəmpleɪt] *v/t* contemplar

con·tem·po·ra·ry [kənˈtempərerɪ] **1** *adj* contemporáneo **2** *n* contemporáneo(-a) *m(f)*

con·tempt [kənˈtempt] desprecio *m*, desdén *m*; **be beneath contempt** ser despreciable

con·temp·ti·ble [kənˈtemptəbl] *adj* despreciable

con·temp·tu·ous [kənˈtemptʊəs] *adj* despectivo

con·tend [kənˈtend] *v/i*: **contend for …** competir por …; **contend with** enfrentarse a

con·tend·er [kənˈtendər] SP, POL contendiente *m/f*; **against champion** aspirante m/f

con·tent¹ ['kɑːntent] n contenido m

con·tent² [kən'tent] **1** adj satisfecho; **I'm quite content to sit here** me contento con sentarme aquí **2** v/t: **content o.s. with** contentarse con

con·tent·ed [kən'tentɪd] adj satisfecho

con·ten·tion [kən'tenʃn] (*assertion*) argumento m; **be in contention for** tener posibilidades de ganar

con·ten·tious [kən'tenʃəs] adj polémico

con·tent·ment [kən'tentmənt] satisfacción f

con·tents ['kɑːntents] npl of house, letter, bag etc contenido m; list: in book tabla f de contenidos

con·test¹ ['kɑːntest] n (*competition*) concurso m; (*struggle, for power*) lucha f

con·test² [kən'test] v/t leadership etc presentarse como candidato a; *decision, will* impugnar

con·tes·tant [kən'testənt] concursante m/f; in competition competidor(a) m(f)

con·text ['kɑːntekst] contexto m; **look at sth in context / out of context** examinar algo en contexto / fuera de contexto

con·ti·nent ['kɑːntɪnənt] n continente m

con·ti·nen·tal [kɑːntɪ'nentl] adj continental

con·tin·gen·cy [kən'tɪndʒənsɪ] contingencia f, eventualidad f

con·tin·u·al [kən'tɪnjʊəl] adj continuo

con·tin·u·al·ly [kən'tɪnjʊəlɪ] adv continuamente

con·tin·u·a·tion [kəntɪnjʊ'eɪʃn] continuación f

con·tin·ue [kən'tɪnjuː] **1** v/t continuar; **to be continued** continuará; **he continued to drink** continuó bebiendo **2** v/i continuar

con·ti·nu·i·ty [kɑːntɪ'njuːətɪ] continuidad f

con·tin·u·ous [kən'tɪnjʊəs] adj continuo

con·tin·u·ous·ly [kən'tɪnjʊəslɪ] adv continuamente, ininterrumpidamente

con·tort [kən'tɔːrt] v/t face contraer; body contorsionar

con·tour ['kɑːntʊr] contorno m

con·tra·cep·tion [kɑːntrə'sepʃn] anticon-

cepción f

con·tra·cep·tive [kɑːntrə'septɪv] n (*device, pill*) anticonceptivo m

con·tract¹ ['kɑːntrækt] n contrato m

con·tract² [kən'trækt] **1** v/i (*shrink*) contraerse **2** v/t illness contraer

con·trac·tor [kən'træktər] contratista m/f; **building contractor** constructora f

con·trac·tu·al [kən'træktʊəl] adj contractual

con·tra·dict [kɑːntrə'dɪkt] v/t statement desmentir; *person* contradecir

con·tra·dic·tion [kɑːntrə'dɪkʃn] contradicción f

con·tra·dic·to·ry [kɑːntrə'dɪktərɪ] adj account contradictorio

con·trap·tion [kən'træpʃn] F artilugio m F

con·tra·ry¹ ['kɑːntrərɪ] **1** adj contrario; **contrary to** al contrario de **2** n: **on the contrary** al contrario

con·tra·ry² [kən'trerɪ] adj (*perverse*) difícil

con·trast **1** n ['kɑːntræst] contraste m; **by contrast** por contraste **2** v/t & v/i [kən'træst] contrastar

con·trast·ing [kən'træstɪŋ] adj opuesto

con·tra·vene [kɑːntrə'viːn] v/t contravenir

con·trib·ute [kən'trɪbjuːt] **1** v/i contribuir (**to** a) **2** v/t money, time, suggestion contribuir con, aportar

con·tri·bu·tion [kɑːntrɪ'bjuːʃn] money contribución f; to political party, church donación f; of time, effort, to debate contribución f, aportación f; to magazine colaboración f

con·trib·u·tor [kən'trɪbjutər] of money donante m/f; to magazine colaborador(a) m(f)

con·trol [kən'troʊl] **1** n control m; **take / lose control of** tomar / perder el control de; **lose control of o.s.** perder el control; **circumstances beyond our control** circunstancias ajenas a nuestra voluntad; **be in control of** controlar; **we're in control of the situation** tenemos la situación controlada or bajo control; **get out of control** descontrolarse; **under control** bajo control; **controls** of air-

C

craft, vehicle controles *mpl; (restrictions)* controles *mpl* **2** *v/t (pret & pp* **controlled**) *(govern)* controlar, dominar; *(restrict, regulate)* controlar; **control o.s.** controlarse

con·trol cen·ter, *Br* **con·trol centre** centro *m* de control

con·trol freak F *persona obsesionada con controlar todo*

con·trolled 'sub·stance [kən'trould] estupefaciente *m*

con·trol·ling 'in·ter·est [kən'troulɪŋ] FIN participación *f* mayoritaria, interés *m* mayoritario

con·trol pan·el panel *m* de control

con·trol tow·er torre *f* de control

con·tro·ver·sial [kɑːntrə'vɜːrʃl] *adj* polémico, controvertido

con·tro·ver·sy ['kɑːntrəvɜːrsɪ] polémica *f*, controversia *f*

con·va·lesce [kɑːnə'les] *v/i* convalecer

con·va·les·cence [kɑːnə'lesns] convalecencia *f*

con·vene [kən'viːn] *v/t* convocar

con·ve·ni·ence [kən'viːnɪəns] conveniencia *f;* **at your / my convenience** a su / mi conveniencia; **all (modern) conveniences** todas las comodidades

con·ve·ni·ence food comida *f* preparada

con·ve·ni·ence store tienda *f* de barrio

con·ve·ni·ent [kən'viːnɪənt] *adj location, device* conveniente; *time, arrangement* oportuno; **it's very convenient living so near the office** vivir cerca de la oficina es muy cómodo; **the apartment is convenient for the station** el apartamento está muy cerca de la estación; **I'm afraid Monday isn't convenient** me temo que el lunes no me va bien

con·ve·ni·ent·ly [kən'viːnɪəntlɪ] *adv* convenientemente; **conveniently located for theaters** situado cerca de los teatros

con·vent ['kɑːnvənt] convento *m*

con·ven·tion [kən'venʃn] *(tradition)* convención *f; (conference)* congreso *m*

con·ven·tion·al [kən'venʃnl] *adj* convencional

con·ven·tion cen·ter palacio *m* de congresos

con·ven·tion·eer [kən'venʃnɪr] congresista *m/f*

◆ **con·verge on** [kən'vɜːrdʒ] *v/t* converger en

con·ver·sant [kən'vɜːrsənt] *adj:* **be conversant with** estar familiarizado con

con·ver·sa·tion [kɑːnvər'seɪʃn] conversación *f;* **make conversation** conversar; **have a conversation** mantener una conversación

con·ver·sa·tion·al [kɑːnvər'seɪʃnl] *adj* coloquial

con·verse ['kɑːnvɜːrs] *n (opposite):* **the converse** lo opuesto

con·verse·ly [kən'vɜːrslɪ] *adv* por el contrario

con·ver·sion [kən'vɜːrʃn] conversión *f*

con·ver·sion ta·ble tabla *f* de conversión

con·vert **1** *n* ['kɑːnvɜːrt] converso(-a) *m(f)* **(to** a) **2** *v/t* [kən'vɜːrt] convertir

con·ver·ti·ble [kən'vɜːrtəbl] *n car* descapotable *m*

con·vey [kən'veɪ] *v/t (transmit)* transmitir; *(carry)* transportar

con·vey·or belt [kən'veɪər] cinta *f* transportadora

con·vict 1 *n* ['kɑːnvɪkt] convicto(-a) *m(f)* **2** *v/t* [kən'vɪkt] LAW: **convict s.o. of sth** declarar a alguien culpable de algo

con·vic·tion [kən'vɪkʃn] LAW condena *f; (belief)* convicción *f*

con·vince [kən'vɪns] *v/t* convencer; **I'm convinced he's lying** estoy convencido de que miente

con·vinc·ing [kən'vɪnsɪŋ] *adj* convincente

con·viv·i·al [kən'vɪvɪəl] *adj (friendly)* agradable

con·voy ['kɑːnvɔɪ] *of ships, vehicles* convoy *m*

con·vul·sion [kən'vʌlʃn] MED convulsión *f*

cook [kuk] **1** *n* cocinero(-a) *m(f);* **I'm a good cook** soy un buen cocinero, cocino bien **2** *v/t* cocinar; **a cooked meal** una comida caliente; **cook the books** F falsificar las cuentas **3** *v/i* cocinar

'cook·book libro *m* de cocina

cook·e·ry ['kukərɪ] cocina *f*

cook·ie ['kʊkɪ] galleta *f*
cook·ing ['kʊkɪŋ] *food* cocina *f*
cool [kuːl] **1** *n*: *keep one's cool* F mantener la calma; *lose one's cool* F perder la calma **2** *adj weather, breeze* fresco; *drink* frío; *(calm)* tranquilo, sereno; *(unfriendly)* frío **3** *v/i of food, interest* enfriarse; *of tempers* calmarse **4** *v/t*: *cool it* F cálmate
◆ **cool down 1** *v/i* enfriarse; *of weather* refrescar; *fig: of tempers* calmarse, tranquilizarse **2** *v/t food* enfriar; *fig* calmar, tranquilizar
cool·ing-'off pe·ri·od fase *f* de reflexión
co·op·e·rate [koʊ'ɑːpəreɪt] *v/i* cooperar
co·op·e·ra·tion [koʊɑːpə'reɪʃn] cooperación *f*
co·op·e·ra·tive [koʊ'ɑːpərətɪv] **1** *n* COM cooperativa *f* **2** *adj* COM conjunto; *(helpful)* cooperativo
co·or·di·nate [koʊ'ɔːrdɪneɪt] *v/t activities* coordinar
co·or·di·na·tion [koʊɔːrdɪ'neɪʃn] coordinación *f*
cop [kɑːp] *n* F poli *m/f* F
cope [koʊp] *v/i* arreglárselas; *cope with* poder con
cop·i·er ['kɑːpɪər] *machine* fotocopiadora *f*
co·pi·lot ['koʊpaɪlət] copiloto *m/f*
co·pi·ous ['koʊpɪəs] *adj* copioso
cop·per ['kɑːpər] *n metal* cobre *m*
cop·y ['kɑːpɪ] **1** *n* copia *f*; *of book* ejemplar *m*; *of record, CD* copia *f*; *(written material)* texto *m*; *make a copy of a file* COMPUT hacer una copia de un archivo **2** *v/t* (*pret & pp copied*) copiar
'cop·y cat F copión (-ona) *m(f)* F, copiota *m/f* F
'cop·y·cat crime delito inspirado en otro
'cop·y·right *n* copyright *m*, derechos *mpl* de reproducción
'cop·y·writ·er *in advertising* creativo(-a) *m(f)* (*de publicidad*)
cor·al ['kɑːrəl] coral *m*
cord [kɔːrd] (*string*) cuerda *f*, cordel *m*; (*cable*) cable *m*
cor·di·al ['kɔːrdʒəl] *adj* cordial
cord·less 'phone ['kɔːrdlɪs] teléfono *m*

inalámbrico
cor·don ['kɔːrdn] cordón *m*
◆ **cordon off** *v/t* acordonar
cords [kɔːrdz] *npl pants* pantalones *mpl* de pana
cor·du·roy ['kɔːrdərɔɪ] pana *f*
core [kɔːr] **1** *n of fruit* corazón *m*; *of problem* meollo *m*; *of organization, party* núcleo *m* **2** *v/t fruit* sacar el corazón a **3** *adj issue, meaning* central
co·ri·an·der ['kɑːriændər] cilantro *m*
cork [kɔːrk] *in bottle* (tapón *m* de) corcho *m*; *material* corcho *m*
'cork·screw *n* sacacorchos *m inv*
corn [kɔːrn] *grain* maíz *m*
cor·ner ['kɔːrnər] **1** *n of page, street* esquina *f*; *of room* rincón *m*; (*bend: on road*) curva *f*; *in soccer* córner *m*, saque *m* de esquina; *in the corner* en el rincón; *I'll meet you on the corner* te veré en la esquina **2** *v/t person* arrinconar; *corner a market* monopolizar un mercado **3** *v/i of driver, car* girar
'cor·ner kick *in soccer* saque *m* de esquina, córner *m*
'corn·flakes *npl* copos *mpl* de maíz
'corn·starch harina *f* de maíz
corn·y ['kɔːrnɪ] *adj* F (*sentimental*) cursi F; *joke* manido
cor·o·na·ry ['kɔːrənerɪ] **1** *adj* coronario **2** *n* infarto *m* de miocardio
cor·o·ner ['kɔːrənər] *oficial encargado de investigar muertes sospechosas*
cor·po·ral ['kɔːrpərəl] *n* cabo *m/f*
cor·po·ral 'pun·ish·ment castigo *m* corporal
cor·po·rate ['kɔːrpərət] *adj* COM corporativo, de empresa; *corporate image* imagen *f* corporativa; *corporate loyalty* lealtad *f* a la empresa
cor·po·ra·tion [kɔːrpə'reɪʃn] (*business*) sociedad *f* anónima
corps [kɔːr] *nsg* cuerpo *m*
corpse [kɔːrps] cadáver *m*
cor·pu·lent ['kɔːrpjʊlənt] *adj* corpulento
cor·pus·cle ['kɔːrpʌsl] corpúsculo *m*
cor·ral [kə'ræl] *n* corral *m*
cor·rect [kə'rekt] **1** *adj* correcto; *time* exacto; *you are correct* tiene razón **2** *v/t*

C

corregir

cor·rec·tion [kə'rekʃn] corrección f

cor·rect·ly [kə'rektlɪ] adv correctamente

cor·re·spond [kɑːrɪ'spɑːnd] v/i (match) corresponderse; **correspond to** corresponder a; **correspond with** corresponderse con; (write letters) mantener correspondencia con

cor·re·spon·dence [kɑːrɪ'spɑːndəns] (matching) correspondencia f, relación f; (letters) correspondencia f

cor·re·spon·dent [kɑːrɪ'spɑːndənt] (letter writer) correspondiente m/f; (reporter) corresponsal m/f

cor·re·spon·ding [kɑːrɪ'spɑːndɪŋ] adj (equivalent) correspondiente

cor·ri·dor ['kɔːrɪdər] in building pasillo m

cor·rob·o·rate [kə'rɑːbəreɪt] v/t corroborar

cor·rode [kə'roʊd] **1** v/t corroer **2** v/i corroerse

cor·ro·sion [kə'roʊʒn] corrosión f

cor·ru·gat·ed 'card·board ['kɑːrəgeɪtɪd] cartón m ondulado

cor·ru·gat·ed 'i·ron chapa f ondulada

cor·rupt [kə'rʌpt] **1** adj corrupto; COMPUT corrompido **2** v/t corromper; (bribe) sobornar

cor·rup·tion [kə'rʌpʃn] corrupción f

cos·met·ic [kɑːz'metɪk] adj cosmético; fig superficial

cos·met·ics [kɑːz'metɪks] npl cosméticos mpl

cos·met·ic 'sur·geon especialista m/f en cirugía estética

cos·met·ic 'sur·ger·y cirugía f estética

cos·mo·naut ['kɑːzmənɔːt] cosmonauta m/f

cos·mo·pol·i·tan [kɑːzmə'pɑːlɪtən] adj city cosmopolitano

cost[1] [kɑːst] **1** n also fig costo m, Span coste m; **at all costs** cueste lo que cueste; **I've learnt to my cost** por desgracia he aprendido **2** v/t (pret & pp **cost**) money, time costar; **how much does it cost?** ¿cuánto cuesta?; **it cost me my health** me costó mi salud

cost[2] [kɑːst] v/t (pret & pp **costed**) FIN proposal, project estimar el costo de

cost and 'freight COM costo or Span coste y flete

Cos·ta Ri·ca ['kɑːstə'riːkə] n Costa Rica

Cos·ta Ri·can ['kɑːstə'riːkən] **1** adj costarricense **2** n costarricense m/f

'cost-con·scious adj consciente del costo or Span coste

'cost-ef·fec·tive adj rentable

'cost, in·sur·ance, freight COM costo or Span coste, seguro y flete

cost·ly [kɑːstlɪ] adj mistake caro

cost of 'liv·ing costo m or Span coste m de la vida

cost 'price precio m de costo or Span coste

cos·tume ['kɑːstuːm] for actor traje m

cos·tume 'jew·el·lery Br, **costume** 'jew·el·ry bisutería f

'cos·y Br → **cozy**

cot [kɑːt] (camp-bed) catre m

cott·age ['kɑːtɪdʒ] casa f de campo, casita f

cot·tage 'cheese queso m fresco

cot·ton ['kɑːtn] **1** n algodón m **2** adj de algodón

◆ **cotton on** v/i F darse cuenta

◆ **cotton on to** v/t F darse cuenta de

◆ **cotton to** v/t F: **I never cottoned to her** nunca me cayó bien

cot·ton 'can·dy algodón m dulce

cot·ton 'wool Br algodón m (hidrófilo)

couch [kaʊtʃ] n sofá m

'couch po·ta·to F teleadicto(-a) m(f) F

cou·chette [kuː'ʃet] litera f

cough [kɑːf] **1** n tos f; to get attention carraspeo m **2** v/i toser; to get attention carraspear

◆ **cough up 1** v/t blood etc toser; F money soltar, Span apoquinar F **2** v/i F (pay) soltar dinero, Span apoquinar F

'cough med·i·cine, 'cough syr·up jarabe m para la tos

could [kʊd] **1** v/aux: **could I have my key?** ¿me podría dar la llave?; **could you help me?** ¿me podrías ayudar?; **this could be our bus** puede que éste sea nuestro autobús; **you could be right** puede que tengas razón; **I couldn't say for sure** no sabría decirlo con seguridad;

he could have got lost a lo mejor se ha perdido; *you could have warned me!* ¡me podías haber avisado! **2** *pret* → *can¹*

coun·cil ['kaʊnsl] *n (assembly)* consejo *m*

'**coun·cil·man** concejal *m*

coun·cil·or ['kaʊnsələr] concejal(a) *m(f)*

coun·sel ['kaʊnsl] **1** *n (advice)* consejo *m*; *(lawyer)* abogado(-a) *m(f)* **2** *v/t course of action* aconsejar; *person* ofrecer apoyo psicológico

coun·sel·ing, *Br* **coun·sel·ling** ['kaʊnslɪŋ] apoyo *m* psicológico

coun·sel·lor *Br*, **coun·sel·or** ['kaʊnslər] *(adviser)* consejero(-a) *m(f)*; *of student* orientador(a) *m(f)*; LAW abogado(-a) *m(f)*

count¹ [kaʊnt] **1** *n (number arrived at)* cuenta *f*; *(action of counting)* recuento *m*; *in baseball, boxing* cuenta *f*; *what is your count?* ¿cuántos has contado?; *keep count of* llevar la cuenta de; *lose count of* perder la cuenta de; *at the last count* en el último recuento **2** *v/i to ten etc* contar; *(be important)* contar; *(qualify)* contar, valer **3** *v/t* contar

♦ **count on** *v/t* contar con

count² [kaʊnt] *nobleman* conde *m*

'**count·down** cuenta *f* atrás

coun·te·nance ['kaʊntənəns] *v/t* tolerar

coun·ter¹ ['kaʊntər] *n in shop* mostrador *m*; *in café* barra *f*; *in game* ficha *f*

coun·ter² ['kaʊntər] **1** *v/t* contrarrestar **2** *v/i (retaliate)* responder

coun·ter³ ['kaʊntər] *adv*: *run counter to* estar en contra de

'**coun·ter·act** *v/t* contrarrestar

coun·ter·at·tack 1 *n* contraataque *m* **2** *v/i* contraatacar

'**coun·ter·bal·ance 1** *n* contrapeso *m* **2** *v/t* contrarrestar, contrapesar

coun·ter'clock·wise *adv* en sentido contrario al de las agujas del reloj

'**coun·ter·es·pi·o·nage** contraespionaje *m*

coun·ter·feit ['kaʊntərfɪt] **1** *v/t* falsificar **2** *adj* falso

'**coun·ter·part** *(person)* homólogo(-a) *m(f)*

coun·ter·pro·duc·tive *adj* contraproduc-

cente

'**coun·ter·sign** *v/t* refrendar

coun·tess ['kaʊntes] condesa *f*

count·less ['kaʊntlɪs] *adj* incontables

coun·try ['kʌntrɪ] *n (nation)* país *m*; *as opposed to town* campo *m*; *in the country* en el campo

coun·try and 'west·ern MUS música *f* country

'**coun·try·man** *(fellow countryman)* compatriota *m*

'**coun·try·side** campo *m*

coun·ty ['kaʊntɪ] condado *m*

coup [kuː] POL golpe *m (de Estado)*; *fig* golpe *m* de efecto

cou·ple ['kʌpl] *n* pareja *f*; *just a couple* un par; *a couple of* un par de

cou·pon ['kuːpɑːn] cupón *m*

cour·age ['kʌrɪdʒ] valor *m*, coraje *m*

cou·ra·geous [kə'reɪdʒəs] *adj* valiente

cou·ra·geous·ly [kə'reɪdʒəslɪ] *adv* valientemente

cou·ri·er ['kʊrɪr] *(messenger)* mensajero(-a) *m(f)*; *with tourist party* guía *m/f*

course [kɔːrs] *n (series of lessons)* curso *m*; *(part of meal)* plato *m*; *of ship, plane* rumbo *m*; *for horse race* circuito *m*; *for golf* campo *m*; *for skiing, marathon* recorrido *m*; *change course* of ship, plane cambiar de rumbo; *of course (certainly)* claro, por supuesto; *(naturally)* por supuesto; *of course not* claro que no; *course of action* táctica *f*; *course of treatment* tratamiento *m*; *in the course of ...* durante ...

court [kɔːrt] *n* LAW tribunal *m*; *(courthouse)* palacio *m* de justicia; SP pista *f*, cancha *f*; *take s.o. to court* llevar a alguien a juicio

'**court case** proceso *m*, causa *f*

cour·te·ous ['kɜːrtɪəs] *adj* cortés

cour·te·sy ['kɜːrtəsɪ] cortesía *f*

'**court·house** palacio *m* de justicia

court 'mar·tial 1 *n* consejo *m* de guerra **2** *v/t* formar un consejo de guerra a

'**court or·der** orden *f* judicial

'**court·room** sala *f* de juicios

'**court·yard** patio *m*

cous·in ['kʌzn] primo(-a) *m(f)*

C

cove [kouv] (*small bay*) cala *f*

cov·er ['kʌvər] **1** *n protective* funda *f*; *of book, magazine* portada *f*; (*shelter*) protección *f*; (*insurance*) cobertura *f*; **covers** *for bed* manta y sábanas *fpl*; **we took cover from the rain** nos pusimos a cubierto de la lluvia **2** *v/t* cubrir

◆ **cover up 1** *v/t* cubrir; *scandal* encubrir **2** *v/i* disimular; **cover up for s.o.** encubrir a alguien

cov·er·age ['kʌvərɪdʒ] *by media* cobertura *f* informativa

cov·er·ing let·ter ['kʌvrɪŋ] carta *f*

cov·ert [kou'vɜːrt] *adj* encubierto

'cov·er-up encubrimiento *m*

cow [kau] vaca *f*

cow·ard ['kauərd] cobarde *m/f*

cow·ard·ice ['kauərdɪs] cobardía *f*

cow·ard·ly ['kauərdlɪ] *adj* cobarde

'cow·boy vaquero *m*

cow·er ['kauər] *v/i* agacharse, amilanarse

co-work·er ['kouwɜːrkər] compañero(a) *m(f)* de trabajo

coy [kɔɪ] *adj* (*evasive*) evasivo; (*flirtatious*) coqueto

co·zy ['kouzɪ] *adj room* acogedor; *job* cómodo

CPU [siːpiːˈjuː] *abbr* (= **central processing unit**) CPU *f* (= unidad *f* central de proceso)

crab [kræb] *n* cangrejo *m*

crack [kræk] **1** *n* grieta *f*; *in cup, glass* raja *f*; (*joke*) chiste *m* (malo) **2** *v/t cup, glass* rajar; *nut* cascar; *code* descifrar; F (*solve*) resolver; **crack a joke** contar un chiste **3** *v/i* rajarse; **get cracking** F poner manos a la obra F

◆ **crack down on** *v/t* castigar severamente

◆ **crack up** *v/i* (*have breakdown*) sufrir una crisis nerviosa; F (*laugh*) desternillarse F

'crack-brained *adj* F chiflado F

'crack·down medidas *fpl* severas

cracked [krækt] *adj cup, glass* rajado; F (*crazy*) chiflado F

crack·er ['krækər] *to eat* galleta *f* salada

crack·le ['krækl] *v/i of fire* crepitar

cra·dle ['kreidl] *n for baby* cuna *f*

craft[1] [kræft] NAUT embarcación *f*

craft[2] [kræft] (*skill*) arte *m*; (*trade*) oficio *m*

crafts·man ['kræftsmən] artesano *m*

craft·y ['kræftɪ] *adj* astuto

crag [kræg] *rock* peñasco *m*, risco *m*

cram [kræm] *v/t* embutir

cramp [kræmp] *n* calambre *m*; **stomach cramp** retorcijón *m*

cramped [kræmpt] *adj room, apartment* pequeño

cramps [kræmps] *npl* calambre *m*; **stomach cramps** retorcijón *m*

cran·ber·ry ['krænberɪ] arándano *m* agrio

crane [kreɪn] **1** *n machine* grúa *f* **2** *v/t*: **crane one's neck** estirar el cuello

crank [kræŋk] *n person* maniático(-a) *m(f)*, persona *f* rara

'crank·shaft cigüeñal *m*

crank·y ['kræŋkɪ] *adj* (*bad-tempered*) gruñón

crash [kræʃ] **1** *n noise* estruendo *m*, estrépito *m*; *accident* accidente *m*; COM barrera *f*, crac *m*; COMPUT bloqueo *m*; **a crash of thunder** un trueno **2** *v/i of car, airplane* estrellarse (*into* con *or* contra); *of thunder* sonar; COM *of market* hundirse, desplomarse; COMPUT bloquearse, colgarse; F (*sleep*) dormir, Span sobar F; **the waves crashed onto the shore** las olas chocaban contra la orilla; **the vase crashed to the ground** el jarrón se cayó con estruendo **3** *v/t car* estrellar

◆ **crash out** *v/i* F (*fall asleep*) dormirse, Span quedarse sobado

'crash bar·ri·er quitamiedos *m inv*

'crash course curso *m* intensivo

'crash di·et dieta *f* drástica

'crash hel·met casco *m* protector

'crash-land *v/i* realizar un aterrizaje forzoso

'crash 'land·ing aterrizaje *m* forzoso

crate [kreit] (*packing case*) caja *f*

cra·ter ['kreitər] *of volcano* cráter *m*

crave [kreiv] *v/t* ansiar

crav·ing ['kreivɪŋ] ansia *f*, deseo *m*; *of pregnant woman* antojo *m*; **I have a craving for ...** me apetece muchísimo ...

crawl [krɒːl] **1** *n in swimming* crol *m*; **at a**

crawl (*very slowly*) muy lentamente **2** *v/i* on floor arrastrarse; *of baby* andar a gatas; (*move slowly*) avanzar lentamente ♦ **crawl with** *v/t* estar abarrotado de

cray·fish ['kreɪfɪʃ] *freshwater* cangrejo *m* de río; *saltwater* langosta *f*

cray·on ['kreɪɑːn] *n* lápiz *m* de color

craze [kreɪz] locura *f* (**for** de); **the latest craze** la última locura *or* moda

cra·zy ['kreɪzɪ] *adj* loco; **be crazy about** estar loco por

creak [kriːk] **1** *n of hinge, door* chirrido *m*; *of floor* crujido *m* **2** *v/i of hinge, door* chirriar; *of floor, shoes* crujir

creak·y ['kriːkɪ] *adj hinge, door* que chirria; *floor, shoes* que cruje

cream [kriːm] **1** *n for skin* crema *f*; *for coffee, cake* nata *f*; (*color*) crema *m* **2** *adj* crema

cream 'cheese queso *m* blanco para untar

cream·er ['kriːmər] (*pitcher*) jarra *f* para la nata; *for coffee* leche *f* en polvo

cream·y ['kriːmɪ] *adj with lots of cream* cremoso

crease [kriːs] **1** *n accidental* arruga *f*; *deliberate* raya *f* **2** *v/t accidentally* arrugar

cre·ate [kriːˈeɪt] *v/t & v/i* crear

cre·a·tion [kriːˈeɪʃn] creación *f*

cre·a·tive [kriːˈeɪtɪv] *adj* creativo

cre·a·tor [kriːˈeɪtər] creador(a) *m(f)*; (*founder*) fundador(a) *m(f)*; **the Creator** REL el Creador

crea·ture ['kriːtʃər] *animal, person* criatura *f*

crèche [kreʃ] *for children* guardería *f* (infantil); REL nacimiento *m*, belén *m*

cred·i·bil·i·ty [kredə'bɪlətɪ] credibilidad *f*

cred·i·ble ['kredəbl] *adj* creíble

cred·it ['kredɪt] **1** *n* FIN crédito *m*; (*honor*) crédito *m*, reconocimiento *m*; **be in credit** tener un saldo positivo; **get the credit for sth** recibir reconocimiento por algo **2** *v/t* (*believe*) creer; **would you credit it!** ¡te lo puedes creer!; **credit an amount to an account** abonar una cantidad en una cuenta

cred·i·ta·ble ['kredɪtəbl] *adj* estimable, honorable

'cred·it card tarjeta *f* de crédito

'cred·it lim·it límite *m* de crédito

cred·i·tor ['kredɪtər] acreedor(a) *m(f)*

'cred·it·wor·thy *adj* solvente

cred·u·lous ['kredʊləs] *adj* crédulo

creed [kriːd] (*beliefs*) credo *m*

creek [kriːk] (*stream*) arroyo *m*

creep [kriːp] **1** *n pej* asqueroso(-a) *m(f)* **2** *v/i* (*pret & pp crept*) moverse sigilosamente

creep·er ['kriːpər] BOT enredadera *f*

creeps [kriːps] *npl* F: **the house / he gives me the creeps** la casa / él me pone la piel de gallina F

creep·y ['kriːpɪ] *adj* F espeluznante F

cre·mate [krɪˈmeɪt] *v/t* incinerar

cre·ma·tion [krɪˈmeɪʃn] incineración *f*

cre·ma·to·ri·um [kreməˈtɔːrɪəm] crematorio *m*

crept [krept] *pret & pp* → **creep**

cres·cent ['kresənt] *n shape* medialuna *f*; **crescent moon** cuarto *m* creciente

crest [krest] *of hill* cima *f*; *of bird* cresta *f*

crest·fal·len *adj* abatido

crev·ice ['krevɪs] grieta *f*

crew [kruː] *n of ship, airplane* tripulación *f*; *of repairmen etc* equipo *m*; (*crowd, group*) grupo *m*, pandilla *f*

'crew cut rapado *m*

'crew neck cuello *m* redondo

crib [krɪb] *n for baby* cuna *f*

crick [krɪk]: **have a crick in the neck** tener tortícolis

crick·et ['krɪkɪt] *insect* grillo *m*

crime [kraɪm] (*offense*) delito *m*; *serious, also fig* crimen *m*

crim·i·nal ['krɪmɪnl] **1** *n* delincuente *m/f*, criminal *m/f* **2** *adj* (*relating to crime*) criminal; (LAW: *not civil*) penal; (*shameful*) vergonzoso; *act* delictivo; **it's criminal** (*shameful*) es un crimen

crim·son ['krɪmzn] *adj* carmesí

cringe [krɪndʒ] *v/i with embarrassment* sentir vergüenza ajena

crip·ple ['krɪpl] **1** *n* (*disabled person*) inválido(-a) *m(f)* **2** *v/t person* dejar inválido; *fig: country, engine* paralizar

cri·sis ['kraɪsɪs] (*pl* **crises** ['kraɪsiːz]) crisis *f inv* crisp [krɪsp] adj weather, air fresco; lettuce, apple, bacon crujiente; new shirt, bills flamante

cri·te·ri·on [kraɪ'tɪrɪən] (standard) criterio m

crit·ic ['krɪtɪk] crítico(-a) m(f)

crit·i·cal ['krɪtɪkl] adj (making criticisms, serious) crítico; moment etc decisivo

crit·i·cal·ly ['krɪtɪklɪ] adv speak etc en tono de crítica; critically ill en estado crítico

crit·i·cism ['krɪtɪsɪzm] crítica f

crit·i·cize ['krɪtɪsaɪz] v/t criticar

croak [krouk] 1 n of frog croar m 2 v/i of frog croar

cro·chet ['krouʃeɪ] 1 n ganchillo m 2 v/t hacer a ganchillo

crock·e·ry ['krɑːkərɪ] vajilla f

croc·o·dile ['krɑːkədaɪl] cocodrilo m

cro·cus ['kroukəs] azafrán m

cro·ny ['krounɪ] F amiguete m/f F

crook [kruk] n ladrón (-ona) m(f); dishonest trader granuja m/f

crook·ed ['krukɪd] adj (not straight) torcido; (dishonest) deshonesto

crop [krɑːp] 1 n also fig cosecha f; plant grown cultivo m 2 v/t (pret & pp cropped) hair cortar; photo recortar

◆ crop up v/i salir

cross [krɑːs] 1 adj (angry) enfadado, enojado 2 n cruz f 3 v/t (go across) cruzar; cross o.s. REL santiguarse; cross one's legs cruzar las piernas; keep one's fingers crossed cruzar los dedos; it never crossed my mind no se me ocurrió 4 v/i (go across) cruzar; of lines cruzarse, cortarse

◆ cross off, cross out v/t tachar

'cross·bar of goal larguero m; of bicycle barra f; in high jump listón m

'cross·check 1 n comprobación f 2 v/t comprobar

cross·coun·try ('ski·ing) esquí m de fondo

crossed 'check, Br crossed 'cheque [krɑːst] cheque m cruzado

cross·ex·am·i'na·tion LAW interrogatorio m

cross·ex'am·ine v/t LAW interrogar

cross·'eyed adj bizco

cross·ing ['krɑːsɪŋ] NAUT travesía f

'cross·roads nsg also fig encrucijada f

'cross·sec·tion of people muestra f representativa

'cross·walk paso m de peatones

'cross·word (puz·zle) crucigrama m

crotch [krɑːtʃ] of person, pants entrepierna f

crouch [krautʃ] v/i agacharse

crow [krou] n bird corneja f; as the crow flies en línea recta

'crow·bar palanca f

crowd [kraud] n multitud f, muchedumbre f; at sports event público m

crowd·ed ['kraudɪd] adj abarrotado (with de)

crown [kraun] 1 n on head, tooth corona f 2 v/t tooth poner una corona a

cru·cial ['kruːʃl] adj crucial

cru·ci·fix ['kruːsɪfɪks] crucifijo m

cru·ci·fix·ion [kruːsɪ'fɪkʃn] crucifixión f

cru·ci·fy ['kruːsɪfaɪ] v/t (pret & pp crucified) also fig crucificar

crude [kruːd] 1 adj (vulgar) grosero; (unsophisticated) primitivo 2 n: crude (oil) crudo m

crude·ly ['kruːdlɪ] adv speak groseramente; made de manera primitiva

cru·el ['kruːəl] adj cruel (to con)

cru·el·ty ['kruːəltɪ] crueldad f (to con)

cruise [kruːz] 1 n crucero m; go on a cruise ir de crucero 2 v/i of people hacer un crucero; of car ir a velocidad de crucero; of plane volar

'cruise lin·er transatlántico m

cruis·ing speed ['kruːzɪŋ] of vehicle velocidad f de crucero; fig: of project etc ritmo m normal

crumb [krʌm] miga f

crum·ble ['krʌmbl] 1 v/t desmigajar 2 v/i of bread desmigajarse; of stonework desmenuzarse; fig: of opposition etc desmoronarse

crum·bly ['krʌmblɪ] adj cookie que se desmigaja; stonework que se desmenuza

crum·ple ['krʌmpl] 1 v/t (crease) arrugar 2 v/i (collapse) desplomarse

crunch [krʌntʃ] 1 n: when it comes to the

C

crunch a la hora de la verdad **2** *v/i of snow, gravel* crujir

cru·sade [kruːˈseɪd] *n also fig* cruzada *f*

crush [krʌʃ] **1** *n (crowd)* muchedumbre *f*; **have a crush on** estar loco por **2** *v/t* aplastar; *(crease)* arrugar; **they were crushed to death** murieron aplastados **3** *v/i (crease)* arrugarse

crust [krʌst] *on bread* corteza *f*

crust·y [ˈkrʌstɪ] *adj bread* crujiente

crutch [krʌtʃ] *for injured person* muleta *f*

cry [kraɪ] **1** *n (call)* grito *m*; **have a cry** llorar **2** *v/t (pret & pp cried) (call)* gritar **3** *v/i (pret & pp cried) (weep)* llorar

♦ **cry out** *v/t & v/i* gritar

♦ **cry out for** *v/t (need)* pedir a gritos

cryp·tic [ˈkrɪptɪk] *adj* críptico

crys·tal [ˈkrɪstl] *n* cristal *m*

crys·tal·lize [ˈkrɪstəlaɪz] **1** *v/t* cristalizar **2** *v/i* cristalizarse

cub [kʌb] cachorro *m*; *of bear* osezno *m*

Cu·ba [ˈkjuːbə] Cuba

Cu·ban [ˈkjuːbən] **1** *adj* cubano **2** *n* cubano(-a) *m(f)*

cube [kjuːb] *shape* cubo *m*

cu·bic [ˈkjuːbɪk] *adj* cúbico

cu·bic ca'pac·i·ty TECH cilindrada *f*

cu·bi·cle [ˈkjuːbɪkl] *(changing room)* cubículo *m*

cu·cum·ber [ˈkjuːkʌmbər] pepino *m*

cud·dle [ˈkʌdl] **1** *n* abrazo **2** *v/t* abrazar

cud·dly [ˈkʌdlɪ] *adj kitten etc* tierno

cue [kjuː] *n for actor etc* pie *m*, entrada *f*; *for pool* taco *m*

cuff [kʌf] **1** *n of shirt* puño *m*; *of pants* vuelta *f*; *(blow)* cachete *m*; **off the cuff** improvisado **2** *v/t (hit)* dar un cachete a

'cuff link gemelo *m*

cul-de-sac [ˈkʌldəsæk] callejón *m* sin salida

cu·li·nar·y [ˈkʌlɪnərɪ] *adj* culinario

cul·mi·nate [ˈkʌlmɪneɪt] *v/i* culminar *(in* en)

cul·mi·na·tion [kʌlmɪˈneɪʃn] culminación *f*

cul·prit [ˈkʌlprɪt] culpable *m/f*

cult [kʌlt] *(sect)* secta *f*

cul·ti·vate [ˈkʌltɪveɪt] *v/t also fig* cultivar

cul·ti·vat·ed [ˈkʌltɪveɪtɪd] *adj person* culto

cul·ti·va·tion [kʌltɪˈveɪʃn] *of land* cultivo *m*

cul·tu·ral [ˈkʌltʃərəl] *adj* cultural

cul·ture [ˈkʌltʃər] *artistic* cultura *f*

cul·tured [ˈkʌltʃərd] *adj (cultivated)* culto

'cul·ture shock choque *m* cultural

cum·ber·some [ˈkʌmbərsəm] *adj* engorroso

cu·mu·la·tive [ˈkjuːmjʊlətɪv] *adj* acumulativo

cun·ning [ˈkʌnɪŋ] **1** *n* astucia *f* **2** *adj* astuto

cup [kʌp] *n* taza *f*; *trophy* copa *f*

cup·board [ˈkʌbərd] armario *m*

'cup fi·nal final *f* de (la) copa

cu·po·la [ˈkjuːpələ] cúpula *f*

cu·ra·ble [ˈkjʊrəbl] *adj* curable

cu·ra·tor [kjuˈreɪtər] conservador(a) *m(f)*

curb [kɜːrb] **1** *n of street* bordillo *m*; *on powers etc* freno *f* **2** *v/t* frenar

cur·dle [ˈkɜːrdl] *v/i of milk* cortarse

cure [kjʊr] **1** *n* MED cura *f* **2** *v/t* MED, *meat* curar

cur·few [ˈkɜːrfjuː] toque *m* de queda

cu·ri·os·i·ty [kjʊrɪˈɑːsətɪ] *(inquisitiveness)* curiosidad *f*

cu·ri·ous [ˈkjʊrɪəs] *adj (inquisitive, strange)* curioso

cu·ri·ous·ly [ˈkjʊrɪəslɪ] *adv (inquisitively)* con curiosidad; *(strangely)* curiosamente; **curiously enough** curiosamente

curl [kɜːrl] **1** *n in hair* rizo *m*; *of smoke* voluta *f* **2** *v/t hair* rizar; *(wind)* enroscar **3** *v/i of hair* rizarse; *of leaf, paper etc* ondularse

♦ **curl up** *v/i* acurrucarse

curl·y [ˈkɜːrlɪ] *adj hair* rizado; *tail* enroscado

cur·rant [ˈkʌrənt] *(dried fruit)* pasa *f* de Corinto

cur·ren·cy [ˈkʌrənsɪ] *money* moneda *f*; **foreign currency** divisas *fpl*

cur·rent [ˈkʌrənt] **1** *n in sea*, ELEC corriente *f* **2** *adj (present)* actual

cur·rent af'fairs, cur·rent e'vents *npl* la actualidad

cur·rent af'fairs pro·gram programa *m* de actualidad

C

'cur·rent ac·count *Br* cuenta *f* corriente
cur·rent·ly ['kʌrəntlɪ] *adv* actualmente
cur·ric·u·lum [kə'rɪkjʊləm] plan *m* de estudios
cur·ric·u·lum vi·tae ['viːtaɪ] *Br* currículum *m* vitae
cur·ry ['kʌrɪ] curry *m*
curse [kɜːrs] **1** *n* (*spell*) maldición *f*; (*swearword*) palabrota *f* **2** *v/t* maldecir; (*swear at*) insultar **3** *v/i* (*swear*) decir palabrotas
cur·sor ['kɜːrsər] COMPUT cursor *m*
cur·so·ry ['kɜːrsərɪ] *adj* rápido, superficial
curt [kɜːrt] *adj* brusco, seco
cur·tail [kɜːr'teɪl] *v/t* acortar
cur·tain ['kɜːrtn] cortina *f*; THEA telón *m*
curve [kɜːrv] **1** *n* curva *f* **2** *v/i* (*bend*) curvarse
cush·ion ['kʊʃn] **1** *n for couch etc* cojín *m* **2** *v/t blow, fall* amortiguar
cus·tard ['kʌstərd] natillas *fpl*
cus·to·dy ['kʌstədɪ] *of children* custodia *f*; **in custody** LAW detenido
cus·tom ['kʌstəm] (*tradition*) costumbre *f*; COM clientela *f*; **it's the custom in France** es costumbre en Francia; **as was his custom** como era costumbre en él; **thank you for your custom** at *shop* gracias por comprar aquí
cus·tom·a·ry ['kʌstəmərɪ] *adj* acostumbrado, de costumbre; **it is customary to ...** es costumbre ...
cus·tom-'built *adj* hecho de encargo
cus·tom-'made *adj* hecho de encargo
cus·tom·er ['kʌstəmər] cliente(-a) *m(f)*
cus·tom·er re'la·tions *npl* relaciones *fpl* con los clientes
cus·tom·er 'serv·ice atención *f* al cliente
cus·toms ['kʌstəmz] *npl* aduana *f*
'cus·toms clear·ance despacho *m* de aduanas
'cus·toms in·spec·tion inspección *f* aduanera
'cus·toms of·fi·cer funcionario(-a) *m(f)* de aduanas
cut [kʌt] **1** *n with knife etc, of garment* corte *m*; (*reduction*) recorte (*in* de); **my hair needs a cut** necesito un corte de pe-

lo **2** *v/t* (*pret & pp* **cut**) cortar; (*reduce*) recortar; *hours* acortar; **get one's hair cut** cortarse el pelo; **I've cut my finger** me he cortado el dedo
♦ cut back **1** *v/i in costs* recortar gastos **2** *v/t staff numbers* recortar
♦ cut down **1** *v/t tree* talar, cortar **2** *v/i in expenses* gastar menos; *in smoking / drinking* fumar / beber menos
♦ cut down on *v/t*: **cut down on the cigarettes** fumar menos; **cut down on chocolate** comer menos chocolate
♦ cut off *v/t with knife, scissors etc* cortar; (*isolate*) aislar; **I was cut off** se me ha cortado la comunicación
♦ cut out *v/t with scissors* recortar; (*eliminate*) eliminar; **cut that out!** F ¡ya está bien! F; **be cut out for sth** estar hecho para algo
♦ cut up *v/t meat etc* trocear
'cut·back recorte *m*
cute [kjuːt] *adj* (*pretty*) guapo, lindo; (*sexually attractive*) atractivo; (*smart, clever*) listo; **it looks really cute on you** eso te queda muy mono
cu·ti·cle ['kjuːtɪkl] cutícula *f*
'cut-off date fecha *f* límite
cut-'price *adj goods* rebajado; *store* de productos rebajados
cut-'throat *adj competition* despiadado
cut·ting ['kʌtɪŋ] **1** *n from newspaper etc* recorte *m* **2** *adj remark* hiriente
cy·ber·space ['saɪbərspeɪs] ciberespacio *m*
cy·cle ['saɪkl] **1** *n* (*bicycle*) bicicleta *f*; (*series of events*) ciclo *m* **2** *v/i* ir en bicicleta
'cy·cle path vía *f* para bicicletas; *part of roadway* carril *m* bici
cy·cling ['saɪklɪŋ] ciclismo *m*
cy·clist ['saɪklɪst] ciclista *m/f*
cyl·in·der ['sɪlɪndər] cilindro *m*
cy·lin·dri·cal [sɪ'lɪndrɪkl] *adj* cilíndrico
cyn·ic ['sɪnɪk] escéptico(-a) *m(f)*, suspicaz *m/f*
cyn·i·cal ['sɪnɪkl] *adj* escéptico, suspicaz
cyn·i·cal·ly ['sɪnɪklɪ] *adv smile, remark* con escepticismo *or* suspicacia
cyn·i·cism ['sɪnɪsɪzm] escepticismo *m*, suspicacia *f*

current affairs program

cy·press ['saɪprəs] ciprés *m*
cyst [sɪst] quiste *m*
Czech [ʧek] **1** *adj* checo; **the Czech**

Republic la República Checa **2** *n person* checo(-a) *m(f)*; *language* checo *m*

D

D

DA *abbr* (= **district attorney**) fiscal *m/f* (del distrito)
dab [dæb] **1** *n small amount* pizca *f* **2** *v/t* (*pret & pp* **dabbed**) (*remove*) quitar; (*apply*) poner
◆ **dab·ble in** *v/t* ser aficionado a
dad [dæd] *talking to him* papá *m*; *talking about him* padre *m*
dad·dy ['dædɪ] *talking to him* papi *m*; *talking about him* padre *m*
daf·fo·dil ['dæfədɪl] narciso *m*
dag·ger ['dægər] daga *f*
dai·ly ['deɪlɪ] **1** *n* (*paper*) diario *m* **2** *adj* diario
dain·ty ['deɪntɪ] *adj* grácil, delicado
dair·y ['derɪ] *on farm* vaquería *f*
'dair·y prod·ucts *npl* productos *mpl* lácteos
dais ['deɪɪs] tarima *f*
dai·sy ['deɪzɪ] margarita *f*
dam [dæm] **1** *n for water* presa *f* **2** *v/t* (*pret & pp* **dammed**) *river* embalsar
dam·age ['dæmɪʤ] **1** *n* daños *mpl*; *fig: to reputation etc* daño *m* **2** *v/t also fig* dañar; **you're damaging your health** estás perjudicando tu salud
dam·ages ['dæmɪʤɪz] *npl* LAW daños *mpl* y perjuicios
dam·ag·ing ['dæmɪʤɪŋ] *adj* perjudicial
dame [deɪm] F (*woman*) mujer *f*, *Span* tía *f* F
damn [dæm] **1** *interj* F ¡mecachis! F **2** *n* F: *I don't give a damn!* ¡me importa un pimiento! F **3** *adj* F maldito F **4** *adv* F muy; *a damn stupid thing* una tontería monumental **5** *v/t* (*condemn*) condenar; *damn it!* F ¡maldita sea! F; *I'm damned if ...* F ya

lo creo que ... F
damned [dæmd] → *damn adj, adv*
damn·ing ['dæmɪŋ] *adj evidence* condenatorio; *report* crítico
damp [dæmp] *adj* húmedo
damp·en ['dæmpən] *v/t* humedecer
dance [dæns] **1** *n* baile *m* **2** *v/i* bailar; *would you like to dance?* ¿le gustaría bailar?
danc·er ['dænsər] bailarín (-ina) *m(f)*
danc·ing ['dænsɪŋ] baile *m*
dan·de·lion ['dændɪlaɪən] diente *m* de león
dan·druff ['dændrʌf] caspa *f*
dan·druff sham·poo champú *m* anticaspa
Dane [deɪn] danés(-esa) *m(f)*
dan·ger ['deɪnʤər] peligro *m*; *be in danger* estar en peligro; *out of danger* of patient estar fuera de peligro; *be in no danger* no estar en peligro
dan·ger·ous ['deɪnʤərəs] *adj* peligroso
dan·ger·ous 'driv·ing conducción *f* peligrosa
dan·ger·ous·ly ['deɪnʤərəslɪ] *adv drive* peligrosamente; *dangerously ill* gravemente enfermo
dan·gle ['dæŋgl] **1** *v/t* balancear **2** *v/i* colgar
Da·nish ['deɪnɪʃ] **1** *adj* danés **2** *n language* danés *m*
'Da·nish (pas·try) pastel *m* de hojaldre (*dulce*)
dare [der] **1** *v/i* atreverse; *dare to do sth* atreverse a hacer algo; *how dare you!* ¡cómo te atreves! **2** *v/t*: *dare s.o. to do sth* desafiar a alguien para que haga algo
dare·dev·il ['derdevɪl] temerario(-a) *m(f)*

dar·ing ['deərɪŋ] *adj* atrevido

dark [dɑːrk] **1** *n* oscuridad *f*; *in the dark* en la oscuridad; *after dark* después de anochecer; *keep s.o. in the dark about sth fig* no revelar algo a alguien **2** *adj* oscuro; *hair* oscuro, moreno; *dark green / blue* verde / azul oscuro

dark·en ['dɑːrkn] *v/i of sky* oscurecerse

dark 'glass·es *npl* gafas *fpl* oscuras, *L.Am.* lentes *fpl* oscuras

dark·ness ['dɑːrknɪs] oscuridad *f*; *in darkness* a oscuras

'dark·room PHOT cuarto *m* oscuro

dar·ling ['dɑːrlɪŋ] **1** *n* cielo *m*; *yes my darling* sí cariño **2** *adj* encantador; *darling Ann, how are you?* querida Ann, ¿cómo estás?

darn[1] [dɑːrn] **1** *n* (*mend*) zurcido *m* **2** *v/t* (*mend*) zurcir

darn[2], **darned** [dɑːrn, dɑːrnd] → *damn adj, adv*

dart [dɑːrt] **1** *n for throwing* dardo *m* **2** *v/i* lanzarse, precipitarse

darts [dɑːrts] *nsg* dardos *mpl*

'dart(s)·board diana *f*

dash [dæʃ] **1** *n punctuation* raya *f*; (*small amount*) chorrito *m*; (MOT: *dashboard*) salpicadero *m*; *make a dash for* correr hacia *f v/i* correr; *I must dash* tengo que darme prisa; *he dashed downstairs* bajó las escaleras corriendo **3** *v/t hopes* frustrar, truncar

♦ **dash off 1** *v/i* irse **2** *v/t* (*write quickly*) escribir rápidamente

'dash·board salpicadero *m*

da·ta ['deɪtə] datos *mpl*

'da·ta·base base *f* de datos

da·ta 'cap·ture captura *f* de datos

da·ta 'pro·cess·ing proceso *m* or tratamiento *m* de datos

da·ta pro'tec·tion protección *f* de datos

da·ta 'stor·age almacenamiento *m* de datos

date[1] [deɪt] *fruit* dátil *m*

date[2] [deɪt] **1** *n* fecha *f*; (*meeting*) cita *f*; (*person*) pareja *f*; *what's the date today?* ¿qué fecha es hoy?, ¿a qué fecha estamos?; *out of date clothes* pasado de moda; *passport* caducado; *up to date*

al día **2** *v/t letter, check* fechar; (*go out with*) salir con; *that dates you* (*shows your age*) eso demuestra lo viejo que eres

dat·ed ['deɪtɪd] *adj* anticuado

daub [dɔːb] *v/t* embadurnar

daugh·ter ['dɔːtər] hija *f*

'daugh·ter-in-law (*pl* **daughters-in-law**) nuera *f*

daunt [dɔːnt] *v/t* acobardar, desalentar

daw·dle ['dɔːdl] *v/i* perder el tiempo

dawn [dɔːn] **1** *n* amanecer *m*, alba *f*; *fig: of new age* albores *mpl* **2** *v/i* amanecer; *it dawned on me that ...* me di cuenta de que ...

day [deɪ] día *m*; *what day is it today?* ¿qué día es hoy?, ¿a qué día estamos?; *day off* día *m* de vacaciones; *by day* durante el día; *day by day* día tras día; *the day after* el día siguiente; *the day after tomorrow* pasado mañana; *the day before* el día anterior; *the day before yesterday* anteayer; *day in day out* un día sí y otro también; *in those days* en aquellos tiempos; *one day* un día; *the other day* (*recently*) el otro día; *let's call it a day!* ¡dejémoslo!

'day·break amanecer *m*, alba *f*

'day care servicio *m* de guardería

'day·dream 1 *n* fantasía *f* **2** *v/i* soñar despierto

'day·dream·er soñador(a) *m(f)*

'day·light luz *f* del día

'day·light 'sav·ing time horario *m* de verano

'day·time: *in the daytime* durante el día

'day trip excursión *m* en el día

daze [deɪz] *n:* *in a daze* aturdido

dazed [deɪzd] *adj* aturdido

daz·zle ['dæzl] *v/t also fig* deslumbrar

DC [diː'siː] *abbr* (= *direct current*) corriente *f* continua; (= *District of Columbia*) Distrito *m* de Columbia

dead [ded] **1** *adj person, plant* muerto; *battery* agotado; *light bulb* fundido; F *place* muerto F; *the phone is dead* no hay línea **2** *adv* F (*very*) tela de F, la mar de F; *dead beat, dead tired* hecho polvo; *that's dead right* tienes toda la razón del mundo **3** *n: the dead* (*dead peo-*

ple) los muertos; *in the dead of night* a altas horas de la madrugada

dead·en ['dedn] *v/t pain, sound* amortiguar

dead 'end *(street)* callejón *m* sin salida

dead-'end job trabajo *m* sin salidas

dead 'heat empate *m*

'dead·line fecha *f* tope; *for newspaper, magazine* hora *f* de cierre; *meet a deadline* cumplir un plazo

'dead·lock *n in talks* punto *m* muerto

dead·ly ['dedlɪ] *adj (fatal)* mortal; F *(boring)* mortal F

deaf [def] *adj* sordo

deaf-and-'dumb *adj* sordomudo

deaf·en ['defn] *v/t* ensordecer

deaf·en·ing ['defnɪŋ] *adj* ensordecedor

deaf·ness ['defnɪs] sordera *f*

deal [diːl] 1 *n* acuerdo *m*; *I thought we had a deal?* creía que habíamos hecho un trato; *it's a deal!* ¡trato hecho!; *a good deal (bargain)* una ocasión; *a good deal (a lot)* mucho; *a great deal of (lots)* mucho(s) 2 *v/t (pret & pp dealt) cards* repartir; *deal a blow to* asestar un golpe a

◆ deal in *v/t (trade in)* comerciar con; *deal in drugs* traficar con drogas

◆ deal out *v/t cards* repartir

◆ deal with *v/t (handle)* tratar; *situation* hacer frente a; *customer, applications* encargarse de; *(do business with)* hacer negocios con

deal·er ['diːlər] *(merchant)* comerciante *m/f*; *(drug dealer)* traficante *m/f*

deal·ing ['diːlɪŋ] *(drug dealing)* tráfico *m*

deal·ings ['diːlɪŋz] *npl (business)* tratos *mpl*

dealt [delt] *pret & pp → deal*

dean [diːn] *of college* decano(-a) *m(f)*

dear [dɪr] *adj* querido; *(expensive)* caro; *Dear Sir* Muy Sr. Mío; *Dear Richard / Margaret* Querido Richard / Querida Margaret; *(oh) dear!, dear me!* ¡oh, cielos!

dear·ly ['dɪrlɪ] *adv love* muchísimo

death [deθ] muerte *f*

'death cer·tif·i·cate certificado *m* de defunción

'death pen·al·ty pena *f* de muerte

'death toll saldo *m* de víctimas mortales

de·ba·ta·ble [dɪ'beɪtəbl] *adj* discutible

de·bate [dɪ'beɪt] 1 *n also* POL debate *m* 2 *v/i* debatir; *I debated with myself whether to go* me debatía entre ir o no ir 3 *v/t* debatir

de·bauch·er·y [dɪ'bɔːtʃərɪ] libertinaje *m*

deb·it ['debɪt] 1 *n* cargo *m* 2 *v/t account* cargar en; *amount* cargar

'deb·it card tarjeta *f* de débito

deb·ris ['debriː] *of building* escombros *mpl*; *of airplane, car* restos *mpl*

debt [det] deuda *f*; *be in debt financially* estar endeudado

debt·or ['detər] deudor(-a) *m(f)*

de·bug [diː'bʌg] *v/t (pret & pp debugged) room* limpiar de micrófonos; COMPUT depurar

dé·but ['deɪbjuː] *n* debut *m*

dec·ade ['dekeɪd] década *f*

dec·a·dence ['dekədəns] decadencia *f*

dec·a·dent ['dekədənt] *adj* decadente

de·caf·fein·at·ed [dɪ'kæfɪneɪtɪd] *adj* descafeinado

de·cant·er [dɪ'kæntər] licorera *f*

de·cap·i·tate [dɪ'kæpɪteɪt] *v/t* decapitar

de·cay [dɪ'keɪ] 1 *n of wood, plant* putrefacción *f*; *of civilization* declive *m*; *in teeth* caries *f inv* 2 *v/i of wood, plant* pudrirse; *of civilization* decaer; *of teeth* cariarse

de·ceased [dɪ'siːst]: *the deceased* el difunto / la difunta

de·ceit [dɪ'siːt] engaño *m*, mentira *f*

de·ceit·ful [dɪ'siːtfəl] *adj* mentiroso

de·ceive [dɪ'siːv] *v/t* engañar

De·cem·ber [dɪ'sembər] diciembre *m*

de·cen·cy ['diːsənsɪ] decencia *f*; *he had the decency to ...* tuvo la delicadeza de ...

de·cent ['diːsənt] *adj* decente; *(adequately dressed)* presentable

de·cen·tral·ize [diː'sentrəlaɪz] *v/t* descentralizar

de·cep·tion [dɪ'sepʃn] engaño *m*

de·cep·tive [dɪ'septɪv] *adj* engañoso

de·cep·tive·ly [dɪ'septɪvlɪ] *adv*: *it looks deceptively simple* parece muy fácil

dec·i·bel ['desɪbel] decibelio *m*

de·cide [dɪ'saɪd] **1** *v/t* decidir **2** *v/i* decidir; *you decide* decide tú; *it's so hard to decide* es tan difícil decidirse

de·cid·ed [dɪ'saɪdɪd] *adj (definite)* tajante

de·cid·er [dɪ'saɪdər]: *this match will be the decider* este partido será el que decida

dec·i·du·ous [dɪ'sɪdʊəs] *adj* de hoja caduca

dec·i·mal ['desɪml] *n* decimal *m*

dec·i·mal 'point coma *f* (decimal)

dec·i·mate ['desɪmeɪt] *v/t* diezmar

de·ci·pher [dɪ'saɪfər] *v/t* descifrar

de·ci·sion [dɪ'sɪʒn] decisión *f*; *come to a decision* llegar a una decisión

de·ci·sion-mak·er: *who's the decision-maker here?* ¿quién toma aquí las decisiones?

de·ci·sive [dɪ'saɪsɪv] *adj* decidido; *(crucial)* decisivo

deck [dek] *of ship* cubierta *f*; *of cards* baraja *f*

'deck·chair tumbona *f*

dec·la·ra·tion [deklə'reɪʃn] *(statement)* declaración *f*

de·clare [dɪ'kler] *v/t (state)* declarar

de·cline [dɪ'klaɪn] **1** *n (fall)* descenso *m*; *in standards* caída *f*; *in health* empeoramiento *m* **2** *v/t invitation* declinar; *decline to comment* declinar hacer declaraciones **3** *v/i (refuse)* rehusar; *(decrease)* declinar; *of health* empeorar

de·clutch [diː'klʌtʃ] *v/i* desembragar

de·code [diː'koʊd] *v/t* descodificar

de·com·pose [diːkəm'poʊz] *v/i* descomponerse

dé·cor ['deɪkɔːr] decoración *f*

dec·o·rate ['dekəreɪt] *v/t with paint* pintar; *with paper* empapelar; *(adorn)* decorar; *soldier* condecorar

dec·o·ra·tion [dekə'reɪʃn] *paint* pintado *m*; *paper* empapelado *m*; *(ornament)* decoración *f*

dec·o·ra·tive ['dekərətɪv] *adj* decorativo

dec·o·ra·tor ['dekəreɪtər] *(interior decorator)* decorador(a) *m(f)*; *with paint* pintor(a) *m(f)*; *with wallpaper* empapelador(a) *m(f)*

de·co·rum [dɪ'kɔːrəm] decoro *m*

de·coy ['diːkɔɪ] *n* señuelo *m*

de·crease 1 *n* ['diːkriːs] disminución *f*, reducción *f* (*in* de) **2** *v/t* [dɪ'kriːs] disminuir, reducir **3** *v/i* [dɪ'kriːs] disminuir, reducirse

de·crep·it [dɪ'krepɪt] *adj car, coat, shoes* destartalado; *person* decrépito

ded·i·cate ['dedɪkeɪt] *v/t book etc* dedicar; *dedicate o.s. to* dedicarse a

ded·i·ca·ted ['dedɪkeɪtɪd] *adj* dedicado

ded·i·ca·tion [dedɪ'keɪʃn] *in book* dedicatoria *f*; *to cause, work* dedicación *f*

de·duce [dɪ'duːs] *v/t* deducir

de·duct [dɪ'dʌkt] *v/t* descontar; *deduct sth from sth* descontar alguien de alguien

de·duc·tion [dɪ'dʌkʃn] *from salary, (conclusion)* deducción *f*

dee·jay ['diːdʒeɪ] F disk jockey *m/f*, Span pincha *m/f* F

deed [diːd] *n (act)* acción *f*, obra *f*; LAW escritura *f*

deem [diːm] *v/t* estimar

deep [diːp] *adj* profundo; *color* intenso; *be in deep trouble* estar metido en serios apuros

deep·en ['diːpn] **1** *v/t* profundizar **2** *v/i* hacerse más profundo; *of crisis, mystery* agudizarse

'deep freeze *n* congelador *m*

'deep-froz·en food comida *f* congelada

'deep-fry *v/t (pret & pp deep-fried)* freír (en mucho aceite)

deep 'fry·er freidora *f*

deer [dɪr] *(pl deer)* ciervo *m*

de·face [dɪ'feɪs] *v/t* desfigurar, dañar

def·a·ma·tion [defə'meɪʃn] difamación *f*

de·fam·a·to·ry [dɪ'fæmətɔːrɪ] *adj* difamatorio

de·fault ['diːfɔːlt] *adj* COMPUT por defecto

de·fec·tive [dɪˈfektɪv] *adj* defectuoso

de·feat [dɪ'fiːt] **1** *n* derrota *f* **2** *v/t* derrotar; *of task, problem* derrotar, vencer

de·feat·ist [dɪ'fiːtɪst] *adj attitude* derrotista

de·fect ['diːfekt] *n* defecto *m*

de·fec·tive [dɪ'fektɪv] *adj* defectuoso

de·fence *etc Br* → *defense etc*

de·fend [dɪ'fend] *v/t* defender

de·fend·ant [dɪ'fendənt] acusado(-a) *m(f)*; *in civil case* demandado(-a) *m(f)*

de·fense [dɪ'fens] defensa *f*; *come to s.o.'s defense* salir en defensa de alguien

de'fense budg·et POL presupuesto *m* de defensa

de'fense law·yer abogado(-a) *m(f)* defensor(a)

de'fense·less [dɪ'fenslɪs] *adj* indefenso

de'fense play·er SP defensa *m/f*

De'fense Se·cre·ta·ry POL ministro(-a) *m(f)* de Defensa; *in USA* secretario *m* de Defensa

de'fense wit·ness LAW testigo *m/f* de la defensa

de·fen·sive [dɪ'fensɪv] **1** *n*: *on the defensive* a la defensiva; *go on the defensive* ponerse a la defensiva **2** *adj* weaponry defensivo; *stop being so defensive!* ¡no hace falta que te pongas tan a la defensiva!

de·fen·sive·ly [dɪ'fensɪvlɪ] *adv* a la defensiva

de·fer [dɪ'fɜːr] *v/t* (*pret & pp* **deferred**) (*postpone*) aplazar, diferir

def·er·ence ['defərəns] deferencia *f*

def·er·en·tial [defə'renʃl] *adj* deferente

de·fi·ance [dɪ'faɪəns] desafío *m*; *in defiance of* desafiando

de·fi·ant [dɪ'faɪənt] *adj* desafiante

de·fi·cien·cy [dɪ'fɪʃənsɪ] (*lack*) deficiencia *f*, carencia *f*

de·fi·cient [dɪ'fɪʃənt] *adj* deficiente, carente; *be deficient in ...* carecer de ...

def·i·cit ['defɪsɪt] déficit *m*

de·fine [dɪ'faɪn] *v/t* word, objective definir

def·i·nite ['defɪnɪt] *adj* date, time, answer definitivo; *improvement* claro; (*certain*) seguro; *are you definite about that?* ¿estás seguro de eso?; *nothing definite has been arranged* no se ha acordado nada de forma definitiva

def·i·nite 'ar·ti·cle GRAM artículo *m* determinado *or* definido

def·i·nite·ly ['defɪnɪtlɪ] *adv* con certeza, sin lugar a dudas

def·i·ni·tion [defɪ'nɪʃn] definición *f*

def·i·ni·tive [dɪ'fɪnətɪv] *adj* definitivo

de·flect [dɪ'flekt] *v/t* desviar; *criticism* distraer; *be deflected from* desviarse de

de·for·est·a·tion [diːfɑːrɪs'teɪʃn] deforestación *f*

de·form [dɪ'fɔːrm] *v/t* deformar

de·for·mi·ty [dɪ'fɔːrmɪtɪ] deformidad *f*

de·fraud [dɪ'frɔːd] *v/t* defraudar

de·frost [diː'frɔːst] *v/t* food, fridge descongelar

deft [deft] *adj* hábil, diestro

de·fuse [diː'fjuːz] *v/t* bomb desactivar; *situation* calmar

de·fy [dɪ'faɪ] *v/t* (*pret & pp* **defied**) desafiar

de·gen·e·rate [dɪ'dʒenəreɪt] *v/i* degenerar; *degenerate into* degenerar en

de·grade [dɪ'greɪd] *v/t* degradar

de·grad·ing [dɪ'greɪdɪŋ] *adj* position, work degradante

de·gree [dɪ'griː] *from university* título *m*; *of temperature, angle, latitude* grado *m*; *there is a degree of truth in that* hay algo de verdad en eso; *a degree of compassion* algo de compasión; *by degrees* gradualmente; *get one's degree* graduarse, *L.Am.* egresar

de·hy·drat·ed [diːhaɪ'dreɪtɪd] *adj* deshidratado

de·ice [diː'aɪs] *v/t* deshelar

de·ic·er [diː'aɪsər] spray descongelador *m*, descongelante *m*

deign [deɪn] *v/i*: *deign to* dignarse a

de·i·ty ['diːɪtɪ] deidad *f*

de·jec·ted [dɪ'dʒektɪd] *adj* abatido, desanimado

de·lay [dɪ'leɪ] **1** *n* retraso *m* **2** *v/t* retrasar; *be delayed* llevar retraso **3** *v/i* retrasarse

del·e·gate ['delɪgət] **1** *n* delegado(-a) *m(f)* **2** ['delɪgeɪt] *v/t* task delegar; person delegar en

del·e·ga·tion [delɪ'geɪʃn] delegación *f*

de·lete [dɪ'liːt] *v/t* borrar; (*cross out*) tachar; *delete where not applicable* táchese donde no corresponda

de·le·tion [dɪ'liːʃn] act borrado *m*; *that deleted* supresión *f*

del·i ['delɪ] → **delicatessen**

de·lib·e·rate 1 *adj* [dɪ'lɪbərət] deliberado, intencionado **2** *v/i* [dɪ'lɪbəreɪt] deliberar de·lib·e·rate·ly [dɪˈlɪbərətlɪ] *adv* deliberadamente, a propósito

del·i·ca·cy [ˈdelɪkəsɪ] delicadeza *f*; *of health* fragilidad *f*; *food* exquisitez *f*, manjar *m*

del·i·cate [ˈdelɪkət] *adj fabric, problem* delicado; *health* frágil

del·i·ca·tes·sen [delɪkəˈtesn] *tienda de productos alimenticios de calidad*

del·i·cious [dɪˈlɪʃəs] *adj* delicioso

de·light [dɪˈlaɪt] *n* placer *m*

de·light·ed [dɪˈlaɪtɪd] *adj* encantado; *I'd be delighted to come* me encantaría venir

de·light·ful [dɪˈlaɪtfəl] *adj* encantador

de·lim·it [diːˈlɪmɪt] *v/t* delimitar

de·lin·quen·cy [dɪˈlɪŋkwənsɪ] delincuencia *f*

de·lin·quent [dɪˈlɪŋkwənt] *n* delincuente *m/f*

de·lir·i·ous [dɪˈlɪrɪəs] *adj* MED delirante; *(ecstatic)* entusiasmado; *she's delirious about the new job* está como loca con el nuevo trabajo

de·liv·er [dɪˈlɪvər] *v/t* entregar, repartir; *message* dar; *baby* dar a luz; *speech* pronunciar

de·liv·er·y [dɪˈlɪvərɪ] *of goods, mail* entrega *f*, reparto *m*; *of baby* parto *m*

de·liv·er·y charge gastos *mpl* de envío

de·liv·er·y date fecha *f* de entrega

de·liv·er·y man repartidor *m*

de·liv·er·y note nota *f* de entrega

de·liv·er·y serv·ice servicio *m* de reparto

de·liv·er·y van furgoneta *f* de reparto

de·lude [dɪˈluːd] *v/t* engañar; *you're deluding yourself* te estás engañando a ti mismo

de·luge [ˈdeljuːdʒ] **1** *n* diluvio *m*; *fig* avalancha *f* **2** *v/t fig* inundar (*with* de)

de·lu·sion [dɪˈluːʒn] engaño *m*; *you're under a delusion if you think ...* te engañas si piensas que ...

de luxe [dəˈlʊks] *adj* de lujo

◆ delve into [delv] *v/t* rebuscar en

de·mand [dɪˈmænd] **1** *n* exigencia *f*; *by union* reivindicación *f*; COM demanda *f*; *in demand* solicitado **2** *v/t* exigir; *(require)* requirir

de·mand·ing [dɪˈmændɪŋ] *adj job* que exige mucho; *person* exigente

de·mean·ing [dɪˈmiːnɪŋ] *adj* degradante

de·ment·ed [dɪˈmentɪd] *adj* demente

de·mise [dɪˈmaɪz] fallecimiento *m*; *fig* desaparición *f*

dem·i·tasse [ˈdemɪtæs] taza *f* de café

dem·o [ˈdemoʊ] *protest* manifestación *f*; *of video etc* maqueta *f*

de·moc·ra·cy [dɪˈmɑːkrəsɪ] democracia *f*

dem·o·crat [ˈdeməkræt] demócrata *m/f*; **Democrat** POL Demócrata *m/f*

dem·o·crat·ic [demeˈkrætɪk] *adj* democrático

dem·o·crat·ic·al·ly [demeˈkrætɪklɪ] *adv* democráticamente

ˈdem·o disk disco *m* de demostración

de·mo·graph·ic [demoʊˈgræfɪk] *adj* demográfico

de·mol·ish [dɪˈmɑːlɪʃ] *v/t building* demoler; *argument* destruir, echar por tierra

dem·o·li·tion [deməˈlɪʃn] *of building* demolición *f*; *of argument* destrucción *f*

de·mon [ˈdiːmən] demonio *m*

dem·on·strate [ˈdemənstreɪt] **1** *v/t* demostrar **2** *v/i politically* manifestarse

dem·on·stra·tion [demənˈstreɪʃn] demostración *f*; *protest* manifestación *f*

de·mon·stra·tive [dɪˈmɑːnstrətɪv] *adj person* extrovertido, efusivo; GRAM demostrativo

dem·on·stra·tor [ˈdemənstreɪtər] *protester* manifestante *m/f*

de·mor·al·ized [dɪˈmɔːrəlaɪzd] *adj* desmoralizado

de·mor·al·iz·ing [dɪˈmɔːrəlaɪzɪŋ] *adj* desmoralizador

de·mote [diːˈmoʊt] *v/t* degradar

de·mure [dɪˈmjʊər] *adj* solemne, recatado

den [den] *(study)* estudio *m*

de·ni·al [dɪˈnaɪəl] *of rumor, accusation* negación *f*; *of request* denegación *f*

den·im [ˈdenɪm] tela *f* vaquera

den·ims [ˈdenɪmz] *npl (jeans)* vaqueros *mpl*

Den·mark [ˈdenmɑːrk] Dinamarca

de·nom·i·na·tion [dɪnɑːmɪˈneɪʃn] *of money* valor *m*; *religious* confesión *f*

de·nounce [dɪˈnaʊns] *v/t* denunciar

dense [dens] *adj smoke, fog* denso; *foliage* espeso; *crowd* compacto; F *(stupid)* corto

dense·ly ['densli] *adv:* **densely populated** densamente poblado

den·si·ty ['densɪtɪ] *of population* densidad *f*

dent [dent] **1** *n* abolladura *f* **2** *v/t* abollar

den·tal ['dentl] *adj* dental; **dental surgeon** odontólogo(-a) *m(f)*

den·ted ['dentɪd] *adj* abollado

den·tist ['dentɪst] dentista *m/f*

den·tist·ry ['dentɪstrɪ] odontología *f*

den·tures ['dentʃərz] *npl* dentadura *f* postiza

de·ny [dɪ'naɪ] *v/t (pret & pp denied) charge, rumor* negar; *right, request* denegar

de·o·do·rant [diːˈoʊdərənt] desodorante *m*

de·part [dɪ'paːrt] *v/i* salir; **depart from** *(deviate from)* desviarse de

de·part·ment [dɪ'paːrtmənt] departamento *m; of government* ministerio *m*

De·part·ment of 'De·fense Ministerio *m* de Defensa

De·part·ment of the In'te·ri·or Ministerio *m* del Interior

De·part·ment of 'State Ministerio *m* de Asuntos Exteriores

de'part·ment store grandes almacenes *mpl*

de·par·ture [dɪ'paːrtʃər] salida *f; of person from job* marcha *f; (deviation)* desviación *f;* **a new departure** *for government, organization* una innovación; *for company* un cambio; *for actor, artist, writer* una nueva experiencia

de'par·ture lounge sala *f* de embarque

de'par·ture time hora *f* de salida

de·pend [dɪ'pend] *v/i* depender; **that depends** depende; **it depends on the weather** depende del tiempo; **I depend on you** dependo de ti

de·pen·da·ble [dɪ'pendəbl] *adj* fiable

de·pen·dant [dɪ'pendənt] → **dependent**

de·pen·dence, de·pen·den·cy [dɪ'pendəns, dɪ'pendənsɪ] dependencia *f*

de·pen·dent [dɪ'pendənt] **1** *n* persona a cargo de otra; **how many dependents**

do you have? ¿cuántas personas tiene a su cargo? **2** *adj* dependiente (**on** de)

de·pict [dɪ'pɪkt] *v/t* describir

de·plete [dɪ'pliːt] *v/t* agotar, mermar

de·plor·a·ble [dɪ'plɔːrəbl] *adj* deplorable

de·plore [dɪ'plɔːr] *v/t* deplorar

de·ploy [dɪ'plɔɪ] *v/t (use)* utilizar; *(position)* desplegar

de·pop·u·la·tion [diːpɑːpjəˈleɪʃn] despoblación *f*

de·port [dɪ'pɔːrt] *v/t* deportar

de·por·ta·tion [diːpɔːrˈteɪʃn] deportación *f*

de·por'ta·tion or·der orden *f* de deportación

de·pose [dɪ'pouz] *v/t* deponer

de·pos·it [dɪ'paːzɪt] **1** *n in bank, of oil* depósito *m; of coal* yacimiento *m; on purchase* señal *f*, depósito *m* **2** *v/t money* depositar, *Span* ingresar; *(put down)* depositar

de'pos·it ac·count *Br* cuenta *f* de ahorro *or* de depósito

dep·o·si·tion [diːpouˈzɪʃn] LAW declaración *f*

dep·ot ['diːpou] *(train station)* estación *f* de tren; *(bus station)* estación *f* de autobuses; *for storage* depósito *m*

de·praved [dɪ'preɪvd] *adj* depravado

de·pre·ci·ate [dɪ'priːʃɪeɪt] *v/i* FIN depreciarse

de·pre·ci·a·tion [dɪpriːʃɪˈeɪʃn] FIN depreciación *f*

de·press [dɪ'pres] *v/t person* deprimir

de·pressed [dɪ'prest] *adj person* deprimido

de·press·ing [dɪ'presɪŋ] *adj* deprimente

de·pres·sion [dɪ'preʃn] MED, *economic* depresión *f; meteorological* borrasca *f*

dep·ri·va·tion [deprɪ'veɪʃn] privación *f*

de·prive [dɪ'praɪv] *v/t* privar; **deprive s.o. of sth** privar a alguien de algo

de·prived [dɪ'praɪvd] *adj* desfavorecido

depth [depθ] profundidad *f; of color* intensidad *f;* **in depth** *(thoroughly)* en profundidad; **in the depths of winter** en pleno invierno; **be out of one's depth** *in water* no tocar el fondo; *fig: in discussion etc* saber muy poco

dep·u·ta·tion [depjʊˈteɪʃn] delegación f

◆ **dep·u·tize for** [ˈdepjʊtaɪz] v/t sustituir

dep·u·ty [ˈdepjʊtɪ] segundo(-a) m(f)

'**dep·u·ty lead·er** vicelíder m/f

de·rail [dɪˈreɪl] v/t hacer descarrilar; **be derailed** of train descarrilar

de·ranged [dɪˈreɪndʒd] adj perturbado, trastornado

de·reg·u·late [dɪˈreɡjʊleɪt] v/t liberalizar, desregular

de·reg·u·la·tion [dɪreɡjʊˈleɪʃn] liberalización f, desregulación f

der·e·lict [ˈderəlɪkt] adj en ruinas

de·ride [dɪˈraɪd] v/t ridiculizar, mofarse de

de·ri·sion [dɪˈrɪʒn] burla f, mofa f

de·ri·sive [dɪˈraɪsɪv] adj burlón

de·ri·sive·ly [dɪˈraɪsɪvlɪ] adv burlonamente

de·ri·so·ry [dɪˈraɪsərɪ] adj amount, salary irrisorio

de·riv·a·tive [dɪˈrɪvətɪv] adj (not original) poco original

de·rive [dɪˈraɪv] v/t obtener, encontrar; **be derived from** of word derivar(se) de

der·ma·tol·o·gist [dɜːrməˈtɑːlədʒɪst] dermatólogo(-a) m(f)

de·rog·a·tory [dɪˈrɑːɡətɔːrɪ] adj despectivo

de·scend [dɪˈsend] 1 v/t descender por; **be descended from** descender de 2 v/i descender; of mood, darkness caer

de·scen·dant [dɪˈsendənt] descendiente m/f

de·scent [dɪˈsent] descenso m; (ancestry) ascendencia f; **of Chinese descent** de ascendencia china

de·scribe [dɪˈskraɪb] v/t describir; **describe sth as sth** definir a algo como algo

de·scrip·tion [dɪˈskrɪpʃn] descripción f

des·e·crate [ˈdesɪkreɪt] v/t profanar

des·e·cra·tion [desɪˈkreɪʃn] profanación f

de·seg·re·gate [diːˈseɡrəɡeɪt] v/t acabar con la segregación racial en

des·ert[1] [ˈdezərt] n also fig desierto m

des·ert[2] [dɪˈzɜːrt] 1 v/t (abandon) abandonar 2 v/i of soldier desertar

de·sert·ed [dɪˈzɜːrtɪd] adj desierto

de·sert·er [dɪˈzɜːrtər] MIL desertor(a) m(f)

de·ser·ti·fi·ca·tion [dɪzɜːrtɪfɪˈkeɪʃn] desertización f

de·ser·tion [dɪˈzɜːrʃn] (abandonment) abandono m; MIL deserción f

des·ert 'is·land isla f desierta

de·serve [dɪˈzɜːrv] v/t merecer

de·sign [dɪˈzaɪn] 1 n diseño m; (pattern) motivo m 2 v/t diseñar; **not designed for heavy use** no está diseñado para ser utilizado constantemente

des·ig·nate [ˈdezɪɡneɪt] v/t person designar; area declarar

de·sign·er [dɪˈzaɪnər] diseñador(a) m(f)

de'sign·er clothes npl ropa f de diseño

de'sign fault defecto m de diseño

de'sign school escuela f de diseño

de·sir·a·ble [dɪˈzaɪrəbl] adj deseable; house apetecible, atractivo

de·sire [dɪˈzaɪr] n deseo m; **I have no desire to see him** no me apetece verle

desk [desk] in classroom pupitre m; in home, office mesa f; in hotel recepción f

'**desk clerk** recepcionista m/f

'**desk di·a·ry** agenda f

'**desk·top** also on screen escritorio m; computer Span ordenador m de escritorio, L.Am. computadora f de escritorio

desk·top 'pub·lish·ing autoedición f

des·o·late [ˈdesələt] adj place desolado

de·spair [dɪˈsper] 1 n desesperación f; **in despair** desesperado 2 v/i desesperarse; **I despair of finding something to wear** he perdido la esperanza de encontrar algo para ponerme

des·per·ate [ˈdespərət] adj desesperado; **be desperate** estar desesperado; **be desperate for a drink / cigarette** necesitar una bebida / un cigarrillo desesperadamente

des·per·a·tion [despəˈreɪʃn] desesperación f; **an act of desperation** un acto de desesperado

des·pic·a·ble [dɪsˈpɪkəbl] adj despreciable

de·spise [dɪˈspaɪz] v/t despreciar

de·spite [dɪˈspaɪt] prep a pesar de

de·spon·dent [dɪˈspɑːndənt] adj abatido, desanimado

des·pot [ˈdespɑːt] déspota m/f

des·sert [dɪˈzɜːrt] postre *m*

des·ti·na·tion [destɪˈneɪʃn] destino *m*

des·tined [ˈdestɪnd] *adj*: **be destined for** *fig* estar destinado a

des·ti·ny [ˈdestɪnɪ] destino *m*

des·ti·tute [ˈdestɪtuːt] *adj* indigente; **be destitute** estar en la miseria

de·stroy [dɪˈstrɔɪ] *v/t* destruir

de·stroy·er [dɪˈstrɔɪər] NAUT destructor *m*

de·struc·tion [dɪˈstrʌkʃn] destrucción *f*

de·struc·tive [dɪˈstrʌktɪv] *adj* destructivo; *child* revoltoso

de·tach [dɪˈtætʃ] *v/t* separar, soltar

de·tach·a·ble [dɪˈtætʃəbl] *adj* desmontable, separable

de·tached [dɪˈtætʃt] *adj* (*objective*) distanciado

de·tach·ment [dɪˈtætʃmənt] (*objectivity*) distancia *f*

de·tail [ˈdiːteɪl] *n* detalle *m*; **in detail** en detalle

de·tailed [ˈdiːteɪld] *adj* detallado

de·tain [dɪˈteɪn] *v/t* (*hold back*) entretener; *as prisoner* detener

de·tain·ee [diːteɪnˈiː] detenido(-a) *m(f)*

de·tect [dɪˈtekt] *v/t* percibir; *of device* detectar

de·tec·tion [dɪˈtekʃn] *of criminal, crime* descubrimiento *m*; *of smoke etc* detección *f*

de·tec·tive [dɪˈtektɪv] detective *m/f*

de·tec·tive nov·el novela *f* policiaca *or* de detectives

de·tec·tor [dɪˈtektər] detector *m*

dé·tente [ˈdeɪtɑːnt] POL distensión *f*

de·ten·tion [dɪˈtenʃn] (*imprisonment*) detención *f*

de·ter [dɪˈtɜːr] *v/t* (*pret & pp* **deterred**) disuadir; **deter s.o. from doing sth** disuadir a alguien de hacer algo

de·ter·gent [dɪˈtɜːrdʒənt] detergente *m*

de·te·ri·o·rate [dɪˈtɪrɪəreɪt] *v/i* deteriorarse; *of weather* empeorar

de·te·ri·o·ra·tion [dɪtɪrɪəˈreɪʃn] deterioro *m*; *of weather* empeoramiento *m*

de·ter·mi·na·tion [dɪtɜːrmɪˈneɪʃn] (*resolution*) determinación *f*

de·ter·mine [dɪˈtɜːrmɪn] *v/t* (*establish*) determinar

de·ter·mined [dɪˈtɜːrmɪnd] *adj* resuelto, decidido; *I'm determined to succeed* estoy decidido a triunfar

de·ter·rent [dɪˈterənt] *n* elemento *m* disuasorio; *act as a deterrent* actuar como elemento disuasorio; *nuclear deterrent* disuasión *f* nuclear

de·test [dɪˈtest] *v/t* detestar

de·test·a·ble [dɪˈtestəbl] *adj* detestable

de·to·nate [ˈdetəneɪt] 1 *v/t* hacer detonar *or* explotar 2 *v/i* detonar, explotar

de·to·na·tion [detəˈneɪʃn] detonación *f*, explosión *f*

de·tour [ˈdiːtʊr] *n* rodeo *m*; (*diversion*) desvío *m*; *make a detour* dar un rodeo

♦ **de·tract from** [dɪˈtrækt] *v/t* *achievement* quitar méritos a; *beauty* quitar atractivo a; *the bad weather didn't detract from their enjoyment* el mal tiempo no impidió que disfrutaran

de·tri·ment [ˈdetrɪmənt]: *to the detriment of* en detrimento de

de·tri·men·tal [detrɪˈmentl] *adj* perjudicial (*to* para)

deuce [duːs] *in tennis* deuce *m*

de·val·u·a·tion [diːvæljuˈeɪʃn] *of currency* devaluación *f*

de·val·ue [diːˈvæljuː] *v/t currency* devaluar

dev·a·state [ˈdevəsteɪt] *v/t* *crops, countryside, city* devastar; *fig: person* asolar

dev·a·stat·ing [ˈdevəsteɪtɪŋ] *adj* devastador

de·vel·op [dɪˈveləp] 1 *v/t film* revelar; *land, site* urbanizar; *activity, business* desarrollar; (*originate*) desarrollar; (*improve on*) perfeccionar; *illness, cold* contraer 2 *v/i* (*grow*) desarrollarse; *develop into* convertirse en

de·vel·op·er [dɪˈveləpər] *of property* promotor(a) *m(f)* inmobiliario(-a)

de·vel·op·ing 'coun·try [dɪˈveləpɪŋ] país *m* en vías de desarrollo

de·vel·op·ment [dɪˈveləpmənt] *of film* revelado *m*; *of land, site* urbanización *f*; *of business, country* desarrollo *m*; (*event*) acontecimiento *m*; (*origination*) desarrollo *m*; (*improving*) perfeccionamiento *m*

de·vice [dɪ'vaɪs] *tool* aparato *m*, dispositivo *m*

dev·il ['devl] *also fig* diablo *m*, demonio *m*

de·vi·ous ['diːvɪəs] *adj (sly)* retorcido

de·vise [dɪ'vaɪz] *v/t* idear

de·void [dɪ'vɔɪd] *adj*: **be devoid of** estar desprovisto de

dev·o·lu·tion [diːvə'luːʃn] POL traspaso *m* de competencias

de·vote [dɪ'vəʊt] *v/t* dedicar (**to** a)

de·vot·ed [dɪ'vəʊtɪd] *adj* son etc afectuoso; **be devoted to s.o.** tener mucho cariño a alguien

dev·o·tee [dɪvəʊ'tiː] entusiasta *m/f*

de·vo·tion [dɪ'vəʊʃn] devoción *f*

de·vour [dɪ'vaʊər] *v/t food, book* devorar

de·vout [dɪ'vaʊt] *adj* devoto

dew [duː] rocío *m*

dex·ter·i·ty [dek'sterətɪ] destreza *f*

di·a·be·tes [daɪə'biːtiːz] *nsg* diabetes *f*

di·a·bet·ic [daɪə'betɪk] **1** *n* diabético(-a) *m(f)* **2** *adj* diabético; *foods* para diabéticos

di·ag·nose ['daɪəgnəʊz] *v/t* diagnosticar; **she has been diagnosed as having cancer** se le ha diagnosticado un cáncer

di·ag·no·sis [daɪəg'nəʊsɪs] (*pl* **diagnoses** [daɪəg'nəʊsiːz]) diagnóstico *m*

di·ag·o·nal [daɪ'ægənl] *adj* diagonal

di·ag·o·nal·ly [daɪ'ægənlɪ] *adv* diagonalmente, en diagonal

di·a·gram ['daɪəgræm] diagrama *m*

di·al ['daɪl] **1** *n* of clock esfera *f*; of instrument cuadrante *m*; TELEC disco *m* **2** *v/t & v/i* (*pret & pp* **dialed**, *Br* **dialled**) TELEC marcar

di·a·lect ['daɪəlekt] dialecto *m*

di·al·ling tone *Br* → **dial tone**

di·a·log, *Br* di·a·logue ['daɪəlɒg] diálogo *m*

di·a·log box COMPUT ventana *f* de diálogo

'di·al tone tono *m* de marcar

di·am·e·ter [daɪ'æmɪtər] diámetro *m*; **a circle 6 cms in diameter** un círculo de 6 cms. de diámetro

di·a·met·ri·cal·ly [daɪə'metrɪkəlɪ] *adv*: **diametrically opposed** diametralmente opuesto

di·a·mond ['daɪmənd] *also in cards* diamante *m*; *shape* rombo *m*

di·a·per ['daɪpər] pañal *m*

di·a·phragm ['daɪəfræm] ANAT, *contraceptive* diafragma *m*

di·ar·rhe·a, *Br* di·ar·rhoe·a [daɪə'riːə] diarrea *f*

di·a·ry ['daɪrɪ] *for thoughts* diario *m*; *for appointments* agenda *f*

dice [daɪs] **1** *n* dado *m*; *pl* dados *mpl* **2** *v/t food* cortar en dados

di·chot·o·my [daɪ'kɒtəmɪ] dicotomía *f*

dic·ta·te [dɪk'teɪt] *v/t* dictar

dic·ta·tion [dɪk'teɪʃn] dictado *m*

dic·ta·tor [dɪk'teɪtər] POL dictador(a) *m(f)*

dic·ta·to·ri·al [dɪktə'tɔːrɪəl] *adj* dictatorial

dic·ta·tor·ship [dɪk'teɪtərʃɪp] dictadura *f*

dic·tion·a·ry ['dɪkʃənerɪ] diccionario *m*

did [dɪd] *pret* → **do**

die [daɪ] *v/i* morir; **die of cancer / Aids** morir de cáncer / sida; **I'm dying to know / leave** me muero de ganas de saber / marchar

◆ **die away** *v/i* of noise desaparecer

◆ **die down** *v/i* of noise irse apagando; of storm amainar; of fire irse extinguiendo; of excitement calmarse

◆ **die out** *v/i* of custom, species desaparecer

die·sel ['diːzl] *fuel* gasoil *m*, gasóleo *m*

di·et ['daɪət] **1** *n* (*regular food*) dieta *f*; *for losing weight, for health reasons* dieta *f*, régimen *m* **2** *v/i to lose weight* hacer dieta or régimen

di·e·ti·tian [daɪə'tɪʃn] experto(-a) *m(f)* en dietética

dif·fer ['dɪfər] *v/i* (*be different*) ser distinto; (*disagree*) discrepar; **the male differs from the female in ...** el macho se diferencia de la hembra por ...

dif·fe·rence ['dɪfrəns] diferencia *f*; (*disagreement*) diferencia *f*, discrepancia *f*; **it doesn't make any difference** (*doesn't change anything*) no cambia nada; (*doesn't matter*) da lo mismo

dif·fe·rent ['dɪfrənt] *adj* diferente, distinto (**from, than** de)

dif·fe·ren·ti·ate [dɪfə'renʃɪeɪt] *v/i* diferenciar, distinguir (**between** entre); ***differentiate between*** *treat differently* establecer diferencias entre

dif·fe·rent·ly ['dɪfrəntlɪ] *adv* de manera diferente

dif·fi·cult ['dɪfɪkəlt] *adj* difícil

dif·fi·cul·ty ['dɪfɪkəltɪ] dificultad *f*; **with difficulty** con dificultades

dif·fi·dence ['dɪfɪdəns] retraimiento *m*

dif·fi·dent ['dɪfɪdənt] *adj* retraído

dig [dɪg] *v/t & v/i* (*pret & pp* **dug**) cavar

◆ **dig out** *v/t* (*find*) encontrar

◆ **dig up** *v/t* levantar, cavar; *information* desenterrar

di·gest [daɪ'dʒest] *v/t also fig* digerir

di·gest·i·ble [daɪ'dʒestəbl] *adj food* digerible

di·ges·tion [daɪ'dʒestʃn] digestión *f*

di·ges·tive [daɪ'dʒestɪv] *adj* digestivo

dig·ger ['dɪgər] *machine* excavadora *f*

dig·it ['dɪdʒɪt] (*number*) dígito *m*; **a 4 digit number** un número de 4 dígitos

di·gi·tal ['dɪdʒɪtl] *adj* digital

dig·ni·fied ['dɪgnɪfaɪd] *adj* digno

dig·ni·ta·ry ['dɪgnɪterɪ] dignatario(-a) *m(f)*

dig·ni·ty ['dɪgnɪtɪ] dignidad *f*

di·gress [daɪ'gres] *v/i* divagar, apartarse del tema

di·gres·sion [daɪ'greʃn] digresión *f*

dike [daɪk] *wall* dique *m*

di·lap·i·dat·ed [dɪ'læpɪdeɪtɪd] *adj* destartalado

di·late [daɪ'leɪt] *v/i of pupils* dilatarse

di·lem·ma [dɪ'lemə] dilema *m*; **be in a dilemma** estar en un dilema

dil·et·tante [dɪle'tæntɪ] diletante *m/f*

dil·i·gent ['dɪlɪdʒənt] *adj* diligente

di·lute [daɪ'luːt] *v/t* diluir

dim [dɪm] **1** *adj room* oscuro; *light* tenue; *outline* borroso, confuso; (*stupid*) tonto; *prospects* remoto **2** *v/t* (*pret & pp* **dimmed**): atenuar; **dim the headlights** poner las luces cortas **3** *v/i* (*pret & pp* **dimmed**) *of lights* atenuarse

dime [daɪm] *moneda de diez centavos*

di·men·sion [daɪ'menʃn] (*measurement*) dimensión *f*

di·min·ish [dɪ'mɪnɪʃ] *v/t & v/i* disminuir

di·min·u·tive [dɪ'mɪnʊtɪv] **1** *n* diminutivo *m* **2** *adj* diminuto

dim·ple ['dɪmpl] hoyuelo *m*

din [dɪn] *n* estruendo *m*

dine [daɪn] *v/i fml* cenar

din·er ['daɪnər] *person* comensal *m/f*; *restaurant* restaurante *m* barato

din·ghy ['dɪŋgɪ] (*small yacht*) bote *m* de vela; (*rubber boat*) lancha *f* neumática

din·gy ['dɪndʒɪ] *adj* sórdido; (*dirty*) sucio

din·ing car ['daɪnɪŋ] RAIL vagón *m* restaurante, coche *m* comedor

'din·ing room comedor *m*

'din·ing ta·ble mesa *f* de comedor

din·ner ['dɪnər] *in the evening* cena *f*; *at midday* comida *f*; (*formal gathering*) cena *f* de gala

'din·ner guest invitado(-a) *m(f)* a cenar

'din·ner jack·et esmoquin *m*

'din·ner par·ty cena *f*

'din·ner serv·ice vajilla *f*

di·no·saur ['daɪnəsɔːr] dinosaurio *m*

dip [dɪp] **1** *n* (*swim*) baño *m*, zambullida *f*; *for food* salsa *f*; (*slope*) inclinación *f*, pendiente *f*; (*depression*) hondonada *f* **2** *v/t* (*pret & pp* **dipped**) meter; **dip the headlights** poner las luces cortas **3** *v/i* (*pret & pp* **dipped**) *of road* bajar

di·plo·ma [dɪ'ploumə] diploma *m*

di·plo·ma·cy [dɪ'plouməsɪ] *also fig* diplomacia *f*

di·plo·mat ['dɪpləmæt] diplomático(-a) *m(f)*

di·plo·mat·ic [dɪplə'mætɪk] *adj also fig* diplomático

dip·lo·mat·i·cal·ly [dɪplə'mætɪklɪ] *adv* de forma diplomática

dip·lo·mat·ic im·mu·ni·ty inmunidad *f* diplomática

dire [daɪr] *adj* terrible; **be in dire need of** necesitar acuciantemente

di·rect [daɪ'rekt] **1** *adj* directo **2** *v/t play, movie, attention* dirigir; **can you direct me to the museum?** ¿me podría indicar cómo se va al museo?

di·rect 'cur·rent ELEC corriente *f* continua

di·rec·tion [dɪ'rekʃn] dirección *f*; **directions** *to a place* indicaciones *fpl*; (*instructions*) instrucciones *fpl*; *for medicine* pos-

D

olo·gía f; *let's ask for directions* preguntemos cómo se va; *directions for use* modo m de empleo

di·rec·tion 'in·di·ca·tor мот intermitente m

di·rec·tive [dɪ'rektɪv] directiva f

di·rect·ly [dɪ'rektlɪ] **1** adv (straight) directamente; (soon) pronto; (immediately) ahora mismo **2** conj en cuanto

di·rec·tor [dɪ'rektər] director(a) m(f)

di·rec·to·ry [dɪ'rektərɪ] directorio m; TELEC guía f telefónica

dirt [dɜːrt] suciedad f

'dirt cheap adj F tirado F

dirt·y ['dɜːrtɪ] **1** adj sucio; (pornographic) pornográfico, obsceno **2** v/t (pret & pp dirtied) ensuciar

dirt·y 'trick jugarreta f; *play a dirty trick on s.o.* hacer una jugarreta a alguien

dis·a·bil·i·ty [dɪsə'bɪlətɪ] discapacidad f, minusvalía f

dis·a·bled [dɪs'eɪbld] **1** n: *the disabled* los discapacitados mpl **2** adj discapacitado

dis·ad·van·tage [dɪsəd'væntɪdʒ] (drawback) desventaja f; *be at a disadvantage* estar en desventaja

dis·ad·van·taged [dɪsəd'væntɪdʒd] adj desfavorecido

dis·ad·van·ta·geous [dɪsædvæn'teɪdʒəs] adj desventajoso, desfavorable

dis·a·gree [dɪsə'griː] v/i of person no estar de acuerdo, discrepar; *let's agree to disagree* aceptemos que no nos vamos a poner de acuerdo

◆ disagree with v/t of person no estar de acuerdo con, discrepar con; of food sentar mal; *lobster disagrees with me* la langosta me sienta mal

dis·a·gree·a·ble [dɪsə'griːəbl] adj desagradable

dis·a·gree·ment [dɪsə'griːmənt] desacuerdo m; (argument) discusión f

dis·ap·pear [dɪsə'pɪr] v/i desaparecer

dis·ap·pear·ance [dɪsə'pɪrəns] desaparición f

dis·ap·point [dɪsə'pɔɪnt] v/t desilusionar, decepcionar

dis·ap·point·ed [dɪsə'pɔɪntɪd] adj desilu-

sionado, decepcionado

dis·ap·point·ing [dɪsə'pɔɪntɪŋ] adj decepcionante

dis·ap·point·ment [dɪsə'pɔɪntmənt] desilusión f, decepción f

dis·ap·prov·al [dɪsə'pruːvl] desaprobación f

dis·ap·prove [dɪsə'pruːv] v/i desaprobar, estar en contra; *disapprove of* desaprobar, estar en contra de

dis·ap·prov·ing [dɪsə'pruːvɪŋ] adj desaprobatorio, de desaprobación

dis·ap·prov·ing·ly [dɪsə'pruːvɪŋlɪ] adv con desaprobación

dis·arm [dɪs'ɑːrm] **1** v/t desarmar **2** v/i desarmarse

dis·ar·ma·ment [dɪs'ɑːrməmənt] desarme m

dis·arm·ing [dɪs'ɑːrmɪŋ] adj cautivador

dis·as·ter [dɪ'zæstər] desastre m

di·sas·ter ar·e·a zona f catastrófica; (fig: person) desastre m

di·sas·trous [dɪ'zæstrəs] adj desastroso

dis·band [dɪs'bænd] **1** v/t disolver **2** v/i disolverse

dis·be·lief [dɪsbə'liːf] incredulidad f; *in disbelief* con incredulidad

disc [dɪsk] (CD) compact m (disc)

dis·card [dɪ'skɑːrd] v/t desechar; boyfriend deshacerse de

di·scern [dɪ'sɜːrn] v/t distinguir, percibir

di·scern·i·ble [dɪ'sɜːrnəbl] adj perceptible

di·scern·ing [dɪ'sɜːrnɪŋ] adj entendido, exigente

dis·charge **1** n ['dɪstʃɑːrdʒ] from hospital alta f; from army licencia f **2** v/t [dɪs-'tʃɑːrdʒ] from hospital dar el alta a; from army licenciar; from job despedir

di·sci·ple [dɪ'saɪpl] religious discípulo m

dis·ci·pli·nar·y [dɪsɪ'plɪnərɪ] adj disciplinario

dis·ci·pline ['dɪsɪplɪn] **1** n disciplina f **2** v/t child, dog castigar; employee sancionar

'disc jock·ey disc jockey m/f, Span pinchadiscos m/f inv

dis·claim [dɪs'kleɪm] v/t negar

dis·close [dɪs'kloʊs] v/t revelar

dis·clo·sure [dɪs'kloʊʒər] revelación f

dis·co ['dɪskou] discoteca *f*

dis·col·or, *Br* **dis·col·our** [dɪs'kʌlər] *v/i* decolorar

dis·com·fort [dɪs'kʌmfərt] (*pain*) molestia *f*; (*embarrassment*) incomodidad *f*

dis·con·cert [dɪskən'sɜːrt] *v/t* desconcertar

dis·con·cert·ed [dɪskən'sɜːrtɪd] *adj* desconcertado

dis·con·nect [dɪskə'nekt] *v/t* desconectar

dis·con·so·late [dɪs'kɑːnsəlæt] *adj* desconsolado

dis·con·tent [dɪskən'tent] descontento *m*

dis·con·tent·ed [dɪskən'tentɪd] *adj* descontento

dis·con·tin·ue [dɪskən'tɪnjuː] *v/t product* dejar de producir; *bus, train service* suspender; *magazine* dejar de publicar

dis·cord ['dɪskɔːrd] MUS discordancia *f*; *in relations* discordia *f*

dis·co·theque ['dɪskətek] discoteca *f*

dis·count 1 *n* ['dɪskaunt] descuento *m* **2** *v/t* [dɪs'kaunt] *goods* descontar; *theory* descartar

dis·cour·age [dɪs'kʌrɪdʒ] *v/t* (*dissuade*) disuadir (*from* de); (*dishearten*) desanimar, desalentar

dis·cour·age·ment [dɪs'kʌrɪdʒmənt] disuasión *f*; (*being disheartened*) desánimo *m*, desaliento *m*

dis·cov·er [dɪ'skʌvər] *v/t* descubrir

dis·cov·er·er [dɪ'skʌvərər] descubridor(a) *m(f)*

dis·cov·e·ry [dɪ'skʌvəri] descubrimiento *m*

dis·cred·it [dɪs'kredɪt] *v/t* desacreditar

dis·creet [dɪ'skriːt] *adj* discreto

dis·creet·ly [dɪ'skriːtlɪ] *adv* discretamente

dis·crep·an·cy [dɪ'skrepənsɪ] discrepancia *f*

dis·cre·tion [dɪ'skreʃn] discreción *f*; *at your discretion* a discreción; *use your discretion* usa tu criterio

dis·crim·i·nate [dɪ'skrɪmɪneɪt] *v/i* discriminar (*against* contra); *discriminate between* (*distinguish*) distinguir entre

dis·crim·i·nat·ing [dɪ'skrɪmɪneɪtɪŋ] *adj* entendido, exigente

di·scrim·i·na·tion [dɪ'skrɪmɪneɪʃn] *sexual, racial etc* discriminación *f*

dis·cus ['dɪskəs] SP *object* disco *m*; *event* lanzamiento *m* de disco

di·scuss [dɪ'skʌs] *v/t* discutir; *of article* analizar

dis·cus·sion [dɪ'skʌʃn] discusión *f*

'**dis·cus throw·er** lanzador(a) *m(f)* de disco

dis·dain [dɪs'deɪn] *n* desdén *m*

dis·ease [dɪ'ziːz] enfermedad *f*

dis·em·bark [dɪsəm'bɑːrk] *v/i* desembarcar

dis·en·chant·ed [dɪsən'tʃæntɪd] *adj*: *disenchanted with* desencantado con

dis·en·gage [dɪsən'geɪdʒ] *v/t* soltar

dis·en·tan·gle [dɪsən'tæŋgl] *v/t* desenredar

dis·fig·ure [dɪs'fɪgər] *v/t* desfigurar

dis·grace [dɪs'greɪs] **1** *n* vergüenza *f*; *it's a disgrace!* ¡qué vergüenza!; *in disgrace* desacreditado **2** *v/t* deshonrar

dis·grace·ful [dɪs'greɪsfəl] *adj behavior, situation* vergonzoso, lamentable

dis·grun·tled [dɪs'grʌntld] *adj* descontento

dis·guise [dɪs'gaɪz] **1** *n* disfraz *m*; *in disguise* disfrazado **2** *v/t voice, handwriting* cambiar; *fear, anxiety* disfrazar; *disguise o.s. as* disfrazarse de; *he was disguised as* iba disfrazado de

dis·gust [dɪs'gʌst] **1** *n* asco *m*, repugnancia *f*; *in disgust* asqueado **2** *v/t* dar asco, repugnar; *I'm disgusted by ...* me da asco *or* me repugna ...

dis·gust·ing [dɪs'gʌstɪŋ] *adj habit, smell, food* asqueroso, repugnante; *it is disgusting that ...* da asco que ..., es repugnante que ...

dish [dɪʃ] (*part of meal, container*) plato *m*

'**dish·cloth** paño *m* de cocina

dis·heart·en·ed [dɪs'hɑːrtnd] *adj* desalentado, descorazonado

dis·heart·en·ing [dɪs'hɑːrtnɪŋ] *adj* descorazonador

di·shev·eled [dɪ'ʃevld] *adj hair, clothes* desaliñado; *person* despeinado

dis·hon·est [dɪs'ɑːnɪst] *adj* deshonesto

dis·hon·est·y [dɪsˈɑːnɪstɪ] deshonestidad f

dis·hon·or [dɪsˈɑːnər] n deshonra f; **bring dishonor on** deshonrar a

dis·hon·o·ra·ble [dɪsˈɑːnərəbl] adj deshonroso

dis·hon·our etc Br → **dishonor** etc

'dish·wash·er person lavaplatos m/f inv; machine lavavajillas m inv, lavaplatos m inv

'dish·wash·ing liq·uid lavavajillas m inv

'dish·wa·ter agua f de lavar los platos

dis·il·lu·sion [dɪsɪˈluːʒn] v/t desilusionar

dis·il·lu·sion·ment [dɪsɪˈluːʒnmənt] desilusión f

dis·in·clined [dɪsɪnˈklaɪnd] adj: **she was disinclined to believe him** no estaba inclinada a creerle

dis·in·fect [dɪsɪnˈfekt] v/t desinfectar

dis·in·fec·tant [dɪsɪnˈfektənt] desinfectante m

dis·in·her·it [dɪsɪnˈherɪt] v/t desheredar

dis·in·te·grate [dɪsˈɪntəgreɪt] v/i desintegrarse; of marriage deshacerse

dis·in·terest·ed [dɪsˈɪntərestɪd] adj (unbiased) desinteresado

dis·joint·ed [dɪsˈdʒɔɪntɪd] adj deshilvanado

disk [dɪsk] also COMPUT disco m; **on disk** en disco

'disk drive COMPUT unidad f de disco

disk·ette [dɪsˈket] disquete m

dis·like [dɪsˈlaɪk] 1 n antipatía f 2 v/t: **she dislikes being kept waiting** no le gusta que la hagan esperar; **I dislike him** no me gusta

dis·lo·cate [ˈdɪsləkeɪt] v/t shoulder dislocar

dis·lodge [dɪsˈlɑːdʒ] v/t desplazar, mover de su sitio

dis·loy·al [dɪsˈlɔɪəl] adj desleal

dis·loy·al·ty [dɪsˈlɔɪəltɪ] deslealtad f

dis·mal [ˈdɪzməl] adj weather horroroso, espantoso; news, prospect negro; person (sad) triste; person (negative) negativo; failure estrepitoso

dis·man·tle [dɪsˈmæntl] v/t desmantelar

dis·may [dɪsˈmeɪ] 1 n (alarm) consternación f; (disappointment) desánimo m 2 v/t consternar

dis·miss [dɪsˈmɪs] v/t employee despedir; suggestion rechazar; idea, possibility descartar

dis·miss·al [dɪsˈmɪsl] of employee despido m

dis·mount [dɪsˈmaʊnt] v/i desmontar

dis·o·be·di·ence [dɪsəˈbiːdɪəns] desobediencia f

dis·o·be·di·ent [dɪsəˈbiːdɪənt] adj desobediente

dis·o·bey [dɪsəˈbeɪ] v/t desobedecer

dis·or·der [dɪsˈɔːrdər] (untidiness) desorden m; (unrest) desórdenes mpl; MED dolencia f

dis·or·der·ly [dɪsˈɔːrdərlɪ] adj room, desk desordenado; mob alborotado

dis·or·gan·ized [dɪsˈɔːrgənaɪzd] adj desorganizado

dis·o·ri·ent·ed [dɪsˈɔːrɪəntɪd] adj desorientado

dis·own [dɪsˈoʊn] v/t repudiar, renegar de

di·spar·ag·ing [dɪˈspærɪdʒɪŋ] adj despreciativo

di·spar·i·ty [dɪˈspærətɪ] disparidad f

dis·pas·sion·ate [dɪˈspæʃənət] adj (objective) desapasionado

di·spatch [dɪˈspætʃ] v/t (send) enviar

di·spen·sa·ry [dɪˈspensərɪ] in pharmacy dispensario m

◆ di·spense with [dɪˈspens] v/t prescindir de

dis·perse [dɪˈspɜːrs] 1 v/t dispersar 2 v/i of crowd dispersarse; of mist disiparse

dis·pir·it·ed [dɪˈspɪrɪtɪd] adj desalentado, abatido

dis·place [dɪsˈpleɪs] v/t (supplant) sustituir

di·splay [dɪˈspleɪ] 1 n muestra f; in store window objetos mpl expuestos; COMPUT pantalla f; **be on display** estar expuesto 2 v/t emotion mostrar; at exhibition, for sale exponer; COMPUT visualizar

di·splay cab·i·net in museum, shop vitrina f

dis·please [dɪsˈpliːz] v/t desagradar, disgustar

dis·plea·sure [dɪsˈpleʒər] desagrado m, disgusto m

dis·po·sa·ble [dɪ'spouzəbl] *adj* desechable; **disposable income** ingreso(s) *m(pl)* disponible(s)

dis·pos·al [dɪ'spouzl] eliminación *f*; **I am at your disposal** estoy a su disposición; **put sth at s.o.'s disposal** poner algo a disposición de alguien

◆ **dis·pose of** [dɪ'spouz] *v/t (get rid of)* deshacerse de

dis·posed [dɪ'spouzd] *adj*: **be disposed to do sth** *(willing)* estar dispuesto a hacer algo; **be well disposed towards** estar bien dispuesto hacia

dis·po·si·tion [dɪspə'zɪʃn] *(nature)* carácter *m*

dis·pro·por·tion·ate [dɪsprə'pɔːrʃənət] *adj* desproporcionado

dis·prove [dɪs'pruːv] *v/t* refutar

dis·pute [dɪ'spjuːt] **1** *n* disputa *f*; *industrial* conflicto *m* laboral **2** *v/t* discutir; *(fight over)* disputarse; **I don't dispute that** eso no lo discuto

dis·qual·i·fi·ca·tion [dɪskwɑːlɪfɪ'keɪʃn] descalificación *f*

dis·qual·i·fy [dɪs'kwɑːlɪfaɪ] *v/t (pret & pp* **disqualified)** descalificar

dis·re·gard [dɪsrə'gɑːrd] **1** *n* indiferencia *f* **2** *v/t* no tener en cuenta

dis·re·pair [dɪsrə'per]: **in a state of disrepair** deteriorado

dis·rep·u·ta·ble [dɪs'repjutəbl] *adj* poco respetable; *area* de mala reputación

dis·re·spect [dɪsrə'spekt] falta *f* de respeto

dis·re·spect·ful [dɪsrə'spektfəl] *adj* irrespetuoso

dis·rupt [dɪs'rʌpt] *v/t train service* trastornar, alterar; *meeting, class* interrumpir

dis·rup·tion [dɪs'rʌpʃn] *of train service* alteración *f*; *of meeting, class* interrupción *f*

dis·rup·tive [dɪs'rʌptɪv] *adj* perjudicial; **he's very disruptive in class** causa muchos problemas en clase

dis·sat·is·fac·tion [dɪssætɪs'fækʃn] insatisfacción *f*

dis·sat·is·fied [dɪs'sætɪsfaɪd] *adj* insatisfecho

dis·sen·sion [dɪ'senʃn] disensión *f*

dis·sent [dɪ'sent] **1** *n* discrepancia *f* **2** *v/i*: **dissent from** disentir de

dis·si·dent ['dɪsɪdənt] *n* disidente *m/f*

dis·sim·i·lar [dɪs'sɪmɪlər] *adj* distinto

dis·so·ci·ate [dɪ'souʃɪeɪt] *v/t* disociar; **dissociate o.s. from** disociarse de

dis·so·lute ['dɪsəluːt] *adj* disoluto

dis·so·lu·tion ['dɪsəluːʃn] POL disolución *f*

dis·solve [dɪ'zɑːlv] **1** *v/t substance* disolver **2** *v/i of substance* disolverse

dis·suade [dɪ'sweɪd] *v/t* disuadir; **dissuade s.o. from doing sth** disuadir a alguien de hacer algo

dis·tance ['dɪstəns] **1** *n* distancia *f*; **in the distance** en la lejanía **2** *v/t* distanciar; **distance o.s. from** distanciarse de

dis·tant ['dɪstənt] *adj place, time, relative* distante, lejano; *(fig: aloof)* distante

dis·taste [dɪs'teɪst] desagrado *m*

dis·taste·ful [dɪs'teɪstfəl] *adj* desagradable

dis·till·er·y [dɪs'tɪləri] destilería *f*

dis·tinct [dɪ'stɪŋkt] *adj (clear)* claro; *(different)* distinto; **as distinct from** a diferencia de

dis·tinc·tion [dɪ'stɪŋkʃn] *(differentiation)* distinción *f*; **hotel / product of distinction** un hotel / producto destacado

dis·tinc·tive [dɪ'stɪŋktɪv] *adj* característico

dis·tinct·ly [dɪ'stɪŋktlɪ] *adv* claramente, con claridad; *(decidedly)* verdaderamente

dis·tin·guish [dɪ'stɪŋgwɪʃ] *v/t* distinguir; **distinguish between X and Y** distinguir entre X e Y

dis·tin·guished [dɪ'stɪŋgwɪʃt] *adj* distinguido

dis·tort [dɪ'stɔːrt] *v/t* distorsionar

dis·tract [dɪ'strækt] *v/t* distraer

dis·trac·tion [dɪ'strækʃn] distracción *f*; **drive s.o. to distraction** sacar a alguien de quicio

dis·traught [dɪ'strɔːt] *adj* angustiado, consternado

dis·tress [dɪ'stres] **1** *n* sufrimiento *m*; **in distress** *of ship, aircraft* en peligro **2** *v/t (upset)* angustiar

dis·tress·ing [dɪ'stresɪŋ] *adj* angustiante

dis'tress sig·nal señal *m* de socorro

dis·trib·ute [dɪ'strɪbjuːt] *v/t* distribuir, repartir; COM distribuir

dis·tri·bu·tion [dɪstrɪ'bjuːʃn] distribución *f*

dis·tri·bu·tion ar·range·ment COM acuerdo *m* de distribución

dis·trib·u·tor [dɪs'trɪbjuːtər] COM distribuidor(a) *m(f)*

dis·trict ['dɪstrɪkt] *(area)* zona *f*; *(neighborhood)* barrio *m*

dis·trict at'tor·ney fiscal *m/f* del distrito

dis·trust [dɪs'trʌst] **1** *n* desconfianza *f* **2** *v/t* desconfiar de

dis·turb [dɪ'stɜːrb] *v/t (interrupt)* molestar; *(upset)* preocupar; **do not disturb** no molestar

dis·turb·ance [dɪ'stɜːrbəns] *(interruption)* molestia *f*; **disturbances** *(civil unrest)* disturbios *mpl*

dis·turbed [dɪ'stɜːrbd] *adj (concerned, worried)* preocupado, inquieto; *mentally* perturbado

dis·turb·ing [dɪ'stɜːrbɪŋ] *adj (worrying)* inquietante; **you may find some scenes disturbing** algunas de las escenas pueden herir la sensibilidad del espectador

dis·used [dɪs'juːzd] *adj* abandonado

ditch [dɪtʃ] **1** *n* zanja *f* **2** *v/t* F *(get rid of)* deshacerse de; *boyfriend* plantar F; *plan* abandonar

dith·er ['dɪðər] *v/i* vacilar

dive [daɪv] **1** *n* salto *m* de cabeza; *underwater* inmersión *f*; *of plane* descenso *m* en picado; F *bar etc* antro *m* F; **take a dive** F *of dollar etc* desplomarse **2** *v/i (pret also dove)* tirarse de cabeza; *underwater* bucear; *of plane* descender en picado

div·er ['daɪvər] *off board* saltador(a) *m(f)* de trampolín; *underwater* buceador(a) *m(f)*

di·verge [daɪ'vɜːrdʒ] *v/i* bifurcarse

di·verse [daɪ'vɜːrs] *adj* diverso

di·ver·si·fi·ca·tion [daɪvɜːrsɪfɪ'keɪʃn] COM diversificación *f*

di·ver·si·fy [daɪ'vɜːrsɪfaɪ] *v/i (pret & pp diversified)* COM diversificarse

di·ver·sion [daɪ'vɜːrʃn] *for traffic* desvío

f; *to distract attention* distracción *f*

di·ver·si·ty [daɪ'vɜːrsətɪ] diversidad *f*

di·vert [daɪ'vɜːrt] *v/t traffic, attention* desviar

di·vest [daɪ'vest] *v/t:* **divest s.o. of sth** despojar a alguien de algo

di·vide [dɪ'vaɪd] *v/t also fig* dividir; **divide 16 by 4** dividir 16 entre 4

div·i·dend ['dɪvɪdend] FIN dividendo *m*; **pay dividends** *fig* resultar beneficioso

di·vine [dɪ'vaɪn] *adj also* F divino

div·ing ['daɪvɪŋ] *from board* salto *m* de trampolín; *(scuba diving)* buceo *m*, submarinismo *m*

'div·ing board trampolín *m*

di·vis·i·ble [dɪ'vɪzəbl] *adj* divisible

di·vi·sion [dɪ'vɪʒn] división *f*

di·vorce [dɪ'vɔːrs] **1** *n* divorcio *m*; **get a divorce** divorciarse **2** *v/t* divorciarse de; **get divorced** divorciarse **3** *v/i* divorciarse

di·vorced [dɪ'vɔːrst] *adj* divorciado

di·vor·cee [dɪvɔːr'siː] divorciado(-a) *m(f)*

di·vulge [daɪ'vʌldʒ] *v/t* divulgar, dar a conocer

DIY [diːaɪ'waɪ] *abbr (= do it yourself)* bricolaje *m*

DI'Y store tienda *f* de bricolaje

diz·zi·ness ['dɪzɪnɪs] mareo *m*

diz·zy ['dɪzɪ] *adj* mareado; **feel dizzy** estar mareado

DJ ['diːdʒeɪ] *abbr (= disc jockey)* disc jockey *m/f*, *Span* pinchadiscos *m/f inv*; *(= dinner jacket)* esmoquin *m*

DNA [diːen'eɪ] *abbr (= deoxyribonucleic acid)* AND *m (= ácido m* desoxirribonucleico)

do [duː] **1** *v/t (pret did, pp done)* hacer; *100 mph etc* ir a; **do one's hair** peinarse; **what are you doing tonight?** ¿qué vas a hacer esta noche?; **I don't know what to do** no sé qué hacer; **do it right now!** hazlo ahora mismo; **have one's hair done** arreglarse el pelo **2** *v/i (pret did, pp done) (be suitable, enough):* **that'll do nicely** eso bastará; **that will do!** ¡ya vale!; **do well** *of business* ir bien; **he's doing well** le van bien las cosas; **well done!**

(*congratulations!*) ¡bien hecho!; *how do you do?* encantado de conocerle **3** *v/aux: do you know him?* ¿lo conoces?; *I don't know* no sé; *do be quick* date prisa, por favor; *do you like Des Moines? - yes I do* ¿te gusta Des Moines? - sí; *he works hard, doesn't he?* trabaja mucho, ¿verdad?; *don't you believe me?* ¿no me crees?; *you do believe me, don't you?* me crees, ¿verdad?; *you don't know the answer, do you? - no I don't* no sabes la respuesta, ¿no es así? - no, no la sé

◆ **do away with** *v/t* (*abolish*) abolir
◆ **do in** *v/t* F (*exhaust*) machacar F; *I'm do- ne in* estoy hecho polvo F
◆ **do out of** *v/t: do s.o. out of sth* timar alguien a algo F
◆ **do up** *v/t* (*renovate*) renovar; *buttons, coat* abrocharse; *laces* atarse
◆ **do with** *v/t: I could do with ...* no me vendría mal ...; *he won't have anything to do with it* (*won't get involved*) no quiere saber nada de ello
◆ **do without 1** *v/i: you'll have to do with- out* te las tendrás que arreglar **2** *v/t* pasar sin

do·cile ['dousəl] *adj* dócil
dock¹ [dɑːk] **1** *n* NAUT muelle *m* **2** *v/i of ship* atracar; *of spaceship* acoplarse
dock² [dɑːk] *n* LAW banquillo *m* (de los acusados)
'**dock·yard** *Br* astillero *m*
doc·tor ['dɑːktər] *n* MED médico *m*; *form of address* doctor *m*
doc·tor·ate ['dɑːktərət] doctorado *m*
doc·trine ['dɑːktrɪn] doctrina *f*
doc·u·dra·ma ['dɑːkjʊdrɑːmə] docudrama *m*
doc·u·ment ['dɑːkjʊmənt] *n* documento *m*
doc·u·men·ta·ry [dɑːkjʊ'mentərɪ] *n program* documental *m*
doc·u·men·ta·tion [dɑːkjumen'teɪʃn] documentación *f*
dodge [dɑːdʒ] *v/t blow, person* esquivar; *issue, question* eludir
doe [dou] *deer* cierva *f*
dog [dɒːg] **1** *n* perro(-a) *m(f)* **2** *v/t* (*pret &*

pp **dogged**) *of bad luck* perseguir
'**dog catch·er** perrero(-a) *m(f)*
dog-eared ['dɒːgɪrd] *adj book* sobado, con las esquinas dobladas
dog·ged ['dɒːgɪd] *adj* tenaz
dog·gie ['dɒːgɪ] *in children's language* perrito *m*
dog·gy bag ['dɒːgɪbæg] *bolsa para las so- bras de la comida*
'**dog·house: be in the doghouse** F haber caído en desgracia
dog·ma ['dɒːgmə] dogma *m*
dog·mat·ic [dɒːg'mætɪk] *adj* dogmático
do-good·er ['duːgʊdər] *pej* buen(a) sa- maritano(-a) *m(f)*
'**dog tag** MIL chapa *f* de identificación
'**dog-tired** *adj* F hecho polvo F
do-it-your·self [duːɪtjər'self] bricolaje *m*
dol·drums ['douldrəmz]: *be in the dol- drums of economy* estar en un bache; *doldrums of person* estar deprimido
◆ **dole out** *v/t* repartir
doll [dɑːl] *toy* muñeca *f*; F *woman* muñeca *f* F
◆ **doll up** *v/t: get dolled up* emperifol- larse
dol·lar ['dɑːlər] dólar *m*
dol·lop ['dɑːləp] *n* F cucharada *f*
dol·phin ['dɑːlfɪn] delfín *m*
dome [doum] *of building* cúpula *f*
do·mes·tic [də'mestɪk] **1** *adj chores* do- méstico, del hogar; *news, policy* nacional **2** *n* empleado(-a) *m(f)* del hogar
do·mes·tic 'an·i·mal animal *m* doméstico
do·mes·ti·cate [də'mestɪkeɪt] *v/t animal* domesticar; *be domesticated of person* estar domesticado
do·mes·tic flight vuelo *m* nacional
dom·i·nant ['dɑːmɪnənt] *adj* dominante
dom·i·nate ['dɑːmɪneɪt] *v/t* dominar
dom·i·na·tion [dɑːmɪ'neɪʃn] dominación *f*
dom·i·neer·ing [dɑːmɪ'nɪrɪŋ] *adj* domi- nante
dom·i·no ['dɑːmɪnou] ficha *f* de dominó; *play dominoes* jugar al dominó
do·nate [dou'neɪt] *v/t* donar
do·na·tion [dou'neɪʃn] donación *f*, dona- tivo *m*; MED donación *f*

D

done [dʌn] pp → **do**

don·key ['dɒŋkı] burro m

do·nor ['dəʊnər] of money, MED donante m/f

do·nut ['dəʊnʌt] dónut m

doo·dle ['du:dl] v/i garabatear

doom [du:m] n (fate) destino m; (ruin) fatalidad f

doomed [du:md] adj project condenado al fracaso; **we are doomed** (bound to fail) estamos condenados al fracaso; (going to die) vamos a morir

door [dɔːr] puerta f; **there's someone at the door** hay alguien en la puerta

'door·bell timbre m

'door·knob pomo m

'door·man portero m

'door·mat felpudo m

'door·step umbral m

'door·way puerta f

dope [dəʊp] **1** n (drugs) droga f; F (idiot) lelo(-a) m(f); F (information) información f **2** v/t drogar

dor·mant ['dɔːrmənt] adj plant aletargado; volcano inactivo

dor·mi·to·ry ['dɔːrmɪtɔːrɪ] dormitorio m (colectivo); (hall of residence) residencia f de estudiantes

dos·age ['dəʊsɪdʒ] dosis f inv

dose [dəʊs] n dosis f inv

dot [dɒt] n punto m; **on the dot** (exactly) en punto

◆ **dote on** [dəʊt] v/t adorar a

dot.com (com·pany) [dɒt'kɑːm] empresa f punto.com

dot·ing ['dəʊtɪŋ] adj: **my doting aunt** mi tía, que tanto me adora

dot·ted line ['dɑːtɪd] línea f de puntos

dou·ble ['dʌbl] **1** n person doble m/f; room habitación f doble **2** adj doble; **inflation is now in double figures** la inflación ha superado ya el 10% **3** adv: **they offered me double what the others did** me ofrecieron el doble que la otra gente **4** v/t doblar, duplicar **5** v/i doblarse, duplicarse; **it doubles as ...** hace también de ...

◆ **double back** v/i (go back) volver sobre sus pasos

◆ **double up** v/i in pain doblarse; (share) compartir habitación

double-'bass contrabajo m

dou·ble-'bed cama f de matrimonio

dou·ble-'breast·ed [dʌbl'brestɪd] adj cruzado

dou·ble-'check v/t & v/i volver a comprobar

dou·ble 'chin papada f

dou·ble-'cross v/t engañar, traicionar

dou·ble 'glaz·ing doble acristalamiento m

dou·ble'park v/i aparcar en doble fila

'dou·ble-quick adj: **in double-quick time** muy rápidamente

'dou·ble room habitación f doble

dou·bles ['dʌblz] in tennis dobles mpl

doubt [daʊt] **1** n duda f; (uncertainty) dudas fpl; **be in doubt** ser incierto; **not be in doubt** estar claro; **no doubt** (probably) sin duda **2** v/t dudar; **we never doubted you** nunca dudamos de ti

doubt·ful ['daʊtfəl] adj remark, look dubitativo; **be doubtful** of person tener dudas; **it is doubtful whether ...** es dudoso que ...

doubt·ful·ly ['daʊtfəlɪ] adv lleno de dudas

doubt·less ['daʊtlɪs] adj sin duda, indudablemente

dough [dəʊ] masa f; F (money) Span pasta f F, L.Am. plata f F

dough·nut ['dəʊnʌt] dónut m

dove¹ [dʌv] also fig paloma f

dove² [dəʊv] pret → **dive**

dow·dy ['daʊdɪ] adj poco elegante

Dow Jones Av·er·age [daʊdʒəʊnz'ævərɪdʒ] índice m Dow Jones

down¹ [daʊn] n (feathers) plumón m

down² [daʊn] **1** adv (downward) (hacia) abajo; **pull the blind down** baja la persiana; **put it down on the table** ponlo en la mesa; **when the leaves come down** cuando se caen las hojas; **cut down a tree** cortar un árbol; **she was down on her knees** estaba arrodillada; **the plane was shot down** el avión fue abatido; **down there** allá abajo; **fall down** caerse; **die down** amainar; **$200 down**

(as deposit) una entrada de 200 dólares; **down south** hacia el sur; **be down** of price, rate haber bajado; of numbers, amount haber descendido; (not working) no funcionar; F (depressed) estar deprimido or con la depre F **2** prep: **run down the stairs** bajar las escaleras corriendo; **the lava rolled down the hill** la lava descendía por la colina; **walk down the street** andar por la calle; **down the corridor** por el pasillo **3** v/t (swallow) tragar; (destroy) derribar

'down·and·out *n* vagabundo(-a) *m(f)*

'down·cast *adj* (dejected) deprimido

'down·fall caída *f*; of person perdición *f*

'down·grade *v/t* degradar; **the hurricane has been downgraded to a storm** el huracán ha sido reducido a la categoría de tormenta

down·heart·ed [daʊn'hɑːrtɪd] *adj* abatido

down'hill *adv* cuesta abajo; **go downhill** *fig* ir cuesta abajo

'down·hill ski·ing descenso *m*

'down·load *v/t* COMPUT descargar, bajar

'down·mark·et *adj* barato

'down pay·ment entrada *f*; **make a down payment on sth** pagar la entrada de algo

'down·play *v/t* quitar importancia a

'down·pour chaparrón *m*, aguacero *m*

'down·right **1** *adj* lie evidente; idiot completo **2** *adv*: **dangerous** extremadamente; stupid completamente

'down·side (disadvantage) desventaja *f*, inconveniente *m*

'down·size **1** *v/t* car reducir el tamaño de; company reajustar la plantilla de **2** *v/i* of company reajustar la plantilla

'down·stairs **1** *adj* del piso de abajo; **my downstairs neighbors** los vecinos de abajo **2** *adv*: **the kitchen is downstairs** la cocina está en el piso de abajo; **I ran downstairs** bajé corriendo

down-to-'earth *adj* approach, person práctico, realista

'down·town **1** *n* centro *m* **2** *adj* del centro **2** *adv*: **I'm going downtown** voy al centro; **he lives downtown** vive en el centro

'down·turn in economy bajón *m*

'down·ward ['daʊnwərd] **1** *adj* descendente **2** *adv* a la baja

doze [doʊz] **1** *n* cabezada *f*, sueño *m* **2** *v/i* echar una cabezada

♦ doze off *v/i* quedarse dormido

doz·en ['dʌzn] docena *f*; **dozens of** F montonadas de F

drab [dræb] *adj* gris

draft [dræft] **1** *n* of air corriente *f*; of document borrador *m*; MIL reclutamiento *m*; **draft (beer)**, **beer on draft** cerveza *f* de barril **2** *v/t* document redactar un borrador de; MIL reclutar

'draft dodg·er prófugo(-a) *m(f)*

draft·ee [dræf'tiː] recluta *m/f*

drafts·man ['dræftsmən] delineante *m/f*

draft·y ['dræftɪ] *adj*: **it's drafty here** hace mucha corriente aquí

drag [dræg] **1** *n*: **it's a drag having to …** F es un latazo tener que … F; **he's a drag** F es un peñazo F; **the main drag** F la calle principal; **in drag** vestido de mujer **2** *v/t* (pret & pp **dragged**) (pull) arrastrar; (search) dragar **3** *v/i* (pret & pp **dragged**) of time pasar despacio; of show, movie ser pesado; **drag s.o. into sth** (involve) meter a alguien en algo; **drag sth out of s.o.** (get information from) arrancar algo de alguien

♦ drag away *v/t*: **drag o.s. away from the TV** despegarse de la TV

♦ drag in *v/t* into conversation introducir

♦ drag on *v/i* (last long time) alargarse

♦ drag out *v/t* (prolong) alargar

♦ drag up *v/t* F (mention) sacar a relucir

drag·on ['drægn] dragón *m*; *fig* ogro *m*

drain [dreɪn] **1** *n* pipe sumidero *m*, desagüe *m*; under street alcantarilla *f*; **a drain on resources** una sangría en los recursos **2** *v/t* water, vegetables escurrir; land drenar; glass, tank, oil vaciar; person agotar **3** *v/t* of dishes escurrir

♦ drain away *v/i* of liquid irse

♦ drain off *v/t* water escurrir

drain·age ['dreɪnɪdʒ] (drains) desagües *mpl*; of water from soil drenaje *m*

'drain·pipe tubo *m* de desagüe

dra·ma ['drɑːmə] (art form) drama *m*, teatro *m*; (excitement) dramatismo *m*; (play:

on TV) drama *m*, obra *f* de teatro

dra·mat·ic [drə'mætɪk] *adj* dramático; *scenery* espectacular

dra·mat·i·cal·ly [drə'mætɪklɪ] *adv say* con dramatismo, de manera dramática; *decline, rise, change etc* espectacularmente

dram·a·tist ['dræmətɪst] dramaturgo(-a) *m(f)*

dram·a·ti·za·tion [dræmətaɪ'zeɪʃn] (*play*) dramatización *f*

dram·a·tize ['dræmətaɪz] *v/t also fig* dramatizar

drank [dræŋk] *pret* → **drink**

drape [dreɪp] *v/t cloth* cubrir; *draped in* (*covered with*) cubierto con

drap·er·y ['dreɪpərɪ] ropajes *mpl*

drapes [dreɪps] *npl* cortinas *fpl*

dras·tic ['dræstɪk] *adj* drástico

draught *Br* → **draft**

draw [drɔː] **1** *n in match, competition* empate *m*; *in lottery* sorteo *m*; (*attraction*) atracción *f* **2** *v/t* (*pret* **drew**, *pp* **drawn**) *picture, map* dibujar; *cart* tirar de; (*curtain*) correr; *in lottery* sortear; *gun, knife* sacar; (*attract*) atraer; (*lead*) llevar; *from bank account* sacar, retirar **3** *v/i* (*pret* **drew**, *pp* **drawn**) dibujar; *in match, competition* empatar; *draw near* acercarse

◆ **draw back 1** *v/i* (*recoil*) echarse atrás **2** *v/t* (*pull back*) retirar

◆ **draw on 1** *v/i* (*approach*) aproximarse **2** *v/t* (*make use of*) utilizar

◆ **draw out** *v/t wallet, money from bank* sacar

◆ **draw up 1** *v/t document* redactar; *chair* acercar **2** *v/i of vehicle* parar

'draw·back desventaja *f*, inconveniente *m*

draw·er[1] [drɔːr] *of desk etc* cajón *m*

draw·er[2] [drɔːr]: *she's a good drawer* dibuja muy bien

'draw·ing ['drɔːɪŋ] dibujo *m*

'draw·ing board tablero *m* de dibujo; *go back to the drawing board fig* volver a empezar otra vez

'draw·ing pin *Br* chincheta *f*

drawl [drɔːl] *n* acento *m* arrastrado

drawn [drɔːn] *pp* → **draw**

dread [dred] *v/t* tener pavor a; *I dread him ever finding out* me da pavor pensar que lo pueda llegar a descubrir; *I dread going to the dentist* me da pánico ir al dentista

dread·ful ['dredfəl] *adj* horrible, espantoso; *it's a dreadful pity you won't be there* es una auténtica pena que no vayas a estar ahí

dread·ful·ly ['dredfəlɪ] *adv* F (*extremely*) terriblemente, espantosamente F; *behave* fatal

dream [driːm] **1** *n* sueño *m* **2** *adj*: *win your dream house!* ¡gane la casa de sus sueños! **3** *v/t* soñar; (*daydream*) soñar (despierto) **4** *v/i* (*daydream*) soñar (despierto); *I dreamt about you last night* anoche soñé contigo

◆ **dream up** *v/t* inventar

◆ **dream·er** ['driːmər] (*daydreamer*) soñador(a) *m(f)*

dream·y ['driːmɪ] *adj voice, look* soñador

drear·y ['drɪrɪ] *adj* triste, deprimente

dredge [dredʒ] *v/t harbor, canal* dragar

◆ **dredge up** *v/t fig* sacar a relucir

dregs [dregz] *npl of coffee* posos *mpl*; *the dregs of society* la escoria de la sociedad

drench [drentʃ] *v/t* empapar; *get drenched* empaparse

dress [dres] **1** *n for woman* vestido *m*; (*clothing*) traje *m*; *he has no dress sense* no sabe vestir(se); *the company has a dress code* la compañía tiene unas normas sobre la ropa que deben llevar los empleados **2** *v/t person* vestir; *wound* vendar; *get dressed* vestirse **3** *v/i* (*get dressed*) vestirse; *well, in black etc* vestir(se) (*in* de)

◆ **dress up** *v/i* arreglarse, vestirse elegante; (*wear a disguise*) disfrazarse (*as* de)

'dress cir·cle piso *m* principal

dress·er ['dresər] (*dressing table*) tocador *f*; *in kitchen* aparador *m*

dress·ing ['dresɪŋ] *for salad* aliño *m*, *Span* arreglo *m*; *for wound* vendaje *m*

dress·ing 'down regaño *m*; *give s.o. a dressing down* regañar a alguien

'dress·ing room *in theater* camerino *m*

'dress·ing ta·ble tocador *f*

'dress·mak·er modisto(-a) *m(f)*

'dress re·hears·al ensayo *m* general

dress·y ['dresɪ] *adj* F elegante

drew [druː] *pret* → **draw**

drib·ble ['drɪbl] *v/i of person, baby* babear; *of water* gotear; SP driblar

dried [draɪd] *adj fruit etc* seco

dri·er [draɪr] → **dryer**

drift [drɪft] **1** *n of snow* ventisquero *m* **2** *v/i of snow* amontonarse; *of ship* ir a la deriva; *(go off course)* desviarse del rumbo; *of person* vagar

♦ **drift apart** *v/i of couple* distanciarse

drift·er ['drɪftər] vagabundo(-a) *m(f)*

drill [drɪl] **1** *n tool* taladro *m*; *exercise* simulacro *m*; MIL instrucción *f* **2** *v/t hole* taladrar, perforar **3** *v/i for oil* hacer perforaciones; MIL entrenarse

dril·ling rig ['drɪlɪŋrɪg] *(platform)* plataforma *f* petrolífera

dri·ly ['draɪlɪ] *adv remark* secamente, lacónicamente

drink [drɪŋk] **1** *n* bebida *f*; **a drink of ...** un vaso de ...; **go for a drink** ir a tomar algo **2** *v/t (pret* drank, *pp* drunk) beber **3** *v/i (pret* drank, *pp* drunk) beber, *L.Am.* tomar; **I don't drink** no bebo

♦ **drink up 1** *v/i (finish drink)* acabarse la bebida **2** *v/t (drink completely)* beberse todo

drink·a·ble ['drɪŋkəbl] *adj* potable

drink 'driv·ing conducción *f* bajo los efectos del alcohol

drink·er ['drɪŋkər] bebedor(a) *m(f)*

drink·ing ['drɪŋkɪŋ]: **I'm worried about his drinking** me preocupa que beba tanto; **a drinking problem** un problema con la bebida

'drink·ing wa·ter agua *f* potable

'drinks ma·chine máquina *f* expendedora de bebidas

drip [drɪp] **1** *n* gota *f*; MED gotero *m*, suero *m* **2** *v/i (pret & pp* dripped) gotear

'drip-dry *adj* que no necesita planchado

drip·ping ['drɪpɪŋ] *adv*: **dripping wet** empapado

drive [draɪv] **1** *n outing* vuelta *f*, paseo *m* (en coche); *(energy)* energía *f*; COMPUT unidad *f*; *(campaign)* campaña *f*; **it's a**

short drive from the station está a poca distancia en coche de la estación; **with left-/right-hand drive** MOT con el volante a la izquierda/a la derecha **2** *v/t (pret* drove, *pp* driven) *vehicle* conducir, *L.Am.* manejar; *(own)* tener; *(take in car)* llevar (en coche); TECH impulsar; **that noise / he is driving me mad** ese ruido / él me está volviendo loco **3** *v/i (pret* drove, *pp* driven) conducir, *L.Am.* manejar; **don't drink and drive** si bebes, no conduzcas; **I drive to work** voy al trabajo en coche

♦ **drive at** *v/t*: **what are you driving at?** ¿qué insinúas?

♦ **drive away 1** *v/t* llevarse en un coche; *(chase off)* ahuyentar **2** *v/i* marcharse

♦ **drive in** *v/t nail* remachar

♦ **drive off** → **drive away**

'drive-in *n (movie theater)* autocine *m*

driv·el ['drɪvl] *n* tonterías *fpl*

driv·en ['drɪvn] *pp* → **drive**

driv·er ['draɪvər] conductor(a) *m(f)*; *Br of train* maquinista *m/f*; COMPUT controlador *m*

'driv·er's li·cense carné *m* de conducir

drive-thru ['draɪvθruː] *restaurante / banco etc* en el que se atiende al cliente sin que salga del coche

'drive·way camino *m* de entrada

driv·ing ['draɪvɪŋ] **1** *n* conducción *f*; **his driving is appalling** conduce *or L.Am.* maneja fatal **2** *adj rain* torrencial

'driv·ing force fuerza *f* motriz

'driv·ing in·struct·or profesor(a) *m(f)* de autoescuela

'driv·ing les·son clase *f* de conducir

'driv·ing li·cence *Br* carné *m* de conducir

'driv·ing school autoescuela *f*

'driv·ing test examen *m* de conducir *or L.Am.* manejar

driz·zle ['drɪzl] **1** *n* llovizna *f* **2** *v/i* lloviznar

drone [droʊn] *n noise* zumbido *m*

droop [druːp] *v/i of plant* marchitarse; **her shoulders drooped** se encorvó

drop [drɑːp] **1** *n* gota *f*; *in price, temperature* caída *f*; **could I have a drop more milk, please?** ¿me podría poner un poquitín más de leche, por favor? **2** *v/t (pret*

& pp **dropped**) object dejar caer; *person from car* dejar; *person from team* excluir; (*stop seeing*) abandonar; *charges, demand etc* retirar; (*give up*) dejar; **drop a line to** mandar unas líneas a 3 *v/i* (*pret & pp* **dropped**) caer, caerse; (*decline*) caer; *of wind* amainar

◆ **drop in** *v/i* (*visit*) pasar a visitar

◆ **drop off 1** *v/t person* dejar; (*deliver*) llevar 2 *v/i* (*fall asleep*) dormirse; (*decline*) disminuir

◆ **drop out** *v/i* (*withdraw*) retirarse; **drop out of school** abandonar el colegio

'drop·out (*from school*) alumno que ha abandonado los estudios; *from society* marginado(-a) *m(f)*

drops [drɑːps] *npl for eyes* gotas *fpl*

drought [draʊt] sequía *f*

drove [droʊv] *pret* → **drive**

drown [draʊn] **1** *v/i* ahogarse **2** *v/t person, sound* ahogar; **be drowned** ahogarse

drow·sy ['draʊzɪ] *adj* soñoliento(-a)

drudg·er·y ['drʌdʒərɪ]: **the job is sheer drudgery** el trabajo es terriblemente pesado

drug [drʌg] **1** *n* MED, *illegal* droga *f*; **be on drugs** drogarse **2** *v/t* (*pret & pp* **drugged**) drogar

'drug ad·dict drogadicto(-a) *m(f)*

'drug deal·er traficante *m/f* (de drogas)

drug·gist ['drʌgɪst] farmacéutico(-a) *m(f)*

'drug·store tienda en la que se venden medicinas, cosméticos, periódicos y que a veces tiene un bar

'drug traf·fick·ing tráfico *m* de drogas

drum [drʌm] *n* MUS tambor *m*; *container* barril *m*

◆ **drum into** *v/t* (*pret & pp* **drummed**): **drum sth into s.o.** meter algo en la cabeza de alguien

◆ **drum up** *v/t*: **drum up support** buscar apoyos

drum·mer ['drʌmər] tambor *m*, tamborilero(-a) *m(f)*

'drum·stick MUS baqueta *f*; *of poultry* muslo *m*

drunk [drʌŋk] **1** *n* borracho(-a) *m(f)* **2** *adj* borracho; **get drunk** emborracharse **3** *pp*

→ **drink**

drunk·en [drʌŋkn] *voices, laughter* borracho; *party* con mucho alcohol

dry [draɪ] **1** *adj* seco; *where alcohol is banned* donde está prohibido el consumo de alcohol **2** *v/t & v/i* (*pret & pp* **dried**) secar

◆ **dry out** *v/i* secarse; *of alcoholic* desintoxicarse

◆ **dry up** *v/i of river* secarse; F (*be quiet*) cerrar el pico F

'dry-clean *v/t* limpiar en seco

'dry clean·er tintorería *f*

'dry-clean·ing (*clothes*): **would you pick up my drycleaning for me?** ¿te importaría recogerme la ropa de la tintorería?

dry·er ['draɪr] *machine* secadora *f*

DTP [diːtiːˈpiː] *abbr* (= **desk-top publishing**) autoedición *f*

du·al ['duːəl] *adj* doble

dub [dʌb] *v/t* (*pret & pp* **dubbed**) *movie* doblar

du·bi·ous ['duːbɪəs] *adj* dudoso; (*having doubts*) inseguro; **I'm still dubious about the idea** todavía tengo mis dudas sobre la idea

duch·ess ['dʌtʃɪs] duquesa *f*

duck [dʌk] **1** *n* pato *m*, pata *f* **2** *v/i* agacharse **3** *v/t one's head* agachar; *question* eludir

dud [dʌd] *n* F (*false bill*) billete *m* falso

due [duː] *adj* (*proper*) debido; **the money due me** el dinero que se me debe; **payment is now due** el pago se debe hacer efectivo ahora; **is there a train due soon?** ¿va a pasar un tren pronto?; **when is the baby due?** ¿cuando está previsto que nazca el bebé?; **he's due to meet him next month** tiene previsto reunirse con él el próximo mes; **due to** (*because of*) debido a; **be due to** (*be caused by*) ser debido a; **in due course** en su debido momento

dues [duːz] *npl* cuota *f*

du·et [duːˈet] MUS dúo *m*

dug [dʌg] *pret & pp* → **dig**

duke [duːk] duque *m*

dull [dʌl] *adj weather* gris; *sound, pain* sordo; (*boring*) aburrido, soso

du·ly ['duːlɪ] *adv* (*as expected*) tal y como

se esperaba; (*properly*) debidamente
dumb [dʌm] *adj* (*mute*) mudo; F (*stupid*)
estúpido; *a pretty dumb thing to do* una
tontería
dumb·found·ed [dʌm'faʊndɪd] *adj* boquiabierto
dum·my ['dʌmɪ] *for clothes* maniquí *m*
dump [dʌmp] **1** *n for garbage* vertedero
m, basurero *m*; (*unpleasant place*) lugar
m de mala muerte **2** *v/t* (*deposit*) dejar;
(*dispose of*) deshacerse de; *toxic waste,
nuclear waste* verter
dump·ling ['dʌmplɪŋ] *bola de masa dulce
o salada*
dune [duːn] duna *f*
dung [dʌŋ] estiércol *m*
dun·ga·rees [dʌŋgə'riːz] *npl* pantalones
mpl de trabajo
dunk [dʌŋk] *v/t in coffee etc* mojar
du·o [duːoʊ] MUS dúo *m*
du·plex (a·part·ment) ['duːpleks] dúplex
m
du·pli·cate 1 *n* ['duːplɪkət] duplicado *m*;
in duplicate por duplicado **2** *v/t* ['duːplɪkeɪt] (*copy*) duplicar, hacer un duplicado
de; (*repeat*) repetir
du·pli·cate 'key llave *f* duplicada
du·ra·ble ['dʊrəbl] *adj material* duradero,
durable; *relationship* duradero
du·ra·tion [dʊ'reɪʃn] duración *f*; *for the
duration of her visit* mientras dure su
visita
du·ress [dʊ'res]: *under duress* bajo coacción
dur·ing ['dʊrɪŋ] *prep* durante
dusk [dʌsk] crepúsculo *m*, anochecer *m*
dust [dʌst] **1** *n* polvo *m* **2** *v/t* quitar el polvo a; *dust sth with sth* (*sprinkle*) espol

vorear algo con algo
'dust cov·er *for book* sobrecubierta *f*
dust·er ['dʌstər] (*cloth*) trapo *m* del polvo
'dust jack·et *of book* sobrecubierta *f*
'dust·pan recogedor *m*
dust·y ['dʌstɪ] *adj* polvoriento
Dutch [dʌtʃ] **1** *adj* holandés; *go Dutch* F
pagar a escote F **2** *n* (*language*) neerlandés *m*; *the Dutch* los holandeses
du·ty ['duːtɪ] deber *m*; (*task*) obligación *f*,
tarea *f*; *on goods* impuesto *m*; *be on duty*
estar de servicio; *be off duty* estar fuera
de servicio
du·ty·'free 1 *adj* libre de impuestos **2** *n*
productos *mpl* libres de impuestos
du·ty·'free shop tienda *f* libre de impuestos
dwarf [dwɔːrf] **1** *n* enano *m* **2** *v/t* empequeñecer
♦ **dwell on** [dwel] *v/t*: *dwell on the past*
pensar en el pasado; *don't dwell on
what he said* no des demasiada importancia a lo que ha dicho
dwin·dle ['dwɪndl] *v/i* disminuir, menguar
dye [daɪ] **1** *n* tinte *m* **2** *v/t* teñir
dy·ing ['daɪɪŋ] *adj person* moribundo; *industry, tradition* en vías de desaparición
dy·nam·ic [daɪ'næmɪk] *adj person* dinámico
dy·na·mism ['daɪnəmɪzm] dinamismo *m*
dy·na·mite ['daɪnəmaɪt] *n* dinamita *f*
dy·na·mo ['daɪnəmoʊ] TECH dinamo *f*, dínamo *f*
dy·nas·ty ['daɪnəstɪ] dinastía *f*
dys·lex·i·a [dɪs'leksɪə] dislexia *f*
dys·lex·ic [dɪs'leksɪk] **1** *adj* disléxico **2** *n*
disléxico(-a) *m(f)*

E

each [iːtʃ] **1** *adj* cada **2** *adv*: *he gave us
one each* nos dio uno a cada uno;

they're $1.50 each valen 1.50 dólares cada uno **3** *pron* cada uno; *each other* el uno al otro; **we love each other** nos queremos

ea·ger ['iːgər] *adj* ansioso; **she's always eager to help** siempre está deseando ayudar

ea·ger 'bea·ver F entusiasta *m/f*

ea·ger·ly ['iːgərlɪ] *adv* ansiosamente

ea·ger·ness ['iːgərnɪs] entusiasmo *m*

ea·gle ['iːgl] águila *f*

ea·gle-eyed [iːgl'aɪd] *adj* con vista de lince

ear[1] [ɪr] *of person, animal* oreja *f*; *sense* oído *m*

ear[2] [ɪr] *of corn* espiga *f*

'ear·ache dolor *m* de oídos

'ear·drum tímpano *m*

'ear·lobe lóbulo *m*

ear·ly ['ɜːrlɪ] **1** *adj* (*not late*) temprano; (*ahead of time*) anticipado; (*farther back in time*) primero; (*in the near future*) pronto; *music* antiguo; **let's have an early supper** cenemos temprano; **in early October** a principios de octubre; **in the early hours of the morning** a primeras horas de la madrugada; **an early Picasso** un Picasso de su primera época; **I'm an early riser** soy madrugador **2** *adv* (*not late*) pronto, temprano; (*ahead of time*) antes de tiempo; **it's too early to say** es demasiado pronto como para poder decir nada; **earlier than** antes que

'ear·ly bird madrugador(a) *m(f)*

ear·mark ['ɪrmɑːrk] *v/t* destinar; **earmark sth for sth** destinar algo a algo

earn [ɜːrn] *v/t salary* ganar; *interest* devengar; *holiday, drink etc* ganarse; **earn one's living** ganarse la vida

ear·nest ['ɜːrnɪst] *adj* serio; **in earnest** en serio

earn·ings ['ɜːrnɪŋz] *npl* ganancias *fpl*

'ear·phones *npl* auriculares *fpl*

'ear-pierc·ing *adj* estrepitoso

'ear·ring pendiente *m*

'ear·shot: within earshot al alcance del oído; **out of earshot** fuera del alcance del oído

earth [ɜːrθ] (*soil*) tierra *f*; (*world, planet*) Tierra *f*; **where on earth ...?** F ¿dónde diablos ...? F

earth·en·ware ['ɜːrθnwer] *n* loza *mpl*

earth·ly ['ɜːrθlɪ] *adj* terrenal; **it's no earthly use** F no sirve para nada

earth·quake ['ɜːrθkweɪk] terremoto *m*

earth-shat·ter·ing ['ɜːrθʃætərɪŋ] *adj* extraordinario

ease [iːz] **1** *n* facilidad *f*; **be at (one's) ease, feel at ease** sentirse cómodo; **feel ill at ease** sentirse incómodo **2** *v/t* (*relieve*) aliviar **3** *v/i of pain* disminuir

◆ **ease off 1** *v/t* (*remove*) quitar con cuidado **2** *v/i of pain* disminuir; *of rain* amainar

ea·sel ['iːzl] caballete *m*

eas·i·ly ['iːzəlɪ] *adv* (*with ease*) fácilmente; (*by far*) con diferencia

east [iːst] **1** *n* este *m* **2** *adj* oriental, este; *wind* del este **3** *adv travel* hacia el este

Eas·ter ['iːstər] Pascua *f*; *period* Semana *f* Santa

Eas·ter 'Day Domingo *m* de Resurrección

'Eas·ter egg huevo *m* de pascua

eas·ter·ly ['iːstərlɪ] *adj* del este

Eas·ter 'Mon·day Lunes *m* Santo

Eas·ter 'Sun·day Domingo *m* de Resurrección

east·ern ['iːstərn] *adj* del este; (*oriental*) oriental

east·er·ner ['iːstərnər] *habitante de la costa oeste estadounidense*

east·ward ['iːstwərd] *adv* hacia el este

eas·y ['iːzɪ] *adj* fácil; (*relaxed*) tranquilo; **take things easy** (*slow down*) tomarse las cosas con tranquilidad; **take it easy!** (*calm down*) ¡tranquilízate!

'eas·y chair sillón *m*

eas·y-go·ing ['iːzɪgoʊɪŋ] *adj* tratable

eat [iːt] *v/t & v/i* (*pret* **ate**, *pp* **eaten**) comer

◆ **eat out** *v/i* comer fuera

◆ **eat up** *v/t* comerse; *fig: use up* acabar con

eat·a·ble ['iːtəbl] *adj* comestible

eat·en ['iːtn] *pp* → **eat**

eau de Co·logne [oʊdəkə'loʊn] agua *f* de colonia

eaves [iːvz] *npl* alero *m*

eaves·drop ['iːvzdrɑːp] *v/i* (*pret & pp*

eavesdropped) escuchar a escondidas
(**on s.o.** alguien)
ebb [eb] *v/i of tide* bajar
◆ **ebb away** *v/i fig of courage, strength* desvanecerse
ec·cen·tric [ɪk'sentrɪk] **1** *adj* excéntrico **2** *n* excéntrico(-a) *m(f)*
ec·cen·tric·i·ty [ɪksen'trɪsɪtɪ] excentricidad *f*
ech·o ['ekoʊ] **1** *n* eco *m* **2** *v/i* resonar **3** *v/t words* repetir; *views* mostrar acuerdo con
e·clipse [ɪ'klɪps] **1** *n* eclipse *m* **2** *v/t fig* eclipsar
e·co·lo·gi·cal [iːkə'lɑːdʒɪkl] *adj* ecológico
e·co·lo·gi·cal·ly [iːkə'lɑːdʒɪklɪ] *adv* ecológicamente
e·co·lo·gi·cal·ly 'friend·ly *adj* ecológico
e·col·o·gist [iː'kɑːlədʒɪst] ecologista *m/f*
e·col·o·gy [iː'kɑːlədʒɪ] ecología *f*
ec·o·nom·ic [iːkə'nɑːmɪk] *adj* económico
ec·o·nom·i·cal [iːkə'nɑːmɪkl] *adj* (*cheap*) económico; (*thrifty*) cuidadoso
ec·o·nom·i·cal·ly [iːkə'nɑːmɪklɪ] *adv* (*in terms of economics*) económicamente; (*thriftily*) de manera económica
ec·o·nom·ics [iːkə'nɑːmɪks] *nsg* (*science*) economía *f*; (*npl: financial aspects*) aspecto *m* económico
e·con·o·mist [ɪ'kɑːnəmɪst] economista *m/f*
e·con·o·mize [ɪ'kɑːnəmaɪz] *v/i* economizar, ahorrar
◆ **economize on** *v/t* economizar, ahorrar
e·con·o·my [ɪ'kɑːnəmɪ] *of a country* economía *f*; (*saving*) ahorro *m*
e'con·o·my class clase *f* turista
e'con·o·my drive intento *m* de ahorrar
e'con·o·my size tamaño *m* económico
e·co·sys·tem ['iːkoʊsɪstm] ecosistema *m*
e·co·tour·ism ['iːkoʊtʊrɪzm] ecoturismo *m*
ec·sta·sy ['ekstəsɪ] éxtasis *m*
ec·sta·t·ic [ɪk'stætɪk] *adj* muy emocionado, extasiado
Ec·ua·dor ['ekwədɔːr] *n* Ecuador
Ec·ua·dore·an [ekwə'dɔːrən] **1** *adj* ecuatoriano **2** *n* ecuatoriano(-a) *m(f)*
ec·ze·ma ['eksmə] eczema *f*
edge [edʒ] **1** *n of knife* filo *m*; *of table, se-*

at, road, cliff borde *m*; *in voice* irritación *f*; **on edge** tenso **2** *v/t* ribetear **3** *v/i* (*move slowly*) acercarse despacio
edge·wise ['edʒwaɪz] *adv* de lado; **I couldn't get a word in edgewise** no me dejó decir una palabra
edg·y ['edʒɪ] *adj* tenso
ed·i·ble ['edɪbl] *adj* comestible
ed·it ['edɪt] *v/t text* corregir; *book* editar; *newspaper* dirigir; TV *program, movie* montar
e·di·tion [ɪ'dɪʃn] edición *f*
ed·i·tor ['edɪtər] *of text, book* editor(a) *m(f)*; *of newspaper* director(a) *m(f)*; *of* TV *program, movie* montador(a) *m(f)*; **sports / political editor** redactor(a) *m(f)* de deportes / política
ed·i·to·ri·al [edɪ'tɔːrɪəl] **1** *adj* editorial **2** *n in newspaper* editorial *m*
EDP [iːdiː'piː] *abbr* (= *electronic data processing*) procesamiento *m* electrónico de datos
ed·u·cate ['edʒəkeɪt] *v/t child* educar; *consumers* concienciar
ed·u·cat·ed ['edʒəkeɪtɪd] *adj person* culto
ed·u·ca·tion [edʒə'keɪʃn] educación *f*; **the education system** el sistema educativo
ed·u·ca·tion·al [edʒə'keɪʃnl] *adj* educativo; (*informative*) instructivo
eel [iːl] anguila *f*
ee·rie ['ɪrɪ] *adj* escalofriante
ef·fect [ɪ'fekt] efecto *m*; **take effect** *of medicine, drug* hacer efecto; **come into effect** *of law* entrar en vigor
ef·fec·tive [ɪ'fektɪv] *adj* (*efficient*) efectivo; (*striking*) impresionante; **effective May 1** a partir del 1 de mayo
ef·fem·i·nate [ɪ'femɪnət] *adj* afeminado
ef·fer·ves·cent [efər'vesnt] *adj* efervescente; *personality* chispeante
ef·fi·cien·cy [ɪ'fɪʃənsɪ] *of person* eficiencia *f*; *of machine* rendimiento *f*; *of system* eficacia *f*
ef·fi·cient [ɪ'fɪʃnt] *adj person* eficiente; *machine* de buen rendimiento; *method* eficaz
ef·fi·cient·ly [ɪ'fɪʃntlɪ] *adv* eficientemente

ef·flu·ent ['efluənt] aguas *fpl* residuales

ef·fort ['efərt] (*struggle, attempt*) esfuerzo *m*; **make an effort to do sth** hacer un esfuerzo por hacer algo

ef·fort·less ['efərtlɪs] *adj* fácil

ef·fron·te·ry [ɪ'frʌntərɪ] desvergüenza *f*

ef·fu·sive [ɪ'fju:sɪv] *adj* efusivo

e.g. [i:'dʒi:] p. ej.

e·gal·i·tar·i·an [ɪɡælɪ'terɪən] *adj* igualitario

egg [eg] huevo *m*; *of woman* óvulo *m*
◆ **egg on** *v/t* incitar

'egg·cup huevera *f*

'egg·head F cerebrito(-a) *m(f)* F

'egg·plant berenjena *f*

'egg·shell cáscara *f* de huevo

'egg tim·er reloj *m* de arena

e·go ['i:gou] PSYCH ego *m*; (*self-esteem*) amor *m* propio

e·go·cen·tric [i:gou'sentrɪk] *adj* egocéntrico

e·go·ism ['i:gou'ɪzm] egoismo *m*

e·go·ist ['i:gou'ɪst] egoísta *m/f*

E·gypt ['i:dʒɪpt] Egipto

E·gyp·tian [ɪ'dʒɪpʃn] **1** *adj* egipcio **2** *n* egipcio(-a) *m(f)*

ei·der·down ['aɪdərdaun] *quilt* edredón *m*

eight [eɪt] ocho

eigh·teen [eɪ'ti:n] dieciocho

eigh·teenth [eɪ'ti:nθ] *n & adj* decimoctavo

eighth [eɪtθ] *n & adj* octavo

eigh·ti·eth ['eɪtɪɪθ] *n & adj* octogésimo

eigh·ty ['eɪtɪ] ochenta

ei·ther ['aɪðər] **1** *adj* cualquiera de los dos; *with negative constructions* ninguno de los dos; (*both*) cada, ambos; **he wouldn't accept either of the proposals** no quería aceptar ninguna de las dos propuestas **2** *pron* cualquiera de los dos; *with negative constructions* ninguno de los dos **3** *adv* tampoco; **I won't go either** yo tampoco iré **4** *conj*: **either ... or** choice o ... o; *with negative constructions* ni ... ni

e·ject [ɪ'dʒekt] **1** *v/t* expulsar **2** *v/i from plane* eyectarse
◆ **eke out** [i:k] *v/t* (*make last*) hacer durar

el [el] → **elevated railroad**

e·lab·o·rate 1 *adj* [ɪ'læbərət] elaborado **2**
v/t [ɪ'læbəreɪt] elaborar **3** *v/i* [ɪ'læbəreɪt] dar detalles

e·lab·o·rate·ly [ɪ'læbəreɪtlɪ] *adv* elaboradamente

e·lapse [ɪ'læps] *v/i* pasar

e·las·tic [ɪ'læstɪk] **1** *adj* elástico **2** *n* elástico *m*

e·las·ti·ca·ted [ɪ'læstɪkeɪtɪd] *adj* elástico

e·las·ti·ci·ty [ɪlæs'tɪsətɪ] elasticidad *f*

e·las·ti·cized [ɪ'læstɪsaɪzd] *adj* elástico

e·lat·ed [ɪ'leɪtɪd] *adj* eufórico

el·at·ion [ɪ'leɪʃn] euforia *f*

el·bow ['elbou] **1** *n* codo *m* **2** *v/t* dar un codazo a; **elbow out of the way** apartar a codazos

el·der ['eldər] **1** *adj* mayor **2** *n* mayor *m/f*; **she's two years my elder** es dos años mayor que yo

el·der·ly ['eldərlɪ] **1** *adj* mayor **2** *n*: **the elderly** las personas mayores

el·dest ['eldəst] **1** *adj* mayor **2** *n* mayor *m/f*; **the eldest** el mayor

e·lect [ɪ'lekt] *v/t* elegir; **elect to do sth** decidir hacer algo

e·lect·ed [ɪ'lektɪd] *adj* elegido

e·lec·tion [ɪ'lekʃn] elección *f*; **call an election** convocar elecciones

e·lec·tion cam·paign campaña *f* electoral

e·lec·tion day día *m* de las elecciones

e·lec·tive [ɪ'lektɪv] *adj* opcional; *subject* optativo

e·lec·tor [ɪ'lektər] elector(a) *m(f)*, votante *m/f*

e·lec·to·ral sys·tem [ɪ'lektərəl] sistema *m* electoral

e·lec·to·rate [ɪ'lektərət] electorado *m*

e·lec·tric [ɪ'lektrɪk] *adj* eléctrico; *fig atmosphere* electrizado

e·lec·tri·cal [ɪ'lektrɪkl] *adj* eléctrico

e·lec·tri·cal en·gi·neer ingeniero(-a) *m(f)* electrónico

e·lec·tri·cal en·gi·neer·ing ingeniería *f* electrónica

e·lec·tric 'blan·ket manta *f or L.Am.* cobija *f* eléctrica

e·lec·tric 'chair silla *f* eléctrica

e·lec·tri·cian [ɪlek'trɪʃn] electricista *m/f*

e·lec·tri·ci·ty [ɪlek'trɪsətɪ] electricidad *f*

e·lec·tric 'ra·zor maquinilla *f* eléctrica

e·lec·tric 'shock descarga f eléctrica

e·lec·tri·fy [ɪ'lektrɪfaɪ] v/t (pret & pp **electrified**) electrificar; fig electrizar

e·lec·tro·cute [ɪ'lektrəkju:t] v/t electrocutar

e·lec·trode [ɪ'lektroʊd] electrodo m

e·lec·tron [ɪ'lektrɑ:n] electrón m

e·lec·tron·ic [ɪlek'trɑ:nɪk] adj electrónico

e·lec·tron·ic da·ta 'pro·ces·sing procesamiento m electrónico de datos

e·lec·tron·ic 'mail correo m electrónico

e·lec·tron·ics [ɪlek'trɑ:nɪks] electrónica f

el·e·gance ['elɪɡəns] elegancia f

el·e·gant ['elɪɡənt] adj elegante

el·e·gant·ly ['elɪɡəntlɪ] adv elegantemente

el·e·ment ['elɪmənt] also CHEM elemento m

el·e·men·ta·ry [elɪ'mentərɪ] adj (rudimentary) elemental

el·e'men·ta·ry school escuela f primaria

el·e'men·ta·ry teacher maestro(-a) m(f)

el·e·phant ['elɪfənt] elefante m

el·e·vate ['elɪveɪt] v/t elevar

el·e·vat·ed 'rail·road ['elɪveɪtɪd] ferrocarril m elevado

el·e·va·tion [elɪ'veɪʃn] (altitude) altura f

el·e·va·tor ['elɪveɪtər] ascensor m

el·e·ven [ɪ'levn] once

el·e·venth [ɪ'levnθ] n & adj undécimo; **at the eleventh hour** justo en el último minuto

el·i·gi·ble ['elɪdʒəbl] adj que reúne los requisitos; **eligible to vote** con derecho al voto; **be eligible to do sth** tener derecho a hacer algo

el·i·gi·ble 'bach·e·lor buen partido m

e·lim·i·nate [ɪ'lɪmɪneɪt] v/t eliminar; poverty acabar con; (rule out) descartar

e·lim·i·na·tion [ɪ'lɪmɪneɪʃn] eliminación f

e·lite [eɪ'li:t] 1 n élite f 2 adj de élite

elk [elk] ciervo m canadiense

e·lipse [ɪ'lɪps] elipse f

elm [elm] olmo m

e·lope [ɪ'loʊp] v/i fugarse con un amante

el·o·quence ['eləkwəns] elocuencia f

el·o·quent ['eləkwənt] adj elocuente

el·o·quent·ly ['eləkwəntlɪ] adv elocuentemente

El Sal·va·dor [el'sælvədɔ:r] n El Salvador

else [els] adv: **anything else?** ¿algo más?; **if you've got nothing else to do** si no tienes nada más que hacer; **no one else** nadie más; **everyone else is going** todos (los demás) van, va todo el mundo; **who else was there?** ¿quién más estaba allí?; **someone else** otra persona; **something else** algo más; **let's go somewhere else** vamos a otro sitio; **or else** si no

else·where ['elswer] adv en otro sitio

e·lude [ɪ'lu:d] v/t (escape from) escapar de; (avoid) evitar; **the name eludes me** no recuerdo el nombre

e·lu·sive [ɪ'lu:sɪv] adj evasivo

e·ma·ci·at·ed [ɪ'meɪsieɪtɪd] adj demacrado

e-mail ['i:meɪl] 1 n correo m electrónico 2 v/t person mandar un correo electrónico a

'e-mail ad·dress dirección f de correo electrónico, dirección f electrónica

e·man·ci·pat·ed [ɪ'mænsɪpeɪtɪd] adj emancipado

e·man·ci·pa·tion [ɪmænsɪ'peɪʃn] emancipación f

em·balm [ɪ'bɑ:m] v/t embalsamar

em·bank·ment [ɪm'bæŋkmənt] of river dique m; RAIL terraplén m

em·bar·go [em'bɑ:rɡoʊ] embargo m

em·bark [ɪm'bɑ:rk] v/i embarcar

♦ embark on v/t embarcarse en

em·bar·rass [ɪm'bærəs] v/t avergonzar; **he embarrassed me in front of everyone** me hizo pasar vergüenza delante de todos

em·bar·rassed [ɪm'bærəst] adj avergonzado; **I was embarrassed to ask** me daba vergüenza preguntar

em·bar·rass·ing [ɪm'bærəsɪŋ] adj embarazoso

em·bar·rass·ment [ɪm'bærəsmənt] embarazo m, apuro m

em·bas·sy ['embəsɪ] embajada f

em·bel·lish [ɪm'belɪʃ] v/t adornar; story exagerar

em·bers ['embərz] npl ascuas fpl

em·bez·zle [ɪm'bezl] v/t malversar

em·bez·zle·ment [ɪmˈbezlmənt] malversación f

em·bez·zler [ɪmˈbezlər] malversador(a) m(f)

em·bit·ter [ɪmˈbɪtər] v/t amargar

em·blem [ˈembləm] emblema m

em·bod·i·ment [ɪmˈbɑːdɪmənt] personificación f

em·bod·y[ɪmˈbɑːdɪ] v/t (pret & pp **embodied**) personificar

em·bo·lism [ˈembəlɪzm] embolia f

em·boss [ɪmˈbɑːs] v/t metal repujar; paper grabar en relieve

em·brace [ɪmˈbreɪs] **1** n abrazo m **2** v/t (hug) abrazar; (take in) abarcar **3** v/i of two people abrazarse

em·broi·der [ɪmˈbrɔɪdər] v/t bordar; fig adornar

em·broi·der·y [ɪmˈbrɔɪdərɪ] bordado m

em·bry·o [ˈembrɪoʊ] embrión m

em·bry·on·ic [embrɪˈɑːnɪk] adj fig embrionario

em·e·rald [ˈemərəld] esmeralda f

e·merge [ɪˈmɜːrdʒ] v/i (appear) emerger, salir; of truth aflorar; **it has emerged that** se ha descubierto que

e·mer·gen·cy [ɪˈmɜːrdʒənsɪ] emergencia f; **in an emergency** en caso de emergencia

emer·gen·cy **'ex·it** salida f de emergencia

e·mer·gen·cy **land·ing** aterrizaje m forzoso

e·mer·gen·cy **serv·ices** npl servicios mpl de urgencia

em·er·y board [ˈemərɪ] lima f de uñas

em·i·grant [ˈemɪgrənt] emigrante m/f

em·i·grate [ˈemɪgreɪt] v/i emigrar

em·i·gra·tion [emɪˈgreɪʃn] emigración f

Em·i·nence [ˈemɪnəns] REL: **His Eminence** Su Eminencia

em·i·nent [ˈemɪnənt] adj eminente

em·i·nent·ly [ˈemɪnəntlɪ] adv sumamente

e·mis·sion [ɪˈmɪʃn] of gases emisión f

e·mit [ɪˈmɪt] v/t (pret & pp **emitted**) emitir; heat, odor desprender

e·mo·tion [ɪˈmoʊʃn] emoción f

e·mo·tion·al [ɪˈmoʊʃənl] adj problems, development sentimental; (full of emotion) emotivo

em·pa·thize [ˈempəθaɪz] v/i: **empathize with** identificarse con

em·pe·ror [ˈempərər] emperador m

em·pha·sis [ˈemfəsɪs] in word acento m; fig énfasis m

em·pha·size [ˈemfəsaɪz] v/t syllable acentuar; fig hacer hincapié en

em·phat·ic [ɪmˈfætɪk] adj enfático

em·pire [ˈempaɪr] imperio m

em·ploy [ɪmˈplɔɪ] v/t emplear; **he's employed as a …** trabaja de …

em·ploy·ee [emplɔɪˈiː] empleado(-a) m(f)

em·ploy·er [emˈplɔɪər] empresario(-a) m(f)

em·ploy·ment [emˈplɔɪmənt] empleo m; (work) trabajo m; **be looking for employment** buscar trabajo

em·ploy·ment a·gen·cy agencia f de colociaciones

em·press [ˈemprɪs] emperatriz f

emp·ti·ness [ˈemptɪnɪs] vacío m

emp·ty [ˈemptɪ] **1** adj vacío; promise vana **2** v/t (pret & pp **emptied**) drawer, pockets vaciar; glass, bottle acabar **3** v/i (pret & pp **emptied**) of room, street vaciarse

em·u·late [ˈemjʊleɪt] v/t emular

e·mul·sion [ɪˈmʌlʃn] paint emulsión f

en·a·ble [ɪˈneɪbl] v/t permitir; **enable s.o. to do sth** permitir a alguien hacer algo

en·act [ɪˈnækt] v/t law promulgar; THEA representar

e·nam·el [ɪˈnæml] n esmalte m

enc abbr (= **enclosure(s)**) documento(s) m(pl) adjunto(s)

en·chant [ɪnˈtʃænt] v/t (delight) encantar

en·chant·ing [ɪnˈtʃæntɪŋ] adj encantador

en·cir·cle [ɪnˈsɜːrkl] v/t rodear

encl abbr (= **en·clo·sure(s)**) documento(s) m(pl) adjunto(s)

en·close [ɪnˈkloʊz] v/t Br in letter adjuntar; area rodear; **please find enclosed …** remito adjunto …

en·clo·sure [ɪnˈkloʊʒər] with letter documento m adjunto

en·core [ˈɑːŋkɔːr] bis m

en·coun·ter [ɪnˈkaʊntər] **1** n encuentro m **2** v/t person encontrarse con; problem, resistance tropezar con en·cour·age [ɪnˈkʌrɪdʒ] v/t animar; *violence* fomentar

en·cour·age·ment [ɪnˈkʌrɪdʒmənt] ánimo *m*

en·cour·ag·ing [ɪnˈkʌrɪdʒɪŋ] *adj* alentador

◆ en·croach on [ɪnˈkrəʊtʃ] v/t *land* invadir; *rights* usurpar; *time* quitar

en·cy·clo·pe·di·a [ɪnsaɪkləˈpiːdɪə] enciclopedia *f*

end [end] 1 *n of journey, month* final *m*; (*extremity*) extremo *m*; (*bottom*) fondo *m*; (*conclusion, purpose*) fin *m*; **at the other end of town** al otro lado de la ciudad; **in the end** al final; **for hours on end** durante horas y horas; **stand sth on end** poner de pie algo; **at the end of July** a finales de julio; **in the end** al final; **put an end to** poner fin a 2 v/t terminar, finalizar 3 v/i terminar

◆ end up v/i acabar

en·dan·ger [ɪnˈdeɪndʒər] v/t poner en peligro

en·dan·gered spe·cies especie *f* en peligro de extinción

en·dear·ing [ɪnˈdɪrɪŋ] *adj* simpático

en·deav·or [ɪnˈdevər] 1 *n* esfuerzo *m* 2 v/t procurar

en·dem·ic [ɪnˈdemɪk] *adj* endémico

end·ing [ˈendɪŋ] final *m*; GRAM terminación *f*

end·less [ˈendlɪs] *adj* interminable

en·dorse [ɪnˈdɔːrs] v/t *check* endosar; *candidacy* apoyar; *product* representar

en·dorse·ment [ɪnˈdɔːrsmənt] *of check* endoso *m*; *of candidacy* apoyo *m*; *of product* representación *f*

end prod·uct producto *m* final

end re·sult resultado *m* final

en·dur·ance [ɪnˈdʊrəns] resistencia *f*

en·dure [ɪnˈdʊər] 1 v/t resistir 2 v/i (*last*) durar

en·dur·ing [ɪnˈdʊrɪŋ] *adj* duradero

end-'us·er usuario(-a) *m(f)* final

en·e·my [ˈenəmɪ] enemigo(-a) *m(f)*

en·er·get·ic [enərˈdʒetɪk] *adj* enérgico

en·er·get·ic·al·ly [enərˈdʒetɪklɪ] *adv* enérgicamente

en·er·gy [ˈenərdʒɪ] energía *f*

'en·er·gy-sav·ing *adj device* que ahorra energía

'e·ner·gy sup·ply suministro *m* de energía

en·force [ɪnˈfɔːrs] v/t hacer cumplir

en·gage [ɪnˈɡeɪdʒ] 1 v/t (*hire*) contratar 2 v/i TECH engranar

◆ engage in v/t dedicarse a

en·gaged [ɪnˈɡeɪdʒd] *adj to be married* prometido; **get engaged** prometerse

en'gaged tone *Br* TELEC señal *f* de ocupado *or Span* comunicando

en·gage·ment [ɪnˈɡeɪdʒmənt] (*appointment, to be married*) compromiso *m*; MIL combate *m*

en'gage·ment ring anillo *m* de compromiso

en·gag·ing [ɪnˈɡeɪdʒɪŋ] *adj smile, person* atractivo

en·gine [ˈendʒɪn] motor *m*

en·gi·neer [endʒɪˈnɪr] 1 *n* ingeniero(-a) *m(f)*; NAUT, RAIL maquinista *m/f* 2 v/t fig: *meeting etc* tramar

en·gi·neer·ing [endʒɪˈnɪrɪŋ] ingeniería *f*

En·gland [ˈɪŋɡlənd] Inglaterra *f*

En·glish [ˈɪŋɡlɪʃ] 1 *adj* inglés(-esa) 2 *n language* inglés *m*; **the English** los ingleses

Eng·lish 'Chan·nel Canal *m* de la Mancha

'En·glish·man inglés *m*

'En·glish·wom·an inglesa *f*

en·grave [ɪnˈɡreɪv] v/t grabar

en·grav·ing [ɪnˈɡreɪvɪŋ] grabado *m*

en·grossed [ɪnˈɡrəʊst] *adj* absorto (**in** en)

en·gulf [ɪnˈɡʌlf] v/t devorar

en·hance [ɪnˈhæns] v/t realzar

e·nig·ma [ɪˈnɪɡmə] enigma *m*

e·nig·mat·ic [enɪɡˈmætɪk] *adj* enigmático

en·joy [ɪnˈdʒɔɪ] v/t disfrutar; **enjoy o.s.** divertirse; **enjoy (your meal)!** ¡que aproveche!

en·joy·a·ble [ɪnˈdʒɔɪəbl] *adj* agradable

en·joy·ment [ɪnˈdʒɔɪmənt] diversión *f*

en·large [ɪnˈlɑːrdʒ] v/t ampliar

en·large·ment [ɪnˈlɑːrdʒmənt] ampliación *f*

en·light·en [ɪnˈlaɪtn] v/t educar

en·list [ɪn'lɪst] **1** v/i MIL alistarse **2** v/t: *I enlisted his help* conseguí que me ayudara

en·liv·en [ɪn'laɪvn] v/t animar

en·mi·ty ['enmətɪ] enemistad f

e·nor·mi·ty [ɪ'nɔːrmətɪ] magnitud f

e·nor·mous [ɪ'nɔːrməs] adj enorme; *satisfaction, patience* inmenso

e·nor·mous·ly [ɪ'nɔːrməslɪ] adv enormemente

e·nough [ɪ'nʌf] **1** adj pron suficiente, bastante; *will $50 be enough?* ¿llegará con 50 dólares?; *I've had enough!* ¡estoy harto!; *that's enough, calm down!* ¡ya basta, tranquilízate! **2** adv suficientemente, bastante; *the bag isn't big enough* la bolsa no es lo suficientemente or bastante grande; *strangely enough* curiosamente

en·quire [ɪn'kwaɪr] → **inquire**

en·raged [ɪn'reɪdʒd] adj enfurecido

en·rich [ɪn'rɪtʃ] v/t enriquecer

en·roll [ɪn'roʊl] v/i matricularse

en·roll·ment [ɪn'roʊlmənt] matrícula f

en·sue [ɪn'suː] v/i sucederse

en suite ['ɑːnswiːt] adj: *en suite bathroom* baño m privado

en·sure [ɪn'ʃʊər] v/t asegurar

en·tail [ɪn'teɪl] v/t conllevar

en·tan·gle [ɪn'tæŋgl] v/t *in rope* enredar; *become entangled in* enredarse en; *become entangled with* *in love affair* liarse con

en·ter ['entər] **1** v/t *room, house* entrar en; *competition* participar en; *person, horse in race* inscribir; *(write down)* escribir; COMPUT introducir **2** v/i entrar; THEA entrar en escena; *in competition* inscribirse **3** n COMPUT intro m

en·ter·prise ['entərpraɪz] *(initiative)* iniciativa f; *(venture)* empresa f

en·ter·pris·ing ['entərpraɪzɪŋ] adj con iniciativa

en·ter·tain [entər'teɪn] **1** v/t *(amuse)* entretener; *(consider: idea)* considerar **2** v/i *(have guests)*: *we entertain a lot* recibimos a mucha gente

en·ter·tain·er [entər'teɪnər] artista m/f

en·ter·tain·ing [entər'teɪnɪŋ] adj entretenido

en·ter·tain·ment [entər'teɪnmənt] entretenimiento m

en·thrall [ɪn'θrɔːl] v/t cautivar

en·thu·si·as·m [ɪn'θuːzɪæzm] entusiasmo m

en·thu·si·ast [ɪn'θuːzɪ'æst] entusiasta m/f

en·thu·si·as·tic [ɪnθuːzɪ'æstɪk] adj entusiasta; *be enthusiastic about sth* estar entusiasmado con algo

en·thu·si·as·tic·al·ly [ɪnθuːzɪ'æstɪklɪ] adv con entusiasmo

en·tice [ɪn'taɪs] v/t atraer

en·tire [ɪn'taɪr] adj entero; *the entire school is going* va a ir todo el colegio

en·tire·ly [ɪn'taɪrlɪ] adv completamente

en·ti·tle [ɪn'taɪtld] v/t: *entitle s.o. to sth* dar derecho a alguien a algo; *be entitled to* tener derecho a

en·ti·tled [ɪn'taɪtld] adj *book* titulado

en·trance ['entrəns] entrada f; THEA entrada f en escena

en·tranced [ɪn'trænst] adj encantado

'en·trance ex·am(·i·na·tion) examen m de acceso

'en·trance fee *(cuota f de)* entrada f

en·trant ['entrənt] participante m/f

en·treat [ɪn'triːt] v/t suplicar; *entreat s.o. to do sth* suplicar a alguien que haga algo

en·trenched [ɪn'trentʃt] adj *attitudes* arraigado

en·tre·pre·neur [ɑːntrəprə'nɜːr] empresario(-a) m(f)

en·tre·pre·neur·i·al [ɑːntrəprə'nɜːrɪəl] adj empresarial

en·trust [ɪn'trʌst] v/t confiar; *entrust s.o. with sth, entrust sth to s.o.* confiar algo a alguien

en·try ['entrɪ] entrada f; *for competition* inscripción f; *in diary etc* entrada f; *no entry* prohibida la entrada; *the winning entry was painted by …* el cuadro ganador fue pintado por …

'en·try form impreso m de inscripción

'en·try·phone portero m automático

'en·try vi·sa visado m

e·nu·me·rate [ɪ'nuːməreɪt] v/t enumerar

en·vel·op [ɪn'veləp] v/t cubrir

en·ve·lope ['envələup] sobre m

en·vi·a·ble ['enviəbl] adj envidiable

en·vi·ous ['enviəs] adj envidioso; **be envious of s.o.** tener envidia de alguien

en·vi·ron·ment [ɪn'vairənmənt] (nature) medio m ambiente; (surroundings) entorno m, ambiente m

en·vi·ron·men·tal [ɪnvairən'mentl] adj medioambiental

en·vi·ron·men·tal·ist [ɪnvairən'mməntə-list] ecologista m/f

en·vi·ron·men·tal·ly 'friend·ly [ɪnvairən'məntəlɪ] adj ecológico, que no daña el medio ambiente

en·vi·ron·men·tal pol'lu·tion contaminación f medioambiental

en·vi·ron·men·tal pro'tec·tion protección f medioambiental

en·vi·rons [ɪn'vairənz] npl alrededores mpl

en·vis·age [ɪn'vɪzɪdʒ] v/t imaginar

en·voy ['envɔɪ] enviado(-a) m(f)

en·vy ['envi] **1** n envidia f; **be the envy of** ser la envidia de **2** v/t (pret & pp **envied**) envidiar; **envy s.o. sth** envidiar a alguien por algo

e·phem·er·al [ɪ'femərəl] adj efímero

ep·ic ['epɪk] **1** n epopeya f **2** adj journey épico; **a task of epic proportions** una tarea monumental

ep·i·cen·ter ['epɪsentr] epicentro m

ep·i·dem·ic [epɪ'demɪk] epidemia f

ep·i·lep·sy ['epɪlepsɪ] epilepsia f

ep·i·lep·tic [epɪ'leptɪk] epiléptico(-a) m(f)

ep·i·lep·tic 'fit ataque m epiléptico

ep·i·log, Br ep·i·logue ['epɪlɑːg] epílogo m

ep·i·sode ['epɪsoud] of story, soap opera episodio m, capítulo m; (happening) episodio m; **let's forget the whole episode** olvidemos lo sucedido

ep·i·taph ['epɪtæf] epitafio m

e·poch ['iːpɑːk] época f

e·poch-mak·ing ['iːpɑːkmeɪkɪŋ] adj que hace época

e·qual ['iːkwl] **1** adj igual; **equal amounts of milk and water** la misma cantidad de leche y de agua; **equal opportunities**

igualdad f de oportunidades; **be equal to** a task estar capacitado para **2** n igual m/f **3** v/t (pret & pp **equaled**, Br **equalled**) (with numbers) equivaler; (be as good as) igualar; **four times twelve equals 48** cuatro por doce, (igual a) cuarenta y ocho

e·qual·i·ty [ɪ'kwɑːlətɪ] igualdad f

e·qual·ize ['iːkwəlaɪz] **1** v/t igualar **2** v/i Br SP empatar

e·qual·iz·er ['iːkwəlaɪzər] Br SP gol m del empate

e·qual·ly ['iːkwəlɪ] adv igualmente; share, divide en partes iguales; **equally, ...** igualmente, ...

e·qual 'rights npl igualdad f de derechos

e·quate [ɪ'kweɪt] v/t equiparar; **equate sth with sth** equiparar algo con algo

e·qua·tion [ɪ'kweɪʒn] MATH ecuación f

e·qua·tor [ɪ'kweɪtər] ecuador m

e·qui·lib·ri·um [iːkwɪ'lɪbrɪəm] equilibrio m

e·qui·nox ['iːkwɪnɑːks] equinoccio m

e·quip [ɪ'kwɪp] v/t (pret & pp **equipped**) equipar; **he's not equipped to handle it** fig no está preparado para llevarlo

e·quip·ment [ɪ'kwɪpmənt] equipo m

eq·ui·ty ['ekwətɪ] FIN acciones fpl ordinarias

e·quiv·a·lent [ɪ'kwɪvələnt] **1** adj equivalente; **be equivalent to** equivaler a **2** n equivalente m

e·ra ['ɪrə] era f

e·rad·i·cate [ɪ'rædɪkeɪt] v/t erradicar

e·rase [ɪ'reɪz] v/t borrar

e·ras·er [ɪ'reɪzər] for pencil goma f (de borrar); for chalk borrador m

e·rect [ɪ'rekt] **1** adj erguido **2** v/t levantar, erigir

e·rec·tion [ɪ'rekʃn] of building etc construcción f; of penis erección f

er·go·nom·ic [ɜːrgoʊ'nɑːmɪk] adj furniture ergonómico

e·rode [ɪ'roud] v/t also fig erosionar

e·ro·sion [ɪ'rouʒn] also fig erosión f

e·rot·ic [ɪ'rɑːtɪk] adj erótico

e·rot·i·cism [ɪ'rɑːtɪsɪzm] erotismo m

er·rand ['erənd] recado m; **run errands** hacer recados

er·rat·ic [ɪˈrætɪk] *adj* irregular; *course* errático

er·ror [ˈerər] error *m*

'er·ror mes·sage COMPUT mensaje *m* de error

e·rupt [ɪˈrʌpt] *v/i of volcano* entrar en erupción; *of violence* brotar; *of person* explotar

e·rup·tion [ɪˈrʌpʃn] *of volcano* erupción *f*; *of violence* brote *f*

es·ca·late [ˈeskəleɪt] *v/i* intensificarse

es·ca·la·tion [eskəˈleɪʃn] intensificación *f*

es·ca·la·tor [ˈeskəleɪtər] escalera *f* mecánica

es·cape [ɪˈskeɪp] **1** *n of prisoner, animal* fuga *f*; *of gas* escape *m*, fuga *f*; **have a narrow escape** escaparse por los pelos **2** *v/i of prisoner, animal, gas* escaparse **3** *v/t*: **the word escapes me** no consigo recordar la palabra

es'cape chute AVIA tobogán *m* de emergencia

es·cort **1** *n* [ˈeskɔːrt] acompañante *m/f*; *guard* escolta *m/f*; **under escort** escoltado **2** *v/t* [ɪˈskɔːrt] escoltar; *socially* acompañar

es·pe·cial [ɪˈspeʃl] → **special**

es·pe·cial·ly [ɪˈspeʃlɪ] *adv* especialmente

es·pi·o·nage [ˈespɪənɑːʒ] espionaje *m*

es·pres·so (cof·fee) [esˈpresoʊ] café *m* exprés

es·say [ˈeseɪ] *n creative* redacción *f*; *factual* trabajo *m*

es·sen·tial [ɪˈsenʃl] *adj* esencial; **the essential thing is …** lo esencial es …

es·sen·tial·ly [ɪˈsenʃlɪ] *adv* esencialmente; fundamentalmente

es·tab·lish [ɪˈstæblɪʃ] *v/t company* fundar; *(create, determine)* establecer; **establish o.s. as** establecerse como

es·tab·lish·ment [ɪˈstæblɪʃmənt] *firm, shop etc* establecimiento *m*; **the Establishment** el orden establecido

es·tate [ɪˈsteɪt] *(area of land)* finca *f*; *(possessions of dead person)* patrimonio *m*

es'tate a·gen·cy *Br* agencia *f* inmobiliaria

es·thet·ic [ɪsˈθetɪk] *adj* estético

es·ti·mate [ˈestɪmət] **1** *n* estimación *f*; *for job* presupuesto *m* **2** *v/t* estimar; **estimated time of arrival** hora *f* estimada de llegada

es·ti·ma·tion [estɪˈmeɪʃn] estima *f*; **he has gone up / down in my estimation** le tengo en más / menos estima; **in my estimation** *(opinion)* a mi parecer

es·tranged [ɪsˈtreɪndʒd] *adj wife, husband* separado

es·tu·a·ry [ˈestʃəwerɪ] estuario *m*

ETA [iːtiːˈeɪ] *abbr* (= **estimated time of arrival**) hora *f* estimada de llegada

etc [etˈsetrə] *abbr* (= **et cetera**) etc (= etcétera)

etch·ing [ˈetʃɪŋ] aguafuerte *m*

e·ter·nal [ɪˈtɜːrnl] *adj* eterno

e·ter·ni·ty [ɪˈtɜːrnətɪ] eternidad *f*

eth·i·cal [ˈeθɪkl] *adj* ético

eth·ics [ˈeθɪks] ética *f*; **code of ethics** código *m* ético

eth·nic [ˈeθnɪk] *adj* étnico

eth·nic 'group grupo *m* étnico

eth·nic mi'nor·i·ty minoría *f* étnica

EU [iːˈjuː] *abbr* (= **European Union**) UE *f* (=Unión *f* Europea)

eu·phe·mism [ˈjuːfəmɪzm] eufemismo *m*

eu·pho·ri·a [juːˈfɔːrɪə] euforia *f*

eu·ro [ˈjuroʊ] euro *m*

Eu·rope [ˈjʊrəp] Europa

Eu·ro·pe·an [jʊrəˈpɪən] **1** *adj* europeo **2** *n* europeo(-a) *m(f)*

Eu·ro·pe·an Com'mis·sion Comisión *f* Europea

Eu·ro·pe·an 'Par·lia·ment Parlamento *m* Europeo

Eu·ro·pe·an plan media pensión *f*

Eu·ro·pe·an 'Un·ion Unión *f* Europea

eu·tha·na·si·a [juːθəˈneɪzɪə] eutanasia *f*

e·vac·u·ate [ɪˈvækjʊeɪt] *v/t* evacuar

e·vade [ɪˈveɪd] *v/t* evadir

e·val·u·ate [ɪˈvæljʊeɪt] *v/t* evaluar

e·val·u·a·tion [ɪvæljuˈeɪʃn] evaluación *f*

e·van·gel·ist [ɪˈvændʒəlɪst] evangelista *m/f*

e·vap·o·rate [ɪˈvæpəreɪt] *v/i of water* evaporarse; *of confidence* desvanecerse

e·vap·o·ra·tion [ɪvæpəˈreɪʃn] *of water* evaporación *f*

e·va·sion [ɪ'veɪʒn] evasión f

e·va·sive [ɪ'veɪsɪv] adj evasivo

eve [iːv] víspera f

e·ven ['iːvn] 1 adj (regular) regular; (level) llano; number par; distribution igualado; **I'll get even with him** me las pagará 2 adv **even bigger / better** incluso or aún mayor / mejor; **not even** ni siquiera; **even so** aun así; **even if** aunque; **even if he begged me** aunque me lo suplicara 3 v/t: **even the score** empatar, igualar el marcador

eve·ning ['iːvnɪŋ] tarde f; after dark noche f; **in the evening** por la tarde / noche; **this evening** esta tarde / noche; **yesterday evening** anoche f; **good evening** buenas fpl noches

'eve·ning class clase f nocturna

'eve·ning dress for woman traje f de noche; for man traje f de etiqueta

eve·ning 'pa·per periódico m de la tarde or vespertino

e·ven·ly ['iːvnlɪ] adv (regularly) regularmente

e·vent [ɪ'vent] acontecimiento m; SP prueba f; **at all events** en cualquier caso

e·vent·ful [ɪ'ventfəl] adj agitado, lleno de incidentes

e·ven·tu·al [ɪ'ventʃʊəl] adj final

e·ven·tu·al·ly [ɪ'ventʃʊəlɪ] adv finalmente

ev·er ['evər] adv: **if I ever hear you ...** como te oiga ...; **have you ever been to Japan?** ¿has estado alguna vez en Japón?; **for ever** siempre; **ever since** desde entonces; **ever since she found out about it** desde que se enteró de ello; **ever since I've known him** desde que lo conozco

ev·er·green ['evərgriːn] n árbol m de hoja perenne

ev·er·last·ing [evər'læstɪŋ] adj love eterno

ev·ery ['evrɪ] adj cada; **I see him every day** le veo todos los días; **you have every reason to ...** tienes toda la razón para ...; **one in every ten** uno de cada diez; **every other day** cada dos días; **every now and then** de vez en cuando

ev·ery·bod·y ['evrɪbɑːdɪ] → **everyone**

ev·ery·day ['evrɪdeɪ] adj cotidiano

ev·ery·one ['evrɪwʌn] pron todo el mundo

ev·ery·thing ['evrɪθɪŋ] pron todo

ev·ery·where ['evrɪwer] adv in or por todos sitios; (wherever) dondequiera que

e·vict [ɪ'vɪkt] v/t desahuciar

ev·i·dence ['evɪdəns] also LAW prueba(s) f(pl); **give evidence** prestar declaración

ev·i·dent ['evɪdənt] adj evidente

ev·i·dent·ly ['evɪdəntlɪ] adv (clearly) evidentemente; (apparently) aparentemente, al parecer

e·vil ['iːvl] 1 adj malo 2 n mal m

e·voke [ɪ'vouk] v/t image evocar

ev·o·lu·tion [iːvə'luːʃn] evolución f

e·volve [ɪ'vɑːlv] v/i evolucionar

ewe [juː] oveja f

ex- [eks] pref ex-

ex [eks] F (former wife, husband) ex m/f F

ex·act [ɪg'zækt] adj exacto

ex·act·ing [ɪg'zæktɪŋ] adj exigente; task duro

ex·act·ly [ɪg'zæktlɪ] adv exactamente; **exactly!** ¡exactamente!

ex·ag·ge·rate [ɪg'zædʒəreɪt] v/t & v/i exagerar

ex·ag·ge·ra·tion [ɪgzædʒə'reɪʃn] exageración f

ex·am [ɪg'zæm] examen m; **take an exam** hacer un examen; **pass / fail an exam** aprobar/ suspender un examen

ex·am·i·na·tion [ɪgzæmɪ'neɪʃn] examen m; of patient reconocimiento m

ex·am·ine [ɪg'zæmɪn] v/t examinar; patient reconocer

ex·am·in·er [ɪg'zæmɪnər] EDU examinador(a) m(f)

ex·am·ple [ɪg'zæmpl] ejemplo m; **for example** por ejemplo; **set a good / bad example** dar buen / mal ejemplo

ex·as·pe·rat·ed [ɪg'zæspəreɪtɪd] adj exasperado

ex·as·pe·rat·ing [ɪg'zæspəreɪtɪŋ] adj exasperante

ex·ca·vate ['ekskəveɪt] v/t excavar

ex·ca·va·tion [ekskə'veɪʃn] excavación f

ex·ca·va·tor ['ekskəveɪtər] excavadora f

ex·ceed [ɪk'siːd] v/t (be more than) exceder; (go beyond) sobrepasar

ex·ceed·ing·ly [ɪk'siːdɪŋlɪ] adj sumamente

ex·cel [ɪk'sel] 1 v/i (pret & pp **excelled**) sobresalir (**at** en) 2 v/t (pret & pp **excelled**): **excel o.s.** superarse a sí mismo

ex·cel·lence ['eksələns] excelencia f

ex·cel·lent ['eksələnt] adj excelente

ex·cept [ɪk'sept] prep excepto; **except for** a excepción de; **except that** sólo que

ex·cep·tion [ɪk'sepʃn] excepción f; **with the exception of** a excepción de; **take exception to** molestarse por

ex·cep·tion·al [ɪk'sepʃnl] adj excepcional

ex·cep·tion·al·ly [ɪk'sepʃnlɪ] adv (extremely) excepcionalmente

ex·cerpt ['eksɜːrpt] extracto m

ex·cess [ɪk'ses] 1 n exceso m; **eat / drink to excess** comer / beber en exceso; **in excess of** superior a 2 adj excesivo

ex·cess 'bag·gage exceso m de equipaje

ex·cess 'fare suplemento m

ex·ces·sive [ɪk'sesɪv] adj excesivo

ex·change [ɪks'tʃeɪndʒ] 1 n intercambio m; **in exchange** a cambio (**for** de) 2 v/t cambiar

ex'change rate FIN tipo m de cambio

ex·ci·ta·ble [ɪk'saɪtəbl] adj excitable

ex·cite [ɪk'saɪt] v/t (make enthusiastic) entusiasmar

ex·cit·ed [ɪk'saɪtɪd] adj emocionado, excitado; sexually excitado; **get excited** emocionarse; **get excited about** emocionarse or excitarse con

ex·cite·ment [ɪk'saɪtmənt] emoción f, excitación f

ex·cit·ing [ɪk'saɪtɪŋ] adj emocionante, excitante

ex·claim [ɪk'skleɪm] v/t exclamar

ex·cla·ma·tion [eksklə'meɪʃn] exclamación f

ex·cla'ma·tion point signo m de admiración

ex·clude [ɪk'skluːd] v/t excluir; possibility descartar

ex·clud·ing [ɪk'skluːdɪŋ] prep excluyendo

ex·clu·sive [ɪk'skluːsɪv] adj exclusivo

ex·com·mu·ni·cate [ekskə'mjuːnɪkeɪt] v/t REL excomulgar

ex·cru·ci·a·ting [ɪk'skruːʃɪeɪtɪŋ] adj pain terrible

ex·cur·sion [ɪk'skɜːrʃn] excursión f

ex·cuse 1 n [ɪk'skjuːs] excusa f 2 v/t [ɪk'skjuːz] (forgive) excusar, perdonar; (allow to leave) disculpar; **excuse s.o. from sth** dispensar a alguien de algo; **excuse me** to get past, interrupting perdone, disculpe; to get attention perdone, oiga

ex·e·cute ['eksɪkjuːt] v/t criminal, plan ejecutar

ex·e·cu·tion [eksɪ'kjuːʃn] of criminal, plan ejecución f

ex·e·cu·tion·er [eksɪ'kjuːʃnər] verdugo m

ex·ec·u·tive [ɪg'zekjutɪv] ejecutivo(-a) m(f)

ex·ec·u·tive 'brief·case maletín m de ejecutivo

ex·ec·u·tive 'wash·room baño m para ejecutivos

ex·em·pla·ry [ɪg'zemplərɪ] adj ejemplar

ex·empt [ɪg'zempt] adj exento; **be exempt from** estar exento de

ex·er·cise ['eksərsaɪz] 1 n ejercicio m; **take exercise** hacer ejercicio 2 v/t muscle ejercitar; dog pasear; caution proceder con; **exercise restraint** controlarse 3 v/i hacer ejercicio

'ex·er·cise bike bicicleta f estática

'ex·er·cise book EDU cuaderno m de ejercicios

ex·ert [ɪg'zɜːrt] v/t authority ejercer; **exert o.s.** esforzarse

ex·er·tion [ɪg'zɜːrʃn] esfuerzo m

ex·hale [eks'heɪl] v/t exhalar

ex·haust [ɪg'zɔːst] 1 n fumes gases mpl de la combustión; pipe tubo m de escape 2 v/t (tire) cansar; (use up) agotar

ex·haust·ed [ɪg'zɔːstɪd] adj (tired) agotado

ex'haust fumes npl gases mpl de la combustión

ex·haust·ing [ɪg'zɔːstɪŋ] adj agotador

ex·haus·tion [ɪg'zɔːstʃn] agotamiento m

ex·haus·tive [ɪg'zɔːstɪv] adj exhaustivo

ex'haust pipe tubo m de escape

ex·hib·it [ɪg'zɪbɪt] 1 n in exhibition objeto

m expuesto **2** *v/t of gallery* exhibir; *of artist* exponer; *(give evidence of)* mostrar

ex·hi·bi·tion [eksɪˈbɪʃn] exposición *f*; *of bad behavior, skill* exhibición *f*

ex·hi·bi·tion·ist [eksɪˈbɪʃnɪst] exhibicionista *m/f*

ex·hil·a·rat·ing [ɪgˈzɪləreɪtɪŋ] *adj* estimulante

ex·ile [ˈeksaɪl] **1** *n* exilio *m*; *person* exiliado(-a) *m(f)* **2** *v/t* exiliar

ex·ist [ɪgˈzɪst] *v/i* existir; **exist on** subsistir a base de

ex·ist·ence [ɪgˈzɪstəns] existencia *f*; **be in existence** existir; **come into existence** crearse, nacer

ex·ist·ing [ɪgˈzɪstɪŋ] *adj* existente

ex·it [ˈeksɪt] **1** *n* salida *f*; THEA salida *f*, mutis *m* **2** *v/i* COMPUT salir

ex·on·e·rate [ɪgˈzɑːnəreɪt] *v/t* exonerar de

ex·or·bi·tant [ɪgˈzɔːrbɪtənt] *adj* exorbitante

ex·ot·ic [ɪgˈzɑːtɪk] *adj* exótico

ex·pand [ɪkˈspænd] **1** *v/t* expandir **2** *v/i* expandirse; *of metal* dilatarse

◆ **expand on** *v/t* desarrollar

ex·panse [ɪkˈspæns] extensión *f*

ex·pan·sion [ɪkˈspænʃn] expansión *f*; *of metal* dilatación *f*

ex·pa·tri·ate [eksˈpætrɪət] **1** *adj* expatriado **2** *n* expatriado(-a) *m(f)*

ex·pect [ɪkˈspekt] **1** *v/t* esperar; *(suppose)* suponer, imaginar(se); *(demand)* exigir **2** *v/i*: **be expecting** *(be pregnant)* estar en estado; *I expect so* eso espero, creo que sí

ex·pec·tant [ɪkˈspektənt] *adj crowd* expectante

ex·pec·tant ˈmoth·er futura madre *f*

ex·pec·ta·tion [ekspekˈteɪʃn] expectativa *f*; *live up to people's expectations of you (demands)* estar a la altura de lo que se espera de uno

ex·pe·dient [ɪkˈspiːdɪənt] *adj* oportuno, conveniente

ex·pe·di·tion [ekspɪˈdɪʃn] expedición *f*

ex·pel [ɪkˈspel] *v/t (pret & pp expelled) person* expulsar

ex·pend [ɪkˈspend] *v/t energy* gastar

ex·pend·a·ble [ɪkˈspendəbl] *adj person*

prescindible

ex·pen·di·ture [ɪkˈspendɪʧər] gasto *m*

ex·pense [ɪkˈspens] gasto *m*; *at great expense* gastando mucho dinero; *at the company's expense* a cargo de la empresa; *a joke at my expense* una broma a costa mía; *at the expense of his health* a costa de su salud

ex·pense ac·count cuenta *f* de gastos

ex·pen·ses [ɪkˈspensɪz] *npl* gastos *mpl*

ex·pen·sive [ɪkˈspensɪv] *adj* caro

ex·pe·ri·ence [ɪkˈspɪrɪəns] **1** *n* experiencia *f* **2** *v/t* experimentar

ex·pe·ri·enced [ɪkˈspɪrɪənst] *adj* experimentado

ex·per·i·ment [ɪkˈsperɪmənt] **1** *n* experimento *m* **2** *v/i* experimentar; *experiment on animals* experimentar con; *experiment with (try out)* probar

ex·per·i·men·tal [ɪksperɪˈmentl] *adj* experimental

ex·pert [ˈekspɜːrt] **1** *adj* experto **2** *n* experto(-a) *m(f)*

ex·pert adˈvice la opinión de un experto

ex·per·tise [ekspɜːrˈtiːz] destreza *f*, pericia *f*

ex·pire [ɪkˈspaɪr] *v/i* caducar

ex·pi·ry [ɪkˈspaɪrɪ] *of lease, contract* vencimiento *m*; *of passport* caducidad *f*

exˈpi·ry date *of food, passport* fecha *f* de caducidad; *be past its expiry date* haber caducado

ex·plain [ɪkˈspleɪn] **1** *v/t* explicar **2** *v/i* explicarse

ex·pla·na·tion [ekspləˈneɪʃn] explicación *f*

ex·plan·a·tor·y [ɪkˈsplænətɔːrɪ] *adj* explicativo

ex·plic·it [ɪkˈsplɪsɪt] *adj instructions* explícito

ex·plic·it·ly [ɪkˈsplɪsɪtlɪ] *adv state* explícitamente; *forbid* terminantemente

ex·plode [ɪkˈsploʊd] **1** *v/i of bomb* explotar **2** *v/t bomb* hacer explotar

ex·ploit¹ [ˈeksplɔɪt] *n* hazaña *f*

ex·ploit² [ɪkˈsplɔɪt] *v/t person, resources* explotar

ex·ploi·ta·tion [eksplɔɪˈteɪʃn] *of person* explotación *f*

ex·plo·ra·tion [eksplə'reɪʃn] exploración f

ex·plor·a·to·ry [ɪk'splɔːrətərɪ] adj surgery exploratorio

ex·plore [ɪk'splɔːr] v/t country etc explorar; possibility estudiar

ex·plor·er [ɪk'splɔːrər] explorador(a) m(f)

ex·plo·sion [ɪk'splouʒn] of bomb, in population explosión f

ex·plo·sive [ɪk'splousɪv] n explosivo m

ex·port ['ekspɔːrt] 1 n action exportación f; item producto m de exportación; **exports** npl exportaciones fpl 2 v/t also COMPUT exportar

'ex·port cam·paign campaña f de exportación

ex·port·er ['ekspɔːrtər] exportador(a) m(f)

ex·pose [ɪk'spouz] v/t (uncover) exponer; scandal sacar a la luz; **he's been exposed as a liar** ha quedado como un mentiroso; **expose sth to sth** exponer algo a algo

ex·po·sure [ɪk'spouʒər] exposición f; PHOT foto(grafía) f

ex·press [ɪk'spres] 1 adj (fast) rápido; (explicit) expreso 2 n train expreso m; bus autobús m directo 3 v/t expresar; **express o.s. well / clearly** expresarse bien / con claridad

ex'press el·e·va·tor ascensor rápido que sólo para en algunos pisos

ex·pres·sion [ɪk'spreʃn] voiced muestra f; phrase, on face expresión f; **read with expression** leer con sentimiento

ex·pres·sive [ɪk'spresɪv] adj expresivo

ex·press·ly [ɪk'spreslɪ] adv state expresamente; forbid terminantemente

ex·press·way [ɪk'spreswei] autopista f

ex·pul·sion [ɪk'spʌlʃn] from school, of diplomat expulsión f

ex·qui·site [ek'skwɪzɪt] adj (beautiful) exquisito

ex·tend [ɪk'stend] 1 v/t house, investigation ampliar; (make wider) ensanchar; (make bigger) agrandar; runway, path alargar; contract, visa prorrogar; thanks, congratulations extender 2 v/i of garden etc llegar

ex·ten·sion [ɪk'stenʃn] to house ampliación f; of contract, visa prórroga f; TELEC extensión f

ex·ten·sion ca·ble cable m de extensión

ex·ten·sive [ɪk'stensɪv] adj damage cuantioso; knowledge considerable; search extenso, amplio

ex·tent [ɪk'stent] alcance m; **to such an extent that** hasta el punto de que; **to a certain extent** hasta cierto punto

ex·ten·u·at·ing cir·cum·stanc·es [ɪk'stenueitiŋ] npl circunstancias fpl atenuantes

ex·te·ri·or [ɪk'stɪrɪər] 1 adj exterior 2 n exterior m

ex·ter·mi·nate [ɪk'stɜːrmɪneɪt] v/t exterminar

ex·ter·nal [ɪk'stɜːrnl] adj (outside) exterior, externo

ex·tinct [ɪk'stɪŋkt] adj species extinguido

ex·tinc·tion [ɪk'stɪŋkʃn] of species extinción f

ex·tin·guish [ɪk'stɪŋgwɪʃ] v/t fire extinguir, apagar; cigarette apagar

ex·tin·guish·er [ɪk'stɪŋgwɪʃər] extintor m

ex·tort [ɪk'stɔːrt] v/t obtener mediante extorsión; **extort money from** extorsionar a

ex·tor·tion [ɪk'stɔːrʃn] extorsión f

ex·tor·tion·ate [ɪk'stɔːrʃənət] adj prices desorbitado

ex·tra ['ekstrə] 1 n extra m; in movie extra m/f 2 adj extra; **meals are extra** las comidas se pagan aparte; **that's $1 extra** cuesta 1 dólar más 3 adv super; **extra strong** extrafuerte; **extra special** muy especial

ex·tra 'charge recargo m

ex·tract[1] ['ekstrækt] n extracto m

ex·tract[2] [ɪk'strækt] v/t sacar; coal, oil, tooth extraer; information sonsacar

ex·trac·tion [ɪk'strækʃn] of oil, coal, tooth extracción f

ex·tra·dite ['ekstrədaɪt] v/t extraditar

ex·tra·di·tion [ekstrə'dɪʃn] extradición f

ex·tra·di·tion trea·ty tratado m de extradición

ex·tra·mar·i·tal [ekstrə'mærɪtl] *adj* extramarital

ex·tra·or·di·nar·i·ly [ekstrɔːrdɪn'erɪlɪ] *adv* extraordinariamente

ex·tra·or·di·na·ry [ɪk'strɔːrdɪnerɪ] *adj* extraordinario

ex·trav·a·gance [ɪk'strævəgəns] *with money* despilfarro *m*; *of claim etc* extravagancia *f*

ex·trav·a·gant [ɪk'strævəgənt] *adj with money* despilfarrador; *claim* extravagante

ex·treme [ɪk'striːm] **1** *n* extremo *m* **2** *adj* extremo; *views* extremista

ex·treme·ly [ɪk'striːmlɪ] *adv* extremadamente, sumamente

ex·trem·ist [ɪk'striːmɪst] extremista *m/f*

ex·tri·cate ['ekstrɪkeɪt] *v/t* liberar

ex·tro·vert ['ekstrəvɜːrt] **1** *adj* extrovertido **2** *n* extrovertido(-a) *m(f)*

ex·u·be·rant [ɪg'zuːbərənt] *adj* exuberante

ex·ult [ɪg'zʌlt] *v/i* exultar

eye [aɪ] **1** *n of person, needle* ojo *m*; **keep an eye on** (*look after*) estar pendiente de; (*monitor*) estar pendiente de, vigilar **2** *v/t* mirar

'eye·ball globo *m* ocular

'eye·brow ceja *f*

'eye-catch·ing *adj* llamativo

'eye·glass·es *npl* gafas *fpl*, *L.Am.* anteojos *mpl*, *L.Am.* lentes *mpl*

'eye·lash pestaña *f*

'eye·lid párpado *m*

'eye·lin·er lápiz *m* de ojos

'eye·sha·dow sombra *f* de ojos

'eye·sight vista *f*

'eye·sore engendro *m*, monstruosidad *f*

'eye strain vista *f* cansada

'eye·wit·ness testigo *m/f* ocular

F

F *abbr* (= *Fahrenheit*) F

fab·ric ['fæbrɪk] (*material*) tejido *m*

fab·u·lous ['fæbjʊləs] *adj* fabuloso, estupendo

fab·u·lous·ly ['fæbjʊləslɪ] *adv rich* tremendamente; *beautiful* increíblemente

fa·çade [fə'sɑːd] *of building, person* fachada *f*

face [feɪs] **1** *n* cara *f*; **face to face** cara a cara; **lose face** padecer una *humillación* **2** *v/t* (*be opposite*) estar enfrente de; (*confront*) enfrentarse a

♦ **face up to** *v/t* hacer frente a

'face-cloth toallita *f*

'face-lift lifting *m*, estiramiento *m* de piel

'face pack mascarilla *f* (*facial*)

face 'val·ue: **take sth at face value** tomarse algo literalmente

fa·cial ['feɪʃl] *n* limpieza *f* de cutis

fa·cil·i·tate [fə'sɪlɪteɪt] *v/t* facilitar

fa·cil·i·ties [fə'sɪlətɪz] *npl* instalaciones *fpl*

fact [fækt] hecho *m*; **in fact, as a matter of fact** de hecho

fac·tion ['fækʃn] facción *f*

fac·tor ['fæktər] factor *m*

fac·to·ry ['fæktərɪ] fábrica *f*

fac·ul·ty ['fækəltɪ] (*hearing etc*), *at university* facultad *f*

fad [fæd] moda *f*

fade [feɪd] *v/i of colors* desteñirse, perder color; *of memories* desvanecerse

fad·ed ['feɪdɪd] *adj color, jeans* desteñido, descolorido

fag[1] [fæg] F (*homosexual*) maricón *m* F

fag[2] [fæg] *Br* F (*cigarette*) pitillo *m* F

Fahr·en·heit ['færənhaɪt] *adj* Fahrenheit

fail [feɪl] **1** *v/i* fracasar; *of plan* fracasar, fallar **2** *n*: **without fail** sin falta

fail·ing ['feɪlɪŋ] *n* fallo *m*

fail·ure ['feɪljər] fracaso *m*; *in exam* suspenso *m*; *I feel such a failure* me siento un fracasado

faint [feɪnt] **1** *adj line, smile* tenue; *smell, noise* casi imperceptible **2** *v/i* desmayarse

faint·ly ['feɪntlɪ] *adv smile, smell* levemente

fair[1] [fer] *n* COM feria *f*

fair[2] [fer] *adj hair* rubio; *complexion* claro; *(just)* justo

fair·ly ['ferlɪ] *adv treat* justamente, con justicia; *(quite)* bastante

fair·ness ['fernɪs] *of treatment* imparcialidad *f*

fai·ry ['ferɪ] hada *f*

'fai·ry tale cuento *m* de hadas

faith [feɪθ] fe *f*, confianza *f*; REL fe *f*

faith·ful ['feɪθfəl] *adj* fiel; *be faithful to one's partner* ser fiel a la pareja

faith·ful·ly ['feɪθfəlɪ] *adv* religiosamente

Falk·land Is·lands ['fɔːklənd] *npl: the Falkland Islands* las Islas Malvinas

fake [feɪk] **1** *n* falsificación *f* **2** *adj* falso **3** *v/t (forge)* falsificar; *(feign)* fingir

fall[1] [fɔːl] *n season* otoño *m*

fall[2] [fɔːl] **1** *v/i (pret fell, pp fallen) of person* caerse; *of government, prices, temperature, night* caer; *it falls on a Tuesday* cae en martes; *fall ill* enfermar, caer enfermo; *I fell off the wall* me caí del muro **2** *n* caída *f*

♦ **fall back on** *v/t* recurrir a

♦ **fall behind** *v/i with work, studies* retrasarse

♦ **fall down** *v/i* caerse

♦ **fall for** *v/t person* enamorarse de; *(be deceived by)* dejarse engañar por; *I'm amazed you fell for it* me sorprende mucho que picaras

♦ **fall out** *v/i of hair* caerse; *(argue)* pelearse

♦ **fall over** *v/i* caerse

♦ **fall through** *v/i of plans* venirse abajo

fal·len ['fɔːlən] *pp → fall*[2]

fal·li·ble ['fæləbl] *adj* falible

'fall·out lluvia *f* radiactiva

false [fɑːls] *adj* falso

false a'larm falsa alarma *f*

false·ly ['fɑːːlslɪ] *adv: be falsely accused*

of sth ser acusado falsamente de algo

false 'start *in race* salida *f* nula

false 'teeth *npl* dentadura *f* postiza

fal·si·fy ['fɑːlsɪfaɪ] *v/t (pret & pp falsified)* falsificar

fame [feɪm] fama *f*

fa·mil·i·ar [fə'mɪljər] *adj* familiar; *get familiar (intimate)* tomarse demasiadas confianzas; *be familiar with sth* estar familiarizado con algo; *that looks familiar* eso me resulta familiar; *that sounds familiar* me suena

fa·mil·i·ar·i·ty [fəmɪlɪ'ærɪtɪ] *with subject etc* familiaridad *f*

fa·mil·i·ar·ize [fə'mɪljəraɪz] *v/t: familiarize o.s. with ...* familiarizarse con ...

fam·i·ly ['fæmɪlɪ] familia *f*

fam·i·ly 'doc·tor médico *m/f* de familia

'fam·i·ly name apellido *m*

fam·i·ly 'plan·ning planificación *f* familiar

fam·i·ly 'plan·ning clin·ic clínica *f* de planificación familiar

fam·i·ly 'tree árbol *m* genealógico

fam·ine ['fæmɪn] hambruna *f*

fam·ished ['fæmɪʃt] *adj* F: *I'm famished* estoy muerto de hambre F

fa·mous ['feɪməs] *adj* famoso; *be famous for ...* ser famoso por ...

fan[1] [fæn] *n (supporter)* seguidor(a) *m(f)*; *of singer, band* admirador(a) *m(f)*, fan *m/f*

fan[2] [fæn] **1** *n electric* ventilador *m; handheld* abanico *m* **2** *v/t (pret & pp fanned) fan o.s.* abanicarse

fa·nat·ic [fə'nætɪk] *n* fanático(-a) *m(f)*

fa·nat·i·cal [fə'nætɪkl] *adj* fanático

fa·nat·i·cism [fə'nætɪsɪzm] fanatismo *m*

'fan belt MOT correa *f* del ventilador

'fan club club *m* de fans

fan·cy ['fænsɪ] **1** *adj (luxurious)* de lujo; *(complicated)* sofisticado **2** *n: as the fancy takes you* como te apetezca; *take a fancy to s.o.* encapricharse de alguien **3** *v/t (pret & pp fancied): do you fancy an ice cream?* ¿te apetece un helado?

fan·cy 'dress disfraz *m*

fan·cy-'dress par·ty fiesta *f* de disfraces

fang [fæŋ] colmillo *m*

'**fan mail** cartas *fpl* de los fans

fan·ta·size ['fæntəsaɪz] *v/i* fantasear (**about** sobre)

fan·tas·tic [fæn'tæstɪk] *adj* (*very good*) fantástico, excelente; (*very big*) inmenso

fan·tas·tic·al·ly [fæn'tæstɪklɪ] *adv* (*extremely*) sumamente, increíblemente

fan·ta·sy ['fæntəsɪ] fantasía *f*

far [fɑːr] *adv* lejos; (*much*) mucho; **far bigger / faster** mucho más grande / rápido; **far away** lejos; **how far is it to …?** ¿a cuánto está …?; **as far as the corner / hotel** hasta la esquina / el hotel; **as far as I can see** tal y como lo veo yo; **as far as I know** que yo sepa; **you've gone too far** *in behavior* te has pasado; **so far so good** por ahora muy bien

farce [fɑːrs] farsa *f*

fare [fer] *n price* tarifa *f*; *actual money* dinero *m*

Far 'East Lejano Oriente *m*

fare·well [fer'wel] *n* despedida *f*

fare'well par·ty fiesta *f* de despedida

far-fetched [fɑːr'fetʃt] *adj* inverosímil, exagerado

farm [fɑːrm] *n* granja *f*

farm·er ['fɑːrmər] granjero(-a) *m(f)*

'**farm·house** granja *f*, alquería *f*

'**farm·ing** ['fɑːrmɪŋ] *n* agricultura *f*

'**farm·work·er** trabajador(a) *m(f)* del campo

'**farm·yard** corral *m*

far-'off *adj* lejano

far·sight·ed [fɑːr'saɪtɪd] *adj* previsor; *optically* hipermétrope

fart [fɑːrt] **1** *n* F pedo *m* F **2** *v/i* F tirarse un pedo F

far·ther ['fɑːðər] *adv* más lejos; **farther away** más allá, más lejos

far·thest ['fɑːðəst] *adv travel etc* más lejos

fas·ci·nate ['fæsɪneɪt] *v/t* fascinar; **be fascinated by …** estar fascinado por …

fas·ci·nat·ing ['fæsɪneɪtɪŋ] *adj* fascinante

fas·ci·na·tion [fæsɪ'neɪʃn] fascinación *f*

fas·cism ['fæʃɪzm] fascismo *m*

fas·cist ['fæʃɪst] **1** *n* fascista *m/f* **2** *adj* fascista

fash·ion ['fæʃn] *n* moda *f*; (*manner*)

modo *m*, manera *f*; **in fashion** de moda; **out of fashion** pasado de moda

fash·ion·a·ble ['fæʃnəbl] *adj* de moda

fash·ion·a·bly ['fæʃnəblɪ] *adv dressed* a la moda

'**fash·ion-con·scious** *adj* que sigue la moda

'**fash·ion de·sign·er** modisto(-a) *m(f)*

'**fash·ion mag·a·zine** revista *f* de modas

'**fash·ion show** desfile *f* de moda, pase *m* de modelos

fast[1] [fæst] **1** *adj* rápido; **be fast** *of clock* ir adelantando **2** *adv* rápido; **stuck fast** atascado; **fast asleep** profundamente dormido

fast[2] [fæst] *n not eating* ayuno *m*

fas·ten ['fæsn] **1** *v/t window, lid* cerrar (*poniendo el cierre*); *dress* abrochar; **fasten sth onto sth** asegurar algo a algo **2** *v/i of dress etc* abrocharse

fas·ten·er ['fæsnər] *for dress, lid* cierre *f*

fast 'food comida *f* rápida

fast-'food 'res·tau·rant restaurante *f* de comida rápida

fast 'for·ward 1 *n on video etc* avance *m* rápido **2** *v/i* avanzar

'**fast lane** *on road* carril *f* rápido; **in the fast lane** *fig: of life* con un tren de vida acelerado

'**fast train** (tren *m*) rápido *m*

fat [fæt] **1** *adj* gordo **2** *n on meat, for baking* grasa *f*

fa·tal ['feɪtl] *adj illness* mortal; *error* fatal

fa·tal·i·ty [fə'tælətɪ] víctima *f* mortal

fa·tal·ly ['feɪtəlɪ] *adv* mortalmente; **fatally injured** herido mortalmente

fate [feɪt] destino *m*

fat·ed ['feɪtɪd] *adj*: **be fated to do sth** estar *predestinado* a hacer algo

'**fat-free** *adj* sin grasas

fa·ther ['fɑːðər] *n* padre *m*; **Father Martin** REL el Padre Martin

Fa·ther 'Christ·mas *Br* Papá *m* Noel

fa·ther·hood ['fɑːðərhʊd] paternidad *f*

'**fa·ther-in-law** (*pl* **fathers-in-law**) suegro *m*

fa·ther·ly ['fɑːðəlɪ] *adj* paternal

fath·om ['fæðəm] *n* NAUT braza *f*

◆ **fathom out** *v/t fig* entender

fa·tigue [fə'tiːg] *n* cansancio *m*, fatiga *f*

fat·so ['fætsoʊ] F gordinflón (-ona) *m(f)* F

fat·ten ['fætn] *v/t animal* engordar

fat·ty ['fætɪ] **1** *adj* graso **2** *n* F (*person*) gordinflón (-ona) *m(f)* F

fau·cet ['fɒːsɪt] *Span* grifo *m*, *L.Am.* llave *f*

fault [fɒːlt] *n* (*defect*) fallo *m*; **it's your/ my fault** es culpa tuya / mía; **find fault with** ... encontrar defectos a ...

fault·less ['fɒːltlɪs] *adj* impecable

fault·y ['fɒːltɪ] *adj goods* defectuoso

fa·vor ['feɪvər] **1** *n* favor *m*; **do s.o. a fa·vor** hacer un favor a alguien; **do me a fa·vor!** (*don't be stupid*) ¡haz el favor!; **in favor of** ... a favor de ...; **be in favor of** ... estar a favor de ... **2** *v/t* (*prefer*) preferir

fa·vo·ra·ble ['feɪvərəbl] *adj reply etc* favorable

fa·vo·rite ['feɪvərɪt] **1** *n* favorito(-a) *m(f)*; *food* comida *f* favorita **2** *adj* favorito

fa·vor·it·ism ['feɪvrɪtɪzm] favoritismo *m*

fa·vour *etc Br* → **favor** *etc*

fax [fæks] **1** *n* fax *m*; **send sth by fax** enviar algo por fax **2** *v/t* enviar por fax: **fax sth to s.o.** enviar algo por fax a alguien

FBI [efbiː'aɪ] *abbr* (= **Federal Bureau of Investigation**) FBI *m*

fear [fɪr] **1** *n* miedo *m*, temor *m* **2** *v/t* temer, tener miedo a

fear·less ['fɪrlɪs] *adj* valiente, audaz

fear·less·ly ['fɪrlɪslɪ] *adv* sin miedo

fea·si·bil·i·ty stud·y [fiːzə'bɪlətɪ] estudio *m* de viabilidad

fea·si·ble ['fiːzəbl] *adj* factible, viable

feast [fiːst] *n* banquete *m*, festín *m*

feat [fiːt] *n* hazaña *f*, proeza *f*

feath·er ['feðər] pluma *f*

fea·ture ['fiːtʃər] **1** *n on face* rasgo *m*, facción *f*; *of city, building, plan, style* característica *f*; *article in paper* reportaje *m*; *movie* largometraje *m*; **make a feature of** ... destacar ... **2** *v/t* **a movie featuring** ... una película en la que aparece ...

'fea·ture film largometraje *m*

Feb·ru·a·ry ['februerɪ] febrero *m*

fed [fed] *pret & pp* → **feed**

fed·e·ral ['fedərəl] *adj* federal

fed·e·ra·tion [fedə'reɪʃn] federación *f*

fed 'up *adj* F harto, hasta las narices F; **be fed up with** ... estar harto *or* hasta las narices de ...

fee [fiː] *of lawyer, doctor, consultant* honorarios *mpl*; *for entrance* entrada *f*; *for membership* cuota *f*

fee·ble ['fiːbl] *adj person, laugh* débil; *attempt* flojo; *excuse* pobre

feed [fiːd] *v/t* (*pret & pp* **fed**) alimentar, dar de comer a

'feed·back *n* reacción *m*; **we'll give you some feedback as soon as possible** le daremos nuestra opinión *or* nuestras reacciones lo antes posible

feel [fiːl] **1** *v/t* (*pret & pp* **felt**) (*touch*) tocar; (*sense*) sentir; (*think*) creer, pensar; **you can feel the difference** se nota la diferencia **2** *v/i* (*pret & pp* **felt**): **it feels like silk / cotton** tiene la textura de la seda / algodón; **your hand feels hot** tienes la mano caliente; **I feel hungry** tengo hambre; **I feel tired** estoy cansado; **how are you feeling today?** ¿cómo te encuentras hoy?; **how does it feel to be rich?** ¿qué se siente siendo rico?; **do you feel like a drink / meal?** ¿te apetece una bebida / comida?; **I feel like going / staying** me apetece ir / quedarme; **I don't feel like it** no me apetece

◆ **feel up to** *v/t* sentirse con fuerzas para

feel·er ['fiːlər] *of insect* antena *f*

'feel·good fac·tor sensación *f* positiva

feel·ing ['fiːlɪŋ] sentimiento *m*; (*sensation*) sensación *f*; **what are your feelings about it?** ¿qué piensas sobre ello?; **I have mixed feelings about him** me inspira sentimientos contradictorios; **I have this feeling that** ... tengo el presentimiento de que ...

feet [fiːt] *pl* → **foot**

fe·line ['fiːlaɪn] *adj* felino

fell [fel] *pret* → **fall**[2]

fel·low ['feloʊ] *n* (*man*) tipo *m*

fel·low 'cit·i·zen conciudadano(-a) *m(f)*

fel·low 'coun·try·man compatriota *m/f*

fel·low 'man prójimo *m*

fel·o·ny ['felənɪ] delito *m* grave

felt [felt] **1** *n* fieltro *m* **2** *pret & pp* → **feel**

felt 'tip, felt-tip 'pen rotulador *m*

fe·male ['fiːmeɪl] **1** *adj animal, plant* hembra; *relating to people* femenino **2** *n of animals, plants* hembra *f*; *person* mujer *f*

fem·i·nine ['feminin] **1** *adj also* GRAM femenino **2** *n* GRAM femenino *m*

fem·i·nism ['feminizm] feminismo *m*

fem·i·nist ['feminist] **1** *n* feminista *m/f* **2** *adj* feminista

fence [fens] *n around garden etc* cerca *f*, valla *f*; F *criminal* perista *m/f*; **sit on the fence** nadar entre dos aguas

◆ **fence in** *v/t land* cercar, vallar

fenc·ing ['fensɪŋ] SP esgrima *f*

fend [fend] *v/i*: **fend for o.s.** valerse por sí mismo

fend·er ['fendər] MOT aleta *f*

fer·ment¹ [fə'ment] *v/i of liquid* fermentar

fer·ment² ['fɜːrment] *n* (*unrest*) agitación *f*

fer·men·ta·tion [fɜːrmen'teɪʃn] fermentación *f*

fern [fɜːrn] helecho *m*

fe·ro·cious [fə'rouʃəs] *adj* feroz

fer·ry ['feri] *n* ferry *m*, transbordador *m*

fer·tile ['fɜːrtəl] *adj* fértil

fer·til·i·ty [fɜːr'tɪlətɪ] fertilidad *f*

fer·til·i·ty drug medicamento *m* para el tratamiento de la infertilidad

fer·ti·lize ['fɜːrtəlaɪz] *v/t* fertilizar

fer·ti·liz·er ['fɜːrtəlaɪzər] *for soil* fertilizante *m*

fer·vent ['fɜːrvənt] *adj admirer* ferviente

fer·vent·ly ['fɜːrvəntlɪ] *adv* fervientemente

fes·ter ['festər] *v/i of wound* enconarse

fes·ti·val ['festɪvl] festival *m*

fes·tive ['festɪv] *adj* festivo; **the festive season** la época navideña, las Navidades

fes·tiv·i·ties [fe'stɪvətɪz] *npl* celebraciones *fpl*

fe·tal ['fiːtl] *adj* fetal

fetch [fetʃ] *v/t person* recoger; *thing* traer, ir a buscar; *price* alcanzar

fe·tus ['fiːtəs] feto *m*

feud [fjuːd] **1** *n* enemistad *f* **2** *v/i* estar enemistado

fe·ver ['fiːvər] fiebre *f*

fe·ver·ish ['fiːvərɪʃ] *adj* con fiebre; *fig*: *excitement* febril

few [fjuː] **1** *adj* (*not many*) pocos; **a few** *things* unos pocos; **quite a few, a good few** (*a lot*) bastantes **2** *pron* (*not many*) pocos(-as); **a few** (*some*) unos pocos; **quite a few, a good few** (*a lot*) bastantes; **few of them could speak English** de ellos muy pocos hablaban inglés

few·er ['fjuːər] *adj* menos; **fewer than ...** menos que ...; *with numbers* menos de ...

fi·an·cé [fɪ'ɑːnseɪ] prometido *m*, novio *m*

fi·an·cée [fɪ'ɑːnseɪ] prometida *f*, novia *f*

fi·as·co [fɪ'æskou] fiasco *m*

fib [fɪb] *n* F bola *f* F

fi·ber ['faɪbər] *n* fibra *f*

'fi·ber·glass *n* fibra *f* de vidrio

fi·ber 'op·tic *adj* de fibra óptica

fi·ber 'op·tics fibra *f* óptica

fi·bre *Br* → **fiber**

fick·le ['fɪkl] *adj* inconstante, mudable

fic·tion ['fɪkʃn] *n* (*novels*) literatura *f* de ficción; (*made-up story*) ficción *f*

fic·tion·al ['fɪkʃnl] *adj* de ficción

fic·ti·tious [fɪk'tɪʃəs] *adj* ficticio

fid·dle ['fɪdl] **1** *n* (*violin*) violín *m*; **it's a fiddle** F (*cheat*) es un amaño **2** *v/i*: **fiddle around with** enredar con; **fiddle around with** enredar con **3** *v/t accounts, result* amañar

fi·del·i·ty [fɪ'delətɪ] fidelidad *f*

fid·get ['fɪdʒɪt] *v/i* moverse; **stop fidgeting!** ¡estáte quieto!

fid·get·y ['fɪdʒɪtɪ] *adj* inquieto

field [fiːld] *also of research etc* campo *m*; *for sport* campo *m*, *L.Am.* cancha *f*; (*competitors in race*) participantes *mpl*; **that's not my field** no es mi campo

field·er ['fiːldər] *in baseball* fildeador(-a) *m(f)*

'field e·vents *npl* pruebas *fpl* de salto y lanzamiento

fierce [fɪrs] *adj animal* feroz; *wind, storm* violento

fierce·ly ['fɪrslɪ] *adv* ferozmente

fi·er·y ['faɪrɪ] *adj* fogoso, ardiente

fif·teen [fɪf'tiːn] quince

fif·teenth [fɪf'tiːnθ] *n & adj* decimoquinto

fifth [fɪfθ] *n & adj* quinto

fif·ti·eth ['fɪftɪɪθ] *n & adj* quincuagésimo

fif·ty ['fɪftɪ] cincuenta

fif·ty-'fif·ty *adv* a medias

fig [fɪg] higo *m*

fight [faɪt] **1** *n* lucha *f*, pelea *f*; (*argument*) pelea *f*; *fig: for survival, championship etc* lucha *f*; *in boxing* combate *m*; **have a fight** (*argue*) pelearse **2** *v/t* (*pret & pp* **fought**) *enemy, person* luchar contra, pelear contra; *in boxing* pelear contra; *disease, injustice* luchar contra, combatir **3** *v/i* (*pret & pp* **fought**) luchar, pelear; (*argue*) pelearse

◆ **fight for** *v/t* one's rights, a cause luchar por

fight·er ['faɪtər] combatiente *m/f*; *airplane* caza *m*; (*boxer*) púgil *m*; **she's a fighter** tiene espíritu combativo

fight·ing ['faɪtɪŋ] *n physical, verbal* peleas *fpl*; MIL luchas *fpl*, combates *mpl*

fig·u·ra·tive ['fɪgjərətɪv] *adj* figurado

fig·ure ['fɪgər] **1** *n figura f*; (*digit*) cifra *f* **2** *v/t* F (*think*) imaginarse, pensar

◆ **figure on** *v/t* F (*plan*) pensar

◆ **figure out** *v/t* (*understand*) entender; *calculation* resolver

'fig·ure skat·er patinador(a) *m(f)* artístico(-a)

'fig·ure skat·ing patinaje *m* artístico

file[1] [faɪl] **1** *n of documents* expediente *m*; COMPUT archivo *m*, fichero *m* **2** *v/t documents* archivar

◆ **file away** *v/t documents* archivar

file[2] [faɪl] *n for wood, fingernails* lima *f*

'file cab·i·net archivador *m*

'file man·ag·er COMPUT administrador *m* de archivos

fi·li·al ['fɪlɪəl] *adj* filial

fill [fɪl] **1** *v/t* llenar; *tooth* empastar, L.Am. emplomar **2** *n*: **eat one's fill** hincharse

◆ **fill in** *v/t form, hole* rellenar; **fill s.o. in** poner a alguien al tanto

◆ **fill in for** *v/t* sustituir a

◆ **fill out 1** *v/t form* rellenar **2** *v/i* (*get fatter*) engordar

◆ **fill up 1** *v/t* llenar (hasta arriba) **2** *v/i of stadium, theater* llenarse

fil·let ['fɪlɪt] *n* filete *m*

fill·ing ['fɪlɪŋ] **1** *n in sandwich* relleno *m*; *in tooth* empaste *m*, L.Am. emplomadura *f* **2** *adj*: **be filling** *of food* llenar mucho

'fill·ing sta·tion estación *f* de servicio, gasolinera *f*

film [fɪlm] **1** *n for camera* carrete *m*; (*movie*) película *f* **2** *v/t person, event* filmar

'film-mak·er cineasta *m/f*

'film star estrella *f* de cine

fil·ter ['fɪltər] **1** *n* filtro *m* **2** *v/t coffee, liquid* filtrar

◆ **filter through** *v/i of news reports* filtrarse

'fil·ter pa·per papel *m* de filtro

'fil·ter tip (*cigarette*) cigarrillo *m* con filtro

filth [fɪlθ] suciedad *f*, mugre *f*

filth·y ['fɪlθɪ] *adj* sucio, mugriento; *language etc* obsceno

fin [fɪn] *of fish* aleta *f*

fi·nal ['faɪnl] **1** *adj* (*last*) último; *decision* final, definitivo **2** *n* SP final *f*

fi·na·le [fɪ'nælɪ] final *m*

fi·nal·ist ['faɪnəlɪst] finalista *m/f*

fi·nal·ize ['faɪnəlaɪz] *v/t plans, design* ultimar

fi·nal·ly ['faɪnəlɪ] *adv* finalmente, por último; (*at last*) finalmente, por fin

fi·nance ['faɪnæns] **1** *n* finanzas *fpl* **2** *v/t* financiar

fi·nan·ces ['faɪnænsɪz] *npl* finanzas *fpl*

fi·nan·cial [faɪ'nænʃl] *adj* financiero

fi·nan·cial·ly [faɪ'nænʃəlɪ] *adv* económicamente

fi·nan·cial 'year *Br* ejercicio *m* económico

fi·nan·cier [faɪ'nænsɪr] financiero(-a) *m(f)*

find [faɪnd] *v/t* (*pret & pp* **found**) encontrar, hallar; **if you find it too hot /cold** si te parece demasiado frío / caliente; **find s.o. innocent /guilty** LAW declarar a alguien inocente / culpable; **I find it strange that ...** me sorprende que ...; **how did you find the hotel?** ¿qué te pareció el hotel?

◆ **find out 1** *v/t* descubrir, averiguar **2** *v/i* (*discover*) descubrir; **can you try to find out?** ¿podrías enterarte?

find·ings ['faɪndɪŋz] *npl of report* conclusiones *fpl*

fine[1] [faɪn] *adj day, weather* bueno; *wine, performance, city* excelente; *distinction, line* fino; **how's that? - that's fine** ¿qué tal está? - bien; **that's fine by me** por mí no hay ningún problema; **how are you? - fine** ¿cómo estás? - bien

fine[2] [faɪn] **1** *n* multa *f* **2** *v/t* multar, poner una multa a

fine-'tooth comb: **go through sth with a fine-tooth comb** revisar algo minuciosamente

fine-'tune *v/t engine, fig* afinar, hacer los últimos ajustes a

fin·ger ['fɪŋgər] **1** *n* dedo *m* **2** *v/t* tocar

'fin·ger·nail *n* uña *f*

'fin·ger·print 1 *n* huella *f* digital *or* dactilar **2** *v/t* tomar las huellas digitales *or* dactilares a

'fin·ger·tip *n* punta *f* del dedo; **have sth at one's fingertips** saberse algo al dedillo

fin·i·cky ['fɪnɪkɪ] *adj person* quisquilloso; *design* enrevesado

fin·ish ['fɪnɪʃ] **1** *v/t* acabar, terminar; **finish doing sth** acabar *or* terminar de hacer algo **2** *v/i* acabar, terminar **3** *n of product* acabado *m; of race* final *f*

◆ **finish off** *v/t* acabar, terminar

◆ **finish up** *v/t food* acabar, terminar; **he finished up liking it** acabó gustándole

◆ **finish with** *v/t boyfriend etc* cortar con

fin·ish·ing line ['fɪnɪʃɪŋ] línea *f* de meta

Fin·land ['fɪnlənd] Finlandia

Finn [fɪn] finlandés (-esa) *m(f)*

Finn·ish ['fɪnɪʃ] **1** *adj* finlandés **2** *n language* finés *m*

fir [fɜːr] abeto *m*

fire [faɪr] **1** *n* fuego *m; electric, gas* estufa *f; (blaze)* incendio *m; (bonfire, campfire etc)* hoguera *f;* **be on fire** estar ardiendo; **catch fire** prender; **set sth on fire, set fire to sth** prender fuego a algo **2** *v/i (shoot)* disparar **(on / at** sobre/a) **3** *v/t* F *(dismiss)* despedir

'fire a·larm alarma *f* contra incendios

'fire·arm arma *f* de fuego

'fire·crack·er petardo *m*

'fire de·part·ment (cuerpo *m* de) bomb-

eros *mpl*

'fire door puerta *f* contra incendios

'fire drill simulacro *m* de incendio; *Br* **'fire en·gine** coche *m* de bomberos

'fire es·cape salida *f* de incendios

'fire ex·tin·guish·er extintor *m*

'fire fight·er bombero (-a) *m(f)*

'fire-guard pantalla *f*, parachispas *m inv; Br* **'fire·man** bombero *m*

'fire·place chimenea *f*, hogar *m*

'fire sta·tion parque *m* de bomberos

'fire truck coche *m* de bomberos

'fire·wood leña *f*

'fire·works *npl* fuegos *mpl* artificiales

firm[1] [fɜːrm] *adj* firme; **a firm deal** un acuerdo en firme

firm[2] [fɜːrm] *n* COM empresa *f*

first [fɜːrst] **1** *adj* primero; **who's first please?** ¿quién es el primero, por favor? **2** *n* primero(-a) *m(f)* **3** *adv* primero; **first of all** *(for one reason)* en primer lugar; **at first** al principio

first 'aid primeros *mpl* auxilios

first-'aid box, first-'aid kit botiquín *m* de primeros auxilios

'first-born *adj* primogénito

first 'class 1 *adj ticket, seat* de primera (clase); *(very good)* excelente **2** *adv travel* en primera (clase)

first 'floor planta *f* baja, *Br* primer piso *m*

first'hand *adj* de primera mano

First 'La·dy *of US* primera dama *f*

first·ly ['fɜːrstlɪ] *adv* en primer lugar

first 'name nombre *m* (de pila)

first 'night estreno *m*

first of'fend·er delincuente *m/f* sin antecedentes

first of'fense primer delito *m*

first-'rate *adj* excelente

fis·cal ['fɪskl] *adj* fiscal

fis·cal 'year año *m* fiscal

fish [fɪʃ] *n (pl fish)* **1** *n* pez *m; to eat* pescado *m;* **drink like a fish** F beber como un cosaco F; **feel like a fish out of water** sentirse fuera de lugar **2** *v/i* pescar

'fish·bone espina *f* (de pescado)

fish·er·man ['fɪʃərmən] pescador *m*

fish·ing ['fɪʃɪŋ] pesca *f*

'fish·ing boat (barco *m*) pesquero *m*

'fish·ing line sedal *m*

'fish·ing rod caña *f* de pescar

'fish stick palito *m* de pescado

fish·y ['fɪʃɪ] *adj* F (*suspicious*) sospechoso

fist [fɪst] puño *m*

fit¹ [fɪt] *n* MED ataque *m*; *a fit of rage / jealousy* un arrebato de cólera / un ataque de celos

fit² [fɪt] *adj physically* en forma; *morally* adecuado; *he's not fit to be President* no está en condiciones ser Presidente; *keep fit* mantenerse en forma

fit³ [fɪt] **1** *v/t* (*attach*) colocar; *these pants don't fit me any more* estos pantalones ya no me entran; *it fits you perfectly* te queda perfectamente **2** *v/i* (*pret* & *pp* **fitted**) *of clothes* quedar bien; *of piece of furniture etc* caber **3** *n*: *it's a good fit of jacket etc* queda bien; *of piece of furniture* cabe bien; *it's a tight fit* no hay mucho espacio

◆ fit in **1** *v/i of person in group* encajar; *it fits in with our plans* encaja con nuestros planes **2** *v/t*: *fit s.o. in into schedule etc* hacer un hueco a alguien

fit·ful ['fɪtfəl] *adj sleep* intermitente

fit·ness ['fɪtnɪs] *physical* buena forma *f*

'fit·ness cen·ter, *Br* 'fit·ness cen·tre gimnasio *m*

fit·ted 'kitch·en ['fɪtɪd] cocina *f* a medida

fit·ted 'sheet sábana *f* ajustable

fit·ter ['fɪtər] *n* técnico(-a) *m(f)*

fit·ting ['fɪtɪŋ] *adj* apropiado

fit·tings ['fɪtɪŋz] *npl* equipamiento *m*

five [faɪv] cinco

fix [fɪks] **1** *n* (*solution*) solución *f*; *be in a fix* F estar en un lío F **2** *v/t* (*attach*) fijar; (*repair*) arreglar, reparar; (*arrange: meeting etc*) organizar; *lunch* preparar; (*dishonestly: match etc*) amañar; *fix sth onto sth* fijar algo a algo; *I'll fix you a drink* te preparé una bebida

◆ fix up *v/t meeting* organizar; *it's all fixed up* está todo organizado

fixed [fɪkst] *adj* fijo

fix·ings ['fɪkɪŋz] *npl* guarnición *f*

fix·ture ['fɪkstʃər] (*in room*) parte fija del mobiliario o la decoración de una habitación

◆ fiz·zle out ['fɪzl] *v/i* F quedarse en nada

fiz·zy ['fɪzɪ] *adj drink* con gas

flab [flæb] *on body* grasa *f*

flab·ber·gast ['flæbərgæst] *v/t* F: *be flabbergasted* quedarse estupefacto *or Span* alucinado F

flab·by ['flæbɪ] *adj muscles etc* fofo

flag¹ [flæg] *n* bandera *f*

flag² [flæg] *v/i* (*pret* & *pp* **flagged**) (*tire*) desfallecer

'flag·pole asta *f* (de bandera)

fla·grant ['fleɪgrənt] *adj* flagrante

'flag·ship *fig* estandarte *m*

'flag·staff asta *f* (de bandera)

'flag·stone losa *f*

flair [fler] *n* (*talent*) don *m*; *have a natural flair for* tener dotes para

flake [fleɪk] *n of snow* copo *m*; *of skin* escama *f*; *of plaster* desconchón *m*

◆ flake off *v/i of skin* descamarse; *of plaster, paint* desconcharse

flak·y ['fleɪkɪ] *adj skin* con escamas; *paint* desconchado

flak·y 'pas·try hojaldre *m*

flam·boy·ant [flæm'bɔɪənt] *adj personality* extravagante

flam·boy·ant·ly [flæm'bɔɪəntlɪ] *adv dressed* extravagantemente

flame [fleɪm] *n* llama *f*; *go up in flames* ser pasto de las llamas

fla·men·co [flə'meŋkou] flamenco *m*

fla·men·co danc·er bailador(a) *m(f)*

flam·ma·ble ['flæməbl] *adj* inflamable

flan [flæn] tarta *f*

flank [flæŋk] **1** *n of horse etc* costado *m*; MIL flanco *m* **2** *v/t* flanquear; *be flanked by* estar flanqueado por

flap [flæp] **1** *n of envelope, pocket* solapa *f*; *of table* hoja *f*; *be in a flap* F estar histérico F **2** *v/t* (*pret* & *pp* **flapped**) *wings* batir **3** *v/i* (*pret* & *pp* **flapped**) *of flag etc* ondear

flare [fler] **1** *n* (*distress signal*) bengala *f*; *in dress* vuelo *m* **2** *v/t*: *flare one's nostrils* hinchar las narices resoplando

◆ flare up *v/i of violence* estallar; *of illness, rash* exacerbarse, empeorar; *of fire* llamear; (*get very angry*) estallar

flash [flæʃ] **1** *n of light* destello *m*; PHOT

flash *m*; *in a flash* F en un abrir y cerrar de ojos; *have a flash of inspiration* tener una inspiración repentina; *a flash of lightning* un relámpago 2 *v/i of light* destellar 3 *v/t flash one's headlights* echar las luces

'flash·back *in movie* flash-back *m*, escena *f* retrospectiva

flash·er ['flæʃər] MOT intermitente *m*

'flash·light linterna *f*; PHOT flash *m*

flash·y ['flæʃɪ] *adj pej* ostentoso, chillón

flask [flæsk] *(hip flask)* petaca *f*

flat¹ [flæt] 1 *adj surface, land* llano, plano; *beer* sin gas; *battery* descargado; *tire* desinflado; *shoes* bajo; MUS bemol; *and that's flat* F y sanseacabó F 2 *adv* MUS demasiado bajo; *flat out work, run, drive* a tope; *the factory is producing flat out* la fábrica está al máximo de su capacidad productiva 3 *n Br (flat tire)* pinchazo *m*

flat² [flæt] *n Br* apartamento *m*, *Span* piso *m*

flat-chest·ed [flæt'tʃestɪd] *adj* plana de pecho

flat·ly ['flætlɪ] *adv refuse, deny* rotundamente

'flat rate tarifa *f* única

flat·ten ['flætn] *v/t land, road* allanar, aplanar; *by bombing, demolition* arrasar

flat·ter ['flætər] *v/t* halagar, adular

flat·ter·er ['flætərər] adulador(a) *m(f)*

flat·ter·ing ['flætərɪŋ] *adj comments* halagador; *color, clothes* favorecedor

flat·ter·y ['flætərɪ] halagos *mpl*, adulación *f*

flat·u·lence ['flætjʊləns] flatulencia *f*

'flat·ware *(cutlery)* cubertería *f*

flaunt [flɔːnt] *v/t* hacer ostentación de, alardear de

flau·tist ['flɔːtɪst] flautista *m/f*

fla·vor *etc Br → flavor etc*

fla·vor ['fleɪvər] 1 *n* sabor *m* 2 *v/t food* condimentar

fla·vor·ing ['fleɪvərɪŋ] *n* aromatizante *m*

fla·vour *etc Br → flavor etc*

flaw [flɔː] *n* defecto *m*, fallo *m*

flaw·less ['flɔːlɪs] *adj* impecable

flea [fliː] *n* pulga *f*

fleck [flek] mota *f*

fled [fled] *pret & pp → flee*

flee [fliː] *v/i (pret & pp* fled*)* escapar, huir

fleece [fliːs] *v/t* F desplumar F

fleet [fliːt] *n* NAUT, *of vehicles* flota *f*

fleet·ing ['fliːtɪŋ] *adj visit etc* fugaz; *catch a fleeting glimpse of* vislumbrar fugazmente a

flesh [fleʃ] *n* carne *f*; *of fruit* pulpa *f*; *meet / see s.o. in the flesh* conocer / ver a alguien en persona

flex [fleks] *v/t muscles* flexionar

flex·i·bil·i·ty [fleksə'bɪlətɪ] flexibilidad *f*

flex·i·ble ['fleksəbl] *adj* flexible; *I'm quite flexible about arrangements, timing* soy bastante flexible

'flex·time ['flekstaɪm] horario *m* flexible

flew [fluː] *pret → fly³*

flick [flɪk] *v/t tail* sacudir; *he flicked a fly off his hand* espantó una mosca que tenía en la mano; *she flicked her hair out of her eyes* se apartó el pelo de los ojos

◆ flick through *v/t book, magazine* hojear

flick·er ['flɪkər] *v/i of light, screen* parpadear

fli·er [flaɪr] *(circular)* folleto *m*

flies [flaɪz] *npl Br on pants* bragueta *f*

flight [flaɪt] *n in airplane* vuelo *m*; *(fleeing)* huida *f*; *not capable of flight* incapaz de volar; *flight (of stairs)* tramo *m* (de escaleras)

'flight at·tend·ant auxiliar *m/f* de vuelo

'flight crew tripulación *f*

'flight deck AVIA cabina *f* del piloto

'flight num·ber número *m* de vuelo

'flight path ruta *f* de vuelo

'flight re·cord·er caja *f* negra

'flight time *departure* hora *f* del vuelo; *duration* duración *f* del vuelo

flight·y ['flaɪtɪ] *adj* inconstante

flim·sy ['flɪmzɪ] *adj structure, furniture* endeble; *dress, material* débil; *excuse* pobre

flinch [flɪntʃ] *v/i* encogerse

fling [flɪŋ] 1 *v/t (pret & pp* flung*)* arrojar, lanzar; *fling o.s. into a chair* dejarse caer en una silla 2 *n* F *(affair)* aventura *f*

◆ flip over [flɪp] *v/i* volcar

◆ flip through *v/t (pret & pp* flipped*)* *magazine* hojear

flip·per ['flɪpər] *for swimming* aleta *f*

flirt [flɜːrt] **1** *v/i* flirtear, coquetear **2** *n* ligón (-ona) *m(f)*

flir·ta·tious [flɜːr'teɪʃəs] *adj* coqueto

float [floʊt] **1** *v/i* flirtear, coquetear

float·ing vot·er ['floʊtɪŋ] votante *m/f* indeciso(-a)

flock [flɑːk] **1** *n of sheep* rebaño *m* **2** *v/i* acudir en masa

flog [flɑːg] *v/t (pret & pp* **flogged**) *(whip)* azotar

flood [flʌd] **1** *n* inundación *f* **2** *v/t of river* inundar

♦ **flood in** *v/i* llegar en grandes cantidades

flood·ing ['flʌdɪŋ] inundaciones *fpl*

'**flood·light** *n* foco *m*

flood·lit ['flʌdlɪt] *adj match* con luz artificial

'**flood wa·ters** *npl* crecida *f*

floor [flɔːr] *n* suelo *m*; *(story)* piso *m*

'**floor·board** *n* tabla *f* del suelo

'**floor cloth** trapo *m* del suelo

'**floor lamp** lámpara *f* de pie

flop [flɑːp] **1** *v/i (pret & pp* **flopped**) dejarse caer; F *(fail)* pinchar F **2** *n* F *(failure)* pinchazo *m* F

flop·py ['flɑːpɪ] *adj ears* caído; *hat* blando; *(weak)* flojo

flop·py ('**disk**) disquete *m*

flor·ist ['flɔːrɪst] florista *m/f*

floss [flɑːs] **1** *n for teeth* hilo *m* dental **2** *v/t*: **floss one's teeth** limpiarse los dientes con hilo dental

flour [flaʊr] harina *f*

flour·ish ['flʌrɪʃ] *v/i of plant* crecer rápidamente; *of business, civilization* florecer, prosperar

flour·ish·ing ['flʌrɪʃɪŋ] *adj business, trade* floreciente, próspero

flow [floʊ] *v/i of liquid* fluir **2** *n* flujo *m*

'**flow·chart** *n* diagrama *m* de flujo

flow·er [flaʊr] **1** *n* flor *f* **2** *v/i* florecer

'**flow·er·bed** parterre *m*

'**flow·er·pot** tiesto *m*, maceta *f*

'**flow·er show** exposición *f* floral

flow·er·y ['flaʊrɪ] *adj pattern* floreado; *style of writing* florido

flown [floʊn] *pp* → **fly³**

flu [fluː] gripe *f*

fluc·tu·ate ['flʌktjʊeɪt] *v/i* fluctuar

fluc·tu·a·tion [flʌktjʊ'eɪʃn] fluctuación *f*

flu·en·cy ['fluːənsɪ] *in a language* fluidez *f*

flu·ent ['fluːənt] *adj*: **he speaks fluent Spanish** habla español con soltura

flu·ent·ly ['fluːəntlɪ] *adv speak, write* con soltura

fluff [flʌf] *material* pelusa *f*

fluff·y ['flʌfɪ] *adj* esponjoso; **fluffy toy** juguete *m* de peluche

fluid ['fluːɪd] *n* fluido *m*

flung [flʌŋ] *pret & pp* → **fling**

flunk [flʌŋk] *v/t* F *subject* suspender, *Span* catear F

flu·o·res·cent [fluˈresnt] *adj light* fluorescente

flur·ry ['flʌrɪ] *of snow* torbellino *m*

flush [flʌʃ] **1** *v/t*: **flush the toilet** tirar de la cadena; **flush sth down the toilet** tirar algo por el retrete **2** *v/i (go red in the face)* ruborizarse; **the toilet won't flush** la cisterna no funciona **3** *adj (level)*: **be flush with ...** estar a la misma altura que ...

♦ **flush away** *v/t*: **flush sth away** *down toilet* tirar algo por el retrete

♦ **flush out** *v/t rebels etc* hacer salir

flus·ter ['flʌstər] *v/t*: **get flustered** ponerse nervioso

flute [fluːt] MUS flauta *f*; *glass* copa *f* de champán

flut·ist ['fluːtɪst] flautista *m/f*

flut·ter ['flʌtər] *v/i of bird, wings* aletear; *of flag* ondear; *of heart* latir con fuerza

fly¹ [flaɪ] *n insect* mosca *f*

fly² [flaɪ] *n on pants* bragueta *f*

fly³ [flaɪ] **1** *v/i (pret* **flew**, *pp* **flown**) *of bird, airplane* volar; *in airplane* volar, ir en avión; *of flag* ondear; **fly into a rage** enfurecerse; **she flew out of the room** salió a toda prisa de la habitación **2** *v/t (pret* **flew**, *pp* **flown**) *airplane* pilotar; *airline* volar con; *(transport by air)* enviar por avión

♦ **fly away** *v/i of bird* salir volando; *of airplane* alejarse

♦ **fly back** *v/i (travel back)* volver en avión

♦ **fly in 1** *v/i of airplane, passengers* llegar

en avión **2** *v/t supplies etc* transportar en avión

◆ **fly off** *v/i of hat etc* salir volando

◆ **fly out** *v/i in* (*en avión*); **when do you fly out?** ¿cuándo os vais?

fly-ing ['flaɪɪŋ] *n* volar *m*

fly-ing 'sau-cer platillo *m* volante

foam [foum] *n on liquid* espuma *f*

foam 'rub-ber gomaespuma *f*

FOB [efou'biː] *abbr* (= *free on board*) franco a bordo

fo-cus ['foukəs] **1** *n of attention*, PHOT foco *m*; **be in focus / out of focus** PHOT estar enfocado / desenfocado **2** *v/t*: *focus one's attention on* concentrar la atención en **3** *v/i* enfocar

◆ **focus on** *v/t problem, issue* concentrarse en; PHOT enfocar

fod-der ['fɑːdər] *n* forraje *m*

fog [fɑːg] *n* niebla *f*

◆ **fog up** *v/i* (*pret & pp fogged*) empañarse

'fog-bound *adj* paralizado por la niebla

fog-gy ['fɑːgɪ] *adj* neblinoso, con niebla; *it's foggy* hay niebla; *I haven't the foggiest idea* no tengo la más remota idea

foi-ble ['fɔɪbl] *n* manía *f*

foil¹ [fɔɪl] *n* papel *m* de aluminio

foil² [fɔɪl] *v/t* (*thwart*) frustrar

fold¹ [fould] **1** *v/t paper etc* doblar; *fold one's arms* cruzarse de brazos **2** *v/i of business* quebrar **3** *n in cloth etc* pliegue *m*

◆ **fold up 1** *v/t* plegar **2** *v/i of chair, table* plegarse

fold² [fould] *n for sheep etc* redil *m*

fold-er ['fouldər] *for documents*, COMPUT carpeta *f*

fold-ing ['fouldɪŋ] *adj* plegable; *folding chair* silla *f* plegable

fo-li-age ['fouliɪdʒ] follaje *m*

folk [fouk] (*people*) gente *f*; *my folks* (*family*) mi familia; *evening folks* F buenas noches, gente F

'folk dance baile *m* popular

'folk mu-sic música *f* folk *or* popular

'folk sing-er cantante *m/f* de folk

'folk song canción *m/f* folk *or* popular

fol-low ['fɑːlou] **1** *v/t* seguir; (*understand*) entender; *follow me* sígueme **2** *v/i logically* deducirse; *it follows from this that ...* de esto se deduce que ...; *you go first and I'll follow* tú ve primero que yo te sigo; *the requirements are as follows* los requisitos son los siguientes

◆ **follow up** *v/t letter, inquiry* hacer el seguimiento de

fol-low-er ['fɑːlouər] seguidor(a) *m(f)*

fol-low-ing ['fɑːlouɪŋ] **1** *adj* siguiente **2** *n people* seguidores(-as) *mpl* (*fpl*); *the following* lo siguiente

'fol-low-up meet-ing reunión *m* de seguimiento

'fol-low-up vis-it *to doctor etc* visita *f* de seguimiento

fol-ly ['fɑːlɪ] (*madness*) locura *f*

fond [fɑːnd] *adj* (*loving*) cariñoso; *memory* entrañable; *he's fond of travel / music* le gusta viajar / la música; *I'm very fond of him* le tengo mucho cariño

fon-dle ['fɑːndl] *v/t* acariciar

fond-ness ['fɑːndnɪs] *for s.o.* cariño *m* (*for* por); *for wine, food* afición *f* (*for* por)

font [fɑːnt] *for printing* tipo *m*; *in church* pila *f* bautismal

food [fuːd] comida *f*

'food chain cadena *f* alimentaria

food-ie ['fuːdɪ] F gourmet *m/f*

'food mix-er robot *m* de cocina

food poi-son-ing ['fuːdpɔɪznɪŋ] intoxicación *f* alimentaria

fool [fuːl] **1** *n* tonto(-a) *m(f)*, idiota *m/f*; *you stupid fool!* ¡estúpido!; *make a fool of o.s.* ponerse en ridículo **2** *v/t* engañar

◆ **fool about, fool around** *v/i* hacer el tonto; *sexually* tener un lío

◆ **fool around with** *v/t knife, drill etc* enredar con algo; *sexually* tener un lío con

'fool-har-dy *adj* temerario

fool-ish ['fuːlɪʃ] *adj* tonto

fool-ish-ly ['fuːlɪʃlɪ] *adv*: *I foolishly ...* cometí la tontería de ...

'fool-proof *adj* infalible

foot [fut] (*pl feet* [fiːt]) *also measurement* pie *m*; *of animal* pata *f*; *on foot* a pie, ca-

F

minando, andando; *I've been on my feet all day* llevo todo el día de pie; *be back on one's feet* estar recuperado; *at the foot of the page / hill* al pie de la página / de la colina; *put one's foot in it* F meter la pata F

foot·age ['fʊtɪdʒ] secuencias *fpl*, imágenes *fpl*

'**foot·ball** *Br* (*soccer*) fútbol *m*; *American style* fútbol *m* americano; *ball* balón *m* or pelota *f* (de fútbol)

'**foot·ball play·er** *American style* jugador(a) *m(f)* de fútbol americano; *Br in soccer* jugador(a) *m(f)* de fútbol, futbolista *m/f*

'**foot·bridge** puente *m* peatonal

foot·er ['fʊtər] *in document* pie *m* de página

foot·hills ['fʊthɪlz] *npl* estribaciones *fpl*

'**foot·hold** *n in climbing* punto *m* de apoyo; *gain a foothold fig* introducirse

foot·ing ['fʊtɪŋ] (*basis*): *put the business back on a secure footing* volver a afianzar la empresa; *lose one's footing* perder el equilibrio; *be on the same/a different footing* estar en igualdad de condiciones; *be on a friendly footing with ...* tener relaciones de amistad con ...

foot·lights ['fʊtlaɪts] *npl* candilejas *fpl*

'**foot·mark** pisada *f*

'**foot·note** nota *f* a pie de página

'**foot·path** sendero *m*

'**foot·print** pisada *f*

'**foot·step** paso *m*; *follow in s.o.'s footsteps* seguir los pasos de alguien

'**foot·stool** escabel *m*

'**foot·wear** calzado *m*

for [fər, fɔːr] *prep* ◇ *purpose, destination etc* para; *a train for ...* un tren para or hacia ...; *clothes for children* ropa para niños; *it's too big / small for you* te queda demasiado grande / pequeño; *here's a letter for you* hay una carta para ti; *this is for you* esto es para ti; *what's for lunch?* ¿qué hay para comer?; *the steak is for me* el filete es para mí; *what is this for?* ¿para qué sirve esto?; *what for?* ¿para qué?

◇ *time* durante; *for three days / two hours* durante tres días / dos horas; *it lasts for two hours* dura dos horas; *please get it done for Monday* por favor tenlo listo (para) el lunes

◇ *distance*: *I walked for a mile* caminé una milla; *it stretches for 100 miles* se extiende 100 millas

◇ (*in favor of*): *I am for the idea* estoy a favor de la idea

◇ (*instead of, in behalf of*): *let me do that for you* déjame que te lo haga; *we are agents for ...* somos representantes de ...

◇ (*in exchange for*) por; *I bought it for $25* lo compré por 25 dólares: *how much did you sell it for?* ¿por cuánto lo vendiste?

for·bade [fər'bæd] *pret* → **forbid**

for·bid [fər'bɪd] *v/t* (*pret* **forbade**, *pp* **forbidden**) prohibir; *forbid s.o. to do sth* prohibir a alguien hacer algo

for·bid·den [fər'bɪdn] **1** *adj* prohibido; *smoking / parking forbidden* prohibido fumar / aparcar **2** *pp* → **forbid**

for·bid·ding [fər'bɪdɪŋ] *adj person, tone, look* amenazador; *rockface* imponente; *prospect* intimidador

force [fɔːrs] **1** *n* fuerza *f*; *come into force of law etc* entrar en vigor; *the forces* MIL las fuerzas **2** *v/t door, lock* forzar; *force s.o. to do sth* forzar a alguien a hacer algo; *force sth open* forzar algo

◆ **force back** *v/t tears* contener

forced [fɔːrst] *adj* forzado

forced 'land·ing aterrizaje *m* forzoso

force·ful ['fɔːrsfəl] *adj argument* poderoso; *speaker* vigoroso; *character* enérgico

force·ful·ly ['fɔːrsfəlɪ] *adv* de manera convincente

for·ceps ['fɔːrseps] *npl* MED fórceps *m inv*

for·ci·ble ['fɔːrsəbl] *adj entry* por la fuerza

for·ci·bly ['fɔːrsəblɪ] *adv* por la fuerza

ford [fɔːrd] *n* vado *m*

fore [fɔːr] *n*: *come to the fore* salir a la palestra

'**fore·arm** antebrazo *m*

fore·bears ['fɔːrberz] *npl* antepasados

mpl

fore·bod·ing [fər'boʊdɪŋ] premonición *f*

'**fore·cast 1** *n* pronóstico *m*; *of weather* pronóstico *m* (del tiempo) **2** *v/t* (*pret & pp* **forecast**) pronosticar

'**fore·court** (*of garage*) explanada *en la parte de delante*

fore·fa·thers ['fɔːrfɑːðərz] *npl* ancestros *mpl*

'**fore·fin·ger** (dedo *m*) índice *m*

'**fore·front**: *be in the forefront of* estar a la vanguardia de

'**fore·gone** *adj*: *that's a foregone conclusion* eso ya se sabe de antemano

'**fore·ground** primer plano *m*

'**fore·hand** *in tennis* derecha *f*

'**fore·head** frente *f*

for·eign ['fɑːrən] *adj* extranjero; *a foreign holiday* unas vacaciones en el extranjero

for·eign af'fairs *npl* asuntos *mpl* exteriores

for·eign 'aid ayuda *f* al exterior

for·eign 'bod·y cuerpo *m* extraño

for·eign 'cur·ren·cy divisa *f* extranjera

for·eign·er ['fɑːrənər] extranjero(-a) *m(f)*

for·eign ex'change divisas *fpl*

for·eign 'lan·guage idioma *m* extranjero

'**For·eign Of·fice** *in UK* Ministerio *m* de Asuntos Exteriores

for·eign 'pol·i·cy política *f* exterior

For·eign 'Sec·re·ta·ry *in UK* Ministro(-a) *m(f)* de Asuntos Exteriores

'**fore·man** capataz *m*

'**fore·most** *adv* principal; *what was foremost in my mind was the worry that …* mi principal preocupación era que …

fo·ren·sic 'medi·cine [fə'rensɪk] medicina *f* forense

fo·ren·sic 'scien·tist forense *m/f*

'**fore·run·ner** predecesor(a) *m(f)*

fore·see *v/t* (*pret* **foresaw**, *pp* **foreseen**) prever

fore·see·a·ble [fər'siːəbl] *adj* previsible; *in the foreseeable future* en un futuro próximo

fore'seen *pp* → **foresee**

'**fore·sight** previsión *f*

for·est ['fɑːrɪst] bosque *m*

for·est·ry ['fɑːrɪstrɪ] silvicultura

'**fore·taste** anticipo *m*

fore'tell *v/t* (*pret & pp* **foretold**) predecir

for·ev·er [fə'revər] *adv* siempre; *it is forever raining here* aquí llueve constantemente; *I will remember this day forever* no me olvidaré nunca de ese día

fore·word ['fɔːrwɜːrd] prólogo *m*

for·feit ['fɔːrfɪt] *v/t* (*lose*) perder; (*give up*) renunciar a

for·gave [fər'geɪv] *pret* → **forgive**

forge [fɔːrdʒ] *v/t* falsificar

♦ **forge ahead** *v/i* progresar rápidamente

forg·er ['fɔːrdʒər] falsificador(a) *m(f)*

forg·er·y ['fɔːrdʒərɪ] falsificación *f*

for·get [fər'get] *v/t* (*pret* **forgot**, *pp* **forgotten**) olvidar; *I forgot his name* se me olvidó su nombre; *forget to do sth* olvidarse de hacer algo

for·get·ful [fər'getfəl] *adj* olvidadizo

for'get-me-not *flower* nomeolvides *m inv*

for·give [fər'gɪv] *v/t & v/i* (*pret* **forgave**, *pp* **forgiven**) perdonar

for·give·ness [fər'gɪvnəs] perdón *m*

for·gi·ven [fər'gɪvn] *pp* → **forgive**

for·got [fər'gɑːt] *pret* → **forget**

for·got·ten [fər'gɑːtn] *pp* → **forget**

fork [fɔːrk] *n for eating* tenedor *m*; *for garden* horca *f*; *in road* bifurcación *f*

♦ **fork out** *v/t & v/i* F (*pay*) apoquinar F

forked *adj tongue* bífido; *stick* bifurcado

fork·lift 'truck carretilla *f* elevadora

form [fɔːrm] **1** *n shape* forma *f*; (*document*) formulario *m*, impreso *m*; *be on / off form* estar / no estar en forma **2** *v/t in clay etc* moldear; *friendship* establecer; *opinion* formarse; *past tense etc* formar; (*constitute*) formar, constituir **3** *v/i* (*take shape, develop*) formarse

form·al ['fɔːrml] *adj* formal; *recognition etc* oficial; *dress* de etiqueta

for·mal·i·ty [fər'mælətɪ] formalidad *f*; *it's just a formality* sólo es una formalidad; *the formalities* las formalidades

for·mal·ly ['fɔːrməlɪ] *adv speak, behave* formalmente; *accepted, recognized* oficialmente

for·mat ['fɔːrmæt] **1** *v/t* (*pret & pp* **for-**

matted) diskette, *document* formatear **2** *n of paper, program etc* formato *m*

for·ma·tion [fɔːrˈmeɪʃn] formación *f*; **formation flying** vuelo *m* en formación

for·ma·tive [ˈfɔːrmətɪv] *adj* formativo; **in his formative years** en sus años de formación

for·mer [ˈfɔːrmər] *adj* antiguo; **the former** el primero; **the former arrangement** la situación de antes

for·mer·ly [ˈfɔːrmərlɪ] *adv* antiguamente

for·mi·da·ble [ˈfɔːrmɪdəbl] *adj personality* formidable; *opponent, task* terrible

for·mu·la [ˈfɔːrmjʊlə] MATH, CHEM, *fig* fórmula *f*

for·mu·late [ˈfɔːrmjʊleɪt] *v/t* (*express*) formular

for·ni·cate [ˈfɔːrnɪkeɪt] *v/i fml* fornicar

for·ni·ca·tion [fɔːrnɪˈkeɪʃn] *fml* fornicación *f*

fort [fɔːrt] MIL fuerte *m*

forth [fɔːrθ] *adv*: **back and forth** de un lado para otro; **and so forth** y así sucesivamente; **from that day forth** desde ese día en adelante

forth·com·ing [ˈfɔːrθkʌmɪŋ] *adj* (*future*) próximo; *personality* comunicativo

'forth·right *adj* directo

for·ti·eth [ˈfɔːrtɪɪθ] *n & adj* cuadragésimo

fort·night [ˈfɔːrtnaɪt] *Br* quincena *f*

for·tress [ˈfɔːrtrɪs] MIL fortaleza *f*

for·tu·nate [ˈfɔːrtʃnət] *adj* afortunado

for·tu·nate·ly [ˈfɔːrtʃnətlɪ] *adv* afortunadamente

for·tune [ˈfɔːrtʃən] (*fate, money*) fortuna *f*; (*luck*) fortuna *f*, suerte *f*; **tell s.o.'s fortune** decir a alguien la buenaventura

'for·tune-tell·er adivino(-a) *m(f)*

for·ty [ˈfɔːrtɪ] cuarenta; **have forty winks** F echarse una siestecilla F

fo·rum [ˈfɔːrəm] *fig* foro *m*

for·ward [ˈfɔːrwərd] **1** *adv* hacia delante **2** *adj pej: person* atrevido **3** *n* SP delantero(-a) *m(f)* **4** *v/t letter* reexpedir

'for·ward·ing ad·dress [ˈfɔːrwərdɪŋ] dirección *f* a la que reexpedir correspondencia

'for·ward·ing a·gent COM transitario(-a) *m(f)*

'for·ward-look·ing *adj* con visión de futuro, moderno

fos·sil [ˈfɑːsəl] fósil *m*

fos·sil·ized [ˈfɑːsəlaɪzd] *adj* fosilizado

fos·ter [ˈfɑːstər] *v/t child* acoger, adoptar (temporalmente); *attitude, belief* fomentar

'fos·ter child niño(-a) *m(f)* en régimen de acogida

'fos·ter home hogar *m* de acogida

'fos·ter par·ents *npl* familia *f* de acogida

fought [fɔːt] *pret & pp →* **fight**

foul [faʊl] **1** *n* SP falta *f* **2** *adj smell, taste* asqueroso; *weather* terrible **3** *v/t* SP hacer (una) falta a

found¹ [faʊnd] *v/t school etc* fundar

found² [faʊnd] *pret & pp →* **find**

foun·da·tion [faʊnˈdeɪʃn] *of theory etc* fundamento *m*; (*organization*) fundación *f*

foun·da·tions [faʊnˈdeɪʃnz] *npl of building* cimientos *mpl*

found·er [ˈfaʊndər] *n* fundador(a) *m(f)*

found·ing [ˈfaʊndɪŋ] *n* fundación *f*

foun·dry [ˈfaʊndrɪ] fundición *f*

foun·tain [ˈfaʊntɪn] fuente *f*

'foun·tain pen pluma *f* (estilográfica)

four [fɔːr] cuatro; **on all fours** a gatas, a cuatro patas

four-let·ter 'word palabrota *f*

four-post·er ('bed) cama *f* de dosel

'four-star *star hotel etc* de cuatro estrellas

four·teen [fɔːrˈtiːn] catorce

four·teenth [fɔːrˈtiːnθ] *n & adj* decimocuarto

fourth [fɔːrθ] *n & adj* cuarto

four-wheel 'drive MOT vehículo *m* con tracción a las cuatro ruedas; *type of drive* tracción *f* a las cuatro ruedas

fowl [faʊl] ave *f* de corral

fox [fɑːks] **1** *n* zorro *m* **2** *v/t* (*puzzle*) dejar perplejo

foy·er [ˈfɔɪər] vestíbulo *m*

frac·tion [ˈfrækʃn] fracción *f*; MATH fracción *f*, quebrado *m*

frac·tion·al·ly [ˈfrækʃnəlɪ] *adv* ligeramente

frac·ture [ˈfræktʃər] **1** *n* fractura *f* **2** *v/t* fracturar; **he fractured his arm** se fracturó el brazo

fra·gile ['frædʒəl] *adj* frágil

frag·ment ['frægmənt] *n* fragmento *m*

frag·men·tar·y ['frægˈməntərɪ] *adj* fragmentario

fra·grance ['freɪgrəns] fragancia *f*

fra·grant ['freɪgrənt] *adj* fragante

frail [freɪl] *adj* frágil, delicado

frame [freɪm] **1** *n of picture, window* marco *m*; *of eyeglasses* montura *f*; *of bicycle* cuadro *m*; **frame of mind** estado *m* de ánimo **2** *v/t picture* enmarcar; **F** *person* tender una trampa a

'frame-up F franquicia *f*

'frame·work estructura *f*; *for agreement* marco *m*

France [fræns] Francia

fran·chise ['fræntʃaɪz] *n for business* franquicia *f*

frank [fræŋk] *adj* franco

frank·furt·er ['fræŋkfɜːrtər] salchicha *f* de Fráncfort

frank·ly ['fræŋklɪ] *adv* francamente; **frankly, it's not worth it** francamente *or* la verdad, no vale la pena

frank·ness ['fræŋknɪs] franqueza *f*

fran·tic ['fræntɪk] *adj* frenético

fran·ti·cal·ly ['fræntɪklɪ] *adv* frenéticamente

fra·ter·nal [frəˈtɜːrnl] *adj* fraternal

fraud [frɔːd] fraude *m*; *person* impostor(a) *m(f)*

fraud·u·lent ['frɔːdjʊlənt] *adj* fraudulento

fraud·u·lent·ly ['frɔːdjʊləntlɪ] *adv* fraudulentamente

frayed [freɪd] *adj cuffs* deshilachado

freak [friːk] **1** *n unusual event* fenómeno *m* anormal; *two-headed person, animal etc* monstruo *m*, monstruosidad *f*; **F** *strange person* bicho *m* raro F; **movie / jazz freak** F un fanático del cine / jazz F **2** *adj wind, storm etc* anormal

freck·le ['frekl] peca *f*

free [friː] **1** *adj i.e. no cost* gratis, gratuito; **are you free this afternoon?** ¿estás libre esta tarde?; **free and easy** relajado; **for free** *travel, get sth* gratis **2** *v/t prisoners* liberar

free·bie ['friːbɪ] F regalo *m*; **as a freebie** de regalo

free·dom ['friːdəm] libertad *f*

free·dom of 'speech libertad *f* de expresión

free·dom of the 'press libertad *f* de prensa

free 'en·ter·prise empresa *f* libre

free 'kick *in soccer* falta *f*, golpe *m* franco

free·lance ['friːlæns] **1** *adj* autónomo, free-lance **2** *adv*: **work freelance** trabajar como autónomo *or* free-lance

free·lanc·er ['friːlænsər] autónomo(-a) *m(f)*, free-lance *m/f*

free·load·er ['friːloʊdər] F gorrón (-ona) *m(f)*

free·ly ['friːlɪ] *adv admit* libremente

free mar·ket e'con·o·my economía *f* de libre mercado

free-range 'chick·en pollo *m* de corral

free-range 'eggs *npl* huevos *mpl* de corral

free 'sam·ple muestra *f* gratuita

free 'speech libertad *f* de expresión

'free·way autopista *f*

free'wheel *v/i on bicycle* ir sin pedalear

free 'will libre albedrío *m*; **he did it of his own free will** lo hizo por propia iniciativa

freeze [friːz] **1** *v/t (pret froze, pp frozen) food, wages, video* congelar; *river* congelar, helar *v/i (pret froze, pp frozen) of water* congelarse, helarse

♦ **freeze over** *v/i of river* helarse

'freeze-dried *adj* liofilizado

freez·er ['friːzər] congelador *m*

freez·ing ['friːzɪŋ] **1** *adj* muy frío; **it's freezing (cold)** *of weather* hace mucho frío; *of water* está muy frío; **I'm freezing (cold)** tengo mucho frío **2** *n*: **10 below freezing** diez grados bajo cero

'freez·ing com·part·ment congelador *m*

'freez·ing point punto *m* de congelación

freight [freɪt] *n* transporte *m*; *costs* flete *m*

'freight car *on train* vagón *m* de mercancías

freight·er ['freɪtər] *ship* carguero *m*; *airplane* avión *m* de carga

'freight train tren *m* de mercancías

French [frentʃ] **1** *adj* francés **2** *n language* francés *m*; **the French** los franceses

French 'bread pan *m* de barra

French 'doors *npl* puerta *f* cristalera

'French fries *npl Span* patatas *fpl or L.Am.* papas *fpl* fritas

'French·man francés *m*

'French·wom·an francesa *f*

fren·zied ['frenzɪd] *adj attack, activity* frenético; *mob* desenfrenado

fren·zy ['frenzɪ] frenesí *m*; **whip s.o. into a frenzy** poner a alguien frenético

fre·quen·cy ['fri:kwənsɪ] *also* RAD frecuencia *f*

fre·quent¹ ['fri:kwənt] *adj* frecuente; **how frequent are the trains?** ¿con qué frecuencia pasan trenes?

fre·quent² [frɪ'kwent] *v/t bar* frecuentar

fre·quent·ly ['fri:kwəntlɪ] *adv* con frecuencia

fres·co ['freskoʊ] fresco *m*

fresh [freʃ] *adj* fresco; *start* nuevo; **don't you get fresh with your mother!** ¡no seas descarado con tu madre!

fresh 'air aire *m* fresco

fresh·en ['freʃn] *v/i of wind* refrescar

◆ freshen up **1** *v/i* refrescarse **2** *v/t room, paintwork* renovar, revivir

fresh·ly ['freʃlɪ] *adv* recién

'fresh·man estudiante *m/f* de primer año

fresh·ness ['freʃnɪs] frescura *f*

'fresh·wa·ter *adj* de agua dulce

fret [fret] *v/i* (*pret & pp* **fretted**) ponerse nervioso, inquietarse

Freud·i·an ['frɔɪdɪən] *adj* freudiano

fric·tion ['frɪkʃn] PHYS rozamiento *m*; *between people* fricción *f*

'fric·tion tape cinta *f* aislante

Fri·day ['fraɪdeɪ] viernes *m inv*

fridge [frɪdʒ] nevera *f*, frigorífico *m*

fried 'egg [fraɪd] huevo *m* frito

fried po'ta·toes *npl Span* patatas *fpl or L.Am.* papas *fpl* fritas

friend [frend] amigo(-a) *m(f)*; **make friends** *of one person* hacer amigos; *of two people* hacerse amigos; **make friends with s.o.** hacerse amigo de alguien

friend·li·ness ['frendlɪnɪs] simpatía *f*

friend·ly ['frendlɪ] *adj atmosphere* agrad-

able; *person* agradable, simpático; (*easy to use*) fácil de usar; *argument, match, relations* amistoso; **be friendly with s.o.** (*be friends*) ser amigo de alguien

'friend·ship ['frendʃɪp] amistad *f*

fries [fraɪz] *npl Span* patatas *fpl or L.Am.* papas *fpl* fritas

fright [fraɪt] susto *m*; **give s.o. a fright** dar un susto a alguien, asustar a alguien; **scream with fright** gritar asustado

fright·en ['fraɪtn] *v/t* asustar; **be frightened** estar asustado, tener miedo; **don't be frightened** no te asustes, no tengas miedo; **be frightened of** tener miedo de

◆ frighten away *v/t* ahuyentar, espantar

fright·en·ing ['fraɪtnɪŋ] *adj noise, person, prospect* aterrador, espantoso

frig·id ['frɪdʒɪd] *adj sexually* frígido

frill [frɪl] *on dress etc* volante *m*; (*fancy extra*) extra *m*

frill·y ['frɪlɪ] *adj* de volantes

fringe [frɪndʒ] *on dress, curtains etc* flecos *mpl*; *Br in hair* flequillo *m*; (*edge*) margen *m*

'fringe ben·e·fits *npl* ventajas *fpl* adicionales

frisk [frɪsk] *v/t* cachear

frisk·y ['frɪskɪ] *adj puppy etc* juguetón

◆ frit·ter away ['frɪtər] *v/t time* desperdiciar; *fortune* despilfarrar

fri·vol·i·ty [frɪ'vɑ:lətɪ] frivolidad *f*

friv·o·lous ['frɪvələs] *adj* frívolo

frizz·y ['frɪzɪ] *adj* hair crespo

frog [frɑːg] rana *f*

'frog·man hombre *m* rana

from [frɑːm] *prep* ◇ *in time* desde; **from 9 to 5 (o'clock)** de 9 a 5; **from the 18th century** desde el siglo XVIII; **from to·day** on a partir de hoy; **from next Tues·day** a partir del próximo martes

◇ *in space* de, desde; **from here to there** de or desde aquí hasta allí; **we drove here from Paris** vinimos en coche desde París

◇ *origin* de; **a letter from Jo** una carta de Jo; **a gift from the management** un regalo de la dirección; **it doesn't say who it's from** no dice de quién es; **I am from New Jersey** soy de Nueva Jer-

sey; *made from bananas* hecho con plátanos
◇ (*because of*): *tired from the journey* cansado del viaje; *it's from overeating* es por comer demasiado

front [frʌnt] 1 n *of building, book* portada f; (*cover organization*) tapadera f; MIL, *of weather* frente m; *in front* delante; *in a race* en cabeza; *the car in front* el coche de delante; *in front of* delante de; *at the front of* en la parte de delante de 2 *adj wheel, seat* delantero 3 *v/t* TV *program* presentar

front 'cov·er portada f
front 'door puerta f principal
front 'en·trance entrada f principal
fron·tier ['frʌntɪr] frontera f; *fig: of knowledge, science* límite m
front 'line MIL línea f del frente
front page *of newspaper* portada f, primera f plana
front page 'news nsg noticia f de portada *or* de primera plana
front 'row primera fila f
front seat 'pas·sen·ger *in car* pasajero(-a) m(f) de delante
front-wheel 'drive tracción f delantera
frost [frɒst] n escarcha f; *there was a frost last night* anoche cayó una helada
'frost·bite congelación f
'frost·bit·ten adj congelado
frost·ed glass ['frɒstɪd] vidrio m esmerilado
frost·ing ['frɒstɪŋ] *on cake* glaseado m
frost·y ['frɒstɪ] adj *weather* gélido; *fig: welcome* glacial
froth [frɒθ] n espuma f
froth·y ['frɒθɪ] adj *cream etc* espumoso
frown [fraʊn] 1 n: *what's that frown for?* ¿por qué frunces el ceño? 2 *v/i* fruncir el ceño
froze [froʊz] pret → *freeze*
fro·zen ['froʊzn] 1 adj *ground, food* congelado; *wastes* helado; *I'm frozen* F estoy helado *or* congelado F 2 pp → *freeze*
fro·zen 'food comida f congelada
fruit [fruːt] fruta f
'fruit cake bizcocho m de frutas
fruit·y ['fruːtfəl] adj *discussions etc* fruc-

tífero
'fruit juice *Span* zumo m *or L.Am.* jugo m de fruta
fruit 'sal·ad macedonia f
frus·trate [frʌ'streɪt] v/t *person, plans* frustrar
frus·trat·ed [frʌ'streɪtɪd] adj frustrado
frus·trat·ing [frʌ'streɪtɪŋ] adj frustrante
frus·tra·tion [frʌ'streɪʃn] frustración f; *sexual frustration* frustración f sexual; *the frustrations of modern life* las frustraciones de la vida moderna
fry [fraɪ] v/t (*pret & pp fried*) freír
'fry·pan sartén f
fuck [fʌk] v/t V *Span* follar con V, *L.Am.* coger V; *fuck!* ¡joder! V; *fuck him!* ¡que se joda! V
♦ fuck off v/i V: *fuck off!* ¡vete a la mierda! V
fuck·ing ['fʌkɪŋ] 1 adj V puto V 2 adv V: *it's fucking crazy* es un estupidez ¡coño!; *it was fucking brilliant!* ¡estuvo de puta madre! V
fu·el ['fjʊəl] 1 n combustible m 2 v/t fig avivar
fu·gi·tive ['fjuːdʒətɪv] n fugitivo(-a) m(f)
ful·fil Br, ful·fill [fʊl'fɪl] v/t *dream* cumplir, realizar; *task* realizar; *contract* cumplir; *feel fulfilled in job, life* sentirse realizado
ful·fill·ing [fʊl'fɪlɪŋ] adj: *I have a fulfilling job* mi trabajo me llena
ful·fil·ment Br, ful·fill·ment [fʊl'fɪlmənt] *of contract etc* cumplimiento m; *moral, spiritual* satisfacción f
full [fʊl] adj lleno; *account, schedule* completo; *life* pleno; *full of* water etc lleno de; *full up* hotel etc, *with food* lleno; *pay in full* pagar al contado
full 'board Br pensión f completa
'full-grown adj completamente desarrollado
'full-length adj *dress* de cuerpo entero; *full-length movie* largometraje m
full 'moon luna f llena
full 'stop Br punto m
full 'time 1 adj *worker, job* a tiempo completo 2 adv *work* a tiempo completo
ful·ly ['fʊlɪ] adv completamente; *describe*

en detalle

fum·ble ['fʌmbl] v/t ball dejar caer

◆ **fumble about** v/i rebuscar

fume [fju:m] v/i: **be fuming** F with anger echar humo F

fumes [fju:mz] npl humos mpl

fun [fʌn] diversión f; **it was great fun** fue muy divertido; **bye, have fun!** ¡adiós, que lo paséis bien!; **for fun** para divertirse; **make fun of** burlarse de

func·tion ['fʌŋkʃn] **1** n (purpose) función f; (reception etc) acto m **2** v/i funcionar; **function as** hacer de

func·tion·al ['fʌŋkʃnl] adj funcional

fund [fʌnd] **1** n fondo m **2** v/t project etc financiar

fun·da·men·tal [fʌndə'mentl] adj fundamental; (crucial) esencial

fun·da·men·tal·ist [fʌndə'mentlɪst] n fundamentalista m/f

fun·da·men·tal·ly [fʌndə'mentlɪ] adv fundamentalmente

fund·ing ['fʌndɪŋ] (money) fondos mpl, financiación f

fu·ne·ral ['fju:nərəl] funeral m

'fu·ne·ral di·rec·tor encargado(-a) m(f) de una funeraria

'fu·ne·ral home funeraria f

fun·gus ['fʌŋgəs] hongos mpl

fu·nic·u·lar ('rail·way) [fju:'nɪkjʊlər] funicular m

fun·nel ['fʌnl] n of ship chimenea f

fun·nies ['fʌnɪz] npl F sección de humor

fun·ni·ly ['fʌnɪlɪ] adv (oddly) de modo extraño; (comically) de forma divertida; **funnily enough** curiosamente

fun·ny ['fʌnɪ] adj (comical) divertido, gracioso; (odd) curioso, raro; **that's not funny** eso no tiene gracia

'fun·ny bone hueso m de la risa

fur [fɜːr] piel f

fu·ri·ous ['fjʊrɪəs] adj (angry) furioso; (intense) furioso, feroz; effort febril; **at a furious pace** a un ritmo vertiginoso

fur·nace ['fɜːrnɪs] horno m

fur·nish ['fɜːrnɪʃ] v/t room amueblar; (supply) suministrar

fur·ni·ture ['fɜːrnɪtʃər] mobiliario m, muebles mpl; **a piece of furniture** un mueble

fur·ry ['fɜːrɪ] adj animal peludo

fur·ther ['fɜːrðər] **1** adj (additional) adicional; (more distant) más lejano; **there's been a further development** ha pasado algo nuevo; **until further notice** hasta nuevo aviso; **have you anything further to say?** ¿tiene algo más que añadir? **2** adv walk, drive más lejos; **further, I want to say ...** además, quiero decir ...; **two miles further (on)** dos millas más adelante **3** v/t cause etc promover

fur·ther·more adv es más

fur·thest ['fɜːrðɪst] **1** adj: **the furthest point north** el punto más al norte; **the furthest stars** las estrellas más lejanas **2** adv más lejos; **this is the furthest north I've ever been** nunca había estado tan al norte

fur·tive ['fɜːrtɪv] adj glance furtivo

fur·tive·ly ['fɜːrtɪvlɪ] adv furtivamente

fu·ry ['fjʊrɪ] (anger) furia f, ira f

fuse [fju:z] **1** n ELEC fusible m **2** v/i ELEC fundirse; **the lights have fused** se han fundido los plomos **3** v/t ELEC fundir

'fuse·box caja f de fusibles

fu·se·lage ['fju:zəlɑːʒ] fuselaje m

'fuse wire fusible m (hilo)

fu·sion ['fju:ʒn] fusión f

fuss [fʌs] n escándalo m; **make a fuss** (complain) armar un escándalo; (behave in exaggerated way) armar un escándalo; **make a fuss of** (be very attentive to) deshacerse en atenciones con

fuss·y ['fʌsɪ] adj person quisquilloso; design etc recargado; **be a fussy eater** ser un quisquilloso a la hora de comer

fu·tile ['fju:tl] adj inútil, vano

fu·til·i·ty [fju:'tɪlətɪ] inutilidad f

fu·ture ['fju:tʃər] **1** n also GRAM futuro m; **in future** en el futuro **2** adj futuro

fu·tures ['fju:tʃərz] npl FIN futuros mpl

'fu·tures mar·ket FIN mercado m de futuros

fu·tur·is·tic [fju:tʃə'rɪstɪk] adj design futurista

fuze [fju:z] → **fuse**

fuzz·y ['fʌzɪ] adj hair crespo; (out of focus) borroso

G

gab [gæb] *n*: **have the gift of the gab** F tener labia F

gab·ble ['gæbl] *v/i* farfullar

◆ **gad about** [gæd] *v/i* (*pret & pp* **gad-ded**) pendonear

gad·get ['gædʒɪt] artilugio *m*, chisme *m*

gaffe [gæf] metedura *f* de pata

gag [gæg] **1** *n over mouth* mordaza *f*; (*joke*) chiste *m* **2** *v/t* (*pret & pp* **gagged**) *also fig* amordazar

gain [geɪn] *v/t* (*acquire*) ganar; *victory* obtener; **gain speed** cobrar velocidad; **gain 10 pounds** engordar 10 libras

ga·la ['gæələ] gala *f*

gal·ax·y ['gæləksɪ] AST galaxia *f*

gale [geɪl] vendaval *m*

gal·lant ['gælənt] *adj* galante

gall blad·der ['gɒːlblædər] vesícula *f* biliar

gal·le·ry ['gælərɪ] *for art* museo *m*; *in theater* galería *f*

gal·ley ['gælɪ] *on ship* cocina *f*

◆ **gal·li·vant around** ['gælɪvænt] *v/i* pendonear

gal·lon ['gælən] galón *m* (*en EE.UU. 3,785 litros, en GB 4,546*); **gallons of tea** F toneladas de té F

gal·lop ['gæləp] *v/i* galopar

gal·lows ['gælouz] *npl* horca *f*

gall·stone ['gɒːlstoun] cálculo *m* biliar

ga·lore [gə'lɔːr] *adj*: **apples / novels galore** manzanas / novelas a montones

gal·va·nize ['gælvənaɪz] *v/t* TECH galvanizar; **galvanize s.o. into activity** hacer que alguien se vuelva más activo

gam·ble ['gæmbl] *v/i* jugar

gam·bler ['gæmblər] jugador(a) *m(f)*

gam·bling ['gæmblɪŋ] *n* juego *m*

game [geɪm] *n* (*sport*) partido *m*; *children's* juego *m*; *in tennis* juego *m*

'game re·serve coto *m* de caza

gang [gæŋ] *of friends* cuadrilla *f*, pandilla *f*; *of criminals* banda *f*

◆ **gang up on** *v/t* compincharse contra

'gang rape **1** *n* violación *f* colectiva **2** *v/t* violar colectivamente

gan·grene ['gæŋgriːn] MED gangrena *f*

gang·ster ['gæŋstər] gángster *m*

'gang war·fare lucha *f* entre bandas

'gang·way pasarela *f*

gaol [dʒeɪl] → **jail**

gap [gæp] *in wall* hueco *m*; *for parking, in figures* espacio *m*; *in time* intervalo *m*; *in conversation* interrupción *f*; *between two people's characters* diferencia *f*

gape [geɪp] *v/i of person* mirar boquiabierto

◆ **gape at** *v/t* mirar boquiabierto a

gap·ing ['geɪpɪŋ] *adj hole* enorme

gar·age [gə'rɑːʒ] *n for parking* garaje *m*; *for gas* gasolinera *f*; *for repairs* taller *m*

gar·bage ['gɑːrbɪdʒ] basura *f*; (*fig: nonsense*) tonterías *fpl*

'gar·bage bag bolsa *f* de la basura

'gar·bage can cubo *m* de la basura

'gar·bage truck camión *m* de la basura

gar·bled ['gɑːrbld] *adj message* confuso

gar·den ['gɑːrdn] jardín *m*

'gar·den cen·ter, *Br* 'gar·den cen·tre vivero *m*, centro *m* de jardinería

gar·den·er ['gɑːrdnər] aficionado(-a) *m(f)* a la jardinería; *professional* jardinero(-a) *m(f)*

gar·den·ing ['gɑːrdnɪŋ] jardinería *f*

gar·gle ['gɑːrgl] *v/i* hacer gárgaras

gar·goyle ['gɑːrgɔɪl] ARCHI gárgola *f*

gar·ish ['gerɪʃ] *adj color* chillón; *design* estridente

gar·land ['gɑːrlənd] *n* guirnalda *f*

gar·lic ['gɑːrlɪk] ajo *m*

gar·lic 'bread pan *m* con ajo

gar·ment ['gɑːrmənt] prenda *f* (de vestir)

gar·nish ['gɑːrnɪʃ] *v/t* guarnecer (**with** con)

gar·ret ['gærɪt] buhardilla *f*

gar·ri·son ['gærɪsn] *n place* plaza *f*; *troops* guarnición *f*

gar·ter ['gɑːrtər] liga *f*

gas [gæs] n gas m; (gasoline) gasolina f, Rpl nafta f

gash [gæʃ] n corte m profundo

gas-ket ['gæskɪt] junta f

gas·o·line ['gæsəliːn] gasolina f, Rpl nafta f

gasp [gæsp] 1 n grito m apagado 2 v/i lanzar un grito apagado; **gasp for breath** luchar por respirar

'gas ped·al acelerador m

'gas pipe·line gasoducto m

'gas pump surtidor m (de gasolina)

'gas stove cocina f de gas 'gas sta·tion gasolinera f, S. Am. bomba f

gas·tric ['gæstrɪk] adj MED gástrico

gas·tric 'flu MED gripe f gastrointestinal

gas·tric 'juices npl jugos mpl gástricos

gas·tric 'ul·cer MED úlcera f gástrica

gate [geɪt] of house, at airport puerta f; made of iron verja f

'gate·crash v/t: **gatecrash a party** colarse en una fiesta

'gate·way also fig entrada f

gath·er ['gæðər] 1 v/t facts, information reunir; **am I to gather that …?** ¿debo entender que …?; **gather speed** ganar velocidad 2 v/i of crowd reunirse

♦ gather up v/t possessions recoger

gath·er·ing ['gæðərɪŋ] n (group of people) grupo m de personas

gau·dy ['gɔːdɪ] adj chillón, llamativo

gauge [geɪdʒ] 1 n indicador m 2 v/t pressure medir, calcular; opinion estimar, evaluar

gaunt [gɔːnt] adj demacrado

gauze [gɔːz] gasa f

gave [geɪv] pret → **give**

gawk·y ['gɔːkɪ] adj desgarbado

gawp [gɔːp] v/i F mirar boquiabierto; **don't just stand there gawping!** ¡no te quedes ahí boquiabierto!

gay [geɪ] 1 n (homosexual) homosexual m, gay m 2 adj homosexual, gay

gaze [geɪz] 1 n mirada f 2 v/i mirar fijamente

♦ gaze at v/t mirar fijamente

GB [dʒiː'biː] abbr (= Great Britain) GB (= Gran Bretaña)

GDP [dʒiːdiː'piː] abbr (= gross domestic **product**) PIB m (= producto m interior bruto)

gear [gɪr] n equipment equipo m; in vehicles marcha f

'gear·box MOT caja f de cambios

'gear le·ver, 'gear shift MOT palanca f de cambios

geese [giːs] pl → **goose**

gel [dʒel] for hair gomina f; for shower gel m

gel·a·tine ['dʒelətiːn] gelatina f

gel·ig·nite ['dʒelɪgnaɪt] gelignita f

gem [dʒem] gema f; (fig: book etc) joya f; (person) cielo m

Gem·i·ni ['dʒemɪnaɪ] ASTR Géminis m/f inv

gen·der ['dʒendər] género m

gene [dʒiːn] gen m; **it's in his genes** lo lleva en los genes

gen·e·ral ['dʒenrəl] 1 n MIL general m; **in general** en general, por lo general 2 adj general

gen·e·ral e'lec·tion elecciones fpl generales

gen·er·al·i·za·tion [dʒenrəlar'zeɪʃn] generalización f; **that's a generalization** eso es generalizar

gen·er·al·ize ['dʒenrəlaɪz] v/i generalizar

gen·er·al·ly ['dʒenrəlɪ] adv generalmente, por lo general; **generally speaking** en términos generales

gen·er·al prac'ti·tion·er médico(-a) m(f) de cabecera or de familia

gen·e·rate ['dʒenəreɪt] v/t generar; a feeling provocar

gen·e·ra·tion [dʒenə'reɪʃn] generación f

gen·e·ra·tion gap conflicto m generacional

gen·e·ra·tor ['dʒenəreɪtər] generador m

ge·ner·ic drug [dʒə'nerɪk] MED medicamento m genérico

gen·e·ros·i·ty [dʒenə'rɑːsətɪ] generosidad f

gen·e·rous ['dʒenərəs] adj generoso

ge·net·ic [dʒɪ'netɪk] adj genético

ge·net·i·cal·ly [dʒɪ'netɪklɪ] adv genéticamente; **genetically modified** crops transgénico; **be genetically modified** estar modificado genéticamente ge·net·ic 'code código *m* genético

ge·net·ic en·gi·neer·ing ingeniería *f* genética

ge·net·ic 'fin·ger·print identificación *f* genética

ge·net·i·cist [dʒɪˈnetɪsɪst] genetista *m/f*, especialista *m/f* en genética

ge·net·ics [dʒɪˈnetɪks] genética *f*

ge·ni·al [ˈdʒiːnjəl] *adj* afable, cordial

gen·i·tals [ˈdʒenɪtlz] *npl* genitales *mpl*

ge·ni·us [ˈdʒiːnjəs] genio *m*

gen·o·cide [ˈdʒenəsaɪd] genocidio *m*

gen·tle [ˈdʒentl] *adj person* tierno, delicado; *touch, detergent* suave; *breeze* suave, ligero; *slope* poco inclinado; **be gentle with it, it's fragile** ten mucho cuidado con él, es frágil

gen·tle·man [ˈdʒentlmən] caballero *m*; **he's a real gentleman** es todo un caballero

gen·tle·ness [ˈdʒentlnɪs] *of person* ternura *f*, delicadeza; *of touch, detergent, breeze* suavidad *f*; *of slope* poca inclinación *f*

gen·tly [ˈdʒentlɪ] *adv* con delicadeza, poco a poco; **a breeze blew gently** sopla una ligera *or* suave brisa

gents [dʒents] *nsg Br toilet* servicio *m* de caballeros

gen·u·ine [ˈdʒenʊɪn] *adj antique* genuino, auténtico; *(sincere)* sincero

gen·u·ine·ly [ˈdʒenʊɪnlɪ] *adv* realmente, de verdad

ge·o·graph·i·cal [dʒɪəˈɡræfɪkl] *adj features* geográfico

ge·og·ra·phy [dʒɪˈɒɡrəfɪ] geografía *f*

ge·o·log·i·cal [dʒɪəˈlɒdʒɪkl] *adj* geológico

ge·ol·o·gist [dʒɪˈɒlədʒɪst] geólogo(-a) *m(f)*

ge·ol·o·gy [dʒɪˈɒlədʒɪ] geología *f*

ge·o·met·ric, ge·o·met·ri·cal [dʒɪəˈmetrɪk(l)] *adj* geométrico

ge·om·e·try [dʒɪˈɒmətrɪ] geometría *f*

ge·ra·ni·um [dʒəˈreɪnɪəm] geranio *m*

ger·i·at·ric [dʒerɪˈætrɪk] **1** *adj* geriátrico **2** *n* anciano(-a) *m(f)*

germ [dʒɜːrm] *also fig* germen *m*

Ger·man [ˈdʒɜːrmən] **1** *adj* alemán **2** *n* *person* alemán (-ana) *m(f)*; *language* alemán *m*

Ger·man 'mea·sles *nsg* rubeola *f*

Ger·man 'shep·herd pastor *m* alemán

Germany [ˈdʒɜːrmənɪ] Alemania

ger·mi·nate [ˈdʒɜːrmɪneɪt] *v/i of seed* germinar

germ 'war·fare guerra *f* bacteriológica

ges·tic·u·late [dʒeˈstɪkjuleɪt] *v/i* gesticular

ges·ture [ˈdʒestʃər] *n also fig* gesto *m*

get [get] *v/t (pret got, pp got, gotten) (obtain)* conseguir; *(fetch)* traer; *(receive: letter, knowledge, respect)* recibir; *(catch: bus, train etc)* tomar, *Span* coger; *(arrive)* llegar; *(understand)* entender; **you can get them at the corner shop** los puedes comprar en la tienda de la esquina; **can I get you something to drink?** ¿quieres tomar algo?; **get tired** cansarse; **get drunk** emborracharse; **I'm getting old** me estoy haciendo mayor; **get the TV fixed** hacer que arreglen la televisión; **get s.o. to do sth** hacer que alguien haga algo; **get to do sth** *(have opportunity)* llegar a hacer algo; **get one's hair cut** cortarse el pelo; **get sth ready** preparar algo; **get going** *(leave)* marcharse, irse; **have got** tener; **he's got a lot of money** tiene mucho dinero; **I have got to study / see him** tengo que estudiar / verlo; **I don't want to, but I've got to** no quiero, pero tengo que hacerlo; **get to know** llegar a conocer

♦ get about *v/i (travel)* viajar; *(be mobile)* desplazarse

♦ get along *v/i (come to party etc)* ir; *with s.o.* llevarse bien; **how are you getting along at school?** ¿cómo te van las cosas en el colegio?; **the patient is getting along nicely** el paciente está progresando satisfactoriamente

♦ get at *v/t (criticize)* meterse con; *(imply, mean)* querer decir

♦ get away **1** *v/i (leave)* marcharse, irse **2** *v/t:* **get sth away from s.o.** quitar algo a alguien

♦ get away with *v/t* salir impune de; **get away with it** salirse con la suya; **she lets** *him get away with anything* le permite todo; *I'll let you get away with it this time* por esta vez te perdonaré

◆ **get back 1** *v/i (return)* volver; *I'll get back to you on that tomorrow* le responderé a eso mañana **2** *v/t (obtain again)* recuperar

◆ **get by** *v/i (pass)* pasar; *financially* arreglárselas

◆ **get down 1** *v/i from ladder etc* bajarse *(from* de); *(duck etc)* agacharse **2** *v/t (depress)* desanimar, deprimir

◆ **get down to** *v/t (start: work)* ponerse a; *get down to the facts* ir a los hechos

◆ **get in 1** *v/i (arrive)* llegar; *to car* subir(se), meterse; *how did they get in? of thieves, mice etc* ¿cómo entraron? **2** *v/t to suitcase etc* meter

◆ **get into** *v/t house* entrar en, meterse en; *car* subir(se) a, meterse en; *computer system* introducirse en

◆ **get off 1** *v/i from bus etc* bajarse; *(finish work)* salir; *(not be punished)* librarse **2** *v/t (remove)* quitar; *clothes, hat, footgear* quitarse; *get off my bike!* ¡bájate de mi bici!; *get off the grass!* ¡no pises la hierba!

◆ **get off with** *v/t: get off with a small fine* tener que pagar sólo una pequeña multa

◆ **get on 1** *v/i to bike, bus, train* montarse, subirse; *(be friendly)* llevarse bien; *(advance: of time)* hacerse tarde; *(become old)* hacerse mayor; *(make progress)* progresar; *how are you getting on with the new subjects?* ¿cómo te va con las nuevas asignaturas?; *it's getting on getting late* se está haciendo tarde; *he's getting on* se está haciendo mayor; *he's getting on for 50* está a punto de cumplir 50 **2** *v/t: get on the bus / one's bike* montarse en el autobús / la bici; *get one's shoes on* ponerse los zapatos; *I can't get these pants on* estos pantalones no me entran

◆ **get out 1** *v/i of car, prison etc* salir; *get out!* ¡vete!, ¡fuera de aquí!; *let's get out of here* ¡salgamos de aquí!; *I don't get out much these days* últimamente no salgo mucho **2** *v/t nail, something jam-*med sacar, extraer; *stain* quitar; *gun, pen* sacar

◆ **get over** *v/t fence etc* franquear; *disappointment* superar; *lover etc* olvidar

◆ **get over with** *v/t* terminar con; *let's get it over with* quitémonoslo de encima

◆ **get through** *v/i on telephone* conectarse; *obviously I'm just not getting through* está claro que no me estoy haciendo entender; *get through to s.o. (make self understood)* comunicarse con alguien

◆ **get up 1** *v/i* levantarse **2** *v/t (climb)* subir

'get·a·way *from robbery* fuga *f*, huida *f*

'get·a·way car coche *m* utilizado en la fuga

'get-to·geth·er reunión *f*

ghast·ly ['gæstlɪ] *adj* terrible

gher·kin ['gɜːrkɪn] pepinillo *m*

ghet·to ['getoʊ] gueto *m*

ghost [goʊst] fantasma *m*

ghost·ly ['goʊstlɪ] *adj* fantasmal

'ghost town ciudad *f* fantasma

ghoul [guːl] macabro(-a) *m(f)*, morboso(-a) *m(f)*

ghoul·ish ['guːlɪʃ] *adj* macabro, morboso

gi·ant ['dʒaɪənt] **1** *n* gigante *m* **2** *adj* gigantesco, gigante

gib·ber·ish ['dʒɪbərɪʃ] F memeces *fpl* F, majaderías *fpl* F

gibe [dʒaɪb] *n* pulla *f*

gib·lets ['dʒɪblɪts] *npl* menudillos *mpl*

gid·di·ness ['gɪdɪnɪs] mareo *m*

gid·dy ['gɪdɪ] *adj* mareado; *feel giddy* estar mareado

gift [gɪft] regalo *m*

gift cer·ti·fi·cate vale *m* de regalo

gift·ed ['gɪftɪd] *adj* con talento

'gift·wrap **1** *n* papel *m* de regalo **2** *v/t (pret & pp giftwrapped)* envolver para regalo

gig [gɪg] F concierto *m*, actuación *f*

gi·ga·byte ['gɪgəbaɪt] COMPUT gigabyte *m*

gi·gan·tic [dʒaɪ'gæntɪk] *adj* gigantesco

gig·gle ['gɪgl] **1** *v/i* soltar risitas **2** *n* risita *f*

gig·gly ['gɪglɪ] *adj* que suelta risitas

gill [gɪl] *of fish* branquia *f*

gilt [gɪlt] *n* dorado *m*; *gilts* FIN valores *mpl* del Estado gim·mick ['gɪmɪk] truco *m*, reclamo *m*

gim·mick·y ['gɪmɪkɪ] *adj* superficial, artificioso

gin [dʒɪn] ginebra *f*; **gin and tonic** gin-tonic *m*

gin·ger ['dʒɪndʒər] **1** *n spice* jengibre *m* **2** *adj cat* color fuego; **he has ginger hair** es pelirrojo

gin·ger 'beer *refresco con sabor a jengibre*

'gin·ger·bread pan *m* de jengibre

gin·ger·ly ['dʒɪndʒərlɪ] *adv* cuidadosamente, delicadamente

gip·sy ['dʒɪpsɪ] gitano(-a) *m(f)*

gi·raffe [dʒɪ'ræf] jirafa *f*

gir·der ['gɜːrdər] *n* viga *f*

girl [gɜːrl] chica *f*; **young girl** niña *f*, chica *f*

'girl·friend *of boy* novia *f*; *of girl* amiga *f*

girl·ie mag·a·zine ['gɜːrlɪ] revista *f* porno

girl·ish ['gɜːrlɪʃ] *adj* de niñas

girl 'scout escultista *f*, scout *f*

gist [dʒɪst] esencia *f*

give [gɪv] *v/t (pret* gave, *pp* given) dar; *as present* regalar; *(supply: electricity etc)* proporcionar; *talk, lecture* dar, pronunciar; *cry, groan* soltar; **give her my love** dale recuerdos (de mi parte); **give s.o. a present** hacer un regalo a alguien

♦ give away *as present* regalar; *(betray)* traicionar; **give o.s. away** descubrirse, traicionarse

♦ give back *v/t* devolver

♦ give in **1** *v/i (surrender)* rendirse **2** *v/t (hand in)* entregar

♦ give off *v/t smell, fumes* emitir, despedir

♦ give onto *v/t (open onto)* dar a

♦ give out **1** *v/t leaflets etc* repartir **2** *v/i of supplies, strength* agotarse

♦ give up **1** *v/t smoking etc* dejar de; **give o.s. up to the police** entregarse a la policía **2** *v/i (stop making effort)* rendirse; **I find it hard to give up** me cuesta mucho dejarlo

♦ give way *v/i of bridge etc* hundirse

give-and-'take toma *m* y daca

giv·en ['gɪvn] *pp* → give

'giv·en name nombre *m* de pila

gla·ci·er ['gleɪʃər] glaciar *m*

glad [glæd] *adj* contento, alegre; **I was glad to see you** me alegré de verte

glad·ly ['glædlɪ] *adv* con mucho gusto

glam·or ['glæmər] atractivo *m*, glamour *m*

glam·or·ize ['glæməraɪz] *v/t* hacer atractivo, ensalzar

glam·or·ous ['glæmərəs] *adj* atractivo, glamoroso

glam·our *Br* → glamor

glance [glæns] **1** *n* ojeada *f*, vistazo *m* **2** *v/i* echar una ojeada *or* vistazo

♦ glance at *v/t* echar una ojeada *or* vistazo a

gland [glænd] glándula *f*

glan·du·lar 'fe·ver ['glændʒələr] mononucleosis *f inv* infecciosa

glare [gler] **1** *n of sun, headlights* resplandor *m* **2** *v/i of headlights* resplandecer

♦ glare at *v/t* mirar con furia a

glar·ing ['glerɪŋ] *adj mistake* garrafal

glar·ing·ly ['glerɪŋlɪ] *adv*: **it's glaringly obvious** está clarísimo

glass [glæs] *material* vidrio *m*; *for drink* vaso *m*

glass 'case vitrina *f*

glass·es *npl* gafas *fpl*, *L.Am.* lentes *mpl*, *L.Am.* anteojos *mpl*

'glass·house invernadero *m*

glaze [gleɪz] *n* vidriado *m*

♦ glaze over *v/i of eyes* vidriarse

glazed [gleɪzd] *adj expression* vidrioso

gla·zi·er ['gleɪzɪr] cristalero(-a) *m(f)*, vidriero(-a) *m(f)*

glaz·ing ['gleɪzɪŋ] cristales *mpl*, vidrios *mpl*

gleam [gliːm] **1** *n* resplandor *m*, brillo *m* **2** *v/i* resplandecer, brillar

glee [gliː] júbilo *m*, regocijo *m*

glee·ful ['gliːfəl] *adj* jubiloso

glib [glɪb] *adj* fácil

glib·ly ['glɪblɪ] *adv* con labia

glide [glaɪd] *v/i of bird, plane* planear; *of piece of furniture* deslizarse

glid·er ['glaɪdər] planeador *m*

glid·ing ['glaɪdɪŋ] *n sport* vuelo *m* sin motor

glim·mer ['glɪmər] **1** *n of light* brillo *m* tenue; **glimmer of hope** rayo *m* de esperanza 2 v/i brillar tenuamente

glimpse [glɪmps] **1** n vistazo m; **catch a glimpse of** vislumbrar **2** v/t vislumbrar

glint [glɪnt] **1** n destello m; **in eyes** centelleo m **2** v/i **of light** destellar; **of eyes** centellear

glis·ten ['glɪsn] v/i relucir, centellear

glit·ter ['glɪtər] v/i resplandecer, destellar

glit·ter·ati npl famosos mpl

gloat [gloʊt] v/i regodearse

◆ **gloat over** v/t regodearse de

glo·bal ['gloʊbl] adj global

glo·bal e'con·o·my economía f global

glo·bal 'mar·ket mercado m global

glo·bal 'war·ming calentamiento m global

globe [gloʊb] (the earth) globo m; (model of earth) globo m terráqueo

gloom [gluːm] (darkness) tinieblas fpl, oscuridad f; (mood) abatimiento m, melancolía f

gloom·i·ly ['gluːmɪlɪ] adv con abatimiento, melancólicamente

gloom·y ['gluːmɪ] adj room tenebroso, oscuro; mood, person abatido, melancólico

glo·ri·ous ['glɔːrɪəs] adj weather, day espléndido, maravilloso; victory glorioso

glo·ry ['glɔːrɪ] n gloria f

gloss [glɑːs] n (shine) lustre m, brillo m; (general explanation) glosa f

◆ **gloss over** v/t pasar por alto

glos·sa·ry ['glɑːsərɪ] n glosario m

'gloss paint pintura f brillante

gloss·y ['glɑːsɪ] **1** adj paper cuché, satinado **2** n magazine revista f en color (en papel cuché o satinado)

glove [glʌv] guante m

'glove com·part·ment in car guantera f

'glove pup·pet marioneta f de guiñol (de guante)

glow [gloʊ] **1** n of light, fire resplandor m, brillo m; in cheeks rubor m **2** v/i of light, fire resplandecer, brillar; of cheeks ruborizarse

glow·er [glaʊr] v/i fruncir el ceño

glow·ing ['gloʊɪŋ] adj description entusiasta

glu·cose ['gluːkoʊs] glucosa f

glue [gluː] **1** n pegamento m, cola f **2** v/t

pegar, encolar; **glue sth to sth** pegar or encolar algo a algo; **be glued to the radio / TV** F estar pegado a la radio / televisión F

glum [glʌm] adj sombrío, triste

glum·ly ['glʌmlɪ] adv con tristeza

glut [glʌt] n exceso m, superabundancia f

glut·ton ['glʌtən] glotón(-ona) m(f)

glut·ton·y ['glʌtənɪ] gula f, glotonería f

GMT [dʒiːem'tiː] abbr (= **Greenwich Mean Time**) hora f del meridiano de Greenwich

gnarled [nɑːrld] adj nudoso

gnat [næt] tipo de mosquito

gnaw [nɔː] v/t bone roer

GNP [dʒiːen'piː] abbr (= **gross national product**) PNB m (= producto m nacional bruto)

go [goʊ] **1** n (try) intento m; **it's my go** me toca a mí; **have a go at sth** (try) intentar algo; (complain about) protestar contra algo; **on the go** en marcha; **in one go** drink, write etc de un tirón **2** v/i (pret **went**, pp **gone**) ir (to a); (leave) irse, marcharse; (work, function) funcionar; (come out: of stain etc) irse; (cease: of pain etc) pasarse; (match: of colors etc) ir bien, pegar; **go shopping / jogging** ir de compras/a hacer footing; **I must be going** me tengo que ir; **let's go!** ¡vamos!; **go for a walk** ir a pasear or a dar un paseo; **go to bed** ir(se) a la cama; **go to school** ir al colegio; **how's the work going?** ¿cómo va el trabajo?; **they're going for $50** (being sold at) se venden por 50 dólares; **hamburger to go** hamburguesa para llevar; **be all gone** (finished) haberse acabado; **go green** ponerse verde; **be going to do sth** ir a hacer algo

◆ **go ahead** v/i **and do sth** seguir adelante; **can I? - sure, go ahead** ¿puedo? - por supuesto, adelante

◆ **go ahead with** v/t plans etc seguir adelante con

◆ **go along with** v/t suggestion aceptar

◆ **go at** v/t (attack) atacar

◆ **go away** v/i of person irse, marcharse; of rain, pain, clouds desaparecer

◆ **go back** v/i (return) volver; (date back)

remontarse; **we go back a long way** nos conocemos desde hace tiempo; **go back to sleep** volver a dormirse

◆ go by v/i *of car, time* pasar

◆ go down v/i *bajar; of sun* ponerse; *of ship* hundirse; **go down well / badly** *of suggestion etc* sentar bien / mal

◆ go for v/t *(attack)* atacar; **I don't much go for gin** no me va mucho la ginebra

◆ go in v/i *to room, house* entrar; *of sun* ocultarse; *(fit: of part etc)* ir, encajar

◆ go in for v/t *competition, race* tomar parte en; **I used to go in for badminton quite a lot** antes jugaba mucho al bádminton

◆ go off 1 v/i *(leave)* marcharse; *of bomb* explotar, estallar; *of gun* dispararse; *of alarm* saltar; *of milk etc* echarse a perder 2 v/t: **I've gone off whisky** ya no me gusta el whisky

◆ go on v/i *(continue)* continuar; *(happen)* ocurrir, pasar; **go on, do it!** *(encouraging)* ¡venga, hazlo!; **what's going on?** ¿qué pasa?

◆ go on at v/t *(nag)* meterse con

◆ go out v/i *of person* salir; *of light, fire* apagarse

◆ go out with v/t *romantically* salir con

◆ go over v/t *(check)* examinar; *(do again)* repasar

◆ go through v/t *illness, hard times* atravesar; *(check)* revisar, examinar; *(read through)* estudiar

◆ go under v/i *(sink)* hundirse; *of company* ir a la quiebra

◆ go up v/i subir

◆ go without 1 v/t *food etc* pasar sin 2 v/i pasar privaciones

goad [gəʊd] v/t pinchar; **goad s.o. into doing sth** pinchar a alguien para que haga algo

'go-a·head 1 n luz f verde; **when we get the go-ahead** cuando nos den la luz verde 2 adj *(enterprising, dynamic)* dinámico

goal [gəʊl] SP *target* portería f, *L.Am.* arco m; SP *point* gol m; *(objective)* objetivo m, meta f

goal·ie ['gəʊlɪ] F portero(-a) m(f), *L.Am.*

arquero(-a) m(f)

'goal·keep·er portero(-a) m(f), guardameta m/f, *Am* arquero(-a) m(f)

'goal kick saque m de puerta

'goal·mouth portería f

'goal·post poste m

goat [gəʊt] cabra f

gob·ble ['gɑːbl] v/t engullir

◆ gobble up v/t engullir

gob·ble·dy·gook ['gɑːbldɪguːk] F jerigonza f F

'go-be·tween intermediario(-a) m(f)

god [gɑːd] dios m; **thank God!** ¡gracias a Dios!; **oh God!** ¡Dios mío!

'god·child ahijado(-a) m(f)

'god·daugh·ter ahijada f

god·dess ['gɑːdɪs] diosa f

'god·fa·ther *also in mafia* padrino m

god·for·sak·en ['gɑːdfərseɪkən] adj *place* dejado de la mano de Dios

'god·moth·er madrina f

'god·pa·rent *man* padrino m; *woman* madrina f

'god·send regalo m del cielo

'god·son ahijado m

go·fer ['gəʊfər] F recadero(-a) m(f)

gog·gles ['gɑːglz] npl gafas fpl

go·ing ['gəʊɪŋ] adj *price etc* vigente; **going concern** empresa f en marcha

go·ings-on [gəʊɪŋz'ɑːn] npl actividades fpl

gold [gəʊld] 1 n oro m 2 adj de oro

gold·en ['gəʊldn] adj *sky, hair* dorado

gold·en 'hand·shake gratificación entregada tras la marcha de un directivo

gold·en 'wed·ding (an·ni·ver·sa·ry) bodas fpl de oro

'gold·fish pez m de colores

'gold mine fig mina f

'gold·smith orfebre m/f

golf [gɑːlf] golf m

'golf ball pelota f de golf

'golf club *organization* club m de golf; *stick* palo m de golf

'golf course campo m de golf

golf·er ['gɑːlfər] golfista m/f

gone [gɑːn] pp → go

gong [gɑːŋ] gong m

good [gʊd] adj bueno; *food* bueno, rico; **a**

good many muchos; **he's good at chess** se le da muy bien el ajedrez; **be good for s.o.** ser bueno para alguien

good-bye [gʊd'baɪ] adiós *m*, despedida *f*; **say goodbye to s.o., wish s.o. goodbye** decir adiós a alguien, despedirse de alguien

'good-for-no-thing *n* inútil *m/f*

Good 'Fri-day Viernes *m inv* Santo

good-hu-mored, *Br* good-hu-moured [gʊd'hjuːmərd] *adj* jovial, afable

good-'look-ing [gʊd'lʊkɪŋ] *adj woman, man* guapo

good-na-tured [gʊd'neɪʃərd] bondadoso

good-ness ['gʊdnɪs] *adj moral* bondad *f*; *of fruit etc* propiedades *fpl*, valor *m* nutritivo; **thank goodness!** ¡gracias a Dios!

goods [gʊdz] *npl* COM mercancías *fpl*, productos *mpl*

good'will buena voluntad *f*

good-y-good-y ['gʊdɪgʊdɪ] *n* F: **she's a real goody-goody** es demasiado buenaza F

goo-ey ['guːɪ] *adj* pegajoso

goof [guːf] *v/i* F meter la pata F

goose [guːs] *n* (*pl* geese [giːs]) ganso *m*, oca *f*

goose-ber-ry ['gʊzberɪ] grosella *f*

'goose bumps *npl* carne *f* de gallina

'goose pim-ples *npl* carne *f* de gallina

gorge [gɔːrdʒ] **1** *n* garganta *f*, desfiladero *m* **2** *v/t*: **gorge o.s. on sth** comer algo hasta hartarse

gor-geous ['gɔːrdʒəs] *adj weather* maravilloso; *dress, hair* precioso; *woman, man* buenísimo; *smell* estupendo

go-ril-la [gə'rɪlə] gorila *m*

gosh [gɑːʃ] *int* ¡caramba!, ¡vaya!

go-'slow huelga *f* de celo

gos-pel ['gɑːspl] *in Bible* evangelio *m*; **it's the gospel truth** es la pura verdad

gos-sip ['gɑːsɪp] **1** *n* cotilleo *m*; *person* cotilla *m/f* **2** *v/i* cotillear

'gos-sip col-umn ecos *mpl* de sociedad

'gos-sip col-um-nist escritor(a) *m(f)* de los ecos de sociedad

gos-sip-y ['gɑːsɪpɪ] *adj letter* lleno de cotilleos

got [gɑːt] *pret & pp* → **get**

got-ten ['gɑːtn] *pp* → **get**

gour-met ['gʊrmeɪ] *n* gastrónomo(-a) *m(f)*, gourmet *m/f*

gov-ern ['gʌvərn] *v/t country* gobernar

gov-ern-ment ['gʌvərnmənt] gobierno *m*

gov-er-nor ['gʌvərnər] gobernador(a) *m(f)*

gown [gaʊn] *long dress* vestido *m*; *wedding dress* traje *m*; *of academic, judge* toga *f*; *of surgeon* bata *f*

grab [græb] *v/t* (*pret & pp* grabbed) agarrar; *food* tomar; **grab some sleep** dormir

grace [greɪs] *of dancer etc* gracia *f*, elegancia *f*; **say grace** bendecir la mesa

grace-ful ['greɪsfəl] *adj* elegante

grace-ful-ly ['greɪsfəlɪ] *adv move* con gracia *or* elegancia

gra-cious ['greɪʃəs] *adj person* amable; *style, living* elegante; **good gracious!** ¡Dios mío!

grade [greɪd] **1** *n quality* grado *m*; EDU curso *m*; (*mark*) nota *f* **2** *v/t* clasificar

'grade cross-ing paso *m* a nivel

'grade school escuela *f* primaria

gra-di-ent ['greɪdɪənt] pendiente *f*

grad-u-al ['grædʒʊəl] *adj* gradual

grad-u-al-ly ['grædʒʊəlɪ] *adv* gradualmente, poco a poco

grad-u-ate ['grædʒʊət] **1** *n* licenciado (-a) *m(f)*; *from high school* bachiller *m/f* **2** *v/i from university* licenciarse, *L.Am.* egresarse; *from high school* sacar el bachillerato

grad-u-a-tion [grædʒʊ'eɪʃn] graduación *f*

graf-fi-ti [grə'fiːtiː] graffiti *m*

graft [græft] **1** *n* BOT, MED injerto *m*; *corruption* corrupción *f* **2** *v/t* BOT, MED injertar

grain [greɪn] grano *m*; *in wood* veta *f*; **go against the grain** ir contra la naturaleza de alguien

gram [græm] gramo *m*

gram-mar ['græmər] gramática *f*

gram-mat-i-cal [grə'mætɪkl] *adj* gramatical

gram-mat-i-cal-ly *adv* gramaticalmente

grand [grænd] **1** *adj* grandioso; F (*very*

good) estupendo, genial **2** *n* F (*$1000*) mil dólares

gran·dad ['grændæd] abuelito *m*

'**grand·child** ['grænd] nieto(-a) *m(f)*

'**grand·daugh·ter** nieta *f*

gran·deur ['grændʒər] grandiosidad *f*

'**grand·fa·ther** abuelo *m*

'**grand·fa·ther clock** reloj *m* de pie

gran·di·ose ['grændɪous] *adj* grandioso

grand 'jur·y jurado *m* de acusación, gran jurado

'**grand·ma** F abuelita *f*, yaya *f* F

'**grand·moth·er** abuela *f*

'**grand·pa** F abuelito *m*, yayo *m* F

'**grand·par·ents** *npl* abuelos *mpl*

grand pi'an·o piano *m* de cola

grand 'slam gran slam *m*

'**grand·son** nieto *m*

'**grand·stand** tribuna *f*

gran·ite ['grænɪt] granito *m*

gran·ny ['grænɪ] F abuelita *f*, yaya *f* F

grant [grænt] **1** *n money* subvención *f* **2** *v/t* conceder; *take sth for granted* dar algo por sentado; *take s.o. for granted* no apreciar a alguien lo suficiente

gran·u·lat·ed sug·ar ['grænʊleɪtɪd] azúcar *m or f* granulado(-a)

gran·ule ['grænjuːl] gránulo *m*

grape [greɪp] uva *f*

'**grape·fruit** pomelo *m*, *L.Am.* toronja *f*

'**grape·fruit juice** *Span* zumo *m* de pomelo, *L.Am.* jugo *m* de toronja

'**grape·vine:** *I've heard on the grapevine that ...* me ha contado un pajarito que ...

graph [græf] gráfico *m*, gráfica *f*

graph·ic ['græfɪk] **1** *adj* (*vivid*) gráfico **2** *n* COMPUT gráfico *m*

graph·ic·al·ly ['græfɪklɪ] *adv describe* gráficamente

graph·ic de'sign·er diseñador(a) *m(f)* gráfico(-a)

♦ **grap·ple with** ['græpl] *v/t attacker* forcejear con; *problem etc* enfrentarse a

grasp [græsp] **1** *n physical* asimiento *m*; *mental* comprensión *m* **2** *v/t physically* agarrar; (*understand*) comprender

grass [græs] *n* hierba *f*

'**grass·hop·per** saltamontes *m inv*

grass 'roots *npl people* bases *fpl*

grass 'wid·ow mujer cuyo marido está a menudo ausente durante largos periodos de tiempo

grass 'wid·ow·er hombre cuya mujer está a menudo ausente durante largos periodos de tiempo

gras·sy ['græsɪ] *adj* lleno de hierba

grate[1] [greɪt] *n metal* parrilla *f*, reja *f*

grate[2] [greɪt] **1** *v/t in cooking* rallar **2** *v/t/i of sound* rechinar

grate·ful ['greɪtfəl] *adj* agradecido; *we are grateful for your help* (le) agradecemos su ayuda; *I'm grateful to him* le estoy agradecido

grate·ful·ly ['greɪtfəlɪ] *adv* con agradecimiento

grat·er ['greɪtər] rallador *m*

grat·i·fy ['grætɪfaɪ] *v/t* (*pret & pp gratified*) satisfacer, complacer

grat·ing ['greɪtɪŋ] **1** *n* reja *f* **2** *adj sound, voice* chirriante

grat·i·tude ['grætɪtuːd] gratitud *f*

gra·tu·i·tous [grəˈtuːɪtəs] *adj* gratuito

gra·tu·i·ty [grəˈtuːɪtɪ] propina *f*, gratificación *f*

grave[1] [greɪv] *n* tumba *f*, sepultura *f*

grave[2] [greɪv] *adj* grave

grav·el ['grævl] *n* gravilla *f*

'**grave·stone** lápida *f*

'**grave·yard** cementerio *m*

♦ **grav·i·tate toward** ['grævɪteɪt] *v/t* verse atraído por

grav·i·ty ['grævətɪ] PHYS gravedad *f*

gra·vy ['greɪvɪ] jugo *m* (de la carne)

gray [greɪ] *adj* gris; *be going gray* encanecer

gray-haired [greɪ'herd] *adj* canoso

'**gray·hound** galgo *m*

graze[1] [greɪz] *v/i of cow etc* pastar, pacer

graze[2] [greɪz] **1** *v/t arm etc* rozar, arañar **2** *n* rozadura *f*, arañazo *m*

grease [griːs] *n* grasa *f*

grease-proof 'pa·per papel *m* de cera *or* parafinado

greas·y ['griːsɪ] *adj food, hands, plate* grasiento; *hair, skin* graso

great [greɪt] *adj grande, before singular noun* gran; F (*very good*) estupendo, genial; *how was it? - great!* ¿cómo fue? -

G

¡estupendo *or* genial!; **great to see you again!** ¡me alegro de volver a verte!

Great 'Brit·ain Gran *Bretaña*

great-'grand·child bisnieto(-a) *m(f)*

great-'grand·daugh·ter bisnieta *f*

great-'grand·fa·ther bisabuelo *m*

great-'grand·moth·er bisabuela *f*

great-'grand·par·ents *npl* bisabuelos *mpl*

great-'grand·son bisnieto *m*

great·ly ['greɪtlɪ] *adv* muy

great·ness ['greɪtnɪs] grandeza *f*

Greece [griːs] Grecia

greed [griːd] *for money* codicia *f; for food* gula *f*, glotonería *f*

greed·i·ly ['griːdɪlɪ] *adv* con codicia; *eat* con gula *or* glotonería

greed·y ['griːdɪ] *adj for food* glotón; *for money* codicioso

Greek [griːk] **1** *adj* griego **2** *n person* griego(-a) *m(f); language* griego *m*

green [griːn] *adj* verde; *environmentally* ecologista, verde

green 'beans *npl* judías *fpl* verdes, *L.Am.* porotos *mpl* verdes, *Mex* ejotes *mpl*

'green belt cinturón *m* verde

'green card *(work permit)* permiso *m* de trabajo

'green·field site terreno *m* edificable en el campo

'green·horn F novato(-a) *m(f)* F

'green·house invernadero *m*

'green·house ef·fect efecto *m* invernadero

'green·house gas gas *m* invernadero

greens [griːnz] *npl* verduras *f*

green 'thumb: **have a green thumb** tener buena mano con la jardinería

greet [griːt] *v/t* saludar

greet·ing ['griːtɪŋ] saludo *m*

'greet·ing card tarjeta *f* de felicitación

gre·gar·i·ous [grɪ'geɪrɪəs] *adj person* sociable

gre·nade [grɪ'neɪd] granada *f*

grew [gruː] *pret → **grow***

grey *Br → **gray***

grid [grɪd] reja *f*, rejilla *f*

'grid·iron SP campo de fútbol americano

'grid·lock *in traffic* paralización *m* del

tráfico

grief [griːf] dolor *m*, aflicción *f*

grief-strick·en ['griːfstrɪkn] *adj* afligido

griev·ance ['griːvəns] queja *f*

grieve [griːv] *v/i* sufrir; **grieve for s.o.** llorar por alguien

grill [grɪl] **1** *n on window* reja *f* **2** *v/t (interrogate)* interrogar

grille [grɪl] reja *f*

grim [grɪm] *adj face* severo; *prospects* desolador; *surroundings* lúgubre

gri·mace ['grɪməs] *n* gesto *m*, mueca *f*

grime [graɪm] mugre *f*

grim·ly ['grɪmlɪ] *adv speak* en tono grave

grim·y ['graɪmɪ] *adj* mugriento

grin [grɪn] **1** *n* sonrisa *f* (amplia) **2** *v/i (pret & pp* **grinned**) sonreír abiertamente

grind [graɪnd] *v/t (pret & pp* **ground**) *coffee* moler; *meat* picar; **grind one's teeth** hacer rechinar los dientes

grip [grɪp] **1** *n*: **he lost his grip on the rope** se le escapó la cuerda; **be losing one's grip** *(losing one's skills)* estar perdiendo el control **2** *v/t (pret & pp* **gripped**) agarrar

gripe [graɪp] **1** *n* F queja *f* **2** *v/i* F quejarse

grip·ping ['grɪpɪŋ] *adj* apasionante

gris·tle ['grɪsl] cartílago *m*

grit [grɪt] **1** *n (dirt)* arenilla *f; for roads* gravilla *f* **2** *v/t (pret & pp* **gritted**): **grit one's teeth** apretar los dientes

grit·ty ['grɪtɪ] *adj* F *book, movie etc* duro F, descarnado

groan [groʊn] **1** *n* gemido *m* **2** *v/i* gemir

gro·cer ['groʊsər] tendero(-a) *m(f)*

gro·cer·ies ['groʊsərɪz] *npl* comestibles *mpl*

gro·cer·y store ['groʊsərɪ] tienda *f* de comestibles *or Mex* abarrotes *mpl*

grog·gy ['grɑːgɪ] *adj* F grogui F

groin [grɔɪn] ANAT ingle *f*

groom [gruːm] **1** *n for bride* novio *m; for horse* mozo *m* de cuadra **2** *v/t horse* almohazar; *(train, prepare)* preparar; **well groomed** *in appearance* bien arreglado

groove [gruːv] ranura *f*

grope [groʊp] **1** *v/i in the dark* caminar a tientas **2** *v/t sexually* manosear

♦ grope for *v/t door handle, the right*

word intentar encontrar

gross [grəʊs] *adj* (*coarse, vulgar*) grosero; *exaggeration* tremendo; *error* craso; FIN bruto

gross do·mes·tic 'prod·uct producto *m* interior bruto

gross na·tion·al 'prod·uct producto *m* nacional bruto

ground[1] [graʊnd] **1** *n* suelo *m*, tierra *f*; (*reason*) motivo *m*; ELEC tierra *f*; **on the ground** en el suelo **2** *v/t* ELEC conectar a tierra

ground[2] [graʊnd] *pret & pp →* **grind**

'ground con·trol control *m* de tierra

'ground crew personal *m* de tierra

ground·ing ['graʊndɪŋ] *in subject* fundamento *m*; **he's had a good grounding in electronics** tiene buenos fundamentos de electrónica

ground·less ['graʊndlɪs] *adj* infundado

ground 'meat carne *f* picada

'ground·nut cacahuete *m*, *L.Am.* maní *m*, *Mex* cacahuate *m*

'ground plan plano *m*

'ground staff SP personal *m* de mantenimiento; *at airport* personal *m* de tierra

'ground·work trabajos *mpl* preliminares

group [gruːp] **1** *n* grupo *m* **2** *v/t* agrupar

group·ie ['gruːpɪ] F grupi *f* F

group 'ther·a·py terapia *f* de grupo

grouse [graʊs] **1** *n* F queja *f* **2** *v/i* F quejarse, refunfuñar

grov·el ['grɑːvl] *v/i fig* arrastrarse

grow [grəʊ] **1** *v/i* (*pret* **grew**, *pp* **grown**) crecer; *of number, amount* crecer, aumentarse; **grow old / tired** envejecer / cansarse **2** *v/t* (*pret* **grew**, *pp* **grown**) *flowers* cultivar

♦ **grow up** *v/i of person, city* crecer; **grow up!** ¡no seas crío!

growl [graʊl] **1** *n* gruñido *m* **2** *v/i* gruñir

grown [grəʊn] *pp →* **grow**

grown-up ['grəʊnʌp] **1** *n* adulto(-a) *m(f)* **2** *adj* maduro

growth [grəʊθ] *of person, economy* crecimiento *m*; (*increase*) incremento *m*; MED bulto *m*

grub [grʌb] *of insect* larva *f*, gusano *m*

grub·by ['grʌbɪ] *adj* mugriento *m*

grudge [grʌdʒ] **1** *n* rencor *m*; **bear s.o. a grudge** guardar rencor a alguien **2** *v/t*: **grudge s.o. sth** *feel envy* envidiar algo a alguien

grudg·ing ['grʌdʒɪŋ] *adj* rencoroso

grudg·ing·ly ['grʌdʒɪŋlɪ] *adv* de mala gana

gru·el·ing, *Br* **gru·el·ling** ['gruːəlɪŋ] *adj* agotador

gruff [grʌf] *adj* seco, brusco

grum·ble ['grʌmbl] *v/i* murmurar, refunfuñar

grum·bler ['grʌmblər] quejica *m/f*

grump·y ['grʌmpɪ] *adj* cascarrabias

grunt [grʌnt] **1** *n* gruñido *m* **2** *v/i* gruñir

guar·an·tee [gærən'tiː] **1** *n* garantía *f*; **guarantee period** periodo *m* de garantía **2** *v/t* garantizar

guar·an·tor [gærən'tɔːr] garante *m/f*

guard [gɑːrd] **1** *n* (*security guard*) guardia *m/f*, guarda *m/f*; MIL guardia *f*; *in prison* guardián (-ana) *m(f)*; **be on one's guard against** estar en guardia contra **2** *v/t* guardar, proteger

♦ **guard against** *v/t* evitar

'guard dog perro *m* guardián

guard·ed ['gɑːrdɪd] *adj reply* cauteloso

guard·i·an ['gɑːrdɪən] LAW tutor(a) *m(f)*

guard·i·an 'an·gel ángel *m* de la guarda

Gua·te·ma·la [gwætə'mɑːlə] *n* Guatemala

Gua·te·ma·lan [gwætə'mɑːlən] **1** *adj* guatemalteco **2** *n* guatemalteco(-a) *m(f)*

guer·ril·la [gə'rɪlə] guerrillero(-a) *m(f)*

guer·ril·la 'war·fare guerra *f* de guerrillas

guess [ges] **1** *n* conjetura *f*, suposición *f* **2** *v/t the answer* adivinar; **I guess so** me imagino *or* supongo que sí; **I guess not** me imagino *or* supongo que no **3** *v/i* adivinar

'guess·work conjeturas *fpl*

guest [gest] invitado(-a) *m(f)*

'guest·house casa *f* de huéspedes

'guest·room habitación *f* para invitados

guf·faw [gʌ'fɔː] **1** *n* carcajada *f*, risotada *f* **2** *v/i* carcajearse

guid·ance ['gaɪdəns] orientación *f*, consejo *m*

guide [gaɪd] **1** *n person* guía *m/f*; *book*

guía f **2** v/t guiar

'guide-book guía f

guid·ed mis·sile ['gaɪdɪd] misil m teledirigido

guide dog Br perro m lazarillo

guid·ed 'tour visita f guiada

guide·lines ['gaɪdlaɪnz] npl directrices fpl, normas fpl generales

guilt [gɪlt] culpa f, culpabilidad f; LAW culpabilidad f

guilt·y ['gɪltɪ] adj also LAW culpable; **be guilty of sth** ser culpable de algo; **have a guilty conscience** tener remordimientos de conciencia

guin·ea pig ['gɪnɪpɪg] conejillo m de Indias, cobaya f; fig conejillo m de Indias

guise [gaɪz] apariencia f; **under the guise of** bajo la apariencia de

gui·tar [gɪ'tɑːr] guitarra f

gui'tar case estuche m de guitarra

gui·tar·ist [gɪ'tɑːrɪst] guitarrista m/f

gui'tar play·er guitarrista m/f

gulf [gʌlf] golfo m; fig abismo m; **the Gulf** el Golfo

Gulf of 'Mex·i·co Golfo m de México

gull [gʌl] bird gaviota f

gul·let ['gʌlɪt] ANAT esófago m

gul·li·ble ['gʌlɪbl] adj crédulo, ingenuo

gulp [gʌlp] **1** n of water etc trago m **2** v/i in surprise tragar saliva

◆ gulp down v/t drink tragar; food engullir

gum[1] [gʌm] in mouth encía f

gum[2] [gʌm] n (glue) pegamento m, cola f; (chewing gum) chicle m

gump·tion ['gʌmpʃn] sentido m común

gun [gʌn] pistol, revolver pistola f; rifle rifle m; cannon cañón m

◆ gun down v/t (pret & pp **gunned**) matar a tiros

'gun·fire disparos mpl

'gun·man hombre m armado

'gun·point: **at gunpoint** a punta de pistola

'gun·shot disparo m, tiro m

'gun·shot wound herida f de bala

gur·gle ['gɜːrgl] v/i of baby gorjear; of drain gorgotear

gu·ru ['guru] fig gurú m

gush [gʌʃ] v/i of liquid manar, salir a chorros

gush·y ['gʌʃɪ] adj F (enthusiastic) efusivo, exagerado

gust [gʌst] ráfaga f

gus·to ['gʌstoʊ] entusiasmo m; **with gusto** con entusiasmo

gust·y ['gʌstɪ] adj weather ventoso, con viento racheado; **gusty wind** viento m racheado

gut [gʌt] **1** n intestino m; F (stomach) tripa f F **2** v/t (pret & pp **gutted**) (destroy) destruir

guts [gʌts] npl F (courage) agallas fpl F

guts·y ['gʌtsɪ] adj F (brave) valiente, con muchas agallas F

gut·ter ['gʌtər] on sidewalk cuneta f; on roof canal m, canalón m

guy [gaɪ] F tipo m F, Span tío m F; **hey, you guys** eh, gente

guz·zle ['gʌzl] v/t tragar, engullir

gym [dʒɪm] gimnasio m

gym·na·si·um [dʒɪm'neɪzɪəm] gimnasio m

gym·nast ['dʒɪmnæst] gimnasta m/f

gym·nas·tics [dʒɪm'næstɪks] gimnasia f

'gym shoes npl zapatillas fpl de gimnasia

gy·nae·col·o·gy etc Br → **gynecology** etc

gy·ne·col·o·gy [gaɪnɪ'kɑːlədʒɪ] ginecología f

gy·ne·col·o·gist [gaɪnɪ'kɑːlədʒɪst] ginecólogo(-a) m(f)

gyp·sy ['dʒɪpsɪ] gitano(-a) m(f)

H

hab·it ['hæbɪt] hábito *m*, costumbre *m*; **get into the habit of doing sth** adquirir el hábito de hacer algo
hab·it·a·ble ['hæbɪtəbl] *adj* habitable
hab·i·tat ['hæbɪtæt] hábitat *m*
ha·bit·u·al [hə'bɪtʊəl] *adj* habitual
hack [hæk] *n poor writer* gacetillero(-a) *m(f)*
hack·er ['hækər] COMPUT pirata *m/f* informático(-a)
hack·neyed ['hæknɪd] *adj* manido
had [hæd] *pret & pp* → **have**
had·dock ['hædək] eglefino *m*
hag·gard ['hægərd] *adj* demacrado
hag·gle ['hægl] *v/i* regatear; **haggle over sth** regatear algo
hail [heɪl] *n* granizo *m*
'hail·stone piedra *f* de granizo
'hail·storm granizada *f*
hair [her] pelo *m*, cabello *m*; *single* pelo *m*; *(body hair)* vello *m*; **have short / long hair** tener el pelo corto / largo
'hair·brush cepillo *m*
'hair·cut corte *m* de pelo; **have a haircut** cortarse el pelo
'hair·do F peinado *m*
'hair·dress·er peluquero(-a) *m(f)*; **at the hairdresser** en la peluquería
'hair·dri·er, 'hair·dry·er secador *m* (de pelo)
hair·less ['herlɪs] *adj* sin pelo
'hair·pin horquilla *f*
hair·pin 'bend curva *f* muy cerrada
hair·rais·ing ['hereɪzɪŋ] *adj* espeluznante
hair re·mov·er [herɪ'muːvər] depilatorio *m*
'hair's breadth *fig*: **by a hair's breadth** por un pelo
hair·split·ting ['hersplɪtɪŋ] *n* sutilezas *fpl*
'hair spray laca *f*
'hair·style peinado *m*
'hair·styl·ist estilista *m/f*, peluquero(-a) *m(f)*
hair·y ['herɪ] *adj arm, animal* peludo; F

(frightening) espeluznante
half [hæf] **1** *n (pl halves* [hævz]) mitad *f*; **half past ten** las diez y media; **half after ten** las diez y media; **half an hour** media hora; **half a pound** media libra; **go halves with s.o. on sth** ir a medias con alguien en algo **2** *adj* medio; **at half price** a mitad de precio **3** *adv* a medias; **half finished** a medio acabar
half 'board *Br* media pensión *f*
half-heart·ed [hæf'hɑːrtɪd] *adj* desganado
half 'time **1** *n* SP descanso *m* **2** *adj*: **half time job** trabajo *m* a tiempo parcial; **half time score** marcador *m* en el descanso
half·way **1** *adj stage, point* intermedio **2** *adv* a mitad de camino
hall [hɔːl] *large room* sala *f*; *(hallway in house)* vestíbulo *m*
Hal·low·e'en [hæloʊ'wiːn] víspera *de* Todos los Santos
halo ['heɪloʊ] halo *m*
halt [hɔːlt] **1** *v/i* detenerse **2** *v/t* detener **3** *n* alto *m*; **come to a halt** detenerse
halve [hæv] *v/t input, costs, effort* reducir a la mitad; *apple* partir por la mitad
ham [hæm] jamón *m*
ham·burg·er ['hæmbɜːrgər] hamburguesa *f*
ham·mer ['hæmər] **1** *n* martillo *m* **2** *v/i*: **hammer at the door** golpear la puerta
ham·mock ['hæmək] hamaca *f*
ham·per[1] ['hæmpər] *n for food* cesta *f*
ham·per[2] *v/t (obstruct)* estorbar, obstaculizar
ham·ster ['hæmstər] hámster *m*
hand [hænd] *n* mano *m*; *of clock* manecilla *f*; *(worker)* brazo *m*; **at hand, to hand** a mano; **at first hand** de primera mano, directamente; **by hand** a mano; **on the one hand ..., on the other hand** por una parte ..., por otra parte; **the work is in hand** el trabajo se está llevando a cabo; **on your right hand** a mano dere-

cha; *hands off!* ¡fuera las manos!; *hands up!* ¡arriba las manos!; *change hands* cambiar de manos; *give s.o. a hand* echar un a mano a alguien
◆ **hand down** v/t transmitir
◆ **hand in** v/t entregar
◆ **hand on** v/t pasar
◆ **hand out** v/t repartir
◆ **hand over** v/t entregar
'hand·bag Br bolso m, L.Am. cartera f
'hand·book manual m
'hand·cuff v/t esposar
hand·cuffs ['hæn(d)kʌfs] npl esposas fpl
hand·i·cap ['hændɪkæp] n desventaja f
hand·i·capped ['hændɪkæpt] adj physically minusválido, disminuido; **handicapped by lack of funds** en desventaja por carecer de fondos
hand·i·craft ['hændɪkræft] artesanía f
hand·i·work ['hændɪwɜːrk] manualidades fpl
hand·ker·chief ['hæŋkərtʃɪf] pañuelo m
han·dle ['hændl] 1 n of door manilla f; of suitcase asa f; of pan, knife mango m 2 v/t goods, difficult person manejar; case, deal llevar, encargarse de; **let me handle this** deja que me ocupe yo de esto
han·dle·bars ['hændlbɑːrz] npl manillar m, L.Am. manubrio m
'hand lug·gage equipaje m de mano
hand·made [hæn(d)'meɪd] adj hecho a mano
'hand·rail barandilla f
'hand·shake apretón m de manos
hands-off [hændz'ɑːf] adj no intervencionista
hand·some ['hænsəm] adj guapo, atractivo
hands-on [hændz'ɑːn] adj práctico; **he has a hands-on style of management** le gusta implicarse en todos los aspectos de la gestión
'hand·writ·ing caligrafía f
hand·writ·ten ['hændrɪtn] adj escrito a mano
hand·y ['hændɪ] adj tool, device práctico; **it's handy for the shops** está muy cerca de las tiendas; **it might come in handy** nos puede venir muy bien

hang [hæŋ] 1 v/t (pret & pp **hung**) picture colgar; person colgar, ahorcar (pret & pp **hanged**) 2 v/i (pret & pp **hung**) colgar; of dress, hair caer, colgar 3 n: **get the hang of sth** F agarrarle el tranquillo a algo F
◆ **hang about** v/i: **he's always hanging about on the street corner** siempre está rondando por la esquina; **hang about a minute!** F ¡un momento!
◆ **hang on** v/i (wait) esperar
◆ **hang on to** v/t (keep) conservar; **do you mind if I hang on to it for a while?** ¿te importa si me lo quedo durante un tiempo?
◆ **hang up** v/i TELEC colgar
han·gar ['hæŋər] hangar m
hang·er ['hæŋər] for clothes percha f
hang glid·er ['hæŋglaɪdər] person piloto m de ala delta; device ala f delta
hang glid·ing ['hæŋglaɪdɪŋ] ala f delta
'hang·o·ver resaca f
◆ **han·ker after** ['hæŋkər] v/t anhelar
han·kie, han·ky ['hæŋkɪ] F pañuelo m
hap·haz·ard [hæp'hæzərd] adj descuidado
hap·pen ['hæpn] v/i ocurrir, pasar, suceder; **if you happen to see him** si por casualidad lo vieras; **what has happened to you?** ¿qué te ha pasado?
◆ **happen across** v/t encontrar por casualidad
hap·pen·ing ['hæpnɪŋ] suceso m
hap·pi·ly ['hæpɪlɪ] adv alegremente; (luckily) afortunadamente
hap·pi·ness ['hæpɪnɪs] felicidad f
hap·py ['hæpɪ] adj feliz, contento; coincidence afortunado
hap·py-go-'luck·y adj despreocupado
'hap·py hour franja horaria en la que las bebidas son más baratas en los bares
har·ass [hə'ræs] v/t acosar; enemy asediar, hostigar
har·assed [hər'æst] adj agobiado
har·ass·ment [hə'ræsmənt] acoso m; **sexual harassment** acoso m sexual
har·bor, Br har·bour ['hɑːrbər] 1 n puerto m 2 v/t criminal proteger; grudge albergar

hard [hɑːrd] *adj* duro; (*difficult*) difícil; *facts, evidence* real; **hard of hearing** duro de oído

'hard-back *n* libro *m* de tapas duras

hard-boiled [hɑːrd'bɔɪld] *adj* egg duro

'hard cop·y copia *f* impresa

'hard core *n* (*pornography*) porno *m* duro

hard 'cur·ren·cy divisa *f* fuerte

hard 'disk disco *m* duro

hard·en ['hɑːrdn] 1 *v/t* endurecer 2 *v/i of glue, attitude* endurecerse

'hard hat casco *m*; (*construction worker*) obrero(-a) *m(f)* (de la construcción)

hard·head·ed [hɑːrd'hedɪd] *adj* pragmático

hard·heart·ed [hɑːrd'hɑːrtɪd] *adj* insensible

hard 'line línea *f* dura; **take a hard line on** adoptar una línea dura en cuanto a

hard'lin·er partidario(-a) *m(f)* de la línea dura

hard·ly ['hɑːrdlɪ] *adv* apenas; **did you agree? - hardly!** ¿estuviste de acuerdo? - ¡en absoluto!

hard·ness ['hɑːrdnɪs] dureza *f*; (*difficulty*) dificultad *f*

hard'sell venta *f* agresiva

hard·ship ['hɑːrdʃɪp] penuria *f*, privación *f*

hard 'up *adj*: **be hard up** andar mal de dinero

'hard·ware ferretería *f*; COMPUT hardware *m*

'hard·ware store ferretería *f*

hard-work·ing [hɑːrd'wɜːrkɪŋ] *adj* trabajador

har·dy ['hɑːrdɪ] *adj* resistente

hare [her] liebre *f*

hare-brained ['herbreɪnd] *adj* alocado

harm [hɑːrm] 1 *n* daño *m*; **it wouldn't do any harm to buy two** por comprar dos no pasa nada 2 *v/t* hacer daño a, dañar

harm·ful ['hɑːrmfəl] *adj* dañino, perjudicial

harm·less ['hɑːrmlɪs] *adj* inofensivo; *fun* inocente

har·mo·ni·ous [hɑːr'moʊnɪəs] *adj* armonioso

har·mo·nize ['hɑːrmənaɪz] *v/i* armonizar

har·mo·ny ['hɑːrmənɪ] MUS, *fig* armonía *f*

harp [hɑːrp] *n* arpa *f*

◆ harp on about *v/t* F dar la lata con F

har·poon [hɑːr'puːn] *n* arpón *m*

harsh [hɑːʃ] *adj criticism, words* duro, severo; *color* chillón; *light* potente

harsh·ly ['hɑːrʃlɪ] *adv* con dureza *or* severidad

har·vest ['hɑːrvɪst] *n* cosecha *f*

hash [hæʃ] F: **make a hash of** fastidiar

hash browns *npl* Span patatas *fpl or* L.Am. papas *fpl* fritas

hash·ish ['hæʃiːʃ] hachís *m*

'hash mark almohadilla *f, el signo* '#'

haste [heɪst] *n* prisa *f*

has·ten ['heɪsn] *v/i*: **hasten to do sth** apresurarse en hacer algo

hast·i·ly ['heɪstɪlɪ] *adv* precipitadamente

hast·y ['heɪstɪ] *adj* precipitado

hat [hæt] sombrero *m*

hatch [hætʃ] *n for serving food* trampilla *f; on ship* escotilla *f*

◆ hatch out *v/i of eggs* romperse; *of chicks* salir del cascarón

hatch·et ['hætʃɪt] hacha *f*; **bury the hatchet** enterrar el hacha de guerra

hate [heɪt] 1 *n* odio *m* 2 *v/t* odiar

ha·tred ['heɪtrɪd] odio *m*

haugh·ty ['hɒːtɪ] *adj* altanero

haul [hɒːl] 1 *n of fish* captura *f; of robbery* botín *m* 2 *v/t* (*pull*) arrastrar

haul·age ['hɒːlɪdʒ] transporte *m*

'haul·age com·pa·ny empresa *f* de transportes

haul·i·er ['hɒːlɪr] transportista *m*

haunch [hɒːntʃ] *of person* trasero *m; of animal* pierna *f*

haunt [hɒːnt] 1 *v/t*: **this place is haunted** en este lugar hay fantasmas 2 *n* lugar *m* favorito

haunt·ing ['hɒːntɪŋ] *adj tune* fascinante

Ha·van·a [hə'vænə] *n* La Habana *f*

have [hæv] 1 *v/t* (*pret & pp* **had**) (*own*) tener ◊ *breakfast, lunch* tomar

◊ **I don't have a TV** no tengo televisión; **can I have a coffee?** ¿me da un café?; **can I have more time?** ¿me puede dar más tiempo?; **do you have …?** ¿tiene …?

◇ *must*: **have (got) to** tener que

◇ *causative*: **I'll have it faxed to you** te lo mandaré por fax; **I'll have have it repaired** haré que lo arreglen; **I had my hair cut** me corté el pelo

◇ *v/aux*: **I have eaten** he comido; **have you seen her?** ¿la has visto?

♦ have back *v/t*: **when can I have it back?** ¿cuándo me lo devolverá?

♦ have on *v/t* (*wear*) llevar puesto; **do you have anything on tonight?** (*have planned*) ¿tenéis algo planeado para esta noche?

ha·ven ['heɪvn] *fig* refugio *m*

hav·oc ['hævək] estragos *mpl*; **play havoc with** hacer estragos en

hawk [hɔːk] *also fig* halcón *m*

hay [heɪ] heno *m*

'hay fe·ver fiebre *f* del heno

haz·ard ['hæzərd] *n* riesgo *m*, peligro *m*

'haz·ard lights *npl* MOT luces *fpl* de emergencia

haz·ard·ous ['hæzərdəs] *adj* peligroso, arriesgado; **hazardous waste** residuos *mpl* peligrosos

haze [heɪz] neblina *f*

ha·zel ['heɪzl] *n tree* avellano *m*

'ha·zel·nut avellana *f*

haz·y ['heɪzɪ] *adj image, memories* confuso, vago; **I'm a bit hazy about it** no lo tengo muy claro

he [hiː] *pron* él; **he is French/a doctor** es francés / médico; **you're funny, he's not** tú tienes gracia, él no

head [hed] **1** *n* cabeza *f*; (*boss, leader*) jefe(-a) *m(f)*; *of school* director(a) *m(f)*; *on beer* espuma *f*; *of nail, line* cabeza *f*; **$15 a head** 15 dólares por cabeza; **heads or tails?** ¿cara o cruz?; **at the head of the list** encabezando la lista; **head over heels** *fall* rodando; *fall in love* locamente; **lose one's head** (*go crazy*) perder la cabeza **2** *v/t* (*lead*) estar a la cabeza de; *ball* cabecear

♦ head for *v/t* dirigirse a *or* hacia

'head·ache dolor *m* de cabeza

'head·band cinta *f* para la cabeza

head·er ['hedər] *in soccer* cabezazo *m*; *in document* encabezamiento *m*

'head·hunt *v/t* COM buscar, captar

'head·hunt·er COM cazatalentos *m/f inv*

head·ing ['hedɪŋ] *in list* encabezamiento *m*

'head·lamp faro *m*

'head·light faro *m*

'head·line *n in newspaper* titular *m*; **make the headlines** saltar a los titulares

'head·long *adv fall* de cabeza

'head·mas·ter director *m*

'head·mis·tress directora *f*

head 'of·fice *of company* central *f*

head-'on **1** *adv crash* de frente **2** *adj crash* frontal

'head·phones *npl* auriculares *mpl*

'head·quar·ters *npl of party, organization* sede *f*; *of army* cuartel *m* general

'head·rest reposacabezas *f inv*

'head·room *under bridge* gálibo *m*; *in car* espacio *m* vertical

'head·scarf pañuelo *m* (para la cabeza)

'head·strong *adj* cabezudo, testarudo

head 'teach·er director(a) *m(f)*

'head wait·er maître *m*

'head·wind viento *m* contrario

head·y ['hedɪ] *adj drink, wine etc* que se sube a la cabeza

heal [hiːl] *v/t* curar

♦ heal up *v/i* curarse

health [helθ] salud *f*; **your health!** ¡a tu salud!

'health club gimnasio *m* (con piscina, pista de tenis, sauna etc)

'health food comida *f* integral

'health food store tienda *f* de comida integral

'health in·sur·ance seguro *m* de enfermedad

'health re·sort centro *m* de reposo

health·y ['helθɪ] *adj person* sano; *food, lifestyle* saludable; *economy* saneado

heap [hiːp] *n* montón *m*

♦ heap up *v/t* amontonar

hear [hɪr] *v/t & v/i* (*pret & pp* **heard**) oír

♦ hear about *v/t*: **have you heard about Mike?** ¿te has enterado de lo de Mike?; **they're bound to hear about it sooner or later** se van a enterar tarde o temprano

◆ **hear from** v/t (*have news from*) tener noticias de

hear·ing ['hɪrɪŋ] oído m; LAW vista f; *his hearing is not so good now* ahora ya no oye tan bien; *she was within hearing / out of hearing* estaba / no estaba lo suficientemente cerca como para oírlo

'**hear·ing aid** audífono m

'**hear·say** rumores mpl; *by hearsay* de oídas

hearse [hɜːrs] coche m fúnebre

heart [hɑːrt] *also fig* corazón m; *of problem* meollo m; *know sth by heart* saber algo de memoria; *hearts in cards* corazones mpl

'**heart at·tack** infarto m

'**heart·beat** latido m

heart·break·ing ['hɑːrtbreɪkɪŋ] adj desgarrador

'**heart·brok·en** adj descorazonado

'**heart·burn** acidez f (de estómago)

'**heart fail·ure** paro m cardíaco

heart·felt ['hɑːrtfelt] adj *sympathy* sincero

hearth [hɑːrθ] chimenea f

heart·less ['hɑːrtlɪs] adj despiadado

heart·rend·ing ['hɑːrtrendɪŋ] adj *plea, sight* desgarrador

'**heart throb** ídolo m

'**heart trans·plant** transplante m de corazón

heart·y ['hɑːrtɪ] adj *appetite* voraz; *meal* copioso; *person* cordial, campechano

heat [hiːt] n calor m

◆ **heat up** v/t calentar

heat·ed ['hiːtɪd] adj *swimming pool* climatizado; *discussion* acalorado

heat·er ['hiːtər] *in room* estufa f; *turn on the heater* in car enciende la calefacción

hea·then ['hiːðn] n pagano(-a) m(f)

heath·er ['heðər] brezo m

heat·ing ['hiːtɪŋ] calefacción f

'**heat·proof**, '**heat·re·sis·tant** adj resistente al calor

'**heat·stroke** insolación f

'**heat·wave** ola f de calor

heave [hiːv] v/t (*lift*) subir

heav·en ['hevn] cielo m; *good heavens!* ¡Dios mío!

heav·en·ly ['hevənlɪ] adj F divino F

heav·y ['hevɪ] adj pesado; *cold, rain, accent, loss* fuerte; *smoker, drinker* empedernido; *loss of life* grande; *bleeding* abundante; *there's heavy traffic* hay mucho tráfico

heav·y-'du·ty adj resistente

heav·y·weight adj SP de los pesos pesados

heck·le ['hekl] v/t interrumpir (*molestando*)

hec·tic ['hektɪk] adj vertiginoso, frenético

hedge [hedʒ] n seto m

hedge·hog ['hedʒhɑːg] erizo m

hedge·row ['hedʒrou] seto m

heed [hiːd] v/t: *pay heed to …* hacer caso de …

heel [hiːl] *of foot* talón m; *of shoe* tacón m

'**heel bar** zapatería f

hef·ty ['heftɪ] adj *weight, suitcase* pesado; *person* robusto

height [haɪt] altura f; *at the height of the season* en plena temporada

height·en ['haɪtn] v/t *effect, tension* intensificar

heir [er] heredero m

heir·ess ['erɪs] heredera f

held [held] pret & pp → **hold**

hel·i·cop·ter ['helɪkɑːptər] helicóptero m

hell [hel] infierno m; *what the hell are you doing / do you want?* F ¿qué demonios estás haciendo / quieres? F: *go to hell!* F ¡vete a paseo! F; *a hell of a lot* F un montonazo F; *one hell of a nice guy* F un tipo muy simpático *or Span* legal F

hel·lo [hə'lou] hola; TELEC ¿sí?, *Span* ¿diga?, *Am* ¿aló?, *Rpl* ¿oigo?, *Mex* ¿bueno?; *say hello to s.o.* saludar a alguien

helm [helm] NAUT timón m

hel·met ['helmɪt] casco m

help [help] 1 n ayuda f; *help!* ¡socorro! 2 v/t ayudar; *just help yourself* to food toma lo que quieras; *I can't help it* no puedo evitarlo; *I couldn't help laughing* no pude evitar reírme

help·er ['helpər] ayudante m/f

help·ful ['helpfəl] adj *advice* útil; *person* servicial help·ing ['helpiŋ] *of food* ración *f*

help·less ['helplıs] *adj* (*unable to cope*) indefenso; (*powerless*) impotente

help·less·ly ['helplıslı] *adv* impotentemente

help·less·ness ['helplısnıs] impotencia *f*

'help screen COMPUT pantalla *f* de ayuda

hem [hem] *n of dress etc* dobladillo *m*

hem·i·sphere ['hemısfır] hemisferio *m*

'hem·line bajo *m*

hem·or·rhage ['hemərıdʒ] **1** *n* hemorragia *f* **2** *v/i* sangrar

hen [hen] gallina *f*

hench·man ['hentʃmən] *pej* sicario *m*

'hen par·ty despedida *f* de soltera

hen·pecked ['henpekt] *adj:* **henpecked husband** calzonazos *mpl*

hep·a·ti·tis [hepə'taıtıs] hepatitis *f*

her [hɜːr] **1** *adj* su; **her ticket** su entrada; **her books** sus libros **2** *pron direct object* la; *indirect object* le; *after prep* ella; *I know her* la conozco; *I gave her the keys* le di las llaves; *I sold it to her* se lo vendí; *this is for her* esto es para ella; *who do you mean? - her* ¿a quién te refieres? - a ella

herb [ɜːrb] hierba *f*

herb(al) 'tea ['ɜːrb(əl)] infusión *f*

herd [hɜːrd] *n* rebaño *m*; *of elephants* manada *f*

here [hır] *adv* aquí; *over here* aquí; *here's to you!* *as toast* ¡a tu salud!; *here you are giving sth* ¡aquí tienes!; *here we are!* *finding sth* ¡aquí está!

he·red·i·ta·ry [hə'redıterı] *adj disease* hereditario

he·red·i·ty [hə'redıtı] herencia *f*

her·i·tage ['herıtıdʒ] patrimonio *m*

her·mit ['hɜːrmıt] ermitaño(-a) *m(f)*

her·ni·a ['hɜːrnıə] MED hernia *f*

he·ro ['hırou] héroe *m*

he·ro·ic [hı'rouık] *adj* heroico

he·ro·i·cal·ly [hı'rouıklı] *adv* heroicamente

her·o·in ['herouın] heroína *f*

'her·o·in ad·dict heroinómano(-a) *m(f)*

her·o·ine ['herouın] heroína *f*

her·o·ism ['herouızm] heroísmo *m*

her·on ['herən] garza *f*

her·pes ['hɜːrpiːz] MED herpes *m*

her·ring ['herıŋ] arenque *m*

hers [hɜːrz] *pron* el suyo, la suya; *hers are red* los suyos son rojos; *that book is hers* ese libro es suyo; *a cousin of hers* un primo suyo

her·self [hɜːr'self] *pron reflexive* se; *emphatic* ella misma; *she hurt herself* se hizo daño; *when she saw herself in the mirror* cuando se vio en el espejo; *he saw it herself* lo vio ella misma; *by herself* (*alone*) sola; (*without help*) ella sola, ella misma

hes·i·tant ['hezıtənt] *adj* indeciso

hes·i·tant·ly ['hezıtəntlı] *adv* con indecisión

hes·i·tate ['hezıteıt] *v/i* dudar, vacilar

hes·i·ta·tion [hezı'teıʃn] vacilación *f*

het·er·o·sex·u·al [hetərou'sekʃuəl] *adj* heterosexual

hey·day ['heıdeı] apogeo *m*

hi [haı] *int* ¡hola!

hi·ber·nate ['haıbərneıt] *v/i* hibernar

hic·cup ['hıkʌp] *n* hipo *m*; (*minor problem*) tropiezo *m*, traspié *m*; *have the hiccups* tener hipo

hick [hık] *pej* F palurdo(-a) *m(f)* F, pueblerino(-a) *m(f)* F

'hick town *pej* F ciudad *f* provinciana

hid [hıd] *pret* → *hide¹*

hid·den ['hıdn] **1** *adj meaning, treasure* oculto **2** *pp* → *hide¹*

hid·den a'gen·da *fig* objetivo *m* secreto

hide¹ [haıd] **1** *v/t* (*pret* *hid*, *pp* *hidden*) esconder **2** *v/i* (*pret* *hid*, *pp* *hidden*) esconderse

hide² *n of animal* escondrijo *m*

hide-and-'seek escondite *m*

'hide·a·way escondite *m*

hid·e·ous ['hıdıəs] *adj* espantoso, horrendo; *person* repugnante

hid·ing¹ ['haıdıŋ] (*beating*) paliza *f*

hid·ing² ['haıdıŋ]: *be in hiding* estar escondido; *go into hiding* esconderse

'hid·ing place escondite *m*

hi·er·ar·chy ['haırɑːrkı] jerarquía *f*

hi-fi ['haıfaı] equipo *m* de alta fidelidad

high [haı] **1** *adj* alto; *wind* fuerte; (*on drugs*) colocado P; *have a very high opi-*

nion of tener muy buena opinión de; **high in the sky** en lo alto; **it is high time you understood** ya va siendo hora de que entiendas **2** n MOT directa f; in statistics máximo m; EDU escuela f secundaria, Span instituto m **3** adv: **that's as high as we can go** eso es lo máximo que podemos ofrecer

'high-brow adj intelectual

'high-chair trona f

high-'class adj de categoría

High 'Court Tribunal m Supremo

high 'div-ing salto m de trampolín

high-'fre-quen-cy adj de alta frecuencia

high-'grade adj de calidad superior

high-hand-ed [haɪ'hændɪd] adj despótico

high-heeled [haɪ'hiːld] adj de tacón alto

'high jump salto m de altura

high-'lev-el adj de alto nivel

'high life buena vida f

'high-light **1** n (main event) momento m cumbre; in hair reflejo m **2** v/t with pen resaltar; COMPUT seleccionar, resaltar

'high-light-er pen fluorescente m

high-ly ['haɪlɪ] adv desirable, likely muy; **be highly paid** estar muy bien pagado; **think highly of s.o.** tener una buena opinión de alguien

high-ly 'strung adj muy nervioso

high per'form-ance adj drill, battery de alto rendimiento

high-pitched [haɪ'pɪtʃt] adj agudo

'high point of life, career punto m culminante

high-pow-ered [haɪ'paʊərd] adj engine potente; intellectual de alto(s) vuelo(s); salesman enérgico

high 'pres-sure **1** n weather altas presiones fpl **2** adj TECH a gran presión; salesman agresivo; job, lifestyle muy estresante

high 'priest sumo sacerdote m

'high school escuela f secundaria, Span instituto m

high so'ci-e-ty alta sociedad f

high-speed 'train tren m de alta velocidad

high 'tech **1** n alta f tecnología **2** adj de alta tecnología

high 'tide marea f alta

high 'wa-ter: **at high water** con la marea alta

'high-way autopista f

'high wire in circus cuerda f floja

hi-jack ['haɪdʒæk] **1** v/t plane, bus secuestrar **2** n of plane, bus secuestro m

hi-jack-er ['haɪdʒækər] of plane, bus secuestrador(a) m(f)

hike[1] [haɪk] **1** n caminata f **2** v/i caminar

hike[2] [haɪk] n in prices subida f

hik-er ['haɪkər] senderista m/f

hik-ing ['haɪkɪŋ] senderismo m

'hik-ing boots npl botas fpl de senderismo

hi-lar-i-ous [hɪ'lerɪəs] adj divertidísimo, graciosísimo

hill [hɪl] colina f; (slope) cuesta f

hill-bil-ly ['hɪlbɪlɪ] F rústico montañés

hill-side ['hɪlsaɪd] ladera f

hill-top ['hɪltɑːp] cumbre f

hill-y ['hɪlɪ] adj con colinas

hilt [hɪlt] puño m

him [hɪm] pron direct object lo; indirect object le; after prep él; **I know him** lo conozco; **I gave him the keys** le di las llaves; **I sold it to him** se lo vendí; **this is for him** esto es para él; **who do you mean? - him** ¿a quién te refieres? - a él

him-self [hɪm'self] pron reflexive se; emphatic él mismo; **he hurt himself** se hizo daño; **when he saw himself in the mirror** cuando se vio en el espejo; **he saw it himself** lo vio él mismo; **by himself** (alone) solo; (without help) él solo, él mismo

hind [haɪnd] adj trasero

hin-der ['hɪndər] v/t obstaculizar, entorpecer

hin-drance ['hɪndrəns] estorbo m, obstáculo m

hind-sight ['haɪndsaɪt]: **with hindsight** a posteriori

hinge [hɪndʒ] n bisagra f

◆ hinge on v/t depender de

hint [hɪnt] n (clue) pista f; (piece of advice) consejo m; (implied suggestion) indirecta f; of red, sadness etc rastro m

hip [hɪp] n cadera f

hip 'pock-et bolsillo m trasero

hip-po-pot-a-mus [hɪpə'pɑːtəməs] hipopótamo *m*

hire [haɪr] *v/t* alquilar

his [hɪz] **1** *adj* su; *his ticket* su entrada; *his books* sus libros **2** *pron* el suyo, la suya; *his are red* los suyos son rojos; *that ticket is his* esa entrada es suya; *a cousin of his* un primo suyo

His·pan·ic [hɪˈspænɪk] **1** *n* hispano(-a) *m(f)* **2** *adj* hispano, hispánico

hiss [hɪs] *v/i of snake, audience* silbar

his·to·ri·an [hɪˈstɔːrɪən] historiador(a) *m(f)*

his·tor·ic [hɪˈstɔːrɪk] *adj* histórico

his·tor·i·cal [hɪˈstɔːrɪk] *adj* histórico

his·to·ry [ˈhɪstərɪ] historia *f*

hit [hɪt] **1** *v/t* (*pret & pp hit*) golpear; (*collide with*) chocar contra; *he was hit by a bullet* le alcanzó una bala; *it suddenly hit me* (*I realized*) de repente me di cuenta; *hit town* (*arrive*) llegar a la ciudad **2** *n* (*blow*) golpe *m*; MUS, (*success*) éxito *m*

◆ **hit back** *v/i physically* devolver el golpe; *verbally, with actions* responder

◆ **hit on** *v/t idea* dar con

◆ **hit out at** *v/t* (*criticize*) atacar

hit-and-run *adj*: *hit-and-run accident* accidente en el que el vehículo causante se da a la fuga

hitch [hɪtʃ] **1** *n* (*problem*) contratiempo *m*; *without a hitch* sin ningún contratiempo **2** *v/t* enganchar; *hitch sth to sth* enganchar algo a algo; *hitch a ride* hacer autoestop **3** *v/i* (*hitchhike*) hacer autoestop

◆ **hitch up** *v/t wagon, trailer* enganchar

'hitch·hike *v/i* hacer autoestop

'hitch·hik·er autoestopista *m/f*

'hitch·hik·ing autoestop *m*

hi-'tech 1 *n* alta tecnología *f* **2** *adj* de alta tecnología

'hit-list lista *f* de blancos

'hit·man asesino *m* a sueldo

hit-or-'miss *adj* a la buena ventura

'hit squad grupo *m* de intervención especial

HIV [eɪtʃaɪˈviː] *abbr* (= *human immunodeficiency virus*) VIH *m* (= virus *m inv* de la inmunodeficiencia *humana*)

hive [haɪv] *for bees* colmena *f*

◆ **hive off** *v/t* (COM: *separate off*) desprenderse de

HIV-'pos·i·tive *adj* seropositivo

hoard [hɔːrd] **1** *n* reserva *f* **2** *v/t* hacer acopio de; *money* acumular

hoard·er [ˈhɔːrdər] acaparador(a) *m(f)*

hoarse [hɔːrs] *adj* ronco

hoax [hoʊks] *n* bulo *m*, engaño *m*; *bomb hoax* amenaza *f* falsa de bomba

hob [hɑːb] *on cooker* placa *f*

hob·ble [ˈhɑːbl] *v/i* cojear

hob·by [ˈhɑːbɪ] hobby *m*, afición *f*

ho·bo [ˈhoʊboʊ] F vagabundo(-a) *m(f)*

hock·ey [ˈhɑːkɪ] (*ice hockey*) hockey *m* sobre hielo

hog [hɑːg] *n* (*pig*) cerdo *m*, *L.Am.* chancho *m*

hoist [hɔɪst] **1** *n* montacargas *m inv*; *manual* elevador *m* **2** *v/t* (*lift*) levantar, subir; *flag* izar; *they hoisted the winner up onto their shoulders* subieron al ganador a hombros

ho·kum [ˈhoʊkəm] F (*nonsense*) tonterías *fpl*; (*sentimental stuff*) cursilería *f*

hold [hoʊld] **1** *v/t* (*pret & pp held*) *in hand* llevar; (*support, keep in place*) sostener; *passport, license* tener; *prisoner, suspect* retener; (*contain*) contener; *job, post* ocupar; *course* mantener; *hold my hand* dame la mano; *hold one's breath* aguantar la respiración; *he can hold his drink* sabe beber; *hold s.o. responsible* hacer a alguien responsable; *hold that ...* (*believe, maintain*) mantener que ...; *hold the line, please* TELEC espere, por favor **2** *n in ship, plane* bodega *f*; *take hold of sth* agarrar algo; *lose one's hold on sth on rope* soltar algo; *on reality* perder el contacto con algo

◆ **hold against** *v/t*: *hold sth against s.o.* tener algo contra alguien

◆ **hold back 1** *v/t crowds* contener; *facts, information* guardar **2** *v/i* (*not tell all*): *I'm sure he's holding back* estoy seguro de que no dice todo lo que sabe

◆ **hold on** *v/i* (*wait*) esperar; *now hold on a minute!* ¡un momento!

◆ **hold on to** *v/t* (*keep*) guardar; *belief* aferrarse a

◆ **hold out 1** v/t hand tender; prospect ofrecer **2** v/i of supplies durar; (survive) resistir, aguantar

◆ **hold up 1** v/t hand levantar; bank etc atracar; (make late) retrasar; **I was held up by the traffic** he llegado tarde por culpa del tráfico; **hold sth up as an example** poner a alguien como ejemplo

◆ **hold with** v/t (approve of): **I don't hold with that sort of behavior** no me parece bien ese tipo de comportamiento

'**hold·all** Br bolsa f

hold·er ['houldər] (container) receptáculo m; of passport, ticket etc titular m/f; of record poseedor(a) m(f)

'**hold·ing com·pa·ny** holding m

'**hold·up** (robbery) atraco m; (delay) retraso m

hole [houl] n in sleeve, wood, bag agujero m; in ground hoyo m

hol·i·day ['hɑːlədeɪ] single day día f de fiesta; period vacaciones fpl; **take a holiday** tomarse vacaciones

Hol·land ['hɑːlənd] Holanda

hol·low ['hɑːloʊ] adj object hueco; cheeks hundido; promise vacío

hol·ly ['hɑːlɪ] acebo m

hol·o·caust ['hɑːləkɔːst] holocausto m

hol·o·gram ['hɑːləgræm] holograma m

hol·ster ['hoʊlstər] pistolera f

ho·ly ['hoʊlɪ] adj santo

Ho·ly 'Spir·it Espíritu m Santo

'**Ho·ly Week** Semana f Santa

home [hoʊm] **1** n casa f; (native country) tierra f; for old people residencia f; **New York is my home** Nueva York es mi hogar; **at home** (in house) en casa; (in country) en mi / su / nuestra tierra; **make yourself at home** ponte cómodo; **at home and abroad** en el país y en el extranjero; **at home** SP en casa; **work from home** trabajar desde casa **2** adv a casa; **go home** ir a casa; to country ir a mi / tu / su tierra; to town, part of country ir a mi / tu / su ciudad

'**home ad·dress** domicilio m

home 'bank·ing telebanca f, banca f electrónica

'**home·com·ing** vuelta f a casa

home com'put·er Span ordenador m, L.Am. computadora f doméstica

home·less ['hoʊmlɪs] adj sin casa; **the homeless** los sin casa

'**home·lov·ing** adj hogareño

home·ly ['hoʊmlɪ] adj (homeloving) hogareño; (not good-looking) feúcho

home'made adj casero

'**home match** partido m en casa

'**home 'mov·ie** película f casera

ho·me·op·a·thy [hoʊmɪ'ɑːpəθɪ] homeopatía f

'**home page** web site página f personal; on web site página f inicial

'**home·sick** adj nostálgico; **be homesick** tener morriña

'**home town** ciudad f natal

home·ward ['hoʊmwərd] adv to own house a casa; to own country a mi país

'**home·work** EDU deberes mpl

'**home·work·ing** COM teletrabajo m

hom·i·cide ['hɑːmɪsaɪd] crime homicidio m; police department brigada f de homicidios

hom·o·graph ['hɑːməgræf] homógrafo m

ho·mo·pho·bi·a [hɑːmə'foʊbɪə] homofobia f

ho·mo·sex·u·al [hɑːmə'sekʃʊəl] **1** adj homosexual **2** n homosexual m/f

Hon·du·ras [hɑːn'dʊrəs] n Honduras

Hon·du·ran [hɑːn'dʊrən] **1** adj hondureño **2** n hondureño(-a) m(f)

hon·est ['ɑːnɪst] adj honrado

hon·est·ly ['ɑːnɪstlɪ] adv honradamente; **honestly!** ¡desde luego!

hon·es·ty ['ɑːnɪstɪ] honradez f

hon·ey ['hʌnɪ] miel f; F (darling) cariño m/f

'**hon·ey·comb** panal m

'**hon·ey·moon** n luna f de miel

honk [hɑːŋk] v/t horn tocar

hon·or ['ɑːnər] **1** n honor m **2** v/t honrar

hon·or·a·ble ['ɑːnrəbl] adj honorable

hon·our etc Br → **honor** etc

hood [hʊd] over head capucha f; over cooker campana f extractora; MOT capó m; F (gangster) matón(-ona) m(f)

hood·lum ['huːdləm] matón(-ona) m(f)

hoof [huːf] casco m

hook [hʊk] gancho *m*; *to hang clothes on* colgador *m*; *for fishing* anzuelo *m*; *off the hook* TELEC descolgado

hooked [hʊkt] *adj* enganchado; *be hooked on sth* on drugs, *fig* estar enganchado a algo

hook·er ['hʊkər] F fulana *f* F

hook·ey ['hʊkɪ] F: *play hookey* hacer novillos, *Mex* irse de pinta, *S. Am.* hacerse la rabona

hoo·li·gan ['huːlɪgən] gamberro(-a) *m(f)*

hoo·li·gan·ism ['huːlɪgənɪzm] gamberrismo *m*

hoop [huːp] aro *m*

hoot [huːt] **1** *v/t horn* tocar **2** *v/i of car* dar bocinazos; *of owl* ulular

hoo·ver® ['huːvər] **1** *n* aspirador *m*, aspiradora *f* **2** *v/t carpets, room* pasar el aspirador por, aspirar

hop¹ [hɑːp] *n plant* lúpulo *m*

hop² [hɑːp] *v/i (pret & pp* **hopped**) saltar

hope [hoʊp] **1** *n* esperanza *f*; *there's no hope of that* no hay esperanza de eso **2** *v/i* esperar; *hope for sth* esperar algo; *we all hope for peace* todos ansiamos la paz **3** *v/t*: *I hope you like it* espero que te guste; *I hope so* eso espero; *I hope not* espero que no

hope·ful ['hoʊpfəl] *adj* prometedor; *I'm hopeful that ...* espero que ...

hope·ful·ly ['hoʊpfəlɪ] *adv say, wait* esperanzadamente; *hopefully he hasn't forgotten* esperemos que no se haya olvidado

hope·less ['hoʊplɪs] *adj position, prospect* desesperado; (*useless: person*) inútil

ho·ri·zon [hə'raɪzn] horizonte *m*

hor·i·zon·tal [hɑːrɪ'zɑːntl] *adj* horizontal

hor·mone ['hɔːrmoʊn] hormona *f*

horn [hɔːrn] *of animal* cuerno *m*; MOT bocina *f*, claxon *m*

hor·net ['hɔːrnɪt] avispón *m*

horn-rimmed 'spec·ta·cles ['hɔːrnrɪmd] *npl* gafas *fpl* de concha

horn·y ['hɔːrnɪ] *adj* F *sexually* cachondo F

hor·o·scope ['hɑːrəskoʊp] horóscopo *m*

hor·ri·ble ['hɑːrɪbl] *adj* horrible; *person* muy antipático

hor·ri·fy ['hɑːrɪfaɪ] *v/t (pret & pp* **horri-fied**) horrorizar; *I was horrified* me quedé horrorizado

hor·ri·fy·ing ['hɑːrɪfaɪɪŋ] *adj* horroroso

hor·ror ['hɑːrər] horror *m*

'hor·ror mov·ie película *f* de terror

hors d'oeu·vre [ɔːr'dɜːrv] entremés *m*

horse [hɔːrs] caballo *m*

'horse·back: *on horseback* a caballo

horse 'chest·nut castaño *m* de Indias

'horse·pow·er caballo *m* (de vapor)

'horse race carrera *f* de caballos

'horse·shoe herradura *f*

hor·ti·cul·ture ['hɔːrtɪkʌltʃər] horticultura *f*

hose [hoʊz] *n* manguera *f*

hos·pice ['hɑːspɪs] hospital *m* para enfermos terminales

hos·pi·ta·ble [hɑː'spɪtəbl] *adj* hospitalario

hos·pi·tal ['hɑːspɪtl] hospital *m*; *go into the hospital* ir al hospital

hos·pi·tal·i·ty [hɑːspɪ'tælətɪ] hospitalidad *f*

host [hoʊst] *n at party, reception* anfitrión *m*; *of TV program* presentador(a) *m(f)*

hos·tage ['hɑːstɪdʒ] rehén *m*; *take s.o. hostage* tomar a alguien como rehén

'hos·tage tak·er persona *f* que toma rehenes

hos·tel ['hɑːstl] *for students* residencia *f*; (*youth hostel*) albergue *m*

hos·tess ['hoʊstɪs] *at party, reception* anfitriona *f*; *on airplane* azafata *f*; *in bar* cabaretera *f*

hos·tile ['hɑːstl] *adj* hostil

hos·til·i·ty [hɑː'stɪlətɪ] *of attitude* hostilidad *f*; *hostilities* hostilidades *fpl*

hot [hɑːt] *adj weather* caluroso; *object, water, food* caliente; (*spicy*) picante; *it's hot of weather* hace calor; *I'm hot* tengo calor; *she's pretty hot at math* F (*good*) es una fenómena con las matemáticas F

'hot dog perrito *m* caliente

ho·tel [hoʊ'tel] hotel *m*

'hot·plate placa *f*

'hot spot *military, political* punto *m* caliente

hour [aʊr] hora *f*

hour·ly ['aʊrlı] *adj*: **at hourly intervals** a intervalos de una hora; **an hourly bus** un autobús que pasa cada hora

house [haʊs] *n* casa *f*; **at your house** en tu casa

'house·boat barco-vivienda *f*

'house·break·ing allanamiento *m* de morada

'house·hold hogar *m*

house·hold 'name nombre *m* conocido

'house hus·band amo *m* de casa

'house·keep·er ama *f* de llaves

'house·keep·ing *activity* tareas *fpl* domésticas; *money* dinero *m* para gastos domésticos

House of Rep·re'sent·a·tives *npl* Cámara *f* de Representantes

house·warm·ing (party) ['haʊswɔːrmıŋ] fiesta *f* de estreno de una casa

'house·wife ama *f* de casa

'house·work tareas *fpl* domésticas

hous·ing ['haʊzıŋ] vivienda *f*; TECH cubierta *f*

'hous·ing con·di·tions *npl* condiciones *fpl* de la vivienda

hov·el ['hɑːvl] chabola *f*

hov·er ['hɑːvər] *v/i of bird* cernerse; *of helicopter* permanecer inmóvil en el aire

'hov·er·craft aerodeslizador *m*, hovercraft *m*

how [haʊ] *adv* cómo; **how are you?** ¿cómo estás?; **how about …?** ¿qué te parece …?; **how about a drink?** ¿te apetece tomar algo?; **how much?** ¿cuánto?; **how much is it?** *of cost* ¿cuánto vale *or* cuesta?; **how many?** ¿cuántos?; **how often?** ¿con qué frecuencia?; **how funny / sad!** ¡qué divertido / triste!

how·ev·er *adv* sin embargo; **however big / rich / small they are** independientemente de lo grandes / ricos / pequeños que sean

howl [haʊl] *v/i of dog* aullido *m*; *of person in pain* alarido *m*; *with laughter* risotada *f*

howl·er ['haʊlər] *(mistake)* error *m* garrafal

hub [hʌb] *of wheel* cubo *m*

'hub·cap tapacubos *m inv*

◆ hud·dle together ['hʌdl] *v/i* apiñarse,

acurrucarse

hue [hjuː] tonalidad *f*

huff [hʌf]: **be in a huff** estar enfurruñado

hug [hʌg] *v/t (pret & pp hugged)* abrazar

huge [hjuːdʒ] *adj* enorme

hull [hʌl] casco *m*

hul·la·ba·loo [hʌləbə'luː] alboroto *m*

hum [hʌm] **1** *v/t (pret & pp hummed)* *song, tune* tararear **2** *v/i (pret & pp hummed)* *of person* tararear; *of machine* zumbar

hu·man ['hjuːmən] **1** *n* humano *m* **2** *adj* humano; **human error** error *m or* fallo *m* humano

hu·man 'be·ing ser *m* humano

hu·mane [hjuː'meın] *adj* humano

hu·man·i·tar·i·an [hjuːmænı'terıən] *adj* humanitario

hu·man·i·ty [hjuː'mænətı] humanidad *f*

hu·man 'race raza *f* humana

hu·man re'sourc·es *npl* recursos *mpl* humanos

hum·ble ['hʌmbl] *adj* humilde

hum·drum ['hʌmdrʌm] *adj* monótono, anodino

hu·mid ['hjuːmıd] *adj* húmedo

hu·mid·i·fi·er [hjuː'mıdıfaır] humidificador *m*

hu·mid·i·ty [hjuː'mıdıtı] humedad *f*

hu·mil·i·ate [hjuː'mılıeıt] *v/t* humillar

hu·mil·i·at·ing [hjuː'mılıeıtıŋ] *adj* humillante

hu·mil·i·a·tion [hjuːmılı'eıʃn] humillación *f*

hu·mil·i·ty [hjuː'mılətı] humildad *f*

hu·mor ['hjuːmər] humor *m*; **sense of humor** sentido *m* del humor

hu·mor·ous ['hjuːmərəs] *adj* gracioso

hu·mour *Br* → humor

hump [hʌmp] **1** *n of camel, person* joroba *f*; *on road* bache *m* **2** *v/t* F *(carry)* acarrear

hunch [hʌntʃ] *n (idea)* presentimiento *m*, corazonada *f*

hun·dred ['hʌndrəd] cien *m*; **a hundred dollars** cien dólares; **hundreds of birds** cientos *or* centenares de aves; **a hundred and one** ciento uno; **two hundred** doscientos

hun·dredth ['hʌndrədθ] n & adj centésimo

'hun·dred·weight 43 kilogramos

hung [hʌŋ] pret & pp → **hang**

Hun·gar·i·an [hʌŋ'gerɪən] **1** adj húngaro **2** n person húngaro(-a) m(f); language húngaro m

Hun·ga·ry ['hʌŋgərɪ] Hungría

hun·ger ['hʌŋgər] n hambre f

hung·'o·ver adj: **be hung-over** tener resaca

hun·gry ['hʌŋgrɪ] adj hambriento; **I'm hungry** tengo hambre

hunk [hʌŋk] n cacho m, pedazo m; F man cachas m inv F

hun·ky·dor·y [hʌŋkɪ'dɔːrɪ] adj F: **everything's hunky-dory** todo va de perlas

hunt [hʌnt] **1** n caza f, búsqueda f **2** v/t animal cazar

♦ hunt for v/t buscar

hunt·er ['hʌntər] cazador(a) m(f)

hunt·ing ['hʌntɪŋ] caza f

hur·dle ['hɜːrdl] SP valla f; (fig: obstacle) obstáculo m

hur·dler ['hɜːrdlər] SP vallista m/f

hur·dles npl SP vallas fpl

hurl [hɜːrl] v/t lanzar

hur·ray [hʊ'reɪ] int ¡hurra!

hur·ri·cane ['hʌrɪkən] huracán m

hur·ried ['hʌrɪd] adj apresurado

hur·ry ['hʌrɪ] **1** n prisa f; **be in a hurry** tener prisa **2** v/i (pret & pp **hurried**) darse prisa

♦ hurry up **1** v/i darse prisa; **hurry up!** ¡date prisa! **2** v/t meter prisa a

hurt [hɜːrt] **1** v/i (pret & pp **hurt**) doler; **does it hurt?** ¿te duele? **2** v/t (pret & pp **hurt**) physically hacer daño a; emotionally herir; **I've hurt my hand** me he hecho daño en la mano; **did he hurt you?** ¿te hizo daño?

hus·band ['hʌzbənd] marido m

hush [hʌʃ] n silencio m; **hush!** ¡silencio!

♦ hush up v/t scandal etc acallar

husk [hʌsk] of peanuts etc cáscara f

hus·ky ['hʌskɪ] adj voice áspero

hus·tle ['hʌsl] **1** n agitación f; **hustle and bustle** ajetreo m **2** v/t person empujar

hut [hʌt] cabaña f, refugio m; workman's cobertizo m

hy·a·cinth ['haɪəsɪnθ] jacinto m

hy·brid ['haɪbrɪd] n híbrido m

hy·drant ['haɪdrənt] boca f de riego or de incendios

hy·drau·lic [haɪ'drɔːlɪk] adj hidráulico

hy·dro·e·lec·tric [haɪdroʊɪ'lektrɪk] adj hidroeléctrico

'hy·dro·foil ['haɪdrəfɔɪl] boat hidroplaneador m

hy·dro·gen ['haɪdrədʒən] hidrógeno m

'hy·dro·gen bomb bomba f de hidrógeno

hy·giene ['haɪdʒiːn] higiene f

hy·gien·ic [haɪ'dʒiːnɪk] adj higiénico

hymn [hɪm] himno m

hype [haɪp] n bombo m

hy·per·ac·tive [haɪpər'æktɪv] adj hiperactivo

hy·per·sen·si·tive [haɪpər'sensɪtɪv] adj hipersensible

hy·per·ten·sion [haɪpər'tenʃn] hipertensión f

hy·per·text ['haɪpərtekst] COMPUT hipertexto m

hy·phen ['haɪfn] guión m

hyp·no·sis [hɪp'noʊsɪs] hipnosis f

hyp·no·ther·a·py [hɪpnoʊ'θerəpɪ] hipnoterapia f

hyp·no·tize ['hɪpnətaɪz] v/t hipnotizar

hy·po·chon·dri·ac [haɪpə'kɑːndriæk] n hipocondríaco(-a) m(f)

hy·poc·ri·sy [hɪ'pɑːkrəsɪ] hipocresía f

hyp·o·crite ['hɪpəkrɪt] hipócrita m/f

hyp·o·crit·i·cal [hɪpə'krɪtɪkl] adj hipócrita

hy·po·ther·mi·a [haɪpoʊ'θɜːrmɪə] hipotermia f

hy·poth·e·sis [haɪ'pɑːθəsɪs] (pl **hypotheses** [haɪ'pɑːθəsiːz]) hipótesis f inv

hy·po·thet·i·cal [haɪpə'θetɪkl] adj hipotético

hys·ter·ec·to·my [hɪstə'rektəmɪ] histerectomía f

hys·te·ri·a [hɪ'stɪrɪə] histeria f

hys·ter·i·cal [hɪ'sterɪkl] adj person, laugh histérico; F (very funny) tronchante F; **become hysterical** ponerse histérico

hys·ter·ics [hɪ'sterɪks] npl ataque f de histeria; (laughter) ataque f de risa

I

I [aɪ] *pron* yo; **I am English/a student** soy inglés / estudiante; **you're crazy, I'm not** tú estás loco, yo no

ice [aɪs] *in drink, on road* hielo *m*; **break the ice** *fig* romper el hielo

◆ **ice up** *v/i of engine, wings* helarse

ice-berg ['aɪsbɜːrg] iceberg *m*

'ice-box nevera *f*, *Rpl* heladera *f*

'ice-break-er *ship* rompehielos *m inv*

'ice cream helado *m*

'ice cream par-lor heladería *f*

'ice cube cubito *m* de hielo

iced [aɪst] *adj drink* helado

iced 'cof-fee café *m* helado

'ice hock-ey hockey *m* sobre hielo

'ice rink pista *f* de hielo

'ice skate patín *m* de cuchilla

'ice skat-ing patinaje *m* sobre hielo

i-ci-cle ['aɪsɪkl] carámbano *m*

i-con ['aɪkɑːn] *also* COMPUT icono *m*

icy ['aɪsɪ] *adj road* con hielo; *surface* helado; *welcome* frío

ID [aɪ'diː] *abbr* (= **identity**) documentación *f*; **have you got any ID on you?** ¿lleva algún tipo de documentación?

idea [aɪ'diːə] idea *f*; **good idea!** ¡buena idea!; **I have no idea** no tengo ni idea; **it's not a good idea to ...** no es buena idea ...

i-deal [aɪ'diːəl] *adj (perfect)* ideal

i-deal-is-tic [aɪdɪə'lɪstɪk] *adj* idealista

i-deal-ly [aɪ'diːəlɪ] *adv*: **ideally situated** en una posición ideal; **ideally, we would do it like this** lo ideal sería que lo hiciéramos así

i-den-ti-cal [aɪ'dentɪkl] *adj* idéntico; **identical twins** gemelos(-as) *mpl* (*fpl*) idénticos(-as)

i-den-ti-fi-ca-tion [aɪdentɪfɪ'keɪʃn] identificación *f*; *papers etc* documentación *f*

i-den-ti-fy [aɪ'dentɪfaɪ] *v/t (pret & pp identified)* identificar

i-den-ti-ty [aɪ'dentətɪ] identidad *f*; **identity card** carné *m* de identidad

i-de-o-log-i-cal [aɪdɪə'lɑːdʒɪkl] *adj* ideológico

i-de-ol-o-gy [aɪdɪ'ɑːlədʒɪ] ideología *f*

id-i-om ['ɪdɪəm] *(saying)* modismo *m*

id-i-o-mat-ic [ɪdɪə'mætɪk] *adj* natural natural

id-i-o-syn-cra-sy [ɪdɪə'sɪŋkrəsɪ] peculiaridad *f*, rareza *f*

id-i-ot ['ɪdɪət] idiota *m/f*, estúpido(-a) *m/f*

id-i-ot-ic [ɪdɪ'ɑːtɪk] *adj* idiota, estúpido

i-dle ['aɪdl] **1** *adj* **if only I wasn't working** desocupado; *(lazy)* vago; *threat* vano; *machinery* inactivo; **in an idle moment** en un momento libre **2** *v/i of engine* funcionar al ralentí

◆ **idle away** *v/t the time etc* pasar ociosamente

i-dol ['aɪdl] ídolo *m*

i-dol-ize ['aɪdəlaɪz] *v/t* idolatrar

i-dyl-lic [ɪ'dɪlɪk] *adj* idílico

if [ɪf] *conj* si; **if only I hadn't shouted at her** ojalá no le hubiera gritado

ig-nite [ɪg'naɪt] *v/t* inflamar

ig-ni-tion [ɪg'nɪʃn] *in car* encendido *m*; **ignition key** llave *m* de contacto

ig-no-rance ['ɪgnərəns] ignorancia *f*

ig-no-rant ['ɪgnərənt] *adj* ignorante; *(rude)* maleducado; **be ignorant of sth** desconocer *or* ignorar algo

ig-nore [ɪg'nɔːr] *v/t* ignorar; COMPUT omitir

ill [ɪl] *adj* enfermo; **fall ill, be taken ill** caer enfermo; **feel ill at ease** no sentirse a gusto, sentirse incómodo

il-le-gal [ɪ'liːgl] *adj* ilegal

il-le-gi-ble [ɪ'ledʒəbl] *adj* ilegible

il-le-git-i-mate [ɪlɪ'dʒɪtɪmət] *adj child* ilegítimo

ill-fat-ed [ɪl'feɪtɪd] *adj* infortunado

il-li-cit [ɪ'lɪsɪt] *adj* ilícito

il-lit-e-rate [ɪ'lɪtərət] *adj* analfabeto

ill-man-nered [ɪl'mænərd] *adj* maleducado

ill-na-tured [ɪl'neɪtʃərd] *adj* malhumorado

ill-ness ['ɪlnɪs] enfermedad *f*

il·log·i·cal [ɪ'lɑːdʒɪkl] adj ilógico

ill-tem·pered [ɪl'tempərd] adj malhumorado

ill'treat v/t maltratar

il·lu·mi·nate [ɪ'luːmɪneɪt] v/t building etc iluminar

il·lu·mi·nat·ing [ɪ'luːmɪneɪtɪŋ] adj remarks etc iluminador, esclarecedor

il·lu·sion [ɪ'luːʒn] ilusión f

il·lus·trate ['ɪləstreɪt] v/t ilustrar

il·lus·tra·tion [ɪlə'streɪʃn] ilustración f

il·lus·tra·tor [ɪlə'streɪtər] ilustrador(a) m(f)

ill 'will rencor m

im·age ['ɪmɪdʒ] imagen f; he's the image of his father es la viva imagen de su padre

'im·age-con·scious adj preocupado por la imagen

i·ma·gi·na·ble [ɪ'mædʒɪnəbl] adj imaginable; the biggest / smallest size imaginable la talla más grande / más pequeña que se pueda imaginar

i·ma·gi·na·ry [ɪ'mædʒɪnərɪ] adj imaginario

i·ma·gi·na·tion [ɪmædʒɪ'neɪʃn] imaginación f; it's all in your imagination son imaginaciones tuyas

i·ma·gi·na·tive [ɪ'mædʒɪnətɪv] adj imaginativo

i·ma·gine [ɪ'mædʒɪn] v/t imaginar, imaginarse; I can just imagine it me lo imagino; you're imagining things son imaginaciones tuyas

im·be·cile ['ɪmbəsiːl] imbécil m/f

IMF [aɪem'ef] abbr (= International Monetary Fund) FMI m (= Fondo m Monetario Internacional)

im·i·tate ['ɪmɪteɪt] v/t imitar

im·i·ta·tion [ɪmɪ'teɪʃn] imitación f; learn by imitation aprender imitando

im·mac·u·late [ɪ'mækjʊlət] adj inmaculado

im·ma·te·ri·al [ɪmə'tɪrɪəl] adj (not relevant) irrelevante

im·ma·ture [ɪmə'tʃʊər] adj inmaduro

im·me·di·ate [ɪ'miːdɪət] adj inmediato; the immediate family los familiares más cercanos; in the immediate neigh-

borhood en las inmediaciones

im·me·di·ate·ly [ɪ'miːdɪətlɪ] adv inmediatamente; immediately after the bank / church justo después del banco / la iglesia

im·mense [ɪ'mens] adj inmenso

im·merse [ɪ'mɜːrs] v/t sumergir; immerse o.s. in sumergirse en

im·mer·sion heat·er [ɪ'mɜːrʃn] calentador m de agua eléctrico

im·mi·grant ['ɪmɪgrənt] n inmigrante m/f

im·mi·grate ['ɪmɪgreɪt] v/i inmigrar

im·mi·gra·tion [ɪmɪ'greɪʃn] inmigración f; Immigration government department (Departamento m de) Inmigración f

im·mi·nent ['ɪmɪnənt] adj inminente

im·mo·bi·lize [ɪ'moʊbɪlaɪz] v/t factory paralizar; person, car inmovilizar

im·mo·bi·liz·er [ɪ'moʊbɪlaɪzər] on car inmovilizador m

im·mod·e·rate [ɪ'mɑːdərət] adj desmedido, exagerado

im·mor·al [ɪ'mɔːrəl] adj inmoral

im·mor·al·i·ty [ɪmɔː'rælɪtɪ] inmoralidad f

im·mor·tal [ɪ'mɔːrtl] adj inmortal

im·mor·tal·i·ty [ɪmɔːr'tælɪtɪ] inmortalidad f

im·mune [ɪ'mjuːn] adj to illness, infection inmune; from ruling, requirement con inmunidad

im'mune sys·tem MED sistema m inmunológico

im·mu·ni·ty [ɪ'mjuːnətɪ] inmunidad f; diplomatic immunity inmunidad f diplomática

im·pact ['ɪmpækt] n impacto m; the warning had no impact on him el aviso no le hizo cambiar lo más mínimo

im·pair [ɪm'per] v/t dañar

im·paired [ɪm'perd] adj: with impaired hearing / sight con problemas auditivos / visuales

im·par·tial [ɪm'pɑːrʃl] adj imparcial

im·pass·a·ble [ɪm'pæsəbl] adj road intransitable

im·passe ['ɪmpæs] in negotiations etc punto m muerto

im·pas·sioned [ɪm'pæʃnd] adj speech, plea apasionado

im·pas·sive [ɪm'pæsɪv] *adj* impasible

im·pa·tience [ɪm'peɪʃəns] impaciencia *f*

im·pa·tient [ɪm'peɪʃənt] *adj* impaciente

im·pa·tient·ly [ɪm'peɪʃəntlɪ] *adv* impacientemente

im·peach[ɪm'piːtʃ] *v/t President* iniciar un proceso de destitución contra

im·pec·ca·ble [ɪm'pekəbl] *adj* impecable

im·pec·ca·bly [ɪm'pekəblɪ] *adv* impecablemente

im·pede [ɪm'piːd] *v/t* dificultar

im·ped·i·ment [ɪm'pedɪmənt] *in speech* defecto *m* del habla

im·pend·ing [ɪm'pendɪŋ] *adj* inminente

im·pen·e·tra·ble [ɪm'penɪtrəbl] *adj* impenetrable

im·per·a·tive [ɪm'perətɪv] **1** *adj* imprescindible **2** *n* GRAM imperativo *m*

im·per·cep·ti·ble [ɪmpər'septɪbl] *adj* imperceptible

im·per·fect[ɪm'pɜːrfekt] **1** *adj* imperfecto **2** *n* GRAM imperfecto *m*

im·pe·ri·al [ɪm'pɪrɪəl] *adj* imperial

im·per·son·al [ɪm'pɜːrsənl] *adj* impersonal

im·per·so·nate[ɪm'pɜːrsəneɪt] *v/t as a joke* imitar; *illegally* hacerse pasar por

im·per·ti·nence [ɪm'pɜːrtɪnəns] impertinencia *f*

im·per·ti·nent [ɪm'pɜːrtɪnənt] *adj* impertinente

im·per·tur·ba·ble [ɪmpər'tɜːrbəbl] *adj* imperturbable

im·per·vi·ous [ɪm'pɜːrvɪəs] *adj*: *impervious to* inmune a

im·pe·tu·ous [ɪm'petʃʊəs] *adj* impetuoso

im·pe·tus ['ɪmpɪtəs] *of campaign etc* ímpetu *m*

im·ple·ment **1** *n* ['ɪmplɪmənt] utensilio *m* **2** *v/t* ['ɪmplɪment] *measures etc* poner en práctica

im·pli·cate ['ɪmplɪkeɪt] *v/t* implicar; *implicate s.o. in sth* implicar a alguien en algo

im·pli·ca·tion [ɪmplɪ'keɪʃn] consecuencia *f*; *the implication is that ...* implica que ...

im·pli·cit[ɪm'plɪsɪt] *adj* implícito; *trust* inquebrantable

im·plore [ɪm'plɔːr] *v/t* implorar

im·ply [ɪm'plaɪ] *v/i* (*pret & pp* **implied**) implicar; *are you implying I lied?* ¿insinúas que mentí?

im·po·lite [ɪmpə'laɪt] *adj* maleducado

im·port ['ɪmpɔːrt] **1** *n* importación *f* **2** *v/t* importar

im·por·tance [ɪm'pɔːrtəns] importancia *f*

im·por·tant [ɪm'pɔːrtənt] *adj* importante

im·por·ter [ɪm'pɔːrtər] importador(a) *m(f)*

im·pose[ɪm'poʊz] *v/t tax* imponer; *impose o.s. on s.o.* molestar a alguien

im·pos·ing [ɪm'poʊzɪŋ] *adj* imponente

im·pos·si·bil·i·ty [ɪmpɑːsɪ'bɪlɪtɪ] imposibilidad *f*

im·pos·si·ble [ɪm'pɑːsɪbəl] *adj* imposible

im·pos·tor [ɪm'pɑːstər] impostor(a) *m(f)*

im·po·tence ['ɪmpətəns] impotencia *f*

im·po·tent ['ɪmpətənt] *adj* impotente

im·pov·e·rished [ɪm'pɑːvərɪʃt] *adj* empobrecido

im·prac·ti·cal [ɪm'præktɪkəl] *adj* poco práctico

im·press[ɪm'pres] *v/t* impresionar; *be impressed by s.o./sth* quedar impresionado por alguien / algo; *I'm not impressed* no me parece nada extraordinario

im·pres·sion[ɪm'preʃn] impresión *f*; (*impersonation*) imitación *f*; *make a good / bad impression on s.o.* causar a alguien buena / mala impresión; *I get the impression that ...* me da la impresión de que ...

im·pres·sion·a·ble [ɪm'preʃənəbl] *adj* influenciable

im·pres·sive [ɪm'presɪv] *adj* impresionante

im·print ['ɪmprɪnt] *n of credit card* impresión *f*

im·pris·on [ɪm'prɪzn] *v/t* encarcelar

im·pris·on·ment [ɪm'prɪznmənt] encarcelamiento *m*

im·prob·a·ble [ɪm'prɑːbəbl] *adj* improbable

im·prop·er [ɪm'prɑːpər] *adj behavior* incorrecto

im·prove [ɪm'pruːv] *v/t & v/i* mejorar

im·prove·ment [ɪm'pruːvmənt] mejora *f*,

mejoría f

im·pro·vise ['ɪmprəvaɪz] v/i improvisar

im·pu·dent ['ɪmpjʊdənt] adj insolente, desvergonzado

im·pulse ['ɪmpʌls] impulso m; **do sth on an impulse** hacer algo impulsivamente

'impulse buy compra f impulsiva

im·pul·sive [ɪm'pʌlsɪv] adj impulsivo

im·pu·ni·ty [ɪm'pju:nətɪ] impunidad f; **with impunity** impunemente

im·pure [ɪm'pjʊr] adj impuro

in [ɪn] 1 prep ◇ en; **in Washington / Milan** en Washington / Milán; **in the street** en la calle; **in the box** en la caja; **put it in your pocket** métetelon el bolsillo; **wounded in the leg / arm** herido en la pierna / el brazo

◇ **in 1999** en 1999; **in two hours** from now dentro de dos horas

◇ (over period of) en; **in the morning** por la mañana; **in the summer** en verano; **in August** en agosto

◇ **in English / Spanish** en inglés / español; **in a loud voice** en voz alta; **in his style** en su estilo; **in yellow** de amarillo

◇ **in crossing the road** (while) al cruzar la calle; **in agreeing to this** (by virtue of) al expresar acuerdo con esto

◇ **in his novel** en su novela; **in Faulkner** en Faulkner

◇ **three in all** tres en total; **one in ten** uno de cada diez 2 adv: **is he in?** at home ¿está en casa?; **is the express in yet?** ¿ha llegado ya el expreso?; **when the diskette is in** cuando el disquete está dentro; **in here** aquí dentro 3 adj (fashionable, popular) de moda; **be in** estar de moda

in·a·bil·i·ty [ɪnə'bɪlɪtɪ] incapacidad f

in·ac·ces·si·ble [ɪnək'sesɪbl] adj inaccesible

in·ac·cu·rate [ɪn'ækjʊrət] adj inexacto

in·ac·tive [ɪn'æktɪv] adj inactivo

in·ad·e·quate [ɪn'ædɪkwət] adj insuficiente

in·ad·vis·a·ble [ɪnəd'vaɪzəbl] adj poco aconsejable

in·an·i·mate [ɪn'ænɪmət] adj inanimado

in·ap·pro·pri·ate [ɪnə'prəʊprɪət] adj re-

mark, thing to do inadecuado, improcedente; choice inapropiado

in·ar·tic·u·late [ɪnɑːr'tɪkjʊlət] adj: **be inarticulate** expresarse mal

in·au·di·ble [ɪn'ɔːdəbl] adj inaudible

in·au·gu·ral [ɪ'nɔːgjʊrəl] adj speech inaugural

in·au·gu·rate [ɪ'nɔːgjʊreɪt] v/t inaugurar

in·born ['ɪnbɔːrn] adj innato

in·breed·ing ['ɪnbriːdɪŋ] endogamia f

inc. abbr (= **incorporated**) S.A. (= sociedad f anónima)

incalculable [ɪn'kælkjʊləbl] adj damage incalculable

in·ca·pa·ble [ɪn'keɪpəbl] adj incapaz; **be incapable of doing sth** ser incapaz de hacer algo

in·cen·di·a·ry de'vice [ɪn'sendɪrɪ] artefacto m incendiario

in·cense[1] ['ɪnsens] n incienso m

in·cense[2] [ɪn'sens] v/t encolerizar

in·cen·tive [ɪn'sentɪv] incentivo m

in·ces·sant [ɪn'sesnt] adj incesante

in·ces·sant·ly [ɪn'sesntlɪ] adv incesantemente

in·cest ['ɪnsest] incesto m

inch [ɪntʃ] n pulgada f

in·ci·dent ['ɪnsɪdənt] incidente m

in·ci·den·tal [ɪnsɪ'dentl] adj sin importancia; **incidental expenses** gastos mpl varios

in·ci·den·tal·ly [ɪnsɪ'dentlɪ] adv a propósito

in·cin·e·ra·tor [ɪn'sɪnəreɪtər] incinerador m

in·ci·sion [ɪn'sɪʒn] incisión f

in·ci·sive [ɪn'saɪsɪv] adj incisivo

in·cite [ɪn'saɪt] v/t incitar; **incite s.o. to do sth** incitar a alguien a que haga algo

in·clem·ent [ɪn'klemənt] adj inclemente

in·cli·na·tion [ɪnklɪ'neɪʃn] (tendency, liking) inclinación f

in·cline [ɪn'klaɪn] v/t: **be inclined to do sth** tender a hacer algo

in·close, in·clos·ure → **enclose, enclosure**

in·clude [ɪn'kluːd] v/t incluir

in·clud·ing [ɪn'kluːdɪŋ] prep incluyendo

in·clu·sive [ɪn'kluːsɪv] 1 adj price total,

global **2** *prep*: *inclusive of* incluyendo, incluido **3** *adv*: *from Monday to Thursday inclusive* de lunes al jueves, ambos inclusive; *it costs $1000 inclusive* cuesta 1.000 dólares todo incluido

in·co·her·ent *adj* incoherente

in·come ['ɪnkəm] ingresos *mpl*

'in·come tax impuesto *m* sobre la renta

in·com·ing ['ɪnkʌmɪŋ] *adj* *tide* que sube; *incoming flight* vuelo *f* que llega; *incoming mail* correo *m* recibido; *incoming calls* llamadas *fpl* recibidas

in·com·pa·ra·ble [ɪn'kɑːmpərəbl] *adj* incomparable

in·com·pat·i·bil·i·ty [ɪnkəmpætɪ'bɪlɪtɪ] incompatibilidad *f*

in·com·pat·i·ble [ɪnkəm'pætɪbl] *adj* incompatible

in·com·pe·tence [ɪn'kɑːmpɪtəns] incompetencia *f*

in·com·pe·tent [ɪn'kɑːmpɪtənt] *adj* incompetente

in·com·plete [ɪnkəm'pliːt] *adj* incompleto

in·com·pre·hen·si·ble [ɪnkɑːmprɪ'hensɪbl] *adj* incomprensible

in·con·cei·va·ble [ɪnkən'siːvəbl] *adj* inconcebible

in·con·clu·sive [ɪnkən'kluːsɪv] *adj* no concluyente

in·con·gru·ous [ɪn'kɑːŋgruəs] *adj* incongruente

in·con·sid·er·ate [ɪnkən'sɪdərət] *adj* desconsiderado

in·con·sis·tent [ɪnkən'sɪstənt] *adj* *argument, behavior* incoherente, inconsecuente; *player* irregular; *be inconsistent with sth* no ser consecuente con algo

in·con·so·la·ble [ɪnkən'souləbl] *adj* inconsolable, desconsolado

in·con·spic·u·ous [ɪnkən'spɪkjuəs] *adj* discreto

in·con·ve·ni·ence [ɪnkən'viːnɪəns] *n* inconveniencia *f*

in·con·ve·ni·ent [ɪnkən'viːnɪənt] *adj* inconveniente, inoportuno

in·cor·po·rate [ɪn'kɔːrpəreɪt] *v/t* incorporar

in·cor·po·rat·ed [ɪn'kɔːrpəreɪtɪd] *adj* COM: *ABC Incorporated* ABC, sociedad *f* anónima

in·cor·rect [ɪnkə'rekt] *adj* incorrecto

in·cor·rect·ly [ɪnkə'rektlɪ] *adv* incorrectamente

in·cor·ri·gi·ble [ɪn'kɑːrɪdʒəbl] *adj* incorregible

in·crease **1** *v/t & v/i* [ɪn'kriːs] aumentar **2** *n* ['ɪnkriːs] aumento *m*

in·creas·ing [ɪn'kriːsɪŋ] *adj* creciente

in·creas·ing·ly [ɪn'kriːsɪŋlɪ] *adv* cada vez más; *we're getting increasingly concerned* cada vez estamos más preocupados

in·cred·i·ble [ɪn'kredɪbl] *adj* (*amazing, very good*) increíble

in·crim·i·nate [ɪn'krɪmɪneɪt] *v/t* incriminar; *incriminate o.s.* incriminarse

in·cu·ba·tor ['ɪŋkjubeɪtər] incubadora *f*

in·cur [ɪn'kɜːr] *v/t* (*pret & pp* *incurred*) *costs* incurrir en; *debts* contraer; *s.o.'s anger* provocar

in·cu·ra·ble [ɪn'kjurəbl] *adj* incurable

in·debt·ed [ɪn'detɪd] *adj*: *be indebted to s.o.* estar en deuda con alguien

in·de·cent [ɪn'diːsnt] *adj* indecente

in·de·ci·sive [ɪndɪ'saɪsɪv] *adj* indeciso

in·de·ci·sive·ness [ɪndɪ'saɪsɪvnɪs] indecisión *f*

in·deed [ɪn'diːd] *adv* (*in fact*) ciertamente, efectivamente; *yes, agreeing* ciertamente, en efecto; *very much indeed* muchísimo; *thank you very much indeed* muchísimas gracias

in·de·fi·na·ble [ɪndɪ'faɪnəbl] *adj* indefinible

in·def·i·nite [ɪn'defɪnɪt] *adj* indefinido; *indefinite article* GRAM artículo *m* indefinido

in·def·i·nite·ly [ɪn'defɪnɪtlɪ] *adv* indefinidamente

in·del·i·cate [ɪn'delɪkət] *adj* poco delicado

in·dent **1** *n* ['ɪndent] *in text* sangrado *m* **2** *v/t* [ɪn'dent] *line* sangrar

in·de·pen·dence [ɪndɪ'pendəns] independencia *f*

In·de'pen·dence Day Día *m* de la Independencia

in·de·pen·dent [ɪndɪˈpendənt] *adj* independiente

in·de·pen·dent·ly [ɪndɪˈpendəntlɪ] *adv* **deal with** por separado; **independently of** al margen de

in·de·scri·ba·ble [ɪndɪˈskraɪbəbl] *adj* indescriptible

in·de·scrib·a·bly [ɪndɪˈskraɪbəblɪ] *adv* indescriptiblemente

in·de·struc·ti·ble [ɪndɪˈstrʌktəbl] *adj* indestructible

in·de·ter·mi·nate [ɪndɪˈtɜːrmɪnət] *adj* indeterminado

in·dex [ˈɪndeks] *n for book* índice *m*

'in·dex card ficha *f*

'in·dex fin·ger (dedo *m*) índice *m*

in·dex-'linked *adj* indexado

In·di·a [ˈɪndɪə] (la) India

In·di·an [ˈɪndɪən] **1** *adj* indio **2** *n from India* indio(-a) *m(f)*, hindú *m/f*; *American* indio(-a) *m(f)*

In·di·an 'sum·mer *in northern hemisphere* veranillo *m* de San Martín; *in southern hemisphere* veranillo *m* de San Juan

in·di·cate [ˈɪndɪkeɪt] **1** *v/t* indicar **2** *v/i when driving* poner el intermitente

in·di·ca·tion [ɪndɪˈkeɪʃn] indicio *m*

in·di·ca·tor [ˈɪndɪkeɪtər] *on car* intermitente *m*

in·dict [ɪnˈdaɪt] *v/t* acusar

in·dif·fer·ence [ɪnˈdɪfrəns] indiferencia *f*

in·dif·fer·ent [ɪnˈdɪfrənt] *adj* indiferente; *(mediocre)* mediocre; **are you totally indifferent to the way I feel?** ¿no te importa lo más mínimo lo que sienta yo?

in·di·ges·ti·ble [ɪndɪˈdʒestɪbl] *adj* indigesto

in·di·ges·tion [ɪndɪˈdʒestʃn] indigestión *f*

in·dig·nant [ɪnˈdɪgnənt] *adj* indignado

in·dig·na·tion [ɪndɪgˈneɪʃn] indignación *f*

in·di·rect [ɪndɪˈrekt] *adj* indirecto

in·di·rect·ly [ɪndɪˈrektlɪ] *adv* indirectamente

in·dis·creet [ɪndɪˈskriːt] *adj* indiscreto

in·dis·cre·tion [ɪndɪˈskreʃn] indiscreción *f*

in·dis·crim·i·nate [ɪndɪˈskrɪmɪnət] *adj* indiscriminado

in·dis·pen·sa·ble [ɪndɪˈspensəbl] *adj* indispensable, imprescindible

in·dis·posed [ɪndɪˈspəʊzd] *adj* (*not well*) indispuesto; **be indisposed** hallarse indispuesto

in·dis·pu·ta·ble [ɪndɪˈspjuːtəbl] *adj* indiscutible

in·dis·pu·ta·bly [ɪndɪˈspjuːtəblɪ] *adv* indiscutiblemente

in·dis·tinct [ɪndɪˈstɪŋkt] *adj* indistinto, impreciso

in·dis·tin·guish·a·ble [ɪndɪˈstɪŋwɪʃəbl] *adj* indistinguible

in·di·vid·u·al [ɪndɪˈvɪdʒʊəl] **1** *n* individuo *m* **2** *adj* individual

in·di·vid·u·a·list [ɪndɪˈvɪdʒʊəlɪst] *adj* individualista

in·di·vid·u·al·ly [ɪndɪˈvɪdʒʊəlɪ] *adv* individualmente

in·di·vis·i·ble [ɪndɪˈvɪzɪbl] *adj* indivisible

in·doc·tri·nate [ɪnˈdɑːktrɪneɪt] *v/t* adoctrinar

in·do·lence [ˈɪndələns] indolencia *f*

in·do·lent [ˈɪndələnt] *adj* indolente

In·do·ne·sia [ɪndəˈniːʒə] Indonesia

In·do·ne·sian [ɪndəˈniːʒən] **1** *adj* indonesio **2** *n person* indonesio(-a) *m(f)*

in·door [ˈɪndɔːr] *adj activities* de interior; *sport* de pista cubierta; *arena* cubierto; *athletics* en pista cubierta

in·doors [ɪnˈdɔːrz] *adv* dentro

in·dorse → **endorse**

in·dulge [ɪnˈdʌldʒ] **1** *v/t o.s., one's tastes* satisfacer **2** *v/i*: **indulge in a pleasure** entregarse a un placer; **if I might indulge in a little joke** si se me permite contar un chiste

in·dul·gent [ɪnˈdʌldʒənt] *adj* indulgente

in·dus·tri·al [ɪnˈdʌstrɪəl] *adj* industrial; **industrial action** acciones *fpl* reivindicativas

in·dus·tri·al dis'pute conflicto *m* laboral

in·dus·tri·al·ist [ɪnˈdʌstrɪəlɪst] industrial *m/f*

in·dus·tri·al·ize [ɪnˈdʌstrɪəlaɪz] **1** *v/t* industrializar **2** *v/i* industrializarse

in·dus·tri·al 'waste residuos *mpl* industriales

in·dus·tri·ous [ɪnˈdʌstrɪəs] *adj* trabajador, aplicado

in·dus·try ['ɪndəstrɪ] industria f

in·ef·fec·tive [ɪnɪ'fektɪv] adj ineficaz

in·ef·fec·tu·al [ɪnɪ'fektʃʊəl] adj person inepto, incapaz

in·ef·fi·cient [ɪnɪ'fɪʃənt] adj ineficiente

in·el·i·gi·ble[ɪn'elɪdʒɪbl] adj: **be ineligible** no reunir las condiciones

in·ept [ɪ'nept] adj inepto

in·e·qual·i·ty [ɪnɪ'kwɑːlɪtɪ] desigualdad f

in·es·ca·pa·ble[ɪnɪ'skeɪpəbl] adj inevitable

in·es·ti·ma·ble [ɪn'estɪməbl] adj inestimable

in·ev·i·ta·ble [ɪn'evɪtəbl] adj inevitable

in·ev·i·ta·bly [ɪn'evɪtəblɪ] adv inevitablemente

in·ex·cu·sa·ble [ɪnɪk'skjuːzəbl] adj inexcusable, injustificable

in·ex·haus·ti·ble [ɪnɪg'zɒːstəbl] adj supply inagotable

in·ex·pen·sive [ɪnɪk'spensɪv] adj barato, económico

in·ex·pe·ri·enced [ɪnɪk'spɪrɪənst] adj inexperto

in·ex·plic·a·ble [ɪnɪk'splɪkəbl] adj inexplicable

in·ex·pres·si·ble [ɪnɪk'spresɪbl] adj joy indescriptible

in·fal·li·ble [ɪn'fælɪbl] adj infalible

in·fa·mous ['ɪnfəməs] adj infame

in·fan·cy ['ɪnfənsɪ] infancia f

in·fant ['ɪnfənt] bebé m

in·fan·tile ['ɪnfəntaɪl] adj pej infantil, pueril

in·fan·try ['ɪnfəntrɪ] infantería f

in·fan·try 'sol·dier soldado m/f de infantería, infante m/f

'in·fant school colegio m de párvulos

in·fat·u·at·ed [ɪn'fæʃʊeɪtɪd] adj: **be infatuated with s.o.** estar encaprichado de alguien

in·fect [ɪn'fekt] v/t infectar; **he infected everyone with his cold** contagió el resfriado a todo el mundo; **become infected** of wound infectarse; of person contagiarse

in·fec·tion [ɪn'fekʃn] infección f

in·fec·tious [ɪn'fekʃəs] adj disease infeccioso; laughter contagioso

in·fer [ɪn'fɜːr] v/t (pret & pp **inferred**) inferir, deducir (**from** de)

in·fe·ri·or [ɪn'fɪrɪər] adj inferior (**to** a)

in·fe·ri·or·i·ty [ɪnfɪrɪ'ɑːrətɪ] in quality inferioridad f

in·fe·ri·or·i·ty com·plex complejo m de inferioridad

in·fer·tile [ɪn'fɜːrtl] adj woman, plant estéril; soil estéril, yermo

in·fer·til·i·ty [ɪnfər'tɪlɪtɪ] esterilidad f

in·fi·del·i·ty [ɪnfɪ'delɪtɪ] infidelidad f

in·fil·trate ['ɪnfɪltreɪt] v/t infiltrarse en

in·fi·nite ['ɪnfɪnət] adj infinito

in·fin·i·tive [ɪn'fɪnətɪv] infinitivo m

in·fin·i·ty [ɪn'fɪnətɪ] infinidad f

in·firm [ɪn'fɜːrm] adj enfermo, achacoso

in·fir·ma·ry [ɪn'fɜːrmərɪ] enfermería f

in·fir·mi·ty [ɪn'fɜːrmətɪ] debilidad f

in·flame [ɪn'fleɪm] v/t despertar

in·flam·ma·ble [ɪn'flæməbl] adj inflamable

in·flam·ma·tion [ɪnflə'meɪʃn] MED inflamación f

in·flat·a·ble[ɪn'fleɪtəbl] adj dinghy hinchable, inflable

in·flate[ɪn'fleɪt] v/t tire, dinghy hinchar, inflar; economy inflar

in·fla·tion [ɪn'fleɪʃən] inflación f

in·fla·tion·a·ry[ɪn'fleɪʃənərɪ] adj inflacionario, inflacionista

in·flec·tion [ɪn'flekʃn] inflexión f

in·flex·i·ble [ɪn'fleksɪbl] adj inflexible

in·flict [ɪn'flɪkt] v/t infligir; **inflict sth on s.o.** infligir algo a alguien

'in-flight adj: **in-flight entertainment** entretenimiento m durante el vuelo

in·flu·ence ['ɪnflʊəns] **1** n influencia f; **be a good / bad influence on s.o.** tener una buena / mala influencia en alguien **2** v/t influir en, influenciar

in·flu·en·tial [ɪnflʊ'enʃl] adj influyente

in·flu·en·za [ɪnflʊ'enzə] gripe f

in·form [ɪn'fɔːrm] **1** v/t informar; **inform s.o. about sth** informar a alguien de algo; **please keep me informed** por favor manténme informado **2** v/i: **inform on s.o.** delatar a alguien

in·for·mal [ɪn'fɔːrməl] adj informal

in·for·mal·i·ty [ɪnfɔːr'mælɪtɪ] informalidad f

in·form·ant [ɪn'fɔːrmənt] confidente m/f

in·for·ma·tion [ɪnfər'meɪʃn] información f; *a piece of information* una información

in·for·ma·tion 'sci·ence informática f

in·for·ma·tion 'sci·en·tist informático(-a) m(f)

in·for·ma·tion tech'nol·o·gy tecnología fpl de la información

in·for·ma·tive [ɪn'fɔːrmətɪv] adj informativo; *you're not being very informative* no estás dando mucha información

in·form·er [ɪn'fɔːrmər] confidente m/f

in·fra·red [ɪnfrə'red] adj infrarrojo

in·fra·struc·ture ['ɪnfrəstrʌktʃər] infraestructura f

in·fre·quent [ɪn'friːkwənt] adj poco frecuente

in·fu·ri·ate [ɪn'fjʊrɪeɪt] v/t enfurecer, exasperar

in·fu·ri·at·ing [ɪn'fjʊrɪeɪtɪŋ] adj exasperante

in·fuse [ɪn'fjuːz] v/i of tea infundir

in·fu·sion [ɪn'fjuːʒn] (herb tea) infusión f

in·ge·ni·ous [ɪn'dʒiːnɪəs] adj ingenioso

in·ge·nu·i·ty [ɪndʒɪ'nuːətɪ] lo ingenioso

in·got ['ɪŋgət] lingote m

in·gra·ti·ate [ɪn'greɪʃɪeɪt] v/t: *ingratiate o.s. with s.o.* congraciarse con alguien

in·grat·i·tude [ɪn'grætɪtuːd] ingratitud f

in·gre·di·ent [ɪn'griːdɪənt] also fig ingrediente m

in·hab·it [ɪn'hæbɪt] v/t habitar

in·hab·it·a·ble [ɪn'hæbɪtəbl] adj habitable

in·hab·i·tant [ɪn'hæbɪtənt] habitante m/f

in·hale [ɪn'heɪl] 1 v/t inhalar 2 v/i when smoking tragarse el humo

in·ha·ler [ɪn'heɪlər] inhalador m

in·her·it [ɪn'herɪt] v/t heredar

in·her·i·tance [ɪn'herɪtəns] herencia f

in·hib·it [ɪn'hɪbɪt] v/t growth impedir; conversation inhibir, cohibir

in·hib·it·ed [ɪn'hɪbɪtɪd] adj inhibido, cohibido

in·hi·bi·tion [ɪnhɪ'bɪʃn] inhibición f

in·hos·pi·ta·ble [ɪnhɑː'spɪtəbl] adj person inhospitalario; city, climate inhóspito

'in-house 1 adj facilities en el lugar de trabajo; *in-house team* equipo m en plantilla 2 adv work en la empresa

in·hu·man [ɪn'hjuːmən] adj inhumano

i·ni·tial [ɪ'nɪʃl] 1 adj inicial 2 n inicial f 3 v/t (write initials on) poner las iniciales en

i·ni·tial·ly [ɪ'nɪʃlɪ] adv inicialmente, al principio

i·ni·ti·ate [ɪ'nɪʃɪeɪt] v/t iniciar

i·ni·ti·a·tion [ɪnɪʃɪ'eɪʃn] iniciación f, inicio m

i·ni·tia·tive [ɪ'nɪʃətɪv] iniciativa f; *do sth on one's own initiative* hacer algo por iniciativa propia

in·ject [ɪn'dʒekt] v/t drug, fuel, capital inyectar

in·jec·tion [ɪn'dʒekʃn] of drug, fuel, capital inyección f

'in-joke: *it's an in-joke* es un chiste que entendemos nosotros

in·jure ['ɪndʒər] v/t lesionar; *he injured his leg* se lesionó la pierna

in·jured ['ɪndʒərd] 1 adj leg lesionado; feelings herido 2 npl: *the injured* los heridos

in·ju·ry ['ɪndʒərɪ] lesión f; wound herida f

'in·ju·ry time SP tiempo m de descuento

in·jus·tice [ɪn'dʒʌstɪs] injusticia f

ink [ɪŋk] tinta f

'ink-jet ('prin·ter) impresora f de chorro de tinta

in·land ['ɪnlənd] adj interior; mail nacional

in-laws ['ɪnlɔːz] npl familia f política

in·lay ['ɪnleɪ] n incrustación f

in·let ['ɪnlet] of sea ensenada f; in machine entrada f

in·mate ['ɪnmeɪt] of prison recluso(-a) m(f); of mental hospital paciente m/f

inn [ɪn] posada f, mesón m

in·nate [ɪ'neɪt] adj innato

in·ner ['ɪnər] adj interior; *the inner ear* el oído interno

in·ner 'cit·y barrios degradados del centro de la ciudad; *inner city decay* degradación m del centro de la ciudad

'in·ner·most adj feelings más íntimo; recess más recóndito

in·ner 'tube cámara *f* (de aire)
in·no·cence ['ɪnəsəns] inocencia *f*
in·no·cent ['ɪnəsənt] *adj* inocente
in·no·cu·ous [ɪ'nɑːkjuəs] *adj* inocuo
in·no·va·tion [ɪnə'veɪʃn] innovación *f*
in·no·va·tive [ɪnə'veɪtɪv] *adj* innovador
in·no·va·tor ['ɪnəveɪtər] innovador(a) *m(f)*
in·nu·me·ra·ble [ɪ'nuːmərəbl] *adj* innumerable
i·noc·u·late [ɪ'nɑːkjuleɪt] *v/t* inocular
i·noc·u·la·tion [ɪ'nɑːkju'leɪʃn] inoculación *f*
in·of·fen·sive [ɪnə'fensɪv] *adj* inofensivo
in·or·gan·ic [ɪnɔːr'gænɪk] *adj* inorgánico
in·pa·tient paciente *m/f* interno(-a)
in·put ['ɪnput] **1** *n into project etc* contribución *f*, aportación *f*; COMPUT entrada *f* **2** *v/t* (*pret & pp* **inputted** *or* **input**) *into project* contribuir, aportar; COMPUT introducir
in·quest ['ɪnkwest] investigación *f* (**into** sobre)
in·quire [ɪn'kwaɪr] *v/i* preguntar; **inquire into sth** investigar algo
in·quir·y [ɪn'kwaɪrɪ] consulta *f*, pregunta *f*; *into rail crash etc* investigación *f*
in·quis·i·tive [ɪn'kwɪzətɪv] *adj* curioso, inquisitivo
in·sane [ɪn'seɪn] *adj person* loco, demente; *idea* descabellado
in·san·i·ta·ry [ɪn'sænɪterɪ] *adj* antihigiénico
in·san·i·ty [ɪn'sænɪtɪ] locura *f*, demencia *f*
in·sa·tia·ble [ɪn'seɪʃəbl] *adj* insaciable
in·scrip·tion [ɪn'skrɪpʃn] inscripción *f*
in·scru·ta·ble [ɪn'skruːtəbl] *adj* inescrutable
in·sect ['ɪnsekt] insecto *m*
in·sec·ti·cide [ɪn'sektɪsaɪd] insecticida *f*
'in·sect re·pel·lent repelente *m* contra insectos
in·se·cure [ɪnsɪ'kjur] *adj* inseguro
in·se·cu·ri·ty [ɪnsɪ'kjurɪtɪ] inseguridad *f*
in·sen·si·tive [ɪn'sensɪtɪv] *adj* insensible
in·sen·si·tiv·i·ty [ɪnsensɪ'tɪvɪtɪ] insensibilidad *f*
in·sep·a·ra·ble [ɪn'seprəbl] *adj* inseparable

in·sert 1 *n* ['ɪnsɜːrt] *in magazine etc* encarte *m* **2** *v/t* [ɪn'sɜːrt] *coin, finger, diskette* introducir, meter; *extra text* insertar; **insert sth into sth** introducir *or* meter algo en algo
in·ser·tion [ɪn'sɜːrʃn] *act* introducción *f*, inserción *f*; *of text* inserción *f*
in·side [ɪn'saɪd] **1** *n of house, box* interior *m*; **somebody on the inside** alguien de dentro; **inside out** del revés; **turn sth inside out** dar la vuelta a algo (*de dentro a fuera*); **know sth inside out** saberse algo al dedillo **2** *prep* dentro de; **inside the house** dentro de la casa; **inside of 2 hours** dentro de 2 horas **3** *adv stay, remain* dentro; *go, carry* adentro; **we went inside** entramos **4** *adj*: **inside information** información *f* confidencial; **inside lane** SP calle *f* de dentro; *on road* carril *m* de la derecha; **inside pocket** bolsillo *m* interior
in·sid·er [ɪn'saɪdər] *persona con acceso a información confidencial*
in·sid·er 'deal·ing FIN uso *m* de información privilegiada
in·sides [ɪn'saɪdz] *npl* tripas *mpl*
in·sid·i·ous [ɪn'sɪdɪəs] *adj* insidioso
in·sight ['ɪnsaɪt]: **this film offers an insight into local customs** esta película permite hacerse una idea de las costumbres locales; **full of insight** muy perspicaz
in·sig·nif·i·cant [ɪnsɪg'nɪfɪkənt] *adj* insignificante
in·sin·cere [ɪnsɪn'sɪr] *adj* poco sincero, falso
in·sin·cer·i·ty [ɪnsɪn'serɪtɪ] falta *f* de sinceridad
in·sin·u·ate [ɪn'sɪnueɪt] *v/t* (*imply*) insinuar
in·sist [ɪn'sɪst] *v/i* insistir; **please keep it, I insist** por favor, insisto en que te lo quedes
♦ **insist on** *v/t* insistir en
in·sis·tent [ɪn'sɪstənt] *adj* insistente
in·so·lent ['ɪnsələnt] *adj* insolente
in·sol·u·ble [ɪn'sɑːljubl] *adj problem* irresoluble; *substance* insoluble
in·sol·vent [ɪn'sɑːlvənt] *adj* insolvente

in·som·ni·a [ɪn'sɑːmnɪə] insomnio *m*

in·spect [ɪn'spekt] *v/t* inspeccionar

in·spec·tion [ɪn'spekʃn] inspección *f*

in·spec·tor [ɪn'spektər] *in factory, of po-lice* inspector(a) *m(f)*; *on buses* revi-sor(a) *m(f)*

in·spi·ra·tion [ɪnspə'reɪʃn] inspiración *f*

in·spire [ɪn'spaɪr] *v/t respect etc* inspirar; *be inspired by s.o./sth* estar inspirado por alguien / algo

in·sta·bil·i·ty [ɪnstə'bɪlɪtɪ] *of character, economy* inestabilidad *f*

in·stall [ɪn'stɔːl] *v/t* instalar

in·stal·la·tion [ɪnstə'leɪʃn] instalación *f*; *military installation* instalación *f* militar

in·stall·ment *Br*, in·stall·ment [ɪn'stɔːl-mənt] *of story*, TV *drama etc* episodio *m*; *payment* plazo *m*

in·stall·ment plan compra *f* a plazos

in·stance ['ɪnstəns] *(example)* ejemplo *m*; *for instance* por ejemplo

in·stant ['ɪnstənt] 1 *adj* instantáneo 2 *n* instante *m*; *in an instant* en un instante

in·stan·ta·ne·ous [ɪnstən'teɪnɪəs] *adj* in-stantáneo

in·stant 'cof·fee café *m* instantáneo

in·stant·ly ['ɪnstəntlɪ] *adv* al instante

in·stead [ɪn'sted] *adv*: *I'll take that one instead* me llevaré mejor ese otro; *would you like coffee instead?* ¿prefe-riría mejor café?; *I'll have coffee ins-tead of tea* tomaré té en vez de café; *he went instead of me* fue en mi lugar

in·step ['ɪnstep] empeine *m*

in·stinct ['ɪnstɪŋkt] instinto *m*

in·stinc·tive [ɪn'stɪŋktɪv] *adj* instintivo

in·sti·tute ['ɪnstɪtuːt] 1 *n* instituto *m*; *for elderly* residencia *f* de ancianos; *for men-tally ill* psiquiátrico *m* 2 *v/t new law* esta-blecer; *inquiry* iniciar

in·sti·tu·tion [ɪnstɪ'tuːʃn] institución *f*; *(setting up)* iniciación *f*

in·struct [ɪn'strʌkt] *v/t (order)* dar ins-trucciones a; *(teach)* instruir; *instruct s.o. to do sth (order)* ordenar a alguien que haga algo

in·struc·tion [ɪn'strʌkʃn] instrucción *f*; *instructions for use* instrucciones *fpl* de uso

in'struc·tion man·u·al manual *m* de in-strucciones

in·struc·tive [ɪn'strʌktɪv] *adj* instructivo

in·struc·tor [ɪn'strʌktər] instructor(a) *m(f)*

in·stru·ment ['ɪnstrumənt] MUS, *tool* ins-trumento *m*

in·sub·or·di·nate [ɪnsə'bɔːrdɪnət] *adj* in-subordinado

in·suf·fi·cient [ɪnsə'fɪʃnt] *adj* insuficiente

in·su·late ['ɪnsəleɪt] *v/t also* ELEC aislar

in·su·la·tion [ɪnsə'leɪʃn] ELEC aislamiento *m*; *against cold* aislamiento *m* (térmico)

in·su·lin ['ɪnsəlɪn] insulina *f*

in·sult 1 *n* ['ɪnsʌlt] insulto *m* 2 *v/t* [ɪn'sʌlt] insultar

in·sur·ance [ɪn'ʃʊrəns] seguro *m*

in'sur·ance com·pa·ny compañía *f* de se-guros, aseguradora *f*

in'sur·ance pol·i·cy póliza *f* de seguros

in'sur·ance pre·mi·um prima *f* (del se-guro)

in·sure [ɪn'ʃʊr] *v/t* asegurar

in·sured [ɪn'ʃʊrd] 1 *adj* asegurado; *be in-sured* estar asegurado 2 *n*: *the insured* el asegurado, la asegurada

in·sur·moun·ta·ble [ɪnsər'maʊntəbl] *adj* insuperable

in·tact [ɪn'tækt] *adj (not damaged)* intac-to

in·take ['ɪnteɪk] *of college etc* remesa *f*; *we have an annual intake of 300 stu-dents* cada año admitimos a 300 alum-nos

in·te·grate ['ɪntɪgreɪt] *v/t* integrar (*into* en)

in·te·grat·ed 'cir·cuit [ɪntɪgreɪtɪd] circui-to *m* integrado

in·teg·ri·ty [ɪn'tegrətɪ] *(honesty)* integri-dad *f*; *a man of integrity* un hombre ín-tegro

in·tel·lect ['ɪntəlekt] intelecto *m*

in·tel·lec·tual [ɪntə'lektʃʊəl] 1 *adj* intelec-tual 2 *n* intelectual *m/f*

in·tel·li·gence [ɪn'telɪdʒəns] inteligencia *f*; *(information)* información *f* secreta

in'tel·li·gence of·fi·cer agente *m/f* del servicio de inteligencia

in'tel·li·gence ser·vice servicio *m* de inteligencia

in·tel·li·gent [ɪn'telɪdʒənt] *adj* inteligente

in·tel·li·gi·ble [ɪn'telɪdʒəbl] *adj* inteligible

in·tend [ɪn'tend] *v/i*: *intend to do sth* tener la intención de hacer algo; *that's not what I intended* esa no era mi intención

in·tense [ɪn'tens] *adj sensation, pleasure, heat, pressure* intenso; *personality* serio

in·ten·si·fy [ɪn'tensɪfaɪ] **1** *v/t* (*pret & pp* ***intensified***) *effect, pressure* intensificar **2** *v/i* (*pret & pp* ***intensified***) intensificarse

in·ten·si·ty [ɪn'tensətɪ] intensidad *f*

in·ten·sive [ɪn'tensɪv] *adj study, training, treatment* intensivo

in·ten·sive 'care (u·nit) MED (unidad *f* de) cuidados *mpl* intensivos

in·ten·sive 'course *of language study* curso *m* intensivo

in·tent [ɪn'tent] *adj*: *be intent on doing sth* (*determined to do*) estar decidido a hacer algo; (*concentrating on*) estar concentrado haciendo algo

in·ten·tion [ɪn'tenʃn] intención *f*; *I have no intention of ...* (*refuse to*) no tengo intención de ...

in·ten·tion·al [ɪn'tenʃənl] *adj* intencionado

in·ten·tion·al·ly [ɪn'tenʃnlɪ] *adv* a propósito, adrede

in·ter·ac·tion [ɪntər'ækʃn] interacción *f*

in·ter·ac·tive [ɪntər'æktɪv] *adj* interactivo

in·ter·cede [ɪntər'siːd] *v/i* interceder

in·ter·cept [ɪntər'sept] *v/t* interceptar

in·ter·change ['ɪntərtʃeɪndʒ] *n of highways* nudo *m* vial

in·ter·change·a·ble [ɪntər'tʃeɪndʒəbl] *adj* intercambiable

in·ter·com ['ɪntərkɑːm] *in office, ship* interfono *m*; *for front door* portero *m* automático

in·ter·course ['ɪntərkɔːrs] *sexual* coito *m*

in·ter·de·pend·ent [ɪntərdɪ'pendənt] *adj* interdependiente

in·ter·est ['ɪntrəst] **1** *n also* FIN interés *m*; *take an interest in sth* interesarse por algo **2** *v/t* interesar; *does that offer interest you?* ¿te interesa esa oferta?

in·ter·est·ed ['ɪntrəstɪd] *adj* interesado;

be interested in sth estar interesado en algo; *thanks, but I'm not interested* gracias, pero no me interesa

in·terest-free 'loan préstamo *m* sin intereses

in·terest·ing ['ɪntrəstɪŋ] *adj* interesante

'in·terest rate tipo *m* de interés

in·ter·face ['ɪntərfeɪs] **1** *n* interface *m*, interfaz *f* **2** *v/i* relacionarse

in·ter·fere [ɪntər'fɪr] *v/i* interferir, entrometerse

◆ **interfere with** *v/t* afectar a; *the lock had been interfered with* alguien había manipulado la cerradura

in·ter·fer·ence [ɪntər'fɪrəns] intromisión *f*; *on radio* interferencia *f*

in·te·ri·or [ɪn'tɪrɪər] **1** *adj* interior **2** *n* interior *m*; *Department of the Interior* Ministerio *m* del Interior

in·te·ri·or 'dec·o·ra·tor interiorista *m/f*, decorador(a) *m(f)* de interiores

in·te·ri·or de'sign interiorismo *m*

in·te·ri·or de'sign·er interiorista *m/f*

in·ter·lude ['ɪntərluːd] *at theater* entreacto *m*, intermedio *m*; *at concert* intermedio *m*; (*period*) intervalo

in·ter·mar·ry [ɪntər'mærɪ] *v/i* (*pret & pp* ***intermarried***) casarse (*con miembros de otra raza, religión o grupo*); *the two tribes intermarried* los dos tribus se casaron entre sí

in·ter·me·di·a·ry [ɪntər'miːdɪərɪ] *n* intermediario

in·ter·me·di·ate [ɪntər'miːdɪət] *adj* intermedio *m*

in·ter·mis·sion [ɪntər'mɪʃn] *in theater* entreacto *m*, intermedio *m*; *in movie theater* intermedio *m*, descanso *m*

in·tern [ɪn'tɜːrn] *v/t* recluir

in·ter·nal [ɪn'tɜːrnl] *adj* interno

in·ter·nal com'bus·tion en·gine motor *m* de combustión interna

in·ter·nal·ly [ɪn'tɜːrnəlɪ] *adv* internamente

In·ter·nal 'Rev·e·nue (Ser·vice) Hacienda *f*, *Span* Agencia *f* Tributaria

in·ter·na·tion·al [ɪntər'næʃnl] **1** *adj* internacional **2** *n match* partido *m* internacional; *player* internacional *m/f*

In·ter·na·tion·al Court of 'Jus·tice Tribunal *m* Internacional de Justicia

in·ter·na·tion·al·ly [ɪntər'næʃnəlɪ] *adv* internacionalmente

In·ter·na·tion·al 'Mon·e·tar·y Fund Fondo *m* Monetario Internacional

In·ter·net ['ɪntərnet] Internet *f*; *on the Internet* en Internet

in·ter·nist [ɪn'tɜːrnɪst] internista *m/f*

in·ter·pret [ɪn'tɜːrprɪt] *v/t* & *v/i* interpretar

in·ter·pre·ta·tion [ɪntɜːrprɪ'teɪʃn] interpretación *f*

in·ter·pret·er [ɪn'tɜːrprɪtər] intérprete *m/f*

in·ter·re·lat·ed [ɪntərrɪ'leɪtɪd] *adj facts* interrelacionado

in·ter·ro·gate [ɪn'terəgeɪt] *v/t* interrogar

in·ter·ro·ga·tion [ɪnterə'geɪʃn] interrogatorio *m*

in·ter·rog·a·tive [ɪntər'rɑːgətɪv] *n* GRAM (forma *f*) interrogativa *f*

in·ter·ro·ga·tor [ɪnterə'geɪtər] interrogador(a) *m(f)*

in·ter·rupt [ɪntər'ʌpt] **1** *v/t speaker* interrumpir **2** *v/i* interrumpir

in·ter·rup·tion [ɪntər'ʌpʃn] interrupción *f*

in·ter·sect [ɪntər'sekt] **1** *v/t* cruzar **2** *v/i* cruzarse

in·ter·sec·tion ['ɪntərsekʃn] *(crossroads)* intersección *f*

in·ter·state ['ɪntərsteɪt] *n* autopista *f* interestatal

in·ter·val ['ɪntərvl] intervalo *m*; *in theater* entreacto *m*, intermedio *m*; *at concert* intermedio *m*

in·ter·vene [ɪntər'viːn] *v/i of person, police etc* intervenir

in·ter·ven·tion [ɪntər'venʃn] intervención *f*

in·ter·view ['ɪntərvjuː] **1** *n* entrevista *f* **2** *v/t* entrevistar

in·ter·view·ee [ɪntərvjuː'iː] *on TV* entrevistado(-a) *m(f)*; *for job* candidato(-a) *m(f)*

in·ter·view·er ['ɪntərvjuːər] entrevistador(a) *m(f)*

in·trude [ɪn'truːd] *v/i* molestar

in·tes·tine [ɪn'testɪn] intestino *m*

in·ti·ma·cy ['ɪntɪməsɪ] *of friendship* intimidad *f*; *sexual* relaciones *fpl* íntimas

in·ti·mate ['ɪntɪmət] *adj* íntimo

in·tim·i·date [ɪn'tɪmɪdeɪt] *v/t* intimidar

in·tim·i·da·tion [ɪntɪmɪ'deɪʃn] intimidación *f*

in·to ['ɪntu] *prep* en; *he put it into his suitcase* lo puso en su maleta; *translate into English* traducir al inglés; *he's into classical music* F *(likes)* le gusta *or* Span le va mucho la música clásica; *he's into local politics* F *(is involved with)* está muy metido en el mundillo de la política local; *when you're into the job* cuando te hayas metido en el trabajo

in·tol·e·ra·ble [ɪn'tɑːlərəbl] *adj* intolerable

in·tol·e·rant [ɪn'tɑːlərənt] *adj* intolerante

in·tox·i·cat·ed [ɪn'tɑːksɪkeɪtɪd] *adj* ebrio, embriagado

in·tran·si·tive [ɪn'trænsɪtɪv] *adj* intransitivo

in·tra·ve·nous [ɪntrə'viːnəs] *adj* intravenoso

in·trep·id [ɪn'trepɪd] *adj* intrépido

in·tri·cate ['ɪntrɪkət] *adj* intrincado, complicado

in·trigue **1** *n* ['ɪntriːg] intriga **2** *v/t* [ɪn'triːg] intrigar; *I would be intrigued to know ...* tendría curiosidad por saber ...

in·trig·u·ing [ɪn'triːgɪŋ] *adj* intrigante

in·tro·duce [ɪntrə'duːs] *v/t* presentar; *new technique etc* introducir; *may I introduce ...?* permítame presentarle a ...; *he introduced me to his wife* me presentó a su esposa; *introduce s.o. to a new sport* iniciar a alguien en un deporte nuevo

in·tro·duc·tion [ɪntrə'dʌkʃn] *to person* presentación *f*; *to a new food, sport etc* iniciación *f*; *in book, of new techniques et* introducción *f*

in·tro·vert ['ɪntrəvɜːrt] *n* introvertido(-a) *m(f)*

in·trud·er [ɪn'truːdər] intruso(-a) *m(f)*

in·tru·sion [ɪn'truːʒn] intromisión *f*

in·tu·i·tion [ɪntuː'ɪʃn] intuición *f*

in·vade [ɪn'veɪd] v/t invadir
in·val·id¹ [ɪn'vælɪd] adj nulo
in·va·lid² ['ɪnvəlɪd] n MED minusváli-
do(-a) m(f)
in·val·i·date [ɪn'vælɪdeɪt] v/t claim, theory
invalidar
in·val·u·a·ble [ɪn'væljubl] adj help, contributor inestimable
in·var·i·a·bly [ɪn'veɪrɪəblɪ] adv (always)
invariablemente, siempre
in·va·sion [ɪn'veɪʒn] invasión f
in·vent [ɪn'vent] v/t inventar
in·ven·tion [ɪn'venʃn] action invención f;
thing invented invento m
in·ven·tive [ɪn'ventɪv] adj inventivo,
imaginativo
in·ven·tor [ɪn'ventər] inventor(-a) m(f)
in·ven·to·ry ['ɪnvəntɔːrɪ] inventario m
in·verse [ɪn'vɜːrs] adj order inverso
in·vert [ɪn'vɜːrt] v/t invertir
in·vert·ed 'com·mas [ɪn'vɜːrtɪd] npl
comillas fpl
in·ver·te·brate [ɪn'vɜːrtɪbrət] n invertebrado m
invest [ɪn'vest] 1 v/t invertir 2 v/i invertir
(in en)
in·ves·ti·gate [ɪn'vestɪgeɪt] v/t investigar
in·ves·ti·ga·tion [ɪnvestɪ'geɪʃn] investigación f
in·ves·ti·ga·tive 'jour·nal·ism [ɪn'vestɪ-
gətɪv] periodismo m de investigación
in·vest·ment [ɪn'vestmənt] inversión f
in'vest·ment bank banco m de inver-
siones
in·ves·tor [ɪn'vestər] inversor(a) m(f)
in·vig·or·at·ing [ɪn'vɪgəreɪtɪŋ] adj climate vigorizante
in·vin·ci·ble [ɪn'vɪnsəbl] adj invencible
in·vis·i·ble [ɪn'vɪzɪbl] adj invisible
in·vi·ta·tion [ɪnvɪ'teɪʃn] invitación f
in·vite [ɪn'vaɪt] v/t invitar; he invited me
out for a meal me invitó a comer
♦ invite in v/t: invite s.o. in invitar a alguien a que entre
in·voice ['ɪnvɔɪs] 1 n factura f 2 v/t customer enviar la factura a
in·vol·un·ta·ry [ɪn'vɑːləntərɪ] adj involuntario
in·volve [ɪn'vɑːlv] v/t hard work, expense

involucrar, entrañar; it would involve
emigrating supondría emigrar; this
doesn't involve you esto no tiene nada
que ver contigo; what does it involve?
¿en qué consiste?; get involved with
sth involucrarse or meterse en algo;
the police didn't want to get involved
la policía no quería intervenir; get involved with s.o. emotionally, romantically
tener una relación sentimental con alguien
in·volved [ɪn'vɑːlvd] adj (complex) complicado
in·volve·ment [ɪn'vɑːlvmənt] in a project,
crime etc participación f, intervención f
in·vul·ne·ra·ble [ɪn'vʌlnərəbl] adj invulnerable
in·ward ['ɪnwərd] 1 adj feeling, smile interior 2 adv hacia dentro
in·ward·ly ['ɪnwərdlɪ] adv por dentro
i·o·dine ['aɪoʊdiːn] yodo m
IOU [aɪoʊ'juː] abbr (= I owe you) pagaré
m
IQ [aɪ'kjuː] abbr (= intelligence quotient) cociente m intelectual
I·ran [ɪ'rɑːn] Irán
I·ra·ni·an [ɪ'reɪnɪən] 1 adj iraní 2 n iraní
m/f
I·raq [ɪ'rɑːk] Iraq, Irak
I·ra·qi [ɪ'rɑːkɪ] 1 adj iraquí 2 n iraquí m/f
Ire·land ['aɪrlənd] Irlanda
i·ris ['aɪrɪs] of eye iris m inv; flower lirio m
I·rish ['aɪrɪʃ] adj irlandés
'I·rish·man irlandés m
'I·rish·wom·an irlandesa f
i·ron ['aɪərn] 1 n substance hierro m; for
clothes plancha f 2 v/t shirts etc planchar
i·ron·ic(al) [aɪ'rɑːnɪk(l)] adj irónico
i·ron·ing ['aɪərnɪŋ] planchado m; do the
ironing planchar
'i·ron·ing board tabla f de planchar
'i·ron·works fundición f
i·ron·y ['aɪrənɪ] ironía f; the irony of it all
is that ... lo irónico del tema es que ...
ir·ra·tion·al [ɪ'ræʃənl] adj irracional
ir·rec·on·ci·la·ble [ɪrekən'saɪləbl] adj irreconciliable
ir·re·cov·e·ra·ble [ɪrɪ'kʌvərəbl] adj irrecuperable

ir·re·gu·lar [ɪˈreɡjʊlər] *adj* irregular

ir·rel·e·vant [ɪˈreləvənt] *adj* irrelevante

ir·rep·a·ra·ble [ɪˈrepərəbl] *adj* irreparable

ir·re·place·a·ble [ɪˈrɪˈpleɪsəbl] *adj object, person* irreemplazable

ir·re·pres·si·ble [ɪrɪˈpresəbl] *adj sense of humor* incontenible; *person* irreprimible

ir·re·proa·cha·ble [ɪrɪˈprəʊtʃəbl] *adj* irreprochable

ir·re·sis·ti·ble [ɪrɪˈzɪstəbl] *adj* irresistible

ir·re·spec·tive [ɪrɪˈspektɪv] *adv*: ***irrespective of*** independientemente de

ir·re·spon·si·ble [ɪrɪˈspɑːnsəbl] *adj* irresponsable

ir·re·trie·va·ble [ɪrɪˈtriːvəbl] *adj* irrecuperable

ir·rev·e·rent [ɪˈrevərənt] *adj* irreverente

ir·rev·o·ca·ble [ɪˈrevəkəbl] *adj* irrevocable

ir·ri·gate [ˈɪrɪɡeɪt] *v/t* regar

ir·ri·ga·tion [ɪrɪˈɡeɪʃn] riego *m*

ir·ri·ga·tion ca·nal acequia *f*

ir·ri·ta·ble [ˈɪrɪtəbl] *adj* irritable

ir·ri·tate [ˈɪrɪteɪt] *v/t* irritar

ir·ri·tat·ing [ˈɪrɪteɪtɪŋ] *adj* irritante

ir·ri·ta·tion [ɪrɪˈteɪʃn] irritación *f*

Is·lam [ˈɪzlɑːm] (el) Islam

Is·lam·ic [ɪzˈlæmɪk] *adj* islámico

is·land [ˈaɪlənd] isla *f*; ***(traffic) island*** isleta *f*

is·land·er [ˈaɪləndər] isleño(-a) *m(f)*

i·so·late [ˈaɪsəleɪt] *v/t* aislar

i·so·lat·ed [ˈaɪsəleɪtɪd] *adj* aislado

i·so·la·tion [aɪsəˈleɪʃn] *of a region* aislamiento *m*; ***in isolation*** aisladamente

i·so·la·tion ward pabellón *m* de enfermedades infecciosas

ISP [aɪesˈpiː] *abbr* (= *Internet service provider*) proveedor *m* de (acceso a) Internet

Is·rael [ˈɪzreɪl] Israel

Is·rae·li [ɪzˈreɪlɪ] 1 *adj* israelí 2 *n person* israelí *m/f*

is·sue [ˈɪʃuː] 1 *n* (*matter*) tema *m*, asunto *m*; *of magazine* número *m*; ***the point at issue*** el tema que se debate; ***take issue with s.o./sth*** discrepar de algo / alguien 2 *v/t coins* emitir; *passports, visa* expedir; *warning* dar; ***issue s.o. with sth*** entregar algo a alguien

IT [aɪˈtiː] *abbr* (= *information technology*) tecnologías *fpl* de la información; ***IT department*** departamento de informática

it [ɪt] *pron as object* lo *m*, la *f*; ***what color is it? - it is red*** ¿de qué color es? - es rojo; ***it's raining*** llueve; ***it's me / him*** soy yo / es él; ***it's Charlie here*** TELEC soy Charlie; ***it's your turn*** te toca; ***that's it!*** (*that's right*) ¡eso es!; (*finished*) ¡ya está!

I·tal·i·an [ɪˈtæljən] 1 *adj* italiano 2 *n person* italiano(-a) *m(f)*; *language* italiano *m*

I·ta·ly [ˈɪtəlɪ] Italia

itch [ɪtʃ] 1 *n* picor *m* 2 *v/i* picar

i·tem [ˈaɪtəm] *in list, accounts,* (*article*) artículo *m*; *on agenda* punto *m*; *of news* noticia *f*

i·tem·ize [ˈaɪtəmaɪz] *v/t invoice* detallar

i·tin·e·ra·ry [aɪˈtɪnərerɪ] itinerario *m*

its [ɪts] *poss adj* su; ***where is its box?*** ¿dónde está su caja?; ***the dog has hurt its leg*** el perro se ha hecho daño en la pata

it's [ɪts] → ***it is, it has***

it·self [ɪtˈself] *pron reflexive* se; ***the dog hurt itself*** el perro se hizo daño; ***the hotel itself is fine*** el hotel en sí (mismo) está bien; ***by itself*** (*alone*) aislado, solo; (*automatically*) solo

i·vo·ry [ˈaɪvərɪ] marfil *m*

i·vy [ˈaɪvɪ] hiedra *f*

J

jab [dʒæb] v/t (pret & pp **jabbed**) clavar;
he jabbed his elbow into my ribs me
clavó el codo en las costillas

jab·ber ['dʒæbər] v/i parlotear

jack [dʒæk] MOT gato m; *in cards* jota f
♦ jack up v/t MOT levantar con el gato

jack·et ['dʒækɪt] (*coat*) chaqueta f; *of book* sobrecubierta f

jack·et po'ta·to Span patata f or L.Am. papa f asada (*con piel*)

'jack·knife 1 n navaja f 2 v/i derrapar (*por la parte del remolque*)

'jack·pot gordo m; *he hit the jackpot* le tocó el gordo

ja·cuz·zi [dʒə'kuːzɪ] jacuzzi m

jade [dʒeɪd] n jade m

jad·ed ['dʒeɪdɪd] adj harto; *appetite* hastiado

jag·ged ['dʒægɪd] adj accidentado

jag·u·ar ['dʒæguər] jaguar m

jail [dʒeɪl] n cárcel f; *he's in jail* está en la cárcel

jam¹ [dʒæm] n *for bread* mermelada f

jam² [dʒæm] 1 n MOT atasco m; F (*difficulty*) aprieto m; *be in a jam* estar en un aprieto 2 v/t (pret & pp **jammed**) (*ram*) meter, embutir; (*cause to stick*) atascar; *broadcast* provocar interferencias en; *be jammed of roads* estar colapsado; *of door, window* estar atascado; *jam on the brakes* dar un frenazo 3 v/i (pret & pp **jammed**) (*stick*) atascarse; *all ten of us managed to jam into the car* nos las arreglamos para meternos los diez en el coche

jam-'packed adj F abarrotado (*with* de)

jan·i·tor ['dʒænɪtər] portero(-a) m(f)

Jan·u·a·ry ['dʒænueri] enero m

Ja·pan [dʒə'pæn] Japón

Jap·a·nese [dʒæpə'niːz] 1 adj japonés 2 n *person* japonés(-esa) m(f); *language* japonés m; *the Japanese* los japoneses

jar¹ [dʒɑːr] n *container* tarro m

jar² [dʒɑːr] v/i (pret & pp **jarred**) *of noise* rechinar; *jar on* rechinar en

jar·gon ['dʒɑːrgən] jerga f

jaun·dice ['dʒɔːndɪs] n ictericia f

jaun·diced ['dʒɔːndɪst] adj fig resentido

jaunt [dʒɔːnt] n excursión f; *go on a jaunt* ir de excursión

jaunt·y ['dʒɔːntɪ] adj desenfadado

jav·e·lin ['dʒævlɪn] (*spear*) jabalina f; *event* (lanzamiento m de) jabalina f

jaw [dʒɔː] n mandíbula f

jay·walk·er ['dʒeɪwɒːkər] peatón(-ona) m(f)

'jay·walk·ing cruzar la calle de manera imprudente

jazz [dʒæz] n jazz m
♦ jazz up v/t F animar

jeal·ous ['dʒeləs] adj celoso; *be jealous of in love* tener celos de; *of riches etc* tener envidia de

jeal·ous·ly ['dʒeləslɪ] adv celosamente; *relating to possessions* con envidia

jeal·ous·y ['dʒeləsɪ] celos mpl; *of possessions* envidia f

jeans [dʒiːnz] npl vaqueros mpl, jeans mpl

jeep [dʒiːp] jeep m

jeer [dʒɪr] 1 n abucheo m 2 v/i abuchear; *jeer at* burlarse de

Jel·lo® ['dʒeloʊ] gelatina f

jel·ly ['dʒelɪ] mermelada f

'jel·ly bean gominola f

'jel·ly·fish medusa f

jeop·ar·dize ['dʒepərdaɪz] v/t poner en peligro

jeop·ar·dy ['dʒepərdɪ]: *be in jeopardy* estar en peligro

jerk¹ [dʒɜːrk] 1 n sacudida f 2 v/t dar un tirón a

jerk² [dʒɜːr] n F imbécil m/f, Span gilipollas m/f inv F

jerk·y ['dʒɜːrkɪ] adj movement brusco

jer·sey ['dʒɜːrzɪ] (*sweater*) suéter m, Span jersey m

jest [dʒest] 1 n broma f; *in jest* en broma

2 v/i bromear

Je·sus ['dʒiːzəs] Jesús

jet [dʒet] 1 n of water chorro m; (nozzle) boquilla f; (airplane) reactor m, avión m a reacción 2 v/i (pret & pp jetted) travel viajar en avión

jet-'black adj azabache

'jet en·gine reactor m

'jet·lag desfase m horario, jet lag m

jet·ti·son ['dʒetɪsn] v/t also fig tirar por la borda

jet·ty ['dʒetɪ] malecón m

Jew [dʒuː] judío(-a) m(f)

jew·el ['dʒuːəl] joya f, alhaja f; fig: person joya f

jew·el·er, Br jew·el·ler ['dʒuːlər] joyero(-a) m(f)

jew·el·lery Br, jew·el·ry ['dʒuːlrɪ] joyas fpl, alhajas fpl

Jew·ish ['dʒuːɪʃ] adj judío

jif·fy ['dʒɪfɪ] F: in a jiffy en un periquete F

jig·saw (puzzle) ['dʒɪgsɔː] rompecabezas m inv, puzzle m

jilt [dʒɪlt] v/t dejar plantado

jin·gle ['dʒɪŋgl] 1 n (song) melodía f publicitaria 2 v/i of keys, coins tintinear

jinx [dʒɪŋks] n gafe m; there's a jinx on this project este proyecto está gafado

jit·ters ['dʒɪtərz] npl F: I got the jitters me entró el pánico or Span canguelo F

jit·ter·y ['dʒɪtərɪ] adj F nervioso

job [dʒɑːb] (employment) trabajo m, empleo m; (task) tarea f, trabajo m; it's not my job to answer the phone no me corresponde a mí contestar el teléfono; I've got a few jobs to do around the house tengo que hacer unas cuantas cosas en la casa; out of a job sin trabajo or empleo; it's a good job you warned me menos mal que me avisaste; you'll have a job (it'll be difficult) te va a costar Dios y ayuda

'job de·scrip·tion (descripción f de las) responsabilidades fpl del puesto

'job hunt v/i: be job hunting buscar trabajo

job·less ['dʒɑːblɪs] adj desempleado, Span parado

job sat·is·fac·tion satisfacción f con el trabajo

jock·ey ['dʒɑːkɪ] n jockey m/f

jog ['dʒɑːg] 1 n: go for a jog ir a hacer jogging or footing 2 v/i (pret & pp jogged) as exercise hacer jogging or footing 3 v/t (pret & pp jogged) jog s.o.'s memory refrescar la memoria de alguien; somebody jogged my elbow alguien me dio en el codo

◆ jog along v/i F ir tirando P

jog·ger ['dʒɑːgər] person persona f que hace jogging or footing; shoe zapatilla f de jogging or footing

jog·ging ['dʒɑːgɪn] jogging m, footing m; go jogging ir a hacer jogging or footing

'jog·ging suit chándal m

john [dʒɑːn] P (toilet) baño m, váter m

join [dʒɔɪn] 1 n juntura f 2 v/i of roads, rivers juntarse; (become a member) hacerse socio 3 v/t (connect) unir; person unirse a; club hacerse socio de; (go to work for) entrar en; of road desembocar en; I'll join you at the theater me reuniré contigo en el teatro

◆ join in v/i participar

◆ join up v/i MIL alistarse

join·er ['dʒɔɪnər] carpintero(-a) m(f)

joint [dʒɔɪnt] 1 n ANAT articulación f; in woodwork junta f; of meat pieza f; F (place) garito m F; of cannabis porro m F, canuto m F 2 adj (shared) conjunto

joint ac'count cuenta f conjunta

joint 'ven·ture empresa f conjunta

joke [dʒook] 1 n story chiste m; (practical joke) broma f; play a joke on gastar una broma a; it's no joke no tiene ninguna gracia 2 v/i bromear

jok·er ['dʒookər] person bromista m/f; F pej payaso(-a) m(f); in cards comodín m

jok·ing ['dʒookɪn]: joking apart bromas aparte

jok·ing·ly ['dʒookɪnlɪ] adv en broma

jol·ly ['dʒɑːlɪ] adj alegre

jolt [dʒoolt] 1 n (jerk) sacudida f 2 v/t (push) somebody jolted my elbow alguien me dio en el codo

jos·tle ['dʒɑːsl] v/t empujar

◆ jot down [dʒɑːt] v/t (pret & pp jotted) apuntar, anotar

jour·nal ['dʒɜ:rnl] (*magazine*) revista *f*; (*diary*) diario *m*

jour·nal·ism ['dʒɜ:rnəlɪzm] periodismo *m*

jour·nal·ist ['dʒɜ:rnəlɪst] periodista *m/f*

jour·ney ['dʒɜ:rnɪ] *n* viaje *m*

jo·vi·al ['dʒoʊvɪəl] *adj* jovial

joy [dʒɔɪ] alegría *f*, gozo *m*

'joy·stick COMPUT joystick *m*

ju·bi·lant ['dʒu:bɪlənt] *adj* jubiloso

ju·bi·la·tion [dʒu:bɪ'leɪʃn] júbilo *m*

judge [dʒʌdʒ] **1** *n* LAW juez *m/f*, jueza *f*; *in competition* juez *m/f*, miembro *m* del jurado **2** *v/t* juzgar; (*estimate*) calcular **3** *v/i* juzgar; *judge for yourself* júzgalo por ti mismo

judg·ment ['dʒʌdʒmənt] LAW fallo *m*; (*opinion*) juicio *m*; *an error of judgment* una equivocación; *he showed good judgment* mostró tener criterio; *against my better judgment* a pesar de no estar convencido; *the Last Judgment* REL el Juicio Final

'Judg(e)·ment Day Día *m* del Juicio Final

ju·di·cial [dʒu:'dɪʃl] *adj* judicial

ju·di·cious [dʒu:'dɪʃəs] *adj* juicioso

ju·do ['dʒu:doʊ] judo *m*

jug·gle [dʒʌgl] *v/t also fig* hacer malabarismos con

jug·gler ['dʒʌglər] malabarista *m/f*

juice [dʒu:s] *n* Span zumo *m*, *L.Am.* jugo *m*

juic·y ['dʒu:sɪ] *adj* jugoso; *news, gossip* jugoso, sabroso

juke·box ['dʒu:kbɑ:ks] máquina *f* de discos

Ju·ly [dʒu:'laɪ] julio *m*

jum·ble ['dʒʌmbl] *n* revoltijo *m*

◆ **jumble up** *v/t* revolver

jum·bo (jet) ['dʒʌmboʊ] jumbo *m*

'jum·bo(-sized) *adj* gigante

jump [dʒʌmp] **1** *n* salto *m*; (*increase*) incremento *m*, subida *f*; *give a jump of surprise* dar un salto **2** *v/i* saltar; (*increase*) dispararse; *you made me jump!* ¡me diste un susto!; *jump to one's feet* ponerse de pie de un salto; *jump to conclusions* sacar conclusiones precipitadas **3** *v/t fence etc* saltar; F (*attack*) asaltar;

jump the lights saltarse el semáforo, pasarse un semáforo en rojo

◆ **jump at** *v/t opportunity* no dejar escapar

jump·er¹ ['dʒʌmpər] *dress* pichi *m*

jump·er² ['dʒʌmpər] SP saltador(a) *m(f)*; *horse* caballo *m* de saltos

jump·y ['dʒʌmpɪ] *adj* nervioso; *get jumpy* ponerse nervioso

junc·tion ['dʒʌŋkʃn] *of roads* cruce *m*

junc·ture ['dʒʌŋktʃər] *fml: at this juncture* en esta coyuntura

June [dʒu:n] junio *m*

jun·gle ['dʒʌŋgl] selva *f*, jungla *f*

ju·ni·or ['dʒu:njər] **1** *adj subordinate* de rango inferior; *younger* más joven **2** *n in rank* subalterno(-a) *m(f)*; *she is ten years my junior* es diez años más joven que yo

ju·ni·or 'high escuela *f* secundaria (*para alumnos de entre 12 y 14 años*)

junk [dʒʌŋk] *n* trastos *mpl*

'junk food comida *f* basura

junk·ie ['dʒʌŋkɪ] F drogata *m/f* F

'junk mail propaganda *f* postal

'junk shop cacharrería *f*

'junk·yard depósito *m* de chatarra

jur·is·dic·tion [dʒʊrɪs'dɪkʃn] LAW jurisdicción *f*

ju·ror ['dʒʊrər] miembro *m* del jurado

ju·ry ['dʒʊrɪ] jurado *m*

just [dʒʌst] **1** *adj law, cause* justo **2** *adv* (*barely*) justo; (*exactly*) justo, justamente; (*only*) sólo, solamente; *have just done sth* acabar de hacer algo; *I've just seen her* la acabo de ver; *just about* (*almost*) casi; *I was just about to leave when ...* estaba a punto de salir cuando ...; *just like that* (*abruptly*) de repente; *just now* (*at the moment*) ahora mismo; *I saw her just now* (*a few moments ago*) la acabo de ver; *just you wait!* ¡ya verás!; *just be quiet!* ¡cállate de una vez!

jus·tice ['dʒʌstɪs] justicia *f*

jus·ti·fi·a·ble [dʒʌstɪ'faɪəbl] *adj* justificable

jus·ti·fia·bly [dʒʌstɪ'faɪəblɪ] *adv* justificadamente

jus·ti·fi·ca·tion [dʒʌstɪfɪ'keɪʃn] justifica-

ción *f*; **there's no justification for behavior like that** ese comportamiento es injustificable *or* no tiene justificación
jus·ti·fy [ˈdʒʌstɪfaɪ] *v/t* (*pret & pp **justified***) *also text* justificar
just·ly [ˈdʒʌstlɪ] *adv* (*fairly*) con justicia; (*rightly*) con razón
◆ **jut out** [dʒʌt] *v/i* (*pret & pp **jutted***) so-

bresalir
ju·ve·nile [ˈdʒuːvənl] **1** *adj crime* juvenil; *court* de menores; *pej* infantil **2** *n fml* menor *m/f*
ju·ve·nile de'lin·quen·cy delincuencia *f* juvenil
ju·ve·nile de'lin·quent delincuente *m/f* juvenil

K

k [keɪ] *abbr* (= **kilobyte**) k (= kilobyte *m*); (= **thousand**) mil
kan·ga·roo [kæŋgəˈruː] canguro *m*
ka·ra·te [kəˈrɑːtɪ] kárate *m*
ka'ra·te chop golpe *m* de kárate
ke·bab [kɪˈbæb] pincho *m*, brocheta *f*
keel [kiːl] NAUT quilla *f*
◆ **keel over** *v/i of structure* desplomarse; *of person* desmayarse
keen [kiːn] *adj* entusiasta, interesado; *interest* gran; *competition* reñido; **she's keen to learn** tiene mucho interés en aprender; **he's keen on football / her** le gusta el fútbol / ella; **I'm not keen on the idea** no me entusiasma la idea; **be keen to do sth** estar muy interesado en hacer algo
keep [kiːp] **1** *n* (*maintenance*) manutención *f*; **for keeps** F para siempre **2** *v/t* (*pret & pp **kept***) guardar; (*not lose*) conservar; (*detain*) entretener; *family* mantener; *animals* tener, criar; **you can keep it** (*it's for you*) te lo puedes quedar; **keep trying!** ¡sigue intentándolo!; **don't keep interrupting!** ¡deja de interrumpirme!; **keep a promise** cumplir una promesa; **keep s.o. company** hacer compañía a alguien; **keep s.o. waiting** hacer esperar a alguien; **he can't keep anything to himself** no sabe guardar un secreto; **I kept the news of the accident to myself** no dije nada sobre el ac-

cidente; **keep sth from s.o.** ocultar algo a alguien; **we kept the news from him** no le contamos la noticia **3** *v/i* (*pret & pp **kept***) *of food, milk* aguantar, conservarse; **keep calm!** ¡tranquilízate!; **keep quiet!** ¡cállate!
◆ **keep away 1** *v/i*: **keep away from that building** no te acerques a ese edificio **2** *v/t*: **keep the children away from the stove** no dejes que los niños se acerquen a la cocina
◆ **keep back** *v/t* (*hold in check*) contener; *information* ocultar
◆ **keep down** *v/t voice* bajar; *costs, inflation* reducir; *food* retener; **keep your voices down in the library** hablen en voz baja en la biblioteca; **tell the kids to keep the noise down** diles a los niños que no hagan tanto ruido; **I can't keep anything down** devuelvo todo lo que como
◆ **keep in** *v/t in school* castigar (*a quedarse en clase*); **the hospital's keeping her in** la tienen en observación
◆ **keep off 1** *v/t* (*avoid*) evitar; **keep off the grass!** ¡prohibido pisar el césped! **2** *v/i*: **if the rain keeps off** si no llueve
◆ **keep on 1** *v/i* continuar; **if you keep on interrupting me** si no dejas de interrumpirme; **keep on trying** sigue intentándolo **2** *v/t*: **the company kept them on** la empresa los mantuvo en el puesto; **keep**

your coat on! *item of clothing* ¡no te quites el abrigo!

◆ **keep on** at *v/t* (*nag*): **my parents keep on at me to get a job** mis padres no dejan de decirme que busque un trabajo

◆ **keep out 1** *v/t*: **it keeps the cold out** protege del frío; **they must be kept out** no pueden entrar **2** *v/i*: **I told you to keep out!** *of a place* ¡te dije que no entraras!; **I would keep out of it if I were you** *of discussion etc* yo en tu lugar no me metería; **keep out** *as sign* prohibida la entrada, prohibido el paso

◆ **keep to** *v/t path* seguir; *rules* cumplir, respetar

◆ **keep up 1** *v/i when walking, running etc* seguir *or* mantener el ritmo (**with** de); **keep up with s.o.** (*stay in touch with*) mantener contacto con alguien **2** *v/t pace* seguir, mantener; *payments* estar al corriente de; *bridge, pants* sujetar

keep·ing [ˈkiːpɪŋ] *n*: **be in keeping with decor** combinar con; **in keeping with promises** de acuerdo con

'**keep·sake** recuerdo *m*

keg [keg] barril *m*

ken·nel [ˈkenl] *n* caseta *f* del perro

ken·nels [ˈkenlz] *npl* residencia *f* canina

kept [kept] *pret & pp* → **keep**

ker·nel [ˈkɜːrnl] almendra *f*

ker·o·sene [ˈkerəsiːn] queroseno *m*

ketch·up [ˈketʃʌp] ketchup *m*

ket·tle [ˈketl] hervidor *m*

key [kiː] **1** *n to door, drawer* llave *f*; *on keyboard, piano* tecla *f*; *of piece of music* clave *f*; *on map* leyenda *f* **2** *adj* (*vital*) clave, crucial **3** *v/t & v/i* COMPUT teclear

◆ **key in** *v/t data* introducir, teclear

'**key·board** COMPUT, MUS teclado *m*

key·board·er COMPUT operador(a) *m(f)*, *persona que introduce datos en el ordenador*

'**key·card** tarjeta *f* (de hotel)

keyed-up [kiːdˈʌp] *adj* nervioso

'**key·hole** ojo *m* de la cerradura

'**key·note** '**speech** discurso *m* central

'**key·ring** llavero *m*

kha·ki [ˈkæki] *adj* caqui

kick [kɪk] **1** *n* patada *f*; **he got a kick out**

of watching them suffer disfrutó viéndoles sufrir; (*just*) **for kicks** F por diversión **2** *v/t* dar una patada a; F *habit* dejar; **I kicked him in the shins** le di una patada en la espinilla **3** *v/i of person* patalear; *of horse, mule* cocear

◆ **kick around** *v/t ball* dar patadas a; F (*discuss*) comentar

◆ **kick in** *v/t* P *money* apoquinar F

◆ **kick off** *v/i* comenzar, sacar de centro; F (*start*) empezar

◆ **kick out** *v/t of bar, company* echar; *of country, organization* expulsar

◆ **kick up** *v/t*: **kick up a fuss** montar un numerito

'**kick·back** F (*bribe*) soborno *m*

'**kick-off** SP saque *m*

kid [kɪd] **1** *n* F (*child*) crío *m* F, niño *m*; **when I was a kid** cuando era pequeño; **kid brother** hermano *m* pequeño; **kid sister** hermana *f* pequeña **2** *v/t* (*pret & pp* **kidded**) F tomar el pelo a F **3** *v/i* (*pret & pp* **kidded**) F bromear; **I was only kidding** estaba bromeando

'**kid·der** [ˈkɪdər] F vacilón *m* F

kid '**gloves**: **handle s.o. with kid gloves** tratar a alguien con guante de seda

kid·nap [ˈkɪdnæp] *v/t* (*pret & pp* **kidnapped**) secuestrar

kid·nap·(p)er [ˈkɪdnæpər] secuestrador *m*

'**kid·nap·(p)ing** [ˈkɪdnæpɪŋ] secuestro *m*

'**kid·ney** [ˈkɪdnɪ] ANAT riñón *m*; *in cooking* riñones *mpl*

'**kid·ney bean** alubia *f* roja de riñón

'**kid·ney ma·chine** MED riñón *m* artificial, máquina *f* de diálisis

kill [kɪl] *v/t* matar; **the drought killed all the plants** las plantas murieron como resultado de la sequía; **I had six hours to kill** tenía seis horas sin nada que hacer; **be killed in an accident** matarse en un accidente, morirse en un accidente; **kill o.s.** suicidarse; **kill o.s. laughing** F morirse de risa F

kil·ler [ˈkɪlər] (*murderer*) asesino *m*; **be a killer** *of disease* ser mortal

kil·ling [ˈkɪlɪŋ] *n* asesinato *m*; **make a killing** F (*lots of money*) forrarse F

kil·ling·ly [ˈkɪlɪŋlɪ] *adv* F: **killingly funny**

para morirse de risa

kiln [kɪln] horno *m*

ki·lo ['ki:lou] kilo *m*

ki·lo·byte ['kɪloubaɪt] COMPUT kilobyte *m*

ki·lo·gram ['kɪlougræm] kilogramo *m*

ki·lo·me·ter, *Br* **ki·lo·me·tre** [kɪ'lɑːmɪtər] kilómetro *m*

kind[1] [kaɪnd] *adj* agradable, amable

kind[2] [kaɪnd] *n* (*sort*) tipo *m*; (*make, brand*) marca *f*; *all kinds of people* toda clase de personas; *I did nothing of the kind!* ¡no hice nada parecido!; *kind of ... sad, lonely, etc* un poco ...; *that's very kind of you* gracias por tu amabilidad

kin·der·gar·ten ['kɪndərgɑːrtn] guardería *f*, jardín *m* de infancia

kind-heart·ed [kaɪnd'hɑːrtɪd] *adj* agradable, amable

kind·ly ['kaɪndlɪ] **1** *adj* amable, agradable **2** *adv* con amabilidad; *kindly don't interrupt* por favor, no me interrumpa; *kindly lower your voice* ¿le importaría hablar más bajo?

kind·ness ['kaɪndnɪs] amabilidad *f*

king [kɪŋ] rey *m*

king·dom ['kɪŋdəm] reino *m*

'**king-size(d)** *adj* F *cigarettes* extralargo; *king-size(d) bed* cama *f* de matrimonio grande

kink [kɪŋk] *n in hose etc* doblez *f*

kink·y ['kɪŋkɪ] *adj* F vicioso

kiosk ['kiːɑːsk] quiosco *m*

kiss [kɪs] **1** *n* beso *m* **2** *v/t* besar **3** *v/i* besarse

kiss of 'life boca *m* a boca, respiración *f* artificial; *give s.o. the kiss of life* hacer a alguien el boca a boca

kit [kɪt] (*equipment*) equipo *m*; *first aid kit* botiquín *m*; *tool kit* caja *f* de herramientas

kitch·en ['kɪtʃɪn] cocina *f*

kitch·en·ette [kɪtʃɪ'net] cocina pequeña

kitch·en 'sink: *you've got everything but the kitchen sink* F llevas la casa a cuestas *f*

kite [kaɪt] cometa *f*

kit·ten ['kɪtn] gatito *m*

kit·ty ['kɪtɪ] *money* fondo *m*

klutz [klʌts] F (*clumsy person*) manazas *m*

F

knack [næk] habilidad *f*; *he has a knack of upsetting people* tiene la habilidad de disgustar a la gente; *I soon got the knack of the new machine* le pillé el truco a la nueva máquina rápidamente

knead [niːd] *v/t dough* amasar

knee [niː] *n* rodilla *f*

'**knee·cap** *n* rótula *f*

kneel [niːl] *v/i* (*pret & pp knelt*) arrodillarse

'**knee-length** *adj* hasta la rodilla

knelt [nelt] *pret & pp → kneel*

knew [nuː] *pret → know*

knick-knacks ['nɪknæks] *npl* F baratijas *fpl*

knife [naɪf] **1** *n* (*pl knives* [naɪvz]) *for food* cuchillo *m*; *carried outside* navaja *f* **2** *v/t* acuchillar, apuñalar

knight [naɪt] *n* caballero *m*

knit [nɪt] **1** *v/t* (*pret & pp knitted*) tejer **2** *v/i* (*pret & pp knitted*) tricotar

◆ **knit together** *v/i of broken bone* soldarse

knit·ting ['nɪtɪŋ] punto *m*

'**knit·ting nee·dle** aguja *f* para hacer punto

'**knit·wear** prendas *fpl* de punto

knob [nɑːb] *on door* pomo *m*; *on drawer* tirador *m*; *of butter* nuez *f*, trocito *m*

knock [nɑːk] **1** *n on door* golpe *m*; (*blow*) golpe *m*; *there was a knock on the door* llamaron a la puerta **2** *v/t* (*hit*) golpear; F (*criticize*) criticar, meterse con F; *he was knocked to the ground* le tiraron al suelo **3** *v/i on the door* llamar

◆ **knock around 1** *v/t* F (*beat*) pegar a **2** *v/i* F (*travel*) viajar

◆ **knock down** *v/t of car* atropellar; *building* tirar; *object* tirar al suelo; F (*reduce the price of*) rebajar

◆ **knock off 1** *v/t* P (*steal*) mangar P **2** *v/i* F (*stop work for the day*) acabar, *Span* plegar F

◆ **knock out** *v/t* (*make unconscious*) dejar K.O.; *of medicine* dejar para el arrastre F; *power lines etc* destruir; (*eliminate*) eliminar

◆ **knock over** *v/t* tirar; *of car* atropellar

'knock·down *adj*: **at a knockdown price** tirado

knock-kneed [nɑːkˈniːd] *adj* patizambo

'knock·out *n in boxing* K.O. *m*

knot [nɑːt] **1** *n* nudo *m* **2** *v/t (pret & pp **knotted**)* anudar

'knot·ty [ˈnɑːtɪ] *adj problem* complicado

know [noʊ] **1** *v/t (pret **knew**, pp **known**) fact, language, how to do sth* saber; *person, place* conocer; *(recognize)* reconocer; **will you let him know that ...?** ¿puedes decirle que ...? **2** *v/i (pret **knew**, pp **known**)* saber; **I don't know** no (lo) sé; **yes, I know** sí, lo sé **3** *n*: **people in the know** los enterados

'know·how pericia *f*

know·ing [ˈnoʊɪŋ] *adj* cómplice

know·ing·ly [ˈnoʊɪŋlɪ] *adv (wittingly)* deliberadamente; *smile etc* con complicidad

'know-it-all F sabiondo F

knowl·edge [ˈnɑːlɪdʒ] conocimiento *m*; **to the best of my knowledge** por lo que sé; **have a good knowledge of ...** tener buenos conocimientos de ...

knowl·edge·a·ble [ˈnɑːlɪdʒəbl] *adj*: **she's very knowledgeable about music** sabe mucho de música

known [noʊn] *pp → know*

knuck·le [ˈnʌkl] nudillo *m*

◆ knuckle down *v/i* F aplicarse F

◆ knuckle under *v/i* F pasar por el aro F

KO [keɪˈoʊ] *(knockout)* K.O.

Ko·ran [kəˈræn] Corán *m*

Ko·re·a [kəˈriːə] Corea

Ko·re·an [kəˈriːən] **1** *adj* coreano **2** *n* coreano(a) *m(f)*; *language* coreano *m*

ko·sher [ˈkoʊʃər] *adj* REL kosher; F legal F

kow·tow [ˈkaʊtaʊ] *v/i* F reverenciar

ku·dos [ˈkjuːdɑːs] reconocimiento *m*, prestigio *m*

L

lab [læb] laboratorio *m*

la·bel [ˈleɪbl] **1** *n* etiqueta *f* **2** *v/t baggage* etiquetar

la·bor [ˈleɪbər] *n (work)* trabajo *m*; *in pregnancy* parto *m*; **be in labor** estar de parto

la·bor·a·to·ry [ˈlæbrətɔʊrɪ] laboratorio *m*

la·bor·a·to·ry tech·ni·cian técnico(-a) *m(f)* de laboratorio

la·bo·ri·ous [ləˈbɔːrɪəs] *adj* laborioso

la·bored [ˈleɪbərd] *adj style, speech* elaborado

la·bor·er [ˈleɪbərər] obrero(-a) *m(f)*

'la·bor u·ni·on sindicato *m*

'la·bor ward MED sala *f* de partos

la·bour *etc Br → labor etc*

lace [leɪs] *n material* encaje *m*; *for shoe* cordón *m*

◆ lace up *v/t shoes* atar

lack [læk] **1** *n* falta *f*, carencia *f* **2** *v/t* carecer de; **he lacks confidence** le falta confianza **3** *v/i*: **be lacking** faltar

lac·quer [ˈlækər] *n for hair* laca *f*

lad [læd] muchacho *m*, chico *m*

lad·der [ˈlædər] *n* escalera *f* (de mano)

la·den [ˈleɪdn] *adj* cargado (**with** de)

la·dies room [ˈleɪdiːz] servicio *m* de señoras

la·dle [ˈleɪdl] *n* cucharón *m*, cazo *m*

la·dy [ˈleɪdɪ] señora *f*

'la·dy·bug mariquita *f*

'la·dy·like *adj* femenino

lag [læg] *v/t (pret & pp **lagged**) pipes* revestir con aislante

◆ lag behind *v/i* quedarse atrás

la·ger [ˈlɑːgər] cerveza *f* rubia

la·goon [ləˈguːn] laguna *f*

laid [leɪd] *pret & pp → lay¹*

laid-back [leɪd'bæk] *adj* tranquilo, despreocupado

lain [leɪn] *pp* → **lie²**

lake [leɪk] *n* lago *m*

lamb [læm] *animal, meat* cordero *m*

lame [leɪm] *adj person* cojo; *excuse* pobre

la-ment [lə'ment] **1** *n* lamento *m* **2** *v/t* lamentar

lam-en-ta-ble ['læməntəbl] *adj* lamentable

lam-i-nat-ed ['læmɪneɪtɪd] *adj surface* laminado; *paper* plastificado

lam-i-nat-ed 'glass cristal *m* laminado

lamp [læmp] lámpara *f*

'lamp-post farola *f*

'lamp-shade pantalla *f* (*de lámpara*)

land [lænd] **1** *n* tierra *f*; *by land* por tierra; *on land* en tierra; *work on the land as farmer* trabajar la tierra **2** *v/t airplane* aterrizar; *job* conseguir **3** *v/i of airplane* aterrizar; *of capsule on the moon* alunizar; *of ball, sth thrown* caer; *it landed right on top of his head* le cayó justo en la cabeza

land-ing ['lændɪŋ] *n of airplane* aterrizaje *m*; *on moon* alunizaje *m*; *of staircase* rellano *m*

'land-ing field pista *f* de aterrizaje

'land-ing gear tren *m* de aterrizaje

'land-ing strip pista *f* de aterrizaje

'land-la-dy *of bar* patrona *f*; *of hostel etc* dueña *f*; *of rented room* casera *f*

'land-lord *of bar* patrón *m*; *of hostel etc* dueño *m*; *of rented room* casero *m*

'land-mark punto *m* de referencia; *fig* hito *m*

land own-er terrateniente *m/f*

land-scape ['lændskeɪp] **1** *n* (*also painting*) paisaje *m* **2** *adv print* en formato apaisado

'land-slide corrimiento *m* de tierras

land-slide 'vic-to-ry victoria *f* arrolladora

lane [leɪn] *in country* camino *m*, vereda *f*; (*alley*) callejón *m*; *MOT* carril *m*

lan-guage ['læŋgwɪdʒ] lenguaje *m*; *of nation* idioma *f*, lengua *f*

'lan-guage lab laboratorio *m* de idiomas

lank [læŋk] *adj hair* lacio

lank-y ['læŋkɪ] *adj person* larguirucho

lan-tern ['læntərn] farol *f*

lap¹ [læp] *n of track* vuelta *f*

lap² [læp] *n of water* chapoteo *m*

◆ **lap up** *v/t* (*pret & pp* **lapped**) *drink, milk* beber a lengüetadas; *flattery* deleitarse con

lap³ [læp] *n of person* regazo *m*

la-pel [lə'pel] solapa *f*

lapse [læps] **1** *n* (*mistake, slip*) desliz *m*; *of time* lapso *m*; *a lapse of attention* un momento de distracción; *a lapse of memory* un olvido **2** *v/i of membership* vencer; *lapse into silence / despair* sumirse en el silencio / la desesperación; *she lapsed into English* empezó a hablar en inglés

lap-top ['læptɑːp] COMPUT ordenador *m* portátil, *L.Am.* computadora *f* portátil

lar-ce-ny ['lɑːrsənɪ] latrocinio *m*

lard [lɑːrd] manteca *f* de cerdo

lar-der ['lɑːrdər] despensa *f*

large [lɑːrdʒ] *adj* grande; *be at large of criminal, wild animal* andar suelto

large-ly ['lɑːrdʒlɪ] *adv* (*mainly*) en gran parte, principalmente

lark [lɑːrk] *bird* alondra *f*

lar-va ['lɑːrvə] larva *f*

lar-yn-gi-tis [lærɪn'dʒaɪtɪs] laringitis *f*

lar-ynx ['lærɪŋks] laringe *f*

la-ser ['leɪzər] láser *m*

'la-ser beam rayo *m* láser

'la-ser print-er impresora *f* láser

lash¹ [læʃ] *v/t with whip* azotar

◆ **lash down** *v/t with rope* amarrar

◆ **lash out** *v/i with fists, words* atacar (*at* a), arremeter (*at* contra)

lash² [læʃ] *n* (*eyelash*) pestaña *f*

lass [læs] muchacha *f*, chica *f*

last¹ [læst] **1** *adj in series* último; (*preceding*) anterior; *last Friday* el viernes pasado; *last but one* penúltimo; *last night* anoche; *last but not least* por último, pero no por ello menos importante **2** *adv at last* por fin, al fin

last² [læst] *v/i* durar

last-ing ['læstɪŋ] *adj* duradero

last-ly ['læstlɪ] *adv* por último, finalmente

latch [lætʃ] *n* pestillo *m*

late [leɪt] **1** *adj: the bus is late again* el

autobús vuelve a llegar tarde; *it's late* es tarde; *it's getting late* se está haciendo tarde; *of late* últimamente, recientemente; *the late 19th/20th century* la última parte del siglo XIX / XX; *in the late 19th/20th century* a finales del siglo XIX / XX **2** *adv arrive, leave* tarde
late·ly ['leɪtlɪ] *adv* últimamente, recientemente
lat·er ['leɪtər] *adv* más tarde; *see you later!* ¡hasta luego!; *later on* más tarde
lat·est['leɪtɪst] *adj news, girlfriend* último
lathe [leɪð] *n* torno *m*
la·ther ['lɑːðər] *n from soap* espuma *f*; *in a lather* (*sweaty*) empapado de sudor
Lat·in ['lætɪn] **1** *adj* latino **2** *n* latín *m*
Lat·in A'mer·i·ca Latinoamérica, América Latina
La·tin A'mer·i·can 1 *n* latinoamericano(-a) *m(f)* **2** *adj* latinoamericano
La·ti·no [læ'tiːnou] **1** *adj* latino **2** *n* latino(-a)
lat·i·tude ['lætɪtuːd] *geographical* latitud *f*; (*freedom to act*) libertad *f*
lat·ter['lætər] **1** *adj* último **2** *n*: *Mr Brown and Mr White, of whom the latter was ...* el Señor *Brown* y el Señor *White*, de quien el segundo *or* este último era ...
laugh [læf] **1** *n* risa *f*; *it was a laugh* F fue genial **2** *v/i* reírse
◆ **laugh at** *v/t* reírse de
'laugh·ing stock *make o.s. a laughing stock* ponerse en ridículo; *become a laughing stock* ser el hazmerreír
laugh·ter ['læftər] risas *fpl*
launch [lɔːntʃ] **1** *n small boat* lancha *f*; *of ship* botadura *f*; *of rocket, new product* lanzamiento *m* **2** *v/t rocket, new product* lanzar; *ship* botar
'launch cer·e·mo·ny ceremonia *f* de lanzamiento
launch-(ing) pad plataforma *f* de lanzamiento
laun·der ['lɔːndər] *v/t clothes* lavar (y planchar); *money* blanquear
laun·dro·mat ['lɔːndrəmæt] lavandería *f*
laun·dry ['lɔːndrɪ] *place* lavadero *m*; *dirty clothes* ropa *f* sucia; *clean clothes* ropa *f* lavada; *do the laundry* lavar la ropa,

Span hacer la colada
lau·rel ['lɑːrəl] laurel *m*
lav·a·to·ry ['lævətɔːrɪ] *place* cuarto *m* de baño, lavabo *m*; *equipment* retrete *m*
lav·en·der ['lævəndər] espliego *m*, lavanda *f*
lav·ish ['lævɪʃ] *adj* espléndido
law [lɔː] ley *f*; *subject* derecho *m*; *be against the law* estar prohibido, ser ilegal
'law court juzgado *m*
law·ful ['lɔːfəl] *adj* legal; *wife* legítimo
law·less ['lɔːlɪs] *adj* sin ley
lawn [lɔːn] césped *m*
'lawn mow·er cortacésped *m*
'law·suit pleito *m*
law·yer ['lɔːjər] abogado(-a) *m(f)*
lax [læks] *adj* poco estricto
lax·a·tive ['læksətɪv] *n* laxante *m*
lay[1] [leɪ] *v/t* (*pret & pp* **laid**) (*put down*) dejar, poner; *eggs* poner; V *sexually* tirarse a V
lay[2] [leɪ] *pret* → **lie**[2]
◆ **lay into** *v/t* (*attack*) arremeter contra
◆ **lay off** *v/t workers* despedir
◆ **lay on** *v/t* (*provide*) organizar
◆ **lay out** *v/t objects* colocar, disponer; *page* diseñar, maquetar
'lay·a·bout F gandul(a) *m(f)* F
'lay-by *on road* área *f* de descanso
lay·er ['leɪər] estrato *m*; *of soil, paint* capa *f*
'lay·man laico *m*
'lay-off despido *m*
◆ **laze around** [leɪz] *v/i* holgazanear
la·zy ['leɪzɪ] *adj person* holgazán, perezoso; *day* ocioso
lb *abbr* (= *pound*) libra *f* (*de peso*)
LCD[elsiːˈdiː] *abbr* (= *liquid crystal display*) LCD, pantalla *f* de cristal líquido
lead[1] [liːd] **1** *v/t* (*pret & pp* **led**) *procession, race* ir al frente de; *company, team* dirigir; (*guide, take*) conducir **2** *v/i* (*pret & pp* **led**) *in race, competition* ir en cabeza; (*provide leadership*) tener el mando; *a street leading off the square* una calle que sale de la plaza; *where is this lea-*

ding? ¿adónde nos lleva esto? **3** *n in race* ventaja *f*; *be in the lead* estar en cabeza; *take the lead* ponerse en cabeza; *lose the lead* perder la cabeza

◆ **lead on** *v/i* (*go in front*) ir delante

◆ **lead up to** *v/t* preceder a; *I wonder what she's leading up to* me pregunto a dónde quiere ir a parar

lead² [liːd] *for dog* correa *f*

lead³ [led] *substance* plomo *m*

lead·ed ['ledɪd] *adj gas* con plomo

lead·er ['liːdər] líder *m*

lead·er·ship ['liːdərʃɪp] *of party etc* liderazgo *m*; *under his leadership* bajo su liderazgo

lead-free ['ledfriː] *adj gas* sin plomo

lead·ing ['liːdɪŋ] *adj runner* en cabeza; *company, product* puntero

lead·ing-edge *adj company* en la vanguardia; *technology* de vanguardia

leaf [liːf] (*pl leaves* [liːvz]) hoja *f*

◆ **leaf through** *v/t* hojear

leaf·let ['liːflət] folleto *m*

league [liːg] liga *f*

leak [liːk] **1** *n in roof* gotera *f*; *in pipe* agujero *m*; *of air, gas* fuga *f*, escape *m*; *of information* filtración *f* **2** *v/i of boat* hacer agua; *of pipe* tener un agujero; *of liquid, gas* fugarse, escaparse

◆ **leak out** *v/i of air, gas* fugarse, escaparse; *of news* filtrarse

leak·y ['liːkɪ] *adj pipe* con agujeros; *boat* que hace agua

lean¹ [liːn] **1** *v/i* (*be at an angle*) estar inclinado; *lean against sth* apoyarse en algo **2** *v/t apoyar*; *lean sth against sth* apoyar algo contra algo

lean² [liːn] *adj meat* magro; *style, prose* pobre, escueto

leap [liːp] **1** *n* salto *m*; *a great leap forward* un gran salto adelante **2** *v/i* (*pret & pp leaped or leapt*) saltar; *he leapt over the fence* saltó la valla; *they leapt into the river* se tiraron al río

leapt [lept] *pret & pp* → **leap**

leap year año *m* bisiesto

learn [lɜːrn] **1** *v/t* aprender; (*hear*) enterarse de; *learn how to do sth* aprender a hacer algo **2** *v/i* aprender

learn·er ['lɜːrnər] estudiante *m/f*

'learn·er driv·er conductor(a) *m(f)* en prácticas

learn·ing ['lɜːrnɪŋ] *n* (*knowledge*) conocimientos *mpl*; *act* aprendizaje *m*

'learn·ing curve curva *f* de aprendizaje; *be on the learning curve* tener que aprender cosas nuevas

lease [liːs] **1** *n* (contrato *m* de) arrendamiento *m* **2** *v/t apartment, equipment* arrendar

◆ **lease out** *v/t apartment, equipment* arrendar

lease 'pur·chase arrendamiento *m* con opción de compra

leash [liːʃ] *for dog* correa *f*

least [liːst] **1** *adj* (*slightest*) menor; *the least amount, money, baggage* menos; *there's not the least reason to …* no hay la más mínima razón para que … **2** *adv* menos **3** *n* lo menos; *he drank the least* fue el que menos bebió; *not in the least surprised* en absoluto sorprendido; *at least* por lo menos

leath·er ['leðər] **1** *n* piel *f*, cuero *m* **2** *adj* de piel, de cuero

leave [liːv] **1** *n* (*vacation*) permiso *m*; *on leave* de permiso **2** *v/t* (*pret & pp left*) *city, place* marcharse de, irse de; *person, food, memory,* (*forget*) dejar; *let's leave things as they are* dejemos las cosas tal y como están; *how did you leave things with him?* ¿cómo quedaron las cosas con él?; *leave s.o./sth alone* (*not touch, not interfere with*) dejar a alguien / algo en paz; *be left* quedar; *there is nothing left* no queda nada; *I only have one left* sólo me queda uno **3** *v/i* (*pret & pp left*) *of person* marcharse, irse; *of plane, train, bus* salir

◆ **leave behind** *v/t intentionally* dejar; (*forget*) olvidarse

◆ **leave on** *v/t hat, coat* dejar puesto; *TV, computer* dejar encendido

◆ **leave out** *v/t word, figure* omitir; (*not put away*) no guardar; *leave me out of this* a mí no me metas en esto 'leav·ing par·ty fiesta f de despedida

lec·ture ['lektʃər] **1** n clase f; *to general public* conferencia f **2** v/i *at university* dar clases (*in* de); *to general public* dar una conferencia

'lec·ture hall sala f de conferencias

'lec·tur·er ['lektʃərər] profesor(a) m(f)

LED [eliː'diː] abbr (= **light-emitting diode**) LED m (= diodo m emisor de luz)

led [led] pret & pp → **lead¹**

ledge [ledʒ] *of window* alféizar f; *on rock face* saliente m

ledg·er ['ledʒər] COM libro m mayor

leek [liːk] puerro m

leer [lɪr] n *sexual* mirada f impúdica; *evil* mirada f maligna

left [left] **1** adj izquierdo **2** n also POL izquierda f; **on the left** a la izquierda; **on the left of sth** a la izquierda de algo; **to the left** *turn, look* a la izquierda **3** adv *turn, look* a la izquierda

left² [left] pret & pp → **leave**

'left-hand adj de izquierda; **on your left-hand side** a tu izquierda; *bend* a la izquierda

left-hand 'drive: **this car is left-hand drive** este coche tiene el volante a la izquierda

left-'handed adj zurdo

left 'lug·gage (of·fice) Br consigna f

'left-overs npl *food* sobras fpl

'left-wing adj POL izquierdista, de izquierdas

leg [leg] *of person* pierna f; *of animal* pata f; **pull s.o.'s leg** tomar el pelo a alguien

leg·a·cy ['legəsɪ] legado m

le·gal ['liːgl] adj legal

le·gal ad'vis·er asesor(a) m(f) jurídico(-a)

le·gal·i·ty [lɪ'gælətɪ] legalidad f

le·gal·ize ['liːgəlaɪz] v/t legalizar

le·gend ['ledʒənd] leyenda f

le·gen·da·ry ['ledʒəndrɪ] adj legendario

le·gi·ble ['ledʒəbl] adj legible

le·gis·late ['ledʒɪsleɪt] v/i legislar

le·gis·la·tion [ledʒɪs'leɪʃn] legislación f

le·gis·la·tive ['ledʒɪslətɪv] adj legislativo

le·gis·la·ture ['ledʒɪslətʃər] POL legislativo m

le·git·i·mate [lɪ'dʒɪtɪmət] adj legítimo

'leg room espacio m para las piernas

lei·sure ['liːʒər] ocio m; **I look forward to having more leisure** estoy deseando tener más tiempo libre; **do it at your leisure** tómate tu tiempo para hacerlo

'lei·sure cen·ter, Br 'lei·sure cen·tre centro m recreativo

'lei·sure·ly ['liːʒəlɪ] adj *pace, lifestyle* tranquilo, relajado

'lei·sure time tiempo m libre

le·mon ['lemən] limón m

le·mon·ade [lemə'neɪd] limonada f

'le·mon juice zumo m de limón, L.Am. jugo de limón

le·mon 'tea té m con limón

lend [lend] v/t (pret & pp **lent**) prestar

length [leŋθ] longitud f; (*piece: of material etc*) pedazo m; **at length** *describe, explain* detalladamente; (*finally*) finalmente

length·en ['leŋθən] v/t alargar

length·y ['leŋθɪ] adj *speech, stay* largo

le·ni·ent ['liːnɪənt] adj indulgente, poco severo

lens [lenz] *of camera* objetivo m, lente f; *of eyeglasses* cristal m; *of eye* cristalino m; (*contact lens*) lente m de contacto, Span lentilla f

'lens cov·er *of camera* tapa f del objetivo

Lent [lent] REL Cuaresma f

lent [lent] pret & pp → **lend**

len·til ['lentl] lenteja f

len·til 'soup sopa f de lentejas

Leo ['liːoʊ] Leo ASTR m/f inv

leop·ard ['lepərd] leopardo m

le·o·tard ['liːoʊtɑːrd] malla f

les·bi·an ['lezbɪən] **1** n lesbiana f **2** adj lésbico, lesbiano

less [les] adv menos; **eat / talk less** comer / hablar menos; **less interesting / serious** menos interesante / serio; **it costs less** cuesta menos; **less than $200** menos de 200 dólares

les·sen ['lesn] **1** v/t disminuir **2** v/i reducirse, disminuir

les·son ['lesn] lección f

let [let] v/t (pret & pp **let**) (*allow*) dejar, permitir; **let s.o. do sth** dejar a alguien hacer algo; **let me go!** ¡déjame!; **let him come in!** ¡déjale entrar!; **let's go / stay** vamos / quedémonos; **let's not argue** no discutamos; **let alone** mucho menos; **let go of sth** of rope, handle soltar algo; **let go of me!** ¡suéltame!

◆ **let down** v/t hair soltarse; blinds bajar; (disappoint) decepcionar, defraudar; dress, pants alargar

◆ **let in** v/t to house dejar pasar

◆ **let off** v/t (not punish) perdonar; from car dejar; **the court let him off with a small fine** el tribunal sólo le impuso una pequeña multa

◆ **let out** v/t of room, building alquilar, Mex rentar; jacket etc agrandar; (groan, yell soltar

◆ **let up** v/i (stop) amainar

le·thal ['liːθl] adj letal

leth·ar·gic [lɪ'θɑːrdʒɪk] adj aletargado, apático

leth·ar·gy ['leθərdʒɪ] sopor m, apatía f

let·ter ['letər] of alphabet letra f; in mail carta f

'let·ter·box buzón m

'let·ter·head (heading) membrete m; (headed paper) papel m con membrete

'let·ter of 'cred·it com carta f de crédito

let·tuce ['letɪs] lechuga f

'let·up: **without a letup** sin interrupción

leu·ke·mia [luː'kiːmɪə] leucemia f

lev·el ['levl] **1** adj field, surface nivelado, llano; in competition, scores igualado; **draw level with s.o.** in race ponerse a la altura de alguien **2** n on scale, in hierarchy, (amount) nivel m; **on the level** F (honest) honrado

lev·el-head·ed [levl'hedɪd] adj ecuánime, sensato

le·ver ['liːvər] **1** n palanca f **2** v/t: **lever sth open** abrir algo haciendo palanca

lev·er·age ['liːvrɪdʒ] apalancamiento m; (influence) influencia f

lev·y ['levɪ] v/t (pret & pp levied) taxes imponer

lewd [luːd] adj obsceno

li·a·bil·i·ty [laɪə'bɪlətɪ] (responsibility) responsabilidad f; (likeliness) propensión f (**to** a)

li·a·ble ['laɪəbl] adj (responsible) responsable (**for** de); **be liable to** (likely) ser propenso a

◆ li·ai·se with [lɪ'eɪz] v/t actuar de enlace con

li·ai·son [lɪ'eɪzɑːn] (contacts) contacto m, enlace m

li·ar [laɪr] mentiroso(-a) m(f)

li·bel ['laɪbl] **1** n calumnia f, difamación f **2** v/t calumniar, difamar

lib·e·ral ['lɪbərəl] adj (broad-minded), POL liberal; (generous: portion etc) abundante

lib·e·rate ['lɪbəreɪt] v/t liberar

lib·e·rat·ed ['lɪbəreɪtɪd] adj liberado

lib·e·ra·tion [lɪbə'reɪʃn] liberación f

lib·er·ty ['lɪbərtɪ] libertad f; **at liberty** of prisoner etc en libertad; **be at liberty to do sth** tener libertad para hacer algo

Li·bra ['liːbrə] ASTR Libra m/f inv

li·brar·i·an [laɪ'breɪrɪən] bibliotecario(-a) m(f)

li·bra·ry ['laɪbrɪ] biblioteca f

Lib·y·a ['lɪbɪə] Libia f

Lib·y·an ['lɪbɪən] **1** adj libio **2** n libio(-a) m(f)

lice [laɪs] pl → louse

li·cence Br → **license 1** n

li·cense ['laɪsns] **1** n permiso m, licencia f **2** v/t autorizar; **be licensed** tener permiso or licencia

'li·cense num·ber (número m de) matrícula f

'li·cense plate of car (placa f de) matrícula f

lick [lɪk] **1** n lamedura f **2** v/t lamer; **lick one's lips** relamerse

lick·ing ['lɪkɪŋ] F (defeat): **we got a licking** nos dieron una paliza F

li·co·rice ['lɪkərɪs] regaliz m

lie[1] [laɪ] **1** n mentira f **2** v/i mentir

lie[2] [laɪ] v/i (pret lay, pp lain) of person estar tumbado; of object estar; (be situated) estar, encontrarse; **lie on your stomach** túmbate boca abajo

◆ **lie down** v/i tumbarse

'lie-in: **have a lie-in** quedarse un rato más en la cama

lieu [luː]: *in lieu of* en lugar de

lieu·ten·ant [lʊ'tenənt] teniente *m/f*

life [laɪf] (*pl* **lives** [laɪvz]) vida *f*; *of machine* vida *f*, duración *f*; *all her life* toda su vida; *that's life!* ¡así es la vida!

'**life belt** salvavidas *m inv*

'**life·boat** *from ship* bote *m* salvavidas; *from land* lancha *f* de salvamento

'**life ex·pec·tan·cy** esperanza *f* de vida

'**life·guard** socorrista *m/f*

'**life his·to·ry** historia *f* de la vida

life im·pris·on·ment cadena *f* perpetua

'**life jack·et** chaleco *m* salvavidas

life·less ['laɪflɪs] *adj* sin vida

life·like ['laɪflaɪk] *adj* realista

'**life·long** de toda la vida

'**life pre·serv·er** salvavidas *m inv*

'**life-sav·ing** *adj medical equipment, drug* que salva vidas

'**life-sized** *adj* de tamaño natural

'**life-threat·en·ing** *adj* que puede ser mortal

'**life·time** vida *f*; *in my lifetime* durante mi vida

lift [lɪft] **1** *v/t* levantar **2** *v/i of fog* disiparse **3** *n* (*Br: elevator*) ascensor *m*; *give s.o. a lift* llevar a alguien (en coche)

♦ **lift off** *v/i of rocket* despegar

'**lift-off** *of rocket* despegue *m*

lig·a·ment ['lɪgəmənt] ligamento *m*

light[1] [laɪt] **1** *n* luz *f*; *in the light of* a la luz de; *have you got a light?* ¿tienes fuego? **2** *v/t* (*pret & pp* **lighted** *or* **lit**) *fire, cigarette* encender; (*illuminate*) iluminar **3** *adj color, sky* claro; *room* luminoso

light[2] [laɪt] **1** *adj* (*not heavy*) ligero **2** *adv*: *travel light* viajar ligero de equipaje

♦ **light up 1** *v/t* (*illuminate*) iluminar **2** *v/i* (*start to smoke*) encender un cigarrillo

'**light bulb** bombilla *f*

light·en[1] ['laɪtn] *v/t color* aclarar

light·en[2] ['laɪtn] *v/t load* aligerar

♦ **lighten up** *v/i of person* alegrarse; *come on, lighten up* venga, no te tomes las cosas tan en serio

light·er ['laɪtər] *for cigarettes* encendedor *m*, *Span* mechero *m*

light-head·ed [laɪt'hedɪd] (*dizzy*) mareado

light-'heart·ed [laɪt'hɑːrtɪd] *adj* alegre

'**light·house** faro *m*

light·ing ['laɪtɪŋ] iluminación *f*

light·ly ['laɪtlɪ] *adv touch* ligeramente; *get off lightly* salir bien parado

light·ness[1] ['laɪtnɪs] *of room, color* claridad *f*

light·ness[2] ['laɪtnɪs] *in weight* ligereza *f*

light·ning ['laɪtnɪŋ]: *a flash of lightning* un relámpago; *they were struck by lightning* les cayó un rayo

'**light·ning con·duc·tor** pararrayos *m inv*

'**light pen** lápiz *m* óptico

'**light·weight** *n in boxing* peso *m* ligero

'**light year** año *m* luz

like[1] [laɪk] **1** *prep* como; *be like s.o.* ser como alguien; *what is she like?* ¿cómo es?; *it's not like him* (*not his character*) no es su estilo **2** *conj* F (*as*) como; *like I said* como dije

like[2] [laɪk] *v/t*: *I like it / her* me gusta; *I would like ...* querría ...; *I would like to ...* me gustaría ...; *would you like to ...?* ¿querrías ...?; *would you like to ...?* ¿querrías ...?; *she likes to swim* le gusta nadar; *if you like* si quieres

like·a·ble ['laɪkəbl] *adj* simpático

like·li·hood ['laɪklɪhʊd] probabilidad *f*; *in all likelihood* con toda probabilidad

like·ly ['laɪklɪ] *adj* (*probable*) probable; *not likely!* ¡ni hablar!

like·ness ['laɪknɪs] (*resemblance*) parecido *m*

'**like·wise** ['laɪkwaɪz] *adv* igualmente; *pleased to meet you - likewise!* encantado de conocerle - ¡lo mismo digo!

lik·ing ['laɪkɪŋ] afición *f* (*for* a); *to your liking* a su gusto; *take a liking to s.o.* tomar cariño a alguien

li·lac ['laɪlək] *flower* lila *f*; *color* lila *m*

li·ly ['lɪlɪ] lirio *m*

li·ly of the 'val·ley lirio *m* de los valles

limb [lɪm] miembro *m*

lime[1] [laɪm] *fruit, tree* lima *f*

lime[2] [laɪm] *substance* cal *f*

lime'green *adj* verde lima

'**lime·light** *be in the limelight* estar en el candelero

lim·it ['lɪmɪt] **1** *n* límite *m*; *within limits*

dentro de un límite; **be off limits** of place ser zona prohibida; **that's the limit!** F ¡es el colmo! F **2** v/t limitar

lim·i·ta·tion [lɪmɪˈteɪʃn] limitación f

lim·it·ed 'com·pa·ny sociedad f limitada

li·mo ['lɪmoʊ] F limusina f

lim·ou·sine ['lɪməziːn] limusina f

limp¹ [lɪmp] adj flojo

limp² [lɪmp] n: **he has a limp** cojea

line¹ [laɪn] n of text, on road, TELEC línea f; of trees fila f, hilera f; of people fila f, cola f; of business especialidad f; **what line are you in?** ¿a qué te dedicas?; **the line is busy** está ocupado, Span está comunicando; **hold the line** no cuelgue; **draw the line at sth** no estar dispuesto a hacer algo; **line of inquiry** línea f de investigación; **line of reasoning** argumentación f; **stand in line** hacer cola; **in line with ...** (conforming with) en las mismas líneas que

line² [laɪn] v/t forrar

◆ **line up** v/i hacer cola

lin·e·ar ['lɪnɪər] adj lineal

lin·en ['lɪnɪn] material lino m; (sheets etc) ropa f blanca

lin·er ['laɪnər] ship transatlántico m

lines·man ['laɪnzmən] SP juez m de línea, linier m

lin·ger ['lɪŋɡər] v/i of person entretenerse; of pain persistir

lin·ge·rie ['lænʒəriː] lencería f

lin·guist ['lɪŋɡwɪst] lingüista m/f; **she's a good linguist** se le dan bien los idiomas

lin·guis·tic [lɪŋˈɡwɪstɪk] adj lingüístico

lin·ing ['laɪnɪŋ] of clothes forro m; of brakes, pipe revestimiento m

link [lɪŋk] **1** n (connection) conexión f; between countries vínculo m; in chain eslabón m **2** v/t conectar

◆ **link up** v/i encontrarse; TV conectar

li·on ['laɪən] león m

lip [lɪp] labio m

'lip·read v/i (pret & pp **lipread** [red]) leer los labios

'lip·stick barra f de labios

li·queur [lɪˈkjʊr] licor m

liq·uid ['lɪkwɪd] **1** n líquido m **2** adj líquido

liq·ui·date ['lɪkwɪdeɪt] v/t assets liquidar; F (kill) cepillarse a F

liq·ui·da·tion [lɪkwɪˈdeɪʃn] liquidación f; **go into liquidation** ir a la quiebra

liq·ui·di·ty [lɪˈkwɪdɪtɪ] FIN liquidez f

liq·uid·ize ['lɪkwɪdaɪz] v/t licuar

liq·uid·iz·er ['lɪkwɪdaɪzər] licuadora f

liq·uor ['lɪkər] bebida f alcohólica

'liq·uor store tienda f de bebidas alcohólicas

lisp [lɪsp] **1** n ceceo m **2** v/i cecear

list [lɪst] **1** n lista f **2** v/t enumerar; COMPUT listar

lis·ten ['lɪsn] v/i escuchar; **I tried to persuade him, but he wouldn't listen** intenté convencerle, pero no me hizo ningún caso

◆ **listen in** v/i escuchar

◆ **listen to** v/t radio, person escuchar

lis·ten·er ['lɪsnər] to radio oyente m/f; **he's a good listener** sabe escuchar

list·ings mag·a·zine ['lɪstɪŋz] guía f de espectáculos

list·less ['lɪstlɪs] adj apático, lánguido

lit [lɪt] pret & pp → **light**¹

li·ter ['liːtər] litro m

lit·e·ral ['lɪtərəl] adj literal

lit·e·ral·ly ['lɪtərəlɪ] adv literalmente

lit·e·ra·ry ['lɪtərerɪ] adj literario

lit·e·rate ['lɪtərət] adj culto; **be literate** saber leer y escribir

lit·e·ra·ture ['lɪtrətʃər] literatura f; about a product folletos mpl, prospectos mpl

li·tre Br → **liter**

lit·ter ['lɪtər] basura f; of animal camada f

'lit·ter bas·ket papelera f

'lit·ter bin cubo m de la basura

lit·tle ['lɪtl] **1** adj pequeño; **the little ones** los pequeños **2** n poco m; **the little I know** lo poco que sé; **a little** un poco; **a little bread / wine** un poco de pan / vino; **a little is better than nothing** más vale poco que nada **3** adv: poco; **little by little** poco a poco; **a little better / bigger** un poco mejor / más grande; **a little before 6** un poco antes de las 6

live¹ [lɪv] v/i vivir

◆ **live on 1** v/t rice, bread sobrevivir a base de **2** v/i (continue living) sobrevivir, vivir

◆ live up: **live it up** pasarlo bien

◆ live up to *v/t* responder a

◆ live with *v/t* vivir con

live² [laɪv] *adj broadcast* en directo; *ammunition* real; *wire* con corriente

live·li·hood ['laɪvlɪhʊd] vida *f*, sustento *m*; **earn one's livelihood** ganarse la vida

live·li·ness ['laɪvlɪnɪs] *of person, music* vivacidad *f*; *of debate* lo animado

live·ly ['laɪvlɪ] *adj* animado

liv·er ['lɪvər] MED, *food* hígado *m*

live·stock ['laɪvstɑːk] ganado *m*

liv·id ['lɪvɪd] *adj (angry)* enfurecido, furioso

liv·ing ['lɪvɪŋ] **1** *adj* vivo **2** *n* vida *f*; **what do you do for a living?** ¿en qué trabajas?; **earn one's living** ganarse la vida; **standard of living** estándar *m* de vida

'liv·ing room sala *f* de estar, salón *m*

liz·ard ['lɪzərd] lagarto *m*

load [loʊd] **1** *n also* ELEC carga *f*; **loads of F** montones de F **2** *v/t car, truck, gun* cargar; *camera* poner el carrete a; COMPUT: *software* cargar (en memoria); **load sth onto sth** cargar algo en algo

load·ed ['loʊdɪd] *adj* F *(very rich)* forrado F; *(drunk)* como una cuba

loaf [loʊf] *n (pl* **loaves** [loʊvz]) pan *m*; **a loaf of bread** una barra de pan, un pan

◆ loaf about *v/i* F gandulear F

loaf·er ['loʊfər] *shoe* mocasín *m*

loan [loʊn] **1** *n* préstamo *m*; **on loan** prestado **2** *v/t* prestar; **loan s.o. sth** prestar algo a alguien

loathe [loʊð] *v/t* detestar, aborrecer

loath·ing ['loʊðɪŋ] odio *m*, aborrecimiento *m*

lob·by ['lɑːbɪ] *n in hotel, theater* vestíbulo *m*; POL lobby *m*, grupo *m* de presión

lobe [loʊb] *of ear* lóbulo *m*

lob·ster ['lɑːbstər] langosta *f*

lo·cal ['loʊkl] **1** *adj* local; **the local people** la gente del lugar; **I'm not local** no soy de aquí **2** *n: the locals* los del lugar; **are you a local?** ¿eres de aquí?

'lo·cal call TELEC llamada *f* local

lo·cal e'lec·tions *npl* elecciones *fpl* municipales

lo·cal 'gov·ern·ment administración *f* municipal

lo·cal·i·ty [loʊ'kælətɪ] localidad *f*

lo·cal·ly ['loʊkəlɪ] *adv live, work* cerca, en la zona; **it's well known locally** es muy conocido en la zona; **they are grown locally** son cultivados en la región

lo·cal 'pro·duce productos *mpl* del lugar

'lo·cal time hora *f* local

lo·cate [loʊ'keɪt] *v/t new factory etc* emplazar, ubicar; *(identify position of)* situar; **be located** encontrarse

lo·ca·tion [loʊ'keɪʃn] *(siting)* emplazamiento *m*; *(identifying position of)* localización *f*; **on location** *movie* en exteriores

lock¹ [lɑːk] *of hair* mechón *m*

lock² [lɑːk] **1** *n on door* cerradura *f* **2** *v/t door* cerrar (con llave)

◆ lock away *v/t* guardar bajo llave

◆ lock in *v/t person* encerrar; **I locked myself in** me quedé encerrado

◆ lock out *v/t of house* dejar fuera

◆ lock up *v/t in prison* encerrar

lock·er ['lɑːkər] taquilla *f*

'lock·er room vestuario *m*

lock·et ['lɑːkɪt] guardapelo *m*

lock·smith ['lɑːksmɪθ] cerrajero(-a) *m(f)*

lo·cust ['loʊkəst] langosta *f*

lodge [lɑːdʒ] **1** *v/t complaint* presentar **2** *v/i of bullet* alojarse

lodg·er ['lɑːdʒər] huésped *m/f*

loft [lɑːft] buhardilla *f*, desván *m*

loft·y ['lɑːftɪ] *adj heights, ideals* elevado

log [lɑːg] *n wood* tronco *m*; *written record* registro *m*

◆ log off *v/i (pret & pp* **logged**) salir

◆ log on *v/i* entrar

◆ log on to *v/t* entrar a

'log·book *captain's* cuaderno *m* de bitácora; *driver's* documentación *f* del vehículo

log 'cab·in cabaña *f*

log·ger·heads ['lɑːgərhedz]: **be at loggerheads** estar enfrentado

lo·gic ['lɑːdʒɪk] lógica *f*

lo·gi·cal ['lɑːdʒɪkl] *adj* lógico

lo·gi·cal·ly ['lɑːdʒɪklɪ] *adv* lógicamente

lo·gis·tics [lə'dʒɪstɪks] logística *f*

lo·go ['loʊgoʊ] logotipo *m*

loi·ter ['lɔɪtər] v/i holgazanear

lol·li·pop ['lɑːlɪpɑːp] piruleta f

Lon·don ['lʌndən] Londres

lone·li·ness ['lounlɪnɪs] of person, place soledad f

lone·ly ['lounlɪ] adj person solo; place solitario

lon·er ['lounər] solitario(-a) m(f)

long[1] [lɔːŋ] **1** adj largo; it's a long way hay un largo camino; it's two feet long mide dos pies de largo; the movie is three hours long la película dura tres horas **2** adv mucho tiempo; don't be long no tardes mucho; 5 weeks is too long 5 semanas son mucho tiempo; will it take long? ¿llevará mucho tiempo?; that was long ago eso fue hace mucho tiempo; long before then mucho antes; before long al poco tiempo; we can't wait any longer no podemos esperar más tiempo; she no longer works here ya no trabaja aquí; so long as (provided) siempre que; so long! ¡hasta la vista!

long[2] [lɔːŋ] v/i: long for sth home echar en falta algo; change anhelar or desear algo; be longing to do sth anhelar or desear hacer algo

long-'dis·tance adj race de fondo; flight de larga distancia; a long-distance phone-call una llamada de larga distancia, una conferencia interurbana

lon·gev·i·ty [lɑːn'dʒevɪtɪ] longevidad f

long·ing ['lɔːŋɪŋ] n anhelo m, deseo m

lon·gi·tude ['lɑːŋgɪtuːd] longitud f

'long jump Br salto m de longitud

'long-range missile de largo alcance; forecast a largo plazo

long-sight·ed [lɔːŋ'saɪtɪd] adj hipermétrope

long-sleeved [lɔːŋ'sliːvd] adj de manga larga

long·'stand·ing adj antiguo

'long-term adj a largo plazo

'long wave RAD onda f larga

'long-wind·ed [lɔːŋ'wɪndɪd] adj prolijo

look [lʊk] **1** n (appearance) aspecto m; (glance) mirada f; give s.o./sth a look mirar a alguien / mirar algo; have a look at sth (examine) echar un vistazo a algo;

can I have a look? ¿puedo echarle un vistazo?; can I have a look around? in shop etc ¿puedo echar un vistazo?; looks (beauty) atractivo m, guapura f **2** v/i mirar; (search) buscar; (seem) parecer; you look tired / different pareces cansado / diferente; he looks about 25 aparenta 25 años; how do things look to you? ¿qué te parece cómo están las cosas?; that looks good tiene buena pinta

◆ **look after** v/t children cuidar (de); property, interests proteger

◆ **look ahead** v/i fig mirar hacia el futuro

◆ **look around 1** v/i mirar **2** v/t museum, city dar una vuelta por

◆ **look at** v/t mirar; (examine) estudiar; (consider) considerar; it depends how you look at it depende de cómo lo mires

◆ **look back** v/i mirar atrás

◆ **look down on** v/t mirar por encima del hombro a

◆ **look for** v/t buscar

◆ **look forward to** v/t estar deseando; I'm looking forward to the vacation tengo muchas ganas de empezar las vacaciones

◆ **look in on** v/t (visit) hacer una visita a

◆ **look into** v/t (investigate) investigar

◆ **look on 1** v/i (watch) quedarse mirando **2** v/t: look on s.o./sth as (consider) considerar a alguien / algo como

◆ **look onto** v/t garden, street dar a

◆ **look out** v/i through, from window etc mirar; (pay attention) tener cuidado; look out! ¡cuidado!

◆ **look out for** v/t buscar; (be on guard against) tener cuidado con

◆ **look out of** v/t window mirar por

◆ **look over** v/t translation revisar, repasar; house inspeccionar

◆ **look round** v/t museum, city dar una vuelta por

◆ **look through** v/t magazine, notes echar un vistazo a, hojear

◆ **look to** v/t (rely on): we look to you for help acudimos a usted en busca de ayuda

◆ **look up 1** v/i from paper etc levantar la mirada; (improve) mejorar; things are looking up las cosas están mejorando

2 v/t *word, phone number* buscar; (*visit*) visitar

◆ **look up to** v/t (*respect*) admirar

'look-out *person* centinela *m*, vigía *m*; *be on the lookout for* estar a la mira

◆ **loom up** [luːm] v/i aparecer (*out of* de entre)

loon·y ['luːnɪ] **1** *n* F chalado(-a) *m(f)* F **2** *adj* F chalado F

loop [luːp] *n* bucle *m*

'loop·hole *in law etc* resquicio *m or* vacío *m* legal

loose [luːs] *adj connection, button* suelto; *clothes* suelto, holgado; *morals* disoluto, relajado; *wording* impreciso; *loose change* suelto *m*, *L.Am.* sencillo *m*; *loose ends of problem, discussion* cabos *mpl* sueltos

loose·ly ['luːslɪ] *adv worded* vagamente

loos·en ['luːsn] v/t *collar, knot* aflojar

loot [luːt] **1** *n* botín *m* **2** v/i saquear

loot·er ['luːtər] saqueador(a) *m(f)*

◆ **lop off** [lɑːp] v/t (*pret & pp* **lopped**) *branch* cortar; podar

lop·sid·ed [lɑːp'saɪdɪd] *adj* torcido; *balance of committee* desigual

Lord [lɔːrd] (*God*) Señor *m*

Lord's 'Prayer padrenuestro *m*

lor·ry ['lɒrɪ] *Br* camión *m*

lose [luːz] **1** v/t (*pret & pp* **lost**) *object, match* perder **2** v/i (*pret & pp* **lost**) sp perder; *of clock* retrasarse; *I'm lost* me he perdido; *get lost!* F ¡vete a paseo!

◆ **lose out** v/i salir perdiendo

los·er ['luːzər] perdedor(a) *m(f)*; *F in life* fracasado(-a) *m(f)*

loss [lɒːs] pérdida *f*; *make a loss* tener pérdidas; *I'm at a loss what to say* no sé qué decir

lost [lɑːst] **1** *adj* perdido **2** *pret & pp* → **lose**

lost-and-'found, *Br* **lost 'prop·er·ty** (*office*) oficina *f* de objetos perdidos

lot [lɑːt]: *the lot* todo; *a lot (of), lots (of)* mucho, muchos; *a lot of books, lots of books* muchos libros; *a lot of butter, lots of butter* mucha mantequilla; *a lot better / easier* mucho mejor / más fácil

lo·tion ['loʊʃn] loción *f*

lot·te·ry ['lɑːtərɪ] lotería *f*

loud [laʊd] *adj voice, noise* fuerte; *music* fuerte, alto; *color* chillón

loud'speak·er altavoz *m*, *L.Am.* altoparlante *m*

lounge [laʊndʒ] *in house* salón *m*

◆ **lounge about** v/i holgazanear

'lounge suit traje *m* de calle

louse [laʊs] (*pl lice* [laɪs]) piojo *m*

lous·y ['laʊzɪ] *adj* F asqueroso F; *I feel lousy* me siento de pena F

lout [laʊt] gamberro *m*

lov·a·ble ['lʌvəbl] *adj* adorable, encantador

love [lʌv] **1** *n* amor *m*; *in tennis* nada *f*; *be in love* estar enamorado (*with* de); *I'm in love with you* estoy enamorado de ti; *fall in love* enamorarse (*with* de); *make love* hacer el amor; *make love to* hacer el amor con; *yes, my love* sí, amor **2** v/t *person, country, wine* amar; *she loves to watch tennis* le encanta ver tenis

'love af·fair aventura *f* amorosa

'love-life vida *f* amorosa

'love let·ter carta *f* de amor

love·ly ['lʌvlɪ] *adj face, hair, color, tune* precioso, lindo; *person, character* encantador; *holiday, weather, meal* estupendo; *we had a lovely time* nos lo pasamos de maravilla

lov·er ['lʌvər] amante *m/f*

lov·ing ['lʌvɪŋ] *adj* cariñoso

lov·ing·ly ['lʌvɪŋlɪ] *adv* con cariño

low [loʊ] **1** *adj bridge, salary, price, voice, quality* bajo; *be feeling low* estar deprimido; *we're low on gas / tea* nos queda poca gasolina / té **2** *n in weather* zona *f* de bajas presiones, borrasca *f*; *in sales, statistics* mínimo *m*

low·brow ['loʊbraʊ] *adj* poco intelectual, popular

low-'cal·o·rie *adj* bajo en calorías

'low-cut *adj dress* escotado

low·er ['loʊər] v/t *to the ground, hemline, price* bajar; *flag* arriar; *pressure* reducir

'low-fat *adj* de bajo contenido graso

'low-key *adj* discreto, mesurado

'low·lands *npl* tierras *fpl* bajas

low·'pres·sure ar·e·a zona *f* de bajas presiones, borrasca *f*

'low sea·son temporada *f* baja

'low tide marea *f* baja

loy·al ['lɔɪəl] *adj* leal, fiel (**to** a)

loy·al·ly ['lɔɪəlɪ] *adv* lealmente, fielmente

loy·al·ty ['lɔɪəltɪ] lealtad *f* (**to** a)

loz·enge ['lɑːzɪndʒ] *shape* rombo *m*; *tablet* pastilla *f*

Ltd *abbr* (= **limited**) S.L. (= sociedad *f* limitada)

lu·bri·cant ['luːbrɪkənt] lubricante *m*

lu·bri·cate ['luːbrɪkeɪt] *v/t* lubricar

lu·bri·ca·tion [luːbrɪ'keɪʃn] lubricación *f*

lu·cid ['luːsɪd] *adj* (*clear, sane*) lúcido

luck [lʌk] suerte *f*; **bad luck** mala suerte; **hard luck!** ¡mala suerte!; **good luck!** ¡buena suerte!

◆ luck out *v/i* F tener mucha suerte

luck·i·ly ['lʌkɪlɪ] *adv* afortunadamente, por suerte

luck·y ['lʌkɪ] *adj person, coincidence* afortunado; *day, number* de la suerte; **you were lucky** tuviste suerte; **she's lucky to be alive** tiene suerte de estar con vida; **that's lucky!** ¡qué suerte!

lu·cra·tive ['luːkrətɪv] *adj* lucrativo

lu·di·crous ['luːdɪkrəs] *adj* ridículo

lug [lʌg] *v/t* (*pret & pp lugged*) arrastrar

lug·gage ['lʌgɪdʒ] equipaje *m*

luke·warm ['luːkwɔːrm] *adj water* tibio, templado; *reception* indiferente

lull [lʌl] **1** *n in storm, fighting* tregua *f*; *in conversation* pausa *f* **2** *v/t*: **lull s.o. into a false sense of security** dar a alguien una falsa sensación de seguridad

lul·la·by ['lʌləbaɪ] canción *f* de cuna, nana *f*

lum·ba·go [lʌm'beɪgoʊ] lumbago *m*

lum·ber ['lʌmbər] *n* (*timber*) madera *f*

lu·mi·nous ['luːmɪnəs] *adj* luminoso

lump [lʌmp] *n of sugar, earth* terrón *m*; (*swelling*) bulto *m*

◆ lump together *v/t* agrupar

lump 'sum pago *m* único

lump·y ['lʌmpɪ] *adj liquid, sauce* grumoso; *mattress* lleno de bultos

lu·na·cy ['luːnəsɪ] locura *f*

lu·nar ['luːnər] *adj* lunar

lu·na·tic ['luːnətɪk] *n* lunático(-a) *m(f)*, loco(-a) *m(f)*

lunch [lʌntʃ] *n* almuerzo *m*, comida *f*; **have lunch** almorzar, comer

'lunch box fiambrera *f*

'lunch break pausa *f* para el almuerzo

'lunch hour hora *f* del almuerzo

'lunch·time hora *f* del almuerzo

lung [lʌŋ] pulmón *m*

'lung can·cer cáncer *m* de pulmón

◆ lunge at [lʌndʒ] *v/t* arremeter contra

lurch [lɜːrtʃ] *v/i of drunk* tambalearse; *of ship* dar sacudidas

lure [lʊr] **1** *n* atractivo *m* **2** *v/t* atraer

lu·rid ['lʊrɪd] *adj color* chillón; *details* espeluznante

lurk [lɜːrk] *v/i of person* estar oculto, estar al acecho

lus·cious ['lʌʃəs] *adj fruit, dessert* jugoso, exquisito; F *woman, man* cautivador

lush [lʌʃ] *adj vegetation* exuberante

lust [lʌst] *n* lujuria *f*

lux·u·ri·ous [lʌg'ʒʊrɪəs] *adj* lujoso

lux·u·ri·ous·ly [lʌg'ʒʊrɪəslɪ] *adv* lujosamente

lux·u·ry ['lʌkʃərɪ] **1** *n* lujo *m* **2** *adj* de lujo

lymph gland ['lɪmfglænd] ganglio *m* linfático

lynch [lɪntʃ] *v/t* linchar

lyr·i·cist ['lɪrɪsɪst] letrista *m/f*

lyr·ics ['lɪrɪks] *npl* letra *f*

M

M [em] *abbr* (= *medium*) M (= talla *f* media)

MA [em'ei] *abbr* (= *Master of Arts*) Máster *m* en Humanidades

ma'am [mæm] señora *f*

mac [mæk] F (*mackintosh*) impermeable *m*

ma·chine [mə'ʃi:n] 1 *n* máquina *f* 2 *v/t with sewing machine* coser a máquina; TECH trabajar a máquina

ma'chine gun *n* ametralladora *f*

ma·chine-'read·a·ble *adj* legible por *Span* el ordenador *or L.Am.* la computadora

ma·chin·e·ry [mə'ʃi:nərɪ] (*machines*) maquinaria *f*

ma·chine trans'la·tion traducción *f* automática

ma·chis·mo [mə'kɪzmou] machismo *m*

mach·o ['mætʃou] *adj* macho

mack·in·tosh ['mækɪntɑ:ʃ] impermeable *m*

mac·ro ['mækrou] COMPUT macro *m*

mad [mæd] *adj* (*insane*) loco; F (*angry*) enfadado; *a mad idea* una idea disparatada; *be mad about* F estar loco por; *drive s.o. mad* volver loco a alguien; *go mad* (*become insane*) volverse loco; F (*with enthusiasm*) volverse loco F; *like mad* F *run, work* como un loco F; *Pa got real mad when I told him* papá se puso hecho una furia cuando se lo conté

mad·den ['mædən] *v/t* (*infuriate*) sacar de quicio

mad·den·ing ['mædnɪŋ] *adj* exasperante

made [meɪd] *pret & pp* → *make*

'mad·house *fig* casa *f* de locos

mad·ly ['mædlɪ] *adv* como loco; *madly in love* locamente enamorado

'mad·man loco *m*

mad·ness ['mædnɪs] locura *f*

Ma·don·na [mə'dɑ:nə] madona *f*

Ma·fi·a ['mɑːfɪə]: *the Mafia* la mafia

mag·a·zine [mægə'zi:n] (*printed*) revista

f

mag·got ['mægət] gusano *m*

Ma·gi ['meɪdʒaɪ] REL: *the Magi* los Reyes Magos

ma·gic ['mædʒɪk] 1 *n* magia *f*; *as if by magic, like magic* como por arte de magia 2 *adj* mágico; *there's nothing magic about it* no tiene nada de mágico

mag·i·cal ['mædʒɪkl] *adj* mágico

ma·gi·cian [mə'dʒɪʃn] *performer* mago(-a) *m(f)*

ma·gic 'spell hechizo *m*

ma·gic 'trick truco *m* de magia

mag·ic 'wand varita *f* mágica

mag·nan·i·mous [mæg'nænɪməs] *adj* magnánimo

mag·net ['mægnɪt] imán *m*

mag·net·ic [mæg'netɪk] *adj* magnético; *fig: personality* cautivador

mag·net·ic 'stripe banda *f* magnética

mag·net·ism ['mægnetɪzm] *of person* magnetismo *m*

mag·nif·i·cence [mæg'nɪfɪsəns] magnificencia *f*

mag·nif·i·cent [mæg'nɪfɪsənt] *adj* magnífico

mag·ni·fy ['mægnɪfaɪ] *v/t* (*pret & pp* *magnified*) aumentar; *difficulties* magnificar

'mag·ni·fy·ing glass lupa *f*

mag·ni·tude ['mægnɪtuːd] magnitud *f*

ma·hog·a·ny [mə'hɑ:gənɪ] caoba *f*

maid [meɪd] (*servant*) criada *f*; *in hotel* camarera *f*

'maid·en name ['meɪdn] apellido *m* de soltera

maid·en 'voy·age viaje *m* inaugural

mail [meɪl] 1 *n* correo *m*; *put sth in the mail* echar algo al correo 2 *v/t letter* enviar (por correo)

'mail·box *also* COMPUT buzón *m*

'mail·ing list lista *f* de direcciones

'mail·man cartero *m*

mail-'or·der cat·a·log, *Br* mail-'or·der cat·a·logue catálogo *m* de venta por correo

mail-'or·der firm empresa f de venta por correo

'mail-shot mailing m

maim [meɪm] v/t mutilar

main [meɪn] adj principal; *she's alive, that's the main thing* está viva, que es lo principal

'main course plato m principal

main 'en·trance entrada f principal

'main-frame *Span* ordenador m central, *L.Am.* computadora f central

'main·land tierra f firme; *on the mainland* en el continente

main·ly ['meɪnlɪ] adv principalmente

main 'road carretera f general

'main street calle f principal

main·tain [meɪn'teɪn] v/t mantener

main·te·nance ['meɪntənəns] mantenimiento m; *pay maintenance* pagar una pensión alimenticia

'main·te·nance costs npl gastos mpl de mantenimiento

'main·te·nance staff personal m de mantenimiento

ma·jes·tic [mə'dʒestɪk] adj majestuoso

ma·jes·ty ['mædʒestɪ] majestuosidad f; *Her Majesty* Su Majestad

ma·jor ['meɪdʒər] 1 adj (*significant*) importante, principal; *in C major* MUS en C mayor 2 n MIL comandante m

♦ major in v/t especializarse en

ma·jor·i·ty [mə'dʒɑːrətɪ] *also* POL mayoría f; *be in the majority* ser mayoría

make [meɪk] 1 n (*brand*) marca f 2 v/t (*pret & pp made*) hacer; *cars* fabricar, producir; *movie* rodar; *speech* pronunciar; (*earn*) ganar; MATH hacer; *two and two make four* dos y dos son cuatro; *make s.o. do sth* (*force to*) obligar a alguien a hacer algo; (*cause to*) hacer que alguien haga algo; *you can't make me do it!* ¡no puedes obligarme a hacerlo!; *make s.o. happy / angry* hacer feliz/ enfadar a alguien; *make a decision* tomar una decisión; *make a telephone call* hacer una llamada telefónica; *made in Japan* hecho en Japón; *make it* (*catch bus, train*) llegar a tiempo; (*come*) ir;

(*succeed*) tener éxito; (*survive*) sobrevivir; *what time do you make it?* ¿qué hora llevas?; *make believe* imaginarse; *make do with* conformarse con; *what do you make of it?* ¿qué piensas?

♦ make for v/t (*go toward*) dirigirse hacia

♦ make off v/i escaparse

♦ make off with v/t (*steal*) llevarse

♦ make out v/t *list* hacer, elaborar; *check* extender; (*see*) distinguir; (*imply*) pretender

♦ make over ceder

♦ make up 1 v/i *of woman, actor* maquillarse; *after quarrel* reconciliarse 2 v/t *story, excuse* inventar; *face* maquillar; (*constitute*) suponer, formar; *be made up of* estar compuesto de; *make up one's mind* decidirse; *make it up* *after quarrel* reconciliarse

♦ make up for v/t compensar por

'make-be·lieve n ficción f, fantasía f

mak·er ['meɪkər] (*manufacturer*) fabricante m

make·shift ['meɪkʃɪft] adj improvisado

make-up ['meɪkʌp] (*cosmetics*) maquillaje m

'make-up bag bolsa f del maquillaje

mal·ad·just·ed [mælə'dʒʌstɪd] adj inadaptado

male [meɪl] 1 adj (*masculine*) masculino; *animal, bird, fish* macho; *male bosses* los jefes varones; *a male teacher* un profesor 2 n *man* hombre m, varón m; *animal, bird, fish* macho m

male 'chau·vin·ism machismo m

male chau·vin·ist 'pig machista m

male 'nurse enfermero m

ma·lev·o·lent [mə'levələnt] adj malévolo

mal·func·tion [mæl'fʌŋkʃn] 1 n fallo m (*in* de) 2 v/i fallar

mal·ice ['mælɪs] malicia f

ma·li·cious [mə'lɪʃəs] adj malicioso

ma·lig·nant [mə'lɪgnənt] adj *tumor* maligno

mall [mɔːl] (*shopping mall*) centro m comercial

mal·nu·tri·tion [mælnuː'trɪʃn] desnutrición f

mal·treat [mæl'triːt] v/t maltratar

mal·treat·ment [mæl'tri:tmənt] maltrato *m*

mam·mal ['mæml] mamífero *m*

mam·moth ['mæməθ] *adj* (*enormous*) gigantesco

man [mæn] **1** *n* (*pl* **men** [men]) hombre *m*; (*humanity*) el hombre; *in checkers* ficha *f* **2** *v/t* (*pret* & *pp* **manned**) *telephones, front desk* atender; *spacecraft* tripular

man·age ['mænɪdʒ] **1** *v/t business* dirigir; *money* gestionar; *suitcase* poder con; *manage to* ... conseguir ... **2** *v/i* (*cope*) arreglárselas

man·age·a·ble ['mænɪdʒəbl] *adj* (*easy to handle*) manejable; (*feasible*) factible

man·age·ment ['mænɪdʒmənt] (*managing*) gestión *f*, administración *f*; (*managers*) dirección *f*; *under his management* bajo su gestión

man·age·ment 'buy-out compra de una empresa por sus directivos

man·age·ment con'sult·ant consultor(a) *m(f)* en administración de empresas

'man·age·ment stud·ies estudios *mpl* de administración de empresas

'man·age·ment team equipo *m* directivo

man·ag·er ['mænɪdʒər] *of hotel, company* director(a) *m(f)*; *of shop, restaurant* encargado(-a) *m(f)*

man·a·ge·ri·al [mænɪ'dʒɪrɪəl] *adj* de gestión; *a managerial post* un puesto directivo

man·ag·ing di'rec·tor director(a) *m(f)* gerente

man·da·rin (**or·ange**) [mændərɪn'(ɔːrɪndʒ)] mandarina *f*

man·date ['mændeɪt] (*authority*) mandato *m*; (*task*) tarea *f*

man·da·to·ry ['mændətɔːrɪ] *adj* obligatorio

mane [meɪn] *of horse* crines *fpl*

ma·neu·ver [mə'nuːvər] **1** *n* maniobra *f* **2** *v/t* maniobrar; *she maneuvered him into giving her the assignment* consiguió convencerle para que le diera el trabajo

man·gle ['mæŋgl] *v/t* (*crush*) destrozar

man·han·dle ['mænhændl] *v/t* mover a la fuerza

man·hood ['mænhʊd] (*maturity*) madur-

ez *f*; (*virility*) virilidad *f*

'man-hour hora-hombre *f*

'man·hunt persecución *f*

ma·ni·a ['meɪnɪə] (*craze*) pasión *f*

ma·ni·ac ['meɪnɪæk] F chiflado(-a) *m(f)* F

man·i·cure ['mænɪkjʊr] manicura *f*

man·i·fest ['mænɪfest] **1** *adj* manifiesto **2** *v/t* manifestar; *manifest itself* manifestarse

ma·nip·u·late [mə'nɪpjəleɪt] *v/t person, bones* manipular

ma·nip·u·la·tion [mənɪpjə'leɪʃn] *of person, bones* manipulación *f*

ma·nip·u·la·tive [mə'nɪpjələtɪv] *adj* manipulador

man'kind la hum*anidad*

man·ly ['mænlɪ] *adj* (*brave*) de hombres; (*strong*) varonil

'man-made *adj fibers, materials* sintético; *crater, structure* artificial

man·ner ['mænər] *of doing sth* manera *f*, modo *m*; (*attitude*) actitud *f*

man·ners ['mænərz] *npl* modales *mpl*; *good / bad manners* buena / mala educación; *have no manners* ser un maleducado

ma·noeu·vre *Br* → **maneuver**

'man·pow·er (*workers*) mano *f* de obra; *for other tasks* recursos *mpl* humanos

man·sion ['mænʃn] mansión *f*

'man·slaugh·ter *Br* homicidio *m* sin premeditación

man·tel·piece ['mæntlpiːs] repisa *f* de chimenea

man·u·al ['mænjʊəl] **1** *adj* manual **2** *n* manual *m*

man·u·al·ly ['mænjʊəlɪ] *adv* a mano

man·u·fac·ture [mænjʊ'fæktʃər] **1** *n* fabricación *f* **2** *v/t equipment* fabricar

man·u·fac·tur·er [mænjʊ'fæktʃərər] fabricante *m*

man·u·fac·tur·ing [mænjʊ'fæktʃərɪŋ] *adj industry* manufacturero

ma·nure [mə'nʊr] estiércol *m*

man·u·script ['mænjʊskrɪpt] manuscrito *m*

man·y ['menɪ] **1** *adj* muchos; *take as many apples as you like* toma todas las manzanas que quieras; *many times*

M

muchas veces; **not many people / taxis** no mucha gente / muchos taxis; **too many problems / beers** demasiados problemas / demasiadas cervezas **2** *pron* muchos; **a great many, a good many** muchos; **how many do you need?** ¿cuántos necesitas?; **as many as 200 are still missing** hay hasta 200 desaparecidos

'man-year año-hombre *m*

map [mæp] mapa *m*

◆ map out *v/t* (*pret & pp* **mapped**) proyectar

ma·ple ['meɪpl] arce *m*

mar [mɑːr] *v/t* (*pret & pp* **marred**) empañar

mar·a·thon ['mærəθɑːn] *race* maratón *m or f*

mar·ble ['mɑːrbl] *material* mármol *m*

March [mɑːrtʃ] marzo *m*

march [mɑːrtʃ] **1** *n* marcha *f* **2** *v/i* marchar

march·er ['mɑːrtʃər] manifestante *mf*

mare [mer] yegua *f*

mar·ga·rine [mɑːrdʒə'riːn] margarina *f*

mar·gin ['mɑːrdʒɪn] *also* COM margen *m*; **by a narrow margin** por un estrecho margen

mar·gin·al ['mɑːrdʒɪnl] *adj* (*slight*) marginal

mar·gin·al·ly ['mɑːrdʒɪnlɪ] *adv* (*slightly*) ligeramente

mar·i·hua·na, mar·i·jua·na [mærɪ'hwɑːnə] marihuana *f*

ma·ri·na [mə'riːnə] puerto *m* deportivo

mar·i·nade [mærɪ'neɪd] *n* adobo *m*

mar·i·nate ['mærɪneɪt] *v/t* adobar, marinar

ma·rine [mə'riːn] **1** *adj* marino **2** *n* MIL marine *m/f*, infante *m/f* de marina

mar·i·tal ['mærɪtl] *adj* marital

mar·i·tal 'sta·tus estado *m* civil

mar·i·time ['mærɪtaɪm] *adj* marítimo

mar·jo·ram ['mɑːrdʒərəm] mejorana *f*

mark[1] [mɑːrk] FIN marco *m*

mark[2] [mɑːrk] **1** *n* señal *f*, marca *f*; (*stain*) marca *f*, mancha *f*; (*sign, token*) signo *m*, señal *f*; (*trace*) señal *f*; EDU nota *f*; **leave one's mark** dejar huella **2** *v/t* (*stain*) manchar; EDU calificar; (*indicate, commemo-*

rate) marcar **3** *v/i of fabric* mancharse

◆ mark down *v/t goods* rebajar

◆ mark out *v/t with a line etc* marcar; (*fig: set apart*) distinguir

◆ mark up *v/t price* subir; *goods* subir de precio

marked [mɑːrkt] *adj* (*definite*) marcado, notable

mark·er ['mɑːrkər] (*highlighter*) rotulador *m*

mar·ket ['mɑːrkɪt] **1** *n* mercado *m*; (*stock market*) bolsa *f*; **on the market** en el mercado **2** *v/t* comercializar

mar·ket·a·ble ['mɑːrkɪtəbl] *adj* comercializable

mar·ket e'con·o·my economía *f* de mercado

'mar·ket for·ces *npl* fuerzas *fpl* del mercado

mar·ket·ing ['mɑːrkɪtɪŋ] marketing *m*

'mar·ket·ing cam·paign campaña *f* de marketing

'mar·ket·ing de·part·ment departamento *m* de marketing

'mar·ket·ing mix marketing mix *m*, *el producto, el precio, la distribución y la promoción*

'mar·ket·ing strat·e·gy estrategia *f* de marketing

mar·ket 'lead·er líder *m* del mercado

'mar·ket·place *in town* plaza *f* del mercado; *for commodities* mercado *m*

mar·ket re'search investigación *m* de mercado

mar·ket 'share cuota *f* de mercado

mark-up ['mɑːrkʌp] margen *m*

mar·ma·lade ['mɑːrməleɪd] mermelada *f* de naranja

mar·quee [mɑːr'kiː] carpa *f*

mar·riage ['mærɪdʒ] matrimonio *m*; *event* boda *f*

'mar·riage cer·tif·i·cate certificado *m* de matrimonio

'mar·riage 'guid·ance coun·se·lor consejero(-a) *m(f)* matrimonial

mar·ried ['mærɪd] *adj* casado; **be married to ...** estar casado con ...

mar·ried 'life vida *f* matrimonial

mar·ry ['mærɪ] *v/t* (*pret & pp* **married**) casarse con; *of priest* casar; **get married** casarse

marsh [mɑːrʃ] pantano *m*, ciénaga *f*

mar·shal ['mɑːrʃl] *n in police* jefe(-a) *m(f)* de policía; *in security service* miembro *m* del servicio de seguridad

marsh·mal·low ['mɑːrʃˈmæloʊ] dulce de consistencia blanda

marsh·y ['mɑːrʃɪ] *adj* pantanoso

mar·tial arts [mɑːrʃl'ɑːrts] *npl* artes *fpl* marciales

mar·tial 'law ley *f* marcial

mar·tyr ['mɑːrtər] mártir *m/f*

mar·tyred ['mɑːrtərd] *adj fig* de mártir

mar·vel ['mɑːrvl] maravilla *f*

◆ **marvel** at *v/t* maravillarse de

mar·vel·ous, *Br* **mar·vel·lous** ['mɑːrvələs] *adj* maravilloso

Marx·ism ['mɑːrksɪzm] marxismo *m*

Marx·ist ['mɑːrksɪst] **1** *adj* marxista **2** *n* marxista *m/f*

mar·zi·pan ['mɑːrzɪpæn] mazapán *m*

mas·ca·ra [mæ'skærə] rímel *m*

mas·cot ['mæskət] mascota *f*

mas·cu·line ['mæskjʊlɪn] *adj* masculino

mas·cu·lin·i·ty [mæskjʊ'lɪnətɪ] *(virility)* masculinidad *f*

mash [mæʃ] *v/t* hacer puré de, majar

mashed po·ta·toes [mæʃt] *npl* puré *m* de patatas *or L.Am.* papas

mask [mæsk] **1** *n* máscara *f; to cover mouth, nose* mascarilla *f* **2** *v/t feelings* enmascarar

'mask·ing tape cinta *f* adhesiva de pintor

mas·och·ism ['mæsəkɪzm] masoquismo *m*

mas·och·ist ['mæsəkɪst] masoquista *m/f*

ma·son ['meɪsn] cantero *m*

ma·son·ry ['meɪsnrɪ] albañilería *f*

mas·que·rade [mæskə'reɪd] **1** *n fig* mascarada *f* **2** *v/i:* **masquerade as** hacerse pasar por

mass¹ [mæs] **1** *n (great amount)* gran cantidad *f; (body)* masa *f; the masses* las masas; **masses of** F un montón de F **2** *v/i* concentrarse

mass² [mæs] REL misa *f*

mas·sa·cre ['mæsəkər] **1** *n* masacre *f*, matanza *f; in sport* paliza *f* **2** *v/t* masa-

crar; F *in sport* dar una paliza a

mas·sage ['mæsɑːʒ] **1** *n* masaje *m* **2** *v/t* dar un masaje en; *figures* maquillar

'mas·sage par·lor, *Br* **'mas·sage parlour** salón *m* de masajes

mas·seur [mæ'sɜːr] masajista *m*

mas·seuse [mæ'sɜːz] masajista *f*

mas·sive ['mæsɪv] *adj* enorme; *heart attack* muy grave

mass 'me·di·a *npl* medios *mpl* de comunicación

mass·pro'duce *v/t* fabricar en serie

mass pro'duc·tion fabricación *f* en serie

mast [mæst] *of ship* mástil *m; for radio signal* torre *f*

mas·ter ['mæstər] **1** *n of dog* dueño *m*, amo *m; of ship* patrón *m;* **be a master of** ser un maestro de **2** *v/t skill, language, situation* dominar

'mas·ter bed·room dormitorio *m* principal

'mas·ter key llave *f* maestra

'mas·ter·ly ['mæstəlɪ] *adj* magistral

'mas·ter·mind 1 *n* cerebro *m* **2** *v/t* dirigir, organizar

Mas·ter of 'Arts Máster *m* en Humanidades

'mas·ter·piece obra *f* maestra

'mas·ter's (de·gree) máster *m*

mas·ter·y ['mæstərɪ] dominio *m*

mas·tur·bate ['mæstərbeɪt] *v/i* masturbarse

mat [mæt] *for floor* estera *f; for table* salvamanteles *m inv*

match¹ [mætʃ] *for cigarette* cerilla *f*, fósforo *m*

match² [mætʃ] **1** *n* SP partido *m; in chess* partida *f;* **be no match for s.o.** no estar a la altura de alguien; **meet one's match** encontrar la horma de su zapato **2** *v/t (be the same as)* coincidir con; *(be in harmony with)* hacer juego con; *(equal)* igualar **3** *v/i of colors, patterns* hacer juego

'match·box caja *f* de cerillas

match·ing ['mætʃɪŋ] *adj* a juego

'match stick cerilla *f*, fósforo *m*

mate [meɪt] **1** n of animal pareja f; NAUT oficial m/f **2** v/i aparearse; *these birds mate for life* estas aves viven con la misma pareja toda la vida

ma·te·ri·al [mə'tɪrɪəl] **1** n (fabric) tejido m; (substance) material m; *materials* materiales mpl **2** adj material

ma·te·ri·al·ism [mə'tɪrɪəlɪzm] materialismo m

ma·te·ri·al·ist [mətɪrɪə'lɪst] materialista m/f

ma·te·ri·al·is·tic [mətɪrɪə'lɪstɪk] adj materialista

ma·te·ri·al·ize [mə'tɪrɪəlaɪz] v/i (appear) aparecer; (come into existence) hacerse realidad

ma·ter·nal [mə'tɜːrnl] adj maternal; *my maternal grandfather* mi abuelo materno

ma·ter·ni·ty [mə'tɜːrnətɪ] maternidad f

ma·ter·ni·ty dress vestido m premamá

ma·ter·ni·ty leave baja f por maternidad

ma·ter·ni·ty ward pabellón m de maternidad

math [mæθ] matemáticas fpl

math·e·mat·i·cal [mæθə'mætɪkl] adj matemático

math·e·ma·ti·cian [mæθəmə'tɪʃn] matemático(-a) m(f)

math·e·mat·ics [mæθ'mætɪks] matemáticas fpl

maths Br → math

mat·i·née ['mætɪneɪ] sesión f de tarde

ma·tri·arch ['meɪtrɪɑːrk] matriarca f

mat·ri·mo·ny ['mætrəmounɪ] matrimonio m

matt [mæt] adj mate

mat·ter ['mætər] **1** n (affair) asunto m; PHYS materia f; *you're only making matters worse* sólo estás empeorando las cosas; *as a matter of course* automáticamente; *as a matter of fact* de hecho; *what's the matter?* ¿qué pasa?; *no matter what she says* diga lo que diga **2** v/i importar; *it doesn't matter* no importa

mat·ter-of-'fact adj tranquilo

mat·tress ['mætrɪs] colchón m

ma·ture [mə'tʃʊr] **1** adj maduro **2** v/i of person madurar; of insurance policy etc

vencer

ma·tu·ri·ty [mə'tʃʊrətɪ] madurez f

maul [mɔːl] v/t of lion, tiger atacar; of critics destrozar

max·i·mize ['mæksɪmaɪz] v/t maximizar

max·i·mum ['mæksɪməm] **1** adj máximo; *it will cost $500 maximum* costará 500 dólares como máximo **2** n máximo m

May [meɪ] mayo m

may [meɪ] v/aux ◊ possibility: *it may rain* puede que llueva; *you may be right* puede que tengas razón; *it may not happen* puede que no ocurra

◆ permission poder; *may I help / smoke?* ¿puedo ayudar / fumar?

may·be ['meɪbɪ] adv quizás, tal vez

'May Day el Primero de Mayo

may·o, may·on·naise ['meɪou, meɪ-'neɪz] mayonesa f

may·or [mer] alcalde m

maze [meɪz] laberinto m

MB abbr (= *megabyte*) MB (= megabyte m)

MBA [embiː'eɪ] abbr (= *Master of Business Administration*) MBA m (= Máster m en Administración de Empresas)

MBO [embiː'ou] abbr (= *management buyout*) compra de una empresa por sus directivos

MC [em'siː] abbr (= *master of ceremonies*) maestro m de ceremonias

MD [em'diː] abbr (= *Doctor of Medicine*) Doctor(a) m(f) en Medicina; (= *managing director*) director(a) m(f) gerente

me [miː] pron direct & indirect object me; after prep mí; *he knows me* me conoce; *he gave me the keys* me dio las llaves; *he sold it to me* me lo vendió; *this is for me* esto es para mí; *who do you mean? - me?* ¿a quién te refieres? - ¿a mí?; *with me* conmigo; *it's me* soy yo; *taller than me* más alto que yo

mead·ow ['medou] prado m

mea·ger, Br mea·gre ['miːgər] adj escaso, exiguo

meal [miːl] comida f; *enjoy your meal* ¡que aproveche!

'**meal·time** hora *f* de comer

mean¹ [miːn] *adj with money* tacaño; (*nasty*) malo, cruel; *that was a mean thing to say* ha estado fatal que dijeras eso

mean² [miːn] **1** *v/t* (*pret & pp* **meant**) (*intend to say*) querer decir; (*signify*) querer decir, significar; *you weren't meant to hear that* no era mi intención que oyeras eso; *mean to do sth* tener la intención de hacer algo; *be meant for* ser para; *of remark* ir dirigido a; *doesn't it mean anything to you?* ¿no te importa para nada? **2** *v/i* (*pret & pp* **meant**): *mean well* tener buena intención

mean·ing ['miːnɪŋ] *of word* significado *m*

mean·ing·ful ['miːnɪfəl] *adj* (*comprehensible*) con sentido; (*constructive*), *glance* significativo

mean·ing·less ['miːnɪŋlɪs] *adj* sin sentido

means [miːnz] *npl financial* medios *mpl*; (*nsg: way*) medio *m*; *a means of transport* un medio de transporte; *by all means* (*certainly*) por supuesto; *by all means check my figures* comprueba mis cifras, faltaría más; *by no means rich / poor* ni mucho menos rico / pobre; *by means of* mediante

meant [ment] *pret & pp* → **mean**²

mean·time ['miːntaɪm] **1** *adv* mientras tanto **2** *n*: *in the meantime* mientras tanto

mean·while ['miːnwaɪl] **1** *adv* mientras tanto **2** *n*: *in the meanwhile* mientras tanto

mea·sles ['miːzlz] *nsg* sarampión *m*

mea·sure ['meʒər] **1** *n* (*step*) medida *f*; *we've had a measure of success* (*certain amount*) hemos tenido cierto éxito **2** *v/t* medir **3** *v/i* medir

◆ **measure out** *v/t area, drink, medicine* medir; *sugar, flour, ingredients* pesar

◆ **measure up** *v/i* estar a la altura (*to* de)

mea·sure·ment ['meʒərmənt] medida *f*; *system of measurement* sistema *m* de medidas

meas·ur·ing jug ['meʒərɪŋ] jarra *m* graduada

'**mea·sur·ing tape** cinta *f* métrica

meat [miːt] carne *f*

'**meat·ball** albóndiga *f*

'**meat·loaf** *masa de carne cocinada en forma de barra de pan que se come fría*

me·chan·ic [mɪ'kænɪk] mecánico(-a) *m(f)*

me·chan·i·cal [mɪ'kænɪkl] *adj also fig* mecánico

me·chan·i·cal en·gi·neer ingeniero(-a) *m(f)* industrial

me·chan·i·cal en·gi·neer·ing ingeniería *f* industrial

me·chan·i·cal·ly [mɪ'kænɪklɪ] *adv also fig* mecánicamente

mech·a·nism ['mekənɪzm] mecanismo *m*

mech·a·nize ['mekənaɪz] *v/t* mecanizar

med·al ['medl] medalla *f*

med·a·list, *Br* **med·al·list** ['medəlɪst] medallista *m/f*

med·dle ['medl] *v/i* entrometerse; *don't meddle with the TV* no enredes con la televisión

me·di·a ['miːdɪə] *npl*: *the media* los medios de comunicación

'**me·di·a cov·er·age** cobertura *f* informativa

'**me·di·a e·vent** acontecimiento *m* informativo

me·di·a 'hype revuelo *m* informativo

'**me·di·a stud·ies** ciencias *fpl* de la información

me·di·an strip [miːdɪən'strɪp] mediana *f*

me·di·ate ['miːdɪeɪt] *v/i* mediar

me·di·a·tion [miːdɪ'eɪʃn] mediación *f*

me·di·a·tor ['miːdɪeɪtər] mediador(a) *m(f)*

med·i·cal ['medɪkl] **1** *adj* médico **2** *n* reconocimiento *m* médico

'**med·i·cal cer·tif·i·cate** certificado *m* médico

'**med·i·cal ex·am·i·na·tion** reconocimiento *m* médico

'**med·i·cal his·to·ry** historial *m* médico

'**med·i·cal pro·fes·sion** profesión *f* médica; (*doctors*) médicos *mpl*

'**med·i·cal re·cord** ficha *f* médica

Med·i·care ['medɪker] *seguro de enfermedad para los ancianos en Estados Unidos* med·i·cat·ed ['medɪkeɪtɪd] adj medicinal

med·i·ca·tion [medɪ'keɪʃn] medicamento m, medicina f; *are you on any medication?* ¿está tomando algún medicamento?

me·di·ci·nal [mɪ'dɪsɪnl] adj medicinal

medi·cine ['medsən] *science* medicina f; (*medication*) medicina f, medicamento m

'med·i·cine cab·i·net botiquín m

med·i·e·val [medɪ'iːvl] adj medieval

me·di·o·cre [miːdɪ'oukər] adj mediocre

me·di·oc·ri·ty [miːdɪ'ɑːkrətɪ] *of work etc, person* mediocridad f

med·i·tate ['medɪteɪt] v/i meditar

med·i·ta·tion [medɪ'teɪʃn] meditación f

Med·i·ter·ra·ne·an [medɪtə'reɪnɪən] 1 adj mediterráneo 2 n: *the Mediterranean* el Mediterráneo

me·di·um ['miːdɪəm] 1 adj (*average*) medio; *steak* a punto 2 n *size* talla f media; (*means*) medio m; (*spiritualist*) médium m/f

me·di·um-sized ['miːdɪəmsaɪzd] adj de tamaño medio

me·di·um 'term: *in the medium term* a medio plazo

'me·di·um wave RAD onda f media

med·ley ['medlɪ] (*assortment*) mezcla f

meek [miːk] adj manso, dócil

meet [miːt] 1 v/t (*pret & pp met*) *by appointment* encontrarse con, reunirse con; *by chance, of eyes* encontrarse con; (*get to know*) conocer; (*collect*) ir a buscar; *in competition* enfrentarse con; (*satisfy*) satisfacer; *meet a deadline* cumplir un plazo 2 v/i (*pret & pp met*) encontrarse; *in competition* enfrentarse; *of committee etc* reunirse; *have you two met?* ¿os conocíais? 3 n SP reunión f

◆ meet with v/t *person, opposition, approval* encontrarse con; *my attempts met with failure* mis intentos fracasaron

meet·ing ['miːtɪŋ] *by chance* encuentro m; *of committee, in business* reunión f; *he's in a meeting* está reunido

'meet·ing place lugar m de encuentro

meg·a·byte ['megəbaɪt] COMPUT megabyte m

mel·an·chol·y ['melənkəlɪ] adj melancólico

mel·low ['melou] 1 adj suave 2 v/i *of person* suavizarse, sosegarse

me·lo·di·ous [mɪ'loudɪəs] adj melodioso

mel·o·dra·mat·ic [melədrə'mætɪk] adj melodramático

mel·o·dy ['melədɪ] melodía f

mel·on ['melən] melón m

melt [melt] 1 v/i fundirse, derretirse 2 v/t fundir, derretir

◆ melt away v/i fig desvanecerse

◆ melt down v/t *metal* fundir

'melt·ing pot ['meltɪŋpɑːt] fig crisol m

mem·ber ['membər] miembro m

Mem·ber of 'Con·gress diputado(-a) m(f)

Mem·ber of 'Par·lia·ment *Br* diputado(-a) m(f)

mem·ber·ship ['membərʃɪp] afiliación f; (*number of members*) número m de miembros; *he applied for membership of the club* solicitó ser admitido en el club

'mem·ber·ship card tarjeta f de socio

mem·brane ['membreɪn] membrana f

me·men·to [me'mentou] recuerdo m

mem·o ['memou] nota f

mem·oirs ['memwɑːrz] npl memorias fpl

'mem·o pad bloc m de notas

mem·o·ra·ble ['memərəbl] adj memorable

me·mo·ri·al [mɪ'mɔːrɪəl] 1 adj conmemorativo 2 n monumento m conmemorativo

Me'mo·ri·al Day Día f de los Caídos

mem·o·rize ['meməraɪz] v/t memorizar

mem·o·ry ['memərɪ] (*recollection*) recuerdo m; (*power of recollection*), COMPUT memoria f; *I have no memory of the accident* no recuerdo el accidente; *have a good / bad memory* tener buena / mala memoria; *in memory of* en memoria de

men [men] pl → *man*

men·ace ['menɪs] 1 n (*threat*) amenaza f; *person* peligro m 2 v/t amenazar

men·ac·ing ['menɪsɪŋ] amenazador

mend [mend] 1 v/t reparar; *clothes* coser, remendar; *shoes* remendar 2 n: *be on the mend after illness* estar recuperándose

me·ni·al ['mi:nɪəl] *adj* ingrato, penoso

men·in·gi·tis [menɪn'dʒaɪtɪs] meningitis *f*

men·o·pause ['menəpɔ:z] menopausia *f*

'men's room servicio *m* de caballeros

men·stru·ate ['menstrʊeɪt] *v/i* menstruar

men·stru·a·tion [menstrʊ'eɪʃn] menstruación *f*

men·tal ['mentl] *adj* mental; F (*crazy*) chiflado F, pirado F

men·tal a'rith·me·tic cálculo *m* mental

men·tal 'cru·el·ty crueldad *f* mental

'men·tal hos·pi·tal hospital *m* psiquiátrico

men·tal 'ill·ness enfermedad *f* mental

men·tal·i·ty [men'tælətɪ] mentalidad *f*

men·tal·ly ['mentəlɪ] *adv* (*inwardly*) mentalmente

men·tal·ly 'hand·i·capped *adj* con minusvalía psíquica

men·tal·ly 'ill *adj*: *be mentally ill* sufrir una enfermedad mental

men·tion ['menʃn] **1** *n* mención *f*; *she made no mention of it* no lo mencionó **2** *v/t* mencionar; *don't mention it* (*you're welcome*) no hay de qué

men·tor ['mentɔ:r] mentor(a) *m(f)*

men·u ['menu:] *for food*, COMPUT menú *m*

mer·ce·na·ry ['mɜːrsɪnərɪ] **1** *adj* mercenario **2** *n* MIL mercenario(-a) *m(f)*

mer·chan·dise ['mɜːrtʃəndaɪz] mercancías *fpl*, *L.Am.* mercadería *f*

mer·chant ['mɜːrtʃənt] comerciante *m/f*

mer·chant 'bank *Br* banco *m* mercantil

mer·ci·ful ['mɜːrsɪfəl] *adj* compasivo, piadoso

mer·ci·ful·ly ['mɜːrsɪfəlɪ] *adv* (*thankfully*) afortunadamente

mer·ci·less ['mɜːrsɪlɪs] *adj* despiadado

mer·cu·ry ['mɜːrkjʊrɪ] mercurio *m*

mer·cy ['mɜːrsɪ] clemencia *f*, compasión *f*; *be at s.o.'s mercy* estar a merced de alguien

mere [mɪr] *adj* mero, simple

mere·ly ['mɪrlɪ] *adv* meramente, simplemente

merge [mɜːrdʒ] *v/i of two lines etc* juntarse, unirse; *of companies* fusionarse

merg·er ['mɜːrdʒər] COM fusión *f*

mer·it ['merɪt] **1** *n* (*worth*) mérito *m*; (*advantage*) ventaja *f*; *she got the job on merit* consiguió el trabajo por méritos propios **2** *v/t* merecer

mer·ry ['merɪ] *adj* alegre; *Merry Christmas!* ¡Feliz Navidad!

'mer·ry-go-round tiovivo *m*

mesh [meʃ] malla *f*

mess [mes] (*untidiness*) desorden *m*; (*trouble*) lío *m*; *I'm in a bit of a mess* estoy metido en un lío; *be a mess of room, desk* estar desordenado; *of hair* estar revuelto; *of situation, s.o.'s life* ser un desastre

◆ mess about, mess around **1** *v/i* enredar **2** *v/t person* jugar con

◆ mess around with *v/t* enredar con; *s.o.'s wife* tener un lío con

◆ mess up *v/t room, papers* desordenar; *task* convertir en una chapuza; *plans, marriage* estropear, arruinar

mes·sage ['mesɪdʒ] *also of movie etc* mensaje *m*

mes·sen·ger ['mesɪndʒər] (*courier*) mensajero(-a) *m(f)*

mess·y ['mesɪ] *adj room, person* desordenado; *job* sucio; *divorce, situation* desagradable

met [met] *pret & pp → meet*

me·tab·o·lism [mətæ'bəlɪzm] metabolismo *m*

met·al ['metl] **1** *adj* metálico **2** *n* metal *m*

me·tal·lic [mɪ'tælɪk] *adj* metálico

met·a·phor ['metəfər] metáfora *f*

me·te·or ['mi:tɪər] meteoro *m*

me·te·or·ic [mi:tɪ'ɔ:rɪk] *adj fig* meteórico

me·te·or·ite ['mi:tɪəraɪt] meteorito *m*

me·te·or·o·log·i·cal [mi:tɪə'lɑːdʒɪkl] *adj* meteorológico

me·te·or·ol·o·gist [mi:tɪə'rɑːlədʒɪst] meteorólogo(-a) *m(f)*

me·te·or·ol·o·gy [mi:tɪə'rɑːlədʒɪ] meteorología *f*

me·ter¹ ['mi:tər] *for gas, electricity* contador *m*; (*parking meter*) parquímetro *m*

me·ter² ['mi:tər] *unit of length* metro *m*

'me·ter read·ing lectura *f* del contador

meth·od ['meθəd] método *m*

me·thod·i·cal [mɪˈθɑːdɪkl] *adj* metódico
me·thod·i·cal·ly [mɪˈθɑːdɪklɪ] *adv* metódicamente
me·tic·u·lous [məˈtɪkjuləs] *adj* meticuloso, minucioso
me·tre *Br* → **meter**[2]
met·ric [ˈmetrɪk] *adj* métrico
me·trop·o·lis [mɪˈtrɑːpəlɪs] metrópolis *f inv*
met·ro·pol·i·tan [metrəˈpɑːlɪtən] *adj* metropolitano
mew [mjuː] → **miaow**
Mex·i·can [ˈmeksɪkən] **1** *adj* mexicano, mejicano **2** *n* mexicano(-a) *m(f)*, mejicano(-a) *m(f)*
Mex·i·co [ˈmeksɪkou] México, Méjico
Mex·i·co 'Cit·y *n* Ciudad *f* de México, *Mex* México, *Mex* el Distrito Federal, *Mex* el D.F.
mez·za·nine (floor) [ˈmezəniːn] entresuelo *m*
mi·aow [miau] **1** *n* maullido *m* **2** *v/i* maullar
mice [maɪs] *pl* → **mouse**
mick·ey mouse [mɪkɪˈmaus] *adj* P *course, qualification* de tres al cuarto P
mi·cro·bi·ol·o·gy [maɪkroubaɪˈɑːlədʒɪ] microbiología *f*
'mi·cro·chip microchip *m*
'mi·cro·cli·mate microclima *m*
mi·cro·cosm [ˈmaɪkroukɑːzm] microcosmos *m inv*
'mi·cro·e·lec·tron·ics microelectrónica *f*
'mi·cro·film microfilm *m*
'mi·cro·or·gan·ism microorganismo *m*
'mi·cro·phone micrófono *m*
mi·cro'pro·ces·sor microprocesador *m*
'mi·cro·scope microscopio *m*
mi·cro·scop·ic [maɪkrəˈskɑːpɪk] *adj* microscópico
'mi·cro·wave oven microondas *m inv*
mid-air [mɪdˈer]: *in midair* en pleno vuelo
mid·day [mɪdˈdeɪ] mediodía *m*
mid·dle [ˈmɪdl] **1** *adj* del medio; *the middle child of five* el tercero de cinco hermanos **2** *n* medio *m*; *it's the middle of the night!* ¡estamos en plena noche!; *in the middle of* of *floor, room* en medio de; *of period of time* a mitad *or* mediados

de; *in the middle of winter* en pleno invierno; *be in the middle of doing sth* estar ocupado haciendo algo
'mid·dle-aged *adj* de mediana edad
'Mid·dle Ages *npl* Edad *f* Media
mid·dle 'class *adj* de clase media; *the middle class(es)* las clases medias
Mid·dle 'East Oriente *m* Medio
'mid·dle·man intermediario *m*
mid·dle 'man·age·ment mandos *mpl* intermedios
'mid·dle 'name segundo nombre *m*
'mid·dle·weight *boxer* peso *m* medio
'mid·dling [ˈmɪdlɪŋ] *adj* regular
mid·field·er [mɪdˈfiːldər] centrocampista *m/f*
midge [mɪdʒ] mosquito *m* (pequeño)
midg·et [ˈmɪdʒɪt] *adj* en miniatura
'mid·night [ˈmɪdnaɪt] medianoche *f*; *at midnight* a medianoche
'mid·sum·mer pleno verano *m*
'mid·way *adv*: *we'll stop for lunch midway* pararemos para comer a mitad de camino; *midway through the meeting* a mitad de la reunión
'mid·week *adv* a mitad de semana
'Mid·west Medio Oeste *m* (de Estados Unidos)
'mid·wife comadrona *f*
'mid·win·ter pleno invierno *m*
might[1] [maɪt] *v/aux* poder, ser posible que; *I might be late* es posible que llegue tarde; *it might rain* puede *or* es posible que llueva; *it might never happen* puede *or* es posible que no ocurra nunca; *he might have left* a lo mejor se ha ido; *you might have told me!* ¡me lo podías haber dicho!
might[2] [maɪt] (*power*) poder *m*, fuerza *f*
might·y [ˈmaɪtɪ] **1** *adj* poderoso **2** *adv* F (*extremely*) muy, cantidad de F
mi·graine [ˈmiːgreɪn] migraña *f*
mi·grant work·er [ˈmaɪgrənt] trabajador(a) *m(f)* itinerante
mi·grate [maɪˈgreɪt] *v/i* emigrar
mi·gra·tion [maɪˈgreɪʃn] emigración *f*
mike [maɪk] F micro *m* F
mild [maɪld] *adj weather, climate* apacible; *cheese, voice* suave; *curry* no muy pic-

ante; *person* afable, apacible

mil·dew ['mɪldu:] moho *m*

mild·ly ['maɪldlɪ] *adv* say sth con suavidad; *spicy* ligeramente; **to put it mildly** por no decir algo peor

mild·ness ['maɪldnɪs] *of weather, voice* suavidad *f*; *of person* afabilidad *f*

mile [maɪl] milla *f*; **be miles better / easier** F ser mil veces mejor / más fácil F

mile·age ['maɪlɪdʒ] millas *fpl* recorridas; **unlimited mileage** kilometraje *m* ilimitado

'mile·stone *fig* hito *m*

mil·i·tant ['mɪlɪtənt] **1** *adj* militante **2** *n* militante *m/f*

mil·i·ta·ry ['mɪlɪterɪ] **1** *adj* militar **2** *n:* **the military** el ejército, las fuerzas armadas

mil·i·ta·ry a'cad·e·my academia *f* militar

mil·i·ta·ry po'lice policía *f* militar

mil·i·ta·ry 'serv·ice servicio *m* militar

mi·li·tia [mɪ'lɪʃə] milicia *f*

milk [mɪlk] **1** *n* leche *f* **2** *v/t* ordeñar

milk 'choc·o·late chocolate *m* con leche

'milk jug jarra *f* de leche

milk of mag·ne·sia leche *f* de magnesia

'milk·shake batido *m*

'milk·y ['mɪlkɪ] *adj with lots of milk* con mucha leche; *made with milk* con leche

Milk·y 'Way Vía *f* Láctea

mill [mɪl] *for grain* molino *m*; *for textiles* fábrica *f* de tejidos

◆ mill about, mill around *v/i* pulular

mil·len·ni·um [mɪ'lenɪəm] milenio *m*

mil·li·gram, *Br* mil·li·gramme ['mɪlɪgræm] miligramo *m*

mil·li·me·ter, *Br* mil·li·me·tre ['mɪlɪmi:tər] milímetro *m*

mil·lion ['mɪljən] millón *m*

mil·lion·aire [mɪljə'ner] millonario(-a) *m(f)*

mime [maɪm] *v/t* representar con gestos

mim·ic['mɪmɪk] **1** *n* imitador(a) *m(f)* **2** *v/t* (*pret & pp* **mimicked**) imitar

mince [mɪns] *v/t* picar

'mince·meat carne *f* picada

mince 'pie empanada *f* de carne picada

mind [maɪnd] **1** *n* mente *f*; **it's uppermost in my mind** es lo que más me preocupa; **it's all in your mind** son imaginaciones

tuyas; **be out of one's mind** haber perdido el juicio; **bear, keep sth in mind** recordar; **I've a good mind to ...** estoy considerando seriamente ...; **change one's mind** cambiar de opinión; **it didn't enter my mind** no se me ocurrió; **give s.o. a piece of one's mind** cantarle a alguien las cuarenta; **make up one's mind** decidirse; **have something on one's mind** tener algo en la cabeza; **keep one's mind on sth** concentrarse en algo **2** *v/t* (*look after*) cuidar (de); (*heed*) prestar atención a; **I don't mind what we do** no me importa lo que hagamos; **do you mind if I smoke?, do you mind my smoking?** ¿le importa que fume?; **would you mind opening the window?** ¿le importaría abrir la ventana?; **mind the step!** ¡cuidado con el escalón!; **mind your own business!** ¡métete en tus asuntos! **3** *v/i:* **mind!** ¡ten cuidado!; **never mind!** ¡no importa!; **I don't mind** no me importa, me da igual

mind-bog·gling ['maɪndbɑ:glɪŋ] *adj* increíble

mind·less ['maɪndlɪs] *adj violence* gratuito

mine¹ [maɪn] *pron* el mío, la mía; **los míos son rojos**; **that book are red los míos son rojos; that book is mine** eso libro es mío; **a cousin of mine** un primo mío

mine² [maɪn] **1** *n for coal etc* mina *f* **2** *v/i:* **mine for** extraer

mine³ [maɪn] **1** *n* (*explosive*) mina *f* **2** *v/t* minar

'mine·field MIL campo *m* de minas; *fig* campo *m* minado

min·er ['maɪnər] minero(-a) *m(f)*

min·e·ral ['mɪnərəl] *n* mineral *m*

'min·e·ral wa·ter agua *f* mineral

'mine·sweep·er NAUT dragaminas *m inv*

min·gle ['mɪŋgl] *v/i of sounds, smells* mezclarse; *at party* alternar

min·i ['mɪnɪ] *skirt* minifalda *f*

min·i·a·ture ['mɪnɪtʃər] *adj* en miniatura

'min·i·bus microbús *m*

min·i·mal ['mɪnɪməl] *adj* mínimo

min·i·mal·ism ['mɪnɪməlɪzm] minimalismo *m*

min·i·mize ['mɪnɪmaɪz] *v/t risk, delay* minimizar, reducir al mínimo; (*downplay*) minimizar, quitar importancia a

min·i·mum ['mɪnɪməm] **1** *adj* mínimo **2** *n* mínimo *m*

min·i·mum 'wage salario *m* mínimo

min·ing ['maɪnɪŋ] minería *f*

'min·i·se·ries TV miniserie *f*

'min·i·skirt minifalda *f*

min·is·ter ['mɪnɪstər] POL ministro(-a) *m(f)*; REL ministro(-a) *m(f)*, pastor(a) *m(f)*

min·is·te·ri·al [mɪnɪ'stɪrɪəl] *adj* ministerial

min·is·try ['mɪnɪstrɪ] POL ministerio *m*

mink [mɪŋk] *animal, fur* visón *m*; *coat* abrigo *m* de visón

mi·nor ['maɪnər] **1** *adj problem, setback* menor, pequeño; *operation, argument* de poca importancia; *aches and pains* leve; *in D minor* MUS en D menor **2** *n* LAW menor *m/f* de edad

mi·nor·i·ty [maɪ'nɑːrətɪ] minoría *f*; *be in the minority* ser minoría

mint [mɪnt] *n herb* menta *f*; *chocolate* pastilla *f* de chocolate con sabor a menta; *hard candy* caramelo *m* de menta

mi·nus ['maɪnəs] **1** *n* (*minus sign*) (signo *m* de) menos *m* **2** *prep* menos; *temperatures of minus 18* temperaturas de 18 grados bajo cero

mi·nus·cule ['mɪnəskjuːl] *adj* minúsculo

min·ute[1] ['mɪnɪt] *of time* minuto *m*; *in a minute* (*soon*) en un momento; *just a minute* un momento

mi·nute[2] [maɪ'nuːt] *adj* (*tiny*) diminuto, minúsculo; (*detailed*) minucioso; *in minute detail* minuciosamente

'mi·nute hand ['mɪnɪt] minutero *m*

mi·nute·ly [maɪ'nuːtlɪ] *adv in detail* minuciosamente; (*very slightly*) mínimamente

min·utes ['mɪnɪts] *npl of meeting* acta(s) *f(pl)*

mir·a·cle ['mɪrəkl] milagro *m*

mi·rac·u·lous [mɪ'rækjʊləs] *adj* milagroso

mi·rac·u·lous·ly [mɪ'rækjʊləslɪ] *adv* milagrosamente

mi·rage ['mɪrɑːʒ] espejismo *m*

mir·ror ['mɪrər] **1** *n* espejo *m*; MOT (espejo *m*) retrovisor *m* **2** *v/t* reflejar

mis·an·thro·pist [mɪ'zænθrəpɪst] misántropo(-a) *m(f)*

mis·ap·pre·hen·sion [mɪsæprɪ'henʃn]: *be under a misapprehension* estar equivocado

mis·be·have [mɪsbə'heɪv] *v/i* portarse mal

mis·be·hav·ior, *Br* **mis·be·hav·iour** [mɪsbə'heɪvɪər] mal comportamiento *m*

mis·cal·cu·late [mɪs'kælkjʊleɪt] *v/t & v/i* calcular mal

mis·cal·cu·la·tion [mɪs'kælkjʊleɪʃn] error *m* de cálculo

mis·car·riage ['mɪskærɪdʒ] MED aborto *m* (espontáneo); *miscarriage of justice* error *m* judicial

mis·car·ry ['mɪskærɪ] *v/i* (*pret & pp miscarried*) *of plan* fracasar

mis·cel·la·ne·ous [mɪsə'leɪnɪəs] *adj* diverso; *put it in the file marked "miscellaneous"* ponlo en la carpeta de "varios"

mis·chief ['mɪstʃɪf] (*naughtiness*) travesura *f*, trastada *f*

mis·chie·vous ['mɪstʃɪvəs] *adj* (*naughty*) travieso; (*malicious*) malicioso

mis·con·cep·tion [mɪskən'sepʃn] idea *f* equivocada

mis·con·duct [mɪs'kɑːndʌkt] mala conducta *f*

mis·con·strue [mɪskən'struː] *v/t* malinterpretar

mis·de·mea·nor, *Br* **mis·de·mea·nour** [mɪsdə'miːnər] falta *f*, delito *m* menor

mi·ser ['maɪzər] avaro(-a) *m(f)*

mis·e·ra·ble ['mɪzrəbl] *adj* (*unhappy*) triste, infeliz; *weather, performance* horroroso

mi·ser·ly ['maɪzərlɪ] *adj person* avaro; *a miserly $150* 150 míseros dólares

mis·e·ry ['mɪzərɪ] (*unhappiness*) tristeza *f*, infelicidad *f*; (*wretchedness*) miseria *f*

mis·fire [mɪs'faɪr] *v/i of joke, scheme* salir mal

mis·fit ['mɪsfɪt] *in society* inadaptado(-a) *m(f)*

mis·for·tune [mɪsˈfɔːrtʃən] desgracia f

mis·giv·ings [mɪsˈgɪvɪŋz] npl recelo m, duda f

mis·guid·ed [mɪsˈgaɪdɪd] adj person equivocado; attempt, plan desacertado

mis·han·dle [mɪsˈhændl] v/t situation llevar mal

mis·hap [ˈmɪshæp] contratiempo m

mis·in·form [mɪsɪnˈfɔːrm] v/t informar mal

mis·in·ter·pret [mɪsɪnˈtɜːrprɪt] v/t malinterpretar

mis·in·ter·pre·ta·tion [mɪsɪntɜːrprɪˈteɪʃn] mala interpretación f

mis·judge [mɪsˈdʒʌdʒ] v/t person, situation juzgar mal

mis·lay [mɪsˈleɪ] v/t (pret & pp mislaid) perder

mis·lead [mɪsˈliːd] v/t (pret & pp misled) engañar

mis·lead·ing [mɪsˈliːdɪŋ] adj engañoso

mis·man·age [mɪsˈmænɪdʒ] v/t gestionar mal

mis·man·age·ment [mɪsˈmænɪdʒmənt] mala gestión f

mis·match [ˈmɪsmætʃ]: there's a mismatch between the two sets of figures los dos grupos de cifras no se corresponden

mis·placed [ˈmɪspleɪst] adj loyalty inmerecido; enthusiasm inoportuno

mis·print [ˈmɪsprɪnt] errata f

mis·pro·nounce [mɪsprəˈnaʊns] v/t pronunciar mal

mis·pro·nun·ci·a·tion [mɪsprənʌnsɪˈeɪʃn] pronunciación f incorrecta

mis·read [mɪsˈriːd] v/t (pret & pp misread) word, figures leer mal; situation malinterpretar

mis·rep·re·sent [mɪsreprɪˈzent] v/t deformar, tergiversar

miss¹ [mɪs]: Miss Smith la señorita Smith; miss! ¡señorita!

miss² [mɪs] 1 n SP fallo m; give sth a miss meeting, party etc no ir a algo 2 v/t target no dar en; emotionally echar de menos; bus, train, airplane perder; (not notice) pasar por alto; (not be present at) perderse; I ducked and he missed me

me agaché y no me dio; you just missed her (she's just left) se acaba de marchar; we must have missed the turnoff nos hemos debido pasar el desvío; you don't miss much! ¡no se te escapa una!; miss a class faltar a una clase 3 v/i fallar

mis·shap·en [mɪsˈʃeɪpən] adj deforme

mis·sile [ˈmɪsəl] arma f arrojadiza; weapon misil m

miss·ing [ˈmɪsɪŋ] adj desaparecido; be missing of person, plane haber desaparecido; the missing money el dinero que falta

mis·sion [ˈmɪʃn] task misión f; people delegación f

mis·sion·a·ry [ˈmɪʃənrɪ] REL misionero(-a) m(f)

mis·spell [mɪsˈspel] v/t escribir incorrectamente

mist [mɪst] neblina f

◆ mist over v/i of eyes empañarse

◆ mist up v/i of mirror, window empañarse

mis·take [mɪˈsteɪk] 1 n error m, equivocación f; make a mistake cometer un error or una equivocación, equivocarse; by mistake por error or equivocación 2 v/t (pret mistook, pp mistaken) confundir; mistake X for Y confundir X con Y

mis·tak·en [mɪˈsteɪkən] 1 adj erróneo, equivocado; be mistaken estar equivocado 2 pp → mistake

mis·ter [ˈmɪstər] → Mr

mis·took [mɪˈstʊk] pret → mistake

mis·tress [ˈmɪstrɪs] lover amante f, querida f; of servant ama f; of dog dueña f, ama f

mis·trust [mɪsˈtrʌst] 1 n desconfianza f (of en) 2 v/t desconfiar de

mist·y [ˈmɪstɪ] adj weather neblinoso; eyes empañado; color borroso

mis·un·der·stand [mɪsʌndərˈstænd] v/t (pret & pp misunderstood) entender mal

mis·un·der·stand·ing [mɪsʌndərˈstændɪŋ] (mistake) malentendido m; (argument) desacuerdo m

mis·use 1 n [mɪsˈjuːs] uso m indebido 2 v/t [mɪsˈjuːz] usar indebidamente

mit·i·ga·ting cir·cum·stances ['mɪtɪgeɪtɪŋ] *npl* circunstancias *fpl* atenuantes
mitt [mɪt] *in baseball* guante *m* de béisbol
mit·ten ['mɪtən] mitón *m*
mix [mɪks] **1** *n* (*mixture*) mezcla *f; cooking*: ready to use preparado *m* **2** *v/t* mezclar; *mix the flour in well* mezclar la harina bien; *cement* preparar **3** *v/i socially* relacionarse
◆ **mix up** *v/t* (*confuse*) confundir (*with* con); (*put in wrong order*) revolver, desordenar; *be mixed up emotionally* tener problemas emocionales; *of figures* estar confundido; *of papers* estar revuelto *or* desordenado; *be mixed up in* estar metido en; *get mixed up with* verse liado con
◆ **mix with** *v/t* (*associate with*) relacionarse con
mixed [mɪkst] *adj feelings* contradictorio; *reactions, reviews* variado
mixed 'mar·riage matrimonio *m* mixto
mix·er ['mɪksər] *for food* batidora *f; drink* refresco *m* (*para mezclar con bebida alcohólica*); *she's a good mixer* es muy sociable
mix·ture ['mɪkstʃər] mezcla *f; medicine* preparado *m*
mix-up ['mɪksʌp] confusión *f*
moan [moʊn] **1** *n of pain* gemido *m* **2** *v/i in pain* gemir
mob [mɑːb] **1** *n* muchedumbre *f* **2** *v/t* (*pret & pp* **mobbed**) asediar, acosar
mo·bile ['moʊbəl] **1** *adj person* con movilidad; (*that can be moved*) móvil; *she's a lot less mobile now* ahora tiene mucha menos movilidad **2** *n* móvil *m*
mo·bile 'home casa *f* caravana
mo·bile 'phone *Br* teléfono *m* móvil
mo·bil·i·ty [mə'bɪlətɪ] movilidad *f*
mob·ster ['mɑːbstər] gángster *m*
mock [mɑːk] **1** *adj* fingido, simulado; *mock-Tudor houses* casas de estilo Tudor simulado; *mock exams / elections* exámenes *mpl*/elecciones *fpl* de prueba **2** *v/t* burlarse de
mock·er·y ['mɑːkərɪ] (*derision*) burlas *fpl*; (*travesty*) farsa *f*
mock-up ['mɑːkʌp] (*model*) maqueta *f*,

modelo *m*
mode [moʊd] (*form*), COMPUT modo *m*; *mode of transportation* medio *m* de transporte
mod·el ['mɑːdl] **1** *adj employee, husband* modélico, modelo; *model boat / plane* maqueta *f* de un barco / avión **2** *n miniature* maqueta *f*, modelo *m*; (*pattern*) modelo *m*; (*fashion model*) modelo *m/f; male model* modelo *m* **3** *v/t: model clothes* trabajar de modelo; *she models swimsuits* trabaja de modelo de bañadores **4** *v/i for designer* trabajar de modelo; *for artist, photographer* posar
mo·dem ['moʊdem] módem *m*
mod·e·rate 1 *adj* ['mɑːdərət] moderado **2** *n* ['mɑːdərət] POL moderado(-a) *m(f)* **3** *v/t* ['mɑːdəreɪt] moderar
mod·e·rate·ly ['mɑːdərətlɪ] *adv* medianamente, razonablemente
mod·e·ra·tion [mɑːdə'reɪʃn] (*restraint*) moderación *f; in moderation* con moderación
mod·ern ['mɑːdn] *adj* moderno; *in the modern world* en el mundo contemporáneo
mod·ern·i·za·tion [mɑːdənaɪ'zeɪʃn] modernización *f*
mod·ern·ize ['mɑːdənaɪz] **1** *v/t* modernizar **2** *v/i of business, country* modernizarse
mod·ern 'lan·guages *npl* lenguas *fpl* modernas
mod·est ['mɑːdɪst] *adj* modesto
mod·es·ty ['mɑːdɪstɪ] modestia *f*
mod·i·fi·ca·tion [mɑːdɪfɪ'keɪʃn] modificación *f*
mod·i·fy ['mɑːdɪfaɪ] *v/t* (*pret & pp* **modified**) modificar
mod·u·lar ['mɑːdʊlər] *adj furniture* por módulos
mod·ule ['mɑːduːl] módulo *m*
moist [mɔɪst] *adj* húmedo
moist·en ['mɔɪsn] *v/t* humedecer
mois·ture ['mɔɪstʃər] humedad *f*
mois·tur·iz·er ['mɔɪstʃəraɪzər] *for skin* crema *f* hidratante
mo·lar ['moʊlər] muela *f*, molar *m*
mo·las·ses [mə'læsɪz] *npl* melaza *f*

mold¹ [mould] *on food* moho *m*

mold² [mould] **1** *n* molde *m* **2** *v/t clay, character* moldear

mold·y ['mouldɪ] *adj food* mohoso *m*

mole [moul] *on skin* lunar *m*

mo·lec·u·lar [mə'lekjulər] *adj* molecular

mol·e·cule ['ma:lɪkju:l] molécula *f*

mo·lest [mə'lest] *v/t child, woman* abusar sexualmente de

mol·ly·cod·dle ['ma:lɪka:dl] *v/t* F mimar, consentir

mol·ten ['moultən] *adj* fundido

mom [ma:m] F mamá *f*

mo·ment ['moumənt] momento *m*; **at the moment** en estos momentos, ahora mismo; **for the moment** por el momento, por ahora

mo·men·tar·i·ly [moumən'terɪlɪ] *adv (for a moment)* momentáneamente; *(in a moment)* de un momento a otro

mo·men·ta·ry ['moumənterɪ] *adj* momentáneo

mo·men·tous [mə'mentəs] *adj* trascendental, muy importante

mo·men·tum [mə'mentəm] cobrar / perder ímpetu

mon·arch ['ma:nərk] monarca *m/f*

mon·ar·chy ['ma:nərkɪ] monarquía *f*

mon·as·tery ['ma:nəsterɪ] monasterio *m*

mo·nas·tic [mə'næstɪk] *adj* monástico

Mon·day ['mʌndeɪ] lunes *m inv*

mon·e·ta·ry ['ma:nɪterɪ] *adj* monetario

mon·ey ['mʌnɪ] dinero *m*; **he's making a lot of money** está ganando mucho dinero

'mon·ey belt faltriquera *f*

'mon·ey-lend·er prestamista *m/f*

'mon·ey mar·ket mercado *m* monetario

'mon·ey or·der giro *m* postal

mon·grel ['mʌngrəl] perro *m* cruzado

mon·i·tor ['ma:nɪtər] **1** *n* COMPUT monitor *m* **2** *v/t* controlar

monk [mʌŋk] monje *m*

mon·key ['mʌŋkɪ] mono *m*; F *child* diablillo *m* F

♦ monkey about with *v/t* F enredar con

'mon·key wrench llave *f* inglesa

mon·o·gram ['ma:nəgræm] monograma *m*

mon·o·grammed ['ma:nəgræmd] con monograma

mon·o·log, *Br* mon·o·logue ['ma:nəla:g] monólogo *m*

mo·nop·o·lize [mə'na:pəlaɪz] *v/t* monopolizar

mo·nop·o·ly [mə'na:pəlɪ] monopolio *m*

mo·not·o·nous [mə'na:tənəs] *adj* monótono

mo·not·o·ny [mə'na:tənɪ] monotonía *f*

mon·soon [ma:n'su:n] monzón *m*

mon·ster ['ma:nstər] *n* monstruo *m*

mon·stros·i·ty [ma:n'stra:sətɪ] monstruosidad *f*

mon·strous ['ma:nstrəs] *adj (frightening, huge)* monstruoso; *(shocking)* escandaloso

month [mʌnθ] mes *m*; **how much do you pay a month?** ¿cuánto pagas al mes?

month·ly ['mʌnθlɪ] **1** *adj* mensual **2** *adv* mensualmente **3** *n magazine* revista *f* mensual

mon·u·ment ['ma:numənt] monumento *m*

mon·u·ment·al [ma:nu'mentl] *adj fig* monumental

mood [mu:d] *(frame of mind)* humor *m*; *(bad mood)* mal humor *m*; *of meeting, country* atmósfera *f*; **be in a good / bad mood** estar de buen / mal humor; **I'm in the mood for a pizza** me apetece una pizza

mood·y ['mu:dɪ] *adj* temperamental; *(bad-tempered)* malhumorado

moon [mu:n] *n* luna *f*

'moon·light **1** *n* luz *f* de luna **2** *v/i* F estar pluriempleado irregularmente; **he's moonlighting as a barman** tiene un segundo empleo de camarero

'moon·lit *adj* iluminado por la luna

moor [mur] *v/t boat* atracar

moor·ing ['murɪŋ] atracadero *m*

moose [mu:s] alce *m* americano

mop [ma:p] **1** *n for floor* fregona *f*; *for dishes* estropajo *m* (*con mango*) **2** *v/t* (*pret & pp mopped*) *floor* fregar; *eyes, face* limpiar

♦ mop up *v/t* limpiar; MIL acabar con

mope [moup] *v/i* estar abatido

M

mor·al ['mɔːrəl] **1** adj moral; *person, behavior* moralista **2** n *of story* moraleja f; *morals* moral f, moralidad f

mo·rale [məˈræl] moral f

mo·ral·i·ty [məˈrælətɪ] moralidad f

mor·bid ['mɔːrbɪd] adj morboso

more [mɔːr] **1** adj más; *there are no more eggs* no quedan huevos; *some more tea?* ¿más té?; *more and more students / time* cada vez más estudiantes / tiempo **2** adv más; *more important* más importante; *more often* más a menudo; *more and more* cada vez más; *more or less* más o menos; *once more* una vez más; *he paid more than $100 for it* pagó más de 100 dólares por él; *he earns more than I do* gana más que yo; *I don't live there any more* ya no vivo allí **3** pron más; *do you want some more?* ¿quieres más?; *a little more* un poco más

more·o·ver [mɔːˈrouvər] adv además, lo que es más

morgue [mɔːrg] depósito m de cadáveres

morn·ing ['mɔːrnɪŋ] mañana f; *in the morning* por la mañana; *this morning* esta mañana; *tomorrow morning* mañana por la mañana; *good morning* buenos días

morn·ing 'sick·ness náuseas fpl matutinas *(típicas del embarazo)*

mo·ron ['mɔːraɪn] F imbécil m/f F, subnormal m/f F

mo·rose [məˈrous] adj hosco, malhumorado

mor·phine ['mɔːrfiːn] morfina f

mor·sel ['mɔːrsl] pedacito m

mor·tal ['mɔːrtl] **1** adj mortal **2** n mortal m/f

mor·tal·i·ty [mɔːrˈtælətɪ] mortalidad f

mor·tar[1] ['mɔːrtər] MIL mortero m

mor·tar[2] ['mɔːrtər] *(cement)* mortero m, argamasa f

mort·gage ['mɔːrgɪdʒ] **1** n hipoteca f, préstamo m hipotecario **2** v/t hipotecar

mor·ti·cian [mɔːrˈtɪʃn] encargado(-a) m(f) de una funeraria

mor·tu·a·ry ['mɔːrtʊerɪ] depósito m de cadáveres

mo·sa·ic [mouˈzeɪɪk] mosaico m

Mos·cow ['maːskau] Moscú

Mos·lem ['muzlm] **1** adj musulmán **2** n musulmán(-ana) m(f)

mosque [maːsk] mezquita f

mos·qui·to [maːsˈkiːtou] mosquito m

moss [maːs] musgo m

moss·y ['maːsɪ] adj cubierto de musgo

most [moust] **1** adj la mayoría de **2** adv *(very)* muy, sumamente; *the most beautiful / interesting* el más hermoso / interesante; *that's the one I like most* ése es el que más me gusta; *most of all* sobre todo **3** pron la mayoría de; *I've read most of her novels* he leído la mayoría de sus novelas; *at (the) most* como mucho; *make the most of* aprovechar al máximo

most·ly ['moustlɪ] adv principalmente, sobre todo

mo·tel [mouˈtel] motel m

moth [maːθ] mariposa f nocturna; *(clothes moth)* polilla f

'moth·ball bola f de naftalina

moth·er ['mʌðər] **1** n madre f **2** v/t mimar

'moth·er·board COMPUT placa f madre

'moth·er·hood maternidad f

Moth·er·ing 'Sun·day → *Mother's Day*

'moth·er-in-law *(pl mothers-in-law)* suegra f

moth·er·ly ['mʌðərlɪ] adj maternal

moth·er-of-'pearl nácar m

'Moth·er's Day Día f de la Madre

'moth·er tongue lengua f materna

mo·tif [mouˈtiːf] motivo m

mo·tion ['mouʃn] **1** n *(movement)* movimiento m; *(proposal)* moción f; *put, set things in motion* poner las cosas en marcha **2** v/t: *he motioned me forward* me indicó con un gesto que avanzara

mo·tion·less ['mouʃnlɪs] adj inmóvil

mo·ti·vate ['moutɪveɪt] v/t *person* motivar

mo·ti·va·tion [moutɪˈveɪʃn] motivación f

mo·tive ['moutɪv] motivo m

mo·tor ['moutər] motor m

'mo·tor·bike moto f

'mo·tor·boat lancha f motora

mo·tor·cade ['moutəkeɪd] caravana f, desfile m de coches

'mo·tor·cy·cle motocicleta f
'mo·tor·cy·clist motociclista m/f
'mo·tor home autocaravana f
mo·tor·ist ['moutərist] conductor(a) m(f), automovilista m/f
'mo·tor me·chan·ic mecánico(-a) m(f) (de automóviles)
'mo·tor rac·ing carreras fpl de coches
'mo·tor·scoot·er vespa® f
'mo·tor ve·hi·cle vehículo m de motor
'mo·tor·way Br autopista f
mot·to ['mɑːtou] lema f
mould etc Br → mold² etc
mound [maund] montículo m
mount [maunt] 1 n (mountain) monte m; (horse) montura f; Mount McKinley el Monte McKinley 2 v/t steps subir; horse, bicycle montar en; campaign, photo montar 3 v/i aumentar, crecer
◆ mount up v/i acumularse
moun·tain ['mauntin] montaña f
'moun·tain bike bicicleta f de montaña
moun·tain·eer [mauntɪ'nɪr] montañero(-a) m(f), alpinista m/f, L.Am. andinista m/f
moun·tain·eer·ing [mauntɪ'nɪrɪŋ] montañismo m, alpinismo m, L.Am. andinismo m
moun·tain·ous ['mauntɪnəs] adj montañoso
mount·ed po'lice [mauntɪd] policía f montada
mourn [mɔːrn] 1 v/t llorar 2 v/i: mourn for s.o. llorar la muerte de alguien
mourn·er ['mɔːrnər] doliente m/f
mourn·ful ['mɔːrnfəl] adj voice, face triste
mourn·ing ['mɔːrnɪŋ] luto m, duelo m; be in mourning estar de luto; wear mourning vestir de luto
mouse [maus] (pl mice [maɪs]) also COMPUT ratón m
'mouse mat COMPUT alfombrilla f
mous·tache → mustache
mouth [mauθ] of person boca f; of river desembocadura f
mouth·ful ['mauθfəl] of food bocado m; of drink trago m
'mouth·or·gan armónica f
'mouth·piece of instrument boquilla f;

(spokesperson) portavoz m/f
'mouth·wash enjuague m bucal, elixir m bucal
'mouth·wa·ter·ing adj apetitoso
move [muːv] 1 n in chess, checkers movimiento m; (step, action) paso m; (change of house) mudanza f; make the first move dar el primer paso; get a move on! F ¡espabílate! F; don't make a move! ¡ni te muevas! 2 v/t object mover; (transfer) trasladar; emotionally conmover; move those papers out of your way aparta esos papeles; move house mudarse de casa 3 v/i moverse; (transfer) trasladarse
◆ move around v/i in room andar; from place to place trasladarse, mudarse
◆ move away v/i alejarse, apartarse; (move house) mudarse
◆ move in v/i to house, neighborhood mudarse; to office trasladarse
◆ move on v/i to another town mudarse; to another job cambiarse; to another subject pasar a hablar de
◆ move out v/i of house mudarse; of area marcharse
◆ move up v/i in league ascender, subir; (make room) correrse
move·ment ['muːvmənt] also organization, MUS movimiento m
mov·ers ['muːvərz] npl firm empresa f de mudanzas; (men) empleados mpl de una empresa de mudanzas
mov·ie ['muːvɪ] película f; go to a movie, the movies ir al cine
mov·ie·go·er ['muːvɪgouər] aficionado(a) m/f al cine
'mov·ie thea·ter cine m, sala f de cine
mov·ing ['muːvɪŋ] adj which can move movible; emotionally conmovedor
mow [mou] v/t grass cortar
◆ mow down v/t segar la vida de
mow·er ['mouər] cortacésped m
MP [em'piː] abbr (= Member of Parliament) Br diputado(-a) m(f); abbr (= Military Policeman) policía m militar
mph [empiː'eɪtʃ] abbr (= miles per hour) millas fpl por hora
Mr ['mɪstər] Sr.
Mrs ['mɪsɪz] Sra.

M

Ms [mɪz] Sra. (*casda o no casada*)

Mt *abbr* (= **Mount**) Monte *m*

much [mʌtʃ] **1** *adj* mucho; *so much money* tanto dinero; *as much ... as ...* tanto ... como **2** *adv* mucho; *I don't like him much* no me gusta mucho; *he's much more intelligent than ...* es mucho más inteligente que ...; *the house is much too large for one person* la casa es demasiado grande para una sola persona; *very much* mucho; *thank you very much* muchas gracias; *I love you very much* te quiero muchísimo; *too much* demasiado; *as much as ...* tanto ... como; *it may cost as much as half a million dollars* puede que haya malversado hasta medio millón de dólares; *I thought as much* eso es lo que pensaba **3** *pron* mucho; *what did she say? - nothing much* ¿qué dijo? - no demasiado

muck [mʌk] (*dirt*) suciedad *f*

mu·cus ['mjuːkəs] mocos *mpl*, mucosidad *f*

mud [mʌd] barro *m*

mud·dle ['mʌdl] **1** *n* lío *m* **2** *v/t person* liar; *you've got the story all muddled* te has hecho un lío con la *historia*

♦ **muddle up** *v/t* desordenar; (*confuse*) liar

mud·dy ['mʌdɪ] *adj* embarrado

mues·li ['mjuːzlɪ] muesli *m*

muf·fin ['mʌfɪn] magdalena *f*

muf·fle ['mʌfl] *v/t* ahogar, amortiguar

♦ **muffle up** *v/i* abrigarse

muf·fler ['mʌflər] MOT silenciador *m*

mug[1] [mʌg] *for tea, coffee* taza *f*; F (*face*) jeta *f* F, *Span* careto *m* F

mug[2] [mʌg] *v/t* (*pret & pp* **mugged**) (*attack*) atracar

mug·ger ['mʌgər] atracador(a) *m(f)*

mug·ging ['mʌgɪŋ] atraco *m*

mug·gy ['mʌgɪ] *adj* bochornoso

mule [mjuːl] *animal* mulo(-a) *m(f)*; (*slipper*) pantufla *f*

♦ **mull over** [mʌl] *v/t* reflexionar sobre

mul·ti·lat·e·ral [mʌltɪ'lætərəl] *adj* POL multilateral

mul·ti·lin·gual [mʌltɪ'lɪŋgwəl] *adj* multilingüe

mul·ti·me·di·a [mʌltɪ'miːdɪə] **1** *n* multimedia *f* **2** *adj* multimedia

mul·ti·na·tion·al [mʌltɪ'næʃnl] **1** *adj* multinacional **2** *n* COM multinacional *f*

mul·ti·ple ['mʌltɪpl] *adj* múltiple

mul·ti·ple 'choice ques·tion pregunta *f* tipo test

mul·ti·ple scle·ro·sis [sklə'rəusɪs] esclerosis *f* múltiple

mul·ti·pli·ca·tion [mʌltɪplɪ'keɪʃn] multiplicación *f*

mul·ti·ply ['mʌltɪplaɪ] **1** *v/t* (*pret & pp* **multiplied**) multiplicar **2** *v/i* (*pret & pp* **multiplied**) multiplicarse

mum·my ['mʌmɪ] *Br* mamá *f*

mum·ble ['mʌmbl] **1** *n* murmullo *m* **2** *v/t* farfullar **3** *v/i* hablar entre dientes

mumps [mʌmps] *nsg* paperas *fpl*

munch [mʌntʃ] **1** *v/t* mascar **2** *v/i* mascar

mu·ni·ci·pal [mjuː'nɪsɪpl] *adj* municipal

mu·ral ['mjʊrəl] mural *m*

mur·der ['mɜːrdər] **1** *n* asesinato *m* **2** *v/t person* asesinar, matar; *song* destrozar

mur·der·er ['mɜːrdərər] asesino(-a) *m(f)*

mur·der·ous ['mɜːrdrəs] *adj rage, look* asesino

murk·y ['mɜːrkɪ] *adj water* turbio, oscuro; *fig* turbio

mur·mur ['mɜːrmər] **1** *n* murmullo *m* **2** *v/t* murmurar

mus·cle ['mʌsl] músculo *m*

mus·cu·lar ['mʌskjʊlər] *adj pain, strain* muscular; *person* musculoso

muse [mjuːz] *v/i* meditar, reflexionar

mu·se·um [mjuː'zɪəm] museo *m*

mush·room ['mʌʃrʊm] **1** *n* seta *f*, hongo *m*; (*button mushroom*) champiñón *m* **2** *v/i* crecer rápidamente

mu·sic ['mjuːzɪk] música *f*; *in written form* partitura *f*

mu·sic·al ['mjuːzɪkl] **1** *adj* musical; *person* con talento para la música **2** *n* musical *m*

'mu·sic·(al) box caja *f* de música

mu·sic·al 'in·stru·ment instrumento *m* musical

mu·si·cian [mjuː'zɪʃn] músico(-a) *m(f)*

mus·sel ['mʌsl] mejillón *m*

must [mʌst] v/aux ◇ necessity tener que, deber; **I must be on time** tengo que or debo llegar a la hora; **do you have to leave now? yes, I must** ¿tienes que marcharte ahora? - sí, debo marcharme; **I mustn't be late** no tengo que llegar tarde, no debo llegar tarde ◇ probability deber de; **it must be about 6 o'clock** deben de ser las seis; **they must have arrived by now** ya deben de haber llegado

mus·tache [mə'stæʃ] bigote m

mus·tard ['mʌstərd] mostaza f

must·y ['mʌstɪ] adj room que huele a humedad; smell a humedad

mute [mjuːt] adj animal mudo

mut·ed ['mjuːtɪd] adj color apagado; criticism débil

mu·ti·late ['mjuːtɪleɪt] v/t mutilar

mu·ti·ny ['mjuːtɪnɪ] **1** n motín m **2** v/i (pret & pp **mutinied**) amotinarse

mut·ter ['mʌtər] v/t & v/i murmurar

mut·ton ['mʌtn] carnero m

mu·tu·al ['mjuːtʃuəl] adj mutuo

muz·zle ['mʌzl] **1** n of animal hocico m; for dog bozal m **2** v/t poner un bozal a; **muzzle the press** amordazar a la prensa

my [maɪ] adj mi; **my house** mi casa; **my parents** mis padres

my·op·ic [maɪ'ɑːpɪk] adj miope

my·self [maɪ'self] pron reflexive me; emphatic yo mismo(-a); **when I saw myself in the mirror** cuando me vi en el espejo; **I saw it myself** lo vi yo mismo; **by myself** (alone) solo; (without help) yo solo, yo mismo

mys·te·ri·ous [mɪ'stɪrɪəs] adj misterioso

mys·te·ri·ous·ly [mɪ'stɪrɪəslɪ] adv misteriosamente

mys·te·ry ['mɪstərɪ] misterio m; **mystery (story)** relato m de misterio

mys·ti·fy ['mɪstɪfaɪ] v/t (pret & pp **mystified**) dejar perplejo

myth [mɪθ] also fig mito m

myth·i·cal ['mɪθɪkl] adj mítico

my·thol·o·gy [mɪ'θɑːlədʒɪ] mitología f

N

nab [næb] v/t (pret & pp **nabbed**) F (take for o.s.) pescar F, agarrar

nag [næg] **1** v/i (pret & pp **nagged**) of person dar la lata **2** v/t (pret & pp **nagged**): **nag s.o. to do sth** dar la lata a alguien para que haga algo

nag·ging ['nægɪŋ] adj person quejica; doubt persistente; pain continuo

nail [neɪl] for wood clavo m; on finger, toe uña f

'nail clip·pers npl cortaúñas m inv

'nail file lima f de uñas

'nail pol·ish esmalte m de uñas

'nail pol·ish re·mov·er quitaesmaltes m inv

'nail scis·sors npl tijeras fpl de manicura

'nail var·nish esmalte m de uñas

na·ive [naɪ'iːv] adj ingenuo

naked ['neɪkɪd] adj desnudo; **to the naked eye** a simple vista

name [neɪm] **1** n nombre m; **what's your name?** ¿cómo te llamas?; **call s.o. names** insultar a alguien; **make a name for o.s.** hacerse un nombre **2** v/t: **they named him Ben** le llamaron Ben

◆ name for v/t: **name s.o. for s.o.** poner a alguien el nombre de alguien

name·ly ['neɪmlɪ] adv a saber

'name·sake tocayo(-a) m(f); homónimo(-a) m(f)

'name·tag on clothing etc etiqueta f

nan·ny ['nænɪ] niñera f

nap [næp] n cabezada f; **have a nap** echar una cabezada

nape [neɪp]: *nape of the neck* nuca *f*

nap·kin ['næpkɪn] (*table napkin*) servilleta *f*; (*sanitary napkin*) compresa *f*

nar·cot·ic [nɑːr'kɑːtɪk] *n* narcótico *m*, estupefaciente *m*

nar'cot·ics a·gent agente *m/f* de la brigada de estupefacientes

nar·rate [nə'reɪt] *v/t* narrar

nar·ra·tion [nə'reɪʃn] (*telling*) narración *f*

nar·ra·tive ['nærətɪv] **1** *n* (*story*) narración *f* **2** *adj poem, style* narrativo

nar·ra·tor [nə'reɪtər] narrador(a) *m(f)*

nar·row ['nærou] *adj street, bed, victory* estrecho; *views, mind* cerrado

nar·row·ly ['nærouli] *adv win* por poco; *narrowly escape sth* escapar por poco de algo

nar·row-mind·ed [nærou'maɪndɪd] *adj* cerrado

na·sal ['neɪzl] *adj voice* nasal

nas·ty ['næstɪ] *adj person, smell* desagradable, asqueroso; *thing to say* malintencionado; *weather* horrible; *cut, wound* feo; *disease* serio

na·tion ['neɪʃn] nación *f*

na·tion·al ['næʃənl] **1** *adj* nacional **2** *n* ciudadano(-a) *m(f)*

na·tion·al 'an·them himno *m* nacional

na·tion·al 'debt deuda *f* pública

na·tion·al·ism ['næʃənəlɪzm] nacionalismo *m*

na·tion·al·i·ty [næʃə'næləti] nacionalidad *f*

na·tion·al·ize ['næʃənəlaɪz] *v/t industry etc* nacionalizar

na·tion·al 'park parque *m* nacional

na·tive ['neɪtɪv] **1** *adj* nativo; *native language* lengua *f* materna **2** *n* nativo(-a) *m(f)*, natural *m/f*; *tribesman* nativo(-a) *m(f)*, indígena *m/f*; *he's a native of New York* es natural de Nueva York

na·tive 'coun·try país *m* natal

na·tive 'speak·er hablante *m/f* nativo(-a)

NATO ['neɪtou] *abbr* (= *North Atlantic Treaty Organization*) OTAN *f* (= Organización *f* del Tratado del Atlántico Norte)

nat·u·ral ['nætʃrəl] *adj* natural; *a natural blonde* una rubia natural

nat·u·ral 'gas gas *m* natural

nat·u·ral·ist ['nætʃrəlɪst] naturalista *m/f*

nat·u·ral·ize ['nætʃrəlaɪz] *v/t: become naturalized* naturalizarse, nacionalizarse

nat·u·ral·ly ['nætʃərəli] *adv* (*of course*) naturalmente; *behave, speak* con naturalidad; (*by nature*) por naturaleza

nat·u·ral 'sci·ence ciencias *fpl* naturales

nat·u·ral 'sci·en·tist experto(-a) *m(f)* en ciencias naturales

na·ture ['neɪtʃər] naturaleza *f*

na·ture re'serve reserva *f* natural

naugh·ty ['nɔːtɪ] *adj* travieso, malo; *photograph, word etc* picante

nau·se·a ['nɔːzɪə] náusea *f*

nau·se·ate ['nɔːzɪeɪt] *v/t* (*fig: disgust*) dar náuseas a

nau·se·at·ing ['nɔːzɪeɪtɪŋ] *adj smell, taste* nauseabundo; *person* repugnante

nau·seous ['nɔːʃəs] *adj* nauseabundo; *feel nauseous* tener náuseas

nau·ti·cal ['nɔːtɪkl] *adj* náutico

'nau·ti·cal mile milla *f* náutica

na·val ['neɪvl] *adj* naval

'na·val base base *f* naval

na·vel ['neɪvl] ombligo *m*

nav·i·ga·ble ['nævɪgəbl] *adj river* navegable

nav·i·gate ['nævɪgeɪt] *v/i in ship, airplane*, COMPUT navegar; *in car* hacer de copiloto

nav·i·ga·tion [nævɪ'geɪʃn] navegación *f*; *in car* direcciónes *fpl*

nav·i·ga·tor ['nævɪgeɪtər] *on ship* oficial *m* de derrota; *in airplane* navegante *m/f*; *in car* copiloto *m/f*

na·vy ['neɪvɪ] armada *f*, marina *f* (de guerra)

na·vy 'blue **1** *n* azul *m* marino **2** *adj* azul marino

near [nɪr] **1** *adv nearer; come a bit nearer* acércate un poco más **2** *prep* cerca de; *near the bank* cerca del banco; *do you go near the bank?* ¿pasa cerca del banco? **3** *adj* cercano, próximo; *the nearest bus stop* la parada de autobús más cercana *or* próxima; *in the near future* en un futuro próximo

near·by [nɪr'baɪ] *adv live* cerca

near·ly ['nɪrlɪ] *adv* casi

near-sight·ed [nɪr'saɪtɪd] *adj* miope

neat [niːt] *adj* ordenado; *whisky* solo, seco; *solution* ingenioso; F *(terrific)* genial F, estupendo F

ne·ces·sar·i·ly ['nesəserəlɪ] *adv* necesariamente

ne·ces·sa·ry ['nesəserɪ] *adj* necesario, preciso; *it is necessary to ...* es necesario ..., hay que ...

ne·ces·si·tate [nɪ'sesɪteɪt] *v/t* exigir, hacer necesario

ne·ces·si·ty [nɪ'sesɪtɪ] *(being necessary)* necesidad *f*; *(something necessary)* necesidad *f*, requisito *m* imprescindible

neck [nek] cuello *m*

neck·lace ['neklɪs] collar *m*

'neck·line *of dress* escote *m*

'neck·tie corbata *f*

née [neɪ] *adj* de soltera

need [niːd] **1** *n* necesidad *f*; *if need be* si fuera necesario; *in need* necesitado; *be in need of sth* necesitar algo; *there's no need to be rude / upset* no hace falta ser grosero /que te enfades **2** *v/t* necesitar; *you'll need to buy one* tendrás que comprar uno; *you don't need to wait* no hace falta que esperes; *I need to talk to you* tengo que *or* necesito hablar contigo; *need I say more?* ¿hace falta que añada algo?

nee·dle ['niːdl] *for sewing, injection, on dial* aguja *f*

'nee·dle·work costura *f*

need·y ['niːdɪ] *adj* necesitado

neg·a·tive ['negətɪv] *adj* negativo; *answer in the negative* dar una respuesta negativa

ne·glect [nɪ'glekt] **1** *n* abandono *m*, descuido *m* **2** *v/t garden, one's health* descuidar, desatender; *neglect to do sth* no hacer algo

ne·glect·ed [nɪ'glektɪd] *adj gardens* abandonado, descuidado; *author* olvidado; *feel neglected* sentirse abandonado

neg·li·gence ['neglɪdʒəns] negligencia *f*

neg·li·gent ['neglɪdʒənt] *adj* negligente

neg·li·gi·ble ['neglɪdʒəbl] *adj quantity, amount* insignificante

ne·go·ti·a·ble [nɪ'goʊʃəbl] *adj salary, contract* negociable

ne·go·ti·ate [nɪ'goʊʃɪeɪt] **1** *v/i* negociar **2** *v/t deal, settlement* negociar; *obstacles* franquear, salvar; *bend in road* tomar

ne·go·ti·a·tion [nɪgoʊʃɪ'eɪʃn] negociación *f*; *be under negotiation* estar siendo negociado

ne·go·ti·a·tor [nɪ'goʊʃɪeɪtər] negociador(a) *m(f)*

Ne·gro ['niːgroʊ] negro(-a) *m(f)*

neigh [neɪ] *v/i* relinchar

neigh·bor ['neɪbər] vecino(-a) *m(f)*

neigh·bor·hood ['neɪbərhʊd] *in town* vecindario *m*, barrio *m*; *in the neighborhood of ...* *fig* alrededor de ...

neigh·bor·ing ['neɪbərɪŋ] *adj house, state* vecino, colindante

neigh·bor·ly ['neɪbərlɪ] *adj* amable

neigh·bour *etc Br* → *neighbor etc*

nei·ther ['niːðər] **1** *adj* ninguno; *neither applicant was any good* ninguno de los candidatos era bueno **2** *pron* ninguno(-a) *m(f)* **3** *adv*: *neither ... nor ...* ni ... ni **4** *conj*: *neither do I* yo tampoco; *neither can I* yo tampoco

ne·on light ['niːuːɪn] luz *f* de neón

neph·ew ['nefjuː] sobrino *m*

nerd [nɜːrd] F petardo(-a) *m(f)*

nerve [nɜːrv] nervio *m*; *(courage)* valor *m*; *(impudence)* descaro *m*; *it's bad for my nerves* me pone de los nervios; *get on s.o.'s nerves* sacar de quicio a alguien

nerve-rack·ing ['nɜːrvrækɪŋ] *adj* angustioso, exasperante

ner·vous ['nɜːrvəs] *adj person* nervioso, inquieto; *twitch* nervioso; *I'm nervous about meeting them* la reunión con ellos me pone muy nervioso

ner·vous 'break·down crisis *f inv* nerviosa

ner·vous 'en·er·gy energía *f*

ner·vous·ness ['nɜːrvəsnɪs] nerviosismo *m*

ner·vous 'wreck manojo *m* de nervios

nerv·y ['nɜːrvɪ] *adj (fresh)* descarado

nest [nest] *n* nido *m*

nes·tle ['nesl] *v/i* acomodarse

net¹ [net] *for fishing, tennis* red *f*

N

net² [net] *adj* price, weight neto
net 'cur·tain visillo *m*
net 'pro·fit beneficio *m* neto
net·tle ['netl] ortiga *f*
'net·work of contacts, cells, COMPUT red *f*
neu·rol·o·gist [nʊˈrɑːlədʒɪst] neurólogo(-a) *m(f)*
neu·ro·sis [nʊˈrəʊsɪs] neurosis *f inv*
neu·rot·ic [nʊˈrɑːtɪk] *adj* neurótico
neu·ter ['nuːtər] *v/t* animal castrar
neu·tral ['nuːtrl] **1** *adj* country neutral; *color* neutro **2** *n* gear punto *m* muerto; *in neutral* en punto muerto
neu·tral·i·ty ['nuːtrælətɪ] neutralidad *f*
neu·tral·ize ['nutrəlaɪz] *v/t* neutralizar
nev·er ['nevər] *adv* nunca; *you're never going to believe this* no te vas a creer esto; *you never promised, did you?* no lo llegaste a prometer, ¿verdad?
nev·er·end·ing *adj* interminable
nev·er·the·less [nevərðəˈles] *adv* sin embargo, no obstante
new [nuː] *adj* nuevo; *this system is still new to me* todavía no me he hecho con este sistema; *I'm new to the job* soy nuevo en el trabajo; *that's nothing new* no es nada nuevo
'new·born *adj* recién nacido
new·com·er ['nuːkʌmər] recién llegado(-a) *m(f)*
new·ly ['nuːlɪ] *adv* (recently) recientemente, recién
new·ly weds [wedz] *npl* recién casados *mpl*
new 'moon luna *f* nueva
news [nuːz] *nsg* noticias *fpl*; *on* TV noticias *fpl*, telediario *m*; *on radio* noticias *fpl*; *that's news to me* no sabía eso
'news a·gen·cy agencia *f* de noticias
'news·a·gent quiosquero(-a) *m(f)*
'news·cast TV noticias *fpl*, telediario *m*; *on radio* noticias *fpl*
'news·cast·er TV presentador(a) *m(f)* de informativos
'news flash flash *m* informativo, noticia *f* de última hora
'newspaper periódico *m*
'news·read·er TV etc presentador(a) *m(f)* de informativos

'news re·port reportaje *m*
'news·stand quiosco *m*
'news·ven·dor vendedor(a) *m(f)* de periódicos
'New Year año *m* nuevo; *Happy New Year!* ¡Feliz Año Nuevo!
New Year's 'Day Día *m* de Año Nuevo
New Year's 'Eve Nochevieja *f*
New York [jɔːrk] **1** *adj* neoyorquino **2** *n*: *New York (City)* Nueva York
New York·er ['jɔːrkər] *n* neoyorquino(-a) *m(f)*
New Zea·land ['ziːlənd] Nueva Zelanda
New Zea·land·er ['ziːləndər] neozelandés(-esa) *m(f)*, neocelandés(-esa) *m(f)*
next [nekst] **1** *adj* in time próximo, siguiente; *in space* siguiente, de al lado; *next week* la próxima semana, la semana que viene; *the next week he came back again* volvió a la semana siguiente; *who's next?* ¿quién es el siguiente? **2** *adv* luego, después; *next, we're going to study ...* a continuación, vamos a estudiar ...; *next to (beside)* al lado de; *(in comparison with)* en comparación con
next 'door **1** *adj* neighbor de al lado **2** *adv* live al lado
next of 'kin pariente *m* más cercano
nib·ble ['nɪbl] *v/t* mordisquear
Nic·a·ra·gua [nɪkəˈrɑːgwə] Nicaragua
Nic·a·ra·guan [nɪkəˈrɑːgwən] **1** *adj* nicaragüense **2** *n* nicaragüense *m/f*
nice [naɪs] *adj* trip, house, hair bonito, L.Am. lindo; *person* agradable, simpático; *weather* bueno, agradable; *meal, food* bueno, rico; *be nice to your sister!* ¡trata bien a tu hermana!; *that's very nice of you* es muy amable de tu parte
nice·ly ['naɪslɪ] *adv* written, presented bien; *(pleasantly)* amablemente
nice·ties ['naɪsətɪz] *npl* sutilezas *fpl*; refinamientos *mpl*; *social niceties* cumplidos *mpl*
niche [niːʃ] *in market* hueco *m*, nicho *m*; *(special position)* hueco *m*
nick [nɪk] *n (cut)* muesca *f*, mella *f*; *in the nick of time* justo a tiempo
nick·el ['nɪkl] níquel *m*; *(coin)* moneda de cinco centavos

'nick·name n apodo m, mote m

niece [niːs] sobrina f

nig·gard·ly ['nɪgərdlɪ] adj amount, person mísero

night [naɪt] noche f; **tomorrow night** mañana por la noche; **11 o'clock at night** las 11 de la noche; **travel by night** viajar de noche; **during the night** por la noche; **stay the night** quedarse a dormir; **a room for 2 nights** una habitación para 2 noches; **work nights** trabajar de noche; **good night** buenas noches; **in the middle of the night** en mitad de la noche

'night·cap drink copa f (tomada antes de ir a dormir)

'night·club club m nocturno, discoteca f

'night·dress camisón m

'night·fall: **at nightfall** al anochecer

'night flight vuelo m nocturno

'night·gown camisón m

night·ie ['naɪtɪ] camisón m

nigh·tin·gale ['naɪtɪŋgeɪl] ruiseñor m

'night·life vida f nocturna

night·ly ['naɪtlɪ] 1 adj: **a nightly event** algo que sucede todas las noches 2 adv todas las noches

'night·mare also fig pesadilla f

'night por·ter portero m de noche

'night school escuela f nocturna

'night shift turno m de noche

'night·shirt camisa f de dormir

'night·spot local m nocturno

'night·time: **at nighttime, in the nighttime** por la noche

nil [nɪl] Br cero

nim·ble ['nɪmbl] adj ágil

nine [naɪn] nueve

nine·teen [naɪn'tiːn] diecinueve

nine·teenth [naɪn'tiːnθ] n & adj decimonoveno

nine·ti·eth ['naɪntɪɪθ] n & adj nonagésimo

nine·ty ['naɪntɪ] noventa

ninth [naɪnθ] n & adj noveno

nip [nɪp] n (pinch) pellizco m; (bite) mordisco m

nip·ple ['nɪpl] pezón m

ni·tro·gen ['naɪtrədʒn] nitrógeno m

no [noʊ] 1 adv no 2 adj: **there's no coffee / tea left** no queda café / té; **I have**

no family / money no tengo familia / dinero; **I'm no linguist / expert** no soy un lingüista / experto; **no smoking / parking** prohibido fumar / aparcar

no·bil·i·ty [noʊ'bɪlətɪ] nobleza f

no·ble ['noʊbl] adj noble

no·bod·y ['noʊbədɪ] pron nadie; **nobody knows** nadie lo sabe; **there was nobody at home** no había nadie en casa

nod [nɑd] 1 n movimiento m de la cabeza 2 v/i (pret & pp **nodded**) asentir con la cabeza

◆ nod off v/i (fall asleep) quedarse dormido

no-hop·er [noʊ'hoʊpər] F inútil m/f F

noise [nɔɪz] ruido m

nois·y ['nɔɪzɪ] adj ruidoso

nom·i·nal ['nɑmɪnl] adj amount simbólico

nom·i·nate ['nɑmɪneɪt] v/t (appoint) nombrar; **nominate s.o. for a post** (propose) proponer a alguien para un puesto

nom·i·na·tion [nɑmɪ'neɪʃn] (appointment) nombramiento m; (proposal) nominación f; **who was your nomination?** ¿a quién propusiste?

nom·i·nee [nɑmɪ'niː] candidato(-a) m(f)

non ... [nɑːn] no ...

non·al·co·hol·ic adj sin alcohol

non·a·ligned adj no alineado

non·cha·lant ['nɑːnʃələːnt] adj despreocupado

non·com·mis·sioned 'of·fi·cer suboficial m/f

non·com'mit·tal adj person, response evasivo

non·de·script ['nɑːndɪskrɪpt] adj anodino

none [nʌn] pron: **none of the students** ninguno de los estudiantes; **none of the water** nada del agua; **there are none left** no queda ninguno; **there is none left** no queda nada

none·the·less [nʌnðə'les] adv sin embargo, no obstante

non·ex'ist·ent adj inexistente

non'fic·tion no ficción f

non·(in)'flam·ma·ble adj incombustible,

no inflamable

non·in·ter·fer·ence, non·in·ter'ven·tion
no intervención *f*

non-'i·ron *adj shirt* que no necesita plancha

'no-no: *that's a no-no* F de eso nada

no-'non·sense *adj approach* directo

non'payment impago *m*

non·pol'lut·ing *adj* que no contamina

non'res·i·dent *n* no residente *m/f*

non·re·turn·a·ble [nɑːnrɪ'tɜːrnəbl] *adj* no
retornable

non·sense ['nɑːnsəns] disparate *m*, tontería *f*; *don't talk nonsense* no digas disparates *or* tonterías; *nonsense, it's easy!* tonterías, ¡es fácil!

non'skid *adj tires* antideslizante

non'slip *adj surface* antideslizante

non'smok·er *person* no fumador(a) *m(f)*

non'stand·ard *adj* no estándar

non'stick *adj pans* antiadherente

non'stop 1 *adj flight, train* directo, sin escalas; *chatter* ininterrumpido **2** *adv fly, travel* directamente; *chatter, argue* sin parar

non'swim·mer: *be a nonswimmer* no saber nadar

non'u·nion *adj* no sindicado

non'vi·o·lence no violencia *f*

non'vi·o·lent *adj* no violento

noo·dles ['nuːdlz] *npl* tallarines *mpl* (chinos)

nook [nʊk] rincón *m*

noon [nuːn] mediodía *m*; *at noon* al mediodía

noose [nuːs] lazo *m* corredizo

nor [nɔːr] *conj* ni; *nor do I* yo tampoco, ni yo

norm [nɔːrm] norma *f*

nor·mal ['nɔːrml] *adj* normal

nor·mal·i·ty [nɔːr'mælətɪ] normalidad *f*

nor·mal·ize ['nɔːrməlaɪz] *v/t relationships* normalizar

nor·mal·ly ['nɔːrməlɪ] *adv (usually)* normalmente; *(in a normal way)* normalmente, con normalidad

north [nɔːrθ] **1** *n* norte *m*; *to the north of* al norte de **2** *adj* norte **3** *adv travel* al norte; *north of* al norte de

North Am·er·i·ca América del Norte, Norteamérica

North Am·er·i·can 1 *n* norteamericano(-a) *m(f)* **2** *adj* norteamericano

north'east *n* nordeste *m*, noreste *m*

nor·ther·ly ['nɔːrðəlɪ] *adj* norte, del norte

nor·thern ['nɔːrðən] norte, del norte

nor·thern·er ['nɔːrðənər] norteño(-a) *m(f)*

North Ko're·a Corea del Norte

North Ko're·an 1 *adj* norcoreano **2** *n* norcoreano(-a) *m(f)*

North 'Pole Polo *m* Norte

north·ward ['nɔːrðwərd] *adv travel* hacia el norte

north·west [nɔːrð'west] *n* noroeste *m*

Nor·way ['nɔːrweɪ] Noruega

Nor·we·gian [nɔːr'wiːdʒn] **1** *adj* noruego **2** *n person* noruego(-a) *m(f)*; *language* noruego *m*

nose [nouz] nariz *m*; *of animal* hocico *m*; *it was right under my nose!* ¡lo tenía delante de mis narices!

◆ **nose about** *v/i* F husmear

'nose·bleed: *have a nosebleed* sangrar por la nariz

nos·tal·gia [nɑː'stældʒɪə] nostalgia *f*

nos·tal·gic [nɑː'stældʒɪk] *adj* nostálgico

nos·tril ['nɑːstrəl] ventana *f* de la nariz

nos·y ['nouzɪ] *adj* F entrometido

not [nɑːt] *adv* no; *not this one, that one* éste no, ése; *not now* ahora no; *not there* no allí; *not like that* así no; *not before Tuesday / next week* no antes del martes / de la próxima semana; *not for me, thanks* para mí no, gracias; *not a lot* no mucho; *it's not ready / allowed* no está listo / permitido; *I don't know* no lo sé; *I am not American* no soy americano; *he didn't help* no ayudó

no·ta·ble ['noutəbl] *adj* notable

no·ta·ry ['noutərɪ] notario(-a) *m(f)*

notch [nɑːtʃ] muesca *f*, mella *f*

note [nout] *n written*, MUS nota *f*; *take notes* tomar notas; *take note of sth* prestar atención a algo

◆ **note down** *v/t* anotar

'note·book cuaderno *m*, libreta *f*; COMPUT *Span* ordenador *m* portátil, *L.Am.* computadora f portátil

not·ed ['nəʊtɪd] adj destacado

'note·pad bloc m de notas

'note·pa·per papel m de carta

noth·ing ['nʌθɪŋ] pron nada; **nothing but** sólo; **nothing much** no mucho; **for nothing** (for free) gratis; (for no reason) por nada; **I'd like nothing better** me encantaría

no·tice ['nəʊtɪs] **1** n on bulletin board, in street cartel m, letrero m; (advance warning) aviso m; in newspaper anuncio m; **at short notice** con poca antelación; **until further notice** hasta nuevo aviso; **give s.o. his / her notice** to quit job despedir a alguien; to leave house comunicar a alguien que tiene que abandonar la casa; **hand in one's notice** to employer presentar la dimisión; **four weeks' notice** cuatro semanas de preaviso; **take notice of sth** observar algo, prestar atención a algo; **take no notice of s.o./sth** no hacer caso de alguien / algo **2** v/t notar, fijarse en

no·tice·a·ble ['nəʊtɪsəbl] adj apreciable, evidente

no·ti·fy ['nəʊtɪfaɪ] v/t (pret & pp notified) notificar, informar

no·tion ['nəʊʃn] noción f, idea f

no·tions ['nəʊʃnz] npl artículos mpl de costura

no·to·ri·ous [nəʊ'tɔːrɪəs] adj de mala fama

nou·gat ['nuːgət] especie de turrón

nought [nɔːt] cero m

noun [naʊn] nombre m, sustantivo m

nour·ish·ing ['nʌrɪʃɪŋ] adj nutritivo

nour·ish·ment ['nʌrɪʃmənt] alimento m, alimentación f

nov·el ['nɑːvl] n novela f

nov·el·ist ['nɑːvlɪst] novelista m/f

no·vel·ty ['nɑːvltɪ] (being new) lo novedoso; (something new) novedad f

No·vem·ber [nəʊ'vembər] noviembre m

nov·ice ['nɑːvɪs] principiante m/f

now [naʊ] adv ahora; **now and again**, **now and then** de vez en cuando; **by now** ya; **from now on** de ahora en adelante; **right now** ahora mismo; **just now** (at this moment) en este momento; (a little while ago) hace un momento; **now, now!** ¡vamos!, ¡venga!; **now, where did I put it?** ¿y ahora dónde lo he puesto?

now·a·days ['naʊədeɪz] adv hoy en día

no·where ['nəʊwer] adv en ningún lugar; **it's nowhere near finished** no está acabado ni mucho menos; **he was nowhere to be seen** no se le veía en ninguna parte

noz·zle ['nɑːzl] boquilla f

nu·cle·ar ['nuːklɪər] adj nuclear

nu·cle·ar 'en·er·gy energía f nuclear

nu·cle·ar 'fis·sion fisión f nuclear

'nu·cle·ar-free adj desnuclearizado

nu·cle·ar 'phys·ics física f nuclear

nu·cle·ar 'pow·er energía f nuclear; POL potencia f nuclear

nu·cle·ar 'pow·er sta·tion central f nuclear

nu·cle·ar re'ac·tor reactor m nuclear

nu·cle·ar 'waste residuos mpl nucleares

nu·cle·ar 'weap·on arma f nuclear

nude [nuːd] **1** adj desnudo **2** n painting desnudo m; **in the nude** desnudo

nudge [nʌdʒ] v/t dar un toque con el codo a

nud·ist ['nuːdɪst] n nudista m/f

nui·sance ['nuːsns] incordio m, molestia f; **make a nuisance of o.s.** dar la lata; **what a nuisance!** ¡qué incordio!

nuke [nuːk] v/t F atacar con armas nucleares

null and 'void [nʌl] adj nulo y sin efecto

numb [nʌm] adj entumecido; emotionally insensible

num·ber ['nʌmbər] **1** n número m; **a number of people** un cierto número de personas **2** v/t (put a number on) numerar

numeral ['nuːmərəl] número m

nu·me·rate ['nuːmərət] adj que sabe sumar y restar

nu·me·rous ['nuːmərəs] adj numeroso

nun [nʌn] monja f

nurse [nɜːrs] enfermero(-a) m(f)

nur·se·ry ['nɜːrsərɪ] guardería f; for plants vivero m

'nur·se·ry rhyme canción f infantil

'nur·se·ry school parvulario m, jardín m

de infancia

'nur·se·ry school teach·er profesor(a) *m(f)* de parvulario

nurs·ing ['nɜːrsɪŋ] enfermería *f*

'nurs·ing home *for old people* residencia *f*

nut [nʌt] nuez *f*; *for bolt* tuerca *f*; *nuts* F *(testicles)* pelotas *fpl* F

'nut·crack·ers *npl* cascanueces *m inv*

nu·tri·ent ['nuːtrɪənt] *n* nutriente *m*

nu·tri·tion [nuːˈtrɪʃn] nutrición *f*

nu·tri·tious [nuːˈtrɪʃəs] *adj* nutritivo

nuts [nʌts] *adj* F *(crazy)* chalado F, pirado F; *be nuts about s.o.* estar coladito por alguien F

'nut·shell: *in a nutshell* en una palabra

nut·ty ['nʌti] *adj taste* a nuez; F *(crazy)* chalado F, pirado F

ny·lon ['naɪlɑːn] **1** *n* nylon *m* **2** *adj* de nylon

O

oak [oʊk] *tree, wood* roble *m*

oar [ɔːr] remo *m*

o·a·sis [oʊˈeɪsɪs] (*pl oases* [oʊˈeɪsiːz]) *also fig* oasis *m inv*

oath [oʊθ] LAW, *(swearword)* juramento *m*; *on oath* bajo juramento

'oat·meal harina *f* de avena

oats [oʊts] *npl* copos *mpl* de avena

o·be·di·ence [oʊˈbiːdɪəns] obediencia *f*

o·be·di·ent [oʊˈbiːdɪənt] *adj* obediente

o·be·di·ent·ly [oʊˈbiːdɪəntli] *adv* obedientemente

o·bese [oʊˈbiːs] *adj* obeso

o·bes·i·ty [oʊˈbiːsɪti] obesidad *f*

o·bey [oʊˈbeɪ] *v/t* obedecer

o·bit·u·a·ry [əˈbɪtʊerɪ] *n* necrología *f*, obituario *m*

ob·ject¹ ['ɑːbdʒɪkt] *n (thing)* objeto *m*; *(aim)* objetivo *m*; GRAM objeto *m*

ob·ject² [əbˈdʒekt] *v/i* oponerse

◆ object to *v/t* oponerse a

ob·jec·tion [əbˈdʒekʃn] objeción *f*

ob·jec·tio·na·ble [əbˈdʒekʃnəbl] *adj* (*unpleasant*) desagradable

ob·jec·tive [əbˈdʒektɪv] **1** *adj* objetivo **2** *n* objetivo *m*

ob·jec·tive·ly [əbˈdʒektɪvli] *adv* objetivamente

ob·jec·tiv·i·ty [əbdʒekˈtɪvəti] objetividad *f*

ob·li·ga·tion [ɑːblɪˈɡeɪʃn] obligación *f*; *be under an obligation to s.o.* tener una obligación para con alguien

ob·lig·a·to·ry [əˈblɪɡətɔːrɪ] *adj* obligatorio

o·blige [əˈblaɪdʒ] *v/t* obligar; *much obliged!* muy agradecido

o·blig·ing [əˈblaɪdʒɪŋ] *adj* atento, servicial

o·blique [əˈbliːk] **1** *adj reference* indirecto **2** *n in punctuation* barra *f* inclinada

o·blit·er·ate [əˈblɪtəreɪt] *v/t city* destruir, arrasar; *memory* borrar

o·bliv·i·on [əˈblɪvɪən] olvido *m*; *fall into oblivion* caer en el olvido

o·bliv·i·ous [əˈblɪvɪəs] *adj*: *be oblivious of sth* no ser consciente de algo

ob·long ['ɑːblɒŋ] *adj* rectangular

ob·nox·ious [əbˈnɑːkʃəs] *adj person* detestable, odioso; *smell* repugnante

ob·scene [əbˈsiːn] *adj* obsceno; *salary, poverty* escandaloso

ob·scen·i·ty [əbˈsenəti] obscenidad *f*

ob·scure [əbˈskjʊr] *adj* oscuro

ob·scu·ri·ty [əbˈskjʊrəti] oscuridad *f*

ob·ser·vance [əbˈzɜːrvns] *of festival* práctica *f*

ob·ser·vant [əbˈzɜːrvnt] *adj* observador

ob·ser·va·tion [ɑːbzəˈveɪʃn] *of nature, stars* observación *f*; *(comment)* observación *f*, comentario *m*

ob·ser·va·to·ry [əb'zɜːrvətɔːrɪ] observatorio *m*

ob·serve [əb'zɜːrv] *v/t* observar

ob·serv·er [əb'zɜːrvər] observador(a) *m(f)*

ob·sess [əb'ses] *v/t* obsesionar; **be obsessed by/with** estar obsesionado con/por

ob·ses·sion [əb'seʃn] obsesión *f*

ob·ses·sive [əb'sesɪv] *adj* obsesivo

ob·so·lete ['ɑːbsəliːt] *adj* obsoleto

ob·sta·cle ['ɑːbstəkl] obstáculo *m*

ob·ste·tri·cian [ɑːbstə'trɪʃn] obstetra *m/f*, tocólogo(-a) *m(f)*

ob·stet·rics [əb'stetrɪks] obstetricia *f*, tocología *f*

ob·sti·na·cy ['ɑːbstɪnəsɪ] obstinación *f*

ob·sti·nate ['ɑːbstɪnət] *adj* obstinado

ob·sti·nate·ly ['ɑːbstɪnətlɪ] *adv* obstinadamente

ob·struct [əb'strʌkt] *v/t road* obstruir; *investigation, police* obstaculizar

ob·struc·tion [əb'strʌkʃn] *on road etc* obstrucción *f*

ob·struc·tive [əb'strʌktɪv] *adj behavior, tactics* obstruccionista

ob·tain [əb'teɪn] *v/t* obtener, lograr

ob·tain·a·ble [əb'teɪnəbl] *adj products* disponible

ob·tru·sive [əb'truːsɪv] *adj* molesto; **the plastic chairs are rather obtrusive** las sillas de plástico desentonan por completo

ob·tuse [əb'tuːs] *adj fig* duro de mollera

ob·vi·ous ['ɑːbvɪəs] *adj* obvio, evidente

ob·vi·ous·ly ['ɑːbvɪəslɪ] *adv* obviamente; **obviously!** ¡por supuesto!

oc·ca·sion [ə'keɪʒn] ocasión *f*

oc·ca·sion·al [ə'keɪʒənl] *adj* ocasional, esporádico; *I like the occasional whisky* me gusta tomarme un whisky de vez en cuando

oc·ca·sion·al·ly [ə'keɪʒnlɪ] *adv* ocasionalmente, de vez en cuando

oc·cult [ə'kʌlt] **1** *adj* oculto **2** *n*: **the occult** lo oculto

oc·cu·pant ['ɑːkjupənt] ocupante *m/f*

oc·cu·pa·tion [ɑːkju'peɪʃn] ocupación *f*

oc·cu·pa·tion·al 'ther·a·pist [ɑːkju'peɪʃnl] terapeuta *m/f* ocupacional

oc·cu·pa·tion·al 'ther·a·py terapia *f* ocupacional

oc·cu·py ['ɑːkjupaɪ] *v/t (pret & pp occupied)* ocupar

oc·cur [ə'kɜːr] *v/i (pret & pp occurred)* ocurrir, suceder; **it occurred to me that ...** se me ocurrió que ...

oc·cur·rence [ə'kʌrəns] acontecimiento *m*

o·cean ['əuʃn] océano *m*

o·ce·a·nog·ra·phy [əuʃə'nɑːgrəfɪ] oceanografía *f*

o'clock [ə'klɑːk]: **at five/six o'clock** a las cinco/seis

Oc·to·ber [ɑːk'təubər] octubre *m*

oc·to·pus ['ɑːktəpəs] pulpo *m*

OD [əu'diː] *v/i* F **OD on** *drug* tomar una sobredosis de

odd [ɑːd] *adj (strange)* raro, extraño; *(not even)* impar; **the odd one out** el bicho raro; **50 odd** cerca de 50

'odd·ball F bicho *m* raro F

odds [ɑːdz] *npl*: **be at odds with sth/s.o.** no concordar con algo/estar peleado con alguien; **the odds are 10 to one** las apuestas están en 10 a 1; **the odds are that ...** lo más probable es que ...; **against all the odds** contra lo que se esperaba

odds and 'ends *npl objects* cacharros *mpl*; *things to do* cosillas *fpl*

'odds-on *adj favorite* indiscutible

o·di·ous ['əudɪəs] *adj* odioso

o·dom·e·ter [əu'dɑːmətər] cuentakilómetros *m inv*

o·dor, *Br* o·dour ['əudər] olor *m*

of [ʌv], [əv] *prep possession* de; **the name of the street/hotel** el nombre de la calle/del hotel; **the color of the car** el color del coche; **the works of Dickens** las obras de Dickens; **five/ten minutes of twelve** las doce menos cinco/diez; **die of cancer** morir de cáncer; **love of money/adventure** amor por el dinero/la aventura; **of the three this is ...** de los tres éste es ...

off [ɑːf] **1** *prep*: **off the main road** *(away*

from) apartado de la carretera principal; (*leading off*) saliendo de la carretera principal; **$20 off the price** una rebaja en el precio de 20 dólares; **he's off his food** no come nada, está desganado **2** *adv*: **be off** of light, TV, machine estar apagado; of brake, lid, top no estar puesto; not at work faltar; on vacation estar de vacaciones; (*canceled*) estar cancelado; **we're off tomorrow** (*leaving*) nos vamos mañana; **I'm off to New York** me voy a Nueva York; **with his pants / hat off** sin los pantalones / el sombrero; **take a day off** tomarse un día de fiesta *or* un día libre; **it's 3 miles off** está a tres millas de distancia; **it's a long way off** in distance está muy lejos; in future todavía queda mucho tiempo; **he got into his car and drove off** se subió al coche y se marchó; **off and on** de vez en cuando **3** *adj*: **the off switch** el interruptor de apagado

of·fence *Br* → offense

of·fend [əˈfend] *v/t* (*insult*) ofender

of·fend·er [əˈfendər] LAW delincuente *m/f*; **offenders will be prosecuted** se procesará a los infractores

of·fense [əˈfens] LAW delito *m*; **take offense at sth** ofenderse por algo

of·fen·sive [əˈfensɪv] **1** *adj* behavior, remark ofensivo; smell repugnante **2** *n* (MIL: attack) ofensiva *f*; **go on(to) the offensive** pasar a la ofensiva

of·fer [ˈɑːfər] **1** *n* oferta *f* **2** *v/t* ofrecer; **offer s.o. sth** ofrecer algo a alguien

off'hand *adj* attitude brusco

of·fice [ˈɑːfɪs] building oficina *f*; room oficina *f*, despacho *m*; position cargo *m*

'of·fice block bloque *m* de oficinas

'of·fice hours *npl* horas *fpl* de oficina

of·fi·cer [ˈɑːfɪsər] MIL oficial *m/f*; in police agente *m/f*

of·fi·cial [əˈfɪʃl] **1** *adj* oficial **2** *n* funcionario(-a) *m(f)*

of·fi·cial·ly [əˈfɪʃlɪ] *adv* oficialmente

of·fi·ci·ate [əˈfɪʃɪeɪt] *v/i*: **with X officiating** con X celebrando la ceremonia

of·fi·cious [əˈfɪʃəs] *adj* entrometido

'off-line *adv* work fuera de línea; **be off-line** of printer etc estar desconectado;

go off-line desconectarse

'off-peak *adj* rates en horas valle, fuera de las horas punta; **offpeak electricity** electricidad *f* en horas valle *or* fuera de las horas punta

'off-sea·son **1** *adj* rates, vacation de temporada baja **2** *n* temporada *f* baja

'off·set *v/t* (*pret & pp* offset) losses, disadvantage compensar

'off·shore *adj* drilling rig cercano a la costa; investment en el exterior

'off·side **1** *adj* wheel etc del lado del conductor **2** *adv* SP fuera de juego

'off·spring of person vástagos *mpl*, hijos *mpl*; of animal crías *fpl*

off-the-'rec·ord *adj* confidencial

'off-white *adj* blancuzco

of·ten [ˈɑːfn] *adv* a menudo, frecuentemente *m*

oil [ɔɪl] **1** *n* for machine, food, skin aceite *m*; petroleum petróleo *m* **2** *v/t* hinges, bearings engrasar

'oil change cambio *m* del aceite

'oil com·pa·ny compañía *f* petrolera

'oil·field yacimiento *m* petrolífero

'oil-fired *adj* central heating de gasóleo *or* fuel

'oil paint·ing óleo *m*

'oil-pro·duc·ing coun·try país *m* productor de petróleo

'oil re·fin·e·ry refinería *f* de petróleo

'oil rig plataforma *f* petrolífera

'oil·skins *npl* ropa *f* impermeable

'oil slick marea *f* negra

'oil tank·er petrolero *m*

'oil well pozo *m* petrolífero

oil·y [ˈɔɪlɪ] *adj* grasiento

oint·ment [ˈɔɪntmənt] ungüento *m*, pomada *f*

ok [oʊˈkeɪ] *adj*, *adv* F **can I? - ok** ¿puedo? - de acuerdo *or* Span vale; **is it ok with you if ...?** ¿te parecería bien si ...?; **does that look ok?** ¿queda bien?; **that's ok by me** por mí, ningún problema; **are you ok?** (*well, not hurt*) ¿estás bien?; **are you ok for Friday?** ¿te va bien el viernes?; **he's ok** (*is a good guy*) es buena persona; **is this bus ok for ...?** ¿este autobús va a ...?

old [ould] *adj* viejo; (*previous*) anterior, antiguo; *an old man / woman* un anciano / una anciana, un viejo / una vieja; *how old are you / is he?* ¿cuántos años tienes / tiene?; *he's getting old* está haciéndose mayor

old age vejez *f*

old-'fash·ioned *adj clothes, style, ideas* anticuado, pasado de moda, *word* anticuado

ol·ive ['ɑlɪv] aceituna *f*, oliva *f*

'ol·ive oil aceite *m* de oliva

O·lym·pic 'Games [ə'lɪmpɪk] *npl* Juegos *mpl* Olímpicos

om·e·let, *Br* **om·e·lette** ['ɑːmlɪt] tortilla *f* (francesa)

om·i·nous ['ɑːmɪnəs] *adj* siniestro

o·mis·sion [ou'mɪʃn] omisión *f*

o·mit [ə'mɪt] *v/t* (*pret & pp omitted*) omitir; *omit to do sth* no hacer algo

om·nip·o·tent [ɑːm'nɪpətənt] *adj* omnipotente

om·nis·ci·ent [ɑːm'nɪsɪənt] *adj* omnisciente

on [ɑːn] **1** *prep* en; *on the table / wall* en la mesa / la pared; *on the bus / train* en el autobús / el tren; *on TV / the radio* en la televisión / la radio; *on Sunday* el domingo; *on the 1st of ...* el uno de ...; *this is on me* (*I'm paying*) invito yo; *have you any money on you?* ¿llevas dinero encima?; *on his arrival / departure* cuando llegue / se marche; *on hearing this* al escuchar esto **2** *adv*: *be on* of *light, TV, computer etc* estar encendido *L.Am.* prendido; *of brake, lid, top* estar puesto; *of meeting etc*: *be scheduled to happen* haber sido acordado; *it's on at 5 am* of *TV program* lo dan *or Span* ponen a las cinco; *what's on tonight?* on *TV etc* ¿qué dan *or Span* ponen esta noche?; (*what's planned?*) ¿qué planes hay para esta noche?; *with his hat on* con el sombrero puesto; *you're on* (*I accept your offer etc*) trato hecho; *that's not on* (*not allowed, not fair*) eso no se hace; *on you go* (*go ahead*) adelante; *walk / talk on* seguir caminando / hablando; *and so on* etcétera; *on and on* talk *etc* sin parar

3 *adj*: *the on switch* el interruptor de encendido

once [wʌns] **1** *adv* (*one time, formerly*) una vez; *once again, once more* una vez más; *at once* (*immediately*) de inmediato, inmediatamente; *all at once* (*suddenly*) de repente; (*all*) *at once* (*together*) al mismo tiempo; *once upon a time there was ...* érase una vez ...; *once in a while* de vez en cuando; *once and for all* de una vez por todas; *for once* por una vez **2** *conj* una vez que; *once you have finished* una vez que hayas acabado

one [wʌn] **1** *number* uno **m 2** *adj* un(a); *one day* un día **3** *pron* uno(-a); *which one?* ¿cuál?; *one by one* enter, deal with uno por uno; *we help one another* nos ayudamos mutuamente; *what can one say / do?* ¿qué puede uno decir / hacer?; *the little ones* los pequeños; *I for one* yo personalmente

one·'off *n* (*unique event, person*) hecho *m* aislado; (*exception*) excepción *f*

one-par·ent 'fam·i·ly familia *f* monoparental

one·self *pron* uno(-a) mismo(-a) *m(f)*; *do sth by oneself* hacer algo sin ayuda; *look after oneself* cuidarse; *be by oneself* estar solo

one-sid·ed [wʌn'saɪdɪd] *adj discussion, fight* desigual

one-track 'mind *hum*: *have a one-track mind* ser un obseso

'one-way street calle *f* de sentido único

'one-way tick·et billete *m* de ida

on·ion ['ʌnjən] cebolla *f*

'on-line *adv* en línea; *go on-line to* conectarse a

'on-line serv·ice COMPUT servicio *m* en línea

on·look·er ['ɑːnlʊkər] espectador(a) *m(f)*, curioso(-a) *m(f)*

on·ly ['ounlɪ] **1** *adv* sólo, solamente; *he was here only yesterday* estuvo aquí ayer mismo; *not only ... but also ...* no sólo *or* solamente ... sino también ...; *only just* por poco **2** *adj* único; *only son* hijo único

'on·set comienzo *m*

'on·side *adv* SP en posición reglamentaria

on-the-job 'train·ing formación *f* continua

on·to ['ɑːntuː] *prep*: **put sth onto sth** poner algo encima de algo

on·ward ['ɑːnwərd] *adv* hacia adelante; **from … onward** de … en adelante

ooze [uːz] **1** *v/i* of *liquid, mud* rezumar **2** *v/t* rezumar; **he oozes charm** rezuma or rebosa encanto

o·paque [oʊ'peɪk] *adj glass* opaco

OPEC ['oʊpek] *abbr* (= **Organization of Petroleum Exporting Countries**) OPEP *f* (= Organización *f* de Países Exportadores de Petróleo)

o·pen ['oʊpən] **1** *adj* (*also honest*) abierto; **in the open air** al aire libre **2** *v/t* abrir **3** *v/i* of *door, shop* abrir; of *flower* abrirse
♦ open up *v/i* of *person* abrirse

o·pen·'air *adj meeting, concert* al aire libre; *pool* descubierto

'o·pen day jornada *f* de puertas abiertas

o·pen-'end·ed *adj contract etc* abierto

o·pen·ing ['oʊpənɪŋ] *in wall etc* abertura *f*; (*beginning*: of *film, novel etc*) comienzo *m*; (*job*) puesto *m* vacante

'o·pen·ing hours *npl* horario *m* de apertura

o·pen·ly ['oʊpənlɪ] *adv* (*honestly, frankly*) abiertamente

o·pen-mind·ed [oʊpən'maɪndɪd] *adj* de mentalidad abierta

o·pen 'plan of·fice oficina *f* de planta abierta

'o·pen tick·et billete *m* abierto

op·e·ra ['ɑːpərə] ópera *f*

'op·e·ra glass·es *npl* gemelos *mpl*, prismáticos *mpl*

'op·e·ra house (teatro *m* de la) ópera *f*

'op·e·ra sing·er cantante *m/f* de ópera

op·e·rate ['ɑːpəreɪt] **1** *v/i* of *company* operar, actuar; of *airline, bus service,* MED operar; of *machine* funcionar (**on** con) **2** *v/t machine* manejar
♦ operate on *v/t* MED operar; **they operated on his leg** le operaron de la pierna

'op·e·rat·ing in·struc·tions *npl* instrucciones *fpl* de funcionamiento

'op·e·rating room MED quirófano *m*

'op·e·rat·ing sys·tem COMPUT sistema *m* operativo

op·e·ra·tion [ɑːpə'reɪʃn] MED operación *f*; of *machine* manejo *m*; **operations** of *company* operaciones *fpl*, actividades *fpl*; **have an operation** MED ser operado

op·e·ra·tor ['ɑːpəreɪtər] TELEC operador(a) *m(f)*; of *machine* operario(-a) *m(f)*; (*tour operator*) operador *m* turístico

oph·thal·mol·o·gist [ɑːfθæl'mɑːlədʒɪst] oftalmólogo(-a) *m(f)*

o·pin·ion [ə'pɪnjən] opinión *f*; **in my opinion** en mi opinión

o'pin·ion poll encuesta *f* de opinión

op·po·nent [ə'poʊnənt] oponente *m/f*, adversario(-a) *m(f)*

op·por·tune ['ɑːpərtuːn] *adj fml* oportuno

op·por·tun·ist [ɑːpər'tuːnɪst] oportunista *m/f*

op·por·tu·ni·ty [ɑːpər'tuːnətɪ] oportunidad *f*

op·pose [ə'poʊz] *v/t* oponerse a; **be opposed to …** estar en contra de …; **John, as opposed to George …** John, al contrario que George …

op·po·site ['ɑːpəzɪt] **1** *adj* contrario; *views, characters, meaning* opuesto; **the opposite side of town / end of the road** el otro lado de la ciudad / el otro extremo de la calle; **the opposite sex** el sexo opuesto **2** *n*: **the opposite of** lo contrario de

op·po·site 'num·ber homólogo(-a) *m(f)*

op·po·si·tion [ɑːpə'zɪʃn] *to plan,* POL oposición *f*; **meet with opposition** encontrar oposición

op·press [ə'pres] *v/t the people* oprimir

op·pres·sive [ə'presɪv] *adj rule, dictator* opresor; *weather* agobiante

opt [ɑːpt] *v/t*: **opt to do sth** optar por hacer algo

op·ti·cal il·lu·sion ['ɑːptɪkl] ilusión *f* óptica

op·ti·cian [ɑːp'tɪʃn] óptico(-a) *m(f)*

op·ti·mism ['ɑːptɪmɪzm] optimismo *m*

op·ti·mist ['ɑːptɪmɪst] optimista *m/f*

op·ti·mist·ic [ɑːptɪ'mɪstɪk] *adj* optimista

op·ti·mist·ic·al·ly [ɑ:ptɪ'mɪstɪklɪ] *adv* con optimismo

op·ti·mum ['ɑ:ptɪməm] **1** *adj* óptimo **2** *n*: *the optimum* lo ideal

op·tion ['ɑ:pʃn] opción *f*

op·tion·al ['ɑ:pʃnl] *adj* optativo

op·tion·al 'ex·tras *npl* accesorios *mpl* opcionales

or [ɔːr] *conj* o; *before a word beginning with the letter o* u ; *or else!* ¡más vale que no llegues tarde, ¡de lo contrario!

o·ral ['ɔːrəl] *adj exam, sex* oral; *hygiene* bucal

or·ange ['ɒrɪndʒ] **1** *adj color* naranja **2** *n fruit* naranja *f*; *color* naranja *m*

'or·ange juice *Span* zumo *m or L.Am.* jugo de naranja

or·ange 'squash naranjada *f*

or·a·tor ['ɔːrətər] orador(a) *m(f)*

or·bit ['ɔːrbɪt] **1** *n of earth* órbita *f*; *send sth into orbit* poner algo en órbita **2** *v/t the earth* girar alrededor de

or·chard ['ɔːrtʃərd] huerta *f* (de frutales)

or·ches·tra ['ɔːrkɪstrə] orquesta *f*

or·chid ['ɔːrkɪd] orquídea *f*

or·dain [ɔːr'deɪn] *v/t* ordenar

or·deal [ɔːr'diːl] calvario *m*, experiencia *f* penosa

or·der ['ɔːrdər] **1** *n* (*command*) orden *f*; (*sequence, being well arranged*) orden *m*; *for goods* pedido *m*; *take s.o.'s order in restaurant* preguntar a alguien lo que va a tomar; *in order to* para; *out of order* (*not functioning*) estropeado; (*not in sequence*) desordenado **2** *v/t* (*put in sequence, proper layout*) ordenar; *goods* pedir, encargar; *meal* pedir; *order s.o. to do sth* ordenar a alguien hacer algo *or* que haga algo **3** *v/i in restaurant* pedir

or·der·ly ['ɔːrdəlɪ] **1** *adj lifestyle* ordenado, metódico **2** *n in hospital* celador(a) *m(f)*

or·di·nal num·ber ['ɔːrdɪnl] (número *m*) ordinal *m*

or·di·nar·i·ly [ɔːrdɪ'nerɪlɪ] *adv* (*as a rule*) normalmente

or·di·nary ['ɔːrdɪnerɪ] *adj* común, normal

ore [ɔːr] mineral, mena *f*

or·gan ['ɔːrgən] ANAT, MUS órgano *m*

or·gan·ic [ɔːr'gænɪk] *adj food* ecológico, biológico; *fertilizer* orgánico

or·gan·i·cal·ly [ɔːr'gænɪklɪ] *adv grown* ecológicamente, biológicamente

or·gan·ism ['ɔːrgənɪzm] organismo *m*

or·gan·i·za·tion [ɔːrgənaɪ'zeɪʃn] organización *f*

or·gan·ize ['ɔːrgənaɪz] *v/t* organizar

or·gan·ized 'crime crimen *m* organizado

or·gan·iz·er ['ɔːrgənaɪzər] *person* organizador(a) *m(f)*

or·gasm ['ɔːrgæzm] orgasmo *m*

O·ri·ent ['ɔːrɪent] Oriente

O·ri·en·tal [ɔːrɪ'entl] **1** *adj* oriental **2** *n* oriental *m/f*

o·ri·en·tate ['ɔːrɪənteɪt] *v/t* (*direct*) orientar; *orientate o.s.* (*get bearings*) orientarse

or·i·gin ['ɑːrɪdʒɪn] origen *m*; *idea / person of Chinese origin* una idea / una persona de origen chino

o·rig·i·nal [ə'rɪdʒənl] **1** *adj* (*not copied, first*) original **2** *n painting etc* original *m*

o·rig·i·nal·i·ty [ərɪdʒən'ælətɪ] originalidad *f*

o·rig·i·nal·ly [ə'rɪdʒənlɪ] *adv* originalmente; (*at first*) originalmente, en un principio

o·rig·i·nate [ə'rɪdʒɪneɪt] **1** *v/t scheme, idea* crear **2** *v/i of idea, belief* originarse; *of family* proceder

o·rig·i·na·tor [ə'rɪdʒɪneɪtər] *of scheme etc* creador(a) *m(f)*; *he's not an originator* no es un creador nato

or·na·ment ['ɔːrnəmənt] adorno *m*

or·na·men·tal [ɔːrnə'mentl] *adj* ornamental

or·nate [ɔːr'neɪt] *adj style, architecture* recargado

or·phan ['ɔːrfn] *n* huérfano(-a) *m(f)*

or·phan·age ['ɔːrfənɪdʒ] orfanato *m*

or·tho·dox ['ɔːrθədɑːks] *adj* REL, *fig* ortodoxo

or·tho·pe·dic [ɔːrθə'piːdɪk] *adj* ortopédico

os·ten·si·bly [ɑː'stensəblɪ] *adv* aparentemente

os·ten·ta·tion [ɑːsten'teɪʃn] ostentación *f*

os·ten·ta·tious [ɑːsten'teɪʃəs] *adj* osten-

O

toso

os·ten·ta·tious·ly [ɑːstenˈteɪʃəslɪ] adv de forma ostentosa

os·tra·cize [ˈɑːstrəsaɪz] v/t condenar al ostracismo

oth·er [ˈʌðər] 1 adj otro; other people might agree puede que otros no estén de acuerdo; the other day (recently) el otro día; every other day / person cada dos días / personas 2 n: the other el otro; the others los otros

oth·er·wise [ˈʌðərwaɪz] adv de lo contrario, si no; (differently) de manera diferente

ot·ter [ˈɑːtər] nutria f

ought [ɔːt] v/aux: I/you ought to know debo / debes saberlo; he / they ought to know debe / deben saberlo; you ought to have done it deberías haberlo hecho

ounce [aʊns] onza f

our [aʊr] adj nuestro m, nuestra f; our brother nuestro hermano; our books nuestros libros

ours [aʊrz] pron el nuestro, la nuestra; ours are red los nuestros son rojos; that book is ours ese libro es nuestro; a friend of ours un amigo nuestro

our·selves [aʊrˈselvz] pron reflexive nos; emphatic nosotros mismos mpl, nosotras mismas fpl; we hurt ourselves nos hicimos daño; when we saw ourselves in the mirror cuando nos vimos en el espejo; we saw it ourselves lo vimos nosotros mismos; by ourselves (alone) solos; (without help) nosotros solos, nosotras mismos

oust [aʊst] v/t from office derrocar

out [aʊt] adv: be out of light, fire estar apagado; of flower estar en flor; (not at home, not in building), of sun haber salido; of calculations estar equivocado; (be published) haber sido publicado; (no longer in competition) estar eliminado; (no longer in fashion) estar pasado de moda; the secret is out el secreto ha sido revelado; out here in Dallas aquí en Dallas; he's out in the garden está en el jardín; (get) out! ¡vete!; (get) out of

my room! ¡fuera de mi habitación!; that's out! (out of the question) ¡eso es imposible!; he's out to win (fully intends to) va a por la victoria

out·board 'mo·tor motor m de fueraborda

'out·break of violence, war estallido m

'out·build·ing edificio m anexo

'out·burst emotional arrebato m, arranque m

'out·cast n paria m/f

'out·come resultado m

'out·cry protesta f

out'dat·ed adj anticuado

out'do v/t (pret outdid, pp outdone) superar

out'door adj toilet, activities, life al aire libre

out'doors adv fuera

out·er [ˈaʊtər] adj wall etc exterior

out·er 'space espacio m exterior

'out·fit clothes traje m, conjunto m; (company, organization) grupo m

'out·go·ing adj flight saliente; personality extrovertido

out'grow v/t (pret outgrew, pp outgrown) old ideas dejar atrás

out·ing [ˈaʊtɪŋ] (trip) excursión f

out'last v/t durar más que

'out·let of pipe desagüe m; for sales punto m de venta

'out·line 1 n of person, building etc perfil m, contorno m; of plan, novel resumen m 2 v/t plans etc resumir

out'live v/t sobrevivir a

'out·look (prospects) perspectivas fpl

'out·ly·ing adj areas periférico

'out·num·ber v/t superar en número

out of prep ◇ motion fuera de; run out of the house salir corriendo de la casa; it fell out of the window se cayó por la ventana

◇ position: 20 miles out of of Detroit a 20 millas de Detroit

◇ cause por; out of jealousy / curiosity por celos / curiosidad

◇ without: we're out of gas / beer no nos queda gasolina / cerveza

◇ from a group de cada; 5 out of 10 5 de

cada 10

out-of-'date *adj* anticuado, desfasado

out-of-the-'way *adj* apartado

'out·pa·tient paciente *m/f* externo(-a)

'out·pa·tients' (**clin·ic**) clínica *f* ambulatoria

'out·per·form *v/t* superar a

'out·put 1 *n of factory* producción *f*; COMPUT salida *f* **2** *v/t* (*pret & pp* **outputted** *or* **output**) (*produce*) producir

'out·rage 1 *n feeling* indignación *f*; *act* ultraje *m*, atrocidad *f* **2** *v/t* indignar, ultrajar; *I was outraged to hear ...* me indignó escuchar que ...

out·ra·geous [aʊtˈreɪdʒəs] *adj acts* atroz; *prices* escandaloso

'out·right 1 *adj winner* absoluto **2** *adv win* completamente; *kill* en el acto

out'run *v/t* (*pret* **outran**, *pp* **outrun**) correr más que

'out·set principio *m*, comienzo *m*; *from the outset* desde el principio *or* comienzo

out'shine *v/t* (*pret & pp* **outshone**) eclipsar

'out·side 1 *adj surface, wall* exterior; *lane* de fuera **2** *adv sit, go* fuera **3** *prep* fuera de; (*apart from*) aparte de **4** *n of building, case etc* exterior *m*; *at the outside* a lo sumo

out·side 'broad·cast emisión *f* desde exteriores

out·sid·er [aʊtˈsaɪdər] *in life* forastero(-a) *m(f)*; *be an outsider in election, race* no ser uno de los favoritos

'out·size *adj clothing* de talla especial

'out·skirts *npl* afueras *fpl*

out'smart → **outwit**

out'stand·ing *adj success, quality* destacado, sobresaliente; *writer, athlete* excepcional; FIN: *invoice, sums* pendiente

out·stretched ['aʊtstretʃt] *adj hands* extendido

out'vote *v/t*: *be outvoted* perder la votación

out·ward ['aʊtwərd] *adj appearance* externo; *outward journey* viaje *m* de ida

out·ward·ly ['aʊtwərdlɪ] *adv* aparentemente

out'weigh *v/t* pesar más que

out'wit *v/t* (*pret & pp* **outwitted**) mostrarse más listo que

o·val ['oʊvl] *adj* oval, ovalado

o·va·ry ['oʊvərɪ] ovario *m*

o·va·tion [oʊˈveɪʃn] ovación *f*; *give s.o. a standing ovation* aplaudir a alguien de pie

ov·en ['ʌvn] horno *m*

'ov·en glove, 'ov·en mitt manopla *f* para el horno

'ov·en·proof *adj* refractario

'ov·en·read·y *adj* listo para el horno

o·ver ['oʊvər] **1** *prep* (*above*) sobre, encima de; (*across*) al otro lado de; (*more than*) más de; (*during*) durante; *she walked over the street* cruzó la calle; *travel all over Brazil* viajar por todo Brasil; *let's talk over a drink / meal* hablemos mientras tomamos una bebida / comemos; *we're over the worst* lo peor ya ha pasado; *over and above* además de **2** *adv*: *be over* (*finished*) haber acabado; *there were just 6 over* sólo quedaban seis; *over to you* (*your turn*) te toca a ti; *over in Japan* allá en Japón; *over here / there* por aquí / allá; *it hurts all over* me duele por todas partes; *painted white all over* pintado todo de blanco; *it's all over* se ha acabado; *over and over again* una y otra vez; *do sth over* (*again*) volver a hacer algo

o·ver·all ['oʊvərɔːl] **1** *adj length* total **2** *adv* (*in general*) en general; *it measures six feet overall* mide en total seis pies

o·ver·alls ['oʊvərɔːlz] *npl Span* mono *m*, *L.Am.* overol *m*

o·ver·awe *v/t* intimidar; *be overawed by s.o./sth* sentirse intimidado por alguien / algo

o·ver·bal·ance *v/i* perder el equilibrio

o·ver·bear·ing *adj* dominante, despótico

'o·ver·board *adv* por la borda; *man overboard!* ¡hombre al agua!; *go overboard for s.o./sth* entusiasmarse muchísimo con alguien / algo

'o·ver·cast *adj day* nublado; *sky* cubierto

o·ver·charge *v/t customer* cobrar de más a

'o·ver·coat abrigo *m*

o·ver'come *v/t* (*pret* **overcame**, *pp* **overcome**) *difficulties*, *shyness* superar, vencer; **be overcome by emotion** estar embargado por la emoción

o·ver'crowd·ed *adj* *train* atestado; *city* superpoblado

o·ver'do *v/t* (*pret* **overdid**, *pp* **overdone**) (*exaggerate*) exagerar; *in cooking* recocer, cocinar demasiado; **you're overdoing things** te estás excediendo

o·ver'done *adj* *meat* demasiado hecho

'o·ver·dose *n* sobredosis *f inv*

'o·ver·draft descubierto *m*; **have an overdraft** tener un descubierto

o·ver'draw *v/t* (*pret* **overdrew**, *pp* **overdrawn**) *account* dejar al descubierto; **be overdrawn** tener un descubierto de 800 dólares

o·ver'dressed *adj* demasiado trajeado

'o·ver·drive MOT superdirecta *f*

o·ver'due *adj*: **his apology was long overdue** se debía haber disculpado hace tiempo; **an overdue alteration** un cambio que había que haber efectuado hace tiempo

o·ver·es·ti·mate *v/t* *abilities*, *value* sobreestimar

o·ver'ex·pose *v/t* *photograph* sobreexponer

'o·ver·flow[1] *n* *pipe* desagüe *m*, rebosadero *m*

o·ver'flow[2] *v/i* *of water* desbordarse

o·ver'grown *adj* *garden* abandonado, cubierto de vegetación; **he's an overgrown baby** es como un niño

o·ver'haul *v/t* *engine*, *plans* revisar

'o·ver·head **1** *adj* *lights*, *railway* elevado **2** *n* FIN gastos *mpl* generales

o·ver'hear *v/t* (*pret & pp* **overheard**) oír por casualidad

o·ver'heat·ed *adj* recalentado

o·ver·joyed [ouvər'dʒɔɪd] *adj* contentísimo, encantado

'o·ver·kill: **that's overkill** eso es exagerar

'o·ver·land **1** *adj* *route* terrestre **2** *adv* *travel* por tierra

o·ver'lap *v/i* (*pret & pp* **overlapped**) *of tiles etc* solaparse; *of periods of time* coincidir; *of theories* tener puntos en común

o·ver'leaf *adv*: **see overleaf** véase al dorso

o·ver'load *v/t* *vehicle*, ELEC sobrecargar

o·ver'look *v/t* *of tall building etc* dominar; (*not see*) pasar por alto

o·ver·ly ['ouvərlı] *adv* excesivamente, demasiado

'o·ver·night *adv* *travel* por la noche; **stay overnight** quedarse a pasar la noche

o·ver'night 'bag bolso *m* de viaje

o·ver'paid *adj*: **be overpaid** cobrar demasiado

'o·ver·pass paso *m* elevado

o·ver·pop·u·lat·ed [ouvə'pɑːpjuleɪtɪd] *adj* superpoblado

o·ver'pow·er *v/t* *physically* dominar

o·ver·pow·er·ing [ouvər'pauɪrŋ] *adj* *smell* fortísimo; *sense of guilt* insoportable

o·ver·priced [ouvər'praɪst] *adj* demasiado caro

o·ver·rat·ed [ouvə'reɪtɪd] *adj* sobrevalorado

o·ver·re'act *v/i* reaccionar exageradamente

o·ver'ride *v/t* (*pret* **overrode**, *pp* **overridden**) anular

o·ver'rid·ing *adj* *concern* primordial

o·ver'rule *v/t* *decision* anular

o·ver'run *v/t* (*pret* **overran**, *pp* **overrun**) *country* invadir; *time* superar; **be overrun with** estar plagado de

o·ver'seas **1** *adv* *live*, *work* en el extranjero; *go* al extranjero **2** *adj* extranjero

o·ver'see *v/t* (*pret* **oversaw**, *pp* **overseen**) supervisar

o·ver'shad·ow *v/t* *fig* eclipsar

'o·ver·sight descuido *m*

o·ver·sim·pli·fi·ca·tion simplificación *f* excesiva

o·ver'sim·pli·fy *v/t* (*pret & pp* **oversimplified**) simplificar en exceso

o·ver'sleep *v/i* (*pret & pp* **overslept**) quedarse dormido

o·ver'state *v/t* exagerar

o·ver'state·ment exageración *f*

o·ver'step *v/t* (*pret & pp* **overstepped**) *fig* traspasar; **overstep the mark** propasarse, pasarse de la raya o·ver·take v/t (pret overtook, pp overtaken) in work, development adelantarse a; Br MOT adelantar

o·ver·throw[1] v/t (pret overthrew, pp overthrown) derrocar

'o·ver·throw[2] n derrocamiento m

'o·ver·time 1 n SP: in overtime en la prórroga 2 adv: work in overtime hacer horas extras

'o·ver·ture ['ouvərtʃur] MUS obertura f; make overtures to establecer contactos con

o·ver·turn 1 v/t vehicle volcar; object dar la vuelta a; government derribar 2 v/i of vehicle volcar

'o·ver·view visión f general

o·ver·weight adj con sobrepeso; be overweight estar demasiado gordo

o·ver·whelm [ouvər'welm] v/t with work abrumar, inundar; with emotion abrumar; be overwhelmed by by response estar abrumado por

o·ver·whelm·ing [ouvər'welmɪŋ] adj feeling abrumador; majority aplastante

o·ver·work 1 n exceso m de trabajo 2 v/i trabajar en exceso 3 v/t hacer trabajar en exceso

owe [ou] v/t deber; owe s.o. $500 deber a alguien 500 dólares; owe s.o. an apology deber disculpas a alguien; how much do I owe you? ¿cuánto te debo?

ow·ing to ['ouɪŋ] prep debido a

owl [aul] búho m

own[1] [oun] v/t poseer; who owns the restaurant? ¿de quién es el restaurante?, ¿quién es el propietario del restaurante?

own[2] [oun] 1 adj propio 2 pron: a car / an apartment of my own mi propio coche/ apartamento; on my / his own yo / él solo

◆ own up v/i confesar

own·er ['ounər] dueño(-a) m(f), propietario(-a) m(f)

own·er·ship ['ounərʃɪp] propiedad f

ox [ɑːks] buey m

ox·ide ['ɑːksaɪd] óxido m

ox·y·gen ['ɑːksɪdʒən] oxígeno m

oy·ster ['ɔɪstər] ostra f

oz abbr (= ounce(s)) onza(s) f(pl)

o·zone ['ouzoun] ozono m

'o·zone lay·er capa f de ozono

P

PA [piː'eɪ] abbr (= personal assistant) secretario(-a) m(f) personal

pace [peɪs] 1 n (step) paso m; (speed) ritmo m 2 v/i: pace up and down pasear de un lado a otro

'pace·mak·er MED marcapasos m inv; SP liebre f

Pa·cif·ic [pə'sɪfɪk]: the Pacific (Ocean) el (Océano) Pacífico

pac·i·fi·er ['pæsɪfaɪər] chupete m

pac·i·fism ['pæsɪfɪzm] pacifismo m

pac·i·fist ['pæsɪfɪst] n pacifista m/f

pac·i·fy ['pæsɪfaɪ] v/t (pret & pp pacified) tranquilizar; country pacificar

pack [pæk] 1 n (backpack) mochila f; of cereal, food, cigarettes paquete m; of cards baraja f 2 v/t item of clothing etc meter en la maleta; goods empaquetar; groceries meter en una bolsa; pack one's bag / suitcase hacer la bolsa / la maleta 3 v/i hacer la maleta

pack·age ['pækɪdʒ] 1 n paquete m; employment package of offers etc condiciones fpl de empleo 2 v/t in packs embalar; idea, project presentar

'pack·age deal for holiday paquete m

'pack·age tour viaje m organizado

pack·ag·ing ['pækɪdʒɪŋ] of product embalaje m; of idea, project presentación f; **it's all packaging** fig es sólo imagen

pack·ed [pækt] adj (crowded) abarrotado

pack·et ['pækɪt] paquete m

pact [pækt] pacto m

pad[1] [pæd] **1** n for protection almohadilla f; for absorbing liquid compresa f; for writing bloc m **2** v/t (pret & pp **padded**) with material acolchar; speech, report meter paja en

pad[2] v/i (move quietly) caminar silenciosamente

pad·ded shoulders ['pædɪd] hombreras fpl

pad·ding ['pædɪŋ] material relleno m; in speech etc paja f

pad·dle ['pædl] **1** n for canoe canalete m, remo m **2** v/i in canoe remar; in water chapotear

pad·dling pool ['pædlɪŋ] piscina f para niños

pad·dock ['pædək] potrero m

pad·lock ['pædlɑːk] **1** n candado m **2** v/t gate cerrar con candado; **I padlocked my bike to the railings** até mi bicicleta a la verja con candado

page[1] [peɪdʒ] n of book etc página f; **page number** número m de página

page[2] [peɪdʒ] v/t (call) llamar; by PA llamar por megafonía; by beeper llamar por el buscapersonas or Span busca

pag·er ['peɪdʒər] buscapersonas m inv, Span busca m

paid [peɪd] pret & pp → **pay**

paid em·ploy·ment empleo m remunerado

pail [peɪl] cubo m

pain [peɪn] dolor m; **be in pain** sentir dolor; **take pains to ...** tomarse muchas molestias por ...; **a pain in the neck** F una lata F, un tostón F

pain·ful ['peɪnfəl] adj dolorido; blow, condition, subject doloroso; (laborious) difícil; **my arm is still very painful** me sigue doliendo mucho el brazo

pain·ful·ly ['peɪnfəli] adv (extremely, acutely) extremadamente

pain·kill·er ['peɪnkɪlər] analgésico m

pain·less ['peɪnlɪs] adj indoloro; **be com-** **pletely painless** doler nada

pains·tak·ing ['peɪnzteɪkɪŋ] adj meticuloso

paint [peɪnt] **1** n pintura f **2** v/t pintar

paint·brush ['peɪntbrʌʃ] large brocha f; small pincel m

paint·er ['peɪntər] decorator pintor(a) m(f) (de brocha gorda); artist pintor(a) m(f)

paint·ing ['peɪntɪŋ] activity pintura f; picture cuadro m

paint·work ['peɪntwɜːrk] pintura f

pair [per] of shoes, gloves, objects par m; of people, animals pareja f

pa·ja·ma 'jack·et camisa f de pijama

pa·ja·ma 'pants pantalón m de pijama

pa·ja·mas [pə'dʒɑːməz] npl pijama m

Pa·ki·stan [pɑːkɪ'stɑːn] Paquistán, Pakistán

Pa·ki·sta·ni [pɑːkɪ'stɑːni] **1** n paquistaní m/f, pakistaní m/f **2** adj paquistaní, pakistaní

pal [pæl] F (friend) amigo(-a) m(f); Span colega m/f F; **hey pal, got a light?** oye amigo or Span tío, ¿tienes fuego?

pal·ace ['pælɪs] palacio m

pal·ate ['pælət] paladar m

pa·la·tial [pə'leɪʃl] adj palaciego

pale [peɪl] adj person pálido; **she went pale** palideció; **pale pink / blue** rosa / azul claro

Pal·es·tine ['pæləstaɪn] Palestina

Pal·es·tin·i·an [pælə'stɪnɪən] **1** n palestino(-a) m(f) **2** adj palestino

pal·let ['pælɪt] palé m

pal·lor ['pælər] palidez f

palm [pɑːm] of hand palma f; tree palmera f

pal·pi·ta·tions [pælpɪ'teɪʃnz] npl MED palpitaciones fpl

pal·try ['pɒːltrɪ] adj miserable

pam·per ['pæmpər] v/t mimar

pam·phlet ['pæmflɪt] for information folleto m; political panfleto m

pan [pæn] **1** n for cooking cacerola f; for frying sartén f **2** v/t (pret & pp **panned**) F (criticize) poner por los suelos F

◆ **pan out** v/i (develop) salir

Pan·a·ma ['pænəmɑː] n Panamá

Pan·a·ma Ca'nal *n*: *the Panama Canal* el Canal de Panamá

Pan·a·ma 'Cit·y *n* Ciudad *f* de Panamá

Pan·a·ma·ni·an [pænə'meɪnɪən] **1** *adj* panameño **2** *n* panameño(-a) *m(f)*

pan·cake ['pænkeɪk] crepe *m*, *L.Am.* panqueque *m*

pan·da ['pændə] (oso *m*) panda *m*

pan·de·mo·ni·um [pændɪ'moʊnɪəm] pandemónium *m*, pandemonio *m*

◆ **pan·der to** ['pændər] *v/t* complacer

pane [peɪn] *of glass* hoja *f*

pan·el ['pænl] panel *m*; *people* grupo *m*, panel *m*

pan·el·ing ['pænlɪŋ] paneles *mpl*; *of ceiling* artesonado *m*

pang [pæŋ]: *pangs of hunger* retortijones *mpl*; *pangs of remorse* remordimientos *mpl*

'pan·han·dle *v/i* F mendigar

pan·ic ['pænɪk] **1** *n* pánico *m* **2** *v/i* (*pret & pp panicked*) ser presa del pánico; *don't panic* ¡que no cunda el pánico!

'pan·ic buy·ing FIN compra *f* provocada por el pánico

'pan·ic sel·ling FIN venta *f* provocada por el pánico

'pan·ic-strick·en presa del pánico

pan·o·ra·ma [pænə'rɑːmə] panorama *m*

pa·no·ra·mic [pænə'ræmɪk] *adj view* panorámico

pan·sy ['pænzɪ] *flower* pensamiento *m*

pant [pænt] *v/i* jadear

pan·ties ['pæntɪz] *npl Span* bragas *fpl*, *L.Am.* calzones *mpl*

pantihose → *pantyhose*

pantihose [pænt] *v/i* jadear

pants [pænts] *npl* pantalones *mpl*

pan·ty·hose ['pæntɪhoʊz] medias *fpl*, pantis *mpl*

pa·pal ['peɪpəl] *adj* papal

pa·per ['peɪpər] **1** *n* papel *m*; (*newspaper*) periódico *m*; *academic* estudio *m*; *at conference* ponencia *f*; (*examination paper*) examen *m*; *papers* (*documents*) documentos *mpl*; *of vehicle* (*identity papers*) papeles *mpl*, documentación *f*; *a piece of paper* un trozo de papel **2** *adj* de papel **3** *v/t room, walls* empapelar

'paperback libro *m* en rústica

paper 'bag bolsa *f* de papel

'paper boy repartidor *m* de periódicos

'paper clip clip *m*

'paper cup vaso *m* de papel

'paperwork papeleo *m*

par [pɑːr] *in golf* par *m*; *be on a par with* ser comparable a; *feel below par* sentirse en baja forma

par·a·chute ['pærəʃuːt] **1** *n* paracaídas *m inv* **2** *v/i* saltar en paracaídas **3** *v/t troops, supplies* lanzar en paracaídas

par·a·chut·ist ['pærəʃuːtɪst] paracaidista *m/f*

pa·rade [pə'reɪd] **1** *n procession* desfile *m* **2** *v/i* desfilar; (*walk about*) pasearse **3** *v/t knowledge, new car* hacer ostentación de

par·a·dise ['pærədaɪs] paraíso *m*

par·a·dox ['pærədɑːks] paradoja *f*

par·a·dox·i·cal [pærə'dɑːksɪkl] *adj* paradójico

par·a·dox·i·cal·ly [pærə'dɑːksɪklɪ] *adv* paradójicamente

par·a·graph ['pærəgræf] párrafo *m*

Par·a·guay ['pærəgwaɪ] *n* Paraguay

Par·a·guay·an [pærə'gwaɪən] **1** *adj* paraguayo **2** *n* paraguayo(-a) *m(f)*

par·al·lel ['pærəlel] **1** *n in geometry* paralela *f*; GEOG paralelo *m*; *fig* paralelismo *m*; *draw a parallel* establecer un paralelismo; *do two things in parallel* hacer dos cosas al mismo tiempo **2** *adj also fig* paralelo **3** *v/t* (*match*) equipararse a

pa·ral·y·sis [pə'ræləsɪs] parálisis *f*

par·a·lyze ['pærəlaɪz] *v/t also fig* paralizar

par·a·med·ic [pærə'medɪk] *n* auxiliar *m/f* sanitario(a)

pa·ram·e·ter [pə'ræmɪtər] parámetro *m*

par·a·mil·i·tar·y [pærə'mɪlɪterɪ] **1** *adj* paramilitar **2** *n* paramilitar *m/f*

par·a·mount ['pærəmaʊnt] *adj* supremo, extremo; *be paramount* ser de importancia capital

par·a·noi·a [pærə'nɔɪə] paranoia *f*

par·a·noid ['pærənɔɪd] *adj* paranoico

par·a·pher·na·li·a [pærəfər'neɪlɪə] parafernalia *f*

par·a·phrase ['pærəfreɪz] *v/t* parafrasear

par·a·pleg·ic [pærə'pliːdʒɪk] *n* parapléjico(-a) *m(f)*

par·a·site ['pærəsaɪt] *also fig* parásito *m*

par·a·sol ['pærəsɒːl] sombrilla *f*

par·a·troop·er ['pærətruːpər] paracaidista *m/f* (*militar*)

par·cel ['paːrsl] *n* paquete *m*

◆ **parcel up** *v/t* empaquetar

parch [paːrtʃ] *v/t* secar; **be parched** F *of person* estar muerto de sed F

par·don ['paːrdn] **1** *n* LAW indulto *m*; **I beg your pardon?** (*what did you say?*) ¿cómo ha dicho?; **I beg your pardon** (*I'm sorry*) discúlpeme **2** *v/t* perdonar; LAW indultar; **pardon me?** ¿perdón?; **pardon me?** ¿qué?

pare [per] *v/t* (*peel*) pelar

par·ent ['perənt] *father* padre *m*; *mother* madre *f*; **my parents** mis padres

'par·ent com·pa·ny empresa *f* matriz

par·ent-'teach·er as·so·ci·a·tion asociación *f* de padres y profesores

pa·ren·the·sis [pə'renθəsɪs] (*pl* **parentheses** [pə'renθəsiːz]) paréntesis *m inv*

par·ish ['pærɪʃ] parroquia *f*

park[1] [paːrk] *n* parque *m*

park[2] *v/t & v/i* MOT estacionar, *Span* aparcar

par·ka ['paːrkə] parka *f*

par·king ['paːrkɪŋ] MOT estacionamiento *m*, *Span* aparcamiento *m*; **no parking** prohibido aparcar

'par·king disc disco *m* (de aparcamiento)

'par·king ga·rage párking *m*, *Span* aparcamiento *m*

'par·king lot estacionamiento *m*, *Span* aparcamiento *m* (al aire libre)

'par·king me·ter parquímetro *m*

'par·king place (plaza *f* de) estacionamiento *or Span* aparcamiento, sitio *m* para estacionar *or Span* aparcar

'par·king tick·et multa *f* de estacionamiento

par·lia·ment ['paːrləmənt] parlamento *m*

par·lia·men·ta·ry [paːrlə'mentərɪ] *adj* parlamentario

pa·role [pə'roul] **1** *n* libertad *f* condicional; **be on parole** estar en libertad condicional **2** *v/t* poner en libertad condicional; **be paroled** salir en libertad condicional

cional

par·rot ['pærət] loro *m*

pars·ley ['paːrslɪ] perejil *m*

part [paːrt] **1** *n* (*portion, area*) parte *f*; (*episode*) parte *f*, episodio *m*; *of machine* pieza *f* (de repuesto); *in play, film* papel *m*; *in hair* raya *f*; **take part in** tomar parte en **2** *adv* (*partly*) en parte; **part American part Spanish** medio americano medio español; **part fact, part fiction** con una parte de realidad y una parte de ficción **3** *v/i* separarse **4** *v/t*: **part one's hair** hacerse la raya

◆ **part with** *v/t* desprenderse de

'part ex·change: **take sth in part exchange** llevarse algo como parte del pago

par·tial ['paːrʃl] *adj* (*incomplete*) parcial; **be partial to** tener debilidad por

par·tial·ly ['paːrʃəlɪ] *adv* parcialmente

par·ti·ci·pant [paːr'tɪsɪpənt] participante *m/f*

par·ti·ci·pate [paːr'tɪsɪpeɪt] *v/i* participar

par·ti·ci·pa·tion [paːrtɪsɪ'peɪʃn] participación *f*

par·ti·cle ['paːrtɪkl] PHYS partícula *f*; (*small amount*) pizca *f*

par·tic·u·lar [pər'tɪkjələr] *adj* (*specific*) particular, concreto; (*demanding*) exigente; *about friends, employees* selectivo; *pej* especial, quisquilloso; **you know how particular she is** ya sabes lo especial que es; **this particular morning** precisamente esta mañana; **in particular** en particular; **it's a particular favorite of mine** es uno de mis preferidos

par·tic·u·lar·ly [pər'tɪkjələrlɪ] *adv* particularmente, especialmente

par·ti·tion [paːr'tɪʃn] **1** *n* (*screen*) tabique *m*; *of country* partición *f*, división *f* **2** *v/t country* dividir

◆ **partition off** *v/t* dividir con tabiques

part·ly ['paːrtlɪ] *adv* en parte

part·ner ['paːrtnər] COM socio(-a) *m(f)*; *in relationship* compañero(-a) *m(f)*; *in tennis, dancing* pareja *f*

part·ner·ship ['paːrtnərʃɪp] COM sociedad *f*; *in particular activity* colaboración *f*

part of 'speech parte *f* de la oración

'part own·er copropietario(-a) *m(f)*

'part-time **1** *adj* a tiempo parcial **2** *adv* work a tiempo parcial

part-'tim·er: *be a part-timer* trabajar a tiempo parcial

par·ty ['pɑːrtɪ] **1** *n* (*celebration*) fiesta *f*; POL partido *m*; (*group of people*) grupo *m*; *be a party to* tomar parte en **2** *v/i* (*pret & pp partied*) F salir de marcha F

pass [pæs] **1** *n for entry*, SP pase *m*; *in mountains* desfiladero *m*; *make a pass at* tirarle los tejos a **2** *v/t* (*hand*) pasar; (*go past*) pasar por delante de; (*overtake*) adelantar; (*go beyond*) sobrepasar; (*approve*) aprobar; *pass an exam* aprobar un examen; *pass sentence* LAW dictar sentencia; *pass the time* pasar el tiempo **3** *v/i of time* pasar; *in exam* aprobar; (*go away*) pasarse

◆ pass around *v/t* repartir

◆ pass away *v/i euph* fallecer, pasar a mejor vida

◆ pass by **1** *v/t* (*go past*) pasar por **2** *v/i* (*go past*) pasarse

◆ pass on **1** *v/t information, book* pasar; *pass on the savings to ...* of supermarket etc revertir el ahorro en ... **2** *v/i* (*euph: die*) fallecer, pasar a mejor vida

◆ pass out *v/i* (*faint*) desmayarse

◆ pass through *v/t town* pasar por

◆ pass up *v/t opportunity* dejar pasar

pass·a·ble ['pæsəbl] *adj road* transitable; (*acceptable*) aceptable

pas·sage ['pæsɪdʒ] (*corridor*) pasillo *m*; *from poem, book* pasaje *m*; *of time* paso *m*

pas·sage·way ['pæsɪdʒweɪ] pasillo *m*

pas·sen·ger ['pæsɪndʒər] pasajero(-a) *m(f)*

'pas·sen·ger seat asiento *m* de pasajero

pas·ser·by [pæsər'baɪ] (*pl passers-by*) transeúnte *m/f*

pas·sion ['pæʃn] pasión *f*; *a crime of passion* un crimen pasional

pas·sion·ate ['pæʃnət] *adj lover* apasionado; (*fervent*) fervoroso

pas·sive ['pæsɪv] **1** *adj* pasivo **2** *n* GRAM (*voz f*) pasiva *f*; *in the passive* en pasiva

'pass mark EDU nota *f* mínima para aprobar

Pass·o·ver ['pæsouvər] REL Pascua *f* de los hebreos

pass·port ['pæspɔːrt] pasaporte *m*

'pass·port control control *m* de pasaportes

pass·word ['pæswɜːrd] contraseña *f*

past [pæst] **1** *adj* (*former*) pasado; *his past life* su pasado; *the past few days* los últimos días; *that's all past now* todo eso es agua pasada **2** *n* pasado; *in the past* antiguamente **3** *prep in position* después de; *it's half past two* son las dos y media; *it's past ten o'clock* pasan de las siete; *it's past your bedtime* hace rato que tenías que haberte ido a la cama **4** *adv*: *run / walk past* pasar

pas·ta ['pæstə] pasta *f*

paste [peɪst] **1** *n* (*adhesive*) cola *f* **2** *v/t* (*stick*) pegar

pas·tel ['pæstl] **1** *n color* pastel *m* **2** *adj* pastel

pas·time ['pæstaɪm] pasatiempo *m*

past 'par·ti·ci·ple GRAM participio *m* pasado

pas·tra·mi [pæ'strɑːmɪ] pastrami *m*, carne de vaca ahumada con especias

pas·try ['peɪstrɪ] *for pie* masa *f*; *small cake* pastel *m*

'past tense GRAM (*tiempo m*) pasado *m*

pas·ty ['peɪstɪ] *adj complexion* pálido

pat [pæt] **1** *n* palmadita *f*; *give s.o. a pat on the back fig* dar una palmadita a alguien en la espalda **2** *v/t* (*pret & pp patted*) dar palmaditas a

patch [pætʃ] **1** *n on clothing* parche *m*; (*area*) mancha *f*; *a bad patch* (*period of time*) un mal momento, una mala racha; *patches of fog* zonas de niebla; *not be a patch on fig* no tener ni punto de comparación con **2** *v/t clothing* remendar

◆ patch up *v/t* (*repair temporarily*) hacer un remiendo a, arreglar a medias; *quarrel* solucionar

patch·work ['pætʃwɜːrk] **1** *n needlework* labor *f* de retazo **2** *adj* hecho de remiendos

patch·y ['pætʃɪ] *quality* desigual; *work, performance* irregular pâ·té [pɑː'teɪ] paté *m*

pa·tent ['peɪtnt] **1** *adj* patente, evidente **2** *n for invention* patente *f* **3** *v/t invention* patentar

pa·tent 'leath·er charol *m*

pa·tent·ly ['peɪtntlɪ] (*clearly*) evidentemente, claramente

pa·ter·nal [pə'tɜːrnl] *relative* paterno; *pride, love* paternal

pa·ter·nal·ism [pə'tɜːrnlɪzm] paternalismo *m*

pa·ter·nal·is·tic [pətɜːrnl'ɪstɪk] *adj* paternalista

pa·ter·ni·ty [pə'tɜːrnɪtɪ] paternidad *f*

path [pæθ] *also fig* camino *m*

pa·thet·ic [pə'θetɪk] *adj invoking pity* patético; F (*very bad*) lamentable F

path·o·log·i·cal [pæθə'lɑːdʒɪkl] *adj* patológico

pa·thol·o·gy [pə'θɑːlədʒɪ] patología *f*

pa·thol·o·gist [pə'θɑːlədʒɪst] patólogo(-a) *m(f)*

pa·tience ['peɪʃns] paciencia *f*

pa·tient ['peɪʃnt] **1** *n* paciente *m/f* **2** *adj* paciente; *just be patient!* ¡ten paciencia!

pa·tient·ly ['peɪʃntlɪ] *adv* pacientemente

pat·i·o ['pætɪoʊ] patio *m*

pat·ri·ot ['pætrɪət] patriota *m/f*

pat·ri·ot·ic [peɪtrɪ'ɑːtɪk] *adj* patriótico

pat·ri·ot·ism ['peɪtrɪətɪzm] patriotismo *m*

pa·trol [pə'troʊl] **1** *n* patrulla *f*; *be on patrol* estar de patrulla **2** *v/t* (*pret & pp patrolled*) *streets, border* patrullar

pa·trol car coche *m* patrulla

pa·trol·man policía *m*, patrullero *m*

pa·trol wag·on furgón *m* policial

pa·tron ['peɪtrən] *of store, movie theater* cliente *m/f*; *of artist, charity etc* patrocinador(a) *m(f)*

pa·tron·ize ['pætrənaɪz] *v/t store* ser cliente de; *person* tratar con condescendencia *or* como a un niño

pa·tron·iz·ing ['pætrənaɪzɪŋ] condescendiente

pa·tron 'saint santo(-a) *m(f)* patrón(-ona), patrón(-ona) *m(f)*

pat·ter ['pætər] **1** *n of rain etc* repiqueteo *m*; F (*of salesman*) parloteo *m* **2** *v/i* repiquetear

pat·tern ['pætərn] *n on wallpaper, fabric* estampado *m*; *for knitting, sewing* diseño *m*; (*model*) modelo *m*; *in behavior, events* pauta *f*

pat·terned ['pætərnd] *adj* estampado

paunch [pɔːntʃ] barriga *f*

pause [pɔːz] **1** *n* pausa *f* **2** *v/i* parar; *when speaking* hacer una pausa **3** *v/t tape* poner en pausa

pave [peɪv] *with concrete* pavimentar; *with slabs* adoquinar; *pave the way for fig* preparar el terreno para

pave·ment ['peɪvmənt] (*Am: roadway*) calzada *f*; (*Br: sidewalk*) acera *f*

pav·ing stone ['peɪvɪŋ] losa *f*

paw [pɔː] **1** *n of animal* pata *f*; F (*hand*) pezuña *f* F **2** *v/t* F sobar F

pawn¹ [pɔːn] *n in chess* peón *m*; *fig* títere *m*

pawn² [pɔːn] *v/t* empeñar

'pawn·bro·ker prestamista *m/f*

'pawn·shop casa *f* de empeños

pay [peɪ] **1** *n* paga *f*, sueldo *m*; *in the pay of* a sueldo de **2** *v/t* (*pret & pp paid*) *employee, sum, bill* pagar; *pay attention* prestar atención; *pay s.o. a compliment* hacer un cumplido a alguien **3** *v/i* (*pret & pp paid*) pagar; (*be profitable*) ser rentable; *it doesn't pay to* ... no conviene ...; *pay for purchase* pagar; *you'll pay for this! fig* ¡me las pagarás!

♦ pay back *v/t person* devolver el dinero a *; loan* devolver

♦ pay in *v/t to bank* ingresar

♦ pay off **1** *v/t debt* liquidar; (*bribe*) sobornar **2** *v/i* (*be profitable*) valer la pena

♦ pay up *v/i* pagar

pay·a·ble ['peɪəbl] *adj* pagadero

'pay check cheque *m* del sueldo

'pay·day día *m* de paga

pay·ee [peɪ'iː] beneficiario(-a) *m(f)*

'pay en·ve·lope sobre *m* con la paga

pay·er ['peɪər] pagador(a) *m(f)* *they are good payers* pagan puntualmente

pay·ment ['peɪmənt] pago *m*

'pay phone teléfono *m* público

'pay·roll *money* salarios *mpl*; *employees* nómina *f*; *be on the payroll* estar en nómina

pay·slip ['peɪslɪp] nómina f (*papel*)

PC [piː'siː] *abbr* (= *personal computer*) PC *m*, *Span* ordenador *m or L.Am.* computadora personal; (= *politically correct*) políticamente correcto

pea [piː] *Span* guisante *m*, *L.Am.* arveja f, *Mex* chícharo *m*

peace [piːs] paz f; (*quietness*) tranquilidad

peace·a·ble ['piːsəbl] *adj person* pacífico

'Peace Corps organización gubernamental estadounidense de ayuda al desarrollo

peace·ful ['piːsfəl] *adj* tranquilo; *demonstration* pacífico

peace·ful·ly ['piːsfəlɪ] *adv* pacíficamente

peach [piːtʃ] *fruit* melocotón *m*, *L.Am.* durazno *m*; *tree* melocotonero *m*, *L.Am.* duraznero *m*

pea·cock ['piːkɑːk] pavo *m* real

peak [piːk] **1** *n of mountain* cima f; *mountain* pico *m*; *fig* clímax *m* **2** *v/i* alcanzar el máximo

'peak hours *npl* horas *fpl* punta

pea·nut ['piːnʌt] cacahuete *m*, *L.Am.* maní *m*, *Mex* cacahuate *m*; **get paid peanuts** F cobrar una miseria F; **that's peanuts to him** F eso es calderilla para él F

pea·nut 'but·ter crema f de cacahuete

pear [per] pera f

pearl [pɜːrl] perla f

peas·ant ['peznt] campesino(-a) *m(f)*

peb·ble ['pebl] guijarro *m*

pe·can ['piːkən] pacana f

peck [pek] **1** *n bite* picotazo *m*; *kiss* besito *m* **2** *v/t bite* picotear; *kiss* dar un besito a

pe·cu·li·ar [pɪ'kjuːljər] *adj* (*strange*) raro; **peculiar to** (*special*) característico de

pe·cu·li·ar·i·ty [pɪkjuːlɪ'ærətɪ] (*strangeness*) rareza f; (*special feature*) peculiaridad f, característica f

ped·al ['pedl] **1** *n of bike* pedal *m* **2** *v/i* (*turn pedals*) pedalear; (*cycle*) recorrer en bicicleta

pe·dan·tic [pɪ'dæntɪk] *adj* puntilloso

ped·dle ['pedl] *v/t drugs* traficar *or* trapichear con

ped·es·tal ['pedəstl] *for statue* pedestal *m*

pe·des·tri·an [pɪ'destrɪən] *n* peatón(-ona) *m(f)*

pe·des·tri·an 'cros·sing paso *m* de peatones

pe·di·at·ric [piːdɪ'ætrɪk] *adj* pediátrico

pe·di·a·tri·cian [piːdɪə'trɪʃn] pediatra *m/f*

pe·di·at·rics [piːdɪ'ætrɪks] pediatría f

ped·i·cure ['pedɪkjʊr] pedicura f

ped·i·gree ['pedɪgriː] **1** *n of animal* pedigrí; *of person* linaje *m* **2** *adj* con pedigrí

pee [piː] *v/i* F hacer pis F, mear F

peek [piːk] **1** *n* ojeada f, vistazo *m* **2** *v/i* echar una ojeada *or* vistazo

peel [piːl] **1** *n* piel f **2** *v/t fruit, vegetables* pelar **3** *v/i of nose, shoulders* pelarse; *of paint* levantarse

◆ **peel off 1** *v/t wrapper etc* quitar; *jacket etc* quitarse **2** *v/i of wrapper* quitarse

peep [piːp] → **peek**

peep·hole ['piːphoʊl] mirilla f

peer[1] [pɪr] *n* (*equal*) igual *m*

peer[2] [pɪr] *v/i* mirar; **peer through the mist** buscar con la mirada entre la niebla; **peer at** forzar la mirada para ver

peeved [piːvd] F mosqueado F

peg [peg] *n for hat, coat* percha f; *for tent* clavija f; **off the peg** de confección

pe·jo·ra·tive [pɪ'dʒɑːrətɪv] *adj* peyorativo

pel·let ['pelɪt] pelotita f; (*bullet*) perdigón *m*

pelt [pelt] **1** *v/t*: **pelt s.o. with sth** tirar algo a alguien **2** *v/i*: **they pelted along the road** F fueron a toda mecha por la carretera F; **it's pelting down** F está diluviando F

pel·vis ['pelvɪs] pelvis f

pen[1] [pen] *n* (*ballpoint pen*) bolígrafo *m*; (*fountain pen*) pluma f (estilográfica)

pen[2] [pen] (*enclosure*) corral *m*

pen[3] [pen] → **penitentiary**

pe·nal·ize ['piːnəlaɪz] *v/t* penalizar

pen·al·ty ['penltɪ] sanción f; SP penalti *m*; **take the penalty** *in soccer* lanzar el penalti

'pen·al·ty ar·e·a SP área f de castigo

'pen·al·ty clause LAW cláusula f de penalización

'pen·al·ty kick (lanzamiento *m* de) penalti *m*

'pen·al·ty 'shoot-out tanda f de penalties

'pen·al·ty spot punto *m* de penalti

pen·cil ['pensɪl] lápiz *m*

pen·cil sharp·en·er sacapuntas *m inv*

pen·dant ['pendənt] (*necklace*) colgante *m*

pend·ing ['pendɪŋ] **1** *prep* en espera de **2** *adj* pendiente; **be pending** *awaiting a decision* estar pendiente; *about to happen* ser inminente

pen·e·trate ['penɪtreɪt] *v/t* (*pierce*) penetrar; *market* penetrar en

pen·e·trat·ing ['penɪtreɪtɪŋ] *adj stare, scream* penetrante; *analysis* exhaustivo

pen·e·tra·tion [penɪ'treɪʃn] penetración *f*; *of defences* incursión *f*; *of market* entrada *f*

'pen friend amigo(-a) *m(f)* por correspondencia

pen·guin ['peŋgwɪn] pingüino *m*

pen·i·cil·lin [penɪ'sɪlɪn] penicilina *f*

pe·nin·su·la [pə'nɪnsʊlə] península *f*

pe·nis ['piːnɪs] pene *m*

pen·i·tence ['penɪtəns] (*remorse*) arrepentimiento *m*

pen·i·tent ['penɪtənt] *adj* arrepentido

pen·i·ten·ia·ry [penɪ'tenʃərɪ] prisión *f*, cárcel *f*

pen·knife ['pennaɪf] navaja *f*

'pen name seudónimo *m*

pen·nant ['penənt] banderín *f*

pen·ni·less ['penɪlɪs] *adj* sin un centavo

pen·ny ['penɪ] penique *m*

'pen pal amigo(-a) *m(f)* por correspondencia

pen·sion ['penʃn] pensión *f*

♦ pension off *v/t* jubilar

'pen·sion fund fondo *m* de pensiones

'pen·sion scheme plan *m* de jubilación

pen·sive ['pensɪv] *adj* pensativo

Pen·ta·gon ['pentəgɑːn]: **the Pentagon** el Pentágono

pen·tath·lon [pen'tæθlən] pentatlón *m*

Pen·te·cost ['pentɪkɑːst] Pentecostés *m*

pent·house ['penthaʊs] ático *m* (*de lujo*)

pent·up ['pentʌp] *adj* reprimido

pe·nul·ti·mate [pe'nʌltɪmət] *adj* penúltimo

peo·ple ['piːpl] *npl* gente *f*; (*individuals*) personas *fpl*; (*nsg: race, tribe*) pueblo *m*; **the people** (*citizens*) el pueblo, los ciudadanos; **the Spanish people** los españoles; **a lot of people think ...** muchos piensan que ...; **people say ...** se dice que ..., dicen que ...

pep·per ['pepər] *spice* pimienta *f*; *vegetable* pimiento *m*

pep·per·mint *sweet* caramelo *m* de menta

pep talk ['peptɔːk]: **give a pep talk** decir unas palabras de aliento

per [pɜːr] *prep* por; **per annum** al año, por año

per·ceive [pər'siːv] *v/t with senses* percibir; (*view, interpret*) interpretar

per·cent [pər'sent] *adv* por ciento

per·cen·tage [pər'sentɪdʒ] porcentaje *m*, tanto *m* por ciento

per·cep·ti·ble [pər'septəbl] *adj* perceptible

per·cep·ti·bly [pər'septəblɪ] *adv* visiblemente

per·cep·tion [pər'sepʃn] *through senses* percepción *f*; *of situation* apreciación *f*; (*insight*) perspicacia *f*

per·cep·tive [pər'septɪv] *adj* perceptivo

perch [pɜːrtʃ] **1** *n for bird* percha *f* **2** *v/i of bird* posarse; *of person* sentarse

per·co·late ['pɜːrkəleɪt] *v/i of coffee* filtrarse

per·co·la·tor ['pɜːrkəleɪtər] cafetera *f* de filtro

per·cus·sion [pər'kʌʃn] percusión *f*

per'cus·sion in·stru·ment instrumento *m* de percusión

pe·ren·ni·al [pə'renɪəl] *n* BOT árbol *m* de hoja perenne

per·fect **1** *n* ['pɜːrfɪkt] GRAM pretérito *m* perfecto **2** *adj* perfecto **3** *v/t* [pər'fekt] perfeccionar

per·fec·tion [pər'fekʃn] perfección *f*; **do sth to perfection** hacer algo a la perfección

per·fec·tion·ist [pər'fekʃnɪst] perfeccionista *m/f*

per·fect·ly ['pɜːrfɪktlɪ] perfectamente; (*totally*) completamente

per·fo·rat·ed ['pɜːrfəreɪtɪd] *adj line* perforado

per·fo·ra·tions [pɜːrfə'reɪʃnz] *npl* perforaciones *fpl*

per·form [pə'fɔːrm] **1** v/t (*carry out*) realizar, llevar a cabo; *of actors, musician etc* interpretar, representar **2** v/i *of actor, musician, dancer* actuar; *of machine* funcionar

per·form·ance [pə'fɔːrməns] *by actor, musician etc* actuación f, interpretación f; *of play* representación f; *of employee* rendimiento m; *of official, company, in sport* actuación f; *of machine* rendimiento m

per'form·ance car coche m de gran rendimiento

per·form·er [pə'fɔːrmər] intérprete m/f

per·fume ['pɜːrfjuːm] perfume m

per·func·to·ry [pər'fʌŋktəri] *adj* superficial

per·haps [pər'hæps] *adv* quizá(s), tal vez; *perhaps it's not too late* puede que no sea demasiado tarde

per·il ['perəl] peligro m

per·il·ous ['perələs] *adj* peligroso

pe·rim·e·ter [pə'rimitər] perímetro m

pe'rim·e·ter fence cerca f

pe·ri·od ['piriəd] periodo m, período m; (*menstruation*) regla f; (*punctuation mark*) punto m; *I don't want to, period!* F ¡no me da la gana y punto! F

pe·ri·od·ic [piri'ɑːdik] *adj* periódico

pe·ri·od·i·cal [piri'ɑːdikl] *n* publicación f periódica

pe·ri·od·i·cal·ly [piri'ɑːdikli] *adv* periódicamente, con periodicidad

pe·riph·e·ral [pə'rifərəl] **1** *adj* (*not crucial*) secundario **2** *n* COMPUT periférico m

pe·riph·e·ry [pə'rifəri] periferia f

per·ish ['periʃ] v/i *of rubber* estropearse, picarse; *of person* perecer

per·ish·a·ble ['periʃəbl] *adj food* perecedero

per·jure ['pɜːrdʒər] v/t: *perjure o.s.* perjurar

per·ju·ry ['pɜːrdʒəri] perjurio m

perk [pɜːrk] *n of job* ventaja f

♦ **perk up 1** v/t animar **2** v/i animarse

perk·y ['pɜːrki] (*cheerful*) animado

perm [pɜːrm] **1** *n* permanente f **2** v/t hacer la permanente; *she had her hair permed* se hizo la permanente

per·ma·nent ['pɜːrmənənt] *adj* permanente

per·ma·nent·ly ['pɜːrmənəntli] *adv* permanentemente

per·me·a·ble ['pɜːrmiəbl] *adj* permeable

per·me·ate ['pɜːrmieit] v/t impregnar

per·mis·si·ble [pər'misəbl] *adj* permisible

per·mis·sion [pər'miʃn] permiso m; *ask s.o.'s permission to ...* pedir permiso a alguien para ...

per·mis·sive [pər'misiv] *adj* permisivo

per·mit ['pɜːrmit] **1** *n* licencia f **2** v/t (*pret & pp permitted*) [pər'mit] permitir; *permit s.o. to do sth* permitir a alguien que haga algo

per·pen·dic·u·lar [pɜːrpən'dikjulər] *adj* perpendicular

per·pet·u·al *adj* perpetuo; *interruptions* continuo

per·pet·u·al·ly [pər'petʃuəli] *adv* constantemente

per·pet·u·ate [pər'petʃueit] v/t perpetuar

per·plex [pər'pleks] v/t dejar perplejo

per·plexed [pər'plekst] *adj* perplejo

per·plex·i·ty [pər'pleksiti] perplejidad f

per·se·cute ['pɜːrsikjuːt] v/t perseguir; (*hound*) acosar

per·se·cu·tion [pɜːrsi'kjuːʃn] persecución f; (*harassment*) acoso m

per·se·cu·tor [pɜːrsi'kjuːtər] perseguidor(a) m(f)

per·se·ver·ance [pɜːrsi'virəns] perseverancia f

per·se·vere [pɜːrsi'vir] v/i perseverar

per·sist [pər'sist] v/i persistir; *persist in* persistir en

per·sis·tence [pər'sistəns] (*perseverance*) perseverancia f; (*continuation*) persistencia f

per·sis·tent [pər'sistənt] *adj person, questions* perseverante; *rain, unemployment etc* persistente

per·sis·tent·ly [pər'sistəntli] *adv* (*continually*) constantemente

per·son ['pɜːrsn] persona f; *in person* en persona

per·son·al ['pɜːrsənl] *adj* (*private*) personal; *life* privado; *don't make personal*

remarks no hagas comentarios personales

per·son·al as·sist·ant secretario(-a) *m(f)* personal

'**per·son·al col·umn** sección *f* de anuncios personales

per·son·al com'put·er *Span* ordenador *m* personal, *L.Am.* computadora *f* personal

per·son·al 'hy·giene higiene *f* personal

per·son·al·i·ty [pɜːrsə'næləti] personalidad *f*; *(celebrity)* personalidad *f*, personaje *m*

per·son·al·ly ['pɜːrsənəli] *adv (for my part)* personalmente; *(in person)* en persona; ***don't take it personally*** no te lo tomes como algo personal

per·son·al 'or·gan·iz·er organizador *m* personal

per·son·al 'pro·noun pronombre *m* personal

per·son·al 'ster·e·o walkman *m* ®

per·son·i·fy [pɜːr'sɑːnɪfaɪ] *v/t (pret & pp **personified**)* personificar

per·son·nel [pɜːrsə'nel] *employees, department* personal *m*

per·son'nel man·a·ger director(a) *m(f)* de personal

per·spec·tive [pər'spektɪv] PAINT perspectiva *f*; ***get sth into perspective*** poner algo en perspectiva

per·spi·ra·tion [pɜːrspɪ'reɪʃn] sudor *m*, transpiración *f*

per·spire [pɜːr'spaɪr] *v/i* sudar, transpirar

per·suade [pər'sweɪd] *v/t person* persuadir; ***persuade s.o. to do sth*** persuadir a alguien para que haga algo

per·sua·sion [pər'sweɪʒn] persuasión *f*

per·sua·sive [pər'sweɪsɪv] persuasivo

per·ti·nent ['pɜːrtɪnənt] *adj fml* pertinente

per·turb [pər'tɜːrb] *v/t* perturbar

per·turb·ing [pər'tɜːrbɪŋ] *adj* perturbador

Pe·ru [pə'ruː] *n* Perú

pe·ruse [pə'ruːz] *v/t fml* leer atentamente

Pe·ru·vi·an [pə'ruːvɪən] **1** *adj* peruano **2** *n* peruano(-a) *m(f)*

per·va·sive [pər'veɪsɪv] *adj influence, ideas* dominante

per·verse [pər'vɜːrs] *adj (awkward)* terco; ***just to be perverse*** sólo para llevar la contraria

per·ver·sion [pər'vɜːrʃn] *sexual* perversión *f*

per·vert ['pɜːrvɜːrt] *n sexual* pervertido(-a) *m(f)*

pes·si·mism ['pesɪmɪzm] pesimismo *m*

pes·si·mist ['pesɪmɪst] pesimista *m/f*

pes·si·mis·tic [pesɪ'mɪstɪk] *adj* pesimista

pest [pest] *pest* plaga *f*; F *person* tostón *m* F

pes·ter ['pestər] *v/t* acosar; ***pester s.o. to do sth*** molestar *or* dar la lata a alguien para que haga algo

pes·ti·cide ['pestɪsaɪd] pesticida *f*

pet [pet] **1** *n animal* animal *m* doméstico *or* de compañía; *(favorite)* preferido(-a) *m(f)* **2** *adj* preferido, favorito **3** *v/t (pret & pp **petted**)* animal acariciar **4** *v/i (pret & pp **petted**)* of couple magrearse F

pet·al ['petl] pétalo *m*

♦ **pe·ter out** ['piːtər] *v/i of rain* amainar; *of rebellion* irse extinguiendo; *of path* ir desapareciendo

pe·tite [pə'tiːt] *adj* chiquito(-a); *size* menudo

pe·ti·tion [pə'tɪʃn] *n* petición *f*

'**pet name** nombre *m* cariñoso

pet·ri·fied ['petrɪfaɪd] *adj person* petrificado; *scream, voice* aterrorizado

pet·ri·fy ['petrɪfaɪ] *v/t (pret & pp **petrified**)* dejar petrificado

pet·ro·chem·i·cal [petroʊ'kemɪkl] *adj* petroquímico

pet·rol ['petrl] *Br* gasolina *f*, *Arg* nafta *f*

pe·tro·le·um [pɪ'troʊlɪəm] petróleo *m*

pet·ting ['petɪŋ] magreo *m* F

pet·ty ['peti] *adj person, behavior* mezquino; *details, problem* sin importancia

pet·ty 'cash dinero *m* para gastos menores

pet·u·lant ['petʃələnt] *adj* caprichoso

pew [pjuː] banco *m (de iglesia)*

pew·ter ['pjuːtər] peltre *m*

phar·ma·ceu·ti·cal [fɑːrmə'suːtɪkl] *adj* farmacéutico

phar·ma·ceu·ti·cals [fɑːmə'suːtɪklz] *npl* fármacos *mpl*

phar·ma·cist ['fɑːrməsɪst] *in store* farmaceútico(-a) *m(f)*

phar·ma·cy ['fɑːrməsɪ] *store* farmacia *f*

phase [feɪz] fase *f*; **go through a difficult phase** atravesar una mala etapa

◆ **phase in** *v/t* introducir gradualmente

◆ **phase out** *v/t* eliminar gradualmente

PhD [piːeɪtʃ'diː] *abbr* (= ***Doctor of Philosophy***) Doctorado *m*

phe·nom·e·nal [fɪ'nɑːmɪnl] *adj* fenomenal

phe·nom·e·nal·ly [fɪ'nɑːmɪnlɪ] *adv* extraordinariamente; *stupid* increíblemente

phe·nom·e·non [fɪ'nɑːmɪnɑːn] fenómeno *m*

phil·an·throp·ic [fɪlən'θrɑːpɪk] *adj* filantrópico

phi·lan·thro·pist [fɪ'lænθrəpɪst] filántropo(-a) *m(f)*

phi·lan·thro·py [fɪ'lænθrəpɪ] filantropía *f*

Phil·ip·pines ['fɪlɪpiːnz] *npl*: ***the Philippines*** las Filipinas

phil·is·tine ['fɪlɪstaɪn] *n* filisteo(-a) *m(f)*

phi·los·o·pher [fɪ'lɑːsəfər] filósofo(-a) *m(f)*

phil·o·soph·i·cal [fɪlə'sɑːfɪkl] *adj* filosófico

phi·los·o·phy [fɪ'lɑːsəfɪ] filosofía *f*

pho·bi·a ['foʊbɪə] fobia *f*

phone [foʊn] **1** *n* teléfono *m*; **be on the phone** have a phone tener teléfono; *be talking* estar hablando por teléfono **2** *v/t* llamar (por teléfono) a **3** *v/i* llamar (por teléfono)

'**phone book** guía *f* (de teléfonos)

'**phone booth** cabina *f* (de teléfonos)

'**phone call** llamada *f* (telefónica)

'**phone card** *Br* tarjeta *f* telefónica

'**phone num·ber** número *m* de teléfono

pho·net·ics [fə'netɪks] fonética *f*

pho·n(e)y ['foʊnɪ] *adj* F falso

pho·to ['foʊtoʊ] *n* foto *f*

'**pho·to al·bum** álbum *m* de fotos

'**pho·to·cop·i·er** fotocopiadora *f*

'**pho·to·cop·y 1** *n* fotocopia *f* **2** *v/t* (*pret & pp **photocopied***) fotocopiar

pho·to·gen·ic [foʊtoʊ'dʒenɪk] *adj* fotogénico

pho·to·graph ['foʊtəgræf] **1** *n* fotografía *f* **2** *v/t* fotografiar

pho·tog·ra·pher [fə'tɑːgrəfər] fotógrafo(-a) *m(f)*

pho·tog·ra·phy [fə'tɑːgrəfɪ] fotografía *f*

phrase [freɪz] **1** *n* frase *f* **2** *v/t* expresar

'**phrase·book** guía *f* de conversación

phys·i·cal ['fɪzɪkl] **1** *adj* físico **2** *n* MED reconocimiento *m* médico

phys·i·cal 'hand·i·cap minusvalía *f* física

phys·i·cal·ly ['fɪzɪklɪ] *adv* físicamente

phys·i·cal·ly 'hand·i·cap·ped disminuido(-a) *m(f)* físico

phy·si·cian [fɪ'zɪʃn] médico(-a) *m(f)*

phys·i·cist ['fɪzɪsɪst] físico(-a) *m(f)*

phys·ics ['fɪzɪks] física *f*

phys·i·o·ther·a·pist [fɪzɪoʊ'θerəpɪst] fisioterapeuta *m/f*

phys·i·o·ther·a·py [fɪzɪoʊ'θerəpɪ] fisioterapia *f*

phy·sique [fɪ'ziːk] físico *m*

pi·a·nist ['pɪənɪst] pianista *m/f*

pi·an·o [pɪ'ænoʊ] piano *m*

pick [pɪk] **1** *n*: ***take your pick*** elige el que prefieras **2** *v/t* (*choose*) escoger, elegir; *flowers, fruit* recoger; ***pick one's nose*** meterse el dedo en la nariz **3** *v/i*: ***pick and choose*** ser muy exigente

◆ **pick at** *v/t*: ***pick at one's food*** comer como un pajarito

◆ **pick on** *v/t* (*treat unfairly*) meterse con; (*select*) elegir

◆ **pick out** *v/t* (*identify*) identificar

◆ **pick up 1** *v/t object* recoger, *Span* coger; *habit* adquirir, *Span* coger; *illness* contraer, *Span* coger; *in car, from ground, from airport etc* recoger; *telephone* descolgar; *language, skill* aprender; (*buy*) comprar; *criminal* detener; ***pick s.o. up*** *sexually* ligar con alguien; ***pick up the tab*** F pagar **2** *v/i* (*improve*) mejorar

pick·et ['pɪkɪt] **1** *n of strikers* piquete *m* **2** *v/t* hacer piquete delante de

'**pick·et fence** valla *f* de estacas

'**pick·et line** piquete *m*

pick·le ['pɪkl] *v/t* encurtir; *fish* poner en escabeche; *meat* poner en adobo

pick·les ['pɪklz] *npl* (*dill pickles*) encurtidos *mpl*

'**pick·pock·et** carterista *m/f*

pick-up (truck) ['pɪkʌp] camioneta *f*

pick-y ['pɪkɪ] *adj* F tiquismiquis F

pic-nic ['pɪknɪk] **1** *n* picnic *m* **2** *v/i* (*pret & pp* **picnicked**) ir de picnic

pic-ture ['pɪktʃər] **1** *n* (*photo*) fotografía *f*; (*painting*) cuadro *m*; (*illustration*) dibujo *m*; (*movie*) película *f*; **on** TV imagen *f*; **keep s.o. in the picture** mantener a alguien al día **2** *v/t* imaginar

'pic-ture book libro *m* ilustrado

pic-ture 'post-card postal *f*

pic-tur-esque [pɪktʃə'resk] *adj* pintoresco

pie [paɪ] pastel *m*

piece [piːs] (*fragment*) fragmento *m*; *component, in board game* pieza *f*; **a piece of pie / bread** un trozo de pastel / una rebanada de pan; **a piece of advice** un consejo; **go to pieces** derrumbarse; **take to pieces** desmontar

♦ **piece together** *v/t broken plate* recomponer; *facts, evidence* reconstruir

piece-meal ['piːsmiːl] *adv* poco a poco

piece-work ['piːswɜːrk] *n* trabajo *m* a destajo

pier [pɪr] *at seaside* malecón *m*

pierce [pɪrs] *v/t* (*penetrate*) perforar; *ears* agujerear

pierc-ing ['pɪrsɪŋ] *adj scream* desgarrador; *gaze* penetrante; *wind* cortante

pig [pɪg] *also fig* cerdo *m*; *greedy* glotón(-a) *m(f)*

pi-geon ['pɪdʒɪn] paloma *f*

'pi-geon-hole 1 *n* casillero *m* **2** *v/t person* encasillar; *proposal* archivar

'pig-gy-bank ['pɪgɪbæŋk] hucha *f*

pig-head-ed [pɪg'hedɪd] *adj* F cabezota F

'pig-pen *also fig* pocilga *f*

'pig-skin piel *f* de cerdo

'pig-tail coleta *f*

pile [paɪl] montón *m*, pila *f*; **a pile of work** F un montón de trabajo F

♦ **pile up 1** *v/i of work, bills* acumularse **2** *v/t* amontonar

piles [paɪlz] *nsg* MED hemorroides *fpl*

pile-up ['paɪlʌp] MOT choque *m* múltiple

pil-fer-ing ['pɪlfərɪŋ] hurtos *mpl*

pil-grim ['pɪlgrɪm] peregrino(-a) *m(f)*

pil-grim-age ['pɪlgrɪmɪdʒ] peregrinación *f*

pill [pɪl] pastilla *f*; **be on the pill** tomar la

píldora

pil-lar ['pɪlər] pilar *m*

pil-lion ['pɪljən] *of motor bike* asiento *m* trasero

pil-low ['pɪloʊ] *n* almohada *f*

'pill-ow-case, 'pil-low-slip funda *f* de almohada

pi-lot ['paɪlət] **1** *n of airplane* piloto *m/f*; *for ship* práctico *m* **2** *v/t airplane* pilotar

'pi-lot scheme plan *m* piloto

pimp [pɪmp] *n* proxeneta *m*, *Span* chulo *m* F

pim-ple ['pɪmpl] grano *m*

pin [pɪn] **1** *n for sewing* alfiler *m*; *in bowling* bolo *m*; (*badge*) pin *m*; ELEC clavija *f*; **safety pin** imperdible *m* **2** *v/t* (*pret & pp* **pinned**) (*hold down*) mantener; (*attach*) sujetar

♦ **pin down** *v/t:* **pin s.o. down to a date** forzar a alguien a concretar una fecha

♦ **pin up** *v/t notice* sujetar con chinchetas

PIN [pɪn] PIN *m* **personal identification number** número *m* de identificación personal

pin-cers ['pɪnsərz] *npl of crab* pinzas *fpl*; *tool* tenazas *fpl*; **a pair of pincers** unas tenazas *fpl*

pinch [pɪntʃ] **1** *n* pellizco *m*; *of salt, sugar etc* pizca *f*; **at a pinch** si no queda otro remedio; **at a pinch** with numbers como máximo **2** *v/t* pellizcar **3** *v/i of shoes* apretar

pine¹ [paɪn] *n tree* pino *m*; *wood* (madera *f* de) pino *m*

pine² [paɪn] *v/i:* **pine for** echar de menos

pine-ap-ple ['paɪnæpl] piña *f*, *L.Am.* ananá(s) *f*

ping [pɪŋ] **1** *n* sonido *m* metálico **2** *v/i* hacer un sonido metálico

ping-pong ['pɪŋpɑːŋ] pimpón *m*, ping-pong *m*

pink [pɪŋk] *adj* rosa

pin-na-cle ['pɪnəkl] *fig* cima *f*

'pin-point determinar

pins and 'nee-dles hormigueo *m*

'pin-stripe *adj* a rayas

pint [paɪnt] pinta *f*, *medida equivalente a 0,473 litros en Estados Unidos o a 0,568 litros en Gran Bretaña*

'pin-up modelo *m/f* de revista
pi·o·neer [paɪə'nɪr] 1 *n* fig pionero(-a) *m(f)* 2 *v/t* ser pionero en
pi·o·neer·ing [paɪə'nɪrɪŋ] *adj* work pionero
pi·ous ['paɪəs] piadoso
pip [pɪp] *n of fruit* pepita *f*
pipe [paɪp] 1 *n for smoking* pipa *f; for water, gas, sewage* tubería *f* 2 *v/t* conducir por tuberías
◆ pipe down *v/i* F cerrar el pico F
piped mu·sic [paɪpt'mjuːzɪk] hilo *m* musical
pipe·line *for oil* oleoducto *m; for gas* gasoducto *m; in the pipeline fig* en trámite
pip·ing hot [paɪpɪŋ'hɑːt] *adj* muy caliente
pi·rate ['paɪrət] 1 *n* pirata *m/f* 2 *v/t software* piratear
Pis·ces ['paɪsiːz] ASTR Piscis *m/f inv*
piss [pɪs] 1 *v/i* F (*urinate*) mear P; *take the piss out of s.o.* P cachondearse de alguien P 2 *n* P (*urine*) meada *f* P
◆ piss off *v/i* P largarse F; *piss off!* P ¡vete al cuerno! P
pissed [pɪst] *adj* P (*annoyed*) cabreado P; *Br* F (*drunk*) borracho, pedo F
pis·tol ['pɪstl] pistola *f*
pis·ton ['pɪstən] pistón *m*
pit [pɪt] *n* (*hole*) hoyo *m;* (*coal mine*) mina *f*
pitch¹ [pɪtʃ] *n* MUS tono *m*
pitch² [pɪtʃ] 1 *v/i in baseball* lanzar la pelota 2 *v/t tent* montar; *ball* lanzar
'pitch black *adj* negro como el carbón
pitch·er¹ ['pɪtʃər] *baseball player* lanzador(a) *m(f)*, pítcher *m/f*
pitch·er² ['pɪtʃər] *container* jarra *f*
pit·e·ous ['pɪtiəs] *adj* patético
pit·fall ['pɪtfɔːl] dificultad *f*
pith [pɪθ] *of citrus fruit* piel *f* blanca
pit·i·ful ['pɪtɪfəl] *adj sight* lastimoso; *excuse, attempt* lamentable
pit·i·less ['pɪtɪləs] *adj* despiadado
pits [pɪts] *npl in motor racing* boxes *mpl*
'pit stop *in motor racing* parada *f* en boxes
pit·tance ['pɪtns] miseria *f*
pit·y ['pɪtɪ] 1 *n* pena *f*, lástima *f; it's a pity that* es una pena *or* lástima que; *what a pity!* ¡qué pena!; *take pity on* compade-

cerse de 2 *v/t* (*pret & pp pitied*) *person* compadecerse de
piv·ot ['pɪvət] *v/i* pivotar
piz·za ['piːtsə] pizza *f*
plac·ard ['plækɑːrd] pancarta *f*
place [pleɪs] 1 *n* sitio *m; in race, competition* puesto *m;* (*seat*) sitio *m*, asiento; *I've lost my place in book* no sé por dónde iba; *at my / his place* en mi / su casa; *in place of* en lugar de; *feel out of place* sentirse fuera de lugar; *take place* tener lugar, llevarse a cabo; *in the first place* (*firstly*) en primer lugar; (*in the beginning*) en principio 2 *v/t* (*put*) poner, colocar; *I know you but I can't quite place you* te conozco pero no recuerdo de qué; *place an order* hacer un pedido
'place mat mantel *m* individual
plac·id ['plæsɪd] *adj* apacible
pla·gia·rism ['pleɪdʒərɪzm] plagio *m*
pla·gia·rize ['pleɪdʒəraɪz] *v/t* plagiar
plague [pleɪg] 1 *n* plaga *f* 2 *v/t* (*bother*) molestar
plain¹ [pleɪn] *n* llanura *f*
plain² [pleɪn] 1 *adj* (*clear, obvious*) claro; (*not fancy*) simple; (*not pretty*) feíllo; (*not patterned*) liso; (*blunt*) directo; *plain chocolate* chocolate amargo 2 *adv* verdaderamente; *it's plain crazy* es una verdadera locura
'plain-clothes: *in plain-clothes* de paisano
plain·ly ['pleɪnlɪ] *adv* (*clearly*) evidentemente; (*bluntly*) directamente; (*simply*) con sencillez; *he's plainly upset* está claro que está enfadado
plain 'spo·ken *adj* directo
plain·tiff ['pleɪntɪf] demandante *m/f*
plain·tive ['pleɪntɪv] *adj* quejumbroso
plan [plæn] 1 *n* (*project, intention*) plan *m;* (*drawing*) plano *m; wedding plans* preparaciones *fpl* para la boda 2 *v/t* (*pret & pp planned*) (*prepare*) planear; (*design*) hacer los planos de; *plan to do sth, plan on doing sth* planear hacer algo 3 *v/i* (*pret & pp planned*) hacer planes
plane¹ [pleɪn] *n* (*airplane*) avión *m*
plane² [pleɪn] *tool* cepillo *m*

P

plan·et ['plænɪt] planeta f

plank [plæŋk] of wood tablón m; fig: of policy punto m

plan·ning ['plænɪŋ] planificación f; **at the planning stage** en fase de estudio

plant¹ [plænt] **1** n planta f **2** v/t plantar

plant² [plænt] n (factory) fábrica f, planta f; (equipment) maquinaria f

plan·ta·tion [plæn'teɪʃn] plantación f

plaque [plæk] on wall, teeth placa f

plas·ter ['plæstər] **1** n on wall, ceiling yeso m **2** v/t wall, ceiling enyesar; **be plastered with** estar recubierto de

plas·ter cast escayola f

plas·tic ['plæstɪk] **1** n plástico m **2** adj (made of plastic) de plástico

plas·tic 'bag bolsa f de plástico

'plas·tic (mon·ey) plástico m, tarjetas fpl de pago

plas·tic 'sur·geon cirujano(-a) m(f) plástico(-a)

plas·tic 'sur·ge·ry cirugía f estética

plate [pleɪt] n for food plato m; (sheet of metal) chapa f; F PHOT placa f

pla·teau ['plætoʊ] meseta f

plat·form ['plætfɔːrm] (stage) plataforma f; of railroad station andén m; fig: political programa f

plat·i·num ['plætɪnəm] **1** n platino m **2** adj de platino

plat·i·tude ['plætɪtuːd] tópico m

pla·ton·ic [plə'tɑːnɪk] adj relationship platónico

pla·toon [plə'tuːn] of soldiers sección f

plat·ter ['plætər] for meat, fish fuente f

plau·si·ble ['plɔːzəbl] adj plausible

play [pleɪ] **1** n in theater, on TV obra f (de teatro); of children, in match, TECH juego m **2** v/i jugar; of musician tocar **3** v/t musical instrument tocar; piece of music interpretar, tocar; game jugar; tennis, football jugar a; opponent jugar contra; (perform: Macbeth etc) representar; particular role interpretar, hacer el papel de; **play a joke on** gastar una broma a

◆ play around v/i F (be unfaithful) acostarse con otras personas

◆ play down v/t quitar importancia a

◆ play up v/i of machine dar problemas;

of child dar guerra

play·act ['pleɪækt] v/i (pretend) fingir

play·boy ['pleɪbɔɪ] playboy m

play·er ['pleɪr] SP jugador(a) m(f); (musician) intérprete m/f; (actor) actor m, actriz f

play·ful ['pleɪfəl] adj punch etc de broma

play·ground ['pleɪgraʊnd] zona f de juegos

'play·group guardería f

play·ing card ['pleɪɪŋkɑːrd] carta f

play·ing field ['pleɪɪŋfiːld] campo m de deportes

play·mate ['pleɪmeɪt] compañero(-a) m(f) de juego

play·wright ['pleɪraɪt] autor(a) m(f)

pla·za ['plɑːzə] for shopping centro m comercial

plc [piːel'siː] abbr (= Br **public limited company**) S.A. f (= sociedad f anónima)

plea [pliː] n súplica f

plead [pliːd] v/i: **plead for mercy** pedir clemencia; **plead guilty/not guilty** declararse culpable/inocente; **she pleaded with me not to go** me suplicó que no fuera

pleas·ant ['pleznt] adj agradable

please [pliːz] **1** adv por favor; **more tea? - yes, please** ¿más té? - sí, por favor; **please do** claro que sí, por supuesto **2** v/t complacer; **please yourself!** ¡haz lo que quieras!

pleased [pliːzd] adj contento; (satisfied) satisfecho; **pleased to meet you** encantado de conocerle; **I'm very pleased to be here** estoy muy contento de estar aquí

pleas·ing ['pliːzɪŋ] adj agradable

pleas·ure ['pleʒər] (happiness, satisfaction, delight) satisfacción f; as opposed to work placer m; **it's a pleasure** (you're welcome) no hay de qué; **with pleasure** faltaría más

pleat [pliːt] n in skirt tabla f

pleat·ed skirt ['pliːtɪd] falda f de tablas

pledge [pledʒ] **1** n (promise) promesa f; (guarantee) compromiso m; (money) donación f; **Pledge of Allegiance** juramento de lealtad a la bandera estadounidense **2** v/t (promise) prometer; (guarantee) comprometerse; *money* donar

plen·ti·ful ['plentɪfəl] *adj* abundante

plen·ty ['plentɪ] (*abundance*) abundancia *f*; **plenty of books / food** muchos libros / mucha comida; **we've got plenty of room** tenemos espacio más que suficiente; **that's plenty** es suficiente; **there's plenty for everyone** hay (suficiente) para todos

pli·a·ble ['plaɪəbl] *adj* flexible

pli·ers ['plaɪərz] *npl* alicates *mpl*; **a pair of pliers** unos alicates

plight [plaɪt] situación *f* difícil

plod [plɑːd] *v/i* (*pret & pp* **plodded**) (*walk*) arrastrarse

◆ **plod on** *v/i* with a job avanzar laboriosamente

plod·der ['plɑːdər] (*at work, school*) persona no especialmente lista pero muy trabajadora

plot[1] [plɑːt] *n* (*land*) terreno *m*

plot[2] [plɑːt] **1** *n* (*conspiracy*) complot *m*; *of novel* argumento *m* **2** *v/t* (*pret & pp* **plotted**) tramar **3** *v/i* (*pret & pp* **plotted**) conspirar

plot·ter ['plɑːtər] conspirador(a) *m(f)*; COMPUT plóter *m*

plough *Br*, **plow** [plaʊ] **1** *n* arado *m* **2** *v/t & v/i* arar

◆ **plow back** *v/t* profits reinvertir

pluck [plʌk] *v/t* eyebrows depilar; *chicken* desplumar

◆ **pluck up** *v/t*: **pluck up courage to ...** reunir el valor para ...

plug [plʌg] **1** *n* for sink, bath tapón *m*; *electrical* enchufe *m*; (*spark plug*) bujía *f*; **give a book a plug** dar publicidad a un libro **2** *v/t* (*pret & pp* **plugged**) *hole* tapar; *new book etc* hacer publicidad de

◆ **plug away at** *v/t* F trabajar con esfuerzo en

◆ **plug in** *v/t* enchufar

plum [plʌm] **1** *n* fruit ciruela *f*; tree ciruelo *m* **2** *adj* F: **plum job** un chollo de trabajo

plum·age ['pluːmɪdʒ] plumaje *m*

plumb [plʌm] *adj* vertical

◆ **plumb in** *v/t* washing machine conectar a la red del agua

plumb·er ['plʌmər] *Span* fontanero(-a)

m(f), *L.Am.* plomero(-a) *m(f)*

plumb·ing ['plʌmɪŋ] (*pipes*) tuberías *fpl*

plume [pluːm] *n* (*feather*) pluma *f*; *of smoke* nube *f*

plum·met ['plʌmɪt] *v/i* of airplane, prices caer en picado

plump [plʌmp] *adj* rellenito

◆ **plump for** *v/t* decidirse por

plunge [plʌndʒ] **1** *n* salto *m*; in prices caída *f*; **take the plunge** dar el paso **2** *v/i* precipitarse; *of prices* caer en picado **3** *v/t* hundir; (*into water*) sumergir; **the city was plunged into darkness** la ciudad quedó inmersa en la oscuridad; **the news plunged him into despair** la noticia lo hundió en la desesperación

plung·ing ['plʌndʒɪŋ] *adj* neckline escotado

plu·per·fect ['pluːpɜːrfɪkt] *n* GRAM pluscuamperfecto *m*

plu·ral ['plʊərəl] **1** *n* plural *m* **2** *adj* plural

plus [plʌs] **1** *prep* más; **I want John plus two other volunteers ...** quiero a John y a otros dos voluntarios **2** *adj* más de; **$500 plus** más de 500 dólares **3** *n* symbol signo *m* más; (*advantage*) ventaja *f* **4** *conj* (*moreover, in addition*) además

plush [plʌʃ] *adj* lujoso

'plus sign signo *m* más

ply·wood ['plaɪwʊd] madera *f* contrachapada

PM [piː'em] *Br abbr* (= **Prime Minister**) Primer(a) *m(f)* Ministro(-a)

p.m. [piː'em] *abbr* (= **post meridiem**) p.m.; **at 3 p.m** a las 3 de la tarde; **at 11 p.m** a las 11 de la noche

pneu·mat·ic [nuː'mætɪk] *adj* neumático

pneu·mat·ic 'drill martillo *m* neumático

pneu·mo·ni·a [nuː'moʊnɪə] pulmonía *f*, neumonía *f*

poach[1] [poʊtʃ] *v/t* (*cook*) hervir

poach[2] [poʊtʃ] *v/t & v/i* (*hunt*) cazar furtivamente; *fish* pescar furtivamente

poached egg [poʊtʃt'eg] huevo *m* escalfado

◆ **poach·er** ['poʊtʃər] *of game* cazador(a) *m(f)* furtivo(a); *of fish* pescador(a) *m(f)* furtivo(a)

P.O. Box [piː'oʊbɑːks] apartado *m* de cor-

P

reos

pock·et ['pɑːkɪt] **1** *n* bolsillo *m*; *line one's pockets* llenarse los bolsillos; *be $10 out of pocket* salir perdiendo 10 dólares **2** *adj radio, dictionary* de bolsillo **3** *v/t* meter en el bolsillo

'**pock·et·book** (*handbag*) bolso *m*; (*wallet*) cartera *f*; (*book*) libro *m* de bolsillo

pock·et '**cal·cu·la·tor** calculadora *f* de bolsillo

'**pock·et·knife** navaja *f*

po·di·um ['poʊdɪəm] podio *m*

po·em ['poʊɪm] poema *m*

po·et ['poʊɪt] poeta *m*; poeta *f*, poetisa *f*

po·et·ic [poʊ'etɪk] *adj* poético

po·et·ic '**jus·tice** justicia *f* divina

po·et·ry ['poʊɪtrɪ] poesía *f*

poign·ant ['pɔɪnjənt] *adj* conmovedor

point [pɔɪnt] **1** *n of pencil, knife* punta *f*; *in competition, argument* punto *m*; (*purpose*) objetivo *m*; (*moment*) momento *m*; *in decimals* coma *f*; *what's the point of telling him?* ¿qué se consigue diciéndoselo?; *the point I'm trying to make ...* lo que estoy intentando decir ...; *at one point* en un momento dado; *that's beside the point* eso no viene a cuento; *be on the point of* estar a punto de; *get to the point* ir al grano; *the point is ...* la cuestión es que ...; *there's no point in waiting / trying* no vale la pena esperar / intentarlo **2** *v/i* señalar con el dedo **3** *v/t*: *he pointed the gun at me* me apuntó con la pistola

◆ **point out** *v/t sights* indicar; *advantages etc* destacar

◆ **point to** *v/t with finger* señalar con el dedo; (*fig: indicate*) indicar

'**point-blank 1** *adj refusal, denial* categórico; *at point-blank range* a quemarropa **2** *adv refuse, deny* categóricamente

point·ed ['pɔɪntɪd] *adj remark* mordaz

point·er ['pɔɪntər] *for teacher* puntero *m*; (*hint*) consejo *m*; (*sign, indication*) indicador *m*

point·less ['pɔɪntləs] *adj* inútil; *it's pointless trying* no sirve de nada intentarlo

'**point of sale** *place* punto *m* de venta; *promotional material* material *m* de promo-

cional

'**point of view** punto *m* de vista

poise [pɔɪz] confianza *f*

poised [pɔɪzd] *adj person* con aplomo

poi·son ['pɔɪzn] **1** *n* veneno *m* **2** *v/t* envenenar

poi·son·ous ['pɔɪzənəs] *adj* venenoso

poke [poʊk] **1** *n* empujón *m* **2** *v/t* (*prod*) empujar; (*stick*) clavar; *he poked his head out of the window* asomó la cabeza por la ventana; *poke fun at* reírse de; *poke one's nose into* F meter las narices en F

◆ **poke around** *v/i* F husmear

pok·er ['poʊkər] *card game* póquer *m*

pok·y ['poʊkɪ] *adj* F (*cramped*) enano, minúsculo

Po·land ['poʊlənd] Polonia *f*

po·lar ['poʊlər] *adj* polar

po·lar bear oso *m* polar *or* blanco

po·lar·ize ['poʊləraɪz] *v/t* polarizar

Pole [poʊl] polaco(-a) *m(f)*

pole[1] [poʊl] *for support* poste *m*; *for tent, pushing things* palo *m*

pole[2] [poʊl] *of earth* polo *m*

'**pole star** estrella *f* polar

'**pole-vault** salto *m* con pértiga

'**pole-vault·er** saltador(a) *m(f)* de pértiga

po·lice [pə'liːs] *n* policía *f*

po·lice car coche *m* de policía

po·lice·man policía *m*

po·lice state estado *m* policial

po·lice sta·tion comisaría *f* (de policía)

po·lice·wo·man (mujer *f*) policía *f*

pol·i·cy[1] ['pɑːlɪsɪ] política *f*

pol·i·cy[2] ['pɑːlɪsɪ] (*insurance policy*) póliza *f*

po·li·o ['poʊlɪoʊ] polio *f*

Pol·ish ['poʊlɪʃ] **1** *adj* polaco **2** *n* polaco *m*

pol·ish ['pɑːlɪʃ] **1** *n* abrillantador *m*; (*nail polish*) esmalte *m* de uñas **2** *v/t* dar brillo a; *speech* pulir

◆ **polish off** *v/t food* acabar, comerse

◆ **polish up** *v/t skill* perfeccionar

pol·ished ['pɑːlɪʃt] *adj performance* brillante

po·lite [pə'laɪt] *adj* educado

po·lite·ly [pə'laɪtlɪ] *adv* educadamente

po·lite·ness [pə'laɪtnɪs] educación *f*

po·lit·i·cal [pə'lɪtɪkl] *adj* político

po·lit·i·cal·ly cor·rect [pə'lɪtɪklɪ kə'rekt] políticamente correcto

pol·i·ti·cian [pɑːlɪ'tɪʃn] político(-a) *m(f)*

pol·i·tics ['pɑːlətɪks] política *f*; *I'm not interested in politics* no me interesa la política; *what are his politics?* ¿cuáles son sus ideas políticas?

poll [poul] **1** *n (survey)* encuesta *f*, sondeo *m*; *the polls (election)* las elecciones; *go to the polls (vote)* acudir a las urnas **2** *v/t people* sondear; *votes* obtener

pol·len ['pɑːlən] polen *m*

'pol·len count concentración *f* de polen en el aire

'poll·ing booth ['poulɪŋ] cabina *f* electoral

'poll·ing day día *m* de las elecciones

poll·ster ['pɑːlstər] encuestador(a) *m(f)*

pol·lu·tant [pə'luːtənt] contaminante *m*

pol·lute [pə'luːt] *v/t* contaminar

pol·lu·tion [pə'luːʃn] contaminación *f*

po·lo ['poulou] SP polo *m*

'po·lo neck *sweater* suéter *m* de cuello alto

'po·lo shirt polo *m*

pol·y·eth·yl·ene [pɑːlɪ'eθɪliːn] polietileno *m*

pol·y·es·ter [pɑːlɪ'estər] poliéster *m*

pol·y·sty·rene [pɑːlɪ'staɪriːn] poliestireno *m*

pol·y·un·sat·u·rat·ed [pɑːliʌn'sætʃəreɪtɪd] *adj* poliinsaturado

pom·pous ['pɑːmpəs] *adj* pomposo

pond [pɑːnd] estanque *m*

pon·der ['pɑːndər] *v/i* reflexionar

pon·tiff ['pɑːntɪf] pontífice *m*

pon·y ['pouni] poni *m*

'pon·y·tail coleta *f*

poo·dle ['puːdl] caniche *m*

pool[1] [puːl] *n (swimming pool)* piscina *f*, *L.Am.* pileta *f*, *Mex* alberca *f*; *of water*, *blood* charco *m*

pool[2] [puːl] *game* billar *m* americano

pool[3] [puːl] **1** *n (common fund)* bote *m*, fondo *m* común **2** *v/t resources* juntar

'pool hall sala *f* de billares

'pool ta·ble mesa *f* de billar americano

poop·ed [puːpt] *adj* F hecho polvo F

poor [pur] **1** *adj* pobre; *(not good)* mediocre, malo; *be in poor health* estar enfermo; *poor old Tony!* ¡pobre(cito) Tony! **2** *n: the poor* los pobres

poor·ly ['purlɪ] **1** *adv* mal **2** *adj (unwell)*: *feel poorly* encontrarse mal

pop[1] [pɑːp] **1** *n noise* pequeño *m* ruido **2** *v/i (pret & pp popped) of balloon etc* estallar **3** *v/t (pret & pp popped) cork* hacer saltar; *balloon* pinchar

pop[2] [pɑːp] **1** *n* MUS pop *m* **2** *adj* pop

pop[3] [pɑːp] F *(father)* papá *m* F

pop[4] [pɑːp] F *(put)* meter

◆ pop in *v/i* F *(make a brief visit)* pasar un momento

◆ pop out *v/i* F *(go out for a short time)* salir un momento

◆ pop up *v/i* F *(appear suddenly)* aparecer

'pop con·cert concierto *m* (de música) pop

pop·corn ['pɑːpkɔːrn] palomitas *fpl* de maíz

pope [poup] papa *m*

'pop group grupo *m* (de música) pop

'pop·py ['pɑːpɪ] amapola *f*

Pop·sicle® ['pɑːpsɪkl] polo *m (helado)*

'pop song canción *f* pop

pop·u·lar ['pɑːpjʊlər] *adj* popular; *contrary to popular belief* contrariamente a lo que se piensa

pop·u·lar·i·ty [pɑːpjʊ'lærətɪ] popularidad *f*

pop·u·late ['pɑːpjʊleɪt] *v/t* poblar

pop·u·la·tion [pɑːpjʊ'leɪʃn] población *f*

porce·lain ['pɔːrsəlɪn] **1** *n* porcelana *f* **2** *adj* de porcelana

porch [pɔːrtʃ] porche *m*

por·cu·pine ['pɔːrkjʊpaɪn] puercoespín *m*

pore [pɔːr] *of skin* poro *m*

◆ pore over *v/t* estudiar detenidamente

pork [pɔːrk] cerdo *m*

porn [pɔːrn] *n* F porno *m*

porn(o) [pɔːrn, 'pɔːrnou] *adj* F porno F

por·no·graph·ic [pɔːrnə'ɡræfɪk] *adj* pornográfico

por·nog·ra·phy [pɔːr'nɑːɡrəfɪ] pornografía *f*

po·rous ['pɔːrəs] *adj* poroso

P

port[1] [pɔːrt] *n town, area* puerto *m*

port[2] [pɔːrt] *adj* (*left-hand*) a babor

por·ta·ble ['pɔːrtəbl] **1** *adj* portátil **2** *n* COMPUT portátil *m*; TV televisión *f* portátil

por·ter ['pɔːrtər] mozo(-a) *m(f)*

port·hole ['pɔːrthoul] NAUT portilla *f*

por·tion ['pɔːrʃn] *n* parte *f*; *of food* ración *f*

por·trait ['pɔːrtreɪt] **1** *n* retrato *m* **2** *adv print* en formato vertical

por·tray [pɔːr'treɪ] *of artist, photographer* retratar; *of actor* interpretar; *of author* describir

por·tray·al [pɔːr'treɪəl] *by actor* interpretación *f*, representación *f*; *by author* descripción *f*

Por·tu·gal ['pɔːrtʃugl] Portugal

Por·tu·guese [pɔːrtʃu'giːz] **1** *adj* portugués **2** *n person* portugués(-esa) *m(f)*; *language* portugués *m*

pose [pouz] **1** *n* (*pretense*) pose *f*; **it's all a pose** no es más que una pose **2** *v/i for artist, photographer* posar; **pose as** hacerse pasar por **3** *v/t*: **pose a problem/a threat** representar un problema / una amenaza

posh [pɑːʃ] *adj Br* F elegante, *pej* pijo

po·si·tion [pə'zɪʃn] **1** *n* posición *f*; (*stance, point of view*) postura *f*; (*job*) puesto *m*, empleo *m*; (*status*) posición *f* (social) **2** *v/t* situar, colocar

pos·i·tive ['pɑːzətɪv] *adj* positivo; **be positive** (*sure*) estar seguro

pos·i·tive·ly ['pɑːzətɪvlɪ] *adv* (*decidedly*) verdaderamente, sin lugar a dudas; (*definitely*) claramente

pos·sess [pə'zes] *v/t* poseer

pos·ses·sion [pə'zeʃn] posesión *f*; **possessions** posesiones *fpl*

pos·ses·sive [pə'zesɪv] *adj person*, GRAM posesivo

pos·si·bil·i·ty [pɑːsə'bɪlətɪ] posibilidad *f*; **there is a possibility that …** cabe la posibilidad de que …

pos·si·ble ['pɑːsəbl] *adj* posible; **the shortest / quickest route possible** la ruta más corto / rápido posible; **the best possible …** el mejor …

possibly ['pɑːsəblɪ] *adv* (*perhaps*) puede

ser, quizás; **that can't possibly be right** no puede ser cierto; **they're doing everything they possibly can** están haciendo todo lo que pueden; **could you possibly tell me …?** ¿tendría la amabilidad de decirme …?

post[1] [poust] *n of wood, metal* poste *m* **2** *v/t notice* pegar; *on notice board* poner; *profits* presentar; **keep s.o. posted** mantener a alguien al corriente

post[2] [poust] **1** *n* (*place of duty*) puesto *m* **2** *v/t soldier, employee* destinar; *guards* apostar

post[3] [poust] **1** *n Br* (*mail*) correo *m* **2** *v/t Br letter* echar al correo

post·age ['poustɪdʒ] franqueo *m*

'**post·age stamp** *fml* sello *m*, *L.Am.* estampilla *f*, *Mex* timbre *m*

post·al ['poustl] *adj* postal

'**post·card** (*tarjeta f*) postal *f*

'**post·code** *Br* código *m* postal

'**post·date** *v/t* posfechar

post·er ['poustər] póster *m*, *L.Am.* afiche *m*

pos·te·ri·or [pɑː'stɪrɪər] *n* (*hum: buttocks*) trasero *m*

pos·ter·i·ty [pɑː'sterətɪ] posteridad *f*; **for posterity** para la posteridad

post·grad·u·ate ['poustgrædʒuət] **1** *n* posgraduado(-a) *m(f)* **2** *adj* de posgrado

post·hu·mous ['pɑːstuməs] *adj* póstumo

post·hu·mous·ly ['pɑːstuməslɪ] *adv* póstumamente

post·ing ['poustɪŋ] (*assignment*) destino *m*

post·mark ['poustmɑːrk] matasellos *m inv*

post·mor·tem [poust'mɔːrtəm] autopsia *f*

'**post of·fice** oficina *f* de correos

post·pone [poust'poun] *v/t* posponer, aplazar

post·pone·ment [poust'pounmənt] aplazamiento *m*

pos·ture ['pɑːstʃər] postura *f*

'**post·war** *adj* de posguerra

pot[1] [pɑːt] *for cooking* olla *f*; *for coffee* cafetera *f*; *for tea* tetera *f*; *for plant* maceta *f*

pot[2] [pɑːt] F (*marijuana*) maría *f* F

po·ta·to [pə'teɪtoʊ] *Span* patata *f*, *L.Am.* papa *f*

po·ta·to chips, *Br* po·ta·to crisps *npl Span* patatas *fpl* fritas, *L.Am.* papas *fpl* fritas

'pot·bel·ly ['pɑːtbelɪ] barriga *f*

po·tent ['poʊtənt] *adj* potente

po·ten·tial [pə'tenʃl] **1** *adj* potencial **2** *n* potencial *m*

po·ten·tial·ly [pə'tenʃəlɪ] *adv* potencialmente

pot·hole ['pɑːthoʊl] *in road* bache *m*

pot·ter ['pɑːtər] *n* alfarero(-a) *m(f)*

pot·ter·y ['pɑːtərɪ] *n* alfarería *f*

pot·ty ['pɑːtɪ] *n for baby* orinal *m*

pouch [paʊtʃ] *(bag)* bolsa *f*; *for tobacco* petaca *f*; *for amunition* cartuchera *f*; *for mail* saca *m*

poul·try ['poʊltrɪ] *birds* aves *fpl* de corral; *meat* carne *f* de ave

pounce [paʊns] *v/i of animal* saltar; *fig* echarse encima

pound¹ [paʊnd] *n weight* libra *f* (453,6 gr)

pound² [paʊnd] *n for strays* perrera *f*; *for cars* depósito *m*

pound³ [paʊnd] *v/i of heart* palpitar con fuerza; **pound on** *(hammer on)* golpear en

pound 'ster·ling libra *f* esterlina

pour [pɔːr] **1** *v/t into a container* verter; *spill* derramar; **pour s.o. some coffee** servir café a alguien **2** *v/i*: **it's pouring (with rain)** está lloviendo a cántaros

◆ pour out *v/t liquid* servir; *troubles* contar

pout [paʊt] *v/i* hacer un mohín

pov·er·ty ['pɑːvərtɪ] pobreza *f*

pov·er·ty-strick·en ['pɑːvərtɪstrɪkn] depauperado

pow·der ['paʊdər] **1** *n* polvo *m*; *for face* polvos *m*, colorete *m* **2** *v/t face* empolvarse

pow·er ['paʊər] **1** *n (strength)* fuerza *f*; *of engine* potencia; *(authority)* poder *m*; *(energy)* energía *f*; *(electricity)* electricidad *f*; **in power** POL en el poder; **fall from power** POL perder el poder **2** *v/t*: **be powered by** estar impulsado por

'pow·er-as·sist·ed steering dirección *f* asistida

'pow·er cut apagón *m*

'pow·er fail·ure apagón *m*

pow·er·ful ['paʊərfəl] *adj* poderoso; *car* potente; *drug* fuerte

pow·er·less ['paʊərlɪs] *adj* impotente; **be powerless to ...** ser incapaz de ...

'pow·er line línea *f* de conducción eléctrica

'pow·er out·age apagón *m*

'pow·er sta·tion central *f* eléctrica

'pow·er steer·ing dirección *f* asistida

'pow·er u·nit fuente *f* de alimentación

PR [piː'ɑːr] *abbr* (= **public relations**) relaciones *fpl* públicas

prac·ti·cal ['præktɪkl] *adj* práctico; *layout* funcional

prac·ti·cal 'joke broma *f* *(que se gasta)*

prac·ti·cal·ly ['præktɪklɪ] *adv* *behave, think* de manera práctica; *(almost)* prácticamente, casi

prac·tice ['præktɪs] **1** *n* práctica *f*; *(rehearsal)* ensayo *m*; *(custom)* costumbre *f*; **in practice** *(in reality)* en la práctica; **be out of practice** estar desentrenado; **practice makes perfect** a base de práctica se aprende **2** *v/i* practicar; *of musician* ensayar; *of footballer* entrenarse **3** *v/t* practicar; *law, medicine* ejercer

prac·tise *Br* → **practice** *v/i & v/t*

prag·mat·ic [præg'mætɪk] *adj* pragmático

prag·ma·tism ['prægmətɪzm] pragmatismo *m*

prai·rie ['prerɪ] pradera *f*

praise [preɪz] **1** *n* elogio *m*, alabanza *f* **2** *v/t* elogiar

'praise·wor·thy *adj* elogiable

prank [præŋk] *n* travesura *f*

prat·tle ['prætl] *v/i* F parlotear F

prawn [prɔːn] gamba *f*

pray [preɪ] *v/i* rezar

prayer [prer] oración *f*

preach [priːtʃ] **1** *v/i in church* predicar; *(moralize)* sermonear **2** *v/t sermon* predicar

preach·er ['priːtʃər] predicador(a) *m(f)*

pre·am·ble [priː'æmbl] preámbulo *m*

pre·car·i·ous [prɪ'kerɪəs] *adj* precario

pre·car·i·ous·ly [prɪ'kerɪəslɪ] *adv* preca-

P

riamente

pre·cau·tion [prɪ'kɔːʃn] precaución *f*; *as a precaution* como precaución

pre·cau·tion·a·ry [prɪ'kɔːʃnrɪ] *adj measure* preventivo

pre·cede [prɪ'siːd] *v/t in time* preceder; *(walk in front of)* ir delante de

pre·ce·dent ['presɪdənt] precedente *m*

pre·ce·ding [prɪ'siːdɪŋ] *adj week, chapter* anterior

pre·cinct ['priːsɪŋkt] *(district)* distrito *m*

pre·cious ['preʃəs] *adj* preciado; *gem* precioso

pre·cip·i·tate [prɪ'sɪpɪteɪt] *v/t crisis* precipitar

pré·cis ['preɪsiː] *n* resumen *m*

pre·cise [prɪ'saɪs] *adj* preciso

pre·cise·ly [prɪ'saɪslɪ] *adv* exactamente

pre·ci·sion [prɪ'sɪʒn] precisión *f*

pre·co·cious [prɪ'kəʊʃəs] *adj child* precoz

pre·con·ceived ['priːkənsiːvd] *adj idea* preconcebido

pre·con·di·tion [priːkən'dɪʃn] condición *f* previa

pred·a·tor ['predətər] *animal* depredador(a) *m(f)*

pred·a·to·ry ['predətɔːrɪ] *adj* depredador

pre·de·ces·sor ['priːdɪsesər] *in job* predecesor(a) *m(f)*; *machine* modelo *m* anterior

pre·des·ti·na·tion [priːdestɪ'neɪʃn] predestinación *f*

pre·des·tined [priː'destɪnd] *adj*: *be predestined to* estar predestinado a

pre·dic·a·ment [prɪ'dɪkəmənt] apuro *m*

pre·dict [prɪ'dɪkt] *v/t* predecir, pronosticar

pre·dict·a·ble [prɪ'dɪktəbl] *adj* predecible

pre·dic·tion [prɪ'dɪkʃn] predicción *f*, pronóstico *m*

pre·dom·i·nant [prɪ'dɑːmɪnənt] *adj* predominante

pre·dom·i·nant·ly [prɪ'dɑːmɪnəntlɪ] *adv* predominantemente

pre·dom·i·nate [prɪ'dɑːmɪneɪt] *v/i* predominar

pre·fab·ri·cat·ed [priː'fæbrɪkeɪtɪd] *adj* prefabricado

pref·ace ['prefɪs] *n* prólogo *m*, prefacio *m*

pre·fer [prɪ'fɜːr] *v/t (pret & pp preferred)* preferir; *prefer X to Y* preferir X a Y; *prefer to do* preferir hacer

pref·e·ra·ble ['prefərəbl] *adj* preferible; *anywhere is preferable to this* cualquier sitio es mejor que éste

pref·e·ra·bly ['prefərəblɪ] *adv* preferentemente

pref·e·rence ['prefərəns] preferencia *f*

pref·er·en·tial [prefə'renʃl] *adj* preferente

pre·fix ['priːfɪks] prefijo *m*

preg·nan·cy ['pregnənsɪ] embarazo *m*

preg·nant ['pregnənt] *adj woman* embarazada; *animal* preñada

pre·heat ['priːhiːt] *v/t oven* precalentar

pre·his·tor·ic [priːhɪs'tɑːrɪk] *adj* prehistórico

pre·judge [priː'dʒʌdʒ] *v/t* prejuzgar, juzgar de antemano

prej·u·dice ['predʒʊdɪs] **1** *n* prejuicio *m* **2** *v/t person* predisponer, influir; *chances* perjudicar

prej·u·diced ['predʒʊdɪst] *adj* parcial, predispuesto

pre·lim·i·na·ry [prɪ'lɪmɪnərɪ] *adj* preliminar

pre·mar·i·tal [priː'mærɪtl] *adj* prematrimonial

pre·ma·ture ['priːmətʊr] *adj* prematuro

pre·med·i·tat·ed [priː'medɪteɪtɪd] *adj* premeditado

prem·i·er ['premɪr] *n (Prime Minister)* primer(a) ministro(-a) *m(f)*

prem·i·ère ['premɪer] *n* estreno *m*

prem·is·es ['premɪsɪz] *npl* local *m*

pre·mi·um ['priːmɪəm] *n in insurance* prima *f*

pre·mo·ni·tion [premə'nɪʃn] premonición *f*, presentimiento *m*

pre·na·tal [priː'neɪtl] *adj* prenatal

pre·oc·cu·pied [priː'ɑːkjʊpaɪd] *adj* preocupado

prep·a·ra·tion [prepə'reɪʃn] preparación *f*; *in preparation for* como preparación a; *preparations* preparativos *mpl*

pre·pare [prɪ'per] **1** *v/t* preparar; *be prepared to do sth (willing)* estar dispuesto a hacer algo; *be prepared for sth (be ex-*

pecting, ready) estar preparado para algo **2** *v/i* prepararse

prep·o·si·tion [prepə'zɪʃn] preposición *f*

pre·pos·ter·ous [prɪ'pɑːstərəs] *adj* ridículo, absurdo

prep school ['prepskuːl] escuela *f* primaria privada

pre·req·ui·site [priː'rekwɪzɪt] requisito *m* previo

pre·scribe [prɪ'skraɪb] *v/t of doctor* recetar

pre·scrip·tion [prɪ'skrɪpʃn] MED receta *f*

pres·ence ['prezns] presencia *f*; **in the presence of** en presencia de, delante de

pres·ence of 'mind presencia *f* de ánimo

pres·ent¹ ['preznt] **1** *adj (current)* actual; **be present** estar presente **2** *n: the present also* GRAM el presente; **at present** en este momento

pres·ent² ['preznt] *n (gift)* regalo *m*

pre·sent³ [prɪ'zent] *v/t* presentar; *award* entregar; *program* presentar; **present s.o. with sth, present sth to s.o.** entregar algo a alguien

pre·sen·ta·tion [prezn'teɪʃn] *to audience* presentación *f*

pres·ent-day [preznt'deɪ] *adj* actual

pre·sent·er [prɪ'zentər] presentador(a) *m(f)*

pres·ent·ly ['prezntlɪ] *adv (at the moment)* actualmente; *(soon)* pronto

'pres·ent tense tiempo *m* presente

pres·er·va·tion [prezər'veɪʃn] conservación *f*; *of standards, peace* mantenimiento *m*

pre·ser·va·tive [prɪ'zɜːrvətɪv] *n* conservante *m*

pre·serve [prɪ'zɜːrv] **1** *n (domain)* dominio *m* **2** *v/t standards, peace etc* mantener; *food, wood* conservar

pre·side [prɪ'zaɪd] *v/i at meeting* presidir; **preside over** *meeting* presidir

pres·i·den·cy ['prezɪdənsɪ] presidencia *f*

pres·i·dent ['prezɪdnt] POL, *of company* presidente(-a) *m(f)*

pres·i·den·tial [prezɪ'denʃl] *adj* presidencial

press [pres] **1** *n: the press* la prensa **2** *v/t button* pulsar, presionar; *(urge)* presio-

nar; *(squeeze)* apretar; *clothes* planchar **3** *v/i:* **press for** presionar para obtener

'press a·gen·cy agencia *f* de prensa

'press con·fer·ence rueda *f or* conferencia *f* de prensa

press·ing ['presɪŋ] *adj* urgente

pres·sure ['preʃər] **1** *n* presión *f*; **be under pressure** estar sometido a presión; **he is under pressure to resign** lo están presionando para que dimita **2** *v/t* presionar

pres·tige [pre'stiːʒ] prestigio *m*

pres·ti·gious [pre'stɪdʒəs] *adj* prestigioso

pre·su·ma·bly [prɪ'zuːməblɪ] *adv* presumiblemente, probablemente

pre·sume [prɪ'zuːm] suponer; **they were presumed dead** los dieron por muertos; **presume to do sth** *fml* tomarse la libertad de hacer algo

pre·sump·tion [prɪ'zʌmpʃn] *of innocence, guilt* presunción *f*

pre·sump·tu·ous [prɪ'zʌmptuəs] *adj* presuntuoso

pre·sup·pose [priːsə'pəʊs] *v/t* presuponer

pre-tax ['priːtæks] *adj* antes de impuestos

pre·tence *Br* → **pretense**

pre·tend [prɪ'tend] *v/t* fingir, hacer como si; *claim* pretender; **pretend to be s.o.** hacerse pasar por alguien; **the children are pretending to be spacemen** los niños están jugando a que son astronautas **2** *v/i* fingir

pre·tense [prɪ'tens] farsa *f*

pre·ten·tious [prɪ'tenʃəs] *adj* pretencioso

pre·text ['priːtekst] pretexto *m*

pret·ty ['prɪtɪ] **1** *adj village, house, fabric etc* bonito, lindo; *child, woman* guapo, lindo **2** *adv (quite)* bastante

pre·vail [prɪ'veɪl] *v/i (triumph)* prevalecer

pre·vail·ing [prɪ'veɪlɪŋ] *adj* predominante

pre·vent [prɪ'vent] *v/t* impedir, evitar; **prevent s.o. (from) doing sth** impedir que alguien haga algo

pre·ven·tion [prɪ'venʃn] prevención *f*

pre·ven·tive [prɪ'ventɪv] *adj* preventivo

pre·view ['priːvjuː] **1** *n of movie, exhibition* preestreno *m* **2** *v/t* hacer la presentación previa de

P

pre·vi·ous ['priːvɪəs] *adj* anterior, previo
pre·vi·ous·ly ['priːvɪəslɪ] *adv* anteriormente, antes
pre-war ['priːwɔːr] *adj* de preguerra, de antes de la guerra
prey [preɪ] **1** *n* presa *f*; **prey to** presa de
◆ prey on *v/t* atacar; *fig: of con man etc* aprovecharse de
price [praɪs] **1** *n* precio *m* **2** *v/t* COM poner precio a
price·less ['praɪslɪs] *adj* que no tiene precio
'price tag etiqueta *f* del precio
'price war guerra *f* de precios
pric·ey ['praɪsɪ] *adj* F carillo F
prick¹ [prɪk] **1** *n pain* punzada *f* **2** *v/t (jab)* pinchar
prick² [prɪk] *n* V *(penis)* polla *f* V, carajo *m* V; V *person Span* gilipollas *m inv* V, *L.Am.* pendejo *m* V
◆ prick up *v/t:* **prick up one's ears** *of dog* aguzar las orejas; *of person* prestar atención
prick·le ['prɪkl] *on plant* espina *f*
prick·ly ['prɪklɪ] *adj beard, plant* que pincha; *(irritable)* irritable
pride [praɪd] **1** *n in person, achievement* orgullo *m*; *(self-respect)* amor *m* propio **2** *v/t:* **pride o.s. on** enorgullecerse de
priest [priːst] sacerdote *m*; *(parish priest)* cura *m*
pri·ma·ri·ly [praɪ'merɪlɪ] *adv* principalmente
pri·ma·ry ['praɪmərɪ] **1** *adj* principal **2** *n* POL elecciones *fpl* primarias
prime [praɪm] **1** *n:* **be in one's prime** estar en la flor de la vida **2** *adj example, reason* primordial; *of prime importance* de suprema importancia
prime 'min·is·ter primer(a) ministro(-a) *m(f)*
'prime time *n* TV horario *m* de mayor audiencia
prim·i·tive ['prɪmɪtɪv] *adj* primitivo
prince [prɪns] príncipe *m*
prin·cess [prɪn'ses] princesa *f*
prin·ci·pal ['prɪnsəpl] **1** *adj* principal **2** *n of school* director(a) *m(f)*; *of university* rector(a) *m(f)*

prin·ci·pal·ly ['prɪnsəplɪ] *adv* principalmente
prin·ci·ple ['prɪnsəpl] principio *m*; **on principle** por principios; **in principle** en principio
print [prɪnt] **1** *n in book, newspaper etc* letra *f*; *(photograph)* grabado *m*; **out of print** agotado **2** *v/t* imprimir; *use block capitals* escribir en mayúsculas
◆ print out *v/t* imprimir
print·ed mat·ter ['prɪntɪd] impresos *mpl*
print·er ['prɪntər] *person* impresor(a) *m(f)*; *machine* impresora *f*; *company* imprenta *f*
print·ing press ['prɪntɪŋpres] imprenta *f*
'print·out copia *f* impresa
pri·or ['praɪr] **1** *adj* previo **2** *prep:* **prior to** antes de
pri·or·i·tize [praɪ'ɔːrətaɪz] *v/t (put in order of priority)* ordenar atendiendo a las prioridades; *(give priority to)* dar prioridad a
pri·or·i·ty [praɪ'ɑːrətɪ] prioridad *f*; **have priority** tener prioridad
pris·on ['prɪzn] prisión *f*, cárcel *f*
pris·on·er ['prɪznər] prisionero(-a) *m(f)*; **take s.o. prisoner** hacer prisionero a alguien
pris·on·er of 'war prisionero(-a) *m(f)* de guerra
pri·va·cy ['prɪvəsɪ] intimidad *f*
pri·vate ['praɪvət] **1** *adj* privado **2** *n* MIL soldado *m/f* raso; **in private** en privado
pri·vate·ly ['praɪvətlɪ] *adv (in private)* en privado; *with one other* a solas; *(inwardly)* para sí; **privately owned** en manos privadas
'pri·vate sec·tor sector *m* privado
pri·va·tize ['praɪvətaɪz] *v/t Br* privatizar
priv·i·lege ['prɪvəlɪdʒ] *(special treatment)* privilegio *m*; *(honor)* honor *m*
priv·i·leged ['prɪvəlɪdʒd] *adj* privilegiado
prize [praɪz] **1** *n* premio *m* **2** *v/t* apreciar, valorar
prize-win·ner ['praɪzwɪnər] premiado(-a) *m(f)*
prize-win·ning ['praɪzwɪnɪŋ] *adj* premiado
pro¹ [prou] *n:* **the pros and cons** los pros

y los contras

pro² [prou] → **professional**

pro³ [prou]: *be pro ...* (*in favor of*) estar a favor de; *the pro Clinton Democrats* los demócratas partidarios de Clinton

prob·a·bil·i·ty [prɑːbəˈbɪlətɪ] probabilidad *f*

prob·a·ble [ˈprɑːbəbl] *adj* probable

prob·a·bly [ˈprɑːbəblɪ] *adv* probablemente

pro·ba·tion [prəˈbeɪʃn] *in job* período *m* de prueba; LAW libertad *f* condicional; *be given probation* ser puesto en libertad condicional

pro·'ba·tion of·fi·cer oficial encargado de la vigilancia de los que están en libertad condicional

pro·'ba·tion pe·ri·od *in job* período *m* de prueba

probe [proub] **1** *n* (*investigation*) investigación *f*; *scientific* sonda *f* **2** *v/t* examinar; (*investigate*) investigar

prob·lem [ˈprɑːbləm] problema *f*; *no problem!* ¡claro!

pro·ce·dure [prəˈsiːdʒər] procedimiento *m*

pro·ceed [prəˈsiːd] *v/i* (*go: of people*) dirigirse; *of work etc* proseguir, avanzar; *proceed to do sth* pasar a hacer algo

pro·ceed·ings [prəˈsiːdɪŋz] *npl* (*events*) actos *mpl*

pro·ceeds [ˈprousiːdz] *npl* recaudación *f*

pro·cess [ˈprɑːses] **1** *n* proceso *m*; *in the process* (*while doing it*) al hacerlo **2** *v/t* *food* tratar; *raw materials, data* procesar; *application* tramitar

pro·ces·sion [prəˈseʃn] desfile *m*; *religious* procesión *f*

pro·claim [prəˈkleɪm] *v/t* declarar, proclamar

prod [prɑːd] **1** *n* empujoncito *m* **2** *v/t* (*pret & pp* **prodded**) dar un empujoncito a; *with elbow* dar un codazo a

prod·i·gy [ˈprɑːdɪdʒɪ]: (*infant*) *prodigy* niño(-a) *m(f)* prodigio

prod·uce¹ [ˈprɑːduːs] *n* productos *mpl* del campo

pro·duce² [prəˈduːs] *v/t* producir; (*manufacture*) fabricar; (*bring out*) sacar

pro·duc·er [prəˈduːsər] productor(a) *m(f)*; (*manufacturer*) fabricante *m/f*

prod·uct [ˈprɑːdʌkt] producto *m*

pro·duc·tion [prəˈdʌkʃn] producción *f*

pro·'duc·tion ca·pac·i·ty capacidad *f* de producción

pro·'duc·tion costs *npl* costos *mpl* de producción

pro·duc·tive [prəˈdʌktɪv] *adj* productivo

pro·duc·tiv·i·ty [prɑːdʌkˈtɪvətɪ] productividad *f*

pro·fane [prəˈfeɪn] *adj language* profano

pro·fess [prəˈfes] *v/t* manifestar

pro·fes·sion [prəˈfeʃn] profesión *f*; *what's your profession?* ¿a qué se dedica?

pro·fes·sion·al [prəˈfeʃnl] **1** *adj* profesional; *turn professional* hacerse profesional **2** *n* profesional *m/f*

pro·fes·sion·al·ly [prəˈfeʃnlɪ] *adv play sport* profesionalmente; (*well, skillfully*) con profesionalidad

pro·fes·sor [prəˈfesər] catedrático(-a) *m(f)*

pro·fi·cien·cy [prəˈfɪʃnsɪ] competencia *f*

pro·fi·cient [prəˈfɪʃnt] competente; (*skillful*) hábil

pro·file [ˈproufaɪl] *of face* perfil *m*

prof·it [ˈprɑːfɪt] **1** *n* beneficio *m* **2** *v/i*: *profit by, profit from* beneficiarse de

prof·it·a·bil·i·ty [prɑːfɪtəˈbɪlətɪ] rentabilidad *f*

prof·it·a·ble [ˈprɑːfɪtəbl] *adj* rentable

'prof·it mar·gin margen *m* de beneficios

pro·found [prəˈfaʊnd] *adj* profundo

pro·found·ly [prəˈfaʊndlɪ] *adv* profundamente, enormemente; *thank, apologize* efusivamente

prog·no·sis [prɑːgˈnoʊsɪs] pronóstico *m*

pro·gram, *Br* **pro·gramme** [ˈprougræm] **1** *n* programa *m* **2** *v/t* (*pret & pp* **programmed**) COMPUT programar

pro·gram·mer [ˈprougræmər] COMPUT programador(a) *m(f)*

pro·gress 1 *n* [ˈprɑːgres] progreso *m*; *make progress* hacer progresos; *in progress* en curso **2** *v/i* [prəˈgres] (*advance in time*) avanzar; (*move on*) pasar; (*make progress*) progresar; *how is the work*

progressing? ¿cómo avanza el trabajo?
pro·gres·sive [prə'gresɪv] adj (*enlightened*) progresista; (*which progresses*) progresivo

pro·gres·sive·ly [prə'gresɪvlɪ] adv progresivamente

pro·hib·it [prə'hɪbɪt] v/t prohibir

pro·hi·bi·tion [prouhɪ'bɪʃn] prohibición f; **during Prohibition** durante la ley seca

pro·hib·i·tive [prə'hɪbɪtɪv] adj *prices* prohibitivo

proj·ect¹ ['prɑːdʒekt] n (*plan, undertaking*) proyecto m; EDU trabajo m; *housing area* barriada f de viviendas sociales

pro·ject² [prə'dʒekt] **1** v/t *movie* proyectar; *figures, sales* calcular **2** v/i (*stick out*) sobresalir

pro·jec·tion [prə'dʒekʃn] (*forecast*) previsión f

pro·jec·tor [prə'dʒektər] *for slides* proyector m

pro·lif·ic [prə'lɪfɪk] adj *writer, artist* prolífico

pro·log, Br **pro·logue** ['proulɑːg] prólogo m

pro·long [prə'lɒːŋ] v/t prolongar

prom [prɑːm] (*school dance*) baile de fin de curso

prom·i·nent ['prɑːmɪnənt] adj *nose, chin* prominente; (*significant*) destacado

prom·is·cu·i·ty [prɑːmɪ'skjuːətɪ] promiscuidad f

pro·mis·cu·ous [prə'mɪskjuəs] adj promiscuo

prom·ise ['prɑːmɪs] **1** n promesa f **2** v/t prometer; **she promised to help** prometió ayudar; **promise sth to s.o.** prometer algo a alguien **3** v/i: **do you promise?** ¿lo prometes?

prom·is·ing ['prɑːmɪsɪŋ] adj prometedor

pro·mote [prə'mout] v/t *employee* ascender; (*encourage, foster*) promover; COM promocionar

pro·mot·er [prə'moutər] *of sports event* promotor(a) m(f)

pro·mo·tion [prə'mouʃn] *of employee* ascenso m; *of scheme, idea*, COM promoción f

prompt [prɑːmpt] **1** adj (*on time*) puntual;

(*speedy*) rápido **2** adv: **at two o'clock prompt** a las dos en punto **3** v/t (*cause*) provocar; *actor* apuntar **4** n COMPUT mensaje m; **go to the c prompt** ir a c:\

prompt·ly ['prɑːmptlɪ] adv (*on time*) puntualmente; (*immediately*) inmediatamente

prone [proun] adj: **be prone to** ser propenso a

pro·noun ['prounaun] pronombre m

pro·nounce [prə'nauns] v/t *word* pronunciar; (*declare*) declarar

pro·nounced [prə'naunst] adj *accent* marcado; *views* fuerte

pron·to ['prɑːntou] adv F ya, en seguida

pro·nun·ci·a·tion [prənʌnsɪ'eɪʃn] pronunciación f

proof [pruːf] n prueba(s) f(pl); *of book* prueba f

prop [prɑːp] **1** v/t (*pret & pp* **propped**) apoyar **2** n THEA accesorio m

♦ **prop up** v/t apoyar

prop·a·gan·da [prɑːpə'gændə] propaganda f

pro·pel [prə'pel] v/t (*pret & pp* **propelled**) propulsar

pro·pel·lant [prə'pelənt] *in aerosol* propelente m

pro·pel·ler [prə'pelər] *of boat* hélice f

prop·er ['prɑːpər] adj (*real*) de verdad; (*fitting*) adecuado; **it's not proper** no está bien; **put it back in its proper place** vuelve a ponerlo en su sitio

prop·er·ly ['prɑːpərlɪ] adv (*correctly*) bien; (*fittingly*) adecuadamente

prop·er·ty ['prɑːpərtɪ] propiedad f; (*land*) propiedad(es) f(pl)

prop·er·ty de·vel·op·er promotor(a) m(f) inmobiliario(a)

proph·e·cy ['prɑːfəsɪ] profecía f

proph·e·sy ['prɑːfəsaɪ] v/t (*pret & pp* **prophesied**) profetizar

pro·por·tion [prə'pɔːrʃn] proporción f; **a large proportion of North Americans** gran parte de los norteamericanos; **proportions** (*dimensions*) proporciones fpl

pro·por·tion·al [prə'pɔːrʃnl] adj proporcional

pro·por·tion·al rep·re·sen·ta·tion POL

representación f proporcional

pro·pos·al [prəˈpouzl] (*suggestion*) propuesta f; *of marriage* proposición f

pro·pose [prəˈpouz] **1** v/t (*suggest*) sugerir, proponer; (*plan*) proponerse **2** v/i (*make offer of marriage*) pedir la mano

prop·o·si·tion [prɑːpəˈzɪʃn] **1** n propuesta f **2** v/t *woman* hacer proposiciones a

pro·pri·e·tor [prəˈpraɪətər] propietario(-a) m(f)

pro·pri·e·tress [prəˈpraɪətrɪs] propietaria f

prose [prouz] prosa f

pros·e·cute [ˈprɑːsɪkjuːt] v/t LAW procesar

pros·e·cu·tion [prɑːsɪˈkjuːʃn] LAW procesamiento m; *lawyers* acusación f; *he's facing prosecution* lo van a procesar

pros·e·cu·tor → *public prosecutor* fiscal m/f

pros·pect [ˈprɑːspekt] **1** n (*chance, likelihood*) probabilidad f; (*thought of something in the future*) perspectiva f; *prospects* perspectivas fpl (de futuro) **2** v/i: *prospect for gold* buscar

pro·spec·tive [prəˈspektɪv] adj potencial

pros·per [ˈprɑːspər] v/i prosperar

pros·per·i·ty [prɑːˈsperətɪ] prosperidad f

pros·per·ous [ˈprɑːspərəs] adj próspero

pros·ti·tute [ˈprɑːstɪtuːt] n prostituta f; *male prostitute* prostituto m

pros·ti·tu·tion [prɑːstɪˈtuːʃn] prostitución f

pros·trate [ˈprɑːstreɪt] adj postrado; *be prostrate with grief* postrado por el dolor

pro·tect [prəˈtekt] v/t proteger

pro·tec·tion [prəˈtekʃn] protección f

pro'tec·tion mon·ey dinero pagado a delincuentes a cambio de obtener protección; *paid to terrorists* impuesto m revolucionario

pro·tec·tive [prəˈtektɪv] adj protector

pro·tec·tive 'cloth·ing ropa f protectora

pro·tec·tor [prəˈtektər] protector(a) m(f)

pro·tein [ˈproutiːn] proteína f

pro·test 1 n [ˈproutest] protesta f [prəˈtest] protestar, quejarse de; (*object to*) protestar contra **3** v/i [prəˈtest] testar

Prot·es·tant [ˈprɑːtɪstənt] **1** n protestante m/f **2** adj protestante

pro·test·er [prəˈtestər] manifestante m/f

pro·to·col [ˈproutəkɑːl] protocolo m

pro·to·type [ˈproutətaɪp] prototipo m

pro·tract·ed [prəˈtræktɪd] adj prolongado, largo

pro·trude [prəˈtruːd] v/i sobresalir

pro·trud·ing [prəˈtruːdɪŋ] adj saliente; *ears, teeth* prominente

proud [praud] adj orgulloso; *be proud of* estar orgulloso de

proud·ly [ˈpraudlɪ] adv con orgullo, orgullosamente

prove [pruːv] v/t demostrar, probar

prov·erb [ˈprɑːvɜːrb] proverbio m, refrán m

pro·vide [prəˈvaɪd] v/t proporcionar; *provide sth to s.o., provide s.o. with sth* proporcionar algo a alguien; *provided (that)* (*on condition that*) con la condición de que, siempre que

◆ **provide for** v/t *family* mantener; *of law etc* prever

prov·ince [ˈprɑːvɪns] provincia f

pro·vin·cial [prəˈvɪnʃl] adj *city* provincial; *pej: attitude* de pueblo, provinciano

pro·vi·sion [prəˈvɪʒn] (*supply*) suministro m; *of law, contract* disposición f

pro·vi·sion·al [prəˈvɪʒnl] adj provisional

pro·vi·so [prəˈvaɪzou] condición f

prov·o·ca·tion [prɑːvəˈkeɪʃn] provocación f

pro·voc·a·tive [prəˈvɑːkətɪv] adj provocador; *sexually* provocativo

pro·voke [prəˈvouk] v/t (*cause, annoy*) provocar

prow [prau] NAUT proa f

prow·ess [ˈprauɪs] proezas fpl

prowl [praul] v/i *of tiger, burglar* merodear

prowl·er [ˈpraulər] merodeador(a) m(f)

prox·im·i·ty [prɑːkˈsɪmətɪ] proximidad f

prox·y [ˈprɑːksɪ] (*authority*) poder m; *person* apoderado(-a) m(f)

prude [pruːd] mojigato(-a) m(f)

pru·dence [ˈpruːdns] prudencia f

pru·dent [ˈpruːdnt] adj prudente

prud·ish ['pru:dɪʃ] *adj* mojigato

prune¹ [pru:n] *n* ciruela *f* pasa

prune² [pru:n] *v/t plant* podar; *fig* reducir

pry [praɪ] *v/i* (*pret & pp* **pried**) entrometerse

◆ pry into *v/t* entrometerse en

PS ['pi:es] *abbr* (= **postscript**) PD (= posdata *f*)

pseu·do·nym ['su:dənɪm] pseudónimo *m*

psy·chi·at·ric [saɪkɪ'ætrɪk] *adj* psiquiátrico

psy·chi·a·trist [saɪ'kaɪətrɪst] psiquiatra *m/f*

psy·chi·a·try [saɪ'kaɪətrɪ] psiquiatría *f*

psy·chic ['saɪkɪk] *adj research* paranormal; *I'm not psychic* no soy vidente

psy·cho·a·nal·y·sis [saɪkouən'æləsɪs] psicoanálisis *m*

psy·cho·an·a·lyst [saɪkou'ænəlɪst] psicoanalista *m/f*

psy·cho·an·a·lyze [saɪkou'ænəlaɪz] *v/t* psicoanalizar

psy·cho·log·i·cal [saɪkə'lɑ:dʒɪkl] *adj* psicológico

psy·cho·log·i·cal·ly [saɪkə'lɑ:dʒɪklɪ] *adv* psicológicamente

psy·chol·o·gist [saɪ'kɑ:lədʒɪst] psicólogo(-a) *m(f)*

psy·chol·o·gy [saɪ'kɑ:lədʒɪ] psicología *f*

psy·cho·path ['saɪkoupæθ] psicópata *m/f*

psy·cho·so·mat·ic [saɪkousə'mætɪk] *adj* psicosomático

PTO [pi:ti:'ou] *abbr* (= **please turn over**) véase al dorso

pub [pʌb] *Br* bar *m*

pu·ber·ty ['pju:bərtɪ] pubertad *f*

pu·bic hair ['pju:bɪk] vello *m* púbico

pub·lic ['pʌblɪk] **1** *adj* público **2** *n*: *the public* el público; *in public* en público

pub·li·ca·tion [pʌblɪ'keɪʃn] publicación *f*

pub·lic 'hol·i·day día *m* festivo

pub·lic·i·ty [pʌb'lɪsətɪ] publicidad *f*

pub·li·cize ['pʌblɪsaɪz] *v/t* (*make known*) publicar, hacer público; COM dar publicidad a

pub·lic 'li·bra·ry biblioteca *f* pública

pub·lic·ly ['pʌblɪklɪ] *adv* públicamente

pub·lic 'pros·e·cu·tor fiscal *m/f*

pub·lic re'la·tions *npl* relaciones públicas *fpl*

'pub·lic school *Br* colegio *m* privado; *Am* colegio *m* público

'pub·lic sec·tor sector *m* público

pub·lish ['pʌblɪʃ] *v/t* publicar

pub·lish·er ['pʌblɪʃər] *person* editor(a) *m(f)*; *company* editorial *f*

pub·lish·ing ['pʌblɪʃɪŋ] industria *f* editorial

'pub·lish·ing com·pa·ny editorial *f*

pud·ding ['pudɪŋ] *Br dish* pudín *m*; *part of meal* postre *m*

pud·dle ['pʌdl] charco *m*

Puer·to Ri·can [pwertou'ri:kən] **1** *adj* portorriqueño, puertorriqueño **2** *n* portorriqueño(-a) *m(f)*, puertorriqueño(-a) *m(f)*

Puer·to Ri·co [pwertou'ri:kou] *n* Puerto Rico

puff [pʌf] **1** *n of wind* racha *f*; *from cigarette* calada *f*; *of smoke* bocanada *f* **2** *v/i* (*pant*) resoplar; *puff on a cigarette* dar una calada a un cigarrillo

puff·y ['pʌfɪ] *adj eyes, face* hinchado

puke [pju:k] **1** *n* P *substance* vomitona *f* P **2** *v/i* P echar la pota P

pull [pul] **1** *n on rope* tirón *m*; F (*appeal*) gancho *m* F; F (*influence*) enchufe *m* F **2** *v/t* (*drag*) arrastrar; (*tug*) tirar de; *tooth* sacar; *pull a muscle* sufrir un tirón en un músculo **3** *v/i* tirar

◆ pull ahead *v/i in race, competition* adelantarse

◆ pull apart *v/t* (*separate*) separar

◆ pull away *v/t* apartar

◆ pull down *v/t* (*lower*) bajar; (*demolish*) derribar

◆ pull in *v/i of bus, train* llegar

◆ pull off *v/t* quitar; *item of clothing* quitarse; F conseguir

◆ pull out **1** *v/t* sacar; *troops* retirar; **2** *v/i of an agreement, of troops* retirarse; *of ship* salir

◆ pull over *v/i* parar en el arcén

◆ pull through *v/i from an illness* recuperarse

◆ pull together **1** *v/i* (*cooperate*) cooperar **2** *v/t*: *pull o.s. together* tranquilizarse

◆ pull up **1** *v/t* (*raise*) subir; *item of clot-*

hing subirse; *plant, weeds* arrancar **2** v/i *of car etc* parar

pul·ley ['pʊlɪ] polea f

pull·o·ver ['pʊloʊvər] suéter m, Span jersey m

pulp [pʌlp] *of fruit* pulpa f; *for paper-making* pasta f

pul·pit ['pʊlpɪt] púlpito m

pul·sate [pʌl'seɪt] v/i *of heart, blood* palpitar; *of music* vibrar

pulse [pʌls] pulso m

pul·ver·ize ['pʌlvəraɪz] v/t pulverizar

pump [pʌmp] **1** n bomba f; (*gas pump*) surtidor m **2** v/t bombear

♦ **pump up** v/t inflar

pump·kin ['pʌmpkɪn] calabaza f

pun [pʌn] juego m de palabras

punch [pʌntʃ] **1** n (*blow*) puñetazo m; *implement* perforadora f **2** v/t *with fist* dar un puñetazo a; *hole, ticket* agujerear

'**punch line** *última frase de un chiste*

punc·tu·al ['pʌŋktʃʊəl] *adj* puntual

punc·tu·al·i·ty [pʌŋktʃʊ'ælətɪ] puntualidad f

punc·tu·al·ly ['pʌŋktʃʊəlɪ] *adv* puntualmente

punc·tu·ate ['pʌŋktʃʊəɪt] v/t puntuar

punc·tu·a·tion ['pʌŋktʃʊ'eɪʃn] puntuación f

punc·tu·a·tion mark signo m de puntuación

punc·ture ['pʌŋktʃər] **1** n perforación f **2** v/t perforar

pun·gent ['pʌndʒənt] *adj* fuerte

pun·ish ['pʌnɪʃ] v/t person castigar

pun·ish·ing ['pʌnɪʃɪŋ] *adj schedule* exigente; *pace* fuerte

pun·ish·ment ['pʌnɪʃmənt] castigo m

punk (rock) ['pʌŋk(rɑːk)] MUS (música f) punk m

pu·ny ['pjuːnɪ] *adj person* enclenque

pup [pʌp] cachorro m

pu·pil¹ ['pjuːpl] *of eye* pupila f

pu·pil² ['pjuːpl] (*student*) alumno(-a) m(f)

pup·pet ['pʌpɪt] *also fig* marioneta f

'**pup·pet gov·ern·ment** gobierno m títere

pup·py ['pʌpɪ] cachorro m

pur·chase¹ ['pɜːrtʃəs] **1** n adquisición f, compra f **2** v/t adquirir, comprar

pur·chase² ['pɜːrtʃəs] (*grip*) agarre m

pur·chas·er ['pɜːrtʃəsər] comprador(a) m(f)

pure [pjʊr] *adj* puro; ***pure new wool*** pura lana f virgen

pure·ly ['pjʊrlɪ] *adv* puramente

pur·ga·to·ry ['pɜːrgətɔːrɪ] purgatorio m

purge [pɜːrdʒ] **1** n *of political party* purga f **2** v/t purgar f

pu·ri·fy ['pjʊrɪfaɪ] v/t (*pret & pp* **purified**) *water* depurar

pu·ri·tan ['pjʊrɪtən] puritano(-a) m(f)

pu·ri·tan·i·cal [pjʊrɪ'tænɪkl] *adj* puritano

pu·ri·ty ['pjʊrɪtɪ] pureza f

pur·ple ['pɜːrpl] *adj* morado

Pur·ple 'Heart MIL medalla concedida a los soldados heridos en combate

pur·pose ['pɜːrpəs] (*aim, object*) propósito m, objeto m; ***on purpose*** a propósito; ***what is the purpose of your visit?*** ¿cuál es el objeto de su visita?

pur·pose·ful ['pɜːrpəsfəl] *adj* decidido

pur·pose·ly ['pɜːrpəslɪ] *adv* decididamente

purr [pɜːr] v/i *of cat* ronronear

purse [pɜːrs] n (*pocket book*) bolso m; Br: *for money* monedero m

pur·sue [pər'suː] v/t *person* perseguir; *career* ejercer; *course of action* proseguir

pur·su·er [pər'suːər] perseguidor(a) m(f)

pur·suit [pər'suːt] (*chase*) persecución f; *of happiness etc* búsqueda f; (*activity*) actividad f; ***those in pursuit*** los perseguidores

pus [pʌs] pus m

push [pʊʃ] **1** n (*shove*) empujón m; ***at the push of a button*** apretando un botón **2** v/t (*shove*) empujar; *button* apretar, pulsar; (*pressurize*) presionar; F *drugs* pasar F, mercadear con; ***be pushed for cash*** F estar pelado F, estar sin un centavo; ***be pushed for time*** F ir mal de tiempo F; ***be pushing 40*** F rondar los 40 **3** v/i empujar

♦ **push ahead** v/i seguir adelante

♦ **push along** v/t *cart etc* empujar

♦ **push away** v/t apartar

♦ **push off 1** v/t *lid* destapar; **2** v/i Br F (*leave*) largarse F

◆ **push on** v/i (*continue*) continuar

◆ **push up** v/t *prices* hacer subir

push·er ['pʊʃər] F *of drugs* camello *m* F

push-up ['pʊʃʌp] flexión *f* (de brazos)

push·y ['pʊʃɪ] *adj* F avasallador, agresivo

puss, pus·sy (**cat**) [pʊs, 'pʊsɪ (kæt)] F minino *m* F

◆ **pussy foot about** ['pʊsɪfʊt] v/i F andarse con rodeos

put [pʊt] v/t (*pret & pp* **put**) poner; *question* hacer; **put the cost at ...** estimar el costo en ...

◆ **put across** v/t *idea etc* hacer llegar

◆ **put aside** v/t *money* apartar, ahorrar; *work* dejar a un lado

◆ **put away** v/t *in closet etc* guardar; *in institution* encerrar; (*be firm*) consumir, cepillarse F; *money* apartar, ahorrar; *animal* sacrificar

◆ **put back** v/t (*replace*) volver a poner

◆ **put by** v/t *money* apartar, ahorrar

◆ **put down** v/t dejar; *deposit* entregar; *rebellion* reprimir; (*belittle*) dejar en mal lugar; **put down in writing** poner por escrito; **put one's foot down** *in car* apretar el acelerador; (*be firm*) plantarse; **put sth down to sth** (*attribute*) atribuir algo a algo

◆ **put forward** v/t *idea etc* proponer, presentar

◆ **put in** v/t meter; *time* dedicar; *request, claim* presentar

◆ **put in for** v/t (*apply for*) solicitar

◆ **put off** v/t *light, radio*, TV apagar; (*postpone*) posponer, aplazar; (*deter*) desalentar; (*repel*) desagradar; **I was put off by the smell** el olor me quitó las ganas; **that put me off shellfish for life** me quitó las ganas de volver a comer marisco

◆ **put on** v/t *light, radio*, TV encender; *L.Am.* prender; *tape, music* poner; *jacket, shoes, eye glasses* ponerse; (*perform*) representar; (*assume*) fingir; **put on make-up** maquillarse; **put on the brake** frenar; **put on weight** engordar; **she's just putting it on** está fingiendo

◆ **put out** v/t *hand* extender; *fire, light* apagar

◆ **put through** v/t: **put s.o. through to s.o.** *on phone* poner a alguien con alguien

◆ **put together** v/t (*assemble, organize*) montar

◆ **put up** v/t *hand* levantar; *person* alojar; (*erect*) levantar; *prices* subir; *poster, notice* colocar; *money* aportar; **put your hands up!** ¡arriba las manos!; **put up for sale** poner en venta

◆ **put up with** v/t (*tolerate*) aguantar

putt [pʌt] v/i SP golpear con el putter

put·ty ['pʌtɪ] masilla *f*

puz·zle ['pʌzl] **1** *n* (*mystery*) enigma *m*; *game* pasatiempos *mpl*; (*jigsaw puzzle*) puzzle *m*; (*crossword puzzle*) crucigrama *m* **2** v/t desconcertar; **one thing puzzles me** hay algo que no acabo de entender

puz·zling ['pʌzlɪŋ] *adj* desconcertante

PVC [piːviːˈsiː] *abbr* (= **polyvinyl chloride**) PVC *m* (= cloruro *m* de polivinilo)

py·ja·mas *Br* → **pajamas**

py·lon ['paɪlən] torre *f* de alta tensión

Q

quack¹ [kwæk] **1** *n of duck* graznido *m* **2** v/i graznar

quack² [kwæk] *n* F (*bad doctor*) matasanos *m/f inv* F

quad·ran·gle ['kwɑːdræŋgl] *figure* cuadrángulo *m*; *courtyard* patio *m*

quad·ru·ped ['kwɑːdruped] cuadrúpedo *m*

quad·ru·ple ['kwɑːdrupl] v/i cuadruplicarse

quad·ru·plets ['kwɑ:druplɪts] *npl* cuatrillizos(-as) *mpl (fpl)*

quads [kwɑ:dz] *npl* F cuatrillizos(-as) *mpl f(fpl)*

quag·mire ['kwɑ:gmaɪr] *fig* atolladero *m*

quail [kweɪl] *v/i* temblar (*at* ante)

quaint [kweɪnt] *adj cottage* pintoresco; (*slightly eccentric: ideas etc*) extraño

quake [kweɪk] **1** *n* (*earthquake*) terremoto *m* **2** *v/i of earth, with fear* temblar

qual·i·fi·ca·tion [kwɑ:lɪfɪ'keɪʃn] *from university etc* título *m*; **have the right qual·ifications for a job** estar bien cualificado para un trabajo

qual·i·fied ['kwɑ:lɪfaɪd] *adj doctor, engineer, plumber etc* titulado; (*restricted*) limitado; **I am not qualified to judge** no estoy en condiciones de poder juzgar

qual·i·fy ['kwɑ:lɪfaɪ] **1** *v/t* (*pret & pp* **qualified**) *of degree, course etc* habilitar; *remark etc* matizar **2** *v/i* (*pret & pp* **qualified**) (*get degree etc*) titularse, *L.Am.* egresar; *in competition* clasificarse; **they qualified for the final** se clasificaron para la final; **that doesn't qualify as ...** eso no cuenta como ...

qual·i·ty ['kwɑ:lətɪ] calidad *f*; (*characteristic*) cualidad *f*

qual·i·ty con·trol control *m* de calidad

qualm [kwɑ:m]: **have no qualms about ...** no tener reparos en ...

quan·da·ry ['kwɑ:ndərɪ] dilema *m*

quan·ti·fy ['kwɑ:ntɪfaɪ] *v/t* (*pret & pp* **quantified**) cuantificar

quan·ti·ty ['kwɑ:ntətɪ] cantidad *f*

quan·tum 'phys·ics ['kwɑ:ntəm] física *f* cuántica

quar·an·tine ['kwɑ:rənti:n] cuarentena *f*

quar·rel ['kwɑ:rəl] **1** *n* pelea *f* **2** *v/i* (*pret & pp* **quarreled**, *Br* **quarrelled**) pelearse

quar·rel·some ['kwɑ:rəlsʌm] *adj* peleón

quar·ry[1] ['kwɑ:rɪ] *in hunt* presa *f*

quar·ry[2] ['kwɑ:rɪ] *for mining* cantera *f*

quart [kwɔ:rt] cuarto *m* de galón

quar·ter ['kwɔ:rtər] cuarto *m*; *25 cents* cuarto *m* de dólar; *part of town* barrio *m*; **a quarter of an hour** un cuarto de hora; **a quarter of 5** las cinco menos cuarto; **a quarter after 5** las cinco y cuar-

to

'quar·ter·back SP quarterback *m*, *en fútbol americano, jugador que dirige el juego de ataque*

quar·ter·'fi·nal cuarto *m* de final

quar·ter·'fi·nal·ist cuartofinalista *m/f*

quar·ter·ly ['kwɔ:rtəlɪ] **1** *adj* trimestral **2** *adv* trimestralmente

'quar·ter·note MUS negra *f*

quar·ters ['kwɔ:rtəz] *npl* MIL alojamiento *m*

quar·tet [kwɔ:r'tet] MUS cuarteto *m*

quartz [kwɔ:rts] cuarzo *m*

quash [kwɑ:ʃ] *v/t rebellion* aplastar, sofocar; *court decision* revocar

qua·ver ['kweɪvər] **1** *n in voice* temblor *m* **2** *v/i of voice* temblar

quay [ki:] muelle *m*

'quay·side muelle *m*

quea·sy ['kwi:zɪ] *adj* mareado; **get queasy** marearse

queen [kwi:n] reina *f*

queen [kwi:n] *bee* abeja *f* reina

queer [kwɪr] *adj* (*peculiar*) raro, extraño

queer·ly ['kwɪrlɪ] *adv* de manera extraña

quell [kwel] *v/t protest, crowd* acallar; *riot* aplastar, sofocar

quench [kwentʃ] *v/t thirst* apagar, saciar; *flames* apagar

que·ry ['kwɪrɪ] **1** *n* duda *f*, pregunta *f* **2** *v/t* (*pret & pp* **queried**) (*express doubt about*) cuestionar; (*check*) comprobar; **query sth with s.o.** preguntar algo a alguien

quest [kwest] busca *f*

ques·tion ['kwestʃn] **1** *n* pregunta *f*; (*matter*) cuestión *f*, asunto *m*; **in question** (*being talked about*) en cuestión; (*in doubt*) en duda; **it's a question of money / time** es una cuestión de dinero / tiempo; **that's out of the question** eso es imposible **2** *v/t person* preguntar a; LAW interrogar; (*doubt*) cuestionar, poner en duda

ques·tion·a·ble ['kwestʃnəbl] *adj* cuestionable, dudoso

ques·tion·ing ['kwestʃnɪŋ] **1** *adj look, tone* inquisitivo **2** *n* interrogatorio *m*

'ques·tion mark signo *m* de interrogación

ques·tion·naire [kwestʃə'ner] cuestionario *m*

queue [kjuː] *n Br* cola *f*

quib·ble ['kwɪbl] *v/i* discutir (*por algo insignificante*)

quick [kwɪk] *adj* rápido; *be quick!* ¡date prisa!; *let's have a quick drink* vamos a tomarnos algo rápidamente; *can I have a quick look?* ¿me dejas echarle un vistazo?; *that was quick!* ¡qué rápido!

quick·ie ['kwɪkɪ]: *have a quickie* F (*quick drink*) tomarse una copa rápida

quick·ly ['kwɪklɪ] *adv* rápidamente, rápido, deprisa

'quick·sand arenas *fpl* movedizas

'quick·sil·ver azogue *m*

quick-wit·ted [kwɪk'wɪtɪd] *adj* agudo

qui·et ['kwaɪət] *adj* tranquilo; *engine* silencioso; *keep quiet about sth* guardar silencio sobre algo; *quiet!* ¡silencio!

◆ qui·et·en down ['kwaɪətn] **1** *v/t children, class* tranquilizar, hacer callar **2** *v/i of children* tranquilizarse, callarse; *of political situation* calmarse

quiet·ly ['kwaɪətlɪ] *adv* (*not loudly*) silenciosamente; (*without fuss*) discretamente; (*peacefully*) tranquilamente; *speak quietly* hablar en voz baja

quiet·ness ['kwaɪətnɪs] *n of voice* suavidad *f*; *of night, street* silencio *m*, calma *f*

quilt [kwɪlt] *on bed* edredón *m*

quilt·ed ['kwɪltɪd] *adj* acolchado

quin·ine ['kwɪniːn] quinina *f*

quin·tet [kwɪn'tet] *mus* quinteto *m*

quip [kwɪp] **1** *n joke* broma *f*; *remark* salida *f* **2** *v/i* (*pret & pp quipped*) bromear

quirk [kwɜːrk] peculiaridad *f*, rareza *f*

quirk·y ['kwɜːrkɪ] *adj* peculiar, raro

quit [kwɪt] **1** *v/t* (*pret & pp quit*) *job* dejar, abandonar; *quit doing sth* dejar de hacer algo **2** *v/i* (*pret & pp quit*) (*leave job*) dimitir; COMPUT salir; *get one's notice to quit* from landlord recibir la notificación de desalojo

quite [kwaɪt] *adv* (*fairly*) bastante; (*completely*) completamente; *not quite ready* no listo del todo; *I didn't quite understand* no entendí bien; *is that right? - not quite* ¿es verdad? - no exactamente; *quite!* ¡exactamente!; *quite a lot* bastante; *quite a few* bastantes; *it was quite a surprise / change* fue toda una sorpresa / un cambio

quits [kwɪts] *adj*: *be quits with s.o.* estar en paz con alguien

quit·ter ['kwɪtər] F *persona que abandona fácilmente*

quiv·er ['kwɪvər] *v/i* estremecerse

quiz [kwɪz] **1** *n* concurso *m* (*de preguntas y respuestas*) **2** *v/t* (*pret & pp quizzed*) interrogar (*about* sobre)

'quiz mas·ter *presentador de un concurso de preguntas y respuestas*

'quiz pro·gram, *Br* 'quiz pro·gramme programa *m* concurso (*de preguntas y respuestas*)

quo·ta ['kwoʊtə] cuota *f*

quo·ta·tion [kwoʊ'teɪʃn] *from author* cita *f*; (*price*) presupuesto *m*

quo'ta·tion marks *npl* comillas *fpl*

quote [kwoʊt] **1** *n from author* cita *f*; (*price*) presupuesto *m*; (*quotation mark*) comilla *f*; *in quotes* entre comillas **2** *v/t text* citar; *price* dar **3** *v/i*: *quote from an author* citar de un autor

R

rab·bi ['ræbaɪ] rabino *m*

rab·bit ['ræbɪt] conejo *m*

rab·ble ['ræbl] chusma *f*, multitud *f*

rab·ble-rous·er ['ræblraʊzər] agitador(a) *m(f)*

ra·bies ['reɪbiːz] *nsg* rabia *f*

rac·coon [rə'ku:n] mapache *m*

race¹ [reɪs] *n of people* raza *f*

race² [reɪs] **1** *n* SP carrera *f*; *the races* horse races las carreras **2** *v/i (run fast)* correr; *he raced through his meal / work* acabó su comida / trabajo a toda velocidad **3** *v/t* correr contra; *I'll race you* te echo una carrera

'race·course hipódromo *m*

'race·horse caballo *m* de carreras

'race riot disturbios *mpl* raciales

'race·track circuito *m*; *for horses* hipódromo *m*

ra·cial ['reɪʃl] *adj* racial; *racial equality* igualdad *f* racial

rac·ing ['reɪsɪŋ] carreras *fpl*

rac·ism ['reɪsɪzm] racismo *m*

ra·cist ['reɪsɪst] **1** *n* racista *m/f* **2** *adj* racista

rack [ræk] **1** *n (for bikes)* barras para aparcar bicicletas; *for bags on train* portaequipajes *m inv*; *for CDs* mueble *m* **2** *v/t*: *rack one's brains* devanarse los sesos

rack·et¹ ['rækɪt] SP raqueta *f*

rack·et² ['rækɪt] *(noise)* jaleo *m*; *(criminal activity)* negocio *m* sucio

ra·dar ['reɪdɑ:r] radar *m*

'ra·dar screen pantalla *f* de radar

'ra·dar trap control *m* de velocidad por radar

ra·di·al 'tire, *Br* ra·di·al 'tyre ['reɪdɪəl] neumático *m* radial

ra·di·ance ['reɪdɪəns] esplendor *m*, brillantez *f*

ra·di·ant ['reɪdɪənt] *adj smile, appearance* resplandeciente, brillante

ra·di·ate ['reɪdɪeɪt] *v/i of heat, light* irradiar

ra·di·a·tion [reɪdɪ'eɪʃn] PHYS radiación *f*

ra·di·a·tor ['reɪdɪeɪtər] *in room, car* radiador *m*

rad·i·cal ['rædɪkl] **1** *adj* radical **2** *n* POL radical *m/f*

rad·i·cal·ism ['rædɪkəlɪzm] POL radicalismo *m*

rad·i·cal·ly ['rædɪklɪ] *adv* radicalmente

ra·di·o ['reɪdɪoʊ] radio *f*; *on the radio* en la radio; *by radio* por radio

ra·di·o·ac·tive [reɪdɪoʊ'æktɪv] *adj* radiactivo

ra·di·o·ac·tive 'waste residuos *mpl* radiactivos

ra·di·o·ac·tiv·i·ty [reɪdɪoʊæk'tɪvətɪ] radiactividad *f*

ra·di·o a'larm radio *f* despertador

ra·di·og·ra·pher [reɪdɪ'ɑ:grəfər] técnico(-a) *m(f)* de rayos X

ra·di·og·ra·phy [reɪdɪ'ɑ:grəfɪ] radiografía *f*

'ra·di·o sta·tion emisora *f* de radio

'ra·di·o tax·i radiotaxi *m*

ra·di·o'ther·a·py radioterapia *f*

rad·ish ['rædɪʃ] rábano *m*

ra·di·us ['reɪdɪəs] radio *m*

raf·fle ['ræfl] *n* rifa *f*

raft [ræft] balsa *f*

raf·ter ['ræftər] viga *f*

rag [ræg] *n for cleaning etc* trapo *m*; *in rags* con harapos

rage [reɪdʒ] **1** *n* ira *f*, cólera *f*; *be in a rage* estar encolerizado; *be all the rage* F estar arrasando F **2** *v/i of storm* bramar

rag·ged ['rægɪd] *adj* andrajoso

raid [reɪd] **1** *n by troops* incursión *f*; *by police* redada *f*; *by robbers* atraco *m*; FIN ataque *m*, incursión *f* **2** *v/t of troops* realizar una incursión en; *of police* realizar una redada en; *of robbers* atracar; *fridge, orchard* saquear

raid·er ['reɪdər] *on bank etc* atracador(a) *m(f)*

rail [reɪl] *n on track* riel *m*, carril *m*; *(handrail)* pasamanos *m inv*, baranda *f*; *for towel* barra *f*; *by rail* en tren

rail·ings ['reɪlɪŋz] *npl around park etc* verja *f*

'rail·road ['reɪlroʊd] ferrocarril *m*

'rail·road sta·tion estación *f* de ferrocarril *or* de tren

'rail·way ['reɪlweɪ] *Br* ferrocarril *m*

rain [reɪn] **1** *n* lluvia *f*; *in the rain* bajo la lluvia **2** *v/i* llover; *it's raining* llueve

'rain·bow arco *m* iris

'rain·check: *can I take a raincheck on that?* F ¿lo podríamos aplazar para algún otro momento?

'rain·coat impermeable *m*

'rain·drop gota *f* de lluvia

R

'rain·fall pluviosidad f, precipitaciones fpl

'rain for·est selva f

'rain·proof adj fabric impermeable

'rain·storm tormenta f, aguacero m

rain·y ['reɪnɪ] adj lluvioso; **it's rainy** llueve mucho

'rain·y sea·son estación f de las lluvias

raise [reɪz] **1** n in salary aumento m de sueldo **2** v/t shelf etc levantar; offer incrementar; children criar; question plantear; money reunir

rai·sin ['reɪzn] pasa f

rake [reɪk] n for garden rastrillo m

♦ rake up v/t leaves rastrillar; fig sacar a la luz

ral·ly ['rælɪ] n (meeting, reunion) concentración f; political mitin m; MOT rally m; in tennis peloteo m

♦ rally round **1** v/i (pret & pp rallied) acudir a ayudar **2** v/t (pret & pp rallied): **rally round s.o.** acudir a ayudar a alguien

ram [ræm] **1** n carnero m **2** v/t (pret & pp rammed) ship, car embestir

RAM [ræm] COMPUT abbr (= **random access memory**) RAM f (= memoria f de acceso aleatorio)

ram·ble ['ræmbl] **1** n walk caminata f, excursión f **2** v/i walk caminar; in speaking divagar; (talk incoherently) hablar sin decir nada coherente

ram·bler ['ræmblər] walker senderista m/f, excursionista m/f

ram·bling ['ræmblɪŋ] **1** n walking senderismo m; in speech divagaciones fpl **2** adj speech inconexo

ramp [ræmp] rampa f; for raising vehicle elevador m

ram·page ['ræmpeɪdʒ] **1** v/i pasar arrasando con todo **2** n: **go on the rampage** pasar arrasando con todo

ram·pant ['ræmpənt] adj inflation galopante

ram·part ['ræmpɑːrt] muralla f

ram·shack·le ['ræmʃækl] adj destartalado, desvencijado

ran [ræn] pret → **run**

ranch [ræntʃ] rancho m

ranch·er ['ræntʃər] ranchero(-a) m(f)

ran·cid ['rænsɪd] adj rancio

ran·cor ['ræŋkər] rencor m

R & D [ɑːrən'diː] abbr (= **research and development**) I+D f (= investigación f y desarrollo)

ran·dom ['rændəm] **1** adj al azar; **random sample** muestra f aleatoria **2** n: **at random** al azar

ran·dy ['rændɪ] adj Br F cachondo F; **it makes me randy** me pone cachondo

rang [ræŋ] pret → **ring²**

range [reɪndʒ] **1** n of products gama f; of gun, airplane alcance m; of voice registro m; of mountains cordillera f; **at close range** de cerca **2** v/i: **range from X to Y** ir desde X a Y

rang·er ['reɪndʒər] guardabosques m/f inv

rank [ræŋk] **1** n MIL, in society rango m; **the ranks** MIL la tropa **2** v/t clasificar

♦ rank among v/t figurar entre

ran·kle ['ræŋkl] v/i doler; **it still rankles (with him)** todavía le duele

ran·sack ['rænsæk] v/t saquear

ran·som ['rænsəm] n rescate m; **hold s.o. to ransom** pedir un rescate por alguien

'ran·som mon·ey (dinero m del) rescate m

rant [rænt] v/i: **rant and rave** despotricar

rap [ræp] **1** n at door etc golpe m; MUS rap m **2** v/t (pret & pp rapped) table etc golpear

♦ rap at v/t window etc golpear

rape¹ [reɪp] **1** n violación f **2** v/t violar

rape² [reɪp] n BOT colza f

'rape vic·tim víctima m/f de una violación

rap·id ['ræpɪd] adj rápido

ra·pid·i·ty [rə'pɪdətɪ] rapidez f

rap·id·ly ['ræpɪdlɪ] adv rápidamente

rap·ids ['ræpɪdz] npl rápidos mpl

rap·ist ['reɪpɪst] violador(a) m(f)

rap·port [ræ'pɔːr] relación f; **we've got a good rapport** nos entendemos muy bien

rap·ture ['ræptʃər]: **go into raptures over** extasiarse con

rap·tur·ous ['ræptʃərəs] adj clamoroso

rare [rer] adj raro; steak poco hecho

rare·ly ['rerlɪ] adv raramente, raras veces

rar·i·ty ['rerətɪ] rareza f

ras·cal ['ræskl] pícaro(-a) m(f)

rash[1] [ræʃ] *n* MED sarpullido *m*, erupción *f* cutánea

rash[2] [ræʃ] *adj* action, behavior precipitado

rash·ly ['ræʃlɪ] *adv* precipitadamente

rasp·ber·ry ['ræzberɪ] frambuesa *f*

rat [ræt] *n* rata *f*

rate [reɪt] **1** *n of exchange* tipo *m*; *of pay* tarifa *f*; (*price*) tarifa *f*, precio *m*; (*speed*) ritmo *m*; *rate of interest* FIN tipo *m* de interés; *at this rate* (*at this speed*) a este ritmo; (*if we carry on like this*) si seguimos así; *at any rate* (*anyway*) en todo caso; (*at least*) por lo menos **2** *v/t*: *rate s.o. as ...* considerar a alguien (como) ...; *rate s.o. highly* tener buena opinión de alguien

rath·er ['ræðər] *adv* bastante; *I would rather stay here* preferiría quedarme aquí; *or would you rather ...?* ¿o preferiría ...?

rat·i·fi·ca·tion [rætɪfɪ'keɪʃn] ratificación *f*

rat·i·fy ['rætɪfaɪ] *v/t* (*pret & pp* **ratified**) ratificar

rat·ings ['reɪtɪŋz] *npl* índice *m* de audiencia

ra·ti·o ['reɪʃɪoʊ] proporción *f*

ra·tion ['ræʃn] **1** *n* ración *f* **2** *v/t supplies* racionar

ra·tion·al ['ræʃənl] *adj* racional

ra·tion·al·i·ty [ræʃə'nælɪtɪ] racionalidad *f*

ra·tion·al·i·za·tion [ræʃənəlaɪ'zeɪʃn] racionalización *f*

ra·tion·al·ize ['ræʃənəlaɪz] **1** *v/t* racionalizar **2** *v/i* buscar una explicación racional

ra·tion·al·ly ['ræʃənlɪ] *adv* racionalmente

'**rat race** *la vida frenética y competitiva*

rat·tle ['rætl] **1** *n noise* traqueteo *m*, golpeteo *m*; *toy* sonajero *m* **2** *v/t chains etc* entrechocar **3** *v/i of chains etc* entrechocarse; *of crates* traquetear

◆ **rattle off** *v/t poem, list of names* decir rápidamente

◆ **rattle through** *v/t* hacer rápidamente

'**rat·tle·snake** serpiente *f* de cascabel

rau·cous ['rɔːkəs] *adj laughter, party* estridente

rav·age ['rævɪdʒ] **1** *n*: *the ravages of time* los estragos del tiempo **2** *v/t* arrasar;

ravaged by war arrasado por la guerra

rave [reɪv] **1** *v/i* (*talk deliriously*) delirar; (*talk wildly*) desvariar; *rave about sth* (*be very enthusiastic*) estar muy entusiasmado con algo **2** *n party* fiesta *f* tecno

rave re'view crítica *f* muy entusiasta

ra·ven ['reɪvn] cuervo *m*

rav·e·nous ['rævənəs] *adj appetite* voraz; *have a ravenous appetite* tener un hambre canina

rav·e·nous·ly ['rævənəslɪ] *adv* con voracidad

ra·vine [rə'viːn] barranco *m*

rav·ing ['reɪvɪŋ] *adv*: *raving mad* chalado

rav·ish·ing ['rævɪʃɪŋ] *adj* encantador, cautivador

raw [rɔː] *adj meat, vegetable* crudo; *sugar* sin refinar; *iron* sin tratar

raw ma·te·ri·als *npl* materias *fpl* primas

ray [reɪ] rayo *m*; *a ray of hope* un rayo de esperanza

raze [reɪz] *v/t*: *raze to the ground* arrasar *or* asolar por completo

ra·zor ['reɪzər] maquinilla *f* de afeitar

'**ra·zor blade** cuchilla *f* de afeitar

re [riː] *prep* COM con referencia a

reach [riːtʃ] **1** *n*: *within reach* al alcance; *out of reach* fuera del alcance **2** *v/t* llegar a; *decision, agreement, conclusion* alcanzar, llegar a; *can you reach it?* ¿alcanzas?, ¿llegas?

◆ **reach out** *v/i* extender el brazo

re·act [rɪ'ækt] *v/i* reaccionar

re·ac·tion [rɪ'ækʃn] reacción *f*

re·ac·tion·ar·y [rɪ'ækʃnrɪ] **1** *n* POL reaccionario(-a) *m(f)* **2** *adj* POL reaccionario

re·ac·tor [rɪ'æktər] *nuclear reactor m*

read [riːd] **1** *v/t* (*pret & pp* **read** [red]) *also* COMPUT leer **2** *v/i* (*pret & pp* **read** [red]) leer; *read to s.o.* leer a alguien

◆ **read out** *v/t aloud* leer en voz alta

◆ **read up on** *v/t* leer mucho sobre, estudiar

rea·da·ble ['riːdəbl] *adj handwriting* legible; *book* ameno

read·er ['riːdər] *person* lector(a) *m(f)*

read·i·ly ['redɪlɪ] *adv admit, agree* de buena gana

read·i·ness ['redɪnɪs]: *in a state of readi-*

ness preparado par actuar; *their readiness to help* la facilidad con la que ayudaron

read·ing ['riːdɪŋ] *activity* lectura *f; take a reading from the meter* leer el contador

'**read·ing mat·ter** lectura *f*

re·ad·just [riːə'dʒʌst] **1** *v/t equipment, controls* reajustar **2** *v/i to conditions* volver a adaptarse

read·'on·ly file COMPUT archivo *m* sólo de lectura

read·'on·ly mem·o·ry COMPUT memoria *f* sólo de lectura

read·y ['redɪ] *adj (prepared)* listo, preparado; *(willing)* dispuesto; *get (o.s.) ready* prepararse; *get sth ready* preparar algo

read·y 'cash dinero *m* contante y sonante

read·y-made *adj stew etc* precocinado; *solution* ya hecho

read·y-to-wear *adj* de confección

real [riːl] *adj* real; *surprise, genius* auténtico; *he's a real idiot* es un auténtico idiota

'**real es·tate** bienes *mpl* inmuebles

'**real es·tate a·gent** agente *m/f* inmobiliario(-a)

re·al·ism ['rɪəlɪzəm] realismo *m*

re·a·list ['rɪəlɪst] realista *m/f*

re·a·lis·tic [rɪə'lɪstɪk] *adj* realista

re·a·lis·tic·al·ly [rɪə'lɪstɪklɪ] *adv* realísticamente

re·al·i·ty [rɪ'ælətɪ] realidad *f*

re·a·li·za·tion [rɪələ'zeɪʃn]: *the realization dawned on me that ...* me di cuenta de que ...

re·a·lize ['rɪəlaɪz] *v/t* darse cuenta de; FIN *(yield)* producir; *(sell)* realizar, liquidar; *I realize now that ...* ahora me doy cuenta de que ...

real·ly ['rɪəlɪ] *adv in truth* de verdad; *big, small* muy; *I am really really sorry* lo siento en el alma; *really?* ¿de verdad?; *not really as reply* la verdad es que no

real 'time *n* COMPUT tiempo *m* real

real-time *adj* COMPUT en tiempo real

re·al·tor ['rɪːltər] agente *m/f* inmobiliario(-a)

re·al·ty ['riːltɪ] bienes *mpl* inmuebles

reap [riːp] *v/t* cosechar

re·ap·pear [riːə'pɪr] *v/i* reaparecer

reappearance [riːə'pɪrəns] reaparición *f*

rear [rɪr] **1** *n* parte *f* de atrás **2** *adj legs* de atrás; *seats, wheels, lights* trasero

rear 'end 1 *n* F *of person* trasero *m* **2** *v/t* MOT F dar un golpe por atrás a

rear 'light *of car* luz *f* trasera

re·arm [riː'ɑːrm] **1** *v/t* rearmar **2** *v/i* rearmarse

'**rear·most** *adj* último

re·ar·range [riːə'reɪndʒ] *v/t flowers* volver a colocar; *furniture* reordenar; *schedule, meetings* cambiar

rear-view 'mir·ror espejo *m* retrovisor

rea·son ['riːzn] **1** *n faculty* razón *f; (cause)* razón *f*, motivo *m; see I listen to reason* atender a razones **2** *v/i: reason with s.o.* razonar con alguien

rea·so·na·ble ['riːznəbl] *adj person* razonable; *a reasonable number of people* un buen número de personas

rea·son·a·bly ['riːznəblɪ] *adv act, behave* razonablemente; *(quite)* bastante

rea·son·ing ['riːznɪŋ] razonamiento *m*

re·as·sure [riːə'ʃʊr] *v/t* tranquilizar; *she reassured us of her continued support* nos aseguró que continuábamos contando con su apoyo

re·as·sur·ing [riːə'ʃʊrɪŋ] *adj* tranquilizador

re·bate ['riːbeɪt] *money back* reembolso *m*

reb·el[1] ['rebl] *n* rebelde *m/f; rebel troops* tropas *fpl* rebeldes

re·bel[2] [rɪ'bel] *v/i (pret & pp rebelled)* rebelarse

reb·el·lion [rɪ'beljən] rebelión *f*

reb·el·lious [rɪ'beljəs] *adj* rebelde

reb·el·lious·ly [rɪ'beljəslɪ] *adv* con rebeldía

reb·el·lious·ness [rɪ'beljəsnɪs] rebeldía *f*

re·bound [rɪ'baʊnd] *v/i of ball etc* rebotar

re·buff [rɪ'bʌf] *n* desaire *m*, rechazo *m*

re·build [riː'bɪld] *v/t (pret & pp rebuilt)* reconstruir

re·buke [rɪ'bjuːk] *v/t* reprender

re·call [rɪ'koːl] *v/t goods* retirar del mercado; *(remember)* recordar

re·cap ['riːkæp] *v/i (pret & pp recapped)*

recapitular

re·cap·ture [riːˈkæptʃər] *v/t* MIL reconquistar; *criminal* volver a detener

re·cede [rɪˈsiːd] *v/i of flood waters* retroceder

re·ced·ing [rɪˈsiːdɪŋ] *adj forehead, chin* hundido; *have a receding hairline* tener entradas

re·ceipt [rɪˈsiːt] *for purchase* recibo *m*; *acknowledge receipt of sth* acusar recibo de algo; *receipts* FIN ingresos *mpl*

re·ceive [rɪˈsiːv] *v/t* recibir

re·ceiv·er [rɪˈsiːvər] *of letter* destinatario(-a) *m(f)*; TELEC auricular *m*; *for radio* receptor *m*; *in tennis* jugador(a) *m(f)* al resto

re·ceiv·er·ship [rɪˈsiːvərʃɪp]: *be in receivership* estar en suspensión de pagos

re·cent [ˈriːsnt] *adj* reciente

re·cent·ly [ˈriːsntlɪ] *adv* recientemente

re·cep·tion [rɪˈsepʃn] recepción *f*; *(welcome)* recibimiento *m*

re·cep·tion desk recepción *f*

re·cep·tion·ist [rɪˈsepʃnɪst] recepcionista *m/f*

re·cep·tive [rɪˈseptɪv] *adj*: *be receptive to sth* ser receptivo a algo

re·cess [ˈriːses] *n in wall etc* hueco *m*; EDU recreo *m*; *of parliament* periodo *m* vacacional

re·ces·sion [rɪˈseʃn] *economic* recesión *f*

re·charge [riːˈtʃɑːrdʒ] *v/t battery* recargar

re·ci·pe [ˈresəpɪ] receta *f*

¹re·ci·pe book libro *m* de cocina, recetario *m*

re·cip·i·ent [rɪˈsɪpɪənt] *of parcel etc* destinatario(-a) *m(f)*; *of payment* receptor(a) *m(f)*

re·cip·ro·cal [rɪˈsɪprəkl] *adj* recíproco

re·cit·al [rɪˈsaɪtl] MUS recital *m*

re·cite [rɪˈsaɪt] *v/t poem* recitar; *details, facts* enumerar

reck·less [ˈreklɪs] *adj* imprudente; *driving* temerario

reck·less·ly [ˈreklɪslɪ] *adv* con imprudencia; *drive* con temeridad

reck·on [ˈrekən] *v/i (think, consider)* estimar, considerar; *I reckon it won't happen* creo que no va a pasar

◆ **reckon on** *v/t* contar con

◆ **reckon with** *v/t*: *have s.o./sth to reckon with* tener que vérselas con alguien / algo

reck·on·ing [ˈrekənɪŋ] estimaciones *fpl*, cálculos *mpl*; *by my reckoning* según mis cálculos

re·claim [rɪˈkleɪm] *v/t land from sea* ganar, recuperar; *lost property, rights* reclamar

re·cline [rɪˈklaɪn] *v/i* reclinarse

re·clin·er [rɪˈklaɪnər] *chair* sillón *m* reclinable

re·cluse [rɪˈkluːs] solitario(-a) *m(f)*

rec·og·ni·tion [rekəgˈnɪʃn] *of state, s.o.'s achievements* reconocimiento *m*; *in recognition of* en reconocimiento a; *be changed beyond recognition* estar irreconocible

rec·og·niz·a·ble [rekəgˈnaɪzəbl] *adj* reconocible

rec·og·nize [ˈrekəgnaɪz] *v/t* reconocer

re·coil [rɪˈkɔɪl] *v/i* echarse atrás, retroceder

rec·ol·lect [rekəˈlekt] *v/t* recordar

rec·ol·lec·tion [rekəˈlekʃn] recuerdo *m*; *I have no recollection of the accident* no me acuerdo del accidente

rec·om·mend [rekəˈmend] *v/t* recomendar

rec·om·men·da·tion [rekəmenˈdeɪʃn] recomendación *f*

rec·om·pense [ˈrekəmpens] *n* recompensa *f*

rec·on·cile [ˈrekənsaɪl] *v/t people* reconciliar; *differences, facts* conciliar; *reconcile o.s. to …* hacerse a la idea de …; *be reconciled of two people* haberse reconciliado

rec·on·cil·i·a·tion [rekənsɪlɪˈeɪʃn] *of people* reconciliación *f*; *of differences, facts* conciliación *f*

re·con·di·tion [riːkənˈdɪʃn] *v/t* reacondicionar

re·con·nais·sance [rɪˈkɑːnɪsns] MIL reconocimiento *m*

re·con·sid·er [riːkənˈsɪdər] **1** *v/t offer, one's position* reconsiderar **2** *v/i*: *won't you please reconsider?* ¿por qué no lo reconsideras, por favor?

re·con·struct [riːkən'strʌkt] v/t reconstruir

rec·ord¹ ['rekɔːrd] n MUS disco m; SP etc récord m; written document etc registro m, documento m; in database registro m; **records** archivos mpl; **say sth off the record** decir algo oficiosamente; **have a criminal record** tener antecedentes penales; **have a good record for sth** tener un buen historial en materia de algo

re·cord² [rɪ'kɔːrd] v/t electronically grabar; in writing anotar

're·cord-break·ing adj récord

re·cor·der [rɪ'kɔːrdər] MUS flauta f dulce

're·cord hold·er plusmarquista m/f

re·cord·ing [rɪ'kɔːrdɪŋ] grabación f

re'cord·ing stu·di·o estudio m de grabación

're·cord play·er tocadiscos m inv

re·count¹ [rɪ'kaʊnt] v/t (tell) relatar

re·count² ['riːkaʊnt] 1 n of votes segundo recuento m 2 v/t (count again) volver a contar

re·coup [rɪ'kuːp] v/t financial losses resarcirse de

re·cov·er [rɪ'kʌvər] 1 v/t sth lost, stolen goods recuperar; composure recobrar 2 v/i from illness recuperarse

re·cov·er·y [rɪ'kʌvərɪ] recuperación f; he has made a good recovery se ha recuperado muy bien

rec·re·a·tion [rekrɪ'eɪʃn] ocio m

rec·re·a·tion·al [rekrɪ'eɪʃnl] adj done for pleasure recreativo

re·cruit [rɪ'kruːt] 1 n MIL recluta m/f; to company nuevo(-a) trabajador(a) 2 v/t new staff contratar

re·cruit·ment [rɪ'kruːtmənt] MIL reclutamiento m; to company contratación f

re'cruit·ment drive MIL campaña f de reclutamiento; to company campaña f de contratación

rec·tan·gle ['rektæŋgl] rectángulo m

rec·tan·gu·lar [rek'tæŋgjʊlər] adj rectangular

rec·ti·fy ['rektɪfaɪ] v/t (pret & pp rectified) rectificar

re·cu·pe·rate [rɪ'kuːpəreɪt] v/i recuperarse

re·cur [rɪ'kɜːr] v/i (pret & pp **recurred**) of error, event repetirse; of symptoms reaparecer

re·cur·rent [rɪ'kʌrənt] adj recurrente

re·cy·cla·ble [riː'saɪkləbl] adj reciclable

re·cy·cle [riː'saɪkl] v/t reciclar

re·cy·cling [riː'saɪklɪŋ] reciclado m

red [red] adj rojo; in the red FIN en números rojos

Red 'Cross Cruz f Roja

red·den ['redn] v/i (blush) ponerse colorado

re·dec·o·rate [riː'dekəreɪt] v/t with paint volver a pintar; with paper volver a empapelar

re·deem [rɪ'diːm] v/t debt amortizar; REL redimir

re·deem·ing feat·ure [rɪ'diːmɪŋ]: his one redeeming feature is that ... lo único que lo salva es que ...

re·demp·tion [rɪ'dempʃn] REL redención f

re·de·vel·op [riːdɪ'veləp] v/t part of town reedificar

red-hand·ed [red'hændɪd] adj: catch s.o. red-handed coger a alguien con las manos en la masa

'red·head pelirrojo(-a) m(f)

red-'hot adj al rojo vivo

red 'let·ter day día m señalado

red 'light at traffic light semáforo m (en) rojo

red 'light dis·trict zona f de prostitución

red 'meat carne f roja

'red·neck F individuo racista y reaccionario, normalmente de clase trabajadora

re·dou·ble [riː'dʌbl] v/t: redouble one's efforts redoblar los esfuerzos

red 'pep·per vegetable pimiento m rojo

red 'tape F burocracia f, papeleo m

re·duce [rɪ'duːs] v/t reducir; price rebajar

re·duc·tion [rɪ'dʌkʃn] reducción f; in price rebaja f

re·dun·dant [rɪ'dʌndənt] adj (unnecessary) innecesario; be made redundant Br at work ser despedido

reed [riːd] BOT junco m

reef [riːf] in sea arrecife m

'reef knot nudo m de rizos

reek [riːk] *v/i* apestar (*of* a)

reel [riːl] *n of film* rollo *m; of thread* carrete *m*

◆ **reel off** *v/t* soltar

re-e'lect *v/t* reelegir

re-e'lec-tion reelección *f*

re-'entry *of spacecraft* reentrada *f*

ref [ref] F árbitro(-a) *m(f)*

re-fer [rɪ'fɜːr] *v/t (pret & pp* **referred**): *refer a decision / problem* **to s.o.** remitir una decisión / un problema a alguien

◆ **refer to** *v/t (allude to)* referirse a; *dictionary etc* consultar

ref-er-ee [refə'riː] SP árbitro(-a) *m(f)*; *(for job)* persona que pueda dar referencias

ref-er-ence ['refərəns] referencia *f;* **with reference to** con referencia a

'ref-er-ence book libro *m* de consulta

'reference li-bra-ry biblioteca *f* de consulta

'ref-er-ence num-ber número *m* de referencia

ref-e-ren-dum [refə'rendəm] referéndum *m*

re-fill ['riːfɪl] *v/t tank, glass* volver a llenar

re-fine [rɪ'faɪn] *v/t oil, sugar* refinar; *technique* perfeccionar

re-fined [rɪ'faɪnd] *adj manners, language* refinado

re-fine-ment [rɪ'faɪnmənt] *to process, machine* mejora *f*

re-fin-e-ry [rɪ'faɪnərɪ] refinería *f*

re-fla-tion ['riːfleɪʃn] reflación *f*

reflect [rɪ'flekt] **1** *v/t light* reflejar; **be reflected in** reflejarse en **2** *v/i (think)* reflexionar

re-flec-tion [rɪ'flekʃn] *in water, glass etc* reflejo *f; (consideration)* reflexión *f*

re-flex ['riːfleks] *in body* reflejo *m*

re-flex re'ac-tion acto *m* reflejo

re-form [rɪ'fɔːrm] **1** *n* reforma *f* **2** *v/t* reformar

re-form-er [rɪ'fɔːrmər] reformador(a) *m(f)*

re-frain¹ [rɪ'freɪn] *v/i fml* abstenerse; **please refrain from smoking** se ruega no fumar

re-frain² [rɪ'freɪn] *n in song, poem* estribillo *m*

re-fresh [rɪ'freʃ] *v/t person* refrescar; **feel refreshed** sentirse fresco

refresh-er course [rɪ'freʃər] curso *m* de actualización *or* reciclaje

re-fresh-ing [rɪ'freʃɪŋ] *adj drink* refrescante; *experience* reconfortante

re-fresh-ments [rɪ'freʃmənts] *npl* refrigerio *m*

re-fri-ge-rate [rɪ'frɪdʒəreɪt] *v/t* refrigerar; **keep refrigerated** conservar refrigerado

re-fri-ge-ra-tor [rɪ'frɪdʒəreɪtər] frigorífico *m*, refrigerador *m*

re-fu-el [riːf'juəl] **1** *v/t airplane* reabastecer de combustible a **2** *v/i of airplane* repostar

ref-uge ['refjuːdʒ] refugio *m;* **take refuge** *from storm etc* refugiarse

ref-u-gee [refjuː'dʒiː] refugiado(-a) *m(f)*

ref'u-gee camp campo *m* de refugiados

re-fund ['riːfʌnd] **1** *n* ['riːfʌnd] reembolso *m;* **give s.o. a refund** devolver el dinero a alguien **2** *v/t* [rɪ'fʌnd] reembolsar

re-fus-al [rɪ'fjuːzl] negativa *f*

re-fuse¹ [rɪ'fjuːz] **1** *v/i* negarse **2** *v/t help, food* rechazar; **refuse s.o. sth** negar algo a alguien; **refuse to do sth** negarse a hacer algo

ref-use² ['refjuːs] *(garbage)* basura *f*

'ref-use col-lec-tion recogida *f* de basuras

'ref-use dump vertedero *m*

re-gain [rɪ'geɪn] *v/t* recuperar

re-gal ['riːgl] *adj* regio

re-gard [rɪ'gɑːrd] **1** *n:* **have great regard for s.o.** sentir gran estima por alguien; **in this regard** en este sentido; **with regard to** con respecto a; *(kind)* **regards** saludos; **give my regards to Paula** dale saludos *or* recuerdos a Paula de mi parte; **with no regard for** sin tener en cuenta **2** *v/t:* **regard s.o./sth as sth** considerar a alguien / algo como algo; **I regard it as an honor** para mí es un honor; **as regards** con respecto a

re-gard-ing [rɪ'gɑːrdɪŋ] *prep* con respecto a

re-gard-less [rɪ'gɑːrdlɪs] *adv* a pesar de todo; **regardless of** sin tener en cuenta

re-gime [reɪ'ʒiːm] *(government)* régimen *m*

re·gi·ment ['redʒɪmənt] n regimiento m

re·gion ['riːdʒən] región f; **in the region of** del orden de

re·gion·al ['riːdʒənl] adj regional

re·gis·ter ['redʒɪstər] **1** n registro m; at school lista f **2** v/t birth, death registrar; vehicle matricular; letter certificar; emotion mostrar; **send a letter registered** enviar una carta por correo certificado **3** v/i at university, for a course matricularse; with police registrarse

re·gis·tered let·ter ['redʒɪstərd] carta f certificada

re·gis·tra·tion [redʒɪ'streɪʃn] registro m; at university, for course matriculación f

re·gis·tra·tion num·ber Br MOT (número m de) matrícula f

re·gret [rɪ'gret] **1** v/t (pret & pp **regretted**) lamentar, sentir **2** n arrepentimiento m, pesar m

re·gret·ful [rɪ'gretfəl] adj arrepentido

re·gret·ful·ly [rɪ'gretfəlɪ] adv lamentablemente

re·gret·ta·ble [rɪ'gretəbl] adj lamentable

re·gret·ta·bly [rɪ'gretəblɪ] adv lamentablemente

reg·u·lar ['regjʊlər] **1** adj regular; (normal, ordinary) normal **2** n at bar etc habitual m/f

reg·u·lar·i·ty [regjʊ'lærətɪ] regularidad f

reg·u·lar·ly ['regjʊlərlɪ] adv regularmente

reg·u·late ['regʊleɪt] v/t regular

reg·u·la·tion [regʊ'leɪʃn] (rule) regla f, norma f

re·hab ['riːhæb] F rehabilitación f

re·ha·bil·i·tate [riːhə'bɪlɪteɪt] v/t ex-criminal rehabilitar

re·hears·al [rɪ'hɜːrsl] ensayo m

re·hearse [rɪ'hɜːrs] v/t & v/i ensayar

reign [reɪn] **1** n reinado m **2** v/i reinar

re·im·burse [riːɪm'bɜːrs] v/t reembolsar

rein [reɪn] rienda f

re·in·car·na·tion [riːɪnkɑːr'neɪʃn] reencarnación f

re·in·force [riːɪn'fɔːrs] v/t structure reforzar; beliefs reafirmar

re·in·forced con·crete [riːɪn'fɔːrst] hormigón m armado

re·in·force·ments [riːɪn'fɔːrsmənts] npl MIL refuerzos mpl

re·in·state [riːɪn'steɪt] v/t person in office reincorporar; paragraph in text volver a colocar

re·it·e·rate [riː'ɪtəreɪt] v/t fml reiterar

re·ject [rɪ'dʒekt] v/t rechazar

re·jec·tion [rɪ'dʒekʃn] rechazo m; **he felt a sense of rejection** se sintió rechazado

re·lapse ['riːlæps] n MED recaída f; **have a relapse** sufrir una recaída

re·late [rɪ'leɪt] **1** v/t story relatar, narrar; **relate sth to sth** connect relacionar algo con algo **2** v/i: **relate to** be connected with estar relacionado con; **he doesn't relate to people** no se relaciona fácilmente con la gente

re·lat·ed [rɪ'leɪtɪd] adj by family emparentado; events, ideas etc relacionado; **are you two related?** ¿sois parientes?

re·la·tion [rɪ'leɪʃn] in family pariente m/f; (connection) relación f; **business / diplomatic relations** relaciones fpl comerciales / diplomáticas

re·la·tion·ship [rɪ'leɪʃnʃɪp] relación f

rel·a·tive ['relətɪv] **1** n pariente m/f **2** adj relativo; **X is relative to Y** X está relacionado con Y

rel·a·tive·ly ['relətɪvlɪ] adv relativamente

re·lax [rɪ'læks] **1** v/i relajarse; **relax!, don't get angry** ¡tranquilízate!, no te enfades **2** v/t muscle, pace relajar

re·lax·a·tion [riːlæk'seɪʃn] relajación f; **what do you do for relaxation?** ¿qué haces para relajarte?

re·laxed [rɪ'lækst] adj relajado

re·lax·ing [rɪ'læksɪŋ] adj relajante

re·lay [riː'leɪ] **1** v/t message pasar; radio, TV signals retransmitir **2** n: **relay (race)** carrera f de relevos

re·lease [rɪ'liːs] **1** n from prison liberación f, puesta f en libertad; of CD etc lanzamiento m; CD, record trabajo m **2** v/t prisoner liberar, poner en libertad; parking brake soltar; information hacer público

rel·e·gate ['relɪgeɪt] v/t relegar

re·lent [rɪ'lent] v/i ablandarse, ceder

re·lent·less [rɪ'lentlɪs] adj (determined) implacable; rain etc que no cesa re·lent·less·ly [rɪ'lentlɪslɪ] *adv* implacablemente; *rain* sin cesar

rel·e·vance ['reləvəns] pertinencia *f*

rel·e·vant ['reləvənt] *adj* pertinente

re·li·a·bil·i·ty [rɪlaɪə'bɪlətɪ] fiabilidad *f*

re·li·a·ble [rɪ'laɪəbl] *adj* fiable; *information* fiable, fidedigna

re·li·a·bly [rɪ'laɪəblɪ] *adv*: *I am reliably informed that* sé de buena fuente que

re·li·ance [rɪ'laɪəns] confianza *f*, dependencia *f*; *reliance on s.o./sth* confianza en alguien / algo, dependencia de alguien / algo

re·li·ant [rɪ'laɪənt] *adj*: *be reliant on* depender de

rel·ic ['relɪk] reliquia *f*

re·lief [rɪ'liːf] alivio *m*; *that's a relief* qué alivio; *in relief* in *art* en relieve

re·lieve [rɪ'liːv] *v/t* *pressure, pain* aliviar; *(take over from)* relevar; *be relieved at news etc* sentirse aliviado

re·li·gion [rɪ'lɪdʒən] religión *f*

re·li·gious [rɪ'lɪdʒəs] *adj* religioso

re·li·gious·ly [rɪ'lɪdʒəslɪ] *adv* *(conscientiously)* religiosamente

re·lin·quish [rɪ'lɪŋkwɪʃ] *v/t* renunciar a

rel·ish ['relɪʃ] **1** *n* *sauce* salsa *f*; *(enjoyment)* goce *m* **2** *v/t* *idea, prospect* gozar con; *I don't relish the idea* la idea no me entusiasma

re·live [riː'lɪv] *v/t* *the past, an event* revivir

re·lo·cate [riːlə'keɪt] *v/i* *of business, employee* trasladarse

re·lo·ca·tion [riːlə'keɪʃn] *of business, employee* traslado *m*

re·luc·tance [rɪ'lʌktəns] reticencia *f*

re·luc·tant [rɪ'lʌktənt] *adj* reticente, reacio; *be reluctant to do sth* ser reacio a hacer algo

re·luc·tant·ly [rɪ'lʌktəntlɪ] *adv* con reticencia

◆ re·ly on [rɪ'laɪ] *v/t* *(pret & pp relied)* depender de; *rely on s.o. to do sth* contar con alguien para hacer algo

re·main [rɪ'meɪn] *v/i* *(be left)* quedar, MATH restar; *(stay)* permanecer

re·main·der [rɪ'meɪndər] **1** *n also* MATH resto *m* **2** *v/t* vender como saldo

re·main·ing [rɪ'meɪnɪŋ] *adj* restante

re·mains [rɪ'meɪnz] *npl* *of body* restos *mpl* *(mortales)*

re·make ['riːmeɪk] *n* *of movie* nueva versión *f*

re·mand [rɪ'mænd] **1** *v/t*: *remand s.o. in custody* poner a alguien en prisión preventiva **2** *n*: *be on remand in prison* estar en prisión preventiva; *on bail* estar en libertad bajo fianza

re·mark [rɪ'mɑːrk] **1** *n* comentario *m*, observación *f* **2** *v/t* comentar, observar

re·mar·ka·ble [rɪ'mɑːrkəbl] *adj* notable, extraordinario

re·mark·a·bly [rɪ'mɑːrkəblɪ] *adv* extraordinariamente

re·mar·ry [riː'mærɪ] *v/i* *(pret & pp remarried)* volver a casarse

rem·e·dy ['remədɪ] *n* MED, *fig* remedio *m*

re·mem·ber [rɪ'membər] **1** *v/t* *s.o., sth* recordar, acordarse de; *remember to lock the door* acuérdate de cerrar la puerta; *remember me to her* dale recuerdos de mi parte **2** *v/i* recordar, acordarse; *I don't remember* no recuerdo, no me acuerdo

re·mind [rɪ'maɪnd] *v/t*: *remind s.o. of sth* recordar algo a alguien; *remind s.o. of s.o.* recordar alguien a alguien; *you remind me of your father* me recuerdas a tu padre

re·mind·er [rɪ'maɪndər] recordatorio *m*; *for payment* recordatorio *m* de pago

rem·i·nisce [remɪ'nɪs] *v/i* contar recuerdos

rem·i·nis·cent [remɪ'nɪsənt] *adj*: *be reminiscent of sth* recordar a algo, tener reminiscencias de algo

re·miss [rɪ'mɪs] *adj* *fml* negligente, descuidado

re·mis·sion [rɪ'mɪʃn] remisión *f*; *go into remission* MED remitir

rem·nant ['remnənt] resto *m*

re·morse [rɪ'mɔːrs] remordimientos *mpl*

re·morse·less [rɪ'mɔːrslɪs] *adj* *person* despiadado; *pace, demands* implacable

re·mote [rɪ'moʊt] *adj* *village, possibility* remoto; *(aloof)* distante; *ancestor* lejano

re·mote 'ac·cess COMPUT acceso *m* remoto

re·mote con'trol control *m* remoto; *for* TV mando *m* a distancia

re·mote·ly [rɪ'moʊtlɪ] *adv related, connected* remotamente; *it's just remotely possible* es una posibilidad muy remota

re·mote·ness [rɪ'moʊtnəs]: *the remoteness of the house* la lejanía *or* lo aislado de la casa

re·mov·a·ble [rɪ'muːvəbl] *adj* de quita y pon

re·mov·al [rɪ'muːvl] eliminación *f*

re·move [rɪ'muːv] *v/t* eliminar; *top, lid* quitar; *coat etc* quitarse; *doubt, suspicion* despejar; *growth, organ* extirpar

re·mu·ner·a·tion [rɪmjuːnə'reɪʃn] remuneración *f*

re·mu·ner·a·tive [rɪ'mjuːnərətɪv] *adj* bien remunerado

re·name [riː'neɪm] *v/t* cambiar el nombre a

ren·der ['rendər] *v/t service* prestar; *render s.o. helpless / unconscious* dejar a alguien indefenso / inconsciente

ren·der·ing ['rendərɪŋ] *of piece of music* interpretación *f*

ren·dez·vous ['rɑːndeɪvuː] *romantic* cita *f*; MIL encuentro *m*

re·new [rɪ'nuː] *v/t contract, license* renovar; *discussions* reanudar; *feel renewed* sentirse como nuevo

re·new·al [rɪ'nuːəl] *of contract etc* renovación *f*; *of discussions* reanudación *f*

re·nounce [rɪ'naʊns] *v/t title, rights* renunciar a

ren·o·vate ['renəveɪt] *v/t* renovar

ren·o·va·tion [renə'veɪʃn] renovación *f*

re·nown [rɪ'naʊn] renombre *m*

re·nowned [rɪ'naʊnd] *adj* renombrado; *be renowned for sth* ser célebre por algo

rent [rent] **1** *n* alquiler *m*; *for rent* se alquila **2** *v/t apartment, car, equipment* alquilar, *Mex* rentar

rent·al ['rentl] *for apartment, for* TV alquiler *m*, *Mex* renta *f*

'rent·al a·gree·ment acuerdo *m* de alquiler

'rent·al car coche *m* de alquiler

rent-'free *adv* sin pagar alquiler

re·o·pen [riː'oʊpn] **1** *v/t* reabrir; *negotiations* reanudar **2** *v/i of theater etc* volver a abrir

re·or·gan·i·za·tion [riːɔːrgənaɪz'eɪʃn] reorganización *f*

re·or·gan·ize [riː'ɔːrgənaɪz] *v/t* reorganizar

rep [rep] COM representante *m/f*, comercial *m/f*

re·paint [riː'peɪnt] *v/t* repintar

re·pair [rɪ'per] **1** *v/t fence, clothes* reparar; *shoes* arreglar **2** *n to fence,* TV reparación *f*; *of shoes* arreglo *m*; *in a good / bad state of repair* en buen / mal estado

re'pair·man técnico *m*

re·pa·tri·ate [riː'pætrɪeɪt] *v/t* repatriar

re·pa·tri·a·tion [riː'pætrɪ'eɪʃn] repatriación *f*

re·pay [riː'peɪ] *v/t (pret & pp repaid) money* devolver; *person* pagar

re·pay·ment [riː'peɪmənt] devolución *f*; *installment* plazo *m*

re·peal [rɪ'piːl] *v/t law* revocar

re·peat [rɪ'piːt] **1** *v/t* repetir; *am I repeating myself?* ¿me estoy repitiendo? **2** *n* TV *program etc* repetición *f*

re·peat 'busi·ness COM negocio *m* que se repite

re·peat·ed [rɪ'piːtɪd] *adj* repetido

re·peat·ed·ly [rɪ'piːtɪdlɪ] *adv* repetidamente, repetidas veces

re·peat 'or·der COM pedido *m* repetido

re·pel [rɪ'pel] *v/t (pret & pp repelled) invaders, attack* rechazar; *insects* repeler, ahuyentar; *(disgust)* repeler, repugnar

re·pel·lent [rɪ'pelənt] **1** *n (insect repellent)* repelente *m* **2** *adj* repelente, repugnante

re·pent [rɪ'pent] *v/i* arrepentirse

re·per·cus·sions [riːpər'kʌʃnz] *npl* repercusiones *fpl*

rep·er·toire ['repərtwɑːr] repertorio *m*

rep·e·ti·tion [repɪ'tɪʃn] repetición *f*

rep·e·ti·tive [rɪ'petɪtɪv] *adj* repetitivo

re·place [rɪ'pleɪs] *v/t (put back)* volver a poner; *(take the place of)* reemplazar, sustituir

re·place·ment [rɪ'pleɪsmənt] *n person* sustituto(-a) *m(f)*; *thing* recambio *m*, reemplazo *m* re·place·ment 'part (pieza *f* de) recambio *m*

re·play ['ri:pleɪ] **1** *n recording* repetición *f* (de la jugada); *match* repetición *f* (del partido) **2** *v/t match* repetir

re·plen·ish [rɪ'plenɪʃ] *v/t container* rellenar; *supplies* reaprovisionar

rep·li·ca ['replɪkə] réplica *f*

re·ply [rɪ'plaɪ] **1** *n* respuesta *f*, contestación *f* **2** *v/t & v/i* (*pret & pp* replied) responder, contestar

re·port [rɪ'pɔ:rt] **1** *n* (*account*) informe *m*; *by journalist* reportaje *m* **2** *v/t facts* informar; *to authorities* informar de, dar parte de; *report a person to the police* denunciar a alguien a la policía; *he is reported to be in Washington* se dice que está en Washington **3** *v/i of journalist* informar; (*present o.s.*) presentarse (*to* ante)
♦ report to *v/t in business* trabajar a las órdenes de

re'port card boletín *m* de evaluación

re·port·er [rɪ'pɔ:rtər] reportero(-a) *m(f)*

re·pos·sess [ri:pə'zes] *v/t* COM embargar

rep·re·hen·si·ble [reprɪ'hensəbl] *adj* recriminable

rep·re·sent [reprɪ'zent] *v/t* representar

rep·re·sen·ta·tive [reprɪ'zentətɪv] **1** *n* representante *m/f*; POL representante *m/f*, diputado(-a) *m(f)/* **2** *adj* (*typical*) representativo

re·press [rɪ'pres] *v/t revolt* reprimir; *feelings, laughter* reprimir, controlar

re·pres·sion [rɪ'preʃn] POL represión *f*

re·pres·sive [rɪ'presɪv] *adj* POL represivo

re·prieve [rɪ'pri:v] **1** *n* LAW indulto *m*; *fig* aplazamiento *m* **2** *v/t prisoner* indultar

rep·ri·mand ['reprɪmænd] *v/t* reprender

re·print ['ri:prɪnt] **1** *n* reimpresión *f* **2** *v/t* reimprimir

re·pri·sal [rɪ'praɪzl] represalia *f*; *take reprisals* tomar represalias; *in reprisal for* en represalia por

re·proach [rɪ'prəʊtʃ] **1** *n* reproche *m*; *be beyond reproach* ser irreprochable **2** *v/t*: *reproach s.o. for sth* reprochar algo a alguien

re·proach·ful [rɪ'prəʊtʃfəl] *adj* de reproc-

he

re·proach·ful·ly [rɪ'prəʊtʃfəlɪ] *adv look* con una mirada de reproche; *say* con tono de reproche

re·pro·duce [ri:prə'du:s], **1** *v/t atmosphere, mood* reproducir **2** *v/i* BIO reproducirse

re·pro·duc·tion [ri:prə'dʌkʃn] reproducción *f*

re·pro·duc·tive [rɪprə'dʌktɪv] *adj* reproductivo

rep·tile ['reptaɪl] reptil *m*

re·pub·lic [rɪ'pʌblɪk] república *f*

re·pub·li·can [rɪ'pʌblɪkn] **1** *n* republicano(-a) *m(f)* **2** *adj* republicano

re·pu·di·ate [rɪ'pju:dɪeɪt] *v/t* (*deny*) rechazar

re·pul·sive [rɪ'pʌlsɪv] *adj* repulsivo

rep·u·ta·ble ['repjʊtəbl] *adj* reputado, acreditado

rep·u·ta·tion [repjʊ'teɪʃn] reputación *f*; *have a good / bad reputation* tener una buena / mala reputación

re·put·ed [rep'jʊtəd] *adj*: *be reputed to be* tener fama de ser

re·put·ed·ly [rep'jʊtədlɪ] *adv* según se dice

re·quest [rɪ'kwest] **1** *n* petición *f*, solicitud *f*; *on request* por encargo **2** *v/t* pedir, solicitar

re·quiem ['rekwɪəm] MUS réquiem *m*

re·quire [rɪ'kwaɪr] *v/t* (*need*) requerir, necesitar; *it requires great care* se requiere mucho cuidado; *as required by law* como estipula la ley; *guests are required to ...* se ruega a los los invitados que ...

re·quired [rɪ'kwaɪrd] *adj* (*necessary*) necesario

re·quire·ment [rɪ'kwaɪrmənt] (*need*) necesidad *f*; (*condition*) requisito *m*

req·ui·si·tion [rekwɪ'zɪʃn] *v/t* requisar

re·route [ri:'ru:t] *v/t airplane etc* desviar

re·run ['ri:rʌn] **1** *n of* TV *program* reposición *f* **2** *v/t* (*pret* reran, *pp* rerun) *tape* volver a poner

re·sched·ule [ri:'ʃedu:l] *v/t* volver a programar

res·cue ['reskju:] **1** *n* rescate *m*; *come to*

s.o.'s rescue acudir al rescate de alguien **2** *v/t* rescatar

'res·cue par·ty equipo *m* de rescate

re·search [rɪˈsɜːrtʃ] *n* investigación *f*

♦ **research into** *v/t* investigar

re·search and de·vel·op·ment investigación *f* y desarrollo

re'search as·sist·ant ayudante *m/f* de investigación

re·search·er [rɪˈsɜːrtʃər] investigador(a) *m(f)*

re'search proj·ect proyecto *m* de investigación

re·sem·blance [rɪˈzembləns] parecido *m*, semejanza *f*

re·sem·ble [rɪˈzembl] *v/t* parecerse a

re·sent [rɪˈzent] *v/t* estar molesto por

re·sent·ful [rɪˈzentfəl] *adj* resentido

re·sent·ful·ly [rɪˈzentfəlɪ] *adv* con resentimiento

re·sent·ment [rɪˈzentmənt] resentimiento *m*

res·er·va·tion [rezərˈveɪʃn] reserva *f*; **I have a reservation** *in hotel, restaurant* tengo una reserva

re·serve [rɪˈzɜːrv] **1** *n* reserva *f*; SP reserva *m/f*; **reserves** FIN reservas *fpl*; **keep sth in reserve** tener algo en la reserva **2** *v/t seat, table* reservar; *judgment* reservarse

re·served [rɪˈzɜːrvd] *adj table, manner* reservado

res·er·voir [ˈrezərvwɑːr] *for water* embalse *m*, pantano *m*

re·shuf·fle [ˈriːʃʌfl] **1** *n* POL remodelación *f* **2** *v/t* POL remodelar

re·side [rɪˈzaɪd] *v/i fml* residir

res·i·dence [ˈrezɪdəns] (*fml: house etc*) residencia *f*; (*stay*) estancia *f*

'res·i·dence per·mit permiso *m* de residencia

'res·i·dent [ˈrezɪdənt] **1** *n* residente *m/f* **2** *adj* (*living in a building*) residente

res·i·den·tial [rezɪˈdenʃl] *adj district* residencial

res·i·due [ˈrezɪduː] residuo *m*

re·sign [rɪˈzaɪn] **1** *v/t position* dimitir de; **resign o.s. to** resignarse a **2** *v/i from job* dimitir

res·ig·na·tion [rezɪgˈneɪʃn] *from job* dimisión *f*; *mental* resignación *f*

re·signed [rɪˈzaɪnd] *adj* resignado; **we have become resigned to the fact that** ... nos hemos resignado a aceptar que ...

re·sil·i·ent [rɪˈzɪliənt] *adj personality* fuerte; *material* resistente

res·in [ˈrezɪn] resina *f*

re·sist [rɪˈzɪst] **1** *v/t* resistir; *new measures* oponer resistencia a **2** *v/i* resistir

re·sist·ance [rɪˈzɪstəns] resistencia *f*

re·sis·tant [rɪˈzɪstənt] *adj material* resistente; **resistant to heat / rust** resistente al calor/a la oxidación

res·o·lute [ˈrezəluːt] *adj* resuelto

res·o·lu·tion [rezəˈluːʃn] resolución *f*; *made at New Year etc* propósito *m*

re·solve [rɪˈzɑːlv] *v/t problem, mystery* resolver; **resolve to do sth** resolver hacer algo

re·sort [rɪˈzɔːrt] *n place* centro *m* turístico; **as a last resort** como último recurso

♦ **resort to** *v/t violence, threats* recurrir a

♦ **re·sound with** [rɪˈzaʊnd] *v/t* resonar con

re·sound·ing [rɪˈzaʊndɪŋ] *adj success, victory* clamoroso

re·source [rɪˈsɔːrs] recurso *m*; **leave s.o. to his own resources** dejar que alguien se las arregle solo

re·source·ful [rɪˈsɔːrsfəl] *adj person* lleno de recursos; *attitude, approach* ingenioso

re·spect [rɪˈspekt] **1** *n* respeto *m*; **show respect to** mostrar respeto hacia; **with respect to** con respecto a; **in this / that respect** en cuanto a esto / eso; **in many respects** en muchos aspectos; **pay one's last respects to s.o.** decir el último adiós a alguien **2** *v/t* respetar

re·spect·a·bil·i·ty [rɪspektəˈbɪlətɪ] respetabilidad *f*

re·spect·a·ble [rɪˈspektəbl] *adj* respetable

re·spect·a·bly [rɪˈspektəblɪ] *adv* respetablemente

re·spect·ful [rɪˈspektfəl] *adj* respetuoso

re·spect·ful·ly [rɪˈspektfəlɪ] *adv* respetuosamente, con respeto

re·spec·tive [rɪˈspektɪv] *adj* respectivo

re·spec·tive·ly [rɪˈspektɪvlɪ] *adv* respectivamente

res·pi·ra·tion [respɪ'reɪʃn] respiración f

res·pi·ra·tor [respɪ'reɪtər] MED respirador m

re·spite ['respaɪt] respiro m; *without respite* sin respiro

re·spond [rɪ'spɑːnd] v/i responder

re·sponse [rɪ'spɑːns] respuesta f

re·spon·si·bil·i·ty [rɪspɑːnsɪ'bɪlətɪ] responsabilidad f; *accept responsibility for* aceptar responsabilidad de; *a job with more responsibility* un trabajo con más responsabilidad

re·spon·si·ble [rɪ'spɑːnsəbl] adj reponsable (*for* de); *job* de responsabilidad

re·spon·sive [rɪ'spɑːnsɪv] adj *brakes* que responde bien; *a responsive audience* una audiencia que muestra interés

rest[1] [rest] **1** n descanso m; *he needs a rest* necesita descansar; *set s.o.'s mind at rest* tranquilizar a alguien **2** v/i descansar; *rest on* of theory, box apoyarse en; *it all rests with him* todo depende de él **3** v/t (*lean, balance*) apoyar

rest[2] [rest]: *the rest* el resto

res·tau·rant ['restrɑːnt] restaurante m

'res·tau·rant car vagón m or coche m restaurante

'rest cure cura f de reposo or descanso

rest·ful ['restfəl] adj tranquilo, relajante

'rest home residencia f de ancianos

rest·less ['restlɪs] adj inquieto; *have a restless night* pasar una mala noche

rest·less·ly ['restlɪslɪ] adv sin descanso

res·to·ra·tion [restə'reɪʃn] restauración f

re·store [rɪ'stɔːr] v/t *building etc* restaurar; (*bring back*) devolver

re·strain [rɪ'streɪn] v/t contener; *restrain o.s.* contenerse

re·straint [rɪ'streɪnt] (*moderation*) moderación f, comedimiento m

re·strict [rɪ'strɪkt] v/t restringir, limitar; *I'll restrict myself to …* me limitaré a …

re·strict·ed [rɪ'strɪktɪd] adj *view* limitado

re·strict·ed 'ar·e·a MIL zona f de acceso restringido

re·stric·tion [rɪ'strɪkʃn] restricción f, limitación f; *place restrictions upon s.o.* imponer restricciones or limitaciones a

alguien

'rest room Am aseo m, servicios mpl

re·sult [rɪ'zʌlt] n resultado m; *as a result of this* como resultado de esto

◆ **result from** v/t resultar de

◆ **result in** v/t tener como resultado

re·sume [rɪ'zjuːm] **1** v/t reanudar **2** v/i continuar

ré·su·mé ['rezumeɪ] currículum m (vitae)

re·sump·tion [rɪ'zʌmpʃn] reanudación f

re·sur·face [riː'sɜːfɪs] **1** v/t *roads* volver a asfaltar **2** v/i (*reappear*) reaparecer

res·ur·rec·tion [rezə'rekʃn] REL resurrección f

re·sus·ci·tate [rɪ'sʌsɪteɪt] v/t resucitar, revivir

re·sus·ci·ta·tion [rɪsʌsɪ'teɪʃn] resucitación f

re·tail ['riːteɪl] **1** adv: *sell sth retail* vender algo al por menor **2** v/i: *retail at …* su precio de venta al público es de …

re·tail·er ['riːteɪlər] minorista m/f

're·tail out·let punto m de venta

're·tail price precio m de venta al público

re·tain [rɪ'teɪn] v/t conservar; *heat* retener

re·tain·er [rɪ'teɪnər] FIN anticipo m

re·tal·i·ate [rɪ'tælɪeɪt] v/i tomar represalias

re·tal·i·a·tion [rɪtælɪ'eɪʃn] represalias fpl; *in retaliation for* como represalia por

re·tard·ed [rɪ'tɑːrdɪd] adj *mentally* retrasado mental

re·think [riː'θɪŋk] v/t (*pret & pp rethought*) replantear

ret·i·cence ['retɪsns] reserva f

ret·i·cent ['retɪsnt] adj reservado

re·tire [rɪ'taɪr] v/i *from work* jubilarse

re·tired [rɪ'taɪrd] adj jubilado

re·tire·ment [rɪ'taɪrmənt] jubilación f

re'tire·ment age edad f de jubilación

re·tir·ing [rɪ'taɪrɪŋ] adj retraído, reservado

re·tort [rɪ'tɔːrt] **1** n réplica f **2** v/t replicar

re·trace [rɪ'treɪs] v/t: *they retraced their footsteps* volvieron sobre sus pasos

re·tract [rɪ'trækt] v/t *claws* retraer; *undercarriage* replegar; *statement* retirar

re·train [riː'treɪn] v/i reciclarse

re·treat [rɪ'triːt] **1** v/i retirarse **2** n MIL retirada *f*; *place* retiro *m*

re·trieve [rɪˈtriːv] *v/t* recuperar

re·triev·er [rɪˈtriːvər] *dog* perro *m* cobrador

ret·ro·ac·tive [retroʊˈæktɪv] *adj law etc* retroactivo

ret·ro·ac·tive·ly [retroʊˈæktɪvlɪ] *adv* con retroactividad

ret·ro·grade [ˈretrəgreɪd] *adj move, decision* retrógrado

ret·ro·spect [ˈretrəspekt]: *in retrospect* en retrospectiva

ret·ro·spec·tive [retrəˈspektɪv] *n* retrospectiva *f*

re·turn [rɪˈtɜːrn] **1** *n to a place* vuelta *f*, regreso *m*; *(giving back)* devolución *f*; COMPUT retorno *m*; *in tennis* resto *m*; *(profit)* rendimiento *m*; *Br ticket* billete *m or L.Am.* boleto *m* de ida y vuelta; *by return (of post)* a vuelta de correo; *many happy returns (of the day)* feliz cumpleaños; *in return for* a cambio de **2** *v/t (give back)* devolver; *(put back)* volver a colocar **3** *v/i (go back, come back)* volver, regresar; *of good times, doubts etc* volver

re·turn 'flight vuelo *m* de vuelta

re·turn 'jour·ney viaje *m* de vuelta

re·u·ni·fi·ca·tion [riːjuːnɪfɪˈkeɪʃn] reunificación *f*

re·u·nion [riːˈjuːnjən] reunión *f*

re·u·nite [riːjuːˈnaɪt] *v/t* reunir

re·us·a·ble [riːˈjuːzəbl] *adj* reutilizable

re·use [riːˈjuːz] *v/t* reutilizar

rev [rev] *n* revolución *f*; *revs per minute* revoluciones por minuto

◆ **rev up** *v/t (pret & pp revved) engine* revolucionar

re·val·u·a·tion [riːvæljuˈeɪʃn] revaluación *f*

re·veal [rɪˈviːl] *v/t (make visible)* revelar; *(make known)* revelar, desvelar

re·veal·ing [rɪˈviːlɪŋ] *adj remark* revelador; *dress* insinuante, atrevido

◆ **rev·el in** [ˈrevl] *v/t (pret & pp reveled, Br revelled)* deleitarse con

rev·e·la·tion [revəˈleɪʃn] revelación *f*

re·venge [rɪˈvendʒ] *n* venganza *f*; *take one's revenge* vengarse; *in revenge for* como venganza por

rev·e·nue [ˈrevənuː] ingresos *mpl*

re·ver·be·rate [rɪˈvɜːrbəreɪt] *v/i of sound* reverberar

re·vere [rɪˈvɪr] *v/t* reverenciar

rev·e·rence [ˈrevərəns] reverencia *f*

Rev·e·rend [ˈrevərənd] REL Reverendo *m*

rev·e·rent [ˈrevərənt] *adj* reverente

re·verse [rɪˈvɜːrs] **1** *adj sequence* inverso; *in reverse order* en orden inverso **2** *n (back)* dorso *m*; MOT marcha *f* atrás; *the reverse (the opposite)* lo contrario **3** *v/t sequence* invertir; *reverse a vehicle* hacer marcha atrás con un vehículo **4** *v/i* MOT hacer marcha atrás

re·vert [rɪˈvɜːrt] *v/i: revert to* volver a

re·view [rɪˈvjuː] **1** *n of book, movie* reseña *f*, crítica *f*; *of troops* revista *f*; *of situation etc* revisión *f* **2** *v/t book, movie* reseñar, hacer una crítica de; *troops* pasar revista a; *situation etc* revisar; EDU repasar

re·view·er [rɪˈvjuːər] *of book, movie* crítico(-a) *m(f)*

re·vise [rɪˈvaɪz] *v/t opinion, text* revisar

re·vi·sion [rɪˈvɪʒn] *of opinion, text* revisión *f*

re·viv·al [rɪˈvaɪvl] *of custom, old style etc* resurgimiento *m*; *of patient* reanimación *f*

re·vive [rɪˈvaɪv] **1** *v/t custom, old style etc* hacer resurgir; *patient* reanimar **2** *v/i of business, exchange rate etc* reactivarse

re·voke [rɪˈvoʊk] *v/t law* derogar; *license* revocar

re·volt [rɪˈvoʊlt] **1** *n* rebelión *f* **2** *v/i* rebelarse

re·volt·ing [rɪˈvoʊltɪŋ] *adj (disgusting)* repugnante

rev·o·lu·tion [revəˈluːʃn] POL revolución *f*; *(turn)* vuelta *f*, revolución *f*

rev·o·lu·tion·a·ry [revəˈluːʃnərɪ] **1** *n* POL revolucionario(-a) *m(f)* **2** *adj* revolucionario

rev·o·lu·tion·ize [revəˈluːʃnaɪz] *v/t* revolucionar

re·volve [rɪˈvɑːlv] *v/i* girar *(around* en torno a)

re·volv·er [rɪˈvɑːlvər] revólver *m*

re·volv·ing 'door [rɪˈvɑːlvɪŋ] puerta *f* giratoria

re·vue [rɪ'vjuː] THEA revista *f*

re·vul·sion [rɪ'vʌlʃn] repugnancia *f*

re·ward [rɪ'wɔːrd] **1** *n* recompensa *f* **2** *v/t financially* recompensar

re·ward·ing [rɪ'wɔːrdɪŋ] *adj experience* gratificante

re·wind [riː'waɪnd] *v/t (pret & pp re-wound) film, tape* rebobinar

re·write [riː'raɪt] *v/t (pret rewrote, pp rewritten)* reescribir

rhe·to·ric ['retərɪk] retórica *f*

rhe·to·ric·al 'ques·tion [rɪ'tɑːrɪkl] pregunta *f* retórica

rheu·ma·tism ['ruːmətɪzm] reumatismo *m*

rhi·no·ce·ros [raɪ'nɑːsərəs] rinoceronte *m*

rhu·barb ['ruːbɑːrb] ruibarbo *m*

rhyme [raɪm] **1** *n* rima *f* **2** *v/i* rimar

rhythm ['rɪðm] ritmo *m*

rib [rɪb] ANAT costilla *f*

rib·bon ['rɪbən] cinta *f*

rice [raɪs] arroz *m*

rich [rɪtʃ] **1** *adj (wealthy)* rico; *food* sabroso; **it's too rich** es muy pesado **2** *n:* **the rich** los ricos

rich·ly ['rɪtʃlɪ] *adv:* **be richly deserved** ser muy merecido

rick·et·y ['rɪkətɪ] *adj* desvencijado

ric·o·chet ['rɪkəʃeɪ] *v/i* rebotar

rid [rɪd]: **get rid of** deshacerse de

rid·dance ['rɪdns] F: **good riddance to her!** ¡espero no volver a verla nunca!

rid·den ['rɪdn] *pp* → **ride**

rid·dle ['rɪdl] **1** *n* acertijo *m* **2** *v/t:* **be riddled with** estar lleno de

ride [raɪd] **1** *n on horse, in vehicle* paseo *m*, vuelta *f*; *(journey)* viaje *m*; **do you want a ride into town?** ¿quieres que te lleve al centro? **2** *v/t (pret rode, pp ridden) horse* montar a; *bike* montar en **3** *v/i (pret rode, pp ridden) on horse* montar; **can you ride?** ¿sabes montar?; **those who were riding at the back of the bus** los que iban en la parte de atrás del autobús

rid·er ['raɪdər] *on horse* jinete *m*, amazona *f*; *on bicycle* ciclista *m/f*; *on motorbike*

motorista *m/f*

ridge [rɪdʒ] *raised strip* borde *m*; *of mountain* cresta *f*; *of roof* caballete *m*

rid·i·cule ['rɪdɪkjuːl] **1** *n* burlas *fpl* **2** *v/t* ridiculizar, poner en ridículo

ri·dic·u·lous [rɪ'dɪkjuləs] *adj* ridículo

ri·dic·u·lous·ly [rɪ'dɪkjuləslɪ] *adv expensive, difficult* terriblemente; **it's ridiculously easy** es facilísimo

rid·ing ['raɪdɪŋ] *on horseback* equitación *f*

ri·fle ['raɪfl] *n* rifle *m*

rift [rɪft] *in earth* grieta *f*; *in party etc* escisión *f*

rig [rɪg] **1** *n (oil rig)* plataforma *f* petrolífera; *(truck)* camión *m* **2** *v/t (pret & pp rigged) elections* amañar

right [raɪt] **1** *adj (correct)* correcto; *(suitable)* adecuado, apropiado; *(not left)* derecho; **it's not right to treat people like that** no está bien tratar así a la gente; **it's the right thing to do** es lo que hay que hacer; **be right** *of answer* estar correcto; *of person* tener razón; *of clock* ir bien; **put things right** arreglar las cosas; **that's right!** ¡eso es!; **that's all right** *doesn't matter* no te preocupes; *when s.o. says thank you* de nada; *is quite good* está bastante bien; **I'm all right** *not hurt* estoy bien; *have got enough* no, gracias; **all right, that's enough!** ¡ahora sí que ya está bien! **2** *adv (directly)* justo; *(correctly)* correctamente; *(not left)* a la derecha; **he broke it right off** lo rompió por completo; **right back in 1982** allá en 1982; **right now** ahora mismo **3** *n civil, legal etc* derecho *m*; *not left*, POL derecha *f*; **on the right** *also* POL a la derecha; **turn to the right, take a right** gira a la derecha; **be in the right** tener razón; **know right from wrong** distinguir lo que está bien de lo que está mal

right·'an·gle ángulo *m* recto; **at right-angles to** en *or* formando ángulo recto con

right·ful ['raɪtfəl] *adj heir, owner etc* legítimo

'right-hand *adj:* **on the right-hand side** a mano derecha

right-hand 'drive *n* MOT vehículo *m* con el volante a la derecha

R

right-hand·ed [raɪt'hændɪd] *adj person* diestro

right-hand 'man mano *f* derecha

right of 'way *in traffic* preferencia *f*; *across land* derecho *m* de paso

right 'wing *n* POL la derecha *f*; SP la banda derecha

right-'wing *adj* POL de derechas

right-wing ex'trem·ism POL extremismo *m* de derechas

right-'wing·er POL derechista *m/f*

rig·id ['rɪdʒɪd] *adj* rígido

rig·or ['rɪgər] *of discipline* rigor *m*; *the rigors of the winter* los rigores del invierno

rig·or·ous ['rɪgərəs] *adj* riguroso

rig·or·ous·ly ['rɪgərəslɪ] *adv check, examine* rigurosamente

rig·our *Br* → **rigor**

rile [raɪl] *v/t* F fastidiar, *Span* mosquear F

rim [rɪm] *of wheel* llanta *f*; *of cup* borde *m*; *of eye glasses* montura *f*

ring[1] [rɪŋ] *n* (*circle*) círculo *m*; *on finger* anillo *m*; *in boxing* cuadrilátero *m*, ring *m*; *at circus* pista *f*

ring[2] [rɪŋ] **1** *n of bell* timbrazo; *of voice* tono *m*; *give s.o. a ring* Br TELEC dar un telefonazo a alguien **2** *v/t* (*pret* **rang**, *pp* **rung**) *bell* hacer sonar **3** *v/i* (*pret* **rang**, *pp* **rung**) *of bell* sonar; *please ring for attention* toque el timbre para que le atiendan

'ring·lead·er cabecilla *m/f*

'ring-pull anilla *f*

rink [rɪŋk] pista *f* de patinaje

rinse [rɪns] **1** *n for hair color* reflejo *m* **2** *v/t* aclarar

ri·ot ['raɪət] **1** *n* disturbio *m* **2** *v/i* causar disturbios

ri·ot·er ['raɪətər] alborotador(a) *m(f)*

'riot police policía *f* antidisturbios

rip [rɪp] **1** *n in cloth etc* rasgadura *f* **2** *v/t* (*pret & pp* **ripped**) *cloth etc* rasgar; *rip sth open* romper algo rasgándolo

◆ **rip off** *v/t* F *customers* robar F, clavar F; (*cheat*) timar

◆ **rip up** *v/t letter, sheet* hacer pedazos

ripe [raɪp] *adj fruit* maduro

rip·en ['raɪpn] *v/i of fruit* madurar

ripe·ness ['raɪpnɪs] *of fruit* madurez *f*

'rip-off *n* F robo *m* F

rip·ple ['rɪpl] *on water* onda *f*

rise [raɪz] **1** *v/i* (*pret* **rose**, *pp* **risen**) *from chair etc* levantarse; *of sun* salir; *of rocket* ascender, subir; *of price, temperature, water* subir **2** *n in price, temperature* subida *f*, aumento *m*; *in water level* subida *f*; *in salary* aumento *m*; *give rise to* dar pie a

ris·en ['rɪzn] *pp* → **rise**

ris·er ['raɪzər]: *be an early riser* ser un madrugador; *be a late riser* levantarse tarde

risk [rɪsk] **1** *n* riesgo *m*, peligro *m*; *take a risk* arriesgarse **2** *v/t* arriesgar; *let's risk it* arriesguémonos

risk·y ['rɪskɪ] *adj* arriesgado

ris·qué [rɪ'skeɪ] *adj* subido de tono

rit·u·al ['rɪtʊəl] **1** *n* ritual *m* **2** *adj* ritual

ri·val ['raɪvl] **1** *n* rival *m/f* **2** *v/t* rivalizar con; *I can't rival that* no puedo rivalizar con eso

ri·val·ry ['raɪvlrɪ] rivalidad *f*

riv·er ['rɪvər] río *m*

'riv·er·bank ribera *f*

'riv·er·bed lecho *m*

Riv·er 'Plate *n*: *the River Plate* el Río de la Plata

'riv·er·side 1 *adj* a la orilla del río **2** *n* ribera *f*, orilla *f* del río

riv·et ['rɪvɪt] **1** *n* remache *m* **2** *v/t* remachar; *rivet sth to sth* unir algo a algo con remaches

riv·et·ing ['rɪvɪtɪŋ] *adj* fascinante

road [roʊd] *in country* carretera *f*; *in city* calle *f*; *it's just down the road* está muy cerca

'road·block control *m* de carretera

'road hog conductor(a) *temerario(-a)*

'road-hold·ing *of vehicle* adherencia *f*, agarre *m*

'road map mapa *m* de carreteras

road 'safe·ty seguridad *f* vial

'road·side: *at the roadside* al borde de la carretera

'road·sign señal *f* de tráfico

'road·way calzada *f*

'road·wor·thy *adj* en condiciones de circular

roam [roʊm] *v/i* vagar

roar [rɔːr] **1** *n of traffic, engine* estruendo *m; of lion* rugido *m; of person* grito *m,* bramido *m* **2** *v/i of engine, lion* rugir; *of person* gritar, bramar; ***roar with laughter*** reírse a carcajadas

roast [roʊst] **1** *n of beef etc* asado *m* **2** *v/t* asar **3** *v/i of food* asarse; ***we're roasting*** nos estamos asando

roast 'beef rosbif *m*

'roast·ing tin [roʊstɪŋ] fuente *f* para asar

roast 'pork cerdo *m* asado

rob [rɑːb] *v/t* (*pret & pp* **robbed**) *person* robar a; *bank* atracar, robar; ***I've been robbed*** me han robado

rob·ber ['rɑːbər] atracador(a) *m(f)*

rob·ber·y ['rɑːbərɪ] atraco *m,* robo *m*

robe [roʊb] *of judge* toga *f; of priest* sotana *f;* (*bathrobe*) bata *f*

rob·in ['rɑːbɪn] petirrojo *m*

ro·bot ['roʊbɑːt] robot *m*

ro·bust [roʊ'bʌst] *adj person, structure* robusto; *material* resistente; ***be in robust health*** tener una salud de hierro

rock [rɑːk] **1** *n roca f; MUS* rock *m;* ***on the rocks*** *of drink* con hielo; ***their marriage is on the rocks*** su matrimonio está en crisis **2** *v/t baby* acunar; *cradle* mecer; (*surprise*) sorprender, impactar **3** *v/i on chair* mecerse; *of boat* balancearse

'rock band grupo *m* de rock

rock 'bot·tom: ***reach rock bottom*** tocar fondo

'rock-bot·tom *adj prices* mínimo

'rock climb·er escalador(a) *m(f)*

'rock climb·ing escalada *f* (en roca)

rock·et ['rɑːkɪt] **1** *n* cohete *m* **2** *v/i of prices etc* dispararse

'rock·ing chair ['rɑːkɪŋ] mecedora *f*

'rock·ing horse caballito *m* de juguete

rock 'n roll [rɑːkn'roʊl] rock and roll *m*

'rock star estrella *f* del rock

rock·y ['rɑːkɪ] *adj beach, path* pedregoso

rod [rɑːd] vara *f; for fishing* caña *f*

rode [roʊd] *pret* → **ride**

ro·dent ['roʊdnt] roedor *m*

rogue [roʊg] granuja *m/f,* bribón(-ona) *m(f)*

role [roʊl] papel *m*

'role mod·el ejemplo *m*

roll [roʊl] **1** *n* (*bread roll*) panecillo *m; of film* rollo *m; of thunder* retumbo *m;* (*list, register*) lista *f* **2** *v/i of ball etc* rodar; *of boat* balancearse **3** *v/t:* ***roll sth into a ball*** hacer una bola con algo; ***roll sth along the ground*** hacer rodar algo por el suelo

◆ **roll over 1** *v/i* darse la vuelta **2** *v/t person, object* dar la vuelta a; (*renew*) renovar; (*extend*) refinanciar

◆ **roll up 1** *v/t sleeves* remangar **2** *v/i* F (*arrive*) llegar

'roll-call lista *f*

roll·er ['roʊlər] *for hair* rulo *m*

'roll·er blade® *n* patín *m* en línea

'roll·er blind persiana *f*

'roll·er coast·er ['roʊlərkoʊstər] montaña *f* rusa

'roll·er skate *n* patín *m* (de ruedas)

'roll·ing pin ['roʊlɪŋ] rodillo *m* de cocina

ROM [rɑːm] COMPUT *abbr* (= ***read only memory***) ROM *f* (= memoria *f* de sólo lectura)

Ro·man ['roʊmən] **1** *adj* romano **2** *n* romano(-a) *m(f)*

Ro·man 'Cath·o·lic 1 *n* REL católico(-a) *m(f)* romano(-a) **2** *adj* católico romano

ro·mance [rə'mæns] (*affair*) aventura *f* (amorosa); *novel* novela *f* rosa; *movie* película *f* romántica

ro·man·tic [roʊ'mæntɪk] *adj* romántico

ro·man·tic·al·ly [roʊ'mæntɪklɪ] *adv:* ***be romantically involved with s.o.*** tener un romance con alguien

roof [ruːf] techo *m,* tejado *m;* ***have a roof over one's head*** tener un techo donde dormir

'roof-rack MOT baca *f*

rook·ie ['rʊkɪ] F novato(-a) *m(f)*

room [ruːm] habitación *f;* (*space*) espacio *m,* sitio *m;* ***there's no room for …*** no hay sitio para …, no cabe …

'room clerk recepcionista *m/f*

'room-mate *sharing room* compañero(-a) *m(f)* de habitación; *sharing apartment* compañero(-a) *m(f)* de apartamento

'room ser·vice servicio *m* de habitaciones

room 'tem·per·a·ture temperatura *f* am-

biente
room·y ['ru:mɪ] *adj house, car etc* espacioso; *clothes* holgado
root [ru:t] *n* raíz *f*; *roots of person* raíces *fpl*
♦ **root for** *v/t* F apoyar
♦ **root out** *v/t (get rid of)* cortar de raíz; *(find)* encontrar
rope [roup] cuerda *f*; *thick* soga *f*; *show s.o. the ropes* F poner a alguien al tanto
♦ **rope off** *v/t* acordonar
ro·sa·ry ['rouzərɪ] REL rosario *m*
rose¹ [rouz] BOT rosa *f*
rose² [rouz] *pret* → **rise**
rose·ma·ry ['rouzmerɪ] romero *m*
ros·trum ['rɑːstrəm] estrado *m*
ros·y ['rouzɪ] *adj cheeks* sonrosado; *future* de color de rosa
rot [rɑːt] **1** *n in wood* putrefacción *f* **2** *v/i (pret & pp rotted) of food, wood* pudrirse; *of teeth* cariarse
ro·ta ['routə] turnos *mpl*; *actual document* calendario *m* con los turnos
ro·tate [rou'teɪt] **1** *v/i of blades, earth* girar **2** *v/t* hacer girar; *crops* rotar
ro·ta·tion [rou'teɪʃn] *around the sun etc* rotación *f*; *do sth in rotation* hacer algo por turnos rotatorios
rot·ten ['rɑːtn] *adj food, wood etc* podrido; *weather, luck* horrible; *that was a rotten trick* ¡qué mala idea!
rough [rʌf] **1** *adj surface, ground* accidentado; *hands, skin* áspero; *voice* ronco; *(violent)* bruto; *crossing* movido; *seas* bravo; *(approximate)* aproximado; *rough draft* borrador *m* **2** *adv: sleep rough* dormir a la intemperie **3** *n in golf* rough *m* **4** *v/t: rough it* apañárselas
♦ **rough up** *v/t* F dar una paliza a
rough·age ['rʌfɪdʒ] *in food* fibra *f*
rough·ly ['rʌflɪ] *adv (approximately)* aproximadamente; *(harshly)* brutalmente; *roughly speaking* aproximadamente
rou·lette [ru:'let] ruleta *f*
round [raund] **1** *adj* redondo; *in round figures* en números redondos **2** *n of mailman, doctor, drinks, competition* ronda *f*; *of toast* rebanada *f*; *in boxing match*

round *m*, asalto *m* **3** *v/t corner* doblar **4** *adv, prep* → **around**
♦ **round off** *v/t edges* redondear; *meeting, night out* concluir
♦ **round up** *v/t figure* redondear (hacia la cifra más alta); *suspects, criminals* detener
round·a·bout ['raundəbaut] **1** *adj route, way of saying sth* indirecto **2** *n Br on road* rotonda *f*, *Span* glorieta *f*
'round-the-world *adj* alrededor del mundo
round 'trip viaje *m* de ida y vuelta
round trip 'tick·et billete *m* or *L.Am.* boleto *m* de ida y vuelta
'round-up *of cattle* rodeo *m*; *of suspects, criminals* redada *f*; *of news* resumen *m*
rouse [rauz] *v/t from sleep* despertar; *interest, emotions* excitar, provocar
rous·ing ['rauzɪŋ] *adj speech, finale* emocionante
route [raut] *n* ruta *f*, recorrido *m*
rou·tine [ru:'ti:n] **1** *adj* habitual **2** *n* rutina *f*; *as a matter of routine* como rutina
row¹ [rou] *n (line)* hilera *f*; *5 days in a row* 5 días seguidos
row² [rou] **1** *v/t boat* llevar remando **2** *v/i* remar
row³ [rau] *n (quarrel)* pelea *f*, discusión *f*; *(noise)* alboroto *m*
row·boat ['roubout] bote *m* de remos
row·dy ['raudɪ] *adj* alborotador, *Span* follonero
roy·al [rɔɪəl] *adj* real
roy·al·ty ['rɔɪltɪ] *royal persons* realeza *f*; *on book, recording* derechos *mpl* de autor
rub [rʌb] *v/t (pret & pp rubbed)* frotar
♦ **rub down** *v/t to clean* lijar
♦ **rub in** *v/t cream, ointment* extender, frotar; *don't rub it in! fig* ¡no me lo restriegues por las narices!
♦ **rub off 1** *v/t dirt* limpiar frotando; *paint etc* borrar **2** *v/i: it rubs off on you* se te contagia
rub·ber ['rʌbər] **1** *n material* goma *f*, caucho *m*; P *(condom)* goma *f* P **2** *adj* de goma *or* caucho
rub·ber 'band goma *f* elástica

rub·ber 'gloves *npl* guantes *mpl* de goma
rub·bish [ˈrʌbɪʃ] basura *f*; *poor quality* basura *f*, porquería *f*; *(nonsense)* tonterías *fpl*; **this radio is rubbish** esta radio es una basura *or* porquería; **don't talk rubbish!** ¡no digas tonterías!
rub·ble [ˈrʌbl] escombros *mpl*
ru·by [ˈruːbɪ] *jewel* rubí *m*
ruck·sack [ˈrʌksæk] mochila *f*
rud·der [ˈrʌdər] timón *m*
rud·dy [ˈrʌdɪ] *adj complexion* rubicundo
rude [ruːd] *adj person, behavior* maleducado, grosero; *language* grosero; **it is rude to ...** es de mala educación ...; **I didn't mean to be rude** no pretendía faltar al respeto
rude·ly [ˈruːdlɪ] *adv (impolitely)* groseramente
rude·ness [ˈruːdnɪs] mala *f* educación, grosería *f*
ruf·fi·an [ˈrʌfɪən] rufián *m*
ruf·fle [ˈrʌfl] **1** *n on dress* volante *m* **2** *v/t hair* despeinar; *clothes* arrugar; *person* alterar, enfadar; **get ruffled** alterarse
rug [rʌg] alfombra *f*; *(blanket)* manta *f* (de viaje)
rug·by [ˈrʌgbɪ] rugby *m*
'rug·by match partido *m* de rugby
'rug·by play·er jugador(a) *m(f)* de rugby
rug·ged [ˈrʌgɪd] *adj scenery, cliffs* escabroso, accidentado; *face* de rasgos duros; *resistance* decidido
ru·in [ˈruːɪn] **1** *n* ruina *f*; **ruins** ruinas *fpl*; **in ruins** *city, building* en ruinas; *of plans, marriage* arruinado **2** *v/t* arruinar; **be ruined** *financially* estar arruinado *or* en la ruina
rule [ruːl] **1** *n of club, game* regla *f*, norma *f*; *of monarch* reinado *m*; *for measuring* regla *f*; **as a rule** por regla general **2** *v/t country* gobernar; **the judge ruled that**

... el juez dictaminó que ... **3** *v/i of monarch* reinar
♦ **rule out** *v/t* descartar
rul·er [ˈruːlər] *for measuring* regla *f*; *of state* gobernante *m/f*
rul·ing [ˈruːlɪŋ] **1** *n* fallo *m*, decisión *f* **2** *adj party* gobernante, en el poder
rum [rʌm] *n drink* ron *m*
rum·ble [ˈrʌmbl] *v/i of stomach* gruñir; *of train in tunnel* retumbar
♦ **rum·mage around** [ˈrʌmɪdʒ] *v/i* buscar revolviendo
'rum·mage sale rastrillo *m* benéfico
ru·mor [ˈruːmər] **1** *n* rumor *m* **2** *v/t*: **it is rumored that ...** se rumorea que ...
rump [rʌmp] *of animal* cuartos *mpl* traseros
rum·ple [ˈrʌmpl] *v/t clothes, paper* arrugar
rump·'steak filete *m* de lomo
run [rʌn] **1** *n on foot* carrera *f*; *in car* viaje *m*; *in tights* carrera *f*; THEA: *of play* temporada *f*; **it has had a three year run** *of play* lleva tres años en cartel; **go for a run** ir a correr; **go for a run in the car** ir a dar una vuelta en el coche; **make a run for it** salir corriendo; **a criminal on the run** un criminal fugado; **in the short / long run** a corto / largo plazo; **a run on the dollar** un movimiento especulativo contra el dólar **2** *v/i (pret ran, pp run) of person, animal* correr; *of river* correr, discurrir; *of paint, make-up* correrse; *of play* estar en cartel; *of engine, machine, software* funcionar; *in election* presentarse; **run for President** presentarse a las elecciones presidenciales; **the trains run every ten minutes** pasan trenes cada diez minutos; **it doesn't run on Saturdays** *of bus, train* no funciona los sábados; **don't leave the tap running** no dejes el grifo abierto; **his nose is running** le moquea la nariz; **her eyes are running** le lloran los ojos **3** *v/t (pret ran, pp run) race* correr; *business, hotel, project etc* dirigir; *software* usar; *(start)* ejecutar; *car* tener; *(use)* usar; **can I run you to the station?** ¿te puedo llevar hasta la estación?; **he ran his eye down the page** echó una ojeada a la página

◆ **run across** v/t (meet) encontrarse con; (find) encontrar

◆ **run away** v/i salir corriendo, huir; from home escaparse

◆ **run down 1** v/t (knock down) atropellar; (criticize) criticar; stocks reducir **2** v/i of battery agotarse

◆ **run into** v/t (meet) encontrarse con; difficulties tropezar con

◆ **run off 1** v/i salir corriendo **2** v/t (print off) tirar

◆ **run out** v/i of contract vencer; of supplies agotarse; **time has run out** se ha acabado el tiempo

◆ **run out of** v/t time, supplies quedarse sin; **I ran out of gas** me quedé sin gasolina; **I'm running out of patience** se me está acabando la paciencia

◆ **run over 1** v/t (knock down) atropellar; **can we run over the details again?** ¿podríamos repasar los detalles otra vez? **2** v/i of water etc desbordarse

◆ **run through** v/t (rehearse, go over) repasar

◆ **run up** v/t debts, large bill acumular; clothes coser

run·a·way ['rʌnəweɪ] n persona que se ha fugado de casa

run·down adj person débil, apagado; part of town, building ruinoso

rung[1] [rʌŋ] of ladder peldaño m

rung[2] [rʌŋ] pp → **ring**[2]

run·ner ['rʌnər] athlete corredor(a) m(f)

run·ner 'beans npl judías fpl verdes, L.Am. porotos mpl verdes, Mex ejotes mpl

run·ner-'up subcampeón(-ona) m(f)

run·ning ['rʌnɪŋ] **1** n SP el correr; (jogging) footing m; of business gestión f **2** adj: **for two days running** durante dos días seguidos

run·ning 'wa·ter agua f corriente

run·ny ['rʌnɪ] adj mixture fluido, líquido; nose que moquea

'run-up SP carrerilla f; **in the run-up to** en el periodo previo a

run·way pista f de aterrizaje / despegue

rup·ture ['rʌptʃər] **1** n ruptura f **2** v/i of pipe etc romperse

ru·ral ['rʊrəl] adj rural

ruse [ruːz] artimaña f

rush [rʌʃ] **1** n prisa f; **do sth in a rush** hacer algo con prisas; **be in a rush** tener prisa; **what's the big rush?** ¿qué prisa tenemos? **2** v/t person meter prisa a; meal comer a toda prisa; **rush s.o. to hospital** llevar a alguien al hospital a toda prisa **3** v/i darse prisa

'rush hour hora f punta

Rus·sia ['rʌʃə] Rusia

Rus·sian ['rʌʃən] **1** adj ruso **2** n ruso(-a) m(f); language ruso m

rust [rʌst] **1** n óxido m **2** v/i oxidarse

rus·tle ['rʌsl] **1** n of silk, leaves susurro m **2** v/i of silk, leaves susurrar

'rust-proof adj inoxidable

rust re·mov·er ['rʌstrɪmuːvər] desoxidante m

rust·y ['rʌstɪ] adj oxidado; **my French is pretty rusty** tengo el francés muy abandonado; **I'm a little rusty** estoy un poco falto de forma

rut [rʌt] in road rodada f; **be in a rut** fig estar estancado

ruth·less ['ruːθlɪs] adj implacable, despiadado

ruth·less·ly ['ruːθlɪslɪ] adv sin compasión, despiadadamente

ruth·less·ness ['ruːθlɪsnɪs] falta f de compasión

rye [raɪ] centeno m

'rye bread pan m de centeno

S

sab·bat·i·cal [sə'bætɪkl] *n year* año *m* sabático; *a 6 month sabbatical* 6 meses de excedencia

sab·o·tage ['sæbətɑːʒ] **1** *n* sabotaje *m* **2** *v/t* sabotear

sab·o·teur [sæbə'tɜːr] saboteador(a) *m(f)*

sac·cha·rin ['sækərɪn] *n* sacarina *f*

sa·chet ['sæʃeɪ] *of shampoo, cream etc* sobrecito *m*

sack [sæk] **1** *n bag* saco *m*; *for groceries* bolsa *f*; *he got the sack* F lo echaron **2** *v/t* echar

sa·cred ['seɪkrɪd] *adj* sagrado

sac·ri·fice ['sækrɪfaɪs] **1** *n* sacrificio *m*; *make sacrifices fig* hacer sacrificios **2** *v/t* sacrificar

sac·ri·lege ['sækrɪlɪdʒ] sacrilegio *m*

sad [sæd] *adj person, face, song* triste; *state of affairs* lamentable, desgraciado

sad·dle ['sædl] **1** *n* silla *f* de montar **2** *v/t horse* ensillar; *saddle s.o. with sth fig* endilgar algo a alguien

sa·dism ['seɪdɪzm] sadismo *m*

sa·dist ['seɪdɪst] sádico(-a) *m(f)*

sa·dis·tic [sə'dɪstɪk] *adj* sádico

sad·ly ['sædlɪ] *adv look, say etc* con tristeza; *(regrettably)* lamentablemente

sad·ness ['sædnɪs] tristeza *f*

safe [seɪf] **1** *adj* seguro; *driver* prudente; *(not in danger)* a salvo; *is it safe to walk here?* ¿se puede andar por aquí sin peligro? **2** *n* caja *f* fuerte

'safe·guard **1** *n* garantía *f*; *as a safeguard against* como garantía contra **2** *v/t* salvaguardar

safe·ly ['seɪflɪ] *adv arrive* sin percances; *(successfully)* sin problemas; *drive* prudentemente; *assume* con certeza

'safe keep·ing: *give sth to s.o. for safe keeping* dar algo a alguien para que lo custodie

safe·ty ['seɪftɪ] seguridad *f*

'safety belt cinturón *m* de seguridad

'safe·ty-con·scious *adj*: *be safety-conscious* tener en cuenta la seguridad

safe·ty 'first prevención *f* de accidentes

'safe·ty pin imperdible *m*

sag [sæg] **1** *n in ceiling etc* combadura *f* **2** *v/i (pret & pp sagged) of ceiling* combarse; *of rope* destensarse; *of tempo* disminuir

sa·ga ['sɑːgə] saga *f*

sage [seɪdʒ] *n herb* salvia *f*

Sa·git·tar·i·us [sædʒɪ'terɪəs] ASTR Sagitario *m/f inv*

said [sed] *pret & pp* → *say*

sail [seɪl] **1** *n of boat* vela *f*; *trip* viaje *m* (en barco); *go for a sail* salir a navegar **2** *v/t yacht* manejar **3** *v/i* navegar; *(depart)* zarpar, hacerse a la mar

'sail·board **1** *n* tabla *f* de windsurf **2** *v/i* hacer windsurf

'sail·board·ing windsurf *m*

'sail·boat barco *m* de vela, velero *m*

sail·ing ['seɪlɪŋ] SP vela *f*

'sail·ing ship barco de vela, velero *m*

sail·or ['seɪlər] *in the navy* marino *m/f*; *in the merchant navy*, SP marinero(-a) *m(f)*; *I'm a good / bad sailor* no me mareo / me mareo con facilidad

saint [seɪnt] santo *m*

sake [seɪk]: *for my sake* por mí; *for the sake of peace* por la paz

sal·ad ['sæləd] ensalada *f*

sal·ad 'dress·ing aliño *m* or aderezo *m* para ensalada

sal·a·ry ['sælərɪ] sueldo *m*, salario *f*

'sal·a·ry scale escala *f* salarial

sale [seɪl] venta *f*; *reduced prices* rebajas *fpl*; *for sale sign* se vende; *is this for sale?* ¿está a la venta?; *be on sale* estar a la venta; *at reduced prices* estar de rebajas

sales [seɪlz] *npl department* ventas *fpl*

'sales clerk *in store* vendedor(a) *m(f)*, dependiente(-a) *m(f)*

'sales fig·ures *npl* cifras *fpl* de ventas

'sales·man vendedor *m*

sales 'man·ag·er jefe(-a) *m(f)* de ventas

'sales meet·ing reunión *f* del departamento de ventas

'sales·wo·man vendedora *f*

sa·lient ['seɪlɪənt] *adj* sobresaliente, destacado

sa·li·va [sə'laɪvə] saliva *f*

salm·on ['sæmən] (*pl salmon*) salmón *m*

sa·loon [sə'luːn] MOT turismo *m*; (*bar*) bar *m*

salt [sɔːlt] 1 *n* sal *f* 2 *v/t food* salar

'salt·cel·lar salero *m*

salt 'wa·ter agua *f* salada

'salt·wa·ter fish pez *m* de agua salada

salt·y ['sɔːltɪ] *adj* salado

sal·u·tar·y ['sæljʊterɪ] *adj experience* beneficioso

sa·lute [sə'luːt] 1 *n* MIL saludo; *take the salute* presidir un desfile 2 *v/t* saludar; *fig* (*hail*) elogiar 3 *v/i* MIL saludar

Sal·va·dor(e)·an [sælvə'dɔːrən] 1 *adj* vadoreño 2 *n* salvadoreño(-a) *m(f)*

sal·vage ['sælvɪdʒ] *v/t from wreck* rescatar

sal·va·tion [sæl'veɪʃn] *also fig* salvación *f*

Sal·va·tion 'Ar·my Ejército *m* de Salvación

same [seɪm] 1 *adj* mismo 2 *pron: the same* lo mismo; *Happy New Year – the same to you* Feliz Año Nuevo – igualmente; *he's not the same any more* ya no es el mismo; *life isn't the same without you* la vida es distinta sin ti; *all the same* (*even so*) aun así; *men are all the same* todos los hombres son iguales; *it's all the same to me* me da lo mismo, me da igual 3 *adv: the same* igual

sam·ple ['sæmpl] *n* muestra *f*

sanc·ti·mo·ni·ous [sæŋktɪ'məʊnɪəs] *adj* mojigato

sanc·tion ['sæŋkʃn] 1 *n* (*approval*) sentimiento *m*, aprobación *f*; (*penalty*) sanción *f* 2 *v/t* (*approve*) sancionar

sanc·ti·ty ['sæŋktətɪ] carácter *m* sagrado

sanc·tu·a·ry ['sæŋktʃʊerɪ] santuario *m*

sand [sænd] 1 *n* arena *f* 2 *v/t with sandpaper* lijar

san·dal ['sændl] sandalia *f*

'sand·bag saco *m* de arena

'sand·blast *v/t* arenar

'sand dune duna *f*

sand·er ['sændər] *tool* lijadora *f*

'sand·pa·per 1 *n* lija *f* 2 *v/t* lijar

'sand·stone arenisca *f*

sand·wich ['sænwɪtʃ] 1 *n Span* bocadillo *m*, *L.Am.* sandwich *m* 2 *v/t: be sandwiched between two ...* estar encajonado entre dos ...

sand·y ['sændɪ] *adj soil* arenoso; *feet, towel etc* lleno de arena; *hair* rubio oscuro; *sandy beach* playa *f* de arena

sane [seɪn] *adj* cuerdo

sang [sæŋ] *pret → sing*

san·i·tar·i·um [sænɪ'terɪəm] sanatorio *m*

san·i·ta·ry ['sænɪterɪ] *adj conditions* salubre, higiénico; *sanitary installations* instalaciones *fpl* sanitarias

'san·i·ta·ry nap·kin compresa *f*

san·i·ta·tion [sænɪ'teɪʃn] (*sanitary installations*) instalaciones *fpl* sanitarias; (*removal of waste*) saneamiento *f*

san·i·ta·tion de·part·ment servicio *m* de limpieza

san·i·ty ['sænɪtɪ] razón *f*, juicio *m*

sank [sæŋk] *pret → sink*

San·ta Claus ['sæntəklɔːz] Papá Noel *m*, Santa Claus *m*

sap [sæp] 1 *n in tree* savia *f* 2 *v/t* (*pret & pp sapped*) *s.o.'s energy* consumir

sap·phire ['sæfaɪr] *n jewel* zafiro *m*

sar·cas·m ['sɑːrkæzm] sarcasmo *m*

sar·cas·tic [sɑːr'kæstɪk] *adj* sarcástico

sar·cas·tic·al·ly [sɑːr'kæstɪklɪ] *adv* sarcásticamente

sar·dine [sɑːr'diːn] sardina *f*

sar·don·ic [sɑːr'dɑːnɪk] *adj* sardónico

sar·don·ic·al·ly [sɑːr'dɑːnɪklɪ] *adv* sardónicamente

sash [sæʃ] *on dress* faja *f*; *on uniform* fajín *m*

sat [sæt] *pret & pp → sit*

Sa·tan ['seɪtn] Satán, Satanás

satch·el ['sætʃl] *for schoolchild* cartera *f*

sat·el·lite ['sætəlaɪt] satélite *m*

'sat·el·lite dish antena *f* parabólica

sat·el·lite T·V televisión *f* por satélite

sat·in ['sætɪn] 1 *adj* satinado 2 *n* satén *m*

sat·ire ['sætaɪr] sátira f

sa·tir·i·cal [sə'tɪrɪkl] adj satírico

sat·i·rist ['sætərɪst] escritor(a) m(f) de sátiras

sat·i·rize ['sætəraɪz] v/t satirizar

sat·is·fac·tion [sætɪs'fækʃn] satisfacción f; *I get satisfaction out of my job* mi trabajo me produce satisfacción; *is that to your satisfaction madam?* fml ¿está a gusto de la señora?

sat·is·fac·to·ry [sætɪs'fæktərɪ] adj satisfactorio; (*just good enough*) suficiente

sat·is·fy ['sætɪsfaɪ] v/t (pret & pp *satisfied*) satisfacer; conditions cumplir; *I am satisfied* (*had enough to eat*) estoy lleno; *I am satisfied that ...* (*convinced*) estoy convencido or satisfecho de que ...; *I hope you're satisfied!* ¡estarás contento!

Sat·ur·day ['sætərdeɪ] sábado m

sauce [sɒːs] salsa f

'sauce·pan cacerola f

sau·cer ['sɒːsər] plato m (*de taza*)

sauc·y ['sɒːsɪ] adj person, dress descarado

Sa·u·di A·ra·bi·a [saʊdɪə'reɪbɪə] Arabia Saudí or Saudita

Sa·u·di A·ra·bi·an [saʊdɪə'reɪbɪən] 1 adj saudita, saudí 2 n saudita m/f, saudí m/f

sau·na ['sɔːnə] sauna f

saun·ter ['sɔːntər] v/i andar sin prisas

saus·age ['sɒːsɪdʒ] salchicha f

sav·age ['sævɪdʒ] 1 adj animal, attack salvaje; criticism feroz 2 n salvaje m/f

sav·age·ry ['sævɪdʒrɪ] crueldad f

save [seɪv] 1 v/t (*rescue*) rescatar, salvar; money, time, effort ahorrar; (*collect*) guardar; COMPUT guardar; goal parar; REL salvar 2 v/i (*put money aside*) ahorrar; SP hacer una parada 3 n SP parada f

♦ **save up for** v/t ahorrar para

sav·er ['seɪvər] person ahorrador(a) m(f)

sav·ing ['seɪvɪŋ] amount saved, activity ahorro m

sav·ings ['seɪvɪŋz] npl ahorros mpl

'sav·ings ac·count cuenta f de ahorros

sav·ings and 'loan caja f de ahorros

'sav·ings bank caja f de ahorros

sa·vior, Br **sa·viour** ['seɪvjər] REL salvador m

sa·vor ['seɪvər] v/t saborear

sa·vor·y ['seɪvərɪ] adj not sweet salado

sa·vour etc Br → **savor** etc

saw[1] [sɒː] 1 n tool serrucho m, sierra f 2 v/t aserrar

saw[2] [sɒː] pret → **see**

♦ **saw off** v/t cortar (con un serrucho)

'saw·dust serrín m, aserrín m

sax·o·phone ['sæksəfoʊn] saxofón m

say [seɪ] 1 v/t (pret & pp **said**) decir; poem recitar; *that is to say* es decir; *what do you say to that?* ¿qué opinas de eso?; *what does the note say?* ¿qué dice la nota?, ¿qué pone en la nota? 2 n: *have one's say* expresar una opinión

say·ing ['seɪɪŋ] dicho m

scab [skæb] on skin costra f

scaf·fold·ing ['skæfəldɪŋ] on building andamiaje m

scald [skɒːld] v/t escaldar

scale[1] [skeɪl] on fish, reptile escama f

scale[2] [skeɪl] 1 n (size) escala f, tamaño m; on thermometer, map, MUS escala f; *on a larger scale* a gran escala; *on a smaller scale* a pequeña escala 2 v/t cliffs etc escalar

♦ **scale down** v/t disminuir, reducir

scale 'draw·ing dibujo m a escala

scales [skeɪlz] npl for weighing báscula f, peso m

scal·lop ['skæləp] n shellfish vieira f

scalp [skælp] n cuero m cabelludo

scal·pel ['skælpl] bisturí m

scam [skæm] F chanchullo m F

scam·pi ['skæmpɪ] gambas fpl rebozadas

scan [skæn] 1 v/t (pret & pp **scanned**) horizon otear; page ojear; COMPUT escanear 2 n of brain escáner m; of fetus ecografía f

♦ **scan in** v/t COMPUT escanear

scan·dal ['skændl] escándalo m

scan·dal·ize ['skændəlaɪz] v/t escandalizar

scan·dal·ous ['skændələs] adj affair, prices escandaloso

Scan·di·na·vi·a [skændɪ'neɪvɪə] Escandinavia

S

scan·ner ['skænər] MED, COMPUT escáner *m*; *for foetus* ecógrafo *m*

scant [skænt] *adj* escaso

scant·i·ly ['skæntɪlɪ] *adv*: *be scantily clad* andar ligero de ropa

scant·y ['skæntɪ] *adj skirt* cortísimo; *bikini* mínimo

scape·goat ['skeɪpgəʊt] cabeza *f* de turco, chivo *m* expiatorio

scar [skɑːr] 1 *n* cicatriz *f* 2 *v/t* (*pret & pp* **scarred**) cicatrizar

scarce [skers] *adj in short supply* escaso; *make o.s. scarce* desaparecer

scarce·ly ['skerslɪ] *adv*: *he had scarcely said it when ...* apenas lo había dicho cuando ...; *there was scarcely anything left* no quedaba casi nada; *I scarcely know her* apenas la conozco

scar·ci·ty ['skersɪtɪ] escasez *f*

scare [sker] 1 *v/t* asustar, atemorizar; *be scared of* tener miedo de 2 *n* (*panic, alarm*) miedo *m*, temor *m*; *give s.o. a scare* dar a alguien un susto

♦ scare away *v/t* ahuyentar

'scare·crow espantapájaros *m inv*

scare·mon·ger ['skermʌŋgər] alarmista *m/f*

scarf [skɑːrf] *around neck, over head* pañuelo *m*; *woollen* bufanda *f*

scar·let ['skɑːrlət] *adj* escarlata

scar·let 'fe·ver escarlatina *f*

scar·y ['skerɪ] *adj sight* espeluznante; *scary music* música de miedo

scath·ing ['skeɪðɪŋ] *adj* feroz

scat·ter ['skætər] 1 *v/t leaflets* esparcir; *seeds* diseminar; *be scattered all over the room* estar esparcido por toda la habitación 2 *v/i of people* dispersarse

scat·ter·brained ['skætərbreɪnd] *adj* despistado

scat·tered ['skætərd] *adj showers, family, villages* disperso

scav·enge ['skævɪndʒ] *v/i* rebuscar; *scavenge for sth* rebuscar en busca de algo

scav·en·ger ['skævɪndʒər] *animal, bird* carroñero *m*; (*person*) persona que busca comida entre la basura

sce·na·ri·o [sɪ'nɑːrɪəʊ] situación *f*

scene [siːn] escena *f*; *of accident, crime etc* lugar *m*; (*argument*) escena *f*, número *m*; *make a scene* hacer una escena, montar un número; *scenes* THEA decorados *mpl*; *jazz / rock scene* mundo del jazz / rock; *behind the scenes* entre bastidores

sce·ne·ry ['siːnərɪ] THEA escenario *m*

scent [sent] *n* olor *m*; (*perfume*) perfume *m*, fragancia *m*

scep·tic *etc Br* → *skeptic etc*

sched·ule ['ʃeduːl] 1 *n of events, work* programa *m*; *of exams* calendario *m*; *for train, work, of lessons* horario *m*; *be on schedule of work* ir según lo previsto; *of train* ir a la hora prevista; *be behind schedule of work, train etc* ir con retraso 2 *v/t* (*put on schedule*) programar; *it's scheduled for completion next month* está previsto que se complete el próximo mes

sched·uled 'flight ['ʃeduːld] vuelo *m* regular

scheme [skiːm] 1 *n* (*plan*) plan *m*, proyecto *m*; (*plot*) confabulación *f* 2 *v/i* (*plot*) confabularse

schem·ing ['skiːmɪŋ] *adj* maquinador

schiz·o·phre·ni·a [skɪtsə'friːnɪə] esquizofrenia *f*

schiz·o·phren·ic [skɪtsə'frenɪk] 1 *n* esquizofrénico(-a) *m(f)* 2 *adj* esquizofrénico

schol·ar ['skɑːlər] erudito(-a) *m(f)*

schol·ar·ly ['skɑːlərlɪ] *adj* erudito

schol·ar·ship ['skɑːlərʃɪp] *scholarly work* estudios *mpl*; *financial award* beca *f*

school [skuːl] escuela *f*, colegio *m*; (*university*) universidad *f*

'school bag (*satchel*) cartera *f*

'school·boy escolar *m*

'school·chil·dren *npl* escolares *mpl*

'school days *npl*; *do you remember your school days?* ¿te acuerdas de cuándo ibas al colegio?

'school·girl escolar *f*

'school·mate compañero *m* de colegio

'school·teach·er maestro(-a) *m(f)*, profesor(a) *m(f)*

sci·at·i·ca [saɪ'ætɪkə] ciática *f*

sci·ence ['saɪəns] ciencia *f*

sci·ence 'fic·tion ciencia f ficción

sci·en·tif·ic [saɪən'tɪfɪk] adj científico

sci·en·tist ['saɪəntɪst] científico(-a) m(f)

scis·sors ['sɪzərz] npl tijeras fpl

scoff[1] [skɑːf] v/t F (eat fast) zamparse F

scoff[2] [skɑːf] v/i (mock) burlarse, mofarse

◆ **scoff at** v/t burlarse de, mofarse de

scold [skoʊld] v/t child, husband regañar

scoop [skuːp] **1** n implement cuchara f; for mud pala f; (story) exclusiva f **2** v/t: **scoop sth into sth** recoger algo para meterlo en algo

◆ **scoop up** v/t recoger

scoot·er ['skuːtər] with motor escúter m; child's patinete m

scope [skoʊp] alcance m; (freedom, opportunity) oportunidad f; **he wants more scope to do his own thing** quiere más libertad para hacer lo que quiere

scorch [skɔːrtʃ] v/t quemar

scorch·ing ['skɔːrtʃɪŋ] adj abrasador

score [skɔːr] **1** n sp resultado m; in competition puntuación f; (written music) partitura f; of movie etc banda f sonora, música f; **what's the score?** sp ¿cómo van?; **have a score to settle with s.o.** tener una cuenta pendiente con alguien; **keep (the) score** llevar el tanteo **2** v/t goal marcar; point anotar; (cut: line) marcar **3** v/i marcar; (keep the score) llevar el tanteo; **that's where he scores** ése es su punto fuerte

'**score·board** marcador m

scor·er ['skɔːrər] of goal goleador(a) m(f); of point anotador(a) m(f); (official score-keeper) encargado del marcador

scorn [skɔːrn] **1** n desprecio m; **pour scorn on sth** despreciar algo, menospreciar algo **2** v/t idea, suggestion despreciar

scorn·ful ['skɔːrnfəl] adj despreciativo

scorn·ful·ly ['skɔːrnfəlɪ] adv con desprecio

Scor·pi·o ['skɔːrpɪoʊ] ASTR Escorpio m/f inv

Scot [skɑːt] escocés(-esa) m(f)

Scotch [skɑːtʃ] (whisky) whisky m escocés

Scotch 'tape® celo m, L.Am. Durex® m

scot-'**free** adv: **get off scot-free** salir impune

Scot·land ['skɑːtlənd] Escocia f

Scots·man ['skɑːtsmən] escocés m

Scots·wom·an ['skɑːtswʊmən] escocesa f

Scot·tish ['skɑːtɪʃ] adj escocés

scoun·drel ['skaʊndrəl] canalla m/f

scour[1] ['skaʊər] v/t (search) rastrear, peinar

scour[2] ['skaʊər] v/t pans fregar

scout [skaʊt] n (boy scout) boy-scout m

scowl [skaʊl] **1** n ceño m **2** v/i fruncir el ceño

scram [skræm] v/i (pret & pp **scrammed**) F largarse F; **scram!** ¡largo!

scram·ble ['skræmbl] **1** n (rush) prisa f **2** v/t message cifrar, codificar **3** v/i (climb) trepar; **he scrambled to his feet** se levantó de un salto

scram·bled '**eggs** ['skræmbld] npl huevos mpl revueltos

scrap [skræp] **1** n metal chatarra f; (fight) pelea f; of food trocito m; of evidence indicio m; of common sense pizca f **2** v/t (pret & pp **scrapped**) plan, project abandonar; paragraph borrar

'**scrap·book** álbum m de recortes

scrape [skreɪp] **1** n on paintwork etc arañazo m **2** v/t paintwork rayar; **scrape a living** apañarse

◆ **scrape through** v/i in exam aprobar por los pelos

'**scrap heap**: **be good for the scrap heap** of person estar para el arrastre; of object estar para tirar

scrap 'met·al chatarra f

scrap 'pa·per papel m usado

scrap·py ['skræpɪ] adj work, writing desorganizado

scratch [skrætʃ] **1** n mark marca f; **have a scratch** to stop itching rascarse; **start from scratch** empezar desde cero; **your work isn't up to scratch** tu trabajo es insuficiente **2** v/t (mark: skin) arañar; (mark: paint) rayar; because of itch rascarse **3** v/i of cat etc arañar; because of itch rascarse

scrawl [skrɔːl] **1** n garabato m **2** v/t garabatear

scraw·ny ['skrɔːnɪ] *adj* escuálido

scream [skriːm] **1** *n* grito *m*; **screams of laughter** carcajadas *fpl* **2** *v/i* gritar

screech [skriːtʃ] **1** *n of tires* chirrido *m*; (*scream*) chillido *m* **2** *v/i of tires* chirriar; (*scream*) chillar

screen [skriːn] **1** *n in room, hospital* mampara *f*; *protective* cortina *f*; *in movie theater* pantalla *f*; COMPUT monitor *m*, pantalla *f* **2** *v/t* (*protect, hide*) ocultar; *movie* proyectar; *for security reasons* investigar

'screen·play guión *m*

'screen sav·er COMPUT salvapantallas *m inv*

'screen test *for movie* prueba *f*

screw [skruː] **1** *n* tornillo *m*; V (*sex*) polvo *m* V **2** *v/t*: **screw sth to sth** atornillar algo a algo; V (*have sex with*) echar un polvo con V; F (*cheat*) timar F

◆ **screw up 1** *v/t eyes* cerrar; *piece of paper* arrugar; F (*make a mess of*) fastidiar F **2** *v/i* F (*make a bad mistake*) meter la pata F

'screw·driv·er destornillador *m*

screwed 'up [skruːdˈʌp] *adj* F *psychologically* acomplejado

'screw top *on bottle* tapón *m* de rosca

screw·y ['skruːɪ] *adj* F chiflado F; *idea, film* descabellado F

scrib·ble ['skrɪbl] **1** *n* garabato *m* **2** *v/t & v/i* garabatear

scrimp [skrɪmp] *v/i*: **scrimp and scrape** pasar apuros, pasar estrecheces

script [skrɪpt] *for movie, play* guión *m*; *form of writing* caligrafía *f*

scrip·ture ['skrɪptʃər] escritura *f*; **the (Holy) Scriptures** las Sagradas Escrituras

'script·writ·er guionista *m/f*

scroll [skroʊl] *n* (*manuscript*) manuscrito *m*

◆ **scroll down** *v/i* COMPUT avanzar

◆ **scroll up** *v/i* COMPUT retroceder

scrounge [skraʊndʒ] *v/t* gorronear

scroung·er ['skraʊndʒər] gorrón(-ona) *m(f)*

scrub [skrʌb] *v/t* (*pret & pp* **scrubbed**) *floors* fregar; *hands* frotar

scrub·bing brush ['skrʌbɪŋ] *for floor* cepillo *m* para fregar

scruff·y ['skrʌfɪ] *adj* andrajoso, desaliñado

scrum [skrʌm] *in rugby* melé *f*

◆ **scrunch up** [skrʌntʃ] *v/t plastic cup etc* estrujar

scru·ples ['skruːplz] *npl* escrúpulos *mpl*

scru·pu·lous ['skruːpjələs] *adj with moral principles* escrupuloso; (*thorough*) meticuloso; *attention to detail* minucioso

scru·pu·lous·ly ['skruːpjələslɪ] *adv* (*meticulously*) minuciosamente

scru·ti·nize ['skruːtɪnaɪz] *v/t* (*examine closely*) estudiar, examinar

scru·ti·ny ['skruːtɪnɪ] escrutinio *m*; **come under scrutiny** ser objeto de investigación

scu·ba div·ing ['skuːbə] submarinismo *m*

scuf·fle ['skʌfl] *n* riña *f*

sculp·tor ['skʌlptər] escultor(a) *m(f)*

sculp·ture ['skʌlptʃər] escultura *f*

scum [skʌm] *on liquid* película *f* de suciedad; (*pej: people*) escoria *f*

sea [siː] *n* mar *m*; **by the sea** junto al mar

'sea·bed fondo *m* marino

'sea·bird ave *f* marina

'sea·far·ing ['siːferɪŋ] *adj nation* marinero

'sea·food marisco *m*

'sea·front paseo *m* marítimo

'sea·go·ing *adj vessel* de altura

'sea·gull gaviota *f*

seal[1] [siːl] *n animal* foca *f*

seal[2] [siːl] **1** *n on document* sello *m*; TECH junta *f*, sello *m* **2** *v/t container* sellar

◆ **seal off** *v/t area* aislar

'sea lev·el: **above sea level** sobre el nivel del mar; **below sea level** bajo el nivel del mar

seam [siːm] *n on garment* costura *f*; *of ore* filón *m*

'sea·man marinero *m*

seam·stress ['siːmstrɪs] modista *f*

'sea·port puerto *m* marítimo

'sea pow·er *nation* potencia *f* marítima

search [sɜːrtʃ] **1** *n* búsqueda *f*; **be in search of** estar en busca de **2** *v/t baggage, person* registrar; **search a place for s.o.** buscar a alguien en un lugar

◆ **search for** v/t buscar

search·ing ['sɜːrtʃɪŋ] adj look escrutador; question difícil

'**search·light** reflector m

'**search par·ty** grupo m de rescate

'**search war·rant** orden f de registro

'**sea·shore** orilla f

'**sea·sick** adj mareado; **get seasick** marearse

'**sea·side** costa f, playa f; **seaside resort** centro m de veraneo costero

sea·son ['siːzn] n (winter, spring etc) estación f; for tourism etc temporada f; **plums aren't in season at the moment** ahora no es temporada de ciruelas

sea·son·al ['siːznl] adj fruit, vegetables del tiempo; employment temporal

sea·soned ['siːznd] adj wood seco; traveler, campaigner experimentado

sea·son·ing ['siːznɪŋ] condimento m

'**sea·son tick·et** abono m

seat [siːt] **1** n in room, bus, plane asiento; in theater butaca f; of pants culera f; **please take a seat** por favor, siéntese **2** v/t (have seating for): **the hall can seat 200 people** la sala tiene capacidad para 200 personas; **please remain seated** por favor, permanezcan sentados

'**seat belt** cinturón m de seguridad

'**sea ur·chin** erizo m de mar

'**sea·weed** alga(s) f(pl)

se·clud·ed [sɪ'kluːdɪd] adj apartado

se·clu·sion [sɪ'kluːʒn] aislamiento m

sec·ond[1] ['sekənd] **1** n of time segundo m **2** adj segundo **3** adv come in en segundo lugar **4** v/t motion apoyar

se·cond[2] [sɪ'kɑːnd] v/t: **be seconded to** ser asignado a

sec·on·da·ry ['sekənderɪ] adj secundario; **of secondary importance** de menor importancia

sec·on·da·ry ed·u·ca·tion educación f secundaria

se·cond 'best adj: **be second best** ser el segundo mejor; inferior ser un segundón; **the second best runner in the school** el segundo mejor corredor del colegio

sec·ond 'big·gest adj: **it is the second biggest company in the area** es la segunda empresa más grande de la zona

sec·ond 'class adj ticket de segunda clase

sec·ond 'floor tercer piso m, Br segundo piso m

'**sec·ond hand** n on clock segundero m

sec·ond·'hand 1 adj de segunda mano **2** adv buy de segunda mano

sec·ond·ly ['sekəndlɪ] adv en segundo lugar

sec·ond·'rate adj inferior

sec·ond 'thoughts: **I've had second thoughts** he cambiado de idea

se·cre·cy ['siːkrəsɪ] secretismo m

se·cret ['siːkrət] **1** n secreto m; **in secret** en secreto **2** adj secreto

se·cret 'a·gent agente m/f secreto

sec·re·tar·i·al [sekrə'terɪəl] adj tasks, job de secretaria

sec·re·tar·y ['sekrəterɪ] secretario(-a) m(f); POL ministro(-a) m(f)

Sec·re·tar·y of 'State in USA Secretario(-a) m(f) de Estado

se·crete [sɪ'kriːt] v/t (give off) segregar; (hide away) esconder

se·cre·tion [sɪ'kriːʃn] secreción f

se·cre·tive ['siːkrətɪv] adj reservado

se·cret·ly ['siːkrətlɪ] adv en secreto

se·cret po'lice policía f secreta

se·cret 'ser·vice servicio m secreto

sect [sekt] secta f

sec·tion ['sekʃn] of book, company, text sección f; of building zona f; of apple parte f

sec·tor ['sektər] sector m

sec·u·lar ['sekjələr] adj laico

se·cure [sɪ'kjur] **1** adj shelf etc seguro; job, contract fijo **2** v/t shelf etc asegurar; s.o.'s help conseguir

se·cu·ri·ty [sɪ'kjurətɪ] seguridad f; for investment garantía f

se·cu·ri·ties mar·ket FIN mercado m de valores

se'cu·ri·ty a·lert alerta f

se'cu·ri·ty check control m de seguridad

se'cu·ri·ty-con·scious adj consciente de la seguridad

se'cu·ri·ty forces npl fuerzas fpl de seguridad

se·cu·ri·ty guard guardia *m/f* de seguridad

se·cu·ri·ty risk *person* peligro *m* (para la seguridad)

se·dan [sɪˈdæn] turismo *m*

se·date [sɪˈdeɪt] *v/t* sedar

se·da·tion [sɪˈdeɪʃn]: **be under sedation** estar sedado

sed·a·tive [ˈsedətɪv] *n* sedante *m*

sed·en·ta·ry [ˈsedənterɪ] *adj job* sedentario

sed·i·ment [ˈsedɪmənt] sedimento *m*

se·duce [sɪˈduːs] *v/t* seducir

se·duc·tion [sɪˈdʌkʃn] seducción *f*

se·duc·tive [sɪˈdʌktɪv] *adj dress* seductor; *offer* tentador

see [siː] *v/t* (*pret* **saw**, *pp* **seen**) ver; (*understand*) entender, ver; *romantically* ver, salir con; **I see** ya veo; **can I see the manager?** ¿puedo ver al encargado?; **you should see a doctor** deberías ir a que te viera un médico; **see s.o. home** acompañar a alguien a casa; **see you!** F ¡hasta la vista!, ¡chao! F

◆ **see about** *v/t* (*look into*): **I'll see about getting it repaired** me encargaré de que lo arreglen

◆ **see off** *v/t at airport etc* despedir; (*chase away*) espantar

◆ **see out** *v/t*: **see s.o. out** acompañar a alguien a la puerta

◆ **see to** *v/t*: **see to sth** ocuparse de algo; **see to it that sth gets done** asegurarse de que algo se haga

seed [siːd] semilla *f*; *in tennis* cabeza *f* de serie; **go to seed** *of person* descuidarse; *of district* empeorarse

seed·ling [ˈsiːdlɪŋ] planta *f* de semillero

seed·y [ˈsiːdɪ] *adj bar, district* de mala calaña

see·ing 'eye dog [ˈsiːɪŋ] perro *m* lazarillo

see·ing (that) [ˈsiːɪŋ] *conj* dado que, ya que

seek [siːk] *v/t* (*pret & pp* **sought**) buscar

seem [siːm] *v/i* parecer; **it seems that ...** parece que ...

seem·ing·ly [ˈsiːmɪŋlɪ] *adv* aparentemente

seen [siːn] *pp* → **see**

seep [siːp] *v/i of liquid* filtrarse

◆ **seep out** *v/i of liquid* filtrarse

see·saw [ˈsiːsɔː] *n* sube y baja *m*

seethe [siːð] *v/i*: **be seething with anger** estar a punto de estallar (de cólera)

'see-through *adj dress, material* transparente

seg·ment [ˈsegmənt] segmento *m*

seg·ment·ed [segˈmentɪd] *adj* segmentado, dividido

seg·re·gate [ˈsegrɪgeɪt] *v/t* segregar

seg·re·ga·tion [segrɪˈgeɪʃn] segregación *f*

seis·mol·o·gy [saɪzˈmɑːlədʒɪ] sismología *f*

seize [siːz] *v/t s.o., s.o.'s arm* agarrar; *opportunity* aprovechar; *of Customs, police etc* incautarse

◆ **seize up** *v/i of engine* atascarse

sei·zure [ˈsiːʒər] MED ataque *m*; *of drugs etc* incautación *f*; *amount seized* alijo *m*

sel·dom [ˈseldəm] *adv* raramente, casi nunca

se·lect [sɪˈlekt] **1** *v/t* seleccionar **2** *adj* (*exclusive*) selecto

se·lec·tion [sɪˈlekʃn] selección *f*; (*choosing*) elección *f*

se'lec·tion pro·cess proceso *m* de selección

se·lec·tive [sɪˈlektɪv] *adj* selectivo

self [self] (*pl* **selves** [selvz]) ego *m*; **my other self** mi otro yo

self-ad·dressed 'en·ve·lope [selfəˈdrest]: **send us a self-addressed envelope** envíenos un sobre con sus datos

self-as'sur·ance confianza *f* en sí mismo

self-as'sured [selfəˈʃʊrd] *adj* seguro de sí mismo

self-ca·ter·ing a'part·ment [selfˈkeɪtərɪŋ] *Br* apartamento *m* or *Span* piso *m* sin servicio de comidas

self-'cen·tered, *Br* self-'cen·tred [selfˈsentərd] *adj* egoísta

self-'clean·ing *adj oven* con autolimpieza

self-con'fessed [selfkənˈfest] *adj*: **he's a self-confessed megalomaniac** se confiesa megalómano

self-'con·fi·dence confianza *f* en sí mismo

self-'con·fi·dent *adj* seguro de sí mismo

self-'con·scious *adj* tímido

self-'con·scious·ness timidez *f*

self-con·tained [selfkən'teɪnd] *adj apartment* independiente

self con'trol autocontrol *m*

self-de'fence *Br*, **self-de'fense** autodefensa *f*; **in self-defence** en defensa propia

self-'dis·ci·pline autodisciplina *f*

self-'doubt inseguridad *f*

self-em·ployed [selfɪm'plɔɪd] *adj* autónomo

self-e'steem autoestima *f*

self-ex'pres·sion autoexpresión *f*

self-'ev·i·dent *adj* obvio

self-'gov·ern·ment autogobierno *m*

self-'in·terest interés *m* propio

self·ish ['selfɪʃ] *adj* egoísta

self·less ['selflɪs] *adj* desinteresado

self-made 'man [self'meɪd] hombre *m* hecho a sí mismo

self-'pit·y autocompasión *f*

self-'por·trait autorretrato *m*

self-pos·sessed [selfpə'zest] *adj* sereno

self-re'li·ant *adj* autosuficiente

self-re'spect amor *m* propio

self-'right·eous [self'raɪʃəs] *adj pej* santurrón, intolerante

self-sat·is·fied [self'sætɪzfaɪd] *adj pej* pagado de sí mismo

self-'ser·vice *adj* de autoservicio

self-ser·vice 'res·tau·rant (restaurante *m*) autoservicio *m*

self-taught [self'tɔːt] *adj* autodidacta

sell [sel] *v/t & v/i* (*pret & pp* **sold**) vender
 ◆ **sell out** *v/i* of *product* agotarse; **we've sold out** se nos ha(n) agotado
 ◆ **sell out of** *v/t* agotar las existencias de
 ◆ **sell up** *v/i* vender todo

'sell-by date fecha *f* límite de venta; **be past its sell-by date** haber pasado la fecha límite de venta

sell·er ['selər] vendedor(a) *m(f)*

sell·ing ['selɪŋ] *n* COM ventas *fpl*

'sell·ing point com ventaja *f*

Sel·lo·tape® ['seləteɪp] *Br* celo *m*, *L.Am.* Durex® *m*

se·men ['siːmən] semen *m*

se·mes·ter [sɪ'mestər] semestre *m*

sem·i ['semɪ] *n* truck camión *m* semirremolque

'sem·i·cir·cle semicírculo *m*

sem·i·cir·cu·lar *adj* semicircular

semi-'co·lon punto y coma

sem·i·con·duc·tor ELEC semiconductor *m*

semi·fi·nal semifinal *f*

semi·fi·nal·ist semifinalista *m/f*

sem·i·nar ['semɪnɑːr] seminario *m*

sem·i·skilled *adj* semicualificado

sen·ate ['senət] senado *m*

sen·a·tor ['senətər] senador(a) *m(f)*; **Senator George Schwarz** el Senador George Schwarz

send [send] *v/t* (*pret & pp* **sent**) enviar, mandar; **the doctor sent him to a specialist** el médico lo envió *or* mandó a un especialista; **send her my best wishes** dale recuerdos de mi parte
 ◆ **send back** *v/t* devolver
 ◆ **send for** *v/t* mandar buscar
 ◆ **send in** *v/t troops, application* enviar, mandar; *next interviewee* hacer pasar
 ◆ **send off** *v/t letter, fax etc* enviar, mandar

send·er ['sendər] *of letter* remitente *m/f*

se·nile ['siːnaɪl] *adj* senil

se·nil·i·ty [sɪ'nɪlətɪ] senilidad *f*

se·ni·or ['siːnjər] *adj* (*older*) mayor; *in rank* superior

se·ni·or 'cit·i·zen persona *f* de la tercera edad

se·ni·or·i·ty [siːnj'ɑːrətɪ] *in job* antigüedad *f*

sen·sa·tion [sen'seɪʃn] sensación *f*

sen·sa·tion·al [sen'seɪʃnl] *adj news, discovery* sensacional

sense [sens] **1** *n* (*meaning, point, hearing etc*) sentido *m*; (*feeling*) sentimiento *m*; (*common sense*) sentido *m* común, sensatez *f*; **in a sense** en cierto sentido; **talk sense, man!** ¡no digas tonterías!; **come to one's senses** entrar en razón; **it doesn't make sense** no tiene sentido; **there's no sense in waiting** no tiene sentido que esperemos **2** *v/t s.o.'s presence* sentir, notar; **I could sense that something was wrong** tenía la sensación de que algo no iba bien

sense·less ['senslɪs] *adj* (*pointless*) absurdo

sen·si·ble ['sensəbl] *adj* sensato; *clothes, shoes* práctico, apropiado

sen·si·bly ['sensəblɪ] *adv* con sensatez; **she wasn't sensibly dressed** no llevaba ropa apropiada

sen·si·tive ['sensɪtɪv] *adj skin, person* sensible

sen·si·tiv·i·ty [sensə'tɪvətɪ] *of skin, person* sensibilidad *f*

sen·sor ['sensər] sensor *m*

sen·su·al ['senʃuəl] *adj* sensual

sen·su·al·i·ty [senʃu'ælətɪ] sensualidad *f*

sen·su·ous ['senʃuəs] *adj* sensual

sent [sent] *pret & pp* → **send**

sen·tence ['sentəns] **1** *n* GRAM oración *f*; LAW sentencia *f* **2** *v/t* LAW sentenciar, condenar

sen·ti·ment ['sentɪmənt] (*sentimentality*) sentimentalismo *m*; (*opinion*) opinión *f*

sen·ti·men·tal [sentɪ'mentl] *adj* sentimental

sen·ti·men·tali·ty [sentɪmen'tælətɪ] sentimentalismo *m*

sen·try ['sentrɪ] centinela *m*

sep·a·rate[1] ['sepərət] *adj* separado; **keep sth separate from sth** guardar algo separado de algo

sep·a·rate[2] ['sepəreɪt] **1** *v/t* separar; **separate sth from sth** separar algo de algo **2** *v/i of couple* separarse

sep·a·rat·ed ['sepəreɪtɪd] *adj couple* separado

sep·a·rate·ly ['sepərətlɪ] *adv pay, treat* por separado

sep·a·ra·tion [sepə'reɪʃn] separación *f*

Sep·tem·ber [sep'tembər] septiembre *m*

sep·tic ['septɪk] *adj* séptico; **go septic** *of wound* infectarse

se·quel ['siːkwəl] continuación *f*

se·quence ['siːkwəns] *n* secuencia *f*; **in sequence** en orden; **out of sequence** en desorden; **the sequence of events** la secuencia de hechos

se·rene [sɪ'riːn] *adj* sereno

ser·geant ['sɑːrdʒənt] sargento *m/f*

se·ri·al [sɪ'rɪəl] *n on* TV, *radio* serie *f*, serial *m*; *in magazine* novela *f* por entregas

se·ri·al·ize [sɪ'rɪəlaɪz] *v/t novel on* TV emitir en forma de serie; *in newspaper* publicar por entregas

'se·ri·al kill·er asesino(-a) *m(f)* en serie

'se·ri·al num·ber *of product* número *m* de serie

'se·ri·al port COMPUT puerto *m* (en) serie

se·ries ['sɪriːz] *nsg* serie *f*

se·ri·ous ['sɪriəs] *adj situation, damage, illness* grave; (*person: earnest*) serio; *company* serio; **I'm serious** lo digo en serio; **we'd better take a serious look at it** deberíamos examinarlo seriamente

se·ri·ous·ly ['sɪriəslɪ] *adv injured* gravemente; **seriously intend to …** tener intenciones firmes de …; **seriously?** ¿en serio? **take s.o. seriously** tomar a alguien en serio

se·ri·ous·ness ['sɪriəsnɪs] *of person* seriedad *f*; *of situation* seriedad *f*, gravedad *f*; *of illness* gravedad *f*

ser·mon ['sɜːrmən] sermón *m*

ser·vant ['sɜːrvənt] sirviente(-a) *m(f)*

serve [sɜːrv] **1** *n* in tennis servicio *m*, saque *m* **2** *v/t food, meal* servir; *customer in shop* atender; *one's country, the people* servir a; **it serves you right** ¡te lo mereces! **3** *v/i* servir; *in tennis* servir, sacar
◆ **serve up** *v/t meal* servir

serv·er ['sɜːrvər] *in tennis* jugador(a) *m(f)* al servicio; COMPUT servidor *m*

ser·vice ['sɜːrvɪs] **1** *n to customers, community* servicio *m*; *for vehicle, machine* revisión *f*; *in tennis* servicio *m*, saque *m*; **services** (*service sector*) el sector servicios; **the services** MIL las fuerzas armadas **2** *v/t vehicle, machine* revisar

'ser·vice ar·e·a área *f* de servicio

'ser·vice charge *in restaurant* servicio *m* (*tarifa*)

'ser·vice in·dus·try industria *f* de servicios

'ser·vice·man MIL militar *m*

'ser·vice pro·vid·er COMPUT proveedor *m* de servicios

'ser·vice sec·tor sector *m* servicios

'ser·vice sta·tion estación *f* de servicio

ser·vi·ette [sɜːrvɪ'et] servilleta *f*

ser·vile ['sɜːrvəl] *adj pej* servil

serv·ing ['sɜːrvɪŋ] *n of food* ración *f*

ses·sion ['seʃn] sesión *f; with boss* reunión *f*

set [set] **1** *n of tools* juego *m; of books* colección *f; (group of people)* grupo *m;* MATH conjunto *m;* (THEA: *scenery)* decorado *m; where a movie is made* plató *m; in tennis* set *m;* **television set** televisor *m;* **a set of dishes** una vajilla; **a set of glasses** una cristalería **2** *v/t (pret & pp* **set)** *(place)* colocar; *movie, novel etc* ambientar; *date, time, limit* fijar; *mechanism, alarm* poner; *clock* poner en hora; *broken limb* recomponer; *jewel* engastar; *(typeset)* componer; **set the table** poner la mesa **3** *v/i (pret & pp* **set)** *of sun* ponerse; *of glue* solidificarse **4** *adj views, ideas* fijo; *(ready)* preparado; **be dead set on sth** estar empeñado en hacer algo; **be very set in one's ways** ser de ideas fijas; **set meal** menú *m* (del día)

◆ **set apart** *v/t* distinguir

◆ **set aside** *v/t material, food* apartar; *money* ahorrar

◆ **set back** *v/t in plans etc* retrasar; **it set me back $400** me salió por 400 dólares

◆ **set off** *v/i on journey* salir **2** *v/t explosion* provocar; *bomb* hacer explotar; *chain reaction* desencadenar; *alarm* activar

◆ **set out 1** *v/i on journey* salir **(for** hacia) **2** *v/t ideas, goods* exponer; **set out to do sth** *(intend)* tener la intención de hacer algo

◆ **set to** *v/i (start on a task)* empezar a trabajar

◆ **set up 1** *v/t new company* establecer; *equipment, machine* instalar; *market stall* montar; *meeting* organizar; F *(frame)* tender una trampa a **2** *v/i in business* emprender un negocio

'set·back contratiempo *m*

set·tee [se'tiː] *(couch, sofa)* sofá *m*

set·ting ['setɪŋ] *n of novel etc* escenario *m; of house* ubicación *f*

set·tle ['setl] **1** *v/i of bird, dust* posarse; *of building* hundirse; *to live* establecerse **2** *v/t dispute, uncertainty* resolver, solucionar; *debts* saldar; *nerves, stomach* calmar; **that settles it!** ¡está decidido!

◆ **settle down** *v/i (stop buying noisy)* tranquilizarse; *(stop wild living)* sentar la cabeza; *in an area* establecerse

◆ **settle for** *v/t (take, accept)* conformarse con

◆ **settle up** *v/i (pay)* ajustar cuentas con

set·tled ['setld] *adj weather* estable

set·tle·ment ['setlmənt] *of claim* resolución *f; of debt* liquidación *f; of dispute* acuerdo *m;* (*payment)* suma *f; of building* hundimiento *m*

set·tler ['setlər] *in new country* colono *m*

'set-up *(structure)* estructura *f;* *(relationship)* relación *f;* F *(frameup)* trampa *f*

sev·en ['sevn] siete

sev·en·teen [sevn'tiːn] diecisiete

sev·en·teenth [sevn'tiːnθ] *n & adj* decimoséptimo

sev·enth ['sevnθ] *n & adj* séptimo

sev·en·ti·eth ['sevntɪɪθ] *n & adj* septuagésimo

sev·en·ty ['sevntɪ] setenta

sev·er ['sevər] *v/t* cortar; *relations* romper

sev·er·al ['sevrl] **1** *adj* varios **2** *pron* varios(-as) *mpl (fpl)*

se·vere [sɪ'vɪr] *adj illness* grave; *penalty, winter, weather* severo; *teacher* estricto

se·vere·ly [sɪ'vɪrlɪ] *adv punish, speak con* severidad; *injured, disrupted* gravemente

se·ver·i·ty [sɪ'verɪtɪ] severidad *f; of illness* gravedad *f*

Se·ville [sə'vɪl] *n* Sevilla

sew [soʊ] *v/t & v/i (pret* **sewed***, pp* **sewn)** coser

◆ **sew on** *v/t button* coser

sew·age ['suːɪdʒ] aguas *fpl* residuales

'sew·age plant planta *f* de tratamiento de aguas residuales, depuradora *f*

sew·er ['suːər] alcantarilla *f*, cloaca *f*

sew·ing ['soʊɪŋ] *skill* costura *f; that being sewn* labor *f*

'sew·ing ma·chine máquina *f* de coser

sewn [soʊn] *pp* → **sew**

sex [seks] *(act, gender)* sexo *m;* **have sex with** tener relaciones sexuales con, acostarse con

sex·ist ['seksɪst] **1** *adj* sexista **2** *n* sexista *m/f* sex·u·al ['sekʃʊəl] adj sexual

sex·u·al as'sault agresión f sexual

sex·u·al ha'rass·ment acoso m sexual

sex·u·al 'in·ter·course relaciones fpl sexuales

sex·u·al·ity [sekʃʊ'ælətɪ] sexualidad f

sex·u·al·ly ['sekʃʊlɪ] adv sexualmente; **sexually transmitted disease** enfermedad f de transmisión sexual

sex·y ['seksɪ] adj sexy inv

shab·bi·ly ['ʃæbɪlɪ] adv dressed con desaliño; treat muy mal, de manera muy injusta

shab·by ['ʃæbɪ] adj coat etc desgastado, raído; treatment malo, muy injusto

shack [ʃæk] choza f

shade [ʃeɪd] **1** n for lamp pantalla f; of color tonalidad f; on window persiana f; **in the shade** a la sombra **2** v/t from sun, light proteger de la luz

shad·ow ['ʃædoʊ] n sombra f

shad·y ['ʃeɪdɪ] adj spot umbrío; character, dealings sospechoso

shaft [ʃæft] TECH eje m, árbol m; of mine pozo m

shag·gy ['ʃægɪ] adj hair, dog greñudo

shake [ʃeɪk] **1** n sacudida f; **give sth a good shake** agitar algo bien **2** v/t (pret **shook**, pp **shaken**) agitar; emotionally conmocionar; **he shook his head** negó con la cabeza; **shake hands** estrechar or darse la mano; **shake hands with s.o.** estrechar or dar la mano a alguien **3** v/i (pret **shook**, pp **shaken**) of voice, building, person temblar

shak·en ['ʃeɪkən] **1** adj emotionally conmocionado **2** pp → **shake**

'shake·up reestructuración f

shak·y ['ʃeɪkɪ] adj table etc inestable; after illness débil; after shock conmocionado; grasp of sth, grammar etc flojo; voice, hand tembloroso

shall [ʃæl] v/aux ◇ future: **I shall do my best** haré todo lo que pueda; **I shan't see them** no los veré

◇ suggesting: **shall we go?** ¿nos vamos?

shal·low ['ʃæloʊ] adj water poco profundo; person superficial

sham·bles ['ʃæmblz] nsg caos m

shame [ʃeɪm] **1** n vergüenza f, Col, Mex, Ven pena f; **bring shame on** avergonzar or Col, Mex, Ven apenar a; **shame on you!** ¡debería darte vergüenza!; **what a shame!** ¡qué pena or lástima! **2** v/t avergonzar, Col, Mex, Ven apenar; **shame s.o. into doing sth** avergonzar a alguien para que haga algo

shame·ful ['ʃeɪmfəl] adj vergonzoso

shame·ful·ly ['ʃeɪmfəlɪ] adv vergonzosamente

shame·less ['ʃeɪmlɪs] adj desvergonzado

sham·poo [ʃæm'puː] **1** n champú m **2** v/t customer lavar la cabeza a; hair lavar

shan·ty town ['ʃæntɪ] Span barrio m de chabolas, Am barriada f

shape [ʃeɪp] **1** n forma f **2** v/t clay modelar; person's life, character determinar; the future dar forma a

shape·less ['ʃeɪplɪs] adj dress etc amorfo

shape·ly ['ʃeɪplɪ] adv figure esbelto

share [ʃer] **1** n parte f; FIN acción f; **I did my share of the work** hice la parte del trabajo que me correspondía **2** v/t feelings, opinions compartir **3** v/i compartir

♦ share out v/t repartir

'share·hold·er accionista m/f

shark [ʃɑːrk] fish tiburón m

sharp [ʃɑːrp] **1** adj knife afilado; mind vivo; pain agudo; taste ácido **2** adv MUS demasiado alto; **at 3 o'clock sharp** a las tres en punto

sharp·en ['ʃɑːrpn] v/t knife afilar; pencil sacar punta a; skills perfeccionar

sharp 'prac·tice triquiñuelas fpl, tejemanejes mpl

shat [ʃæt] pret & pp → **shit**

shat·ter ['ʃætər] **1** v/t glass hacer añicos; illusions destrozar **2** v/i of glass hacerse añicos

shat·tered ['ʃætərd] adj F (exhausted) destrozado F, hecho polvo F; (very upset) destrozado F

shat·ter·ing ['ʃætərɪŋ] adj news, experience demoledor, sorprendente

shave [ʃeɪv] **1** v/t afeitar **2** v/i afeitarse **3** n afeitado m; **have a shave** afeitarse; **that was a close shave** ¡le faltó un pelo!

◆ **shave off** v/t beard afeitar; *from piece of wood* rebajar

shav·en ['ʃeɪvn] adj head afeitado

shav·er ['ʃeɪvər] electric máquinilla f de afeitar (eléctrica)

shav·ing brush ['ʃeɪvɪŋ] brocha f de afeitar

'**shav·ing soap** jabón m de afeitar

shawl [ʃɔːl] chal m

she [ʃiː] pron ella; **she is German/a student** es alemana / estudiante; **you're funny, she's not** tú tienes gracia, ella no

shears [ʃɪrz] npl for gardening tijeras fpl (de podar); for sewing tijeras fpl (grandes)

sheath [ʃiːθ] n for knife funda f; contraceptive condón m

shed¹ [ʃed] v/t (pret & pp shed) blood, tears derramar; leaves perder; **shed light on** fig arrojar luz sobre

shed² [ʃed] n cobertizo m

sheep [ʃiːp] (pl sheep) oveja f

'**sheep·dog** perro m pastor

sheep·herd·er ['ʃiːphɜːrdər] pastor m

sheep·ish ['ʃiːpɪʃ] adj avergonzado

'**sheep·skin** adj lining (de piel) de borrego

sheer [ʃɪr] adj madness, luxury puro, verdadero; hell verdadero; drop, cliffs escarpado

sheet [ʃiːt] for bed sábana f; of paper hoja f; of metal chapa f, plancha f; of glass hoja f, lámina f

shelf [ʃelf] (pl shelves [ʃelvz]) estante m; **shelves** estanterías fpl

shell [ʃel] 1 n of mussel etc concha f; of egg cáscara f; of tortoise caparazón m; MIL proyectil m; **come out of one's shell** fig salir del caparazón 2 v/t peas pelar; MIL bombardear (con artillería)

'**shell·fire** fuego m de artillería

'**shell·fish** marisco m

shel·ter ['ʃeltər] 1 n refugio m; (bus shelter) marquesina f 2 v/i from rain, bombing etc refugiarse 3 v/t (protect) proteger

shel·tered ['ʃeltərd] adj place resguardado; **lead a sheltered life** llevar una vida protegida

shelve [ʃelv] v/t fig posponer

shep·herd ['ʃepərd] n pastor m

sher·iff ['ʃerɪf] sheriff m/f

sher·ry ['ʃerɪ] jerez m

shield [ʃiːld] 1 n escudo m; sports trophy trofeo m (en forma de escudo); TECH placa f protectora; of policeman placa f 2 v/t (protect) proteger

shift [ʃɪft] 1 n cambio m; (period of work) turno m 2 v/t (move) mover; stains etc eliminar 3 v/i (move) moverse; (change) trasladarse, desplazarse; of wind cambiar; **he was shifting!** F iba a toda mecha F

'**shift key** COMPUT tecla f de mayúsculas

'**shift work** trabajo m por turnos

'**shift work·er** trabajador(a) m(f) por turnos

shift·y ['ʃɪftɪ] adj pej sospechoso

shil·ly-shal·ly ['ʃɪlɪʃælɪ] v/i (pret & pp shilly-shallied) F titubear

shim·mer ['ʃɪmər] v/i brillar; of roads in heat reverberar

shin [ʃɪn] n espinilla f

shine [ʃaɪn] 1 v/i (pret & pp shone) brillar; fig: of student etc destacar (at en) 2 v/t (pret & pp shone): **could you shine a light in here?** ¿podrías alumbrar aquí? 3 n on shoes etc brillo m

shin·gle ['ʃɪŋgl] on beach guijarros mpl

shin·gles ['ʃɪŋglz] nsg MED herpes m

shin·y ['ʃaɪnɪ] adj surface brillante

ship [ʃɪp] 1 n barco m, buque m 2 v/t (pret & pp shipped) (send) enviar; by sea enviar por barco

ship·ment ['ʃɪpmənt] (consignment) envío m

'**ship·own·er** naviero(-a) m(f), armador(a) m(f)

ship·ping ['ʃɪpɪŋ] n (sea traffic) navíos mpl, buques mpl; (sending) envío m; (sending by sea) envío m por barco

'**ship·ping com·pa·ny** (compañía f) naviera f

ship·ping costs npl gastos mpl de envío

ship'shape adj ordenado, organizado

'**ship·wreck** 1 n naufragio m 2 v/t: **be shipwrecked** naufragar

'**ship·yard** astillero m

S

shirk [ʃɜːrk] v/t eludir

shirk·er ['ʃɜːrkər] vago(-a) m(f)

shirt [ʃɜːrt] camisa f; **in his shirt sleeves** en mangas de camisa

shit [ʃɪt] 1 n P mierda f P; **I need a shit** tengo que cagar P 2 v/i (pret & pp **shat**) P cagar P 3 interj P mierda P

shit·ty ['ʃɪtɪ] adj F asqueroso F; **I feel shitty** me encuentro de pena F

shiv·er ['ʃɪvər] v/i tiritar

shock [ʃɑːk] 1 n shock m, impresión f; ELEC descarga f; **be in shock** MED estar en estado de shock 2 v/t impresionar, dejar boquiabierto; **I was shocked by the news** la noticia me impresionó or dejó boquiabierto; **an artist who tries to shock his public** un artista que intenta escandalizar a su público

'shock ab·sorb·er [əb'sɔːrbər] MOT amortiguador m

shock·ing ['ʃɑːkɪŋ] adj behavior, poverty impresionante, escandaloso; F prices escandaloso; F weather, spelling terrible

shock·ing·ly ['ʃɑːkɪŋlɪ] adv behave escandalosamente

shod·dy ['ʃɑːdɪ] adj goods de mala calidad; behavior vergonzoso

shoe [ʃuː] zapato m

'shoe·horn n calzador m

'shoe·lace cordón m

'shoe·mak·er zapatero(-a) m(f)

'shoe men·der zapatero(-a) m(f) remendón(-ona)

'shoe·store zapatería f

'shoe·string: **do sth on a shoestring** hacer algo con cuatro duros

shone [ʃɑːn] pret & pp → shine

◆ shoo away [ʃuː] v/t children, chicken espantar

shook [ʃʊk] pret → shake

shoot [ʃuːt] 1 n BOT brote m 2 v/t (pret & pp **shot**) disparar; and kill matar de un tiro; movie rodar; **shoot s.o. in the leg** disparar a alguien en la pierna

◆ shoot down v/t airplane derribar; fig: suggestion echar por tierra

◆ shoot off v/i (rush off) irse deprisa

◆ shoot up v/i of prices dispararse; of children crecer mucho; of new suburbs,

buildings etc aparecer de repente; F of drug addict chutarse F

shoot·ing 'star ['ʃuːtɪŋ] estrella f fugaz

shop [ʃɑːp] 1 n tienda f; **talk shop** hablar del trabajo 2 v/i (pret & pp **shopped**) comprar; **go shopping** ir de compras

shop·keep·er ['ʃɑːkiːpər] tendero(-a) m(f)

shop·lift·er ['ʃɑːplɪftər] ladrón(-ona) m(f) (en tienda)

shop·lift·ing ['ʃɑːplɪftɪŋ] n hurtos mpl (en tiendas)

shop·per ['ʃɑːpər] person comprador(a) m(f)

shop·ping ['ʃɑːpɪŋ] items compra f; **I hate shopping** odio hacer la compra; **do one's shopping** hacer la compra

'shop·ping bag bolsa f de la compra

'shop·ping cen·ter, Br 'shop·ping cen-tre centro m comercial

'shop·ping list lista f de la compra

'shop·ping mall centro m comercial

shop 'stew·ard representante m/f sindical

shop 'win·dow escaparate m, L.Am. vidriera f, Mex aparador m

shore [ʃɔːr] orilla f; **on shore** (not at sea) en tierra

short [ʃɔːrt] 1 adj corto; in height bajo; **it's just a short walk** está a poca distancia a pie; **we're short of fuel** nos queda poco combustible; **he's not short of ideas** no le faltan ideas; **time is short** hay poco tiempo 2 adv: **cut short** vacation, meeting interrumpir; **stop a person short** hacer pararse a una persona; **go short of** pasar sin; **in short** en resumen

short·age ['ʃɔːrtɪdʒ] escasez f, falta f

short 'cir·cuit n cortocircuito m

short·com·ing ['ʃɔːrtkʌmɪŋ] defecto m

'short cut atajo m

short·en ['ʃɔːrtn] v/t dress, hair, vacation acortar; chapter, article abreviar; work day reducir

short·en·ing ['ʃɔːrtnɪŋ] n grasa utilizada para hacer masa de pastelería

'short·fall déficit m

'short·hand n taquigrafía f

short·hand·ed [ʃɔːrt'hændɪd] adj falto de

personal
short-lived ['ʃɔːrtlɪvd] *adj* efímero
short·ly ['ʃɔːrtlɪ] *adv* (*soon*) pronto; *shortly before / after* justo antes / después
short·ness ['ʃɔːrtnɪs] *of visit* brevedad *f*; *in height* baja *f* estatura
shorts [ʃɔːrts] *npl* pantalones *mpl* cortos, shorts *mpl*; *underwear* calzoncillos *mpl*
short·sight·ed [ʃɔːrt'saɪtɪd] *adj* miope; *fig* corto de miras
short-sleeved ['ʃɔːrtsliːvd] *adj* de manga corta
short-staffed [ʃɔːrt'stæft] *adj* falto de personal
short 'sto·ry relato *m or* cuento corto
short-tem·pered [ʃɔːrt'tempərd] *adj* irascible
'short-term *adj* a corto plazo
'short time: *be on short time of workers* trabajar a jornada reducida
'short wave onda *f* corta
shot¹ [ʃɑːt] *from gun* disparo *m*; (*photograph*) fotografía *f*; (*injection*) inyección *f*; *be a good / poor shot* tirar bien / mal; *he accepted like a shot* aceptó al instante; *he ran off like a shot* se fue como una bala
shot² [ʃɑːt] *pret & pp* → **shoot**
'shot·gun escopeta *f*
should [ʃʊd] *v/aux*: *what should I do?* ¿qué debería hacer?; *you shouldn't do that* no deberías hacer eso; *that should be long enough* debería ser lo suficientemente largo; *you should have heard him!* ¡tendrías que haberle oído!
shoul·der ['ʃoʊldər] *n* ANAT hombro *m*
'shoul·der bag bolso *m* (de bandolera)
'shoul·der blade omóplato *m*, omoplato *m*
'shoul·der strap *of brassiere, dress* tirante *m*; *of bag* correa *f*
shout [ʃaʊt] 1 *n* grito *m* 2 *v/t & v/i* gritar
◆ **shout at** *v/t* gritar a
shout·ing ['ʃaʊtɪŋ] *n* griterío *m*
shove [ʃʌv] 1 *n* empujón *m* 2 *v/t & v/i* empujar
◆ **shove in** *v/i in line* meterse empujando
◆ **shove off** *v/i* F (*go away*) largarse F
shov·el ['ʃʌvl] 1 *n* pala *f* 2 *v/t*: *shovel*

snow off the path retirar a paladas la nieve del camino
show [ʃoʊ] 1 *n* THEA espectáculo *m*; TV programa *m*; *of emotion* muestra *f*; *on show at exhibition* expuesto, en exposición 2 *v/t* (*pret showed, pp shown*) *passport, ticket* enseñar, mostrar; *interest, emotion* mostrar; *at exhibition* exponer; *movie* proyectar; *show s.o. sth, show sth to s.o.* enseñar *or* mostrar algo a alguien 3 *v/i* (*pret showed, pp shown*) (*be visible*) verse; *what's showing at ...? of movie* qué ponen en el ...?
◆ **show around** *v/t* enseñar; *he showed us around* nos enseñó la casa / el edificio *etc*
◆ **show in** *v/t* hacer pasar a
◆ **show off** 1 *v/t skills* mostrar 2 *v/i pej* presumir, alardear
◆ **show up** 1 *v/t shortcomings etc* poner de manifiesto; *don't show me up in public* (*embarrass*) no me avergüences en público 2 *v/i* (*be visible*) verse; F (*arrive, turn up*) aparecer
'show busi·ness el mundo del espectáculo
'show·case *n* vitrina *f*; *fig* escaparate *m*
'show·down enfrentamiento *m*
show·er ['ʃaʊər] *n* 1 *n of rain* chaparrón *m*, chubasco *m*; *to wash* ducha *f*, *Mex* regadera *f*; (*party*) *fiesta con motivo de un bautizo, una boda etc., en la que los invitados llevan obsequios*; *take a shower* ducharse 2 *v/i* ducharse 3 *v/t*: *shower s.o. with compliments / praise* colmar a alguien de cumplidos / alabanzas
'show·er cap gorro *m* de baño
'show·er cur·tain cortina *f* de ducha
'show·er-proof *adj* impermeable
'show·jump·ing concurso *m* de saltos
shown [ʃoʊn] *pp* → **show**
'show-off *n pej* fanfarrón(-ona) *m(f)*
'show·room sala *f* de exposición *f*; *in showroom condition* como nuevo
show·y ['ʃoʊɪ] *adj jacket, behavior* llamativo
shrank [ʃræŋk] *pret* → **shrink¹**
shred [ʃred] 1 *n of paper etc* trozo *m*; *of fabric* jirón *m*; *there isn't a shred of evi-*

dence no hay prueba alguna **2** v/t (pret & pp **shredded**) paper hacer trizas; in cooking cortar en tiras

shred·der ['ʃredər] for documents trituradora f (de documentos)

shrewd [ʃruːd] adj person astuto; judgment, investment inteligente

shrewd·ness ['ʃruːdnɪs] of person astucia f; of decision inteligencia f

shriek [ʃriːk] **1** n alarido m, chillido m **2** v/i chillar

shrill [ʃrɪl] adj estridente, agudo

shrimp [ʃrɪmp] gamba f; larger Span langostino m, L.Am. camarón m

shrine [ʃraɪn] santuario m

shrink¹ [ʃrɪŋk] v/i (pret **shrank**, pp **shrunk**) of material encoger(se); level of support etc reducirse

shrink² [ʃrɪŋk] n F (psychiatrist) psiquiatra m/f

'shrink-wrap v/t (pret & pp **shrink-wrapped**) envolver en plástico adherente

'shrink-wrap·ping material plástico adherente para envolver

shriv·el ['ʃrɪvl] v/i of skin arrugarse; of leaves marchitarse

Shrove Tues·day [ʃroʊv] martes m inv de Carnaval

shrub [ʃrʌb] arbusto m

shrub·ber·y ['ʃrʌbərɪ] arbustos mpl

shrug [ʃrʌg] **1** n: ... he said with a shrug ... dijo encogiendo los hombros **2** v/i (pret & pp **shrugged**) encoger los hombros **3** v/t (pret & pp **shrugged**): **shrug one's shoulders** encoger los hombros

shrunk [ʃrʌŋk] → **shrink¹**

shud·der ['ʃʌdər] **1** n of fear, disgust escalofrío m; of earth, building temblor m **2** v/i of fear, disgust estremecerse; of earth, building temblar; **I shudder to think** me estremezco de pensar

shuf·fle ['ʃʌfl] **1** v/t cards barajar **2** v/i in walking arrastrar los pies

shun [ʃʌn] v/t (pret & pp **shunned**) rechazar

shut [ʃʌt] v/t & v/i (pret & pp **shut**) cerrar

◆ **shut down 1** v/t business cerrar; computer apagar **2** v/i of business cerrarse; of computer apagarse

◆ **shut off** v/t cortar

◆ **shut up** v/i F (be quiet) callarse; **shut up!** ¡cállate!

shut·ter ['ʃʌtər] on window contraventana f; PHOT obturador m

'shut·ter speed PHOT tiempo m de exposición

shut·tle ['ʃʌtl] v/i: **shuttle between** of bus conectar; of airplane hacer el puente aéreo entre

'shut·tle·bus at airport autobús m de conexión

'shut·tle·cock SP volante m

'shut·tle ser·vice servicio m de conexión

shy [ʃaɪ] adj tímido

shy·ness ['ʃaɪnɪs] timidez f

Si·a·mese 'twins [saɪə'miːz] npl siameses mpl (fpl)

sick [sɪk] adj enfermo; sense of humor morboso, macabro; society enfermo; **be sick of** (fed up with) estar harto de

sick·en ['sɪkn] **1** v/t (disgust) poner enfermo **2** v/i: **be sickening for sth** estar incubando algo

sick·en·ing ['sɪknɪŋ] adj stench nauseabundo; behavior, crime repugnante

'sick leave baja f (por enfermedad); **be on sick leave** estar de baja

sick·ly ['sɪklɪ] adj person enfermizo; color pálido

sick·ness ['sɪknɪs] enfermedad f; (vomiting) vómitos mpl

side [saɪd] n of box, house, field lado m; of mountain ladera f, vertiente f; of person costado m; SP equipo m; **take sides** (favor one side) tomar partido (**with** por); **I'm on your side** estoy de parte tuya; **side by side** uno al lado del otro; **at the side of the road** al lado de la carretera; **on the big / small side** un poco grande / pequeño

◆ **side with** v/t tomar partido por

'side·board aparador m

'side·burns npl patillas fpl

'side dish plato m de acompañamiento

'side ef·fect efecto m secundario

'side·light MOT luz f de posición

'side·line 1 n actividad f complementaria **2** v/t: **feel sidelined** sentirse marginado 'side·step v/t (pret & pp **sidestepped**) fig evadir

'side street bocacalle f

'side·track v/t distraer; **get sidetracked** distraerse

'side·walk acera f, Rpl vereda f, Mex banqueta f

side·walk 'caf·é terraza f

side·ways ['saɪdweɪz] adv de lado

siege [si:dʒ] sitio m; **lay siege to** sitiar

sieve [sɪv] n tamiz m

sift [sɪft] v/t flour tamizar; data examinar a fondo

◆ sift through v/t details, data pasar por el tamiz

sigh [saɪ] 1 n suspiro m; **heave a sigh of relief** suspirar de alivio 2 v/i suspirar

sight [saɪt] n vista f; (power of seeing) vista f, visión f; **sights** of city lugares mpl de interés; **he can't stand the sight of blood** no aguanta ver sangre; **I caught sight of him just as ...** lo vi justo cuando ...; **know by sight** conocer de vista; **within sight of** a la vista de; **as soon as the car was out of sight** en cuanto se dejó de ver el coche; **what a sight you look!** ¡qué pintas llevas!; **lose sight of** objective etc olvidarse de

sight·see·ing ['saɪtsi:ɪŋ] n: **we like sight-seeing** nos gusta hacer turismo; **go sightseeing** hacer turismo

'sight·see·ing tour visita f turística

sight·seer ['saɪtsi:ər] turista m/f

sign [saɪn] 1 n señal f; outside shop, on building cartel m, letrero m; **it's a sign of the times** es un signo de los tiempos que corren 2 v/t & v/i firmar

◆ sign in v/i registrarse

◆ sign up v/i (join the army) alistarse

sig·nal ['sɪɡnl] 1 n señal f; **send out all the wrong signals** dar a una impresión equivocada 2 v/i of driver poner el intermitente

sig·na·to·ry ['sɪɡnətɔːri] n signatario(-a) m(f), firmante m/f

sig·na·ture ['sɪɡnətʃər] n firma f

sig·na·ture 'tune sintonía f

sig·net ring ['sɪɡnɪt] sello m (anillo)

sig·nif·i·cance [sɪɡ'nɪfɪkəns] importan-

cia f, relevancia f

sig·nif·i·cant [sɪɡ'nɪfɪkənt] adj event etc importante, relevante; (quite large) considerable

sig·nif·i·cant·ly [sɪɡ'nɪfɪkəntli] adv larger, more expensive considerablemente

sig·ni·fy ['sɪɡnɪfaɪ] v/t (pret & pp **signified**) significar, suponer

'sign lan·guage lenguaje m por señas

'sign·post señal f

si·lence ['saɪləns] 1 n silencio m; **in silence** work, march en silencio; **silence!** ¡silencio! 2 v/t hacer callar

si·lenc·er ['saɪlənsər] on gun silenciador m

si·lent ['saɪlənt] adj silencioso; movie mudo; **stay silent** (not comment) permanecer callado

sil·hou·ette [sɪluː'et] n silueta f

sil·i·con ['sɪlɪkən] silicio m

sil·i·con 'chip chip m de silicio

sil·i·cone ['sɪlɪkoʊn] silicona f

silk [sɪlk] 1 n seda f 2 adj shirt etc de seda

silk·y ['sɪlki] adj hair, texture sedoso

sil·li·ness ['sɪlɪnɪs] tontería f, estupidez f

sil·ly ['sɪli] adj tonto, estúpido

si·lo ['saɪloʊ] silo m

sil·ver ['sɪlvər] 1 n metal, medal plata f; (silver objects) (objetos mpl de) plata f 2 adj ring de plata; hair canoso

sil·ver·plat·ed [sɪlvər'pleɪtɪd] adj plateado

sil·ver·ware ['sɪlvərwer] plata f

sil·ver 'wed·ding bodas fpl de plata

sim·i·lar ['sɪmɪlər] adj parecido, similar; **be similar to** ser parecido a, parecerse a

sim·i·lar·i·ty [sɪmɪ'lærəti] parecido m, similitud f

sim·i·lar·ly ['sɪmɪlərli] adv de la misma manera

sim·mer ['sɪmər] v/i in cooking cocer a fuego lento; **be simmering** (with rage) estar a punto de explotar

◆ simmer down v/i tranquilizarse

sim·ple ['sɪmpl] adj (easy, not fancy) sencillo; person simple

sim·ple-mind·ed [sɪmpl'maɪndɪd] adj pej simplón

sim·pli·ci·ty [sɪm'plɪsəti] of task, design

S

sencillez f, simplicidad f

sim·pli·fy ['sɪmplɪfaɪ] v/t (pret & pp **simplified**) simplificar

sim·plis·tic [sɪm'plɪstɪk] adj simplista

sim·ply ['sɪmplɪ] adv sencillamente; **it is simply the best** es sin lugar a dudas el mejor

sim·u·late ['sɪmjʊleɪt] v/t simular

sim·ul·ta·ne·ous [saɪml'teɪnɪəs] adj simultáneo

sim·ul·ta·ne·ous·ly [saɪml'teɪnɪəslɪ] adv simultáneamente

sin [sɪn] **1** n pecado m **2** v/i (pret & pp **sinned**) pecar

since [sɪns] **1** prep desde; **since last week** desde la semana pasada **2** adv desde entonces; **I haven't seen him since** no lo he visto desde entonces **3** conj in expressions of time desde que; (seeing that) ya que, dado que; **since you left** desde que te marchaste; **since I have been living here** desde que vivo aquí; **since you don't like it** ya que or dado que no te gusta

sin·cere [sɪn'sɪr] adj sincero

sin·cere·ly [sɪn'sɪrlɪ] adv sinceramente; **I sincerely hope he appreciates it** espero de verdad que lo aprecie; **Yours sincerely** atentamente

sin·cer·i·ty [sɪn'serətɪ] sinceridad f

sin·ful ['sɪnfʊl] adj person pecador; things pecaminoso; **it is sinful to ...** es pecado ...

sing [sɪŋ] v/t & v/i (pret **sang**, pp **sung**) cantar

singe [sɪndʒ] v/t chamuscar

sing·er ['sɪŋər] cantante m/f

sin·gle ['sɪŋgl] **1** adj (sole) único, solo; (not double) único; (not married) soltero m; **there wasn't a single mistake** no había ni un solo error; **in single file** en fila india; **single currency** moneda única **2** n MUS sencillo m; (single room) habitación f individual; person soltero(-a) m(f); Br ticket billete m or L.Am. boleto m de ida; **holidays for singles** vacaciones para gente sin pareja; **singles** in tennis individuales mpl

♦ **single out** v/t (choose) seleccionar;

(distinguish) distinguir

sin·gle-breast·ed [sɪŋgl'brestɪd] adj recto, con una fila de botones

sin·gle-'hand·ed [sɪŋgl'hændɪd] **1** adj en solitario **2** adv en solitario

sin·gle-mind·ed [sɪŋgl'maɪndɪd] adj determinado, resuelto

Sin·gle 'Mar·ket Mercado m Único

sin·gle 'moth·er madre f soltera

sin·gle 'pa·rent padre m/madre f soltero(-a)

sin·gle pa·rent 'fam·i·ly familia f monoparental

sin·gle 'room habitación f individual

sin·gu·lar ['sɪŋgjʊlər] **1** adj GRAM singular **2** n GRAM singular m; **in the singular** en singular

sin·is·ter ['sɪnɪstər] adj siniestro; sky amenazador

sink [sɪŋk] **1** n in kitchen fregadero m; in bathroom lavabo m **2** v/i (pret **sank**, pp **sunk**) of ship, object hundirse; of sun ponerse; of interest rates, pressure etc descender, bajar; **he sank onto the bed** se tiró a la cama **3** v/t (pret **sank**, pp **sunk**) ship hundir; funds investir

♦ **sink in** v/i of liquid penetrar; **it still hasn't really sunk in** of realization todavía no lo he asumido

sin·ner ['sɪnər] pecador(a) m(f)

si·nus ['saɪnəs] seno m (nasal)

si·nus·i·tis [saɪnə'saɪtɪs] MED sinusitis f

sip [sɪp] **1** n sorbo m **2** v/t (pret & pp **sipped**) sorber

sir [sɜːr] señor m; **excuse me, sir** perdone, caballero

si·ren ['saɪrən] sirena f

sir·loin ['sɜːrlɔɪn] solomillo m

sis·ter ['sɪstər] hermana f

'sis·ter-in-law (pl **sisters-in-law**) cuñada f

sit [sɪt] **1** v/i (pret & pp **sat**) estar sentado; (sit down) sentarse **2** v/t (pret & pp **sat**) exam presentarse a

♦ **sit down** v/i sentarse

♦ **sit up** v/i in bed incorporarse; (straighten back) sentarse derecho; (wait up at night) esperar levantado

sit·com ['sɪtkɑːm] telecomedia f, comedia *f* de situación

site [saɪt] **1** *n* emplazamiento *m*; *of battle* lugar *m* **2** *v/t new offices etc* situar

sit·ting ['sɪtɪŋ] *n of committee, court, for artist* sesión *f*; *for meals* turno *m*

'sit·ting room sala *f* de estar, salón *m*

sit·u·at·ed ['sɪtʊeɪtɪd] *adj* situado

sit·u·a·tion [sɪtʊ'eɪʃn] situación *f*

six [sɪks] seis

six·teen [sɪks'tiːn] dieciséis

six·teenth [sɪks'tiːnθ] *n & adj* decimosexto

sixth [sɪksθ] *n & adj* sexto

six·ti·eth [sɪkstɪɪθ] *n & adj* sexagésimo

six·ty ['sɪkstɪ] sesenta

size [saɪz] tamaño *m*; *of loan* importe *m*; *of jacket* talla *f*; *of shoes* número *m*

◆ **size up** *v/t* evaluar, examinar

size·a·ble ['saɪzəbl] *adj house, order* considerable; *meal* copioso

siz·zle ['sɪzl] *v/i* chisporrotear

skate [skeɪt] **1** *n* patín *m* **2** *v/i* patinar

skate·board ['skeɪtbɔːrd] *n* monopatín *m*

skate·board·er ['skeɪtbɔːrdər] *persona que patina en monopatín*

skate·board·ing ['skeɪtbɔːrdɪŋ] patinaje *m* en monopatín

skat·er ['skeɪtər] patinador(a) *m(f)*

skat·ing ['skeɪtɪŋ] *n* patinaje *m*

'skat·ing rink pista *f* de patinaje

skel·e·ton ['skelɪtn] esqueleto *m*

'skel·e·ton key llave *f* maestra

skep·tic ['skeptɪk] escéptico(-a) *m(f)*

skep·ti·cal ['skeptɪkl] *adj* escéptico

skep·ti·cism ['skeptɪsɪzm] escepticismo *m*

sketch [sketʃ] **1** *n* boceto *m*, esbozo *m*; THEA sketch *m* **2** *v/t* bosquejar

'sketch·book cuaderno *m* de dibujo

sketch·y ['sketʃɪ] *adj knowledge etc* básico, superficial

skew·er ['skjʊər] *n* brocheta *f*

ski [skiː] **1** *n* esquí *m* **2** *v/i* esquiar

'ski boots *npl* botas *fpl* de esquí

skid [skɪd] **1** *n of car* patinazo *m*; *of person* resbalón *m* **2** *v/i* (*pret & pp* **skidded**) *of car* patinar; *of person* resbalar

ski·er ['skiːər] esquiador(a) *m(f)*

ski·ing ['skiːɪŋ] esquí *m*

'ski in·struc·tor monitor(a) *m(f)* de esquí

skil·ful *etc Br* → **skillful** *etc*

'ski lift remonte *m*

skill [skɪl] destreza *f*, habilidad *f*

skilled [skɪld] *adj* capacitado, preparado

skilled 'work·er trabajador(a) *m(f)* cualificado

'skill·ful ['skɪlfəl] *adj* hábil, habilidoso

skill·ful·ly ['skɪlfəlɪ] *adv* con habilidad *or* destreza

skim [skɪm] *v/t* (*pret & pp* **skimmed**) *surface* rozar; *milk* desnatar, descremar

◆ **skim off** *v/t the best* escoger

◆ **skim through** *v/t text* leer por encima

skimmed 'milk [skɪmd] leche *f* desnatada *or* descremada

skimp·y ['skɪmpɪ] *adj account etc* superficial; *dress* cortísimo; *bikini* mínimo

skin [skɪn] **1** *n* piel *f* **2** *v/t* (*pret & pp* **skinned**) despellejar, desollar

'skin div·ing buceo *m* (en bañador)

skin·flint ['skɪnflɪnt] F agarrado(a) *m(f)* F, roñoso(-a) *m(f)*

'skin graft injerto *m* de piel

skin·ny ['skɪnɪ] *adj* escuálido

'skin-tight *adj* ajustado

skip [skɪp] **1** *n* (*little jump*) brinco *m*, saltito *m* **2** *v/i* (*pret & pp* **skipped**) brincar **3** *v/t* (*pret & pp* **skipped**) (*omit*) pasar por alto

'ski pole bastón *m* de esquí

skip·per ['skɪpər] NAUT patrón(-ona) *m(f)*, capitán (-ana) *m(f)*; *of team* capitán(-ana) *m(f)*

'ski re·sort estación *f* de esquí

skirt [skɜːrt] *n* falda *f*

'ski run pista *f* de esquí

'ski tow telesquí *m*

skull [skʌl] cráneo *m*

skunk [skʌŋk] mofeta *f*

sky [skaɪ] cielo *m*

'sky·light claraboya *f*

'sky·line horizonte *m*

'sky·scrap·er ['skaɪskreɪpər] rascacielos *m inv*

slab [slæb] *of stone* losa *f*; *of cake etc* trozo *m* grande

slack [slæk] *adj rope* flojo; *work* descuidado; *period* tranquilo; **discipline is**

very slack no hay disciplina

slack·en ['slækn] *v/t rope, pace* aflojar; *pace*

◆ **slacken off** *v/i of trading, pace* disminuir

slacks [slæks] *npl* pantalones *mpl*

slain [sleɪn] *pp* → **slay**

slam [slæm] **1** *v/t* (*pret & pp* **slammed**) *door* cerrar de un golpe **2** *v/i* (*pret & pp* **slammed**) *of door* cerrarse de golpe

◆ **slam down** *v/t* estampar

slan·der ['slændər] **1** *n* difamación *f* **2** *v/t* difamar

slan·der·ous ['slændərəs] *adj* difamatorio

slang [slæŋ] argot *m*, jerga *f*; *of a specific group* jerga *f*

slant [slænt] **1** *v/i* inclinarse **2** *n* inclinación *f*; *given to a story* enfoque *m*

slant·ing ['slæntɪŋ] *adj roof* inclinado; *eyes* rasgado

slap [slæp] **1** *n* (*blow*) bofetada *f*, cachete *m* **2** *v/t* (*pret & pp* **slapped**) dar una bofetada *or* un cachete a; **slap s.o. in the face** dar una bofetada a alguien

'slap-dash *adj* chapucero

slash [slæʃ] **1** *n* (*cut*) corte *m*, raja *f*; *in punctuation* barra *f* **2** *v/t skin etc* cortar; *prices, costs* recortar drásticamente; **slash one's wrists** cortarse las venas

slate [sleɪt] *n* pizarra *f*

slaugh·ter ['slɔːtər] **1** *n of animals* sacrificio *m*; *of people, troops* matanza *f* **2** *v/t animals* sacrificar; *people, troops* masacrar

'slaugh·ter·house *for animals* matadero *m*

Slav [slɑːv] *adj* eslavo

slave [sleɪv] *n* esclavo(-a) *m(f)*

'slave-driv·er F negrero(-a) *m(f)* F

slay [sleɪ] *v/t* (*pret* **slew**, *pp* **slain**) asesinar

slay·ing ['sleɪɪŋ] (*murder*) asesinato *m*

sleaze [sliːz] POL corrupción *f*

slea·zy ['sliːzɪ] *adj bar* sórdido; *person de* mala calaña

sled, sledge [sled, sledʒ] *n* trineo *m*

'sledge ham·mer mazo *m*

sleep [sliːp] **1** *n* sueño *m*; **go to sleep** dormirse; **I need a good sleep** necesito dor-

mir bien; **I couldn't get to sleep** no pude dormirme **2** *v/i* (*pret & pp* **slept**) dormir

◆ **sleep in** *v/i* (*have a long lie*) dormir hasta tarde

◆ **sleep on** *v/t*: **sleep on sth** *decision* consultar algo con la almohada

◆ **sleep with** *v/t* (*have sex with*) acostarse con

sleep·i·ly ['sliːpɪlɪ] *adv*: **say sth sleepily** decir algo medio dormido

'sleep·ing bag ['sliːpɪŋ] saco *m* de dormir

'sleep·ing car RAIL coche *m* cama

'sleep·ing pill somnífero *m*, pastilla *f* para dormir

sleep·less ['sliːplɪs] *adj*: **have a sleepless night** pasar la noche en blanco

'sleep walk·er sonámbulo(-a) *m(f)*

'sleep walk·ing sonambulismo *m*

sleep·y ['sliːpɪ] *adj* adormilado, somnoliento; *town* tranquilo; **I'm sleepy** tengo sueño

sleet [sliːt] *n* aguanieve *f*

sleeve [sliːv] *of jacket etc* manga *f*

sleeve·less ['sliːvlɪs] *adj* sin mangas

sleigh [sleɪ] *n* trineo *m*

sleight of 'hand [slaɪt] juegos *mpl* de manos

slen·der ['slendər] *adj figure, arms* esbelto; *income, margin* escaso; *chance* remoto

slept [slept] *pret & pp* → **sleep**

slew [sluː] *pret* → **slay**

slice [slaɪs] **1** *n of bread* rebanada *f*; *of cake* trozo *m*; *of salami, cheese* loncha *f*; *fig: of profits etc* parte *f* **2** *v/t loaf etc* cortar (en rebanadas)

sliced 'bread [slaɪst] pan *m* de molde en rebanadas; **the greatest thing since sliced bread** F lo mejor desde que se inventó la rueda F

slick [slɪk] **1** *adj performance* muy logrado; (*pej: cunning*) con mucha labia **2** *n of oil* marea *f* negra

slid [slɪd] *pret & pp* → **slide**

slide [slaɪd] **1** *n for kids* tobogán *m*; PHOT diapositiva *f* **2** *v/i* (*pret & pp* **slid**) deslizarse; *of exchange rate etc* descender **3** *v/t* (*pret & pp* **slid**) deslizar

slid·ing 'door [slaɪdɪŋ] puerta *f* corredera

slight [slaɪt] **1** *adj person, figure* menudo; (*small*) pequeño; *accent* ligero; *I have a slight headache* me duele un poco la cabeza; *no, not in the slightest* no, en absoluto

slight·ly ['slaɪtlɪ] *adv* un poco

slim [slɪm] **1** *adj* delgado; *chance* remoto **2** *v/i* (*pret & pp* **slimmed**): *I'm slimming* estoy a dieta

slime [slaɪm] (*mud*) lodo *m*; *of slug etc* baba *f*

slim·y ['slaɪmɪ] *adj liquid* viscoso; *river bed* lleno de lodo

sling [slɪŋ] **1** *n for arm* cabestrillo *m* **2** *v/t* (*pret & pp* **slung**) F (*throw*) tirar

slip [slɪp] **1** *n on ice etc* resbalón *m*; (*mistake*) desliz *m*; *a slip of paper* un trozo de papel; *a slip of the tongue* un lapsus; *give s.o. the slip* dar esquinazo a alguien **2** *v/i* (*pret & pp* **slipped**) *on ice etc* resbalar; *of quality etc* empeorar; *he slipped out of the room* se fue de la habitación sigilosamente **3** *v/t* (*pret & pp* **slipped**) (*put*): *he slipped it into his briefcase* lo metió en su maletín sigilosamente; *it slipped my mind* se me olvidó

◆ **slip away** *v/i of time* pasar; *of opportunity* esfumarse; (*die quietly*) morir tranquilamente

◆ **slip off** *v/t jacket etc* quitarse

◆ **slip on** *v/t jacket etc* ponerse

◆ **slip out** *v/i* (*go out*) salir (sigilosamente)

◆ **slip up** *v/i* equivocarse

slipped 'disc [slɪpt] hernia *f* discal

slip·per ['slɪpər] zapatilla *f* (*de estar por casa*)

slip·per·y ['slɪpərɪ] *adj surface, road* resbaladizo; *fish* escurridizo

slip·shod ['slɪpʃɑːd] *adj* chapucero

'slip-up (*mistake*) error *m*

slit [slɪt] **1** *n* (*tear*) raja *f*; (*hole*) rendija *f*; *in skirt* corte *m* **2** *v/t* (*pret & pp* **slit**) abrir; *slit s.o.'s throat* degollar a alguien

slith·er ['slɪðər] *v/i* deslizarse

sliv·er ['slɪvər] trocito *m*; *of wood, glass* astilla *f*

slob [slɑːb] *pej* dejado(-a) *m/f*, guarro(-a) *m/f*

slob·ber ['slɑːbər] *v/i* babear

slog [slɑːg] *n* paliza *f*

slo·gan ['slougən] eslogan *m*

slop [slɑːp] *v/t* (*pret & pp* **slopped**) derramar

slope [sloup] **1** *n of roof, handwriting* inclinación *f*; *of mountain* ladera *f*; *built on a slope* construido en una pendiente **2** *v/i* inclinarse; *the road slopes down to the sea* la carretera baja hasta el mar

slop·py ['slɑːpɪ] *adj* descuidado; *too sentimental* sensiblero

slot [slɑːt] **1** *n* ranura *f*; *in schedule* hueco *m*

◆ **slot in 1** *v/t* (*pret & pp* **slotted**) introducir **2** *v/i* (*pret & pp* **slotted**) encajar

'slot ma·chine *for cigarettes, food* máquina *f* expendedora; *for gambling* máquina *f* tragaperras

slouch [slautʃ] *v/i*: *don't slouch* ponte derecho

slov·en·ly ['slʌvnlɪ] *adj* descuidado

slow [slou] *adj* lento; *be slow of clock* ir retrasado

◆ **slow down 1** *v/t work, progress* restrasar; *traffic, production* ralentizar **2** *v/i in walking, driving* reducir la velocidad; *of production etc* relantizarse; *you need to slow down in lifestyle* tienes que tomarte las cosas con calma

'slow-down *in production* ralentización *f*

slow·ly ['sloulɪ] *adv* despacio, lentamente

slow 'mo·tion: *in slow motion* a cámara lenta

slow·ness ['slounɪs] lentitud *f*

'slow-poke F tortuga *f* F

slug [slʌg] *n animal* babosa *f*

slug·gish ['slʌgɪʃ] *adj* lento

slum [slʌm] *n* suburbio *m*, arrabal *m*

slump [slʌmp] **1** *n in trade* desplome *m* **2** *v/i economically* desplomarse, hundirse; (*collapse: of person*) desplomarse

slung [slʌŋ] *pret & pp* → **sling**

slur [slɜːr] **1** *n on s.o.'s character* difamación *f* **2** *v/t* (*pret & pp* **slurred**) *words* arrastrar

slurp [slɜːrp] *v/t* sorber

S

slurred [slɜːrd] adj: *his speech was slurred* habló arrastrando las palabras

slush [slʌʃ] nieve f derretida; (*pej: sentimental stuff*) sensiblería f

'**slush fund** fondo m para corruptelas

slush·y ['slʌʃɪ] adj *snow* derretido; *movie, novel* sensiblero or trivialidades

slut [slʌt] *pej* fulana f

sly [slaɪ] adj ladino; *on the sly* a escondidas

smack [smæk] **1** n: *a smack on the bottom* un azote; *a smack in the face* una bofetada **2** v/t *child* pegar; *bottom* dar un azote en

small ['smɔːl] adj pequeño, *L.Am.* chico

small 'change cambio m, suelto m, *L.Am.* sencillo m

small 'hours npl madrugada f

small·pox ['smɔːlpɑːks] viruela f

'**small print** letra f pequeña

'**small talk**: *make small talk* hablar de banalidades or trivialidades

smart [smɑːrt] **1** adj (*elegant*) elegante; (*intelligent*) inteligente; *pace* rápido; *get smart with* hacerse el listillo con **2** v/i (*hurt*) escocer

'**smart ass** F sabelotodo m/f F

'**smart card** tarjeta f inteligente

♦ **smart·en up** ['smɑːrtn] v/t *appearance* mejorar; *room* arreglar

smart·ly ['smɑːrtlɪ] adv *dressed* con elegancia

smash [smæʃ] **1** n *noise* estruendo m; (*car crash*) choque m; *in tennis* smash m, mate m **2** v/t *break* hacer pedazos or añicos; *he smashed the toys against the wall* estrelló los juguetes contra la pared; *he smashed his fist on the table* dio un puñetazo en la mesa; *smash sth to pieces* hacer algo añicos **3** v/i *break* romperse; *the driver smashed into ...* el conductor se estrelló contra ...

♦ **smash up** v/t *place* destrozar

smash 'hit F exitazo m F

smat·ter·ing ['smætərɪŋ] *of a language* nociones fpl

smear ['smɪr] **1** n *of ink* borrón m; *of paint* mancha f; MED citología f; *on character* difamación f **2** v/t *character* difamar;

smear X over Y untar or embadurnar Y de X

'**smear cam·paign** campaña f de difamación

smell [smel] **1** n olor m; *it has no smell* no huele a nada; *sense of smell* sentido m del olfato **2** v/t oler **3** v/i unpleasantly oler (mal); (*sniff*) olfatear; *you smell of beer* hueles a cerveza; *it smells good* huele bien

smell·y ['smelɪ] adj apestoso; *she had smelly feet* le olían los pies; *it's so smelly in here!* ¡qué mal huele aquí!

smile [smaɪl] **1** n sonrisa f **2** v/i sonreír

♦ **smile at** v/t sonreír a

smirk [smɜːrk] **1** n sonrisa f maligna **2** v/i sonreír malignamente

smog [smɑːg] niebla f tóxica

smoke [smoʊk] **1** n humo m; *have a smoke* fumarse un cigarrillo **2** v/t *cigarettes* fumar; *bacon* ahumar **3** v/i *of person* fumar

smok·er ['smoʊkər] *person* fumador(a) m(a)

smok·ing ['smoʊkɪŋ]: *smoking is bad for you* fumar es malo; *no smoking sign* prohibido fumar

'**smok·ing com·part·ment** RAIL compartimento m de fumadores

smok·y ['smoʊkɪ] adj *room, air* lleno de humo

smooth [smuːð] **1** adj *surface, skin* liso, suave; *sea* en calma; (*peaceful*) tranquilo; *ride, drive* sin vibraciones; *transition* sin problemas; *pej: person* meloso **2** v/t *hair* alisar

♦ **smooth down** v/t with sandpaper etc alisar

♦ **smooth out** v/t *paper, cloth* alisar

♦ **smooth over** v/t: *smooth things over* suavizar las cosas

smooth·ly ['smuːðlɪ] adv *without any problems* sin incidentes

smoth·er ['smʌðər] v/t *flames* apagar, sofocar; *person* asfixiar; *smother s.o. with kisses* comerse a alguien a besos; *he smothered the bread with jam* cubrió or embardurnó el pan de mermelada

smol·der, *Br* **smoul·der** ['smoʊldər] v/i of

fire arder (*los rescoldos*); *fig: with anger* arder de rabia; *fig: with desire* arder en deseos

smudge [smʌdʒ] **1** *n of paint* mancha *f; of ink* borrón *m* **2** *v/t ink* emborronar; *paint* difuminar

smug [smʌg] *adj* engreído

smug·gle ['smʌgl] *v/t* pasar de contrabando

smug·gler ['smʌglər] contrabandista *m/f*

smug·gling ['smʌglɪŋ] contrabando *m*

smug·ly ['smʌglɪ] *adv* con engreimiento *or* suficiencia

smut·ty ['smʌtɪ] *adj joke, sense of humor* obsceno

snack [snæk] *n* tentempié *m*, aperitivo *m*

'**snack bar** cafetería *f*

snag [snæg] *n* (*problem*) inconveniente *m*, pega *f*

snail [sneɪl] *n* caracol *m*

snake [sneɪk] *n* serpiente *f*

snap [snæp] **1** *n* chasquido *m*; PHOT foto *f* **2** *v/t* (*pret & pp* **snapped**) *break* romper **3** *v/i* (*pret & pp* **snapped**) *break* romperse; ***none of your business, she snapped*** no es asunto tuyo, saltó **4** *adj decision, judgment* rápido, súbito

◆ **snap up** *v/t bargains* llevarse

snap fast·en·er ['snæpfæsnər] automático *m*, corchete *m*

snap·py ['snæpɪ] *adj person, mood* irascible; *decision, response* rápido; (*elegant*) elegante

'**snap·shot** foto *f*

snarl [snɑːrl] **1** *n of dog* gruñido *m* **2** *v/i* gruñir

snatch [snætʃ] **1** *v/t* arrebatar; (*steal*) robar; (*kidnap*) secuestrar; ***snatch sth from s.o.*** arrebatar algo a alguien **2** *v/i*: ***don't snatch*** no lo agarres

◆ **snatch at** *v/t* intentar agarrar

snaz·zy ['snæzɪ] *adj* F vistoso, *Span* chulo F

sneak [sniːk] **1** *n* (*telltale*) chivato(-a) *m(f)* **2** *v/t* (*remove, steal*) llevarse; ***sneak a glance at*** mirar con disimulo a **3** *v/i* (*tell tales*) chivarse; ***sneak into the room*** entrar a la habitación a hurtadillas

sneak·ers ['sniːkərz] *npl* zapatillas *fpl* de

deporte

sneak·ing ['sniːkɪŋ] *adj*: ***have a sneaking suspicion that ...*** sospechar que ...

sneak·y ['sniːkɪ] *adj* F (*crafty*) ladino, cuco F

sneer [snɪr] **1** *n* mueca *f* desdeñosa **2** *v/i* burlarse (***at*** de)

sneeze [sniːz] **1** *n* estornudo *m* **2** *v/i* estornudar

snick·er ['snɪkər] **1** *n* risita *f* **2** *v/i* reírse (*en voz baja*)

sniff [snɪf] **1** *v/i to clear nose* sorberse los mocos; *of dog* olfatear **2** *v/t* (*smell*) oler; *of dog* olfatear

snip [snɪp] *n* F (*bargain*) ganga *f*

snip·er ['snaɪpər] francotirador(a) *m(f)*

sniv·el ['snɪvl] *v/i* gimotear

snob [snɑːb] presuntuoso(-a) *m(f)*

snob·ber·y ['snɑːbərɪ] presuntuosidad *f*

snob·bish ['snɑːbɪʃ] *adj* presuntuoso

snoop [snuːp] *n* fisgón(-ona) *m(f)*

◆ **snoop around** *v/i* fisgonear

snoot·y ['snuːtɪ] *adj* presuntuoso

snooze [snuːz] **1** *n* cabezada *f*; ***have a snooze*** echar una cabezada **2** *v/i* echar una cabezada

snore [snɔːr] *v/i* roncar

snor·ing ['snɔːrɪŋ] *n* ronquidos *mpl*

snor·kel ['snɔːrkl] *n* snorkel *m*, tubo *m* para buceo

snort [snɔːrt] *v/i of bull, person* bufar, resoplar

snout [snaʊt] *of pig, dog* hocico *m*

snow [snoʊ] **1** *n* nieve *f* **2** *v/i* nevar

◆ **snow under** *v/i*: ***be snowed under*** estar desbordado

'**snow·ball** bola *f* de nieve

'**snow·bound** *adj* aislado por la nieve

'**snow chains** *npl* MOT cadenas *fpl* para la nieve

'**snow·drift** nevero *m*

'**snow·drop** campanilla *f* de invierno

'**snow·flake** copo *m* de nieve

'**snow·man** muñeco *m* de nieve

'**snow·plow** quitanieves *f inv*

'**snow·storm** tormenta *f* de nieve

snow·y ['snoʊɪ] *adj weather* de nieve; *roads, hills* nevado

snub [snʌb] **1** *n* desaire **2** *v/t* (*pret & pp*

snubbed) desairar

snub-nosed ['snʌbnoʊzd] *adj* con la nariz respingona

snug [snʌg] *adj* (*tight-fitting*) ajustado; *we are nice and snug in here* aquí se está muy a gusto

◆ **snug·gle down** ['snʌgl] *v/i* acurrucarse

◆ **snug·gle up to** *v/t* acurrucarse contra

so [soʊ] **1** *adv* tan; *it was so easy* fue tan fácil; *I'm so cold* tengo tanto frío; *that was so kind of you* fue muy amable de tu parte; *not so much* no tanto; *so much easier* mucho más fácil; *you shouldn't eat / drink so much* no deberías comer / beber tanto; *I miss you so* te echo tanto de menos; *so am / do I* yo también; *so is she / does she* ella también; *and so on* etcétera **2** *pron*: *I hope / think so* eso espero / creo; *you didn't tell me - I did so* no me lo dijiste - sí que lo hice; *50 or so* unos 50 **3** *conj for that reason* así que; *in order that* para que; *I got up late and so I missed the train* me levanté tarde y por eso perdí el tren; *so (that) I could come too* para que yo también pudiera venir; *so what?* F ¿y qué? F

soak [soʊk] *v/t* (*steep*) poner en remojo; *of water, rain* empapar

◆ **soak up** *v/t liquid* absorber; *soak up the sun* tostarse al sol

soaked [soʊkt] *adj* empapado; *be soaked to the skin* estar calado hasta los huesos

soak·ing (*wet*) [soʊkɪŋ] *adj* empapado

so-and-so ['soʊənsoʊ] F (*unknown person*) fulanito *m*; (*euph: annoying person*) canalla *m/f*

soap [soʊp] *for washing* jabón *m*

'soap (op·e·ra) telenovela *f*

soap·y ['soʊpɪ] *adj water* jabonoso

soar [sɔːr] *v/i of rocket etc* elevarse; *of prices* dispararse

sob [sɑːb] **1** *n* sollozo *m* **2** *v/i* (*pret & pp* **sobbed**) sollozar

so·ber ['soʊbər] *adj* (*not drunk*) sobrio; (*serious*) serio

◆ **sober up** *v/i*: *he sobered up* se le pasó la borrachera

so-'called *adj* (*referred to as*) así llamado; (*incorrectly referred to as*) mal llamado

soc·cer ['sɑːkər] fútbol *m*

'soc·cer hoo·li·gan hincha *m* violento

so·cia·ble ['soʊʃəbl] *adj* sociable

so·cial ['soʊʃl] *adj* social

so·cial 'dem·o·crat socialdemócrata *m/f*

so·cial·ism ['soʊʃəlɪzm] socialismo *m*

so·cial·ist ['soʊʃəlɪst] **1** *adj* socialista **2** *n* socialista *m/f*

so·cial·ize ['soʊʃəlaɪz] *v/i* socializar (*with* con)

'soc·ial life vida *f* social

so·cial 'sci·ence ciencia *f* social

'so·cial work trabajo *m* social

'so·cial work·er asistente(-a) *m(f)* social

so·ci·e·ty [sə'saɪətɪ] sociedad *f*

so·ci·ol·o·gist [soʊsɪ'ɑːlədʒɪst] sociólogo(-a) *m(f)*

so·ci·ol·o·gy [soʊsɪ'ɑːlədʒɪ] sociología *f*

sock[1] [sɑːk] *for wearing* calcetín *m*

sock[2] [sɑːk] **1** *n* (*punch*) puñetazo *m* **2** *v/t* (*punch*) dar un puñetazo a

sock·et ['sɑːkɪt] *for light bulb* casquillo *m*; *of arm* cavidad *f*; *of eye* cuenca *f*; *Br electrical* enchufe *m*

so·da ['soʊdə] (*soda water*) soda *f*; (*ice-cream soda*) refresco de soda con helado

sod·den ['sɑːdn] *adj* empapado

so·fa ['soʊfə] sofá *m*

'so·fa-bed sofá cama *m*

soft [sɑːft] *adj voice, light, color, skin* suave; *pillow, attitude* blando; *have a soft spot for* tener una debilidad por

'soft drink refresco *m*

'soft drug droga *f* blanda

soft·en ['sɑːfn] **1** *v/t position* ablandar; *impact, blow* amortiguar **2** *v/i of butter, ice cream* ablandarse, reblandecerse

soft·ly ['sɑːftlɪ] *adv* suavemente

soft 'toy peluche *m*

soft·ware ['sɑːftwer] software *m*

sog·gy ['sɑːgɪ] *adj* empapado

soil [sɔɪl] **1** *n* (*earth*) tierra *f* **2** *v/t* ensuciar

so·lar 'en·er·gy ['soʊlər] energía *f* solar

'so·lar pan·el panel *m* solar

'solar system sistema *m* solar

sold [soʊld] *pret & pp* → **sell**

sol·dier ['soʊldʒər] soldado *m*

◆ **soldier on** v/i seguir adelante; **we'll ha-ve to soldier on without her** nos las ten-dremos que arreglar sin ella

sole[1] [soʊl] n of foot planta f; of shoe suela f

sole[2] [soʊl] adj único

sole·ly ['soʊlɪ] adv únicamente

sol·emn ['sɑːləm] adj solemne

so·lem·ni·ty [sə'lemnətɪ] solemnidad f

sol·emn·ly ['sɑːləmlɪ] adv solemnemente

so·lic·it [sə'lɪsɪt] v/i of prostitute abordar clientes

so·lic·i·tor [sə'lɪsɪtər] Br abogado(-a) m(f) (que no aparece en tribunales)

sol·id ['sɑːlɪd] adj sólido; (without holes) compacto; gold, silver macizo; **a solid hour** una hora seguida

sol·i·dar·i·ty [sɑːlɪ'dærətɪ] solidaridad f

so·lid·i·fy [sə'lɪdɪfaɪ] v/i (pret & pp **solidified**) solidificarse

sol·id·ly ['sɑːlɪdlɪ] adv built sólidamente; in favor of sth unánimemente

so·lil·o·quy [sə'lɪləkwɪ] soliloquio f

sol·i·taire [sɑːlɪ'ter] card game solitario m

sol·i·ta·ry ['sɑːlɪterɪ] adj life, activity solitario; (single) único

sol·i·ta·ry con'fine·ment prisión f incomunicada

sol·i·tude ['sɑːlɪtuːd] soledad f

so·lo ['soʊloʊ] 1 n MUS solo m 2 adj en solitario

so·lo·ist ['soʊloʊɪst] solista m/f

sol·u·ble ['sɑːljubl] adj substance, problem soluble

so·lu·tion [sə'luːʃn] solución f (**to** a); (mixture) solución f

solve [sɑːlv] v/t problem solucionar, resolver; mystery resolver; crossword resolver, sacar

sol·vent ['sɑːlvənt] adj financially solvente

som·ber, Br **som·bre** ['sɑːmbər] adj (dark) oscuro; (serious) sombrío

some [sʌm] 1 adj: **would you like some water / cookies?** ¿quieres agua / galletas?; **some countries** algunos países; **I gave him some money** le di (algo de) dinero; **some people say that ...** hay quien dice ... 2 pron: **some of the group** parte del grupo; **would you like some?** ¿quieres?; **milk? - no thanks, I've got some** ¿leche? - gracias, ya tengo 3 adv (a bit): **we'll have to wait some** tendremos que esperar algo or un poco

some·bod·y ['sʌmbədɪ] pron alguien

'some·day adv algún día

'some·how adv (by one means or another) de alguna manera; (for some unknown reason) por alguna razón; **I've never liked him somehow** por alguna razón u otra nunca me cayó bien

'some·one pron → **somebody**

'some·place adv → **somewhere**

som·er·sault ['sʌmərsɔːlt] 1 n salto mortal 2 v/i dar un salto mortal

'some·thing pron algo; **would you like something to drink / eat?** ¿te gustaría beber / comer algo?; **is something wrong?** ¿pasa algo?

'some·time adv: **let's have lunch sometime** quedemos para comer un día de éstos; **sometime last year** en algún momento del año pasado

'some·times ['sʌmtaɪmz] adv a veces

'some·what adv un tanto

'some·where 1 adv en alguna parte or algún lugar 2 pron: **let's go to somewhere quiet** vamos a algún sitio tranquilo; **I was looking for somewhere to park** buscaba un sitio donde aparcar

son [sʌn] hijo m

so·na·ta [sə'nɑːtə] MUS sonata f

song [sɒŋ] canción f

'song·bird pájaro m cantor

'song·writ·er cantautor(a) m(f)

'son-in-law (pl **sons-in-law**) yerno m

'son·net ['sɑːnɪt] soneto m

soon [suːn] adv pronto; **how soon can you be ready to leave?** ¿cuándo estarás listo para salir?; **he left soon after I arrived** se marchó al poco de llegar yo; **can't you get here any sooner?** ¿no podrías llegar antes?; **as soon as** tan pronto como; **as soon as possible** lo antes posible; **sooner or later** tarde o temprano; **the sooner the better** cuanto antes mejor

soot [sʊt] hollín m

S

soothe [suːð] v/t calmar

so·phis·ti·cat·ed [səˈfɪstɪkeɪtɪd] adj sofisticado

so·phis·ti·ca·tion [səˈfɪstɪkeɪʃn] sofisticación f

soph·o·more [ˈsɑːfəmɔːr] estudiante m/f de segundo año

sop·py [ˈsɑːpɪ] adj F sensiblero

so·pra·no [səˈprænou] n singer soprano m/f; voice voz f de soprano

sor·did [ˈsɔːrdɪd] adj affair, business sórdido

sore [sɔːr] 1 adj (painful) dolorido; F (angry) enojado, Span mosqueado F; is it sore? ¿duele?; I'm sore all over me duele todo el cuerpo 2 n llaga f

sor·row [ˈsɑːrou] n pena f

sor·ry [ˈsɑːrɪ] adj (sad: day, sight) triste; (I'm) sorry! apologizing ¡lo siento!; I'm sorry that I didn't tell you sooner lamento no habértelo dicho antes; I was so sorry to hear of her death me dio mucha pena oír lo de su muerte; (I'm) sorry but I can't help le siento pero no puedo ayudar; I won't be sorry to leave here no me arrepentiré de irme de aquí; I feel sorry for her siento pena or lástima por ella; be a sorry sight ofrecer un espectáculo lamentable

sort [sɔːrt] 1 n clase f, tipo m; sort of F un poco, algo; is it finished? - sort of F ¿está acabado? - más o menos 2 v/t ordenar, clasificar; COMPUT ordenar

◆ sort out v/t papers ordenar, clasificar; problem resolver, arreglar

SOS [esouˈes] SOS m; fig llamada f de auxilio

so-'so adv F así así F

sought [sɔːt] pret & pp → seek

soul [soul] REL, fig: of a nation etc alma f; character personalidad f; the poor soul el pobrecillo

sound¹ [saund] 1 adj (sensible) sensato; (healthy) sano; sleep profundo 2 adv: be sound asleep estar profundamente dormido

sound² [saund] 1 n sonido m; (noise) ruido m 2 v/t (pronounce) pronunciar; MED auscultar; sound one's horn tocar la bo-

cina 3 v/i: that sounds interesting parece interesante; she sounded unhappy parecía triste

◆ sound out v/t sondear; I sounded her out about the idea sondeé a ver qué le parecía la idea

'sound card COMPUT tarjeta f de sonido

'sound ef·fects npl efectos mpl sonoros

sound·ly [ˈsaundlɪ] adv sleep profundamente; beaten rotundamente

'sound·proof adj insonorizado

'sound·track banda f sonora

soup [suːp] sopa f

'soup bowl cuenco m

souped-up [suːptˈʌp] adj F trucado

'soup plate plato m sopero

'soup spoon cuchara f sopera

sour [saur] adj apple, orange ácido, agrio; milk cortado; comment agrio

source [sɔːrs] n fuente f; of river nacimiento m; (person) fuente f

'sour cream nata f agria

south [sauθ] 1 adj sur, del sur 2 n sur m; the south of al sur de 3 adv al sur; south of al sur de

South 'Af·ric·a Sudáfrica

South 'Af·ri·can 1 adj sudafricano 2 n sudafricano(-a) m(f)

South A·mer·i·ca Sudamérica, América del Sur

South A·mer·i·can 1 adj sudamericano 2 n sudamericano(-a) m(f)

south'east 1 n sudeste m, sureste m 2 adj sudeste, sureste 3 adv al sudeste or sureste; southeast of al sudeste de

south'east·ern adj del sudeste

south·er·ly [ˈsʌðərlɪ] adj wind sur, del sur; direction sur

south·ern [ˈsʌðərn] adj sureño

south·ern·er [ˈsʌðərnər] sureño(-a) m(f)

south·ern·most [ˈsʌðərnmoust] adj más al sur

South 'Pole Polo m Sur

south·ward [ˈsauθwərd] adv hacia el sur

south·'west 1 n sudoeste m, suroeste m 2 adj sudoeste, suroeste 3 adv al sudoeste or suroeste; southwest of al sudoeste or suroeste de

south'west·ern adj del sudoeste or suroeste

sou·ve·nir [suːvəˈnɪr] recuerdo *m*

sove·reign [ˈsɑːvrɪn] *adj state* soberano

sove·reign·ty [ˈsɑːvrɪntɪ] *of state* soberanía *f*

So·vi·et [ˈsouviət] *adj* soviético

So·vi·et 'U·nion Unión *f* Soviética

sow[1] [sau] *n* (*female pig*) cerda *f*, puerca *f*

sow[2] [sou] *v/t* (*pret* **sowed**, *pp* **sown**) *seeds* sembrar

sown [soun] *pp* → **sow**[2]

'soy bean [sɔɪ] semilla *f* de soja

soy 'sauce salsa *f* de soja

space [speɪs] *n* espacio *m*

◆ **space out** *v/t* espaciar

'space-bar COMPUT barra *f* espaciadora

'space·craft nave *f* espacial

'space·ship nave *f* espacial

'space shut·tle transbordador *m* espacial

'space sta·tion estación *f* espacial

'space·suit traje *m* espacial

spa·cious [ˈspeɪʃəs] *adj* espacioso

spade [speɪd] *for digging* pala *f*; **spades** *in card game* picas *fpl*

'spade·work *fig* trabajo *m* preliminar

spa·ghet·ti [spəˈgetɪ] *nsg* espaguetis *mpl*

Spain [speɪn] España

span [spæn] *v/t* (*pret & pp* **spanned**) abarcar; *of bridge* cruzar

Span·iard [ˈspænjərd] español(a) *m*(*f*)

Span·ish [ˈspænɪʃ] **1** *adj* español **2** *n language* español *m*; **the Spanish** los españoles

spank [spæŋk] *v/t* azotar

spank·ing [ˈspæŋkɪŋ] azotaina *f*

span·ner [ˈspænər] *Br* llave *f*

spare [sper] **1** *v/t*: **can you spare me $50?** ¿me podrías dejar 50 dólares?; **we can't spare a single employee** no podemos prescindir ni de un solo trabajador; **can you spare the time?** ¿tienes tiempo?; **I have time to spare** me sobra el tiempo; **there were 5 to spare** sobraban cinco **2** *adj pair of glasses, set of keys* de repuesto; **do you have any spare cash?** ¿no te sobrará algo de dinero? **3** *n* recambio *m*, repuesto *m*

spare 'part pieza *f* de recambio *or* repuesto

spare 'ribs *npl* costillas *fpl* de cerdo

spare 'room habitación *f* de invitados

spare 'time tiempo *m* libre

spare 'tire, *Br* **spare 'tyre** MOT rueda *f* de recambio *or* repuesto

spar·ing [ˈsperɪŋ] *adj* moderado; **be sparing with** no derrochar

spar·ing·ly [ˈsperɪŋlɪ] *adv* con moderación

spark [spɑːrk] *n* chispa *f*

spar·kle [ˈspɑːrkl] *v/i* destellar

spar·kling 'wine [ˈspɑːrklɪŋ] vino *m* espumoso

'spark plug bujía *f*

spar·row [ˈspærou] gorrión *m*

sparse [spɑːrs] *adj vegetation* escaso

sparse·ly [ˈspɑːrslɪ] *adv*: **sparsely populated** poco poblado

spar·tan [ˈspɑːrtn] *adj room* espartano

spas·mod·ic [spæzˈmɑːdɪk] *adj* intermitente

spat [spæt] *pret & pp* → **spit**

spate [speɪt] *fig* oleada *f*

spa·tial [ˈspeɪʃl] *adj* espacial

spat·ter [ˈspætər] *v/t*: **the car spattered mud all over me** el coche me salpicó de barro

speak [spiːk] **1** *v/i* (*pret* **spoke**, *pp* **spoken**) hablar (**to** con); (*make a speech*) dar una charla; **we're not speaking (to each other)** (*we've quarreled*) no nos hablamos; **speaking** TELEC al habla **2** *v/t* (*pret* **spoke**, *pp* **spoken**) *foreign language* hablar; **she spoke her mind** dijo lo que pensaba

◆ **speak for** *v/t* hablar en nombre de

◆ **speak out** *v/i*: **speak out against injustice** denunciar la injusticia

◆ **speak up** *v/i* (*speak louder*) hablar más alto

speak·er [ˈspiːkər] *at conference* conferenciante *m*/*f*; (*orator*) orador(a) *m*(*f*); *of sound system* altavoz *m*, *L.Am.* altoparlante *m*; *of language* hablante *m*/*f*

spear [spɪr] lanza *f*

spear·mint [ˈspɪrmɪnt] hierbabuena *f*

spe·cial [ˈspeʃl] *adj* especial; **be on special** estar de oferta

spe·cial ef·fects *npl* efectos *mpl* espe-

S

ciales

spe·cial·ist ['speʃlɪst] especialista m/f

spe·cial·ize ['speʃəlaɪz] v/i especializarse (in en)

spe·cial·ly ['speʃlɪ] adv → **especially**

spe·cial·i·ty [speʃɪ'ælətɪ] Br, spe·cial·ty ['speʃəltɪ] especialidad f

spe·cies ['spiːʃiːz] nsg especie f

spe·cif·ic [spə'sɪfɪk] adj específico

spe·cif·i·cal·ly [spə'sɪfɪklɪ] adv específicamente

spec·i·fi·ca·tions [spesɪfɪ'keɪʃnz] npl of machine etc especificaciones fpl

spec·i·fy ['spesɪfaɪ] v/t (pret & pp specified) especificar

spe·ci·men ['spesɪmən] muestra f

speck [spek] of dust, soot mota f

specs [speks] npl F (spectacles) gafas fpl, L.Am. lentes mpl

spec·ta·cle ['spektəkl] (impressive sight) espectáculo m; (a pair of) spectacles unas gafas, L.Am. unos lentes

spec·tac·u·lar [spek'tækjʊlər] adj espectacular

spec·ta·tor [spek'teɪtər] espectador(a) m(f)

spec·ta·tor sport deporte m espectáculo

spec·trum ['spektrəm] fig espectro m

spec·u·late ['spekjʊleɪt] v/i also FIN especular

spec·u·la·tion [spekjʊ'leɪʃn] also FIN especulación f

spec·u·la·tor ['spekjʊleɪtər] FIN especulador(a) m(f)

sped [sped] pret & pp → **speed**

speech [spiːtʃ] (address) discurso m; in play parlamento m; (ability to speak) habla f, dicción f; (way of speaking) forma f de hablar

'speech de·fect defecto m del habla

speech·less ['spiːtʃlɪs] adj with shock, surprise sin habla; I was left speechless me quedé sin habla

'speech ther·a·pist logopeda m/f

'speech ther·a·py logopedia f

'speech writ·er redactor(a) m(f) de discursos

speed [spiːd] 1 n velocidad f; (promptness) rapidez f; at a speed of 150 mph

a una velocidad de 150 millas por hora 2 v/i (pret & pp sped) run correr; drive too quickly sobrepasar el límite de velocidad; we were speeding along íbamos a toda velocidad

◆ speed by v/i pasar a toda velocidad

◆ speed up 1 v/i of car, driver acelerar; when working apresurarse 2 v/t process acelerar

'speed·boat motora f, planeadora f

'speed bump resalto m (para reducir la velocidad del tráfico), Arg despertador m, Mex tope m

speed·i·ly ['spiːdɪlɪ] adv con rapidez

speed·ing ['spiːdɪŋ] n: fined for speeding multado por exceso de velocidad

'speed·ing fine multa f por exceso de velocidad

'speed lim·it on roads límite m de velocidad

speed·om·e·ter [spiː'dɑːmɪtər] velocímetro m

'speed trap control m de velocidad por radar

speed·y ['spiːdɪ] adj rápido

spell¹ [spel] 1 v/t word deletrear how do you spell ...? ¿cómo se escribe ... ? 2 v/i deletrear

spell² [spel] n (period of time) periodo m, temporada; I'll take a spell at the wheel te relevaré un rato al volante

'spell·bound adj hechizado

'spell·check COMPUT: do a spellcheck on pasar el corrector ortográfico a

'spell·check·er COMPUT corrector m ortográfico

spell·ing ['spelɪŋ] ortografía f

spend [spend] v/t (pret & pp spent) money gastar; time pasar

'spend·thrift n pej derrochador(a) m(f)

spent [spent] pret & pp → spend

sperm [spɜːrm] espermatozoide m; (semen) esperma f

'sperm bank banco m de esperma

'sperm count recuento m espermático

sphere [sfɪr] also fig esfera f; sphere of influence ámbito m de influencia

spice [spaɪs] n (seasoning) especia f

spic·y ['spaɪsɪ] adj food con especias;

(*hot*) picante

spi·der ['spaɪdər] araña *f*

'spi·der·web telaraña *f*, tela *f* de araña

spike [spaɪk] *n* pincho *m*; *on running shoe* clavo *m*

spill [spɪl] **1** *v/t* derramar **2** *v/i* derramarse **3** *n* derrame *m*

spin¹ [spɪn] **1** *n* (*turn*) giro *m* **2** *v/t* (*pret & pp* **spun**) hacer girar **3** *v/i* (*pret & pp* **spun**) *of wheel* girar, dar vueltas; *my head is spinning* me da vueltas la cabeza

spin² [spɪn] *v/t wool, cotton* hilar; *web* tejer

◆ spin around *v/i of person, car* darse la vuelta

◆ spin out *v/t* alargar

spin·ach ['spɪnɪdʒ] espinacas *fpl*

spin·al ['spaɪnl] *adj* de la columna vertebral

spin·al 'col·umn columna *f* vertebral

spin·al 'cord médula *f* espinal

'spin doc·tor F asesor encargado de dar la mejor prensa posible a un político o asunto

'spin-dry *v/t* centrifugar

spin-'dry·er centrifugadora *f*

spine [spaɪn] *of person, animal* columna *f* vertebral; *of book* lomo *m*; *on plant, hedgehog* espina *f*

spine·less ['spaɪnlɪs] *adj* (*cowardly*) débil

'spin-off producto *m* derivado

spin·ster ['spɪnstər] solterona *f*

spin·y ['spaɪnɪ] *adj* espinoso

spi·ral ['spaɪrəl] **1** *n* espiral *f* **2** *v/i* (*rise quickly*) subir vertiginosamente

spi·ral 'stair·case escalera *f* de caracol

spire [spaɪr] aguja *f*

spir·it ['spɪrɪt] *n* espíritu *m*; (*courage*) valor *m*; *in a spirit of cooperation* con espíritu de cooperación

spir·it·ed ['spɪrɪtɪd] *adj* (*energetic*) enérgico

'spir·it lev·el nivel *m* de burbuja

spir·its¹ ['spɪrɪts] *npl* (*alcohol*) licores *mpl*

spirits² ['spɪrɪts] *npl* (*morale*) la moral; *be in good / poor spirits* tener la moral alta / baja

spir·i·tu·al ['spɪrɪtʃʊəl] *adj* espiritual

spir·it·u·al·ism ['spɪrɪtʃəlɪzm] espiritismo *m*

spir·it·u·al·ist ['spɪrɪtʃəlɪst] *n* espiritista *m/f*

spit [spɪt] *v/i* (*pret & pp* **spat**) *of person* escupir; *it's spitting with rain* está chispeando

◆ spit out *v/t food, liquid* escupir

spite [spaɪt] *n* rencor *m*; *in spite of* a pesar de

spite·ful ['spaɪtfəl] *adj* malo, malicioso

spite·ful·ly ['spaɪtfəlɪ] *adv* con maldad *or* malicia

spit·ting 'im·age ['spɪtɪŋ]: *be the spitting image of s.o.* ser el vivo retrato de alguien

splash [splæʃ] **1** *n small amount of liquid* chorrito *m*; *of color* mancha *f* **2** *v/t person* salpicar; *the car splashed mud all over me* el coche me salpicó de barro **3** *v/i chapotear*; *of water* salpicar

◆ splash down *v/i of spacecraft* amerizar

◆ splash out *v/i in spending* gastarse una fortuna

'splash·down amerizaje *m*

splen·did ['splendɪd] *adj* espléndido

splen·dor, *Br* splen·dour ['splendər] esplendor *m*

splint [splɪnt] *n* MED tablilla *f*

splin·ter ['splɪntər] **1** *n* astilla *f* **2** *v/i* astillarse

'splin·ter group grupo *m* escindido

split [splɪt] **1** *n damage* raja *f*; (*disagreement*) escisión *f*; (*division, share*) reparto *m* **2** *v/t* (*pret & pp* **split**) *damage* rajar; *logs* partir en dos; (*cause disagreement in*) escindir; (*share*) repartir **3** *v/i* (*pret & pp* **split**) (*tear*) rajarse; (*disagree*) escindirse

◆ split up *v/i of couple* separarse

split per·son'al·i·ty PSYCH doble personalidad *f*

split·ting ['splɪtɪŋ] *adj*: *splitting headache* dolor *m* de cabeza atroz

splut·ter ['splʌtər] *v/i* farfullar

spoil [spɔɪl] *v/t* estropear, arruinar

'spoil·sport F aguafiestas *m/f inv* F

spoilt [spɔɪlt] *adj child* consentido, mimado; *be spoilt for choice* tener mucho

S

donde elegir

spoke[1] [spəuk] *of wheel* radio *m*

spoke[2] [spəuk] *pret* → **speak**

spo·ken ['spəukən] *pp* → **speak**

spokes·man ['spəuksmən] portavoz *m*

spokes·per·son ['spəukspɜːrsən] portavoz *m/f*

spokes·wom·an ['spəukswumən] portavoz *f*

sponge [spʌndʒ] *n* esponja *f*
♦ **sponge off, sponge on** *v/t* F vivir a costa de

'**sponge cake** bizcocho *m*

spong·er ['spʌndʒər] F gorrón(-ona) *m(f)* F

spon·sor ['spɑːnsər] **1** *n* patrocinador *m* **2** *v/t* patrocinar

spon·sor·ship ['spɑːnsərʃɪp] patrocinio *m*

spon·ta·ne·ous [spɑːn'teɪnɪəs] *adj* espontáneo

spon·ta·ne·ous·ly [spɑːn'teɪnɪəslɪ] *adv* espontáneamente

spook·y ['spuːkɪ] *adj* F espeluznante, terrorífico

spool [spuːl] *n* carrete *m*

spoon [spuːn] *n* cuchara *f*

'**spoon-feed** *v/t* (*pret & pp* **spoonfed**) *fig* dar todo mascado a

spoon·ful ['spuːnful] cucharada *f*

spo·rad·ic [spə'rædɪk] *adj* esporádico

sport [spɔːrt] *n* deporte *m*

sport·ing ['spɔːrtɪŋ] *adj* deportivo; ***a sporting gesture*** un gesto deportivo

'**sports car** [spɔːrts] (coche *m*) deportivo *m*

'**sports·coat** chaqueta *f* de sport

sports 'jour·nal·ist periodista *m/f* deportivo(-a)

'**sports·man** deportista *m*

'**sports med·i·cine** medicina *f* deportiva

'**sports news** *nsg* noticias *fpl* deportivas

'**sports page** página *f* de deportes

'**sports·wear** ropa *f* de deporte

'**sports·wom·an** deportista *f*

sport·y ['spɔːrtɪ] *adj person* deportista; *clothes* deportivo

spot[1] [spɑːt] (*pimple etc*) grano *m*; (*part of pattern*) lunar *m*; ***a spot of ...*** (*a little*)

algo de ..., un poco de ...

spot[2] [spɑːt] (*place*) lugar *m*, sitio *m*; **on the spot** (*in the place in question*) en el lugar; (*immediately*) en ese momento; ***put s.o. on the spot*** poner a alguien en un aprieto

spot[3] [spɑːt] *v/t* (*pret & pp* **spotted**) (*notice*) ver; (*identify*) ver, darse cuenta de

spot 'check *n* control *m* al azar; ***carry out spot check checks*** llevar a cabo controles al azar

spot·less ['spɑːtlɪs] *adj* inmaculado, impecable

'**spot·light** *n* foco *m*

spot·ted ['spɑːtɪd] *adj fabric* de lunares

spot·ty ['spɑːtɪ] *adj with pimples* con granos

spouse [spaus] *fml* cónyuge *m/f*

spout [spaut] **1** *n* pitorro *m* **2** *v/i of liquid* chorrear **3** *v/t* F soltar F

sprain [spreɪn] **1** *n* esguince *m* **2** *v/t* hacerse un esguince en

sprang [spræn] *pret* → **spring**[3]

sprawl [sprɔːl] *v/i* despatarrarse; *of city* expandirse; ***send s.o. sprawling*** *of punch* derribar de un golpe

sprawl·ing ['sprɔːlɪŋ] *adj city, suburbs* en expansión

spray [spreɪ] **1** *n of sea water, from fountain* rociada *f*; *for hair* spray *m*; *container* aerosol *m*, spray *m* **2** *v/t* rociar; ***spray sth with sth*** rociar algo de algo

'**spray-gun** pistola *f* pulverizadora

spread [spred] **1** *n of disease, religion etc* propagación *f*; F (*big meal*) comilona F *f* **2** *v/t* (*pret & pp* **spread**) (*lay*) extender; *butter, jelly* untar; *news, rumor* difundir; *disease* propagar; *arms, legs* extender **3** *v/i* (*pret & pp* **spread**) *of disease, fire* propagarse; *of rumor, news* difundirse; *of butter* extenderse, untarse

'**spread·sheet** COMPUT hoja *f* de cálculo

spree [spriː] F: ***go (out) on a spree*** ir de juerga; ***go on a shopping spree*** salir a comprar a lo loco

sprig [sprɪg] *n* ramita *f*

spright·ly ['spraɪtlɪ] *adj* lleno de energía

spring[1] [sprɪŋ] *n* (*season*) primavera *f*

spring[2] [sprɪŋ] *n* (*device*) muelle *m*

spring³ [sprıŋ] **1** *n* (*jump*) brinco *m*, salto *m*; (*stream*) manantial *m* **2** *v/i* (*pret* **sprang**, *pp* **sprung**) brincar, saltar; **spring from** proceder de; **he sprang to his feet** se levantó de un salto

'**spring·board** trampolín *m*

spring 'chick·en *hum*: **she's no spring chicken** no es ninguna niña

spring-'clean·ing limpieza *f* a fondo

'**spring·time** primavera *f*

spring·y ['sprıŋı] *adj mattress, ground* mullido; *walk* ligero; *piece of elastic* elástico

sprin·kle ['sprıŋkl] *v/t* espolvorear; **sprinkle sth with sth** espolvorear algo con algo

sprin·kler ['sprıŋklər] *for garden* aspersor *m*; *in ceiling* rociador *m* contra incendios

sprint [sprınt] **1** *n* esprint *m*; SP carrera *f* de velocidad **2** *v/i* (*run fast*) correr a toda velocidad; *of runner* esprintar

sprint·er ['sprıntər] SP esprínter *m/f*, velocista *m/f*

sprout [spraʊt] **1** *v/i of seed* brotar **2** *n*: (**Brussels**) **sprouts** coles *fpl* de Bruselas

spruce [spruːs] *adj* pulcro

sprung [sprʌŋ] *pp* → **spring³**

spry [spraı] *adj* lleno *m* de energía

spun [spʌn] *pret & pp* → **spin¹**

spur [spɜːr] *n* espuela *f*; *fig* incentivo; **on the spur of the moment** sin pararse a pensar

◆ **spur on** *v/t* (*pret & pp* **spurred**) (*encourage*) espolear

spurt [spɜːrt] **1** *n in race* arrancada *f*; **put on a spurt** acelerar **2** *v/i of liquid* chorrear

sput·ter ['spʌtər] *v/i of engine* chisporrotear

spy [spaı] **1** *n* espía *m/f* **2** *v/i* (*pret & pp* **spied**) espiar **3** *v/t* (*pret & pp* **spied**) (*see*) ver

◆ **spy on** *v/t* espiar

squab·ble ['skwɑːbl] **1** *n* riña *f* **2** *v/i* reñir

squal·id ['skwɒlıd] *adj* inmundo, miserable

squal·or ['skwɒlər] inmundicia *f*

squan·der ['skwɒndər] *v/t money* despilfarrar

square [skwer] **1** *adj in shape* cuadrado; **square miles** millas cuadradas **2** *n also* MATH cuadrado *m*; *in town* plaza *f*; *in board game* casilla *f*; **we're back to square one** volvemos al punto de partida

◆ **square up** *v/i* hacer cuentas

square 'root raíz *f* cuadrada

squash¹ [skwɑːʃ] *n vegetable* calabacera *f*

squash² [skwɑːʃ] *n game* squash *m*

squash³ [skwɑːʃ] *v/t* (*crush*) aplastar

squat [skwɑːt] **1** *adj person, build* chaparro; *figure, buildings* bajo **2** *v/i* (*pret & pp* **squatted**) *sit* agacharse; **squat in a building** ocupar ilegalmente un edificio

squat·ter ['skwɑːtər] ocupante *m/f* ilegal, Span okupa *m/f* F

squeak [skwiːk] **1** *n of mouse* chillido *m*; *of hinge* chirrido *m* **2** *v/i of mouse* chillar; *of hinge* chirriar; *of shoes* crujir

squeak·y ['skwiːkı] *adj hinge* chirriante; *shoes* que crujen; *voice* chillón

'**squeak·y clean** *adj* F bien limpio

squeal [skwiːl] **1** *n* chillido; **there was a squeal of brakes** se oyó una frenada estruendosa **2** *v/i* chillar; *of brakes* armar un estruendo

squeam·ish ['skwiːmıʃ] *adj* aprensivo

squeeze [skwiːz] **1** *n of hand, shoulder* apretón *m* **2** *v/t* (*press*) apretar; (*remove juice from*) exprimir

◆ **squeeze in** *v/t to a car etc* meterse a duras penas **2** *v/t* hacer hueco para

◆ **squeeze up** *v/i to make space* apretarse

squid [skwıd] calamar *m*

squint [skwınt] *n*: **she has a squint** es estrábica, tiene estrabismo

squirm [skwɜːrm] *v/t* retorcerse

squir·rel ['skwırl] *n* ardilla *f*

squirt [skwɜːrt] **1** *v/t* lanzar un chorro de **2** *n* F *pej* canijo(-a) *m(f)* F, mequetrefe *m/f* F

St *abbr* (= **saint**) Sto; Sta (= santo *m*; santa *f*); (= **street**) c/ (= calle *f*)

stab [stæb] **1** *n* F intento *m*; **have a stab at sth** intentar algo **2** *v/t* (*pret & pp* **stabbed**) apuñalar

sta·bil·i·ty [stə'bılətı] estabilidad *f*

sta·bil·ize [ˈsteɪbılaɪz] **1** *v/t prices, boat*

estabilizar **2** v/i of prices etc estabilizarse

sta·ble¹ ['steɪbl] n for horses establo m

sta·ble² ['steɪbl] adj estable; patient's condition estacionario

stack [stæk] **1** n (pile) pila f; (smokestack) chimenea f; **stacks of** F montones de F **2** v/t apilar

sta·di·um ['steɪdɪəm] estadio m

staff [stæf] npl (employees) personal m; (teachers) profesorado m; **staff are not allowed to …** los empleados no tienen permitido …

staf·fer ['stæfər] empleado(-a) m(f)

'**staff·room** in school sala f de profesores

stag [stæg] ciervo m

stage¹ [steɪdʒ] in life, project etc etapa f

stage² [steɪdʒ] **1** n THEA escenario m; **go on the stage** hacerse actor / actriz **2** v/t play escenificar, llevar a escena; demonstration llevar a cabo

stage 'door entrada f de artistas

'**stage fright** miedo m escénico

'**stage hand** tramoyista m/f

stag·ger ['stægər] **1** v/i tambalearse **2** v/t (amaze) dejar anonadado; coffee breaks etc escalonar

stag·ger·ing ['stægərɪŋ] adj asombroso

stag·nant ['stægnənt] adj also fig estancado

stag·nate [stæg'neɪt] v/i fig estancarse

stag·na·tion [stæg'neɪʃn] estancamiento m

'**stag par·ty** despedida f de soltero

stain [steɪn] **1** n (dirty mark) mancha f; for wood tinte m **2** v/t (dirty) manchar; wood teñir **3** v/i of wine etc manchar, dejar mancha; of fabric mancharse

stained-glass 'win·dow [steɪnd] vidriera f

stain·less 'steel ['steɪnlɪs] n acero m inoxidable

'**stain re·mov·er** [rɪ'muːvər] quitamanchas m inv

stair [ster] escalón m; **the stairs** la(s) escalera(s)

'**stair·case** escalera(s) f(/pl)

stake [steɪk] **1** n of wood estaca f; when gambling apuesta f; (investment) participación f; **be at stake** estar en juego **2** v/t

tree arrodrigar; money apostar; reputation jugarse; person ayudar (económicamente)

stale [steɪl] adj bread rancio; air viciado; fig: news viejo

'**stale·mate** in chess tablas fpl (por rey ahogado); fig punto m muerto

stalk¹ [stɔːk] n of fruit, plant tallo m

stalk² [stɔːk] v/t (follow) acechar; person seguir

stalk·er ['stɔːkər] persona que sigue a otra obsesivamente

stall¹ [stɔːl] n at market puesto m; for cow, horse casilla f

stall² [stɔːl] **1** v/i of vehicle, engine calarse; of plane entrar en pérdida; (play for time) intentar ganar tiempo **2** v/t engine calar; person retener

stal·li·on ['stæljən] semental m

stalls [stɔːlz] npl patio m de butacas

stal·wart ['stɔːlwərt] adj support, supporter incondicional

stam·i·na ['stæmɪnə] resistencia f

stam·mer ['stæmər] **1** n tartamudeo m **2** v/i tartamudear

stamp¹ [stæmp] **1** n for letter sello m, L.Am. estampilla f, Mex timbre m; device tampón m; mark made with device sello m **2** v/t sellar; **stamped addressed envelope** sobre m franqueado con la dirección

stamp² [stæmp] v/t: **stamp one's feet** patear

◆ **stamp out** v/t (eradicate) terminar con

'**stamp col·lec·ting** filatelia f

'**stamp col·lec·tion** collección f de sellos or L.Am. estampillas or Mex timbres

'**stamp col·lec·tor** coleccionista m/f de sellos or L.Am. estampillas or Mex timbres

stam·pede [stæm'piːd] **1** n of cattle etc estampida f; of people desbandada f **2** v/i of cattle etc salir de estampida; of people salir en desbandada

stance [stæns] (position) postura f

stand [stænd] **1** n at exhibition puesto m, stand m; (witness stand) estrado m; (support, base) soporte m; **take the stand** LAW subir al estrado **2** v/i (pret & pp **stood**) of *building* encontrarse, hallarse; *as opposed to sit* estar de pie; (*rise*) ponerse de pie; *did you notice two men standing near the window?* ¿viste a dos hombres al lado de la ventana?; *there was a large box standing in the middle of the floor* había una caja muy grande en mitad del suelo; *the house stands at the corner of ...* la casa se encuentra en la esquina de ...; *stand still* quedarse quieto; *where do you stand with Liz?* ¿cual es tu situación con Liz? **3** *v/t* (*pret & pp* **stood**) (*tolerate*) aguantar, soportar; (*put*) colocar; *you don't stand a chance* no tienes ninguna posibilidad; *stand s.o. a drink* invitar a alguien a una copa; *stand one's ground* mantenerse firme

◆ **stand back** *v/i* echarse atrás

◆ **stand by 1** *v/i* (*not take action*) quedarse sin hacer nada; (*be ready*) estar preparado **2** *v/t person* apoyar; *decision* atenerse a

◆ **stand down** *v/i* (*withdraw*) retirarse

◆ **stand for** *v/t* (*tolerate*) aguantar; (*represent*) significar

◆ **stand in for** *v/t* sustituir

◆ **stand out** *v/i* destacar

◆ **stand up 1** *v/i* levantarse **2** *v/t* F plantar F

◆ **stand up for** *v/t* defender; *stand up for yourself!* ¡defiéndete!

◆ **stand up to** *v/t* hacer frente a

stan·dard ['stændərd] **1** *adj* (*usual*) habitual **2** *n* (*level of excellence*) nivel *m*; TECH estándar *m*; *be up to standard* cumplir el nivel exigido; *not be up to standard* estar por debajo del nivel exigido; *my parents set very high standards* mis padres exigen mucho

stan·dard·ize ['stændərdaɪz] *v/t* normalizar

stan·dard of 'li·ving nivel *m* de vida

'**stand·by 1** *n ticket* billete *m* stand-by; *be on standby* estar en stand-by *or* en lista de espera **2** *adv fly* con un billete standby

'**stand·by pas·sen·ger** pasajero(-a) *m(f)* en stand-by *or* en lista de espera

stand·ing ['stændɪŋ] *n in society etc* pos-

ición *f*; (*repute*) reputación *f*; *a musician / politician of some standing* un reputado músico / político; *a relationship of long standing* una relación establecida hace mucho tiempo

'**stand·ing room**: *standing room only* no quedan asientos

stand·off·ish [stænd'ɑːfɪʃ] *adj* distante

'**stand·point** punto *m* de vista

'**stand·still**: *be at a standstill* estar paralizado; *bring to a standstill* paralizar

stank [stæŋk] *pret →* **stink**

sta·ple¹ ['steɪpl] *n foodstuff* alimento *m* básico

sta·ple² ['steɪpl] **1** *n* (*fastener*) grapa *f* **2** *v/t* grapar

sta·ple 'di·et dieta *f* básica

'**sta·ple gun** grapadora *f* industrial

sta·pler ['steɪplər] grapadora *f*

star [stɑːr] **1** *n also person* estrella *f* **2** *v/t* (*pret & pp* **starred**) *of movie* estar protagonizado por **3** *v/i* (*pret & pp* **starred**) *in movie*: *Depardieu starred in ...* Depardieu protagonizó ...

'**star·board** *adj* de estribor

starch [stɑːrtʃ] *in foodstuff* fécula *f*

stare [ster] **1** *n* mirada *f* fija **2** *v/i* mirar fijamente; *stare at* mirar fijamente

'**star·fish** estrella *f* de mar

stark [stɑːrk] **1** *adj landscape* desolado; *reminder, picture etc* desolador; *in stark contrast to* en marcado contraste con **2** *adv*: *stark naked* completamente desnudo

star·ling ['stɑːrlɪŋ] estornino *m*

star·ry ['stɑːrɪ] *adj night* estrellado

star·ry-eyed [stɑːrɪ'aɪd] *adj person* cándido, ingenuo

Stars and 'Stripes la bandera estadounidense

start [stɑːrt] **1** *n* (*beginning*) comienzo *m*, principio *m*; *of race* salida *f*; *get off to a good / bad start* empezar bien / mal; *from the start* desde el principio; *well, it's a start!* bueno, ¡algo es algo! **2** *v/i* empezar, comenzar; *of engine, car* arrancar; *starting from tomorrow* a partir de mañana **3** *v/t* empezar, comenzar; *engine,* *car* arrancar; *business* montar; **start to do sth, start doing sth** empezar *or* comenzar a hacer algo; **he started to cry** se puso a llorar

start·er ['stɑ:rtər] (*part of meal*) entrada *f*, entrante *m*; *of car* motor *m* de arranque

'start·ing point punto *m* de partida

'start·ing sal·a·ry sueldo *m* inicial

start·le ['stɑ:rtl] *v/t* sobresaltar

start·ling ['stɑ:rtlɪŋ] *adj* sorprendente, asombroso

starv·a·tion [stɑ:r'veɪʃn] inanición *f*, hambre *f*

starve [stɑ:rv] *v/i* pasar hambre; **starve to death** morir de inanición *or* hambre; **I'm starving** F me muero de hambre F

state¹ [steɪt] 1 *n* (*condition, country*) estado *m*; **the States** (los) Estados Unidos 2 *adj capital etc* estatal, del estado; *banquet etc* de estado

state² [steɪt] *v/t* declarar

'State De·part·ment Departamento *m* de Estado, *Ministerio de Asuntos Exteriores*

state·ment ['steɪtmənt] declaración *f*; (*bank statement*) extracto *m*

state of e'mer·gen·cy estado *m* de emergencia

state-of-the-'art *adj* modernísimo

states·man ['steɪtsmən] hombre *m* de estado

state 'troop·er policía *m/f* estatal

state 'vis·it visita *f* de estado

stat·ic (e·lec·'tric·i·ty) ['stætɪk] electricidad *f* estática

sta·tion ['steɪʃn] 1 *n* RAIL estación *f*; RAD emisora *f*; TV canal *m* 2 *v/t guard etc* apostar; **be stationed in** *of soldier* estar destinado en

sta·tion·a·ry ['steɪʃnəri] *adj* parado

sta·tion·er ['steɪʃənər] papelería *f*

sta·tion·er·y ['steɪʃənəri] artículos *mpl* de papelería

sta·tion 'man·ag·er RAIL jefe *m* de estación

'sta·tion wag·on ranchera *f*

sta·tis·ti·cal [stə'tɪstɪkl] *adj* estadístico

sta·tis·ti·cal·ly [stə'tɪstɪkli] *adv* estadísticamente

sta·tis·ti·cian [stætɪs'tɪʃn] estadístico(-a) *m(f)*

sta·tis·tics [stə'tɪstɪks] (*nsg: science*) estadística *f*; (*npl: figures*) estadísticas *fpl*

stat·ue ['stætʃu:] estatua *f*

Stat·ue of 'Lib·er·ty Estatua *f* de la Libertad

sta·tus ['steɪtəs] categoría *f*, posición *f*; **women want equal status with men** las mujeres quieren igualdad con los hombres

'sta·tus bar COMPUT barra *f* de estado

'sta·tus sym·bol símbolo *m* de estatus

stat·ute ['stætʃu:t] estatuto *m*

staunch [stɔ:ntʃ] *adj supporter* incondicional; *friend* fiel

stay [steɪ] 1 *n* estancia *f*, *L.Am.* estadía *f* 2 *v/i in a place* quedarse; *in a condition* permanecer; **stay in a hotel** alojarse en un hotel; **stay right there!** ¡quédate ahí!; **stay put** no moverse

◆ **stay away** *v/i*: **tell the children to stay away** diles a los niños que no se acerquen

◆ **stay away from** *v/t* no acercarse a

◆ **stay behind** *v/i* quedarse

◆ **stay up** *v/i* (*not go to bed*) quedarse levantado

stead·i·ly ['stedɪli] *adv improve etc* constantemente

stead·y ['stedi] 1 *adj* (*not shaking*) firme; (*continuous*) continuo; *beat* regular; *boyfriend* estable 2 *adv*: **they've been going steady for two years** llevan saliendo dos años; **steady on!** ¡un momento! 3 *v/t* (*pret & pp* **steadied**) afianzar; *voice* calmar

steak [steɪk] filete *m*

steal [sti:l] 1 *v/t* (*pret* **stole**, *pp* **stolen**) *money etc* robar 2 *v/i* (*pret* **stole**, *pp* **stolen**) (*be a thief*) robar; **he stole into the bedroom** entró furtivamente en la habitación

'stealth bomb·er [stelθ] bombardero *m* invisible

stealth·y ['stelθi] *adj* sigiloso

steam [sti:m] 1 *n* vapor *m* 2 *v/t food* cocinar al vapor

◆ **steam up** *v/i of window* empañarse

steamed up [stiːmd'ʌp] *adj* F enojado, *Span* mosqueado F

steam-er ['stiːmər] *for cooking* olla *f* para cocinar al vapor

'steam i-ron plancha *f* de vapor

steel [stiːl] 1 *n* acero m 2 *adj* (*made of steel*) de acero

'steel-work-er trabajador(a) *m(f)* del acero

'steel-works acería *f*

steep¹ [stiːp] *adj hill etc* empinado; F: *prices* caro

steep² [stiːp] *v/t* (*soak*) poner en remojo

stee-ple ['stiːpl] torre *f*

'stee-ple-chase *in athletics* carrera *f* de obstáculos

steep-ly ['stiːplɪ] *adv*: **climb steeply** *of path* subir pronunciadamente; *of prices* dispararse

steer¹ [stɪr] *n animal* buey m

steer² [stɪr] *v/t car* conducir, *L.Am.* manejar; *boat* gobernar; *person* guiar; *conversation* llevar

steer-ing ['stɪrɪŋ] *n* MOT dirección *f*

'steer-ing wheel volante m, *S. Am.* timón m

stem¹ [stem] *n of plant* tallo m; *of glass* pie m; *of pipe* tubo m; *of word* raíz *f*

♦ stem from *v/t* (*pret* & *pp* **stemmed**) derivarse de

stem² [stem] *v/t* (*block*) contener

'stem-ware [*'stemwer*] cristalería *f*

stench [stentʃ] *n* peste *f*, hedor m

sten-cil ['stensɪl] 1 *n* plantilla *f* 2 *v/t* (*pret* & *pp* **stenciled**, *Br* **stencilled**) *pattern* estarcir

step [step] 1 *n* (*pace*) paso m; (*stair*) escalón m; (*measure*) medida *f*; **step by step** paso a paso 2 *v/i* (*pret* & *pp* **stepped**): **step on sth** pisar algo; **step into a puddle** pisar un charco; **I stepped back** di un paso atrás; **step forward** dar un paso adelante

♦ step down *v/i from post etc* dimitir

♦ step up *v/t* (*increase*) incrementar

'step-broth-er hermanastro m

'step-daugh-ter hijastra *f*

'step-fa-ther padrastro m

'step-lad-der escalera *f* de tijera

'step-moth-er madrastra *f*

step-ping stone ['stepɪŋ] pasadera *f*; *fig* trampolín m

'step-sis-ter hermanastra *f*

'step-son hijastro m

ster-e-o ['sterɪoʊ] *n* (*sound system*) equipo m de música

ster-e-o-type ['sterɪoʊtaɪp] *n* estereotipo m

ster-ile ['sterəl] *adj* estéril

ster-il-ize ['sterəlaɪz] *v/t woman* esterilizar; *equipment* esterilizar

ster-ling ['stɜːrlɪŋ] *n* FIN libra *f* esterlina

stern¹ [stɜːrn] *adj* severo

stern² [stɜːrn] *n* NAUT popa *f*

stern-ly ['stɜːrnlɪ] *adv* con severidad

ster-oids ['sterɔɪdz] *npl* esteroides *mpl*

steth-o-scope ['steθəskoʊp] fonendoscopio m, estetoscopio m

Stet-son® ['stetsn] sombrero m de vaquero

ste-ve-dore ['stiːvədɔːr] estibador(a) *m(f)*

stew [stuː] *n* guiso m

stew-ard ['stuːərd] *n on plane* auxiliar m de vuelo; *on ship* camarero m; *at demonstration, meeting* miembro m de la organización

stew-ard-ess [stuːər'des] *on plane* auxiliar *f* de vuelo; *on ship* camarera *f*

stewed [stuːd] *adj apples, plums* en compota

stick¹ [stɪk] *n* palo m; *of policeman* porra *f*; (*walking stick*) bastón m; **live out in the sticks** F vivir en el quinto pino F, vivir en el campo

stick² [stɪk] 1 *v/t* (*pret* & *pp* **stuck**) *with adhesive* pegar; F (*put*) meter 2 *v/i* (*pret* & *pp* **stuck**) (*jam*) atascarse; (*adhere*) pegarse

♦ stick around *v/i* F quedarse

♦ stick by *v/t* F apoyar, no abandonar

♦ stick out *v/i* (*protrude*) sobresalir; (*be noticeable*) destacar; **his ears stick out** tiene las orejas salidas

♦ stick to *v/t* (*adhere to*) pegarse a; F (*keep to*) seguir; F (*follow*) pegarse a F

♦ stick together *v/i* mantenerse unidos

♦ stick up *v/t poster, leaflet* pegar

◆ **stick up for** v/t F defender
stick·er ['stɪkər] pegatina f
'**stick-in-the-mud** F aburrido(-a) m(f) F, soso(-a) m(f)
stick·y ['stɪkɪ] adj hands, surface pegajoso; label adhesivo
stiff [stɪf] **1** adj cardboard, manner rígido; brush, penalty, competition duro; muscle, body agarrotado; mixture, paste consistente; drink cargado **2** adv: **be scared stiff** F estar muerto de miedo F; **be bored stiff** F aburrirse como una ostra F
stiff·en ['stɪfn] v/i of person agarrotarse
◆ **stiffen up** v/i of muscle agarrotarse
stiff·ly ['stɪflɪ] adv con rigidez; fig forzadamente
stiff·ness ['stɪfnəs] of muscles agarrotamiento m; fig: of manner rigidez f
sti·fle ['staɪfl] v/t yawn, laugh reprimir, contener; criticism, debate reprimir
sti·fling ['staɪflɪŋ] adj sofocante; **it's stifling in here** hace un calor sofocante aquí dentro
stig·ma ['stɪgmə] estigma m
sti·let·tos [stɪ'letoʊz] npl shoes zapatos mpl de tacón de aguja
still[1] [stɪl] **1** adj (not moving) quieto; with no wind sin viento; **it was very still** no wind no soplaba nada de viento **2** adv: **keep still!** ¡estáte quieto!; **stand still!** ¡no te muevas!
still[2] [stɪl] adv (yet) todavía, aún; (nevertheless) de todas formas; **do you still want it?** ¿todavía or aún lo quieres?; **she still hasn't finished** todavía or aún no ha acabado; **I still don't understand** sigo sin entenderlo; **she might still come** puede que aún venga; **they are still my parents** siguen siendo mis padres; **still more** (even more) todavía más
'**still·born** adj: **be stillborn** nacer muerto
still 'life naturaleza f muerta, bodegón m
stilt·ed ['stɪltɪd] adj forzado
stim·u·lant ['stɪmjʊlənt] estimulante m
stim·u·late ['stɪmjʊleɪt] v/t person estimular; growth, demand estimular, provocar
stim·u·lat·ing ['stɪmjʊleɪtɪŋ] adj estimulante

stim·u·la·tion [stɪmjʊ'leɪʃn] estimulación f
stim·u·lus ['stɪmjʊləs] (incentive) estímulo m
sting [stɪŋ] **1** n from bee, jellyfish picadura f **2** v/t (pret & pp **stung**) of bee, jellyfish picar **3** v/i (pret & pp **stung**) of eyes, scratch escocer
sting·ing ['stɪŋɪŋ] adj remark, criticism punzante
sting·y ['stɪndʒɪ] adj F agarrado F, rácano F
stink [stɪŋk] **1** n (bad smell) peste f, hedor m; F (fuss) escándalo f; **kick up a stink** F armar un escándalo F **2** v/i (pret **stank**, pp **stunk**) (smell bad) apestar; F (be very bad) dar asco
stint [stɪnt] n temporada f; **do a stint in the army** pasar una temporada en el ejército
◆ **stint on** v/t F racanear F
stip·u·late ['stɪpjʊleɪt] v/t estipular
stip·u·la·tion [stɪpjʊ'leɪʃn] estipulación f
stir [stɜːr] **1** n: **give the soup a stir** darle vueltas a la sopa; **cause a stir** causar revuelo **2** v/t (pret & pp **stirred**) remover, dar vueltas a **3** v/i (pret & pp **stirred**) of sleeping person moverse
◆ **stir up** v/t crowd agitar; bad memories traer a la memoria
stir-'cra·zy adj F majareta F
'**stir-fry** v/t (pret & pp **stir-fried**) freír rápidamente y dando vueltas
stir·ring ['stɜːrɪŋ] adj music, speech conmovedor
stir·rup ['stɪrəp] estribo m
stitch [stɪtʃ] **1** n in sewing puntada f; in knitting punto m; **stitches** MED puntos mpl; **be in stitches** laughing partirse de risa; **have a stitch** tener flato **2** v/t sew coser
◆ **stitch up** v/t wound coser, suturar
stitch·ing ['stɪtʃɪŋ] (stitches) cosido m
stock [stɑːk] **1** n (reserves) reservas fpl; COM of store existencias fpl; (animals) ganado m; FIN acciones mpl; for soup etc caldo m; **in stock** en existencias; **out of stock** agotado; **take stock** hacer balance **2** v/t COM (have) tener en existen-

cias; COM (*sell*) vender

◆ **stock up on** *v/t* aprovisionarse de

'**stock·breed·er** ganadero(-a) *m(f)*

'**stock·brok·er** corredor(a) *m(f)* de bolsa

'**stock cube** pastilla *f* de caldo concentrado

'**stock ex·change** bolsa *f* (de valores)

'**stock·hold·er** accionista *m/f*

stock·ing ['stɑːkɪŋ] media *f*

stock·ist ['stɑːkɪst] distribuidor(a) *m(f)*

'**stock mar·ket** mercado *m* de valores

'**stock mar·ket crash** crack *m* bursátil

'**stock·pile 1** *n* of food, weapons reservas *fpl* **2** *v/t* acumular

'**stock·room** almacén *m*

stock-'still *adv*: **stand stock-still** quedarse inmóvil

'**stock·tak·ing** inventario *m*

'**stock·y** ['stɑːkɪ] *adj* bajo y robusto

stodg·y ['stɑːdʒɪ] *adj food* pesado

sto·i·cal ['stoʊɪkl] *adj* estoico

sto·i·cism ['stoʊɪsɪzm] estoicismo *m*

stole [stoʊl] *pret* → **steal**

stol·en ['stoʊlən] *pp* → **steal**

stom·ach ['stʌmək] **1** *n* estómago *m*, tripa *f* **2** *v/t* (*tolerate*) soportar

'**stom·ach·ache** dolor *m* de estómago

stone [stoʊn] *n* piedra *f*; *in fruit* hueso *m*

stoned [stoʊnd] *adj* F (*on drugs*) colocado F

stone-'deaf *adj*: **be stone-deaf** estar más sordo que una tapia

'**stone·wall** *v/i* F andarse con evasivas

ston·y ['stoʊnɪ] *adj ground, path* pedregoso

stood [stuːd] *pret & pp* → **stand**

stool [stuːl] (*seat*) taburete *m*

stoop[1] [stuːp] **1** *n*: **have a stoop** estar encorvado **2** *v/i* (*bend down*) agacharse

stoop[2] [stuːp] *n* (*porch*) porche *m*

stop [stɑːp] **1** *n* for train, bus parada *f*; **come to a stop** detenerse; **put a stop to** poner fin a **2** *v/t* (*pret & pp* **stopped**) (*put an end to*) poner fin a; (*prevent*) impedir; (*cease*) parar; *person in street* parar; *car, bus, train, etc: of driver* detener; *check* bloquear; **stop doing sth** dejar de hacer algo; **it has stopped raining** ha parado *or* dejado de llover; **I stopped**

her from leaving impedí que se fuera **3** *v/i* (*pret & pp* **stopped**) (*come to a halt*) pararse, detenerse; *in a particular place: of bus, train* parar

◆ **stop by** *v/i* (*visit*) pasarse

◆ **stop off** *v/i* hacer una parada

◆ **stop over** *v/i* hacer escala

◆ **stop up** *v/t sink* atascar

'**stop·gap** solución *f* intermedia

'**stop·light** (*traffic light*) semáforo *m*; (*brake light*) luz *m* de freno

'**stop·o·ver** *n* parada *f*; *in air travel* escala *f*

stop·per ['stɑːpər] *for bath, bottle* tapón *m*

stop·ping ['stɑːpɪŋ]: **no stopping** *sign* prohibido estacionar

'**stop sign** (señal *f* de) stop *m*

'**stop·watch** cronómetro *m*

stor·age ['stɔːrɪdʒ] almacenamiento *m*; **put sth in storage** almacenar algo; **be in storage** estar almacenado

'**stor·age ca·pac·i·ty** COMPUT capacidad *f* de almacenamiento

'**stor·age space** espacio *m* para guardar cosas

store [stɔːr] **1** *n* tienda *f*; (*stock*) reserva *f*; (*storehouse*) almacén *m* **2** *v/t* almacenar; COMPUT guardar

'**store·front** fachada *f* de tienda

'**store·house** almacén *m*

'**store·keep·er** tendero(-a) *m(f)*

'**store·room** almacén *m*

sto·rey *Br* → **story**[2]

stork [stɔːrk] cigüeña *f*

storm [stɔːrm] *n* tormenta *f*

'**storm drain** canal *m* de desagüe

'**storm warn·ing** aviso *m* de tormenta

storm 'win·dow contraventana *f*

storm·y ['stɔːrmɪ] *adj weather, relationship* tormentoso

sto·ry[1] ['stɔːrɪ] (*tale*) cuento *m*; (*account*) historia *f*; (*newspaper article*) artículo *m*; F (*lie*) cuento *m*

sto·ry[2] ['stɔːrɪ] *of building* piso *m*, planta *f*

stout [staʊt] *adj person* relleno, corpulento; *boots* resistente; *defender* valiente

stove [stoʊv] *for cooking* cocina *f*, Col,

Mex, Ven estufa *f; for heating* estufa *f*
stow [stǝʊ] *v/t* guardar
◆ **stow away** *v/i* viajar de polizón
'**stow·a·way** *n* polizón *m*
strag·gler ['stræglǝr] rezagado(-a) *m(f)*
straight [streɪt] **1** *adj line, back* recto; *hair* liso; *(honest, direct)* franco; *whisky* solo; *(tidy)* en orden; *(conservative)* serio; *(not homosexual)* heterosexual; **be a straight A student** sacar sobresaliente en todas las asignaturas; **keep a straight face** contener la risa **2** *adv (in a straight line)* recto; *(directly, immediately)* directamente; *(clearly)* con claridad; **stand up straight!** ¡ponte recto!; **look s.o. straight in the eye** mirar a los ojos de alguien; **go straight** F *of criminal* reformarse; **give it to me straight** F dímelo sin rodeos; **straight ahead** *be situated* todo derecho; *walk, drive* todo recto; *look* hacia delante; **carry straight on** *of driver etc* seguir recto; **straight away, straight off** en seguida; **straight out** directamente; **straight up** *without ice* solo
straight·en ['streɪtn] *v/t* enderezar
◆ **straighten out** *v/t situation* resolver; F *person* poner por el buen camino **2** *v/i of road* hacerse recto
◆ **straighten up** *v/i* ponerse derecho
straight'for·ward *adj (honest, direct)* franco; *(simple)* simple
strain[1] [streɪn] **1** *n on rope* tensión *f; on engine, heart* esfuerzo *m; on person* agobio *m* **2** *v/t fig: finances, budget* crear presión en; **strain one's back** hacerse daño en la espalda; **strain one's eyes** forzar la vista
strain[2] [streɪn] *v/t vegetables* escurrir; *oil, fat etc* colar
strain[3] [streɪn] *n of virus* cepa *f*
strained [streɪnd] *adj relations* tirante
strain·er ['streɪnǝr] *for vegetables etc* colador *m*
strait [streɪt] estrecho *m*
strait-laced [streɪt'leɪst] *adj* mojigato
strand[1] [strænd] *n of wool, thread* hebra *f; a strand of hair* un pelo
strand[2] [strænd] *v/t* abandonar; **be stranded** quedarse atrapado *or* tirado

strange [streɪndʒ] *adj (odd, curious)* extraño, raro; *(unknown, foreign)* extraño
strange·ly ['streɪndʒlɪ] *adv (oddly)* de manera extraña; **strangely enough** aunque parezca extraño
strang·er ['streɪndʒǝr] *(person you don't know)* extraño(-a) *m(f)*, desconocido(-a) *m(f)*; **I'm a stranger here myself** yo tampoco soy de aquí
stran·gle ['stræŋgl] *v/t person* estrangular
strap [stræp] *n of purse, watch* correa *f; of brassiere, dress* tirante *m; of shoe* tira *f*
◆ **strap in** *v/t (pret & pp strapped)* poner el cinturón de seguridad a
◆ **strap on** *v/t* ponerse
strap·less ['stræplɪs] *adj* sin tirantes
stra·te·gic [strǝ'tiːdʒɪk] *adj* estratégico
strat·e·gy ['strætǝdʒɪ] estrategia *f*
straw[1] [strɔː] *material* paja *f; that's the last straw!* ¡es la gota que colma el vaso!
straw[2] [strɔː] *for drink* pajita *f*
straw·ber·ry ['strɔːberɪ] *fruit* fresa *f*, *S. Am.* frutilla *f*
stray [streɪ] **1** *adj animal* callejero; *bullet* perdido **2** *n dog* perro *m* callejero; *cat* gato *m* callejero **3** *v/i of animal, child* extraviarse, perderse; *fig: of eyes, thoughts* desviarse
streak [striːk] **1** *n of dirt, paint* raya *f; in hair* mechón *m; fig: of nastiness etc* vena *f* **2** *v/i move quickly* pasar disparado
streak·y ['striːkɪ] *adj* veteado
stream [striːm] **1** *n* riachuelo *m; fig: of people, complaints* oleada *f; come on stream* entrar en funcionamiento **2** *v/i: there were tears streaming down my face* me bajaban ríos de lágrimas por la cara; **people streamed out of the building** la gente salía en masa
stream·er ['striːmǝr] serpentina *f*
'**stream·line** *v/t fig* racionalizar
'**stream-lined** *adj car, plane* aerodinámico; *fig: organization* racionalizado
street [striːt] calle *f*
'**street·car** tranvía *f*
'**street·light** farola *f*
'**street peo·ple** *npl* los sin techo
'**street value** *of drugs* valor *m* en la calle
'**street-walk·er** F prostituta *f*

'street·wise *adj* espabilado

strength [streŋθ] fuerza *f*; (*fig: strong point*) punto *m* fuerte; *of friendship etc* solidez *f*; *of emotion* intensidad *f*; *of currency* fortaleza *f*

strength·en ['streŋθn] 1 *v/t muscles, currency* fortalecer; *bridge* reforzar; *country, ties, relationship* consolidar 2 *v/i of bonds, ties* consolidarse; *of currency* fortalecerse

stren·u·ous ['strenjuəs] *adj* agotador

stren·u·ous·ly ['strenjuəslɪ] *adv deny* tajantemente

stress [stres] 1 *n* (*emphasis*) énfasis *m*; (*tension*) estrés *m*; *on syllable* acento *m*; *be under stress* estar estresado 2 *v/t* (*emphasize: syllable*) acentuar; *importance etc* hacer hincapié en; *I must stress that ...* quiero hacer hincapié en que ...

stressed 'out [strest] *adj* F estresado

stress·ful ['stresfəl] *adj* estresante

stretch [stretʃ] 1 *n land, water* extensión *m*; *of road* tramo *m*; *at a stretch* (*non-stop*) de un tirón 2 *adj fabric* elástico 3 *v/t material, income* estirar; F *rules* ser flexible con; *he stretched out his hand* estiró la mano; *my job stretches me* mi trabajo me obliga a esforzarme 4 *v/i to relax muscles, reach sth* estirarse; (*spread*) extenderse; *of fabric* estirarse, dar de sí

stretch·er ['stretʃər] camilla *f*

strict [strɪkt] *adj* estricto

strict·ly ['strɪktlɪ] *adv* con rigor; *it is strictly forbidden* está terminantemente prohibido

strid·den ['strɪdn] *pp* → *stride*

stride [straɪd] 1 *n* zancada *f*; *take sth in one's stride* tomarse algo con tranquilidad; *make great strides fig* avanzar a pasos agigantados 2 *v/i* (*pret* *strode*, *pp* *stridden*) caminar dando zancadas

stri·dent ['straɪdnt] *adj also fig* estridente

strike [straɪk] 1 *n of workers* huelga *f*; *in baseball* strike *m*; *of oil* descubrimiento *m*; *be on strike* estar en huelga; *go on strike* ir a la huelga 2 *v/i* (*pret & pp* *struck*) *of workers* hacer huelga; (*attack*)

atacar; *of disaster* sobrevenir; *of clock* dar las horas; *the clock struck three* el reloj dio las tres 3 *v/t* (*pret & pp* *struck*) (*hit*) golpear; *fig: of disaster* sacudir; *match* encender; *oil* descubrir; *didn't it ever strike you that ...?* ¿no se te ocurrió que ...?; *she struck me as being ...* me dio la impresión de ser ...

♦ strike out 1 *v/t* tachar; *in baseball* eliminar a, *L.Am.* ponchar 2 *v/i in baseball* quedar eliminado, *L.Am.* poncharse

'strike·break·er esquirol(a) *m(f)*

strik·er ['straɪkər] (*person on strike*) huelguista *m/f*; *in soccer* delantero(-a) *m(f)*

strik·ing ['straɪkɪŋ] *adj* (*marked*) sorprendente, llamativo; (*eye-catching*) deslumbrante

string [strɪŋ] *n also of violin, racket etc* cuerda *f*; *strings musicians* la sección de cuerda; *pull strings* mover hilos; *a string of* (*series*) una serie de

♦ string along 1 *v/i* (*pret & pp* *strung*) F apuntarse 2 *v/t* (*pret & pp* *strung*) F: *string s.o. along* dar falsas esperanzas a alguien

♦ string up *v/t* F colgar

stringed 'in·stru·ment [strɪŋd] instrumento *m* de cuerda

strin·gent ['strɪndʒnt] *adj* riguroso

'string play·er instrumentista *m/f* de cuerda

strip [strɪp] 1 *n of land* franja *f*; *of cloth* tira *f*; (*comic strip*) tira *f* cómica 2 *v/t* (*pret & pp* *stripped*) (*remove*) quitar; (*undress*) desnudar; *strip s.o. of sth* despojar a alguien de algo 3 *v/i* (*pret & pp* *stripped*) (*undress*) desnudarse; *of stripper* hacer striptease

'strip club club *m* de striptease

stripe [straɪp] raya *f*; *indicating rank* galón *m*

striped [straɪpt] *adj* a rayas

'strip joint F → *strip club*

strip·per ['strɪpər] artista *m/f* de striptease; *male stripper* artista *m* de striptease

'strip show espectáculo *m* de striptease

strip'tease striptease *m*

strive [straɪv] v/i (pret **strove**, pp **striven**)
esforzarse; **strive to do sth** esforzarse
por hacer algo; **strive for** luchar por

striv·en ['strɪvn] pp → **strive**

strobe (light) [stroʊb] luz f estroboscó-
pica

strode [stroʊd] pret → **stride**

stroke [stroʊk] **1** n MED derrame m cerebral; *when writing* trazo m; *when painting*
pincelada f; (*style of swimming*) estilo m;
stroke of luck golpe de suerte; **she never does a stroke (of work)** no pega ni
golpe **2** v/t acariciar

stroll [stroʊl] **1** n paseo m **2** v/i caminar

stroll·er ['stroʊlər] *for baby* silla f de paseo

strong [strɔːŋ] adj fuerte; *structure* resistente; *candidate* claro, con muchos posibilidades; *support, supporter, views, objection* firme; *tea, coffee* cargado, fuerte

'strong·hold *fig* baluarte m

strong·ly ['strɔːŋlɪ] adv fuertemente, rotundamente

strong-mind·ed [strɔːŋ'maɪndɪd] adj decidido

'strong point (punto m) fuerte m

'strong·room cámara f acorazada

strong-willed [strɔːŋ'wɪld] adj tenaz

strove [stroʊv] pret → **strive**

struck [strʌk] pret & pp → **strike**

struc·tur·al ['strʌktʃərl] adj estructural

struc·ture ['strʌktʃər] **1** n (*something
built*) construcción f; *of novel, society
etc* estructura f **2** v/t estructurar

strug·gle ['strʌgl] **1** n lucha f **2** v/i *with a
person* forcejear; (*have a hard time*) luchar; **they struggled for the gun** force-
jearon por conseguir la pistola; **he was
struggling with the door** tenía problemas para abrir la puerta; **struggle
to do sth** luchar por hacer algo

strum [strʌm] v/t (pret & pp **strummed**)
guitar rasguear

strung [strʌŋ] pret & pp → **string**

strut [strʌt] v/i (pret & pp **strutted**) pavonearse

stub [stʌb] **1** n *of cigarette* colilla f; *of
check* matriz f; *of ticket* resguardo m **2**
v/t (pret & pp **stubbed**): **stub one's**

toe darse un golpe en el dedo (del pie)

◆ stub out v/t apagar (apretando)

stub·ble ['stʌbl] *on man's face* barba f incipiente

stub·born ['stʌbərn] adj *person* testarudo, terco; *defense, refusal, denial* tenaz,
pertinaz

stub·by ['stʌbɪ] adj regordete

stuck [stʌk] **1** pret & pp → **stick²** **2** adj F:
be stuck on s.o. estar colado por alguien
F

stuck-'up adj F engreído

stu·dent ['stuːdnt] *at high school* alum-
no(-a) m(f); *at college, university* estudiante m/f

stu·dent 'nurse estudiante m/f de enfermería

stu·dent 'teach·er profesor(a) m(f) en
prácticas

stu·di·o ['stuːdɪoʊ] *of artist, sculptor* estudio m; (*film studio*, TV *studio*) estudio m,
plató m

stu·di·ous ['stuːdɪəs] adj estudioso

stud·y ['stʌdɪ] **1** n estudio m; (*room*)
(cuarto m de) estudio m **2** v/t & v/i (pret
& pp **studied**) estudiar

stuff [stʌf] **1** n (*things*) cosas fpl **2** v/t *turkey* rellenar; **stuff sth into sth** meter algo dentro de algo

stuffed 'toy [stʌft] muñeco m de peluche

stuff·ing ['stʌfɪŋ] relleno m

stuff·y ['stʌfɪ] adj *room* cargado; *person*
anticuado, estirado

stum·ble ['stʌmbl] v/i tropezar

◆ stumble across v/t toparse con

◆ stumble over v/t tropezar con; *words*
trastrabillarse con

stum·bling-block ['stʌmblɪŋ] escollo m

stump [stʌmp] **1** n *of tree* tocón m **2** v/t *of
question, questioner* dejar perplejo

◆ stump up v/t F aflojar, *Span* apoquinar

stun [stʌn] v/t (pret & pp **stunned**) *of
blow* dejar sin sentido; *of news* dejar atónito *or* de piedra

stung [stʌŋ] pret & pp → **sting**

stunk [stʌŋk] pp → **stink**

stun·ning ['stʌnɪŋ] adj (*amazing*) increíble, sorprendente; (*very beautiful*) impo-

nente

stunt [stʌnt] *n for publicity* truco *m; in movie* escena *f* peligrosa

'stunt·man *in movie* doble *m*, especialista *m*

stu·pe·fy ['stu:pɪfaɪ] *v/t (pret & pp **stupefied**)* dejar perplejo

stu·pen·dous [stu:'pendəs] *adj* extraordinario

stu·pid ['stu:pɪd] *adj* estúpido; **what a stupid thing to say I do!** ¡qué estupidez!

stu·pid·i·ty [stu:'pɪdətɪ] estupidez *f*

stu·por ['stu:pər] aturdimiento *m*

stur·dy ['stɜːrdɪ] *adj person* robusto; *table, plant* resistente

stut·ter ['stʌtər] *v/i* tartamudear

sty [staɪ] *for pig* pocilga *f*

style [staɪl] *n* estilo *m;* (*fashion*) moda *f;* **go out of style** pasarse de moda

styl·ish ['staɪlɪʃ] *adj* elegante

styl·ist ['staɪlɪst] (*hair stylist*) estilista *m/f*

sub·com·mit·tee ['sʌbkəmɪtɪ] subcomité *m*

sub·com·pact (**car**) [sʌb'kɑːmpækt] *utilitario de pequeño tamaño*

sub·con·scious [sʌb'kɑːnʃəs] *adj* subconsciente; **the subconscious** (**mind**) el subconsciente

sub·con·scious·ly [sʌb'kɑːnʃəslɪ] *adv* inconscientemente

sub·con·tract [sʌbkɑːn'trækt] *v/t* subcontratar

sub·con·trac·tor [sʌbkɑːn'træktər] subcontratista *m/f*

sub·di·vide [sʌbdɪ'vaɪd] *v/t* subdividir

sub·due [səb'du:] *v/t rebellion, mob* someter, contener

sub·dued [səb'du:d] *adj* apagado

sub·head·ing ['sʌbhedɪŋ] subtítulo *m*

sub·hu·man [sʌb'hju:mən] *adj* inhumano

sub·ject 1 *n* ['sʌbdʒɪkt] (*topic*) tema *m;* (*branch of learning*) asignatura *f*, materia *f*; GRAM sujeto *m; of monarch* súbdito(-a) *m(f)*; **change the subject** cambiar de tema **2** *adj* ['sʌbdʒɪkt]: **be subject to** *have tendency to* ser propenso a; *be regulated by* estar sujeto a; **subject to availability** *of goods* promoción válida hasta fin de existencias **3** *v/t* [səb-

'dʒekt] someter

sub·jec·tive [səb'dʒektɪv] *adj* subjetivo

sub·junc·tive [səb'dʒʌŋktɪv] *n* GRAM subjuntivo *m*

sub·let ['sʌblet] *v/t (pret & pp **sublet**)* realquilar

sub·ma·chine gun metralleta *f*

sub·ma·rine ['sʌbməri:n] submarino *m*

sub·merge [səb'mɜːrdʒ] **1** *v/t* sumergir **2** *v/i of submarine* sumergirse

sub·mis·sion [səb'mɪʃn] (*surrender*) sumisión *f; to committee etc* propuesta *f*

sub·mis·sive [səb'mɪsɪv] *adj* sumiso

sub·mit [səb'mɪt] **1** *v/t (pret & pp **submitted**) plan, proposal* presentar **2** *v/i (pret & pp **submitted**)* someterse

sub·or·di·nate [sə'bɔːrdɪneɪt] **1** *adj employee, position* subordinado **2** *n* subordinado(-a) *m(f)*

sub·poe·na [sə'piːnə] **1** *n* citación *f* **2** *v/t person* citar

♦ **sub·scribe to** [səb'skraɪb] *v/t magazine etc* suscribirse a; *theory* suscribir

sub·scrib·er [səb'skraɪbər] *to magazine* suscriptor(a) *m(f)*

sub·scrip·tion [səb'skrɪpʃn] suscripción *f*

sub·se·quent ['sʌbsɪkwənt] *adj* posterior

sub·se·quent·ly ['sʌbsɪkwəntlɪ] *adv* posteriormente

sub·side [səb'saɪd] *v/i of flood waters* bajar; *of high winds* amainar; *of building* hundirse; *of fears, panic* calmarse

sub·sid·i·a·ry [səb'sɪdɪerɪ] *n* filial *f*

sub·si·dize ['sʌbsɪdaɪz] *v/t* subvencionar

sub·si·dy ['sʌbsɪdɪ] subvención *f*

♦ **sub·sist on** *v/t* subsistir a base de

sub·sis·tence 'farm·er [səb'sɪstəns] agricultor(a) *m(f)* de subsistencia

sub·sis·tence lev·el nivel *m* mínimo de subsistencia

sub·stance ['sʌbstəns] (*matter*) sustancia *f*

sub·stan·dard [sʌb'stændərd] *adj performance* deficiente; *shoes, clothes* con tara

sub·stan·tial [səb'stænʃl] *adj* sustancial, considerable

sub·stan·tial·ly [səb'stænʃlɪ] *adv* (*considerably*) considerablemente; (*in essence*) sustancialmente, esencialmente

S

sub·stan·ti·ate [səbˈstænʃɪeɪt] *v/t* probar

sub·stan·tive [səbˈstæntɪv] *adj* significativo

sub·sti·tute [ˈsʌbstɪtuːt] **1** *n for person* sustituto(-a) *m(f)*; *for commodity* sustituto *m*; SP suplente *m/f* **2** *v/t* sustituir, reemplazar; **substitute X for Y** sustituir Y por X **3** *v/i*: **substitute for s.o.** sustituir a alguien

sub·sti·tu·tion [sʌbstɪˈtuːʃn] (*act*) sustitución *f*; **make a substitution** SP hacer un cambio *or* sustitución

sub·ti·tle [ˈsʌbtaɪtl] *n* subtítulo *m*

sub·tle [ˈsʌtl] *adj* sutil

sub·tract [səbˈtrækt] *v/t number* restar

sub·urb [ˈsʌbɜːrb] zona *f* residencial de la periferia

sub·ur·ban [səˈbɜːrbən] *adj housing* de la periferia; *attitudes, lifestyle* aburguesado

sub·ver·sive [səbˈvɜːrsɪv] **1** *adj* subversivo **2** *n* subversivo(-a) *m(f)*

sub·way [ˈsʌbweɪ] metro *m*

sub ˈze·ro [zɪˈroʊ] *adj* bajo cero

suc·ceed [səkˈsiːd] **1** *v/i* (*be successful*) tener éxito; *to throne* suceder en el trono; **succeed in doing sth** conseguir hacer algo **2** *v/t* (*come after*) suceder

suc·ceed·ing [səkˈsiːdɪŋ] *adj* siguiente

suc·cess [səkˈses] éxito *m*; **be a success** *of book, play, idea* ser un éxito; *of person* tener éxito

suc·cess·ful [səkˈsesfəl] *adj person* con éxito; **be successful in business** tener éxito en los negocios; **be successful in doing sth** lograr hacer algo

suc·cess·ful·ly [səkˈsesfəlɪ] *adv* con éxito

suc·ces·sion [səkˈseʃn] sucesión *f*; **three days in succession** tres días seguidos

suc·ces·sive [səkˈsesɪv] *adj* sucesivo

suc·ces·sor [səkˈsesər] sucesor(a) *m(f)*

suc·cinct [səkˈsɪŋkt] *adj* sucinto

suc·cu·lent [ˈsʌkjʊlənt] *meat, fruit* suculento

suc·cumb [səˈkʌm] *v/i* (*give in*) sucumbir

such [sʌtʃ] **1** *adj* (*of that kind*) tal; **such men are dangerous** los hombres así son peligrosos; **I know of many such cases** conozco muchos casos así; **don't**

make such a fuss no armes tanto alboroto; **I never thought it would be such a success** nunca imaginé que sería un éxito tal; **such as** como; **there is no such word as** ... no existe la palabra ... **2** *adv* tan; **as such** como tal

suck [sʌk] **1** *v/t candy etc* chupar; **suck one's thumb** chuparse el dedo **2** *v/i* P: **it sucks** (*is awful*) es una mierda P

◆ **suck up 1** *v/t* absorber **2** *v/i* F: **suck up to s.o.** hacer la pelota a alguien

suck·er [ˈsʌkər] F (*person*) primo(-a) *m/f* F, ingenuo(-a) *m/f*; F (*lollipop*) piruleta *f*

suc·tion [ˈsʌkʃn] succión *f*

sud·den [ˈsʌdn] *adj* repentino; **all of a sudden** de repente

sud·den·ly [ˈsʌdnlɪ] *adv* de repente

suds [sʌdz] *npl* (*soap suds*) espuma *f*

sue [suː] *v/t* demandar

suede [sweɪd] *n* ante *m*

suf·fer [ˈsʌfər] **1** *v/i* (*be in great pain*) sufrir; (*deteriorate*) deteriorarse; **be suffering from** sufrir **2** *v/t loss, setback, heart attack* sufrir

suf·fer·ing [ˈsʌfərɪŋ] *n* sufrimiento *m*

suf·fi·cient [səˈfɪʃnt] *adj* suficiente

suf·fi·cient·ly [səˈfɪʃntlɪ] *adv* suficientemente

suf·fo·cate [ˈsʌfəkeɪt] **1** *v/i* asfixiarse **2** *v/t* asfixiar

suf·fo·ca·tion [sʌfəˈkeɪʃn] asfixia *f*

sug·ar [ˈʃʊgər] **1** *n* azúcar *m or f*; **how many sugars?** ¿cuántas cucharadas de azúcar? **2** *v/t* echar azúcar a; **is it sugared?** ¿lleva azúcar?

ˈsug·ar bowl azucarero *m*

ˈsug·ar cane caña *f* de azúcar

sug·gest [səˈdʒest] *v/t* sugerir; **I suggest that we stop now** sugiero que paremos ahora

sug·ges·tion [səˈdʒestʃən] sugerencia *f*

su·i·cide [ˈsuːɪsaɪd] suicidio *m*; **commit suicide** suicidarse

suit [suːt] **1** *n* traje *m*; *in cards* palo *m* **2** *v/t of clothes, color* sentar bien a; **suit yourself!** F ¡haz lo que quieras!; **be suited for sth** estar hecho para algo

suit·a·ble [ˈsuːtəbl] *adj partner, words, clothing* apropiado, adecuado; *time* apropiado

sui·ta·bly [ˈsuːtəblɪ] *adv* apropiadamente, adecuadamente

'suit·case maleta *f, L.Am.* valija *f*

suite [swiːt] *of rooms,* MUS suite *f; furniture* tresillo *m*

sul·fur [ˈsʌlfər] azufre *m*

sul·fur·ic ac·id [sʌlˈfjuːrɪk] ácido *m* sulfúrico

sulk [sʌlk] *v/i* enfurruñarse; *be sulking* estar enfurruñado

sulk·y [ˈsʌlkɪ] *adj* enfurruñado

sul·len [ˈsʌlən] *adj* malhumorado, huraño

sul·phur *etc Br* → **sulfur** *etc*

sul·try [ˈsʌltrɪ] *adj climate* sofocante, bochornoso; *sexually* sensual

sum [sʌm] *(total)* total *m,* suma *f; (amount)* cantidad *f; in arithmetic* suma *f; a large sum of money* una gran cantidad de dinero; *sum insured* suma *f* asegurada; *the sum total of his efforts* la suma de sus esfuerzos

◆ **sum up 1** *v/t (pret & pp summed) (summarize)* resumir; *(assess)* catalogar **2** *v/i (pret & pp summed)* LAW recapitular

sum·mar·ize [ˈsʌməraɪz] *v/t* resumir

sum·ma·ry [ˈsʌmərɪ] *n* resumen *m*

sum·mer [ˈsʌmər] verano *m*

sum·mit [ˈsʌmɪt] *of mountain* cumbre *f,* cima *f;* POL cumbre *f*

'sum·mit meet·ing → **summit**

sum·mon [ˈsʌmən] *v/t staff, ministers* llamar; *meeting* convocar

◆ **summon up** *v/t: he summoned up his strength* hizo acopio de fuerzas

sum·mons [ˈsʌmənz] *nsg* LAW citación *f*

sump [sʌmp] *for oil* cárter *m*

sun [sʌn] sol *m; in the sun* al sol; *out of the sun* a la sombra; *he has had too much sun* le ha dado demasiado el sol

'sun·bathe *v/i* tomar el sol

'sun·bed cama *f* de rayos UVA

'sun·block crema *f* solar de alta protección

'sun·burn quemadura *f* (del sol)

'sun·burnt *adj* quemado (por el sol)

Sun·day [ˈsʌndeɪ] domingo *m*

'sun·dial reloj *m* de sol

sun·dries [ˈsʌndrɪz] *npl* varios *mpl*

sung [sʌŋ] *pp* → **sing**

'sun·glass·es *npl* gafas *fpl or L.Am.* anteojos *mpl* de sol

sunk [sʌŋk] *pp* → **sink**

sunk·en [ˈsʌŋkn] *adj ship, cheeks* hundido

sun·ny [ˈsʌnɪ] *adj day* soleado; *disposition* radiante; *it is sunny* hace sol

'sun·rise amanecer *m*

'sun·set atardecer *m,* puesta *f* de sol

'sun·shade sombrilla *f*

'sun·shine sol *m*

'sun·stroke insolación *f*

'sun·tan bronceado *m; get a suntan* broncearse

su·perb [suˈpɜːrb] *adj* excelente

su·per·fi·cial [suːpərˈfɪʃl] *adj* superficial

su·per·flu·ous [suˈpɜːrfluəs] *adj* superfluo

su·per'hu·man *adj efforts* sobrehumano

su·per·in·tend·ent [suːpərɪnˈtendənt] *of apartment block* portero(-a) *m(f); Br of police* inspector(a) *m(f)* jefe

su·pe·ri·or [suːˈpɪrɪər] **1** *adj (better)* superior; *pej: attitude* arrogante **2** *n in organization* superior *m*

su·per·la·tive [suːˈpɜːrlətɪv] **1** *adj superb* excelente **2** *n* GRAM superlativo *m*

su·per'mar·ket supermercado *m*

su·per'nat·u·ral 1 *adj powers* sobrenatural **2** *n: the supernatural* lo sobrenatural

su·per'pow·er POL superpotencia *f*

su·per·son·ic [suːpərˈsɑːnɪk] *adj flight, aircraft* supersónico

su·per·sti·tion [suːpərˈstɪʃn] superstición *f*

su·per·sti·tious [suːpərˈstɪʃəs] *adj person* supersticioso

su·per·vise [ˈsuːpərvaɪz] *v/t class* vigilar; *workers* supervisar; *activities* dirigir

su·per·vi·sor [ˈsuːpərvaɪzər] *at work* supervisor(a) *m(f)*

sup·per [ˈsʌpər] cena *f, L.Am.* comida *f*

sup·ple [ˈsʌpl] *adj person* ágil; *limbs, material* flexible

sup·ple·ment [ˈsʌplɪmənt] *(extra pay-*

ment) suplemento *m*

sup·pli·er [sə'plaɪər] COM proveedor *m*

sup·ply [sə'plaɪ] **1** *n* suministro *m*, abastecimiento *m*; **supply and demand** la oferta y la demanda; **supplies** of food provisiones *fpl*; **office supplies** material *f* de oficina **2** *v/t* (*pret & pp* **supplied**) *goods* suministrar; **supply s.o. with sth** suministrar algo a alguien; **be supplied with ...** venir con ...

sup·port [sə'pɔːrt] **1** *n for structure* soporte *m*; (*backing*) apoyo *m* **2** *v/t building, structure* soportar, sostener; *financially* mantener; (*back*) apoyar

sup·port·er [sə'pɔːrtər] partidario/(-a) *m(f)*; *of football team etc* seguidor(a) *m(f)*

sup·port·ive [sə'pɔːrtɪv] *adj* comprensivo; **be supportive** apoyar (**toward, of** a)

sup·pose [sə'pouz] *v/t* (*imagine*) suponer; **I suppose so** supongo (que sí); **you are not supposed to ...** (*not allowed to*) no deberías ...; **it is supposed to be delivered today** (*be meant to*) se supone que lo van a entregar hoy; **it's supposed to be very beautiful** *is said to be* se supone que es hermosísimo

sup·pos·ed·ly [sə'pouzɪdlɪ] *adv* supuestamente

sup·pos·i·to·ry [sə'pɑːzɪtɔːrɪ] MED supositorio *m*

sup·press [sə'pres] *v/t rebellion etc* reprimir, sofocar

sup·pres·sion [sə'preʃn] represión *f*

su·prem·a·cy [suː'preməsɪ] supremacía *f*

su·preme [suː'priːm] *adj* supremo

sur·charge ['sɜːrtʃɑːrdʒ] *n* recargo *m*

sure [ʃʊr] **1** *adj* seguro; **I'm not sure** no estoy seguro; **be sure about sth** estar seguro de algo; **make sure that ...** asegurarse de que ... **2** *adv*: **sure enough** efectivamente; **it sure is hot today** F vaya calor que hace F; **sure!** ¡claro!

sure·ly ['ʃʊrlɪ] *adv* (*gladly*) claro que sí; **surely you don't mean that!** ¡ no lo dirás en serio!; **surely somebody knows** alguien tiene que saberlo

sure·ty ['ʃʊrətɪ] *for loan* fianza *f*, depósito *m*

surf [sɜːrf] **1** *n on sea* surf *m* **2** *v/t*: **surf the Net** navegar por Internet

sur·face ['sɜːrfɪs] **1** *n of table, object, water* superficie *f*; **on the surface** *fig* a primera vista **2** *v/i of swimmer, submarine* salir a la superficie; (*appear*) aparecer

'sur·face mail correo *m* terrestre

'surf·board tabla *f* de surf

surf·er ['sɜːrfər] *on sea* surfista *m/f*

surf·ing ['sɜːrfɪŋ] surf *m*; **go surfing** ir a hacer surf

surge [sɜːrdʒ] *n in electric current* sobrecarga *f*; *in demand etc* incremento *m* repentino

◆ **surge forward** *v/i of crowd* avanzar atropelladamente

sur·geon ['sɜːrdʒən] cirujano/(-a) *m(f)*

sur·ge·ry ['sɜːrdʒərɪ] cirugía *f*; **undergo surgery** ser intervenido quirúrgicamente

sur·gi·cal ['sɜːrdʒɪkl] *adj* quirúrgico

sur·gi·cal·ly ['sɜːrdʒɪklɪ] *adv* quirúrgicamente

sur·ly ['sɜːrlɪ] *adj* arisco, hosco

sur·name ['sɜːrneɪm] apellido *m*

sur·mount [sər'maunt] *v/t difficulties* superar

sur·pass [sər'pæs] *v/t* superar

sur·plus ['sɜːrpləs] **1** *n* excedente *m* **2** *adj* excedente

sur·prise [sər'praɪz] **1** *n* sorpresa *f*; **it came as no surprise** no me sorprendió **2** *v/t* sorprender; **be / look surprised** estar / parecer sorprendido

sur·pris·ing [sər'praɪzɪŋ] *adj* sorprendente; **it's not surprising that ...** no me sorprende que ...

sur·pris·ing·ly [sər'praɪzɪŋlɪ] *adv* sorprendentemente

sur·ren·der [sə'rendər] **1** *v/i of army* rendirse **2** *v/t* (*hand in: weapons etc*) entregar **3** *n* rendición *f*; (*handing in*) entrega *f*

sur·ro·gate 'moth·er ['sʌrəgət] madre *f* de alquiler

sur·round [sə'raund] **1** *v/t* rodear; **surrounded by** rodeado de *or* por **2** *n of picture etc* marco *m*

sur·round·ing [sə'raundɪŋ] *adj* circundante

sur·round·ings [sə'raʊndɪŋz] *npl of village* alrededores *mpl*; *(environment)* entorno *m*

sur·vey ['sɜːrveɪ] **1** *n* ['sɜːrveɪ] *of modern literature etc* estudio *m*; *of building* tasación *f*, peritaje; *poll* encuesta *f* **2** *v/t* [sər'veɪ] *(look at)* contemplar; *building* tasar, peritar

sur·vey·or [sɜːr'veɪr] tasador(a) *m(f) or* perito (-a) *m(f)* de la propiedad

sur·viv·al [sər'vaɪvl] supervivencia *f*

sur·vive [sər'vaɪv] **1** *v/i* sobrevivir; **how are you? – I'm surviving** ¿cómo estás? – voy tirando; **his two surviving daughters** las dos hijas que aún viven **2** *v/t accident, operation* sobrevivir a; *(outlive)* sobrevivir

sur·vi·vor [sər'vaɪvər] superviviente *m/f*; **he's a survivor** *fig* es incombustible

sus·cep·ti·ble [sə'septəbl] *adj emotionally* sensible, susceptible; **be susceptible to the cold / heat** ser sensible al frío / calor

sus·pect 1 *n* ['sʌspekt] sospechoso(-a) *m(f)* **2** *v/t* [sə'spekt] *person* sospechar de; *(suppose)* sospechar

sus·pect·ed [sə'spektɪd] *adj murderer* presunto; *cause, heart attack etc* supuesto

sus·pend [sə'spend] *v/t (hang)* colgar; *from office, duties* suspender

sus·pend·ers [sə'spendərz] *npl for pants* tirantes *mpl*, S. Am. suspensores *mpl*

sus·pense [sə'spens] *Span* suspense *m*, L.Am. suspenso *m*

sus·pen·sion [sə'spenʃn] MOT, *from duty* suspensión *f*

sus'pen·sion bridge puente *m* colgante

sus·pi·cion [sə'spɪʃn] sospecha *f*

sus·pi·cious [sə'spɪʃəs] *adj (causing suspicion)* sospechoso; *(feeling suspicion)* receloso, desconfiado; **be suspicious of** sospechar de

sus·pi·cious·ly [sə'spɪʃəslɪ] *adv behave* de manera sospechosa; *ask* con recelo *or* desconfianza

sus·tain [sə'steɪn] *v/t* sostener

sus·tain·a·ble [sə'steɪnəbl] *adj* sostenible

swab [swɑːb] *material* torunda *f*; *test* muestra *f*

swag·ger ['swægər] *n*: **walk with a swagger** caminar pavoneándose

swal·low¹ ['swɑːloʊ] **1** *v/t liquid, food* tragar, tragarse **2** *v/i* tragar

swal·low² ['swɑːloʊ] *n bird* golondrina *f*

swam [swæm] *pret* → **swim**

swamp [swɑːmp] **1** *n pantano m* **2** *v/t*: **be swamped with** estar inundado de

swamp·y ['swɑːmpɪ] *adj* pantanoso

swan [swɑːn] cisne *m*

swap [swɑːp] **1** *v/t (pret & pp swapped)* cambiar; **swap sth for sth** cambiar algo por algo **2** *v/i (pret & pp swapped)* hacer un cambio

swarm [swɔːrm] **1** *n of bees* enjambre *m* **2** *v/i*: **the town was swarming with …** la ciudad estaba abarrotada de …

swar·thy ['swɔːrðɪ] *adj face, complexion* moreno

swat [swɑːt] *v/t (pret & pp swatted) insect, fly* aplastar, matar

sway [sweɪ] **1** *n (influence, power)* dominio *m* **2** *v/i* tambalearse

swear [swer] **1** *v/i (pret swore, pp sworn) (use swearword)* decir palabrotas *or* tacos; **swear at s.o.** insultar a alguien; **I swear** lo juro **2** *v/t (pret swore, pp sworn) (promise)*, LAW jurar

◆ **swear in** *v/t witnesses etc* tomar juramento a

'swear·word palabrota *f*, taco *m*

sweat [swet] **1** *n sudor m*; **covered in sweat** empapado de sudor **2** *v/i* sudar

'sweat·band banda *f* (en la frente); *on wrist* muñequera *f*

sweat·er ['swetər] suéter *m*, Span jersey *m*

'sweat·shirt sudadera *f*

sweat·y ['swetɪ] *adj hands* sudoroso

Swede [swiːd] sueco(-a) *m(f)*

Swe·den ['swiːdn] Suecia *f*

Swe·dish ['swiːdɪʃ] **1** *adj* sueco **2** *n* sueco *m*

sweep [swiːp] **1** *v/t (pret & pp swept) floor, leaves* barrer **2** *n (long curve)* curva *f*

◆ **sweep up** *v/t mess, crumbs* barrer

sweep·ing ['swiːpɪŋ] *adj statement* demasiado generalizado; *changes* radical

S

sweet [swiːt] *adj taste, tea* dulce; F (*kind*) amable; F (*cute*) mono

sweet and 'sour *adj* agridulce

'sweet-corn maíz *m*, *S. Am.* choclo *m*

sweet-en ['swiːtn] *v/t drink, food* endulzar

sweet-en-er ['swiːtnər] *for drink* edulcorante *m*

'sweet-heart novio(-a) *m(f)*

swell [swel] **1** *v/i of wound, limb* hincharse **2** *adj* F (*good*) genial F, fenomenal F **3** *n of the sea* oleaje *m*

swell-ing ['swelɪŋ] *n* MED hinchazón *f*

swel-ter-ing ['sweltərɪŋ] *adj heat, day* sofocante

swept [swept] *pret & pp* → **sweep**

swerve [swɜːrv] *v/i of driver, car* girar bruscamente, dar un volantazo

swift [swɪft] *adj* rápido

swim [swɪm] **1** *v/i* (*pret* **swam**, *pp* **swum**) nadar; **go swimming** ir a nadar; **my head is swimming** me da vueltas la cabeza **2** *n* baño *m*; **go for a swim** ir a darse un baño

swim-mer ['swɪmər] nadador(a) *m(f)*

swim-ming ['swɪmɪŋ] natación *f*

'swim-ming cos-tume traje *m* de baño, bañador *m*

'swim-ming pool piscina *f*, *Mex* alberca *f*, *Rpl* pileta *f*

swin-dle ['swɪndl] **1** *n* timo *m*, estafa *f* **2** *v/t* timar, estafar; **swindle s.o. out of sth** estafar algo a alguien

swine [swaɪn] F (*person*) cerdo(-a) *m(f)* F

swing [swɪŋ] **1** *n* oscilación *f*; *for child* columpio *m*; **swing to the Democrats** giro favorable a los Demócratas **2** *v/t* (*pret & pp* **swung**) balancear; *hips* menear **3** *v/i* (*pret & pp* **swung**) balancearse; (*turn*) girar; *of public opinion etc* cambiar

swing-'door puerta *f* basculante *or* de vaivén

Swiss [swɪs] **1** *adj* suizo **2** *n person* suizo(-a) *m(f)*; **the Swiss** los suizos

switch [swɪtʃ] **1** *n for light* interruptor *m*; (*change*) cambio *m* **2** *v/t* (*change*) cambiar de **3** *v/t* (*change*) cambiar

◆ **switch off** *v/t lights, engine, PC, TV* apa-

gar

◆ **switch on** *v/t lights, engine, PC, TV* encender, *L.Am.* prender

'switch-board centralita *f*, *L.Am.* conmutador

'switch-o-ver *to new system* cambio *m* (**to** a)

Swit-zer-land ['swɪtsərlənd] Suiza

swiv-el ['swɪvl] *v/i* (*pret & pp* **swiveled**, *Br* **swivelled**) *of chair, monitor* girar

swol-len ['swoʊlən] *adj* hinchado

swoop [swuːp] *v/i of bird* volar en picado

◆ **swoop down on** *v/t prey* caer en picado sobre

◆ **swoop on** *v/t of police etc* hacer una redada contra

sword [sɔːrd] espada *f*

'sword-fish pez *f* espada

swore [swɔːr] *pret* → **swear**

sworn [swɔːrn] *pp* → **swear**

swum [swʌm] *pp* → **swim**

swung [swʌŋ] *pret & pp* → **swing**

syc-a-more ['sɪkəmɔːr] plátano *m* (*árbol*)

syl-la-ble ['sɪləbl] sílaba *f*

syl-la-bus ['sɪləbəs] plan *m* de estudios

sym-bol ['sɪmbl] símbolo *m*

sym-bol-ic [sɪm'bɑːlɪk] *adj* simbólico

sym-bol-ism ['sɪmbəlɪzm] simbolismo *m*

sym-bol-ist ['sɪmbəlɪst] simbolista *m/f*

sym-bol-ize ['sɪmbəlaɪz] *v/t* simbolizar

sym-met-ri-c(al) [sɪ'metrɪk] *adj* simétrico

sym-me-try ['sɪmətrɪ] simetría *f*

sym-pa-thet-ic [sɪmpə'θetɪk] *adj* (*showing pity*) compasivo; (*understanding*) comprensivo; **be sympathetic toward a person / an idea** simpatizar con una persona / idea

◆ **sym-pa-thize with** ['sɪmpəθaɪz] *v/t person, views* comprender

sym-pa-thiz-er ['sɪmpəθaɪzər] POL simpatizante *m/f*

sym-pa-thy ['sɪmpəθɪ] (*pity*) compasión *f*; (*understanding*) comprensión *f*; **don't expect any sympathy from me!** no esperes que te compadezca

sym-pho-ny ['sɪmfənɪ] sinfonía *f*

'sym-pho-ny or-ches-tra orquesta *f* sinfónica

symp·tom ['sɪmptəm] *also fig* síntoma *f*

symp·to·mat·ic [sɪmptə'mætɪk] *adj*: **be symptomatic of** *fig* ser sintomático de

syn·chro·nize ['sɪŋkrənaɪz] *v/t* sincronizar

syn·o·nym ['sɪnənɪm] sinónimo *m*

sy·non·y·mous [sɪ'nɑːnɪməs] *adj* sinónimo; **be synonymous with** *fig* ser sinónimo de

syn·tax ['sɪntæks] sintaxis *f inv*

syn·the·siz·er ['sɪnθəsaɪzər] MUS sintetizador *m*

syn·thet·ic [sɪn'θetɪk] *adj* sintético

syph·i·lis ['sɪfɪlɪs] sífilis *f*

Syr·i·a ['sɪrɪə] Siria

Syr·i·an ['sɪrɪən] **1** *adj* sirio **2** *n* sirio(-a) *m(f)*

sy·ringe [sɪ'rɪndʒ] *n* jeringuilla *f*

syr·up ['sɪrəp] almíbar *m*

sys·tem ['sɪstəm] *also* COMPUT sistema *f*; **the braking system** el sistema de frenado; **the digestive system** el aparato digestivo

sys·te·mat·ic [sɪstə'mætɪk] *adj* sistemático

sys·tem·at·i·cal·ly [sɪstə'mætɪklɪ] *adv* sistemáticamente

sys·tems 'an·a·lyst ['sɪstəmz] COMPUT analista *m/f* de sistemas

T

tab [tæb] *n for pulling* lengüeta *f*; *in text* tabulador *m*; *bill* cuenta *f*; **pick up the tab** pagar (la cuenta)

ta·ble ['teɪbl] *n* mesa *f*; *of figures* cuadro *m*

'ta·ble·cloth mantel *m*

'table lamp lámpara *f* de mesa

table of 'con·tents índice *m* (de contenidos)

'ta·ble·spoon *object* cuchara *f* grande; *quantity* cucharada *f* grande

ta·blet ['tæblɪt] MED pastilla *f*

'ta·ble ten·nis tenis *m* de mesa

tab·loid ['tæblɔɪd] *n newspaper* periódico *m* sensacionalista (*de tamaño tabloide*)

ta·boo [tə'buː] *adj* tabú *inv*

ta·cit ['tæsɪt] *adj* tácito

ta·ci·turn ['tæsɪtɜːrn] *adj* taciturno

tack [tæk] **1** *n* (*nail*) tachuela *f* **2** *v/t* (*sew*) hilvanar **3** *v/i of yacht* dar bordadas

tack·le ['tækl] **1** *n* (*equipment*) equipo *m*; SP entrada *f*; **fishing tackle** aparejos *mpl* de pesca **2** *v/t* SP entrar a; *problem* abordar; *intruder* hacer frente a

tack·y ['tækɪ] *adj paint, glue* pegajoso; F (*cheap, poor quality*) chabacano, *Span* hortera F; *behavior* impresentable

tact [tækt] tacto *m*

tact·ful ['tæktfəl] *adj* diplomático

tact·ful·ly ['tæktfəlɪ] *adv* diplomáticamente

tac·tic·al ['tæktɪkl] *adj* táctico

tac·tics ['tæktɪks] *npl* táctica *f*

tact·less ['tæktlɪs] *adj* indiscreto

tad·pole ['tædpoʊl] renacuajo *m*

tag [tæg] *n* (*label*) etiqueta *f*

◆ tag along *v/i* (*pret & pp* **tagged**) pegarse

tail [teɪl] *n of bird, fish* cola *f*; *of mammal* cola *f*, rabo *m*

'tail·back *Br* caravana *f*

'tail light luz *f* trasera

tai·lor ['teɪlər] *n* sastre *m*

tai·lor-made [teɪlər'meɪd] *adj suit, solution* hecho a medida

'tail·pipe *of car* tubo *m* de escape

'tail·wind viento *m* de cola

taint·ed ['teɪntɪd] *adj food* contaminado; *reputation* empañado

Tai·wan [taɪ'wɑn] Taiwán

Tai·wan·ese [taɪwən'iːz] **1** *adj* taiwanés **2** *n* taiwanés(-esa) *m(f)*; *dialect* taiwanés *m*

take [teɪk] *v/t* (*pret* **took**, *pp* **taken**) (*remove*) llevarse; *Span* coger; (*steal*) llevarse; (*transport, accompany*) llevar; (*accept: money, gift, credit cards*) aceptar; (*study: maths, French*) hacer, estudiar; (*photograph, photocopy*) hacer, sacar; (*exam, degree*) hacer; (*shower*) darse; (*stroll*) dar; (*medicine, s.o.'s temperature, taxi*) tomar; (*endure*) aguantar; *how long does it take?* ¿cuánto tiempo lleva?; *I'll take it when shopping* me lo llevo; *it takes a lot of courage* se necesita mucho valor

◆ **take after** *v/t* parecerse a

◆ **take apart** *v/t* (*dismantle*) desmontar; *F* (*criticize*) hacer pedazos; *F* (*reprimand*) echar una bronca a *F*; *F in physical fight* machacar *F*

◆ **take away** *v/t* *pain* hacer desaparecer; (*remove: object*) quitar; MATH restar; *take sth away from s.o.* quitar algo a alguien

◆ **take back** *v/t* (*return: object*) devolver; *person* llevar de vuelta; (*accept back: husband etc*) dejar volver; *that takes me back* of *music, thought etc* me trae recuerdos

◆ **take down** *v/t from shelf* bajar; *scaffolding* desmontar; *trousers* bajarse; (*write down*) anotar, apuntar

◆ **take in** *v/t* (*take indoors*) recoger; (*give accommodation to*) acoger; (*make narrower*) meter; (*deceive*) engañar; (*include*) incluir

◆ **take off 1** *v/t clothes, hat* quitarse; *10% etc* descontar; (*mimic*) imitar; (*cut off*) cortar; *take a day / week off* tomarse un día / una semana de vacaciones **2** *v/i of airplane* despegar, *L.Am.* decolar; (*become popular*) empezar a cuajar

◆ **take on** *v/t job* aceptar; *staff* contratar

◆ **take out** *v/t from bag, pocket* sacar; *tooth* sacar, extraer; *word from text* quitar, borrar; *money from bank* sacar; *insurance policy* suscribir; *he took her out to dinner* la llevó a cenar; *take the dog out* sacar al perro a pasear; *take the kids out to the park* llevar a los niños

al parque; *don't take it out on me!* ¡no la pagues conmigo!

◆ **take over 1** *v/t company etc* absorber, adquirir; *tourists took over the town* los turistas invadieron la ciudad **2** *v/i of new management etc* asumir el cargo; *of new government* asumir el poder; (*do sth in s.o.'s place*) tomar el relevo

◆ **take to** *v/t* (*like*): *how did they take to the new idea?* ¿qué les pareció la nueva idea?; *I immediately took to him* me cayó bien de inmediato; *he has taken to getting up early* le ha dado por levantarse temprano; *she took to drink* se dio a la bebida

◆ **take up** *v/t carpet etc* levantar; (*carry up*) subir; (*shorten: dress etc*) acortar; *hobby* empezar a hacer; *subject* empezar a estudiar; *offer* aceptar; *new job* comenzar; *space, time* ocupar; *I'll take you up on your offer* aceptaré tu oferta

'**take-home pay** salario *m* neto

'**take-off** *of airplane* despegue *m*, *L.Am.* decolaje *m*; (*impersonation*) imitación *f*

'**take·o·ver** COM absorción *f*, adquisición *f*

'**take·o·ver bid** oferta *f* pública de adquisición, OPA *f*

tak·en ['teɪkən] *pp* → **take**

ta·kings ['teɪkɪŋz] *npl* recaudación *f*

tal·cum pow·der ['tælkəmpaʊdər] polvos *mpl* de talco

tale [teɪl] cuento *m*, historia *f*

tal·ent ['tælənt] talento *m*

tal·ent·ed ['tæləntɪd] *adj* con talento; *she's very talented* tiene mucho talento

'**tal·ent scout** cazatalentos *m inv*

talk [tɔːk] **1** *v/i* hablar; *can I talk to ...?* ¿podría hablar con ...?; *I'll talk to him about it* hablaré de tema con él **2** *v/t English etc* hablar; *talk business / politics* hablar de negocios / de política; *talk s.o. into sth* persuadir a alguien para que haga algo **3** *n* (*conversation*) charla *f*, *C.Am.*, *Mex* plática *f*; (*lecture*) conferencia *f*, *give a talk on sth* dar una conferencia sobre algo; charla *f*; *talks* negociaciones *fpl*; *he's all talk pej* habla mucho y no hace nada

◆ **talk back** *v/i* responder, contestar

◆ **talk down to** v/t hablar con aires de superioridad a

◆ **talk over** v/t hablar de, discutir

talk·a·tive ['tɔːkətɪv] adj hablador

talk·ing-to ['tɔːkɪŋtuː] sermón *m*, rapapolvo *m*; **give s.o. a good talking-to** echar a alguien un buen sermón *or* rapapolvo

'**talk show** programa *m* de entrevistas

tall [tɔːl] adj alto; **it is ten meters tall** mide diez metros de alto

tall 'or·der: that's a tall order eso es muy difícil

tall 'sto·ry cuento *m* chino

tal·ly ['tælɪ] **1** *n* cuenta *f* **2** v/i (*pret & pp* **tallied**) cuadrar, encajar

◆ **tally with** v/t cuadrar con, encajar con

tame [teɪm] adj *animal* manso, domesticado; *joke etc* soso

◆ **tam·per with** ['tæmpər] v/t *lock* intentar forzar; *brakes* tocar

tam·pon ['tæmpɑːn] tampón *m*

tan [tæn] **1** *n from sun* bronceado *m*; **get a tan** ponerse moreno; (*color*) marrón *m* claro **2** v/i (*pret & pp* **tanned**) *in sun* broncearse **3** v/t (*pret & pp* **tanned**) *leather* curtir

tan·dem ['tændəm] (*bike*) tándem *m*

tan·gent ['tændʒənt] MATH tangente *f*

tan·ge·rine [tændʒə'riːn] mandarina *f*

tan·gi·ble ['tændʒɪbl] adj tangible

tan·gle ['tæŋgl] *n* lío *m*, maraña *f*

◆ **tangle up: get tangled up** *of string etc* quedarse enredado

tan·go ['tæŋgoʊ] *n* tango *m*

tank [tæŋk] *for water* depósito *m*, tanque *m*; *for fish* pecera *f*; MOT depósito *m*; MIL, *for skin diver* tanque *m*

tank·er ['tæŋkər] *truck* camión *m* cisterna; *ship* buque *m* cisterna; *for oil* petrolero *m*

'**tank top** camiseta *f* sin mangas

tan·ned [tænd] adj moreno, bronceado

Tan·noy® ['tænɔɪ] megafonía *f*

tan·ta·liz·ing ['tæntəlaɪzɪŋ] adj sugerente

tan·ta·mount ['tæntəmaʊnt] adj: **be tantamount to** equivaler a

tan·trum ['tæntrəm] rabieta *f*

tap [tæp] **1** *n* grifo *m*, *L.Am.* llave *f* **2** v/t

(*pret & pp* **tapped**) (*knock*) dar un golpecito en; *phone* intervenir

◆ **tap into** v/t *resources* explotar

'**tap dance** *n* claqué *m*

tape [teɪp] **1** *n* cinta *f* **2** v/t *conversation etc* grabar; *with sticky tape* pegar con cinta adhesiva

'**tape deck** pletina *f*

'**tape drive** COMPUT unidad *f* de cinta

'**tape meas·ure** cinta *f* métrica

tap·er ['teɪpər] v/i estrecharse

◆ **taper off** v/i *of production, figures* disminuir

'**tape re·cor·der** magnetofón *m*, *L.Am.* grabador *m*

'**tape re·cor·ding** grabación *f* (magnetofónica)

'**tape·worm** tenia *f*, solitaria *f*

tar [tɑːr] *n* alquitrán *m*

tar·dy ['tɑːrdɪ] adj tardío

tar·get ['tɑːrgɪt] **1** *n in shooting* blanco *m*; *for sales, production* objetivo *m* **2** v/t *market* apuntar a

'**tar·get 'au·di·ence** audiencia *f* a la que está orientado el programa

'**tar·get date** fecha *f* fijada

'**tar·get 'fig·ure** cifra *f* objetivo

'**tar·get group** COM grupo *m* estratégico

'**tar·get mar·ket** mercado *m* objetivo

tar·iff ['tærɪf] (*price*) tarifa *f*; (*tax*) arancel *m*

tar·mac ['tɑːrmæk] *for road surface* asfalto *m*; *at airport* pista *f*

tar·nish ['tɑːrnɪʃ] v/t *metal* deslucir, deslustrar; *reputation* empañar

tar·pau·lin [tɑːr'pɔːlɪn] lona *f* (*impermeable*)

tart¹ [tɑːrt] *n* tarta *f*, pastel *m*

tart² [tɑːrt] *n* F *woman* fulana *f* F

tar·tan ['tɑːrtn] tartán *m*

task [tæsk] tarea *f*

'**task force** *for a special job* equipo *m* de trabajo; MIL destacamento *m*

tas·sel ['tæsl] borla *f*

taste [teɪst] **1** *n* gusto *m*; *of food etc* sabor *m*; **he has no taste** tiene mal gusto **2** v/t *also fig* probar

T

taste·ful ['teɪstfəl] *adj* de buen gusto

taste·ful·ly ['teɪstfəlɪ] *adv* con buen gusto

taste·less ['teɪstlɪs] *adj food* insípido; *remark* de mal gusto

tast·ing ['teɪstɪŋ] *of wine* cata *f*, degustación *f*

tast·y ['teɪstɪ] *adj* sabroso, rico

tat·tered ['tætərd] *adj clothes* andrajoso; *book* destrozado

tat·ters ['tætərz]: *in tatters clothes* hecho jirones; *reputation, career* arruinado

tat·too [tə'tuː] *n* tatuaje *m*

tat·ty ['tætɪ] *adj* sobado, gastado

taught [tɔːt] *pret & pp* → **teach**

taunt [tɔːnt] **1** *n* pulla *f* **2** *v/t* mofarse de

Taur·us ['tɔːrəs] ASTR Tauro *m/f inv*

taut [tɔːt] *adj* tenso

taw·dry ['tɔːdrɪ] *adj* barato, cursi

tax [tæks] **1** *n* impuesto *m*; *before / after tax* sin descontar / descontando impuestos **2** *v/t people* cobrar impuestos a; *product* gravar

tax·a·ble 'in·come ingresos *mpl* gravables

ta·x·a·tion [tæk'seɪʃn] *(act of taxing)* imposición *f* de impuestos; *(taxes)* fiscalidad *f*, impuestos *mpl*

'tax avoid·ance elusión *f* legal de impuestos

'tax brack·et banda *f* impositiva

'tax de·duct·i·ble *adj* desgravable

'tax eva·sion evasión *f* fiscal

'tax free *adj* libre de impuestos

'tax haven paraíso *m* fiscal

tax·i ['tæksɪ] *n* taxi *m*

'tax·i dri·ver taxista *m/f*

tax·ing ['tæksɪŋ] *adj* difícil, arduo

'tax in·spec·tor inspector(a) *m(f)* de Hacienda

'tax·i rank, 'tax·i stand parada *f* de taxis

'tax·pay·er contribuyente *m/f*

'tax re·turn *form* declaración *f* de la renta

'tax year año *m* fiscal

TB [tiː'biː] *abbr* (= **tuberculosis**) tuberculosis *f*

tea [tiː] *drink* té *m*; *meal* merienda *f*

tea·bag ['tiːbæg] bolsita *f* de té

teach [tiːtʃ] **1** *v/t* (*pret & pp* **taught**) *person, subject* enseñar; *teach s.o. to do sth* enseñar a alguien a hacer algo **2**

v/i (*pret & pp* **taught**): *I taught at that school* di clases en ese colegio; *he always wanted to teach* siempre quiso ser profesor

tea·cher ['tiːtʃər] *at primary school* maestro(-a) *m(f)*; *at secondary school, university* profesor(a) *m(f)*

tea·cher 'train·ing formación *f* pedagógica, magisterio *m*

tea·ching ['tiːtʃɪŋ] *profession* enseñanza *f*, docencia *f*

'tea·ching aid material *m* didáctico

'tea cloth paño *m* de cocina

'tea·cup taza *f* de té

'tea drink·er bebedor(a) *m(f)* de té

teak [tiːk] teca *f*

'tea leaf hoja *f* de té

team [tiːm] equipo *m*

'team·mate compañero(-a) *m(f)* de equipo

team 'spir·it espíritu *m* de equipo

'team·ster ['tiːmstər] camionero(-a) *m(f)*

'team·work trabajo *m* en equipo

'tea·pot tetera *f*

tear[1] [ter] **1** *n in cloth etc* desgarrón *m*, rotura *f* **2** *v/t* (*pret tore*, *pp torn*) *paper, cloth* rasgar; *be torn between two alternatives* debatirse entre dos alternativas **3** *v/i* (*pret tore*, *pp torn*) (*run fast, drive fast*) ir a toda velocidad

♦ **tear down** *v/t poster* arrancar; *building* derribar

♦ **tear out** *v/t* arrancar

♦ **tear up** *v/t paper* romper, rasgar; *agreement* romper

tear[2] [tɪr] *in eye* lágrima *f*; *burst into tears* echarse a llorar; *be in tears* estar llorando

tear·drop ['tɪrdrɑːp] lágrima *f*

tear·ful ['tɪrfəl] *adj* lloroso

'tear gas gas *m* lacrimógeno

tease [tiːz] *v/t person* tomar el pelo a, burlarse de; *animal* hacer rabiar

tea serv·ice, 'tea set servicio *m* de té

'tea·spoon *object* cucharilla *f*; *quantity* cucharadita *f*

'tea strain·er colador *m* de té

teat [tiːt] teta *f*

'tea to·wel *Br* paño *m* de cocina

tech·ni·cal ['teknɪkl] *adj* técnico
tech·ni·cal·i·ty [teknɪ'kælətɪ] (*technical nature*) tecnicismo *m*; LAW detalle *m* técnico
tech·ni·cal·ly ['teknɪklɪ] *adv* técnicamente
tech·ni·cian [tek'nɪʃn] técnico(-a) *m(f)*
tech·nique [tek'niːk] técnica *f*
tech·no·log·i·cal [teknə'lɑːdʒɪkl] *adj* tecnológico
tech·nol·o·gy [tek'nɑːlədʒɪ] tecnología *f*
tech·no·phob·i·a [teknə'foʊbɪə] rechazo *m* de las nuevas tecnologías
ted·dy bear ['tedɪber] osito *m* de peluche
te·di·ous ['tiːdɪəs] *adj* tedioso
tee [tiː] *n* in golf tee *m*
teem [tiːm] *v/i*: **be teeming with rain** llover a cántaros; **be teeming with tourists / ants** estar abarrotado de turistas / lleno de hormigas
teen·age ['tiːneɪdʒ] *adj* fashions adolescente, juvenil; **teenage boy / girl** un adolescente / una adolescente
teen·ag·er ['tiːneɪdʒər] adolescente *m/f*
teens [tiːnz] *npl* adolescencia *f*; **be in one's teens** ser un adolescente; **reach one's teens** alcanzar la adolescencia
tee·ny ['tiːnɪ] *adj* F chiquitín F
teeth [tiːθ] *pl* → **tooth**
teethe [tiːð] *v/i* echar los dientes
'teething problems *npl* problemas *fpl* iniciales
tee·to·tal [tiː'toʊtl] *adj* person abstemio
tee·to·tal·er [tiː'toʊtlər] abstemio(-a) *m(f)*
tel·e·com·mu·ni·ca·tions [telɪkəmjuːnɪ'keɪʃnz] telecomunicaciones *fpl*
tel·e·gram ['telɪgræm] telegrama *m*
tel·e·graph pole ['telɪgræf] poste *m* telegráfico
tel·e·path·ic [telɪ'pæθɪk] *adj* telepático; **you must be telepathic!** ¡debes tener telepatía!
te·lep·a·thy [tɪ'lepəθɪ] telepatía *f*
tel·e·phone ['telɪfoʊn] **1** *n* teléfono *m*; **be on the telephone** (*be speaking*) estar hablando por teléfono; (*possess a phone*) tener teléfono **2** *v/t* person telefonear, llamar por teléfono a **3** *v/i* telefonear, lla-

mar por teléfono
'tel·e·phone bill factura *f* del teléfono
'tel·e·phone book guía *f* telefónica, listín *m* telefónico
'tel·e·phone booth cabina *f* telefónica
'tel·e·phone call llamada *f* telefónica
'tel·e·phone con·ver·sa·tion conversación *f* por teléfono or telefónica
'tel·e·phone di·rec·to·ry guía *f* telefónica, listín *m* telefónico
'tel·e·phone ex·change central *f* telefónica, centralita *f*
'tel·e·phone mes·sage mensaje *m* telefónico
'tel·e·phone num·ber número *m* de teléfono
tel·e·pho·to lens [telɪ'foʊtoʊlenz] teleobjetivo *m*
tel·e·sales ['telɪseɪlz] televentas *fpl*
tel·e·scope ['telɪskoʊp] telescopio *m*
tel·e·thon ['telɪθɑːn] maratón *m* benéfico televisivo
tel·e·vise ['telɪvaɪz] *v/t* televisar
tel·e·vi·sion ['telɪvɪʒn] televisión *f*; set televisión *f*, televisor *m*; **on television** en *or* por (la) televisión; **watch television** ver la televisión
'tel·e·vi·sion au·di·ence audiencia *f* televisiva
'tel·e·vision pro·gram programa *m* televisivo
'tel·e·vision set televisión *f*, televisor *m*
'tel·e·vision stu·di·o estudio *m* de televisión
tell [tel] **1** *v/t* (*pret & pp* **told**) story contar; lie decir, contar; **I can't tell the difference** no veo la diferencia; **tell s.o. sth** decir algo a alguien; **don't tell Mom** no se lo digas a mamá; **could you tell me the way to …?** ¿me podría decir por dónde se va a …?; **tell s.o. to do sth** decir a alguien que haga algo; **you're telling me!** F ¡a mí me lo vas a contar! **2** *v/i* (*pret & pp* **told**) (*have effect*) hacerse notar; **the heat is telling on him** el calor está empezando a afectarle; **time will tell** el tiempo lo dirá
tell·er ['telər] cajero(-a) *m(f)*
tell·ing ['telɪŋ] *adj* contundente

tell·ing 'off regañina *f*

tell·tale ['telteɪl] **1** *adj signs* revelador **2** *n* chivato(-a) *m(f)*

temp [temp] **1** *n employee* trabajador(a) *m(f)* temporal **2** *v/i* hacer trabajo temporal

tem·per ['tempər] (*bad temper*) mal humor *m*; **be in a temper** estar de mal humor; **keep one's temper** mantener la calma; **lose one's temper** perder los estribos

tem·pe·ra·ment ['tempromant] temperamento *m*

tem·pe·ra·men·tal [tempro'mentl] *adj* (*moody*) temperamental

tem·pe·rate ['tempərət] *adj* templado

tem·pe·ra·ture ['tempratʃər] temperatura *f*; (*fever*) fiebre *f*; **have a temperature** tener fiebre

tem·ple[1] ['templ] REL templo *m*

tem·ple[2] ['templ] ANAT sien *f*

tem·po ['tempou] tempo *m*

tem·po·rar·i·ly [tempə'rerɪlɪ] *adv* temporalmente

tem·po·ra·ry ['tempərerɪ] *adj* temporal

tempt [tempt] *v/t* tentar

temp·ta·tion [temp'teɪʃn] tentación *f*

tempt·ing ['temptɪŋ] *adj* tentador

ten [ten] diez

te·na·cious [tɪ'neɪʃəs] *adj* tenaz

te·nac·i·ty [tɪ'næsɪtɪ] tenacidad *f*

ten·ant ['tenənt] *of building* inquilino(-a) *m(f)*; *of farm, land* arrendatario *m*

tend[1] [tend] *v/t* (*look after*) cuidar (de)

tend[2] [tend]: **tend to do sth** soler hacer algo; **tend toward sth** tender hacia algo

ten·den·cy ['tendənsɪ] tendencia *f*

ten·der[1] ['tendər] *adj* (*sore*) sensible, delicado; (*affectionate*) cariñoso, tierno; *steak* tierno

ten·der[2] ['tendər] *n* COM oferta *f*

ten·der·ness ['tendərnɪs] (*soreness*) dolor *m*; *of kiss etc* cariño *m*, ternura *f*

ten·don ['tendən] tendón *m*

ten·nis ['tenɪs] tenis *m*

'ten·nis ball pelota *f* de tenis

'ten·nis court pista *f* de tenis; cancha *f* de tenis

'ten·nis pla·yer tenista *m/f*

'ten·nis rack·et raqueta *f* de tenis

ten·or ['tenər] MUS tenor *m*

tense[1] [tens] *n* GRAM tiempo *m*

tense[2] [tens] *adj muscle, moment* tenso; *voice, person* tenso, nervioso

◆ tense up *v/i* ponerse tenso

ten·sion ['tenʃn] *of rope* tensión *f*; *in atmosphere, voice* tensión *f*, tirantez *f*; *in film, novel* tensión *f*

tent [tent] tienda *f*

ten·ta·cle ['tentəkl] tentáculo *m*

ten·ta·tive ['tentətɪv] *adj move, offer* provisional

ten·ter·hooks ['tentərhʊks]: **be on tenterhooks** estar sobre ascuas

tenth [tenθ] **1** *adj* décimo **2** *n* décimo *m*, décima parte *f*; *of second, degree* décima *f*

tep·id ['tepɪd] *adj water, reaction* tibio

term [tɜːrm] *in office etc* mandato *m*; EDU trimestre *m*; (*condition*) término *m*, condición *f*; (*word*) término *m*; **be on good / bad terms with s.o.** llevarse bien / mal con alguien; **in the long / short term** a largo / corto plazo; **come to terms with sth** llegar a aceptar algo

ter·mi·nal ['tɜːrmɪnl] **1** *n at airport, for buses, for containers* terminal *f*; ELEC, COMPUT terminal *m*; *of battery* polo *m* **2** *adj illness* terminal

ter·mi·nal·ly ['tɜːrmɪnəlɪ] *adv*: **terminally ill** en la fase terminal de una enfermedad

ter·mi·nate ['tɜːrmɪneɪt] **1** *v/t contract* rescindir; *pregnancy* interrumpir **2** *v/i* finalizar

ter·mi·na·tion [tɜːrmɪ'neɪʃn] *of contract* rescisión *f*; *of pregnancy* interrupción *f*

ter·mi·nol·o·gy [tɜːrmɪ'nɑːlədʒɪ] terminología *f*

ter·mi·nus ['tɜːrmɪnəs] *for buses* final *m* de trayecto; *for trains* estación *f* terminal

ter·race ['terəs] terraza *f*

ter·ra cot·ta [terə'kɑːtə] *adj* de terracota

ter·rain [te'reɪn] terreno *m*

ter·res·tri·al [te'restrɪəl] **1** *n* terrestre *m* **2** *adj television* por vía terrestre

ter·ri·ble ['terəbl] *adj* terrible, horrible

ter·ri·bly ['terəblɪ] *adv* (*very*) tremendamente

ter·rif·ic [təˈrɪfɪk] *adj* estupendo

ter·rif·i·cal·ly [təˈrɪfɪklɪ] *adv* (*very*) tremendamente

ter·ri·fy [ˈterɪfaɪ] *v/t* (*pret & pp* **terrified**) aterrorizar; **be terrified** estar aterrorizado

ter·ri·fy·ing [ˈterɪfaɪɪŋ] *adj* aterrador

ter·ri·to·ri·al [terɪˈtɔːrɪəl] *adj* territorial

ter·ri·to·ri·al 'wa·ters *npl* aguas *fpl* territoriales

ter·ri·to·ry [ˈterɪtɔːrɪ] territorio *m*; *fig* ámbito *m*, territorio *m*

ter·ror [ˈterər] terror *m*

ter·ror·ism [ˈterərɪzm] terrorismo *m*

ter·ror·ist [ˈterərɪst] terrorista *m*

'ter·ror·ist at·tack atentado *m* terrorista

'ter·ror·ist or·gan·i·za·tion organización *f* terrorista

ter·ror·ize [ˈterəraɪz] *v/t* aterrorizar

terse [tɜːrs] *adj* tajante, seco

test [test] **1** *n* prueba *f*; *academic, for driving* examen *m* **2** *v/t* probar, poner a prueba

tes·ta·ment [ˈtestəmənt] *to s.o.'s life etc* testimonio *m*; **Old / New Testament** REL Viejo / Nuevo Testamento *m*

'test-drive *v/t* (*pret* **test-drove**, *pp* **test-driven**) *car* probar en carretera

tes·ti·cle [ˈtestɪkl] testículo *m*

tes·ti·fy [ˈtestɪfaɪ] *v/i* (*pret & pp* **testified**) LAW testificar, prestar declaración

tes·ti·mo·ni·al [testɪˈmoʊnɪəl] *n* referencias *fpl*

tes·ti·mo·ny [ˈtestɪmənɪ] LAW testimonio *m*

'test tube tubo *m* de ensayo, probeta *f*

'test-tube ba·by niño(-a) *m(f)* probeta

tes·ty [ˈtestɪ] *adj* irritable

te·ta·nus [ˈtetənəs] tétanos *m*

teth·er [ˈteðər] **1** *v/t* *horse* atar **2** *n* correa *f*; **be at the end of one's tether** estar a la punto de perder la paciencia

text [tekst] texto *m*

'text·book libro *m* de texto

tex·tile [ˈtekstəl] textil

tex·ture [ˈtekstʃər] textura *f*

Thai [taɪ] **1** *adj* tailandés **2** *n person* tailandés(-esa) *m(f)*; *language* tailandés *m*

Thai·land [ˈtaɪlænd] Tailandia

than [ðæn] *adv* que; **bigger / faster than me** más grande / más rápido que yo; **more than 50** más de 50

thank [θæŋk] *v/t* dar las gracias a; **thank you** gracias; **no thank you** no, gracias

thank·ful [ˈθæŋkfəl] *adj* agradecido; **we have to be thankful that ...** tenemos que dar gracias de que ...

thank·ful·ly [ˈθæŋkfəlɪ] *adv* (*luckily*) afortunadamente

thank·less [ˈθæŋklɪs] *adj task* ingrato

thanks [θæŋks] *npl* gracias *fpl*; **thanks!** ¡gracias!; **thanks to** gracias a

Thanks·giv·ing (Day) [θæŋksˈgɪvɪŋdeɪ] Día *m* de Acción de Gracias

that [ðæt] **1** *adj* ese *m*, esa *f*; *more remote* aquel *m*, aquella; **that one** ése **2** *pron* ése *m*, ésa; *more remote* aquél *m*, aquella *f*; **what is that?** ¿qué es eso?; **who is that?** ¿quién es ése?; **that's mine** ése es mío; **that's tea** es té; **that's very kind** qué amable; **I think that ...** creo que ...; **the person / car that you see** el coche / la persona que ves **3** *adv* (*so*) tan; **that big / expensive** tan grande / caro

thaw [θɔː] *v/i of snow* derretirse, fundirse; *of frozen food* descongelarse

the [ðə] el, la; *plural* los, las; **the sooner the better** cuanto antes, mejor

the·a·ter [ˈθɪətər] teatro *m*

'the·a·ter crit·ic crítico *m* teatral

the·a·tre *Br* → **theater**

the·at·ri·cal [θɪˈætrɪkl] *also fig* teatral

theft [θeft] robo *m*

their [ðer] *adj* su; (*his or her*) su; **their brother** su hermano; **their books** sus libros

theirs [ðerz] *pron* el suyo, la suya; **theirs are red** los suyos son rojos; **that book is theirs** ese libro es suyo; **a friend of theirs** un amigo suyo

them [ðem] *pron direct object* los *mpl*, las *fpl*; *indirect object* les; *after prep* ellos *mpl*, ellas *fpl*; **I know them** los / las conozco; **I gave them the keys** les di las llaves; **I sold it to them** se lo vendí; **he lives with them** vive con ellos / ellas; **if a person asks for help, you should help them** him / her si una persona pide ayuda, hay que ayudarla

theme [θi:m] tema *m*

'theme park parque *m* temático

'theme song tema *m* musical

them·selves [ðem'selvz] *pron reflexive* se; *emphatic* ellos mismos *mpl*, ellas mismas *fpl*; **they hurt themselves** se hicieron daño; **when they saw themselves in the mirror** cuando se vieron en el espejo; **they saw it themselves** lo vieron ellos mismos; **by themselves** *(alone)* solos; *(without help)* ellos solos, ellos mismos

then [ðen] *adv (at that time)* entonces; *(after that)* luego, después; *deducing* entonces; **by then** para entonces

the·o·lo·gian [θɪə'loudʒɪən] teólogo *m*

the·ol·o·gy [θɪ'ɑːlədʒɪ] teología *f*

the·o·ret·i·cal [θɪə'retɪkl] *adj* teórico

the·o·ret·i·cal·ly [θɪə'retɪklɪ] *adv* en teoría

the·o·ry ['θɪrɪ] teoría *f*; **in theory** en teoría

ther·a·peu·tic [θerə'pjuːtɪk] *adj* terapéutico

ther·a·pist ['θerəpɪst] terapeuta *m/f*

ther·a·py ['θerəpɪ] terapia *f*

there [ðer] *adv* allí, ahí, allá; **over there** allí, ahí, allá; **down there** allí *or* ahí *or* allá abajo; **there is / are ...** hay ...; **there is / are not ...** no hay ...; **there you are** *giving sth* aquí tienes; *finding sth* aquí está; *completing sth* ya está; **there and back** ida y vuelta; **it's 5 miles there and back** entre ida y vuelta hay cinco millas; **there he is!** ¡ahí está!; **there, there!** ¡venga!

there·a·bouts [ðerə'bauts] *adv* aproximadamente

there·fore [ðerfɔːr] *adv* por (lo) tanto

ther·mom·e·ter [θər'mɑːmɪtər] termómetro *m*

ther·mos flask ['θɜːrməs] termo *m*

ther·mo·stat ['θɜːrməstæt] termostato *m*

these [ðiːz] **1** *adj* estos(-as) **2** *pron* éstos *mpl*, éstas *fpl*

the·sis ['θiːsɪs] *(pl theses* ['θiːsiːz]) tesis *f inv*

they [ðeɪ] *pron* ellos *mpl*, ellas *fpl*; **they are Mexican** son mexicanos; **they're**

going, but we're not ellos van, pero nosotros no; **if anyone looks at this, they will see that ...** si alguien mira esto, verá que ...; **they say that ...** dicen que ...; **they are going to change the law** van a cambiar la ley

thick [θɪk] *adj soup* espeso; *fog* denso; *wall, book* grueso; *hair* poblado; *crowd* compacto; F *(stupid)* corto; **it's 3 cm thick** tiene 3 cm de grosor

thick·en ['θɪkən] *v/t sauce* espesar

thick·set ['θɪkset] *adj* fornido

thick·skinned [θɪk'skɪnd] *adj fig* insensible

thief [θiːf] *(pl thieves* [θiːvz]) ladrón(-ona) *m(f)*

thigh [θaɪ] muslo *m*

thim·ble ['θɪmbl] dedal *m*

thin [θɪn] *adj person* delgado; *hair* ralo, escaso; *soup* claro; *coat, line* fino

thing [θɪŋ] cosa *f*; **things** *(belongings)* cosas *fpl*; **how are things?** ¿cómo te va?; **it's a good thing you told me** menos mal que me lo dijiste; **what a thing to do / say!** ¡qué barbaridad!

thing·um·a·jig ['θɪŋʌmədʒɪg] F *object* chisme *m*; *person* fulanito *m*

think [θɪŋk] *v/t & v/i (pret & pp thought)* pensar; *hold an opinion* pensar, creer; **I think so** creo que sí; **I don't think so** creo que no; **I think so too** pienso lo mismo; **what do you think?** ¿qué piensas o crees?; **what do you think of it?** ¿qué te parece?; **I can't think of anything more** no se me ocurre nada más; **think hard!** ¡piensa más!; **I'm thinking about emigrating** estoy pensando en emigrar

◆ **think over** *v/t* reflexionar sobre

◆ **think through** *v/t* pensar bien

◆ **think up** *v/t* plan idear

'think tank grupo *m* de expertos

thin·skinned [θɪn'skɪnd] *adj* sensible

third [θɜːrd] **1** *adj* tercero **2** *n* tercero(a) *m(f)*; *fraction* tercio *m*, tercera parte *f*

third·ly ['θɜːrdlɪ] *adv* en tercer lugar

third 'par·ty tercero *m*

third-par·ty in'sur·ance seguro *m* a terceros

third 'per·son GRAM tercera persona *f*

'**third-rate** *adj* de tercera, de pacotilla F
Third 'World Tercer Mundo *m*
thirst [θɜːrst] sed *f*
thirst·y ['θɜːrstɪ] *adj* sediento; *be thirsty* tener sed
thir·teen [θɜːr'tiːn] trece
thir·teenth [θɜːr'tiːnθ] *n & adj* decimotercero
thir·ti·eth ['θɜːrtɪɪθ] *n & adj* trigésimo
thir·ty ['θɜːrtɪ] treinta
this [ðɪs] **1** *adj* este *m*, esta *f*; *this one* éste **2** *pron* esto *m*, esta *f*; *this is good* esto es bueno; *this is ... introducing s.o.* éste / ésta es ...; TELEC soy ... **3** *adv*: *this big / high* así de grande / de alto
thorn [θɔːrn] espina *f*
thorn·y ['θɔːrnɪ] *adj* also *fig* espinoso
thor·ough ['θɜːrou] *adj search* minucioso; *knowledge* profundo; *person* concienzudo
thor·ough·bred ['θɜːroubred] *horse* purasangre *m*
thor·ough·ly ['θɜːroulɪ] *adv* completamente; *clean up* a fondo; *search* minuciosamente; *I'm thoroughly ashamed* estoy avergonzadísimo
those [ðouz] **1** *adj* esos *mpl*, esas *fpl*; *more remote* aquellos *mpl*, aquellas *fpl* **2** *pron* ésos *mpl*, ésas *fpl*; aquéllos *mpl*, aquéllas *mpl*
though [ðou] **1** *conj* (*although*) aunque; *as though* como si **2** *adv* sin embargo; *it's not finished though* pero no está acabado
thought[1] [θɔːt] *single* idea *f*; *collective* pensamiento *m*
thought[2] [θɔːt] *pret & pp* → **think**
thought·ful ['θɔːtfəl] *adj* pensativo; *book* serio; (*considerate*) atento
thought·less ['θɔːtlɪs] *adj* desconsiderado
thou·sand ['θauznd] mil *m*; *thousands of* miles de; *a thousand and ten* mil diez
thou·sandth['θauzndθ] *n & adj* milésimo
thrash [θræʃ] *v/t* golpear, dar una paliza a; SP dar una paliza a
◆ **thrash about** *v/i with arms etc* revolverse
◆ **thrash out** *v/t solution* alcanzar

thrash·ing ['θræʃɪŋ] *also* SP paliza *f*
thread [θred] **1** *n* hilo *m*; *of screw* rosca *f* **2** *v/t needle* enhebrar; *beads* ensartar
thread·bare ['θredber] *adj* raído
threat [θret] amenaza *f*
threat·en ['θretn] *v/t* amenazar
threat·en·ing ['θretnɪŋ] *adj* amenazador
three [θriː] tres
three-'quart·ers tres cuartos *mpl*
thresh [θreʃ] *v/t corn* trillar
thresh·old ['θreʃhould] *of house, new age* umbral *m*; *on the threshold of* en el umbral *or* en puertas de
threw [θruː] *pret* → **throw**
thrill [θrɪl] **1** *n* emoción *f*, estremecimiento *m* **2** *v/t*: *be thrilled* estar entusiasmado
thril·ler ['θrɪlər] *movie* película *f* de *Span* suspense *or* L.Am. suspenso; *novel* novela *f* de *Span* suspense *or* L.Am. suspenso
thrill·ing ['θrɪlɪŋ] *adj* emocionante
thrive [θraɪv] *v/i of plant* medrar, crecer bien; *of business, economy* prosperar
throat [θrout] garganta *f*
'**throat loz·enge** pastilla *f* para la garganta
throb [θrɑːb] **1** *n of heart* latido *m*; *of music* zumbido *m* **2** *v/i* (*pret & pp* **throbbed**) *of heart* latir; *of music* zumbar
throm·bo·sis [θrɑːm'bousɪs] trombosis *f*
throne [θroun] trono *m*
throng [θrɑːŋ] *n* muchedumbre *f*
throt·tle ['θrɑːtl] **1** *n on motorbike* acelerador *m*; *on boat* palanca *f* del gas; *on motorbike* mango *m* del gas **2** *v/t* (*strangle*) estrangular
◆ **throttle back** *v/i* desacelerar
through [θruː] **1** *prep* ◇ (*across*) a través de; *go through the city* atravesar la ciudad
◇ (*during*) durante; *through the winter / summer* durante el invierno / verano; *Monday through Friday* de lunes a viernes
◇ (*by means of*) a través de, por medio de; *arranged through him* acordado por él **2** *adv*: *wet through* completamente

T

mojado; **watch a film through** ver una película de principio a fin; **read a book through** leerse un libro de principio a fin 3 *adj*: **be through** *of couple* haber terminado; *(have arrived: of news etc)* haber llegado; **you're through** TELEC ya puede hablar; **I'm through with ...** *(finished with)* he terminado con ...

'through flight vuelo *m* directo

through-out [θruː'aʊt] **1** *prep* durante, a lo largo de **2** *adv* *(in all parts)* en su totalidad

'through train tren *m* directo

throw [θroʊ] **1** *v/t* (*pret* threw, *pp* thrown) tirar; *of horse* tirar, desmontar; *(disconcert)* desconcertar; *party* dar **2** *n* lanzamiento *m*; **it's your throw** te toca tirar

◆ throw away *v/t* tirar, *L.Am.* botar

◆ throw off *v/t* *jacket etc* quitarse rápidamente; *cold etc* deshacerse de

◆ throw on *v/t* *clothes* ponerse rápidamente

◆ throw out *v/t* *old things* tirar, *L.Am.* botar; *from bar, job, home* echar; *from country* expulsar; *plan* rechazar

◆ throw up **1** *v/t* *ball* lanzar hacia arriba; **throw up one's hands** echarse las manos a la cabeza **2** *v/i* *(vomit)* vomitar

'throw-a-way *adj* *remark* insustancial, pasajero; *(disposable)* desechable

'throw-in SP saque *m* de banda

thrown [θroʊn] *pp* → throw

thru [θruː] → through

thrush [θrʌʃ] *bird* zorzal *m*

thrust [θrʌst] *v/t* (*pret & pp* thrust) *(push hard)* empujar; *knife* hundir; **thrust sth into s.o.'s hands** poner algo en las manos de alguien; **thrust one's way through the crowd** abrirse paso a empujones entre la multitud

thud [θʌd] *n* golpe *m* sordo

thug [θʌɡ] *n* matón *m*

thumb [θʌm] **1** *n* pulgar *m* **2** *v/t*: **thumb a ride** hacer autoestop

'thumb·tack ['θʌmtæk] chincheta *f*

thump [θʌmp] **1** *n* *blow* porrazo *m*; *noise* golpe *m* sordo **2** *v/t* person dar un porrazo a; **thump one's fist on the table** pegar un puñetazo en la mesa **3** *v/i* *of heart* latir con fuerza; **thump on the door** aporrear la puerta

thun·der ['θʌndər] *n* truenos *mpl*

thun·der·ous ['θʌndərəs] *adj* applause tormenta *f*

thun·der·storm ['θʌndərstɔːrm] tormenta *f* (con truenos)

'thun·der·struck *adj* atónito

thun·der·y ['θʌndərɪ] *adj* weather tormentoso

Thurs·day ['θɜːrzdeɪ] jueves *m inv*

thus [ðʌs] *adv* *(in this way)* así

thwart [θwɔːrt] *v/t* person, plans frustrar

thyme [taɪm] tomillo *m*

thy·roid gland ['θaɪrɔɪdɡlænd] (glándula *f*) tiroides *m inv*

tick [tɪk] **1** *n of clock* tictac *m*; *in text* señal *f* de visto bueno **2** *v/i of clock* hacer tictac

tick·et ['tɪkɪt] *for bus, train, lottery* billete *m*, *L.Am.* boleto *m*; *for airplane* billete *m*, *L.Am.* pasaje *m*; *for theater, concert, museum* entrada *f*, *L.Am.* boleto *m*; *for speeding etc* multa *f*

'ti·cket col·lec·tor revisor(a) *m(f)*

'ti·cket in·spec·tor revisor(a) *m(f)*

'ti·cket ma·chine máquina *f* expendedora de billetes

'ti·cket of·fice *at station* mostrador *m* de venta de billetes; THEA taquilla *f*, *L.Am.* boletería *f*

tick·ing ['tɪkɪŋ] *noise* tictac *m*

tick·le ['tɪkl] **1** *v/t* person hacer cosquillas a **2** *v/i of material* hacer cosquillas; **stop that, you're tickling!** ¡para ya, me haces cosquillas!

tick·lish ['tɪklɪʃ] *adj* person tener cosquillas

ti·dal wave ['taɪdlweɪv] maremoto *m* (ola)

tide [taɪd] marea *f*; **high tide** marea alta; **low tide** marea baja; **the tide is in / out** la marea está alta / baja

◆ tide over *v/t*: **20 dollars will tide me over** 20 dólares me bastarán

ti·di·ness ['taɪdɪnɪs] orden *m*

ti·dy ['taɪdɪ] *adj* ordenado

◆ tidy away *v/t* (*pret & pp* tidied) guardar

◆ tidy up **1** *v/t* room, shelves ordenar; **tidy o.s. up** arreglarse **2** *v/i* recoger

tie [taɪ] **1** n (*necktie*) corbata f; SP (*even result*) empate m; **he doesn't have any ties** no está atado a nada **2** v/t knot hacer, atar; hands atar; **tie two ropes together** atar dos cuerdas **3** v/i SP empatar

◆ **tie down** v/t also fig atar

◆ **tie up** v/t person, laces atar; boat amarrar; hair recoger; **I'm tied up tomorrow** (*busy*) mañana estaré muy ocupado

tier [tɪr] of hierarchy nivel m; in stadium grada f

ti·ger ['taɪgər] tigre m

tight [taɪt] **1** adj clothes ajustado, estrecho; security estricto; (*hard to move*) apretado; (*properly shut*) cerrado; (*not leaving much time*) justo de tiempo; F (*drunk*) como una cuba F **2** adv hold fuerte; shut bien

tight·en ['taɪtn] v/t screw apretar; control endurecer; security intensificar; **tighten one's grip on sth** on rope etc asir algo con más fuerza; on power etc incrementar el control sobre algo

◆ **tighten up** v/i in discipline, security ser más estricto

tight-fist·ed [taɪt'fɪstɪd] adj agarrado

tight·ly ['taɪtlɪ] adv → **tight**

tight·rope ['taɪtroʊp] cuerda f floja

tights [taɪts] npl Br medias fpl, pantis mpl

tile [taɪl] on floor baldosa f; on wall azulejo m; on roof teja f

till[1] [tɪl] → **until**

till[2] [tɪl] n (*cash register*) caja f (registradora)

till[3] [tɪl] v/t soil labrar

tilt [tɪlt] **1** v/t inclinar **2** v/i inclinarse

tim·ber ['tɪmbər] madera f (de construcción)

time [taɪm] tiempo m; (*occasion*) vez f; **time is up** se acabó (el tiempo); **for the time being** por ahora, por el momento; **have a good time** pasarlo bien; **have a good time!** ¡que lo paséis bien!; **what's the time?, do you have the time?** ¿qué hora es?; **the first time** la primera vez; **four times** cuatro veces; **time and again** una y otra vez; **all the time** todo el rato; **two / three at a time** de dos en dos / de tres en tres; **at the same time** speak,

reply etc a la vez; (*however*) al mismo tiempo; **in time** con tiempo; **on time** puntual; **in no time** en un santiamén

'time bomb bomba f de relojería

'time clock in factory reloj m registrador

'time-con·sum·ing adj que lleva mucho tiempo

'time dif·fer·ence diferencia f horaria

'time-lag intervalo m

'time lim·it plazo m

time·ly ['taɪmlɪ] adj oportuno

time out SP tiempo m muerto

tim·er ['taɪmər] device temporizador m; person cronometrador m

'time-sav·ing n ahorro m de tiempo

'time-scale of project plazo m (de tiempo)

'time switch temporizador m

'time-warp salto m en el tiempo

'time zone huso m horario

tim·id ['tɪmɪd] adj tímido

tim·ing ['taɪmɪŋ] of dancer sincronización f; of actor utilización f de las pausas y del ritmo; **the timing of the announcement was perfect** el anuncio due realizado en el momento perfecto

tin [tɪn] metal estaño m; Br (*can*) lata f

tin·foil ['tɪnfɔɪl] papel m de aluminio

tinge [tɪndʒ] n of color, sadness matiz m

tin·gle ['tɪŋgl] n hormigueo m

◆ **tin·ker with** ['tɪŋkər] v/t enredar con

tin·kle ['tɪŋkl] n of bell tintineo m

tin·sel ['tɪnsl] espumillón m

tint [tɪnt] **1** n of color matiz m; in hair tinte m **2** v/t hair teñir

tint·ed ['tɪntɪd] glasses con un tinte; paper coloreado

ti·ny ['taɪnɪ] adj diminuto, minúsculo

tip[1] [tɪp] n of stick, finger punta f; of mountain cumbre f; of cigarette filtro m

tip[2] [tɪp] **1** n advice consejo m; money propina f **2** v/t (*pret & pp tipped*) waiter etc dar propina a

◆ **tip off** v/t avisar

◆ **tip over** v/t jug volcar; liquid derramar; **he tipped water all over me** derramó agua encima mío

tipped [tɪpt] adj cigarettes con filtro

Tipp-Ex® n Tipp-Ex m

T

tip·py-toe['tɪpɪtou]: *on tippy-toe* de puntillas

tip·sy ['tɪpsɪ] *adj* achispado

tire¹[taɪr] *n* neumático *m*, *L.Am.* llanta *f*

tire²[taɪr] **1** *v/t* cansar, fatigar **2** *v/i* cansarse, fatigarse; *he never tires of telling the story* nunca se cansa de contar la *his*-*toria*

tired [taɪrd] *adj* cansado, fatigado; *be ti*-*red of s.o./sth* estar cansado de algo / de alguien

tired·ness['taɪrdnɪs] cansancio *m*, fatiga *f*

tire·less ['taɪrlɪs] *adj efforts* incansable, infatigable

tire·some['taɪrsəm] *adj (annoying)* pesado

tir·ing ['taɪrɪŋ] *adj* agotador

tis·sue ['tɪʃuː] ANAT tejido *m*; *(handker*-*chief)* pañuelo *m* de papel, Kleenex® *m*

'tis·sue pa·per papel *m* de seda

tit¹ [tɪt] *bird* herrerillo *m*

tit² [tɪt]: *give s.o. tit for tat* pagar a alguien con la misma moneda

tit³ [tɪt] V *(breast)* teta *f* V

ti·tle ['taɪtl] *of novel, person etc* título *m*; LAW título *m* de propiedad

'ti·tle-hold·er *sp* campeón(-ona) *m(f)*

tit·ter ['tɪtər] *v/i* reírse tontamente

to[tu:] *unstressed* [tə] **1** *prep a*: *to Japan / Chicago* a Japón / Chicago; *let's go to my place* vamos a mi casa; *walk to the station* camina a la estación; *to the north / south of ...* al norte / sur de ...; *give sth to s.o.* dar algo a alguien; *from Monday to Wednesday* de lunes a miércoles; *from 10 to 15 people* de 10 a 15 personas **2** *with verbs*: *to speak, to shout* hablar, chillar; *learn to swim* aprender a nadar; *nice to eat* sabroso; *too heavy to carry* demasiado pesado para llevarlo; *to be honest with you ...* para ser sincero ... **3** *adv*: *to and fro* de un lado para otro

toad [toud] *n* sapo *m*

toad·stool ['toudstu:l] seta *f* venenosa

toast [toust] **1** *n* pan *m* tostado; *drinking* brindis *m inv*; *propose a toast to s.o.* proponer un brindis en honor de alguien

2 *v/t drinking* brindar por

toast·er ['toustər] tostador(a) *m(f)*

to·bac·co [tə'bækou] tabaco *m*

to·bog·gan [tə'bɑːgən] *n* tobogán *m*

to·day [tə'deɪ] hoy

tod·dle ['tɑːdl] *v/i of child* dar los primeros pasos

tod·dler ['tɑːdlər] niño *m* pequeño

to·do [tə'duː] F revuelo *m*

toe[tou] **1** *n* dedo *m* del pie; *of shoe* puntera *f* **2** *v/t*: *toe the line* acatar la disciplina

toe·nail ['touneɪl] uña *f* del pie

to·geth·er [tə'geðər] *adv* juntos(-as); *mix two drinks together* mezclar dos bebidas; *don't all talk together* no hablen todos a la vez

toil [tɔɪl] *n* esfuerzo *m*

toi·let ['tɔɪlɪt] *place* cuarto *m* de baño, servicio *m*; *equipment* retrete *m*; *go to the toilet* ir al baño

'toi·let pa·per papel *m* higiénico

toil·et·ries['tɔɪlɪtrɪz] *npl* artículos *mpl* de tocador

'toi·let roll rollo *m* de papel higiénico

to·ken['toukən] *(sign)* muestra *f*; *for gam*-*bling* ficha *f*; *(gift token)* vale *m*

told [tould] *pret & pp* → *tell*

tol·e·ra·ble ['tɑːlərəbl] *adj pain etc* soportable; *(quite good)* aceptable

tol·e·rance ['tɑːlərəns] tolerancia *f*

tol·e·rant ['tɑːlərənt] *adj* tolerante

tol·e·rate ['tɑːləreɪt] *v/t noise, person* tolerar; *I won't tolerate it!* ¡no lo toleraré!

toll¹ [toul] *v/i of bell* tañer

toll² [toul] *n (deaths)* mortandad *f*, número *m* de víctimas

toll³ [toul] *n for bridge, road* peaje *m*; TELEC tarifa *f*

'toll booth cabina *f* de peaje

'toll-free *adj* TELEC gratuito

'toll road carretera *f* de peaje

to·ma·to [tə'meɪtou] tomate *m*, *Mex* jitomate *m*

to·ma·to 'ketch·up ketchup *m*

to·ma·to 'sauce*for pasta etc* salsa *f* de tomate

tomb [tu:m] tumba *f*

tom·boy['tɑːmbɔɪ] niña *f* poco femenina

tomb·stone [ˈtuːmstoʊn] lápida f

tom·cat [ˈtɑːmkæt] gato m

to·mor·row [təˈmɔːroʊ] mañana; *the day after tomorrow* pasado mañana; *tomorrow morning* mañana por la mañana

ton [tʌn] tonelada f (*907 kg*)

tone [toʊn] *of color, conversation* tono m; *of musical instrument* timbre m; *of neighborhood* nivel m; *tone of voice* tono m de voz

◆ **tone down** v/t *demands, criticism* bajar el tono de

ton·er [ˈtoʊnər] npl tóner m

tongs [tɑːŋz] npl tenazas fpl; *for hair* tenacillas fpl de rizar

tongue [tʌŋ] n lengua f

ton·ic [ˈtɑːnɪk] MED tónico m

'ton·ic (wa·ter) (agua f) tónica f

to·night [təˈnaɪt] esta noche

ton·sil [ˈtɑːnsl] amígdala f

ton·sil·li·tis [tɑːnsəˈlaɪtɪs] amigdalitis f

too [tuː] adv (*also*) también; (*excessively*) demasiado; *me too* yo también; *too big / hot* demasiado grande / caliente; *too much rice* demasiado arroz; *eat too much* comer demasiado

took [tʊk] pret → **take**

tool [tuːl] herramienta f

toot [tuːt] v/t F tocar

tooth [tuːθ] (pl **teeth** [tiːθ]) diente m

'tooth·ache dolor m de muelas

'tooth·brush cepillo m de dientes

tooth·less [ˈtuːθlɪs] adj desdentado

'tooth·paste pasta f de dientes, dentífrico m

'tooth·pick palillo m

top [tɑːp] 1 n *of mountain* cima f; *of tree* copa f; *of wall, screen, page* parte f superior; (*lid: of bottle etc*) tapón m; *of pen* capucha f; *clothing* camiseta f, top m; (MOT: *gear*) directa f; *on top of* encima de, sobre; *at the top of the page* en la parte superior de la página; *at the top of the mountain* en la cumbre; *the top of the class / league* person, team ser el primero de la clase / de la liga; *get to the top* of company, mountain llegar a la cumbre; *of mountain*; *be over the top* (*exaggerated*) ser una exagera-

ción 2 adj branches superior; floor de arriba, último; management, official alto; player mejor; speed, note máximo 3 v/t (pret etc pp **topped**): **topped with ... of cake etc** con una capa de ... por encima

◆ **top up** v/t glass, tank llenar

top 'hat sombrero m de copa

top 'heav·y adj sobrecargado en la parte superior

top·ic [ˈtɑːpɪk] tema m

top·ic·al [ˈtɑːpɪkl] adj de actualidad

top·less [ˈtɑːplɪs] adj en topless

top·most [ˈtɑːpmoʊst] adj branches, floor superior

top·ping [ˈtɑːpɪŋ] on pizza ingrediente m

top·ple [ˈtɑːpl] 1 v/i derrumbarse 2 v/t government derrocar

top 'se·cret adj altamente confidencial

top·sy·tur·vy [tɑːpsɪˈtɜːrvɪ] adj (*in disorder*) desordenado; world al revés

torch [tɔːrtʃ] with flame antorcha f

tore [tɔːr] pret → **tear**[1]

tor·ment 1 n [ˈtɔːrment] tormento m 2 v/t [tɔːrˈment] person, animal atormentar; *tormented by doubt* atormentado por la duda

torn [tɔːrn] pp → **tear**[1]

tor·na·do [tɔːrˈneɪdoʊ] tornado m

tor·pe·do [tɔːrˈpiːdoʊ] 1 n torpedo m 2 v/t also fig torpedear

tor·rent [ˈtɑːrənt] also fig torrente m; of lava colada f

tor·ren·tial [təˈrenʃl] adj rain torrencial

tor·toise [ˈtɔːrtəs] tortuga f

tor·ture [ˈtɔːrtʃər] 1 n tortura f 2 v/t torturar

toss [tɑːs] 1 v/t ball lanzar, echar; rider desmontar; salad remover; *toss a coin* echar a cara o cruz 2 v/i: *toss and turn* dar vueltas

to·tal [ˈtoʊtl] 1 n total m 2 adj sum, amount total; disaster rotundo, completo; idiot de tomo y lomo; stranger completo 3 v/t F car cargarse F; *the truck was totaled* el camión quedó destrozado

to·tal·i·tar·i·an [toʊtælɪˈterɪən] adj totalitario

to·tal·ly [ˈtoʊtəlɪ] adv totalmente

tote bag [ˈtoʊtbæg] bolsa f grande

T

tot·ter ['tɑːtər] v/i of person tambalearse

touch [tʌtʃ] **1** n toque m; sense tacto m; **lose touch with s.o.** perder el contacto con alguien; **keep in touch with s.o.** mantenerse en contacto con alguien; **we kept in touch** seguimos en contacto; **be out of touch** no estar al corriente; **the leader was out of touch with the people** el líder estaba desconectado de lo que pensaba la gente; **in touch** SP fuera **2** v/t tocar; emotionally conmover **3** v/i tocar; of two lines etc tocarse

♦ touch down v/i of airplane aterrizar; SP marca un ensayo

♦ touch on v/t (mention) tocar, mencionar

♦ touch up v/t photo retocar; sexually manosear

touch·down ['tʌtʃdaun] of airplane aterrizaje m; SP touchdown m, ensayo m

touch·ing ['tʌtʃɪŋ] adj conmovedor

touch·line ['tʌtʃlaɪn] SP línea f de banda

'touch screen pantalla f táctil

touch·y ['tʌtʃɪ] adj person susceptible

tough [tʌf] adj person, meat, punishment duro; question, exam difícil; material resistente, fuerte

♦ tough·en up v/t person hacer más fuerte

'tough guy F tipo m duro F

tour [tur] **1** n of museum etc recorrido m; of area viaje m (**of** por); of band ecc gira f **2** v/t area recorrer **3** v/i of band etc estar de gira

'tour guide guía m/f turístico(-a)

tour·i·sm ['turɪzm] turismo m

tour·i·st ['turɪst] turista m/f

'tour·ist at·trac·tion atracción f turística

'tour·ist in·dus·try industria f turística

'tour·ist (in·for·ma·tion) of·fice oficina f de turismo

'tour·ist sea·son temporada f turística

tour·na·ment ['turnəmənt] torneo m

'tour op·er·a·tor operador m turístico

tous·led ['tauzld] adj hair revuelto

tow [tou] **1** v/t car, boat remolcar **2** n: **give s.o. a tow** remolcar a alguien

♦ tow away v/t car llevarse

to·ward [tɔːrd] prep hacia; **we are wor-** **king toward a solution** estamos intentando encontrar una solución

tow·el ['tauəl] toalla f

tow·er ['tauər] n torre m

♦ tower over v/t of building elevarse por encima de; of person ser mucho más alto que

town [taun] ciudad f

town 'cen·ter centro m de la ciudad / del pueblo

town 'coun·cil ayuntamiento m

town 'hall ayuntamiento m

'tow·rope cuerda f para remolcar

tox·ic ['tɑːksɪk] adj tóxico

tox·ic 'waste residuos mpl tóxicos

tox·in ['tɑːksɪn] BIO toxina f

toy [tɔɪ] juguete m

'toy store juguetería f, tienda f de juguetes

♦ toy with v/t object juguetear con; idea darle vueltas a

trace [treɪs] **1** n of substance resto m **2** v/t (find) localizar; (follow: footsteps of) seguir el rastro a; (draw) trazar

track [træk] n (path) senda f, camino; for horses hipódromo m; for dogs canódromo m; for cars circuito m; for athletics pista f; on CD canción f, corte m; RAIL vía f; **track 10** RAIL vía 10; **keep track of sth** llevar la cuenta de algo

♦ track down v/t localizar

'track·suit chándal m

trac·tor ['træktər] tractor m

trade [treɪd] **1** n (commerce) comercio m; (profession, craft) oficio m **2** v/i (do business) comerciar; **trade in sth** comerciar en algo **3** v/t (exchange) intercambiar; **trade sth for sth** intercambiar algo por algo

♦ trade in v/t when buying entregar como parte del pago

'trade fair feria f de muestras

'trade·mark marca f registrada

'trade mis·sion misión f comercial

trad·er ['treɪdər] comerciante m

trade 'se·cret secreto m de la casa, secreto m comercial

trades·man ['treɪdzmən] (plumber etc) electricista, fontanero / plomero etc

tra·di·tion [trə'dɪʃn] tradición *f*

tra·di·tion·al [trə'dɪʃnl] *adj* tradicional

tra·di·tion·al·ly [trə'dɪʃnlɪ] *adv* tradicionalmente

traf·fic ['træfɪk] *n* on roads, in drugs tráfico *m*

♦ **traffic in** *v/t* (*pret & pp* **trafficked**) *drugs* traficar con

'**traf·fic cir·cle** rotonda *f*, *Span* glorieta

'**traf·fic cop** F poli *m* de tráfico F

'**traf·fic is·land** isleta *f*

'**traf·fic jam** atasco *m*

'**traf·fic light** semáforo *m*

'**traf·fic po·lice** policía *f* de tráfico

'**traf·fic sign** señal *f* de tráfico

tra·ge·dy ['trædʒɪk] tragedia *f*

tra·gic ['trædʒɪk] *adj* trágico

trail [treɪl] **1** *n* (path) camino *m*, senda *f*; of blood rastro *m* **2** *v/t* (follow) seguir la pista de; (tow) arrastrar **3** *v/i* (lag behind) ir a la zaga

trail·er ['treɪlər] pulled by vehicle remolque *m*; (mobile home) caravana *f*; of film avance *m*, tráiler *m*

train[1] [treɪn] *n* tren *m*; **go by train** ir en tren

train[2] [treɪn] **1** *v/t* team, athlete entrenar; employee formar; dog adiestrar **2** *v/i* of team, athlete entrenarse; of teacher etc formarse

train·ee [treɪ'niː] aprendiz(a) *m(f)*

train·er ['treɪnər] SP entrenador(a) *m(f)*; of dog adiestrador(a) *m(f)*

train·ers ['treɪnərz] *npl* Br shoes zapatillas *fpl* de deporte

train·ing ['treɪnɪŋ] of new staff formación *f*; SP entrenamiento *m*; **be in training** SP estar entrenándose; **be out of training** SP estar desentrenado

'**train·ing course** cursillo *m* de formación

'**train·ing scheme** plan *m* de formación

'**train sta·tion** estación *f* de tren

trait [treɪt] rasgo *m*

trai·tor ['treɪtər] traidor(a) *m(f)*

tramp [træmp] **1** *n* (vagabond) vagabundo(-a) *m(f)* **2** *v/i* caminar con pasos pesados

tram·ple ['træmpl] *v/t* pisotear; **be trampled to death** morir pisoteado; **be tram-**

pled underfoot ser pisoteado

♦ **trample on** *v/t* person, object pisotear

tram·po·line ['træmpoliːn] cama *f* elástica

trance [træns] trance *m*; **go into a trance** entrar en trance

tran·quil ['træŋkwɪl] *adj* tranquilo

tran·quil·i·ty [træŋ'kwɪlətɪ] tranquilidad *f*

tran·quil·iz·er ['træŋkwɪlaɪzər] tranquilizante *m*

trans·act [træn'zækt] *v/t* deal negociar

trans·ac·tion [træn'zækʃn] action transacción *f*; deal negociación *f*

trans·at·lan·tic [trænzət'læntɪk] *adj* transatlántico

tran·scen·den·tal [trænsen'dentl] *adj* trascendental

tran·script ['trænskrɪpt] transcripción *f*

trans·fer 1 *v/t* [træns'fɜːr] (*pret & pp* **transferred**) transferir **2** *v/i* (*pret & pp* **transferred**) in traveling hacer transbordo; from one language to another pasar **3** *n* ['trænsfɜːr] transferencia *f*; in travel transbordo *m*; of money transferencia *f*

trans·fer·a·ble [træns'fɜːrəbl] *adj* ticket transferible

'**trans·fer fee** for football player traspaso *m*

trans·form [træns'fɔːrm] *v/t* transformar

trans·form·a·tion [trænsfər'meɪʃn] transformación *f*

trans·form·er [træns'fɔːrmər] ELEC transformador *m*

trans·fu·sion [træns'fjuːʒn] transfusión *f*

tran·sis·tor [træn'zɪstər] transistor *m*; (radio) transistor *m*, radio *m* transistor

tran·sit ['trænzɪt]: **in transit** en tránsito

tran·si·tion [træn'sɪʒn] transición *f*

tran·si·tion·al [træn'sɪʒnl] *adj* de transición

'**tran·sit lounge** at airport sala *f* de tránsito

'**trans·it pas·sen·ger** pasajero *m* en tránsito

trans·late [træns'leɪt] *v/t & v/i* traducir

trans·la·tion [træns'leɪʃn] traducción *f*

trans·la·tor [træns'leɪtər] traductor(a) *m(f)*

trans·mis·sion [trænz'mɪʃn] of news, program emisión *f*; of disease transmisión *f*; MOT transmisión *f*

trans·mit [trænz'mɪt] *v/t* (*pret & pp* **transmitted**) *news, program* emitir; *disease* transmitir

trans·mit·ter [trænz'mɪtər] *for radio*, TV emisora *f*

trans·par·en·cy [træns'pærənsɪ] PHOT diapositiva *f*

trans·par·ent [træns'pærənt] *adj* transparente; (*obvious*) obvio

trans·plant 1 *v/t* [træns'plænt] MED transplantar **2** *n* ['trænsplænt] MED transplante *m*

trans·port 1 *v/t* [træn'spɔːrt] *goods, people* transportar **2** *n* ['trænspɔːrt] *of goods, people* transporte *m*

trans·por·ta·tion [trænspɔːr'teɪʃn] *of goods, people* transporte *m*; *means of transportation* medio *m* de transporte; *public transportation* transporte *m* público; *Department of Transportation* Ministerio *m* de Transporte

trans·ves·tite [træns'vestaɪt] travestí *m*, travestido *m*

trap [træp] **1** *n* trampa *f*; *set a trap for s.o.* tender una trampa a alguien **2** *v/t* (*pret & pp* **trapped**) atrapar; *be trapped* by *enemy, flames, landslide etc* quedar atrapado

trap·door ['træpdɔːr] trampilla *f*

tra·peze [trə'piːz] trapecio *m*

trap·pings ['træpɪŋz] *npl of power* parafernalia *f*

trash [træʃ] (*garbage*) basura *f*; (*poor product*) bazofia *f*; (*despicable person*) escoria *f*

trash·can [træʃkæn] cubo *m* de la basura

trash·y ['træʃɪ] *adj goods, novel* barato

trau·mat·ic [trə'mætɪk] *adj* traumático

trau·ma·tize ['trɔːmətaɪz] *v/t* traumatizar

trav·el ['trævl] **1** *n* viajes *mpl*; *do you like travel?* ¿te gusta viajar?; *on my travels* en mis viajes **2** *v/i* (*pret & pp* **traveled**, *Br* **travelled**) viajar **3** *v/t miles* viajar, recorrer

'**trav·el a·gen·cy** agencia *f* de viajes

'**trav·el a·gent** agente *m* de viajes

'**trav·el bag** bolsa *f* de viaje

trav·el·er, *Br* **trav·el·ler** ['trævələr] viaje-

ro(-a) *m*(*f*)

'**trav·el·er's check**, *Br* '**trav·el·ler's che·que** cheque *m* de viaje

'**trav·el ex·penses** *npl* gastos *mpl* de viaje

'**trav·el in·sur·ance** seguro *m* de asistencia en viaje

'**trav·el pro·gram**, *Br* '**trav·el pro·gramme** *on* TV *etc* programa *m* de viajes

'**trav·el-sick** *adj* mareado

trawl·er ['trɒːlər] (barco *m*) arrastrero *m*

tray [treɪ] bandeja *f*

treach·er·ous ['tretʃərəs] *adj* traicionero

treach·er·y ['tretʃərɪ] traición *f*

tread [tred] **1** *n* pasos *mpl*; *of staircase* huella *f* (del peldaño); *of tyre* dibujo *m* **2** *v/i* (*pret* **trod**, *pp* **trodden**) andar; *mind where you tread* cuida dónde pisas

◆ **tread on** *v/t s.o.'s foot* pisar

trea·son ['triːzn] traición *f*

trea·sure ['treʒər] **1** *n* tesoro *m*; *person* tesoro *m* **2** *v/t gift etc* apreciar mucho

trea·sur·er ['treʒərər] tesorero(-a) *m*(*f*)

Trea·sur·y De·part·ment ['treʒərɪ] Ministerio *m* de Hacienda

treat [triːt] **1** *n* placer; *it was a real treat* fue un auténtico placer; *I have a treat for you* tengo una sorpresa agradable para ti; *it's my treat* (*I'm paying*) yo invito **2** *v/t* tratar; *treat s.o. to sth* invitar a alguien a algo

treat·ment ['triːtmənt] tratamiento *m*

treat·y ['triːtɪ] tratado *m*

tre·ble[^1] ['trebl] *n* MUS soprano *m*

tre·ble[^2] ['trebl] **1** *adv*: *treble the price* el triple del precio **2** *v/i* triplicarse

tree [triː] árbol *m*

trem·ble ['trembl] *v/i* temblar

tre·men·dous [trɪ'mendəs] *adj* (*very good*) estupendo; (*enormous*) enorme

tre·men·dous·ly [trɪ'mendəslɪ] *adv* (*very*) tremendamente; (*a lot*) enormemente

trem·or ['tremər] *of earth* temblor *m*

trench [trentʃ] trinchera *f*

trend [trend] tendencia *f*; (*fashion*) moda *f*

trend·y ['trendɪ] *adj* de moda; *views* moderno

tres·pass ['trespæs] *v/i* entrar sin autorización; *no trespassing* prohibido el paso

◆ **trespass on** *v/t s.o.'s land* entrar sin autorización en; *s.o.'s privacy* entrometerse en

tres·pass·er ['trespæsər] intruso(-a) *m(f)*

tri·al ['traiəl] LAW juicio *m*; *of equipment* prueba *f*; **be on trial** LAW estar siendo juzgado; **have sth on trial** *equipment* tener algo a prueba

tri·al 'pe·ri·od periodo *m* de prueba

tri·an·gle ['traiæŋgl] triángulo *m*

tri·an·gu·lar [trai'æŋgjulər] *adj* triangular

tribe [traib] tribu *f*

tri·bu·nal [trai'bju:nl] tribunal *m*

tri·bu·ta·ry ['tribjətəri] *of river* afluente *m*

trick [trik] **1** *n* (*to deceive, knack*) truco *m*; **play a trick on s.o.** gastar una broma a alguien **2** *v/t* engañar; **trick s.o. into doing sth** engañar a alguien para que haga algo

trick·e·ry ['trikəri] engaños *mpl*

trick·le ['trikl] **1** *n* hilo *m*, reguero *m*; *fig: of money* goteo *m* **2** *v/i* gotear, escurrir

trick·ster ['trikstər] embaucador(a) *m(f)*

trick·y ['triki] *adj* (*difficult*) difícil

tri·cy·cle ['traisikl] triciclo *m*

tri·fle ['traifl] *n* (*triviality*) nadería *f*

tri·fling ['traifliŋ] *adj* insignificante

trig·ger ['trigər] *n on gun* gatillo *m*; *on camcorder* disparador *m*

◆ **trigger off** *v/t* desencadenar

trim [trim] **1** *adj* (*neat*) muy cuidado; *figure* delgado **2** *v/t* (*pret & pp* **trimmed**) *hair, hedge* recortar; *budget, costs* recortar, reducir; (*decorate: dress*) adornar **3** *n* (*light cut*) recorte *m*; **just a trim, please** *to hairdresser* corte sólo las puntas, por favor; **in good trim** en buenas condiciones

trim·ming ['trimiŋ] *on clothes* adorno *m*; **with all the trimmings** *dish* con la guarnición clásica; *car* con todos los extras

trin·ket ['triŋkit] baratija *f*

tri·o ['tri:ou] MUS trío *m*

trip [trip] **1** *n* (*journey*) viaje *m* **2** *v/i* (*pret & pp* **tripped**) (*stumble*) tropezar **3** *v/t* (*pret & pp* **tripped**) (*make fall*) poner

la zancadilla a

◆ **trip up 1** *v/t* (*make fall*) poner la zancadilla a; (*cause to go wrong*) confundir **2** *v/i* (*stumble*) tropezar; (*make a mistake*) equivocarse

tripe [traip] mondongo *m*, *Span* callos *mpl*

trip·le ['tripl] → **treble²**

trip·lets ['triplits] *npl* trillizos *mpl*

tri·pod ['traipa:d] PHOT trípode *m*

trite [trait] *adj* manido

tri·umph ['traiʌmf] *n* triunfo *m*

triv·i·al ['triviəl] *adj* trivial

triv·i·al·i·ty [trivi'æləti] trivialidad *f*

trod [tra:d] *pret* → **tread**

trod·den ['tra:dn] *pp* → **tread**

trol·ley ['tra:li] (*streetcar*) tranvía *f*

trol·ley·bus ['tra:libʌs] trolebús *m*

trom·bone [tra:m'boun] trombón *m*

troops [tru:ps] *npl* tropas *fpl*

tro·phy ['troufi] trofeo *m*

trop·ic ['tra:pik] trópico *m*

trop·i·cal ['tra:pikl] *adj* tropical

trop·ics ['tra:piks] *npl* trópicos *mpl*

trot [tra:t] *v/i* (*pret & pp* **trotted**) trotar

trou·ble ['trʌbl] **1** *n* (*difficulties*) problema *m*, problemas *mpl*; (*inconvenience*) molestia *f*; (*disturbance*) conflicto *m*, desorden *m*; **go to a lot of trouble to do sth** complicarse mucho la vida para hacer algo; **no trouble!** no es molestia; **get into trouble** meterse en líos **2** *v/t* (*worry*) preocupar, inquietar; (*bother, disturb*) molestar

'**trou·ble-free** *adj* sin complicaciones

'**trou·ble-mak·er** alborotador(a) *m(f)*

'**trou·ble·shoot·er** (*mediator*) persona encargada de resolver problemas

'**trou·ble·shoot·ing** resolución *f* de problemas

trou·ble·some ['trʌblsəm] *adj* problemático

trou·sers ['trauzərz] *npl* pantalones *mpl*

trout [traut] (*pl* **trout**) trucha *f*

tru·ant ['tru:ənt]: **play truant** hacer novillos, *Mex* irse de pinta, *S. Am.* hacerse la rabona

truce [tru:s] tregua *f*

truck [trʌk] camión *m*

T

'truck driv·er camionero(-a) m(f)

'truck farm huerta f

'truck farm·er horticultor(a) m(f)

'truck stop restaurante m de carretera

trudge [trʌdʒ] **1** v/i caminar fatigosamente **2** n caminata f

true [truː] adj verdadero, cierto; friend, American auténtico; **come true** of hopes, dream hacerse realidad

trul·y ['truːlɪ] adv verdaderamente, realmente; **Yours truly** le saluda muy atentamente

trum·pet ['trʌmpɪt] trompeta f

trum·pet·er ['trʌmpɪtər] trompetista m/f

trunk [trʌŋk] of tree, body tronco m; of elephant trompa f; (large case) baúl m; of car maletero m, C.Am., Mex cajuela f, Rpl baúl m

trunks [trʌŋks] npl Br for swimming bañador m

trust [trʌst] **1** n confianza f; FIN fondo m de inversión **2** v/t confiar en

trusted ['trʌstɪd] adj de confianza

trust·ee [trʌsˈtiː] fideicomisario(-a) m(f)

trust·ful, trust·ing ['trʌstful, 'trʌstɪŋ] adj confiado

trust·wor·thy ['trʌstwɜːrðɪ] adj de confianza

truth [truːθ] verdad f

truth·ful ['truːθfəl] adj person sincero; account verdadero

try [traɪ] **1** v/t (pret & pp tried) probar; LAW juzgar; **try to do sth** intentar hacer algo, tratar de hacer algo **2** v/i (pret & pp tried): **he didn't even try** ni siquiera lo intentó; **you must try harder** debes esforzarte más **3** n intento m; **can I have a try?** ¿puedo probar?; at doing sth ¿puedo intentarlo?

◆ try on v/t clothes probar

◆ try out v/t new machine, new method probar

try·ing ['traɪɪŋ] adj (annoying) molesto, duro

T-shirt ['tiːʃɜːrt] camiseta f

tub [tʌb] (bath) bañera f, L.Am. tina f; for liquid cuba f; for yoghurt, ice cream envase m

tub·by ['tʌbɪ] adj rechoncho

tube [tuːb] tubo m

tube·less ['tuːblɪs] adj tire sin cámara de aire

tu·ber·cu·lo·sis [tuːbɜːrkjəˈloʊsɪs] tuberculosis f

tuck [tʌk] **1** n in dress pinza f **2** v/t (put) meter

◆ tuck away v/t (put away) guardar; F (eat quickly) zamparse F

◆ tuck in **1** v/t children arropar; sheets remeter **2** v/i (start eating) ponerse a comer

◆ tuck up v/t sleeves etc remangar; **tuck s.o. up in bed** meter a alguien en la cama

Tues·day ['tuːzdeɪ] martes m inv

tuft [tʌft] of hair mechón m; of grass mata f

tug [tʌg] **1** n (pull) tirón m; NAUT remolcador m **2** v/t (pret & pp tugged) (pull) tirar de

tu·i·tion [tuːˈɪsn] clases fpl

tu·lip ['tuːlɪp] tulipán m

tum·ble ['tʌmbl] v/i caer, caerse

tum·ble-down ['tʌmbldaʊn] adj destartalado

tum·ble-dry·er ['tʌmbldraɪr] secadora f

tum·bler ['tʌmblər] for drink vaso m; in circus acróbata m/f

tum·my ['tʌmɪ] F tripa f F, barriga f F

'tum·my ache dolor m de tripa or barriga

tu·mor ['tuːmər] tumor m

tu·mult ['tuːmʌlt] tumulto m

tu·mul·tu·ous [tuːˈmʌltʃʊəs] adj tumultuoso

tu·na ['tuːnə] atún m

tune [tuːn] **1** n melodía f; **be in tune** of instrument estar afinado; **sing in tune** cantar sin desafinar; **be out of tune** of singer desafinar; of instrument estar desafinado **2** v/t instrument afinar

◆ tune in v/i Radio, TV sintonizar

◆ tune in to v/t Radio, TV sintonizar (con)

◆ tune up **1** v/i of orchestra, players afinar **2** v/t engine poner a punto

tune·ful ['tuːnfəl] adj melodioso

tun·er ['tuːnər] hi-fi sintonizador m

tune-up ['tuːnʌp] of engine puesta f a punto

tun·nel ['tʌnl] n túnel m

tur·bine ['tɜːrbaɪn] turbina f

tur·bu·lence ['tɜːrbjələns] *in air travel* turbulencia *f*

tur·bu·lent ['tɜːrbjələnt] *adj* turbulento

turf [tɜːrf] césped *m*; *piece* tepe *m*

Turk [tɜːrk] turco(-a) *m(f)*

Tur·key ['tɜːrkɪ] Turquía

tur·key ['tɜːrkɪ] pavo *m*

Turk·ish ['tɜːrkɪʃ] **1** *adj* turco **2** *n language* turco *m*

tur·moil ['tɜːrmɔɪl] desorden *m*, agitación *f*

turn [tɜːrn] **1** *n (rotation)* vuelta *f*; *in road* curva *f*; *junction* giro *m*; *in vaudeville* número *m*; *take turns in doing sth* turnarse para hacer algo; *it's my turn* me toca a mí; *it's not your turn yet* no te toca todavía; *take a turn at the wheel* turnarse para conducir *or L.Am.* manejar; *do s.o. a good turn* hacer un favor a alguien **2** *v/t wheel* girar; *corner* dar la vuelta; *turn one's back on s.o.* dar la espalda a alguien **3** *v/i of driver, car, wheel* girar; *of person: turn around* volverse; *turn left / right here* gira aquí a la izquierda/a la derecha; *it has turned sour / cold* se ha cortado / enfriado; *it turned blue* se volvió *or* puso azul; *he has turned 40* ha cumplido cuarenta años

◆ **turn around 1** *v/t object* dar la vuelta a; *company* dar un vuelco a; (COM: *deal with*) procesar, preparar **2** *v/i of person* volverse, darse la vuelta; *of driver* dar la vuelta

◆ **turn away 1** *v/t (send away)* rechazar; *the doorman turned us away* el portero no nos dejó entrar **2** *v/i (walk away)* marcharse; *(look away)* desviar la mirada

◆ **turn back 1** *v/t edges, sheets* doblar **2** *v/i of walkers etc* volver; *in course of action* echarse atrás

◆ **turn down** *v/t offer, invitation* rechazar; *volume, TV, heating* bajar; *edge, collar* doblar

◆ **turn in 1** *v/i (go to bed)* irse a dormir **2** *v/t to police* entregar

◆ **turn off 1** *v/t TV, engine* apagar; *tap* cerrar; *heater* apagar; *it turns me off* F *sexually* me quita las ganas F **2** *v/i of car, driver* doblar

◆ **turn on 1** *v/t TV, engine, heating* encender, *L.Am.* prender; *tap* abrir; F *sexually* excitar F **2** *v/i of machine* encenderse, *L.Am.* prenderse

◆ **turn out 1** *v/t lights* apagar **2** *v/i: it turned out well* salió bien; *as it turned out* al final; *he turned out to be …* resultó ser …

◆ **turn over 1** *v/i in bed* darse la vuelta; *of vehicle* volcar, dar una vuelta de campana **2** *v/t (put upside down)* dar la vuelta a; *page* pasar; FIN facturar

◆ **turn up 1** *v/t collar* subirse; *volume, heating* subir **2** *v/i (arrive)* aparecer

turn·ing ['tɜːrnɪŋ] giro *m*

'turn·ing point punto *m* de inflexión

tur·nip ['tɜːrnɪp] nabo *m*

'turn·out *of people* asistencia *f*

'turn·o·ver FIN facturación *f*; *staff turnover* rotación *f* de personal

'turn·pike autopista *f* de peaje

'turn sig·nal *on car* intermitente *m*

'turn·stile torniquete *m (de entrada)*

'turn·ta·ble *of record player* plato *m*,

tur·quoise ['tɜːrkwɔːz] *adj* turquesa

tur·ret ['tʌrɪt] *of castle* torrecilla *f*; *of tank* torreta *f*

tur·tle ['tɜːrtl] tortuga *f* (marina)

tur·tle·neck 'sweater suéter *m* de cuello alto

tusk [tʌsk] colmillo *m*

tu·tor ['tuːtər] *at university* tutor *m*; *(private) tutor* profesor(a) *m(f)* particular

tu·xe·do [tʌk'siːdou] esmoquin *m*

TV [tiː'viː] televisión *f*; *on TV* en la televisión

T'V din·ner menú *m* precocinado

T'V guide guía *f* televisiva

T'V pro·gram programa *m* de televisión

twang [twæŋ] **1** *n in voice* entonación *f* nasal **2** *v/t guitar string* puntear

tweez·ers ['twiːzərz] *npl* pinzas *fpl*

twelfth [twelfθ] *n & adj* duodécimo

twelve [twelv] doce

twen·ti·eth ['twentɪɪθ] *n & adj* vigésimo

twen·ty ['twentɪ] veinte

twice [twaɪs] *adv* dos veces; *twice as much* el doble

T

twid·dle ['twɪdl] v/t dar vueltas a; **twiddle one's thumbs** holgazanear

twig [twɪg] n ramita f

twi·light ['twaɪlaɪt] crepúsculo m

twin [twɪn] gemelo m

'twin beds npl camas fpl gemelas

twinge [twɪndʒ] of pain punzada f

twin·kle ['twɪŋkl] v/i of stars parpadeo m; of eyes brillo m

twin 'room habitación f con camas gemelas

'twin town ciudad f hermana

twirl [twɜːrl] 1 v/t hacer girar 2 n of cream etc voluta f

twist [twɪst] 1 v/t retorcer; **twist one's ankle** torcerse el tobillo 2 v/i of road, river serpentear 3 n in rope, road vuelta f; in plot, story giro m inesperado

twist·y ['twɪstɪ] adj road serpenteante

twit [twɪt] F memo(-a) m(f) F

twitch [twɪtʃ] 1 n nervous tic m 2 v/i (jerk) moverse (ligeramente)

twit·ter ['twɪtər] v/i of birds gorjear

two [tuː] dos; **the two of them** los dos, ambos

two-faced ['tuːfeɪst] adj falso

'two-piece (woman's suit) traje m

'two-stroke adj engine de dos tiempos

two-way 'traf·fic tráfico m en dos direcciones

ty·coon [taɪˈkuːn] magnate m

type [taɪp] 1 n (sort) tipo m, clase f; **what type of ...?** ¿qué tipo or clase de ...? 2 v/i (use a keyboard) escribir a máquina 3 v/t with a typewriter mecanografiar, escribir a máquina

type·writ·er ['taɪpraɪtər] máquina f de escribir

ty·phoid ['taɪfɔɪd] fiebre f tifoidea

ty·phoon [taɪˈfuːn] tifón m

ty·phus ['taɪfəs] tifus m

typ·i·cal ['tɪpɪkl] adj típico; **that's typical of you / him!** ¡típico tuyo / de él!

typ·i·cal·ly ['tɪpɪklɪ] adv típicamente; **typically American** típicamente americano

typ·ist ['taɪpɪst] mecanógrafo(-a) m(f)

ty·ran·ni·cal [tɪˈrænɪkl] adj tiránico

ty·ran·nize ['tɪrənaɪz] v/t tiranizar

ty·ran·ny ['tɪrənɪ] tiranía f

ty·rant ['taɪrənt] tirano(-a) m(f)

tyre Br → tire[1]

U

ug·ly ['ʌglɪ] adj feo

UK [juːˈkeɪ] abbr (= **United Kingdom**) RU m (= Reino m Unido)

ul·cer ['ʌlsər] úlcera f; in mouth llaga f

ul·ti·mate ['ʌltɪmət] adj (final) final; (basic) esencial; **the ultimate car** (best, definitive) lo último en coches

ul·ti·mate·ly ['ʌltɪmətlɪ] adv (in the end) en última instancia

ul·ti·ma·tum [ʌltɪˈmeɪtəm] ultimátum m

ul·tra·sound ['ʌltrəsaʊnd] MED ultrasonido m; (scan) ecografía f

ul·tra·vi·o·let [ʌltrəˈvaɪələt] adj ultravioleta

um·bil·i·cal cord [ʌmˈbɪlɪkl] cordón m umbilical

um·brel·la [ʌmˈbrelə] paraguas m inv

um·pire ['ʌmpaɪr] n árbitro m; in tennis juez m/f de silla

ump·teen [ʌmpˈtiːn] adj F miles de F

UN [juːˈen] abbr (= **United Nations**) ONU f (= Organización f de las Naciones Unidas)

un·a·ble [ʌnˈeɪbl] adj: **be unable to do sth** (not know how to) no saber hacer algo; (not be in a position to) no poder hacer algo

un·ac·cept·a·ble [ʌnəkˈseptəbl] adj inaceptable; *it is unacceptable that* es inaceptable que

un·ac·count·a·ble [ʌnəˈkaʊntəbl] *adj* inexplicable

un·ac·cus·tomed [ʌnəˈkʌstəmd] *adj: be unaccustomed to sth* no estar acostumbrado a algo

un·a·dul·ter·at·ed [ʌnəˈdʌltəreɪtɪd] *adj* (*fig: absolute*) absoluto

un·A·mer·i·can [ʌnəˈmerɪkən] *adj* poco americano; *activities* antiamericano

u·nan·i·mous [juːˈnænɪməs] *adj verdict* unánime; *be unanimous on* ser unánime respecto a algo

u·nan·i·mous·ly [juːˈnænɪməslɪ] *adv vote, decide* unánimemente

un·ap·proach·a·ble [ʌnəˈprəʊtʃəbl] *adj person* inaccesible

un·armed [ʌnˈɑːrmd] *adj person* desarmado; *unarmed combat* combate *m* sin armas

un·as·sum·ing [ʌnəˈsuːmɪŋ] *adj* sin pretensiones

un·at·tached [ʌnəˈtætʃt] *adj* (*without a partner*) sin compromiso, sin pareja

un·at·tend·ed [ʌnəˈtendɪd] *adj* desatendido; *leave sth unattended* dejar algo desatendido

un·au·thor·ized [ʌnˈɒːθəraɪzd] *adj* no autorizado

un·a·void·a·ble [ʌnəˈvɔɪdəbl] *adj* inevitable

un·a·void·a·bly [ʌnəˈvɔɪdəblɪ] *adv: unavoidably detained* entretenerse sin poder evitarlo

un·a·ware [ʌnəˈwer] *adj: be unaware of* no ser consciente de

un·a·wares [ʌnəˈwerz] *adv* desprevenido; *catch s.o. unawares* agarrar *or Span* coger a alguien desprevenido

un·bal·anced [ʌnˈbælənst] *adj also* PSYCH desequilibrado

un·bear·a·ble [ʌnˈberəbl] *adj* insoportable

un·beat·a·ble [ʌnˈbiːtəbl] *adj team* invencible; *quality* insuperable

un·beat·en [ʌnˈbiːtn] *adj team* invicto

un·be·knownst [ʌnbɪˈnəʊnst] *adj: unbeknownst to her* sin que ella lo supiera

un·be·lie·va·ble [ʌnbɪˈliːvəbl] *adj also* F increíble; *he's unbelievable* F (*very good / bad*) es increíble

un·bi·as(s)ed [ʌnˈbaɪəst] *adj* imparcial

un·block [ʌnˈblɑːk] *v/t pipe* desatascar

un·born [ʌnˈbɔːrn] *adj* no nacido

un·break·a·ble [ʌnˈbreɪkəbl] *adj plates* irrompible; *world record* inalcanzable

un·but·ton [ʌnˈbʌtn] *v/t* desabotonar

un·called-for [ʌnˈkɒːldfɔːr] *adj: be uncalled-for* estar fuera de lugar

un·can·ny [ʌnˈkænɪ] *adj resemblance* increíble, asombroso; *skill* inexplicable; (*worrying: feeling*) extraño, raro

un·ceas·ing [ʌnˈsiːsɪŋ] *adj* incesante

un·cer·tain [ʌnˈsɜːrtn] *adj future, origins* incierto; *be uncertain about sth* no estar seguro de algo; *what will happen? - it's uncertain* ¿qué ocurrirá? - no se sabe

un·cer·tain·ty [ʌnˈsɜːrtntɪ] *adj* incertidumbre *f*; *there is still uncertainty about his health* todavía hay incertidumbre en torno a su estado de salud

un·checked [ʌnˈtʃekt] *adj: let sth go unchecked* no controlar algo

un·cle [ˈʌŋkl] *tío m*

un·com·for·ta·ble [ʌnˈkʌmftəbl] *adj chair, hotel* incómodo; *feel uncomfortable about sth about decision etc* sentirse incómodo con algo; *I feel uncomfortable with him* me siento incómodo con él

un·com·mon [ʌnˈkɑːmən] *adj* poco corriente, raro; *it's not uncommon* no es raro *or* extraño

un·com·pro·mis·ing [ʌnˈkɑːmprəmaɪzɪŋ] *adj* inflexible

un·con·cerned [ʌnkənˈsɜːrnd] *adj* indiferente; *be unconcerned about s.o./sth* no preocuparse por alguien / algo

un·con·di·tion·al [ʌnkənˈdɪʃnl] *adj* incondicional

un·con·scious [ʌnˈkɑːnʃəs] *adj* MED, PSYCH inconsciente; *knock unconscious* dejar inconsciente; *be unconscious of sth* (*not aware*) no ser consciente de algo

un·con·trol·la·ble [ʌnkənˈtrəʊləbl] *adj anger, children* incontrolable; *desire* ̕ controlable, irresistible

un·con·ven·tion·al [ʌnkən'venʃnl] *adj*
poco convencional

un·co·op·er·a·tive [ʌnkoʊ'ɑːpərətɪv] *adj*:
be uncooperative no estar dispuesto a
colaborar

un·cork [ʌn'kɔːrk] *v/t* **bottle** descorchar

un·cov·er [ʌn'kʌvər] *v/t* **remove cover
from** destapar; **plot, ancient remains** descubrir

un·dam·aged [ʌn'dæmɪdʒd] *adj* intacto

un·daunt·ed [ʌn'dɔːntɪd] *adj* impertérrito; **carry on undaunted** seguir impertérrito

un·de·cid·ed [ʌndɪ'saɪdɪd] *adj* **question**
sin resolver; **be undecided about s.o./-
sth** estar indeciso sobre alguien / algo

un·de·ni·a·ble [ʌndɪ'naɪəbl] *adj* innegable

un·de·ni·a·bly [ʌndɪ'naɪəblɪ] *adv* innega-
blemente

un·der ['ʌndər] **1** *prep* **(beneath)** debajo
de, bajo; **(less than)** menos de; **under
the water** bajo el agua; **it is under review / investigation** está siendo revisa-
do / investigado **2** *adv* **(anesthetized)**
anestesiado

un·der·age *adj*: **underage drinking** el
consumo de alcohol por menores de
edad

'un·der·arm *adv*: **throw a ball underarm**
lanzar una pelota soltándola por debajo
de la altura del hombro

'un·der·car·riage tren *m* de aterrizaje

'un·der·cov·er *adj* **agent** secreto

un·der·cut *v/t* (*pret & pp* **undercut**) COM
vender más barato que

'un·der·dog *n*: **support the underdog**
apoyar al más débil

un·der·done *adj* **meat** poco hecho

un·der·es·ti·mate *v/t* subestimar

un·der·ex·posed *adj* PHOT subexpuesto

un·der·fed *adj* malnutrido

un·der·go *v/t* (*pret* **underwent**, *pp* **under-
gon[e]** *surgery*, **treatment** ser sometido a;
...s sufrir; **the hotel is under...**
...rbishment se están efectuan-
...nes en el hotel

...ate *Br* estudiante *m/f* uni-

versitario(-a) (**todavía no licenciado(a)**)

'un·der·ground **1** *adj* **passages** etc subterráneo; POL **resistance, newpaper** etc
clandestino **2** *adv* **work** bajo tierra; **go
underground** POL pasar a la clandestini-
dad

'un·der·growth maleza *f*

un·der·hand *adj* **(devious)** poco honrado

un·der·lie *v/t* (*pret* **underlay**, *pp* **under-
lain**) **(form basis of)** sostener

un·der·line *v/t* **text** subrayar

un·der·ly·ing *adj* **causes, problems** subyacente

un·der·mine *v/t* **s.o.'s position, theory**
minar, socavar

un·der·neath [ʌndər'niːθ] **1** *prep* debajo
de, bajo **2** *adv* debajo

'un·der·pants *npl* calzoncillos *mpl*

'un·der·pass **for pedestrians** paso *m* subterráneo

un·der·priv·i·leged [ʌndər'prɪvɪlɪdʒ]
adj desfavorecido

un·der·rate *v/t* subestimar, infravalorar

'un·der·shirt camiseta *f*

un·der·sized [ʌndər'saɪzd] *adj* demasiado pequeño

'un·der·skirt enaguas *fpl*

un·der·staffed [ʌndər'stæft] *adj* sin suficiente personal

un·der·stand [ʌndər'stænd] **1** *v/t* (*pret &
pp* **understood**) entender, comprender;
language entender; **I understand that
you ...** tengo entendido que ...; **they
are understood to be in Canada** se cree
que están en Canadá **2** *v/i* (*pret & pp* **understood**) entender, comprender

un·der·stand·able [ʌndər'stændəbl] *adj*
comprensible

un·der·stand·ably [ʌndər'stændəblɪ] *adv*
comprensiblemente

un·der·stand·ing [ʌndər'stændɪŋ] **1** *adj*
person comprensivo **2** *n of problem, situation* interpretación *f*; (*agreement*)
acuerdo *m*; **on the understanding that
...** (*condition*) a condición de que ...

'un·der·state·ment *n*: **that's an under-
statement** ¡y te quedas corto!

un·der·take *v/t* (*pret* **undertook**, *pp* **un-
dertaken**) **task** emprender; **undertake**

to do sth (*agree to*) encargarse de hacer algo

un·der·tak·er [ˈʌndərˈteɪkər] *Br* encargado *m* de una funeraria

'un·der·tak·ing (*enterprise*) proyecto *m*, empresa *f*; ***give an undertaking to do sth*** comprterse a hacer algo

un·der·val·ue *v/t* infravalorar

'un·der·wear ropa *f* interior

un·der·weight *adj*: ***be underweight*** pesar menos de lo normal

'un·de·rworld *criminal* hampa *f*; *in mythology* Hades *m*

un·der·write *v/t* (*pret* **underwrote**, *pp* **underwritten**) FIN asegurar, garantizar

un·de·served [ʌndɪˈzɜːrvd] *adj* inmerecido

un·de·sir·a·ble [ʌndɪˈzaɪrəbl] *adj* *features, changes* no deseado; *person* indeseable; ***undesirable element*** persona *f* problemática

un·dis·put·ed [ʌndɪˈspjuːtɪd] *adj* *champion, leader* indiscutible

un·do [ʌnˈduː] *v/t* (*pret* **undid**, *pp* **undone**) *parcel, wrapping* abrir; *buttons, shirt* desabrochar; *shoelaces* desatar; *s.o. else's work* deshacer

un·doubt·ed·ly [ʌnˈdaʊtɪdlɪ] *adv* indudablemente

un·dreamt-of [ʌnˈdremtəv] *adj* *riches* inimaginable

un·dress [ʌnˈdres] **1** *v/t* desvestir, desnudar; ***get undressed*** desvestirse, desnudarse **2** *v/i* desvestirse, desnudarse

un·due [ʌnˈduː] *adj* (*excessive*) excesivo

un·du·ly [ʌnˈduːlɪ] *adv* *punished, blamed* injustamente; (*excessively*) excesivamente

un·earth [ʌnˈɜːrθ] *v/t* descubrir; *ancient remains* desenterrar

un·earth·ly [ʌnˈɜːrθlɪ] *adv*: ***at this unearthly hour*** a esta hora intempestiva

un·eas·y [ʌnˈiːzɪ] *adj* *relationship, peace* tenso; ***feel uneasy about*** estar inquieto por

un·eat·a·ble [ʌnˈiːtəbl] *adj* incomible

un·e·co·nom·ic [ʌniːkəˈnɑːmɪk] *adj* antieconómico, no rentable

un·ed·u·cat·ed [ʌnˈedʒəkeɪtɪd] *adj* inculto, sin educación

un·em·ployed [ʌnɪmˈplɔɪd] *adj* desempleado, *Span* parado

un·em·ploy·ment [ʌnɪmˈplɔɪmənt] desempleo *m*, *Span* paro *m*

un·end·ing [ʌnˈendɪŋ] *adj* interminable

un·e·qual [ʌnˈiːkwəl] *adj* desigual; ***be unequal to the task*** no estar a la altura de lo que requiere el trabajo

un·er·ring [ʌnˈerɪŋ] *adj* *judgment, instinct* infalible

un·e·ven [ʌnˈiːvn] *adj* *quality* desigual; *surface, ground* irregular

un·e·ven·ly [ʌnˈiːvnlɪ] *adv* *distributed, applied* de forma desigual; ***be unevenly matched*** *of two contestants* no estar en igualdad de condiciones

un·e·vent·ful [ʌnɪˈventfəl] *adj* *day, journey* sin incidentes

un·ex·pec·ted [ʌnɪkˈspektɪd] *adj* inesperado

un·ex·pec·ted·ly [ʌnɪkˈspektɪdlɪ] *adv* inesperadamente, de forma inesperada

un·fair [ʌnˈfer] *adj* injusto; ***that's unfair*** eso no es justo

un·faith·ful [ʌnˈfeɪθfəl] *adj* *husband, wife* infiel; ***be unfaithful to s.o.*** ser infiel a alguien

un·fa·mil·i·ar [ʌnfəˈmɪljər] *adj* desconocido, extraño; ***be unfamiliar with sth*** desconocer algo

un·fas·ten [ʌnˈfæsn] *v/t* *belt* desabrochar

un·fa·vo·ra·ble, *Br* **un·fa·vou·ra·ble** [ʌnˈfeɪvərəbl] *adj* desfavorable

un·feel·ing [ʌnˈfiːlɪŋ] *adj* *person* insensible

un·fin·ished [ʌnˈfɪnɪʃt] *adj* inacabado; ***leave sth unfinished*** dejar algo sin acabar

un·fit [ʌnˈfɪt] *adj*: ***be unfit*** *physically* estar en baja forma; ***be unfit to eat*** no ser apto para el consumo; ***be unfit to drink*** no ser potable; ***he's unfit to be a parent*** no tiene lo que se necesita para ser padre

un·fix [ʌnˈfɪks] *v/t part* soltar, desmontar

un·flap·pa·ble [ʌnˈflæpəbl] *adj* F impasible

un·fold [ʌnˈfoʊld] **1** *v/t* *sheets, letter* desdoblar; *one's arms* descruzar **2** *v/i of* *story etc* desarrollarse; *of view* abrirse

un·fore·seen [ʌnfɔr'siːn] *adj* imprevisto

un·for·get·ta·ble [ʌnfər'getəbl] *adj* inolvidable

un·for·giv·a·ble [ʌnfər'gɪvəbl] *adj* imperdonable; ***that was unforgivable of you*** eso ha sido imperdonable

un·for·tu·nate [ʌn'fɔːrtʃənət] *adj people* desafortunado; *event* desgraciado; *choice of words* desafortunado, desacertado; ***that's unfortunate for you*** has tenido muy mala suerte

un·for·tu·nate·ly [ʌn'fɔːrtʃənətlɪ] *adv* desgraciadamente

un·found·ed [ʌn'faʊndɪd] *adj* infundado

un·friend·ly [ʌn'frendlɪ] *adj person* antipático; *place* desagradable; *welcome* hostil; *software* de difícil manejo

un·fur·nished [ʌn'fɜːrnɪʃt] *adj* sin amueblar

un·god·ly [ʌn'gɑːdlɪ] *adj*: ***at this ungodly hour*** a esta hora intempestiva

un·grate·ful [ʌn'greɪtfəl] *adj* desagradecido

un·hap·pi·ness [ʌn'hæpɪnɪs] infelicidad *f*

un·hap·py [ʌn'hæpɪ] *adj person, look* infeliz; *day* triste; *customer etc* descontento

un·harmed [ʌn'hɑːrmd] *adj* ileso; ***be unharmed*** salir ileso

un·health·y [ʌn'helθɪ] *adj person* enfermizo; *conditions, food, economy* poco saludable

un·heard-of [ʌn'hɜːrdəv] *adj* inaudito

un·hurt [ʌn'hɜːrt] *adj*: ***be unhurt*** salir ileso

un·hy·gi·en·ic [ʌnhaɪ'dʒiːnɪk] *adj* antihigiénico

u·ni·fi·ca·tion [juːnɪfɪ'keɪʃn] unificación *f*

u·ni·form ['juːnɪfɔːrm] **1** *n* uniforme *m* **2** *adj* uniforme

u·ni·fy ['juːnɪfaɪ] *v/t (pret & pp **unified**)* unificar

u·ni·lat·er·al [juːnɪ'lætərəl] *adj* unilateral

un·i·ma·gi·na·ble [ʌnɪ'mædʒɪnəbl] *adj* inimaginable

un·i·ma·gi·na·tive [ʌnɪ'mædʒɪnətɪv] *adj* sin imaginación

un·im·por·tant [ʌnɪm'pɔːrtənt] *adj* poco importante

un·in·hab·i·ta·ble [ʌnɪn'hæbɪtəbl] *adj* inhabitable

un·in·hab·it·ed [ʌnɪn'hæbɪtɪd] *adj building* deshabitado; *region* desierto

un·in·jured [ʌn'ɪndʒərd] *adj*: ***be uninjured*** salir ileso

un·in·tel·li·gi·ble [ʌnɪn'telɪdʒəbl] *adj* ininteligible

un·in·ten·tion·al [ʌnɪn'tenʃnl] *adj* no intencionado; ***sorry, that was unintentional*** lo siento, ha sido sin querer

un·in·ten·tion·al·ly [ʌnɪn'tenʃnlɪ] *adv* sin querer

un·in·te·rest·ing [ʌn'ɪntrəstɪŋ] *adj* sin interés

un·in·ter·rupt·ed [ʌnɪntə'rʌptɪd] *adj sleep, two hours' work* ininterrumpido

u·nion ['juːnjən] POL unión *f*; *(labor union)* sindicato *m*

u·nique [juː'niːk] *adj* único

u·nit ['juːnɪt] unidad *f*; ***unit of measurement*** unidad *f* de medida; ***power unit*** fuente *f* de alimentación

u·nit 'cost COM costo *m or Span* coste *m* unitario *or* por unidad

u·nite [juː'naɪt] **1** *v/t* unir **2** *v/i* unirse

u·nit·ed [juː'naɪtɪd] *adj* unido

U·nit·ed 'King·dom Reino *m* Unido

U·nit·ed 'Na·tions Naciones *fpl* Unidas

U·nit·ed 'States (of A·mer·i·ca) Estados *mpl* Unidos (de América)

u·ni·ty ['juːnətɪ] unidad *f*

u·ni·ver·sal [juːnɪ'vɜːrsl] *adj* universal

u·ni·ver·sal·ly [juːnɪ'vɜːrsəlɪ] *adv* universalmente

u·ni·verse ['juːnɪvɜːrs] universo *m*

u·ni·ver·si·ty [juːnɪ'vɜːrsətɪ] **1** *n* universidad *f*; ***he is at university*** está en la universidad **2** *adj* universitario

un·just [ʌn'dʒʌst] *adj* injusto

un·kempt [ʌn'kempt] *adj appearance* descuidado; *hair* revuelto

un·kind [ʌn'kaɪnd] *adj* desagradable, cruel

un·known [ʌn'noʊn] **1** *adj* desconocido **2** *n*: ***a journey into the unknown*** un viaje hacia lo desconocido

un·lead·ed [ʌn'ledɪd] *adj* sin plomo

un·less [ən'les] *conj* a menos que, a no ser

que; *don't say anything unless you're sure* no digas nada a menos que *or* a no ser que estés seguro

un·like [ʌn'laɪk] *prep (not similar to)* diferente de; *it's unlike him to drink so much* él no suele beber tanto; *that photograph is so unlike you* has salido completamente diferente en esa fotografía

un·like·ly [ʌn'laɪklɪ] *adj (improbable)* improbable; *explanation* inverosímil; *he is unlikely to win* es improbable *or* poco probable que gane

un·lim·it·ed [ʌn'lɪmɪtɪd] *adj* ilimitado

un·list·ed [ʌn'lɪstɪd] *adj*: *be unlisted* no aparecer en la guía telefónica

un·load [ʌn'loud] *v/t* descargar

un·lock [ʌn'lɑːk] *v/t* abrir

un·luck·i·ly [ʌn'lʌkɪlɪ] *adv* desgraciadamente, por desgracia

un·luck·y [ʌn'lʌkɪ] *adj day, choice* aciago, funesto; *person* sin suerte; *that was so unlucky for you!* ¡qué mala suerte tuviste!

un·manned [ʌn'mænd] *adj spacecraft* no tripulado

un·mar·ried [ʌn'mærɪd] *adj* soltero

un·mis·ta·ka·ble [ʌnmɪ'steɪkəbl] *adj* inconfundible

un·moved [ʌn'muːvd] *adj*: *he was unmoved by her tears* sus lágrimas no lo conmovieron

un·mu·si·cal [ʌn'mjuːzɪkl] *adj person* sin talento musical; *sounds* estridente

un·nat·u·ral [ʌn'nætʃrəl] *adj* anormal; *it's not unnatural to be annoyed* es normal estar enfadado

un·ne·ces·sa·ry [ʌn'nesəserɪ] *adj* innecesario

un·nerv·ing [ʌn'nɜːrvɪŋ] *adj* desconcertante

un·no·ticed [ʌn'noutɪst] *adj*: *it went unnoticed* pasó desapercibido

un·ob·tain·a·ble [ʌnəb'teɪnəbl] *adj goods* no disponible; TELEC desconectado

un·ob·tru·sive [ʌnəb'truːsɪv] *adj* discreto

un·oc·cu·pied [ʌn'ɑːkjʊpaɪd] *adj building, house* desocupado; *post* vacante

un·of·fi·cial [ʌnə'fɪʃl] *adj* no oficial; *this

is still unofficial but ...* esto todavía no es oficial, pero ...

un·of·fi·cial·ly [ʌnə'fɪʃlɪ] *adv* extraoficialmente

un·or·tho·dox [ʌn'ɔːrθədɑːks] *adj* poco ortodoxo

un·pack [ʌn'pæk] **1** *v/t* deshacer **2** *v/i* deshacer el equipaje

un·paid [ʌn'peɪd] *adj work* no remunerado

un·pleas·ant [ʌn'pleznt] *adj* desagradable; *he was very unpleasant to her* fue muy desagradable con ella

un·plug [ʌn'plʌg] *v/t (pret & pp unplugged)* TV, *computer* desenchufar

un·pop·u·lar [ʌn'pɑːpjələr] *adj* impopular

un·pre·ce·den·ted [ʌn'presɪdentɪd] *adj* sin precedentes; *it was unprecedented for a woman to ...* no tenía precedentes que una mujer ...

un·pre·dict·a·ble [ʌnprɪ'dɪktəbl] *adj person, weather* imprevisible, impredecible

un·pre·ten·tious [ʌnprɪ'tenʃəs] *adj person, style, hotel* modesto, sin pretensiones

un·prin·ci·pled [ʌn'prɪnsɪpld] *adj* sin principios

un·pro·duc·tive [ʌnprə'dʌktɪv] *adj meeting, discussion* infructuoso; *soil* improductivo

un·pro·fes·sion·al [ʌnprə'feʃnl] *adj* poco profesional

un·prof·i·ta·ble [ʌn'prɑːfɪtəbl] *adj* no rentable

un·pro·nounce·a·ble [ʌnprə'naunsəbl] *adj* impronunciable

un·pro·tect·ed [ʌnprə'tektɪd] *adj borders* desprotegido, sin protección; *unprotected sex* sexo *m* sin preservativos

un·pro·voked [ʌnprə'voukt] *adj attack* no provocado

un·qual·i·fied [ʌn'kwɑːlɪfaɪd] *adj worker, doctor etc* sin titulación

un·ques·tio·na·bly [ʌn'kwestʃnəblɪ] *adv (without doubt)* indiscutiblemente

un·ques·tion·ing [ʌn'kwestʃnɪŋ] *adj attitude, loyalty* incondicional

un·rav·el [ʌn'rævl] *v/t (pret & pp unravel-*

ed, *Br* **unravelled**) *string, knitting* desenredar; *mystery, complexities* desentrañar

un·rea·da·ble [ʌnˈriːdəbl] *adj book* ilegible

un·re·al [ʌnˈrɪəl] *adj* irreal; **this is unreal!** F ¡esto es increíble! F

un·re·al·is·tic [ʌnrɪəˈlɪstɪk] *adj* poco realista

un·rea·so·na·ble [ʌnˈriːznəbl] *adj person* poco razonable, irrazonable; *demand, expectation* excesivo, irrazonable; **you're being unreasonable** no estás siendo razonable

un·re·lat·ed [ʌnrɪˈleɪtɪd] *adj issues* no relacionado; *people* no emparentado

un·re·lent·ing [ʌnrɪˈlentɪŋ] *adj* implacable

un·re·li·a·ble [ʌnrɪˈlaɪəbl] *adj car, machine* poco fiable; *person* informal

un·rest [ʌnˈrest] malestar *m*; (*rioting*) disturbios *mpl*

un·re·strained [ʌnrɪˈstreɪnd] *adj emotions* incontrolado

un·road·wor·thy [ʌnˈroʊdwɜːrðɪ] *adj* que no está en condiciones de circular

un·roll [ʌnˈroʊl] *v/t carpet, scroll* desenrollar

un·ru·ly [ʌnˈruːlɪ] *adj* revoltoso

un·safe [ʌnˈseɪf] *adj* peligroso; **it's unsafe to drink / eat** no se puede beber / comer

un·san·i·tar·y [ʌnˈsænɪterɪ] *adj conditions, drains* insalubre

un·sat·is·fac·to·ry [ʌnsætɪsˈfæktərɪ] *adj* insatisfactorio

un·sa·vo·ry [ʌnˈseɪvərɪ] *adj person, reputation* indeseable; *district* desagradable

un·scathed [ʌnˈskeɪðd] *adj* (*not injured*) ileso; (*not damaged*) intacto

un·screw [ʌnˈskruː] *v/t top* desenroscar; *shelves, hooks* desatornillar

un·scru·pu·lous [ʌnˈskruːpjələs] *adj* sin escrúpulos

un·self·ish [ʌnˈselfɪʃ] *adj* generoso

un·set·tled [ʌnˈsetld] *adj issue* sin decidir; *weather, stock market, lifestyle* inestable; *bills* sin pagar

un·shav·en [ʌnˈʃeɪvn] *adj* sin afeitar

un·sight·ly [ʌnˈsaɪtlɪ] *adj* horrible, feo

un·skilled [ʌnˈskɪld] *adj* no cualificado

un·so·cia·ble [ʌnˈsoʊʃəbl] *adj* insociable

un·so·phis·ti·cat·ed [ʌnsəˈfɪstɪkeɪtɪd] *adj person, beliefs* sencillo; *equipment* simple

un·sta·ble [ʌnˈsteɪbl] *adj* inestable

un·stead·y [ʌnˈstedɪ] *adj hand* tembloroso; *ladder* inestable; **be unsteady on one's feet** tambalearse

un·stint·ing [ʌnˈstɪntɪŋ] *adj* generoso; **be unstinting in one's efforts / generosity** no escatimar esfuerzos / generosidad

un·stuck [ʌnˈstʌk] *adj*: **come unstuck** F *of plan etc* irse al garete F

un·suc·cess·ful [ʌnsəkˈsesfəl] *adj writer etc* fracasado; *candidate* perdedor; *party, attempt* fallido; **he tried but was unsuccessful** lo intentó sin éxito

un·suc·cess·ful·ly [ʌnsəkˈsesfəlɪ] *adv try, apply* sin éxito

un·suit·a·ble [ʌnˈsuːtəbl] *adj partner, film, clothing* inadecuado; *thing to say* inoportuno

un·sus·pect·ing [ʌnsəsˈpektɪŋ] *adj* confiado

un·swerv·ing [ʌnˈswɜːrvɪŋ] *adj loyalty, devotion* inquebrantable

un·think·a·ble [ʌnˈθɪŋkəbl] *adj* impensable

un·ti·dy [ʌnˈtaɪdɪ] *adj room, desk* desordenado; *hair* revuelto

un·tie [ʌnˈtaɪ] *v/t knot, laces, prisoner* desatar

un·til [ənˈtɪl] **1** *prep* hasta; **from Monday until Friday** desde el lunes hasta el viernes; **I can wait until tomorrow** puedo esperar hasta mañana; **not until Friday** no antes del viernes; **it won't be finished until July** no estará acabado hasta julio **2** *conj* hasta que; **can you wait until I'm ready?** ¿puedes esperar hasta que esté listo?; **they won't do anything until you say so** no harán nada hasta que (no) se lo digas

un·time·ly [ʌnˈtaɪmlɪ] *adj death* prematuro

un·tir·ing [ʌnˈtaɪrɪŋ] *adj efforts* incansable

un·told [ʌn'toʊld] *adj suffering* indecible; *riches* inconmensurable; *story* nunca contado

un·trans·lat·a·ble [ʌntræns'leɪtəbl] *adj* intraducible

un·true [ʌn'truː] *adj* falso

un·used[1] [ʌn'juːzd] *adj goods* sin usar

un·used[2] [ʌn'juːst] *adj:* **be unused to sth** no estar acostumbrado a algo; **be unused to doing sth** no estar acostumbrado a hacer algo

un·u·su·al [ʌn'juːʒl] *adj* poco corriente; *it is unusual ...* es raro *or* extraño ...

un·u·su·al·ly [ʌn'juːʒəlɪ] *adv* inusitadamente; *the weather's unusually cold* hace un frío inusual

un·veil [ʌn'veɪl] *v/t memorial, statue etc* desvelar

un·well [ʌn'wel] *adj* indispuesto, mal; **be unwell** sentirse indispuesto *or* mal

un·will·ing [ʌn'wɪlɪŋ] *adj* poco dispuesto, reacio; **be unwilling to do sth** no estar dispuesto a hacer algo, ser reacio a hacer algo

un·will·ing·ly [ʌn'wɪlɪŋlɪ] *adv* de mala gana, a regañadientes

un·wind [ʌn'waɪnd] **1** *v/t* (*pret & pp* **unwound**) *tape* desenrollar **2** *v/i* (*pret & pp* **unwound**) *of tape* desenrollarse; *of story* irse desarrollando; F (*relax*) relajarse

un·wise [ʌn'waɪz] *adj* imprudente

un·wrap [ʌn'ræp] *v/t* (*pret & pp* **unwrapped**) *gift* desenvolver

un·writ·ten [ʌn'rɪtn] *adj law, rule* no escrito

un·zip [ʌn'zɪp] *v/t* (*pret & pp* **unzipped**) *dress etc* abrir la cremallera de; COMPUT descomprimir

up [ʌp] **1** *adv position* arriba; *movement* hacia arriba; *up in the sky / up on the roof* (arriba) en el cielo / tejado; *up here / there* aquí / allí arriba; **be up** (*out of bed*) estar levantado; *of sun* haber salido; (*be built*) haber sido construido, estar acabado; *of shelves* estar montado; *of prices, temperature* haber subido; (*have expired*) haberse acabado; *what's up?* F ¿qué pasa?; **up to the year 1989** hasta

el año 1989; *he came up to me* se me acercó; *what are you up to these days?* ¿qué es de tu vida?; *what are those kids up to?* ¿qué están tramando esos niños?; **be up to something** (**bad**) estar tramando algo; *I don't feel up to it* no me siento en condiciones de hacerlo; *it's up to you* tú decides; *it is up to them to solve it* (*their duty*) les corresponde a ellos resolverlo; *be up and about after illness* estar recuperado **2** *prep: further up the mountain* más arriba de la montaña; *he climbed up a tree* se subió a un árbol; *they ran up the street* corrieron por la calle; *the water goes up this pipe* el agua sube por esta tubería; *we traveled up to Chicago* subimos hasta Chicago **3** *n:* **ups and downs** altibajos *mpl*

'up·bring·ing educación *f*

'up·com·ing *adj* (*forthcoming*) próximo

up'date[1] *v/t file, records* actualizar; **update s.o. on sth** poner a alguien al corriente de algo

'up·date[2] *n* actualización *f*; *can you give me an update on the situation?* ¿me puedes poner al corriente de la situación?

up'grade *v/t computers etc* actualizar; (*replace with new versions*) modernizar; *product* modernizar; **upgrade s.o. to business class** cambiar a alguien a clase ejecutiva

up·heav·al [ʌp'hiːvl] *emotional* conmoción *m*; *physical* trastorno *m*; *political, social* sacudida *f*

up·hill 1 *adv* [ʌp'hɪl] *walk* cuesta arriba **2** *adj* ['ʌphɪl] *struggle* arduo, difícil

up'hold *v/t* (*pret & pp* **upheld**) *traditions, rights* defender, conservar; (*vindicate*) confirmar

up·hol·ster·y [ʌp'hoʊlstərɪ] (*coverings of chairs*) tapicería *f*; (*padding of chairs*) relleno *m*

'up·keep *of buildings, parks etc* mantenimiento *m*

'up·load *v/t* COMPUT cargar

up'mar·ket *adj restaurant, hotel* de categoría

up·on [ə'pɑːn] *prep* → **on**

up·per ['ʌpər] *adj part of sth* superior; *stretches of a river* alto; *deck* superior, de arriba

up·per 'class *adj accent, family* de clase alta

up·per 'clas·ses *npl* clases *fpl* altas

'up·right 1 *adj citizen* honrado **2** *adv sit* derecho

'up·right ('pi·an·o) *piano m* vertical

'up·ris·ing levantamiento *m*

'up·roar (*loud noise*) alboroto *m*; (*protest*) tumulto *m*

up'set 1 *v/t* (*pret & pp* **upset**) *drink, glass* tirar; *emotionally* disgustar **2** *adj emotionally* disgustado; **get upset about sth** disgustarse por algo; **have an upset stomach** tener el estómago mal

up'set·ting *adj* triste

'up·shot (*result, outcome*) resultado *m*

up·side 'down *adv* boca abajo; **turn sth upside down** *box etc* poner algo al revés *or* boca abajo

up'stairs 1 *adv* arriba **2** *adj room* de arriba

'up·start advenedizo(-a) *m(f)*

'up·stream *adv* río arriba

'up·take FIN respuesta *f* (**of** a); **be quick / slow on the uptake** F ser / no ser muy espabilado F

'up·tight *adj* F (*nervous*) tenso; (*inhibited*) estrecho

up-to-'date *adj information* actualizado; *fashions* moderno

'up·turn *in economy* mejora *f*

up·ward ['ʌpwərd] *adv fly, move* hacia arriba; **upward of 10,000** más de 10.000

u·ra·ni·um [juˈreɪnɪəm] *n* uranio *m*

ur·ban ['ɜːrbən] *adj* urbano

ur·ban·i·za·tion [ɜːrbənaɪˈzeɪʃn] urbanización *f*

ur·chin ['ɜːrtʃɪn] golfillo(-a) *m(f)*

urge [ɜːrdʒ] **1** *n* impulso *m*; **I felt an urge to hit her** me entraron ganas de pegarle; **I have an urge to do something new** siento la necesidad de hacer algo nuevo **2** *v/t*: **urge s.o. to do sth** rogar a alguien que haga algo

◆ **urge on** *v/t* (*encourage*) animar

ur·gen·cy ['ɜːrdʒənsɪ] *of situation* urgen-

cia *f*

ur·gent ['ɜːrdʒənt] *adj job, letter* urgente; **be in urgent need of sth** necesitar algo urgentemente; **is it urgent?** ¿es urgente?

u·ri·nate ['jurəneɪt] *v/i* orinar

u·rine ['jurɪn] orina *f*

urn [ɜːrn] urna *f*

U·ru·guay ['jurəgwaɪ] *n* Uruguay

U·ru·guay·an [jurəˈgwaɪən] **1** *adj* uruguayo **2** *n* uruguayo(-a) *m(f)*

us [ʌs] *pron* nos; *after prep* nosotros(-as); **they love us** nos quieren; **she gave us the keys** nos dio las llaves; **he sold it to us** nos lo vendió; **that's for us** eso es para nosotros; **who's that? - it's us** ¿quién es? - ¡somos nosotros!

US [juːˈes] *abbr* (= **United States**) EE.UU. *mpl* (= Estados *mpl* Unidos)

USA [juːesˈeɪ] *abbr* (= **United States of America**) EE.UU. (= Estados Unidos)

us·a·ble ['juːzəbl] *adj* utilizable; **it's not usable** no se puede utilizar

us·age ['juːzɪdʒ] uso *m*

use 1 *v/t* [juːz] *tool, word* utilizar, usar; *skills, knowledge, car* usar; *a lot of gas* consumir; *pej: person* utilizar; **I could use a drink** F no me vendría mal una copa **2** *n* [juːs] uso *m*, utilización *f*; **be of great use to s.o.** ser de gran utilidad para alguien; **it's of no use to me** no me sirve; **is that of any use?** ¿eso sirve para algo?; **it's no use** no sirve de nada; **it's no use trying / waiting** no sirve de nada intentarlo / esperar

◆ **use up** *v/t* agotar

used¹ [juːzd] *adj car etc* de segunda mano

used² [juːst] *adj*: **be used to s.o./sth** estar acostumbrado a alguien / algo; **get used to s.o./sth** acostumbrarse a alguien / algo; **be used to doing sth** estar acostumbrado a hacer algo; **get used to doing sth** acostumbrarse a hacer algo

used³ [juːst]: **I used to like him** antes me gustaba; **they used to meet every Saturday** solían verse todos los sábados

use·ful ['juːsfl] *adj* útil

use·ful·ness ['juːsflnɪs] utilidad *f*

use·less ['juːslɪs] *adj* inútil; *machine,*

computer inservible; **be useless** F *person* ser un inútil F; **it's useless trying** (*there's no point*) no vale la pena intentarlo

us·er ['juːzər] *of product* usuario

us·er-'friend·ly *adj software, device* de fácil manejo

ush·er ['ʌʃər] *n* (*at wedding*) persona que se encarga de indicar a los asistentes dónde se deben sentar

◆ **usher in** *v/t new era* anunciar

ush·er·ette [ʌʃə'ret] acomodadora *f*

u·su·al ['juːʒl] *adj* habitual, acostumbrado; **as usual** como de costumbre; **the usual, please** lo de siempre, por favor

u·su·al·ly ['juːʒəlɪ] *adv* normalmente; **I**

usually start at 9 suelo empezar a las 9

u·ten·sil [juː'tensl] utensilio *m*

u·te·rus ['juːtərəs] útero *m*

u·til·i·ty [juː'tɪlətɪ] (*usefulness*) utilidad *f*; **public utilities** servicios *mpl* públicos

u·til·ize ['juːtɪlaɪz] *v/t* utilizar

ut·most ['ʌtmoʊst] **1** *adj* sumo **2** *n*: **do one's utmost** hacer todo lo posible

ut·ter ['ʌtər] **1** *adj* completo, total **2** *v/t sound* decir, pronunciar

ut·ter·ly ['ʌtərlɪ] *adv* completamente, totalmente

U-turn ['juːtɜːrn] cambio *m* de sentido; **do a U-turn** *fig: in policy etc* dar un giro de 180 grados

V

va·can·cy ['veɪkənsɪ] *at work* puesto *m* vacante

va·cant ['veɪkənt] *adj building* vacío; *position* vacante; *look, expression* vago, distraído

va·cant·ly ['veɪkəntlɪ] *adv* distraídamente

va·cate [veɪ'keɪt] *v/t room* desalojar

va·ca·tion [veɪ'keɪʃn] *n* vacaciones *fpl*; **be on vacation** estar de vacaciones; **go to ... on vacation** ir de vacaciones a ...

va·ca·tion·er [veɪ'keɪʃənər] turista *m/f*; *in summer* veraneante *m/f*

vac·cin·ate ['væksɪneɪt] *v/t* vacunar; **be vaccinated against ...** estar vacunado contra ...

vac·cin·a·tion [væksɪ'neɪʃn] *action* vacunación *f*; (*vaccine*) vacuna *f*

vac·cine ['væksiːn] vacuna *f*

vac·u·um ['vækjʊəm] **1** *n* PHYS, *fig* vacío *m* **2** *v/t floors* pasar el aspirador por, aspirar

'vac·u·um clean·er aspirador *m*, aspiradora *f*

'vac·u·um flask termo *m*

vac·u·um-'packed *adj* envasado al vacío

vag·a·bond ['vægəbɑːnd] vagabundo(-a) *m(f)*

va·gi·na [və'dʒaɪnə] vagina *f*

va·gi·nal ['vædʒɪnl] *adj* vaginal

va·grant ['veɪgrənt] vagabundo(-a) *m(f)*

vague [veɪg] *adj* vago; **he was very vague about it** no fue muy preciso

vague·ly ['veɪglɪ] *adv answer,* (*slightly*) vagamente; *possible* muy poco

vain [veɪn] **1** *adj person* vanidoso; *hope* vano **2** *n*: **in vain** en vano; **their efforts were in vain** sus esfuerzos fueron en vano

val·en·tine ['væləntaɪn] *card* tarjeta *f* del día de San Valentín; **Valentine's Day** día de San Valentín *or* de los enamorados

val·et **1** *n* ['væleɪ] *person* mozo *m* **2** *v/t* ['vælət] *car* lavar y limpiar

'val·et ser·vice *for clothes* servicio *m* de planchado; *for cars* servicio *m* de lavado y limpiado

val·iant ['væljənt] *adj* valiente, valeroso

val·iant·ly ['væljəntlɪ] *adv* valientemente, valerosamente

val·id ['vælɪd] *adj* válido

val·i·date ['vælɪdeɪt] *v/t with official stamp* sellar; *s.o.'s alibi* dar validez a

va·lid·i·ty [və'lɪdətɪ] validez *f*

val·ley ['vælɪ] valle *m*

val·u·a·ble ['væljubl] **1** *adj* valioso **2** *n*: *valuables* objetos *mpl* de valor

val·u·a·tion [vælju'eɪʃn] tasación *f*, valoración *f*

val·ue ['vælju:] **1** *n* valor *m*; *be good value* ofrecer buena relación calidad-precio; *get value for money* recibir una buena relación calidad-precio; *rise / fall in value* aumentar / disminuir de valor **2** *v/t s.o.'s friendship, one's freedom* valorar; *I value your advice* valoro tus consejos; *have an object valued* pedir la valoración *or* tasación de un objeto

valve [vælv] válvula *f*

van [væn] camioneta *f*, furgoneta *f*

van·dal ['vændl] vándalo *m*, gamberro(-a) *m(f)*

van·dal·ism ['vændəlɪzm] vandalismo *m*

van·dal·ize ['vændəlaɪz] *v/t* destrozar (*intencionadamente*)

van·guard ['vænɡɑːrd] vanguardia *f*; *be in the vanguard of fig* estar a la vanguardia de

va·nil·la [və'nɪlə] **1** *n* vainilla *f* **2** *adj* de vainilla

van·ish ['vænɪʃ] *v/i* desaparecer

van·i·ty ['vænətɪ] *of person* vanidad *f*

'van·i·ty case neceser *m*

van·tage point ['væntɪdʒ] *on hill etc* posición *f* aventajada

va·por ['veɪpər] vapor *m*

va·por·ize ['veɪpəraɪz] *v/t of atomic bomb, explosion* vaporizar

'va·por trail *of airplane* estela *f*

va·pour *Br* → **vapor**

var·i·a·ble ['verɪəbl] **1** *adj* variable **2** *n* MATH, COMPUT variable *f*

var·i·ant ['verɪənt] *n* variante *f*

var·i·a·tion [verɪ'eɪʃn] variación *f*

var·i·cose 'vein ['værɪkous] variz *f*

var·ied ['verɪd] *adj* variado

va·ri·e·ty [və'raɪətɪ] (*variedness, type*)

variedad *f*; *a variety of things to do* (*range, mixture*) muchas cosas para hacer

var·i·ous ['verɪəs] *adj* (*several*) varios; (*different*) diversos

var·nish ['vɑːrnɪʃ] **1** *n for wood* barniz *m*; *for fingernails* esmalte *m* **2** *v/t wood* barnizar; *fingernails* poner esmalte a, pintar

var·y ['verɪ] **1** *v/i* (*pret & pp varied*) variar; *it varies* depende **2** *v/t* (*pret & pp varied*) variar

vase [veɪz] jarrón *m*

vas·ec·to·my [və'sektəmɪ] vasectomía *f*

vast [væst] *adj desert, knowledge* vasto; *number, improvement* enorme

vast·ly ['væstlɪ] *adv* enormemente

VAT [viːeɪ'tiː, væt] *Br abbr* (= *value-added tax*) IVA *m* (= *impuesto m sobre el valor añadido*)

Vat·i·can ['vætɪkən]: *the Vatican* el Vaticano

vau·de·ville ['vɒːdvɪl] *adj* vodevil *m*

vault[1] [vɒːlt] *n in roof* bóveda *f*; *vaults* (*cellar*) sótano *m*; *of bank* cámara *f* acorazada

vault[2] [vɒːlt] **1** *n* SP salto *m* **2** *v/t beam etc* saltar

VCR [viːsiː'ɑːr] *abbr* (= *video cassette recorder*) aparato *m* de *Span* vídeo *or* *L.Am.* video

VDU [viːdiː'juː] *abbr* (= *visual display unit*) monitor *m*

veal [viːl] ternera *f*

veer [vɪr] *v/i* girar, torcer

ve·gan ['viːɡn] **1** *n* vegetariano(-a) *m(f)* estricto (-a) (*que no come ningún producto de origen animal*) **2** *adj* vegetariano estricto

vege·ta·ble ['vedʒtəbl] hortaliza *f*; *vegetables* verduras *fpl*

ve·ge·tar·i·an [vedʒɪ'terɪən] **1** *n* vegetariano(-a) *m(f)* **2** *adj* vegetariano

ve·ge·tar·i·an·ism [vedʒɪ'terɪənɪzm] vegetarianismo *m*

veg·e·ta·tion [vedʒɪ'teɪʃn] vegetación *f*

ve·he·mence ['viːəməns] vehemencia *f*

ve·he·ment ['viːəmənt] *adj* vehemente

ve·he·ment·ly ['viːəməntlɪ] *adv* vehementemente

ve·hi·cle ['viːɪkl] *also fig* vehículo *m*

veil [veɪl] **1** *n* velo *m* **2** *v/t* cubrir con un velo

vein [veɪn] ANAT vena *f*; *in this vein* fig en este tono

Vel·cro® ['velkrəʊ] velcro *m*

ve·loc·i·ty [vɪ'lɒsətɪ] velocidad *f*

vel·vet ['velvɪt] *n* terciopelo *m*

vel·vet·y ['velvɪtɪ] *adj* aterciopelado

ven·det·ta [ven'detə] vendetta *f*

vend·ing ma·chine ['vendɪŋ] máquina *f* expendedora

vend·or ['vendər] LAW parte *f* vendedora

ve·neer [və'nɪr] *on wood* chapa *f*; *of politeness etc* apariencia *f*, fachada

ven·e·ra·ble ['venərəbl] *adj* venerable

ven·e·rate ['venəreɪt] *v/t* venerar

ven·e·ra·tion [venə'reɪʃn] veneración *f*

ven·e·re·al dis·ease [vɪ'nɪrɪəl] enfermedad *f* venérea

ve·ne·tian 'blind persiana *f* veneciana

Ven·e·zue·la [veniz'weɪlə] *n* Venezuela

Ven·e·zue·lan [veniz'weɪlən] **1** *adj* venezolano **2** *n* venezolano(-a) *m(f)*

ven·geance ['vendʒəns] venganza *f*; *with a vengeance* con ganas

ven·i·son ['venɪsn] venado *m*

ven·om ['venəm] *also fig* veneno *m*

ven·om·ous ['venəməs] *adj snake* venenoso; *fig* envenenado

vent [vent] *n for air* respiradero *m*; *give vent to feelings* dar rienda suelta a

ven·ti·late ['ventɪleɪt] *v/t* ventilar

ven·ti·la·tion [ventɪ'leɪʃn] ventilación *f*

ven·ti·la·tion shaft pozo *m* de ventilación

ven·ti·la·tor ['ventɪleɪtər] ventilador *m*; MED respirador *m*

ven·tril·o·quist [ven'trɪləkwɪst] ventrilocuo(-a) *m(f)*

ven·ture ['ventʃər] **1** *n (undertaking)* iniciativa *f*; COM empresa *f* **2** *v/i* aventurarse

ven·ue ['venjuː] *for meeting* lugar *m*; *for concert* local *m*, sala *f*

ve·ran·da [və'rændə] porche *m*

verb [vɜːrb] verbo *m*

verb·al [vɜːrbl] *adj (spoken)* verbal

verb·al·ly ['vɜːrbəlɪ] *adv* de palabra

ver·ba·tim [vɜːr'beɪtɪm] *adv* literalmente

ver·dict ['vɜːrdɪkt] LAW veredicto *m*; *what's your verdict?* ¿qué te parece?,

¿qué opinas?

verge [vɜːrdʒ] *n of road* arcén *m*; *be on the verge of ruin* estar al borde de; *tears* estar a punto de

◆ **verge on** *v/t* rayar en

ver·i·fi·ca·tion [verɪfɪ'keɪʃn] *(checking)* verificación *f*; *(confirmation)* confirmación *f*

ver·i·fy ['verɪfaɪ] *v/t (pret & pp verified)* *(check)* verificar; *(confirm)* confirmar

ver·mi·cel·li [vɜːrmɪ'tʃelɪ] *nsg* fideos *mpl*

ver·min ['vɜːrmɪn] *npl* bichos *mpl*, alimañas *fpl*

ver·mouth [vɜːr'muːθ] vermut *m*

ver·nac·u·lar [vər'nækjələr] *n* lenguaje *m* de la calle

ver·sa·tile ['vɜːrsətəl] *adj* polifacético, versátil

ver·sa·til·i·ty [vɜːrsə'tɪlətɪ] polivalencia *f*, versatilidad *f*

verse [vɜːrs] verso *m*

versed [vɜːrst] *adj: be well versed in a subject* estar muy versado en una materia

ver·sion ['vɜːrʃn] versión *f*

ver·sus ['vɜːrsəs] *prep* SP, LAW contra

ver·te·bra ['vɜːrtɪbrə] vértebra *f*

ver·te·brate ['vɜːrtɪbreɪt] *n* vertebrado(-a) *m(f)*

ver·ti·cal ['vɜːrtɪkl] *adj* vertical

ver·ti·go ['vɜːrtɪgəʊ] vértigo *m*

ver·y ['verɪ] **1** *adv muy*; *was it cold? - not very* ¿hizo frío? - no mucho; *the very best* el mejor de todos **2** *adj: at that very moment* en ese mismo momento; *that's the very thing I need (exact)* eso es precisamente lo que necesito; *the very thought (mere)* sólo de pensar en; *right at the very top / bottom* arriba / al fondo del todo

ves·sel ['vesl] NAUT buque *m*

vest [vest] chaleco *m*

ves·tige ['vestɪdʒ] vestigio *m*; vestigio *m*

vet[1] [vet] *n (veterinary surgeon)* veterinario(-a) *m(f)*

vet[2] [vet] *v/t (pret & pp vetted)* *applicants etc* examinar, investigar

vet[3] [vet] MIL veterano(-a) *m(f)*

vet·e·ran ['vetərən] **1** *n* veterano(-a) *m(f)*

V

2 *adj* veterano

vet·e·ri·nar·i·an [vetərə'neriən] veterinario(-a) *m(f)*

ve·to ['vi:tou] **1** *n* veto *m* **2** *v/t* vetar

vex [veks] *v/t* (*concern, worry*) molestar, irritar

vexed [vekst] *adj* (*worried*) molesto, irritado; *the vexed question of* la polémica cuestión de

vi·a ['vaiə] *prep* vía

vi·a·ble ['vaiəbl] *adj* viable

vi·brate [vai'breit] *v/i* vibrar

vi·bra·tion [vai'breiʃn] vibración *f*

vic·ar ['vikər] vicario *m*

vic·ar·age ['vikərɪdʒ] vicaría *f*

vice[1] [vais] vicio *m*; *the problem of vice* el problema del vicio

vice[2] *Br* → **vise**

vice 'pres·i·dent vicepresidente(-a) *m(f)*

'vice squad brigada *f* antivicio

vi·ce ver·sa [vais'vɜːrsə] *adv* viceversa

vi·cin·i·ty [vi'sinəti] zona *f*; *in the vicinity of ...* the church *etc* en las cercanías de ...; *$500 etc* rondando ...

vi·cious ['viʃəs] *adj* dog fiero; *attack, temper, criticism* feroz

vi·cious 'cir·cle círculo *m* vicioso

vi·cious·ly ['viʃəsli] *adv* con brutalidad

vic·tim ['viktim] víctima *f*

vic·tim·ize ['viktimaiz] *v/t* tratar injustamente

vic·tor ['viktər] vencedor(a) *m(f)*

vic·to·ri·ous [vik'tɔːriəs] *adj* victorioso

vic·to·ry ['viktəri] victoria *f*; *win a victory over ...* obtener una victoria sobre ...

vid·e·o ['vidiou] **1** *n* Span vídeo *m*, L.Am. video *m*; *have X on video* tener a X en Span vídeo *or* L.Am. video **2** *v/t* grabar en Span vídeo *or* L.Am. video

'vid·e·o cam·e·ra videocámara *f*

vid·e·o cas'sette videocasete *m*

'vid·e·o con·fer·ence TELEC videoconferencia *f*

'vid·e·o game videojuego *m*

'vid·e·o·phone videoteléfono *m*

'vid·e·o re·cord·er aparato *m* de Span vídeo *or* L.Am. video

'vid·e·o re·cord·ing grabación *f* en Span

vídeo *or* L.Am. video

'vid·e·o·tape cinta *f* de Span vídeo *or* L.Am. video

vie [vai] *v/i* competir

Vi·et·nam [viet'nɑːm] Vietnam

Vi·et·nam·ese [vietnɑ'mi:z] **1** *adj* vietnamita **2** *n* vietnamita *m/f*; *language* vietnamita *m*

view [vju:] **1** *n* vista *f*; *of situation* opinión *f*; *in view of* teniendo en cuenta; *be on view of paintings* estar expuesto al público; *with a view to* con vistas a **2** *v/t events, situation* ver, considerar; TV program, house ver **3** *v/i* (*watch* TV) ver la televisión

view·er ['vju:ər] TV telespectador(a) *m(f)*

'view·find·er PHOT visor *m*

'view·point punto *m* de vista

vig·or ['vigər] (*energy*) vigor *m*

vig·or·ous ['vigərəs] *adj* shake vigoroso; *person* enérgico; *denial* rotundo

vig·or·ous·ly ['vigərəsli] *adv* shake con vigor; *deny, defend* rotundamente

vig·our *Br* → **vigor**

vile [vail] *adj* smell asqueroso; *thing to do* vil

vil·la ['vilə] chalet *m*; *in the country* villa *f*

vil·lage ['vilidʒ] pueblo *m*

vil·lag·er ['vilidʒər] aldeano(-a) *m(f)*

vil·lain ['vilən] malo(a) *m(f)*

vin·di·cate ['vindikeit] *v/t* (*show to be correct*) dar la razón a; (*show to be innocent*) vindicar; *I feel vindicated* los hechos me dan ahora la razón

vin·dic·tive [vin'diktiv] *adj* vengativo

vin·dic·tive·ly [vin'diktivli] *adv* vengativamente

vine [vain] vid *f*

vin·e·gar ['vinigər] vinagre *m*

vine·yard ['vinjɑːrd] viñedo *m*

vin·tage ['vintidʒ] **1** *n of wine* cosecha *f* **2** *adj* (*classic*) clásico *m*

vi·o·la [vi'oulə] MUS viola *f*

vi·o·late ['vaiəleit] *v/t* violar

vi·o·la·tion [vaiə'leiʃn] violación *f*; (*traffic violation*) infracción *f*

vi·o·lence ['vaiələns] violencia *f*; *outbreak of violence* estallido de violencia

vi·o·lent ['vaiələnt] *adj* violento; *have a*

violent temper tener muy mal genio

vi·o·lent·ly ['vaɪələntlɪ] *adv react* violentamente; *object* rotundamente; **fall violently in love with s.o.** enamorarse perdidamente de alguien

vi·o·let ['vaɪələt] *n color, plant* violeta *f*

vi·o·lin [vaɪə'lɪn] violín *m*

vi·o·lin·ist [vaɪə'lɪnɪst] violinista *m/f*

VIP [viːaɪ'piː] *abbr* (= **very important person**) VIP *m*

vi·per ['vaɪpər] *snake* víbora *f*

vi·ral ['vaɪrəl] *adj infection* vírico, viral

vir·gin ['vɜːrdʒɪn] virgen *m/f*

vir·gin·i·ty [vɜːr'dʒɪnətɪ] virginidad *f*; **lose one's virginity** perder la virginidad

Vir·go ['vɜːrgoʊ] ASTR Virgo *m/f inv*

vir·ile ['vɪrəl] *adj man* viril; *prose* vigoroso

vi·ril·i·ty [vɪ'rɪlətɪ] virilidad *f*

vir·tu·al ['vɜːrtʃʊəl] *adj* virtual

vir·tu·al·ly ['vɜːrtʃʊəlɪ] *adv* (*almost*) virtualmente, casi

vir·tu·al re·al·i·ty realidad *f* virtual

vir·tue ['vɜːrtʃuː] virtud *f*; **in virtue of** en virtud de

vir·tu·o·so [vɜːrtʃuː'oʊzoʊ] MUS virtuoso(-a) *m(f)*

vir·tu·ous ['vɜːrtʃʊəs] *adj* virtuoso

vir·u·lent ['vɪrʊlənt] *adj* virulento

vi·rus ['vaɪrəs] MED, COMPUT virus *m inv*

vi·sa ['viːzə] visa *f*, visado *m*

vise [vaɪs] torno *m* de banco

vis·i·bil·i·ty [vɪzə'bɪlətɪ] visibilidad *f*

vis·i·ble ['vɪzəbl] *adj object, difference* visible; *anger* evidente; **not visible to the naked eye** no ser visible a simple vista

vis·i·bly ['vɪzəblɪ] *adv different* visiblemente; **he was visibly moved** estaba visiblemente conmovido

vi·sion ['vɪʒn] *also* REL visión *f*

vis·it ['vɪzɪt] **1** *n* visita *f*; **pay a visit to the doctor/dentist** visitar al doctor/dentista; **pay s.o. a visit** hacer una visita a alguien **2** *v/t* visitar

vis·it·ing card ['vɪzɪtɪŋ] tarjeta *f* de visita

'vis·it·ing hours *npl at hospital* horas *fpl* de visita

vis·it·or ['vɪzɪtər] (*guest*) visita *f*; (*tourist*), *to museum etc* visitante *m/f*

vi·sor ['vaɪzər] visera *f*

vis·u·al ['vɪʒʊəl] *adj* visual

vis·u·al 'aid medio *m* visuale

vis·u·al dis'play u·nit monitor *m*

vis·u·al·ize ['vɪʒʊəlaɪz] *v/t* visualizar; (*foresee*) prever

vis·u·al·ly ['vɪʒʊlɪ] *adv* visualmente

vis·u·al·ly im'paired *adj* con discapacidad visual

vi·tal ['vaɪtl] *adj* (*essential*) vital; **it is vital that ...** es vital que ...

vi·tal·i·ty [vaɪ'tælətɪ] *of person, city etc* vitalidad *f*

vi·tal·ly ['vaɪtəlɪ] *adv*: **vitally important** de importancia vital

vi·tal 'or·gans *npl* órganos *mpl* vitales

vi·tal sta'tis·tics *npl of woman* medidas *fpl*

vit·a·min ['vaɪtəmɪn] vitamina *f*

'vit·a·min pill pastilla *f* vitamínica

vit·ri·ol·ic [vɪtrɪ'ɑːlɪk] *adj* virulento

vi·va·cious [vɪ'veɪʃəs] *adj* vivaz

vi·vac·i·ty [vɪ'væsətɪ] vivacidad *f*

viv·id ['vɪvɪd] *adj color* vivo; *memory, imagination* vívido

viv·id·ly ['vɪvɪdlɪ] *adv* (*brightly*) vivamente; (*clearly*) vívidamente

V-neck ['viːnek] cuello *m* de pico

vo·cab·u·la·ry [voʊ'kæbjʊlərɪ] vocabulario *m*

vo·cal ['voʊkl] *adj to do with the voice* vocal; *expressing opinions* ruidoso; **a vocal opponent** un declarado adversario

'vo·cal cords *npl* cuerdas *fpl* vocales

'vo·cal group MUS grupo *m* vocal

vo·cal·ist ['voʊkəlɪst] MUS vocalista *m/f*

vo·ca·tion [və'keɪʃn] (*calling*) vocación *f*; (*profession*) profesión *f*

vo·ca·tion·al [və'keɪʃnl] *adj guidance* profesional

vod·ka ['vɑːdkə] vodka *m*

vogue [voʊg] moda *f*; **be in vogue** estar en boga

voice [vɔɪs] **1** *n* voz *f* **2** *v/t opinions* expresar

'voice mail correo *m* de voz

void [vɔɪd] **1** *n* vacío *m* **2** *adj*: **void of** carente de

vol·a·tile ['vɑːlətəl] *adj personality,*

V

moods cambiante; *markets* inestable

vol·ca·no [vɑːlˈkeɪnou] volcán *m*

vol·ley [ˈvɑːlɪ] *n of shots* ráfaga *f*; *in tennis* volea *f*

'vol·ley·ball voleibol *m*, balonvolea *m*

volt [voult] voltio *m*

volt·age [ˈvoultɪdʒ] voltaje *m*

vol·ume [ˈvɑːljəm] volumen *m*; *of container* capacidad *f*; *of book* volumen *m*, tomo *m*

vol·ume con·trol control *m* del volumen

vol·un·tar·i·ly [vɑːlənˈterɪlɪ] *adv* voluntariamente

vol·un·ta·ry [ˈvɑːləntərɪ] *adj* voluntario

vol·un·teer [vɑːlənˈtɪr] **1** *n* voluntario(-a) *m(f)* **2** *v/i* ofrecerse voluntariamente

vo·lup·tu·ous [vəˈlʌptʃuəs] *adj woman, figure* voluptuoso

vom·it [ˈvɑːmət] **1** *n* vómito *m* **2** *v/i* vomitar

◆ **vomit up** *v/t* vomitar

vo·ra·cious [vəˈreɪʃəs] *adj appetite* voraz

vo·ra·cious·ly [vəˈreɪʃəslɪ] *also fig* vorazmente

vote [vout] **1** *n* voto *m*; *have the vote (be entitled to vote)* tener el derecho al voto **2**

v/i POL votar; *vote for / against* votar a favor / en contra **3** *v/t*: *they voted him President* lo votaron presidente; *they voted to stay behind* votaron (a favor de) quedarse atrás

◆ **vote in** *v/t new member* elegir en votación

◆ **vote on** *v/t issue* someter a votación

◆ **vote out** *v/t of office* rechazar en votación

vot·er [ˈvoutər] POL votante *m/f*

vot·ing [ˈvoutɪŋ] POL votación *f*

'vot·ing booth cabina *f* electoral

◆ **vouch for** [vautʃ] *v/t truth of sth* dar fe de; *person* responder por

vouch·er [ˈvautʃər] vale *m*

vow [vau] **1** *n* voto *m* **2** *v/t*: *vow to do sth* prometer hacer algo

vow·el [vaul] vocal *f*

voy·age [ˈvɔɪɪdʒ] *n* viaje *m*

vul·gar [ˈvʌlgər] *adj person, language* vulgar, grosero

vul·ne·ra·ble [ˈvʌlnərəbl] *adj to attack, criticism* vulnerable

vul·ture [ˈvʌltʃər] buitre *m*

W

wad [wɑːd] *n of paper, absorbent cotton etc* bola *f*; *a wad of $100 bills* un fajo de billetes de 100 dólares

wad·dle [ˈwɑːdl] *v/i of duck* caminar; *of person* anadear

wade [weɪd] *v/i* caminar en el agua

◆ **wade through** *v/t book, documents* leerse

wa·fer [ˈweɪfər] *cookie* barquillo *m*; REL hostia *f*

'wa·fer-thin *adj* muy fino

waf·fle¹ [ˈwɑːfl] *n to eat* gofre *m*

waf·fle² [ˈwɑːfl] *v/i* andarse con rodeos

wag [wæg] **1** *v/t (pret & pp wagged)* tail,

finger menear **2** *v/i (pret & pp wagged) of tail* menearse

wage¹ [weɪdʒ] *v/t*: *wage war* hacer la guerra

wage² [weɪdʒ] *n* salario *m*, sueldo *m*; *wages* salario *m*, sueldo *m*

'wage earn·er asalariado(-a) *m(f)*

'wage freeze congelación *f* salarial

'wage ne·go·ti·a·tions *npl* negociación *f* salarial

'wage pack·et *fig* salario *m*, sueldo *m*

wag·gle [ˈwægl] *v/t hips* menear; *ears, loose screw etc* mover

wag·on, *Br* **wag·on** [ˈwægən] RAIL va-

gón m; **be on the wagon** F haber dejado
la bebida

wail [weɪl] **1** n of person, baby gemido m;
of siren sonido m, aullido m **2** v/i of person, baby gemir; of siren sonar, aullar

waist [weɪst] cintura f

'waist·coat Br chaleco m

'waist·line cintura f

wait [weɪt] **1** n espera f; **I had a long wait
for a train** esperé mucho rato al tren **2** v/i
esperar; **have you been waiting long?**
¿llevan mucho rato esperando? **2** v/t:
don't wait supper for me no me esperéis
a cenar; **wait table** trabajar de camarero

◆ **wait for** v/t esperar; **wait for me!** ¡es-
peradme!

◆ **wait on** v/t (serve) servir; (wait for) esperar

◆ **wait up** v/i esperar levantado

wait·er ['weɪtər] camarero m

wait·ing ['weɪtɪŋ] n espera f; **no waiting
sign** señal f de prohibido estacionar

'wait·ing list lista f de espera

'wait·ing room sala f de espera

wait·ress ['weɪtrɪs] camarera f

waive [weɪv] v/t right renunciar; requirement no aplicar

wake[1] [weɪk] **1** v/i (pret woke, pp woken):
wake (up) despertarse **2** v/t (pret woke,
pp woken): **wake (up)** despertar

wake[2] [weɪk] n of ship estela f; **in the
wake of** fig tras; **missionaries followed in
the wake of the explorers** a los explo-
radores siguieron los misioneros

'wake-up call: **could I have a wake-up
call at 6.30?** ¿me podrían despertar a
las 6.30?

Wales [weɪlz] n Gales

walk [wɒk] **1** n paseo m; longer caminata
f; (path) camino m; **it's a long / short
walk to the office** hay una caminata /
un paseo hasta la oficina; **go for a walk**
salir a dar un paseo, salir de paseo; **it's a
five-minute walk** está a cinco minutos a
pie **2** v/i caminar, andar; **she walked
over to the window** se acercó a la ventana; **I walked over to her place** fui a su
casa **3** v/t dog sacar a pasear; **walk the
streets** (walk around) caminar por las

calles

◆ **walk out** v/i of spouse marcharse; from
theater etc salir; (go on strike) declararse
en huelga

◆ **walk out on** v/t: **walk out on s.o.** abandonar a alguien

walk·er ['wɒkər] (hiker) excursionista
m/f; for baby, old person andador m;
be a slow / fast walker caminar or andar
despacio / rápido

walk·ie-'talk·ie [wɒkɪ'tɒkɪ] walkie-talk-
ie m

walk-in 'clos·et vestidor m, armario m
empotrado

walk·ing ['wɒkɪŋ] n (hiking) excursionis-
mo m; **walking is one of the best forms
of exercise** caminar es uno de los mejores ejercicios; **it's within walking distance** se puede ir caminando or andando

'walk·ing stick bastón m

'walk·ing tour visita f a pie

'Walk·man® walkman m

'walk-out n (strike) huelga f

'walk-over (easy win) paseo m

'walk-up n apartamento en un edificio sin
ascensor

wall [wɒl] external, fig muro m; of room
pared m; **go to the wall** of company quebrar; **drive s.o. up the wall** F hacer que
alguien se suba por las paredes

wal·let ['wɑlɪt] cartera f

wal·lop ['wɒləp] **1** n F blow tortazo m F,
galletazo m F **2** v/t F dar un golpetazo a F;
opponent dar una paliza a F

'wall·pa·per **1** n papel m pintado **2** v/t empapelar

wall-to-wall 'car·pet Span moqueta f,
L.Am. alfombra f

wal·nut ['wɒlnʌt] nuez f; tree, wood nogal m

waltz [wɒlts] n vals m

wan [wɑn] adj face pálido m

wan·der ['wɑndər] v/i (roam) vagar,
deambular; (stray) extraviarse; **my attention began to wander** empecé a dis-
traerme

◆ **wander around** v/i deambular, pasear

wane [weɪn] v/i of interest, enthusiasm
decaer, menguar

W

wan·gle ['wæŋgl] *v/t* F agenciarse F

want [wɑ:nt] **1** *n*: **for want of** por falta de **2** *v/t* querer; (*need*) necesitar; **want to do sth** querer hacer algo; **I want to stay here** quiero quedarme aquí; **do you want to come too? - no, I don't want to come** ¿quieres venir tú también? - no, no quiero; **you can have whatever you want** toma lo que quieras; **it's not what I wanted** no es lo que quería; **she wants you to go back** quiere que vuelvas; **he wants a haircut** necesita un corte de pelo **3** *v/i*: **he wants for nothing** no le falta nada

'want ad anuncio *m* por palabras (*buscando algo*)

want·ed ['wɑ:ntɪd] *adj by police* buscado por la policía

want·ing ['wɑ:ntɪŋ] *adj*: **the team is wanting in experience** al equipo le falta experiencia

wan·ton ['wɑ:ntən] *adj* gratuito

war [wɔ:r] *n also fig* guerra *f*; **be at war** estar en guerra

war·ble ['wɔ:rbl] *v/i of bird* trinar

ward [wɔ:rd] *n in hospital* sala *f*; *child* pupilo(-a) *m(f)*

◆ **ward off** *v/t blow* parar; *attacker* rechazar; *cold* evitar

war·den ['wɔ:rdn] *of prison* director(-a) *m(f)*, alcaide(sa) *m(f)*; *Br of hostel* vigilante *m/f*

'ward·robe *for clothes* armario *m*; (*clothes*) guardarropa *m*

ware·house ['werhaʊs] almacén *m*

'war·fare guerra *f*

'war·head ojiva *f*

war·i·ly ['werɪlɪ] *adv* cautelosamente

warm [wɔ:rm] **1** *adj hands, room, water* caliente; *weather, welcome* cálido; *coat* de abrigo; **it's warmer than yesterday** hace más calor que ayer **2** *v/t* → **warm up**

◆ **warm up 1** *v/t* calentar **2** *v/i* calentarse; *of athlete etc* calentar

warm-heart·ed ['wɔ:rmhɑ:rtɪd] *adj* cariñoso, simpático

warm·ly ['wɔ:rmlɪ] *adv welcome, smile* calurosamente; **warmly dressed** abrigado

warmth [wɔ:rmθ] *calor m; of welcome,*

smile calor *m*, calidez *m*

'warm-up SP calentamiento *m*

warn [wɔ:rn] *v/t* advertir, avisar

warn·ing ['wɔ:rnɪŋ] *n* advertencia *f*, aviso *m*; **without warning** sin previo aviso

warp [wɔ:rp] **1** *v/t wood* combar; *character* corromper **2** *v/i of wood* combarse

warped [wɔ:rpt] *adj fig* retorcido

'war·plane avión *m* de guerra

war·rant ['wɔ:rənt] **1** *n* orden *f* judicial **2** *v/t* (*deserve, call for*) justificar

war·ran·ty ['wɔ:rəntɪ] (*guarantee*) garantía *f*; **be under warranty** estar en garantía

war·ri·or ['wɔ:rɪər] guerrero(-a) *m(f)*

'war·ship buque *m* de guerra

wart [wɔ:rt] verruga *f*

'war·time tiempos *mpl* de guerra

war·y ['werɪ] *adj* cauto, precavido; **be wary of** desconfiar de

was [wʌz] *pret* → **be**

wash [wɑ:ʃ] **1** *n* lavado *m*; **have a wash** lavarse; **that shirt needs a wash** hay que lavar esa camisa **2** *v/t* lavar **3** *v/i* lavarse

◆ **wash up** *v/i* (*wash one's hands and face*) lavarse

wash·a·ble ['wɑ:ʃəbl] *adj* lavable

'wash·ba·sin, 'wash·bowl lavabo *m*

'wash·cloth toallita *f*

washed out [wɑ:ʃt'aʊt] *adj* agotado

wash·er ['wɑ:ʃər] *for faucet etc* arandela *f*; → **washing machine**

wash·ing ['wɑ:ʃɪŋ] (*clothes washed*) ropa *f* limpia; (*dirty clothes*) ropa *f* sucia; **do the washing** lavar la ropa, hacer la colada

wash·ing ma·chine lavadora *f*

wash·ing-'up liq·uid *Br* lavavajillas *m inv*

'wash·room lavabo *m*, aseo *m*

wasp [wɑ:sp] *insect* avispa *f*

waste [weɪst] **1** *n* desperdicio *m*; *from industrial process* desechos *mpl*; **it's a waste of time / money** es una pérdida de tiempo / dinero **2** *adj* residual; **waste land** erial *m* **3** *v/t* derrochar; *money* gastar; *time* perder

◆ **waste away** *v/i* consumirse

'waste dis·pos·al (unit) trituradora *f* de basuras

W

waste·ful ['weɪstfəl] *adj* despilfarrador, derrochador

'**waste·land** erial *m*

waste-'pa·per papel *m* usado

waste-pa·per 'bas·ket papelera *f*

'**waste pipe** tubería *f* de desagüe

'**waste prod·uct** desecho *m*

watch [wɑːtʃ] **1** *n timepiece* reloj *m*; **keep watch** hacer la guardia, vigilar **2** *v/t film*, TV ver; (*look after*) vigilar **3** *v/i* mirar, observar

◆ **watch for** *v/t* esperar

◆ **watch out** *v/i* tener cuidado; **watch out!** ¡cuidado!

◆ **watch out for** *v/t* tener cuidado con

watch·ful ['wɑːtʃfəl] *adj* vigilante

'**watch·mak·er** relojero(-a) *m(f)*

wa·ter ['wɒːtər] **1** *n* agua *f*; **waters** NAUT aguas *fpl* **2** *v/t plant* regar **3** *v/i*: **my eyes are watering** me lloran los ojos; **my mouth is watering** se me hace la boca agua

◆ **water down** *v/t drink* aguar, diluir

'**water can·non** cañón *m* de agua

'**wa·ter·col·or**, *Br* '**wa·ter·col·our** acuarela *f*

'**wa·ter·cress** berro *m*

watered 'down ['wɒːtərd] *adj fig* dulcificado

'**wa·ter·fall** cascada *f*, catarata *f*

wa·ter·ing can ['wɒːtərɪŋ] regadera *f*

'**wa·ter·ing hole** *hum* bar *m*

'**wa·ter lev·el** nivel *m* del agua

'**wa·ter lil·y** nenúfar *m*

'**wa·ter·line** línea *f* de flotación

wa·ter·logged ['wɒːtərlɑːgd] *adj earth*, *field* anegado; *boat* lleno de agua

'**wa·ter main** tubería *f* principal

'**wa·ter·mark** filigrana *f*

'**wa·ter mel·on** sandía *f*

'**wa·ter pol·lu·tion** contaminación *f* del agua

'**wa·ter po·lo** waterpolo *m*

'**wa·ter·proof** *adj* impermeable

'**wa·ter·shed** *fig* momento *m* clave

'**wa·ter·side** *n* orilla *f*; **at the waterside** en la orilla

'**wa·ter·ski·ing** esquí *m* acuático

'**wa·ter·tight** *adj compartment* estanco;

fig irrefutable

'**wa·ter·way** curso *m* de agua navegable

'**wa·ter·wings** *npl* flotadores *mpl* (*para los brazos*)

wa·ter·works F: **turn on the waterworks** ponerse a llorar como una magdalena F

wa·ter·y ['wɒːtərɪ] *adj* aguado

watt [wɑːt] vatio *m*

wave[1] [weɪv] *n in sea* ola *f*

wave[2] [weɪv] **1** *n of hand* saludo *m* **2** *v/i with hand* saludar con la mano; **wave to s.o.** saludar con la mano a alguien **3** *v/t flag etc* agitar

'**wave·length** RAD longitud *f* de onda; **be on the same wavelength** *fig* estar en la misma onda

wa·ver ['weɪvər] *v/i* vacilar, titubear

wav·y ['weɪvɪ] *adj hair*, *line* ondulado

wax [wæks] *n for floor*, *furniture* cera *f*; *in ear* cera *f*, cerumen

way [weɪ] **1** *n* (*method*) manera *f*, forma *f*; (*manner*) manera *f*, modo *m*; (*route*) camino *m*; **I don't like the way he behaves** no me gusta cómo se comporta; **can you tell me the way to ...?** ¿me podría decir cómo se va a ...?; **this way** (*like this*) así; (*in this direction*) por aquí; **by the way** (*incidentally*) por cierto, a propósito; **by way of** (*via*) por; (*in the form of*) a modo de; **in a way** (*in certain respects*) en cierto sentido; **be under way** haber comenzado, estar en marcha; **give way** MOT ceder el paso; (*collapse*) ceder; **give way to** (*be replaced by*) ser reemplazado por; **have one's** (**own**) **way** salirse con la suya; **OK, we'll do it your way** de acuerdo, lo haremos a tu manera; **lead the way** abrir (el) camino; *fig* marcar la pauta; **lose one's way** perderse; **be in the way** (*be an obstruction*) estar en medio; **it's on the way to the station** está camino de la estación; **I was on my way to the station** iba camino de la estación; **no way!** ¡ni hablar!, ¡de ninguna manera!; **there's no way he can do it** es imposible que lo haga **2** *adv* F (*much*): **it's way too soon to decide** es demasiado pronto como para decidir; **they are way behind with their work** van atrasadísimos en el trabajo

way 'in entrada *f*

way of 'life modo *m* de vida

way 'out *n* salida *f*; *fig: from situation* salida *f*

we [wiː] *pron* nosotros *mpl*, nosotras *fpl*; *we are the best* somos los mejores; *they're going, but we're not* ellos van, pero nosotros no

weak [wiːk] *adj* débil; *tea, coffee* poco cargado

weak·en ['wiːkn] **1** *v/t* debilitar **2** *v/i* debilitarse

weak·ling ['wiːklɪŋ] *morally* cobarde *m/f*; *physically* enclenque *m/f*

weak·ness ['wiːknɪs] debilidad *f*; *have a weakness for sth* (*liking*) sentir debilidad por algo

wealth [welθ] riqueza *f*; *a wealth of* abundancia de

wealth·y ['welθɪ] *adj* rico

wean [wiːn] *v/t* destetar

weap·on ['wepən] arma *f*

wear [wer] **1** *n*: *wear (and tear)* desgaste *m*; *clothes for everyday / evening wear* ropa *f* de diario / de noche **2** *v/t* (*pret wore, pp worn*) (*have on*) llevar; (*damage*) desgastar **3** *v/i* (*pret wore, pp worn*) (*wear out*) desgastarse; (*last*) durar

◆ **wear away 1** *v/i* desgastarse **2** *v/t* desgastar

◆ **wear down** *v/t* agotar

◆ **wear off** *v/i of effect, feeling* pasar

◆ **wear out 1** *v/t* (*tire*) agotar; *shoes* desgastar **2** *v/i of shoes, carpet* desgastarse

wea·ri·ly ['wɪrɪlɪ] *adv* cansinamente

wear·ing ['werɪŋ] *adj* (*tiring*) agotador

wea·ry ['wɪrɪ] *adj* cansado

weath·er ['weðər] **1** *n* tiempo *m*; *what's the weather like?* ¿qué tiempo hace?; *be feeling under the weather* estar pachucho **2** *v/t crisis* capear, superar

'weath·er-beat·en *adj* curtido

'weath·er chart mapa *m* del tiempo

'weath·er fore·cast pronóstico *m* del tiempo

'weath·er·man hombre *m* del tiempo

weave [wiːv] **1** *v/t* (*pret wove, pp woven*) tejer **2** *v/i* (*pret wove, pp woven*) *move* zigzaguear

web [web] *of spider* tela *f*; *the Web* COMPUT la Web

webbed 'feet patas *fpl* palmeadas

'web page página *f* web

'web site sitio *m* web

wed·ding ['wedɪŋ] boda *f*

'wed·ding an·ni·ver·sa·ry aniversario *m* de boda

'wed·ding cake pastel *m or* tarta *f* de boda

'wed·ding day día *f* de la boda

'wed·ding dress vestido *m* de boda *or* novia

'wed·ding ring anillo *m* de boda

wedge [wedʒ] **1** *n to hold sth in place* cuña *f*; *of cheese etc* trozo *m* **2** *v/t*: *wedge a door open* calzar una puerta para que se quede abierta

Wed·nes·day ['wenzdeɪ] miércoles *m inv*

weed [wiːd] **1** *n* mala hierba **2** *v/t* escardar

◆ **weed out** *v/t* (*remove*) eliminar; *candidates* descartar

'weed-kill·er herbicida *m*

weed·y ['wiːdɪ] *adj* F esmirriado, enclenque

week [wiːk] semana *f*; *a week tomorrow* dentro de una semana

'week·day día *m* de la semana

week'end fin *m* de semana; *on the weekend* el fin de semana

week·ly ['wiːklɪ] **1** *adj* semanal **2** *n magazine* semanario *m* **3** *adv* semanalmente

weep [wiːp] *v/i* (*pret & pp wept*) llorar

'weep·ing wil·low sauce *m* llorón

weep·y ['wiːpɪ] *adj*: *be weepy* estar lloroso

wee-wee 1 *n* F pipí *m*; *do a wee-wee* hacer pipí **2** *v/i* F hacer pipí

weigh[1] [weɪ] **1** *v/t* pesar **2** *v/i* pesar; *how much do you weigh?* ¿cuánto pesas?

weigh[2] [weɪ] *v/t*: *weigh anchor* levar anclas

◆ **weigh down** *v/t* cargar; *be weighed down with bags* ir cargado con; *worries* estar abrumado por

◆ **weigh on** *v/t* preocupar

◆ **weigh up** *v/t* (*assess*) sopesar

weight [weɪt] peso *m*; *put on weight* engordar, ganar peso; *lose weight* adelgazar, perder peso

◆ **weight down** *v/t* sujetar *(con pesos)*

'weight·less ['weɪtləs] *adj* ingrávido

'weight·less·ness ['weɪtləsnəs] ingravidez *f*

'weight·lift·er levantador(a) *m(f)* de pesas

'weight·lift·ing halterofilia *f*, levantamiento *m* de pesas

weight·y ['weɪtɪ] *adj (fig: important)* serio

weir [wɪr] presa *f (rebasadero)*

weird [wɪrd] *adj* extraño, raro

weird·ly ['wɪrdlɪ] *adv* extrañamente

weird·o ['wɪrdoʊ] *n* F bicho *m* raro F

wel·come ['welkəm] **1** *adj* bienvenido; *you're welcome!* ¡de nada!; *you're welcome to try some* prueba algunos, por favor **2** *n* bienvenida *f* **3** *v/t* guests etc dar la bienvenida a; *fig: decision etc* acoger positivamente

weld [weld] *v/t* soldar

weld·er ['weldər] soldador(a) *m(f)*

wel·fare ['welfer] bienestar *m*; *financial assistance* subsidio *m* estatal; *be on welfare* estar recibiendo subsidios del Estado

'wel·fare check *cheque con el importe del subsidio estatal*

wel·fare 'state estado *m* del bienestar

'wel·fare work trabajo *m* social

'wel·fare work·er asistente *m/f* social

well¹ [wel] *n for water, oil* pozo *m*

well² ¹ *adv* bien; *as well (too)* también; *as well as (in addition to)* así como; *it's just as well you told me* menos mal que me lo dijiste; *very well* muy bien; *well, well!* surprise ¡caramba!; *well ... uncertainty, thinking* bueno …; *you might as well spend the night here* ya puestos quédate a pasar la noche aquí; *you might as well throw it out* yo de ti lo tiraría **2** *adj*: *be well* estar bien; *how are you? - I'm very well* ¿cómo estás? - muy bien; *feel well* sentirse bien; *get well soon!* ¡ponte bueno!, ¡que te mejores!

well-'bal·anced *adj* person, diet equilibrado

well-be'haved *adj* educado

well-'be·ing bienestar *m*

well-'built *adj also euph* fornido

well-'done *adj meat* muy hecho

well-'dressed *adj* bien vestido

well-'earned *adj* merecido

well-'heeled *adj* F adinerado, Span con pasta F

well-in'formed *adj* bien informado

well-'known *adj fact* conocido; *person* conocido, famoso

well-'made *adj* bien hecho

well-'man·nered *adj* educado

well-'mean·ing *adj* bienintencionado

well-'off *adj* acomodado

well-'paid *adj* bien pagado

well-'read *adj*: *be well-read* haber leído mucho

well-'timed *adj* oportuno

well-to-'do *adj* acomodado

'well-wish·er admirador(a) *m(f)*

well-'worn *adj* gastado

Welsh [welʃ] **1** *adj* galés **2** *n language* galés; *the Welsh* los galeses

went [went] *pret* → **go**

wept [wept] *pret* & *pp* → **weep**

were [wer] *pret* → **be**

west [west] **1** *n* oeste *m*; *the West (Western nations)* Occidente *m*; *(western part of a country)* el oeste **2** *adj* del oeste; *west Africa* África occidental **3** *adv* travel hacia el oeste; *west of* al oeste de

West 'Coast *of USA* Costa *f* Oeste

West 'In·di·an **1** *adj* antillano **2** *n* antillano(-a) *m(f)*

West In·dies ['ɪndɪz] *npl: the West Indies* las Antillas

west·er·ly ['westərlɪ] *adj wind* del oeste; *direction* hacia el oeste

west·ern ['westərn] **1** *adj* occidental; *Western* occidental **2** *n movie* western *m*, película *f* del oeste

West·ern·er ['westərnər] occidental *m/f*

west·ern·ized ['westərnaɪzd] *adj* occidentalizado

west·ward ['westwərd] *adv* hacia el oeste

wet [wet] *adj* mojado; *(damp)* húmedo; *(rainy)* lluvioso; *get wet* mojarse; *wet paint as sign* recién pintado; *be wet*

through estar empapado

wet 'blan·ket F aguafiestas *m/f inv*

'wet suit *for diving* traje *m* de neopreno

whack [wæk] **1** *n* F *(blow)* porrazo *m* F; F *(share)* parte *f* 2 *v/t* F dar un porrazo a F

whacked [wækt] *adj* F hecho polvo F

whale [weɪl] ballena *f*

whal·ing ['weɪlɪŋ] caza *f* de ballenas

wharf [wɔːrf] *n* embarcadero *m*

what [wɑːt] **1** *pron* qué; *what is that?* ¿qué es eso?; *what is it?* ¿qué es it, que want) ¿qué quieres?; *what?* *(what do you want)* ¿qué?; *(what did you say)* ¿qué?, ¿cómo?; *astonishment* ¿qué?; *what about some dinner?* ¿os apetece cenar?; *what about heading home?* ¿y si nos fuéramos a casa?; *what for?* *(why)* ¿para qué?; *so what?* ¿y qué?; *what is the book about?* ¿de qué trata el libro?; *take what you need* toma lo que te haga falta **2** *adj* qué; *what university are you at?* ¿en qué universidad estás?; *what color is the car?* ¿de qué color es el coche?

what·ev·er [wɑːt'evər] **1** *pron*: *I'll do whatever you want* haré lo que quieras; *whatever gave you that idea?* ¿se puede saber qué te ha dado esa idea?; *whatever the season* en cualquier estación; *whatever people say* diga lo que diga la gente **2** *adj* cualquier; *you have no reason whatever to worry* no tienes por qué preocuparte en absoluto

wheat [wiːt] trigo *m*

whee·dle ['wiːdl] *v/t*: *wheedle sth out of s.o.* camelar algo a alguien

wheel [wiːl] **1** *n* rueda *f*; *(steering wheel)* volante *m* **2** *v/t bicycle* empujar **3** *v/i of birds* volar en círculo

◆ **wheel around** *v/i* darse la vuelta

'wheel·bar·row carretilla *f*

'wheel·chair silla *f* de ruedas

'wheel clamp cepo *m*

wheeze [wiːz] *n* resoplido *m*

when [wen] **1** *adv* cuándo; *when do you open?* ¿a qué hora abren? **2** *conj* cuando; *when I was a child* cuando era niño

when·ev·er [wen'evər] *adv (each time)* cada vez que; *call me whenever you like*

llámame cuando quieras; *I go to Paris whenever I can afford it* voy a París siempre que me lo puedo permitir

where [wer] **1** *adv* dónde; *where from?* ¿de dónde es?; *where to?* ¿a dónde? **2** *conj* donde; *this is where I used to live* aquí es donde vivía antes

where·a·bouts [werə'bauts] **1** *adv* dónde **2** *npl nothing is known of his whereabouts* está en paradero desconocido

where·as *conj* mientras que

wher·ev·er [wer'evər] **1** *conj* dondequiera que; *sit wherever you like* siéntate donde prefieras **2** *adv* dónde

whet [wet] *v/t (pret & pp whetted)* appetite abrir

wheth·er ['weðər] *conj* si; *I don't know whether to tell him or not* no sé si decírselo o no; *whether you approve or not* te parezca bien o que

which [wɪtʃ] **1** *adj* qué; *which one is yours?* ¿cuál es tuyo? **2** *pron interrogative* cuál; *relative* que; *take one, it doesn't matter which* toma uno, no importa cuál

which·ev·er [wɪtʃ'evər] **1** *adj*: *whichever color you choose* elijas el color que elijas **2** *pron*: *whichever you like* el que quieras; *use whichever of the methods you prefer* utiliza el método que prefieras

whiff [wɪf] *(smell)* olorcillo *m*

while [waɪl] **1** *conj* mientras; *(although)* si bien **2** *n* rato *m*; *a long while* un rato largo; *for a while* durante un tiempo; *I lived in Tokyo for a while* viví en Tokio una temporada; *I'll wait a while longer* esperaré un rato más

◆ **while away** *v/t* pasar

whim [wɪm] capricho *m*

whim·per ['wɪmpər] **1** *n* gimoteo *m* **2** *v/i* gimotear

whine [waɪn] *v/i of dog* gimotear; F *(complain)* quejarse

whip [wɪp] **1** *n* látigo *m* **2** *v/t (pret & pp whipped) (beat)* azotar; *cream* batir, montar; F *(defeat)* dar una paliza a F

◆ **whip out** *v/t* F sacar rápidamente

◆ **whip up** *v/t (arouse)* agitar; F *meal* improvisar

'whipped cream [wɪpt] nata *f* montada

whip·ping ['wɪpɪŋ] (*beating*) azotes *mpl*; F (*defeat*) paliza *f* F

'whip·round F colecta *f*; *have a whip-round* hacer una colecta

whirl [wɜːrl] 1 *n*: *my mind is in a whirl* me da vueltas la cabeza 2 *v/i* dar vueltas

'whirl·pool *in river* remolino *m*; *for relaxation* bañera *f* de hidromasaje

whirr [wɜːr] *v/i* zumbar

whisk [wɪsk] 1 *n kitchen implement* 2 *v/t eggs* batir

◆ whisk away *v/t* retirar rápidamente

whis·kers ['wɪskərz] *npl of man* patillas *fpl*; *of animal* bigotes *mpl*

whis·key, whis·ky ['wɪskɪ] whisky *m*

whis·per ['wɪspər] 1 *n* susurro *m*; (*rumor*) rumor *m* 2 *v/i* susurrar 3 *v/t* susurrar

whis·tle ['wɪsl] 1 *n* sound silbido *m*; *device* silbato *m* 2 *v/t & v/i* silbar

white [waɪt] 1 *n color* blanco *m*; *of egg* clara *f*; *person* blanco(-a) *m(f)* 2 *adj* blanco; *her face went white* se puso blanca

white 'Christ·mas Navidades *fpl* blancas

white 'cof·fee *Br* café *m* con leche

white-col·lar 'work·er persona que trabaja en una oficina

'White House Casa *f* Blanca

white 'lie mentira *f* piadosa

white 'meat carne *f* blanca

'white·wash 1 *n* cal *f*; *fig* encubrimiento *m* 2 *v/t* encalar

white 'wine vino *m* blanco

whit·tle ['wɪtl] *v/t wood* tallar

◆ whittle down *v/t* reducir

whiz(z) [wɪz] *n*: *be a whiz(z) at* F ser un genio de

◆ whizz by, whizz past *v/i of time, car* pasar zumbando

'whizz·kid F joven *m/f* prodigio

who [huː] *pron interrogative* ¿quién?; *relative* que; *who do you want to speak to?* ¿con quién quieres hablar?; *I don't know who to believe?* no sé a quién creer

who·dun·(n)it [huː'dʌnɪt] *libro o película centrados en la resolución de un caso*

who·ev·er [huː'evər] *pron* quienquiera; *whoever can that be calling at this time of night?* ¿pero quién llama a estas horas de la noche?

whole [hoʊl] 1 *adj* entero; *the whole town / country* toda la ciudad / todo el país; *he drank / ate the whole lot* se lo bebió / comió todo; *it's a whole lot easier / better* es mucho más fácil / mucho mejor 2 *n* totalidad *f*; *the whole of the United States* la totalidad de los Estados Unidos; *on the whole* en general

whole-heart·ed [hoʊl'hɑːrtɪd] *adj* incondicional

whole-heart·ed·ly [hoʊl'hɑːrtɪdlɪ] *adv* incondicionalmente

whole·meal 'bread pan *m* integral

'whole·sale 1 *adj* al por mayor; *fig* indiscriminado 2 *adv* al por mayor

whole·sal·er ['hoʊlseɪlər] mayorista *m/f*

whole·some ['hoʊlsəm] *adj* saludable, sano

whol·ly ['hoʊlɪ] *adv* completamente

whol·ly owned 'sub·sid·i·ar·y subsidiaria *f* en propiedad absoluta

whom [huːm] *pron fml* quién; *whom did you see?* ¿a quién vio?; *the person to whom I was speaking* la persona con la que estaba hablando

whoop·ing cough ['huːpɪŋ] tos *f* ferina

whop·ping ['wɑːpɪŋ] *adj* F enorme

whore [hɔːr] *n* prostituta *f*

whose [huːz] 1 *pron interrogative* de quién; *relative* cuyo(-a); *whose is this?* ¿de quién es esto?; *a country whose economy is booming* un país cuya economía está experimentando un boom 2 *adj* de quién; *whose bike is that?* ¿de quién es esa bici?

why [waɪ] *adv interrogative* por qué; *relative* por qué; *that's why* por eso; *why not?* ¿por qué no?

wick [wɪk] pabilo *m*

wick·ed ['wɪkɪd] *adj* malvado, perverso

wick·er ['wɪkər] *adj* de mimbre

wick·er 'chair silla *f* de mimbre

wick·et ['wɪkɪt] *in station, bank etc* ventanilla *f*

wide [waɪd] *adj* ancho; *experience, range*

W

amplio; **be 12 feet wide** tener 12 pies de ancho

wide a'wake *adj* completamente despierto

wide·ly ['waɪdlɪ] *adv used, known* ampliamente

wid·en ['waɪdn] **1** *v/t* ensanchar **2** *v/i* ensancharse

wide-'o·pen *adj* abierto de par en par

wide-'rang·ing *adj* amplio

'**wide·spread** *adj* extendido, muy difundido

wid·ow ['wɪdoʊ] *n* viuda *f*

wid·ow·er ['wɪdoʊər] viudo *m*

width [wɪdθ] anchura *f*, ancho *m*

wield [wiːld] *v/t weapon* empuñar; *power* detentar

wife [waɪf] (*pl* **wives** [waɪvz]) mujer *f*, esposa *f*

wig [wɪg] peluca *f*

wig·gle ['wɪgl] *v/t* menear

wild [waɪld] **1** *adj animal* salvaje; *flower* silvestre; *teenager, party* descontrolado; (*crazy: scheme*) descabellado; *applause* arrebatado; **be wild about ...** (*keen on*) estar loco por ...; **go wild** (*express enthusiasm*) volverse loco; (*become angry*) ponerse hecho una furia; **run wild** *of children* descontrolarse **2** *n*: **the wilds** los parajes remotos

wil·der·ness ['wɪldərnɪs] (*empty place*) desierto *m*, yermo *m*; (*fig: garden etc*) jungla *f*

'**wild·fire**: **spread like wildfire** extenderse como un reguero de pólvora

wild-'goose chase búsqueda *f* infructuosa

'**wild·life** flora *f* y fauna; **wildlife program** TV documental *m* sobre la naturaleza

wild·ly ['waɪldlɪ] *adv applaud* enfervorizadamente; **I'm not wildly enthusiastic about the idea** la idea no me emociona demasiado

wil·ful *Br* → **willful**

will¹ [wɪl] *n* LAW testamento *m*

will² [wɪl] *n* (*willpower*) voluntad *f*

will³ [wɪl] *v/aux*: **I will let you know tomorrow** te lo diré mañana; **will you be there?** ¿estarás allí?; **I won't be back until**

late volveré tarde; **you will call me, won't you?** me llamarás, ¿verdad?; **I'll pay for this - no you won't** esto lo pago yo - no, ni hablar; **the car won't start** el coche no arranca; **will you tell her that ...?** ¿le quieres decir que ...?; **will you have some more tea?** ¿quiere más té?; **will you stop that!** ¡basta ya!

will·ful ['wɪlfl] *adj person* tozudo, obstinado; *action* deliberado, intencionado

will·ing ['wɪlɪŋ] *adj* dispuesto

will·ing·ly ['wɪlɪŋlɪ] *adv* gustosamente

will·ing·ness ['wɪlɪŋnɪs] buena disposición *f*

wil·low ['wɪloʊ] sauce *m*

'**will·pow·er** fuerza *f* de voluntad

wil·ly-nil·ly [wɪlɪ'nɪlɪ] *adv* (*at random*) a la buena de Dios

wilt [wɪlt] *v/i of plant* marchitarse

wi·ly ['waɪlɪ] *adj* astuto

wimp [wɪmp] F enclenque *m/f* F, blandengue *m/f* F

win [wɪn] **1** *n* victoria *f*, triunfo *m* **2** *v/t* & *v/i* (*pret* & *pp* **won**) ganar

◆ **win back** *v/t* recuperar

wince [wɪns] *v/i* hacer una mueca de dolor

winch [wɪntʃ] *n* torno *m*, cabestrante *m*

wind¹ [wɪnd] **1** *n* viento *m*; (*flatulence*) gases *mpl*; **get wind of ...** enterarse de ... **2** *v/t*: **be winded** quedarse sin respiración

wind² [waɪnd] **1** *v/i* (*pret* & *pp* **wound**) zigzaguear; serpentear; **wind around** enrollarse en **2** *v/t* (*pret* & *pp* **wound**) enrollar

◆ **wind down 1** *v/i of party etc* ir finalizando **2** *v/t car window* bajar, abrir; *business* ir reduciendo

◆ **wind up 1** *v/t clock* dar cuerda a; *car window* subir, cerrar; *speech, presentation* finalizar; *business, affairs* concluir; *company* cerrar **2** *v/i* (*finish*) concluir; **wind up in hospital** acabar en el hospital

'**wind·bag** F cotorra *f* F

'**wind·fall** *fig* dinero *m* inesperado

wind·ing ['waɪndɪŋ] *adj* zigzagueante, serpenteante

'wind in·stru·ment instrumento *m* de viento

'wind·mill molino *m* de viento

win·dow ['wɪndoʊ] *also* COMPUT ventana *f*; *of car* ventana *f*, ventanilla *f*; *in the window of store* en el escaparate *or* L.Am. la vidriera

'win·dow box jardinera *f*

'win·dow clean·er *person* limpiacristales *m/f inv*

'win·dow·pane cristal *f* (*de una ventana*)

'win·dow seat *on plane, train* asiento *m* de ventana

'win·dow-shop *v/i* (*pret & pp window-shopped*): *go window-shopping* ir de escaparates *or* L.Am. vidrieras

'win·dow-sill ['wɪndoʊsɪl] alféizar *m*

'wind·pipe tráquea *f*

'wind·screen *Br*, 'wind·shield parabrisas *m inv*

'wind·shield wip·er limpiaparabrisas *inv*

'wind·surf·er *person* windsurfista *m/f*; *board* tabla *f* de windsurf

'wind·surf·ing el windsurf

wind·y ['wɪndɪ] *adj* ventoso; *a windy day* un día de mucho viento; *it's very windy today* hoy hace mucho viento; *it's getting windy* está empezando a soplar el viento

wine [waɪn] vino *m*

'wine bar *bar especializado en vinos*

'wine cel·lar bodega *f*

'wine glass copa *f* de vino

'wine list lista *f* de vinos

'wine mak·er viticultor(a) *m(f)*

'wine mer·chant comerciante *m/f* de vinos

win·ery ['waɪnərɪ] bodega *f*

wing [wɪŋ] *n* ala *f*; SP lateral *m/f*, extremo *m/f*

'wing·span envergadura *f*

wink [wɪŋk] 1 *n* guiño *m*; *I didn't sleep a wink* F no pegué ojo 2 *v/i of person* guiñar, hacer un guiño; *wink at s.o.* guiñar *or* hacer un guiño a alguien

win·ner ['wɪnər] ganador(a) *m(f)*, vencedor(a) *m(f)*; *of lottery* acertante *m/f*

win·ning ['wɪnɪŋ] *adj* ganador

'win·ning post meta *f*

win·nings ['wɪnɪŋz] *npl* ganancias *fpl*

win·ter ['wɪntər] *n* invierno *m*

win·ter 'sports *npl* deportes *mpl* de invierno

win·try ['wɪntrɪ] *adj* invernal

wipe [waɪp] *v/t* limpiar; *tape* borrar

◆ wipe out *v/t* (*kill, destroy*) eliminar; *debt* saldar

wip·er ['waɪpər] → *windshield wiper*

wire [waɪr] *n* alambre *m*; ELEC cable *m*

wire·less ['waɪrlɪs] radio *f*

wire 'net·ting tela *f* metálica

wir·ing ['waɪrɪŋ] *n* ELEC cableado *m*

wir·y ['waɪrɪ] *adj person* fibroso

wis·dom ['wɪzdəm] *of person* sabiduría *f*; *of action* prudencia *f*, sensatez *f*

'wis·dom tooth muela *f* del juicio

wise [waɪz] *adj* sabio; *action, decision* prudente, sensato

'wise·crack *n* F chiste *m*, comentario *m* gracioso

'wise guy *pej* sabelotodo *m*

wise·ly ['waɪzlɪ] *adv act* prudentemente, sensatamente

wish [wɪʃ] 1 *n* deseo *m*; *best wishes* un saludo cordial; *make a wish* pedir un deseo 2 *v/t* desear; *I wish that you could stay* ojalá te pudieras quedar; *wish s.o. well* desear a alguien lo mejor; *I wished him good luck* le deseé buena suerte 3 *v/i*: *wish for* desear

'wish·bone espoleta *f*

wish·ful 'think·ing ['wɪʃfəl] ilusiones *fpl*; *that's wishful thinking on her part* que no se haga ilusiones

wish·y-wash·y ['wɪʃɪwɑːʃɪ] *adj person* anodino; *color* pálido

wisp [wɪsp] *of hair* mechón *m*; *of smoke* voluta *f*

wist·ful ['wɪstfəl] *adj* nostálgico

wist·ful·ly ['wɪstfəlɪ] *adv* con nostalgia

wit [wɪt] (*humor*) ingenio *m*; *person* ingenioso(-a) *m(f)*; *be at one's wits' end* estar desesperado; *keep one's wits about one* mantener la calma; *be scared out of one's wits* estar aterrorizado

witch [wɪʃ] bruja *f*

'witch·hunt *fig* caza *f* de brujas

W

with [wɪð] *prep* con; **shivering with fear** temblando de miedo; **a girl with brown eyes** una chica de ojos castaños; **are you with me?** (*do you understand*) ¿me sigues?; **with no money** sin dinero

with·draw [wɪð'drɔː] **1** *v/t* (*pret* **withdrew**, *pp* **withdrawn**) *complaint, money, troops* retirar **2** *v/i* (*pret* **withdrew**, *pp* **withdrawn**) *of competitor, troops* retirarse

with·draw·al [wɪð'drɔːəl] *of complaint, application, troops* retirada *f*; *of money* reintegro *m*

with'draw·al symp·toms *npl* síndrome *m* de abstinencia

with·drawn [wɪð'drɔːn] *adj person* retraído

with·er [ˈwɪðər] *v/i* marchitarse

with'hold *v/t* (*pret & pp* **withheld**) *information* ocultar; *payment* retener; *consent* negar

with'in *prep* (*inside*) dentro de; *in expressions of time* en menos de; **within five miles of home** a cinco millas de casa; **we kept within the budget** no superamos el presupuesto; **it is well within your capabilities** lo puedes conseguir perfectamente; **within reach** al alcance de la mano

with'out *prep* sin; **without looking / asking** sin mirar / preguntar

with'stand *v/t* (*pret & pp* **withstood**) resistir, soportar

wit·ness [ˈwɪtnɪs] **1** *n* testigo *m/f* **2** *v/t accident, crime* ser testigo de; *signature* firmar en calidad de testigo

'wit·ness stand estrado *m* del testigo

wit·ti·cism [ˈwɪtɪsɪzm] comentario *m* gracioso *or* agudo

wit·ty [ˈwɪtɪ] *adj* ingenioso, agudo

wob·ble [ˈwɑːbl] *v/i* tambalearse

wob·bly [ˈwɑːblɪ] *adj* tambaleante

wok [wɑːk] wok *m*, sartén típica de la cocina china

woke [woʊk] *pret* → **wake¹**

wok·en [ˈwoʊkn] *pp* → **wake¹**

wolf [wʊlf] **1** *n* (*pl* **wolves** [wʊlvz]) *animal* lobo *m*; (*fig: womanizer*) don juan *m* **2** *v/t*: **wolf (down)** engullir

'wolf whis·tle *n* silbido *m*

'wolf-whis·tle *v/i*: **wolf-whistle at s.o.** silbar a alguien (*como piropo*)

wom·an [ˈwʊmən] (*pl* **women** [ˈwɪmɪn]) mujer *f*

wom·an 'doc·tor médica *f*

wom·an 'driv·er conductora *f*

wom·an·iz·er [ˈwʊmənaɪzər] mujeriego(-a) *m(f)*

wom·an·ly [ˈwʊmənlɪ] *adj* femenino

wom·an 'priest mujer *f* sacerdote

womb [wuːm] matriz *f*, útero *m*

wom·en [ˈwɪmɪn] *pl* → **woman**

wom·en's lib [wɪmɪnz'lɪb] la liberación de la mujer

wom·en's lib·ber [wɪmɪnz'lɪbər] partidario(-a) *m(f)* de la liberación de la mujer

won [wʌn] *pret & pp* → **win**

won·der [ˈwʌndər] **1** *n* (*amazement*) asombro *m*; **no wonder!** ¡no me sorprende!; **it's a wonder that ...** es increíble que ... **2** *v/i* preguntarse; **I've often wondered about that** me he preguntado eso a menudo **3** *v/t* preguntarse; **I wonder if you could help** ¿le importaría ayudarme?

won·der·ful [ˈwʌndərfəl] *adj* maravilloso

won·der·ful·ly [ˈwʌndərfəlɪ] *adv* (*extremely*) maravillosamente

won't [woʊnt] → **will³**

wood [wʊd] *n* madera *f*; *for fire* leña *f*; (*forest*) bosque *m*

wood·ed [ˈwʊdɪd] *adj* arbolado

wood·en [ˈwʊdn] *adj* (*made of wood*) de madera

wood·peck·er [ˈwʊdpekər] pájaro *m* carpintero

'wood·wind MUS sección *f* de viento de madera

'wood·work carpintería *f*

wool [wʊl] lana *f*

wool·en, *Br* wool·len [ˈwʊlən] **1** *adj* de lana **2** *n* prenda *f* de lana

word [wɜːrd] **1** *n* palabra *f*; **I didn't understand a word of what she said** no entendí nada de lo que dijo; **is there any word from ...?** ¿se sabe algo de ...?; **I've had word from my daughter** (*news*) he recibido noticias de mi hija;

W

you have my word tienes mi palabra; **have words** *(argue)* discutir; **have a word with s.o.** hablar con alguien; **the words** *of song* la letra **2** *v/t article, letter* redactar

word·ing ['wɜːrdɪŋ]: **the wording of a letter** la redacción de una carta

word 'pro·cess·ing procesamiento *m* de textos

word 'pro·ces·sor *software* procesador *m* de textos

wore [wɔːr] *pret* → **wear**

work [wɜːrk] **1** *n (job)* trabajo *m*; *(employment)* trabajo *m*, empleo *m*; *out of work* desempleado, *Span* en el paro; **be at work** estar en el trabajo; **I go to work by bus** voy al trabajo en autobús **2** *v/i of person* trabajar; *of machine, (succeed)* funcionar; **how does it work?** *of device* ¿cómo funciona? **3** *v/t employee* hacer trabajar; *machine* hacer funcionar, utilizar

◆ **work off** *v/t bad mood, anger* desahogarse de; *flab* perder haciendo ejercicio

◆ **work out 1** *v/t problem, puzzle* resolver; *solution* encontrar, hallar **2** *v/i at gym* hacer ejercicios; *of relationship etc* funcionar, ir bien

◆ **work out to** *v/t (add up to)* sumar

◆ **work up** *v/t appetite* abrir; **work up enthusiasm** entusiasmarse; **get worked up** *(get angry)* alterarse; *(get nervous)* ponerse nervioso

work·a·ble ['wɜːrkəbl] *adj solution* viable

work·a·hol·ic [wɜːrkə'hɑːlɪk] *n* F *persona obsesionada con el trabajo*

work·er ['wɜːrkər] trabajador(a) *m(f)*; **she's a good worker** trabaja bien

'work·day *(hours of work)* jornada *f* laboral; *(not a holiday)* día *m* de trabajo

'work·force trabajadores *mpl*

'work hours *npl* horas *fpl* de trabajo

work·ing ['wɜːrkɪŋ] *n* funcionamiento *m*

'work·ing class clase *f* trabajadora

'work·ing-class *adj* de clase trabajadora

'work·ing con·di·tions *npl* condiciones *fpl* de trabajo

'work·ing 'day → **workday**

'work·ing hours → **work hours**

'work·ing 'knowl·edge conocimientos *mpl* básicos

'work·ing 'moth·er madre *f* que trabaja

'work·load cantidad *f* de trabajo

'work·man obrero *m*

'work·man·like *adj* competente

'work·man·ship factura *f*, confección *f*

work of 'art obra *f* de arte

'work·out sesión *f* de ejercicios

'work per·mit permiso *m* de trabajo

'work·shop *(also seminar)* taller *m*

'work sta·tion estación *f* de trabajo

'work·top encimera *f*

world [wɜːrld] mundo *m*; **the world of computers / the theater** el mundo de la informática / del teatro; **out of this world** F sensacional

World 'Cup Mundial *m*, Copa *f* del Mundo

world·ly ['wɜːrldlɪ] *adj* mundano

world-'class *adj* de categoría mundial

world-'fa·mous *adj* mundialmente famoso

world 'pow·er potencia *f* mundial

world 're·cord récord *m* mundial *or* del mundo

world 'war guerra *f* mundial

'world·wide **1** *adj* mundial **2** *adv* en todo el mundo

worm [wɜːrm] *n* gusano *m*

worn [wɔːrn] *pp* → **wear**

worn-'out *adj shoes, carpet, part* gastado; *person* agotado

wor·ried ['wʌrɪd] *adj* preocupado

wor·ried·ly ['wʌrɪdlɪ] *adv* con preocupación

wor·ry ['wʌrɪ] **1** *n* preocupación *f* **2** *v/t (pret & pp worried)* preocupar **3** *v/i (pret & pp worried)* preocuparse; **don't worry, I'll get it!** ¡no te molestes, ya respondo yo!

wor·ry·ing ['wʌrɪɪŋ] *adj* preocupante

worse [wɜːrs] **1** *adj* peor; **get worse** empeorar **2** *adv* peor

wors·en ['wɜːrsn] *v/i* empeorar

wor·ship ['wɜːrʃɪp] **1** *n* culto *m* **2** *v/t (pret & pp worshipped)* adorar, rendir culto a; *fig* adorar

worst [wɜːrst] **1** *adj & adv* peor **2** *n*: **the**

worst lo peor; *if the worst comes to the worst* en el peor de los casos

worst-case scen·a·ri·o el peor de los casos

worth [wɜːrθ] *adj*: *$20 worth of gas* 20 dólares de gasolina; *be worth ... in monetary terms* valer ...; *the book's worth reading* valer la pena leer el libro; *be worth it* valer la pena

worth·less ['wɜːrθlɪs] *adj person* inútil; *be worthless of object* no valer nada

worth·while *adj* que vale la pena; *be worthwhile* valer la pena

worth·y ['wɜːrðɪ] *adj* digno; *cause* justo; *be worthy of (deserve)* merecer

would [wʊd] *v/aux*: *I would help if I could* te ayudaría si pudiera; *I said that I would go* dije que iría; *I told him I would not leave unless ....* le dije que no me iría a no ser que ...; *would you like to go to the movies?* ¿te gustaría ir al cine?; *would you mind if I smoked?* ¿le importa si fumo?; *would you tell her that ...?* ¿le podrías decir que ...?; *would you close the door?* ¿podrías cerrar la puerta?; *I would have told you but ...* te lo habría dicho pero ...; *I would not have been so angry if ...* no me habría enfadado tanto si ...

wound[1] [wuːnd] **1** *n* herida *f* **2** *v/t with weapon, remark* herir

wound[2] [waʊnd] *pret & pp* → **wind**[2]

wove [woʊv] *pret* → **weave**

wov·en ['woʊvn] *pp* → **weave**

wow [waʊ] *int* ¡hala!

wrap [ræp] *v/t (pret & pp wrapped) parcel, gift* envolver; *he wrapped a scarf around his neck* se puso una bufanda al cuello

◆ **wrap up** *v/i against the cold* abrigarse

wrap·per ['ræpər] envoltorio *m*

wrap·ping ['ræpɪŋ] envoltorio *m*

'wrap·ping pa·per papel *m* de envolver

wrath [ræθ] ira *f*

wreath [riːθ] corona *f* de flores

wreck [rek] **1** *n* restos *mpl*; *be a nervous wreck* ser un manojo de nervios **2** *v/t ship* hundir; *car* destrozar; *plans, marriage* arruinar

wreck·age ['rekɪdʒ] *of car, plane* restos *mpl*; *of marriage, career* ruina *f*

wreck·er ['rekər] grúa *f*

wreck·ing com·pa·ny ['rekɪŋ] empresa *f* de auxilio en carretera

wrench [rentʃ] **1** *n tool* llave *f* **2** *v/t (pull)* arrebatar; *wrench one's wrist* hacerse un esguince en la muñeca

wres·tle ['resl] *v/i* luchar

◆ **wrestle with** *v/t problems* combatir

wres·tler ['reslər] luchador(a) *m(f)* (de lucha libre)

wres·tling ['reslɪŋ] lucha *f* libre

'wres·tling match combate *m* de lucha libre

wrig·gle ['rɪgl] *v/i (squirm)* menearse; *along the ground* arrastrarse; *into small space* escurrirse

◆ **wriggle out of** *v/t* librarse de

◆ **wring out** *v/t (pret & pp wrung) cloth* escurrir

wrin·kle ['rɪŋkl] **1** *n* arruga *f* **2** *v/t clothes* arrugar **3** *v/i of clothes* arrugarse

wrist [rɪst] muñeca *f*

'wrist watch reloj *m* de pulsera

writ [rɪt] LAW mandato *m* judicial

write [raɪt] **1** *v/t (pret wrote, pp written)* escribir; *check* extender **2** *v/i (pret wrote, pp written)* escribir

◆ **write down** *v/t* escribir, tomar nota de

◆ **write off** *v/t debt* cancelar, anular; *car* destrozar

writ·er ['raɪtər] escritor(a) *m(f)*; *of book, song* autor(a) *m(f)*

'write-up reseña *f*

writhe [raɪð] *v/i* retorcerse

writ·ing ['raɪtɪŋ] *words, text* escritura *f*; *(hand-writing)* letra *f*; *in writing* por escrito

'writ·ing desk escritorio *m*

'writ·ing pa·per papel *m* de escribir

writ·ten ['rɪtn] *pp* → **write**

wrong [rɒŋ] **1** *adj answer, information* equivocado; *decision, choice* erróneo; *be wrong of person* estar equivocado; *of answer* ser incorrecto; *morally* ser injusto; *what's wrong?* ¿qué pasa?; *there is something wrong with the car* al coche le pasa algo; *you have the wrong*

number TELEC se ha equivocado **2** *adv*
mal; **go wrong** *of person* equivocarse;
of marriage, plan etc fallar **3** *n* mal *m*;
right a wrong deshacer un entuerto;
he knows right from wrong sabe distinguir entre el bien y el mal; **be in the
wrong** tener la culpa

wrong·ful ['rɒːŋfəl] *adj* ilegal
wrong·ly ['rɒːŋlɪ] *adv* erróneamente
wrote [rout] *pret* → **write**
wrought 'i·ron [rɔːt] hierro *m* forjado
wrung [rʌŋ] *pret & pp* → **wring**
wry [raɪ] *adj* socarrón

X, Y

xen·o·pho·bi·a [zenou'foubɪə] xenofobia
f
X-ray ['eksreɪ] **1** *n* rayo *m* X; *picture* radiografía *f* **2** *v/t* radiografiar, sacar un radiografía de
xy·lo·phone [zaɪlə'foun] xilofón *m*

yacht [jɑːt] yate *m*
yacht·ing ['jɑːtɪŋ] vela *f*
yachts·man ['jɑːtsmən] navegante *m/f*
(*en embarcación de vela*)
Yank [jæŋk] F yanqui *m/f*
yank [jæŋk] *v/t* tirar de
yap [jæp] *v/i* (*pret & pp* **yapped**) *of small
dog* ladrar (*con ladridos agudos*); F (*talk
a lot*) parlotear F, largar F
yard¹ [jɑːrd] *of prison, institution etc* patio *m*; *behind house* jardín *m*; *for storage*
almacén *m* (*al aire libre*)
yard² [jɑːrd] *measurement* yarda *f*
'yard·stick patrón *m*
yarn [jɑːrn] *n* (*thread*) hilo *m*; F (*story*) ba-
tallita *f* F
yawn [jɔːn] **1** *n* bostezo *m* **2** *v/i* bostezar
year [jɪr] año *m*; **I've know her for years**
la conozco desde hace años; **we were in
the same year** *at school* éramos del mismo curso; **be six years old** tener seis
años (de edad)
year·ly ['jɪrlɪ] **1** *adj* anual **2** *adv* anualmente
yearn [jɜːrn] *v/i* anhelar
♦ **yearn for** *v/t* ansiar
yearn·ing ['jɜːrnɪŋ] *n* anhelo *m*

yeast [jiːst] levadura *f*
yell [jel] **1** *n* grito *m* **2** *v/i* gritar **3** *v/t* gritar
yel·low ['jelou] **1** *n* amarillo *m* **2** *adj* amarillo
yel·low 'pag·es *npl* páginas *fpl* amarillas
yelp [jelp] **1** *n* aullido *m* **2** *v/i* aullar
yes [jes] *int* sí; **she said yes** dijo que sí
'yes·man *pej* pelotillero *m*
yes·ter·day ['jestərdeɪ] **1** *adv* ayer; **the
day before yesterday** anteayer; **yesterday afternoon** ayer por la tarde **2** *n* ayer
m
yet [jet] **1** *adv* todavía, aún; **as yet** aún,
todavía; **have you finished yet?** ¿has
acabado ya?; **he hasn't arrived yet** todavía *or* aún no ha llegado; **is he here yet?
- not yet** ¿ha llegado ya? - todavía *or* aún
no; **yet bigger / longer** aún más grande /
largo; **the fastest one yet** el más rápido
hasta el momento **2** *conj* sin embargo;
yet I'm not sure sin embargo no estoy
seguro
yield [jiːld] **1** *n from fields etc* cosecha *f*;
from investment rendimiento *m* **2** *v/t
fruit, good harvest* proporcionar; *interest*
rendir, devengar **3** *v/i* (*give way*) ceder;
of driver ceder el paso
yo·ga ['jougə] yoga *m*
yog·hurt ['jougərt] yogur *m*
yolk [jouk] yema *f*
you [juː] *pron singular* tú, *L.Am.* usted,
Rpl, C.Am. vos; *formal* usted; *plural:
Span* vosotros, vosotras, *L.Am.* ustedes;

formal ustedes; **you are clever** eres / es inteligente; **do you know him?** ¿lo conoces / conoce?; **you go, I'll stay** tú ve / usted vaya, yo me quedo; **never know** nunca se sabe; **you have to pay** hay que pagar; **exercise is good for you** es bueno hacer ejercicio

young [jʌŋ] *adj* joven

young·ster ['jʌŋstər] joven *m/f*

your [jʊr] *adj singular:* tu, *L.Am.* su; *formal* su; *plural: Span* vuestro, *L.Am.* su; *formal* su; **your house** tu / su casa; **your books** tus / sus libros

yours [jʊrz] *pron singular* el tuyo, la tuya, *L.Am.* el suyo, la suya; *formal* el suyo, la suya; *plural* el vuestro, la vuestra, *L.Am.* el suyo, la suya; *formal* el suyo, la suya; **a friend of yours** un amigo tuyo / suyo / vuestro; **yours ...** *at end of letter* un saludo

your·self [jʊr'self] *pron reflexive* te, *L.Am.* se; *formal* se; *emphatic* tú mismo *m*, tú misma *f*, *L.Am.* usted mismo, usted misma; *Rpl, C.Am.* vos mismo, vos misma; *formal* usted mismo, usted misma; **did you hurt yourself?** ¿te hiciste / se hizo daño?; **when you see yourself in the**

mirror cuando te ves / se ve en el espejo; **by yourself** *(alone)* solo; *(without help)* tú solo, tú mismo, *Rpl, C.Am.* vos solo, vos mismo, *Am* usted solo, usted mismo; *formal* usted solo, usted mismo

your·selves [jʊr'selvz] *pron reflexive* os, *L.Am.* se; *formal* se; *emphatic* vosotros mismos *mpl*, vosotras mismas *fpl*, *Am* ustedes mismos, ustedes mismas; *formal* ustedes mismos, ustedes mismas; **did you hurt yourselves?** ¿os hicisteis / se hicieron daño?; **when you see yourselves in the mirror** cuando os veis / se ven en el espejo; **by yourselves** *(alone)* solos; *(without help)* vosotros solos, *Am* ustedes solos, ustedes mismos; *formal* ustedes solos, ustedes mismos

youth [juːθ] *n* juventud *f*; *(young man)* joven *m/f*

'youth club club *m* juvenil

youth·ful ['juːθfəl] *adj* joven; *fashion, idealism* juvenil

'youth hos·tel albergue *m* juvenil

Yu·go·sla·vi·a [juːgəˈslɑːvɪə] Yugoslavia

Yu·go·sla·vi·an [juːgəˈslɑːvɪən] **1** *adj* yugoslavo **2** *n* yugoslavo(-a) *m(f)*

yup·pie ['jʌpɪ] F yupi *m/f*

Z

zap [zæp] *v/t (pret & pp* **zapped***)* F (COMPUT: *delete)* borrar; *(kill)* liquidar F; *(hit)* golpear; *(send)* enviar
◆ **zap along** *v/i* F *(move fast)* volar F

zapped [zæpt] *adj* F *(exhausted)* hecho polvo F

zap·per ['zæpər] *for changing TV channels* telemando *m*, mando *m* a distancia

zap·py ['zæpɪ] *adj* F *car, pace* rápido; *(lively, energetic)* vivo

zeal [ziːl] celo *m*

ze·bra ['zebrə] cebra *f*

ze·ro ['zɪrou] cero *m*; **10 degrees below**

zero 10 bajo cero

ze·ro 'growth crecimiento *m* cero
◆ **zero in on** *v/t (identify)* centrarse en

zest [zest] entusiasmo *m*

zig·zag ['zɪgzæg] **1** *n* zigzag *m* **2** *v/i (pret & pp* **zigzagged***)* zigzaguear

zilch [zɪltʃ] F nada de nada

zinc [zɪŋk] cinc *m*

zip [zɪp] *Br* cremallera *f*
◆ **zip up** *v/t (pret & pp* **zipped***) dress, jacket* cerrar la cremallera de; COMPUT compactar

'zip code código *m* postal

zip·per ['zɪpər] cremallera *f*

zit [zɪt] F *on face* grano *m*

zo·di·ac ['zoudiæk] zodiaco *m*; **signs of the zodiac** signos *mpl* del zodiaco

zom·bie ['zɑːmbɪ] F (*idiot*) estúpido(-a) *m(f)* F; **feel like a zombie** (*exhausted*) sentirse como un zombi

zone [zoun] zona *f*

zonked [zɑːŋkt] *adj* P (*exhausted*) molido P

zoo [zuː] zoo *m*

zo·o·log·i·cal [zuːəˈlɑːdʒɪkl] *adj* zoológico

zo·ol·o·gist [zuːˈɑːlədʒɪst] zoólogo(-a) *m(f)*

zo·ol·o·gy [zuːˈɑːlədʒɪ] *v/i* F (*move fast*) ir zumbando F

zoom [zuːm] *v/i* F (*move fast*) ir zumbando F

♦ **zoom in on** *v/t* PHOT hacer un zoom sobre

zoom 'lens zoom *m*

zuc·chi·ni [zuːˈkiːnɪ] calabacín *m*

Z

Spanish verb conjugations

In the following conjugation patterns verb stems are shown in normal type and verb endings in *italic* type. Irregular forms are indicated by **bold** type.

Notes on the formation of tenses.

The following stems can be used to generate derived forms.

Stem forms	Derived forms
I. From the **Present indicative**, *3rd pers sg* (mand*a*, vend*e*, recib*e*)	**Imperative** *2nd pers. sg* (¡mand*a*! ¡vend*e*! ¡recib*e*!)
II. From the **Present subjunctive**, *2nd* and *3rd pers sg* and all plural forms (mand*es*, mand*e*, mand*emos*, mand*éis*, mand*en* – vend*as*, vend*a*, vend*amos*, vend*áis*, vend*an* – recib*as*, recib*a*, recib*amos*, recib*áis*, recib*an*)	**Imperative** *1st pers pl*, *3rd pers sg* and *pl* as well as the negative imperative of the *2nd pers sg* and *pl* (no mand*es*, mand*e* Vd., mand*emos*, no mand*éis*, mand*en* Vds. – no vend*as*, vend*a* Vd., vend*amos*, no vend*áis*, vend*an* Vds. – no recib*as* *etc*)
III. From the **Preterite**, *3rd pers pl* (mand*aron*, vend*ieron*, recib*ieron*)	a) **Imperfect Subjunctive I** by changing …*ron* to …*ra* (mand*ara*, vend*iera*, recib*iera*) b) **Imperfect Subjunctive II** by changing …*ron* to …*se* (mand*ase*, vend*iese*, recib*iese*) c) **Future Subjunctive** by changing …*ron* to …*re* (mand*are*, vend*iere*, recib*iere*)
IV. From the **Infinitive** (mand*ar*, vend*er*, recib*ir*)	a) **Imperative** *2nd pers pl* by changing …*r* to …*d* (mand*ad*, vend*ed*, recib*id*) b) **Present participle by** changing …*ar* to …*ando*, …*er* and …*ir* to …*iendo* (or sometimes …*yendo*) (mand*ando*, vend*iendo*, recib*iendo*) c) **Future** by adding the *Present* tense endings of **haber** (mand*aré*, vend*eré*, recib*iré*) d) **Conditional** by adding the *Imperfect* endings of **haber** (mand*aría*, vend*ería*, recib*iría*)

V. From the **Past participle** (mand*ado*, vend*ido*, recib*ido*)	all **compound tenses** by placing a form of ***haber*** or ***ser*** in front of the participle.

First Conjugation

⟨**1a**⟩ mandar. No change to the written or spoken form of the stem.

Simple tenses

Indicative

	Present	**Imperfect**	**Preterite**
sg	mand*o*	mand*aba*	mand*é*
	mand*as*	mand*abas*	mand*aste*
	mand*a*	mand*aba*	mand*ó*
pl	mand*amos*	mand*ábamos*	mand*amos*
	mand*áis*	mand*abais*	mand*asteis*
	mand*an*	mand*aban*	mand*aron*

	Future	**Conditional**
sg	mand*aré*	mand*aría*
	mand*arás*	mand*arías*
	mand*ará*	mand*aría*
pl	mand*aremos*	mand*aríamos*
	mand*aréis*	mand*aríais*
	mand*arán*	mand*arían*

Subjunctive

Present		**Imperfect I**	**Imperfect II**
sg	mand*e*	mand*ara*	mand*ase*
	mand*es*	mand*aras*	mand*ases*
	mand*e*	mand*ara*	mand*ase*
pl	mand*emos*	mand*áramos*	mand*ásemos*
	mand*éis*	mand*arais*	mand*aseis*
	mand*en*	mand*aran*	mand*asen*

	Future	**Imperative**
sg	mand*are*	—
	mand*ares*	mand*a* (no mand*es*)
	mand*are*	mand*e* Vd.
pl	mand*áremos*	mand*emos*
	mand*areis*	mand*ad* (no mand*éis*)
	mand*aren*	mand*en* Vds.

Infinitive: mand*ar*
Present participle: mand*ando*
Past participle: mand*ado*

Compound tenses

1. **Active forms:** the conjugated form of **_haber_** is placed before the *Past participle* (which does not change):

Indicative

Perfect	*he* mand*ado*	**Future perfect**	*habré* mand*ado*
Pluperfect	*había* mand*ado*	**Past conditional**	*habría* mand*ado*
Past anterior	*hube* mand*ado*		

Past infinitive	*haber* mand*ado*	**Past gerundive**	*habiendo* mand*ado*

Subjunctive

Perfect	*haya* mand*ado*	**Future perfect**	*hubiere* mand*ado*
Pluperfect	*hubiera* mand*ado*		
	hubiese mand*ado*		

2. **Passive forms:** the conjugated form of **_ser_** (or **_haber_**) is placed before the *Past participle* (which does not change):

Indicative

Present	*soy* mand*ado*	**Past anterior**	*hube sido* mand*ado*
Imperfect	*era* mand*ado*	**Future**	*seré* mand*ado*
Preterite	*fui* mand*ado*	**Future perfect**	*habré sido* mand*ado*
Perfect	*he sido* mand*ado*	**Conditional**	*sería* mand*ado*
Pluperfect	*había sido* mand*ado*	**Past conditional**	*habría sido* mand*ado*

Infinitive		Gerundive	
Present	*ser* mand*ado* etc	**Present**	*siendo* mand*ado*
Past	*haber sido* mand*ado*	**Past**	*habiendo sido* mand*ado*

Subjunctive

Present	*sea* mand*ado*	**Pluperfect**	*hubiera sido* man*dado*
			hubiese sido mand*ado*
Imperfect	*fuera* mand*ado*		
	fuese mand*ado*		
Future	*fuere* mand*ado*	**Future perfect**	*hubiere sido* mand*ado*
Past	*haya sido* mand*ado*		

	Infinitive	Present Indicative	Present Subjunctive	Preterite

⟨**1b**⟩ **cambiar.** Model for all *...iar* verbs, unless formed like *variar* ⟨1c⟩.

	cambio	cambie	cambié
	cambias	cambies	cambiaste
	cambia	cambie	cambió
	cambiamos	cambiemos	cambiamos
	cambiáis	cambiéis	cambiasteis
	cambian	cambien	cambiaron

⟨**1c**⟩ **variar.** *i* becomes *í* when the stem is stressed.

	varío	varíe	varié
	varías	varíes	variaste
	varía	varíe	varió
	variamos	variemos	variamos
	variáis	variéis	variasteis
	varían	varíen	variaron

⟨**1d**⟩ **evacuar.** Model for all *...uar* verbs, unless formed like *acentuar* ⟨1e⟩.

	evacuo	evacue	evacué
	evacuas	evacues	evacuaste
	evacua	evacue	evacuó
	evacuamos	evacuemos	evacuamos
	evacuáis	evacuéis	evacuasteis
	evacuan	evacuen	evacuaron

⟨**1e**⟩ **acentuar.** *u* becomes *ú* when the stem is stressed.

	acentúo	acentúe	acentué
	acentúas	acentúes	acentuaste
	acentúa	acentúe	acentuó
	acentuamos	acentuemos	acentuamos
	acentuáis	acentuéis	acentuasteis
	acentúan	acentúen	acentuaron

⟨**1f**⟩ **cruzar.** Final *z* in the stem becomes *c* before *e*. Model for all *...zar* verbs.

	cruzo	cruce	crucé
	cruzas	cruces	cruzaste
	cruza	cruce	cruzó
	cruzamos	crucemos	cruzamos
	cruzáis	crucéis	cruzasteis
	cruzan	crucen	cruzaron

	Infinitive	Present Indicative	Present Subjunctive	Preterite

⟨1g⟩ **tocar.** Final *c* in the stem becomes *qu* before *e*. Model for all ...*car* verbs.

		Present Indicative	Present Subjunctive	Preterite
		to*co*	to**qu**e	to**qu**é
		to*cas*	to**qu**es	to*caste*
		to*ca*	to**qu**e	to**c**ó
		to*camos*	to**qu**emos	to*camos*
		to*cáis*	to**qu**éis	to*casteis*
		to*can*	to**qu**en	to*caron*

⟨1h⟩ **pagar.** Final *g* in the stem becomes *gu* (*u* is silent) before *e*. Model for all ...*gar* verbs.

		pa*go*	pa**gu**e	pa**gu**é
		pa*gas*	pa**gu**es	pa*gaste*
		pa*ga*	pa**gu**e	pa*gó*
		pa*gamos*	pa**gu**emos	pa*gamos*
		pa*gáis*	pa**gu**éis	pa*gasteis*
		pa*gan*	pa**gu**en	pa*garon*

⟨1i⟩ **fraguar.** Final *gu* in the stem becomes *gü* before *e* (*u* with dieresis is pronounced). Model for all ...*guar* verbs.

		frag*uo*	frag**ü**e	frag**ü**é
		frag*uas*	frag**ü**es	frag*uaste*
		frag*ua*	frag**ü**e	frag*uó*
		frag*uamos*	frag**ü**emos	frag*uamos*
		frag*uáis*	frag**ü**éis	frag*uasteis*
		frag*uan*	frag**ü**en	frag*uaron*

⟨1k⟩ **pensar.** Stressed *e* in the stem becomes *ie*.

		p**ie**ns*o*	p**ie**nse	pens*é*
		p**ie**ns*as*	p**ie**nses	pens*aste*
		p**ie**ns*a*	p**ie**nse	pens*ó*
		pens*amos*	pensemos	pens*amos*
		pens*áis*	penséis	pens*asteis*
		p**ie**ns*an*	p**ie**nsen	pens*aron*

⟨1l⟩ **errar.** Stressed *e* in the stem becomes *ye* (because it comes at the beginning of the word).

		yerr*o*	**ye**rre	err*é*
		yerr*as*	**ye**rres	err*aste*
		yerr*a*	**ye**rre	err*ó*
		err*amos*	erremos	err*amos*
		err*áis*	erréis	err*asteis*
		yerr*an*	**ye**rren	err*aron*

	Infinitive	Present Indicative	Present Subjunctive	Preterite

⟨1m⟩ **contar.** Stressed *o* of the stem becomes *ue* (*u* is pronounced).

		cuento	cuente	conté
		cuentas	cuentes	contaste
		cuenta	cuente	contó
		contamos	contemos	contamos
		contáis	contéis	contasteis
		cuentan	cuenten	contaron

⟨1n⟩ **agorar.** Stressed *o* of the stem becomes *üe* (*u* with dieresis is pronounced).

		agüero	agüere	agoré
		agüeras	agüeres	agoraste
		agüera	agüere	agoró
		agoramos	agoremos	agoramos
		agoráis	agoréis	agorasteis
		agüeran	agüeren	agoraron

⟨1o⟩ **jugar.** Stressed *u* in the stem becomes *ue*; final *g* of the stem becomes *gu* before *e*: (see ⟨1h⟩); *conjugar, enjugar* and *enjugarse* are regular.

		juego	juegue	jugué
		juegas	juegues	jugaste
		juega	juegue	jugó
		jugamos	juguemos	jugamos
		jugáis	juguéis	jugasteis
		juegan	jueguen	jugaron

⟨1p⟩ **estar.** *Present indicative 1st pers sg in …oy*, otherwise regular, but note the stressed *a*; the *Present subjunctive* has a stress on the *e* in the endings (apart from *1st pers pl*); *Preterite etc as* ⟨21⟩. Otherwise regular.

		estoy	esté	estuve
		estás	estés	estuviste
		está	esté	estuvo
		estamos	estemos	estuvimos
		estáis	estéis	estuvisteis
		están	estén	estuvieron

⟨1q⟩ **andar.** *Preterite and derived forms like* estar *as in* ⟨21⟩. *Otherwise regular.*

		ando	ande	anduve
		andas	andes	anduviste
		anda	ande	anduvo
		andamos	andemos	anduvimos
		andáis	andéis	anduvisteis
		andan	anden	anduvieron

Infinitive	Present Indicative	Present Subjunctive	Preterite

⟨1r⟩ **dar.** *Present indicative 1st pers sg in …oy,* otherwise regular. *Present subjunctive 1st* and *3rd pers sg* takes an accent. *Preterite etc* follow the regular second conjugation. Otherwise regular.

	doy	dé	di
	das	des	diste
	da	dé	dio
	damos	demos	dimos
	dáis	deis	disteis
	dan	den	dieron

Second Conjugation

⟨2a⟩ **vender.** No change to the written or spoken form of the stem.

Simple tenses

Indicative

	Present	**Imperfect**	**Preterite**
sg	vend*o*	vend*ía*	vend*í*
	vend*es*	vend*ías*	vend*iste*
	vend*e*	vend*ía*	vend*ió*
pl	vend*emos*	vend*íamos*	vend*imos*
	vend*éis*	vend*íais*	vend*isteis*
	vend*en*	vend*ían*	vend*ieron*

	Future	**Conditional**
sg	vend*eré*	vend*ería*
	vend*erás*	vend*erías*
	vend*erá*	vend*ería*
pl	vend*eremos*	vend*eríamos*
	vend*eréis*	vend*eríais*
	vend*erán*	vend*erían*

Subjunctive

	Present	**Imperfect I**	**Imperfect II**
sg	vend*a*	vend*iera*	vend*iese*
	vend*as*	vend*ieras*	vend*ieses*
	vend*a*	vend*iera*	vend*iese*
pl	vend*amos*	vend*iéramos*	vend*iésemos*
	vend*áis*	vend*ierais*	vend*ieseis*
	vend*an*	vend*ieran*	vend*iesen*

	Future	**Imperative**
sg	vend*iere*	—
	vend*ieres*	vend*e* (no vend*as*)
	vend*iere*	vend*a* Vd.
pl	vend*iéremos*	vend*amos*
	vend*iereis*	vend*ed* (no vend*áis*)
	vend*ieren*	vend*an* Vds.

Infinitive: vend*er*
Present participle: vend*iendo*
Past participle: vend*ido*

Compound tenses

Formed with the *Past participle* together with **haber** and **ser**, see ⟨1a⟩.

Infinitive	Present Indicative	Present Subjunctive	Preterite

⟨2b⟩ **vencer.** Final *c* of the stem becomes *z* bevore *a* and *o*. Model for all ...*cer* verbs where the ...*cer* is proceded by a consonant.

	venzo	venza	vencí
	vences	venzas	venciste
	vence	venza	venció
	vencemos	venzamos	vencimos
	vencéis	venzáis	vencisteis
	vencen	venzan	vencieron

⟨2c⟩ **coger.** Final *g* of the stem becomes *j* before *a* and *o*. Model for all ...*ger* verbs.

	cojo	coja	cogí
	coges	cojas	cogiste
	coge	coja	cogió
	cogemos	cojamos	cogimos
	cogéis	cojáis	cogisteis
	cogen	cojan	cogieron

⟨2d⟩ **merecer.** Final *c* of the stem becomes *zc* before *a* and *o*.

	merezco	merezca	merecí
	mereces	merezcas	mereciste
	merece	merezca	mereció
	merecemos	merezcamos	merecimos
	merecéis	merezcáis	merecisteis
	merecen	merezcan	merecieron

⟨2e⟩ **creer.** Unstressed *i* between two vowels becomes *y*. Past participle: *creído*. Present participle: *creyendo*.

	creo	crea	creí
	crees	creas	creíste
	cree	crea	creyó
	creemos	creamos	creímos
	creéis	creáis	creísteis
	creen	crean	creyeron

⟨2f⟩ **tañer.** Unstressed *i* is omitted after *ñ* and *ll*; compare ⟨3h⟩ Present participle: *tañendo*.

	taño	taña	tañí
	tañes	tañas	tañiste
	tañe	taña	taño
	tañemos	tañamos	tañimos
	tañéis	tañáis	tañisteis
	tañen	tañan	tañeron

	Infinitive	Present Indicative	Present Subjunctive	Preterite

⟨2g⟩ **perder.** Stressed *e* in the stem becomes *ie*; model for many other verbs.

	pierdo	pierda	perdí
	pierdes	pierdas	perdiste
	pierde	pierda	perdió
	perdemos	perdamos	perdimos
	perdéis	perdáis	perdisteis
	pierden	pierdan	perdieron

⟨2h⟩ **mover.** Stressed *o* in the stem becomes *ue*. ...*olver* verbs form their *Past participle* with ...*uelto*.

	muevo	mueva	moví
	mueves	muevas	moviste
	mueve	mueva	movió
	movemos	movamos	movimos
	movéis	mováis	movisteis
	mueven	muevan	movieron

⟨2i⟩ **oler.** Stressed *o* in the stem becomes *hue*... (when it comes at the beginning of the word).

	huelo	huela	olí
	hueles	huelas	oliste
	huele	huela	olió
	olemos	olamos	olimos
	oléis	oláis	olisteis
	huelen	huelan	olieron

⟨2k⟩ **haber.** Many irregular forms. In the *Future* and *Conditional* the *e* after the stem *hab*... is dropped. Future: *habré*. Imperative *2nd pers sg*: *he*.

	he	haya	hube
	has	hayas	hubiste
	ha	haya	hubo
	hemos	hayamos	hubimos
	habéis	hayáis	hubisteis
	han	hayan	hubieron

⟨2l⟩ **tener.** Irregular in most forms. In the *Future* and *Conditional* the *e* coming after the stem is dropped and a *d* is inserted. Future: *tendré*. Imperative *2nd pers sg*: *ten*.

	tengo	tenga	tuve
	tienes	tengas	tuviste
	tiene	tenga	tuvo
	tenemos	tengamos	tuvimos
	tenéis	tengáis	tuvisteis
	tienen	tengan	tuvieron

	Infinitive	Present Indicative	Present Subjunctive	Preterite

⟨2m⟩ **caber.** Irregular in many forms. In the *Future* and *Conditional* the *e* coming after the stem is dropped. Future: *cabré.*

	quep*o*	quep*a*	cup*e*
	cab*es*	quep*as*	cup*iste*
	cab*e*	quep*a*	cup*o*
	cab*emos*	quep*amos*	cup*imos*
	cab*éis*	quep*áis*	cup*isteis*
	cab*en*	quep*an*	cup*ieron*

⟨2n⟩ **saber.** Irregular in many forms. In the *Future* and *Conditional* the *e* coming after the stem is dropped. Future: *sabré.*

	sé	sep*a*	sup*e*
	sab*es*	sep*as*	sup*iste*
	sab*e*	sep*a*	sup*o*
	sab*emos*	sep*amos*	sup*imos*
	sab*éis*	sep*áis*	sup*isteis*
	sab*en*	sep*an*	sup*ieron*

⟨2o⟩ **caer.** In the *Present* …*ig*… is inserted after the stem. Unstressed *i* between vowels changes to *y* as with ⟨2e⟩. Past participle: *caído.* Present participle: *cayendo.*

	ca*igo*	ca*iga*	ca*í*
	ca*es*	ca*igas*	ca*íste*
	ca*e*	ca*iga*	ca*yó*
	ca*emos*	ca*igamos*	ca*ímos*
	ca*éis*	ca*igáis*	ca*ísteis*
	ca*en*	ca*igan*	ca*yeron*

⟨2p⟩ **traer.** In the *Present* …*ig*… is inserted after the stem. The *Preterite* ends in …*je.* In the *Present participle i* changes to *y.* Past participle: *traído.* Present participle: *trayendo.*

	tra*igo*	tra*iga*	tra*je*
	tra*es*	tra*igas*	tra*jiste*
	tra*e*	tra*iga*	tra*jo*
	tra*emos*	tra*igamos*	tra*jimos*
	tra*éis*	tra*igáis*	tra*jisteis*
	tra*en*	tra*igan*	tra*jeron*

	Infinitive	Present Indicative	Present Subjunctive	Preterite

⟨2q⟩ **valer.** In the *Present* …*g*… is inserted after the stem. In the *Future* and *Conditional* the *e* coming after the stem is dropped and a …*d*… inserted. Future: *valdré*.

val*go*	val*ga*	val*í*	
val*es*	val*gas*	val*iste*	
val*e*	val*ga*	val*ió*	
val*emos*	val*gamos*	val*imos*	
val*éis*	val*gáis*	val*isteis*	
val*en*	val*gan*	val*ieron*	

⟨2r⟩ **poner.** …*g*… is inserted in the *Present*. Irregular in the *Preterite* and *Past participle*. In the *Future* and *Conditional* the *e* coming after the stem is dropped and a …*d*… inserted. Future: *pondré*. Past participle: *puesto*. Imperative *2nd pers sg*: *pon*.

pon*go*	pon*ga*	pus*e*	
pon*es*	pon*gas*	pus*iste*	
pon*e*	pon*ga*	pus*o*	
pon*emos*	pon*gamos*	pus*imos*	
pon*éis*	pon*gáis*	pus*isteis*	
pon*en*	pon*gan*	pus*ieron*	

⟨2s⟩ **hacer.** In the *1st* person of the *Present Indicative* and *Subjunctive g* replaces *c*. Irregular in the *Preterite* and *Past participle*. In the *Future* and *Conditional* the *ce* is dropped. In the *Imperative sg* just the stem is used with …*c* changing to …*z*. Future: *haré*. Imperative *2nd pers sg*: *haz*. Past participle: *hecho*.

ha*go*	ha*ga*	hic*e*	
hac*es*	ha*gas*	hic*iste*	
hac*e*	ha*ga*	hiz*o*	
hac*emos*	ha*gamos*	hic*imos*	
hac*éis*	ha*gáis*	hic*isteis*	
hac*en*	ha*gan*	hic*ieron*	

⟨2t⟩ **poder.** Stressed *o* in the stem changes to …*ue*… in the *Present* and the *Imperative*. Irregular in the *Preterite* and *Present participle*. In the *Future* and *Conditional* the *e* coming after the stem is dropped. Future: *podré*. Present participle: *pudiendo*.

pued*o*	pued*a*	pud*e*	
pued*es*	pued*as*	pud*iste*	
pued*e*	pued*a*	pud*o*	
pod*emos*	pod*amos*	pud*imos*	
pod*éis*	pod*áis*	pud*isteis*	
pued*en*	pued*an*	pud*ieron*	

	Infinitive	Present Indicative	Present Subjunctive	Preterite

⟨2u⟩ **querer.** Stressed *e* in the stem changes to *ie* in the *Present* and *Imperative*. Irregular in the *Preterite*. In the *Future* and *Conditional* the *e* coming after the stem is dropped. Future: *querré*.

	quiero	quiera	quise
	quieres	quieras	quisiste
	quiere	quiera	quiso
	queremos	queramos	quisimos
	queréis	queráis	quisisteis
	quieren	quieran	quisieron

⟨2v⟩ **ver.** *Present indicative 1st pers sg, Present subjunctive* and *Imperfect* are formed on the stem *ve*…, otherwise formation is regular using the shortened stem *v*… Irregular in the *Past participle*. Past participle: *visto*.

	veo	vea	vi
	ves	veas	viste
	ve	vea	vio
	vemos	veamos	vimos
	veis	veáis	visteis
	ven	vean	vieron

659

Infinitive	Present Indicative	Present Subjunctive	Imperfect Indicative	Preterite

⟨2w⟩ **ser.** Totally irregular with several different stems being used. Past participle: *sido*. Imperative *2nd pers sg: sé. 2nd pers pl: sed.*

	soy	sea	era	fui
	eres	seas	eras	fuiste
	es	sea	era	fue
	somos	seamos	éramos	fuimos
	sois	seáis	erais	fuisteis
	son	sean	eran	fueron

⟨2x⟩ **placer.** Used almost exclusively in the *3rd pers sg.* Irregular forms: *Present subjunctive plega* and *plegue* egue as well as *plazca; Preterite plugo* (or *plació*), *pluguieron* (or *placieron*); *Imperfect subjunctive pluguiera, pluguiese* (or *placiera, placiese*); *Future subjunctive pluguiere* (or *placiere*).

⟨2y⟩ **yacer.** Used mainly on gravestones and so used primarily in the *3rd pers.* The *Present indicative 1st pers sg* and *Present subjunctive* have three forms. The *Imperative* is regular; just the stem with *c* changing to *z*. *Present indicative: yazco, yazgo, yago, yaces* etc; *Present subjunctive: yazca, yazga, yaga* etc; *Imperative yace* and *yaz.*

⟨2z⟩ **raer.** The regular forms of the *Present indicative 1st pers sg* and *Present subjunctive* are less common than the forms with inserted *...ig...* as in ⟨2o⟩: *raigo, raiga*; but also *rayo, raya* (less common). Otherwise regular.

⟨2za⟩ **roer.** As well as their regular forms the *Present indicative 1st pers sg* and *Present subjunctive* have the less common forms: *roigo, roiga, royo, roya.*

Third Conjugation

⟨3a⟩ **recibir.** No change to the written or spoken form of the stem.

Simple tenses

Indicative

	Present	**Imperfect**	**Preterite**
sg	recibo	recibía	recibí
	recibes	recibías	recibiste
	recibe	recibía	recibió
pl	recibimos	recibíamos	recibimos
	recibís	recibíais	recibisteis
	reciben	recibían	recibieron

	Future	**Conditional**
sg	recibiré	recibiría
	recibirás	recibirías
	recibirá	recibiría
pl	recibiremos	recibiríamos
	recibiréis	recibiríais
	recibirán	recibirían

Subjunctive

	Present	**Imperfect I**	**Imperfect II**
sg	reciba	recibiera	recibiese
	recibas	recibieras	recibieses
	reciba	recibiera	recibiese
pl	recibamos	recibiéramos	recibiésemos
	recibáis	recibierais	recibieseis
	reciban	recibieran	recibiesen

	Future	**Imperative**
sg	recibiere	—
	recibieres	recibe (no recibas)
	recibiere	reciba Vd.
pl	recibiéremos	recibamos
	recibiereis	recibid (no recibáis)
	recibieren	reciban Vds.

Infinitive: recibir
Present participle: recibiendo
Past participle: recibido

Compound tenses

Formed with the *Past participle* together with **haber** and **ser**, see ⟨1a⟩.

	Infinitive	Present Indicative	Present Subjunctive	Preterite
⟨3b⟩	esparcir. Final *c* of the stem becomes *z* before *a* and *o*.			
		esparzo	esparza	esparcí
		esparces	esparzas	esparciste
		esparce	esparza	esparció
		esparcimos	esparzamos	esparcimos
		esparcís	esparzáis	esparcisteis
		esparcen	esparzan	esparcieron
⟨3c⟩	dirigir. Final *g* of the stem becomes *j* before *a* and *o*.			
		dirijo	dirija	dirigí
		diriges	dirijas	dirigiste
		dirige	dirija	dirigió
		dirigimos	dirijamos	dirigimos
		dirigís	dirijáis	dirigisteis
		dirigen	dirijan	dirigieron
⟨3d⟩	distinguir. Final *gu* of the stem becomes *g* before *a* and *o*.			
		distingo	distinga	distinguí
		distingues	distingas	distinguiste
		distingue	distinga	distinguió
		distinguimos	distingamos	distinguimos
		distinguís	distingáis	distinguisteis
		distinguen	distingan	distinguieron
⟨3e⟩	delinquir. Final *qu* of the stem becomes *c* before *a* and *o*.			
		delinco	delinca	delinquí
		delinques	delincas	delinquiste
		delinque	delinca	delinquió
		delinquimos	delincamos	delinquimos
		delinquís	delincáis	delinquisteis
		delinquen	delincan	delinquieron
⟨3f⟩	lucir. Final *c* of the stem becomes *zc* before *a* and *o*.			
		luzco	luzca	lucí
		luces	luzcas	luciste
		luce	luzca	lució
		lucimos	luzcamos	lucimos
		lucís	luzcáis	lucisteis
		lucen	luzcan	lucieron

662

	Infinitive	Present Indicative	Present Subjunctive	Preterite

⟨3g⟩ **concluir.** A *y* is inserted after the stem unless the ending begins with *i*. Past participle: *concluido*. Present participle: *concluyendo*.

concluyo	concluya	concluí
concluyes	concluyas	concluiste
concluye	concluya	concluyó
concluimos	concluyamos	concluimos
concluís	concluyáis	concluisteis
concluyen	concluyan	concluyeron

⟨3h⟩ **gruñir.** Unstressed *i* is dropped after *ñ*, *ll* and *ch*. Likewise *mullir: mulló, mulleron, mullendo; henchir: hinchó, hincheron, hinchendo* Present participle: *gruñendo*.

gruño	gruñes	gruñe
gruñimos	gruñís	gruñen
gruña	gruñí	gruñas
gruñiste	gruña	gruñó
gruñamos	gruñimos	gruñáis
gruñisteis	gruñan	gruñeron

⟨3i⟩ **sentir.** Stressed *e* of the stem becomes *ie*; unstressed *e* remains unchanged before endings starting with *i*, but before other endings it changes to ...*i*...; likewise *adquirir*: stressed *i* of the stem becomes *ie*; unstressed *i* remains unchanged in all forms. Present participle: *sintiendo*.

siento	sienta	sentí
sientes	sientas	sentiste
siente	sienta	sintió
sentimos	sintamos	sentimos
sentís	sintáis	sentisteis
sienten	sientan	sintieron

⟨3k⟩ **dormir.** Stressed *o* of the stem becomes *ue*; unstressed *o* is unchanged when the ending starts with *i*; otherwise it changes to ...*u*... Present participle: *durmiendo*.

duermo	duerma	dormí
duermes	duermas	dormiste
duerme	duerma	durmió
dormimos	durmamos	dormimos
dormís	durmáis	dormisteis
duermen	duerman	durmieron

	Infinitive	Present Indicative	Present Subjunctive	Preterite

⟨3l⟩ **medir.** The *e* of the stem is kept if the ending contains an *i*. Otherwise it changes to ...*i*... whether stressed or unstressed. Present participle: *midiendo*.

mid*o*	mid*a*	med*í*
mid*es*	mid*as*	med*iste*
mid*e*	mid*a*	mid*ió*
med*imos*	mid*amos*	med*imos*
med*ís*	mid*áis*	med*isteis*
mid*en*	mid*an*	mid*ieron*

⟨3m⟩ **reír.** As *medir* ⟨3l⟩; when *e* changes to *i* any second *i* belonging to the ending is dropped. Past participle: *reído*. Present participle: *riendo*.

rí*o*	rí*a*	reí
rí*es*	rí*as*	reí*ste*
rí*e*	rí*a*	rió
rei*mos*	ri*amos*	reí*mos*
reí*s*	ri*áis*	reí*steis*
rí*en*	rí*an*	rieron

⟨3n⟩ **erguir.** As *medir* in the *Present indicative*, *Subjunctive* and *Imperative*. Other forms follow *sentir* with initial *ie*... changing to *ye*... Present participle: *irguiendo*. Imperative: *irgue, yergue*.

irg*o*, yerg*o*	irg*a*, yerg*a*	*erguí*
irg*ues*, yerg*ues*	irg*as*, yerg*as*	erg*uiste*
irg*ue*, yerg*ue*	irg*a*, yerg*a*	irg*uió*
erg*uimos*	irg*amos*, yerg*amos*	erg*uimos*
erg*uís*	irg*áis*, yerg*áis*	erg*uisteis*
irg*uen*, yerg*uen*	irg*an*, yerg*an*	irg*uieron*

⟨3o⟩ **conducir.** Final *c* of the stem, as with *lucir* ⟨3f⟩, becomes *zc* before *a* and *o*. *Preterite* is irregular with ...*je*.

conduz*co*	conduz*ca*	conduj*e*
conduz*ces*	conduz*cas*	conduj*iste*
conduz*ce*	conduz*ca*	conduj*o*
conduz*imos*	conduz*camos*	conduj*imos*
conduz*ís*	conduz*cáis*	conduj*isteis*
conduz*cen*	conduz*can*	conduj*eron*

Infinitive	Present Indicative	Present Subjunctive	Preterite

⟨3p⟩ **decir.** In the *Present* and *Imperative* e and i are changed, as with *medir*; in the *Present indicative 1st pers sg* and in the *Present subjunctive* c becomes g. Irregular *Future* and *Conditional* based on a shortened *Infinitive*. *Preterite* has je. Future: *diré*. Past participle: *dicho*. Present participle: *diciendo*. Imperative *2nd pers sg*: *di*.

di**g**o	di**g**a	di**je**
di**c**es	di**g**as	di**j**iste
di**c**e	di**g**a	di**j**o
de**c**imos	di**g**amos	di**j**imos
de**c**ís	di**g**áis	di**j**isteis
di**c**en	di**g**an	di**j**eron

⟨3q⟩ **oír.** In the *Present indicative 1st pers sg* and *Present subjunctive* ...ig... is inserted after the o... of the stem. Unstressed ...i... changes to ...y... when coming between two vowels. Past participle: *oído*. Present participle: *oyendo*.

o**ig**o	o**ig**a	oí
o**y**es	o**ig**as	oíste
o**y**e	o**ig**a	o**y**ó
o**í**mos	o**ig**amos	oímos
oís	o**ig**áis	oísteis
o**y**en	o**ig**an	o**y**eron

⟨3rk⟩ **salir.** In the *Present indicative 1st pers sg* and the *Present subjunctive* a ...g... is inserted after the stem. In the *Future* and *Conditional* the i is replaced by d. Future: *saldré*. Imperative: *2nd pers sg*: *sal*.

sal**g**o	sal**g**a	salí
sal**e**s	sal**g**as	saliste
sal**e**	sal**g**a	salió
sal**i**mos	sal**g**amos	salimos
sal**í**s	sal**g**áis	salisteis
sal**e**n	sal**g**an	salieron

Infinitive	Present Indicative	Present Subjunctive	Imperfect Indicative	Preterite

⟨3s⟩ **venir.** In the *Present* two changes: either a ...*g*... is inserted after the stem or *e, ie* and *i* follow the same changes as *sentir*. In the *Future* and *Conditional* the *i* is dropped and replaced by *d*. Future: *vendré*. Present participle: *viniendo*. Imperative *2nd pers sg*: *ven*.

ven*go*	ven*ga*	ven*ía*	vin*e*
vien*es*	ven*gas*	ven*ías*	vin*iste*
vien*e*	ven*ga*	ven*ía*	vin*o*
ven*imos*	ven*gamos*	ven*íamos*	vin*imos*
ven*ís*	ven*gáis*	ven*íais*	vin*isteis*
vien*en*	ven*gan*	ven*ían*	vin*ieron*

⟨3t⟩ **ir.** Totally irregular with several different stems being used. Present participle: *yendo*

voy	**vaya**	**iba**	**fui**
vas	**vayas**	**ibas**	**fuiste**
va	**vaya**	**iba**	**fue**
vamos	**vayamos**	**íbamos**	**fuimos**
vais	**vayáis**	**ibais**	**fuisteis**
van	**vayan**	**iban**	**fueron**

Imperative: **ve** (no **vayas**), **vaya** Vd, **vamos**, **id** (no **vayáis**), **vayan** Vds.

Notas sobre el verbo inglés

a) Conjugación

1. **El tiempo presente** tiene la misma forma que el infinitivo en todas las personas menos la **3ª** del singular; en ésta, se añade una *-s* al infinitivo, p.ej. *he brings*, o se añade *-es* si el infinitivo termina en sibilante (ch, sh, ss, zz), p.ej. *he passes*. Esta *s* tiene dos pronunciaciones distintas: tras consonante sorda se pronuncia sorda, p.ej. *he paints* [peɪnts]; tras consonante sonora se pronuncia sonora, *he sends* [sendz]; *-es* se pronuncia también sonora, sea la *e* parte de la desinencia o letra final del infinitivo, p.ej. *he washes* [wɑˈʃɪz], *he urges* [ˈɜːrdʒɪz]. Los verbos que terminan en *-y* la cambian en *-ies* en la tercera persona, p.ej. *he worries, he tries*, pero son regulares los verbos que en el infinitivo tienen una vocal delante de la *-y*, p.ej. *he plays*. El verbo *to be* es irregular en todas las personas: *I am, you are, he is, we are, you are, they are*. Tres verbos más tienen forma especial para la tercera persona del singular: *do-he does, go-he goes, have-he has*.

   En los demás tiempos, todas las personas son iguales. **El pretérito y el participio del pasado** se forman añadiendo *-ed* al infinitivo, p.ej. *I passed, passed*, o añadiendo *-d* a los infinitivos que terminan en *-e*, p.ej. *I faced, faced*. (Hay muchos verbos irregulares: v. abajo). Esta *-(e)d* se pronuncia generalmente como [t]: *passed* [pæst], *faced* [feɪst]; pero cuando se añade a un infinitivo que termina en consonante sonora o en sonido consonántico sonoro o en *r*, se pronuncia como [d]: *warmed* [wɔːrmd], *moved* [muːvd], *feared* [fɪrd]. Si el infinitivo termina en *-d* o *-t*, la desinencia *-ed* se pronuncia [ɪd]. Si el infinitivo termina en *-y*, ésta se cambia en *-ie*, antes de añadirse la *-d*: *try-tried* [traɪd], *pity-pitied* [pɪtɪd]. **Los tiempos compuestos del pasado** se forman con el verbo auxiliar *have* y el participio del pasado, como en español: **perfecto** *I have faced*, **pluscuamperfecto** *I had faced*. Con el verbo auxiliar *will* (*shall*) y el infinitivo se forma **el futuro**, p.ej. *I shall face*; y con el verbo auxiliar *would* (*should*) y el infinitivo se forma **el condicional**, p.ej. *I should face*. En cada tiempo existe además una forma continua que se forma con el verbo *be* (= estar) y el participio del presente (v. abajo): *I am going, I was writing, I had been staying, I shall be waiting*, etc.

2. **El subjuntivo** ha dejado casi de existir en inglés, salvo en algún caso especial (*if I were you, so be it, it is proposed that a vote be taken*, etc.). En el presente, tiene en todas las personas la misma forma que el infinitivo, *that I go, that he go*, etc.

3. **El participio del presente** y **el gerundio** tienen la misma forma en inglés, añadiéndose al infinitivo la desinencia *-ing*: *painting, sending*. Pero 1) Los verbos cuyo infinitivo termina en *-e* muda la pierden al añadir *-ing*, p.ej. *love-loving, write-writing* (excepciones que conservan la *-e*: *dye-dyeing, singe-singeing*); 2) El participio del presente de los verbos *die, lie, vie*, etc. se escribe *dying, lying, vying*, etc.

4. Existe una clase de verbos ligeramente irregulares, que terminan en consonante simple precedida de vocal simple acentuada; en éstos, antes de añadir la desinencia -*ing* o -*ed*, se dobla la consonante:

lob	lob*bed*	lob*bing*	compel	compel*led*	compel*ling*
wed	wed*ded*	wed*ding*	control	control*led*	control*ling*
beg	beg*ged*	beg*ging*	bar	bar*red*	bar*ring*
step	step*ped*	step*ping*	stir	stir*red*	stir*ring*
quit	quit*ted*	quit*ting*			

Los verbos que terminan en -*l*, -*p*, aunque precedida de vocal átona, tienen doblada la consonante en los dos participios en el inglés escrito en Gran Bretaña, aunque no en el de Estados Unidos:

travel	trave*led*,	trave*ling*,
	Br travel*led*,	*Br* travel*led*

Los verbos que terminan en -*c* la cambian en -*ck* al añadirse las desinencias -*ed*, -*ing*:

traffic	traffi*cked*	traffi*cking*

5. La voz pasiva se forma exactamente como en español, con el verbo *be* y el participio del pasado: *I am obliged, he was fined, they will be moved,* etc.

6. Cuando se dirige uno directamente a otra(s) persona(s) en inglés se emplea únicamente el pronombre *you. You* se traduce por el *tú, vosotros, usted* y *ustedes* del español.

b) Los verbos irregulares ingleses

Se citan las tres partes principales de cada verbo: infinitivo, pretérito, participio del pasado.

alight - alighted, alit - alighted, alit
arise - arose - arisen
awake - awoke - awoken, awaked
be (am, is, are) - was (were) been
bear - bore - borne
beat - beat - beaten
become - became - become
begin - began - begun
behold - beheld - beheld
bend - bent - bent
beseech - besought, beseeched - besought, beseeched
bet - bet, betted - bet, betted
bid - bid - bid
bind - bound - bound
bite - bit - bitten
bleed - bled - bled

blow - blew - blown
break - broke - broken
breed - bred - bred
bring - brought - brought
broadcast - broadcast - broadcast
build - built - built
burn - burnt, burned - burnt, burned
burst - burst - burst
bust - bust(ed) - bust(ed)
buy - bought - bought
cast - cast - cast
catch - caught - caught
choose - chose - chosen
cleave (*cut*) - clove, cleft - cloven, cleft
cleave (*adhere*) - cleaved - cleaved
cling - clung - clung

come - came - come	keep - kept - kept
cost (v/i) - cost - cost	kneel - knelt, kneeled - knelt, kneeled
creep - crept - crept	know - knew - known
crow - crowed, crew - crowed	lay - laid - laid
cut - cut - cut	lead - led - led
deal - dealt - dealt	lean - leaned, leant - leaned, leant
dig - dug - dug	leap - leaped, leapt - leaped, leapt
do - did - done	learn - learned, learnt - learned, learnt
draw - drew - drawn	leave - left - left
dream - dreamt, dreamed - dreamt,	lend - lent - lent
dreamed	let - let - let
drink - drank - drunk	lie - lay - lain
drive - drove - driven	light - lighted, lit - lighted, lit
dwell - dwelt, dwelled - dwelt,	lose - lost - lost
dwelled	make - made - made
eat - ate - eaten	mean - meant - meant
fall - fell - fallen	meet - met - met
feed - fed - fed	mow - mowed - mowed, mown
feel - felt - felt	pay - paid - paid
fight - fought - fought	plead - pleaded, pled - pleaded, pled
find - found - found	prove - proved - proved, proven
flee - fled - fled	put - put - put
fling - flung - flung	quit - quit(ted) - quit(ted)
fly - flew - flown	read - read [red] - read [red]
forbear - forbore - forborne	rend - rent - rent
forbid - forbad(e) - forbidden	rid - rid - rid
forecast - forecast(ed) - forecast(ed)	ride - rode - ridden
forget - forgot - forgotten	ring - rang - rung
forgive - forgave - forgiven	rise - rose - risen
forsake - forsook - forsaken	run - ran - run
freeze - froze - frozen	saw - sawed - sawn, sawed
get - got - got, gotten	say - said - said
give - gave - given	see - saw - seen
go - went - gone	seek - sought - sought
grind - ground - ground	sell - sold - sold
grow - grew - grown	send - sent - sent
hang - hung, (v/t) hanged - hung,	set - set - set
(v/t) hanged	sew - sewed - sewed, sewn
have - had - had	shake - shook - shaken
hear - heard - heard	shear - sheared - sheared, shorn
heave - heaved, NAUT hove	shed - shed - shed
heaved, NAUT hove	shine - shone - shone
hew - hewed - hewed, hewn	shit - shit(ted), shat - shit(ted), shat
hide - hid - hidden	shoe - shod - shod
hit - hit - hit	shoot - shot - shot
hold - held - held	show - showed - shown
hurt - hurt - hurt	shrink - shrank - shrunk

shut - shut - shut
sing - sang - sung
sink - sank - sunk
sit - sat - sat
slay - slew - slain
sleep - slept - slept
slide - slid - slid
sling - slung - slung
slink - slunk - slunk
slit - slit - slit
smell - smelt, smelled - smelt, smelled
smite - smote - smitten
sow - sowed - sown, sowed
speak - spoke - spoken
speed - sped, speeded - sped, speeded
spell - spelt, spelled - spelt, spelled
spend - spent - spent
spill - spilt, spilled - spilt, spilled
spin - spun, span - spun
spit - spat - spat
split - split - split
spoil - spoiled, spoilt - spoiled, spoilt
spread - spread - spread
spring - sprang, sprung - sprung
stand - stood - stood
stave - staved, stove - staved, stove
steal - stole - stolen
stick - stuck - stuck
sting - stung - stung

stink - stunk, stank - stunk
strew - strewed - strewed, strewn
stride - strode - stridden
strike - struck - struck
string - strung - strung
strive - strove - striven
swear - swore - sworn
sweep - swept - swept
swell - swelled - swollen
swim - swam - swum
swing - swung - swung
take - took - taken
teach - taught - taught
tear - tore - torn
tell - told - told
think - thought - thought
thrive - throve - thriven
throw - threw - thrown
thrust - thrust - thrust
tread - trod - trodden
understand - understood - understood
wake - woke, waked - woken, waked
wear - wore - worn
weave - wove - woven
wed - wed(ded) - wed(ded)
weep - wept - wept
wet - wet(ted) - wet(ted)
win - won - won
wind - wound - wound
wring - wrung - wrung
write - wrote - written

Numbers – Numerales

Cardinal Numbers – Números cardinales

0	*zero*, Br tb *nought* cero	40	*forty* cuarenta
1	*one* uno, una	50	*fifty* cincuenta
2	*two* dos	60	*sixty* sesenta
3	*three* tres	70	*seventy* setenta
4	*four* cuatro	80	*eighty* ochenta
5	*five* cinco	90	*ninety* noventa
6	*six* seis	100	*a hundred, one hundred* cien(to)
7	*seven* siete	101	*a hundred and one* ciento uno
8	*eight* ocho	110	*a hundred and ten* ciento diez
9	*nine* nueve	200	*two hundred* doscientos, -as
10	*ten* diez	300	*three hundred* trescientos, -as
11	*eleven* once	400	*four hundred* cuatrocientos, -as
12	*twelve* doce	500	*five hundred* quinientos, -as
13	*thirteen* trece	600	*six hundred* seiscientos, -as
14	*fourteen* catorce	700	*seven hundred* setecientos, -as
15	*fifteen* quince	800	*eight hundred* ochocientos, *-as*
16	*sixteen* dieciséis	900	*nine hundred* novecientos, -as
17	*seventeen* diecisiete	1000	*a thousand, one thousand* mil
18	*eighteen* dieciocho	1959	*one thousand nine hundred and fifty-nine* mil novecientos cincuenta y nueve
19	*nineteen* diecinueve		
20	*twenty* veinte	2000	*two thousand* dos mil
21	*twenty-one* veintiuno	1 000 000	*a million, one million* un millón
22	*twenty-two* veintidós	2 000 000	*two million* dos millones
30	*thirty* treinta		
31	*thirty-one* treinta y uno		

Notas:

i) In Spanish numbers a comma is used for decimals:

    1.25   **one point two five**   una coma veinticinco

ii) A period is used where, in English, we would use a comma:

    1.000.000 = 1,000,000

    Numbers like this can also be written using a space instead of a comma:

    1 000 000 = 1,000,000

Ordinal Numbers – Números ordinales

1st	*first*	1°	primero
2nd	*second*	2°	segundo
3rd	*third*	3°	tercero
4th	*fourth*	4°	cuarto
5th	*fifth*	5°	quinto
6th	*sixth*	6°	sexto
7th	*seventh*	7°	séptimo
8th	*eighth*	8°	octavo
9th	*ninth*	9°	noveno, nono
10th	*tenth*	10°	décimo
11th	*eleventh*	11°	undécimo
12th	*twelfth*	12°	duodécimo
13th	*thirteenth*	13°	decimotercero
14th	*fourteenth*	14°	decimocuarto
15th	*fifteenth*	15°	decimoquinto
16th	*sixteenth*	16°	decimosexto
17th	*seventeenth*	17°	decimoséptimo
18th	*eighteenth*	18°	decimoctavo
19th	*nineteenth*	19°	decimonoveno, decimonono
20th	*twentieth*	20°	vigésimo
21st	*twenty-first*	21°	vigésimo prim(er)o
22nd	*twenty-second*	22°	vigésimo segundo
30th	*thirtieth*	30°	trigésimo
31st	*thirty-first*	31°	trigésimo prim(er)o
40th	*fortieth*	40°	cuadragésimo
50th	*fiftieth*	50°	quincuagésimo
60th	*sixtieth*	60°	sexagésimo
70th	*seventieth*	70°	septuagésimo
80th	*eightieth*	80°	octogésimo
90th	*ninetieth*	90°	nonagésimo
100th	*hundredth*	100°	centésimo
101st	*hundred and first*	101°	centésimo primero
110th	*hundred and tenth*	110°	centésimo décimo
200th	*two hundredth*	200°	ducentésimo
300th	*three hundredth*	300°	trecentésimo
400th	*four hundredth*	400°	cuadringentésimo
500th	*five hundredth*	500°	quingentésimo
600th	*six hundredth*	600°	sexcentésimo
700th	*seven hundredth*	700°	septingentésimo
800th	*eight hundredth*	800°	octingentésimo
900th	*nine hundredth*	900°	noningentésimo
1000th	*thousandth*	1000°	milésimo
2000th	*two thousandth*	2000°	dos milésimo
1,000,100th	*millionth*	1 000 100°	millonésimo
2,000,000th	*two millionth*	2 000 000°	dos millonésimo

Fractions and other Numerals – Números quebrados y otros

¹/₂	*one half, a half*	medio, media
1¹/₂	*one and a half*	uno y medio
2¹/₂	*two and a half*	dos y medio
¹/₃	*one third, a third*	un tercio, la tercera parte
²/₃	*two thirds*	· dos tercios, las dos terceras partes
¹/₄	*one quarter, a quarter*	un cuarto, la cuarta parte
³/₄	*three quarters*	tres cuartos, las tres cuartas partes
¹/₅	*one fifth, a fifth*	un quinto
3⁴/₅	*three and four fifths*	tres y cuatro quintos
¹/₁₁	*one eleventh, an eleventh*	un onzavo
⁵/₁₂	*five twelfths*	cinco dozavos
¹/₁₀₀₀	*one thousandth, a thousandth*	un milésimo
	seven times as big, seven times bigger	siete veces más grande
	twelve times more	doce veces más
	first(ly)	en primer lugar
	second(ly) etc	en segundo lugar
7 + 8 = 15	*seven and (or plus) eight are (or is) fifteen*	siete y (or más) ocho son quince
10 − 3 = 7	*ten minus three is seven, three from ten leaves seven*	diez menos tres resta siete, de tres a diez van siete
2 × 3 = 6	*two times three is six*	dos por tres son seis
20 ÷ 4 = 5	*twenty divided by four is five*	veinte dividido por cuatro es cinco

Dates – Fechas

1996	*nineteen ninety-six*	mil novecientos noventa y seis
2005	*two thousand (and) five*	dos mil cinco

the 10th of November, November 10 (ten)
el diez de noviembre, el 10 de noviembre

the 1st of March, March 1 (first)
el uno de marzo, *L.Am.* **el primero de marzo, el 1o de marzo**

Headword in blue Lema en azul	**A·mer·i·ca** [əˈmerɪkə] *continent* América; *USA* Estados *mpl* Unidos
Examples and phrases in ***bold, italics*** Ejemplos y frases en ***negrita*** y ***cursiva***	**i·deal·ly** [aɪˈdiːəlɪ] *adv*: ***ideally situated*** en una posición ideal; ***ideally, we would*** ***do it like this*** lo ideal sería que lo hicié- ramos así
Translation in normal characters with gender shown in *italics* Traducción en caracteres normales con el género en *cursiva*	**'break·down** *of vehicle, machine* avería *f*; *of talks* ruptura *f* ; (*nervous breakdown*) crisis *f inv* nerviosa; *of figures* desglose *m*
Indicating words in *italics* Indicadores semánticos en *cursiva*	**busi·ness** [ˈbɪznɪs] negocios *mpl*; (*com-* *pany*) empresa *f*; (*sector*) sector *m*; (*af-* *fair, matter*) asunto *m*; *as subject of study* empresariales *fpl*; ***on business*** de nego- cios; ***that's none of your business!*** ¡no es asunto tuyo!; ***mind your own busi-*** ***ness!*** ¡no te metas en lo que no te impor- ta!
International Phonetic Alphabet Transcripción fonética	**in·sult 1** *n* [ˈɪnsʌlt] insulto *m* **2** *v/t* [ɪnˈsʌlt] insultar
Hyphenation points Indicación de división silábica	**con·sum·er 'con·fi·dence** confianza *f* de los consumidores
Stress shown in headwords ' identifica la sílaba acentuada	**'mov·ie thea·ter** cine *m*, sala *f* de cine